Critical acclaim for Diaries: Into Politics

'Pure joy. All Christmas presents chosen, all "Book of the Year" dilemmas solved – this is the book of the year, the decade, the millennium. Forget all the cavils about whether these diaries are as good as the first volume, or whether they might have been improved by Alan Clark had he lived – we must simply thank our lucky stars that we have them. The only question now is whether Clark is the greatest English diarist of the 20th century or merely one of the top five'   Lynn Barber, *Daily Telegraph*

'As I read on, I came to cherish Clark. For, while he was undoubtedly a bounder and an idler, he emerges from this book as a classic minor character who would have been thoroughly at home among the dramatis personae of Restoration comedy, named, perhaps, Mr Sneerwell'   Gerald Kaufman, *The Times*

'In the end, Alan Clark and his diaries are engaging and tolerable because we will not, cannot, grant him the thing he most wants from his audience – we cannot take him seriously ... The diaries of the high-minded and consistent cannot be nearly as amusing'   Andrew Marr, *Observer*

'Those of us who knew and loved him immediately recognise an utterly authentic portrait of the man. In his writings, no prisoners are taken, no fear is shown of causing offence. Presumably, given the first-class editing job, they were even ruder beforehand ... You could not get away with inventing Alan Clark in a work of fiction'   Simon Heffer, *Daily Mail*

'A great deal to enjoy ... The principal target of Alan Clark's feline dissection – mesmerically untrustworthy, cackhandedly ambitious, by turns unctuously sycophantic and coldheartedly backstabbing – is, of course, Clark himself. How he relishes each description of his own perfidy! ... when the earnest, self-serving memoirs of countless Prime Ministers are gathering dust, the diaries of Alan Clark will still be read with glee ... He also has a novelist's eye for detail ... like Jane Austen, he is able to perceive the larger significance in apparently humdrum activities'   Craig Brown, *Mail on Sunday*

'A vastly entertaining writer. His diaries of his years as a junior minister have granted him a kind of immortality ... All the familiar ingredients are here – disdain for his constituents and the lower orders generally; alternate cynicism about the House of Commons and ecstasy when he got to hear the sound of his own voice, which he did as a super-jingo during the Falklands War; together with yearnings, often frustrated at this period apparently, for more sex' Max Hastings, *Evening Standard*

Alan Clark, MP for Plymouth (Sutton) 1974–1992 and Kensington and Chelsea, 1997–1999, was Minister of Trade, 1986–1989, and Minister of State, Ministry of Defence, 1989–1992. He made his reputation as a historian with *The Donkeys: A History of the BEF in 1915*, followed by *The Fall of Crete, Barbarossa: The Russian-German Conflict, 1941–45* and *Aces High: The War in the Air over the Western Front 1914–1918*. He also published three novels. In 1973 he edited the private diaries of Viscount Lee of Fareham, *A Good Innings*. After quitting the House of Commons in 1992 he published the first volume of his *Diaries* the following year. His political history, *The Tories: The Conservatives and the Nation State, 1922–1997* appeared in 1998. Alan Clark was married with two sons. He lived until his death in 1999 at Saltwood Castle, Kent. The second volume of his diaries *Into Politics*, was published posthumously in 2000.

Ion Trewin, the editor, is Editor-in-Chief of a London publisher. He was previously Literary Editor of *The Times*.

By Alan Clark

Bargains at Special Prices: A novel

The Donkeys: A History of the BEF in 1915

Summer Season: A novel

The Fall of Crete

Barbarossa: The Russian–German
Conflict, 1941–1945

The Lion Heart: A tale of the war in Vietnam

Aces High: the War in the Air
over the Western Front 1914–1918

A Good Innings: The private papers
of Viscount Lee of Fareham (edited)

Suicide of the Empires:
The Eastern Front, 1914–1918

Diaries: In Power, 1983–1992

The Tories: Conservatives and the
Nation State, 1922–1997

Diaries: Into Politics, 1972–1982

Back Fire: A Passion for Cars and Motoring

DIARIES
Into Politics
1972–1982

ALAN CLARK

Edited, with Introduction
and Notes, by Ion Trewin

PHŒNIX

A PHOENIX PAPERBACK

First published in Great Britain in 2000
by Weidenfeld & Nicolson
This paperback edition published in 2001
by Phoenix,
an imprint of Orion Books Ltd,
Orion House, 5 Upper Saint Martin's Lane,
London WC2H 9EA

A CIP catalogue reference for this book
is available from the British Library.

ISBN 0 75381 414 5

Typeset by Selwood Systems, Midsomer Norton

Printed in Great Britain by
Clays Ltd, St Ives plc

'Sometimes lacking in charity; often trivial, occasionally lewd, cloyingly sentimental, repetitious, whingeing and imperfectly formed. For some readers the entries may seem to be all of these things. But they are real diaries.'

Alan Clark
Diaries, 1993

CONTENTS

ILLUSTRATIONS

A section of photographs from the Clark family albums appears between pages 198 and 199.

GLOSSARY

FAMILY

Jane

James – AC's elder son (aka 'Boy', 'Jamie')

Andrew – AC's younger son (aka 'Tip', 'Tip-book', 'Tup', 'Cin', 'Lilian')

Colette – AC's sister (aka 'Celly')

Colin – AC's brother (aka 'Col')

Lord Clark – (aka Bonny papa) – AC's father, Kenneth Clark

B'Mama (aka Bonny mama) – AC's mother, Jane Clark

Nolwen, Comtesse de Janzé – AC's stepmother

STAFF AND ESTATE

Cradduck – gardener at Saltwood

Eddie – groundsman at Saltwood

Lindley – Lord Clark's butler at the Garden House

Nanny (aka 'Greenwood') – nanny to James and Andrew, and living in a grace and favour cottage on the Saltwood estate

Gangster and Grandee – beagles

Tom – Jack Russell terrier

George – a tame jackdaw at Saltwood

Eva – Jane's Rottweiler

Angus – black labrador

OFFICE

Sue – first secretary at the House of Commons
Veronica – secretary at the House of Commons
Alison – secretary at the House of Commons

SOME CARS AND RELATED MATTERS

(Many of the cars mentioned in this volume are transitory purchases
    which AC sold on; they are usually identified within the text)

Wee Bob – mechanic to Christopher Selmes' (qv)
The Mews – composite name for various vintage car dealers'
    establishments in Queen's Gate, London
Coys – dealers in classic cars

600 – Mercedes
550A Spyder – Porsche ex von Frankenberg Mille Miglia
The black SS100 – owned by AC since his undergraduate days
The 'little white' – Mercedes 230 SL
K10 – 1979 Chevrolet
OLA – Datsun 240Z, belonging to James
Chapron – the Citroen, the *decapotable*, belonging to Jane
The Mehari – a little plastic truck with an air-cooled engine and a
    very light footprint used for clearing glass clippings and prunings
    from the garden because it does not mark the lawn.
The Locomobile – an old chain-driven racing car of 1908
THEBUS – 'the bus' – Transit van
Winter Car – 1967 Chevrolet Impala
Summer Car – 1967 Chevrolet Impala convertible
The Mickey – 2CV
Winifred – Morris 8 (see p. 343)
Bang Bang – R Type Continental (see p. 66)
Osprey and Atco – lawn mowers at Saltwood

HOUSES AND LOCATIONS

SALTWOOD CASTLE

Various rooms: the Great Library; the Tower Office; the Green Room
    (the Clarks' informal sitting room in the old staff wing)

Garden House (GH) – a large bungalow, designed by John King in the old kitchen garden in the grounds of Saltwood, for Lord and Lady Clark, when they moved out of the castle in 1971.

Sandling – the railway station for Saltwood

Gossie Bank – a steep climb at the far end of Grange Farm, Saltwood

The Seeds – a large arable field at Grange Farm, Saltwood

The Bailey (inner and outer) – the two courtyards (see also lawns)

Courtneys, sometimes Courtenays (aka the Secret Garden)

SEEND PARK

Broomhayes (aka Cherry Cottage) – near Devizes in Wiltshire; retained by the Clarks when they moved to Saltwood.

RYE

Watchbell Street – including No 11, where the Clarks lived after they married

BRATTON–CLOVELLY

Town Farm – another early home; in west Devon, about three-quarters of an hour's drive north of Plymouth

ZERMATT

Châlet Caroline – the Clarks' house in the village, which they built at the end of the 1950s

Trift – an inn at an early stage in the ascent to the Rothornhutte

ALBANY

B5 Lower/Upper – Piccadilly chambers shared at various times by AC and Lord Clark. The Upper, more an attic, had once been servants' quarters.

HOUSE OF COMMONS

Dean's Yard – mainly offices for secretaries, by Westminster Abbey

East Cloisters (or simply Cloisters) – where AC had an office from
   1977

PLYMOUTH

Alma Road and Headland Park – at different times the headquarters
   of Sutton Conservative Association

SLANG
(Family sayings and shorthand expressions dotted about the text)

ACHAB – (lit.) 'anything can happen at backgammon', a saying
   originally from 'the Room' at Brooks's where games can swing
   at a late stage on an unpredictable run of the dice, used often as a
   consolation in times of depression. Adaptable in other
   circumstances, substituting 'politics' for 'backgammon' for instance

Ash eating – self-inflicted penance

Piccolo – a minor but telling triumph.

Thompson – defecation

Sadismoid – virtually the same as sadistically, though less *transitive* in
   meaning; the suffic – moid, or moidly is often attached to
   adjectives

Satisly – arousing satisfaction, inducing complacency

Greywater – diarrhoea

Naylor-Leylandish – named after the aquiline features of Sir Vivian
   Naylor-Leyland.

BHLH – a description of perfect male dress sense, right for the
   specific occasion. The initials were those of Basil Liddell-Hart,
   one of AC's heroes, who also invariably dressed immaculately.

'w' – walk, as in going for a walk

Tinky – diminutive, insignificant

ABBREVIATIONS

NAMES

AC – Alan Clark
CH – Charles, Charles Howard
CS – Christopher (aka 'Daisy') Selmes
IG – Ian Gow
RJ – Robert Rhodes James and, sometimes, Roy Jenkins
MT – Margaret Thatcher

ACRONYMS

BHLH– see Slang (above)
CGT – Capital Gains Tax
o/d – overdraft
CPC – Conservative Political Centre
EDM – Early Day Motion
F&GP– Financial and General Purposes Committee (usually of the Plymouth Sutton constituency association)
MLR – Minimum Lending Rate
OLA – see Cars (above)
PQ – Parliamentary Question
ST J – St James' Club, at Coventry House, Piccadilly until 1975, when it merged with Brooks's in St James's Street
SE – Stock Exchange
UBS – Union Bank Suisse

UCH – University College Hospital, London
TSW – Television South West
VGL – very good looking
WD – 'wet' dream

INTRODUCTION

TO THIS EDITION

Many begin diaries, few sustain them. Alan Clark, though, was a stayer. At his death, in September 1999, he had been keeping his without a break for forty-four years. Originally written without any thought of publication, in 1993 he plundered them for a volume covering his spell as a junior minister in successive Thatcher governments.[1] This contains the most authoritative – and enthralling – contemporaneous account of Margaret Thatcher's downfall.

Following the huge success of the first volume (praised and likened to 'Chips' Channon's great journals, into which he rarely failed to dip with his early morning tea),[2] Alan at first considered a sequel, to be called 'The Wilderness Years' – about what happened after he retired from the Commons at the 1992 general election, or 'Matrix Churchill and all that', as he said in a letter. By the new year of 1999 his situation had changed. He was, after all, a Member of Parliament again.[3] Far better, he argued, to go back to the moment he entered politics, which was also, for another reason, a landmark year. A further volume, which might be called 'From Wilderness to Opposition', would come later.

From the late 1960s he had been trying to gain selection as parliamentary candidate for a safe Conservative seat, an ambition finally achieved in 1972. At the same time his father gave him Saltwood Castle overlooking Hythe in Kent with the English Channel beyond.

---

[1] Originally titled, quite simply, *Diaries*, they start in 1983 and close in 1991. In 2001 they were reissued in a new paperback edition as *Diaries: In Power*.

[2] At the time of writing more than 300,000 copies have been sold.

[3] For the Kensington and Chelsea constituency, elected at the 1997 general election.

Politics absorbed Alan for the rest of his life; Saltwood would be his principal and adored home. The die was cast.

At the time this volume opens Alan was forty-three and married with two children. The elder son of Kenneth Clark, who had been the youngest Director of the National Gallery, and his wife Jane, he had twin siblings, Colin and Colette. The family were affluent, their wealth stemming from the Clark cotton thread business in Paisley (Kenneth Clark's great-great-grandfather invented the wooden spool or bobbin). Alan was too young to serve in the Second World War (he celebrated his seventeenth birthday less than four weeks before VE-Day), but he remained proud for the rest of his life that he managed to enlist in the Household Cavalry training regiment before the war was over. His interest in military history (particularly of the twentieth century) had already been awakened.

He was educated at Eton and Oxford, where he spent three happy if hedonistic years at Christ Church reading modern history under Hugh Trevor-Roper. In his address at the memorial service for Alan at St Margaret's, Westminster, in February 2000, Euan Graham recalled their first meeting in the coffee shop opposite Balliol College in 1948, which led to his being asked by Alan to drive him to Stroud in a Buick Roadster convertible. It transpired that Alan had lost his licence for the 'relatively trivial offence' of allowing a girl to drive the car while sitting on his lap, leaving him to work the pedals. To a ripple of knowing laughter from the St Margaret's congregation, Euan Graham acknowledged that there in a single story two of Alan's pleasures were combined.

It took many years for Alan to discover his true vocation. Ten months after becoming an MP – in January 1975 – it was still something of a surprise. 'My real problem is that at the age [he was forty-six] when most people start "slowing up" I suddenly gain a job – having been in retirement from the age of twenty-seven.' After Oxford he served with the Royal Auxiliary Air Force whilst reading for the Bar and qualifying, with difficulty, as a barrister. Although he did not practise, he served briefly as judge's marshal on the south-eastern assize. He went on to augment some family money by working for a company trading in cars, particularly vintage and classic cars (an interest that he would keep up), and playing the Stock Exchange.

With a brilliant mind, this was hardly enough to keep him occupied. He inherited his father's interest and knowledge in art, but never seriously thought of following in his footsteps. He had, however, also

inherited Kenneth Clark's facility for, and pleasure in, writing and by
the mid-1950s was keeping a journal. In 1960 his first novel *Bargains
at Special Prices* – set in the City of London and with its echoes of
early Evelyn Waugh – was published as Number 13[1] in Hutchinson's
New Authors imprint. The novel's publication was not without its
drama: the first printing of 4,000 copies had to be pulped because of
legal threats from a stockbrokers, which claimed that it was the
fictitious firm mocked in the novel. Alan had to pay the publisher's
costs, but when the novel finally came out with the name changed a
few weeks later it received widespread acclaim. Leonard Russell in
the *Sunday Times* wrote: 'Mr Clark's very funny and instructive novel
will be gulped down like a glass of champagne by the army of
newcomers to stock market speculation,' V. S. Naipaul in the *New
Statesman* observed that 'his dialogue is delightful' and The *Observer*
critic noted that he had 'a briskly original wit'. This was followed in
1963, but less successfully, by *Summer Season*. Alan completed one
further novel, *The Lion Heart*, with a Vietnam war setting which
originally started life as a work of non-fiction. It was eventually
published in 1969.

By this time, writing and his interest in military matters had combined in the first of three superlative campaign histories: *The Donkeys:
A History of the British Expeditionary Force in 1915*, which on its
publication in 1961 was to make his reputation as a military historian,
but amid torrents of controversy. 'Eloquent and painful', wrote George
Malcolm Thomson in the *Evening Standard*. 'Clark leaves the impression that vanity and stupidity were the main ingredients of the
massacres of 1915. He writes searingly and unforgettably.'[2] Next came
The Fall of Crete, followed in 1965 by *Barbarossa: The Russian-German
Conflict, 1941–1945*. He toyed with a number of further projects,
including a history of NATO, a life of Lloyd George and a study of
modern Conservatism;[3] but he failed to make the delivery dates and
his long-time literary agent, Michael Sissons, would arrange the
cancellation of contracts and the return of the advances. This literary

---

[1] The number 13 has considerable significance within the Clark family: not only was AC
   himself born on 13 April 1928, his elder son James on 13 February 1960, and his
   grandson Angus on 13 November 1997, but his father's birthday was on 13 July 1903.
[2] Even more than a quarter of a century later, in 1989, when AC was hoping for ministerial
   preferment from Trade to Defence, as Armed Forces Minister, he knew that the 'Army
   brass won't have me because of *The Donkeys*' (24 July 1989).
[3] Eventually written and published in 1998 as *The Tories: Conservatives and the Nation State
   1922–1997*, it was also the basis of a television series.

life still left him unfulfilled. It was not a full-time career.

Whereas his father's politics were firmly to the left, Alan had an intellectual affinity with the right: by 1972 this meant patriotism, the Monday Club, voicing an enthusiasm (not a reverence) for the views of Enoch Powell,[1] but a distaste for many of the political views of Edward Heath, not least firm opposition to what was then known as the 'Common Market'; he was, though, also a member of the Bow Group. He had started looking for a parliamentary seat in the late 1960s: a litany of constituency names sprinkles his notebooks: Norwood, Swindon, Ashchurch, Weston, Havant, Langstone among many others. Early in 1972 a new name emerges: Plymouth Sutton.

By then Alan had been married for fourteen years. He had met Jane Beuttler when he was twenty-eight and she was fourteen. They wed two years later. Their honeymoon ranged wide: on the train to Switzerland he continually worried that she might not like one of his favourite landscapes; they toured the battlefields of the First World War as he was already researching *The Donkeys* (to which she contributed the maps, her interwined initials in the corner being the only clue to their origins); and they visited old haunts along the Mediterranean, where they met Alan's oldest friend, John Pollock, and his patronne, Constance Mappin.[2] Back in England they bought a cob farmhouse at Bratton-Clovelly in west Devon, about three-quarters of an hour's drive to the north of Plymouth. Its position would prove significant politically. Their other early homes included Alan's bachelor house in Watchbell Street, Rye, not far along the south coast from Saltwood, and several properties at Seend in Wiltshire. Their elder son James was born in 1960, followed by Andrew in 1962.

Alan need not have worried about Jane's feelings for Switzerland and together they soon built a chalet in Zermatt, the Châlet Caroline (Jane's first name). In London Alan shared with his father the use of a set at Albany in Piccadilly.

---

[1] Was AC ever a 'Powellite'? In a letter to David Butler, who was compiling his study of the February 1974 election, AC admits that at the time he was looking for a seat he was 'much more closely identified with Monday Club/Powellite sympathies' than he was to become once at Westminster.

[2] 'Jane and I stayed with them at Positano,' AC recalled (*Diaries*, 16 February 1985). 'Christina [a girl friend who had been living in AC's house when he became engaged to Jane] turned up, and a farcical triangular sub-plot developed with Milo Cripps's [later the 4th Baron Parmoor] boyfriend 'Barry' falling for her, and tears shed all round.'

In 1951 Kenneth Clark had moved to Saltwood. He and his wife knew this part of Kent from before the war when they owned a country house close to Philip Sassoon's Port Lympne, where they were frequent visitors. He bought the castle and its grounds from the estate of Lady Conway of Allington, who had restored it with the help of a distinguished medieval architect, Philip Tilden. A previous owner was the father of W. F. (Bill) Deedes, MP, who had been a Minister in Harold Macmillan's second government, and during much of the currency of these diaries was editor of the *Daily Telegraph* and a valued patron for Alan's journalism. Kenneth Clark had continued Lady Conway's restoration, adding, in particular, the bookcases to the Great Library, and it was in the adjoining study that he wrote his later books, including *Civilisation* (the television series of the same name led to him being known informally, but affectionately, as 'Lord Clark of Civilisation'). Alan recalled in a 1980 diary entry the peak days of his parents' occupation 'when it was teeming with staff and beautiful meals arrived on cue.' In 1971, and approaching seventy, Kenneth Clark decided to hand over the castle to his elder son and move to the Garden House, a bungalow he had built in the Saltwood grounds. He took Lindley, his butler, with him, but he and Lady Clark found it difficult to sever the Saltwood knot, and as Alan also relates in his journals, tensions often ran high.

Following Alan's death there was much speculation that no further volumes of his diaries could be published, because his handwriting was said to be impossible to read. The publication of this present volume is testament to the unreliability of such speculation. Much depended on how tired, or how stressed Alan was at the time of writing, as well as the quality of paper on which he wrote, whether he used fountain pen, ballpoint, feltnib or pencil and where he did his writing (train journeys, for instance, do not lend themselves to legibility). And once he had started regularly taking the current volume with him to Westminster he deliberately chose what he called 'a crabbed hand' just in case it was mislaid (indeed later volumes carry the firm injunction on the front cover – REWARD IF FOUND).

Many fans of the published *Diaries* have, though, wondered what all the fuss was about, citing the endpapers printed in the hardback edition, which reproduce entries in an elegant and readable hand. As his editor and publisher for the first volume of *Diaries* in 1993, maybe this is the place to make a confession. Although the content of those endpapers was taken from actual journals of the period, the reproductions were precisely that. Alan made fair copies of a number of entries, and took considerable pleasure in ensuring that each entry appeared to end with an unresolved cliff-hanger at the foot of the page. Of the reviewers, as Alan himself recorded with glee, it was Robert Harris (author of *Enigma*) who first noticed that these entries were a bonus as they do not appear in the published *Diaries* themselves.

Early in 1972 Alan neared the end of his current manuscript volume and was concerned to discover that 'those useful, blue cloth-bound plain-sheeted loose-leaf binders', which he had been using since the beginning – what we might today call an A5 ringbinder – were, *of course*, 'no longer being made.' Rummaging around in the library at Saltwood he turned up a barely used visitors book, bound in crimson-lake leather with 'Katoomba' stamped in gold leaf on the front. Katoomba was the name given by his grandfather to his yachts, and – particularly pleasing to Alan, who enjoyed the symmetry – the few signatures this volume contained started in the year of his father's birth (1903).

'It seems appropriate enough [he wrote] for the new set of journals – Katoomba has long been an evocative name for me[1] and I have all the models: it is good quality paper and there is plenty of space – heaven knows what the pages will (fore) tell or even if I will live to complete them.'

'Katoomba' lasted until 1975, to be followed by a large hardback 'legal' notebook left over from his law studies. With lined paper, it was identified by him, thanks to its binding, as 'the black book'. Through the 1980s he used government-issue hardback A4 note-books. The paper was appalling – 'horrible "austerity" book', he called the first one – and, on the whole, his writing was worse.

Although one page of a 1945 diary survives in which he records – he was seventeen – seeing a show at the Adelphi Theatre, London called *The Love Racket* with the 'uproariously funny' comedian Arthur Askey, the first volume proper begins in 1955. Even in those early days he rarely let more than a couple of weeks go by without making an entry. More usually he would write once a week, a review of the past seven

---

[1] As Kenneth Clark relates in the first volume of his autobiography, *Another Part of the Wood*, the name came from Australia's Blue Mountains, which his father had visited in his teens.

days. By the 1980s – particularly when Parliament was in session – he was often writing daily. Over the decade covered by this second volume I estimate that I have drawn from approximately 500,000 words of the original. The style of his writing evolved, as can be seen in this volume: there is the note (with verb and personal pronoun noticeable by their absence), the simple narrative record, and, finally, the more elaborate set-piece, often with substantial quantities of dialogue, where the sheer pleasure in writing is very apparent. In content the diary was also a confessional and the fact that he kept it going over the best part of five decades demonstrates how important it was to him, no matter the pressures.

During his first election campaign – in February 1974 – he used a W. H. Smith appointments diary – a page a day – which also became the journal for the October 1974 election. In the helter-skelter of campaigning these entries are often little more than brief notes, and on his arrival at Westminster, to judge from the content, he rarely took 'Katoomba' to the Commons or to the Dean's Yard office by Westminster Abbey, where his secretary was lodged. The trusty 'W. H. Smith' (being A5 in size and therefore more portable) continued to do occasional double-duty and includes a short account of his maiden speech on 30 April. But his Westminster journal keeping is haphazard. He has, for instance, not left us with his thoughts on the overthrowing of Edward Heath, following the Tories' defeat at the second 1974 election, and the arrival of Margaret Thatcher as the Conservative leader. However his appreciation of the uncertain future of Heath may be read in his account of a telephone conversation during that election campaign with Bernard (Jack) Weatherill, the Tories' deputy chief whip. Thatcher as possible leader had been mentioned as early as March.

Occasionally, though, he felt compelled to seize the minute, writing on House of Commons notepaper before slipping or stapling the page into the appropriate spot; sometimes entries were even jotted into his engagement diary and later transcribed. The 1975 Common Market debate is one such. But the 1974–79 Labour government – although it had its moments, particularly towards its close – demonstrated to Alan that, with a social life being regularly reduced to tatters as a result of a tedious number of all-night sittings, being a junior back-bench opposition MP was not much fun. He craved power, power for a Tory government, and advancement for himself.

Throughout this period his writing continued, but more often at weekends, when he would retire to the Great Hall at Saltwood or to the garden, perhaps, at Bratton. We may have less politics than in the later journals, but away from Westminster his days are rich and complicated. He gives us life as he experiences it: he is insatiably attracted to a pretty face, he suffers chronic hypochondria (like his father), can't resist dealing in cars (or on the Stock Exchange), is close to bankruptcy and experiences gambling disasters at backgammon that show an addictive streak. But when he strays it is always to Jane, to his sons and to Saltwood that he returns.

Much was to change in 1979. The general election in May – Alan again dragged out the 'W. H. Smith' as his election journal – saw Alan's majority double, to 11,000, and the Tories returned to government, with Margaret Thatcher as Prime Minister. Even as a backbencher, some of Alan's hopes were fulfilled and the tone of his diaries changed: he realised how much he enjoyed being of the party in government, reporting what he saw, heard and was increasingly part of, as well as musing on his own hopes and ambitions. And by the autumn he had devised a solution for his diary. The manuscript book continued, but he also started dictating Westminster entries to his secretary, which considerably increased the political content. For this volume I have drawn on both.

The original published *Diaries* began with the death of his father, the general election of 1983 and Alan's elevation to ministerial rank. Appropriately this current volume concludes the previous year with the political event that secured Margaret Thatcher's position – the victorious Falklands campaign, which through his military interest and knowledge gave Alan lasting political prominence and presaged his long-desired advancement. At Saltwood, too, life was about to change with the first major sign of his father's mortality, a stroke that immobilised him in the summer of 1982. But, as Alan planned before his death, this volume begins ten years before: Plymouth beckons politically and Saltwood is the new family home.

Ion Trewin
March 2001

EDITOR'S NOTE

Footnotes give the present and past – but rarely future – positions of individuals, usually at their first appearance. Nor is an MP's political allegiance listed except where this may be unclear from the text.

AC's occasional inconsistencies in style, dates, capitalisation and even English grammar, have sometimes been left as written. I have followed his own practice and where appropriate silently edited passages.

IT

1972

Centre of gravity moving inexorably to Saltwood. Only pause for thought – where the hell do the years go? Cradduck[1] (naturally) can't get possession of his cottage – and there is nowhere else – *quelle est la solution? . . . averme?* (Gamelin with Churchill May 1940 . . . *'ou est la masse de manoeuvre?'*) Very heavy expenditure looking at interior. Hence dilemma. How far to go? What degree of compromise, or not, between having it as a sort of show-place for summer and occasional smart weekends and living at Broomhayes?[2] Or living there with the whole caboosh, cars, trading, dogs, peacocks. And then, even while we are there I think it might be more 'sensible' in the Victorian part, keeping the medieval part as a show area. Real thing is, it's lovely with the boys, but when they are away, then I rather dread the *existence solitaire* (just) the two of us. If only we could have another baby!

On the financial front, still trading like crazy, though taking profits too soon I don't doubt. Periodic waves of 'panic' at my gearing cause me to shorten the line. 'Garaging' (huh!) a lot of the profits by putting them in cars (Isotta, 540U, Ferrari 375, D-Type), but could well have a car sale in October. The objective must be ELIMINATION OF ALL DEBTS.

Had this concept of a bank (Central Line Investment Management and Banking) charging $1\frac{1}{4}$ per account. Charles[3] very keen on the idea. I think this might be something (big) to go for – but very hard work, capital expenditure, office in the City.

'Daisy'[4] on the phone, ill, in Paris. 'I'm terribly worried that you're going to waste all that money (from the field) Alan ...' So am I.[5] I

---

[1] Head gardener at Saltwood from 1951–1980.

[2] The house at Seend where the Clarks were living before the move to Saltwood.

[3] Charles Howard, a motoring friend who also regularly played backgammon with AC.

[4] Christopher (aka 'Daisy') Selmes, a friend of many years standing, who had made a fortune in the City.

[5] AC was selling the cricket field to the south of Saltwood, and houses were planned on part of it, but the builders went bankrupt. The cricket club bought its corner. A quarter of a century later, in 1998, AC was able to buy back the field as a wedding anniversary present for Jane.

am resorting to the primitive technique, *caching* it in different hollow trees like a squirrel and his nuts; the other school is concentrate, Rommel, turn it into 500[1] this year.

Politics too, that spurious sense of activity (without achievement). Plymouth Sutton – sounds promising and a spy in the camp who told me already more than I ever got out of that shower at Ashchurch. But I've seen too much of those constituency fixings to be sanguine about my own prospects.

As for Langstone, incredibly the tables have *again* turned; poor old Lloyd really looks done for now, having lost all his 'list' at the AGM and slightly gone off his rocker, discussing the agent, stopping surgeries etc.[2] But will they wear me? The bulk of the Executive – no; imprisoned, I should say, by their own guilt. Pity because I do want to get in.

Saltwood   *Saturday, 6 May*

Still not properly unpacked here, many things not 'come to hand' as yet, packing cases in the upper hall etc. *Absolutely* no decoration at all (to my parents' puzzlement . . . 'is Al just going to sell the whole thing to an institution?' etc), but, in fact, adjusting 'quite well' to the change; boys seem reasonably all right at school though dear Cin a bit lonely in break which is giving him light anxiety-asthma.

Plymouth Sutton is a situation of considerable promise. My spy (Graham Butland[3]) has leaked all the questions so I am dutifully preparing fluent, moving answers. He has given me the names of the others short-listed and will meet me on Saturday morning to disclose how Friday's interviewees fared and see if there are any questions I want posed! Still Langstone to fall back on, but I am no longer sanguine there.

Went to Bratton on Wednesday of last week prior to going on to Plymouth. How lovely and soft and restful the West Country is! And

---

[1] Throughout his diaries, when referring to financial sums, AC often leaves off the final '000'. In this case he means £500,000.

[2] AC was being intemperate: Sir Ian Lloyd (Kt 1986) may have had problems with the Portsmouth Langstone constituency association, but it wasn't long before he was selected by nearby Havant in 1974, which he represented until 1992.

[3] A member of the Plymouth Sutton Conservative Association committee.

how evocative of those early distant happy days with Jane and the babies and the blue Oldsmobile. Now we hardly have time to breathe, but I can still get a great draught of peace when I am at Bratton-Clovelly. Whether it would still be the same if I was an MP down there, I don't know.

Duke of Cornwall Hotel, Plymouth   *Friday, 12 May*

I sit at a table in the bay window of a comfortable room in this old-fashioned hotel. Tomorrow I have a preliminary interview for the 'safest' of the three Plymouth seats. This afternoon I have been in reconnaissance.

I first visited Plymouth ten years ago, when I collected Jane and new-born Andrew from the maternity ward at Freedom Fields hospital whither she had been rushed by ambulance from Bratton in the bitter winter of 1962. There are some fine buildings in a hard grey stone, almost granite; especially along the Hoe where Nancy Astor[1] had a grand house. Also tracts of rubble-covered wasteland where the planners have not yet built over the bomb damage.

Hard to understand, this, as it is more than thirty years since the great Luftwaffe raids of April 1941 when the whole population would, at nightfall, trek out on the Yelverton road and camp on Dartmoor. My father, who sometimes comes up with strange, but usually accurate, pieces of useless information told me quite some time ago that Plymouth was 'the most corrupt city in Britain' – which may explain it.

There are now three parliamentary divisions. I had been advised by the Central Office list of 'Drake', a marginal, and applied. A short while afterward I was gratified to receive a telephone call from two complete strangers, who were on the Executive Council of the third seat, entitled 'Sutton' by the Boundaries Commission, out of homage to Nancy, but in fact taking in a large swathe of Heseltine's former

[1] Nancy Astor (wife of the 2nd Viscount Astor) and her husband had a lengthy association with the city. She became the first woman to take her seat in the House of Commons when she was elected MP for the Sutton division in 1919 (a seat her husband had previously held). She retired in 1945.

Tavistock constituency[1] and thus, putatively, very Conservative. 'Forget Drake' they said, 'it's a marginal. Go for Sutton.'

Apparently, but unsurprisingly, Central Office have their eye on the place and wish to make sure that it ends up in 'the right hands'. But there are some on the Executive of the new seat who don't like this idea.

As the preliminary interviews, which started at 4pm, are taking place in this actual building there is much to observe. I have been sitting with a tea tray in front of me since half past three. I am clean-shirted and in a light tweed suit. My features are composed, set you could say, into an expression at the same time fresh and obliging.

A big chap, fifty-ish, balding, spectacles, sat about three tables away. He too appeared to be waiting. Was he the Chairman? Practically anybody could be the chairman at this stage, it seemed. Or at least the Treasurer, or the Vice-chairman. Silently ingratiating, I endeavoured to radiate good will.

Several times I caught him looking at me. Curiously, but *cholerically*. Finally he lumbered over – 'Mr Fowler?'

'No.' Some sixth sense told me not to identify myself.

Just before four o'clock he shambled off up the main staircase – clearly to attend, in all probability to supervise, the selection process.

Scattered about the room sat other candidates. Two of them greeted each other with braying declarations, plainly false, of affection and respect. Standard Party Conference templates; i.e. not very big, not very masculine. Spectacles, new-looking suits, tightly-knotted ties. For much of the time I looked at the ceiling – but *intelligently*, like Richthofen's dog, Moritz.

Only one of these characters was actually seen back down stairs by an escorting bigwig. I recognised Michael Howard, much plugged in the broadsheet press as *thrusting*, a barrister, a high-flyer certain to enter the new Parliament, etc.[2]

The bigwig held him in 'politician's grip'; one hand holding his, the other on Howard's elbow. Not necessarily a good sign, more

---

[1] Michael Heseltine, MP for Tavistock since 1966. Rather than fight one of the reorganised seats in west or south-west Devon, he took the opportunity presented by the changes in constituency boundaries to find a seat nearer London. At the February 1974 election he was elected MP for Henley.

[2] Michael Howard had unsuccessfully fought Liverpool Edgehill in 1966 and 1970. In fact AC was wrong in his forecast. Howard did not finally enter the Commons until 1983, when he won the Folkestone and Hythe seat, thereby becoming the Clarks' Member of Parliament, as Saltwood is in the constituency.

usually an indicator of impending betrayal of some kind.

However – 'Well done', I overheard. 'You'll be hearing from us very shortly ...'

That's that, then. All sewn up. Except, who the hell is 'Mr Fowler'[1]?

Saltwood   *Saturday, 27 May*

The Plymouth interview was a great success.

Graham Butland and David Holmes[2] brought the crib of the set questions to my germ –, as opposed to smoke-filled room. Euphoria and might even have carried the whole thing on the spot – but (according to Graham) a serious decline set in over the weekend; certainly I took an instant dislike to that little 'christian' sub-agent,[3] with his long, but grey-streaked hair – and he reciprocated and spread it round. Apparently 'nigger in the woodpile' was Betty Easton[4] – curious as I should have thought she would be a push-over; I answered her question (about tactics) at greater length than any other. Only explanation I can think of is she now wants Fowler (ex Adley, adopted somewhere else[5]) and sees me as a threat. Next step is a 'cocktail party' for wives, the speech and Q&A session – the very idea makes my stomach turn over. My chances rated low. But anything-can-happen-in backgammon/politics. Throw 4x4, 1x1, 6x6; Fowler gets adopted elsewhere etc. I must press on – that special elation I felt on the Plymouth train after the interview, one is quite charged. Else I am just doomed to sit here, grumblingly reading about those dreadful appeasement collapses of our society (just like 1937–39, with the mass of the party appallingly disreputable in their private complacency) and declining. Lines all over my face. Girls don't even look twice.

---

[1] Norman Fowler, MP for Nottingham South since 1970, but his seat would be disappearing at the next general election as a result of the boundary revisions.

[2] Like Butland a leading light in the Sutton Conservative Association.

[3] P.J. Latimer, the Sutton association agent.

[4] Mrs R.M. Easton, a pillar in Plymouth Conservative circles, who later became the city's Lord Mayor; married to Rodney Easton.

[5] Robert Adley had been MP for Bristol North-East since 1970, but with boundary revisions needed a new seat. The Sutton favourite until selected for Christchurch and Lymington.

Saltwood   *Wednesday, 14 June*

Went to Plymouth for the 'lives' after some shrewd publicity in *The Times*[1] and a huddled but productive conference in mid-week in Horrabridge with my contacts. The previous days had been consumed by incredible driving sagas (*ae?*), picking up the Cadillac at Soton, bringing it to Saltwood, down to Broomhayes, to Bratton (stopped twice by police), then over to Plymouth and back.

That evening I was dead flat. The speech a flop, response tepid. We went to bed early, in daylight, and slept 'more tired than I have been before or since ...'

But next day, the good news. Voting was 10. 11. 9 for Fowler, Hunt, Clark. Final stage now scheduled for Friday, 30 June at Duke of Cornwall Hotel. For a few hours thought I am going to make it. All the Devon-Bratton-Tuppish-Colwyn Bay pent-up magic must be activated to bring it about. But by now losing confidence. Key element, the speech.

Saltwood   *Wednesday, 21 June*

Poor night following refusal of planning permission on field – tho' almost with relief I thought ... 'now no obligation to try to be an MP'.

Darling 'Boy' upstairs with bad chickenpox – 'outside' possibility of encephalitis, which has reduced me to a total jelly.

Alan Cleverley rang to say that it was being put about that [Alan was] 'throwing his money around trying to buy the Constituency ...'

---

[1] As early as 1968 *The Times* Diary column had revealed AC's political ambitions (the offer of an unnamed seat which failed to materialise); on 2 June 1972, under the heading 'Sutton hoo-hah', it disclosed that the Sutton association had upset Tory Central Office by proposing that candidates be invited to show their paces at a dinner or dance. Instead they substituted the 'lives', informal get-togethers with their spouses. AC was in a shortlist of five that also included two future Cabinet ministers: Norman Fowler and David Hunt, national chairman of the Young Conservatives. Fowler, thanks in part to being an MP already, was seen as the front-runner, AC as 'the most obvious alternative', although, said *The Times*, 'he seems to be suffering from his Monday Club tag at a time when he is viewed in the Monday Club as soft on Rhodesia.'

Bad augury. If God inspires me that evening I can go between them (Fowler & Hunt) that I know.

Saltwood   *Thursday, 22 June*

'Mounting' opposition to development of the cricket field, a likelihood of council throwing it out; sale of Woodfall Street[1] fallen through; heavily overbought in SE with 'climate' moving against me. Obviously heading for a bad trough – hold tight, stay calm and systematic and try to see it through. Nothing really matters if dear Boy is preserved OK.

Saltwood   *Saturday, 1 July*

Yesterday was the most memorable of my life with the exception of James being born on 13 II 60.

Of course it is easy enough now to look back and say that I knew I'd get it – all the Bratton magic, the fore-ordained aspect of it all. I can only say that the moment when Tom Bridges[2] gestured to Doc Mac and Howard Davies to console the other two – well! Like a Miss World contestant for a few minutes I couldn't believe it was actually happening to me, and didn't what you might call 'come to' until the Press were taking pictures and data. Then there was the 'repeat convivial' down in the bar. I was on air. Talking to Tom about how 'fairly' the election had been done; slit-eyedly warning M (what's-his-name?); sincerely agreeing with the Macmillans;[3] then a final post-mortem in the street with David Holmes and Graham Butland. At last up to darling Jane who received one in triumph, a *nuit guise* from *sheer elation*.

The next day the early train, and off at Westbury to pick up the

---

[1] London property in SW3, originally owned by Jane Clark, its sale is a running saga through these pages.
[2] The Sutton association chairman.
[3] Dr John Macmillan [Doc Mac] and his wife Pat, members of the Sutton committee, became the Clarks' closest constituency friends.

Bira.[1] It broke down outside Marlborough and I walked for about
two miles to a phone box, stumbling in my buckled candidate shoes
on the hot (though intermittently cloudy) July day. I didn't mind at
all; my mind just went over and over the wonderful fabulous fact that
I had been adopted for a safe seat. Confidence totally restored in
myself and in God's help – if you deserve it. It was the God question
that won it for me, that clinched it. Before I had my turn, on arrival
in room 24, I had opened the bible for a snap quotation, got the
miracle of the loaves and fishes.[2]

There is a long road ahead, if I am to do everything I wish, I am
still a little late – but Oh! I have got two months – the adoption not
till September. Get everything tidied and sorted, build up strength,
regenerate.

Saltwood   *Wednesday, 19 July*

Last night during the great summer storm that woke us three times I
felt a strange, but powerful sense of depression, an impossibility of
looking forward, almost as if there was a death imminent (like Jason's[3]).
This may be a reaction from the intense happiness of the last 2½ weeks
(it seems an age) which I can still rekindle in all its intensity by reading
that item in *The Times* of July 3[4].

At least the new series[5] can open with an achievement, a *real* turning
point. I was worried that we were going to run out of paper and book
and things still the same – purposeless, frustrating, impossibility of
getting interviewed while all the good seats were slowly absorbed by
the huge demand. Jane, I know, was if not losing heart then at last

[1] Bentley, originally owned by and named after Prince Bira.
[2] Norman Fowler was eventually selected for Sutton Coldfield, which he won in the
    February 1974 general election. David Hunt had a rockier road: chosen not long after
    as Tory candidate at the neighbouring – and more marginal – Plymouth Drake
    constituency, he was rejected at his adoption meeting after criticising Enoch Powell at
    the party conference two weeks before. He did not finally become a Tory MP (for the
    Wirral) until a by-election in 1976.
[3] Jane Clark's yellow labrador. The day he was run over and killed by a milk lorry she
    had a premonition that something terrible was going to happen.
[4] Announcing AC's selection.
[5] As described in the Introduction, AC had just started using the 'Katoomba' volume in
    which to keep his diary.

questioning (and not always silently) the whole waste of time. And so much better than getting Langstone with a permanent bad taste in the air: qv Peter Rees[1] (intoned solemnly at dinner), '... if you have a marginal seat your enemies are the Socialists. But in a safe seat – your enemies are Conservatives.'

Saltwood   *Thursday, 3 August*

Somewhat depressed – what's it all in aid of? Just want to be civilised and scholarly and mean in these surroundings, 'working' the place for cash, a little lechery, keeping fit, some b'gammon in London, a little trading in the Mews. Key thing to protect the boys (Tip worryingly asthmatic lately, in spite of visit to quiet-spoken homeopathic doctor). In fact now faced with massive prospects of 'commitment' building up to crazy level after election.

Zermatt   *Friday, 25 August*

One of those days when just everything is falling in at once. Incredibly hot and sunny – yet no point in it really, it took too much yesterday going to the Schönbuhl Hut. Today sitting about disconsolate. ('Daisy' here and plying one with drink in between *ludicrous* deep blaspheming.) Depressed, shaken by Correlli Barnett's *The Collapse of British Power*.[2] Lilian so pale and round-shouldered. He *must* do his exercises daily. 'Daisy' successfully jeering at what I am making on the stock market. Jane crying because the children are so rude. I was briefly hysterical in response this morning in the hall, after a bad night in the dressing room; absurd, unbelievable how I am losing money at backgammon against 'Daisy'. And finally of course, and most ominous, being de-gazumped over the cricket field. A fitting little problem

---

[1] Peter Rees, QC, MP for Dover since 1970 and a sounding board for AC's political ambitions.

[2] This disturbing study of the decline of British influence between the two world wars by a leading British historian had just been published.

(BUT REMEMBER SUTTON! Although plenty of time for that to go sour before the adoption meeting.)

Saltwood   *Sunday, 17 September*

A note of my adoption meeting at the Duke on Friday (15th):

We had spent the previous two days at Carlyon Bay, delightful, evocative, appropriate. I had done the traditional clamber along the rocks to my old sunbathing place of 1947, and walked down the road to the 'Riviera Club' which I so well remember when I used to go up and down in the black SS100 and that woman, greyish, semi-crazy in her big Buick cabriolet. At high tide I rolled up my trousers and walked about that hard, granulated sand. I stood first on the long rock at the western end that one never notices at low tide and watched the waves come streaming in, and felt Carlyon Bay's momentous evocation. Nearly thirty years ago – but it could have been five – the burgeoning sexual desire, the endless hot days, the happy certainty that the future could only hold excellence and pleasure.

Left the speech-making/learning a little late and had a demi-panic at lunch in the hot enclosed front lawn at Bratton. However recovered, washed my hair and did my stuff in the Duke ball-room. First mike since Havant dinner way back – and I got a hang-up half way through. Lesson, don't get slack about prepositions. Link passages *must* be learned by heart.

Speech centred on violence, but all the publicity went to my answers on the Asians afterwards.[1] Gloom by many on the platform, Latimer, Easton, Bridges among them, but *response* from the hall; stayed till the bitter end beer drinking. A good feeling. Afterwards Peter Latimer reproached me for a 'Monday Club speech' instead of a political generality.

---

[1] 'The Tory Party should capitalise on the public outcry against the coming influx of Ugandan Asians and ban all further coloured immigration', was how the *Western Morning News* reported AC's remarks next morning.

Zermatt   *Tuesday, 3 October*

Over here for a couple of days to ruminate. I had been looking forward to this, hoping for some lovely high walks with the rocks dark against navy-blue sky, but my peace of mind somewhat spoiled by the sad death on Saturday evening walk with Col,[1] of dear Grandee.[2] Evidently he had a stroke (similar to that attack of paralysis which he suffered about three weeks ago in the kitchen) and drowned in the stream in the far valley, the one I am trying to get from Ann, but she is resisting.

I didn't give it a thought at first when they started a slight hue and cry, he has so often been lost before and the last I had seen of him, quite close to home, with his nose to the ground picking up a scent. But when dinner-time came and he still hadn't turned up I knew, secretly, the worst. We had walked the full round of the Wakefield Trust that evening, and at the top of the crest I had lifted the fence for the beagles to go underneath. Gangster went straight through, but Grandee stopped and thanked me – he *always* thanked one, but this was something special, quite soppy, he put both his paws up and almost looked unhappy (as I now realise looking back). Then he went on seemingly jolly as ever. But he had been saying good-bye. I am so glad he did.

Jane looked for him by the lights of the Mehari, while I was watching *The Two Ronnies* (mediocre), then after a silent supper we went out again and I found him in the stream, very near where I had last seen him with his fine glossy coat quite dry, rigid in the 'show' position, but his poor little muzzle choked and jammed with mud and grass. I do hope he didn't struggle for too long, didn't feel abandoned. We brought him back, and dug the grave straight away, by the Barbican where he can keep an eye on the comings and goings.

How I hate that moment when the earth goes down on the body (he was shrouded in his red blanket with his steel dish and dinner buried beside him). One must have faith, but haunting me is the endless journey, faster than the speed of light, of the soul into infinity.

Anyhow the death of the beagle reminded me very forcibly (and Heaven knows, it is never very far below the surface) of how very vulnerable we all are; those lovely boys and, just lately, the old-head-

---

[1] AC's brother, Colin.
[2] Grandee and Gangster, the beagles.

of-the-house has been somewhat breathless and suffering from back
pain and potential dizziness. Hope not heading for a great bleak
autumn and winter of hypochondria like '63. Yet, looking back, just
as today's 'appeasement' of violence etc is nothing as bad as that of
the '30s (vide Correlli Barnett) so one forgets how awful that Bratton
hypochondriac effect was, how concerned I was that I was punished.
Ah well.[1]

Saltwood   *Saturday, 21 October*

Back after a very wearing week. Monday Truro (on night train) for
driving disqualification. Six months. Bah! Tuesday up again plus Jane
for night at the Howards (lose £120 to Charles), early train to
Plymouth for WAC[2] lunch. Had sudden late thought, tribute to Dame
Joan,[3] paid it fulsomely and rewarded by excellent quote in *Western
Morning News*. Friday down to Plymouth for Girls School speech in
afternoon. They universally hostile and brainwashed into a whole
series of 'progressive' clichés. The fattish, not unattractive one (Sally)
questioned one tenaciously about colour and then the dark one raving
on about general Tory principles, continuing with tea and cakes in
the common room afterwards. The dark one had done the vote-
of-thanks, very prettily, as she stood, and I had warmed to her
acknowledging our mutual hostility; but that night in the sleeper back
I nearly had a WD playing around with her and getting increasingly
'hot'. This has made me very keen to see her again. I wonder if she
felt it at all?

   Then on to Bratton, and a momentary *crise* because Jane locked the
Bentley doors with the keys inside, entailing scrabbling with knives
and copper wires; hair wash, change and in to Lewtrenchard (dinner

---

[1] AC's father wrote in his memoirs about his own experiences of hypochondria, which
   had their origins, he suggests, in what the French call '*accidie, maladie des moines*': 'For
   some years I believed intermittently, but with absolute conviction, that I was dying of
   paralysis. Like the greatest of my fellow sufferers, Dr Johnson, I went for immensely
   long walks, in the hope that the fatigue would comfort me ... but nothing could get
   the idea out of my head. My own hypochondria was deep rooted enough to reappear
   two or three times in later life.' (*Another Part of the Wood*.)
[2] Women's Advisory Committees of the three Plymouth constituency Conservative
   associations.
[3] Joan Vickers, MP for Devonport since 1955 (DBE, 1964).

dance). Not a *great* success, eg I wasn't introduced properly (if at all), my speech (by Jane's account) lacked 'punch', and I did only one dance to two-step rhythm – it, in fact, being a waltz. Was somewhat depressed – people at Crownhill totally clueless, one of them saying it was 'a dicey seat' etc; but particularly by universal hostility at Plymouth High. Are the young really like this?

A girl, a slim dedicated Marxist, asked me why I was like I was, what motivated me. 'Because I am British,' I said, 'because I want to advance and protect the British people.' 'So what's so special about the British?' she answered, 'what makes them so different from everybody else?' Well I could have answered that what makes them different from anyone else, is the capacity they seem to have for producing at every level of society, people like yourself who ask a question like that. But I get a dark foreboding, sometimes; I feel it at Saltwood as people encroach more and more, with higher sense of justification, on the boundaries and fences – 'it's not right that something so important/ beautiful/interesting/historic should belong to one man ...' There are the boys with their patriotic instincts quite natural, also the sense of privilege and assurance – but will they be able to hold it or will they be crushed before they get an innate strength and cunning such as I have? And what does the future hold for me? How far will I go? Will I be assassinated, or die venerated and venerable, or crabbed and embittered? I don't want to die anyway, at all, and hope it's a long way off.

Must not neglect the physical by the way. This bloody back of mine always lurking inhibiting me from doing all the exercises I need. Stomach at last weakening, ravaged lines (in some lights) on face. On Thursday last week went for a run along the front in my new track suit, did 3km+ by the 2CV speedo and plunged in the sea – felt marvellous. Now the week has changed course. High winds and drizzle, pool temperature 52°.

Saltwood   *Thursday, 26 October*

Extremely depressed. Compounded by fatigue (down to Seend, then London and backgammon – inc tournament – financially disastrous of course). The autumn, the late autumn nearly always affects me like this – another bright beautiful happy year gone; can another ever be the same, is it the decline from now on? Terrible weakness of arms and shoulders, also less spring going upstairs, must have some way round the back trouble so as to try and build up a little 'peck' and shape.

Poor Gangster now terribly slow and creaky and stumbly on the walks. It doesn't seem so long ago that he had that beautiful galloping movement, so much better than poor dear Grandee's Beatrix-Potter lollop. It is so depressing, the inevitable, inexorable decline of physical healing and prowess – the most obvious, the most implacable evidence of the slowly approaching grave imminently closer with each turn of the globe.

Also lowered by Ann refusing to sell the valley, blast her. I think of that beautiful romantic hidden valley, and it lowers me that it should be owned by someone who is only holding on for 'Chunnel' appreciation.[1]

Also, *inevitably*, complications on the sale of the cricket pitch. Now apparent (2 days before completion) that C. Club lease must be surrendered. Club secretary on holiday. Also doubted on whether partial completion desirable, to gain benefit of selling on. Absolutely stretched to the limit with Hoare & Co and expensive cars (Campbell Mercedes etc) coming in on Monday. Gloomy.

Saltwood   *Friday, 17 November*

Just back, very tired and drawn (lines really gone cataclysmically into the face this year, one of those deep seismic coups that alter one's appearance, like their first onset in 1951) from the candidates' conference at St Stephen's Club.

Turned up at the Conference. Status (political majority) of course important – tho' I believe probably not so much, if at all, once one is in the House. Francis Pym[2] gave first lecture. V formidable, somewhat humourless, a particularly exhausted face. A giver of 'short shrift'. I asked him a question and he barked his answer (it related to inexperience and loyalty, hm!). 'I don't know you. I expect I will know

---

[1] AC's suspicion about the Channel Tunnel proved quite untrue. The stone that marks his grave came from the valley.

[2] Francis Pym, MP for Cambridgeshire since 1961 and Chief Whip since 1970.

you ...' Then we had Terence Higgins,[1] cheeky, bright little expert on VAT. Drinks in the bar and I chatted up Webster;[2] he even offered me a cigar. Hard to tell what he was thinking. I may have given too much away, about the Monday Club, Sutton's desire for independence etc. After lunch I dozed in an armchair at the back.

In the evening, drinks and dinner, the PM spoke.[3] Excellent, fluent, tho' obviously tired. Occasional flashes of dry wit. A bit political with the questions – particularly that on strikers' benefits. Afterwards caught the eye of that little piece and she asked 'what sort of seat' Sutton was. 'Winnable' said Doreen, who was with her – quite put me out and I left the St Stephen's rather depressed and tired.

Saltwood   *Sunday, 26 November*

Gloomily contemplating collapsing looks and physique; derelict sex-life; continuing state of flux on field hence total standstill on such things as decorating, improving, protecting Saltwood. Purchase of the great 38/250 ex Malcolm Campbell, a most important car, means must rationalise down to eight in the collection, plus a few favourites (such as the XK) plus trading oddments. Can get by with a bit of scratching, sell about 20,000 worth of cars, possibly Woodfall. Still a whole list of the outgoings: the shop for little Mrs Clarke,[4] various bills on cars, overdrafts. Only consolation, Zermatt almost eliminated so 'v'-sign to UBS[5] at last; they even have security somewhat diminished by expiring of permits etc. Thinking of death, disease, famine and bankers' orders.

---

[1] Terence Higgins, MP for Worthing since 1964, he had not long been Financial Secretary to Treasury.
[2] Sir Richard Webster, Director of Organisation, Conservative Central Office since 1966.
[3] Edward Heath, MP for Bexley since 1950, Leader of the Conservative Party since 1965 and Prime Minister since 1970.
[4] The Clarks were buying the shop in Saltwood village.
[5] Union Bank Suisse, which had loaned money to AC to build the Clarks' Zermatt chalet.

All Souls, Oxford   *[No date] November*

John's[1] Scout has brought me tea and digestive biscuits. The room is comfortable, but not warm.

Yesterday I was in confident form. I had been invited to address a Bow Group dinner, black tie, good claret (or so I would assume), F.E. Smith in his early days. My apotheosis. But the Bow Group are just a bunch of arse-lickers really. Creepy little aspirant candidates who tremble at the thought, still less the sound of someone Right Wing. And they have one other thing in common, namely that they all want to enter Parliament. In the past they used to shun me, probably on instruction from Central Office, but now here I am with, having been adopted for Plymouth Sutton, something of an *edge*. Plus the delight of being based in the Warden's lodging. Plus with a black Bentley convertible parked in the quad.

Dear John. I remember walking with his affectionate arm draped around me in Brewer Street on a summer evening in 1948, when I was a clever but *extremely* feckless undergraduate, and his saying that perhaps I really 'ought' to have a shot at becoming a Fellow. It was rather lovely, this diffident homosexual advance, and I was complimented, like I used to be at Eton; though not, of course, in the slightest bit 'aroused'. At the time I didn't like the sound of All Souls. No girls and no racy company. But quite soon afterwards I regretted having done nothing. I'm sure John could have fixed, or demi-fixed, it for me. Although his advice on preparing for the exam – '*Re*-(sic)-read Ranke's *History of the Popes*' – was a little daunting.

John had always, though, a certain private sense of mischief for which he was notorious and of which his guests expected at least one ritual demo. This time it took me completely by surprise. Freshly bathed and in a black tie I had meandered into the Warden's drawing room, hoping for a *firm* gin and tonic before going down to Hall and meeting the (presumably mixed) Bow Groupers. There, standing by the piano looking quite beautifully bouffed and powdered, was Harold Macmillan,[2] an old friend of John (John had worked for him against

---

[1] John Sparrow, Warden of All Souls College, Oxford, whom AC had known since his childhood.

[2] Harold Macmillan, now aged seventy-eight, had been Chancellor of Oxford University since 1960. He was Prime Minister for six years from 1957 and retired from active politics at the 1964 general election.

Rab[1] when the question of succession had arisen in 1956) and clearly the guest of honour that evening at high table (a grander dinner than the one I was to attend).

'Ah,' said John. 'Here's Alan Clark. He is proposing to stand for Parliament ...'

I simpered, deferentially offered my hand.

'... on a platform that advocates denying the franchise to persons of the Jewish persuasion.'

Macmillan neither smiled nor frowned. Very, very briefly he looked at me. Pale hooded eyes. No point, I judged, in saying anything, although it was so monstrous that I got a short *fou-rire*. 'I'm talking to the Bow Group,' I offered weakly.

Saltwood   *Sunday, 3 December*

Now the 'prophet's' visit. Powell[2] down for the day to chat, advise and hold forth! He was benevolent, articulate, by no means cagey, but somehow impenetrable. I *really* don't know what he thought of me – though clearly 'raw', naïve, inexperienced etc were among them. He cautioned me against too high a degree of personal commitment to the Conservatives in Sutton; also against saying things outside the Party line prior to the election ... 'as a candidate you have no constitutional position'. Would not say how he hoped to attain power, '... the Lord will provide.' Right, he often is, clever he undoubtedly is, but whether he has that sheer finishing touch which Conservatives have to have to get to the top I don't know.

At least I started his car for him, forcing him (to everyone's amazement) to give up the driving seat after many ineffectual yur-yurrings (vet with *chien méchant*) and it fired second time.

---

[1] R.A. ['Rab'] Butler had twice hoped to become leader of the Conservative Party: in 1956 when Anthony Eden resigned from ill-health in the aftermath of Suez; and in 1963, when Macmillan resigned (ill-health again, but prematurely as it turned out) and Lord Home was chosen. Home renounced his peerage and as Sir Alec Douglas-Home became Prime Minister. Butler was now Master of Trinity College, Cambridge.

[2] Enoch Powell, MP for Wolverhampton SW since 1950. AC shared many of his views, particularly on immigration.

Poor James *again* broke his leg today – allegedly green stick, but low
down in the ankle and causing him a lot of pain. His fault – he had
been skiing *beautifully* on the Rothorn and Tuftern, then full of
confidence on his new Atomics, but led, far too fast, on the road and
fell just before Patrilav. I came round the corner and he was howling.
When I noticed, I broke down, and cried, screamed, blamed poor
Tip, who, it turned out wasn't really (much) to blame as James was
miles ahead.

Tip and I left Jane with him and skied down, self crying out loud –
'it seems an age', telephoned from Sunegga, up again, skied down just
as they were loading him on, terribly pale and shaking. Apparently it
won't be so long as the last one, but bang goes the training session,
the session that was going to get him really set up and boost his
confidence and health. Yesterday he was so languid that I bawled him
out in the evening, and today dear little chap he was good as gold,
starting by calling up with our tea.

I was in a filthy temper yesterday – no proper lunch, low-grade
intercourse with banks, brokers etc. Still, no right to grizzle the way
I did, and was still grumpy (until tight) at the Tenne that evening.

Still, all one can say is it *could* have been worse; I thought it was,
much worse and prayed – but hopelessly – to God let it be all right
and he did as well as we could expect. Don't know when you are well
off, Clark. Be conservative, orderly, don't over-reach. Must follow
through, get everything set up so that if I go boys will have ready-
made structure waiting to take-over.

1973

A month gone by. 'Daisy' came for Christmas and it went as well as could be expected, he not so glittering and effervescent as formerly and so less attractive. Kindly gave me a PIII catalogue[1] (bought from Charles Howard), but a little too homosexual now, less interesting, more boasting. Christmas itself quite good. Got Jane a gold-bar in her stocking. Then two set-backs. My back briefly popped when bending down to undo my shoes leaving me crazily twisted and immobilised. I caught a short, sharp cold from the silly, titty little masseuse.

We decided to go home early, and the day before our departure James went to have his confirmatory x-ray which revealed that the bone had slipped a bit and should be reset under a general anaesthetic. We returned to the surgery later that night (he had to wait some hours for the food, water to be digested). Naturally he was apprehensive. The hall of Gentinettas's[2] was dimly lit, noone was about. Slowly the personnel gathered, junior actors first, and a nurse gave him an Atropine injection in the behind – unheralded and unwelcome. Then it deteriorated fast: the two specialists wrenched the plaster off, muttering imprecations at their predecessor who had put it on so tightly. James – horrified – gasped and groaned with pain and simulated pain. Madame Gentinetta played her part in the 'you-must-be-brave' role as she prepared the gas. When they finally put James under we retired, Jane broke down in the waiting-room and I couldn't stand it, but took our things back to the chalet where Tip had already retired (he was incubating flu).

The next day we travelled.

Tremendous longueurs in Brig where we had four hours to wait because I had to catch Previdoli before the UBS closed.

Tip was drowsy and flushed. Boy drawn and apprehensive. That waitress came over, she really waits in the 2ieme classe, but she recognised me, *still* (although, as is the way, she seemed much altered and aged and only her aura identified her). I took a walk, and my footsteps led me, although in the dark, out of the town and up the hill to where, so suddenly, it becomes the Simplon Pass. My mind worked freely back to that first time in the middle fifties – the XK, the brown Dienst (what a sturdy little car that was), the grey,

---

[1] Rolls-Royce Phantom.
[2] The Zermatt doctors.

honeymoon Dienst, the Citroen Safari, the blue 220, the silver
Porsche, the '600'. In the early days that sudden happy realisation, on
the return journey, that one was back in the clear air of beloved
Switzerland; good-looking, seething with youth in the Buffet at Brig,
but, as she said, 'bourgeois devil'. No need of company to reassure
me (all that finally extinguished by the enforced solitary 'messing' at
Eton).

The rest of the journey was a misery as Tip ran a high temperature
and deteriorated at nightmare speed so that one had to give penicillin
from the emergency pack. Once arrived, he made an amazing recovery – but what a reversal! Jane got flu, then I got it; or was/is it flu?
A highly violent upper respiratory infection, leading to at least one
day of feverish coma, but had it to shake-off. Got horribly depressed,
achingly so, as I contemplated the scene. Rung up by Graham Butland
this evening with news that 'some disgust' in the constituency at my
non-publicity/attendances. All bound up with life pattern for this
year.

Saltwood   *Wednesday, 14 February*

Dreadful blustery day, cold snow showers whip-lashing. Tip back in
bed, very peaky and lost weight with those strange evening temperatures – could be a hang-over from his 2nd dose of flu, but both
boys (telepathically) questioned one closely about TB last night. Oh
dear. James now out of plaster, but much scarred by his experiences –
said yesterday at breakfast 'I am giving up skiing'. I suppose he will
recover once he gets the feel of it again, I remember it took me years
to get over my fear of soft snow after cracking my ankle at Wengen.

Now here I am at a chaotic desk, having given up my intention of
a five-day break in Zermatt, and determined to restore some order in
a 'Mens Sana' 4 days here. I cannot decide whether to go forward or
backward on either cars or property, ie do I buy from Danny the
Blower $4\frac{1}{2}$ and the 3 litre on BE tyres or do I retrench, take my money
on the Benz and just keep the small collection? Do I press forward
and buy the nursery and the Payne site in Prospect Road and offer
the whole (ie plus Newmans and Baileys) for 120? Or do I just take
the 35 for Newmans and back of Baileys and de-escalate?

Had a fairly beastly exchange with Hoare's over stumping up for the Benz. Change of attitude on their part, made me feel uncomfortable, has the cricket field money been dissipated quite so quickly?

All these things have generated massive decision-headaches. Also, fairly heavy political activity (not before time). Fortunately had a piccolo success at the Bickleigh Down meeting on the eve of the Western Area Conference. The food, though, was terrible. Feminine company negligible except for the young daughter of that ridiculous ego-woman from Tavistock who boldly hung about – were we establishing a rapport? In the lift she said (2ⁿᵈ day) 'This can't hold eight people, surely?' 'Bags I stand next to you if it does,' I said. From that time on our relations improved.

Am prepared to buy the Constituency the East End club, but Graham Butland went slit-eyed. 'Association wouldn't want to be tied to a candidate through the Club.' Of course one major flaw does hang over one – *actually losing the seat!*

Saltwood   *Saturday, 31 March*

Glorious day (as usual) emphasising deep gloom and malaise. Indigestion night (first for years) and today Andrew – who has been very well until just recently in one of his pale, prowling listlessly, hanging-around-and-trying-to-catch-my-eye conditions which are obviously pre-temperature. This to give 'full house' of troubles and complicate – or indeed abort – Spanish trip itself desperately close in the is-it-quite-reliable '600' following an incomplete rushed job at Mercedes, a mad drive to Plymouth and back for Papa's Romney lecture and canvassing. Am going through disappointing phase at Plymouth, not seen enough, enough publicity etc; people openly saying they will vote Liberal. Finally broken with Valeri/Ali.[1]

---

[1] Variously described as 'the coven', the 'blondes', and the 'i's' – three girls (the third was Joei) related to each other by blood whom AC knew for many years.

Benalmadena   *Sunday, 8 April*

Arrived last night after wearing drive – hands blistered from holding the big white plastic wheel (of the '600') for hour after hour. Beuttler[1] villa very nice, marvellous growth – wisteria etc. Interior improved by decent English furniture. Spain revolting, though individual Spaniards reasonably anxious to please. Architecture, pollution, simply awful.

Journey out was plagued by blocked fuel filters. Changed at Paris, inspected at Bordeaux, packed up in Madrid rush-hour. Total nightmare sequence supervened (memorable land-mark in horror experience) no tools, no language, no *garages*, 7.30pm and sweating, *no map* (so no idea where we were etc etc). Pleasant shop-owner, obliging taximan etc brought apparent relief in due time, though further intervening horrors (mechanic trying to butcher the '600', me wondering where Jane and the children had got to – after blithely packing them into taxi and saying 'Excelsior', calling on totally strange man's flat and asking for telephone directory etc.) before at last oasis of Ifa Hotel.

Here money insulation worked. Food, service (Mercedes mechanic came out next day, changed filter etc). Back on the road at 11am and great heat drive. Andrew had been sick the day before but gamely pulled round. James however incredibly stressed and puffy-looking, slit-eyed and soft-spoken. I have worried on so many holidays about him and it 'turning out all right', but this time seems even worse, with this morning him just listlessly reading, looking terrible with recurrence of watch allergy spot on his wrist. We shared a room in the Ifa and I thought how much I loved him, just getting pleasure from looking at his little top notch of hair showing above the sheets.

Talking about air-travel (I had postulated different planes for the return journey) he said touchingly but alarmingly, that he rather we all die together; he was near to tears. The next morning I tried to explain that the line must go on, that one day one of us must do something for his country that merited a column as high as Nelson's.

While writing weather has deteriorated. Now totally overcast and windy. Grey-watered twice, feeling sickish. Lost God-knows-how-much weight, sunken cheeks, match-stick forearms. Query cancer? How are we going to get home?[2]

---

[1] The home in Spain of Jane Clark's parents.

[2] AC provided the answer (written in December from memory) in what he called 'The Sequel': 'In fact we devised a route using entirely trains and sleepers; spending a day

Saltwood   *Wednesday, 16 May*

Nothing done, everything growing like crazy, tho' Cradduck still keeping garden looking fabulous. No drive, car parks, toilets, signs, garages *or any decoration at all* – visits start on May 28. American party on June 11. Headache.

I am concerned that relations with my parents may be deteriorating.

They were standing on the lower terrace. My mama *exceedingly* dreamy, of both tone and deportment. She swayed at a lavender bush. Then, turning to Jane, 'I never told Cradduck to cut that back'.

'But I employ Cradduck now, Mama.' I spoke very gently. In fact the shrub had barely been cut back at all.

'It's all wrong; all wrong.' Pulling at my father's cardigan (it was a very hot afternoon but he was wearing a cardigan) she set off back towards the bridge. He, sensing this was something not to be drawn into, smiled and mumbled.

That was yesterday. This morning we were in Canterbury. When we returned Mrs Yeo[1] said that they had both been over and 'gone upstairs'.

This has happened a great many times since my parents moved out. They lie awake in the Garden House and brood on the various items of 'contents' that they left behind. I think, but cannot be sure, that there was even a sort of verbal protocol agreed at the time of the conveyance that they should reserve a right of selection for items for which a 'need' became apparent. At the time it would have been graceless, as well as ill-judged, for me to turn this down. Already quite a few things, mainly books, they have retrieved.

Sometimes Lindley[2] (who fancies himself as an *antiquaiere manqué*) is sent over in the car to collect objects, which whenever practicable, he does without referring to us.

Anyway, this morning my father apparently made off with a very nice early XIXc whalebone box about a foot in diameter which carried charming ink-engraved Eskimo drawings of seals and hunters.

(again) at the Ifa – already forgotten by the staff in spite of being tipped massively. Memorable was the old-fashioned dining-car out of Madrid to Paris via Bordeaux. The great brown mountainsides in the failing light and the small station halts with their oil-lamp interiors and Goya-like attendants in upturned coat collars. How wonderful travel must have been when restricted to the few – the Grand Tour!'

[1] Mrs Yeo, housekeeper, who came with the Clarks from Seend.
[2] Lindley, the butler at the Garden House.

Jane loved this box, and was very upset. I found myself getting cross. I telephoned to the Garden House. My mother answered.

'So sorry we missed you this morning.'

'Papa had to come over and find a book.'

'He appears also to have taken the whalebone box which was in the dressing room.'

'Papa has always *loved* that box.'

'In that case why did he leave it behind when you made over the contents?'

My father took over. 'Oh God, God, don't say you are really making a fuss about the box?'

'No of course I'm not making a fuss. If you want the box, you must have the box. Jane is in tears, that doesn't matter at all. But ...' (I must *not* be so icy in tone, it's only one stage off bellowing in rage.) '... mightn't it be a good idea if we worked out exactly what is left here which still belongs to you ...?'

'I'll bring it straight back; I'll bring it back over now, immediately. Take, take, take ...'

Then Mama came on. 'How can you do this to Papa? All he wanted was that box ...'

'Keep the bloody box. I just would like to know what else he must have ...'

I went for a walk around the garden. An exquisitely beautiful evening, and all the birds singing goodnight.

Bratton   *Friday, 1 June*

'Prowling' about, came across the blue and white push-chair, Jolly's and almost wept as I recalled 'More Run' and the oggley-oggley noise 'Boy' made going round past Dick's hens. What did I feel so sad about? Would I was back then, I suppose, to play it again – yet I have been incredibly lucky, the inability to have more children the only blight.

Saltwood   *Saturday, 16 June*

Randily tired after a glorious hot day – about the fifteenth in succession – spent lounging around the pool, sneaking lecherous looks
at Andy, swimming nude, playing backgammon with Charles (won
£66) and admiring the incredible beauty of the place with the peacocks and the full foliage of the trees with the roses just about to burst.
An exquisite *douceur-de-vivre*. Also calm at having got out of the way
of three parties – US drinks here on Tues, Sutton 'workers' on Wed,
a R-R Enthusiasts send-off last night.

The Americans were 'numerous'; they strayed over the walls etc,
'most gracious of you' ... mumbled 'Doc' Goodman in his white
dinner jacket; some thought I was an Earl; they were uncertain of
how to address Jane. The Sutton workers were divine as always, my
speech started well, but got a bit guccky.

Shot at some intruders last night. Now over to office for 1½ (if I'm
lucky) hours on the telephone.

Broomhayes   *Sunday, 5 August*

Here on the way back from Bratton/Plymouth. Wet weekend and
winds; everyone rather pale. First, reasons for being low. Back, after
apparently slightly improving, very painful as both 'low back pain' *and*
no deviation of tightening down R. side and buttocks which makes
it agony in bed by about 5am. Apparently this is an osteo-arthritic
symptom and (I suspect) irreversible. My father in his memoirs says
that growing old (like growing up) is the progress from one *shelf* to
another, not a gradual ascent or descent, and with this new variant of
my back 'trouble' I have now descended another shelf. Another
reason, worried, in a kind of hopeless way, about the boys – particularly
James – being so sort of rotten and anarchic, languidly lacking in
initiative and yet very ready to take offence. In fact, noticeably poorer
in quality than one or even two years ago. James 'gets away with
things' (being quick and fly in retort) too easily and that coupled with
natural laziness leads him to dodge anything in the slightest bit arduous.
Yet without nourishment his intelligence, initiative, eagerness will all
wither. He's such a dear, I do hope it 'turns out all right'. I don't
quite know what I ought to do.

Third reason: the 'Liberal revival'. They are simply picking off the
safe seats in the by-elections. Ludicrous. May be different in a General
Election,[1] although at present so much momentum that looks bad –
certainly Sutton no longer a cake-walk, a three-corner marginal that
needs a lot of work. Very fortunately Banks[2] a little pimple of a
candidate really, chosen when the whole thing was just a joke, and
now they are lumbered with him, hair-lip and all – 'sympathy vote'
John Miller[3] quietly asserted during dinner. I've lost quite a bit of
money playing b'gammon lately. Suppose I'm all-square, having been
nearly £1,500 up at one stage this year.

Saltwood   *Saturday, 26 August*

Sitting in the Great Hall with 'low back pain' and stiffness (following
some fairly severe am-I-dying?-panics earlier this week including
'numb-foot' bringing the Citroen – dear Citroen – back from Wee
Bob heavily laden with Derby spares at night. Depressed about endless
pressures on time. So much to do on so many fronts – would really like
three-week holiday at the Corte just slumped in the deck-chair with
a series of good books – but not a hope. Plymouth always lurking,
not to mention Castle openings.

The fine weather proceeds, endlessly. Lounging (discontentedly)
by the pool this afternoon I started grousing to Jane about my plight
and, with her usual combination of wit and good sense, she tried to
sort me out. First rightly pointing to how much I already had, that to
most men was just greedy. Quite right, I must connect within my own
parameters. Then said – think how much 'time' spend sunbathing, no
wonder you're short of it.

Rightly pointed out that I am: (a) Relaxed millionaire and superimposing on that; (b) Gov. St Thomas' Hospital;[4] (c) Parliamentary

---

[1] The previous Thursday the Liberals won by-elections in two hitherto safe Conservative
seats: Isle of Ely (Clement Freud overturned a Conservative majority of 9,606 to win
by 1,470) and Ripon (where the Conservative majority of 12,064 became a Liberal
majority of 690 for David Austick). At the February 1974 general election Freud
retained his seat; Austick lost his.

[2] Simon Banks, Liberal candidate, who fought the seat in two elections

[3] John Miller, a member of the St James' Club.

[4] AC had been a Governor of London's St Thomas's Hospital since 1969, thanks to the
chairman, Hiram Winterbotham, a friend of Kenneth Clark's since the 1930s.

candidate for distant seat; (d) stately-home-owner; (e) car-dealer; (f) fighting single-handed battles with Council, developing property etc.

And yet if I was your (c) and (d), with just a little of (e) thrown in, there would be nothing creative going back; nothing in value for all that God has given one. I still think I should go flat out, go for the Monday Club choice, take in the whole lot, National Front and all.

I suppose it is this that really fills me with gloom – the prospect of sacrificing probably for ever, certainly until I am too old to enjoy it, the happy celebration of a secure and lazy family life for the unrelenting grind of a mission. Yet, I suppose I must do it. I checked on 'Boy', wanting to help him, but only realising too late that he was now ready to board and to stand on his own. Perhaps my back/leg is to show me the same here.

Zermatt   *Thursday, 6 September*

End of nice therapeutic week here enjoying the lovely air, sunshine and hill walks. *Just* managing the latter tho' back really no better, especially that frightful tightening down the R-side, and morning pains. But did achieve at least one memorable, and new, expedition to the Spitzflüh col while accompanied by dear, active, and incredibly fit young Tip. I could look down both the Tasch and Findeln valleys. I remember Euan[1] and I had turned back on this one some five or so years back when one came to the rock fall and the huge stones through which dear Tip guided me like a little goat by ably spotting the cairns. Otherwise fittish, tho' waist definitely showing first signs now as ability to do exercises virtually non-existent (even the mildest course of week one yoga makes me feel totally battered/supine). For the first time in my life, totally brown all over, buttocks, crotch, everything. Now somewhat apprehensive of 'next stage'.

Returning to financial problems – purchase of Newton Farm [in Cornwall] at 101 has used up whole P2 reserve[2] and at a time when pressed by grotesquely high interest rates (16%) and building 'improvements' at the Castle, both internal and external, and building of garages. Toy with idea of selling all flash cars, being left just with 'enthusiasts' stable – although somewhat of a pity just after beautiful

---

[1] Euan Graham, a friend since Oxford.
[2] A reserve fund from the sale of a Rolls-Royce P2 and other cars.

garages built. Might raise 100 that way. Also somewhat depressed prospect of work/boredom/reproaches in constituency; will my health return to being '100 per cent'; and, quite deeply, by James's failure to get into Eton.[1] Definitely in decline, visibly no new interests and the old ones being pursued less energetically. Tonight he is in disgrace after spilling – disastrously – bottle of unwashable ink in the sitting-room. Somehow I feel that second breaking of the leg was an important watershed, and release, for us all, and for him in particular.

What can I do about this? Should I send them to boarding school? How can I help both to excel and develop their interests and their sense of responsibility?

Bratton   *Monday, 17 September*

Good and bad. Back quite suddenly seems to have 'turned the corner' due, I suspect, to yoga. But generally seem to be hitting little (hopefully not about to be big) bad patch. Cradduck ill, allegedly glandular fever, and unlikely to be back in harness this year, if ever. Finance light, while the works accumulate around the castle, and my parents make comments on the telephone [which] seep back to me. Poor little darling Jane holding the fort at Saltwood (and opening *alone* tomorrow). I fear somehow that yet more blows will fall.

Been working very hard (for me) these last 10 days in the constituency. Did heavy canvassing this afternoon in the rain, scoring (I think) a good mark with Betty [Easton]. Also improving relations with Piggy Williams.[2]

Great Library, Saltwood   *Saturday, 13 October*

In my father's study and maudlin on an empty stomach with suspected latent salmonella – result of one mouthful of an appalling 'steak sandwich' at a road-side pub in Preston on the way back from the Blackpool conference.

---

[1] He had been accepted, but ploughed Common Entrance.
[2] Lyndon Williams, known as 'Piggy', the current Sutton agent.

Isn't Blackpool appalling, loathsome . . .? Impossible to get even a
piece of bread and cheese, or a decent cup of tea; dirt, squalor, shanty-
town broken pavements with pools of water lying in them – on the
Promenade – vulgar common 'primitives' drifting about in groups or
standing, loitering, prominently. The conference, not a specially happy
one. Bullying of the Right by the Heathites (self again not called; fifth
conference in a row). Heseltine, Peter Walker[1] wouldn't speak to
me; Sara Morrison[2] and Richard Webster chilly; even Ian Gilmour[3]
amusingly changing the subject. I *suppose* it will be all right on the
night. Williams has arranged a sequence of open-air meetings at which
I will have to perform. Apprehensive as to (a) my complete ignorance
of the 'answers' – ie all those balls statistics about the 'over eighties',
and the standard of living, and (b) letting down the Sutton crowd.
Their usual delegates came to Blackpool, but the dinner was more
subdued, fortunately the presence of the Turners (ie Osborne-
Turners) plus Williams and Mary-Rose offered lightning-conductors.

Went on television for *Points West* BBC and hope did some good,
though not plugging the Party line. Valeri there plus usual accoutrements of regularised intimacy which make me so jealous (in this case
a geriatric Great-Uncle in Holy Orders who is presumably being
cultivated for a hand-out). Really, too much. If one could paraphrase
Haig's epigram on Derby – the only good thing, incidentally, that the
F-M ever did – 'she is like a feather cushion, carrying the imprint of
the last person to roll on her.'[4]

Various other matters conspire to prevent me looking as smooth
and relaxed as, say, Heseltine: Tip still gets a lot of asthma, inc. *every*
Sunday without fail; crazy expenditure with three different contractors
now going full blast on the interior. We can *just* carry it, but long-
term prosperity heavily dependent on sale at a profit of Newton Farm

[1] Peter Walker, MP for Worcester since 1961, now Secretary of State for Trade and
Industry.

[2] The Morrisons were at this time a powerhouse within the Conservative Party. The
Hon. Sara Morrison, whose husband Charles had been MP for Devizes since 1964,
was in her second year as chairman of the party organisation; her father-in-law, Lord
Margadale, was, before being elevated to the Lords as a Baron, MP for Salisbury 1942–
64; she herself was the daughter of Viscount Long and Laura, Duchess of Marlborough;
and her brother-in-law, Peter Morrison, had been personal assistant to Peter Walker
and had just been selected as candidate for Chester.

[3] Ian Gilmour, MP for Norfolk Central since 1962, had been rising fast through the
junior ministerial ranks at Defence since 1970. Edited *The Spectator* (1954–59).

[4] Haig wrote to his wife in January 1918: that Derby bore 'the marks of the last person
who sat on him.'

(allegedly people still interested 'from the leisure aspect, Mr Clark' – who want to turn it into a golf course). Another heavy blow would be disqualification following the unsuccessful chase by PC James of the 550 Spyder on the Oxford bypass. 'That'll cut your capers' said Valeri, which it will; it will also make canvassing, and visiting much more exhausting, not to mention the strain of (2) school runs and life for Jane.

Saltwood   *Sunday, 11 November*

On top of all the crazy expenditure, just bought a beautiful Alma-Tadema at Sotheby's for £9,000 – suddenly got a demand for £28,000 to pay my father's Capital Gains Tax on the transfer of Saltwood.

Saltwood   *Wednesday, 14 November*

I have now been the prospective Parliamentary candidate in Plymouth for more than a year. I suppose it's all going to be ok. People, not just in Plymouth but at various kinds of political function keep saying 'You'll be all right'; by which, I suppose, they mean 'you will win the seat'. But I don't like the word 'safe'. Perhaps because I am super-stitious, or just wary of hubris. When Brian Somebody, a tiresome left-wing Fellow at All Souls, told [John Sparrow] that he wanted a 'long sabbatical' to go into Parliament and John inquired as to the putative constituency . . . said . . . 'It's a safe seat, of course.'

  To which John retorted, 'Safe? Safe . . .? Oh, you mean *unopposed*?'

  But I've got this feeling I'm not absolutely a billion percent welcome in this outfit; not, at least, in its present 'configuration'.

  Heigh ho. More fool them, I say.

Zermatt   *Wednesday, 19 December*

Lower than ever, after quite a good day yesterday. Had taken pain-killing drug (Distalgesic – sinisterly indicated for 'malignant conditions ... allowing the administration of morphine to be postponed') the previous night, after much intermittent waking at 5.50am and was puffily creased that morning, but after lunch, bathed, took evening walk and thought perhaps really getting better. Night virtually pain free (including 3.50am) until just before 6 when agony. However, fought through without Distal. Pain wouldn't go on pre-breakfast walk for papers and persisted until mid-day. After tea new site in side/hip coupled with pins-and-needles even while breathless walking. Now miserably sitting, with lowest Christmas since 1963 in prospect – only want to return to England, start serious medical treatment – Rowntree [family doctor] or homeopathy.

On my walk this morning looked with real longing at the perfect snow and piste of the little 'Home National'. It is a real deprivation for me not to be able to ski. All my fitness 'program' jeopardised. I must be in shape when I return at Easter – for the Election tone-up.

Zermatt   *Wednesday, Boxing Day*

A very good Christmas. Skied on the last day at Zermatt, and not such a disaster as might have been (though awful moment of side slipping – virtually didn't turn to the R at all). Back quite 'good' on the return journey. And since then have been almost too busy to 'dwell' on it although being very light or walks with Col and on the first of these I thought maybe I was going to be struck down with paralysis – like my poor mother, post-stroke in UCH with her left side paralysed and hopelessly depressed. She returns tomorrow by ambulance to the Hythe nursing home and then (putatively) to the Garden House and a regime with special beds, chairs and apparatus that can only end when she dies, but may project into the future for a very long time. My feeling – what a loss, ie 'loss' = 'nuisance' to us. But Jane, with her real *goodness* of nature, said quite naturally and spontaneously that we must all look after her as well as we can and hope that she never feels discarded or neglected before she dies.

1974

Low and grumpy and self-pitying after a late night, punishment at Aspinalls[1] losing £460 and bringing up my total losses to £820 certain. So now have 'given up b'gammon' following a self-denial chucking (or being chucked) by the 'i's and superimposing a certain amount of pure masochism – 'not drinking again until I have paid off all the money I owe ...' etc.

Prospect is gloomy, and not enhanced by my poor back: skiing being so handicapped; also the prospect of my poor Mama fading away in the nursing home though with her mind still beautifully clear and wittily cynical in the best style. What an irony that she so often feigned, for reasons of convenience, slurred speech and detachment – should now be quite literally stricken with it. What a cautionary tale for us all!

1974 is not going to be good – though how bad remains to be seen.

In tremendous form yesterday morning at prospect of election(!) on anti-union platform – v. good for Sutton prospects. Now total reversal; Heath lost his nerve at the last moment that afternoon, morale shattered,[2] John Miller took £96 off me at tea, I got drunk – boringly sitting between Harold Lever[3] and John Miller at Jimmy's[4] dinner and then lost £90 to Martin Summers and £570 to Harold after the cruel last 32 game when I had a 5.2 6.1 3.1 1.1 2.2 or any 4 for a certain victory. In an absolutely *furious* temper.

Jane tested me when I got back – 'you're never here' etc. We were

---

[1] John Aspinall founded a series of London clubs beginning with the Clermont in Berkeley Square. AC and Aspinall had first met at Oxford. In these diaries he is usually referred to as 'Aspers'.

[2] The Prime Minister threatened to call a general election if the miners' union, the NUM, failed to settle their pay claim.

[3] Harold Lever, Labour MP for Manchester Cheetham since 1950 (Manchester Exchange, 1945–50). Originally a barrister, he was a minister under Harold Wilson and chairman of the Public Accounts Committee in 1970.

[4] James (Jimmy) Goldsmith, a successful businessman, of Anglo-French parentage, chairman of Générale Occidentale SA Paris, and a friend of long-standing of AC's.

walking along the old railway line. Vowed to give up b'gammon.

Worried, too, naggingly, about my mother who is dying – each so-called 'good' day is so noticeably inferior to its predecessor. I'm not giving her enough time – she only really brightens up at all when I come in, and talks quite intelligently. Is irritated by my father who, in turn, can't understand her.

B5 Albany   *Friday, 25 January*

I was in Lister's[1] waiting room. One of my teeth aches periodically, and when I bend over I can feel a pulse in it. This must be bad. I have a feeling that you can get absolutely fearful, *terminal* blood poisoning from a bad tooth. Even if this is unlikely I do not want 'trouble' over the Election.

At the far end of the room an old gentleman wearing a mac was stooped over a *Times* which he rustled and page-turned in a rather ego, demonstrative, manner. Silvery hair, pebble-lens specs. Suddenly I realised who it was – *Uncle Harold*! – and walked across. I thought it more prudent not to remind him of our last meeting [see page 19] thinking in any case that mutual embarrassment and (in his case) very poor vision would occlude the recollection. 'Sir, can I introduce myself? Alan Clark, I am the prospective parliamentary candidate for Plymouth Sutton.'

'My dear boy! Well done, well done. Nancy Astor's old seat, well I never, sit down . . .' etc. He was incredible. Lucid, compos, clear and incisive of speech. Said the Election would be a disaster – 'The working class will see it as a loyalty vote . . .'; that there should be an Energy ministry with sweeping powers; that the miners had to be bought off until North Sea oil came on stream; that it should not be difficult to outmanoeuvre Len Murray;[2] that McGahey[3] wasn't popular in the TUC; that the real agitator was (*Scrimgeour* was it? – the words came thick and fast and I was transfixed[4]); that it was urgent to find

---

[1] AC's dentist.
[2] Len Murray, General Secretary of the TUC since 1973 (he had been with the TUC since 1947).
[3] Mick McGahey, Scottish miners' leader.
[4] Presumably Arthur Scargill, although, as President of the Yorkshire NUM, he was only just coming to prominence.

some way of reassuring the middle classes who were puzzled and that we ought to be talking now to the Liberal Party. Thorpe[1] was a 'show-off' and unreliable, but could probably be enlisted from flattery . . .

On and on did Macmillan speak. I have never listened to anyone so compelling, and with such sense of history. Lister's nurse appeared at the door and said he was ready, but I sent her away. What has happened to the Conservatives? How could they possibly ignore this man, so sage and so authoritative? I have already received ten tons of bumf from Central Office, most of it useless and unreadable. I don't see how we can actually *lose* this Election, or at least how I can lose it, but the whole encounter was rather unsettling. I wish I had not waited so long before going into politics, and could ingratiate myself with Uncle Harold, and defend him from ambitious and scheming mediocrities. Is it really too late? I suppose so.

I had quite forgotten about my tooth, which anyway took hardly a minute. But I don't like the high-speed drill. You can sometimes smell burning, so the frictional heat must be frightful. The accompanying water jet does not cool the 'cavity' but simply sloshes around in the mouth.

Saltwood   *Saturday, 2 February*

Sitting at my desk in office with stacks of paper all round – mainly invitations to great rash of ward AGMs – with moderate wind (now blowing for over a month) rocking the towers, vacuum-extracting the contents of the cars when a door is opened, making any gardening, tidying etc, much less leisurely pottering, impossible.

Absolutely choc-a-bloc with things to do – the whole of next week pre-empted by Plymouth and still quagmire of unfinished work, decision, correspondence. Must get away to Zermatt for a few days. Noticed to my alarm that tip of penis now not so receptive to sensation even after four days.

---

[1] Jeremy Thorpe, MP for Devon North since 1959; succeeded Jo Grimond as Leader of the Liberal Party, 1967.

Bratton   *Monday, 11 February*

Pretty twitchy, let's face it. Election ON – and DON'T WANT TO
LOSE! Definitely nervous about 'Public meetings', cavalcades, school
mums, ebb of confidence at half-way stage. Back tightened right up
after securing the 3-litre Cherrybum [Bentley] last Sunday – though
not yet crippled and trying to keep at bay with yoga and bells. Already
extremely haggard and strained – though put off going to Zermatt by,
in the end perhaps fortuitously (do I mean fortunately?) loss of
passport. Not sleeping very well, waking in the middle of the night
feeling incredibly tired etc. Also worried about Jamie (strange diffused
fatigue/nervous symptoms) and Andrew, not growing.

Heigh ho for future entries.

Bratton   *Thursday, 14 February*

The Campaign is On! With Jane to Guildhall to hand in nomination
papers; went to wrong door so kept everyone waiting, the ludicrous
stilted formality with Labour Mayor. Pouring rain. Went out to
Plympton Police to show documents. Canvassed a little in Embankment Road on way back (not bad). Saw exactly three voters, two
solid Tory and unshakeable smart-alec woman, a common-market.
Down to Ashley Drive to meet some pensioners. Some sour looks en
route as we sped by in Land-Rover, self repeating, inanely – or so it
seemed – 'Hello, everybody, this is your Conservative candidate.
Please vote for me on Feb 28, vote AC, vote Conservative.'

Thankfully back to Bratton for pasty supper (wrong sort of pastry).

Bratton   *Friday, 22 February*

Graham seemed reasonably calm about result, but I don't like talking
about 'when you're in the House etc.' Shattering of the make-believe
too close.

It was agreed how much of a threat the Liberals are. Actually I
think they are a threat, but don't want confirmation of this opinion.
Just as I forecast, today in the Broadway *quite different*. Instead of people

smiling and wishing good luck, pinioned by a few grumblers.

This evening, Liberals showing 20% in the polls. All those fools at Alma Road now echoing my own words: 'the whole Liberal tide flows etc.' This evening for the first time really thought perhaps am going to lose this seat after all – total disaster; struck off by Sir Richard Webster instantly etc etc The whole of that period since May 71 wasted, all that hubris . . .

I remember the exact spot where I was going to lose. I went quite faint and dry-mouthed. It was crossing the car park to that ridiculous little lady in the Club when Kay suddenly said it was 'dicey'.

Rang Saltwood and James, whom I'm missing terribly.

Bratton   *Tuesday, 26 February*

Morale improved by Graham late last night. '. . . when you wake up on Friday morning you'll be a Member of Parliament.' Straight to Alma Road where L.K.Way[1] poo-poohed idea of Liberal victory – 'see you in London, 6 March'. Confidence returned. Took many plaudits and then on to an excellent curry restaurant with Jane. Nothing to drink so lit a small Rössli cigar

11pm. Back in bed with a piece of fruit-cake and the latest *Motor Sport*. One of the best days so far.

After lunch and a short sleep (8 minutes approx) out to Lipson Gardens (couldn't find it) and some scattered calling. Knocked off too early. Piggy [Williams] approached me – 'What do you think, really,' he asked. '50/50,' I replied. Ideas totally shot, useless. Graham very Ladbroke – we're 5/4 on.

Tea at Duke. I remark saying to Jane, 'The reason I'm in such a state is because I think I actually *am* going to lose, and I'm dreading the speeches.' The thought of winning returned for a split second when the *Sunday Times* rang, said '. . . interviewing about 40 people who will be *new faces in the House* . . .' Bob now says majority 3,000 (*far* too tight).

---

[1] L.K.Way, lobby correspondent of Plymouth's daily paper, the *Western Morning News*.

Bratton   *Friday, 1 March*

Toured (very cold) in the Land-Rover, thanking people. A delicious moment, when testing my speaker, said: 'This is your Conservative *candidate* speaking ...' 'Member of Parliament, you twit,' said Graham.[1]

Zermatt   *Saturday, 2 March*

Must be reckoned the pinnacle so far.

I have always to worry about something, of course, so am now worrying about Tip who we have brought out here 'on' a fierce tetracycline (adult) dose after bronchitis in our absence in the last week of the election. He's still a bit peaky and soft-spoken and really hasn't grown at all by comparison with the pillar in our bedroom.[2] Oh dear, I do so adore the little chap, and want him to feel himself, fine and confident.

But otherwise ... Elected, with a majority that even the most optimistic had not expected, 8,104. Back seems to have virtually cleared up. I look back with amazement at those pre-Christmas entries, at here, recall those tormented hours between 5.30–8.30. Now, a real base to build on.

Must repeat (1) my conviction that I had lost, starting from that second Saturday unhappy in Plymstock, a feeling which became congenital so that the *idea* of winning became totally remote. (2) That frightful last day, twenty-eighth, going round the polling stations and committee rooms. Certainty of defeat when I looked at the Mt Gould polling day returns, all of which showed *total* vote up, Conservative vote down (what possible confirmation) and the grey, evasive looks of the Party workers. And yet one had to carry on, still on and on in the dark, so late that we missed dinner at the Duke, until after one of the longest days of my life, Graham rang to say come on over, you got 41 per cent of the total (actually it was 43 per cent). (3) Finally, the smell of victory, the moment I was in the chamber, the palpable excess of votes with the dreaded middle cross:

---

[1] Sutton result: AC, 21,649 votes; Fletcher (Labour), 13,545; Banks (Liberal),12,683.
[2] Used down the years by the Clarks to measure the growth of James and Andrew.

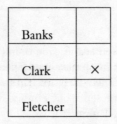

Banks	
Clark	×
Fletcher	

and the fabulous sight of the trays in the middle – the most convincing of all ways of showing it, with our blocks going up and up, and still being counted on 'our' tables.

The General Election on 28 February
    Conservative: 296; Labour: 301; Liberal: 14. Others: Ulster Unionists: 11; Scottish Nationalists: 7; Plaid Cymru: 2; others: 4

Train to Plymouth   *Thursday, 7 March*

Fabulous day of lingering euphoria and luxuriation in being MP.

Started with climb of Summerhouse Hill in glorious spring morning. Then *just* caught 11.18 from Ashford (driving there in little borrowed Triumph 1500 of my parents) still wearing anorak and check trousers/ pink shirt.

Changed and showered and to House. Collected huge bundles of (miscellaneous) mail and through to Euan's office[1] where he got me *monstrously* drunk; then drifted around the Palace of Westminster peeping and pottering, and observing massive available perks; drink in Strangers Bar and to (quite good) lunch. Hailed in Strangers dining room with incredible hurrahs by Jeremy Thorpe, more guardedly by David Steel. Then spent rest of afternoon 'walking off' drink going round various Sergeant-at-Arms type offices drawing vouchers etc.

---

[1] Euan Graham, AC's friend from Oxford days, had been Principal Clerk of Private Bills, House of Lords, since 1961.

Saltwood   *Sunday, 10 March*

After the euphoria the depression. Jane found the invitation from Ali (though fortunately not her letter) and she took it out on James – I didn't realise this at the time – and then had a very late night. Probably saved from row then by presence of Celly and, to a lesser extent Nick.[1] This morning she (and James) still in a filthy temper while Lilian pinched and pale and incredible nose-blowing coughing (which embarrasses me with Barham [doctor], against whose advice I took him to Zermatt last Saturday, which seems an age ago).

To Jane at breakfast I said 'your only real motivation, whether subconscious or conscious, the only yardstick by which you judge things, is whether I am more or less likely to get people to go to bed with me ...' and developed the theme. She cried when I tried to console her. We were interrupted by the back door bell, it was Tim, calling for James. Went and tidied around in the dressing room, with Andrew soft-spokenly helping me with my ties, then over to the Garden House, to find my mother in tears, my father his usual crotchety self, raspingly he made me 'accept' the use of Albany. Andrew deteriorating by the minute, nose-blowing etc.

Also aware on this lovely fine spring morning of the great weight of undone duties ranging from paperwork (eg Meeson[2]) to Saltwood (notices etc, garage) to bills. Financial stringency looms with disallowing of loan interest (probably), plus inevitability of Labour victory in next election.[3]

---

[1] Nick Beuttler, Jane's brother.

[2] Accountant.

[3] AC found himself at Westminster as a backbench MP for a party in opposition, with neither Conservatives nor Labour having an overall majority. Edward Heath, as 'the Prime Minister in possession' (related AC in *The Tories*) and leading a party boasting 1,200,000 more votes than Labour (but five fewer seats), had spent 'five painful days' attempting to 'form' an administration. Jeremy Thorpe, leader of the Liberals (6,000,000 votes, but only 14 seats), demanded nothing less than proportional representation to turn their future voting strength into seats; Heath offered no more than a Speaker's Conference to examine the question of electoral reform. The coalition did not happen, Heath resigned and Harold Wilson became Prime Minister leading a minority Labour government.

Plymouth train   *Friday, 15 March*

Down on the 1.30, suspect slightly flu-bound and picked up Johnny Hannam.[1] (For a few minutes he didn't know who I was.). We sat at lunch together. Self-medicating generously, talked of politics throughout the meal to the grumpy consternation of a *New Statesman*-reading geriatric opposite. Quite a nice chap, interesting and helpful. Concepted Margaret Thatcher as possible successor to Heath.

Saltwood   *Monday, 25 March*

A glorious still spring day, the sun warm – tanning if one could be out all day – and so much to do in the place if one could get down to it – fences, cutting, hedging, etc.

Been going great guns in politics: on ITN, BBC West, *This Week*, Radio 4, all arising, more or less, from the article in the *Sunday Times*.[2] Sometimes, I think, fabulous; a new face, just the right combination of attitudes, appeal etc. Rommel. Press on and on. At others I feel so far to go, such parlous resources, what a waste of the lovely weather and possessions and XVIIIc freedom. My morale suffered from mutterings at Plymouth (reported to me); Dunstone,[3] needless to say, plus letter from Sir Henry Studholme[4] in *Western Morning News*. Bloody fools had none of them read the *ST* itself, only L.K.Way's extracts.

---

[1] John Hannam, MP for Exeter since 1970.
[2] Under the heading 'Tory Party needs a rethink, but where are the thinkers?', AC was highly critical of the party machine, its reliance on the findings of opinion pollsters in formulating an image and packaging policy; he also attacked Tory Central Office for its condemnation 'amounting in the later years almost to a witch-hunt' of all expressions of dissent, particularly those who supported Enoch Powell's views. It was widely seen as a brave, if foolhardy view to voice, not least by a new MP.
[3] A Sutton constituency ward chaired by Mrs H.O'N. (Nan) Howard.
[4] Sir Henry Studholme, 1st Bt, MP for Tavistock, 1942–66, part of whose constituency was redistributed into Sutton.

Albany   *Thursday, 28 March*

Lunched with feisty old backbencher from Gillingham (Kent).[1] 'Oh, you're Alan Clark ... I've heard a lot about you.' 'All of it good, I hope,' I retorted, composing my face into a fresh, anxious-to-please expression. He then did a sort of 'Do-you-mind-old-boy' preliminary and said '... a certain amount of resentment ... don't push it too hard, lie low for a bit' etc. Crusty old cove.

Saltwood   *Sunday, 31 March*

Over in the Great Hall in somewhat melancholy and reflective frame of mind. A fine morning and the first over here this year, taking advantage of the long light and the delicious monastic atmosphere. Not as tranquil as I should have liked with interruptions (a) from my father (b) from Gangster parked in the red chinz armchair, scratching/whining periodically and then barking later.

   Gloomy about constant encroachment on parkland by public, growing tendency to think 'amazing for one person to have so much land ...' actually vouchsafed by a young person whom I evicted (with three others) this afternoon. Came up by car (naturally) and went to tip of escarpment – presumably to smoke 'joints'; went off shouting leftish sentiments and slogans. Have spent huge sums in fencing and security, but still holes, fighting a losing battle; in the end will be down to the original fortified defence line of Outer and Inner Bailey. Are we (J & I and the boys) an etiolated rearguard? The French nobility in 1788? At that appalling dinner party last night every single person was 'progressive'. The good-living/thinking jealousy substitute for the deprived (sexually and materially) professional classes.

   From time to time during the day – heavily persuaded by dep-redations on tool locker, missing funnel etc etc – thought much to do here just with the cars, the estate, *preserving* so that the boys can carry on. I just don't know what will emerge from the House, but time is terribly diminished – weekends are bliss. All the *notices*, opening decisions etc here are still undone. Yet cannot shirk. I have a debt to God who has worked my miracle for me. At least, making extra time for fitness and rest by cutting out b'gammon.

---

[1] Frederick Burden, first elected MP for Gillingham in 1950.

Albany   *Tuesday, 30 April*

Put in to do my 'maiden' today.[1] Sat in Chamber for quite a time, with 'everyone on board most helpful',[2] Spencer Le Marchant coming up and arranging my place in the order. Rose to my feet and spoke clearly and, I believe, it was appreciated once the House realised what I was doing – quite wittily. Interesting thing is both Spencer, and Tony Berry, who summed up (still slightly shaking and shimmering as of old) I knew at various stages of the education process.[3]

Saltwood   *Friday, 7 June*

A very low day. Extremely tired (did late night at Aspinalls) and awoke as unpleasant thoughts slotted into place (1) b'gammon losses last night £470; (ii) Valeri out of my life; (iii) Jimmy Goldsmith warnings about world slump. My mind was racing as to how reduce o/d and then came crashing in on top of this the recollection that CGT also (of minimum 30) is needed shortly.

My parents low; my mother now deteriorated again, although still beautifully poised and witty; talk of wealth tax, obliteration of the 'gentry', look round at the unbelievable driving up of protest sympathies by the press for the IRA and hunger strikers etc.

Given up b'gammon ... statistical analysis shows it just is too expensive.

---

[1] AC chose the debate on the Channel Tunnel, that project being so close to Saltwood (as he declared to the House), if not his constituency, but in his speech he gave a foretaste of his views from Defence, through patriotism to continental Europe, when he reminded the House that the country had always been protected from invasion by the English Channel. An attack would be by 'blitzkrieg, a lightning strike', and its most likely form would now be a parachute landing 'to seize the tunnel head and defend it for a short enough period for the invader to pass through the tunnel and completely bypass our natural protection.' And, he added, that if the tunnel went ahead a fail-safe system should be installed allowing for its instant demolition.

[2] From one of AC's favourite books, Evelyn Waugh's *The Ordeal of Gilbert Pinfold*, a copy of which he kept by his bedside in Zermatt.

[3] Spencer Le Marchant, MP for High Peak, Derbyshire since 1970, and an Opposition Whip since the election. Another Old Etonian, like Anthony Berry, MP for Southgate since 1964.

Albany   *Sunday, 9 June*

Heading for an exceptionally bad night, I should think. Great long
periods just brooding – cutting out birds, drink and backgammon
should have helped, but actually depression so acute that great long
totally uncreative periods supervene when the mind just rambles. Also
being needlessly grumpy and beastly to Jane.

Just as I was changing a mass of gawpers started pouring through
the arch, re-reviving all my neuroses about the unstoppable tide (my
nightmare of them all coming *down* the stairs at Saltwood with me
pluckingly trying to collect a few 20p's).

H of C Library   *Wednesday, 12 June*

Low, and hot. Can't take my coat off, it seems, although I did so once
before I was cowed. Walking with Tim Sainsbury[1] from the Gents to
the Lobby and Margaret Thatcher[2] materialised and gushingly, 'Hello
Tim we've missed you ...' etc. He dropped me like a bit of parrot
shit, naturally. Then, aggravatingly, *missed a Division*. Was in committee
room 13 listening with great interest to Ulster leader Willie Craig[3]
telling how Heath had not replied to telegram from West[4] – 'see you
at the swearing-in'. Made *no* effort to get their support and save
Conservatives. (Perhaps just as well.) Anyhow the bell went, and we
finally shuffled off, a terrific longueurs getting into the lobby. 'Mr
Thomas'[5] suddenly yelled 'Lock the doors' – most irritating of all, to
miss a vote when actually *in* the Palace, indeed *in* the Chamber!

---

[1] Hon Timothy Sainsbury, MP for Hove since November 1973.
[2] Margaret Thatcher, MP for Finchley since 1959. Secretary of State for Education from
    1970 until the general election. Her name was increasingly mentioned as a possible
    successor to Edward Heath as party leader as Conservatives regrouped following the
    February defeat.
[3] William Craig, MP for East Belfast since the General Election. Leader of the Ulster
    Vanguard Party since 1973.
[4] Henry William West, MP for Fermanagh and South Tyrone since the general election
    and leader of the Ulster Unionist Party. When Heath had been trying to form a
    government immediately after the election, as well as parlaying with the Liberals he
    also had brief but abortive discussions about a pact with the Ulster Unionists.
[5] George Thomas, MP (Labour) for Cardiff West since 1950 (Cardiff Central, 1945–50),
    had been Deputy Speaker since the general election. His ringing Welsh tones were
    swiftly making their presence felt in the Chamber.

Yesterday (instead of the House), when I was lying up on the castle's terrace/battlement walk (new spot, just this side of Thorpe's[1]), did absolutely no good tan-wise, but suddenly realised the enormity of the interest charges running against me – 87 + 63 = 150 or £20,000 a year, or £500 a week. Must stop the drain and can only do so by selling cars.

Is it going to be easy to sell cars? CH very gloomy. Money drying up fast. From time to time, as I drive about in my blue Bentley – to which I am very attached, 'MP's car' – I think what a personification of Privilege I am. Silk shirts, beautiful suits, write a cheque or sign an Amex for anything you want; chambers in Albany, castle in Kent, châlet in Zermatt, credit accounts everywhere, the Parliamentary pass to flash. Press the button, the machine will respond. Total confidence. How easy to be pleasant – that calm inner assurance of superiority (like I have sometimes noticed with people who are very good at Judo, the way they move quietly and confidently in crowds). Well, could it be in jeopardy? I got the aerial photos of Saltwood today, thought God what a wonderful place, worth hanging on to, and preserving for the boys.

Bratton-Clovelly   *Thursday, 13 June*

Sitting, utterly pole-axed in the garden in a deckchair.

Seem to have had only 5/6 hours sleep every night this week, late whipping in the House, too much to drink. Incredibly, the adrenalin does keep me going during the week, but this afternoon after sleeper down, trudging around Plymouth – as Porsche in garage.

Bratton delicious, tranquil. What a place to recharge one's batteries. Chief worry is money, impossibility of selling *anything* it seems. Bonny mama not well again. Losing ground.

---

[1] Thorpe's Tower, which looks out over the Barbican Gate, the main entrance to Saltwood.

Dean's Yard   *Wednesday, 17 July*

Reflecting on most unwelcome position, the evidence of (sic) which has been building up for some time, that not only am I in a very uncomfortable financial situation – but that I totally mismanaged (from optimism, *folie de grandeur*, total lack of Scotch canniness, gross miscalculations of economic symptoms and also sheer inability, or at least unwillingness to *count*) the one last great get-out deal, namely the sale of the cricket field.

This could have got me permanently out of debt and allowed consolidation with a lot of excess assets on a well diversified earnings basis – rents, royalties, salaries, public visits. Really, after earlier reverses one would think that lesson had been learned. It *has* been learned now. Just pray I can impart it to James and Tip – one can never entirely, of course, but even *some* of it would help. Now one has to set more modest goals and they will take longer to fulfil, whereas it could have been done 'at a stroke'. Also means giving up some things I like, eg Lago-Talbot and D-type. (If – and it is a bit of an 'if' because these are days of great panic and depression – I sell them, should get my o/d down below 20.) The days of limitless cash flow are over.

Saltwood   *Sunday, 21 July*

For first time, coming back in sleeper from Plymouth, did not feel that delicious sense of relief and anticipation – the mirror-image of the towers reflected in the water as you come through the Barbican, generated anxiety instead of calming. The whole structure unchanged with absurd signs of wealth and stability but as the hot summer days (now shortening) slip by the bills accumulate, so far without *any* sales to relieve them. This has had the effect of reducing, at last, adrenalin flow (contentment must be an ingredient to get a proper flow, I think). And last night I went down with a summer cold, first cold for eighteen months. During the night an enormous chunk of the north curtain wall slid down, and will cost £12–14,000 to repair. I remember talking to my old pal Euan Graham in a bar in the House of Lords last week, and he told me how as well as being by-passed for the long-awaited promotion he had been cut out of his mother's will – 'when one thing hits you, they all do.'

Darling Jamie going to Cranwell today to RAF Camp with various flying activities. Things could get so much worse, couldn't they? I mean we are still painfully blessed and golden (*d'orée*). Yesterday evening, before the cold took hold, I swam a double length of the moat, naked, in the warm sunlight, looking up at the tower, then drove the Ghost with Tip to Dungeness, where there's an old (but interesting) wreck.

Saltwood   *Monday, 5 August*

Conceivably, the last day of the old regime.[1] Not impossible that by the winter I shall be (a) wiped out and (b) lost my seat. I sometimes seriously think of how much I could get out to Zermatt (Bavarian Redoubt) before actually going under. A few objects and pictures out – Degas, Bull, snuff-boxes, some Moores and Sutherlands etc. But how would one live in the long term? On reflection, must preserve Saltwood, so it can be run 'as a business'.

Later

Am I a Renaissance Prince, a philosopher, or a big ageing dud? Looking back at all those lost opportunities of money-making, starting with the waste of the first £15,000 my father gave me in 1948, like properties in Rye (going for nothing), the Torridon Estate (£40,000 in 1964, now ½ million I suppose). And yet when I go and plump for something like Newton it becomes a lemon at once – although I'm sure strategically it must be right.

Fortified by two things – first how all that really matters is the boys' health and survival and how lucky we are, second how God *did* work his miracle for Plymouth Sutton. *That* was the real achievement, *that* is what must be built on. Easy to recharge the batteries with Zermatt and Bratton ... and exercise. I've learnt my lesson about financial speculation at last having been through fire – forget it. Security you can (still) attain. So, thank-you-God-for-any-good-luck and hold on

---

[1] The House of Commons had risen for the summer recess; everyone expected that Harold Wilson, the Prime Minister, would call an election in the autumn in an endeavour to get an overall working majority.

to what you've got, a happy family and fulfilment of your secret – and apparently impossible – ambition.

Charing Cross   *Thursday, 19 September*

Confident (Sutton *not* on the *Guardian* list of marginals).[1]

I went off to face Hoare's, going through the Temple. Seen in a top front room. First dear old Q. Hoare to soften me up, then 'Dick' Hoare – the head man. That was clearly his designed role, but it so happens we took an intense dislike to one another. He's determined to 'get' me, I can feel that; enjoyed bullying me to sell assets – regardless of right price or no. Made some acid quips while Q. Hoare muddled the figures from time to time. At the end (circa 5.30) dear old Q. Hoare asked me if I would like a whisky (!) Have got till 1 April next year (due to Q. Hoare's shuffling – originally in two stages with Christmas the first).[2]

Everything happening at once, ie financial collapse *and* having to fight an election. Waking early with all these worries. Fool, Clark, to have repeated your errors on such a huge scale.

Duke of Cornwall Hotel, Plymouth[3]   *Saturday, 28 September*

It was icy in (or rather on) the Land-Rover this evening. There is no proper rail along the top of the cab so I have to 'steady myself', fingers blue-numbed, by clutching at the tiny and sharp-edged guttering. As I sway about, the hand held microphone will suddenly and unpredictably emit a piercing howl. Why? It seems to have something to do with proximity to metal, at least that's my theory.

You can't talk through it, and it will suddenly cut in *while* you are talking or, even more disconcertingly, for no apparent reason whatever while one is benignly surveying a narrow street crowded with shoppers.

---

[1] The general election had been called for 11 October.
[2] Despite the severity of Hoare's stipulations, the Clarks retained accounts with the bank.
[3] As in February, AC was to use 'The Duke' as his base for the October campaign.

Some, very, very few of these folk smile or wave. Most avoid my eye, or start up conversations with each other.

Sod them, I say. What the hell are they doing shopping anyway, on a Tuesday? People who are spending money in shops ought to be Conservative, surely?

I feel myself to be getting 'out of sorts'.

'Firm Government – but Fair Government'.

Umpteen times have I called this out. A simple enough phrase. So simple, indeed, as to be devoid of meaning or even inference. Yet all too easy to get, in some perverse way, tied around one's tongue. We were driving in those streets that lead uphill from Plymstock to Hooe, there was practically no one about and Jane accelerated. The wind made my eyes water uncontrollably, and for some reason I started a longer discourse and *affected a Devonian accent.*

She jammed on the brakes. 'What *are* you doing? You just make yourself utterly ridiculous.'

Back here I ordered and consumed a lot of tea and buttered toast (both arrived tepid) in the lounge. I am depressed, irritated, suffering from exhaustion. Even in the 'good' areas the electorate are flinty-faced. What's going on?

Bratton   *Thursday, 3 October*

The dear old boy conducting me round Mt Gould – very efficiently – won my heart by suddenly saying: 'Of course you're the one, the one with fire in you.'

Later Jack Weatherill[1] came on the phone: 'How's it going?'

'So so, only.'

'No I mean this Coalition idea.[2] Are you getting it across?'

'They won't understand. It's far too late to start trying to sell that . . .'

---

[1] Bernard (Jack) Weatherill, MP for Croydon NE since 1964. A whip in government and opposition (he had been Opposition deputy chief whip since February 1974). Such were his skills with the more independent-minded Conservative members that he was known, not always affectionately, as 'the shits' whip'.

[2] At mid-point, Tory strategists, at the behest of Edward Heath, came up with the notion that to appeal 'over the heads' of the Labour Party to 'people of good will' might save a number of seats.

'Well, that's the line. Do your best.'

'Look, Jack, we're not going to get anywhere while Ted is leading us. He's had it.'

'Later. That comes later. Leave it for the moment.'

Odd. Particularly that last sentence. Actually, I think we are going to lose, again. And that will be one of the exciting things about the new House. Getting a real change.

Saltwood   *Saturday, 12 October*

Back last night after a (foreshortened) tour of Sutton with the loud-speaker (just did a 'blast' outside the Eastons' house so that they would hear me – for alibi reasons). A glance at the *Evening Standard* was enough to show that Plymouth results were *exceptionally* bad[1] – many safe seats had *increased* their majorities. Only consolation was that of course, most of Liberals had also been slashed. But undeniable bitterness of dejection, or at least personal brush off – all those letters, all that charm. Also uncomfortably concerned that it undermines my personal activities as a right-winger and also, of course, in the Association itself. As Saltwood towers loomed up in the headlights Jane said, 'What a wonderful place.' How I agreed. But dared not say, how much in peril it is. Must take steps at virtually any price, to shift it across into the Trust, and there was that letter from Hoare's: will-you-come-in-straight-away?

Concocted a formula to get one to sleep, of selling the plot adjacent in Zermatt for 90,000 (!). I passed out in bed at 10.30 and woke at 11.20. This gave me back a bit of confidence again, a determination to concentrate on exercises, library, eschew late nights, b'gammon, the Mews etc. Clearheadedly see this through. 'No relaxation without implementation.'

The General Election on 11 October
   Conservative: 276; Labour: 319; Liberal: 13. Others: Ulster Unionists:
   10; Scottish Nationalists: 11; Plaid Cymru: 3; others: 3

---

[1] Sutton result: AC, 20,457 votes; Priestley (Labour), 15,269; Banks (Liberal), 10,131. AC's majority, 5,188 (February, 8,104).

Zermatt   *Thursday, 17 October*

In Zermatt briefly, and depressed to find the old magic almost gone.
Bavarian Redoubt now seems tricky, a cul-de-sac. Brought some
snuff-boxes out and put them in a box in safe in back – but it's 'the
addresses' isn't it? Only point as a *recuperative* tonic, a temporary
refuge. Exile would be very sad. Key principle must be to SAVE
SALTWOOD – still with its potential barely touched in so many
ways.

Gloomy, too, about politics. Absolutely nil contact about the leadership this time, no phoning, no TV, no articles. In desperation, have
sent out 53 invitations to a party at Albany as understandably all MPs
long for some social contact. Can feel – perhaps with some element
of paranoia – latent hostility in Association at Plymouth. They just
longing to get cracking when the Chelmer rules start laying down
conditions about living in the constituency, etc. (When papers interview '... at his family home, Saltwood Castle in Kent', can imagine
Rodney Easton snorting and grunting and slapping his paper down.)
Pine for Folkestone, and wrote to 'Albert' (who sent me a telegram,
although I had veto'd sending him one).[1] Was rewarded by an instant
invitation to address the AGM of their CPC (!) I don't know whether
I would get Folkestone or not – the very idea of chaotic selection
committee ordeal is sheer trauma – but I sometimes think I will never
fight an election in Plymouth again.

Saltwood   *Thursday, 31 October*

Been in a state of considerable 'nervosity' all day. Waves of angst wash
over me at the Hoare's indebtedness (wake every morning at 4am for
about ¾ hr of panic). Also Lenin-stadium type cramp-angst at so
much to resolve:

   (1) Constantly losing and long mucked-up at b'gammon (which I
        love, and am addicted to)
   (2) Virtually ignored in the House this time – in spite of our quite
        jolly and successful performances

---

[1] Albert Costain, MP for Folkestone since 1959. Now in his mid-sixties the question of
   when he might retire and whether AC might succeed him would recur.

(3) Rows – sic – with parents being against my advantage over possible – indeed vital – money-raising sales

(4) Feeling tired cold and looking strangely pressured with hair now degenerating in quality as well as colour and density

(5) Sick of Plymouth – will quit journeys and the sleeper etc – and their introspective minuscule horizons

(6) Badly need energy and will-power to concentrate on problems this winter

Saltwood   *Saturday, 16 November*

Filled with gloom and foreboding as market continues to slide (Coats at $\underline{26^1}$), probability of yet another Arab/Israeli war with total collapse of industry, currency etc (not to mention 'Nuclear Exchange'). November is a terrible month, the equivalent of 3.10am during the night.

Desmond Corcoran[2] coming down this morning. Have prayed to God I make the right decisions.[3]

Saltwood   *Sunday, 8 December*

Reasonably randy and eating ok, but yesterday had a real shock on seeing myself on TV. Unbelievably livid, gaunt, puffy and balding – looked older than the Bishop of London who came on later. *Must* start regime *now*. Exercises, early nights, hair washes, sleep after lunch when possible, cut down on drink. Will 'report back' on this.

---

[1] A stock long-held by AC and in considerable quantities. It had been at a year high of 74. Coats had amalgamated with the Clark cotton thread business, J & J Clark in 1896.

[2] Desmond Corcoran – from the Lefevre Gallery in Mayfair.

[3] AC's comment at foot of entry: 'I was very trembly to start with, but got 31,000 for nine pictures'.

1975

Saltwood *Friday, 3 January 1975*[1]

Have been terribly depressed these last few days. Christmas (which, thanks to Jane's efforts was as usual great fun; 'Daisy' down, and bought, among others, Phantom III from him for 8.5; thin (as usual loathsomely like at Bratton in '63) and said 'you've got a lot greyer'. Only too true, alas. Have got much more continuously tired; slowly catching one, wearing one down in the incessant pressure on time. I no longer have the capacity to extend the day indefinitely – as I used to do; getting up incredibly early to do the great long-range drive or 'missing' a night, but quickly repairing. The time in Zermatt was wonderful – though James's nerve gone, poor dear, and he hates skiing. Tip on the other hand very good potential. But I felt no oxygen boost on getting back – for the first time.

Saltwood *Sunday, 12 January*

Got back today. Nanny had cleaned the place fantastically, throughout, and our fears that various vandalisms would occur proved unfounded. Even the 'No Parking' notice sensibly erect outside the Barbican, and Cradduck's stripping of the ivy from the walls over the Bailey gate most successful. Of the various anticipated disasters only one – the euthanasia of Gangster – took place as predicted. I'm sorry that I couldn't be there to bid him goodbye. But he's buried next to Grandee. And I will always remember the Beagles and their period of great physical prowess, particularly Dartmoor (that time I lost them on the twin boggy ridges that stretched out towards Meldon) and Salisbury Plain (chasing the prototype Chieftain[2]) because it coincided with the longer period of contentment and tranquillity (at Seend) in my own life.

Reasonable (and unexpected) aura of contentment in spite of letter from the Tate semi-reneging on Saltonstall.[3] Beautifully insulated here in panelled library with log fire.

But much will be decided this year. 'Survival' yes, but there must

---

[1] AC heads this page: START OF 'SURVIVAL YEAR'.
[2] The Chieftain was to become the British army's principal tank of the Cold War era.
[3] *The Saltonstall Family*, c1636–7, by David Des Granges.

also be a platform built, because if I don't get established in '76 there can be no further attainment of my goals without a miracle. Thought on the walk this evening how would really be quite content to be just stately-home-owner, dealer and b'gammon-man; last night woke in the wagon-lit feeling tired and wondered if now really too old. My age does seem to have jumped one this last year.

Dean's Yard   *Friday, 17 January*

'Punishment' phase. Lost £1320 to Goldsmith/Slater/Zilkhan at a £40 chou[1] at Lyall Street after Aspers'(only moderate) 'talk' to Bow Group last night. Jane rightly tested me for no constituency visits, no publicity, far too much old cars. *Absolutely nothing* in the papers about me for nearly six weeks, don't open constituency letters any more, no questions tabled, no intervention, no time to work up speeches, complaints about showing my face in Plymouth – haven't even signed all the election thankyou letters yet! Now very tired indeed (7.30 train tomorrow) with cold symptoms.[2]

Saltwood   *Monday, 24 March*

Threatening position welling up in Plymouth. As I somehow suspected Larry Speare[3] undergone total personality change as chairman – head cropped, unsmilingly and *folie de grandeur*. He'd already shown incipient signs of this at the AGM with his *very* reserved compliments and injunctions to 'help the name of Sutton forward'. Then last Thursday, totally dry-minded and fatigued (I had driven down flat out that morning in the 230 SL, spurting out oil through a misplaced

---

[1] Chou is the abbreviation for Chouette, a backgammon game in which more than two players participate.

[2] AC is silent on the change in party leadership, which was about to take place. In the first ballot of Conservative MPs on 4 February, Margaret Thatcher gained 130 votes to Edward Heath's 119, with 16 for the backbencher Hugh Fraser. Heath resigned as leader. A week later Thatcher, with 146 votes, gained an overall majority over four Shadow Cabinet colleagues: William Whitelaw (79 votes), Geoffrey Howe and James Prior (19 each) and John Peyton (11).

[3] Lawrence Speare, a significant member of the Sutton Conservative Association and sometime chairman.

filter cap) he told/warned me of possibility of not being readopted due to having been anti-Heath, anti Referendum. That evening, at the F&GP he, fortunately, 'clashed' with Rodney Easton; but if he, Easton and Speare started ganging up (Nazi-Soviet non-aggression pact) then one would be in trouble, left only with Dunstone (doubtful) and Efford and Sutton.

Saltwood   *Thursday, 10 April*

A note of the last day of the Common Market (approval) – or whatever it should be called – debates.

Entertainment, indeed History, promised with Heath, Powell *and* Heffer[1] all hoping-to-catch-the-eye. Walked up the aisle and turned right past Heath, occupying the prime position in corner seat. He bronzé in grey suit, check shirt (semi-Heseltine outfit) but rather more pinched, less ripplingly. Ugh! What a purse-mouth (*'Bonjours ...'*) he made as I momentarily swished him. Humphrey Atkins[2] smiled in friendly fashion, though. Had John Stradling Thomas[3] already told him that I was going to vote anti? John himself uneasily asked me if I had 'read Margaret's speech'. Oh yes, I said, splendid stuff (I hadn't); of course if she told me to vote 'for' I would. But I welcomed the 'free' vote in order to make my little personal statement. Gloomily he accepted this.

Front bench jammed solid. 'Throng' at the Bar. Heath spoke, reasonably competent and without notes, in the 'Coningsby position' (or hand in d/b jacket pocket). For a second, when he was speaking about sovereignty, I could have interrupted him, but it passed.

'Where's Margaret?' asked nasty little Tony Nelson of Chichester.[4] 'He listened to *her* speech.'

'But wasn't very polite about it,' I said. He looked cross at this.

---

[1] Eric Heffer, MP for Liverpool Walton since 1964, and a leading left-winger.

[2] Humphrey Atkins, MP for Spelthorne since 1970 (Merton and Morden, 1955–1970) and opposition chief whip. Earlier he had a spell as secretary to the Conservative Parliamentary Defence Committee. Deputy and ultimately government chief whip, 1973–74.

[3] John Stradling Thomas, MP for Monmouth since 1970 and an opposition whip.

[4] Tony Nelson, elected MP for Chichester in October 1974, previously with N.M. Rothschild.

The Heath 5th column cheered loudly when he sat down. He was followed, immediately by Enoch! Tortured, baleful, intense, he stood only a few feet away from me, on the same row the other side of the gangway. Spoke well, gestured pointedly. Heath interrupted him three times, having to unfortunately twist his neck and his eyes round and was slightly worsted. Enoch very good and moving and made one feel *all right* about voting anti. 'That's one of the good ones', came from one of Dennis's group as I walked through afterwards and sexy little Miss Horseface (I don't recall her name, but took Dick's place at Lincoln)[1] seductively said 'I didn't know you were an anti.'[2]

Went back to St J and got into b'gammon game, and ended losing again – £226. When I collected my mail Dennis Skinner[3] was standing near. I had to give my name to an unknown PO official. 'Alan Clark'. . . 'The goal scorer,' said D. 'You scored one last night.' 'Not enough of us,' I answered. In the tea-room queue I said, 'I'd rather live in a socialist Britain than one ruled by a lot of fucking foreigners.' He seemed surprised as well as pleased.

Saltwood   *Sunday, 11 May*

An evocative date. The great German offensive across the Low Countries in 1940, Churchill gets the premiership, the die is cast in the country's fight to the death. And, five years later, VE Day, with its illusions that took so long to disperse.

And here is my own life, its 'serious', ambitious, political and however-you-like-to-call-it side so emphatically biased by those experiences, well over half-way through, even deducting the childhood years. I've got ten – *tennish* – more years active, eight as an 'active buffer', the remainder as a sage. That's always assuming freedom/deliverance from the screech of brakes, sickening thud and

---

[1] Margaret Jackson (later better known by her married name Beckett) had regained the Lincoln seat for Labour in October 1974 after the sitting MP, Dick Taverne, defected to the SDP.

[2] AC was one of a small number of Tories to vote against, but their stance was overshadowed by Eric Heffer, who was dismissed as Minister of State, Department of Industry, for not supporting the Government.

[3] Dennis Skinner, MP for Bolsover since 1970 ('good working-class mining stock', *Who's Who* entry) and already a left-winger with a reputation for parliamentary repartee.

rending of metal from the head-on crash over the brow of the hill. Now that the 550A Spyder is roadable I often take it out on fine evenings. So intoxicatingly fast and agile – but so vulnerable. Going onto the slightly blind hump-back of the A20 Sandling Bridge I visualised (as so often) that horrid impact. Have I recorded that nightmare spin in the 230 SL that night when I was unscathed? Let us hope it means that 'what is written, is written'.

Saltwood   *Sunday, 18 May*

Had a relatively slack week, but precious little achieved. Tide turned at b'gammon, at last, and pulled in about £700, totally eliminating losses to Charles and producing a surplus of £100+. Also frenzied dealing in 'leaders' has produced a big surplus – but of course one false move and good deals can be undone – vide Bass, sold one hour too late at a loss of £400. Fast as one consolidates, though, past debts pile up; not only the Saltwood curtain wall and the lesser items like tidying up round the new garages etc, but a sudden 'shock' need: £2–4,000 to pay for brochures. The brochures themselves are very good.

Tremendous long-term investment possibilities for Saltwood. My father (according to Col) now clutches his head and says 'I can't understand why one bought it ... madness.' He strangely distant and crotchety – possibly sale of Sutherlands[1] has something to do with it, but, as I said, it's now 'come and get one, Larsen'.

Dean's Yard   *Tuesday, 27 May*

A certain delicious calmness – one of the first really tranquil entries for nearly a year – since the enormity of the financial crisis and the threat to Saltwood came home. Working up in my (new) 'collegiate' quarters on the quad – Abbey Garden – on a long summer evening. Sent £18,000 odd to Hoare's today, now bringing o/d to agreed April 1st limit and reductions. More to follow. The magic moment when the deeds are returned to me not so far away.

---

[1] Graham Sutherland sketched and painted a number of portraits of Kenneth Clark

What is to be the outcome of the terrible decline of the country –
the total absence of leadership and inspiration in the Conservative
Party? In 1939 at least we had Fighter Command and the Navy, and
Winston around. Now we have nothing. My windows here are filthy,
dirtier even than at Saltwood. *US News and World Report*[1] quite right –
whole thing tatty, bad-tempered, lazy, in collapse. Yet of course there
is no crisis; everyone flush with money. When will the recovery come?
And how?

Yet even as I write this, I feel – too slack, too easygoing. In the
train the other evening I thought perhaps I should go the whole way,
stand as National Front candidate, a *switch* if the Plymouth Association
kicks me out. Or is the very thought that I am 'waiting for the call' a
concealment of my natural laziness?

After two days very successful openings, fired by the cash flow, the
possibilities. One of the few 'enterprises' unlikely to be troubled even
by the envy, the jealousies all around us. I also have these romantic
fantasies of the besieged aristocracy. 1791. I do hope the boys will
catch on in the end. James in particular is unbelievably idle about it
at the moment. He has passed through girls (for the moment) and
drink (largely speaking) and now is obsessed by driving. He had
cleaned the Bang Bang[2] meticulously during 'garage invigilation' on
the public days. Last night Tuppy suddenly cocked an ear and said,
'that's the Bang Bang engine . . .' I looked out of the door and saw it
going down the drive – James was turning it prior to putting it in the
garage. I waited in the shadow of the Barbican. The car came back,
turned in the car park gate and then out back down the drive! I knew
what would follow and sure enough an engine opened up (so like an
aero-engine it sounds) and the lights clearly shone charging up Sandy
Lane! I got the Land-Rover, but by then he was already returning.
Oh dear, I do love 'Boy' so much, in spite of all his bolshiness of
growing up. I do dread his having a motor accident. I must train and
nurture him on the road. He wants to go to Lydden[3] and one might
do that.

---

[1] This American news magazine had compared the Britain of the 1970s – unfavourably –
with the 'swinging sixties' period.

[2] R Type Bentley Continental, the only Continental to be recorded stolen in the 1950s.
Written off, it was rebodied by Bradley Brothers into a cut-down two-seater.

[3] Motor-racing track off the A2 north-west of Dover.

Saltwood   *Thursday, 29 May*

Recess. Heard dawn chorus start up after 4 struck – quite beautiful
and magical – dropped back to sleep. Woke again 7am. Grey water,
made tea, dressed, wakey-wakey'd boys, last minute Thompson before
taking boys to Sandling. Annoyed, at Sandling, by that shirty little
rotting-dog man in a white Renault who always blocks the wrong
place, but did nothing. Letter from Sir Gilbert Longden in *Daily
Telegraph* about me. Still mildly pleased to see myself as 'Mr Alan Clark
MP'.[1]

Evening of one of the two hottest days we're likely to get this year.
Absolutely cloudless, without a breath of wind. Boy out for a party at
St Mary's Bay; usual mixed emotions of jealousy/frustration at the
two 'maidens' (heavily-built, but one somewhat shy and lecherous I
would think) and worry at his using the 1100, which has already been
put in a ditch once. He is to return at 11pm so there will be a half
hour of anxiety. I construct the fantasy of the Lancaster sortie in
Bomber Command.

I feel 'calmer' this summer than last. The total 'apres moi le deluge'
atmosphere ameliorated by velour of semi-solvency. But I also feel
older, creakier. Political weaknesses remain with a dead loss situation
in Parliament – no committees, no work, no activity.

Albany   *Tuesday, 29 July*

Sun pouring through windows, a.m., as this memorable summer goes
on, and on and on. Ever since April have been woken (either here or
at Saltwood) by squares of light moving slowly across the wall, from
5am – or whenever – and longed, with various degrees of yearning,
for a few happy open-air days swimming and working out of doors
to take advantage of a memorable summer that will never, in my lifetime, be repeated. Finally this morning, FED UP with still being stuck
in Commons – and next week too, due to pressure of 'business'.

---

[1] Sir Gilbert Longden, retired in February 1974 after 24 years as MP for South West
Herts. In his letter he was agreeing with AC's view that it was the duty of all
Conservatives to resist socialist politics which 'opposed our liberties, prosperity and
security.'

Summer will be de facto over when we are finally released as at present just mooching around in the lobbies, whips wildly inaccurate with their '... in about an hour ...' estimates. As yet plans not clear – Venice and Chalet? Or vintage rally to Lagenburg (I'm lightly sweating as I write this, by the way at 9.05 am, as in Venice.) Not much point in leaving Saltwood I don't think, until v late, end September. But then bad luck on boys' school hols. James now so grown up, still incredibly beautiful. His girl-friend shaggeable though tall. I don't know what they're doing, but they go quite 'far' as I caught them out-of-sight in the Cadillac on Sunday night. Dear Boy. Tip still tiny, it seems, and unchanged mentally or physically. I hope this isn't worrying him – it does me occasionally.

Saltwood, Great Hall (7pm)   *Saturday, 9 August*

The sun, almost horizontal now, autumn-level, slides across Courtenays, through dirty leaded panes covered with ivy leaves. The library, oppressively stuffy, the whole place ... just a few dandelions – or are they buttercups? The trees all dying on Tanners Hill. *Enfin le chef des champs!* But strangely fatigued and depressed. Can work and write over here till light fails, and much to record, but *incredibly* lethargic and sleepy. Perhaps too much sun (now pleasantly brown all over, and couldn't change colour any more like that hot summer – I suppose it was 1948 – in St John Street at Oxford), not enough protein in diet etc. Virility? Totally impotent.

Must try and sublimate, NO ALCOHOL. Had got completely conditioned by late whip nights to not needing so much sleep – could easily play b'gammon till 2 in the morning or drive down to Saltwood after midnight – but at a price of stiffness and bufferdom and receding hairline and advancing waistline when I think back to how long I kept up the early night, ultra-fit regime. That's what I owe my present condition to.

Saltwood   *Tuesday, 12 August*

By the pool, and still suffering tension in spite of rest and holidays. Derek Priston,[1] very soft-spokenly, asked if I could give *three* (!) Saturdays to attend 'flower shows' etc. Usual sort of 'people asking when your next surgery ...' type mornings turned out to be two separate women wanting to ego about women's rights/lib and Rhianon Wheeldon's 'cleaner' who'd been to Butlins where the food was very bad. Then fell back on 'pub-crawl' suggestions – GAAH! Only five days down from the House and already being pestered.

Saltwood   *Monday, 18 August*

Valeri totally disappeared; 1st phone call v. passionate; 2nd caught me at desk (impossible to talk properly); 3rd from phone box at Ritz (interrupted by Eva); 4th *missed* me by '2 minutes', given untraceable number. Since then total silence.

Zermatt   *Sunday, 7 September*

A greyish, dampish day. Queens departed – 'Daisy' now much more embittered, less effervescent, Geoffrey still splendid, but a little distant. James out here with Peter and incredibly VGL and so *tall*. He did the Mettelhorn yesterday, being dangerously late back so I contemplated getting the helicopter. Light failing and told 'only 5 minutes left' to decide, and then just as I was deciding it should go, a call, 'your son has been found and is at the Edelweiss Hotel' and the sighs of relief.

Tip looks also most pleasing now after a 'shaky' start with his blow wave and cowboy boots, whose purchase so enraged 'Boy'.

And what am I going back to?

---

[1]Derek Priston ran AC's two 1974 election campaigns; becoming full-time agent the following year.

Saltwood   *Saturday, 13 September*

More or less decided and broke the news to Jane – who took it very philosophically – to 'stand down in Sutton'. At this range, it simply isn't possible to satisfy the (insatiable) demands of the Conservative 'workers'.

Draft press release
SUTTON MP STANDS DOWN

'Mr Alan Clark, Member of Parliament for the Sutton division of Plymouth, said in a statement: It is with my great regret that . . . for family reasons . . . I shall not be standing for re-election for the Sutton Division . . . I will of course continue to represent and defend the rights of my constituents who have so loyally supported me in two elections . . .'

Cherry Cottage, Seend   *Saturday, 20 September*

Taking a couple of days 'off' here after a Plymouth session (Jane did the Gymkhana while I went to the Tory Reform Group inaugural – Peter Walker's Private Army).

As always at Seend – even when looking through the rattling windows of the train back from Plymouth – filled with an almost pleasurable melancholy. All the elms are dying – the great trees of the 'clump', or magic circle and the huge sentinels that stood beside the different gateways are absolutely stripped leaving the jackdaws puzzled and nervy. This afternoon I stripped an enormous hunk of bark off and stood it in the courtyard shed as a remembrance.

Saltwood   *Thursday, 25 September*

Last night, just before putting out the light, was talking about hypochondria with Jane. Said mine had virtually disappeared with so many other preoccupations. But morning hypochondria takes its place and comes flooding in – waking me at 3.30 (finally putting light on and peeing at 4.15). Realisation that crazy interest charges still absorbing all capital inflow this year. And now nothing left 'if Newton fails to sell'. Got about one year left before real crunch and Saltwood not yet transferred to Trust as hoping to retain under my own hand. I suppose triggered off by 'session' with Meeson in underground interview room in the deserted Commons yesterday which saw one year interest cheque on £20,000 to Hoare's due and he advised me to sell off Newton for what I could get (shades of 'Dick' Hoare). Thought no more about it at the time, didn't brood, that is to say, but sub-consciously must have been affected by TV film of my father's Edwardian childhood, how much of those riches had gone and how I threw away the last – or at least the penultimate – chance of setting up independent solvency by letting that field money just drift away.

Dean's Yard   *Tuesday, 30 September*

Sat here doing letters feeling incredibly tired and old and Russell Fairgrieve[1] came in – he's not a specially pretty man and less so since becoming a whip. 'Had a holiday?' he barked. No. 'Why not?' – he was crazy – ' . . . not much chance of one now, none at all'. I felt very depressed. Gosh, I would like the deck-chair by the sparkling Med, I thought – now missed it for four years. Bad situation – feeling absolutely dead-beat at end of long vac before night whipping starts.

H o C Library   *Monday, 13 October*

Start of the new term. A certain sleepy tranquillity – in spite of pressures, but this to some extent induced by 'opting out'. Usual slight feeling of being useless, overlooked, passed by. That little prick Michael Latham *already* up on the screen, gabbling (presumably about

---

[1] Russell Fairgrieve, MP for West Aberdeenshire since 1974.

housing)[1] ... Loathsome, oily Leon Brittan[2] grinning nervously at everyone (but not at me; freezes up puzzledly). Speaker wouldn't call me to ask a question – gosh one's heart races after trying to get an impromptu question in. House was pleasingly crowded for Stonehouse[3] who made an appearance starting somewhat grey, portly, tho' still handsome 'at the bar' while a welter of inconclusive points of order were bandied to and fro, then withdrawn.

Multiple source of gloom/resignation, low testosterone level.

I think just *no money* is being paid out anywhere at moment. Perhaps reaction and relief after James's accident is making me less jumpy about this than I should be – but dread the long grey envelope 'Private and Confidential' from C. Hoare & Co calling me to order.. And already saddled by inability to cheque-write – that beautiful, important Hooper PI, a true Indian original. Not to mention 'hesitation' or mistiming on quite tiny items like a new pair of shoes, paying for my suits. Both Jane and I have used our 'Res' of £20 notes, and already raiding the Christie's envelope.

Second, discontented with non-schnazziness of Plymouth. Too far away, same old faces fussing and conspiring. The slow resentment at not living in will build-up and they'll try and throw me out in the end – so surely better to pre-empt and go out on a 'Dear Larry ... Dear Alan' exchange for family reasons now, rather than wait until I really am too old (ie after next election). Jim Coote[4] at Conference said: 'You've got an oily little sod as an agent, a mad gypsy as chairman and a nutter as treasurer.' Exaggerating of course, but I know what he means.

---

[1] Like AC, Michael Latham entered the Commons in February 1974 (for Melton), but unlike AC quickly became a committee man and was now a vice-chairman of the Conservative Parliamentary Housing Committee and a member of several other House committees.

[2] Leon Brittan, MP for Cleveland and Whitby since February 1974. A barrister and former chairman of the Bow Group (and editor of its magazine *Crossbow*).

[3] John Stonehouse, MP for Walsall North since February 1974 (Wednesbury 1957–74). Postmaster-General and then Minister of Posts and Telecommunications in Harold Wilson's second government, fell from grace having faked his own death (missing presumed drowned). He was eventually found in Australia, brought back to Britain and faced charges of forgery, theft and conspiracy. He died in 1988.

[4] A Conservative Party official from Central Office.

Bratton   *Saturday, 13 December*

Terribly low and depressed. Went 'to pieces' last week, ie staying up late, working the body (and the purse), bad decisions, back failure. Lost £140 to Charles, then £100 to Lever, then £250 to Colin Slater, lured by 'Catto' into disastrous loss on Plessey ('rights' issue suddenly announced 24 hours after bull position opened). Very disappointed by failure to get elected as vice-chairman Defence Committee, so scrapped speech on cuts; very low and disconsolate feeling while Geoffrey Pattie[1] swept into secretary-ship.

Meanwhile down at Bratton beautiful cob barn almost beyond repair with tin roof flapping and water running down and wasting away the cob. I just don't have the time to spruce up Bratton – and what's the point anyway? Broomhayes must have a higher priority. In the defence of the empire it's like Australia – ie sentiment, but no economic or power reasons.

Plymouth still bickering and whispering. Larry Speare now gone, Derek Priston temporarily in the ascendant (I am going to have to say something about this tonight at – ugh – the Plymstock Community Centre). Apparently I was a bit 'sneery' (!) on TV and then heard a muddled account of how someone from Drake had been asking how I compared with, say, Peter Mills[2] – bloody cheek.

Will make one last effort to speak in economic debate on Wednesday. Try and control activities, wait for 'turnup'.

Albany, B5 Lower   *Tuesday, 23 December*

Really flying at tree-top height with only one engine at *top of the valley* (!) Bought a beautiful SI Hooper from Charles and had to cheque-write today (another 3+). Also ought really to get Valeri her coat (2), plus inspected latest tax liabilities from Meeson to cripple the New Year. Went round to the House to make a couple of free calls.

---

[1] Geoffrey Pattie, MP for Chertsey and Walton since February 1974 and secretary of the Conservative Parliamentary Aviation Committee since 1974.
[2] Peter Mills, MP for Devon West since February 1974 (Torrington 1964–74).

Saltwood   *Sunday, 28 December*

Given the fact that we are all well and fine (though self oldish – more in feeling than appearance I'm happy to believe) this is the blackest post-Christmas yet. Or should I say *bleakest*; please God don't give me a really black one!

This morning up and read *Express* before breakfast – Heseltine heavily plugged in Crossbencher and talk of 'an election in '76' (thus pre-empting any move from Plymouth – and discarding 'second preference' with Costain and Folkestone). Fact is, this year has seen a steady erosion, dissipation of the position. All I have done is survive – by familiar technique of throwing pats of butter on the surface.

Finance – worse off; o/d only minimally better. Shares all gone, plus some lovely cars.

Politics – no progress. Original promise worn off, 'blackballed' from Defence Committee (bungled security-slip, which Pattie seized). Again 'if only' ... I should have beavered like crazy in defence field – *every* question time, badgered Defence chiefs etc etc.

One major drain this year, looking back: how unlucky I've been at b'gammon. Resolved: NO MORE THIS YEAR (ie 76), except Aspers with 1x1 and Lever on 3–1 ies.[1]

Zermatt   *Wednesday, 31 December*

Year end, and gathering strength. *Very* slight improvement in health and morale. But my personal resolution for the next Christmas: I just bloody well won't have any debts at all – but of course if intention hangs fire that won't be possible. This is the one difference from last year – Newton *is* saleable.

Sitting at my desk with a heavy heart. On top: the ineradicable, obsessional worry about money. Just what am I going to do when we get back, faced with instant outgoings like mortgage on Silks cottages,

---

[1] Aspinall and Lever, both extremely good players, would give AC a handicap by allowing him to start a game with the throw of double ones (1x1) or 3–1 (3–1 ies).

school fees, stock exchange, *plus* balance to be paid Zermatt for the
delightful 2-door Shadow. Immediate decision on 'culling' rest of
collection to bare minimum – but will these be dissipated, when I
meant to concentrate them in the Classic car a/c? One side effect of
this obsession is growing identity of salvation with Hitler in 1943,
that carries with it unhappy overtones of inevitability.

1976

Central Fact finally agreed today: Hoare's insisting on a reduction [of o/d] to 100 by 1st April – ie in less than two months, effectively, from 100 + 35 + 26. Reduced me to a *total* tension blubber, with slight headache, waves of fatigue and then sudden, crazy snapping-out of it, back into realisation of possible total collapse. God knows what kind of a night I'm going to have. At least I don't drink or take pills to combat this.

Need all my energy and testosterone to cope with the Central Fact. Second occurrence, which also seemed to have a kind of pre-destinational quality in forcing me to determine life pattern was the strange accidental delivery by postman of Mama's draft will (!), 1976 model, which one opened, read, took to H of C library and photo-copied and then reposted in a WC2 pillar-box (!). It was a nasty, cold document; no bequests – other than to the British Museum and to servants; Celly got the old clothes and Col and I (it said me, but clearly a mis-print for Col) got the residue after everything (including B5) to Papa. Dealt with Col at 25% of what the other gets, but as he points out, it is an ominous indication and fact is one will get *nothing* over and above what one can steal – odd bits of silver and objects …

Back from Plymouth, and the walk on Summerhouse Hill with Col … This will be the week of the crunch – seeing Norman Reid[1] and Evelyn Joll[2] about sales … also had to decide about Alma-Tadema.

Incredibly tired and lined. No strength at all it seems, and back so feeble – did some 'wooding' this morning, with the Land-Rover and back semi-went almost at once.

---

[1] Sir Norman Reid, Director of the Tate Gallery since 1964.
[2] Evelyn Joll, a director of Agnew's, the Bond Street picture dealers.

Contemplate the exhausting list of sundries ... then the enormous pile of bills – just now trumped by Meeson demanding £2,700 and the Swiss return not yet sealed still less filed with Meeson – a sword of Damocles for the autumn.

Must record the visit to the Tate last Monday. Parked 'the little white', and the Indian lady at reception made me wait, before a youngish assistant appeared and took me up a spiral staircase to the Director's landing. She studied me intently at one point and I thought, somehow, like a nurse looking at a patient going to the theatre or surgeon for examination. In the curious white ultra-modernism reception room we sat down, and in a very short time I realised that Reid was expecting me to ask more money for the Saltonstall (while I was apprehensive that he might be going to renege). So, lying, that I had been offered $100,000, ie £50,000, we went through the pretence of working out what I would save in CGT by selling to the Tate and settled at £48,000. On air I descended the spiral staircase and had a wonderful dinner at Brooks's,[1] lost £170 to Kennedy and then collapsed in bed.

Since then some misgivings and still has to go to Trustees for confirmation.

Saltwood   *Wednesday, 18 February*

Ill (today) and strangely apprehensive – as if about to panic all the time – supposing N. Reid defaults on Saltonstall? ... No more gambling or b'gammon until *out of debt*. Difficult decision, but major operation justifies it.

---

[1] The St James' Club had the previous year merged with Brooks's in St James's Street. Where the St James' was 'cosmopolitan, artistic, boisterous', Brooks's was 'old-fashioned, almost Whiggish', according to the Brooks's historian.

Saltwood   *Thursday, 19 February*

Delicious spring day, first hint of warmth in the sun after fog, and
absolutely still. Charles Jerdein[1] rang to say the German would *not* pay
more for Alma Tadema so deal off (I had gambled on asking for 'any'
increase on £11,000), took this as a bad, bad indicator. Dread the
Tate trustees procrastinating. Walked round and round the battlements
in an inner panic, thinking of this beautiful place, the sale, the whole
collapse. Joined by Jane; didn't communicate it to her of course, but
we continued to drift about absorbing the beauty of the place. This is
real torture, let us hope it is the aversion therapy. Please God see me
through this.

Dean's Yard   *Tuesday, 24 February*

Cleared to the extent of the Trustees confirming Saltonstall – so that
will eliminate number 2 loan with Hoare's.

Albany, B5 Lower, 6am   *Friday, 5 March*

Woke early – as one does post Zurich and listened to the delight of
blackbird singing. Terribly sad that with all my pressure and odious
responsibilities I am cutting myself off even from nature. Got cheque
for Saltonstall, but felt sick opening envelope in the Commons' phone
box. Kept thinking of the quality of the painting, the shock of the
blank wall – I went into the Music Room on my return. Didn't give
a fuck for the rubbish I sold Desmond (though it is vitally important
he bought it), but this a bad week.

---

[1] Charles Jerdein, art dealer and friend.

Albany, B5   *Friday, 19 March*

This morning woke absolutely *frantic* about being wiped out. Balance of Saltonstall consumed in serving interest charges of £8,750. Hoare's letter yesterday morning with firm refusal to release Castle deeds; and then Mr McGrath of Hoare's on the phone asking 'what about steps' being taken to reduce no 2 loan, 'partners meeting' etc. Went to bed v. tired and woke with the knowledge that unless I can get the Saltwood deeds away from them *somehow* have got exactly six months left until next demand.

H of C Library   *Tuesday, 13 April*

Birthday boy. Woke several times in the night and with the glorious Albany blackbird looked from the mattress on the floor (my father has taken all the furniture) and this reinforced the dream of being wiped out. The bailiffs had been in and taken everything.

Fact is cash run out – nothing left to live on. Also 24 light to Hoare's limit, 44 light for release of Saltwood deeds. Get intermittent waves of panic – all my means of relieving indebtedness are in goods – supposing corporate collapse and nobody (ie Desmond and co) will *buy* goods?

Going to see Desmond now, to see what can be raised. Tortured schemes thresh around – did I do a 'scheme of arrangement' with Barclays or Clydesdale?

Strange morning – picked up by Winston in the lobby and asked to a lunch with him 'for' Averell Harriman; I think he said 'my stepfather' so may see Pam[1] again – not since the golden days in Cannes and then once, fleetingly, in the Ritz when she was with some Greeks.

These ironies please me. But God please don't let me go right under. How my health and appearance stood up to these stresses I don't know.

---

[1] Pamela Harriman (née Digby) married first Randolph Churchill, by whom she had a son, Winston, MP for Stretford since 1970. She later married the American theatrical and film producer, Leland Hayward, and, following his death in 1971, the American statesman, Averell Harriman. She became a leading light in the Democratic Party and a legendary Washington hostess.

Saltwood   *Tuesday, 20 April*

What could have been a grotesque weekend was lightened by
Desmond agreeing to take another 34 of pictures and then, on Thursday eve, came a call to say Newton had sold for 40!

Friday night however strange waking with minuscule pee and
faintly peppermint throat. Thought nothing of it, though frightfully
tired and stiff the next day. However kept busy as we are 'opening' for
the first time – though took two hours off for intensive sun bathing
by greenhouse. Blushingly, at supper, I said I had 'sunstroke' temp
99.8. Poorish night. Next day struggled on gamely in 'Hadleigh'[1]
clothes for public – a little Italianish girl I gave a peacock feather
to – and feeling rotten. Went to bed in 'summer double', awaking
intermittently with progressive deterioration – or so it seemed – 100
at 2.30am.

Saltwood   *Saturday, 24 April*

'On the mend' physically, after really awful nights of muck-sweat,
minute tortured dribblings, and fear of galloping prostate cancer.

Great Hall, Saltwood   *Saturday, 1 May*

Back on the night train after the usual crowded surgery, fluffing of
constituency opportunities and late, late curry dinner. Also talk of
early election, *the whole bloody time.* Must write to Albert (difficult
letter to compose) about Folkestone possibility.

A fine, but cold day with no disasters in the waiting post (Smiler
etc), but by now feeling *incredibly tired*, it swept on me about 4pm
while I was polishing the Dienst. God, what a lot of polishing there
is to do on the cars. If I just polished and gardened the whole day
would go by. Even so, 'much better'.

---

[1] The Clarks had been much taken by an ITV television series of that title, starring Gerald
Harper as an immaculately-dressed country squire, with a Monteverdi 375L sports car
and living at the stately if at times expensive to keep up Melford Park.

Albany, B5   *Tuesday, 4 May*

Another glorious morning. Does London have the finest weather in England? Always look out of that little lavatory window behind the Corinthian columns of the R.A.[1]

I had walked into Chamber last night for a minute and stood by Chair as Joel Barnett[2] was saying that 'Heritage Houses' can now also have a fund to protect them, ie if only I can do my bit, Saltwood Estate can be a candidate and passed on in perpetuity. Rushed out and phoned Jane who said '. . . it makes it all seem worthwhile'.

Later

For first time starting to feel *really* on the run. Not even getting *anything* done in politics, never going into the Chamber, cancelling three engagements in a week. Obsessed with fall of the Reich. This is 1944, one year left.

H o C Library   *Monday, 10 May*

Incredibly hot and stuffy, though sitting by open window. Today (actually took place on Saturday) one of those lucky breaks – tipped by George Hutchinson[3] for instant inclusion in 'shadow cabinet'. Suddenly felt fine, burgeoning.

Port Lympne   *Thursday, 3 June*

Drove over here to my favourite spot in the whole of E Kent – one of the most evocative in the world – and shortly to vanish for ever. I sit on the terrace where one would occasionally get tea <u>limone</u>, and indescribably thin cucumber sandwiches before being sent back up to

---

[1] The Clark apartment at Albany backs onto the Royal Academy.
[2] Joel Barnett, MP for Heywood and Royton since 1964, Chief Secretary to the Treasury since 1974.
[3] George Hutchinson, political columnist in *The Times*.

'Bellers'.[1] Can still look through the glass doors at that marbled, Moorish interior, black and white floors and arched ceilings. Totally still outside, but trees now grown enormously, hemming it in, better even than in Philip's heyday. The place has *slept* for 30 years, noone lived in it since Philip died, nothing disturbed. At any moment Philip could come out and call – to this day I can hear his drawl. And in time it will be over-run, damaged irretrievably by the tramping public with their toffee papers and the Kleenexes.[2]

As I pottered about at Saltwood this morning, realised hadn't been up to London for a week – so hadn't needed any cash. Yet cash dribbling in from public – if only 'indebtedness eliminated', could submit very happily. Will I ever emerge? I remember calmly going to Hoare's when it was 190 and trying to borrow *another* 20 to buy Selmes' car and business! Have got until October – or possibly till next April (2nd half year interest) then – explosion. Unless 'House in order' first.

H o C Library   *Monday, 14 June*

Best part of the evening was chat on terrace with Tom Swain[3] and (leftish) little northerner. This latter chappie had come up and said to Tom: 'Ah, thee's courting with the storm-troopers, eh?' That pleased me.

---

[1] Bellers, a house used by AC's family in the 1930s, was close to Port Lympne, the magnificent country home of Sir Philip Sassoon, MP for Hythe and for much of the 1930s the highly influential Under-Secretary of State for Air and chairman of the board of the National Gallery (hence his original links with the Clark family). His mother was a Rothschild. To the designs of Sir Herbert Baker, he started building Port Lympne just before the First World War, lavishing upon it his enormous knowledge of art, furniture, china and old silver. He died in 1939 after a short illness and not yet sixty. Port Lympne was commandeered by the RAF during the Second World War.

[2] AC, happily, was proved wrong. He recommended Port Lympne to John Aspinall who bought it and its 275 acres for £360,000. Aspinall restored the house and used the grounds for a zoo park to complement his original zoo near Canterbury.

[3] Tom Swain, MP for Derbyshire NE since 1959, a former miner.

H o C   *Tuesday, 22 June*

Another glorious evening – every day has been fine, Friesian weather, except needless to say the two days of the weekend.

Sitting in a new perch I've discovered, theoretically allocated to a member of the staff and (tidily) congested with his gear, it is pleasingly situated in a corner, the last one before the non-smoking room, beside no fewer than three open windows, so that the lazy fresh river smells of wet varnish and tidal aromas come in together with the sounds of the chuggy engines of tugs and pleasure craft and the occasional guffaw from the terrace below.

Apparently now heading for two filthy nights of intermittent voting on Land Tax committee stage. Had a very late night last night at the Clermont after late 11.45ish 2nd vote. Ran into Benson and after shocking start 'took command' and relieved him of £160. This gave me palpable pleasure. But they do drain one, these late nights. I went home for a couple of hours and, as I lay by the pool, thought how diminished (by earlier standards) was my sexuality. Always in the past I would get erotic sensations lying out after a 'dip'. Short of food and sleep of course – that strange affliction at Easter (exactly two months ago), had something to do with it. And strange after effects, practically off alcohol for virtually six weeks.

Just a note from dinner at Saltwood for Norman Tebbit: 'Many would like you as Folkestone's next MP . . .', one woman said. Jane, with her usual good sense just replied flatly: '. . . many wouldn't.' And certainly balance of that number hasn't necessarily shifted in my favour since being in 'Parly'.

Great Hall, Saltwood   *Saturday, 26 June*

Sitting, at 8.14pm, at the end of the long table, with only a towel around my waist. What a wonderful room this is! A college library, a castle library all to oneself. For the first time for at least a year (and then it was only for a few brief weeks) I do not wake early each morning and worry about money.

H of C Library   *Tuesday, 29 June*

Absolutely dead whacked by heat, swimming and commuting. Chucked a city lunch to hang on at Saltwood (drove down last night after the vote in the Bira with the windscreen flat and got 'stye' in right eye).

'Daisy' came over on his way to Boulogne/St Trop with a good-looking (G Peck, Anthony Perkins) American student. I said to him '... God if I was that age, and looked like that *and* an MP you wouldn't see me for steam.'

Zermatt   *Saturday, 4 September*

Out here in poor shape. Really *alarmed* at appearance last night. Yet again trying the Zapata moustache, which adds to haggardness. What's the point? On arrival got letter from UBS in the C. Hoare & Co style wanting Sw FR 17,000 immediately, and this morning opened (quite by chance) something from La Suisse apparently noticing that house had not been insured since April and premium of 1,200 Sw overdue.

Also a little depressed about leaving James at home – as he is himself. Going through one of those phases – only gets excited when talking about aeroplanes – of which he is incredibly knowledgeable, better even than I was in 1939. Mercedes 300 car ran badly, roughly at best (though no Mercedes is ever completely perfect to drive). Sad? Next year will probably be in Citroen convertible. James rather gloomily said 'our cars get shabbier and shabbier'.

Zermatt   *Monday, 6 September*

Politically an autumn of application. Allotted three committees: finance, home affairs, defence. Work required in constituency minimum to keep it in play until April/May – ie unlikely actually wanting to sack me before next election or, slightly less easy, seeking to give a reasonable reference. If APC[1] quits [Folkestone] in January

---

[1] AC's journal code for Albert Costain.

trying

OK

will put in, the die is cast. If he fights next election so will I – he can't fight on after that, so the question of the new boundaries doesn't really apply anyway.

Genuinely excited and keen to get back to the House. Ladbroke apparently giving *evens* on a coalition by 1st Jan. I *must* lay against that. Tories all chattering and yearning about an early election. Personally I don't see it. Why? How can it come about? PMs' call elections when they think they are going to win, not in order to commit hari kari. But the gossip and *jockeying* will be fun.

Albany   *Wednesday, 13 October*

Was sipping my EMT and reading *Chips* (for 3rd or 4th time) and got to bit when – 4 November 52 – he recalled Eisenhower's victory in US Presidential Election. Remember on that same 'box-spring', on which I have entertained Pam, Drew, Renny, Marge etc, hearing the news on that same day in '52 with feelings of disgust (was I more Liberal in those days?).[1] Reflected really that my life style hardly altered, I mean still chasing girls and still in debt.

Back at the House, usual cock-up on voting. Whipped at 3.30, but first vote at 7.45pm. As a result lost £96 to Charles at Coys.

Dined with Robin Cooke,[2] sparkling, in the Harcourt Room. Good food, interesting – although younger than me he has been in the House with Mac and Chips.[3] Seemed sanguine enough about his chances to move on to South Dorset, but Associations are such shits.[4] Little chat with APC in the lobby – he enigmatically withholding as always – said my 'image' is against me, among locals etc. New Association elections in March and 'clean sweep' coming. 'Lucky him!' Jane brightly quipped, 'people will just play musical chairs.' Robin

---

[1] In an entry for 4 November 1980, AC adds: 'at the time I was a Stevenson supporter, faintly rebellious and reading, not very successfully, bar finals.'
[2] Robert [Robin] Cooke, MP for Bristol West, since 1957.
[3] Harold Macmillan retired as Bromley's MP in 1964; Sir Henry ('Chips') Channon died in 1958 while MP for Southend West.
[4] AC showed prescience in this entry; Cooke was not selected for S. Dorset, even though the retiring MP was his father-in-law, Evelyn King. He only returned to Parliament as Special Advisor on the Palace of Westminster to the Secretary of State for the Environment. S. Dorset chose Lord Cranborne as its candidate.

Cooke said: 'In a summer of a bygone age ... and so even you, if it comes to that.'

Yes, and so soon after the excitement of returning feel totally flat and neglected. Nobody speaks to me, no invitations, people seem to avoid my eye in the lobby.

Perhaps all that Robin said to me and what Chips wrote about England dying.[1] And yet ... I think of James and Andrew, the young who could still be taken. What is the key?

H of C Library   *Wednesday, 10 November*

Still feeling incredibly tired – constantly having to catch breath. Aftermath of heavy head-cold over weekend; late nights – H Lever last night £100 – travelling, missing meals etc.

Yesterday filthy nadir (hopefully). (1) Took deadly dose of Rontgens at fucking Panoramachest x-ray. Wanted to get up and go when bloody titty nurse in immaculate white overalls put on huge lead caps and went behind screen, but was already too tired to do so. (2) letter telling me of F&GP [at Sutton]: trouble about not answering letters and Nan Howard[2] took this up (! Groan). (3) Great 'out' as Desoutter collapsed and either lose £3000 or take them up – UGH!

Plymouth: my God! With memory of Robin Cooke in my mind, must wait until after AGM and then systematically court Folkestone officers. If 'snap' election would get in for Plymouth, if not then Folkestone option must be taken. Total shits they are – no purpose in life other than to bicker and backbite – degrade everything above a certain level of mediocrity.

---

[1] 8 May 1952: 'The England I wooed and won and love still, is dying; thus I am determined to enjoy what remains to me of it and of life here: the few declining years, the few rapidly diminishing thousands of pounds; if I survive the collapse of the country or of my personal fortune, I shall slip off to some remote part of sun-lit California to die – on my American income, so far untouched, or rather unimpaired. Perhaps I can look for another five years.' (*Chips: The Diaries of Sir Henry Channon.*)

[2] Mrs H.O'N. Howard, chairman of Sutton's Dunstone ward.

Saltwood   *Sunday, 14 November*

Very nice last night and woken this morning about 8am by banging noises at main door. 'Lady Clark died last night'. Jane and I dressed quickly, hoping to beat Col. Found my father 'in tremendous form' wiping mouth with back of hand, having just eaten brown egg and grapefruit, little tray in library.

Spoke briefly and inconclusively, then next went in to see Mama, signalling to Jane *not* to come. Apprehensive about pulling back the sheet, but found her face composed, determined, rather beautiful, not in any way distorted (my father had quite unnecessarily, and alarmingly, said, ' ... the body does undergo certain changes by now ... etc') Jane came in, and as we agreed about her expression – Jane said 'she hasn't given up' – I started briefly crying and she also.

Went back to breakfast. Rang Celly and put her mind at rest about Mama's appearance. Then Col – he wouldn't come over. Changed into black and went up to Cenotaph on green where Jane meant to be laying wreath. Small crowd expected. Jane did her stuff quite well and I spoke to a few (prospective) constituents. Back, briefly to GH, where Father turned up, looking like death warmed up.

After spaghetti lunch snoozed on upright sofa in green room while Jane went over to GH to keep Celly company and (apparently) go through the jewellery. She ran back after an hour – I had woken, washed my face – with a few very insignificant items. We took a walk, much plagued as usual on Sundays by ogling, loutish public who won't say 'Good afternoon' even. After a good tea, Col arrived. We chatted a bit and I walked him up and down, explaining that he won't get anything, as my Father will block my mother's estate and leave his own to his new wife.[1] This made Col very gloomy (later that evening he rang and said he had spoken to Celly about the will and it was a c1971 model!).[2]

My father came over for dinner, shuffling but compos. Only drank 'a little claret', talked, but without much warmth. Wonder how long he will last? Rang Jamie late. He was a bit low, and made lower by news of Granny. Dear Boy, how I love him. God please protect us.

---

[1] AC was in no doubt that his father would remarry and soon.

[2] In a later note he added that he had just read his mother's last will (sent by the Clydesdale): 'She did leave everything to me ... the fact that she did so is a tremendous liberation for me ... the way in which she died fills us with grief and affection.'

Train to Waterloo   *Saturday, 20 November*

After three days feeling really awful, incredibly tired – out-of-breath (radiation disease?); utterly depressed by present condition, nullity of will, futility of H of C, losses on SE, bolshiness of Hoare & Co, and bloodiness of Plymouth constituency.

Shadow Cab 'shuffle' still giving hope, as Heseltine not promoted.

Albany, B5   *Wednesday, 8 December*

Very depressed by end-of-an-era symptom. Fucking H. Lever quite batted me to bits. I lost £350 between 6 and 9pm. I don't say I'll give the game up. But I *must* prove I'm not addicted, so will see how long I can go. Euphoria of Home Affairs Committee victory already wearing off. (Good publicity, plus photo, in *Evening Herald* will just infuriate Plymouth schemers rather than conciliate them). Really, the top priority should be devoted to politics. I'm just not being single-minded enough. I'm using the House as a kind of club/ringside seat/status enhancer, *not* as a central mission.

1977

A YEAR OF TRAVAIL

Indebtedness:	Saltwood to Trust for Jane etc
	Pension Fund
Politics:	Pamphlet on law and order as CPC booklet
B'Gammon:	REDUCED RATION (£64 a week)
Girls:	Mens (presumably) – in cupo sano. Yoga
	[mens sana in corpore sana]

Zermatt   *Saturday, 1 January 1977*

Sometimes gloomily see myself as Hemingway, 'Ernst' in Hotchner book.[1] Best years gone by etc. But at least I don't drink. Seem, in fact, strangely, suspiciously fit and non-tired compared with dragged out days at the House.

What can I do about the House? This year I must have a go. It is impossible to get called. [Speaker] Thomas simply will *not* notice me.

I must –
(a) plan questions seriously. Defence. Home. Foreign. Europe. Chancellor. PM – all got edges. Now I have no excuse for lack of confidence, or fucking sarcasm for that matter.
(b) Sit in for every Question Time until Easter Recess.

This is last chance for 'impact'. It is 1977. Pretty bullish year, three books to write, and Saltwood to improve. Something's got to give and I suppose it will be b'gammon and sex – with the blondes away.

Saltwood Library   *Sunday, 16 January*

Eight days back and peculiar 'improvements'. Are they attributable to that head or helmet that I bought at Christie's? Decided last night that it was bringing me luck following Jane recounting to me (on the phone on Tuesday night) her curious experience of hearing the Yellow

---

[1] A.E. Hotchner's *Papa Hemingway*, an account of the author's friendship with the American writer, had been widely acclaimed.

Room door opening in the middle of the night and lying frozen in terror. The next day she moved the head *into* the Yellow Room thinking (quite rightly) that it might have been trying to communicate. We both agreed how 'powerful' it is. And who knows it might – there is no reason why not that I know – have been here in the past.

What an incredible, marvellous, romantic place Saltwood is, and how I am wedded to it. I must have a little *cache* at Zermatt just in case, a few period things, a kind of mothball fleet in Northern California or Canada, but my roots are here in this glorious piece of English medieval history.

Anyhow, events: done a lot of car-trading and full of enjoyment at this. Hoping to make money by setting up a Sothebys sale and also building up of a private trading stock of mascots etc.

Had a big win off CH plus a series of little, canny ones from 'the school' so comfortably in surplus for first week (£252). And Jerdein offered 11.6 for the Alma-Tadema! On top of this a 'cunning' talk with Sam Alder and he offered 27 for Woodfall St!!

Albany, B5   *Thursday, 27 January*

There are few nicer things than sitting in bed, drinking up strong Indian tea, and reading Chips' diaries – which loosen the mind, and cause reflection. Just reached (or rather re-reached for the umpteenth time) that passage when he has been caught out, and Rab gone to Education, '... a bad mistake',[1] Chips thought, wrongly, and how the Commons seemed to have changed focus. But concerned to see that Chips of 44 felt himself alone and still more by his reference to Richard Wood as Halifax's 'immense auburn young subaltern'.[2]

There he was in the proportional representation debate yesterday on his gammy leg on the front bench below (my place). Don Pontificatore. 'It's all balls, isn't it?' I said to Tony Fell,[3] who was sitting on the cross-bench on the Labour side within earshot of Dennis

---

[1] 18 July 1941: 'Winston offered him the Board of Education which he accepted willingly. A mistake, I think, as he is now in a back-water.' (*Chips: The Diaries of Henry Channon*, edited by Robert Rhodes James.)

[2] 14 September 1943. Wood, MP for Bridlington since 1950, was the second son of Chamberlain's foreign secretary, Lord Halifax. He had been wounded in action later in 1943 and retired aged 23.

[3] Anthony Fell, MP for Yarmouth (Norfolk) since 1970 (also 1951–66).

Skinner. 'Yes, the most total utter bloody crap,' he answered. Both Skinner and Wood tittered.

Saltwood   *Sunday, 6 February*

Watched Enoch on TV – quite by chance. Jane spotted that he had already been on for fifteen minutes. Quite wonderful. His clarity of speech and thought, his administrative experience, his living and incomparable patriotism and they ignore him. I remember that after one of my articles in the *Telegraph* Dennis Skinner said to me – 'you'll end up in despair, like me.'

Speaking to the Folkestone YCs on Monday. Will I be able to get Folkestone? If I do, that will be the real temptation in the wilderness. Because I can either be the local squire, ringside seat, boring buffer, or go flat out with a secure base at last, having learned all my lessons from the last few years.

Billy Wallace died of cancer ... aah.[1]

East Cloisters   *Wednesday, 9 February*

Sitting in my new desk at E. Cloisters after losing £88 to Charles at Coys (tho' still up on him this year).

Miss the blonde family[2] and being mocked on all sides. That (v. pretty) little blonde assistant to the camera team refused to be 'mistaken' and thus didn't acknowledge the dozen red roses I sent to her. Jane (Australian) said 'you're older than her Daddy.' What in hell am I going to do?

Depressed by James talking about getting his pilot's licence this summer. Oh dear! Will there never be an end to those anxieties? Quite amazingly he said: 'Grandpapa never says to *you* – '... you must be in by 11pm' etc.

---

[1] Billy Wallace, the millionaire son of Euan Wallace, a former MP and wartime adviser to George VI, and part of Princess Margaret's circle from the 1950s. He and AC had known each other since Eton.
[2] The coven had moved away without warning.

H o C   *Tuesday, 15 February*

Got back for Anthony's (Avon[1]) memorial service [in Westminster Abbey]. MPs, badly treated, packed into a little side pew in the North Lantern, while the main part was kept open until the last minute (for whom?) then thrown open to a weird showering – mainly Palace of Westminster staff, with a smattering of late-coming MPs, eg Pattie. I was glad to sit next to Angus Maude in a row with Airey Neave and Sir John Hall.[2] The old school. A few nameless slugs were there, such as Michael Hamilton[3] who pretends (not difficult) to be very stupid. Some days I think the Parliamentary Party is three-fifths duck-shit. Walked back alone, aggressive, with the music of Handel's *Saul* ringing in my ears. It's unusual, and nice, not to have heard a fine piece of music before.

Plymouth train 7.30am   *Friday, 18 March*

Reflect on how shattered, *épuisé*, I am. It is not so long ago that with nothing to do after tea I would go for a walk on the Hoe and do half hour exercise in my room. My face *very* lined. Given to long periods of lost concentration, just glazedly reflecting. Has all my physical capital been spent? I am going through a change of life. I must not alter. But I'm *so* low on testosterone. A beautiful new girl would put that right – will I ever meet one?

H of C   *Wednesday, 23 March*

Appalling punishment (b'gammon) on Monday night – lost £800. Will go and do some yoga at Albany.

At the Bow Group dinner Heath rambled 'down memory lane' then finally got into his theme about '... a realignment, moderate

---

[1] Anthony Eden, Earl of Avon, had not enjoyed good health since his resignation as Prime Minister in 1957 following Suez. He had died on 14 January.

[2] Angus Maude, MP for Stratford-upon-Avon since 1963 (Ealing South 1950–58) ; Airey Neave, MP for Abingdon since 1953; Sir John Hall, MP for Wycombe since 1952.

[3] Michael Hamilton, MP for Salisbury since 1965.

grouping of the centre . . .' etc. *No!* people shouted. 'Tripe!' I shouted
from my traditional place at the end of the table.

Heath obviously still trying to play some cards, because I was
listening to the somewhat diffuse – and halting speech by Margaret
this afternoon – House v. full and she in a black suit with white
collar/blouse – when Norman Lamont[1] came in and stood by me at
the Bar of the House, did a 'whatsappen'd? whatsappen'd?' Apparently
Steel[2] interrupted his fund-raising lunch with Heath with a desperate
phone call about something. Actually Callaghan,[3] blandly in
command, had clearly whipped them up. I peered down the benches,
was glad to see signs of receding hairline, high spots at the temples, of
the odious Heseltine.

H o C   *Tuesday, 29 March*

Policeman coming up to serve summons at Brighton with possibility
of optional endorsement (!!)

Total depression. Tip going to Germany tomorrow, and will miss
him. Is Boy to go to Sandhurst? I couldn't arrange the visit. The way,
upperclass ADC to 'Sir Philip' or 'The General'. Who are his friends
going to be?

Spoke in the House last night about Air Raid Shelters (there aren't
any) and frightened myself. Sat down to deafening silence. Plymouth
crumbling. Will I get Folkestone? Old and grey-looking.

To add to the burden – Stradling Thomas suggested I maintained
an anti P-R group in the parliamentary party. Must start catching the
eye. Breathe deeply.

---

[1] Norman Lamont, MP for Kingston-upon-Thames since 1972.
[2] David Steel, MP for Roxburgh, Selkirk and Peebles since 1965; Leader of the Liberal
Party since 1976.
[3] James Callaghan, MP for Cardiff South-East since 1950 (South Cardiff, 1945–50), had
succeeded Harold Wilson as Prime Minister in 1976.

Saltwood   *Monday, 4 April*

My father over last night and grumpily teasing about his will – left James 'the clock' which is in Great Hall study and belongs to me anyway!

Saltwood   *Monday, 25 April*

'Boy' going back to Le Rosey.[1] Hardly seem to have seen him these hols except briefly between biking bouts, only to shout at him for being untidy or idle. Just that one pleasing half hour at Blade's after the dentist. And, I suppose, this was his last holidays as a schoolboy as I have to arrange his Sandhurst interviews etc for the autumn and his plans to go America in the summer. Exposed all this time to more and more perils – plus the obsessive desire to 'race'.

Albany   *Thursday, 28 April*

Had interview yesterday with Margaret Thatcher for first time. She sat, china-blue. Almost *too* text-book sincere. No intimacy. The half-finished sentences, the implied assumption, that mixture of Don, Colonel-of-the-Regiment, 'Library', which one gets from almost every other member of the Shadow – Pym, Willie,[2] Gilmour – even the lower rank like Paul Channon[3] and William Clark[4] – totally absent.

Actually the *point* of my call, which at one time had looked so promising was to explain that the anti-PR strength would *not* be adequate as the Labourites would not join us in the lobby. 'Only 130,

---

[1] Le Rosey, the oldest private school in Switzerland with pupils from all over the world, and, uniquely, two campuses, at Le Rolle for spring and autumn, and at Gstaad for winter.
[2] William (Willie) Whitelaw, MP for Penrith since 1955.
[3] Paul Channon, son of 'Chips', succeeded his father as MP for Southend West in 1959; deputy leader of the Conservative delegation to the WEU and the Council of Europe since 1976.
[4] William Clark, MP for Croydon South since February 1974 (E Surrey, 1970–74), joint deputy chairman, Conservative Party Organisation since 1975.

Alan, what worries me . . .' 'Another 80 with you, of course,' I said and mumbled.

I also slightly fluffed it when she was talking about Callaghan's soft-centre – good for publicity, but inadequate underneath. Instead of saying 'like Heseltine', I mumbled something about 'I could mention a few like that in our party'. She looked startled. There were silences and she mentioned Defence – I half got going when we were interrupted.

H o C   *Tuesday, 21 June*

Summertime in the Library of the House; could go to bed early after some sherrys and white wine and sleep 14 hours – but instead, faced with 'until this business is concluded, which could be at a very late hour . . .' so further harrowing of the body.

Still shampoo'd my hair at Albany after an All-bran box there on return from a day out to Seend. Oh how Cherry Cottage has been exposed, its character altered, by the loss of the Great Elms in the clump. I pottered about in the orchard, *recherché du temps perdu* as always at Seend, thinking of the high spots – my happiest period.

Had my triumph in the House last week – getting both sides to laugh at my 'quip' as the *Telegraph* called it about 'anyone who has been to Eton . . . has already served the equivalent of five years in gaol.'[1] Actually, of course, it was really Miscampbell's[2] idea and I just moved fast enough. Miscampbell put it out during Heffer tirade; I gathered courage during Molloy's[3] follow-up and then stood – as I was close the Speaker called me, almost in surprise – it really was a piccolo triumph, *prolonged* laughter with people leaning down the benches to congratulate me, and so on. A little H of C moment.

---

[1] To which Merlyn Rees, the Home Secretary replied: 'There is one difference – in prison they learn to read and write.'

[2] Norman Miscampbell, MP for Blackpool North since 1962.

[3] William Molloy, MP for Ealing North since 1964.

Albany B5   *Tuesday, 12 July*

Ex-morning tea and reasonably euphoric – though *mouvementé*.

Must record the drive back in THEBUS, splendid on Autoroute and Alp alike, even though grossly loaded with dear 'Boy's' kit, stereo etc. The great, unusual heat of the Le Rosey garden party (certain shades of Verdon Hill in *Hemlock and After*[1]) with Boy going round getting his book signed by his chums ... 'See you ... keep in touch ... etc etc ...' The dress standard bum-boys. David Niven[2] *very* well preserved. Certain beautifully-dressed beauties.

Back at Saltwood, Le Rosey inflections already fading, though having given him, as he rightly said after going into Blades on his own, total confidence.

That week was, of course, the week of the heatwave. I say 'of course' because I was locked into the standing committee on Bill Benyon's Abortion Bill. Curtains drawn to shield us from the sun, endlessly Zombie-like, eating the occasional rock-cake in the corridor or muck-sweating making phone calls from that little, very open phone there.

At night sleeping, perhaps too much absentee sleeping, in committee room 7 where I had found a tiny curved leather armchair, and putting two others in a row could make a sort of couch. Woken in the night by muffled bangings and clatterings and at dawn found that Dr Jeremy Bray, of wealth tax fame (he appeared to be suffering from hay fever)[3] had built up a camp bed in the corner. Every two hours or so we were roused by the amiable but somewhat limited poison-dwarf Ian Campbell (Lab)[4] 'on whip' who kept going on whisky.

Saltwood, Great Hall Study   *Thursday, 11 August*

First actual day of the hols! ie weekday, fine, and *not* having to go up on the 2.52, or whatever. Did some dictating – including writing a personal letter of apology to little Mrs Williams of Bernice Terrace,

[1] Angus Wilson's 1952 novel.
[2] David Niven, the actor, lived in Switzerland and had daughters at the school.
[3] Jeremy Bray, MP for Motherwell since October 1974 (Middlesbrough West 1962–70).
[4] Ian Campbell, MP for Dunbartonshire West since 1970.

who I had shouted at in surgery last Friday. Then did Villa Mauresque getaway by the pool.

After tea I walked with Jane into Ann's valley. I looked at the long, burgeoning August countryside. Trees absurdly overblown, grass long and with pale brown seed pods, everything dry and felt calm – no real anxieties except 'Boy'; but just a whiff of afternoon of one's life. Stiff, energy still down, totally disenchanted. The coven disappeared, and no chance of 'getting off with' anyone else – not to that extent anyhow! And even the coven don't send one, make one's heart thump, like they used to.

Twenty years. On – I shall be 69, rising to become a sage (I do hope I have grandchildren). Back – it was 1957. The year I went bankrupt for the first time and the Clydesdale refused to cash my cheque. I was sleeping with R. (intermittently) and subsisting, no more, at 11 Watchbell Street. At some point I remember being interviewed for a job as a British Leyland salesman in Los Angeles. But of course I was hopelessly 'boyish'. Even after we were married, I used to go to Hastings and prance up and down the promenade trying to pick up girls.

At any rate, I must hold my physique now: see how much I can recover in this long recess and try not to slip back.

Saltwood   *Saturday, 27 August*

C. Hoare & Co letter this morning – always sent to spoil one's weekend. Debts now total £80,000 AGAIN.

Reading David Irving's brilliant, stylish but scholarly biography of Hitler.[1] I remember in that curious white living room of his flat with all its files and things the only time we met when he told me – 'there won't be a dry eye at the end of my next book'. Certainly I find it very unsettling.

---

[1] *Hitler's War* had just been published.

Zermatt   *Sunday, 4 September*

Returned from a great 24 hrs journey to the Mettelhorn with Cin.
He was superb (though nearly collapsed on the initial ascent last night
to Trift) – made the tent, cooked the food, supervised the fires. It was
lovely in the tent – though disappointingly ramshackle as usual. A
long, long climb to the summit – five hours and the last steps on the
Tower were torture. At the peak I twice dropped off in Rodin's
'thinking' position. Got a 'suntan' walking back across the snowfield.

Albany   *Saturday, 12 November*

Saturday morning, a pre-breakfast, post 'Chips', waiting to catch the
11.30 – is there one on a Saturday morning in winter? – for Plymouth
and 'on the spot' ego-fest by County Councillor Lake, as she calls
herself, in Cattedown followed by business-woman dinner black tie
at Duke and Armistice Service. *Oh* how these fucking Plymouth
things drain one (as Heseltine warned me they would). As I sit here
now, decided finally to make the announcement almost immediately
after the next election that will not stand again there. This should give
me three minimum more years without these pressures. Catch is,
what if Albert [Costain] makes last-minute announcement *this* time.
Personally I don't think he will, is chattily delivered to become deputy
speaker or something.[1]

On Sunday we were committed, somewhat reluctantly, to go to
the Dedication of Standards service and general ceremonies in Hythe
(British Legion). Actually it was lovely. Uplifting service – brilliant
address by new vicar of St Leonards: 'Old men dream dreams; young
men see visions', and he recited the names off the monuments and
then the battle honours. Afterwards to the new BL hall – a piece of
cake, as I said to Jane. The sort of thing one would have sat eight
hours in the Plymouth train to do and all one had to do is to climb
back into the Land-Rover and drive for five minutes!

Thursday a little House of Commons episode: I had my nomination
paper for Secretary of Home Affairs and wanted two signatures. House

---

[1] In fact Costain fought another election (1979) and only retired from Folkestone in 1983.
His successor was none other than Michael Howard (see entry 12 May 1972).

virtually deserted, but saw Mayhew, Brooke, Rhodes J and Cope[1] having a jolly dinner; wished I could have joined them instead of being stuck with Oscar Murton[2] who told me at great length about his wife's death from cancer.

Got up and interrupted them and waved my paper. Some badinage (as I thought). Cope signed reluctantly, Rho J to my amazement, actually *wouldn't*, shuffled and said something about 'I've signed so many already, I can't remember' etc, passed it to Brooke who was just preparing an excuse when Mayhew came to my rescue and signed with a flourish.

I thought I had good relations with Rho J. Two historians together in the House. Mystified. It's always hard to realise how many people hate/are jealous/turned off/by me.

'Winter Desk' East Cloisters   *Thursday, 17 November*

Last night as I was talking with Paul Channon in the lobby I noticed how strangely *shiny*, high gloss one might say, were the insides of his ears.

Short-sighted, I looked closer first one side then the other thinking he was wearing some kind of plastic, 'concealed' deaf aid. Apparently not.

Later, driving to the 10 o'clock vote I saw the aftermath of a horrible accident in Piccadilly. The ambulance parked *against* the traffic, by the dreaded St James' Club Island, where the intermittent screech of brakes would disturb one's nights in those front rooms. The stretchers and the red blankets: I was reminded of this now hearing the late night sirens of rushing police cars – that sound always makes me conscious, I ask myself 'where are the boys?'

---

[1] Patrick Mayhew, MP for Tunbridge Wells since February 1974; Peter Brooke, MP for Cities of London and Westminster since a by-election in February 1977; Robert Rhodes James, editor of AC's beloved *Chips*, and MP for Cambridge since 1976; John Cope, MP for South Gloucestershire since February 1974.

[2] Oscar Murton, MP for Poole since 1964, Deputy Speaker 1976–79. His wife had died earlier that year.

Saltwood   *Sunday, 4 December*

I took the train down to Plymouth, where it was mildly cold and was glad of the Winter Car, MoT'd by Mumford. At surgery was rung by Linda Bertram (always one of the 'never-seem-to-see-you' brigade) who said that 'they' had all been waiting at the Blue Peacock (wherever the hell *that* is) for me to turn up and do some canvassing for Eileen Smith at Efford. How was I to know? 'Oh, we thought you'd come into the office and pick up the message.' One more black spot chalked up. The constituents took up my time; then, again, Mr Johnson came in for a chat, a serious chat (I still haven't done *last* fortnightly surgery bumf!). What with Linda Bertram's phone call – she finally pinned me down to do *walkabout* – ugh!! – all next Saturday morning, and a little fireman[1] I had noticed sitting rather resentfully in the waiting room with his tall but attractive wife in her head-scarf, I was late getting to the Duke – no time for a bath – for the CPC dinner. Bought a comb from the receptionist and gloomily inspected my stubbly face – fortunately my battery razor was in the suitcase for a quick chopping for the next meeting – and went ashen-faced down to Room 31 (the original interview room for stage 1 of the Sutton Selection Committee).

I wasn't absolutely happy about it from the start. A little red wine (I drank as much as I could of this). Of course I spotted immediately the shit one – something about each ward electing a representative to liase between the Member and his constituents. I 'good-naturedly' suggested that it should be discussed at the F&GP or the Executive. The session rumbled on, after a bit getting somewhat perilously philosophical with my talking about the Conservatives being the party of appeasement, and 'declaring' for the National Front – I got *so* irritated by Kay Mansfield trying to say we were going to lose votes to the NF – 'there won't be a candidate against me,' I said. She still didn't get the point. '. . . because they know I'm the nearest thing they're ever likely to get to an MP.'

Little Jack Courtney made a kind of grumpy comment about not trying to ride two horses at once. However this thing had almost dragged to its close and the chairman was just about to start, did in fact mumble 'Ladies and Gentlemen . . .' when Jack got up and 'straight-forwardly' said he wanted to refer to 'Question Seven' – I

---

[1] Firemen were on their first nationwide strike in support of pay claim.

couldn't believe my ears when he went much further than I thought
possible (although I knew it was going to be bad) – said I visited the
constituency 'so seldom' etc etc. Massive and flagrant. Asked for more
walkabouts. I suppose I didn't defend myself as well as I might have
done. Noone rushed to defend me from the floor, I might say. I should
have said I've been there every weekend since the recess. I had been
talking for quarter hour and all I wanted to do was scream 'fuck off
you little runt ...' and leave Plymouth never to return. That's Mt
Gould down the plug. It is probably the result of a whispering
campaign to denigrate me by comparison with Janet.[1] At first I
thought because it made it easier for Janet to shine, lately I realise so
that Janet can slide across and take my place in the redrawn boundaries.
Ha Ha! I just can't wait for the election to be over and I can bugger
home for keeps.

Fact is there isn't a single person I can trust. Even John Dobell[2]
looked slightly distant and remote, though proper and 'correct'. The
fact is, they've decided I was not getting publicity, sorry *impact*, from
the first moment, and nothing I will do will alter that. I had noticed
that little rat-skunk Courtney standing awhile on the steps of the
Duke when I arrived, and something *told* me that he was being
conspiratorial in some way. Haven't seen you for months, he kept
saying. Perhaps my irritation showed as I mocked him lightly about
catching cold. Anyway, things will never be quite the same. Will I just
be able to hold out through till the election? Yes, probably, because I
have (a) recourse to a special meeting (b) threat of standing against as
anti-common market/NF.

Albany   *Friday, 9 December*

Been v depressed these last few days. So much to do. My briefcase
goes back and forth on the train, stuffed and gasping with endless
little folded bits of paper many of them, I don't doubt, dealing with
engagements and grievances that I am missing and ducking.

---

[1] Janet Fookes, MP for Plymouth Drake since 1974 (Merton and Morden, 1970–74).
[2] John Dobell, sometime chairman of the Sutton Conservative Association and chief whip
of the Conservative group on Plymouth City Council, he had parliamentary ambitions,
trying unsuccessfully to gain the party nomination for both Drake and Devonport.

Real sadness is that some of the *taste* is going from things I like. This is a sign of age. Saltwood itself, early morning tea, the cars. Only the House retains its unique appeal, the Chamber, the tea-room, good company at dinner (as last night with Gow and Straubenzee[1]). Left preparation of my speech on pay and conditions far too late – usual story. Margaret will be there, but entries must take priority. Actually would have been totally low, but call from the coven this morning gave nig burst of adrenalin.

Duke of Cornwall Hotel, Plymouth   *Saturday, 10 December*

Feeling (and looking) v old and creaky. Looked at old entries a year back and saw *nothing* really achieved in House (in fact lost ground, in a 'disappointment' on PR). A year gone by, and older. Still owe about 40 plus fearful Zermatt debts and no books tackled at all.

John Dobell calling for special meeting of Executive Council to 'question me about my attitude to the National Front.' Gach!

---

[1] Ian Gow, MP for Eastbourne since February 1974. William van Straubenzee, MP for Wokingham since 1959.

1978

Frightful pain in arm and wrist – those evening attacks are now the norm though, touch wood, nights are not so bad.

Rang 'Boy' and not too happy about him. In fact, there's a good 'Boy' scare building up: he was talking 'yeh man' to such an extent that I had to reprimand him – 'don't use that "y'know" interjection ...' etc. He was cross at the prospect of coming back to go to the Rolls-Royce school (I thought I was so clever in getting him into an early vacancy there after their putting one off until July) – but for the first time, particularly when signing off, his voice lacked that special spontaneous affection – 'God bless you too', which I can still hear him say when he was at Rosey even, and in other places.

Rang Jane immediately, and of course she remembered it too from *her* conversation with him last Sunday. The gulf had opened. 'We've become parents,' I said, instead of family, elder bro or sister. I might be wrong. He might recover, snap out of it. Oh dear I said (speaking to Jane), 'much love to Tip.' Good old Tip ... 'I know what you *mean*,' she said. 'Oh dear, let's hear no more.' God, how I wish that we could.

Perhaps I'm being punished for my total indifference to my poor father's plight (into Sister Agnes today for a prostatectomy, and still under the anaesthetic).

Just back from Oxford after talked to small – later grew larger – audience of Monday Club in upstairs room at Union. Kept thinking of Saltwood, Jane and all's well, and almost immediately the sudden pain of the realising Jane in Spain (Bertie[1] died last night), and Tip quite alone with Nanny. No warmth, no decent food then. Got to see my father tomorrow. Apparently he is 'somewhat muddled', and already overshadowed by Nolwen, who has grey water.[2]

---

[1] Jane's father.
[2] Nolwen, Countess de Janzé, who had married Lord Clark the previous year.

Saltwood   *Sunday, 29 January*

General condition no better. Concentration and creative ability much inhibited, also my *cold hand*. I love this damp new weather, don't object to it at all, but no strength to do anything.

Did at least get over the hurdle of the Executive Council meeting where Radford Ward (who else?) were to raise the question of my attitude to the National Front. It was one of those evenings that might have gone nasty if I had played along with their rules, ie let myself get into a flap and on the defensive. There was a slight – no, more than slight – atmosphere of lion-taming, if not witch-hunt. Fortunately I had got there in time to get my 'pulls' of the 'report-back' leaflet from the printer and these distributed on people's chairs so could first 'defuse' the situation by referring to these.

I noticed, throughout this earlier phase, an unknown figure *not* smiling or unbending at all and obviously in a state of extreme nervous suppressed attention. Finally he put, extremely gravely, his question about 'what is the Party's attitude to . . . that disease . . . the National Front?' I dodged it, by citing my election to the Home Affairs Committee, and the meeting broke up, some relieved, some thwarted.

Earlier, at my surgery, two real NF members had come in, for a chat. And I thought how good they were, and how brave is the minority, in a once great country, who still keep alive the tribal essence.

Met Boy at the station last night, and quite marvellous he looked in his belted Kardigan bought that morning at 'Drakes' and having globally travelled back by Swissair, bronzed and strong. But the fact is, he's 'gone'. This year he's suddenly discovered his independence, all in a total rush, far more than at Rosey, or more than the time we left him behind at Zermatt. He wants to go back there and then to South Africa where he thinks he will make his fortune (I have to keep stopping to hold my hand to warm it up – shades of Gavin Maxwell)[1] and so one has accepted this – I don't, can't, any longer allow myself to fuss all the time that he's out and away and so on. I mean at this moment he's driving up to London in the Datsun, and formerly I'd have been scared stiff; now I'm just numb.

---

[1] The author Gavin Maxwell (*Ring of Bright Water*) suffered endless symptoms of ill-health, including circulatory problems.

Saltwood   *Sunday, 12 February*

I just said to Jane – 'will there ever be a moment, a long lazy tranquil
moment when lying in a chaise-longue (by a slip of the tongue I said
wheel-chair) I can laughingly read through these terrible gloomy
winter entries?'
    'Not till you retire from Parliament,' she said.
    'But what if I have to retire from ill-health?'

Saltwood   *Thursday, 23 February*

Had a bad night and rang Jane for Peter Morrison's 'new' osteopath –
'Johnnie Johnson' – thought, give him a try. Fighting a latent cold
with Redoxon. Tracked him down at his block of flats at Peckham.
He's an American (baldish) and in one of those Dr Kildare half white
jackets. A very long session in which he produced every magical
'click' and a great deal of flannel. One very effective double-click of
the neck side-ways. Lizard-eyes, wouldn't look one in the face.
    Had a bath after the 11 o'clock vote and an intermittent night –
fraught with anxiety at total seizing up again. Johnson had diffused
the pain, but not reduced its intensity potential. Felt really awful this
morning. Twice (once at Albany, once after getting to House) seriously
thought of ringing Jane, getting her to come up to drive me down.

Later
I see my father and Nolwen taking a walk, and see myself in the
main – 'waxen-facedly lying and inoperable.'
    Please please God make me better soon.

Saltwood   *Wednesday, 8 March*

Tip talked to me thoughtfully about his exams. Today we had a letter
from G, following his careers interview. I felt almost faint reading it,
sickish. Talk of 'asthma may effect his entry into the Para Regt' etc.
Don't want him to be blighted by asthma, and don't *really* want him

to go into the Parachute Regt. Ideally would like him to have a marsh farm, I suppose.

Bratton   *Saturday, 18 March*

A sad melancholy – accentuated by accumulated fatigue.

I went to see Rowntree [London doctor] on Tuesday, 'You're playing your last card' said Jane, smiling; saw him at 6pm after a *very* bad day, stab pains, longish bouts of 'nerves' 99° temperature etc. He very splendid and calming, confirmed Beth's[1] diagnosis of 'bronchial nevritis' and prescribed heavily, saying if not better in 10 days – take a month off(!)

Felt better at once, of course, and went and bombed at Brooks's; two v. good days. Yesterday had to drive down from London via Plymouth on constituency matters and today very sleepy and aching and *looking awful* with the vile and ludicrous Primrose Ball hanging over us. Had felt so good that seriously contemplated Zermatt for Easter – but today not so sure, as deep, though remote, shoulder ache and cold had shown that all was not well. For the first time in the mirror, *qualitative* changes – most notably shape of body and shoulders (positively remedial) and hair at side – frizzled and sprouting, not sleek.

Depressed too, by something Rowntree said about Mama's 'awful last illness' – and suddenly realised she had committed suicide – hence all the notes and the tidy way it was done. Presumably got the medicine to do it via Kathy or what, I don't know. So even that last sneer was unjustified.

Here, barn falling down, garden neglected – though roof and interior of farmhouse still v. good. But no passage to the old 'nursery' wing and our double. Just the players, and the distant memory of 'Bubbington'[2] lying gurgling with pleasure at being called in the morning, and the dreaded change-over from Farex to orange-juice!

On Thursday in the Commons realised that I was being virtually ignored. 'Messed alone' at dinner and watched Marcus Kimball[3] being

---

[1] Beth Evans-Smith, friend and physiotherapist.
[2] Nickname for James when he was a baby.
[3] Marcus Kimball, MP for Gainsborough since 1956.

dined at Humphrey Atkins' table. That serene corporate instinct which the House unfailingly exercises acknowledged fact that since return (ie Christmas) I have done NOTHING.

Saltwood   *Thursday, 23 March*

Back this evening after a 'day trip' to Norwich to do a discussion with Neil Kinnock[1] in *Arena* (Anglia TV).

NK talked virtually non-stop on the way back. Has a high opinion of himself, but was non-specific about his views for reforming the Labour movement/party. Wants to make changes, but is, I suspect, being gradually checked by the system. Claims to have been offered office three times and contested his reaction with that of Bob Cryer.[2] Said PM was temporarily under Jay's influence,[3] and that Jay got Owen his job rather than the other way round.[4] We discussed Labour's performance. According to NK, 'in leadership contests the Right always wins' (what about Wilson?). Said if Callaghan won another term he would groom his successor – either Owen or Will Rodgers, or possibly someone called Cunningham[5] who I don't even know by sight.

Health would be steadily rising if Barham [doctor] hadn't phoned yesterday and said for insurance purposes he had to 'submit a report' to the Norwich Union – did I mind? With a sinking feeling, I said: 'I've got nothing to conceal'. 'Just that trouble with your constituents,' he reminded me. So was now gloomily waiting for either (a) refusal from Norwich or (b) request for 'fuller examination' of prostate etc.

---

[1] Neil Kinnock, Labour MP for Bedwellty since 1970. A rising young star of the party, who was about to be elected for the first time to Labour's National Executive.

[2] Robert Cryer, Labour MP for Keighley since February 1974.

[3] Peter Jay, son of Douglas Jay, Labour MP (for Battersea North since 1946) and former Minister, had been appointed British ambassador in Washington in May 1977; the Prime Minister was, coincidentally, his father-in-law.

[4] David Owen, MP for Devonport since 1974 (Sutton 1966–74) was Minister of State at Foreign and Commonwealth Office when he was surprise choice as Foreign Secretary in 1977, following the death of Anthony Crosland.

[5] David Owen, and William Rodgers, Labour MP for Stockton North, would quit the Labour Party as two of the 'Gang of Four' who founded the Social Democratic Party in 1981 (the others were Shirley Williams and Roy Jenkins); Jack Cunningham, Labour MP for Whitehaven since 1970.

Saltwood   *Saturday, 25 March*

This evening feeling not to bad 'in myself', took 2CV down to St
Leonards to see when Easter Services and if possibility of a really early
communion. Church empty, though warm and light. Walked about,
read prayers, said a brief contemplative prayer. Realised that at 50 *must*
have 'affairs in order', a conference at which I can explain whole
thing to Jane and James and Andrew. Especially <u>no o/d</u>. Why do I
still shrink from this?

Saltwood   *Friday, 7 April*

'Supervising' darling Jane clearing out the pool today. Will I ever
again bronzedly be leaping in and out?

Saltwood   *Monday, 24 April*

Yesterday quite good, and played piano in evening.

Today Barham came, listened, pronounced 'quite clear' and now
returned to question of x-ray. We could fit it in any time this week –
so why not today! Fixed, on the spot, with Dr W at St Saviours. So,
going down there this evening. In my imagination have already
compounded his explanation – non fiction, nothing to worry about.
And my reaction – resigning, selling up, being an invalid.

Saltwood   *Tuesday, 25 April*

'Cleared' by the fresh-faced and almost smiling Dr W. As I arrived at
St Saviours, parked, went up the steps and into the hospital smells, I
realised how awful to be ill, demi-terminal or declining. Best die like
Maurice[1] in one's own bed after a jolly good dinner.

---

[1] Maurice Bowra, Warden of Wadham College, Oxford, who died in 1972.

H o C Library   *Tuesday, 2 May*

Empty stomach – this bloody syndrome of not eating when away from home (compounded by crazy yellow tongue and bilious feeling due, presumably, to being on massive penicillin). Sole substance since breakfast when felt too ill to broach a fried egg, a danish bun with the blind shop steward in the cafeteria.

Ray Mawby[1] tells me the election will be on 12 October – just as well to get it over this year; Plymouth might have become too hot – but September will not be tranquil.

Vitality so diminished. Outgoings continuing to accumulate at Saltwood. Political plan obviously nil – coming up in the Summer Car this afternoon Jane said: 'How much longer are you going to be an MP? . . . . you work frightfully hard at it, you don't really seem to be getting anything out of it.' I dissimulated. How could I confess that to give up would be to discard my perennial obsession, the vision that has been with me always, the certainty that I would be called to lead?

But when one's energy goes, *one* goes.

Jane at Saltwood, nursing Angus's wound.[2] He had his tumour removed today poor darling. Why does a tumour form? And he was so well and fine. Why have the operation? Will we be faced with this dilemma? So many decisions and commitments. And time, it seems, so terribly constrained.

Saltwood   *Sunday, 7 May*

Last night 'Boy' stayed in and played the piano and the organ. Remembered his playing the organ in the pink room at Seend. At one point woke in the night with a start and noted it was his last night and full day at home before going to South Africa.[3] Monday is a hellish day for me – when do I say goodbye to Jamie?

---

[1] Ray Mawby, Conservative MP for Totnes since 1955.
[2] Angus, the Clarks' black labrador.
[3] James was to dive on the wreck of the *Sacramento*.

East Cloisters   *Wednesday, 17 May*

'Painkilling drugs' a thing of the past. Can slump in chairs, as normal; can double-click fingers of right hand; today for the first time not cold hand first thing this morning.

House Library   *Wednesday, 14 June*

Wonderfully well-feeling; colonial appearance (weight to new 'high' of 11.6$\frac{1}{2}$).

Albany   *Thursday, 22 June*

At PM's Q's John Wells,[1] unexpectedly sitting on the 'Baronets' Bench', asked me bluntly if I wanted Maidstone after he'd gone. Said yes and he replied he could fix it. Would have been on air in previous times, but now ... Especially after seeing what happened to Robin Cooke. Still it allows one a little more peace of mind.

Saltwood   *Friday, 14 July*

End of line in the Commons. First Finance Bill Committee, then Devolution, endless 3-line whips in stuffy conditions. Impossible to 'get anywhere'. Yesterday in the western constituency members committee John Peyton[2] went semi-crazy when I said I was the Anti-Common Market candidate.

---

[1] John Wells, MP for Maidstone since 1959. AC was right to take the offer sceptically as Wells did not finally resign until 1987
[2] John Peyton, MP for Yeovil since 1951, Minister of Transport 1970–74.

Plymouth train [start of recess]   *Friday, 4 August*

Really loathe Plymouth now, but can't chuck as less likely to get Folkestone due to age, passage of time.

Trouble is I just adore the House of Commons. I am seduced by its gossipy, club-like regimental atmosphere and love also the delicious karate-type confidence that being an MP gives me. Last night, called in to collect my razor and already the whole place in sepulchral hibernating gloom – just a few dim chandeliers and 'revealed' lights. Everything locked. Did a quick phone-call to Jane from the cheekie-chappie phone in the twilit Members' Lobby and thought how no life will be throbbing here until 24 October and how much I shall miss it. Two attendants (dim flat-capped sort) emerged from the gloom and flashed their backs on me.

Ashford train   *Wednesday, 9 August*

Going up to London in a state of 'hurry-tension' as the Americans call it. Worried about jaw. Suddenly began to bleed in different places when driving back in the Land-Rover around about Canterbury.

Saltwood   *Sunday, 20 August*

This was our one relaxed happy day (qv last year same date) all by the pool, even Jane. In the evening, Jane and Boy had a row – I forget what about – but at least it proved one could still do it.

Saltwood   *Sunday, 27 August*

Only four more days of the season left. Saltwood looking incredible, practically never better with the new Atco definitely on top of the lawn. Still not really *relaxing*.

Politics dead – tho' election coming in time to save my bacon. Will probably not get a job with MT if the Tories win at all, still doubtful.

Zermatt   *Sunday, 3 September*

Early part of journey blighted by darling Jane very peaky and low about George[1] – who, I was privately convinced, must be dead – missing since breakfast the day before we left, and reported that evening down at the garage by the Military Canal! However, on arrival rang Mrs C, who said he had been brought back by 'Monty' (small world) who had a little boy called 'George' and had called for him that evening, and George had appeared!

Saltwood   *Sunday, 10 September*

Back last night after two very pleasant days driving across France. Delicious dinner in clip joint ** restaurant at Arbois. The Chapron went beautifully – being pressed in the last stage at continuous 160–170kph and running out of petrol, legally, in the customs shed at Calais.

Then, deterioration: missed 7 o'clock boat. Customs kept us waiting an hour and was foiled of a row by being let straight through. Arrived extremely shocked to find George [the jackdaw] had 'gone on Friday'. Greenwood white and grim. Supped on tepid tomato soup and walked into office (11.30pm), masses of useless mail. Livid with James – who was, needless to say, 'out' for the night with the Land-Rover – also I suspect not having nurtured George as he should. Paced about and ate a bit of Nan Howard's (very good) fruit cake and half a mug of hot milk. Slept poorly with Angus taking up most of the room, it seemed.

Morning wet and windy. No sign of George.

---

[1] George was a tame jackdaw, not the first, or the last, to adopt Saltwood. They were usually reared by the Clarks after falling from their nests as chicks.

Albany   *Wednesday, 20 September*

Walked through St James's Park to the House of Commons to pick
up the Chev and make some phone calls. I did reflect how very lucky
I am to be a member of the Privileged Classes, and how *filthily* (in
Michael's[1] phrase) 90% of the rest of the population still live.

Plymouth train   *Tuesday, 3 October*

Letter from some member of the Conservative Assoc asking if Margaret T could come down and do a walkabout in Plympton St Mary's
to put it on the map!

Saltwood 'winter office'   *Saturday, 14 October*

A certain delicious freedom about having forsaken b'gammon
(presently owe Brooks's £888) and been chucked by the blondes.

Plymouth train   *Monday, 16 October*

Set-back when James asked me about the Cloud (in kitchen last night
as I gloomily prepared to go up to London for night prior to catching
9.30 – which I'm on now – to go to 'sit-in' on council meeting about
taxis). 'Sold,' I said. 'What did you get for it?' 'It went in a deal with
the Bi-carb. 'You have sold the Bi-carb?' He was absolutely shattered,
went quite red and eyes filled with tears. If he'd been baby James he'd
have blubbed. 'Now we've got nothing to do rallies in, except the
Bira.' Boy had been driving the Bira that very evening, and didn't
like it – though was too polite to say so – just said it was undergeared,
which it is grossly.

---

[1] Michael Briggs – old friend.

Saltwood   *Monday, 23 October*

Last night George came back via a call from the train-driver's house
after he had been trying to get into their children's window (his wife,
as I always suspected, being extremely pretty). Althou' sleek he is very
subdued and today was hardly off his 'perch' on top of the open
kitchen door all day. Incredible, though, that he is still alive and that,
however torpid, he did make a bid for freedom, do hope one can
rehabilitate him.

Duke of Cornwall Hotel, Plymouth   *Friday, 27 October*

Came down on the sleeper, as arrangements cocked up for the
Constituency Bazaar, which I was also expected to open to the usual
crowd of sullen, impatient and uncomprehending bargain-hunters,
instead of, as I had agreed, doing the draw at 2.30. 'If you blew in at
4.30 (sic) the locals would feel snubbed.' Incredible. And when will
it be possible to escape?

Berwick by-election result this morning[1] told me by the fierce,
heavily-built sleeping-car attendant who, I reckon, stole my replica
Cartier watch. So perhaps there will be another long parliament, with
the constant threat of a new election.

House Library   *Tuesday, 7 November*

Woke this morning to usual 'wah' weather: ie blue sky, crisp autumn
day, wind fresh. Used last bit of china in Albany (white jug) to drink
my tea. Did some dictating and phoning with Veronica[2] (she looking
quite attractive and pert-breasted in her silk dress yesterday). Decided
to make a bolt for it and took train to Saltwood, but after an omelette

---

[1] Caused by the death of the Labour MP John P. Mackintosh, elected in October 1974.
   Labour hung on to the seat, despite by-election reverses elsewhere during James
   Callaghan's premiership, giving the new MP, John Home Robertson, a majority of
   3,112.
[2] Veronica, new Westminster secretary.

lunch and in Mehari to collect wood realised *couldn't* absent myself, too much of an opting out.

Have felt somewhat ignored and 'passed over' at this return, and feel prospects gradually slipping away; talk in the papers of possible 'promotion' for Heseltine etc.

Poor old John Davies resigned today.[1] Everything lovely at Salt-wood, so much to do, such glorious prospects. I could live forever doing things to the Estate, the cars, writing etc. Sadly I caught the 4.52 back up, dozing intermittently and glancing through Sedgwick's *All the Pre-war Bentleys*, a sort of *Huntingdonshire Cabmen* of '30s society.[2]

Why am I so lazy here and composition essential. I excuse b'gam-mon by saying I must have some relaxation – am going round to St J now. But actually it's an addiction and a destructive one.

Plymouth train   *Friday, 10 November*

Looked sadly out of the window at the beaches and rocks after Dawlish. Sun streaks down, but almost deserted. Oh for the open days with the blondes or better, even, with little children, baby sons. Has that gone from one's life for ever? Oh for those days when you realise you're going over the brow of the hill and you will never, again, set eyes on that distant, so long receding range of sunny hills and vineyards.

Saltwood   *Friday, 24 November*

Some shoulder pain and *cold hand*, but this morning a fabulous experi-ence. Flew again with James, in the little '150' as one climbed high over Rye I could see Rye Harbour, the little boats, and the garage that used to be the 'Big' garden, and then we climbed high – into the clouds, a range of strato-cumulus like 'over Italy' from Trockener

---

[1] John Davies had been Director-General, Confederation of British Industry, before becoming an MP (for Knutsford) in 1970. He served both Heath (in government) and Thatcher (in opposition). Then suffered a brain tumour. He died in 1979.

[2] J.B.Morton ('Beachcomber' of the *Daily Express*), conceived his imaginary *The List of Huntingdonshire Cabmen* to epitomise avid scholarship.

Steg. Fantastic beautiful moving experience as great cloud valleys rushed past and towering cliffs loomed over us ... To think that my son, whom I used to kiss goodnight in his cot in that little room, was now piloting me in this fairyland.

On the way back, my mind miles away on 'George', James suddenly said/shouted, 'Daddy, what are you doing!' and I rammed some cheeky red-coloured, but new Peugeot 104 from behind, seconds later a Yank in a blue Ford ran into us! And what's more I'm in the Chapron!!! Set-back. It must go back to Chapron that's all. Darling Jane took it very calmly, but I was shattered – old person accident – also wondered about whether I might have aggravated my 'whiplash' injury.

Saltwood   *Sunday, 10 December*

I still haven't honoured my part of the bargain with God – to acknowledge and research defence book if George came back. Only God could have sent him back in that curious indirect way that didn't quite betoken a miracle, and yet, the more one thinks of it ...

Saltwood   *Wednesday, 27 December*

Saying goodbye to James, off to California – mislaid his passport!

1979

Heavy pain from shoulder, weak wrist etc, but still not so ghastly as last year. After a baddish night did a morning's estate work . . .

I looked round the crowded House and thought – 'in fifty years' time everyone here is going to be dead.' I looked at Hugh Fraser[1] gangling weightlossedly out of the Chamber. Then I looked at John, *Sir* John Langford-Holt[2] next to me, spare and greying, though aquiline Naylor-Leylandish features still remained in vestige. How good-looking he must have been, and charming. What unfulfilled promise when he was adopted some 30 years ago.

Will I be able to break out, either careerwise or healthwise to restore and rebuild?

Back from Plymouth. More or less decided to 'go quickly'. But at breakfast when I told Jane she didn't reply – ominous. When I tackled her with this she said: 'I thought you always said "Never resign".' Yes, quite right, I did. I think solution is try and get snap adoption at AGM. Failing that just the 'gentleman' act holding out as long as possible. Might do a deal with Larry Speare, ask him up to House.

All the same, as the prospect of losing the House re-appears I am shocked and appalled by how little I have done, how much opportunity I have wasted these last four years.

I've got £83,000 in my bag! Quite literally draft for 65 on Cézanne deal and 18 from Paymaster for NPG portraits.[3] Now we never thought we'd get here again, so the lesson of the field money must be

---

[1] Hugh Fraser, MP for Stone and Staffordshire since 1950 (Stone 1945–50) had married Lady Antonia Pakenham (better known by her married name), the daughter of Lord and Lady Longford (as they would become).

[2] Sir John Langford-Holt, MP for Shrewsbury since 1945.

[3] Portraits and sketches of AC's father by Graham Sutherland.

applied. I'm also aware that it is net figure only. Must add up liabilities/
debts and reduce all. Then work things out to see how to distribute
assets.

Albany   *Wednesday, 14 March*

Savoured today the first pleasure of writing a 'surprised-not-to-have-
heard-from-you' note to C. Hoare & Co who I had written to a week
ago asking for exact figures with which to pay off my overdraft.
Dropped it in by hand on way back from cigar-plus lunch.

Saltwood   *Monday, 26 March*

Getting deeds back from Hoare's *is* within my grasp now.

B5, Albany   *Thursday, 29 March*

Tension-headache day. Election date announced for 3 May so self
building on that, also James making decision-decision on does he go
to Air Corps or Cavalry, had to ring up War Office about 'buying
out' etc etc. Gosh it doesn't seem so long since I was *paid* to go into
Household Cavalry and then got out (we were at Lugano) in '46.

Poor dear Veronica said I '... looked terribly harassed', jarred one
every time she opened her mouth.

Had tea, envying all my colleagues with good seats, hoping we
don't have another hung parliament. God how I loathe the Election
campaign! Back to Brooks's to get dinner, then to House to pick up
papers, then to bed and catch 7.30 train to Plymouth.

Plymouth train   *Friday, 30 March*

Loathe election prospect. Slight doubt about adoption meeting, even, but presumably will be ok. Filthy to be away from the estate and dear George also will pine and whose features I want to get shining and give some fresh air to. I think a lot about George, and love the way he taps on his box when I am on the phone; he even hears my voice right down the passage and into the Green Room.

'Boy' going to Pirbright[1] on 17 April, the day the campaign 'starts in earnest'. This preferable, I think, to Army Air Corps, but involves US trip in summer (expensive and dangerous). Dear 'Boy' is so ravishing looking and maddening and engaging. Jane and I agreed on the phone that all we can do is grin-and-bear-it. Become dear old ga-gas.

Of course if I get through the election (happily with majority up) and if Cons have a good majority, then one can at last concentrate on South East, both estate and 'constituency' (will do that anyway, regardless, but less secure if majority 'teeny'). But in a sense isn't this almost dropping-out, the SE concept? Just wanting to retain the Commons as a Club? The inescapable moments of time, receding hair-line, bags under eyes (new development). But 'neck' has cured itself, a great help.

Key factor, though, is elimination of dandruff.

Saltwood   *Friday, 6 April*

Tory lead now down to 6%. Realise it will be gradually whittled away and will lose my seat or the majority halved.

Bratton   *Friday, 13 April (Birthday boy)*

Calmer than might be expected at this 'break' in the campaign, but out here, almost resigned to humiliation at polls (must admit not

---

[1] Headquarters of the army training regiment of the Brigade of Guards.

relishing the re-count!). Wouldn't mind all *that* much just being a stately-home owner.

Teeth seem to be cracking up. Also eyes still get puffy. But basically not feeling bad. A bit stiff, can get quite unpleasant twinges from shoulder if, eg, turning round while holding up phone.

Being 51 makes me feel quite lecherous.

That evening: a lovely relaxed day at Bratton – cleaning windows and paint and planning to revive it substantially, possibly to 'full Bloomsbury'.[1] Only relief in recurrent gloom, Jack the baker, saying sing-song, 'all grown up, all grown up, gone away' about the boys.

Saltwood   *Easter Sunday, 15 April*

Saltwood 'smiling'. Tortoises all woke up, tipped their box over and were released in Courtenays. My 'eye' (left-side) a little suspect. Irritated and slightly stye-borne, but otherwise fine and randy. Gloom about beloved 'Boy'. On the phone last night he recounted how his Zermatt friend in the Scots Guards had just come out of Pirbright and told him how hateful it was: '4 hours sleep, and people paid to be nasty to you ...'

This gave me a bad night. Cheered up a bit in the morning and thought 'what is written is written.' In the sunlight evening gloom of the 'formal' part of the Castle, I still get these terrible forebodings: Kipling and his son at Loos, Weld-Smith, even, of Seend Manor and his son on Blenheims.

Also filled with loathing of the Electorate. Those filthy carriages on the trip down yesterday which annoyed Jane so much, is the nation completely rotten? Yes, and has been since 1916. In the war we were saved by the middle classes who flew the Spitfires and manned the cruisers and frigates.

---

[1] The Clarks did in fact turn Bratton into a miniature Charleston. After the house was sold the Bloomsbury doors were returned to Saltwood.

Saltwood   *Easter Monday, 16 April*

In a state of *désoeuvré* apprehension. My R eye now irritating definitely; would worry over this, but must get election out of the way (very depressed about this, Labour bound to win – at least in Plymouth, it seems). Still foremost worry is darling 'Boy' going in tomorrow to the Pirbright crusher. A little soft-spoken about his coming ordeal. He may be going deliberately to 'flunk'. I don't know. It would be fabulous if he can get through and the world would be his oyster; but in a way thank God for the election to take my mind off it, otherwise I would be worrying non-stop.

   This really will be the last entry until after the (re) count. Yeh yeh!

Bratton   *Sunday, 22 April*

In spite of terrible anxiety about 'Boy' plus gloom/apprehension over Polls (today showing our lead down to 5½ – ie dead heat and looking awful), am slyly, insistently *grossly* randy as one can only be at Bratton with its soft centre and lazy atmosphere. Can't ignore my fears about James – though it puts into scale one's fear about finally losing seat.

Bratton   *Sunday 29 April*

Cheered up by Graham Butland ringing on my return: the *Independent*[1] forecasting a clear sweep for Tories in West Country!

Bratton   *Monday, 30 April*

Met L.K. Way, who said (he wasn't especially friendly) that he had two 'nasty points' to put to me: (1) Large Liberal vote to be pivotal (I know); and (2) influx of 8,000 new voters (I know). Indeed I had

---

[1] West Country Sunday newspaper, published in Plymouth.

been ready to greet him with: 'Leslie, this is a Labour seat' etc. Quickly
I tried to deflect him. But feeling very anxious.

The General Election on 3 May
    Conservative: 339; Labour: 269; Liberal: 11. Others: 16

Saltwood   *Monday, 7 May*

Mrs Thatcher (or Mrs Carrington, as Papa amusingly – muddledly –
called her) has announced her Cabinet, and I'm not in, anywhere.
Don't specially mind, though resentful of Pattie being in so high up
and Hayhoe[1] (of all people) getting the Army. Wouldn't take a PPS
or couldn't take 'disabled' or 'energy'. Lovely to have freedom of the
Commons, consolidated at Plymouth,[2] and the summer before us.

But particularly bad-tempered and martyred, so in essence a little
schizophrenic, I suppose. Noone has been in touch. Where are the
blondes? Did they send the 'AC rules OK' telegram, must have? But
where are they? Sod them too.

B5, Albany   *Wednesday, 16 May*

And still the mood of euphoria persists. Waking very early. And ready
to take on anything. B'gammon – balls to it. Cars – barely interested;
quite happy with the 'gentlemanly' old SI, so reserved in its dark
green, a 2CV, and the two sports models, SG for 'recreation'. The
House consumes me and pumps me with adrenalin – like playing
game after difficult game in a major tournament.

---

[1] Geoffrey Pattie had been Parliamentary Under-Secretary of State, RAF since the general
    election; Barney Hayhoe, MP for Brentford and Isleworth since February 1974 (Heston
    and Isleworth 1970–74) the same but for the Army.
[2] Sutton result: AC, 28,892 votes; Priestley (Labour), 17,605; Scannell (Liberal), 6,225.
    AC majority: 11,287.

Dean's Yard   *Thursday, 24 May*

Didn't make '22' Exec. All PPS's and Whips now announced. Euphoria pretty well extinct. Article in *Telegraph* by Wellbeloved[1] (of all people) stating how RAF run-down. Felt I should answer this, and had brainwave of checking with Pattie: been washing the dishes after breakfast for an hour waiting for him to ring back, gloomily reflecting on contrast. There was I washing dishes. There was he (*pace* his aide) 'in conference with the chiefs of staff'.

Saltwood   *Saturday, 9 June*

One more little notch on James' separation – last night was the first ever that he has been in England and we didn't know where he was. Had a bad scare with skin condition on back, itchy, 'boils', flushes etc. Hypochondria far from dormant. Also what is to happen to 'Boy'? He appeared yesterday in his *ludicrous* spastic US uniform which he had bought at the Military Vehicle rally.

Folkestone Station   *Tuesday, 26 June*

Late for case (when it was expected I would lose my licence) as went to old court, and back to new one. In the little interview room I suddenly realised that I might lose it for a little while. However when I entered the court the Clerk of the Court said: one of the magistrates is known to you, have you any objection? ... eh! 'None whatever,' I replied delightedly. And in due time, *very* narrowly, she declared that there were *special circumstances* which allowed them not to disqualify.

---

[1] James Wellbeloved, Labour MP for Erith and Crayford since 1965, who held the same post at Defence as Pattie until the election.

E Cloisters   *Thursday, 19 July*

So clapped out. After that one glorious 'flare-up' in June pretty girls
no longer look at me. Am drear, waxen-faced with short haircut (but
not 'boyish'). I noticed how drear, too, the whips (Newton and
Wakeham[1]) looked, and yesterday I saw Rhodes-James slumped in
that tiny niche by the phone in the tea-room corridor, his obsessively
ambitious features glazed-over. He wasn't on the phone, he wasn't
moving at all. I thought he might be stuck there indefinitely right
through the recess, and this made me grin, momentarily.

Albany   *Friday, 20 July*

Headache on side of head – right. Is it John Davies or toothache?

East Cloisters   *Monday, 22 October*

Complaining to Michael McNair-Wilson about not having a pair,
and he said – more or less – 'You've been passed finally by, why
bother, you don't need to conform ...' *Why* am I in this condition?
Immediately he tried to placate me, but as I said, they've (the Whips)
got so many candidates they want to accommodate – or rather were
accommodating – that they're only too delighted to cross someone
off their list.

Saltwood   *Sunday, 4 November*

Miss 'Boy' more than I admit.[2] Realised last night that I couldn't play
the piano until he was back (he played it – and the organ – on his last
night). Last night Col said that '... £8,000 was the size of most

---

[1] Antony (Tony) Newton, MP for Braintree since February 1974; John Wakeham, MP
for Maldon since February 1974.
[2] Off to flying-school.

people's overdraft (!)' Jane flinched, and so did I. Agreed that my father will live another five years – which puts a *totally* different complexion on everything.

House of Commons   *Thursday, 15 November*

Met the (reputedly) senior correspondent of *Pravda* in the Strangers' Lobby for lunch. I was feeling ghastly – fourth day of filthy cold – and had taken the precaution of downing a quick pink gin first. The man, Strelnikov by name, had the appearance of a standard KGB 'heavy' of mature years. He started extremely nervous (uncertainty and the prospect of having to use their own initiative always makes Soviet officials, of any rank, very apprehensive). However once he realised that I was not trying to persuade or blackmail him into defecting the atmosphere lightened. The reason I prefer the Russians to the Chinese and at some point in the conversation I even said this, is because their natural human responses – jollity, gloom etc – are never far below the surface with the exceptions of a few clam-faced Commissars, whom ordinary Russians loathe anyway.

I emphasised that this was the moment for the Soviet Union to make a real gesture of conventional disarmament as once the deployment of the new generation of 'theatre' nuclear missiles gets under away it would be more difficult. He did not demur when I said that the Brezhnev gesture of withdrawing 1,000 tanks was meaningless as we all knew they were obsolete and this was part of the normal re-equipment programme.

He fidgeted a great deal and heaved himself about in his seat starting every sentence with the words 'Mr Clark' pronounced in a curious glottal Slavic manner. From time to time I lightened the conversation by asking him about his war experiences noticing that he was both pleased and disconcerted at my accurate knowledge of fronts, Commanders and conditions (he told me that he had been invalided out after being wounded during an air attack on the Mius Front in 1943 having taken part in the great retreat across Caucasus.) Of course there may still be a file on me at the Soviet Embassy relating to my brief flirtation with Vinnikof during the time that I was writing *Barbarossa* and I may be irredeemably persona non grata as a result.

The House then got stuck into one of those days which follow long periods of torpor and ennui that conform to Fred Hoyle's theory of the concatenation of the Universe. For we had, more or less simultaneously, the Chancellor's announcement of a 17 per cent bank rate i.e. 21 per cent overdrafts and a clutch of publicity-seeking Labour MPs each trying to beat the other to the draw (Dennis Skinner, I am glad to say, just beat Christopher Price.[1] The two were standing together and Skinner made it on a 'Point of Order') raising the matter of Anthony Blunt's treachery.[2] This was a lucky break for Geoffrey [Howe][3] because the whole Blunt affair diverted attention from the really alarming manner in which our economy seems to be conducted. He came to the '22' committee and the atmosphere was mildly critical. I asked the question which, perhaps fortunately, the Speaker had not called me to ask at the time of the statement – namely if we had really cut public expenditure then we would not need such devastatingly high interest rates.

Earlier at the '22' I made an announcement on behalf of the Home Secretary about the Immigration rules brief. I spoke clearly, slowly and bossily and this reminded me of how I would really like to be a Whip (*vide* Chips). This is second best from the original concept of galloping across the countryside on a white horse, drawn sword in hand rousing the populace, but I would settle for it, especially as it would give me a good excuse for handing in my notice at Plymouth.

House of Commons   *Wednesday, 21 November*

Ian Gow[4] is a very assiduous attender of Committees. In the last two days I have noticed him at the special meeting of the Finance Committee when the Chancellor came to explain the MLR increase, at the Legal Committee when the Attorney General was defending

---

[1] Christopher Price, MP for Lewisham West since February 1974 (Birmingham Perry Bar, 1966–70).

[2] Anthony Blunt, former Surveyor of Pictures to George VI and Queen Elizabeth II, had been unmasked as the 'Fourth Man' in the group of Cambridge spies (Maclean, Burgess, Philby etc) who betrayed Britain to the Soviet Union.

[3] Geoffrey Howe, MP for Surrey East since 1974 (Bebington, 1964–66; Reigate, 1970–74), Chancellor of the Exchequer since the general election after four years as opposition Treasury spokesman.

[4] Ian Gow, MP for Eastbourne since February 1974, and Parliamentary Private Secretary to Margaret Thatcher since May 1979.

the Protection of Information Act, at the Home Affairs Committee immediately afterwards when the Blunt affair was being discussed and tonight he was at the regular meeting of the Finance Committee when Gordon Pepper[1] addressed them.

By chance I had taken tea alone in one of the armchairs at the far end of the Members' Tea Room instead of convivially at the table. This was because I was exhausted having spent the latter part of the afternoon tramping the streets of Battersea looking for a garage 'with flat over' for the coven. I was reading the financial columns of the *Guardian*, which contained a critique of a speech made by Pepper the previous day to the Society of Investment Analysts.

It is always nice to have a crib and I decided, unusually for me, to attend the Finance Committee that evening. Forearmed (the piece was by Hamish McRae[2]) I was able to ask him a penetrating question about the way in which the recent gilt sales by the Bank had been bungled. So penetrating was it that he became flustered, asked several times if we were off-the-cuff, looked around the room in an exaggeratedly conspiratorial way etc. When it came his answer was more or less unintelligible – the only part I could understand was that Mullens, the Government broker, had spent the last month wining and dining various directors of the Clearing banks. Anyhow I noticed Ian rise from his seat and pad silently around the outer perimeter of the crowded Committee table ... I did not look round although everybody watches Ian wherever he goes because it is thought (rightly or wrongly – I suspect wrongly) that the Prime Minister confides in him and values his opinion.

He stopped behind my chair and tapped me very lightly on the shoulder bending forward and, speaking almost inaudibly, asked if I would come and have dinner. We left immediately, before the Committee rose, and as everybody watched us go out I was reminded of Oliver Lyttelton's[3] story about the French broker who had done one of the Rothschilds a good turn and asked him for a tip on the Bourse. Rothschild said, 'I never give tips, but what I will do is walk across the floor in your company.' This experience was repeated when we went briefly to the Smoking Room. At the corner table by the bar

---

[1] Noted member of the monetarist priesthood. Senior partner in Greenwells and gilt-edge expert.

[2] Hamish McRae, financial editor of *The Guardian* since 1975.

[3] Oliver Lyttelton (created 1st Viscount Chandos, 1954), member of Churchill's war cabinet, industrialist and first chairman of National Theatre Board.

sat Ted Heath, bolt upright in a dinner jacket and having (apparently) had a special snow rinse on his hair which he now wears *en brosse*.

We drove to the Cavalry Club in the green Bentley and Ian ordered copious quantities of Tio Pepe, white Burgundy, Claret etc. I was soon surrounded by a number of half full glasses which I had no intention of emptying. He told me how the Prime Minister and the Treasury team were anxious that no real cuts in public spending had yet been made. He said she was out-numbered three to one in the cabinet. On her side were Howe, Biffen, Nott, Maude, Joseph.[1] The remaining 18 were mutely or vociferously hostile. (Prior[2] – whom Ian loathes – and Walker are her principal opponents.)

Later
I had a piccolo House of Commons triumph this evening. Sat through the Blunt debate (why in hell was Rhodes James called *first* from the back benches to propound his mouldy clichés). Willie Hamilton and Leadbitter[3] were the best. At 9.03pm – with everybody comfortably settled down for the wind-ups I rose – alone – and was called.

A crowded House, a *full* House! And the PM leaning forward in what Ian [Gow][4] calls the 'Blue Peter' position. I put my questions – none of them particularly welcome – and, regrettably, applauded more from the Labour benches. But without an exception (the – unsolicited – joke that anyone who knows anything about the KGB will verify that the Russian controllers in Kensington change every two years) I got a good feeling. The first time that Margaret T has heard me speak since she turned round and looked at me during my 'maiden'. Technique improved since then.

---

[1] John Biffen, MP for Oswestry since 1961, and now Chief Secretary to the Treasury under Howe; John Nott, MP for St Ives (Cornwall) since 1966 and now Secretary of State for Trade; Angus Maude, Paymaster-General; Sir Keith Joseph, MP for Leeds North-East since 1956 and now Secretary of State for Industry.

[2] James Prior, MP for Lowestoft since 1959, now Secretary of State for Employment.

[3] William (Willie) Hamilton, MP for Fife Central since 1974 (Fife West, 1950–74); Edward (Ted) Leadbitter, MP for the Hartlepools since 1964.

[4] Ian Gow has been PPS to Mrs Thatcher since May 1979.

House of Commons   *Tuesday, 27 November*

I was talking to Tony Royle, eminently sensible, never seen him in a flap (ex SAS, I think).[1] But he can be very forthright, no words minced. 'Look at the people round her,' he said. 'Carrington – hates her; Prior – hates her; Gilmour – hates her; Heseltine[2] – hates her; Walker – loathes her, makes no secret of it; Willie – completely even-handed, would never support her against the old gang; Geoffrey Howe – no personal loyalties – durable politburo man, will serve under anyone. The only people committed to Margaret are Angus Maude, John Biffen and Keith Joseph and the last two are so tortured intellectually as to cast doubt on their stability in a crisis.'

I paraphrase his analysis, but it brought home to one how precarious her position is and what a disaster was the assassination of Airey Neave[3] whose subtlety and insight would have helped to out-manoeuvre these quislings. Royle pointed out that the real danger would be that a mass sacking or resignation of the old guard heavies (nominally arising out of 'attitudes' to incomes policy or enforcement of measures disciplining a recalcitrant union) would create an alternative Cabinet and one which would naturally be expected to open its doors to the ageing, sulky, shapeless but still expectant Edward Heath. And that with such weight and so many 'names' it was a danger that more than half the Parliamentary Party might be drawn off to fill their wagons. Margaret would be left with a few young (and presumably discredited) monetarists such as Nott and Lawson[4] and a rabble of African Rightists, Hastings, Winterton[5] etc and the '92'.[6]

---

[1] Anthony Royle, MP for Richmond since 1959. He had served in the Life Guards at the very end of the war, ending up in the 21st Special Air Service regiment (TA), 1948–51.

[2] Michael Heseltine had been Secretary of State for the Environment since the general election.

[3] On 30 March 1979, the day after the announcement of the general election that would bring the Conservatives back to power, the party's Northern Ireland spokesman, and a close confidant of Margaret Thatcher, was murdered in the Palace of Westminster by a car bomb; the INLA, a republican splinter group, claimed responsibility.

[4] Nigel Lawson, MP for Blaby since February 1974, and now Financial Secretary to the Treasury under Geoffrey Howe.

[5] Stephen Hastings, MP for Mid-Bedfordshire since 1960; Nicholas Winterton, MP for Macclesfield since 1971.

[6] The '92' took its name from the London home (92 Cheyne Walk) of its first chairman, Sir Patrick Wall, MP for Haltemprice since 1954, with the main aim of keeping the Conservative Party conservative. Margaret Thatcher dined with the committee in

House of Commons   *Thursday, 6 December*

Last night I spoke, again, on the protectionist theme. And intervened to make my point. Again 'exposed' before Mrs T! These days I interrupt with total confidence. But must be careful not to become an Adley (ie discounted before he even opens his mouth).

1978 and in her first government she appointed six of its members as ministers, most notably Norman Tebbit.

1980

Back a fortnight – it seems like three months!

Antony Buck[1] and John Wells down for the weekend with their wives. Hospitality was lavish – too lavish in the event – as all the guests drank too much and Aspinall, who came over for dinner, became extremely combative and made a great deal of noise. No scope for statesman-like discussions.

Buck refused to go to bed at 2am when everyone else had dispersed and steered me back to the study 'for a last whisky'. He repeated several times the concept of an ideal arrangement whereby he was Secretary of State for Defence and I was Minister, '. . . or perhaps the other way round'.

'No, no,' I said, 'don't be ridiculous.'

Actually, there is not the slightest chance of his being promoted. Like little Winston, whose sexual athletics are being luridly recounted in two rival tabloid papers at this moment, he is a 'has-been'. In his cups Buck mumbled resentfully about Winston having three weeks off from the Whip to go to Cambodia, but I see that W. had to get Minnie[2] out of the way when all this dirt was being made public and the trip was really a kind of leaving present from the Whips Office.

I drank ginger ale (which, in the glass, looks like a medium strength whisky). Buck said 'goodnight' from time to time and made one or two efforts to rise to his feet, but slumped back (he was sitting in the corner of Bonny mama's red sofa). Finally he made it and *reeled* off upstairs.

The long-term purpose of the weekend was to create a 'good impression' to John Wells of the set-up; of my suitability to succeed

---

[1] Antony Buck, MP for Colchester since 1961, chairman of the Conservative Defence Committee since 1979 and thus AC's 'boss', AC being co-secretary with Robert Atkins, MP for Preston North since 1979. AC was convinced that he specialised in defence as the British Aerospace factory manufacturing the Panavia Tornado was situated in his constituency (his majority of 27 was the smallest in the House).

[2] Winston Churchill, MP for Stretford since 1970, married Mary Caroline d'Erlanger in 1964; the marriage was dissolved in 1997.

him when he retires etc., probably less certain. JW did not drink as much as the others and was somewhat inscrutable.

Cloisters   *Tuesday, 5 February*

I asked a supplementary of Mark Carlisle[1] today on the assisted places scheme and the subject simmered on for the rest of Question Time. It must be crazy to tamper with this at the same time as they are presiding over the dismemberment of British heavy industry. If he condemns the bright child to the drudgery of the state system without hope or escape there will be no one to take advantage of the new slim-line economy if we finally bring it off. I took ten minutes off and strolled out into the Members' Lobby where Ian Gow was prowling. He asked me if I had a question in mind (the Prime Minister was due to start answering in ten minutes time).

'Nothing special,' I said. 'Anything I can do for you?'

Out of the corner of his mouth he said, 'Ask when they are going to put some teeth into the Employment Act.'

I know that Ian loathes Prior and never ceases to complain about him, but what I found worrying was that the Prime Minister is so isolated in Cabinet that she has to send her PPS out into the Lobby to try and raise support at random from backbenchers at Question Time. I warned him that I might not get in as the Speaker had already called me once on a supplementary and my name was not on the Order Paper. Sure enough there was an enormous crowd and although I got to my feet repeatedly I was not called. However, Bill Clark, so recently and deservedly knighted,[2] got in with a similar question and I assume this had also been planted.

---

[1] Mark Carlisle, MP for Runcorn since 1964, Secretary for State for Education since 1979.
[2] Sir William Clark, MP for Croydon South since 1974 (E Surrey 1970–74), and former vice-chairman of the Conservative Party, knighted in New Year's honours list.

E Cloisters   *Early morning, Wednesday, 20 February*

I said something to Jamie on the lines of 'I wish I were you ... I'd
know what I'd do all right ...' etc. 'So would I', half to himself, very
much implying – if you were dead I'd get going etc ...

   Actually, little does he know, we're still highly strapped. Interest
charges – I can barely think about them. Oh how I pine for the open
air, nature, return of vitality, happy times with Jane; some days the
heat here is so oppressive, the air stale, and only triangles of blue sky
are perceptible through the leaded panes. I can't do anything after
lunch, virtually for the rest of the day, I'm so drowsy.

Albany (later)
Dined with Tony Buck. The occasional flash of wit. Towards the end
of the evening he confided in me that Rhodes James disapproved very
strongly of my 'reputation', how badly I treated my wife, mumbled
something about Valeri. All total balls, and I am extremely annoyed
considering RJ has been to Saltwood and never reciprocated in any
way. Also slightly disconcerting is that RJ has obviously been spreading
this around for years.

   Afterwards, decided on spur of moment, although frightfully tired –
kept looking at myself in mirror and thought somewhat pale and
bigheaded, with thick neck and domed effect as hair continues to
recede – to go to a late party given by Peter Tapsell[1] in his chambers
at Albany 'for' Dr Savimbi.[2] When I arrived (an hour late) the doctor
was on his feet, on the window sill in fact, addressing the multitude.
And most effectively he did it. These Africans are extremely formidable. There is something very impressive about the powerful
orator, immaculately dressed, who has only lately arrived from the
Bush and who that very evening was flying back to Luanda and the
Kalashnikovs. I said all this when I shook his hand.

---

[1] Peter Tapsell, MP for Horncastle since 1966 (Nottingham West, 1959–64).
[2] Leader of the anti-communist FNLA guerrilla movement in Angola.

Saltwood   *Saturday, 23 February*

A glorious sunny spring day after much rain.

Absurdly frantic with *pressure on time*. Whole night/morning thrown out by James doing (even for him) exceptional young-person night disturbances finally going to bed at twenty minutes to five – *GROAN!* Jane and I had heart-rending discussion about it in the small hours.

This morning, staggering with fatigue, I went out to the Barbican. Wouldn't I have about 1,000 *days* left before I was a buffer? 1,000 days to put affairs in order, finances in shape, car collection disciplined, châlet paid off – everything – plus a *HOLIDAY* with dear Jane.

Albany   *Tuesday, 26 February*

Yesterday evening, feeling very tetchy and harassed with so many pressures, correspondence in arrears, tax statements behind, children wayward and *désoeuvré*, though lovable, walking up the deserted Smoking Corridor I saw Rhodes James in the distance approaching me from the dining-room end. I stopped and looked at the ticker tape. Donnishly acid, he said, 'I saw you featured in the *Sunday Times* yesterday ...'[1]

'Featured means fornicate, Robert,' I said.

He affected not to hear, muttered something about, '... had visions of you picking coal with your little pick.'

'Like Candy,' I said. I don't think he got the allusion.[2]

I had been a little apprehensive about my reception this morning as colleagues do hate one getting publicity unless it is overly scandalous and retarding But most people quite jolly. Those who disapprove as, eg Costain, just twinklingly, or icily, as their mood may be, 'very good photograph of you in yesterday's paper.'

---

[1] Headlined 'The "civilised" Tory Tribunite', the profile drew attention to the similarity of AC's views to those of the Labour left wing: favouring 'import controls, complete withdrawal from the EEC,' although his expressed 'guarded admiration' for Bismarck and Hitler, the profile suggested, was 'to tease his unlikely new friends in the Tribune Group.'

[2] Candy was the nubile, blond *demi-vierge* in Terry Southern's 1964 novel of the same name, who at one stage found herself at a coal face alongside the lecherous Grindle. Candy whiled away the hours picking at the face with an ice pick, laying minuscule fragments on her silk head-square which she had spread on the ground.

Not having any appetite I decided to go and listen to the Prime Minister being interviewed by Robin Day. She was wonderful and very glamorous looking, though slightly spoilt the effect with over-much ocular grimacing.

To such an extent that I worried that she might have got a blob of mascara into her eye and was alarmed, at some camera angles, to see a tell-tale red glow therein. As always she let out a few impromptus, notably the revelation that Jim Prior was 'very, very sorry' for his indiscretion.[1]

There was still three-quarters of an hour left before the vote and I thought I ought to eat something. I couldn't face the dining room, so went down to the cafeteria. I was chatting to Tony Buck and David Madel[2] at their table when I saw Ian Gow come in, almost immediately followed by the Prime Minister who stood alone at the counter waiting to be served. I rushed up and congratulated her on the programme and Ian invited me to join them. I told the Prime Minister that a guffaw had gone round the television room when she said that she had found Ian Gilmour's speeches 'scintillating'.

Almost coquettishly she reminded me of her other comment ... 'something in there for everyone.' Peter Hordern[3] joined us during the meal and was grave, thoughtful and 'correct' about financial matters. But I could see the Prime Minister preferred gossip. Ian grinned benignly as I joked about Prior's reproof and her breaching for the first time the notion that she might 'think about considering whether to withhold our EEC budget contributions'.

But goodness, she is *so* beautiful; made up to the nines of course, for the television programme, but still quite bewitching, as Eva Peron must have been. I could not take my eyes off her and after a bit she, quite properly, would not look me in the face and I detached myself from the group with the excuse that I was going up to heckle Michael Foot[4] who was doing the winding-up for Labour.

---

[1] Some days before Prior, Secretary of State for Employment, had 'leaked' to the lobby that the chairman of British Steel 'would have to be replaced ... as soon as the strike was over.'

[2] David Madel, MP for South Bedfordshire since 1970.

[3] Peter Hordern, MP for Horsham and Crawley since 1974 (Horsham 1964–74), a member of the Public Accounts Committee and the Executive of the 1922 Committee, and before entering politics a member of the Stock Exchange.

[4] Michael Foot, MP for Ebbw Vale since 1960 (Devonport 1945–55); the successor to James Callaghan as Leader of the Labour Party later in the year.

After the 10 o'clock vote I walked back to Albany and at the lower crossing place in St James's Street I saw two shadowy forms, elderly, decrepit even; but with a strange Episcopal authority, in their great black cloaks. The traffic – as always at that hour – made up of drunks and car thieves, was travelling at a colossal speed, so I helped them make it to the first island. I saw to my delight that one of them was Harold Macmillan, wearing his long-range multi-focals that look like sections of a glass rolling pin.[1]

'Are you going, sir, to Pratt's or Brooks's,' I asked him. 'The Carlton,' he replied tersely and shuffled off. But then paused, turned and called after me, 'It's too late for Pratt's anyway,' and waved an enormous half-hunter watch. 'They will be shut.'

A pleasant evening. Two Prime Ministers in the space of an hour and a half. Odd, how I keep meeting Uncle Harold when I least expect it.

Saltwood   *Sunday, 2 March*

If I don't make it by the next reshuffle it's withdrawal, but as the reshuffle now looks to be deferred until Christmas I get a nasty feeling that this is going to be one of the fullest summers.

Back shows no sign of healing – haven't been able to touch my toes for nearly two months.

Cloisters   *Tuesday, 18 March*

I was munching my buns at a table in the Tea Room when Jim Lester[2] came and sat down holding a lot of papers. I used to think he was rather objectionable, but I will say that he has been very effective from the box at Question Time – one of the successes among the junior 'wetter' appointments.

---

[1] Macmillan had celebrated his eighty-sixth birthday a fortnight before.
[2] James (Jim) Lester, MP for Beeston since February 1974; Parliamentary Under-Secretary of State for Employment since 1979.

I touched on the subject of import controls with Lester and asked him what his 'boss' thought. Somewhat to my surprise he answered that, '. . . he (Jim Prior) is in such hot water at the moment that I would not think he would want to put his head above the parapet on anything else.' The reference to hot water quite surprised me. Some correspondents give the impression that Prior is virtually autonomous, with so much backing in the Cabinet that the Lady hardly dares to approach him. But Lester's timidity was quite genuine.

Saltwood   *Wednesday, 19 March*

Oooh – the pressures! A frightfully depressing day yesterday. *Missed* through sheer spontaneity (ie overloaded memory bank with appointments and obligations) the joint meeting of Industry and Trade with Nott and Joseph. Nearly missed, too, the little conspiratorial meeting chaired by Dick Body[1] – but after my arrival I was clearly the most authoritative person there – to organise the anti-EEC EDM at Ian Gow's behest.

Swallow Room totally collapsed – roof not draining at all. Such filthy weather, combination of freezing fog *and* high wind (how can that be?) day after day of wet pavement. My shoulder/arm quite objectionable – doesn't like slumping in chairs or turning. Perhaps too many rail journeys.

Albany   *Thursday, 20 March*

Joei now gone mad; rings only making threats – it's a highly innocuous, run-of-the-mill heterosexual tale, but I suppose it could 'sell' – eg scandal about MPs is news and would certainly screw any career prospects. Just think of formula: 'I do not under any circumstances discuss my relations with the ladies. I am a gentleman, not a hairdresser.'

---

[1] Richard Body, MP for Holland with Boston since 1966, member of the Commons Select Committee on Agriculture since 1979.

Also medium-term worries, like what about Broomhayes? What is beloved 'Boy' going to do next? Do I/can I sell the Moore bust to pay off the chalet etc?

Saltwood   *Friday, 28 March*

Back for the weekend – we had cancelled Zermatt, I hope not disappointing 'Boy' so as to get to grips with the Estate and papers. Although somewhat tired and crotchety (Ali totally withdrawn, sod it, paid that £·5 for nothing) did steel myself to Osprey the Bailey. Saltwood just starting to 'smile', but so much to do, so many small deteriorations: why is the moat still losing water? Did a last walk in failing light, thinking about Andrew coming back from the geography field trip and going straight on out to Zermatt We, in spite of being rascally 'young' and non-bufferish, bore them. I stood at the yard gates and looked across at the dark mass of the Great Hall and Courtenays, the moon almost full. Are we to be driven for the next five years, slaving away to keep the place going – for what? Will our grandchildren want it anyway? Quite suddenly and unexpectedly my daily horoscope said that the next two years are going to be 'unsettled'.

Zermatt   *Saturday, 12 April*

Julian Amery dined last night. A little heavier than formerly; said he skied better in the afternoons and drank a litre (!) of wine at lunch. We spoke non-stop about political matters until midnight. He is well *versé* in foreign affairs. He doesn't acknowledge flattery. He sees things somewhat apocalyptically especially in the mid-East. Wants to get an expeditionary force (still), to south Iran to offer as 'alternative' Iranian government. Sounds a bit cloudy to me, shades of South Vietnam etc.

But interesting, as always, historically. Threw light, at first hand, on the celebrated 'Cipriani' incident.[1] Confided that Willie Whitelaw[2] had told him how he intended to 'smash' the Unionist Party when he was Secretary of State for NI. At breakfast, Andrew cunningly said 'was there much talk about the reshuffle?' Not really, but Julian too agreed that everyone in the Cabinet loathes the PM, is out to do her down. Sole exceptions Biffen (too distracted) and possibly (my addition) John Nott; himself somewhat constrained by his own leadership expectations long-term. Howe now a contender, has advanced massively since the budget – though God knows why.

Cloisters   *Monday, 14 April*

In the lobby for a 3-line vote I was joking with George Gardiner and Tony Marlow (bad company in establishment terms).[3] Marlow was trying to get me to sign an E.D.M. and I declined jokingly, asserting that I only signed them '... on Europe and animal welfare'. General laughter and as I turned away I saw the Prime Minister approaching in conversation with Raison.[4] Raison's expression, as always, was grave and humourless, but as hers was relatively amiable and her distance away from me less than three feet, I quickly composed my features and framed a deferential smile. To my great alarm she looked straight through me, her own expression altering to one of icy disdain. I am worried about this. What have I done wrong? We enjoyed very good relations immediately after Christmas and I was optimistic. I suppose I was too brown; being brown indicates idleness and (at this time of the year) foreign holidays. Albeit in our case an exceedingly

---

[1] Elsewhere AC records as follows, circa late 1979: Anthony Royle 'told an interesting story of Heath's loathing of Julian Amery and, through his personification, the old Whites', that 'magic circle' strain in the Tory Party. In the early 1950s Julian and friends were having drinks on the terrace of the Cipriani in Venice when Heath appeared in gym shoes and made some gauche remark which Amery, slightly tight, tore to pieces and then held up the fragments for his cronies to laugh at. Heath never forgave him and still suspects that every Member of the Parliamentary Party from that ambience is waiting to do the same thing.'

[2] William Whitelaw, after four years as Opposition home affairs spokesman, had been Home Secretary since 1979.

[3] George Gardiner, MP for Reigate and Banstead since February 1974; Antony (Tony) Marlow, MP for Northampton North since 1979.

[4] Timothy Raison, MP for Aylesbury since 1970, Minister of State, Home Office since 1979.

short one.[1] Also my laughter may have been too loud. There was something in the Prime Minister's manner that reminded me of my mother, who also hated loud laughter, and it put her in a bad mood.

Cloisters   *Friday, 18 April*

On Wednesday night I was feeling ghastly and was dropping a 1 mg tablet of Redoxon into a glass of mineral water at the Smoking Room bar when Peter Morrison *volunteered* that he could 'help' with a pair the following day, Thursday. An unprecedented suggestion – was I really looking that ill? But on Friday morning I realised why: there had been a revolt of 37 back-benchers against a provision of the Employment Bill and he had wanted to get me out of the way, or save me embarrassment? Nothing in this place is what it seems. The Machiavellian undercurrents, the need to be permanently on one's guard, to know how to read the codes and smoke signals; how to assess people's real motives, and discount their superficial courtesies and protestations – is what makes the game here so fascinating.

Headland Park, Plymouth   *Saturday, 19 April*

Sitting in this mouldy little 'headquarters' – conveniently walking distance from the station though – just a year since the middle of the election campaign when all was whiz and fizz and I used to shut myself in here and lech at Veronica opposite. There, facing me on the table is one of the election car stickers – did I really look like that only a year ago?

Now time for a last *reflectif* to close the 'black book'. I don't want to make it sound too melodramatic, God is so good to me in waves. But it must be sadder, this note, than the close of earlier volumes.

Even the Katoomba 'red book' which saw the dizzy spiral down from 1972 'too good to be true' to 1974, 'a bailiff at the door'. The testosterone was higher. In the train coming down this afternoon I sat most of the time in that special melancholy that comes from separation,

---

[1] The Clarks had been in Zermatt for five days.

parting almost with a loved one. Realised it was not the 'blondes' – partly because I can't believe it has really happened (had a 'click' call only last week) and half of me looks forward to the rows and reconciliations, the other half is heedless enough (now) to quite enjoy the 'siege'. No, the loved one who has gone is 'Boy'. Have lately (as last night) been waking and worrying about him; (a) that he is destroying his substance; (b) that he finds us so boring – he didn't have a single meal with us the whole time he was in Zermatt and the last two nights he couldn't even face sleeping under the same roof – (c) what the hell is he going to do?

Then I can't deny the physical decline that has occurred in the last five years. It's partly the passing of time – the weekends are so precious; partly the sheer fatigue accumulated by back pain, rheumatics etc that cut down on – and virtually eliminated – exercises. I can't run and I doubt if I could really do Summerhouse Hill without feeling awful. I have had the ticket for the Berkeley swimming pool now for two years and have never used it.

Financially these have been appalling times. I don't really miss the Moore bust, only a showing-off colour, but haven't yet told Jane who didn't want it to be sold (not realising the extent to which one was still in hock on Zermatt). The half Cézanne deal is a mystery – where the hell did it all go? On doing the rooms (although the Great Hall still leaks and drips ominously) and the kitchen and wood system, school fees and heavy expenditure on 'Boy'. Had to sell the Bira – and this with the windfall of Dennis Wright's[1] could get us nominally 'straight'. Even so, as darling Jane who so nobly struggles now with the VAT books laments, output still rages ahead of input, or 'coin'. We can only last a certain amount of time longer and I would say my father is good for at least another four years.

Politically, one might say I have advanced, or at least consolidated. I would have said that I have made *considerable* progress in this new parliament – with my confident interventions, better relationship with the whips, distinct and lucid and insistent advocacy of protectionism – being 'noted' by even John Biffen and 'The Lady' – but all of a sudden 'The Lady' has gone cold, freezing cold on me. Ian Gow, too, seems to be avoiding me in the lobby.

I've catalogued these random impressions, not all by any means. But it's maudlin really, isn't it? The full, full life. One is never content,

---

[1] Cottage in Saltwood village.

but think of poor Nanny, nothing to do but walk slowly in Hythe and listen to what people say. I thank God for the incredible variety and privilege he has bestowed on me, also for strength to take advantage of it. God? I hardly ever speak to him now, except for the ritual 'touch wood' of thanks on my knees before getting into bed.

One last epic memory of the period the great dice against the two super bikes in the green Porsche turbo. Cin was with me and I'm glad of that, as so many of my hopes are now with him.

Thank God for keeping us all so fine, for saving Jamie in his aeroplane and virtually curing Tip of asthma, for still giving me 'highs' and inspiring dear Bonny mama to leave me her fortune.

Cloisters   *Monday, 21 April*

At a loose end I went to the European Affairs Committee. I am due on Welsh Radio the following morning to talk about Carter and United States 'sanctions' against Iran and as Europe is plainly feeble and divided on this subject I thought I might pick up some tips. Ian Gow came in and sat at the far side of the room. On impulse I went over to him and asked him if he was free for dinner.

'Sadly not,' he replied. 'What are you doing after this?'

This was good, but unfortunately I had the Home Affairs Committee at 6 p.m. and as we were due to discuss the Bristol riots I could hardly shirk it.

'Come to my room at 5.30,' he said.

We sat in the leather chairs of the PPS's room. As always he was serious, attentive and conveyed that special sense of urgency and concern of which he is a master. I plunged straight in.

'I say, am I in the Prime Minister's bad books at the moment?'

'No, no, not at all . . .'

'I just seem to detect a certain *frisson* . . .'

'Oh no, she has a very high opinion of you, you are one of her . . .'

'Say no more, no, no, please say no more', I held up my hand in the time honoured Trevor-Roper gesture.[1]

---

[1] Hugh Trevor-Roper, now Lord Dacre, had been AC's tutor at Christ Church and had a special characteristic wave of the hand which he used indiscriminately to halt praise or criticism, or to dismiss argument.

I went straight into the topic of the 'rebel' votes against various aspects of the Employment Bill. It was immediately plain that Gow was anxious to encourage them, 'I can assure you that if you should vote in that lobby it would not make the slightest difference to your standing or reputation' (he only just stopped himself from saying 'career prospects'). He speaks quite openly about hostility between Prior and the Prime Minister. I said that Prior was probably more frightened of dismissal than might appear to those who see him in day to day action in the Cabinet Room and told the story of my conversation with Jim Lester in the Tea Room last month. Gow said that if he were to be sacked he would be more dangerous as a focus of old Heathites and progressives on the backbenches. I said that I hoped the Prime Minister realised the full extent of the armory of weapons at her disposal and how she had nothing to fear provided she realised that whatever happened – short of a defeat on a vote of confidence – she was in power, personally, for another $3\frac{1}{2}$ years. 'It is very difficult to promulgate any policy without the agreement of the Cabinet,' said Gow. 'Well the obvious answer to that is to change the Cabinet,' I replied, 'but I agree there are strategic considerations.'

I told the story that Ray Whitney[1] had recounted to me about how he was so offended by Prior's jokes and criticism of the Prime Minister, with Hayhoe acting as feedman, that he had walked out of a dinner party. Hayhoe is a classic example of a wet and a fifth columnist in a job to which he is totally ill-suited without status of any kind that might make his sacking difficult – and anyway I know I could do the job (Minister of Defence for the Army) better than he does.

'We have never had this conversation,' said Ian. 'Of course not,' I said. Somebody tried the door, we both looked round guilty and I got up to go. Ian unlocked the door and Tony Royle walked in.

'Six of the best,' I said, 'I hope you have got your telephone directory in place.'

The door closed behind him with the key turned.

---

[1] Raymond (Ray) Whitney, MP for Wycombe since 1978.

Cloisters   *Thursday, 24 April*

I was lunching in the Members' Dining Room with two nonentities (I cannot remember their names) when the Chief Whip[1] came and sat at our table.

Conversation strayed round to the events of the previous evenings.[2]

'Don't you think,' I said, foolishly (why did I say this?) '. . . that the list of rebels last night was qualitatively superior to that of the night before?'

'I never consider there is any quality among those who vote against their own government,' he said icily.

Unhappily I tried to be flippant, but it was no good. He was not friendly. I fear I have lost much ground. The Chief Whip fulminated about others (I know Gerry Neale[3] was among them from what he told me) who had voted against on a three-liner the previous week without any warning or apology afterwards. I left the table early and bolted to the Members' Post Office where I scribbled out a full, but I fear largely illegible, letter of apology which I then rushed through to the Chief Whip's office in the hope that it would greet him on his desk on his return from his meal.

House of Commons   *Monday / Tuesday, 28 / 29 April*

Horrible 'austerity' book[4] opens with gloom.

Woken last night by the Albany blackbird, so glad he is still around, he went off quite quietly, almost as soon as the chorus started.

I thought through the various 'last times'. This thing I have. There is, is bound logically to be, a 'last time' you do everything before you die. The first times you know about; they may be good or they may be bad. Sometimes they mirror first times, sometimes they overlap. I mean the first time you are impotent does not immediately follow the last time you have sexual intercourse (in my own case 1955 and . . .

---

[1] Michael Jopling, MP for Westmorland since 1964, Chief Whip since 1979.

[2] The 'rebellions' on the Employment Bill. The number of back benchers voting against the Government had increased from 37 the previous Thursday, to 45 on Tuesday and to 48 the following evening.

[3] Gerrard (Gerry) Neale, MP for North Cornwall since 1979.

[4] New journal, as described in Introduction.

open). But the last time you don't know, not really know because there is always hope, until much later.

When the boys were tiny I used to go up to their room and kiss them goodnight, always with Jane, and this was lovely, the very best part of the whole day. Then Jane dropped out and I used to tell a story (the 'Badgers', the 'Tidy Pig' etc), and this was even better. Then that stopped (to much protestation, some of it slightly formalised) as a punishment for 'tinkling' behind the cupboard on the top floor at the Manor. I think I still did occasionally tell a story, as a treat only for a bit, although often urged to I never wrote them down and can remember very few, only the theft of the cartridges for Guy Fawkes day in full – but a little, dimly, of the kidnapping on the *Hesperides*. Anyway, the next stage was just saying 'goodnight' and perhaps a little chat with them in bed; then with them standing, and dressed in their room; then often downstairs or in the corridor; finally (in James's case) *they* had to check in with *us*.

I composed the letter, which I still have to put on paper, to Tip, both explaining how much I love him and how I agonised when he was tiny. James always outshone him. He wants a black GTI. I can't refuse, because he never asks (until now) for anything. But of course it's even more like OLA – much more – and much faster (because OLA, being as it were 'vintage' imposes its own discipline). I hope to pose certain restrictions – no dicing? – not over 70 etc.

Later
It was the second day of the Defence White Paper debate, for which I had put in a special plea to the Speaker stating my reasons. Although I had asked him to help I suspect that Carol Mather[1] deliberately spoilt my chances. Chris Patten[2] a bumptious but intelligent little careerist was called in my place. I am in bad odour with the whips. And their memory is long. A great nuisance as I thought I had been 'mending my fences'.

---

[1] Carol Mather, MP for Esher since 1970, Defence Whip since 1979.
[2] Chris Patten, MP for Bath since 1979.

Saltwood   *Monday, 5 May*

Jane stays lovely, always bright, happy and has lovely grey eyes and magic powers of observation. She 'found' a Miro in the drawer in the library table yesterday looking through old Christmas cards.

As I closed the Bailey this evening I couldn't help thinking – I really am getting quite a bit older. My physique didn't change at all from 20–30, very, very little from 30–40, and tiny bit faster from 40–45. But the last seven years have been devastating. Is it my life-style? The Commons? It is certainly coinciding with it. I am using up my reserves so that when I am 60 I will actually be like someone of 60.

Saltwood   *Thursday, 8 May*

The Iranian Sanctions Bill is being rushed through the House. Total balls of course from beginning to end, and can only do harm. Tam Dalyell[1] did an incredible job filibustering, speaking for up to two hours at a time without ever being irrelevant or out of order.

I was in a dilemma – and not one of conscience. There was a running two-line whip with the likelihood of votes every three hours or so to get 'closures'. I have no pair and the last thing I wanted was another rumpled night on the back seat of the Chev. I hung around in the early stages and made interjections, also a short speech in which, interalia, I consolidated my position on the US Embassy black list by referring to the President [Carter] as, 'the worst incumbent of the White House since President Harding'. Ioan Evans, the amiable, but presumably lecherous and corrupt, Tribune M.P. for Aberdare,[2] was also taking part in the early stages of the debate. I sensed he would probably want to go about eleven and asked him for a pair. But he would not break his arrangement with Michael Hamilton. 'I will give you a name though boyoo', he then said, 'I will give you a name'.

'Yes, yes', I was over eager.

'Donald Coleman',[3] he said.

I went straight to the Whips' Office and gave some cock and bull

---

[1] Tam Dalyell, Labour MP for West Lothian since 1962.
[2] Ioan Evans, MP for Aberdare since February 1974.
[3] Donald Coleman, MP for Neath since 1964.

story about having arranged a pair yesterday and forgot to register it. They were firm that it had to be registered with Peter Morrison (the implacable pairing whip who, if he had his way, would never register *any* pairs). I knew better than this, so I sought out dear Bob Boscawen[1] and told him that although I had voted with the Government the previous evening I was speaking in favour of a number of amendments and to save embarrassment I thought it would be better if I was paired at this Committee Stage and could he tell Peter.

Later that night at the 'Business' vote (exempt from pairing arrangements) Peter Morrison actually told me to shut up and desist from taking part in the debate. He tried to claim that although I was paired on the amendments I should still attend to vote in the 'closures'. But I was not going to have any of that and went home to bed.

It is hellish not having a pair, I am going to run out of tricks like this in the end. I *must* write to the next Labour candidate for a safe seat at a by-election.

H o C, Committee Room   *Tuesday, 13 May*

Almost fell asleep at Brooks's dinner, solitary on Perrier water. We had to be back in the committee room by 9 'on the dot'. As I blew the two-pressure horn on the little 'Mickey' I was reminded, suddenly, of driving back from the Lavingtons, having been, in all probability with the beagles on Salisbury Plain. Fifteen years ago! What a decline in one's physique, sexuality, appearance. Could I recover? Or rather *how far* could I recover?

Albany   *Monday, 19 May*

I awoke this morning and decided to pick a fight with Willie Whitelaw. I am sick of him. I am pretty sure he does not like me and I suspect that he has a big influence in the higher counsels of the Party. I have long admired his intuition and political skills, but I read over the weekend that the Home Office was actually increasing the grant to

---

[1] Robert (Bob) Boscawen, MP for Wells since 1970, a whip since 1979.

the Voluntary Services Unit, an outfit devoted exclusively, it seems, to funding subversive activities and concerning which I had asked a number of pretty taut questions when we were in Opposition. I thought this was really too much.

However, in politics we are all in the kaleidoscope; give the thing a kick, or even a light tap and it may change out of all recognition. And later that day when I was in the Tea Room eating a rock bun and preparing myself to raise the VSU question aggressively at the Home Affairs Committee in five minutes time, up came Ted Gardner[1] and asked if I would chair the new sub-committee which Willie had asked to be set up to look at the question of Civil Defence. I realised at once that this could be a very useful rung on the ladder. In Committee Ted approaches these things in a very circumlocutory way. I do not know whether he had second thoughts or doubts of any kind, but he almost failed to manage to announce it to the Committee, who nonetheless applauded loudly, led by Hugh Fraser.

Mary Whitehouse[2] had been invited to address us that day and everyone had forgotten. After waiting in the corridor for half an hour she somewhat deferentially tried to get in and had to be shown out and kept waiting for a further fifteen minutes.

So far so good. After the Committee had dispersed little Jim Pawsey, a real cheeky-chappie complete with glasses and bustling papers, stayed behind and we discussed what we were to do. Ted had suggested that I invite Pawsey[3] to be secretary as he had made a lot of mileage on this subject, asked an enormous number of P.A.s etc. He believes it will make his career, and let him go on believing this as he will gladly shoulder the leg work. However, there were hurdles to be leapt.

That evening we were invited to attend a joint meeting with officers of the Defence Committee in Willie's room behind the Speaker's Chair at 10.30 p.m. It was immediately apparent that Willie, dressed in a 'slub' silk dinner jacket, had had too much to drink. I know of old that when his skin is livid, and he carries his head in that special one-sided gait he is fighting hard to beat off the depressant effects of many, many millilitres per centilitre; and sure enough he very quickly got 'on the bellow', recounted an exchange between himself and

---

[1] Edward (Ted) Gardner, MP for South Fylde since 1970.
[2] Mary Whitehouse, President of the National Viewers' and Listeners' Association since 1980. Articulate upholder of conservatism and decency in the media.
[3] James (Jim) Pawsey, MP for Rugby since 1979.

General Creasey[1] in which they appeared to have both been completely uninhibited. Creasey had called Willie a wet and a shit. Willie had apparently shouted 'fuck you' in public and followed up with, 'I hated you when you were in Northern Ireland, I have always hated you and I hate you now.'

By the time we came to actually discuss the arrangements for the Civil Defence enquiry he had become totally lost. All he had done was to repeat at great length twice or three times over his reasons for deferring the Review (our numbers were constantly being swelled by the arrival of various delegates who had been sent for at thirty minutes staggered intervals). When Ted finally got round to the subject of the sub-committee having been promulgated and that I had been appointed to chair it the news went down like a lead balloon. The whole room was furious and Willie was put out – blustered that we would not have time to report before he published his own Review (not half we won't, I will take care of that). Poor little Jimmy Pawsey foolishly and youthfully suggested that I should make a statement. Willie affected not to hear and shouted this down. I was sly because I knew that I had already released the news to the Press Association and the London heavies and that I was going on radio the following morning so they could not get rid of me or change the plan.

Afterwards in the Members' Lobby the odious Atkins came up to me and said, 'It looks as if your committee is going to have only one member.'

I had already had to put off at least half a dozen applicants since it was promulgated that afternoon and said as much. He switched immediately and asked if he could join. But I made a non-committal reply.

Got to bed at 1.20 a.m. and will be woken by an alarm call from the BBC at 6.15 a.m.

---

[1] General Sir Timothy Creasey, Commander-in-Chief, UK Land Forces, had been GOC, Northern Ireland, 1977–79.

Albany   *Tuesday, 20 May*

In the Lobby, Ian Gow, in a dinner jacket, gave me a slightly beady
look. I was meant to be at a Reception at No. 10, but had felt so tired
that I could not be bothered to change and had spent most of the
previous hour dozing in a chair in the Library. However, I abandoned
RJ and pelted after Ian, 'to whom do I address my apologies, I don't
think I have a dinner jacket in London, don't wish to be discourteous
by attending improperly dressed'.

He pressed me to come, insisted, said he would take me in his own
car. 'The Prime Minister would be absolutely furious if you don't
come,' he said. He is such a dear. I ran down and put on a white shirt
and joined him in the Mini which was parked (as he often amusingly
does) on the space 'reserved for the disabled' in Star Court. Charles
Fletcher-Cooke[1] – always good company – was already in the car
though, naturally, wearing a dinner jacket.

The moment we got to No. 10 Ian abandoned us, whizzing into
his own office on the ground floor.

There were *very* few people at the Reception who were not in
dinner jackets. I have a high confidence level, but it was not too good.
However, the Prime Minister did not express disapproval and when she
introduced me to Dr Kurt Waldheim[2], she actually said, 'Something –
something, something' ('specialises in', was it? the noise in the room
was deafening) 'defence'. This I suppose was encouraging. Stumblingly I muttered about my new committee.

Dr Waldheim inclined his head. I do not know what he thought
of things. The 'Reception' seemed to me rather inchoate not to say
disorderly. The Prime Minister herself was rather *waxen*-faced and
disconcertingly broad in the beam as she sometimes can be. She must
not 'go dowager'. That would detract a lot. But how does she sustain
her interest on those occasions? My God, when I am Prime Minister
I will never go to receptions.

---

[1] Charles Fletcher-Cooke, MP for Darwen since 1951.
[2] Dr Kurt Waldheim, Secretary-General of the United Nations since 1972.

Saltwood   *Saturday, 31 May*

We have had some wonderful summer days. Unfortunately the filling
of the pool delayed by the wait for the (new) plastic bubble cover that
was meant to keep the heat in and the leaves out. Pool only just
reaching the top and no swimming yet.

Last night I worried about James (what else??) who had walked off
after dinner. Tip-toed down about midnight and found him in the
Green Room. We looked at the atlas of the British Empire in 1935 –
all gone, in 40 years, all of it. And he told me that his friends said
the Sea-Harrier was still not fitted with HUD [Head Up Display].
Depressing.

Albany   *Tuesday, 17 June*

I've been in vile mood all day. A new List has been published. Michael
McNair-Wilson,[1] as always, was languid and mocking. 'The "K's" are
really flying around, aren't they?'

Michael went on to suggest that Freddy Burden's was 'post-
humous'.[2]

Now we are stuck on some long, rambling, useless 2-liner. So
drained by the horrible fetid air, tight shoes, suits rumpling. I had a
full day here, getting in before 9 a.m., then realised at 7 p.m., when
'the world' was slacking off and putting on its slippers that I still had
another five hours – minimum – to go.

Was feeling randily expectant as Nanny had told me the previous
day that someone 'well-spoken and cheeky' had rung and said that (as
it were) 'Mimi Schluckleberger will dine with you on Wednesday
night.'

The phone rang as I was making cocoa; Ali; I knew Valeri was
there. Suddenly *she* snatched the phone and said, all Lausanne-station-
voice, 'you stupid little bastard' twice and rang off. I was scared and

---

[1] Michael McNair-Wilson, MP for Newbury since February 1974 (Walthamstow East,
1969–74), PPS to the Ministry of Agriculture.
[2] Frederick Burden finally retired from the House in 1983 after 43 years representing
Gillingham. He died in 1987.

thought of bolting; went down and told 'Shea'[1] not to let anyone in.
Was somehow randily expectant, in spite of it. However, Ali rang and
said (late, about 10.30) that 'she' was livid, got it in for me, was going
to get Bodoni to work me over etc.

Ugh. Totally dry mouthed.

I rang Janey. She had had *two* tours, bless her. And that morning
had mowed the Bailey herself, because if Cradduck had seen Eddie
on the new (sit-down) Atco [mower] he'd have been hysterical with
rage. But what's the point of employing two gardeners if the *chatelaine*
has to do the work herself? I wish I was at Saltwood.

Earlier, the mood in the Cloisters was light-headed. The talk strayed
to by-elections, and I invited wagers for my betting book.

Gerry Neale pretended to be shocked. So, camply, did Michael
although it was he who started the whole thing off by saying that he
had a 'horror' of going up to the main gents for a quiet crap, opening
the cubicle door and finding Alan Glyn[2] sprawled across the 'pedestal',
jaw hanging open, eyes rolled round in their sockets. I am offering 11
to 4 on Freddy Burden (must be favourite), 5 to 4 against Graham
Page,[3] 2 to 1 Glyn, 3 to 1 Costain and 4 to 1 (an interesting outsider)
Hugh Rossi.[4] It's the shortish, fattish, tense-ish ones who go first.[5]

Saltwood   *Tuesday, 24 June*

First day of a lovely long weekend, full of promise. I was on Gossie
most of the morning. Burning hot sunshine, and chasing Tom almost
as hard work as beagling. The soil on the bank is very sandy. Not pure
sand, which would be dangerous of course, and put the Jack Russell
in peril when, as he does most often, he goes underground. He was
out of sight for almost an hour, though occasionally I could hear him

---

[1] A porter at Albany.

[2] Dr Alan Glyn, MP for Windsor since 1970.

[3] Sir Graham Page, MP for Crosby since 1953. Died 1981.

[4] Hugh Rossi, MP for Hornsey since 1966, Minister of State for Social Security and the
Disabled since 1981. Not a good bet. Rossi out-lived them all.

[5] In fact Glyn (d. 1997) was to outlive Sir Michael McNair-Wilson by more than six
years. As previous entries have shown, AC had a vested interest in the future of Albert
Costain whose constituency included Saltwood. Costain died in 1987.

barking. Tom 'makes free' with the warrens, going in at one hole and coming out at another. Which must be a bore for any resident rabbits. Watership Down with a difference.

When I got back there was no sign of Jane. Nanny was disapproving. Apparently a young, unidentified, female had been on the telephone. 'Is Al there?' Nanny doesn't think people outside the family should call me 'Al'. When offered Jane instead the caller hung up.

Nanny drawing on fifty years of experience both Up-, and Down-, stairs, said that she was *'well-spoken, but cheeky'*.

'Was she in a call-box?' Didn't know.

Could something tiresome be about to happen? Damn, damn, blast, etc.

Saltwood   *Sunday, 6 July*

Have been, for the last week, extremely *apprehensive*; heavy depression, alternating with fear both short and long-term.

Started on Monday night; foolishly stripped off at Brooks's, played a little b'gammon losing £100 to Villiers and Burnett (but if I can't play with them, then I really have given up).

Dined at Julian Amery's house in Eaton Square. The most *beautiful* library, L-shaped, using the whole depth of the house (which is virtually next door to Henry Wilson, shot on his doorstep by the IRA in 1920) and abutting on a particularly marvellous conservatory just filled with old bushes and plastic bowls. Meant to be for the Crown Prince of Jordan, who didn't show up. Offered champagne, I asked if it could be mixed with orange juice. Julian demurred, said it was 'rather good'. My God it was. Greedily I drank as many glasses as I could. Of the guests I can only remember one, recently beknighted captain of industry. Odious, bullying and livid to be faced with a pipsqueak back-bencher. I didn't give a fuck. During dinner (good wine served by intoxicated, English, man-servant) I heard him asking Julian who I was, and instantly ... being given ... 'Lord Clark'.

However, to return to main theme. Had quite a longish session with Desmond Corcoran who was very reluctant to stump up £5,000 on security of Miro (looking rather grand in its bright gold frame, but apparently unsaleable). However he did so, repayment deferred until 30 September.

Cloisters   *Monday, 7 July*

Fortunately nothing in any of the Dailies today 'following up' yesterday's horror item in the *News of the World*.

Willie Hamilton caught me in the Lobby just after the afternoon
vote.[1] Somewhat pale and put out, he tried to assert that he had not
given my name to anybody, claimed that he had written to the *News
of the World* and insisted that they apologise, etc. 'It will be interesting
to see if they print my letter,' he said. (You bet it will.) He is rattled
about the affair and, indeed, may well have been trapped into giving
my name either by an adroit reporter or by Winston or Nick Winterton. I do not put much value to what he says, but at least it is
something to have him nominally on my side and not out to cause
more trouble.

Later in the evening I was walking down the Smoking Room
Corridor to go towards the dining room and have some dinner when
St John-Stevas,[2] purple shirted as always, hailed me; 'What is all this
about you and Princess Margaret? ...' I told him the story. It is
amazing how many people read *News of the World*. I never see it from
one quarter to the next. Stevas tried to get me to say who it was who
had originally expressed disapproval and did not like it when I would
not. I wandered on into the Dining Room. Most of the tables were
either full or with people obviously finishing a meal over their coffee.
Hal Miller, who was sitting at that long table by the window which
is notorious for its dreadful service, hailed me almost with a note of
desperation in his voice. He was alone with a huge, but unidentified
female companion, presumably a peeress. It was apparent that she was
exceedingly the worse for drink. A cross between Bonny mama and
Christabel Aberconway on a bad day. She ground away at us and
naturally neither of the two bad-tempered waitresses came anywhere
near. Then Ian Gow came in, beaming as always, and suggested joining
us at which prospect naturally we first brightened then, as he turned
away and announced that he was going to bring the Prime Minister,
blenched.

---

[1] Under the heading 'Willie and his Palace mole' AC was implicated in being the
alleged intermediary between a royal equerry and the anti-monarchist Hamilton, who
suggested he lay off the Queen Mother (approaching her eightieth birthday) and
concentrate on Princess Margaret instead.

[2] Norman St John-Stevas, MP for Chelmsford since 1964, Chancellor of the Duchy of
Lancaster, Leader of the House of Commons and Minister for the Arts since 1979.

The Prime Minister duly arrived and was immediately pinned by the giant washerwoman (who turned out from a *sotto voce* enquiry to Ian, who was on my left, to be Dame Hornsby-Smith[1]). On and on she huskily rambled consuming no fewer than four chain-lit Philip Morris filters during her soliloquy, and all the time the Prime Minister looked at her with an expression of rapt fascination and sympathy, occasionally nodding her head in agreement or making a polite interjection to show how closely she was following the story (itself a long untidy affair about precedence of Privy Councillors at a dinner and how Hornsby-Smith ended up going into the room on the arm of the Duke of Edinburgh).

At intervals Gow suggested, far from inaudibly, that there was a division in the Lords. Then, smoothly, Hornsby-Smith shifted across from anecdote to current affairs. She described the present state of play in the Lords regarding the passage of Clause 7 the following day.[2] It is quite clear that due to Labour abstentions and other bungling it is, to use Hornsby-Smith's phrase, 'going to be a very dicy affair'. As she said this some sixth sense made me look up from the tablecloth at the Prime Minister who simultaneously did the same thing and we exchanged a conspiratorial look. Not a wink, but a look into the iris of the eye – very exciting.

Earlier the Prime Minister had seemed to be going out of her way to be friendly and said how she had told Ian, 'that is Alan's voice ...' when I had been showing encouragement in the hurly burly that surrounded the announcement of our restricted pay increase and in particular how I had barracked Edward du Cann's pompous and unpopular short speech.[3]

In the fullness of time, there *was* a division in the Lords and Hornsby-Smith heaved herself to her feet and disappeared. I told the Prime Minister that there was not another Premier in history who would have shown so much attention and good nature and adroitly she semi-rebuked me, said what a wonderful person Pat Hornsby-Smith was and how tragic it was to see her like this, how she had had cancer of the throat, etc. I must say that if she has had cancer of the throat she has certainly adopted a very curious kind of homoeopathy to eradicate it.

[1] Patricia Hornsby-Smith, MP for Chislehurst 1950–66 (1970–February 74), DBE 1961, Life Peer 1974. She died in 1985.

[2] In the Employment Bill, a clause relating to trade union membership.

[3] Edward du Cann, MP for Taunton since 1956; chairman 1922 Committee since 1972.

The Prime Minister lingered at our table for nearly an hour and there was much anecdote and good natured gossip. She was completely relaxed and delightful – buoyed, I don't doubt, by the MORI poll which shows her in the lead for the very first time ever.

At the end, Ian, also in high good humour, dated me for dinner for the following evening and I rushed away to ring up Jane in the highest of spirits. During the phone conversation the division bell rang and coming up from the Lobby I again saw the Prime Minister, but this time talking most intimately tête-à-tête to Geoffrey Pattie, who always makes me jealous, although I recognise his concept of defence for the UK is probably the soundest in the Government.

Saltwood   *Wednesday, 9 July*

More girl trouble.

Someone rang at the House and asked for an appointment. Alison told me that she was calling back which she did on the dot of 4.15. Clearly going to put the bite on. I icily shook. Went and dug out a senior police officer – useless. Gave mouldy advice, wouldn't get me bugging kit; said Yard 'would only supply it if I preferred charges ...' etc. Dived about the place in a state of high anxiety and found myself sitting next to Nick Budgen[1] and confided in him. He wasn't much use, but did give one name – Jonathan Aitken.[2] Caught Jonathan in the lobby at the 10 o'clock vote. He said he was at a dinner, but pressed me to come along; I demurred; it turned out he was with a bird at some flat ... He was calming, gave good advice. Trysted me for next morning at his (incredibly) sumptuous Saudi Arabian offices. We discussed tactics, then round to 'counter-spy' shop for a 'recorder brief-case'. Tried to settle for smaller (lapel-type) recorder, but trial showed defective workmanship. Walked out as couldn't get discount, then, with just 20 minutes to spare back and bought it. (Amexing it.)

Briefly experimented, centred it on my desk and up to lobby (no sign of the police, I may say). She was waiting, *very* pale ... out to the Harcourt Room. Oh she was so silly, wasn't she ... eased gently into the subject – no hint of pressure, almost as if she had been warned

---

[1] Nicholas Budgen, MP for Wolverhampton South-West since February 1974.
[2] Jonathan Aitken, MP for Thanet East since February 1974.

against being recorded. Strictly according to schedule good old Jonathan A turned up to testify that he had seen us together. Finally she came out with it – wanted £5,000. 'Certainly,' I said – 'you can have £5,000.' I don't think she thought her victory would be so easy; she mellowed and allowed the occasional sparkle to shine through – so much so that at the end, and feeling generous ... I invited her to come 'round the block' in the Cadillac. This, however, she declined. I was greatly relieved. Put me in the clear, a 'good omen', acted as a signing off gesture.

Later that afternoon, in the lobby, I told Jonathan I had agreed to pay her £5,000. Amusingly he said, 'I should have offered her £4,000 and the briefcase.'

Cloisters   *Thursday, 10 July*

Met her (less good mood this time) and 'handed over'. She a bit waspish – 'it's only gnat's piss to you' etc.

Bratton-Clovelly   *Saturday, 12 July*

Out here very late after a 'meet-the-Member' party. Dear Jane came down and I met her train in the hired, colourless, Vauxhall Cavalier. I said, 'we'll have to stay till ten.' She said, 'nine.' I didn't make my piccolo speech until 9.20. Left as soon as one decently could after that. Eileen clearly disappointed. This morning I said, 'perhaps we should have stayed for the washing up.' 'No, the Heseltines always left after half an hour,' she replied.

Meeting of the Executive on 25 July – 'West MP on the carpet ...'. Have rehearsed my little, 'I have nothing to say' speech in which I end by saying '... and I bid you goodnight', and pick up the Aitken briefcase and walk out.

Saltwood   *Thursday, 14 August*

Broke off to help Jane move the new broody, then, impromptu, to
clear out the 'junior' hen house; then spray Winifred's radiator grill
(very effective); then go back to clean out 'senior' or matrix hen
house. Very hot and muggy. Decided, while struggling on major sell-
off, for a 'tight ship' plan from now on.

Saltwood   *Monday, 1 September*

Apprehensive about James – 'not come in' yesterday, according to Mr
Thingummy of Turner Aviation. Was there something 'strange' about
his voice? At least he's not 'missing' on a flight, but worried about
him being terrified in a bar. This gave me a bad night, as did the
knowledge that I have exactly one day left to complete my Petty
Expense form and my desk just is a total mess and shambles, floor
hasn't been hoovered for twelve months.

Zermatt   *Saturday, 6 September*

Went up on the Wednesday before we left to dine with Ian Gow. He
was late, and I drank two 'Bucks fizz' at the Cavalry Club. Gave me
the impression, somehow, that he was not quite at the centre as much.
Gloomily said, 'I won't be doing this next year . . .' or something to
that effect. Then later, when I returned to the subject, he said how I
would be a 'perfect' successor, in so many ways but 'too senior'. What
does that mean? (Other than for 'senior' read 'unsuitable'). Awful
already to be in a position when that oblique, but damning compliment
can be paid – not forgetting that 'senior' is the Latin for 'older'. Have
I, in my concentration on the House, undermined some of my other
positions – most noticeably, of course, the virtual, tacit, 'writing-off'
of the constituency. Looks at present as if I won't be able to 'open the
season' with Stan Radford's 'at home' on the twentieth as I will be at
the Rhine Army manoeuvres.

Saltwood   *Tuesday, 14 October*

We did two days at conference – struck standard Brighton typhoon weather, wind sucking with extractor force down those little side streets that lead off at right angles on to 'Royal Parade' (or whatever it's called). Was being 'done' by Thames TV as one of the subjects in *Westminster Man* and so followed around by cameramen. Invited on to platform for Civil Defence debate and 'mentioned' by Leon Brittan (unusual). *Naturally* no Plymouthians in the hall at the time. Still, this gave me enough confidence to ride through them at the dreaded 'W. Area cocktail party' that evening.

We came back after tea on Wednesday and have had a lovely 'free', or shirking week. Jamie returned the next day with lots of lovely presents and quite unchanged, though slightly on a down on his looks. Andrew and I got the Locomobile going and it was incredible, the most exciting thing I have driven since the Lago-Talbot and Andrew is very enthused and helpful.

Cloisters   *Monday, 27 October*

A series of coincidences started to build up today into quite an interesting 'situation'.

Getting to the Palace too late for lunch but feeling rather flu-ey I turned into the Smoking Room for a glass of Malvern water into which I plopped my massive 1 mg tablet of effervescent Redoxon. John Langford-Holt[1] was sitting reading the paper in an otherwise almost deserted room. I sat down beside him and tried to steer the subject to the question of the cuts. He was not especially communicative and kept raising his newspaper as a protective screen. I was really getting nowhere when the Chief Whip [Michael Jopling] came in. He hovered, and then sat down with us.

'We were talking about various subjects appertaining to defence matters,' I said.

'It did just cross my mind that you might have been doing that.'

---

[1] Sir John Langford-Holt, Chairman of the all-party Select Committee for Defence since 1979.

He was clearly in a very anxious condition about the whole thing. I told him that I believed the Party would probably accept the cuts provided they were attached to sweeping and equivalent reductions in other departments, but they would not be acceptable if defence was singled out in isolation on account of its previous (so-called) immunity. He seemed especially interested in all this and very anxious to please. I had to take my place for Prayers because it had suddenly struck me that I ought to ask Heseltine a Plymouth–Plymouth–Plymouth question about the housing moratorium when he made his statement about the ban on council house building, and you have a better chance of being called on such an occasion if you are there to bow to the Speaker when he comes in for Prayers. I duly put the question, which was mildly critical and related to penalising under-spending councils along with the massive over-spenders in the Labour heartlands.

For some reason Ted was in the Chamber, sitting in his usual place, which is three away from me, but with no one between us. To my amazement, as I sat down he swivelled massively in his seat (though retaining two fingers in the famous 'V' position against his right cheek) and said, 'At last you're beginning to learn something', then swivelled ponderously back and stared ahead. I simpered acknowledgement (a mistake) but said nothing. What on earth can he have meant? At first sight it seemed to be a compliment, but on reflection I suppose it wasn't. What I suppose he meant was: 'all of you idiots who voted for The Lady are now beginning to realise the mess you are getting yourselves into'.

As I left the Chamber Bob Boscawen buttonholed me and said in a *very* conspiratorial way that he wanted to see me privately. Heavens! Thoughts of having been caught in some frightful misdemeanour flashed through my mind. In the past when whips have said this it has been to issue a reprimand for such offences as smashing a telephone or having more than the correct quota of cars in the underground car park. I suggested the Tea Room, but he demurred, it was too public (!). I *had* to eat, having missed lunch, so insisted that we go to the Pugin Room where I know that the patisserie are rather good. He, too, wanted to question me about the Party's attitude to the defence cuts and I repeated what I had said earlier to Michael. I got the feeling that Boscawen was trying to lead me on to various light indiscretions which might have helped to form an opinion about my attitudes to general issues prevailing.

'That is one of the people giving us the most trouble,' he muttered to himself as someone got up and left the Pugin Room. Too short-sighted to see who it was I said 'Who?'

'Peter Walker' he muttered, *very* inaudibly. I was interested in this because it is unusual for whips to criticise individual members of the Cabinet;[1] they always pretend we are one big happy family.

Cloisters   *Tuesday, 28 October*

There was an urgent message this morning to meet in Francis Pym's[2] room at 2 p.m. (i.e. before Questions). But the discussion was very light, being confined simply to tactics and a quick survey of the Order Paper. Certainly not as orderly or effective as those pre-question meetings which we always used to have with Willie on Home Office days, when we were in Opposition. However, Francis did express his wish for someone to ask a question about the moratorium, which I duly did, thus getting another opportunity to plug Plymouth on two successive days. Perchance I had received only that morning a letter from a firm of metal painters, a long rambling complaint, itself virtually unanswerable, but to which, by coincidence one could give the semblance of instant action.

That evening at 6 p.m. we again met, this time at Francis' room in the Ministry of Defence. The MoD building always reminds me of a large rather run-down teaching hospital with miles of beaten-up lino, smelling of Dettol, institutional beige paint, strip-lighting etc. The impression is heightened by the shambolic arrangements at the main door where a few 'security' guards, either in their late 50s and, plainly, suffering from a variety of degenerative diseases, or younger versions, pasty and overweight with hair over their collars, lolled about. Our arrival coincided with an outward collection of mail. Trolleys of loaded mail bags were being pushed, with much forced bonhomie (but not always very effectively) through the special 'secure' swing doors. It reminded me of those endless loads of hospital laundry that used to be run out through the basement doors at St Thomas' when I, inevitably arriving late, used to try and take a short cut from the

---

[1] Peter Walker, Minister of Agriculture since 1979.
[2] Francis Pym had been Secretary of State for Defence since 1979.

governors' car park to whichever distant committee room where, as Chairman-designate, I was being awaited by a group of peevish consultants.

It did not take long for me to realise that the substance of *this* meeting was in fact very significant. What in effect Francis was saying was that he was going to resign if any further cuts were forced on him. In his declamation he managed to include a number of coded asides about his doubts on existing Government or, as he called it, 'Treasury' policy. As I listened to this I realised exactly how significant Francis' resignation could be, as he is the only person who can take such a step without splitting the Party. If it were done by Prior or Walker then they would accumulate a coterie of 'wets' – but still be in a substantial minority for the Parliamentary Party. If by John Biffen or Geoffrey Howe, the same would be true except that their personal following would consist of discredited and resentful monetarists. Only Francis could combine the old Heathite gang, those who are resentful of cuts in public spending, *plus* the Union Jack Right who will go to the stake on defence and law-and-order issues.

It was not only that he was candid about his own intentions, he was also indiscreet about who supported him in Cabinet – Carrington, Gilmour and Soames.[1] There was a good deal of diffuse talk – the meeting went on for $1\frac{1}{2}$ hours – and certain tentative suggestions that articles should be written to the *Daily Telegraph* etc.

So blinding was my vision of what Francis ought to do and the possibilities that were open to him, that I resolved to stay behind after the meeting and have a quick word. Unfortunately, though, this was not practicable as two of his Ministers (Geoffrey Pattie and Barney Hayhoe) hung back. Accordingly, I walked back to the House with the other members of the Committee. All seemed perplexed, and certainly did not fully appreciate the significance, in Party terms, of what we had been told.

---

[1] Lord Carrington, Foreign Secretary since 1979 and Lord Soames, Lord President of the Council and Leader of the House of Lords since 1979, were the two most influential Conservatives in the Lords. Ian Gilmour had been Lord Privy Seal since 1979.

Cloisters   *Wednesday, 29 October*

I had told Hal Miller[1] that I would quite like to have a private word
with Francis today if possible. He said that he thought that the
Secretary of State would not be in the Commons at all that day as he
was still entertaining the Italian Defence Minister.

Just before dinner I had a drink with Ian Gow in the Smoking
Room and warned him of the very grave possible consequences, as I
believed, of Francis' resignation. He looked glum. 'Are you telling
me that the Secretary of State is seriously considering a threat of this
kind if he fails to get his way?'

'Yes, I am,' I replied.

Ian made some routine noises in defence of the Treasury. His
monetarism runs very deep, and of course his commitment to the
defence field is not particularly strong, certainly does not compare
with his obsessive identification with the Treasury heartland. Still, I
feel that I had to do my duty as one of his part-time informers.

Just before the ten o'clock vote Hal Miller caught me in the
Members' Lobby and said that Francis would, after all, be able to see
me for a couple of minutes afterwards if I waited outside the 'Aye'
lobby. I duly hung around until it was almost empty. Still no Francis.
The trouble when one is waiting to catch a colleague is that others –
most people are a bit tight by that time of the evening – try and get
into conversation, tell one scraps of gossip, etc. I was simultaneously
fending off dear John Wells who wanted to invite Andrew to go
shooting with him on Saturday, and I was conscious of Ian Gow
hovering (I did not want him to see me in conclave with Francis).
Then the Secretary of State, round-shouldered as ever and wearing a
dinner jacket, finally emerged through the division doors. Better leave
it, I thought. I was getting cold feet. But Hal spotted me and waved
at me to come over.

'Can I see you quite privately?' I asked. We turned right into the
long corridor that cuts down towards the Speaker's Room. Even there
it seemed a seething mass of people bellowing and eavesdropping. I
made some variant of Oliver Lyttelton's joke about the trenches, '. . .
too many people', with which he agreed. He seemed quite benevolent
so, encouraged, I told him that speaking as a historian I felt obliged

---

[1] Hilary (Hal) Miller, MP for Bromsgrove and Redditch since February 1974, PPS to
the Defence Secretary since 1979.

to put a case to him, but that I would neither invite nor even expect him to comment. He looked a little wary at this, but I pressed on.

'If you should finally get pushed into the position where you have to resign...'

'Which I certainly hope I do not have to,' he interjected.

'... you must realise that you are the only person who can take such a step without splitting the Party and that you would, in fact, have a broad franchise, spreading right across from those who are opposed to public spending to include those who, like myself, are sometimes depicted as being on the right. And the likelihood is that you would be Prime Minister in two years time.'

As I finished the concluding sentence the effect was electric. A huge slug of adrenalin visibly shot through his system. Far from dismissing me (as, e.g., Willie might have done) his manner became very intense. 'Come upstairs to my room,' he said, and we turned round and went to the stairs, pushing past three people who were all waiting to see him, including Hal and Keith Speed.[1] Once we got into his room I could see he was highly excited about what I had to say. I developed the theme; explaining that if The Lady were to crash within the next 18 months, there was no need to have a general election, but obviously the Party would have to find a new Leader and were he to resign now and on this issue he would be incomparably better placed than anyone else to unite it. I also pointed out that in the last 18 months of a Parliament it was far easier to alter course and frame election-winning policies if the personalities identified with the old and unpopular ones had disappeared. Francis was very attentive, claimed that his only feelings were for the Party and the Country, etc., etc. But plainly he was greatly encouraged, indeed fortified by the concept which I had put to him. I cannot believe it had not occurred to him; but he is so cautious he probably had not taken any *soundings* and was cheered to get some back-bench encouragement from a (probably) unexpected source. Hal is amiable but too bluff and 'straight' to see things long.

What a rich, endlessly varied and exciting world politics is for those who are addicted to it. And how inextricably woven are the different strands of greed, ambition, cowardice and idealism. No one's motives are pure; certainly not mine.

---

[1] Keith Speed, MP for Ashford since October 1974, and Minister for the Navy since 1979.

Albany, B5   *Tuesday, 4 November*

With a free evening I drifted into Pratt's, having taken the precaution of dressing beautifully in a new Blade's suit, pale pink cotton shirt, etc. Three incredibly boring buffers occupying the middle table, dressed à la Macmillan in cardigans making desultory conversation, and ill-informed comments on politics. The cooking remains execrable, not that any of the members seem to have palates. The English upper classes really are unspeakably awful. Were they always like this, or is the country in its decline because they have changed character, or have they changed character and become rebarbative and introverted (as well as stupid) because the country is in decline and they can do nothing about it?

I went back to Brooks's and had quite an amusing dinner, although too much claret, with James Vance-White, who told me how Euan's aunt had recovered from her deathbed at the age of 96, revoked the power of attorney which she had arrogated, and was now beadily going through the cheque stubs.

Saltwood   *Sunday, 16 November*

John Erickson[1] says Russians are going into Yugoslavia soon, and identified 'hit' units in SW order of battle, so that requires major strategic think-out. I drove Jane back up to London in Winter Car and asked her where she would like the shelter, Bratton or Saltwood. She prefers Saltwood, I think rightly, although am apprehensive of Dungeness explosion.[2]

Cloisters   *Tuesday, 25 November*

Yesterday the Chancellor made a 'statement on economic policy' (generally hailed by the press as a 'package', with all the uncomfortable evocation of that word). Very unsatisfactory. He gabbled through an

---

[1] John Erickson, military historian specialising on the Soviet military.
[2] Dungeness nuclear power station being south-west across the bay from Saltwood.

unintelligible Treasury brief, couched in their most obscure jargon, then came to the point. Only £1 billion further cuts in public expenditure – of which £200 million were to come from Defence – in other words £800 million was coming from all other sectors combined. So the shortfall had to come from revenue, in the form of increased 'contributions' under National Insurance. The net effect is that the workers are going to get less in the righthand column of their payslips, while the so-called Social Wage remains intact. This is precisely contrary to the theme in which our campaign was presented and a rejection of the endorsement we received from the electorate last year.

At the very end of his statement the Chancellor announced, with what for him was presumably meant to be a flourish, but which came out in Evelyn Waugh's phrase, '. . . more in the tones of a nanny than a Master-at-Arms',[1] that interest rates would be reduced by 2 per cent. This cut in interest rates is totally unjustified by the present state of the money supply or public sector borrowing and the measures that the Chancellor had described would not be becoming operative until next year anyway. It is perfectly plain that Government policy is now seriously off course – with consequences that can only be bad both for the Party and the country.

Later that evening I went to Willie's room on Ted Gardner's instructions in order to 'have a drink with' Leon Brittan and Tim Raison as Willie was allegedly absent. I duly turned up at 7 p.m. and found that not only had the time been changed, but that Willie was there in conclave with his two Ministers and that prick John Patten. What the hell was he doing there? I later found out that he had taken Esmond Bulmer's place as PPS.[2] He is so ambitious that he squeaks when he walks, and cannot manage to smile at any colleague inferior in rank in case he compromises himself in some way.

I see that George Morton[3] pleaded guilty today of an act of gross indecency in a gents in Manchester and was fined £25. Simultaneously his constituency chairman announced that he had complete confidence in him and that it was a 'private matter'. God alive, I would only have to be seen with a blonde on the front seat and the Plymouth

[1] Evelyn Waugh's *The Ordeal of Gilbert Pinfold*.
[2] John Patten, MP for Oxford since 1979, had been appointed a PPS to Brittan and Raison, succeeding Esmond Bulmer, MP for Kidderminster since February 1974.
[3] George Morton, Labour MP for Manchester Moss Side since July 1978.

Association would demand an instant vote of no confidence. Some people have all the luck.[1]

In low spirits I went to the Finance Committee meeting in Room 14 at 6 p.m. There were fewer colleagues present than I had expected. John Biffen sat at the end of the platform, radiating gloom, with his head in his hands. Up got the Chancellor and re-gabbled. He reconfirmed, also, the impression that he had really lost control of policy and events. It is the first time that I have ever been to a Party committee attended by a minister or shadow minister who has been more or less openly heckled *sotto voce*, sniggering asides, etc. I sat next to Esmond Bulmer (a good centrist fellow) and he asked a critical question. In front of me sat Tim Sainsbury who did likewise and periodically exchanged an incredulous and mocking commentary with William Waldegrave[2] who sat on my right. Every speaker was in one way or another critical, being led off by Terence Higgins[3] who, although utterly wet on racial matters, is extremely hard lined on monetary ones. The Chancellor was fielding the questions in batches of three which made it easier for him to dissimulate. But the general impression remained of an authority seriously diminished.

I left the meeting early as I had promised to get home and help Jane with the VAT and there was no whip.

Cloisters   *Wednesday, 26 November*

The *Daily Mail* ran a huge front page editorial about the manner in which the Government is falling down on all its policies and pledges and urged the Prime Minister, though not, in my view, strongly or prominently enough, to purge her Cabinet and return to the straight and narrow. At breakfast Jane reinforced this with her own pure common sense views laced with wisdom from working class people like Eddie and Peggy. What the hell *is* going on? I have had no fewer than five telephone messages from Plymouth Sound asking me to call

---

[1] Morton's career as an MP ended, however, at the 1983 general election.
[2] William Waldegrave, MP for Bristol West since 1979.
[3] Terence Higgins, chairman of several Commons committees and a member of the executive of the 1922 Committee.

them back. But I won't do so as there simply is not a comment that I can make on the present state of affairs that would not sound subversive or demoralised.

Later, walking across the Members' Lobby I saw Ian Gow, and asked him if I could have a moment. As always he was delightfully attentive and we went down to the Terrace, which was deserted. Up and down we paced in the biting East wind. What was dangerous, and almost unprecedented, I told him (as if he needed telling), was that the Prime Minister and the Treasury team in combination had been defeated in Cabinet. We all knew that she had made an error of judgement in weighting her Cabinet so heavily with passé Heathites when it was first formed under the scrutiny of Atkins, Thorneycroft and Whitelaw.[1] But was not the theory that by retaining all the Treasury posts for her own supporters she would in the last resort be able to get her way on economic policy? In fact, this did not last and she is now being defeated even on this selected battlefield. No wonder she looks so wan (though still beautiful) and sits with her head bowed at Question Time.

It is clear that The Lady is now well and truly beleaguered. I urged Ian to press her to stand alone, appeal to the country, stage a night of the long knives,[2] stressed that there was still time left for a ruthless policy to pay off. What I cannot make out is to what extent Ian's expressed views reflected his own prejudices, and what he believes to be mine; and to what extent they present a true picture of The Lady's own misgivings and anxieties. One must always remember that she is, must be, a more adroit politician than sometimes appears. Perhaps she, being plagued by inner feelings of insecurity, and being determined to hold on to her position, is consciously trimming now.

In the Tea Room Tony Newton and David Mellor[3] came and sat at the table. Tony asked me what I thought about 'the position'. But I would not answer. One can do too much public declamation, particularly at a table in the Tea Room where there are two whips present. I made various high sounding generalities about the import-

---

[1] Humphrey Atkins, since 1979, Secretary of State for Northern Ireland; Lord Thorneycroft, former Minister in Macmillan and Douglas-Home governments; chairman of the Conservative Party since 1975.

[2] As Harold Macmillan had done on 13 July 1963, when he dismissed six Cabinet Ministers. AC observed, 'butchery on this scale unprecedented in the annals of the party.' (The Tories)

[3] Tony Newton was Whip to the Finance Committee; David Mellor, MP for Putney since 1979.

ance of everyone keeping their heads down, and one not being indiscreet, etc.

After leaving the Tea Room I was caught again by Tony Newton in the corridor leading down to the telephone lobby and the Members' Staircase, and I was again asked what I thought. I told him that we were going through the sound barrier and there was a lot of buffeting; either we slow down and settle for a quiet life, or we accelerate it and hope to break through into serene, but supersonic, tranquillity. Then, I said (always tell people what you think they want to hear) that I was an old-fashioned Tory, that Geoffrey would have to go, but that on the whole my choice for the succession would be Francis. I said I hated saying this because of the implied disloyalty to The Lady and her policies, but these were being so badly mismanaged at the moment that they were doing more harm than good. As I anticipated he agreed, sounding both relieved and elated. 'I am sure that there are a very large number of people who agree with you but don't yet like to say so . . .'

I hope that by my two conversations today I have maintained confidential links with both camps in the Parliamentary Party. We shall see.

Saltwood   *Tuesday, 2 December*

And *still* we are ground down (though not yet, fortunately, in the lower millstones of God's foundry). Yesterday Barclays produced a most insulting letter giving (effectively) three weeks notice to put account in credit. Signed cheque on C. Hoare & Co. and sent down by hand. This means CH is 25+ and then the loan (now down to 20) and also the Clydesdale at 20. *But* Westminster is out of the way and now Barclays. How the hell do I raise the 65 to get completely clear? Had a bad night, early waking etc. Fictionalised with collapse of Italian front.

After five years of financial crisis and seven of intolerable interest charges, it is, I suppose, a miracle that I am still with the major structure intact. But in 1975, if you'd told me 'you've' got to hold on for five years . . . I'd have said (a) I can't and (b) 'it' can't be as along as that.

Cloisters   *Wednesday, 3 December*

Headache/dizzy this morning. Blood pressure? More likely combination hangover, stuffy night, but it remains manically cold.

Went to a 'grand' dinner party at the Royal Academy last night; Jane came up for it, wore her blue dress and masses of pearls and looked ravishing. Patrick Lindsay[1] was host, we had expected 150 people bellowing and filthy food – actually only 24, ultra posh, Jocelyn Stevens[2] and Teddy Hall[3] only people without titles; Jane sat between Cranborne (future Marquess[4]) and Dalkeith (ditto Duke[5]). The pretty, and somewhat confident and *sly* Countess of Halifax sat on my right. Looking at her ghastly red-face husband I thought she ought to be ready for a bit of *interest*, but later on, as we engaged in private view of the Chatsworth 'treasures' I noticed the young Duke of Roxburghe[6] (who I had earlier taken to be a young Naylor-Leyland) with his arm around her.

Bratton   *Saturday, 6 December*

Drove down yesterday in the K10, against a 40–50 mph headwind *the whole way*. Petrol consumption slightly under 10 mpg – don't think I've got any car to do this since the Bi-carb. Last bit in pouring rain. On way back into Plymouth was stopped by police, just out of nastiness really. I quickly pulled rank, but after opening the bazaar in the Guildhall (where I put on a most good-tempered show) I had to go back to Crownhill police station. The officer was probing with his questions about how long the vehicle had been in the country etc.

This put me 'out of sorts' and I was only just getting back into smooth waters (sic) by the fuel gauge not having moved, due to gentle driving, when there was a message from Nanny to ring back (although, all credit to her, she did say 'Boys all right').

---

[1] Director of Christie's.
[2] Jocelyn Stevens, former editor of *Queen*, had been deputy chairman and managing director of Express Newspapers since 1977.
[3] Edward (Teddy) Hall, portrait painter.
[4] of Salisbury.
[5] of Buccleuch.
[6] Guy David Innes-Ker had succeeded to the title in 1974. He married Lady Jane Meriel Grosvenor in 1977 (they would divorce in 1990).

'Now here's some bad news for you . . .' she stated with relish; then recounted how my father had come over with Mrs Sly[1] and taken over 30 books from the library. V. depressing. He is such a shit, so sly and weak, without the *slightest* concept of succession and the boys. Also, with each fresh move, Nolwen increases her hold on him and spreads her tendrils through the Estate.

Both Jane and Nanny urge me to 'speak out'. It's not moral scruple, or cowardice, that prevents me doing so, God knows; simply a residual calculation that there is more to lose than to gain by so doing. Furthermore, his action does somewhat clear the decks for my right to the Cézanne still-life drawing with which I intend to obliterate indebtedness, and restart the 'calculus'.

Will see what happens, but I don't like the look of things (broke off for a minute to visualise kicking her down that last stone flight of steps at Saltwood . . . 'oh Nolwen, I *am* sorry, how awful etc . . .'). So I was again in a bad mood for a fete, this time the Bratton one.

Cloisters   *Wednesday, 10 December*

Won the election for vice-chairman of the Defence Cttee today. I was reasonably confident, as I know I get quite a little vote from the centre, now, Party venerables and others. It's no good just having the Left or Right 'whipped' vote behind you. You have to be able to pick up something from the uncommitted. Conversely, of course, it's no use *just* being one of the uncommitted because however well-liked you are, you are bound to get squeezed between the two – so many people delete every name on the slate except the one printed on their 'whip'. This was what happened to Nick Budgen in the Finance Cttee yesterday – now everybody regrets it, but that's no use to him – and to Ivan Lawrence[2] in Home Affairs on Monday. I think there was an element of this in the fact that I defeated poor, pleasant (but clever) Julian Critchley[3] instead of, as I had hoped and expected, little Winston. One doesn't like advancing to office over the corpses of one's friends, but that's show business.

---

[1] Her real name was Slythe. She acted as librarian to Lord Clark.
[2] Ivan Lawrence, MP for Burton since February 1974.
[3] Julian Critchley, MP for Aldershot since 1974 (Aldershot and North Hants, 1970–74).

Afterwards, I caught sight of Adam Raphael[1] in the lobby and taxed him with his extraordinary theory that the likeliest 'candidates' in a reshuffle were Francis, Ian Gilmour and Norman St J Stevas. But no, this was his assessment on the basis of a hard tip. He told me that all three, who were used to talking to him freely, had been bitterly offended. Raphael's theory is that Francis will be moved to Leader of the House, Norman dropped or, more likely, sent to Education in place of Mark Carlisle who will *definitely* be going (everyone seems agreed on that). But anyway what about this dam' reshuffle? The Lady appears to have got into a face-loss situation here, ie whatever she does will be an I-told-you-so, so she is just holding on. When there was an official briefing, printed in the *Sunday Telegraph* about three weeks ago that '. . . there will be no Ministerial changes for at least six (or was it twelve?) months . . .' I got a few laughs in the tea-room by saying that this meant they were imminent. Now I'm not so sure. Raphael thinks that it may be the Treasury team that goes, and not of their own volition.

Cloisters   *Thursday, 11 December*

Treasury questions. Peter Shore[2] up for the first time and not much use. Fumbled and almost lost the place in what were virtually mini-speeches. Geoffrey H much more confident than formerly (God knows why) and more mellifluous than the First Secretary who has presently a voice that is at the same time hoarse and low-volume (shades of Bonar Law?). Biffen still in his new *persona* more aggressive than formerly and used the word 'damned', as in damned sure, and was instantly rebuked by the Speaker.

At the start of Business Questions there was a scuffling noise and a massive thump at the bar of the House. The Chief Whip,[3] carrying papers, had fallen flat on his face. 'A slip', presumably (to quote one of Harry Carpenter's over-used phrases) as he doesn't drink. He was livid.

---

[1] Adam Raphael, political correspondent of *The Observer* since 1976.
[2] Peter Shore, MP for Stepney and Poplar since 1974 (Stepney, 1964–74) had just moved from Foreign Affairs to become opposition spokesman on Treasury matters.
[3] Michael Jopling, MP for Westmorland since 1964, Chief Whip since 1979.

A little later, who should be called but 'Sir Harold Wilson'.[1] Amazing. He stood erect and slim (cancer-slim one could say) in a beautifully pressed blue suit, in contrast to his usual rumpled and hunted demeanour, and asked a question about his Report on the City's institutions. Down memory lane, with that curious flat nasal twang, that I used to hear so often and so maddeningly at PM's questions when we were in opposition. A certain sadismoid pleasure as I reflected on how the roles were reversed in more than one sense.

That evening we were on a running three liner from 7 p.m. I slipped out to Brooks's for a little backgammon after the first vote, and there in the bar was Roy Jenkins,[2] fat, puffy and unhappily ingratiating. I made some bantering remarks about the Big Push, threw a few scraps of Commons gossip around. He did *not* want to have intercourse.

Fifteen more votes that night. Horrible torture of the fabric and substance. Finally in bed for 2 hrs sleep at 6.45 a.m. I have to be up tomorrow for the Brandt Report debate.

Cloisters   *Friday, 12 December*

Sat right through the Brandt Report without getting called. Disappointment as I had a lovely debunking speech ready, quoting the late and great Ernie Bevin: '... I've been here all night and all I've 'eard is bloody clitches'. No breakfast, no lunch. I did the Christmas card list on my lap, periodically making objectionable interruptions.

At other times I brooded. This autumn there have been a lot of upsets in Committee elections, and *every* person who has lost their seat – Knox (employment), Hicks, Dykes (Europe), Bruce-Gardyne (Finance), Lawrence (Home Affairs), and Critchley and Atkins (Defence) have all taken it *very* badly.[3] Dear Nick Budgen is the only one who has shown any *tenu* at all.

---

[1] Harold Wilson, MP for Huyton since 1950 (Ormskirk 1945–50), Prime Minister 1964–70, 1974–76. Knight of the Garter 1976.

[2] Roy Jenkins, President of the European Commission since 1977, having been a Labour MP since 1948.

[3] David Knox, MP for Leek since 1970; Robert Hicks, MP for Bodmin since 1970; Hugh Dykes, MP for Harrow East since 1970; Jock Bruce-Gardyne, MP for Knutsford since 1979 (South Angus 1964–74).

Saltwood   *Saturday, 13 December*

Saltwood just not a haven at the moment. Untidyness as piled papers seems even worse (like indebtedness) than when one began.

My father *distrait* on the phone (this is tricky as he is going to get my Cézanne letter this week – ugh[1]). Also have a loose front tooth, obviously going to pack up over Christmas or in Zermatt.

Saltwood   *Sunday, 21 December*

Walked out on the steps and looked at the full moon behind the trees. Very cold, but clear. Had spoken to C, who had agreed to meet me at Albany tomorrow to discuss Cézanne still-life. Looked around, and up at the towers. Am I, at last, some £500,000 later, really going to own it all, unencumbered? Will have to do a *really* careful think through at the turn of the year.

---

[1] The incomplete draft of AC's letter begins: 'Dearest Papa, this is bad, I'm afraid...'

1981

Apprehensive as freedom from worry poor – only really brighten up when talking about my o/d being paid off – appearance *not* improving, and then this evening blow fell: RESHUFFLE.

And, monstrously, not announced what it was in detail, just that it will be announced later this evening! Took one totally by surprise. A sad blow for me. I had never really expected to get into government at formation, but hoped and felt that I had made enough general ground in the interim; friendship with Ian Gow, giving notice of questions etc. Perhaps I had, then blew it just recently.

Recalled how I had prayed for George to come back and promised that if he did I would do my Defence Study. He did come, and I didn't. One's relationship with God shouldn't be like that. I should be grateful for everything that he has given me, accept that what-is-written-is-written. But I still have this residual hope, belief, that I can do something for my country. What must I do to deserve it and pave the way? Perhaps this year should be much more political.

Had a very bad night – compounded (of course) by rage at once again boys not coming in until 1 a.m. Thought we would just go back to England today. I felt so sad at losing the 'double', perhaps finally both my love and friendship with the boys – reduced to Bonny papa's state, i.e. more or less of a nuisance, but got to keep in with him for inheritance purposes – and any possibility of doing something for my country. Woke, dragged up from 4 hours sleep at about 6.15 in a kind of 'was-it-really-a-dream?' recollection, and its certain dreamlike qualities – Biffen to Trade, Nott to Defence, John Patten a minister (as a gesture to the new intake etc). No, it was not a dream.[1] I still feel *very* uneasy about 1981. 'Flagellation Year' its provisional title.

---

[1] In Mrs Thatcher's first reshuffle, appointments also included Francis Pym as Leader of the House (succeeding Norman St John-Stevas), thereby proving Adam Raphael's tip (see 10 December) correct. John Patten moved to Northern Ireland Office as Parliamentary Under-Secretary of State.

Saltwood   *Saturday, 10 January*

Got back today. Tip-book had forgotten to phone Nanny and so we
were driven up from the docks by a dear-old-boy ('old coach man')
who remembered bringing my father up – 'your old [sic] father', he
called him – for 8/6d. I gave him £4. Actually, I suppose that is about
right, a ×8 depreciation since 1952?

The dogs gave us a lovely welcome. Children substitute really, the
illusion complete with Nanny in charge. Looked through the mail,
incredibly dull, only pleasurable indication of new regime, just fucking
boring all round. Last a/c of Hoare's still being kept in credit by
income. Looked at the Whip, and got really quite angry as I think of
these bloody people just bossing us around. *Waddington*[1] a minister;
that self-same little tick who blocked me from going to Europe or
whatever it was. Goodlad a whip, Goodlad of all people![2] The stock
example of an MP who looks like a pig and did NOTHING. Much
of the flavour will be diminished from the House I suspect.

Cloisters   *Monday, 12 January*

I saw Patrick Mayhew and congratulated him on his promotion; he
has been moved from Employment back to the Home Office.

'Aren't you glad I stopped you from resigning?' I asked. 'Well it is
not over yet,' he said. More or less conveying that the appointment
of John Nott (or John 'Nit' as poor Norman so injudiciously called
him) was an indication that still further and more savage cuts were in
store. Patrick cheered me by grinding his teeth at the quality of the
junior promotions – 'all whips and wets'.

Ivor Stanbrook[3] quite predictably had also agreed, said it was an
insult to people like himself who had been in the House for so long
that someone like John Patten should be made a Minister after two
years. But he was defeatist. Said, 'You cannot do anything, it will look
like sour grapes.'

---

[1] David Waddington, MP for Clitheroe since 1979; now a Parliamentary Under-Secretary
of State, Department of Employment.
[2] Alastair Goodlad, MP for Northwich since February 1974.
[3] Ivor Stanbrook, MP for Orpington since 1970.

I spent the morning dictating my vitriolic analysis of the reshuffle which I sent to Paul Johnson with a copy to Bill Deedes. I have some doubts and pensées d'escalier, perhaps it was too aggressively expressed – a fault of mine – perhaps it was unwise to quote that small, but I believe significant, experience as an example.

I delivered letters of commiseration to poor Norman and Jim Lester[1] who although very left, always performs well at the Despatch Box. Tony Buck came up to me and suggested a drink(!). 'Tea,' I replied formally, at which his face fell. Conversation was somewhat stilted as neither wanted to be the first to admit how disappointed he was at being left out of the reshuffle. It was quite clear that he deliberately arranged a meeting with the Prime Minister for the previous week, but later cancelled at her request, at a time when he knew I would be away and which would allow him to 'impress' her without being overshadowed. (Hal Miller later told me that AB and Victor Goodhew[2] were the only two able to go to that meeting.) AB made a specific point of asking me to give him 'an hour or so' briefing about weapons systems and so forth before we see The Lady on Wednesday week. The only interesting thing was that Ian Gow had been absolutely furious at my article in the *Telegraph* (as expected) although whether that had anything to do with subsequent events I do not know.

On my way back through the Lobby I was talking to David Hunt[3] who said that John Nott was very anxious to meet the officers of the Defence Committee at the earliest opportunity, he didn't want it thought that he was coming in with 'a pair of scissors', he would take some time before coming to decisions, and so forth. Hunt also said, 'You are a very odd lot, aren't you?' 'What do you mean?' I said. 'Well, I mean, you represent all shades of the Party.' (Silly ass) All these wets think only in terms of 'shades', whether people are right or left, or whatever the case may be.

While we were talking poor Jim Lester came up to us and blow me if he didn't burst into tears (presumably for the eighteenth time). He was very brown, but looking awful. Fancy being told of your dismissal over the telephone while on holiday in Switzerland.

---

[1] Lester had been a junior minister at Department of Employment.
[2] Victor Goodhew, MP for St Albans since 1959; vice-chairman of the Conservative Defence Committee since 1974.
[3] David Hunt had followed John Nott from Trade to Defence as his PPS.

I had been dictating letters until ten past three, but had foresight to put in a Prayer Card as I knew my place would be kept free for Prime Minister's PQ's.

Incidentally, I noticed that for the first time Ian Lloyd had 'shown respect' by leaving a space for me to put my card in, even though he had got to the bench earlier that morning. In the past he has always squabbled with Emery[1] for the place one up from me and if Emery got there before him he would always put one on my seat. I was gratified to see that although Emery had got there before him he had for the first time left my place vacant and put his card on the seat below mine. It will be interesting to see if, when he is pre-empted by Lloyd, Emery does the same.

Just before going in I had soaked myself with Vetiver, even so this did not attract the attention of the former Leader of the House who I noticed was standing at the bar when I entered. (Nick Winterton was putting a long rambling question and because of his position at the end of the front bench it would have been out of order to have walked past him to our places.) When Nick sat down Norman 'made his entry' with that curious mincing step of his. I was glad to see that he got massive applause – not all of it ironic by any means – from the Opposition.

Later, in the course of Questions he was sorely tried by the Prime Minister who said how glad she was that the Arts were no longer an independent ministry, etc. But he did not rise.

I then went into the Tea Room, hopeful of getting some gossip. Maddeningly one large table was already completely full of the young and eager, all of them in an animated condition. However, Hal Miller came up and indicated that he would like a word. We moved over to the armchairs on the other side of the screen and I started to eat the Ryvita sandwiches – I had not lunched – which Jane had sent with me in the train. Hal is still very concerned about Defence matters. Said that they were all relying on me as being the only person of real quality on the Defence Committee – 'Winston is a non-starter; Victor is, err, inscrutable (I admire the neutral adjective) and Buck is bone idle.'

It turned out that one reason why Hal was irritated with Buck was

---

[1] Peter Emery, MP for Honiton since 1967 (Reading 1959–66).

because Buck had asked him for a brief before the meeting with the Prime Minister (just as yesterday he had asked me for one).

I was much cheered talking to Hal (one always likes compliments anyway) and particularly by the fact that Francis was still taking a general interest in things and watching from afar. Later that afternoon I had a brief chat with Tony Royle who told me that he had heard in Pratt's the previous night that Francis was very dejected at his transfer. I talked Tony up about Francis as much as I could, hoping that it would get back to him as Tony, he told me, was meeting Francis that very evening. Hal stressed that the situation was very grave, that it was complete nonsense to say that John Nott was going to take his time before coming to any decision. Hal Miller also said that the decision was so close that, by the time we saw the Prime Minister, it would already have been taken, and much of our meeting would be lost. However, he told me that one element of the decision had been to reinforce the Army at the expense of the Navy and indeed, the original title of the White Paper had been to lay emphasis on the need to reinforce the Central Front (i.e. the one place where it is very unlikely that the Russians will ever attack).

I am meeting Buck this evening and undertook to force him to send a letter by hand to the Prime Minister asking that no final decision should be made until after her meeting with the officers of the Defence Committee.

Went round to Norman Shaw North for the meeting in AB's Room to discuss our tactics for the Prime Minister and Nott. A dear little secretary with very short hair and enormous ovoid glasses – rather like Dora in the Library, but less flat and intellectual. I had not seen her before, but she giggled amiably. Buck, I thought, rather hunted and *chétif*. It was almost as if he had overheard the conversation between Hal Miller and myself a couple of hours earlier in which Hal had more or less said how much Francis would have preferred me to be Chairman of the Committee. Neither of the Committee secretaries were present and Winston was rather more subdued than usual. I let them do the talking, then suggested that Tony should write immediately to the Prime Minister expressing the hope and assumption that nothing would be decided before our meeting with her. He agreed that this was a good idea. We spent some time discussing tactics, but none of the other three seemed to realise that a simple rigid defence of existing spending targets is not enough. What we have to do is steer the Department into a general scrutiny of our defence commitments and make sure that they come up with the right conclusions. Winston, for example, wanted to take £2 billion off the Social Security budget and bang it straight into the RAF. Lovely, but in terms of political *realismus* so impracticable as to put everything else that we argue into disrepute. I also raised with them the question of a possible 'demonstration' (i.e. abstaining in the lobbies). This had not really occurred to them either, but the more they thought about it the more they liked it. I emphasised the need for complete secrecy at this stage. Abstention on the defence estimates – which is what we are talking about, in effect, will only be significant if practised by at least forty colleagues. Easier to drum this up after the reshuffle than before, but still an up-hill task when it comes to the point.

I returned to the House and went into the Smoking Room. Julian Amery was holding court in the corner table between the bar and the fireplace. He was in good form. I noticed George Brown[1] and one or two Labour MPs in the outer circle.

'Now Alan, we are just agreeing that we are all hand-to-heart behind the Prime Minister in her economic policies, but the trouble is we don't know what these are, can you tell us?'

This is not a good sign, this kind of irreverence from senior and respected Privy Counsellors on the Right of the Party, and later that evening in the Lobby poor Nick Budgen told me how terribly depressed he was. He told me that the Prime Minister was an *au fond* popularist and that she was trimming. We agreed that both Geoffrey Howe and Leon Brittan had not a political principle between them and that they would soon get the ship round on its new course.

I started to get steamed up about the junior appointments in the reshuffle, but Nick did not take as extreme a view as I did.

'All bland,' he said, 'they are all bland men without identifiable personalities, this is to be the keynote of the Government from now on.'

When I got back to the Library I saw bright, intelligent, able little Robin Cook from Edinburgh North, who was always a very keen and very well informed interrogator of Ministers in the defence field, but has been promoted by Mr Foot to a shadow Treasury job. I

---

[1] George Brown, former Labour MP and Minister in Harold Wilson's 1964–70 government, took the title Lord George-Brown on being made a life peer in 1970.

congratulated him. I remarked ruefully that talent was being better used in the Labour Party than in our own. He said that this was due to Michael's innovations. He cited the example of Tam Dalyell[1], saying that he was absolutely brilliant, then adding somewhat to my surprise, '... but he is unreliable'.

'Unreliable? What do you mean?'

'Well, he sometimes goes his own way, you cannot rely on him always to speak to the ministerial brief. Which is a good thing of course,' he said hurriedly, but unconvincingly.

Cloisters   *Wednesday, 14 January*

I went into the Smoking Room to get some Malvern water for my fizzy Redoxon and George Brown was there alone drinking a double whisky (it was 11.10 a.m.) and smoking a large cigar. While we were in Zermatt Nanny had told us that she had heard him on the radio saying that The Lady would be dumped by the Conservative Party this year, and having noticed him on the periphery of Julian's group last night (perhaps he had never left the Smoking Room and been there all night), I asked him about this.

GB said that she had got things hopelessly wrong, was still doing trivial things that made her unpopular, but in fact turning her primary policies round so that the basic objectives such as reducing inflation etc. would not be met. He told me that he had written an article saying something to this effect for last Sunday's *Express*, but John Junor had turned it down. Apparently, the Prime Minister had had a special meeting of about six editors to try and subdue criticism, but, of course, as George Brown said, this is highly unpopular with all the other editors who have not been invited along.

I suggested that it was apparent that The Lady was already trying to slither out of her difficulties and he agreed. The telephone went and he was summoned back to one of the bars in the Lords(!). I walked down the corridor with him and mentioned the junior promotions – of which he was fully aware and agreed with my judgement. 'She is making exactly the same mistake as Wilson, trying to please everybody and particularly those who distrust her.'

---

[1] Tam Dalyell, opposition spokesman on science since 1980.

'She has included all her own bully boys,' I said.

'Yes, a great mistake.'

I asked him who he thought the next Leader would be and he said Francis or Jim, '. . . but if I was a Conservative I would prefer Francis.'

Cloisters   *Monday, 19 January*

I received a very friendly reply from Ian Gow, totally disclaiming any disapproval of my celebrated article in the *Daily Telegraph*[1] before Christmas.

Am I paranoid about this? I don't think so. There was no doubt that The Lady cut me dead on the night of Monday 15 December and that for some weeks IG was extremely chilly. However, in politics one can never admit these things and it is easier to turn, or pretend to have turned, the blind eye. This evening, just as I was dictating letters at my desk the telephone rang and it was IG's secretary suggesting dinner. We agreed to meet at 7 p.m., but, in fact, there was a vote then and afterwards I had to go to the Home Secretary's room along with other officers of the Committee. Willie, as always bellowing and small-eyed, lost his temper briefly and alarmingly when Ted Gardner repeated my having raised the question of 'No Go' Reggae areas for black people, police timidity in breaking up parties and so on. Willie thundered and blundered about his Ministry being loaded with so many responsibilities he would find himself 'at breaking point' etc.

However, I held my ground saying, 'This is not a question of Ministerial responsibility for all-night parties.'

This got a bit of a laugh and lightened the atmosphere, just as well because I went on to say that if the police had acted on the complaints that neighbours made a number of lives could have been saved. Willie undertook to talk to the Commissioner about this – but I rather doubt if he will.

I found Ian in the Smoking Room and he took me to the Savoy. Really, his driving in his little blue Mini is now completely berserk. He delights in it, and it makes one's hair stand on end – particularly as he is not a specially skilful driver. At one point as we screamed along

---

[1] On defence policy.

the Embankment (it was pouring with rain) I envisaged a terrible accident with the tiny Mini somersaulting across the dual carriageway, an incandescent fireball. He told me that he sometimes drove the Prime Minister in the car with a detective sitting in the back.

We indulged in small-talk in the new, or rather revealed, foyer with its delightful art-nouveau décor and onyx columns, practically deserted. Over the food he returned to the question of the letter and then almost immediately we got to discussing the junior appointments. He defended these as best he could. I grumbled though that so many appointments had come from the Whips' Office, '. . . we would all like to be Whips'.

'Would you like to be a Whip?' he said sharply.

'I would rather be a Whip than nothing,' I replied.

He muttered something about how hard they worked and I agreed. Then he said, 'Who do you think should succeed me as the Prime Minister's secretary?'

'Very difficult,' I replied. 'I very much hope that you are not going to stand down.' (On looking back I see that this was rather tactless as he would not stand down but be promoted and given a department of his own).

'Would you do it?'

'Nothing I would like more outside the Cabinet itself.'

'But how would Jane take it?' he said.

We talked a bit about wives living in the country etc. I tried hard to steer the subject away from this as (perhaps wrongly) I did not want to appear to be too keen. I do not know how much power he has to recommend his successor or – same thing – how much attention the Leader would pay to what he says. But of course the more I thought about it the more excited I became. He told me that there would definitely be another reshuffle in September and I inferred that it would be then that he would get a department of his own and other changes would be made.

So there it is, one is quickly forced back by a combination of bribes and compulsion into towing the line, being a good boy, etc. I do not quite know what I should do to make myself, or perhaps confirm myself, as being the most suitable over the next six months. I did write him a short note afterwards thanking him for the dinner and saying that what appealed to me most about being a Whip was the intelligence-gathering, rather than the disciplinary function. One lives in hope, but this one seems almost too good to be true.

Cloisters   *Thursday, 22 January*

I wrote to Bill Deedes today explaining why I thought that the time
was not quite right for another article on Defence issues until John
Nott had had time to settle himself in as I did not wish to seem to be
harrying him. I thought it might be an idea to enclose a personal note
telling him that Ian had intimated to me that I might succeed him
and enlist his help. I wrote the letter and was just about to put it in
with the other text (but in a separate envelope) when something made
me telephone Jane. She was doubtful about the wisdom of the
idea, reminded me that someone (I honestly cannot remember
who) said that you could not completely trust Bill Deedes and
rightly pointed out that you could not trust *anyone* in politics.
Anyway, never put anything in writing she said. If you must, go
and see him.

I rang the *Telegraph*, fearing that he would not come in on a Friday,
or that he had already left for the country. However, he was somewhere
in the building and I drove round in the 2CV and weaved my way
round through various corridors (they appear to be involved in some
kind of redecoration). He received me, as he always does, with great
warmth. The moment we were alone I told him of the conversation,
asking, if he possibly had an opportunity, if he could be of any help.
Bill was very enthusiastic, said she badly needed somebody, I would
do the job excellently and so on.

I was buoyed up by this, but when I told Jane later she was rather
dismissive, said he was far too experienced not to say that, whatever
his private feelings might have been.

On the way from the *Telegraph* building to Brooks's, where I was
going to meet Euan, and driving somewhat *Frenchly* I just failed to
slip inside a red Hillman as he accelerated away from a pedestrian
crossing. The occupants immediately put on police caps and flagged
me down. They insisted I take a breath test. 'If this bag changes colour
one iota I will give you £100,' I said. Of course, looking back I now
see that might have been constituted as an overture for a bribe.
However, fortunately the celebrated 'crystals' did not alter colour at
all. It is somewhat alarming though as one puffs down the plastic tube
to see them darkening. This is simply the moisture in one's breath
and not the alcohol content, which in my case was nil. All the same,
I noted that the division of the colour beyond which a positive reading
is indicated and a blood or urine test follows seemed very high up the

Saltwood Castle in the mid-1970s.

AC and his father walk in front of the moat with Jane, Andrew and James.

Plymouth, February 1974.
At a function during AC's
first election campaign:
Derek Priston, the agent,
is on AC's left, and Tom
Bridges, the chairman,
next to him.

AC beat off the challenge
of the Labour candidate,
Brian Fletcher (here seen
with AC at the Guildhall
after the count), to win
the Sutton division by
8,104 votes.

A photo call with Jane
for AC's election address.

Before the October 1974 election, with his fellow Plymouth Conservative candidates, Dame Joan Vickers (left), who was endeavouring to win back Devonport from Labour's David Owen, and Janet Fookes, who was defending a slender majority at Drake. On the day, Labour emerged 20 seats ahead of the Conservatives. David Owen increased his majority; Janet Fookes only just scraped back by 34 votes. AC's majority fell to 5,188.

AC disliked microphones, having had a nasty experience with one many years before when trying to gain the Conservative nomination at Havant.

In August 1974, AC, Jane and their younger son Andrew traversed all eighteen miles of Sutton's constituency boundary in a sponsored walk, picking up supporters for stretches along the way.

Very different vintages of cars at Saltwood: AC drives 'the Antique'. In 1974 the family pose for a pre-autumn election shot with the Citroen Mehari, recently acquired.

The 'prophet's visit' – in December 1972, Enoch Powell and his wife Pam lunched at Saltwood after AC had been selected as prospective Conservative candidate for Sutton.

George, the jackdaw, takes a painful peck at AC's ear.

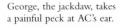

At Zermatt: AC's father on his only visit in 1977 – it was not a success, and there is no mention of it in the diary. Andrew (above), like James, was a keen skier.

Above 'Yet again trying the Zapata moustache, which adds to haggardness. What's the point?' It was shaved off at Zermatt. (September 1972)

Above right AC with Bonny Mama outside the newly-built Garden House at Saltwood in 1972.

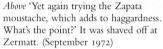

Above At Benalmadena in Spain in April 1973, the home of Jane's parents, Bertie and Pam Beuttler (centre): James and Andrew are in the foreground (left and right). 'Spain revolting,' wrote AC, 'though individual Spaniards reasonably anxious to please. Architecture, pollution, simply awful.'

Above On skimming duties at Saltwood's pool, built in 1973.

Right The Clark family at Saltwood in early 1980: Andrew holds Tom the Jack Russell, AC's stepmother Nolwen sits between Jane and his father.

AC has his arm around the shoulders of Mrs R.M. (Betty) Easton, a formidable figure in the affairs of the Sutton constituency. She later went on to be Lord Mayor of Plymouth.

The 1979 election saw AC returned with his largest majority yet in Sutton: 11,287. The Conservatives, under Margaret Thatcher, won 339 seats, Labour, 269 and the Liberals, 11.

His Westminster secretary, Veronica – seen here at the constituency headquarters – joined the campaign.

Among party workers in Sutton. The Clarks at a Plympton St Mary buffet dance, with Lawrence Speare, often a thorn in AC's side, on his right.

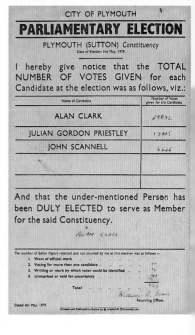

CITY OF PLYMOUTH

PARLIAMENTARY ELECTION

PLYMOUTH (SUTTON) *Constituency*
Date of Election 3rd May, 1979.

I hereby give notice that the TOTAL NUMBER OF VOTES GIVEN for each Candidate at the election was as follows, viz.:

Name of Candidate	Number of Votes given for the Candidate
ALAN CLARK	28842
JULIAN GORDON PRIESTLEY	17605
JOHN SCANNELL	6226

And that the under-mentioned Person has been DULY ELECTED to serve as Member for the said Constituency.

ALAN CLARK

The number of Ballot Papers rejected and not counted by me at this election was as follows :—
1. Want of official mark ... ...
2. Voting for more than one candidate 99
3. Writing or mark by which voter could be identified ... 12
4. Unmarked or void for uncertainty 141

Total 225

William E. Evans
Returning Officer.

Dated 4th May, 1979.   Printed and Published in Devon by G Underhill (Plymouth) Ltd.

The all-party delegation to the Falklands in October 1982 included Antony Buck (on AC's right) and Roy Mason (foreground).

AC meets the Falklands Governor, Rex Hunt.

No signs that a few months earlier a war had been fought here.

AC in the Falklands
in front of a crashed
Argentinian Pucara.

R.A.F. FORM 1185
(Revised June 1974)

ROYAL AIR FORCE
BAGGAGE LABEL

NAME:- ALAN CLARK M.P.

DESTINATION

FLIGHT No.
2386

WEIGHT

LB.

PORT STANLEY
VIA
ASCENSION ISLAND

THIS PORTION TO BE DETACHED AND PLACED IN THE
BAGGAGE BY THE OWNER.

IF THIS BAGGAGE IS FOUND IT IS
TO BE SENT TO:-

NAME:-
ADDRESS:- HOUSE of COMMONS
LONDON

No. 242-12-20

PC 56 8385 5/79   SEE OVER

tube; I got the impression that not much of a drink would get one into trouble.

A little later that evening I went downstairs into Pratt's, which was empty except for, sitting heavily and gloomily in one of those upright circular leather chairs, holding a whisky and soda dark as a piece of mahogany veneer, the Home Secretary.

'Ah, Alan', he said, not greeting me with any great warmth.

'I have just been breathalysed,' I said mischievously (breathalysed invariably means '. . . and produced a positive reading').

But the Home Secretary was very splendid, thundered and spluttered, said it was monstrous, where did it happen, on what grounds did they stop me . . . To my delight I realised that he was angry with the police at breathalysing me, not the other way round. I told him that the test had been completely negative and he was almost disappointed. I think that he might well have done something about it if it had been positive. The Drinker's Union.

Saltwood   *Saturday, 24 January*

Things *consistently calmer* with 'indebtedness eliminated'. But real thriller at the moment is IG's mention of the possibility of my taking his place (!!!). Jane and I think of nothing, talk of little else. Of course it must, I suppose, still be reckoned an ambition. But like getting reported in the *Eton Chronicle* as having got my House Colours (in 1944) even though I hadn't (though deserving it) it is a most timely and magical compensation.

What a coup to overtake, with the most sensational of all ladders, everyone else! The third or fourth most powerful person in the parliamentary party! How they will all cringe and creep! And how well will I do it. A 'posting' – darling little Jane said.

I think of my clothes – a series of dark grey suits and waistcoats with the gold watch chain, grandpapa's, in morning, and BHLH in evening with dark blue. Blue shirts in morning, white in evening. Always Eau de Cologne and Turkish cigarettes in the offices. Also a terrace party in May, constituents from Plymouth and Folkestone (!), colleagues and carefully chosen people. Oh, bliss! But also has more serious possibilities. It would still leave all doors open. On to the FO (with a knighthood), then back to Lord Privy Seal (general duties), then Defence, the Home Office and the leadership election. Truly in politics, as in backgammon, anything is possible.

Jane has some muddled idea (but naturally could not find the paper in which she had seen it, although the whole house is choked with old daily papers) that, in fact, Ian's departure was fairly imminent, as she had read something about some impending honours. The more I think about it the more I realise he would not have been taking 'soundings' if the decision was as far away as I had first thought it was when he mentioned it more or less in the same breath as a September reshuffle.

I spent a lot of time jogging backwards over various tactical mistakes I had made, notably writing to him that handwritten letter in which I qualified my reasons for wanting to be a whip. This must have been a tactical mistake. I was *far* too lukewarm at the time that he mentioned the PPS possibility and then I suppose, in the abstruse code in which one uses to communicate on such matters, my letter about the whip's job will have been interpreted as an oblique way of saying that it was that which I had my eye on rather than the PPSship.

After some torment I decided to write, yet again, to Ian, affirming both my total readiness to serve and making a general request of advice on how to conduct myself. Jane agreed with this course of action. Then I changed my mind and decided to write a formal letter expressing my readiness to serve and an informal letter with a request for advice and enclose the two in the same envelope. However, partly because time was pressing (due to the last collection from Saltwood Post Office), I decided to confine myself to the formal letter of readiness to serve. I wrote it on Saltwood writing paper, did not use a House of Commons envelope, but paid for the stamp (!), marked it 'strictly private' and sealed it using the big James II silver seal of the lion on to which my grandfather had grafted the family crest. I sent the letter to Downing Street as I know that is his first port of call in the mornings.

Cloisters   *Monday, 26 January*

Made an intervention today, though not as intemperate as I had originally intended, criticising Keith Joseph personally, and the principle, for meekly paying up another £1bn. to British Leyland. The

Lady was sitting in the Chamber, and I do not know whether such an intervention increased or diminished my chances of favour, but at least I had warned her about it the previous week. I used the word 'insouciance' which may have been a mistake as some of the Opposition laughed and as it was a serious moment one did not want it to be devalued.

At the Home Affairs Committee Nick Budgen coolly and clearly criticised the Home Office failure to apply objective standards in determining nationality in the new Bill which is to start tomorrow – 'presumably because they are fearful of offending fashionable opinion'. What a splendid, fearless and thoroughly valuable chap he is; no wonder Willie loathes him so much.

Cloisters   *Tuesday, 27 January*

To my gratification I find that my criticism of Keith Joseph got very wide coverage – twice on the radio and reported in full in every paper. Far from diminishing its effectiveness the use of the word insouciance seems to have pleased people. These tiny trivialities which seem to determine whether something is effective or not are very hard to predict.

There was a strange messenger on the Letter Board who did not recognise me and so the internal mail may have been accumulating there for some time. Just after tea I saw my light was on and with considerable alarm noticed that one of the letters on the Board was marked 'First Lord of the Treasury' in the top right-hand corner, which always means Downing Street. I took it away to a quiet corner of the passage which leads down to the Telephone Lobby and, conscious of an accelerating heart rate, tore it open. Inside was *another* envelope, also marked '10 Downing Street' and endorsed 'Private and Confidential' (shades of Ruth Lee and Arthur's communication with Ll G!).[1] I opened the second envelope and inside was a very short note:

'My dear Alan, Thank you so much for your letter of 24 January. You were not dreaming and I am glad to have your note for my file. We will have a further word. Yours ever.'

---

[1] AC had edited the memoirs of Arthur Lee, *A Good Innings* (Murray, 1975).

This very tiny little note at least confirmed that I have not been fantasising as there is documental evidence on both sides of the exchange. Indeed, just looking at Ian's text one can see no possible reason as to why it should be marked 'Strictly Private' and put into two envelopes unless the idea remains a real possibility.

Later, at the Burke Club Dinner, dull and poorly attended and conversation *exclusively* devoted to the Social Democratic Centre Party, Shirley Williams ad nauseam.[1] I did not please people by asserting that the whole thing was balls, no one would vote for them, they would blow themselves out, quarrel, sub-divide, etc. long before the general election. At the very end we went round the table discussing what were the Government's 'achievements' to date. The only one I could think of was, as I put it, that we really have succeeded in putting a lot of people out of work. (Unhappy, indeed Japanese, laughter all round the room, particularly from Lord St Oswald who I suspect to be an old school centrist.) Wedgwood Benn is absolutely right, the Trade Union Movement is disciplined by the fear of being put on the dole and this is a considerable, though brutal, achievement.

Saltwood   *Friday, 20 February*

Reading *Ancestral Voices*, Jim Lees-Milne's[2] volume I, for which I have been searching for two years since first hooked on *Prophesying Peace*. That in itself makes one experience all those beautiful gifted or interesting people – either dead (Nancy Mitford, Cecil Beaton, Eddy [Sackville-West] etc) or just tired old husks. I recollect 'bumping' into poor J L-M coming out of Brooks's the other day. That generation *can't* really communicate. I used to think, naively, that I would always be able to do so with our boys, but I really know better now.

---

[1] Roy Jenkins, David Owen, William Rodgers and Shirley Williams had just announced the formation of the SDP, a new force in left-of-centre politics.

[2] James Lees-Milne published a series of his diaries that began during the Second World War when he travelled the country on behalf of the National Trust.

Cloisters   *Wednesday, 25 February*

A letter in *The Times* today signed by the four 'Wiltshire Wets', Morrison, Hamilton, Walters and Needham,[1] 'calling' for the Government to change course, insisting on 'moderating' (you have to get that word in) the strength of sterling etc. As Jane rightly observed, the letter will have been written by Sara Morrison, Heath's scrawny *éminence noire* at Central Office in the old days, and she will have got poor old Charlie to sign it and rope in the others.

Who are they? Well, Dennis is the least objectionable of the quartet. Said to have an overpowering attraction for the ladies – such powers are very seldom apparent to those of the same sex as the person alleged to have them, and Walters is no exception to this rule.

Then Needham, absolutely odious. He is really the Earl of Kilmorey, but so anxious to appear proletarian that he affects not to use his title and I actually heard him in the Tea Room boasting of having shot 'eighteen pheasant', when even the most parvenu stockbroker is, or should be, taught at his first shoot to score the birds in brace.

Michael Hamilton I have always disliked, but he is much *réclamé* among the wets. He dresses old-school with a stiff collar and blue shirt, usually a brigade tie, never has a hair out of place and invariably smoking Virginia cigarettes through a long black holder ('Winchester Cathedral', etc). We had a narrower escape than I like to contemplate from his being made Chief Whip instead of Michael Jopling, and indeed it might even happen if the regime changes. He is an extremely malicious man and in conversation with me, which I avoid as much as possible, he usually makes a guardedly offensive reference to my father. I suppose he assumes that this causes me pain. Those who know me better could enlighten him.

Nonetheless, there is no doubt that the Party is in poor shape. Much divided among itself. The wets want to go back to full Heathism, the dries are livid at all these extravagant grants to the nationalised industries; others, like myself, are deeply gloomy about the absence of an industrial, or indeed any other kind of, strategy, and the way we seem to be reacting *ad hoc* and in panic to instant crises.

Just after 12.30 p.m. I set off to the Savoy, sharing a taxi with Mark

---

[1] Charles Morrison, MP for Devizes since 1964, Michael Hamilton (Salisbury), Dennis Walters, MP for Westbury since 1964 and Richard Needham, MP for Chippenham since 1979.

Lennox-Boyd, Jack Page and poor old dried-up Paddy Wall,[1] rattled, disappointed and unfriendly in his now rather obvious hair-piece. Jack Page told us how his secretary, Daphne Hickson, elderly and prudish, had been rung up by an irate woman who had asked her who she was, how old she was etc. and told her that she suspected her husband of having affairs with other women and had found her name, Daphne Hickson and the House of Commons extension, written on a piece of paper. Flushing (one suspects), Miss Hickson explained that she worked for a senior backbencher and can only assume that the person in question had a problem and had this number given him for referring. There was a long silence and the aggrieved wife said 'thank you' in a most sinister way. Presumably yet another piece had fallen into place in her jig-saw.

At the door we were greeted by little George Jellicoe.[2] He was just as rubbery as I remembered him in 1965 when he called in at the Chalet and tried to push Sue[3] into a cupboard. He indicated having remembered the incident by asking me if I had 'been skiing' lately. I seem to remember he had to resign a government position about two years ago for some other sexual misdemeanour, but has again bounced back, which helps to prove the generally accepted rule that constant sexual activity has a rejuvenating effect.

The Prime Minister delivered, in her beautiful melodious tones, a rather trite message about the importance of technology, innovation, etc. I suspect that it will not be reported in the papers at all. [It wasn't.] She is off to see President Reagan and I hope will be well received as she needs a bit of relaxation and a boost to her morale.

While I was signing my letters in the Cloisters Michael McNair-W. engaged me in conversation. He said that the morale of the Party had never been lower, that David Howell should have resigned immediately, and that this view was widely felt.[4] I must say that on reflection I agree with this, and indeed think it would have been tactically prudent for The Lady to insist that he do so. Unusually for him, Michael went down the list of Cabinet ministers arguing that

---

[1] Mark Lennox-Boyd, MP for Morecambe and Lonsdale since 1979; John (Jack) Page, MP for Harrow West since 1960; Sir Patrick Wall (Haltemprice).

[2] Earl Jellicoe, a Minister in the Macmillan, Douglas-Home and Heath governments, now President of the Parliamentary and Scientific Committee, whose lunch it was.

[3] Sue Davis was an au pair girl looking after AC's children.

[4] David Howell, MP for Guildford since 1966, and Secretary of State for Energy since 1979, had been seen by Tory backbenchers as giving way to striking coal miners.

Joseph, useless; Biffen complacent, suffering from male men-
opause; Howe 'had had it'. Gently he worked it round to the thesis
that only Walker, Prior, Pym and Jopling still had their credibility
intact.

H'mm. Not wishing either to put him off or encourage him at this
stage, I made some complimentary remarks about Patrick Jenkin[1] for
whom I have a considerable regard as a bland and highly competent
fixer. Michael agreed, said that Patrick could always be relied on to
do as he was told. But who would tell him what? Michael went on
to say (and I judge it came from Peter Walker himself from the very
low tone and anxious guilty looks round the room that accompanied
it) that the Prime Minister was now governing on a purely day-to-
day basis, making decisions on impulse and without forethought. 'Just
like Eden during the Suez Crisis' he said. I simply nodded. 'Margaret's
credibility has gone you know,' he said, 'and once her credibility has
gone she is a pushover.'

I did not like the sound of this. Playing the *agent provocateur* I
suggested, 'Once she becomes a pushover, perhaps she ought to *be*
pushed over?' He became very excited, shifted about in his seat, etc.
This is the first time that I have actually heard it said, in relatively
neutral and centrist quarters, that it might be advisable to rid ourselves
of The Lady, although I do not doubt that it has often been discussed
in the privy counsels of the extreme left of the Party and I did myself
mention it as a possibility when I had my talk with Francis Pym.

Cloisters   *Tuesday, 3 March*

I sat throughout the Trident Debate today and made my long deferred
speech recommending the withdrawal of the Rhine Army. The House
was thinly attended, but not as empty as it usually is at that hour (7.50
p.m.) and I was gratified to note that quite a few people from both
sides came in and stood at the bar while I was talking. Enoch 'hear-
hear'ed' energetically throughout, which is always encouraging and it
was extremely 'well received' by everybody present. Unless one dis-
poses of power (which I do not) congratulations from colleagues are

---

[1] Patrick Jenkin, MP for Wanstead and Woodford since 1964, and Secretary of State for
  Industry since January (Social Services, 1979–81).

rare and so all the more welcome. I even got a note from the Chair, delivered immediately by one of the badge messengers, expressing appreciation and ending 'well done indeed.'

Cloisters   *Wednesday, 4 March*

Balls-aching news. The constituency have suddenly decided to hold a 'really important' Wine and Cheese and have booked the tennis court at Saltram for Saturday 6 June. Betty [Easton] rang and asked if I would arrange for a 'really important speaker' to come down and attend ('Alan Clark to invite a personality ...'). I have been caught like that before. You simply cannot win; if the 'really important speaker' dazzles everybody then they ask themselves why they are lumbered with a nonentity as their own Member of Parliament; if he disappoints, they blame you for having invited a dreary guest. Rather stuffily I said that all speaking engagements had to be made through the Central Office network.

In addition, this and 11 July are the only two Saturdays that we are absolutely committed to Saltwood, as Jane has invited the whole regional hierarchy of the St John's Ambulance Brigade to have their AGM and a fete at the Castle. She will have to be there and she told me that Peggy had expressed a wish that I could also be in attendance, '... so that people could see his other side (!).'

However, as I ground my teeth thinking about this, I realised that the only way out was in fact to short-circuit the Central Office procedure, personally invite a 'really important speaker' and sim-ultaneously explain that neither she nor I could manage 6 June. Francis was the obvious choice and much later on that evening I found Hal in the Speaker's Corridor and fell into conversation with him. H. seemed to think that the invitation would be welcome and also reminded me that I had invited F. to dine with the Defence Committee at some point before Easter. I said I would still be delighted to do this, but rather thought that all his responsibilities in his new field had crowded this out. We fell to talking about general matters.

H. started a little restrained, said that Francis was playing his cards close to the chest and so on. But he soon loosened up. Very slowly we walked down the deserted corridor towards the Speaker's office, our voices sinking lower and lower. We were both talking out of the corners of our mouths, like convicts in the exercise yard. In the Library Corridor we finally came to a halt, leaning against the serried ranks of calf-bound reports of the East India Company.

It is clear that Francis is still on the rampage. Hal told me that there was another 'blockbuster' on the way (for blockbuster I read keynote speech criticising present trends in policy). He also told me that F. had blocked the new provisions for sickness benefit payment in the Legislation Committee of the Cabinet, even though, as Chairman, he was out-voted in that Committee. It is not so long ago that I remembered Ian at dinner delivering a brilliant defence of these provisions when he asked the assembled company why it was right that *they* should have to pay sickness benefit for one of *his* employees when that person fell ill.

Cautiously, I brought the subject round to changes in personalities as well as policies. Hal said that these had to be radical and the need for them was urgent. F.'s great objection (one of them) to The Lady is that she is such a bad butcher, and the dismissal of Normie [St John-Stevas] was held up to ridicule. I forbore to mention that the people *she* wanted to butcher were very different from his own list and might in all probability include himself. Hal quoted to me Francis saying 'it is easy to be a good butcher. All you need is a sharp knife and a thick apron.'

Systematically H. ran through the names of those to be purged – Geoffrey – to go to the Woolsack as soon as possible; it was agreed he could not be demeaned, had performed excellent services for the Party etc, etc. Willie – time expired, too unpredictable and blubbery. I warned Hal that there was very serious trouble brewing if W. tried to impose any sort of bill, in whatever form, to shorten prison sentences or let people out of jail early, and he agreed completely. And if it should be the occasion of W.'s resigning – so be it. Keith – now totally bonkers and a liability. Biffen – as I have remarked earlier in this journal, has suffered[1] a change of life and was now useless. Lawson – universally loathed. Everybody wants *his* head. Hal agreed that David Howell should have resigned. But, hey, just a minute, aren't these all the names that are meant to be supporting The Lady in Cabinet?

Naturally, I didn't say this. Then followed the discussion of who was to take their place. Somewhat disconcertingly Hal suggested

---

[1] AC's comment: For 'suffered' possibly read 'enjoyed', as he had just got married.

Terence Higgins as Chancellor.[1] I mumbled something about the
Party might be restive if so senior a job was filled from the back
benches, even by someone with previous experience. But then who
the hell should it be. Nott? Too scatty, we both agreed and this tallies
with Ian's verdict when we walked on the Terrace last summer. It had
to be Francis. And then Home Secretary, he suggested Peter Walker.
I said no, too grand and would lend weight to his claims for the
succession, 'you must always put your rivals in places where circumstances and the passage of time will be discrediting them by the
time any possible leadership contest could come up'. Hal gave me a
very quizzical look indeed when I said this, but I think he liked it,
and I hoped it would be repeated.

A better solution was to make Peter Walker Minister of Labour and
have Jim Prior at the Home Office, then the leadership contest would
be a 'natural choice'. We both of us agreed that given such a choice
the Party would be bound to choose Francis – which made it easy to
be generous.

With the question of junior appointments we were moving closer
to home and I judged it tactful to tail the conversation off. But we
are very short of senior talent. H. did not like the idea of promoting
Patrick Jenkin, agreed that Michael Jopling might be brought into the
Cabinet with a Department, but *his* successor presented difficulties.
Tony Kershaw[2] possibly. I mentioned Michael Hamilton and got the
reaction that I hoped, namely, one of total rejection.

Cloisters   *Thursday, 5 March*

I asked a supplementary of the Home Secretary today. A lot of anti-
NF stuff was being bandied about apropos of Willie's decision to ban
their march next week. That lazy, greasy slob, John Hunt,[3] stuck in a
question about right-wing publications. 'What about the black ones,'
I interjected. The Speaker very splendidly and exceptionally called
me *after* the Opposition Front Bench had sat down when, by rights,

---

[1] Terence Higgins, although a Minister in Edward Heath's government, had only briefly
    served Margaret Thatcher, as Opposition spokesman for Trade until 1976.
[2] Anthony Kershaw, MP for Stroud since 1955; chairman of the Commons Select
    Committee on Foreign Affairs since 1979.
[3] John Hunt, MP for Ravensbourne since 1974 (Bromley 1964–74).

he should have moved on to the next question. This is what I said:

'Can my right hon. Friend think of anything more overtly racist and criminal, or a clearer demonstration of a breakdown in public order, than the behaviour of the young blacks in the march through Southwark on Monday, when they broke into and damaged shops, terrorised the white population and shouted objectionable slogans about the monarchy to try to provoke the police? . . .'

This was quite a dodgy opening and the fun lay in seeing if one could stand up for the whole passage.

'. . . Will he not recognise that he has to be seen as being completely even-handed or else he will simply add to the very discontent that gives rise to the organisations that Labour Members find so objectionable?'

The House held its breath for a second and then applauded, almost with relief, when I emphasised the necessity for being 'even-handed' etc. Amazingly the other side were silent and half-way through I saw The Lady settling into her place. I hope she enjoyed it. I am completely bomb-happy with Willie now. He has done enormous damage to the Tory Party over the years with his obsessional regard for the *Guardian* vote. Sunningdale[1] was the most outrageous example. But he is at it the whole time, chipping away at our traditional values. After the way he shouted at me and Ivor Stanbrook I realised I could never mend my fences with him. From my conversation with others I feel that he is unlikely to stay the course and I am now enjoying my new recklessness.

I had a quick talk with Adam Raphael, who was so very well informed about our last reshuffle, and trailed the idea of the changes which Hal had discussed with me last night (though without of course attributing). He took a more realistic line, said that The Lady was far tougher than we realised, could not possibly tolerate the wholesale massacre of all her old court, etc. No, I don't think she could. But, of course, the unspoken corollary in my conversation with Hal was that she too was expendable.

---

[1] Was AC's recollection at fault? 'Sunningdale' was an agreement about a cross-party executive for Northern Ireland reached in December 1973 at the Civil Service training college of that name in Surrey. However, perhaps he was referring to the controversial talks between Whitelaw and the Provisional IRA that took place in July 1972 at the London home of Paul Channon, then a junior minister at the Northern Ireland Office?

Cloisters   *Monday, 9 March*

Tim Raison is even more of a leftie on racial matters than Willie. I
remember him being put up to make the anti-Enoch speech at the
Blackpool Conference in 1971. And also the way he behaved on
immigration 'hardship' cases before the Home Affairs Committee
clipped his wings. This evening he was talking to us about the
Nationality Bill. I suddenly got sick of the sneering way in which he
was referring to people of 'British stock' who would be made ineli-
gible to transmit their nationality by descent because of their living or
working abroad. (He is constantly sticking in little weasel amendments
that elevate the status of the coloured 'citizens' and, by exclusion,
penalise our own good people.)

I said all the convolutions attaching to the Nationality Bill sprang
from the basic fact of political cowardice in tackling the question of
colour head-on. Afterwards Nick Budgen gave quite a funny imitation
of me, '. . . and honestly I can not be bothered to conceal either my
Etonian drawl or my intention to offend and insult . . . so you can just
take it or leave it.' This will certainly be passed on to Willie with
relish both by the whips, the PPS and the Minister. On thinking it
over I am not sure that this self-indulgence was wise, although I have
very little respect for him or desire to please. We shall see.

Cloisters   *Tuesday, 10 March – Budget Day*

I walked into the Chamber at five minutes past ten and found the
benches submerged in a positive snowstorm of place cards; nowhere
at all left on the front bench and very few on the one behind. A quick
scan of the cards showed that they were all heavies and entitled to sit
there, except for Anthony Beaumont-Dark.[1] I put my card in his usual
place on the second row and telephoned him. Tactfully, I explained
that one sat on the Baronet's Bench by invitation; that splendid man
though he was he did not quite qualify for a day as important as
Budget Day. I suggested that he and I swapped cards. I must say that
he took it very well and agreed to do so. He claimed that he was
simply doing it out of friendship. This does not fool me for a minute

---

[1] Anthony Beaumont-Dark, MP for Selly Oak since 1979.

of course, but I am gratified that he should think that I am sufficiently important to make it desirable for him to accede to my request.

I lunched in the Dining Room and there was a certain amount of what is known as good-natured chaff. I was at the corner table by the cold buffet, Jean's table (goodness Jean really is getting *so* old and shaky, though still massively dyed, powdered and trussed. I feel the moment is very near when she will be called to her father's 'in harness' hopefully upsetting a dish of scalding soup over Michael Heseltine). I was at a rather dull table, Alex Fletcher[1] and a couple of new Scots MPs – and I inferred from their conversation that they were none of them particularly enamoured of The Lady's policies. Next door sat a more interesting trio, Robert R.J., Jim Prior, and Kenneth Baker.[2] On their way out they stopped and chatted to us. I said I hoped that the intimations of gloom were a double bluff and in fact there might be some 'good news' in the Budget. Jim Prior leant over my chair and said, 'Has it not occurred to you that the rumours of badness are simply to soften you up for something even worse?'

And sure enough the Chancellor was quite uncompromisingly 'firm'. His figures were pretty horrific where they related to the old targets which, of course, had all been wildly overshot, but as soon as he said that tax allowances were not being raised I realised that it was all hard line. That ass Winterton shouted, 'you must be joking' when the Chancellor announced an extra 20p on a gallon of petrol. Although the Gallery described him as wearing a 'sober' grey suit, it seemed rather louche to me. Like his old boss, Ted Heath, Geoffrey Howe affects a curiously opaque café-au-lait complexion. A combination, presumably, of sun lamp and TV studio foundation cream.

Afterwards there was a brief scuffle with the local lobby correspondents. What the hell could I say to them? I 'deplored' the rise in petrol prices, made some anodyne remark about the small business fund and the cut in MLR, then shot up to the Finance Committee.

Here the Chancellor was getting quite a tough time. Cormack,[3] ever an assiduous band-waggoneer, claimed that this measure would ensure that we lost the next election unless corrected. Terence Higgins had led off, perhaps carrying at the back of his mind my flattering suggestion to him (following my conversation with Hal Miller) that

---

[1] Alexander Fletcher, MP for Edinburgh North since 1973.

[2] Kenneth Baker, MP for St Marylebone since 1970, a Junior Minister at Department of Industry since January.

[3] Patrick Cormack, MP for Staffordshire SW since 1974 (Cannock 1970–74).

he was a preferred candidate to take GH's place. Maxwell-Hyslop[1] was crotchety in the extreme about the petrol price rise, '... if I could have the Chancellor's attention for a moment ...' when G.H. bent briefly over to pick up an aside from Lawson.

I really felt I had had enough of the Budget and politics for one day and wanted to get home and see Andrew, who has just returned from Zermatt. But on the telephone Jane was so insistent that I simply could not walk out on the '92' Dinner scheduled for that evening without leaving a formal apology with somebody, that I got the feeling that I really ought to stay up for it. And sure enough in the Tea Room corridor, Jill Knight[2] told me that there was a 'whip' out on attendance at the dinner.

Edward du Cann spoke only briefly and said little of interest. Throughout the meal I had been in conversation with George Gardiner who was talking of forming a Conservative 'Manifesto' group. I asked him if he spoke often to the Prime Minister. He said very seldom, although some weeks ago he had spent three hours with her at Downing Street and she had cooked him and Ian Gow supper. Rather disconcertingly he said: 'Now that you and I no longer have any hopes of office ...' (Oy, just a minute!) and used this as justification for our taking a more positively critical role. One lesson I *have* learned, and I learned it very early on, is do not go high profile in 'positively critical' roles of *anyone*. As if by thought-reading (our conversation took place before E. du C's speech) Edward du Cann made scornful reference to the idea of a Conservative Manifesto Group, said one must communicate with one's whips.

Bob Dunn, who is a decent chap, that attractive combination of a quiet but intelligent Catholic,[3] said that there was not a single whip who could be trusted and he would not dream of talking to his whip about anything concerning his real anxieties. Little John Townend[4] remade a point about the closed shop and encouraged by Ian's presence – he was scribbling away – I switched from my original intention to warn the group about WW's plan to legislate for shorter prison sentences and made a pungent attack on Jim Prior, saying that his remarks (apropos the young girl who was sacked forcibly for not

---

[1] Robert (Robin) Maxwell-Hyslop, MP for Tiverton since 1960.
[2] Jill Knight, MP for Edgbaston since 1966.
[3] Robert Dunn, MP for Dartford since 1979, and Parliamentary Under-Secretary of State for Education and Science since January.
[4] John Townend, MP for Bridlington since 1979.

joining a union[1]) that, 'in the last resort you cannot force anybody to employ someone if you do not want to' were, in my opinion, the most dishonest ever made by any politician in my hearing – and that is saying quite a lot. Of course, the wretched local authority sacked her not because they did not want her, but because they were obliged to by NALGO.

I left early because I wanted to get the last train down from Waterloo. But I heard later that Patrick Wall, who always cocks up everything, had forced a resolution through at the last minute to send a deputation to see the Chief Whip and 'express our views'. This seemed to me extremely illjudged and the following day I sent MJ a letter disassociating myself from it.

Cloisters   *Thursday, 12 March*

Sitting at my desk this morning Bob Boscawen came over looking very solemn and leaned across in that special whip's conspiratorial way and said it was time to steady the banks and not rock the boat, etc; it would be good if I said something to that effect at the '22. All the evidence of a Whip's panic.

I had a question down to the Prime Minister and thought of saying something about the closed shop, asking her if she agreed how unfortunate it would be that a representative of her Government should be defending the closed shop before the European Court of Human Rights at that very moment. As is my practice, I slipped a note in to Ian's office saying that I had this in mind. Just before Question Time an answer was delivered saying that this was not the moment to do so.

So naturally I felt very complacent when Michael McNair-Wilson, who does not adopt this practice of early warning, launched into a great ramble on the same subject and got a lot of his facts wrong. The Lady let him down very gently, but I could not resist showing him Ian's letter afterwards, particularly as I had said to him before lunch that I was number 4 on the list for the Prime Minister and had he any suggestions.

The '22, as so often happens, when everybody anticipates harsh

[1] Joanna Harris, a poultry inspector employed by the Metropolitan Borough of Sandwell.

words and many declamations, was a damp squib. Peter Tapsell sat prominently, with his watering eyes and negroid hair, exuding a desire for martyrdom. But no one even glanced at him.[1]

The level of debate was personified by poor old John Stokes[2] who, relishing his big moment, got up and announced – and only someone of his ineffable complacency could have combined membership of one regiment (The Royal Fusiliers) with enunciating the motto of another – 'Steady the Buffs'. 'Buffers', I whispered to Esmond Bulmer, who was sitting beside me.

Cloisters   *Friday, 13 March*

Last night we went to dinner with Jock Bruce-Gardyne at his little house in Kelso Place. Talk about impoverished dons! The diners were separated at simple tables and overflowed into what was apparently a ground floor bedroom, as I had a wash basin with chromium taps next to me and bumped my elbow on it from time to time. Paper table cloths and napkins and cheap steel cutlery. I have this terrible handicap of a very low boredom threshold and compensated later in the evening by being rude to a soldier called Ramsbotham,[3] who I believe, has some sort of senior command in Northern Ireland. But like all soldiers he regards the Rhine Army as his raison d'être and wants to sink the navy in order to save money.

We left early (but not early enough) to drive to Exeter where I was meant to be lunching with the Chief Constable and his colleagues. Blinding rain and a headwind, I had to stop and phone a message of apology for being late via a startled emergency officer from one of the M5 telephone posts. John Alderson, as always, almost too good to be true, like a very distinguished and expensive General Practitioner with his white hair, dark eyebrows and soothing bed-side manner. He desperately wants to be the next-in-command of the 'Met.' and I

---

[1] Tapsell had called, on the evening of the Budget announcement, for the Chancellor's dismissal as having lost the confidence of the City of London.

[2] John Stokes, MP for Halesowen and Stourbridge since 1974 (Oldbury and Halesowen, 1970–74).

[3] General David Ramsbotham, Commander, 39 Infantry Brigade since 1978.

talked to him at length about his plans.[1] He makes a point of talking to me because of my position on the Home Affairs Committee. He must have been sad that I was late as I noticed from the place cards that he had originally put me opposite him at table, later substituted by Peter Mills.

Saltwood   *Saturday, 14 March*

Last night we had the dreaded AGM. Following my instructions there were, once again, no questions. Knowing how their minds work, there is always a danger that a lunatic may strike at such an event, as that stupid prick Jack Courtney did and catching me completely by surprise some three years ago at Frank and Rhianon's CPC Supper. In fact, it was very poorly attended and everybody was as friendly as could be expected. (In Betty's case that means not much.) I gave a 'rallying' speech, although forgot to read out a long list of subject headings which Alison had carefully prepared for me.

Saltwood   *Sunday, 15 March*

All the Sunday papers carried reference to the fact that after the Budget The Lady had gone into the Tea Room on what was variously described as a 'search and destroy mission'. I know from direct personal experience that this is total nonsense. She and Ian came in, separated and The Lady sat down next to me at one of the large tables at which were also present Michael Shersby, John Stokes and two others who I cannot remember.[2] Conversation was totally banal, as it usually is on such occasions and the habitual standard of sycophancy was not moderated in the least. After about twenty minutes, they both got up from their respective seats and sauntered out.

---

[1] John Alderson, Chief Constable of Devon and Cornwall since 1973, had been in the 'Met' in the 1960s. He did not return.

[2] Michael Shersby, MP for Uxbridge since 1972.

Brocklebank-Fowler staged his defection today.[1] The air was already heavy with rumour about the number of colleagues who were going to abstain or vote against the petrol tax. Michael Spicer[2] told me before lunch that it was going to be a 'surprisingly close thing'. I thought, but kept it to myself, that the only time I had ever known it a surprisingly close thing was the celebrated no-confidence vote that brought down Callaghan's Government in 1979. Usually when it comes to the point the Government of the day always wins more comfortably than people in their excitement estimate for.

J. Prior opened the debate adopting that well-known technique of the moderates of bellowing any point concerning which his conscience made him uneasy. He was followed by Eric Varley,[3] who, although a very nice man with a lot of sound instincts, cannot speak or even read particularly well and did a lot of mispronunciation, gasping (presumably from nervousness), losing his place, etc. Then we had Norman St John-Stevas, mellifluous, reasonable and without any bitterness. Then Enoch, who was perfectly brilliant – what a superb Chancellor he would make – totally demolishing Peter Shore's speech the previous day when he had argued for reflation. Rhodes-James ostentatiously groaned and left the Chamber the moment Enoch rose to speak, but a large number of others came in while he was speaking and by the end the Chamber was almost completely full.

Then up spoke Brocklebank, pretty objectionable stuff it was, much laced with reference to electoral reform, third world and so on, then in a rather stilted little display he walked down the gangway from his own place and over to the front bench right opposite me, where, mysteriously, all the Tribunites had disappeared except Russell Kerr,[4] who was still asleep, and the Social Democrats were sitting on one another's laps. Poor nice Roddy Maclennan got up to make way for Brocklebank. The whole House roared with laughter, which was not the reaction intended by the Social Democrats. Various members leant

---

[1] Christopher Brocklebank-Fowler, MP for Norfolk NW since 1974 (King's Lynn 1970–74), crossed the floor and joined the Social Democrats.

[2] Michael Spicer, MP for South Worcestershire since February 1974.

[3] Eric Varley, MP for Chesterfield since 1964, and a Minister in the Wilson and Callaghan governments.

[4] Russell Kerr, MP for Feltham and Heston since 1974 (Feltham 1966–74).

across to try and shake his hand, one of them, John Roper,[1] actually missed three times.

Afterwards, Jim Prior came into the Tea Room and said that he thought Brocklebank had made a 'very good speech'. I have reported this to Ian Gow.

Cloisters   *Thursday, 19 March*

Just as I was going into Prime Minister's Questions Jonathan Aitken caught me in the Lobby and told me that he had been talking to Chapman Pincher, who was now going to 'blow' the whole story of Roger Hollis[2] and the penetration of MI5 by the KGB. As I sat in my place waiting for the Prime Minister I chatted intermittently about it to Peter Hordern, who confirmed my view that it could have the most damaging effect on the Government.

At 3.14 p.m. on the digital clock (i.e. with less than a minute to go) I scuttled up the aisle in the stooping position, turned left up the gangway and push-stumbled my way along the bench behind Ian's place. I whispered to him that the whole Hollis affair was going to blow at the weekend and did he know, should I have a quiet word with him afterwards? He indicated assent and I went back to my place.

When we met in his room it was clear that he did not have any idea of who Hollis was. ('Where is Hollis at the moment ...' etc.) I sketched in the background briefly, said that I felt the Prime Minister ought to be forewarned in case she did not know. Security scandals always seem to bounce up and hit governments when they start to get a little shaky. Although, of course, I did not say this.

On my way back from the Prime Minister's room I was caught by Adam Raphael in the Members' Lobby. He told me that he felt conspiracies to displace the Prime Minister were now becoming quite flagrant; that she has made so many powerful enemies (the Governor of the Bank of England, Chairman of the CBI, etc.) and that he regarded her as being highly vulnerable if the policies did not start to show results

---

[1] Robert (Roddy) Maclennan (Caithness and Sutherland since 1966) and John Roper (Farnworth since 1970) had both crossed the floor from the Labour benches to join the SDP.

[2] Sir Roger Hollis, Director-General of MI5, 1956–65, was alleged to be the 'Fifth Man' among the Cambridge spies. Subsequent historians disagreed.

during the summer. But we both agreed that the 'wets' were useless –
not called 'wet' for nothing. Raphael said that the unanimity of speeches
last weekend arose simply because each in turn had been 'screamed' at
by the Prime Minister and told to go out and do something.

AR went on to say that this was going to be the theme of his article
this Sunday, coupled with the implication that Francis Pym was the
obvious choice of successor. I suggested that he kept Francis Pym's
name out of the article as it would be dangerous to draw attention to
him at this stage, his own reputation being so high, that people would
pay special credence to what he was saying and so on. AR mumbled
something about flattery did not make any difference, he must stick
to his theme, but he would do it very carefully.

So, I had to go back to IG and warn him of this also. I felt that the
Prime Minister should be forewarned of a text which might come as a
disagreeable shock to her. Ian nodded gloomily, but made no comment.

Later, when I got home, I thought it would also be appropriate to
telephone Francis and let him know as he, too, might appreciate a
word of warning, as there was always the risk that The Lady might
read the piece first, ring him up and scream at him without his
knowing what it was all about. 'But what can I do,' he said plaintively.
Nothing, I agreed, but it was just as well to be forewarned.

Saltwood   *Sunday 22 March*

I see that George Gardiner[1] has got a lead item on the front page of the
Sunday Express 'denouncing' members of the Cabinet who intend to
stage a coup against the Prime Minister. I assume that he was tipped off
by IG immediately after I had left him on Thursday and they agreed
that a pre-emptive attack of this kind was probably the best defence. In
actual fact AR's article did have the Francis Pym reference toned down
so low as to be almost unrecognisable (so hereto I can take, I believe,
personal credit for influencing the course of events). But Michael Jones
in the *Sunday Times* also bandied the question of a coup around on the
front page; so it is clearly a lobby discussion point at the moment.

---

[1] George Gardiner, MP for Reigate and Banstead since February 1974, previously a
    political journalist.

Saltwood   *Monday, 23 March*

A rejuvenating experience today. Sitting in my place for (boring) Employment questions, I allowed my eye to range along the gallery opposite. Lots of birds and birdettes. On the far edge of the front bench, where it joins the Members' Gallery, sat a blonde. I looked up at her, wearing my glasses, she briefly returned my gaze; haughty, composed. I took off my glasses, chatted on with the boys (JB-D[1] and Tony Fell). My thoughts became obsessive. I contemplated going upstairs and sitting beside her – clearly impossible and ludicrous. Well, anyway, let's have a good old stare ... put on my glasses again and stared. Same routine. She *was* strangely attractive in the true sense. Went back to talking and joking with the lads. Then thought, well, sod it, let's go up to the gallery, 'have a look round'.

To reach it you have to go through various colleagues' offices, the door opening *in* towards you as you step out (to an incredible view and acoustics, incidentally). I went over and sat beside her noticing with a faint pang of anxiety that she seemed rather young, not to say child-like, and under-nourished. And yet in that subtle, secret way that one's animal senses tell one, not *rebarbatif*.

After a few seconds in which I gained my confidence by waving and grimacing at B-D and Fell below, I said 'How're you enjoying it? Is it frightfully boring?'

'Oh ... not yet' she answered (!). With each step surmounted, as in all seductions, retreat by either party becomes more difficult than advance. We chatted, I joked. To my delight I noticed she was very, very pretty. Mouth and eyes terrific; skin a little puppy-spotted. She did not mind, indeed *initiated* remarks and questions. Also she leaned towards me at intervals when not quite 'catching' what I had said. Finally emboldened, I said, 'Come and have some tea'. (Willie had been taking PM's questions and Heseltine had got up. She said she was quite keen on him, but having seen him close to was disappointed.)

'Yes, I'd love to' (with some disclaimer about having to be back). A marvellous, ecstatic moment, comparable almost to getting into bed for the first time – indeed more perfect as less fraught – as I unhooked the ropes and she skipped through into our gallery and off we went!

---

[1] John Biggs-Davison, MP for Epping Forest since 1974 (Chigwell, 1955–74).

Tea in the members' cafeteria. Gosh she was pretty! On the way back she said, 'I like this place'.

'I hope you'll come again', I said.

We exchanged phone numbers in the gallery (as Division Bell was ringing) and I kissed her hand. Super.

That great big booby Geoffrey Dickens[1] rose at Question Time and put a classic 'own goal' point to Francis Pym, aggressively asking about seating accommodation for the public, or something of that kind. The Speaker called him with that special weary inflection that his voice carries when he does not at all wish the Member concerned to speak, but he sees no way to avoid it (in this case because no other Member of the House of Commons was on his feet at the time). Actually, I am getting rather a taste for Geoffrey Dickens. He is a big fellow, with a red face and tiny eyes and mouth. He dyes his hair a dark reddish brown, sweats profusely and his suits are rumpled. (The 'familiar' pinstripe suit, in journalists' code.) But he boxed heavy-weight in the Army and put Don Cockell on the floor – no mean feat and explains why he is such a good dancer – verily, he is the personification of the 'Sapper' cliché, 'the big man moved with amazing speed'.

Cloisters   *Wednesday, 1 April*

I did not make an entry for the Monday, when I rang the bird from the gallery, Jessica by name, and she gave 'blanket' refusal – '. . . I'm terribly busy' etc, and how low this made me.

Went to Sotheby's this morning to tie up the deal for my introductory commission on the Clark Collection Sale. There was David Westmorland[2] looking a little less confidently polished than in former years; I noticed that his hand shook when he was folding the documents. But of course the great advantage of Sothebys is that they have discarded all pretence – unlike Christie's – of being *gentlemanly*. We construct a deal and do not waste time on the veneers. Col pronounced a sound dictum about the upper classes in such circs: 'When you do a deal with a New York Jew, or even an Italian, there is a kind of

---

[1] Geoffrey Dickens, MP for Huddersfield West since 1979.
[2] The Earl of Westmorland, chairman of Sotheby's since 1980.

residual acceptance that although they are trying to get the better of you, they hope to leave you with just enough satisfaction and self-esteem to come back for a bit more of the same later on. But with the English aristocracy they simply want to take you for as much as they possibly can and hope you drop dead the next day.' However, in our case it was Greek meets Greek. I am getting £12,500 down on an introductory commission for the whole sale of £180,000. To avoid tricky questions about special interest, breach of equity etc., it is being presented (quite legitimately) on a purchase of the copyright to the tapes which I am cutting with my father in which he describes the items in the collection and how he acquired them.

Then to the curry lunch at India House. A good, but not outstanding array of dishes – not in the class of the Kundon for example. I sat between Roddy Maclennan and some dear old Labour war-horse whose name I do not know, who stuffed himself in silence and drank his free wine. *Not* an active Member, but whereas I despise such people in our own Party, in Labour I understand and sympathise. These are dear old boys, living in terraced houses in God knows what heavy-industrial conurbation, bruised and battered by monotonous years on the shop floor and low-key conspiracies in the smoke-filled rooms of the lower reaches of the Trade Union Movement. They have earned their – quite literally – 'free lunch'. RM was interesting about the Social Democrats, thoroughly agreed that the Liberals were poison and should be avoided. A nice intelligent man, but *wet*.

Around the huge 'U' shaped table there were at least 60 acceptances. That fat slob John Hunt appeared to be chairing the proceedings and sitting on the right of the High Commissioner, himself a poor-person's Onassis with silvery hair and immensely thick thorn-rimmed spectacles. On the other side sat Julius Silverman, always said to be the King Street paymaster of the Labour Party CP sleepers,[1] but of late rather somnolent and grey-complexioned. He frequently disturbs me in the non-smoking end of the Commons Library with his exceptionally heavy snoring. Other characters stood out, including a very stylish Guru with white hair and beard at the top table and an unpleasant bearded communist, who sat opposite me, who appeared to be something to do with the Foreign Office.

---

[1] 14 King Street, London, WC2, headquarters of the British Communist Party. Julius Silverman, MP for Birmingham Erdington 1945–55 and since 1974 (Aston, 1955–74).

The High Commissioner was spectacularly incomprehensible in his speech of welcome, except when he suddenly slipped into overdrive and began to denounce – most tactlessly it seemed to me – the Prime Minister's attitudes to foreign aid, arming Afghan rebels, and the Redeployment Force. Then, after he sat down, up got little John Hunt again and announced that an Indian 'pop singer' had been asked along at the last moment and would entertain us. Immediately, up bobbed the Guru and made a longish, jabbering speech explaining the virtues of a plain, middle-aged lady, quite acceptable in appearance, but no beauty, who also rose and plucked meditatively at an enormous guitar, while the Guru was jabbering. She then walked down to the end of the room where a king-size microphone was located and alternately spoke and sang clearly and attractively. A curious and unexpected end to a rather jolly lunch.

Cloisters   *Monday, 13 April*

Dined at Downing Street after a really frightful day of trivial but insistent pressures – compounded by that special sense of angst and frailty that affects one on one's birthday. No cards or tributes (fortunately I am not on *The Times* list. I say 'fortunately' because I do not like people knowing how old I am).

I was exhausted, as there was a tube strike and no cabs so earlier I had to *walk*, carrying a full two gallon can of petrol, from the House of Commons to Albemarle Street where I finally got a taxi by *force majeure* and then on to Sussex Gardens where the faithful Citroen had puttered to a halt on Friday while I rushed to catch the Plymouth train. The only bonus was that she had stood unharmed and unticketed on a resident's parking space throughout the weekend. She started instantly, as always, and I drove her back to the Albany so that Jane could use her to pick me up at the Commons. Then I walked *again* from Albany to the House of Commons. I got back just in time for the Home Affairs Committee which was briefly, and bellowingly (invariably a sign of guilt and apprehension), addressed by Willie on the subject of the Brixton Riots. The Party's reaction is not as strong on this as I would have hoped.

Earlier I had asked a question, following the Statement, regarding police equipment and police considerations of reinforcement. This, as the *Guardian* rightly spotted, Willie deliberately chose to mis-understand. But the police understood it very well and were pleased. Two of them on the Westminster staff congratulated me immediately afterwards. I have really come to the conclusion that Willie is the most subversive member of the entire Cabinet and practically the worst Home Secretary we have had this century with the possible exception of Roy Jenkins. He is an arch appeaser and lives only for crumbs of praise swept from the table of the National Council for Civil Liberties.

We arrived at Number 10 a little late, after the Rumanians had made their entry. Filing up the stairs I noticed a few stars, like Michael Foot, Keith Joseph, John Biffen, Michael Havers[1] etc., so was glad to realise that it was not a 2nd or 3rd XI affair. Not having done this before I did not know how good the drink would be at dinner, so hastily and greedily downed three dry sherries off the itinerant salvers while talking and joking with Biffen. His wife, Sarah, is surprisingly young and pretty to wed someone so staid and avuncular.

Julian Amery, now the complete senior statesman, heavy in girth and ludicrously empurpled, introduced me to the Rumanian Ambas-sador as (his excellency spoke only the language of the Corps Diplomatic) 'Un de que brillants de nos jeunes députés'. The Ambas-sador was tall, handsome and corrupt looking, very much the old, Mdme Lupescu[2] school. No ascetic nonsense about people's courts etc.

On the way into dinner each person was handed a map of the *placement* with a little red hand indicating their own name. The table was an inverted 'U' and I sat down at the end between a blonde in a red dress and a rather matronly lady in a blue chiffon blouse who turned out to be Jane Parsons, one of the original Number 10 boiler-room girls (to use Harold Evans' expression).[3] She told me that she had been there for 35 years and had served under nine Prime Ministers, starting with Attlee. Naturally, Macmillan was easily her favourite and as he is also mine we got on top hole. This was just as well, as at the

---

[1] Michael Havers, MP for Wimbledon since 1970, Attorney-General since 1979.

[2] Madame Lupescu, mistress of King Carol of Rumania in the 1940s, was always a favourite character of AC and in *Barbarossa* he told how, in 1945, a convoy of fourteen motorcars was needed to move her luggage out of Bucharest when the Russians invaded.

[3] At the time AC was reading *Downing Street Diary*, Sir Harold Evans' book on life at Number 10 under Harold Macmillan, 1957–63, when he was the Prime Minister's official spokesman.

halfway stage I had foolishly and mischievously 'got on the wrong side of' the blonde in the red dress.

It happened like this. She turned out to be a German and I, having reluctantly and timorously consumed the sea-food cocktail, had turned away the second course which was a minute and delicious looking poussin stuffed with grapes. (After all 85 per cent of all chicken is supposed to contain salmonella bacteria isn't it?) I told the waitress I would just have vegetables. The waitress was sympathetic, but the blonde said rather haughtily,

'Are you a vegetarian?'

'Yes, like the Führer.'

She affected not to know that Hitler had been a vegetarian and I elaborated on Frau Maziali and the delightful vegetarian dishes she would prepare for him. I could see that this was not going down very well and so, partly to provoke, I said, 'He was ahead of his time in that as in so many other things.'

'What other things?'

Well here I am afraid my precise memory fades, but I did construct some sentence, clear in syntax but ambivalent in meaning, about the genetic need for racial purity. Then, seeing how shocked she was, developed it. I had not anticipated the intensity of her reaction. Her eyes filled with tears, she kept looking at me in horror and saying, 'You are appalling, I think you are appalling, how can you represent people and say these things,' etc.

I gave as good as I got, said that was she really condemning me for my opinions – because she certainly could not condemn me for my actions. Was it not as wrong to condemn people for their opinions as it was for their race or the colour of their skin?

I switched my attention to the young lady opposite, a kind of demi-cutie called (as I was to discover later) Clara Hauser. She was engaged in conversation with John Bayley. This was dear dotty John Bayley who is married to Iris Murdoch and who I remember meeting at the Stones at Long Bredy in those carefree distant days of the sixties when Jane and I used to drive about in the Jaguar and spend long weekends with our friends in Dorset. John Bayley said something about late nights and I said how much I loathed them.

'You look very tired,' said the girl.

'Oh, do I?', I answered (I never like this).

'Yes,' she answered, 'absolutely devastated.' Not -ing, but -ed. This was really too much.

I turned my attention to Jane Parsons and kept it there for the rest of the meal. Actually, it may have been an ill-wind as the following day Jane suggested that I might have been put next to Jane Parsons as part of a scrutiny process for Ian's succession. However, this has faded so dim that I hardly think about it any longer, although as he is still there the vacancy presumably remains.

Ian and I, and Michael Havers left together for the vote, Ian complaining bitterly about Hauser (the demi-cutie's father) who had been sitting near him during dinner and apparently propounding a stream of Marxist and subversive sentiments. After the Division we went to Ian's room and watched The Lady do a TV interview with Alastair Burnet. Ian had been apprehensive about this, but I did not think it such a disaster, although she was very strained and intense in her expression – quite different from her demeanour at the dinner.

Afterwards we returned to Downing Street. Ian had told me to wait behind until the other guests had left, but I did not do so and we took our leave at the same time as our own Ambassador in Bucharest who wanted a lift to Grosvenor House. I swished him round there in the S2 (always be nice to Ambassadors as they can be so helpful when one is travelling), but the effect may have been somewhat spoiled if the trade plates, that were lying on the back seat, were noticed.

Cloisters   *Tuesday, 5 May*

I dined with little Winston and Julian Amery at White's. The old school. Julian is very clever, with a nice command of language and an attractive and deep rooted cynicism. If he were Prime Minister (which he was expected to be, and should have been – if the whole Macmillan succession had not been warped by the intrusion of the Heath/Walker syndrome and the 'new' Conservative Party) he would certainly have had me in his Cabinet. But I was alarmed to note that he seemed to be getting a tiny bit ga-ga and, as I recorded at the Downing Street dinner, he is putting on weight alarmingly fast. He is also obsessively, dottily, anti-Soviet and pro-Zionist.

Little Winston has mellowed, perhaps on Julian's advice.

White's is not as nice as Pratt's. Conversation is more inhibited. We were joined by a piggish and I suspect a slightly infradig member who the wine waiter referred to as 'commander', and later by Lord

226 MAY 1981

Cowdray[1] to whom the years have lent a superficial benevolence. But below the surface he remains just as nasty as ever. I was not 'respectful' to him, which to my pleasure I could sense him resenting. He spoke with pride and affection about his dreadful, hirsute, smelly son and how he had rented a helicopter to bring his wife's hairdresser from London to Bordeaux.

Cloisters *Monday, 11 May*

Willie is quite changed. He has lost over two stone. But it is not a cancer loss, it arises out of a regime, a purging. His skin is clear where formerly it was blotchy and his eyes water less. Ostentatiously he refuses drink. Like the Reichs Marshall (though of course not on that scale), he has made a tremendous effort of will and kicked the habit.

But why? He should be amiably, but sozzledly tottering towards an Indian summer in the Lords. Instead he is slim, vigorous, attentive and, most unexpected of all, amiable.

What is he preparing himself for? 'Crossbencher', who has also noted this, wrote some idiotic piece in the *Sunday Express* to the effect that Willie's sole purpose was to defend the Prime Minister at every possible moment. Total balls of course. I find the whole thing rather disconcerting.

Saltwood *Thursday, 14 May*

I am drinking *far too much*.

Yesterday
1 bloody mary
1 glass wine } lunch

2 glasses red wine
2 glasses white wine } dinner
1 vintage port

---

[1] Lord Cowdray, former chairman of S. Pearson & Son, owner of, among other things, the *Financial Times*.

Day before	3 glasses wine	dinner
Before that	wine and port	

Cloisters   *Monday, 18 May*

The *Daily Telegraph* carried the most appalling scare headlines about 'slashing' the Navy, getting rid of the three-deck cruisers and the marines etc. Jane quite rightly worked me up into a rage about this and I left early for the Commons where I suspected that there would be plenty of action.

The phone had been ringing all weekend with journalists asking for my comments on Keith Speed's speech to his 'constituents' about running down the Navy.[1] To my mingled gratification and alarm, I saw myself described in two of the Sunday newspapers as *Chairman* of the Defence Committee. I suppose it is a tribute to my personality that most people in and out of the Party think I am the Chairman, but this annoys Tony [Buck].

Poor little Speed, whom I used to hold in some contempt, dating back I think, to the time when, as a junior minister for the Environment, he addressed the Conservative College at Swinton and was so muddled and inarticulate that at the back of the room I started giving a running imitation of him, to the delectation of various YCs who were grouped there. We were all candidates at that time, but since then he has what is known as 'come on' and I know that he has been in despair over the options for some weeks. It was only last Thursday that Tony and I saw him in New Palace Yard as he got out of his official car (almost for the last time, as it turned out). He implied that he was on the point of resignation, then, and looked grey and distraught.

Actually, if I had really had my head screwed on I would have understood the significance of what he was saying at that chance meeting and deliberately gone low-profile on the 'storm' that had inevitably to follow his speech. I would then have been in a strong position as one of his potential successors.

---

[1] Keith Speed had served in the Royal Navy and was appointed Minister for the Navy in 1979.

As soon as I got to the Commons it was clear that Keith's number was up. The whips were spreading it around that he had been 'disloyal' and senior backbenchers were echoing this with the view that he had 'mismanaged' things – should have resigned simultaneously etc.

Almost immediately after I got in I had to do a broadcast on the *World at One* programme and that evening I went on television twice. It is so easy, even for someone relatively experienced like myself, to allow the journalists to lead one on into rather extreme, or at least excessive, comments. As the whole thing was rumour anyway, I suppose I may have overdone it, but colleagues who had heard the broadcast were enthusiastic. Although, in some cases, of course, this could have been tinged with satisfaction at my so obviously putting the kyebosh on my own chances.

In the evening we had the celebrated and long-postponed dinner for Francis Pym and the old officers of the Defence Committee. The postponement had been due to my own spasticity in not getting the original invitations confirmed. But as it happened, it was almost theatrically timely. Someone, presumably Buck himself, had told the press, and the *Evening Standard* featured it as a major item, putting the word 'coincidence' in double quotes.

I made sure that the food would be good and the wine excellent (on the previous Thursday I had won £70 playing backgammon with Lord Armstrong[1] and this led to my credit in the restaurant). We had two bottles of white burgundy and three of excellent claret and Francis became mellow and benevolent – except towards little Winston, with whom he was sharp; 'you are obsessed by your grandfather and comparisons with his period' etc. Winston is *so* thick skinned, is he simple? Francis was not particularly 'loyal' and I exploited my host's prerogative to enunciate one or two personal aversions, Keith Joseph, Nigel Lawson – which I knew he would share. But I would not say that anything very spectacular came out of the meeting except 'goodwill' and we all know what a soft currency that is.

I had kept a place at the table for Hal Miller[2] but he did not turn up as he was making his resignation speech on the floor of the House at that time. Just in case Francis asked me to take Hal's place I rang

---

[1] William Henry Cecil John Robin Watson-Armstrong, 3rd Baron, an underwriting member of Lloyd's.
[2] Hal Miller resigned from his position as PPS to the Chancellor of the Duchy of Lancaster in protest at the Government's attitude to the private steel sector.

Jane to clear it with her that I would, as tactfully as I could, say no. It is the second or third most important PPS in the House, but although I like Francis and hold him in high regard, the drudgery of mucking around with the business of the House does not appeal to me. The right answer, but I am not sure if I would have the courage to give it, is 'ask me again when you are Prime Minister'.

Cloisters   *Tuesday, 19 May*

Yesterday I had written to Tony with copies to all the other officers and the Defence Whip apologising for constantly being referred to as 'Chairman' of our Committee.

So I really was alarmed this morning to see that *The Times* carried in its lead item on the front page not only a report of our having dined with Francis, but a full quote of my combative question, saying that we cannot indefinitely support British Leyland while being asked to make brutal economies in the defence sector, 'as *Chairman* of the Defence Committee'.

There was a phone message from Buck asking me to meet him and Victor Goodhew in the Smoking Room at 12.45 p.m. We should have co-ordinated our line in this afternoon's debate, but in fact the Smoking Room is such a bad place for meetings of this kind that very little was decided except that the officers should ask for an audience with the Prime Minister immediately. I thought this was ill-judged as well as being rather offensive. Clearly protocol demands that we wait until the debate has run its course and all the openings and wind-ups have been heard. Winston of course is so crazy that he wants to charge in immediately with imputations of bad faith, etc. To my surprise Buck, who should be somewhat warier, was also in favour of an immediate meeting *and* telling the press that we were asking for this. Not a good idea.

I listened to Nott and Keith Speed, then the debate seemed to run out of steam somewhat and I went up to the Deputy Speaker and took my name off the list. Perhaps this was a tactical error as I was in fact quite high up on it and it might have been helpful, in more than one sense, if I had made a temperate and constructive speech.

Cloisters   *Wednesday, 20 May*

I have lost count of the number of people who have come up to me
and asked me if I am going to be the next Navy Minister. There was
a rumour going round the Press Gallery yesterday afternoon and
Elinor Goodman (*Financial Times*) said that she had heard it. The Lady
can hardly appoint someone who publicly congratulated the speech
of the person she has just dismissed, but the rumour did momentarily
get some substance when Sir Raymond Gower[1] approached me in
the Tea Room queue this morning and said, in that special senior
backbencher's undertone, that he understood I was the new Minister.
He is one of those people, like Marcus Kimball and Timothy Kitson,[2]
who have an extraordinarily efficient bush telegraph. Also when I
told Spencer [Le Marchant] that I was going to speak this afternoon
he looked rather uneasy, more or less said 'I would not if I were you.'
Perhaps he too knows something?

There are cruel disappointments in the House of Commons at every
turn and their piquancy is aggravated by the hot-house atmosphere in
which one's hopes can soar.

Cloisters   *Thursday, 21 May*

I left the House about 6.00 p.m. and ran into Nick St Germans[3] at
Brooks's and we played backgammon until half past eight. He used to
be a very dangerous international player, but he must be in his late
sixties now and although he knows all the old prize fighter's tricks he
occasionally makes a soft move. However, he had amazingly good
dice and to my great irritation I lost a lot of money. The same
syndrome as when playing Harold Lever – who is not nearly as good
as he thinks either.

We had dinner late and at the corner table sat Norman St John-
Stevas and friends. About halfway through the meal Nick started
complaining that he had seen Heseltine in Pratt's one evening and
who the hell had brought him in? For some reason he had got it into

[1] Sir Raymond Gower, MP for Barry since 1951.
[2] Sir Timothy Kitson, MP for Richmond, Yorks since 1959.
[3] Nicholas Elliot, 9th Earl of St Germans.

his head that it might be Norman. I thought this very unlikely and so
popped over to interrupt their meal and ask him.

'Lord St Germans is very concerned because he thinks you brought
Michael into Pratt's. I have told him this is highly unlikely, will you
confirm?'

'Michael who?'

'Michael Heseltine.'

'Michael *Heseltine?* Good God, I would never take him anywhere.'

Norman, who was clearly a bit bored, moved over to our table
and dazzled with his bright tales, quips and anecdotes. He is one of
those people whose brain is that much faster than my own and can
have a slightly stilting effect. Maurice and John[1] both used
to do it.

Norman told me that he thought Buck would be the choice for
Navy Minister; also that there was no sign of a let up in The Lady's
hard-line policies, that the opposition in the Cabinet was ineffectual –
'they are not called wets for nothing'. I had forgotten that he was the
origin of this very shrewd judgement which, naturally, did not please
anybody. He told me how terrifying The Lady could be, and of one
spectacular row that they had had, with her pacing up and down the
room screaming at him. Were they alone, I asked? Only Willie, he
had replied, but he was slumped in a sofa and said nothing from start
to finish.

Later, we moved on to Pratt's where Nick generated an atmosphere
congenial to Norman by recounting how his father was something-
or-other in the Household to six monarchs in succession. The boys
took the brunt of Nick's reminiscences and Norman continued to
confide in me out of the corner of his mouth. He said he was
determined to remain in politics; that the Queen had been perfectly
charming to him when he surrendered the seals of office and said
what a horrific business politics was; that the Queen Mother had
made a point of inviting him to dinner a few days later and then not
letting him leave after the meal and so on.

I was impressed by him. He is delightful company. But I am afraid
the Tory Party will only tolerate someone as eccentric and witty as
he is if they (a) dispose of real personal power and (b) offer the prospect

---

[1] Maurice Bowra, Warden of Wadham College, Oxford, 1932–71; John Sparrow, Warden
of All Souls College, Oxford, 1950–78.

of patronage. And I fear that in his heart Norman realises that this is
true.

Saltwood   *Wednesday, 27 May*

At this moment I have got what darling Jane called 'reshuffle chum-
blies'. Still no Navy Minister appointed . . . Buck still tipped. Wouldn't
mind this as the Party wouldn't specially like it and I should then be
able to be Chairman [of Defence Committee]. A flat election, anyway.
But of course even better if I could get the Ministry myself. Really
impose reform, impress the House and The Lady and be moved to
Secretary of State when Nott becomes Chancellor.

The great thing about politics is that at any time one can throw
double 4's. I am unlucky at backgammon and psychic. I have this
capacity to psyche my opponent into throwing the shots I've thought
of. Alas, it has got to stop. I've said this a great many times. Now I
have decided on it.

Finally there is the 'question' of *The Gems of Brazil*. It started a year
ago when I saw a Mallets ad – presumably for the 'Two Humming
Birds' – identified the artist and forget his name . . . 'An American'.
Then last year, after his good job on the Fantin [Latour] I got Valentine[1]
to get them cleaned. He brought them back – very satisfactory;
they really looked nice, rich, decorators' items and with a certain
'something'. I was glad to have them. Then on his second visit, at the
end of the evening, he produced a colour ad from (as it were) the
American Connoisseur showing the 'Two Humming Birds' – possibly
the same picture that I had seen earlier at Mallets – and identifying
the artist as Martin Johnson Heade. I lost the reference and Valentine
left the next day.

Then, coming back on the train from Paris, after changing out of
the sleeper, with *The Times* bought at the Gare du Nord, I saw
Geraldine Norman quip that 'American artists of the XIXc are now
worth more per square inch of canvas than any other except Cézanne
and Rembrandt'; she gave a few artists and prices, among them
'Martin Johnson Heade'. I *still* didn't twig. Not for some days until I
rang Valentine and asked for a copy of the ad. Yes it was. Then it

---

[1] Valentine Gould, conservation adviser and old friend of the Clarks.

moved quite fast. I contacted the shop by phone, and they told me
... sold at $40,000, would now ask 50 or even 75. Contacted West
Central reference library and looked up Theodore Stebbings Junior's
book and found out that these were the 16 missing paintings done in
Brazil for the 'Chrome Lithographs' and later sold to Sir Morton Peto
(Valentine had told me that on the back, when cleaning them, he had
discerned the word 'Peto').

Took them round to Desmond – exaggerating the story of Martin
Johnson Heade and a provisional 'price' was 'agreed' of $1.2m.

I could hardly, can hardly, don't really, believe that this is actually
happening. And now Desmond seems to have gone cold (total radio
silence). Am so tired, depressed and martyred, but hourly remind
oneself that one has got 16 highly important and interesting missing
items by a very valuable XIXc American artist. In the slides they look
incredible, so skilful and touching, the 'Luminist' school. Jane rightly
said they were a present from George and the birds, and that we ought
to keep two.[1]

Continued Saturday

We go to bed *so* late, and Angus got us up so early that I am *averaging*
$6-6\frac{1}{4}$ hrs sleep a night! The Estate endlessly demanding. It is only
because it is steadily, insistently summer raining that I have been able
to spare the evening in the Gt Hall writing this text. So, am ash eating.
The motto is 'can't afford it'. Not drinking (!) now $2\frac{1}{2}$ days. No
b'gammon. Sod the cars '... not interested, old boy.' Will try to get
Alison to keep the blondes at bay. The Philosopher Prince – *reflectif*.
But thanking God, none-the-less. I said on the 'w': 'I'm certainly not
going to Zermatt this September.'

'At the present rate,' said Jane, 'one probably won't be alive by
September.'

'Probably alive, but in hospital and on drip-feed.'

She rebuked me, and rightly. We are enormously, colossally lucky.
Such a glorious place, such possessions, fulfilment and security. I am
enjoying my martyrdom – St Gregory; and may God continue to
protect us in the future.

---

[1] Heade (1819–1904) visited South America in the early 1860s to paint the humming
birds for *The Gems of Brazil*. It is thought that he did twenty paintings in all. In the
end the Clarks sold their sixteen.

Cloisters   *Tuesday, 2 June*

I went to the House to try out the new breakfast arrangements which
have been set up by Charles Irving[1] for those of us too lazy or
incompetent to make our own. 'I am just an unhappy bachelor', I had
said to Charles before the Recess and, to do him credit, he quite
enjoyed the joke. He, of course, being a 'confirmed' one.

On the way across the Lobby I ran into Hal Miller and we indulged
in our routine grumble about how time was slipping past and how
things were not really coming right etc. We agreed that it was impossible to get rid of The Lady and, indeed, would be politically highly
dangerous. But it was equally difficult to get *through* to her or to
suggest/impose the necessary changes in personnel. Hal told me that
he still saw Francis and spoke intimately with him. But I got the
impression that the Cabinet is a muddled, leaderless and unhappy lot.
There are shadows of the closing years of the Heath administration,
though painted in starker colours. The principal difference being that
Ted was a rude and arrogant flobbo without an ounce of patriotism
in his body; whereas The Lady is the most wonderful person and
could still work miracles.

Saltwood   *Thursday, 11 June*

Idly thinking of taking a sabbatical next year. 'Castle closed for repairs.'
Selling the *Gems* does induce a certain feeling of tranquillity. I don't
think so much about Bonny papa dying. In fact quite the reverse, I
want him to live on and annoy Nolwen.

Cloisters   *Friday, 12 June*

I believe that these last few days have been the ones when I finally (or
is it first?) realised that I was not going to get any office or preferment
whatever.

---

[1] Charles Irving, MP for Cheltenham since October 1974; Chairman of Select Com-
    mittee on Catering since 1979.

Spurred on by Jane, I had felt it my duty to caution the Prime Minister against putting in Heseltine as Chairman of the Party. This is a perennial threat, much bandied about by the media from time to time and had been trailed on the front page of the *Sunday Telegraph* last weekend. Also, interestingly, with Norman Tebbit's name. T, too, is completely ruthless and ambitious, but in some way not quite so odious as Heseltine, not so totally synthetic and opportunist. I remember first warning dear Airey about Heseltine and explaining that once installed as Chairman he would try and change, or covertly encourage the changing, of the rules governing election of the Party leader. Because of course the Parliamentary Party would never give him a majority. But if we widened our franchise as have the Labour Party and the Liberals, he would have a chance.

It seemed to me that I should repeat this to the PM. All the more so as the Government is, remains, an 'Unhappy Ship'. It is impossible to predict the outcome in politics. The scene can change with nightmare speed in a matter of weeks, and at any time.

Anyhow, I rang Ian on Thursday morning and asked if I could have five minutes with the Prime Minister, '. . . in your presence of course', as what I had to say might have been embarrassing if relayed at second-hand. To his great credit he asked no questions, and after a split-second interval, looking at the engagement book, said 'Come to my room at ten to four, she will see you as soon as she comes out'.

Earlier that afternoon I had been asked to a 'discussion' on Defence at Central Office (!) with two visiting Americans, stereotype hawk heavies from the military-industrial lobby who were touring Europe on a promotion trip for their new glossy magazine, *Military Science*. We sat down in the 'international Conference Room', myself at the head of the table and the two Americans, much encumbered by recording equipment of various kinds on either side, and two willowy, but unsympathetic, middle-rank twits from Central Office in attendance.

The session was quite fun as I was able to dazzle with my specialised knowledge of weaponry – something they would certainly not have got from any other member of the Committee – and hard-boiled attitude to 'relationships' etc.

When they produced an enormous tape-recorder, one of the CO twits left the room in a panic, presumably to ring up MOD. I became more and more reckless in my answers. The remaining CO twit/spy finally interjected feebly, 'Why don't you ask us about the Labour

Party's attitude to Defence?' Typically spastic reaction by an unthinking little toad. If they wanted to know about the Labour Party's Defence policy there was nothing to stop them having a meeting with my counterpart on the Labour side, I said. They agreed. As well as recording the whole interview, one of them constantly clicked and clucked with an expensive looking Pentax. Presumably it will all be published in a forthcoming issue.

I had to cut it short, with the pompous – but perfectly genuine excuse – that I was going to see the Prime Minister. Full of adrenalin I pranced across the pavements from Smith Square. Then followed a long wait in Ian's office. Vast numbers of whisky bottles covered his desk, awaiting the Prime Minister's signature on the label, and outside in the hallway a few backbenchers hung around. I saw Michael Brown and Colin Shepherd[1] waiting to carry away their trophies which would presumably be auctioned or raffled at constituency bazaars.

After 4 p.m. numbers of those identikit 'private secretaries' in grey suits, horn-rimmed spectacles and supercilious manner – are they civil servants, party officials, research assistants or what? – piss off I wanted to shout at them. Finally, The Lady emerged. I could tell from her special rustling, clucking movements that she was not going to stop. 'I have got an ambassador waiting,' she said, 'put it off until next week when we have got *longer.*' Coquettish, debby almost.

She disappeared with the identikit and Ian called me into the long room. *He* seemed in a bit of a hurry too. I explained my misgivings about the prospective choice for the Party Chairman. Ian told me that he had warned The Lady about eighteen months ago that he believed Heseltine was a threat to her, but now he thought that this was less true. I agreed that Heseltine had lost ground in the last year, but warned him of how quickly things could turn around again. IG made the perfectly valid point that the Party would be still less likely to accept changes in the election system when they could see what a mess Labour had got themselves into in experimenting with it.

I followed him out into the Central Lobby where he shook me off. My relations with IG seem a little more distant at the present time. This was a distinct impression and it depressed me for the rest of the day.

That evening Michael McNair-Wilson twitted me endlessly (he

---

[1] Michael Brown, MP for Brigg and Scunthorpe since 1979; Colin Shepherd, MP for Hereford since October 1974.

knows how vulnerable I am on this) with the fact that I had been
making a good impression and 'yet again' had 'said something' that
had spoilt it all. What *can* he be referring to? I have only spoken once
in the last fortnight – on MPs pay. Was it that? It may have been.
Sadistic teasing. Perhaps he is a closet queen; it is always slightly
suspicious when men get married late in life to women with teenage
children and then have none of their own, isn't it? 'One thing I can
tell you, Alan', he said, smiling gloatingly, 'with absolute certainty,
and that is that you will never be Navy Minister.' I went to bed
exceedingly depressed.

Cloisters   *Monday, 15 June*

The weekend papers are full of forecasts that the Government are
contemplating major 'strategic' changes in policy. But what did it all
boil down to? Building the Channel Tunnel. I ask you. One is moved
to despair. They have cocked the thing up solidly for two years and
are now proposing to win the election on an inflationary programme
of public works. Depression both personal and general drags at one.

At 6 p.m. there was a combined meeting of the Defence and Foreign
Affairs Committees at No. 10. I left ample time (too ample as it turned
out) as I decided to go along Birdcage Walk and up Clive Steps. A
young, plump, personable, but unco-operative policewoman refused
to let me through the gate so I had to go all the way round again,
breaking at intervals into apprehensive and flustered pounding (which
is the best verb I can describe jogging fully dressed). As I came into
the hall of Number 10 the major domo took pleasure in telling me
that they had already gone up. Panic! Am I in an accident-prone
phase?
    However, although the backbenchers were assembled in the White
Drawing Room, the Ministers had not yet appeared. Little (and he is
little) Carrington came in first, very bronzed and la-di-dah. I do not
think it is paranoia, I think he really does loathe me. The majority of
people rose to their feet as he came in. I did not, nor did Peter
Bottomley[1], and at the far end of the room I was glad to see that

---
[1] Peter Bottomley, MP for Greenwich, Woolwich West since 1975.

Victor Goodhew had also remained seated, although he has a heart condition of course, which gives him an excuse. Notters was next in, as always slightly rattled and gangling. He is the embodiment of high rank *without* gravitas.

The Lady came in and sat down on the yellow silk sofa on which Carrington had perched himself. There took place one of those curious, almost petty, but completely feminine, scenes which remind me of my mother. We all had drinks in our hands. Carrington had put his on a minute coffee table beside the right arm of the yellow silk sofa. The Lady had nowhere to put hers but an empty chair immediately on her left. Just as we were about to begin she called to Ian, who was at the far end of the room, and asked him to bring her a table for her glass. Ian was fussed by this, there was no table in sight or accessible. As he looked round Carrington got the message and got up. Against a background of 'no, no Peter', etc. he removed his glass, put it on the mantelpiece, picked up the small table and stooping carried it round the sofa and put it down by the Prime Minister's left hand. I enjoyed this, not least because I could see that he did not. *What* a bore for all those men in the Cabinet to have as their leader not only a woman, but a woman who, whether subtly or overtly, insists on being treated as such.

Tony Buck led off, rambling, incoherent almost. I could see members of the Cabinet getting fidgety. The contributions were exceedingly disparate and, perhaps deliberately, the red herring of the Israeli raid trailed repeatedly across our proceedings. Winston hogged the floor, as always, and spoke again and again. Twice he actually tried to shout down The Lady, holding on so that they were speaking simultaneously for quite a long time before her voice actually won through. She made no commitments, told us nothing we did not know already. The standard, somewhat banal lecture. A purely cosmetic exercise.

This evening the small, but select black tie dinner in Dining Room 'C' for Hinch[1]. A disparate lot, some distinguished, some less so. Quintin[2], Julian Amery and John Peyton among the heavies, Hal Miller and myself representing those of lighter weight. Many had

---

[1] Victor Montagu, formerly Viscount Hinchinbrooke and MP for S. Dorset 1941–62, when he succeeded his father as 10th Earl of Sandwich, but disclaimed his peerage. He celebrated his seventy-fifth birthday on 24 July.

[2] Quintin Hogg, Lord Hailsham of St Marylebone and Lord Chancellor since 1979.

heard of the dinner and (apparently) been offended by not having been invited. Peter Thorneycroft had excused himself on thinnish grounds. Cranborne,[1] who had accepted, never turned up and his shrivelled grapefruit stood reproachfully in front of his *placement* card throughout the meal. Speeches were made, and reciprocated. Hinch sat looking pink and benevolent, but stooped. The leading personal example – of which there are always plenty – of someone who needlessly and pointlessly sodded up his political career out of sheer bad judgement. I could not help reflecting that many of the tributes were all the more heartfelt by an unspoken vein of at-least-I-did-not-get-it-that-wrong-ery in the speaker's mind.

Saltwood   *Saturday, 4 July*

Sitting in the Great Hall – always lovely in here on summer evenings. The only remaining place in the estate where one can reach a truly contemplative state. I prefer it to my father's study. I love the high, high hammerbeam roof, the swallows darting excitedly in and out, the looming presence of so many books that I will never, could never, read.

Cloisters   *Monday, 6 July*

Today's papers are full of accounts of the rioting. Simultaneous outbreaks in different parts of London, Liverpool, Manchester, etc. Apparently, the police have taken very heavy casualties in Liverpool. All this was totally predictable once it was apparent that the people who rioted in St Pauls, Bristol had been handled with kid-gloves at the time and those few who had been arrested were discharged without penalty by the courts. Indeed, I am surprised that it has taken so long for the practice to spread. The Scarman Enquiry into the Brixton Riots has not helped of course, with his constant sniping at the police and dreary toleration of endless monologues about social deprivation, etc.

---

[1] Lord Cranborne, MP for S. Dorset since 1979; heir to 6th Marquess of Salisbury.

Willie is down to make a Statement and will then be attending the Home Affairs Committee to elaborate. I am deeply gloomy; that man will sell out anything. He is an arch-appeaser, but cunning with it – a combination of Horace Wilson and Horatio Bottomley.

Cloisters   *Tuesday, 7 July*

Today is the debate on the Defence White Paper. I would quite like to speak, but I gather the list is enormous. However, I will sit it out and, hopefully, get on the record with a few interventions.

Later, as I was walking back from the Tea Room, I thought I should just check with the Speaker if I had any chance, and my steps took me through the deserted 'Aye' lobby. I heard my name called and IG sidled up beside me. 'Ted is going to speak,' he said.

'Oh really, is he going to be objectionable?'

'I should think inevitably,' he said. 'Can you do anything about it?'

'Yes,' I answered. 'He only sits a couple of places from me. I will find a good time to interrupt him, leave it to me.'

Having an official assignment and sense of importance I went back to my seat.

In the fullness of time Ted got up and started off. When he came to the bit about renewing our presence East of Suez I forced him to give way. Everyone listens to Ted's speeches in the expectation of, and more or less exclusively for, some critical reference veiled or otherwise to The Lady and her Government. But this speech seemed to be perfectly clean.

'I have been listening with great attention to my Honourable Friend,' I said, 'and most of us would agree that what he has said *so far . . .*' (lip curling); I went on to point out that the withdrawal East of Suez had been carried out by his Government. It was a carelessly-phrased intervention and it allowed him to slap me down, as in fact it was *implemented* by the Labour Government. I should have said, 'was *decided* upon by . . .' etc.

Anyway, I sat down, conscious of the fact that I had not covered myself with glory, and listened to the rest of his speech. It was extremely good, slightly isolationist and with a number of ingenious suggestions for arms control negotiations. Sometimes I think that Ted is really rather marvellous. After he had finished, I popped out and wrote a little handwritten note of appreciation. In it I more or less admitted that I had been put up to it, 'you know how these things are arranged'. At the time some great grey cloud exuded warning as it hung over the desk. This was pure sneaking and trouble-making. I lightened it with a benign reference to that charming little piece that he wrote about his childhood at Bexhill and popped it straight on to the Board.

Much later I was still in my place when Ted, still in his pale, pale grey suit, returned for the winding up. With a thrill of horror I saw that he was holding my note in his hand. He opened it, read it and very slowly and deliberately put it back into the envelope. As usual his face was totally expressionless. Was he offended? I had a sudden nightmare that he would take it straight to the Chief Whip and complain.[1]

This has been a very bad day in which the Government, and The Lady in particular, have taken a lot of punishment. Yesterday Willie blundered and bellowed his way through the Statement about the riots in Toxteth and Southall and then came and talked to the Committee. As Nick Budgen so percipiently remarked to me afterwards, Willie, to whom the concept of strategic thinking or the national advantage are completely alien, was preoccupied with the narrow political point as to how the House would accept the fact that CS Gas had been used for the first time in Britain (very effectively as it turned out in Toxteth). He was plagued too by a minor worry, namely that the quality of the 'protective headgear' to be issued to the police might prove to be sub-standard and (although of course he did not articulate any of this) the Public Accounts Committee might ask questions later. 'The best is the enemy of the good', he kept repeating.

At Question Time today it was apparent that the Labour Party had pulled themselves together and decided to make the most of this unexpected bonus. It could have gone either way. Law and order situations usually rebound to the credit of the Tory Party in electoral terms, but in this case, either by accident or design, they hit on the notion of attributing the civil disturbance to unemployment. Totally

---

[1] In fact some days later AC received a very polite and appreciative note from Edward Heath, thanking him for his letter and saying that he 'quite understood'. However, sequels with a wider impact were to follow later.

spurious of course – 'There are no riots in Consett, are there?' I shouted from my seat, but as it was repeated from all quarters on the opposite side of the Chamber they came to realise that they had hit on something. They bashed away at Willie all through Home Office questions and by the time The Lady rose to do her bit they were in fine fettle.

The principal danger of this is a political one, and I find it menacing in the extreme. Most of the press, and indeed, most of the Cabinet, have been waiting for 'rioting' to follow The Lady's economic policies. Now that they have got rioting – though for different reasons – they are delighted to be able to link the two and use it to proselytise their own arguments. That toad Prior has apparently already said that unemployment '... has something to do with it' in order to raise money for his maniac ego-boosting Youth Employment schemes. *The Times* has published Peter Walker's Open Letter to the Prime Minister about young unemployed in Brixton. Of course this was originally printed in 1976, and I well remember the rubbery little shit making that very speech on the subject from that place next to me on the Front Bench below the gangway at that time. But bringing it up to date was another flagrant expression of the treachery in which he specialises.

This really is the Tory Party at its worst; a few senior politicians, who feel themselves thwarted, are combining to use a disastrous national crisis to advance their own personal ambitions. It is also desperately dangerous, as if we lose even our identification with law and order, we have no electoral cards left to play whatever. The high point of our prestige came at the time when the SAS broke the siege at Princes Gate. Yet all the majority of the Cabinet want to do now is buy their way out of the trouble in compensation, grants to the inner cities, etc. etc.

I do not think it is exaggerating to say that if this continues the Government, or at any rate The Lady, could very easily fall on the issue. If the disturbances maintain their present pitch she could be forced into consultations with leaders of other parties, followed rapidly by a coalition.

Saltwood   *Saturday, 11 July*

We gave a grand dinner party for Aspinall's Ball at Port Lympne.
Edward and Fiona Montagu, Jonathan Aitken and his wife, Lolicia (or
Lutz as, disconcertingly, appears to be her nickname),[1] also Jonathan
Guinness[2] with his wife and two of his sons, Valentine and Sebastian.
One of these latter never combed his hair or took off his overcoat, as
far as I could see, throughout the weekend, but was quite sympathetic
nevertheless.

The food was delicious and the table almost overloaded with
Meissen, solid silver, Venetian glass, etc. I gave them two magnums of
Batailley '61, as well as much other good stuff. They polished off a
full bottle of Cockburn '55.

Aspinall promised that his Ball would be the most expensive since
Charlie Bestigui in Venice in 1951. He had boy scouts holding torches
of pitch the whole way down the drive and girl guides doing the same
thing on the walk up from the car park. The floodlighting was
spectacular and the flower arrangements quite incredible. Everything
had been done on a kind of nothing-but-the-best principle, and there
were literally vats of caviare, surrounding polar bears carved out of
ice etc. I noticed faces from the past: Vivian Naylor-Leyland, still
consorting with the young, I saw. His face seemed curiously swollen
and stricken and his speech impaired. Surely, he is still too young to
have had a tiny occlusion?

Unfortunately, the weather was a touch too cold and although we
wandered in the grounds and climbed Philip's Great Steps behind the
Tea Garden, we were driven back into the marquee in the early hours.
Frank Williams[3] joined us at our table. I must say that I liked him
better this time. I thought he was a phoney patriot and simply beating
the drum because he was making money out of the rôle, but his
indignation at the rioting and the softness of our responses was totally
genuine, as was his simple incomprehension of the difficulties of
operating inside the Tory Party, if you are a 'reactionary'. His presence
was a great coup for the boys, whom he promised tickets for the British

[1] 'Lutz' was the name of the SS Commandant at the Colditz Camp where AC's son,
James, had worked the previous summer.
[2] Lord Montagu of Beaulieu and his second wife; Jonathan Guinness, former chairman
of the Monday Club, and his second wife.
[3] Frank Williams, founded Frank Williams Racing Cars in 1975. His number one driver,
Carlos Reutermann, was at that time leading the World Championship.

Grand Prix. Befuddled by drink I muddled up Carlos Reutermann and Ronnie Peterson which, I could see, embarrassed Andrew, although he was very sweet about it and helped me correct my mistake.

Jane and I spent most of the time sitting on stone seats in the garden or walking in the more secluded regions (naturally most of the guests simply turned left and went straight down to the marquee where they stuffed themselves with as much free food and drink as they could for four hours).

We wondered how Port Lympne was taking it. I know, because I went there as a child and because Sybil[1] showed me the visitors book, just how much of a centre it was on every summer weekend for twenty years, and of course tonight's party was not really grand in the full sense. The boys, who stayed until the bitter end, told me that there was one person there being referred to as 'Your Royal Highness', who was 'covered in rocks' and Jane told me that she spotted quite a lot of good jewellery. But au fond it was an unselective 20 per cent of café society, a leavening of aristocratic gamblers, from whom Aspinall had won large sums twenty years earlier, and an unfortunately high number of more shadowy figures, presumably Mafia, or 'multinational', who have access to enormous bank accounts.

Yet the presentation was tasteful, no vulgarity whatever, except in the sheer abundance. It was sad too, Gatsby-like in its transience, because poor old Aspers has no money at all, not in the real sense; he could go broke overnight. The great house with all its memories and evocations, that had slept for so long, then drowsed uncomfortably in the last two years while the public trampled about its gardens and ground floor, had been put into a time machine – but a synthetic one: it had not really been awakened, simply put on a life support system that was turned off again at 5 a.m.

---

[1] Marchioness of Cholmondeley, sister of Philip Sassoon, who built Port Lympne.

Cloisters   *Monday, 13 July*

Willie is coming again to the Home Affairs Committee. He must not
be allowed to get away with it this time. As I was crossing the Lobby,
David Rose of ITN came up to me and said, 'On Lobby terms, what
would you most like to get from Mr Whitelaw at the Home Affairs
Committee meeting this evening?'

'On Lobby terms,' I replied, 'what *I* would most like is for him to
announce that he had put his office at the Prime Minister's disposal.'

Cloisters   *Thursday, 16 July*

I suppose today was the high point of my social life to date – in so far
as that depends upon my status as a politician. As I boasted to Charles
Howard, 'I have got the Queen at four, the Prime Minister at six, and
a private dinner with the American Ambassador at eight ...' 'Watch
out it is not God at midnight,' he answered, quite wittily.

It was my first time in the Buck House garden, although to get to
it we walked through that courtyard where I remember dismounting
for the great Armstrong-Jones wedding ball in 1959, when Dukey
tried to pick up Jane. Vast numbers of people, most of them in ill-
fitting and low quality morning dress, with stained and dog-eared
grey toppers. The garden is rather featureless, although the beds and
borders are most densely planted and the edges crazily clipped. The
south side of the Palace is undistinguished in yellow sandstone and a
bit of a muddle, rather like the northern aspect of Ston Easton.[1] The
tea was delicious, a sort of Indian Hukwa, and so was the fruit cake.
Other items, like the drop scones and most of the patisserie were less
good.

We joined the line to catch a glimpse of the Royals and seeing
Tony Buck I mischievously asked him if he was going to dinner with
the Americans that night (they had marked the invitation 'in honour
of Mr and Mrs John Nott'). He was startled and angry to hear about
it, almost more so than I had anticipated. Said he would complain,
etc.

---

[1] Ston Easton Park, near Bristol, which the Clarks nearly bought in 1964 and which was
subsequently sold to William Rees-Mogg, Editor of *The Times*.

We sheered off to another part of the line. The Queen slowly made her way along, preceded by a posse of buffers in slightly better-fitting morning dress than the majority of the guests, and made conversation with certain selected invitees – the statutory person in a wheel chair with bearded mentor etc. When you see the Queen in the flesh she is always smaller and more beautifully made up than one remembers. She was wearing a white silk coat (like Jane) and a navy blue straw hat. We had to leave early as I had been warned that there might be trouble at the '22 Committee concerning the press releases from the Home Affairs meetings which Willie had addressed. But in fact nothing was raised and we went on to Downing Street, arriving with the first guests.

The Lady, although as always enthusiastic in her greeting, struck me as being a little bit triste and blotchy, which I recognise as being one of her stress symptoms. The room was full of MPs and their wives and really rather dull, although in the yellow drawing room I was glad to be able to point out to Jane the actual coffee table which had been a prop in the events of Monday, 15 June. Notters was already in his black tie and so we shot back to the Albany in order to dress up for the Americans.

It always takes longer to get to Regents Park than one anticipates. I was using the old green Bentley as my faithful 2CV is presently immobilised with a puncture. The custodian at the gate said, 'The name must be Clark', from which we inferred (rightly) that we were the last to arrive.

The Ambassadress greeted us, tall and distinguished looking, but not as tall and distinguished as her husband, whom I liked immediately. He has that special quiet authority which very, very rich Americans carry, and I was amused to note that he did not specially respond to my ritual diplomatic praises of the President. He perked up a bit, however, when I talked to him about the Bond Market and where it was going.

The food was quite good, but the drink egregious in the extreme. The gins and tonics were long, but weak. The white wine thin, the claret restricted. This did not matter to me, but I do recognise it as being a potential handicap in some company. A number of speeches were exchanged and I was delighted to hear the Ambassador say that 'We have the whole defence department here this evening ...' (!) How *did* I get on to that invitation list? All the Ministers were there and the PPS, but I was the only officer of the Committee. Perhaps it was Frank Cooper or Arthur Hockaday[1] who fixed it, as I have got on well with them and – hopefully – impressed them at the Wehrkunde and Chatham House Conferences. Or was it one of those muddles which occur from time to time, as when *The Times* printed me as being 'Chairman' of the Committee? I told Geoffrey Pattie that Buck was going to complain. 'That will be a change,' he snorted.

Saltwood   *Saturday, 18 July*

A lovely family day. Both boys around, and divine.

The [*Gems of Brazil*] cash – 950 US is already on deposit in UBS Brig. Due to emerge at 960 (or 910 ex Desmond) on 3 August. It is agonising to dispense any of it, as it edges its way up so close to the big 'M' – I mean this in *cash*, that's really quite good at any time, and particularly now.

Cloisters   *Tuesday, 21 July*

Very surprisingly, England won the test match [against Australia] by 18 runs when Willis took 8 wickets for 43 in just over the hour. Charlie Morrison, deaf and gangling and ill-disposed, got up at PM's Questions and made a characteristically awful intervention. As he can neither compose nor articulate a perfectly normal English sentence, he was unable to get through even his opening words of congratulation to the English Test side without furtively glancing down at his notes. 'Reading,' everybody bellowed with ritual glee. Then he came to the tricky bit. 'Was not this a good example of change of tactics,' he asked, 'which we might emulate?' In fact it was very much less clear than this and brought in some muddled reference to change of *captains* also. So the lobby went abuzz with the news that he had recommended – as may well have been his intention – a change of captain. That is to say, by inference, of substituting Prior for The Lady.

---

[1] Sir Frank Cooper, Permanent Under-Secretary of State. Sir Arthur Hockaday, Second Permanent Under-Secretary of State, Ministry of Defence.

Charles M. is absolutely dreadful. The rotten *old* school, as opposed
to the poncey opportunist new wave. Many upper-class Conservative
MPs, like Gilmour and Whitelaw, allow their feelings of guilt to
intrude on their decisions – but at least Ian is highly intelligent and
Willie is cunning. C. Morrison has conned the majority into thinking
that he is 'nice'.

In the evening I had my end of term dinner with Ian Gow. I got
to Pratt's early and ordered half a bottle of champagne, which I
thought we could split. However, 'George' poured the whole bottle
into a large silver tankard and set it in front of me; very healthy and
reviving. Shortly afterwards, Jonathan Aitken came down the stairs,
followed a little later by Bill Benyon.[1] They enjoyed the fact that I
had sent William Pitt[2] (sic) a telegram yesterday telling him to 'hold
firm, ... this is what Liberalism is all about,' etc. and signed it, 'Ten
gay Party workers in Datchet'.

Ian arrived a little late, having walked across the Park. I noticed
that he had lost weight and he seemed nervous. He is smoking a great
deal. He reproached Benyon, or 'Buckingham', as he calls him, for
advocating selective reflation. Jonathan and I also argued for this,
although I was more candid. 'You have got to bribe the electorate,
buy the votes,' I said, 'in order to get you through the next election.
It is far too early to start now, but it is something that you must carry
in your mind when you plan the '83 Budget.' IG was shocked by
this, genuinely shocked I think. 'You are an innocent', I told him, 'a
complete babe in arms.' How can someone who is so good at his
job and so very alert to political undercurrents and attitudes in the
Parliamentary Party have standards of integrity that make him so
dangerously vulnerable in policy matters? Fortunately, I think that
The Lady is more realistic.

We moved on from Pratt's and had a tête-à-tête meal at Brooks's.
IG mellowed with a good bottle of claret and became less edgy. He
told me that The Lady was completely unperturbed (personally I

[1] William Benyon, MP for Buckingham since 1970.
[2] The vacancy for the Croydon North West by-election was the subject of vicious behind
the scenes in-fighting between the SDP and the Liberals. By an unwritten agreement
it was the Liberals' 'turn' to field the candidate and they already had one in place,
William Pitt. In political terms Pitt was a nonentity who had already lost his deposit
twice contesting that seat. He was a member of the Lambeth Housing Committee and
a supporter of Gay Rights. Shirley Williams, who was the SDP favourite to contest
the seat, and had the backing of David Steel, the Liberal leader, was blocked by
determined resistance from Liberals at local level.

doubt this) and determined to press on. He asked me who should be Chairman of the Party. I simply could not make a convincing suggestion. He mentioned the two leading contenders, Heseltine and Tebbit, and added a third, Tom King. A bit light on charisma and bell-ringing I told him. He looked gloomy. Was there anyone in the Lords? he asked. 'Here we are, knowing the Party as we do,' he said, 'and we cannot think of a single candidate of whom we could wholeheartedly approve.' I did not answer.

At some point I remember telling him that he must take a department soon. He liked my saying this, but I still have the feeling that he would like to stay where he is for the whole Parliament. And yet it was exactly a year ago, when we dined at the end of the 1980 term at the Cavalry Club, that he gave the impression of being fed up and on the point of departure. IG said there would be a major reshuffle in the autumn and that The Lady would be bringing in many of her friends. I laughed and said that I did not believe it. IG became very concerned. 'Oh no,' he said, 'you wait and see, you won't be disappointed, I guarantee that.' Whether he meant me personally, or objectively, I do not know. But I rather fear the latter as earlier he had been digressing on the Chief Whip's power of veto.

We had been talking about people who had been left out or disappointed and I had mentioned Iain Sproat[1] and how good he was and how I thought he was turning sour from having been so completely overlooked. IG was indiscreet about two other figures whom he has always defended in the past. Carrington, he said, was 'a bad influence'. I remember getting my head bitten off when I had trailed this particular idea on previous occasions. Then the subject of poor Tony Buck came up. I told Ian of how angry Tony had been at my being invited to the Ambassador's dinner, and he more or less said that Tony was self-evidently passé. 'You cannot be in his company for more than two minutes without him reminding you that he was at one point Minister for the Navy.' I am glad somebody else has noticed this. In contrast, I pointed out that dear Geoffrey Johnson-Smith, who does not drink, is completely on the ball, and never mentions his (much longer) period as Minister for the Army.[2] Ian agreed,

---

[1] Iain Sproat, MP for Aberdeen South since 1970.

[2] Geoffrey Johnson-Smith, MP for East Grinstead since 1965. He had spent nearly two years at the MoD in the early 1970s.

and it is possible that Geoffrey J-S. might get something in the reshuffle.

What I did not manage to break into was the manner in which the Cabinet split over the riot measures. Although I did notice that Ian was much less resolute in his defence of Willie than previously. Most of the meal we spent gossiping; for example, he told me that [Robert] Atkins' wife, whom one would expect to be a bright young trollop, was in fact extraordinarily plain and *common*.

I drove him back in the green Bentley, which he greatly liked, and we blew the siren going down Birdcage Walk (which he did not like).

Cloisters   *Wednesday, 22 July*

The Lady came to the 1922 Committee and to suit her convenience we sat one hour earlier than usual, at 5 p.m. It was not a happy occasion. The mood of the Committee was gloomy, sepulchral almost. The Lady was 'lackluster' (as the *Wall Street Journal* describes, every day, the bond market).

Edward du Cann, that master of the coded message, who conceals the dagger in his toga until the very last moment, ended by saying that '... although a week is a long time in politics, two years is a very short time until a general election ...'. And everyone got the message – although of course du Cann is nothing like as powerful or as influential as he was in 1974–75 when he was manoeuvring the '22 to overturn Ted.

Saltwood   *Thursday, 23 July*

July fatigue/gloom. Everything should be lovely, but there is, in some sense, too much of it. If I were to write down the *good* things they would be:

Total solvency for the first time ever, nil indebtedness and $\frac{3}{4}$m in US, giving 100 US per annum.

Both boys lovely and settled in what they want to do.

Reasonably high status in H of C.

Hobbies – cars, writing, restoring – all give pleasure.

'Active' and in good health.

Cloisters   *Friday, 24 July*

The House sat all night and those who were not on their feet had been told to return by 8 a.m. for a 'closure'. Needless to say, there was no vote, but I had a cup of coffee while waiting with Jim Lester, who told me that he thought the Prime Minister would announce her reshuffle immediately we rose as a tactical device to muffle the sounds of protest – many people being away on holiday, lobby correspondents in the South of France, etc. I do not believe it. I do not think there will be a radical reshuffle and such as there is will, I think, take place in September and be conformist in the extreme.

This view was confirmed to me by Michael McNair-W., who also said that Peter Walker had told him that Quintin (whom I have always suspected of being disloyal) said that The Lady was like Herbert Hoover and would lead us to such a defeat that we would be out of office for thirty years.

While McNair W. and I were gossiping, Boscawen went through the office and on through the cloister buttoning up his collar and told us we should be in our places for the Prime Minister who was going to present the Queen's response to the Loyal Address on the occasion of The Wedding. Apparently, this was the first time that a Prime Minister had done this since Attlee.

Just in time I got to my seat. The Lady looked rather small and nervous and, as always, very feminine. I hope she noticed me. She could hardly fail to as the bench was empty except for myself and Fell.

A note of farce was introduced because immediately afterwards that idiot Steen[1] got up and declaimed a petition about sex shops in general and in his constituency in particular. The preamble was detailed and explicit about what these shops do and purvey, unnecessarily so, and unfortunate at that time in the morning.

---

[1] Anthony Steen, MP for Liverpool, Wavertree since February 1974.

Saltwood   *Friday, 31 July*

The weather this summer has been appalling. Usually I swim every day once the pool has been filled – this year less than six times I should think. As I swam 'powerful strokes' the other day I said to Jane: 'The truth is I'm not a Renaissance Prince any longer.' I have a little spare tyre, which flaps over my belt when I'm sitting down. My canine tooth is very short and discoloured and can give the impression of a gap.

Saltwood   *Monday, 14 September*

It's ages since I made an entry. The House went down at the end of July, just petered out really with the last three days on running two-liners. But discipline had 'gone' and I gave Bunny a case of (cheapish) white burgundy and told him to 'carry' me.

August was consumed, as it always is, with openings. One thinks one has the mornings free, and I made grandiose programmes for fixed hours at my desk – which was an incredible shambles – Alison came down a couple of times a week and I did a minimum, or modicum, of constituency correspondence. We would sit on the front steps under the portcullis so as to catch the sun (the sun shone every day in August) and hear the telephone, and at intervals fierce little gusts or eddies of draught would whirl the papers around, sometimes carrying them out onto the gravel, to my irritation.

The sun has shone every day since the wedding of the Prince of Wales on the 29 July, and the pool temperature is still over 70°, but this last fortnight I don't seem to have had nearly as much time to myself, and 'on the land' as I would have wished. On the day after Bank Holiday I had to be in Plymouth at 10 a.m. for a day's voyage on *Valiant*. These jaunts are always clogged by members of the Peerage *with nothing to do*. Usual quota of dear (and not so dear, the Welsh ones are the worst) old boys, plus Earl Fortescue. I've never seen him before. We didn't take to each other, as he was obviously uncomfortable about 'placing' me. This is a factor which always affects my relations with the huntin' & shootin' upper classes. Jane even mentioned it this morning when, discussing the reshuffle (of which more, much more, below), I said that I had no protector, and how much Willie disliked and distrusted me.

My God, it's nasty in a submarine. They submerge as soon as they leave port and may stay at sea for *months*, not surfacing again until they return to their home port. The viruses and bacteria go round and round in the ventilation (sic) system which recycles the stale air through some acidifier that 'purifies' it. The heat in the engine room (115°), the lurking menace of the reactor, which needs four people constantly monitoring its evil dials, the claustrophobia, not just of being submerged in the deep, but of sheer confinement, of having nowhere to which one could retreat for any level of privacy at all. The only area, curiously, with any sense of space is the torpedo room in the bows, and firing the torpedoes or 'fish' as they call them (we staged a mock attack) is exhilarating.

Most of the time it was painfully boring – like going round the laundry at St Thomas's (which is, of course, in the basement), and it was all I could do to stop myself nodding off here, there and everywhere that our stooping, shuffling tour came to a halt. Once we had surfaced again for our return into the Sound, I insisted on going up into the 'Fin' as the Conning Tower is now called. And that was marvellous. One climbed up this narrow, wet – the whole fin is flooded while the boat is submerged – iron ladder, some 30 feet up and there one is, in this iron balcony, with the black hull below, foam pouring off her as she cleaves the waters at seventeen knots.

The only other MPs on board were David Hunt: still putting on weight, but reasonably amiable; and poor Neville Trotter[1] who works so hard and has so much defence expertise and is always being passed over. On the platform of Plymouth Station I said something about the reshuffle. I can't remember his exact reply, but it was very much to the effect that all junior appointments were made by the Chief Whip and so (implied) I didn't have a chance, a view which had been most unwelcomely also propagated by Peter Hennessy,[2] one of my August visitors who had let it go almost as an aside.

I reflected on this gloomily last night and throughout this morning as the reshuffle, or reconstruction as it has been in some quarters predicted, gets (apparently) under way. Long-heralded, like some ponderous offensive by the Russian Army, and preceded by much

---

[1] Neville Trotter, MP for Tynemouth since February 1974.
[2] Peter Hennessy, Whitehall correspondent of *The Times* since 1976.

leaking and counter-leaking chiefly by the protagonists of Prior and Tebbit, it has of recent days appeared that The Lady is going to get her way, and purge the wets, as Ian promised me she would when we dined at Brooks's just before the House rose. But I am afraid, I kind of *know* that I am going to be left out. As Jane percipiently observed, the Whips would have rung by now '... to check on your where-abouts'.

I had been looking forward to today as little Graham Turner, mole-like journalist famous for his in-depth articles for the *Sunday Telegraph*, was due to pay me a special visit to collect material for an article he is doing for pre-Conference Sunday on the state of the Party. I waited around all morning and the phone rang less and less frequently. Faint, very faint hopes with the earlier calls which turned out to be Col, muddled cashier at UBS and other dimnesses. After about noon was totally silent. I had put chairs out on lawn, but drizzle started. I got a bottle of Yquem '67 on the ice – the first this year – but it turned out he didn't drink. I was made slightly late fetching him at Folkestone station as I had to combine this with dropping dear, amiable but *slow* Mrs Dewsbury and at the last minute decided to change out of my ultra-casual denim shirt and kickers into more Hadleighfied kit.

We sat in the red library. The Yquem smoothly did its work on an empty stomach and I sparkled. But perhaps the interview went on a little too long and my tight rein relaxed (I am often, but on each occasion too late, reminded of Tim Rathbone's comment, 'Al should realise that there is more to politics than being amusing'). All the time I was unhappily aware that the phone was silent. Completely silent.

I took Graham Turner to Sandling at 4.30 and from the platform he telephoned, with much clicking and crashing of 10p pieces, to Ian Gilmour of all people! Confirmation that he (Ian), Soames and Carlisle had all been sacked.[1] Other changes '... still going on'.

With a heavy heart I drove back to Saltwood. By now I must have had it. We listened to the hourly bulletins on the news, but little else came across. That evening I re-watched *Cabaret*,[2] which kept me diverted. After that wonderful, uplifting scene in the beer garden, when the young SA boy leads the singing of 'Tomorrow Belongs to Me' I switched off and went to bed.

---

[1] Ian Gilmour, Lord Privy Seal since 1979; Lord Soames, Leader of the House of Lords since 1979; Mark Carlisle, Education Secretary since 1979.

[2] *Cabaret*, film with Liza Minelli, of the Kander and Ebb 1966 musical based on Christopher Isherwood's *Goodbye to Berlin* stories.

Albany   *Saturday, 19 September*

I see no prospect of a political breakthrough. One can enjoy the *spectacle*, and the intrigue – though with a little less confidence and authority than when a job was in prospect, but I will have 'to consider my position'. I will choose the appropriate moment when we are reassembled and ask IG why, say, I did not get Philip Goodhart's job.[1]

Saltwood   *Saturday, 3 October*

This morning a wonderful rainbow, a complete one from the Great Hall to Thorpes, perfect and defined. Both boys at home (James did a lot of exotic solo flying in his helicopter last week) and still safe. They have chosen their terribly dangerous callings. Is it this that gives me unhappy angst – and will I ever be free of it?

Blackpool   *Tuesday, 13 October*

Ted Heath has been making a number of fierce attacks on The Lady and her Government, clearly timed to provoke a crisis at the Conference which opens at Blackpool today. Last night he was appearing on *Panorama* with David Dimbleby and I put off my dinner in order to watch him, which I did in Charles Jerdein's bedroom, Charles very nobly agreeing to forgo the first episode of *Brideshead Revisited*[2] on to which he switched his video machine. To my great alarm – though a sixth sense warned me of this – Ted, when questioned about the Dirty Tricks, concerning which he had mentioned a number, cited a distinguished journalist, who admitted to having been fed misinformation, and a Member of Parliament, who quite recently had been put up to interrupt one of his speeches but later retracted and apologised [see entry for 7 July 1981].

---

[1] Philip Goodhart, MP for Beckenham since 1957; had lost his position as a junior minister at Defence after only eight months.
[2] Television adaptation of Evelyn Waugh's novel proved an enormous critical and commercial success.

I rang Jane later from Aspers and told her this and she giggled. But of course she does not know the whole story, namely that I *had* been put up to it and by no less a person than IG. I slept uneasily, conscious of the fact that all my skills of tact and improvisation could be severely taxed in the days to come.

Cloisters   *Monday, 19 October*

The House of Commons at its worst. Dull, fetid, everyone discontented and *chétif*. We prowled about morosely in our blue suits (many of them, my own included, rather shiny). The whips hadn't the face to publish a three-liner on the first day back, so they played their usual trick of calling a running two-line and then putting a footnote to say that the Opposition were 'believed to be' on three-line and that Members are asked to 'verify their pairing arrangements'.

As a result, most people were in attendance and all were ill-tempered. At tea Francis said gloomily, looking up at the annunciator screen as we waited for the third division of the day, that it seemed as if we had never been away, never had any holiday at all. One might have expected to find the place seething with intrigue and dissent. But no. As can sometimes happen with the Parliamentary Party, it is such an obvious subject that no one refers to it.

Bored, I resumed my sly and smearing tactics. The previous day's *Observer* had carried an article by Simon Hoggart in which he reported Ivor Stanbrook as, 'calling for' Willie's resignation at a public meeting. I composed a letter to Ted,[1] expressing the view that this was very bad manners and inappropriate for an officer of the Committee and that he send Willie a note protesting our loyalty. For my own purposes, in the hope that it would retain some residual favour with Willie, whom I expected to see after the Home Affairs Committee that evening, I lodged a copy of it with Roger Sims, his PPS. *Et tu Brute* – but what the hell.

This evening I thought of absenting myself for three hours and playing Backgammon at Brooks's. I got as far as the garage and – rarely for me – my conscience spoke. I felt I really *could not* take off

---

[1] Edward Gardner, Chairman of the Conservative Home Affairs Committee.

quite so early in the session. In any case, I have given up backgammon, haven't I?

Sadly, I trailed back upstairs and, as I was crossing the Members' Lobby, George Gardiner asked me if I was thinking of standing against Tony Buck for the Defence Chair. I hummed and hahed. It is always tricky opposing a friend – especially if you are not certain of the outcome. Then I had a brainwave. Why not ask David Hunt, that way I could both gauge the mood of the Whips Office and of the Secretary of State, whose PPS he was until recently.

Somewhat to my surprise Hunt said that the move would be very welcome, gave me the impression that the Whips Office would support it. 'It will be interesting to see how effective this support is,' I said. 'One reason I was asking you was that I had wanted Phil Goodhart's job and had been told by three people, including one in the Whips' Office [Nick Budgen], that John Nott had opposed the appointment as he thought that I would obstruct the renewed cuts that he is going to have to impose on the Services.'

Hunt denied this with real vigour, said that Nott did not know anything about the change until the last moment and was very upset to have lost Philip. He more or less said that the Whips had chopped Philip because he was inarticulate at Question Time.

I was uplifted by this, even though, as Jane astutely observed when I told her the following morning (I left early and went down to Saltwood for the day): 'You cannot trust any of them. It is just their little way of consoling for not getting a job.'

Cloisters   *Wednesday, 21 October*

I had dinner as the guest of General Dynamics, one of their little promotional meetings to 'sell', in the widest sense, the cruise missile. I do not go for leftist phrases, particularly their reckless use of the adjective 'obscene'. But I must say that I did find it highly unpalatable, the casual, sanitised manner in which all these thrusting young executives talk about this deadly, dangerous – but still profoundly unsatisfactory – weapons system. The top man, who was called Ray Jones, had put me on his right and I noticed that he smoked five cigarettes before I had finished my melon. I was glad to have to leave early.

I then walked up Horseferry Road to the St Stephen's Club where the '92' was in conclave to sort out the Committee appointments. No one was particularly enthusiastic about supporting me for the Defence Chair and I was mildly amused to note Winston (who I suppose, nominally, is the rightful claimant) huffing and puffing and proposing Phil Goodhart and Victor Goodhew in turn. The trouble is that there were at least five people in the room who felt that the Chair was rightfully theirs. By tradition, Defence appointments carry a great deal of prestige on the backbenches and there is a feeling, which may very well do me considerable damage in the election, that they should be reserved for Party elders or ex-Ministers.

Cloisters   *Thursday, 22 October*

Today I am meant to be in Taunton, or more accurately, Bishop's Lydeard at 7.30 p.m. How in hell am I meant to get to Bishop's Lydeard, and more particularly, how to get back to London?

I cannot bear staying with people, unless it is Scottish baronial, or Philip Sassoon baroque. Why did I accept in the first place? These dates seem so distant and innocuous, particularly when they are separated by the sunlit plains of the summer recess. I tried to get out of it a fortnight ago, told Alison to send my apologies, excuse the whipping system, etc. But no, Edward du Cann [Taunton's MP] cornered me on Monday, insisting.

I had told John Cope, the pairing Whip, that I really 'did not mind' if I was confined to the Palace of Westminster all day and all night on Thursday. He was surprised, but affected to understand. I just hope that he did not let on to E. du C. because in the fullness of time I heard from the Whips' Office that I could not leave.

And so here I am working at my desk, instead of training the substance of a 350-mile round trip to talk on a subject which, to us in Government, is at present slightly embarrassing. I suppose this means that I am not a professional politician, but at least it allows me to hear Weinberger[1] (who is coming to attend a Lord's Committee and the 1922 Committee) and, hopefully, to go to the BRM sale which Christie's are staging at Motorfair.

---

[1] Caspar Weinberger, US Secretary of State for Defense.

Later

I was sitting next to Charles Morrison in Pratt's when his brother, Peter,[1] came and sat down beside me. We avoided politics during the meal, but he invited me back to his house to watch the Croydon by-election result.[2] I said I wanted to go to bed early, but he muttered something about 'wanting a gossip' as well and I always fall for this.

Peter lives in a narrow terraced house just off Warwick Way, where I remember some tortured nights prior to my wedding in 1958, staying in a back room. It was drearily, but not particularly cheaply decorated, the walls hung with old dealers' dredge-ups, little oils of XVII century maritime scenes, etc. Bookshelves one degree lower – 'runs' of Walter Scott and Dickens bound in plastic imitation leather and (presumably) photo-printed pages. Peter chatted away about the state of the Party, name-dropped, referred to his father's great wisdom, etc. etc.

I have never been specially keen on Lord Margadale as I attribute – perhaps wrongly – the very heavy sentence I received at Steeple Ashton Magistrates Court, for driving without lights in 1971, to the fact that he took an instant dislike to me. (He was attending the court in his capacity as High Sheriff that day.) Later, he suffered the curse of the Gnome for his actions, when a policeman, quite properly, apprehended him for being slumped over his own steering wheel smelling copiously of drink etc. He was disqualified for a year and moved, more or less permanently, to Scotland.

Peter is unrepentantly pro-Lady and I noted the various light smears with which he daubed her possible successors, including Francis Pym and Peter Carrington – never been in the House, did not know how to conduct himself at Question Time, etc. At intervals I murmured that he was bound to be Chief Whip very soon – he did not dissimulate.

Peter also spoke a great deal about his relations with his Civil Servants, how friendly and attentive he was to them, and yet how firm. Once we were tuned into the television commentaries he produced his red despatch box and rustled papers, but this was plainly for show only.

---

[1] Peter Morrison, younger son of Lord Margadale, promoted to Junior Minister at the Department of Employment, in the September reshuffle.
[2] Won by the SDP/Liberal Alliance candidate William Pitt.

If it was all meant to make me jealous I suppose it succeeded. It would be nice to be a Minister and I am grumpy – sometimes very cross – at not being one.

Saltwood   *Sunday, 25 October*

It was a week ago yesterday that Albert Costain publicly announced that he was not going to stand again for Folkestone. I do not know why, but I get the impression that my position is very much weaker than it was two years ago. I do not seem to know anyone in the Association, and it seems ages since I had a speaking engagement down there. In the past I could never go anywhere without somebody asking why I wasn't the MP yet.

Yesterday we saw Beth[1] in the street. 'Are you putting up?' she said. I said I was and asked her round for drinks today to talk about it.

However, when she arrived she avoided the subject until the very last minute. Then, more or less said that I was too much disliked locally by people I had been rude to, thrown off the grounds, etc. I am not sure if I think this is all that important, or indeed incorrectable by personal contact, but it was lowering nonetheless. It must be said, too, that Beth is nowhere near the centre of the Association (not, for example, the way Graham Butland was in the Plymouth Association in 1972).

She did not even know the name of the new chairman or any of the officers. She said everyone loathed Bunting[2] and wanted to get rid of him and I agreed that Bunting's enmity is not as disastrous as it might be if he was widely liked and respected. But he could still be obstructive in an administrative way, losing particulars, delaying applications, etc.

I had already decided to give a posh weekend, have Anthony Royle down and precede the dinner the previous evening with a drinks party for all the local big wigs. Beth agreed that this would be a good idea. A bit obvious I feel. But there is no harm in that.

---

[1] Mrs Evans-Smith, the physiotherapist who treated AC for his back trouble, was an officer of the Saltwood and Newington Ward of the Folkestone Conservative Association.
[2] George Bunting, local constituency agent.

Cloisters   *Monday, 26 October*

I am worried about poor old Tony Buck as it is already getting back to me that he is 'taking it badly' that I should be opposing him for the Chair of the Defence Committee. There was a message from him this morning via Alison that he would like to 'have a talk about it'. And this afternoon, Victor Goodhew told me that Tony had already been ringing round complaining, saying that I was a chum. We agreed on policy, he couldn't understand it, etc. etc.

Later that evening I heard the door open half way through the Home Affairs Committee and, turning round a few seconds later, who should be there but Tony. I sent him a placatory note and suggested that we had a drink afterwards. He was simultaneously nervous and unfriendly, although superficial courtesies were maintained. I said that there was nothing personal in it, it was no more significant than a game of billiards. He rambled on, '... always recommended that you should be a Minister, seem to agree about everything, regarded you as a chum, etc. etc.'. All very awkward. I was saved prolonged embarrassment by the Division Bell, after which the officers of the Home Affairs Committee had to go and see Willie.

Willie was slimmer (still!) and younger looking. His hair was cut and brilliantined down. Despite his ordeal at the Conference he looked fifteen years younger. He made a point of greeting me, so presumably Roger Sims did show him the copy of my note about Ivor Stanbrook, which I had taken the precaution of letting him see but which he had not acknowledged.

At the seven o'clock division John Nott came up to me in the Lobby and said: 'I hear you are putting up.'

'Yes, I am,' I said. 'Can I see you privately about it for a minute?'

I told him that Tony was very upset, put me in a difficult position, what did he think?

'I could not possibly comment, you must understand I could not, it would be quite wrong for me to say anything.'

'In that case, why did you raise the subject?' I said.

'Well, if you will not repeat this to anyone, I must not really, should not say anything...'

'No, of course I won't.'

'Well, I think you should put up.'

'Thanks. In that case I will.'

An encouraging little exchange, I suppose, but like the pledged support from Hunt in the Whips Office, I don't know how much use it will be. Tony is a dear old thing and very popular and has already started spreading the word round, that I-always-knew-he-was-a-shit syndrome. I thought I might get Julian Critchley to put up as well, and split the nice-person-vote, but he would not do this because he was a friend of Tony and because Tony had already complained to him about my disloyalty. There is reference in this diary to Hal Miller when he was PPS to Francis, implying that I should be Chairman, and so I do not think JN was just trying to console me for not getting a junior defence position in the reshuffle. But the hard arithmetic of the ballot box may tell a different story.

That evening I dined at Pratt's. John Colville[1] was there. Every time I meet him (which is not often) I think he is (a) over-rated, (b) snobbish and (c) not specially bright or nice. He name-dropped massively (surely not necessary at Pratt's?), but did tell one little story illustrating his poor judgement. After the general election in 1959 Harold Macmillan asked him at a private dinner whether it would be a good idea if he (H.M.) 'gave up', having set the Party and the country on the road to peace and prosperity, etc. etc. Foolishly and tactlessly Colville said that he thought he should, said that it would be a seignorial gesture, that the whole country would rise to the nobility of it, his place in history assured, etc. etc. Naturally, Macmillan was furious and did not speak to him again for five years.

Cloisters   *Thursday, 29 October*

Halfway through Prime Minister's Questions Tony Royle came and sat beside me. He had already refused our weekend invitation and, as is the way in politics, did not reveal his principal motive until we had been talking for some time. He said that he had heard rumours that I had put my name in for Folkestone. 'Not true,' I replied. Nor is it, although Vivienne Hepworth, the *Western Evening Herald* correspondent, had been fussing me all day yesterday about how the rumour was 'all over Plymouth'.

Like everybody else, including John Lacy (area agent, S.E. Area),

[1] Sir John Colville, private secretary to Churchill during the Second World War and again 1951–55; also to the Queen when Princess Elizabeth.

Tony tried to talk me out of it, said I would get into frightful difficulties with Plymouth etc.

'I know, I know,' I replied, grinning. As indeed I do. I know all these things, but still think that I will do it, just for the thrills and spills. Afterwards, I suspected that he probably had felt it more tactful not to accept my invitation for the weekend for the very reason that he suspected he might be being set up as a tacit sponsor of my candidature. In fact, this was not my principal intention. I simply wanted him to see Saltwood, and to see how appropriate its setting was for the future MP.

As a matter of fact today I feel so flat, dejected, tired, and stuffy that I hardly want to continue at Westminster at all, and have not even got the energy to campaign properly for the Defence Chair, which is essential for my political plans in 1982.

Plymouth train   *Friday, 30 October*

I must admit I like the Plymouth express. The 3 hour journey is almost too short as one comfortably rolls along suspended from communication or pressure, travelling *free* and closeted with one's papers. I must look at my career prospects. How bad will they be when the dream goes – for good I mean, and people push past?

Incidentally, what is perfectly clear is that my 'intimate' with IG and The Lady has blown. They know the truth about the Dirty Tricks letter!

Trouble is, have lost zing and no adrenalin. A back number. The lobby correspondents no longer approach me as I walk across the lobby.

Bratton   *Saturday, 7 November*

Beleaguered at Bratton, I watched the birds, tits and blackbirds from the first floor window. A blackbird worked his way right along the path, getting at the leaves and poking at wormholes. Afterwards I went out and looked at his handiwork and a very good job he has done. How much better one understands birds after George and how

I feel for them with the giant benefits they bring us.

Couldn't make the fire light; only place and time in the year when it is always earlier than you expect when you look at your watch. 'En Garçon' as Jane has to lay the wreath at Saltwood tomorrow, while I had constituency engagements on Friday, Saturday, Sunday and Monday. Armistice weekend (as I call it) is always loaded.

On the Friday I had undertaken to 'talk to' the F&GP of the Association about 'my intentions' regarding Folkestone and Hythe, and they were summoned to Headland Park, the dingy, peeling, and dry-and-wet-rot smelling, terrace headquarters off North Hill, at 6 p.m.

Mrs Ayres, the secretary, who Jane maintains is well disposed, but is unquestionably slightly mad, specialises in the jarring phrase, almost Nanny-like in its wince-making property. One of her favourites is: 'People are asking when is your next surgery . . .' – invariably uttered within twenty-four hours of the last one – and she had fixed up an 'emergency' surgery for me that evening at 5 p.m.

The Paddington train was late and the traffic frightful. It is not only in London that everyone stops work on a Friday at 3.45 p.m. My first call was on dear nice loyal, but slightly dotty Kay (should be spelt with an 'F') Hamlyn, who was having trouble with access over Railway Property behind her house. Glumly we examined the site, accompanied by a minute and choleric man in a tweed jacket whom she introduced as 'Colonel Hamlyn, my former husband . . .'. He boomed and bellowed and claimed to have three thousand acres at Bridestowe. He repeated the boast several times over tea, but he certainly didn't *look* like a millionaire, not even one of the Q-ship class, and poor Kay's house was dreadfully humble; mouldy and faded to a degree, with the Embankment road traffic thundering past, making the windows shake.

I had to stay for tea – 'We blend our own, you know, we learned how to do this when we were stationed in India . . . such happy times', etc. The 'Colonel' stayed demi-petulant – 'Kay, will you let me speak?' he kept saying, even when she was perfectly silent.

Anyway, the upshot of all this was that I did not get back to Headland Park until 5.30 p.m. Mendicants everywhere. Worse than an ordinary surgery: a little old lady who wanted to sue the Housing Association because she had fallen over a lump of concrete; a 'Bikey' who wanted to argue the case against crash helmets – these were not emergencies! I ground my teeth. Soon, down below, I could hear the

F&GP assembling. They had no 'other business' to discuss and would not wish to be kept waiting.

My problem was, how to finesse the hand. Of course I would prefer to sit for Folkestone. Bigger majority (even), less travelling, easier to socialise, new faces, honeymoon period, etc. As I left London, on one of those lovely dry sunny November mornings when you can kick the leaves, I thought I really am fed up with this. I go on getting older and my precious time is being used up doing bugger all, just moving or waiting or deferring to the egos of others.

The night before I had come across Tony Royle and Albert Costain talking in the Lobby – 'We were just speaking about you.' Ugh. Tony and I went to a private corner and he gave me a 'fatherly' talking to. Albert had said I hadn't a chance, they would never choose the laird, wanted someone he just stopped himself saying 'younger', substituted 'more in touch with ordinary people'. Utter balls of course. Why should it be legitimate to 'discriminate' against the rich and well-educated, when heavy penalties are attached to doing so against the black, the fat, the homosexual, the handicapped, the female, etc. etc.

I was quite prepared, I said, to answer the charge of carpet bagging. Wasn't I deliberately making the sacrifice of throwing up a safe seat, putting everything at risk, simply for the honour of representing my home division, the place where I had spent my childhood, my own children had been brought up? He mellowed slightly. Perhaps if I did it *cleanly*, notified my own people of my intention not to stand ... As he said this I thought of that draft letter of resignation, first written in 1976, and a great weight seemed to lift. How wonderful, and yet how sad! But how tempting!

But then Tony's brow furrowed again. What if I *was* adopted in spite of everything, and then Albert died suddenly and there had to be a by-election? 'Two by-elections', I said. He looked unhappy. 'Your name will be mud in the Party.' But still he is a friend. The bond of the upper classes, pretty thin on the ground, even on the back benches of the Tory Party. He said he would have a word with the agent on Monday, make some enquiries. 'The Agent hates me.' Worse and worse. He'd speak to the chairman, ring him up.

But all this, and the fact that no one in Folkestone *has* been beating a path to my door, has lowered my estimate of my chances. And so, at the meeting of the Plymouth F&GP, I funked it. When Mr Boyette asked me which I would prefer, '... if both were in the hand', I paused reflectively for a long time (knowing full well which was my *real* preference) then said emphatically 'Plymouth'.

Several of them, real dears, clapped. John Arnaud led the testimonials, very splendidly saying that it didn't matter that I wasn't living there. Mike Gregory also came down on my side though with a few qualifications, and Wally Rowland, a well-known Vicar of Bray, also came out pro, though with the coded disclaimer that it might be better *for me* to change. Only that little gnomeprick Jack Courtney said that the matter ought to be 'referred back to the wards.' So we ended friends, with my position here greatly consolidated. Any sign of trouble in the future and I can always refer to that meeting as justifying (a) my fighting all the way, and (b) threatening to stand in any case as Independent-Conservative – against-the-Common-Market or whatever.

All the same I felt a somewhat heavy heart after they had all dispersed. *It might have been.* I am not really *of* Plymouth, and I don't know how much longer I can keep up the pretence.

Cloisters   *Wednesday, 11 November*

Oh dear! A decision, followed by an indecision, followed by a contradiction, followed by a referral.

This afternoon I was scheduled to present the British Safety Standards Award to one of my constituents in the Cholmondeley Room of the Lords. Alison booked me to go down there at 12 noon, but I found that the actual presentation did not take place until 1.30 p.m. Apprehensive of my boredom threshold I went back upstairs and drifted along the Lords Corridor to Euan's room where we started opening my present from M. Goisot,[1] the Sauvignon, of which I had bought him a case. It was at room temperature, but we nonetheless drank copiously. Soon we were joined by some of his colleagues, Derek Rippengal,[2] who is always held up as being the cleverest man in the Palace of Westminster; and then by that grave, handsome bachelor, James Vance-White. Later still, in popped little John Webb,

---

[1] M. Goisot, proprietor of a vineyard at St. Brie from which the Clarks import their house wine.

[2] Derek Rippengal, Counsel to Chairman of Committees, House of Lords since 1977.

somewhat chubbier of countenance than formerly and still very fidgety.

What a jolly lot they are. We sparkled and scintillated. At intervals the popping sound of a cork could be heard, and reheard. These little lunch-time parties are a more or less regular feature of those comfortable bay-windowed offices that look out on to Parliament Square and I, perhaps fortunately, do not go to them as often as I should like. And, indeed, my thoughts strayed from time to time to the mass of Safety Council activists waiting in the Cholmondeley Room.

Finally, a little unsteady of gait, I detached myself from the committee of Established drinkers in the Lords and went and sought out my constituent.

He was a splendid man, a Mr Robins, who had served thirty-three years in the Air Force, including three as a POW after being shot down in a Halifax over Berlin in 1943. I questioned him closely about his experiences and he enjoyed 'shooting a line', as he called it. In the fullness of time I presented him with the award, but made the mistake (as I now see) of speaking to him quietly, as person to person, as we held up the diploma (which was huge) while the photographers clicked and flashed. I should, of course, have bellowed my words of praise so that all and sundry could hear. I noticed that all the other MPs that followed me also spoke *sotto voce*, but it was Mr Robins' big day and I think he would have appreciated it.

Later that afternoon, and still somewhat 'irresponsible', I ran into David Owen. He, too, seemed to be tight – or was this my imagination? He spoke very freely and indiscreetly about political arrangements in Plymouth. He had not seen my statement about standing and believed, or affected to believe, that I had said I was not standing. David launched into a great speech about how I was bound to lose Sutton, how strong the SDP were in Plymouth and how he would really quite like it if I did move, strongly suggesting that I did, etc.

It surprised me that he should be leaving Devonport and if he was, that he should not fight Drake, which looked a better bet. But no, he warned me in the most good-natured terms that I would be 'taken to the cleaners' in Sutton. I was jaunty and blithe. But after he had gone I stole into the Library and looked up the relative percentages of the two seats (Sutton and Folkestone). There is really very little to choose, as in both cases the Conservatives polled approximately 50 per cent in 1979 and approximately 45 per cent in 1974. The percentage points are in every case slightly in favour of Folkestone, where the Labour and Liberal vote is identical in size. But these figures are very much 'at the margin'. David had promised that he would send me a copy of the analysis which his department are doing on the different seats and this may be interesting.

However, it did make me more uneasy than I showed. I suppose it *is* conceivable that one might lose Plymouth Sutton, though God knows what that means for the size and fate of the Tory Party in the country. I cannot think of anything more boring than having to slave away there being nice to everyone for another two years and then lose – that is not part of the bargain at all.

But then *immediately* after this little episode I walked into the Members' Lobby, where I was hailed by Tony Royle. He told me that, as he had promised, he had spoken to the Chairman at Folkestone and that, in fact, he (the Chairman) was not ill-disposed to my candidature and that although no guarantees could be made, I would certainly have a 'good run' if I put in. This is too vexing. Particularly as Tony said that both he and the Chairman and Albert all agreed that it was essential that I should write to my own constituency and 'completely clear the decks' with them.

Now what the hell am I going to do? I suppose that I must proceed with Folkestone. But of course it is more difficult in one sense because of last week's 'statement' in Plymouth. Fortunately though they are not selecting until January. This means that the 'statement' will have bought a little time, quietened the thing down and allow me to write the letter of resignation over the Christmas holiday.

In the meantime I have got to look more closely at the situation in Folkestone and revert to the plan of having a great baronial party before Christmas, somewhat on Astor lines, more official, that is to say, than social. I telephoned Jane to ask her to book the bell ringers for the first Saturday evening in December.[1] Jane, bless her, gave a kind of spluttering giggle at this volte-face. She asked me very pertinently whether I was not making the same mistake, in political terms, that I had already made in the bond market. Namely of switching out of one great lump into another, just as the first one was about to fructify. I am afraid there may be something in this.

---

[1] A group of locals in the Saltwood area who play a (limited) repertoire of musical tunes on handbells.

Cloisters   *Tuesday, 17 November*

I am pretty sure that I have got the Defence Chair in the bag. Both Ian Gilmour and Nigel Fisher said that they would be voting for me and this must be a good augury. With friends and supporters on the Left and in the Centre, coupled with a good single 'word of mouth' (earlier I had seen Patrick Mayhew at tea and he said unequivocally: 'You'll get it'), plus the deployed strength of the '92, I should be invincible.

I stayed on late at my desk and checked through my personal canvass list. I am sending reminders to about twenty-five people who have given me a verbal assurance, and another twenty whom I have been unable to contact, but whom I regard as certain supporters, have received a different type of letter which went on their board this morning. Out of this I should trawl a vote of about 60 and the '92, getting 100 plus out of a total available franchise of approximately 200. It is inconceivable that 200 colleagues will actually vote in the election and so even with 'wastage' I should be home and dry.

Dick Body's secretary came in and said that Buck was in a frightful state, cursing and shouting in his office, always at the gin bottle etc. Poor old Tony, I feel kind of awful about it, but that's Show Business.

Cloisters   *Wednesday, 18 November*

We assembled in Room 10. Little David Trippier[1] started to say something in his flat northern tones about how he thought I was probably doing the right thing ... etc. Knowing that he would vote against me I said, 'No, no, no, all the officers must vote for Tony (grand seigneur!).' As I looked round the room I noted complacently that my supporters predominated. A whip (I cannot remember which one) handed me a pile of ballot papers. I marked one and distributed a few others while holding on to the pile. Unfortunately, Tony was sitting next to me, otherwise I might have succumbed to a reckless impulse to 'vote often.' As it was when I went up with my ballot paper to the return pile I did manage, surreptitiously, to vote once more. I am sure Buck didn't see, but little Neil Thorne was watching

---

[1] David Trippier, MP for Rossendale since 1979.

me closely.[1] At the table I made a joking remark to Tristan Garel-Jones, who takes the 'wet' whip, but had assured me that he would vote for me. He was actually in the process of marking his ballot paper, but doing it so heavily masked by other papers which he was pressing over the names, that it was impossible to see what he was doing. Buck was also leaning over his shoulder and I don't doubt that he had given him assurances too. Now he found himself in difficulties.

These committee elections are a shambles. Perhaps just as well, I thought, although I was rather alarmed when Buck said: 'You have voted three times.' Supposing Neil Thorne had seen me cheat? Was Buck going to make a scene? He seemed good natured, though on edge. I thought my majority would be so huge that I could, if he insisted, readily submit to a recount, excluding my own ballot paper. But the thing died down. Bob Boscawen handed over the ballot papers to Tony Berry who took them outside and we listened, not very attentively, to some boring Group Captain from the RUSI, who was telling us how to 'combat' CND. Then Bob Boscawen came back. He had the result. I didn't catch his eye, although he was only a few feet away from me. Relaxedly I stretched my legs out below the desk; a sidelong glance at Buck showed that he was both sweating *and* smoking.

Then, in between the end of the talk by the Group Captain and the taking of questions, Boscawen announced, in an extremely flat tone, the result – Antony Buck has been elected.

I felt like one of those characters in melodrama who scream 'No, No!' or 'I can't *believe* it.' Little Winston, returned unopposed in his post as Vice-Chairman, and sitting on the top table, grinned wolfishly and sought most blatantly and gloatingly to catch my eye, which, naturally, I did not let him do. I had, of course, made instant and ritual obeisance to Tony and congratulated him. What the hell had happened? Perhaps Berry, who loathes me and had, I believe, black-mailed me for the Whips' Office, had subtracted the necessary number of ballot papers on the way back to the Chief's office where the count took place? This would have been divine punishment for my shiftily voting twice, just as God always punishes one, instantly, for cheating in a backgammon game. Perhaps some of the '92 had in fact voted anti? Little Winston certainly. Very probably Patrick Wall, who has been jealous of my expertise in defence matters ever since I entered

---

[1] Neil Thorne, MP for Ilford South since 1979.

the House; Nick Bonsor,[1] who thinks I snubbed him when he was trying to make the running on the Civil Defence Committee last year. Dear old 'Tone', has, of course, no enemies. He is the personification of '... always has a cheery word for everyone around him'.

Oh dear, though, how very flat making. I slipped away and telephoned Jane who, as always, was sweet, loyal and indignant.

Cloisters   *Thursday, 19 November*

I was sitting in the Committee Room Corridor dictating an introduction to the *Time* and *Life* World War II series, when I noticed Ian Gow walking towards us at the far end. Alison and I always go up to this corridor when we have to dictate anything that is not simply constituency material as there is so much eavesdropping and mischief-making in the Cloister office.

My relations with IG have been cool in the extreme since we returned. Cool on my side from a combination of resentment of being passed over in the reshuffle and guilt at my role in the Ted Heath/'Dirty Tricks' scandal that broke during the Party Conference. On his side, I had assumed that guilt and resentment were also present, though for symmetrically opposite reasons, namely guilt for not having pushed my case at the time of the reshuffle and resentment at my having spilt the beans to Ted. Privately I had written off our relationship and resigned myself to a purely Party role – another reason why I was feeling so depressed about my defeat for the Defence Chair.

I continued dictating and assumed that he would walk past with no more than a courteous acknowledgement. He is an exceedingly courteous man and I am sorry that our friendship has been spoiled. We have had two incidents in the past, but this time things were different. However, he stopped, put his hand on my shoulder and asked me if I would dine that evening. For a moment I feared that it might be one of those terrible strained affairs, when The Lady and one or two other backbenchers are also present and conversation is artificial, but, as it were, competitively banal. No, he suggested the Cavalry Club, so I knew that it would be 'intimate'. After he had

---

[1] Sir Nicholas Bonsor (4th Bt), MP for Nantwich since 1979.

gone I went to telephone Jane. What was I to say to him? I was glad
to have overtures made to me so soon after my recent setback, but
simple words of consolation would not be enough. Jane took a very
strong line, spoke most articulately about the injustice of promoting
so many duds; said that The Lady, for all her qualities, was a prisoner
of circumstance, of communist civil servants, fudging and cowardly
ministers, establishment and, for all her fine words, 'consensus' pressures. Jane said she had only realised the extent of this and started to
lose heart after that dinner at Downing Street when that little prick
Graham ... was still in position in her Questions Office, even though
he was unashamedly (and against all regulations) a committed Labour
supporter and had inspired many of the sneers and smears in the 1979
campaign.

IG drove me to the Cavalry Club in his blue Mini – now definitely
showing the effects of the almost continuous traffic thrashing it has
suffered in the last four years. If anything this made the ride, on wet
roads, even more alarming than usual.

On the way he asked various routine questions about morale in
Plymouth, spoke unhappily about Crosby (he had been the previous
day),[1] described how our candidate was now completely shell-
shocked, would not meet the press, could not bring himself to talk to
strangers etc. etc. Ian said that the candidate, when asked hostile or
even faintly awkward questions, would only answer, 'no comment'.
This is particularly unfortunate as politicians are meant to 'comment'
on everything, and to say 'no comment' invariably means that personal
dirty linen is being washed, or threatens to be washed.

I had hoped to avoid drinking too much, as I knew myself to be in
a gloomy, critical and self-pitying condition. I did not want to warm
up too soon under Ian's hospitality. While we were in the bar we
talked in a melancholy way about the opportunities that had been lost
in the first two years. Ian agreed that the Chancellor's difficulties were
never so acute, that our old objectives of controlling the money
supply and public spending were virtually unattainable. It required a
Herculean effort, even to control their rate of growth – which was
already far higher than it had been in 1979. We agreed that indexing
was the real obstruction to wiping out inflation. If we had de-indexed
immediately, at the outset, everything – public servants' pensions,

---

[1] Crosby by-election, caused by the death of Sir Graham Page, where one of the SDP's
'Gang of Four', Shirley Williams, was standing.

benefits, the whole lot, there would have been a tremendous outcry and eighteen months of hardship, but the prospects now would be very good. But now . . .

We were made late in getting to our table by three incredible boozers who were the only other occupants of the bar. One of them cornered Ian and said: 'I always used to see photographs of you standing near the Prime Minister and now I do not see them any more. Are you in disgrace?' We kept them at bay for a bit, Ian being more polite and attentive than I. But this man (I thought and assumed he was a high-ranking Cavalry officer, but actually it turned out that he was a salesman 'in' tubular steel scaffolding) kept saying, 'I never see you photographed next to the Prime Minister now, why not?' and pushing his face aggressively forward. Finally, Ian said to him: 'It is a matter of complete indifference to me whether you see photographs of me next to the Prime Minister or not,' and we went up to take our table.

He asked me about the Defence Committee elections. I explained the background (even though he probably knew it), and that I had been encouraged by the Whips' Office, the existing Secretary of State and the former Secretary of State. Buck had complained to Ian, possibly even hoping that Ian would restrain me. However, I was interested to hear that, according to Ian, he had made reference to a 'nice' note that I had written to him, although Ian is so skilful and subtle in his approach that he could well have been mentioning this in order to heal any possible bad feelings between Buck and myself. From what I hear of Buck's remarks and comments in other quarters in the run-up to the election, I rather doubt if these were particularly friendly to me.

Gow said: 'The thing about Tony is that he is someone who simply cannot resign himself to the fact that he will (lowering his voice) never hold office again.' I said to Ian that this was as good a moment as any for me to ask him, in all candour, if he could tell me, confirm my suspicions, that the same was true of myself, only I left out, of course, 'again'.

This, clearly, was the point which he had been working round to. Immediately, he started to talk very fast, avoiding a direct 'yes' or 'no' answer. He first drew the analogy with his own experience. Said that John Stanley,[1] on the two occasions when the Shadow Ministers had

---

[1] John Stanley, MP for Tonbridge and Malling, was the Prime Minister's PPS, 1976–79,

been shuffled, had sought him out and said that he was sorry that he (Gow) had not been included, that the Prime Minister had great things in store for him, etc. Ian said, as I knew, that he had nothing to do with the first administration, he had only been called in at a late stage. He *had* sat in on both the January and September reshuffles where the junior posts were effectively apportioned by a quartet consisting of the Prime Minister, the Chief Whip, Willie, and himself in a simple advisory role. He said that it was so difficult as so many factors had to be reconciled. So and so would make too much trouble if kicked out, so and so had to remain for reasons of balance, so and so had to be treated mercifully because he was getting divorced, so and so had to be brought forward to encourage the 1979 intake. So and so, etc . . .

He said, somewhat to my surprise, that Michael [Jopling] had 'had a good opinion' of me, that in September he had talked of my possibly being a Whip, that on both occasions my name had been discussed favourably. He repeated his assurance that if he were 'sacked', he would, without hesitation, recommend me to the Prime Minister as his successor (this was something of a relief because I had feared that the Dirty Tricks episode had ruined that possibility once and for all, although I am now as certain as can be that Ian himself will go the full term of the Parliament in the Prime Minister's service).

Who then was blocking me? It must be Willie? Ian did not give a very clear answer. Ominously he said that some things I had done had irritated Willie. Willie had 'told' him (I think this is balls and that, in fact, Willie had objected, or at least demurred, when my name came up at both these meetings). Willie cannot bear being criticised.

I asked if I had been blackballed in the Whips' Office, as there are only two people there who would do it. Berry would do it in any case. Gummer, if he could, but he is such an oily little creep, he might not have done.[1] Ian mumbled and gave the impression that there had not been a blackballing in the Whips Office, but that other conditions supervened. I suppose it was at this point that they had decided to put in Nick Budgen and this may well have been Willie's doing as the appointment of Budgen has effectively silenced one of Willie's most tiresome critics.

---

while the Conservatives were in Opposition. When the Government was formed he became a Junior Minister at Environment and remained in obscurity.

[1] John Selwyn Gummer, MP for Eye since 1979, and recently made a junior government whip.

Nevertheless, it was a consummate performance. Ian managed to convey to me that my chances of promotion still remained very strong – and certainly it was a relief to hear that Michael, if not an ally, then at least was not an opponent. And yet ... if one looks at the thing objectively it is simply not good enough being told that one's name was actively *considered* twice. It is, irritatingly, just enough to keep one in line for a little longer (which was obviously the intention).

When I told Jane that evening she said that at least it was a kind of compliment that he had to search me out so soon after the Defence Committee defeat and give me three hours on my own. At least it means that they are still afraid of me, she said. But in some ways I felt like a sucker who had called a meeting to try and get his money back and then being conned into investing a further £15,000.

It was only much later when the significance of a peculiar category in Ian's list of factors-that-had-to-be-taken-into-account suddenly dawned on me, 'so and so was going through a divorce'. Of course. That was Jerry Wiggin,[1] who had got Phil Goodhart's job which everybody recognised was rightfully mine. Perhaps it is as well that I had not picked it up at the time, but now I realise why he included it.

.

Cloisters   *Tuesday, 24 November*

Today had another ghastly experience. November is a horrible month, it always brings me disasters. Losses on the Stock Exchange and at the backgammon tables, personal setbacks, snubs, reminders of advancing years, material deterioration and other horrors. Early, at 8.15 a.m. I rang Ian Gow, in obedience to his letter of the previous evening in which he had asked me to 'talk' to him about Prime Minister's Questions where I was number two on the list, and first Conservative. Mindful of our improved relations and the encouragement he had given me last Friday, I said that I would do whatever I was told. He said he would call me back at my desk before 10.00 a.m.

I remained at my desk until five past one and he finally came through and gave me a verbative question about small businesses. Ugh. I loathe small businesses – and big ones if it comes to that – and would

---

[1] Jerry Wiggin, MP for Weston-super-Mare since 1969, the new Parliamentary Under-Secretary of State for the Armed Forces.

greatly have preferred something in my own field. However, I learned it by heart (as I thought) and prepared to do my duty. Michael White wrote a perfect account [in the *Guardian*] of what happened, which I can embellish by saying, first, that at the cries of 'oh' I was not in the least put out, indeed I toyed with the House, relishing that the impact of what I was going to say would be even greater; second, that The Lady did really grit her teeth as she straightened me out.

This is appalling. I have lost my key-elective position in the Party and now I have firmly embedded myself in The Lady's long memory as an incompetent.

'*Not* your finest hour, Alan,' sneered that creep McNair-Wilson in the Tea Room queue just afterwards. What is left for me! A lingering death? Or should I blaze away regardless?

Perhaps, now, I would do better if The Lady were evicted.

Cloisters   *Thursday, 26 November*

Everything is dreadfully depressing. Clearly the SDP are going to win Crosby. How fickle and spastic the electorate are. How gullible, to be duped by someone as scatty and shallow as Shirley Williams. And in today's papers there is the Scarman Report, with its ritual 'we are all guilty' and its call for positive discrimination (i.e., discrimination on the grounds of *colour* against white people and in favour of black). In other words, where a white person is better qualified and more suitable they should nonetheless be rejected in favour of a black person – 'in the interests of racial harmony', as the DPP put it when he withdrew the prosecution from the fourteen defendants in the Bristol Riot Trial.

On Tuesday in the Tea Room, when I was still smarting from my rout at Prime Minister's Questions, Ted Gardner approached me *sotto voce* and said that Willie was determined to include the executive power of release in the new Criminal Justice Act. He personally was doubtful about it, etc. etc, but Willie had already warned the officers at the Home Affairs Committee meeting on Monday (this had been put off from 7 p.m. to 10 p.m. and I had not been told about it).

Willie is obsessed, to the exclusion of practically everything else, by the dangers of a prison riot due to over-crowding, having to come to the House and make a Statement, etc. He thinks, rightly or wrongly, that by reducing the prison population he will make this less likely.

And also, of course, he secretly likes the idea of earning some plaudits from the *Guardian*, and other makers of received opinion, for a 'progressive' penal measure. Willie, for some reason, is very jittery about Kilroy-Silk,[1] perhaps because he usually occupies the corner seat below the gangway and is only a short distance away from him, perhaps because Kilroy-Silk articulates views and feelings which Willie sometimes secretly shares. At any rate, Willie accords him far more respect than he does any other members of the Opposition.

I simply cannot let this go through unchecked. It is a great nuisance as we know that it is Willie who is actually obstructing my promotion – not that *that* has not gone down the drain anyway now – but I still feel that I must articulate rightish opinion on this issue to him.

I contemplated having a word with Michael Jopling, prefacing it with the disclaimer that I knew Willie objected to me personally, but of course I had a great respect for him, etc. etc. and still nonetheless felt that this view should be expressed, etc. etc. Then thought it would probably be better if I went and saw Willie himself, although by chance I did briefly see Michael in the Tea Room and managed to score both by saying this and that I intended to go and see Willie immediately.

I went back into the Chamber and listened in a desultory way to the Law and Order debate on a Liberal motion. The wets on our side were prominent, although there was one very good speech by Dudley Smith.[2] After a bit I slid along the benches and asked Roger Sims if he could arrange a short meeting with Willie, and this was duly effected for 7 p.m.

Willie, of course, is a terrific operator. He was effusive when he greeted me: 'So good of you … so glad you were re-elected … I really mean that,' etc. etc. He led off and gabbled massively about his plans for prison building, raged at the Governor of Wormwood Scrubs for spilling the beans in the press and so forth. Whenever I tried to speak Willie said: 'Yes' gravely and fixed me with his oyster eyes. The substance of our agreement I set out in a letter, ostensibly for Roger Sims, but really for Willie's eyes, the following morning. Fortunately, Willie is more amenable to persuasion on this since his painful experiences at Party Conference than formerly. I do not know that the

---

[1] Robert Kilroy-Silk, Member of Parliament for Ormskirk, considered by AC to be extremely left-wing, member of the Select Committee on Home Affairs.

[2] Dudley Smith, MP for Warwick and Leamington since 1968 (Brentford and Chiswick 1959–66).

assurances that he gave me will amount to much, but I did my best.

Plymouth train   *Friday, 27 November*

Filled with 'set-backs' – my failure to get the Defence chair (which seemed to me to be 'in the bag', my cocking-up of the 'set' PM's questions and now today, devastatingly dear, beloved Tip-book's rejection by RCB.[1]

I just don't understand this; like Jane I am *shitted* by it, shitted *for him*, who so genuinely and unbelievably against all the odds triumphed at Pirbright and 'swotted up' for his lecturette. I was so proud, with all his new friends, and circle and prospects. What a blow it must be for him. What now? I somehow feel that whatever job he gets he will always think wistfully of the Guards. As will I. I will hardly be able to look at a Guards detachment, just as soon, it seems, I will never be able to cross Westminster Bridge again or drive round Parliament Square.

I will telephone Jerry Wiggin and see if he can get the papers from RCB – which could give us some help perhaps.

Saltwood   *Sunday, 29 November*

Still very depressed. I specially left Lilian a note last night to make sure he came up and said 'goodnight'. Excuse being that I wanted the copy of the *Motor* with the year's road tests in it. He didn't although James did. I lay awake for ages hoping he might and thought of my old age when it will be not hours, but days that I will wait sadly for a visit from the boys.

The Winter Office is so nice, but like everything and everywhere, it needs tidying, attention, TIME. A fine day, but cold, cold, and with a keen wind. Before breakfast darling Jane had 'hysterics' because the kitchen fire wouldn't light. I wish, I really do wish, I could find some way of saving her some of the drudgery. A minute ago I

---

[1] Andrew retook his RCB (Regular Commissions Board) the following year and passed. He would join the Life Guards, rise to the rank of Major and retire in 1994.

went into the kitchen and she was brillo-scrubbing the bottom of a saucepan.

At breakfast I grumbled something about the Deeds not being in the Deed-box.[1] She pointed out that she had not got the time to clear out the safe – with VAT two weeks behind, Christmas shopping to do, all the food for the party *and* the dinner to prepare, plus Christmas in prospect – and anyway from the bedroom window she could see ten vehicles 'standing out'. Perfectly true.

Cloisters   *Thursday, 3 December*

In some strange way I continue to warm to Ted Heath, who these days sits only one place away from me. David Howell had made a singularly inept and colourless presentation of the case for allowing heavy, or hea*vier*, juggernauts to free range over the roads of the Kingdom and the House was restive. Criticisms came from every side, although after about a half hour they had retained a repetitive quality. In an effort to produce something new Richard Mitchell[2], now of the SDP, raised the question of the dangers presented by static juggernauts at night – 'particularly as they are usually parked outside houses belonging to persons other than the driver.'

It was a case of the big-man-move-with-surprising-speed. Although he inclined his head very slightly, and his smile was arched and lethargic. Ted's reaction was instantaneous, faster than anyone else on our bench. 'That is a very insulting thing to say about lorry drivers,' he said to us, 'that they are always parked outside other people's houses at night.' Genuinely funny and unexpected.

---

[1]Although, surprisingly, AC makes no mention in his journal, all indebtedness to C. Hoare & Co. had finally been cleared a year before. The deeds arrived back at Saltwood on 23 December 1980.
[2]Richard Mitchell, Labour MP for Southampton, Itchen from 1971 (Southampton Test 1966–71) until joining the SDP earlier in the year.

Cloisters   *Tuesday, 8 December*

Lunched with Frank Johnson.[1] He is so quick and alert and youthfully intelligent; delightful company.

'There is an incredibly beautiful waitress who sometimes serves this table,' he said, nervously apprehensive. And our luck was in and she materialised, an absolutely devastating honey-blonde of about twenty-two; incredible, faultless in appearance, but when she spoke, utterly anaphrodisiac, ridiculous hockey-girl voice, 'Righty-ho,' Betje-manesque.

Frank pretended he wanted to talk about the Tory Party, but he really prefers to talk about the Nazis, concerning whom he is curious, but not, of course, sympathetic. Yes, I told him, I was a Nazi, I really believed it to be the ideal system, and that it was a disaster for the Anglo-Saxon races and for the world that it was extinguished. He both gulped and grinned, 'But surely, er, you mean . . . (behaving like an unhappy interviewer in *Not the Nine O'Clock News* after, e.g., Pamela Stephenson had said something frightfully shocking) . . . ideally in terms of administrative and economic policy . . . you cannot really, er . . .' Oh yes, I told him, I was completely committed to the whole philosophy. The blood and the violence was an essential ingredient of its strength, the heroic tradition of cruelty every bit as powerful and a thousand times more ancient than the Judaeo-Christian ethic.

Even he, I think, was slightly shocked. How can you say such a thing? he kept repeating. Meaning, not how can you say such a thing, but how do you dare put it into words. 'You might be quoted in Atticus.' I said I didn't care and, anyway, I had already been quoted as saying this very thing in Atticus.[2] He agreed, he and Hitchens had talked about it at the time and just like everyone here they took refuge in the convention that Alan-doesn't-really-mean-it. He-only-says-it-to-shock, etc. Frank said that people simply will not allow the reality that a 'toff' could be serious about these views, whereas if they were being expressed by someone like Tony Marlow or Nicholas Winterton, he would be ostracised.

The only time we talked about the Tory Party was when we both spontaneously at the same moment expressed our growing admiration

---

[1] Frank Johnson, Parliamentary sketch writer on *The Times*.

[2] AC was profiled in the *Sunday Times* Atticus column by Christopher Hitchens in February, 1980.

for Ted. I said that it was not necessarily his policies – although these were being expressed in a much more sensible and original style than of old – but his whole personal demeanour was creditable. He had been through the furnace, of rejection and contempt, and emerged unalloyed. Frank agreed. As ardent Heath-haters of old we felt that such a change was a credit to our objectivity.

Later that afternoon in the Economics Debate Ted spoke very brilliantly, ranging far and wide, a relaxed demolition job. He even managed to turn Enoch on the ropes when The Prophet, his own features contorted with fury, told Ted to 'take that grin off your face.' 'The Rt. Hon. gentleman can ask me to do many things, but that is not one of them,' said Ted, and the House roared with laughter in support.

Cloisters   *Wednesday, 9 December*

The Chef had sent a message, as I require him to do, that there was fresh lobster and so I left Brooks's early and went back to the House Dining Room at 9 p.m. Ian Gow was at the other end of the table I joined at which were also seated two Whips (John Stradling Thomas and John Cope), and two Ministers (Lynda Chalker[1] and Tom King[2]). Very ostentatiously and splendidly he passed me across the text of a Question that he wanted me to table for the Prime Minister on a 'set' subject – the accession of Portugal to the EEC. This was particularly loyal and kind of him so soon after my appalling gaffe over the *Morning/Daily Star*. He is *very* good at healing wounds, however slight and even when self-inflicted. When he got up to pay his bill I followed him into the corridor and gave him the amusing news, which I had discovered on Monday evening when I took Andrew to Pratt's, that both Peter Walker and Michael Heseltine had been black-balled. As Jane had said when I told her, this was practically the only encouraging bit of news in the last six months. What a splendid bastion of ancient squirearchical values that place is, that it should even these days feel

---

[1] Lynda Chalker, MP for Wallasey since February 1974, a junior Minister at Health and Social Security since 1979.
[2] Tom King, MP for Bridgwater since 1970, Local Government Minister since 1979.

strong enough to black-ball two up-and-coming Privy Councillors and members of the Cabinet!

However, things then turned nasty for, as we paced along the corridor, Ian told me that little Albert Costain had been making trouble about my intentions regarding Folkestone. Ian said it would be a 'snub' to people who 'had worked so long and loyally for me at election time, also the fact that I had abandoned them would "weigh very heavily" with the Selection Committee.' Sod, sod, sod, sod. Not only was this a tiresome thing to hear from such a source, but it also illuminated Ian's deviousness. Quite feline he is, or rather like some Russian Grandmaster, seeing always many moves ahead. Just as the reason he had taken me out to dinner the night after my defeat for the Defence Chair was not primarily to console me, but just as much (I suspect) because he already perceived my somewhat tetchy manner when I had questioned the Prime Minister about referenda the previous week and, knowing that I was number two on her list the following week, felt obliged to ensure that I didn't use that position to make trouble. And similarly his open impression of friendship and trust at the dinner table was designed to put me in a good mood before he warned off my overtures to the Folkestone constituency.

Cloisters   *Thursday, 10 December*

I had a mini-triumph today, and quite unexpected. The fascination of the House of Commons is that one can never be certain in one's prediction of the outcome of events, even from hour to hour.

I had been placed at very short notice on the Committee of the Local Government (Miscellaneous Provisions) Bill and went in neither having read the Bill, nor attended any stage of the debates on the floor. To my alarm and amazement I noticed that the very first amendment was being put by the likeable, but low-key, Shirley Summerskill,[1] requiring the Government to license pop festivals – and Raison, dutifully reading his Home Office brief, was actually resisting this! I rose in my seat and made a totally impromptu speech, referring to the closet trendiness in the Conservative Party and the absurdity of

---

[1] Dr Shirley Summerskill, MP for Halifax since 1964, and Opposition front bench shadow spokesman on Home Affairs.

resisting such a reasonable amendment. Colleagues pricked up their ears, abandoned their correspondence and it soon became plain to the Front Bench and the Whip that there was not the slightest chance of saving the clause after it was put to a vote. So now pop festivals will have to be licensed. One of those tiny little episodes for which one can claim credit – like me blocking the Local Government (again!) Ethnic Groups Grants Bill in 1979.

Saltwood   *Saturday, 12 December*

London has been snowbound all week. Lovely by the logfire – but not as relaxed as could be, hidden stress. I've totally lost interest in Plymouth, that's the fact. Don't bother with press releases any more, or any kind of self-promotion. I don't know anyone in Plymouth other than a few narrow Conservatives. I suppose it might be recoverable with 18 months dedication in the run-up; but can I afford the time? Have I the inclination? I must leave some record, and it should really be my big philosophico-historical treatise – can only do this with the Commons research facilities available. But everyone warns me against trying for Folkestone including, most recently and most disconcertingly, Ian Gow.

Drawing directly on from that there is our party next Saturday – the celebrated local benefit, now coming off in a rather different atmosphere to that which one had planned; people definitely wary, more suspicious. So much so that I said to Jane, only half in jest, that one should not put in for Folkestone at all, *but* announce an (sic) intention not to stand again in Plymouth. This would leave one free to apply for some of the other local seats (Rye, Maidstone etc). Much depends on the answers – in deeds as well as words – to my letter last week to IG. I would, though, be very sorry to miss the wheeling-and-dealing of the opening days of the new Parliament.

Saltwood   *Saturday, 19 December*

Our party for the local nobs. Much anxiety about who would or
would not come, how the hell we identify them anyway, etc. Masses
of flowers and greenery everywhere, log fires blazing in every fireplace
and – for the first time in fifty years – upper and lower halls properly
lit, as I had raided the Great Library and brought back a number of
lamp standards. Jane valiantly changed plugs throughout the morning
from three-pin to two-pin so that we could use all Mr Paine's old
sockets put in in the early '50s. No fuses blew and the place looked
wonderful.

First to arrive (and, incidentally, the last to leave) was the editor of
the *Folkestone Herald* and his *very* young and pretty wife. He, a little
Welshman with dark curly hair, not as unfriendly as I had feared. Soon
they were pouring in. To get over the identification problem we had
posted William[1] at the door in order to take guests' names and
announce them. Jane and I stood in the lower hall and directed guests
to the upper hall where Sarah and James handed them champagne.
Thereafter they drifted about, most of them finding their way into
the Library where soon a comforting roaring noise built up.

We had two set-pieces. First was the arrival of my father and
Nolwen. He, very ga-ga and tottery (deliberately so, I suspect, like
Harold Macmillan often is), was kind of wheeled across the Library
by William who kept saying: 'Make way for his Lordship; his Lordship
here wants to get to his chair,' etc. This went well and my father's
eccentricities were much appreciated. Examples, when Sarah, who
looked very glamorous, came near them with a plate of canapés,
Nölwen introduced her, 'This is James' girlfriend . . .' A look of great
pain spread over my father's features. All he said was, 'Oh dear.' I
singled out and introduced a number of big-wigs. As each one
approached, my father writhed and groaned. Sometimes he seemed
almost to be holding up his hands with an expression of defensive
panic, like those celebrated pictures of the Hungarian secret policemen
being ushered out of their barracks before being mown down in the
uprising of 1956. Curiously, though, this went quite well.

Everybody seemed contented and appreciative and, at just the right
moment, the ringers of hand bells arrived (one of them, I noticed,

---

[1] 'William' had served Mrs Brown, a neighbour of the Clarks, as butler for many years
and after her death he used to help at Saltwood on social occasions.

being that attractive blonde from whom I had bought crab apple jelly at the St John's fête the previous Saturday). They rang their bells, to the tune of a number of familiar Christmas carols, very prettily. It was a happy and nostalgic sound as it echoed off the gothic tracery of the lower hall and I saw poor Peggy,[1] looking drawn and beautiful in a black dress, put her head round the pillar of the top corridor leading from the dining room. Was she thinking of her dear dead Robert? I fear she must have been.

The chairman of the Association arrived very late. He drank a great deal and gabbled. He is a shameless 'wet' ... Why didn't MPs speak out? It was time to turn the tide, etc. I have seldom heard these arguments put so badly. He stayed until the very end, leaving simultaneously with the editor of the local paper. Indeed, in all but the narrowly medical sense, he was a complete spastic. I cannot make out whether this is a good or bad thing from the point of view of my own interests.

Saltwood   *Wednesday, 23 December*

Today we went to Jock Massereene's party (black tie) for not local – as ours – but county nobs.[2] Icy cold, the Hall of Chilham, standard medieval conditions as Jock had broken the central heating that morning and a huge oak tree blazed in the eight-foot fireplace, scorching those who stood near it, while those guests who stood at receding radii from twenty to sixty feet shivered and could see the steam from their breath as they spoke.

Guests, mainly worthy and rich rather than smart in the Chips sense. I saw Etonian chums like Robin Leigh-Pemberton[3] and Adrian Swire[4]. But Billy Rees-Davies[5] struck a raffish note and in some manner admirably contrived to have the three prettiest women in the

---

[1] Peggy Wilson, wife of the Head Gardener at Saltwood, who worked for the Clarks. Her younger son, Robert, worked as a keeper at John Aspinall's zoo at Canterbury and had been killed by a rogue tiger the previous year.

[2] Viscount Massereene and Ferrard, a friend of AC's with whom he shared an interest in animal welfare.

[3] Robin Leigh-Pemberton, chairman of the National Westminster Bank and Lord Lieutenant-elect of Kent.

[4] Adrian Swire, chairman of John Swire & Son since 1966.

[5] William Rees-Davies, MP for Thanet West since 1974 (Isle of Thanet 1953–74).

room around him and hanging on his words. Perhaps he enjoys that mysterious gift of being able to compel female attendance which William Orpen described so vividly in *Onlooker in France.*

We carried plates of food, which was delicious, '... all come in from mee estates in Scotland,' said Jock, into one of the ante-chambers and I found myself in conversation with a well-ish preserved blonde lady in her 50s who (something-something) living at Leeds.

'Did you know Olive Bailey?' I said to her.

'I am her daughter.'

Unabashed I immediately asked her about David Margesson,[1] who is the subject of fascination by me as he was Chief Whip at the time that the Tory Party had all the right decisions available to it as options and made all the wrong ones. But she clammed up and wouldn't say anything wider than that 'David-was-so-sweet-to-everyone . . .' etc.

Bill Deedes and I had a long chat. We agreed that the miners strike was the key battle ground on which a spectacular victory could turn the tide of public opinion in favour of the Government. The Lady must *not* give in on this. Unpopular though she is at the moment, she could not be loathed as much as Arthur Scargill. All at once we could redeem our pledges 'to do something' about the unions.

Cloisters   *Thursday, 24 December*

Number two for the Prime Minister and, inspired by my conversation with Bill Deedes the previous evening, I had composed a form of supplementary that invited her to stand firm against the miners. There were frantic messages from Ian all over the boards asking me to get in touch with him. But in the light of the earlier débâcle I did not consult but simply sent him a note setting out in general terms the sort of question I intended to ask about the miners. Still greater panic, messages everywhere, whips and runners on the look-out for me all over the Palace. A scribbled note arrived. '*Don't* say anything about the miners. Ask a question about Poland.'

Hastily I improvised. It seemed that everyone had been requested

---

[1] David Margesson (1st Viscount). Legendary Tory Chief Whip from 1931; appointed Secretary of State for War by Churchill in December 1940, but made the scapegoat after the fall of Singapore in 1942.

to ask about Poland and by the time I rose there was very little left to say except the rather obvious point that suspension of aid would harm the Polish people who seemed more deserving of sympathy than retribution. This whole Polish business is a balls-up. Those cretinous hard-liners baying for blood. Their advice is the precise mirror obverse of Jeremy Thorpe's celebrated suggestion that the 'V' Bombers should be used to devastate the Rhodesian railway system.

Saltwood   *Boxing Sunday, 1981*

Lowered by the decline in the quality of my looks. My face now fat – I can feel it in the neck and cheeks when I wash in cold water, and all those double chins and neck creases. On Christmas Eve I went down and tried to contact the Rev Woods about times of services.[1] Just as I arrived an enormous congregation of worthies started leaving, filed out and down the steps of St Leonards Church, not *one*, or rather only one, a foxy-faced blonde, looked at one, even out of curiosity.

God, yes. How moving the *Brideshead* film was, because of course Lady Marchmain won, in the end. And the drama of that moment when C went in to 'talk' to him, and tried to persuade him to see the priest! I would convert, I would love to convert, if there was someone sympathetic I could talk to.

I wondered what's happened to 'Desmond'?[2]

---

[1] The Reverend Canon Norman Woods officiated at AC's funeral, with the Reverend Canon Reg Humphriss of Saltwood.

[2] Desmond Hazelhurst, friend of the Beuttlers, who left the army to become a priest.

1982

First day of the New Year – ORDER AND SECURITY. Not especially inspiring objectives but if we set certain relatively moderate resolutions, to be adhered to, improvements may occur within the frame (sic).

A little more care of fitness, figure and appearance. New Lesley & Roberts suits and San Marco shirting shall help here, plus shampooing, brilliantine, 'smell' etc. (I wonder if the Shadow will materialise from Michael Walker.)[1]

A general 'watching brief' in politics. The die is not yet cast with Folkestone, but looking unlikely. This will impose extra loading in Plymouth for a 'resurgence', but not impossible.

Total financial security now, but must hope in the finish to throw 4x4.

We were reading the papers at breakfast when I suddenly looked up to find a very curious strained expression on Jane's face. As she looked at 'Crossbencher' she started reading '... tea at Saltwood Castle ... don't come round,' as I moved panically across to read over her shoulder. I sat down. There was an item, not especially hostile, and certainly not inaccurate, about my designs on the Folkestone Constituency. H'm.

First day back. The House lovely and welcoming in its embrace. A number of invitations to go on radio and television in pursuance of my dispute with Alderson about Special Branch files. (He has done me a good turn by threatening me with a two-year prison sentence, which gives the exchanges extra piquancy.) Jane amusingly said this

---

[1] AC had fantasised over Christmas buying this Rolls Royce 'just to keep in London for suits, scents and cigars.'

morning: 'You must face the fact that there are quite a lot of people dotted about who would be quite glad to see you put away for two years.'

At the Home Affairs Committee I made a long and withering attack on Willie for his pusillanimous attitude to the demands of law and order hardliners. Ian Gow, who had come in just in time to hear this in its entirety, came round and sat on the platform beside me at the end and asked me to go to the Smoking Room. 'I cannot, I have to go to Willie's room at 6.45 p.m. and if I don't go he will swing something at the Officers and be able to say "I didn't warn you because you weren't there," as he invariably does.' We agreed to postpone it, but it was a good sign.

Willie was thinnish, pale and slightly rattled. Ted Gardner very loyally did not 'shop' me, stated my views as broadly being those of the Committee 'as a whole'. And, luckily for me, Roger Sims had not been in attendance – although I assume that toad John Major[1] will report my attack. And, of course, Donald Thompson[2] will report it to the Chief Whip. In spite of having lost weight Willie has gone off a bit. Indeed, he gave the impression of not knowing, on occasion, his arse from his elbow. Said mugging was not a crime of violence (even his own Ministers were startled at this), that the dismissed Chief Constable had a right of appeal. 'Who to?' I asked. 'Oh no, not a right of appeal exactly, but could make a lot of trouble,' and so on.

That evening I dined at Pratt's. Michael Ancram[3] had brought in Robert Atkins and so we could have a laugh together about the 'Crossbencher' item. Of course, we dislike each other quite strongly – a true example of 'incompatibility'. He has an unpleasant, cruel face, and I am certain that he is by inclination and instinct a subversive. But I must admit that he does have a very fast wit. The Earl of Cathcart, as always, was at the dining room table. Told who he was, Atkins made some instant witticism about his being patron of Teddy Taylor.[4] We discussed the question of office, and both Ancram and Atkins paid

---

[1] John Major, MP for Huntingdonshire since 1979, recently appointed PPS to Ministers of State at the Home Office.

[2] Donald Thompson, MP for Sowerby since 1979, Whip to the Home Affairs Committee.

[3] Michael Ancram, the Earl of Ancram, MP for Edinburgh South since 1979 (Berwickshire and E. Lothian February–October 1974).

[4] Edward (Teddy) Taylor, an effective and uncompromising right-winger, much disliked by a section of the Party, including Robert Atkins. MP for Southend East since 1980 (Glasgow Cathcart, 1964–79). The Earl of Cathcart, a professional senior soldier (retired) and now a deputy speaker, House of Lords.

me compliments, said I should be in the Government – why wasn't I? etc. 'How the hell should I know?' I could say, though, with absolute conviction that I would never take anything in Education, the DHSS, or any PPSship, except the Prime Minister or Leader of the House.

Cloisters   *Tuesday, 19 January*

A message from a young girl reporter on the *Folkestone Herald* about the Crossbencher item. I had to give a good deal of thought to this. I said it would be a great honour, etc. etc., but my own Association had decided that they wanted me to stay in Plymouth and (key phrase, which required a lot of brain-racking), *unless they changed their mind*, there was nothing further that I could do or say.

She also asked me various questions about my row with Alderson, and on the whole seemed well disposed. But we will have to wait and see what the papers say on Saturday.

Saltwood   *Sunday, 31 January*

Decisions, hmm. Can no longer avoid the 'crunch' (sic) of *going for* Folkestone (which means abandoning Plymouth) or standing aside. Beth and Wilf came round and talked. All right as far as it goes, but of course they have *no* idea of how politics operate, very little idea about how a constituency association works. When I recall the skill and care which Graham put into fixing the result at Plymouth my heart sank at the scale of the task which was in prospect. We talked each other up into a state of mutual confidence. Of course I would really be far and away the best candidate for the division, but I always remember Jane's dry comment when I triumphantly read out that letter from some woman who had been arranging a flower show, or whatever it was, '... many would like you to be Folkestone's next MP.'

All Jane said was: 'Many wouldn't.'

The only point of any substance that emerged was how influential the Margarys were. It was suggested that I go and see them.

I telephoned Lympne Castle. An elderly but not particularly accommodating voice answered and said in somewhat peremptory tones that
they were out to lunch. I rang again at 5 p.m. and they had still not
returned. I finally caught Harry Margary at 7 p.m. and without any
preamble asked him if I could come over and have a chat. He hesitated
fractionally, then assented.

I have not been inside the private quarters of Lympne Castle since
Murray Payne's[1] day and the quality of the furnishings had deteriorated
considerably: worn, but not tasteful, chintzes, Benares brass warming
pans, etc. I had forgotten how unpleasant the Margarys are. Exactly
the sort of people with whom a mutual antipathy develops instantly.
Harry motioned me to sit between them. They had a faintly conspiratorial look as of two people going to enjoy themselves at their
victim's expense. I opened the bowling by asking if either of them
(note the use of the word 'either') were proposing to apply for the
vacancy caused by Albert's retirement. Fluttering disclaimers. 'But we
have a problem ...' said Deirdre Margary, echoed by her nasty
husband. They explained that their son (I didn't even know there was
such a person) was going to stand. Subsequent enquiries showed that
he was a watery stockbroker who seldom came to Kent and who had
in the distant past been Chairman of the local Young Conservatives.
'Well clearly you must support him,' etc. etc., I could not get out fast
enough. No point in wasting any more time.

Harry Margary didn't want to let me off so lightly, rambled a bit
about his massive work at Shepway Council. Dutifully I paid appropriate tribute. They warned me off to some extent but there was no
intimacy of any kind, indeed only the bare minimum of good manners.

Cloisters   *Monday, 1 February*

At some point last week in the queue in the Tea Room (I cannot
remember which day) I fell into conversation with the Whip to the
Home Affairs Committee, Donald Thompson. I repeated to him
Paddy Mayhew's complaint to me about the proceedings of the
Committee. Later I said that it is my personal opinion that in his

---

[1] Air Commodore Murray Payne, DFC, who was married to Hilma Howard de Walden
and lived at Lympne Castle in the early fifties.

present position Willie is an 'electoral liability'. I thought Thompson looked a bit unhappy at this; and this is unusual for a Whip, who has been trained to hide his feelings and look alert and expectant at all expressions of opinion, however deviant. But I thought no more of it. I am now absolutely certain that Willie has been told – whether direct by Donald Thompson or (more likely) by John Major, who has always loathed me.

I had a quick word after Questions with Michael Jopling, told him the position, how embarrassing it was and suggested that he tick off Donald Thompson to make sure it doesn't happen again. My real motive was that he would bear this in mind and, hopefully, discount it when Willie next expressed his antipathy and disapproval. Michael was very grave and sympathetic, said that Willie had been getting a lot of flak lately; we must build up his confidence; that he was absolutely indispensable to the Prime Minister, always supported her etc. etc. Said: 'Anything you can do to help in this respect . . .' More or less said, in other words, that it was for me to try and repair the damage.

Later that evening I went into the Smoking Room with Tony Buck and was frozen out of Willie's circle with that technique at which he is such a master. Buck and I sat adjoining but were pointedly excluded, even with the tacit connivance of Ian Gow, who was also in the group, from the jollity and conversation. A little later we were joined by Billy Rees-Davies, making it a real duds table. Tony, who is a genuine habituated social and political climber, became increasingly uneasy and kept looking over to their table. It got worse when we rose to leave. With split-second timing (i.e. just as I had my hand on the door but Tony was a couple of paces behind) Willie hailed Tony with that great roar of greeting and hauled him over into the group.

I worried quite a lot about this, but curiously it had the effect of making me feel I ought to stay on at Plymouth and not take any risks. If Willie and I are going to be openly at war it means he can always block my advancement but, equally, with no longer any restraints on my being *really* objectionable towards him. As there was no vote that evening I journeyed thoughtfully homeward.

When I got back I told Jane both about my interview with the Chief and about Willie's behaviour in the Smoking Room. She got the point at once, said that it was the 'sign' we had been waiting for. 'You must stay on just so as to deprive him of the satisfaction of knowing, until the last possible moment, that you won't be coming back.' I agreed, said it was just like my determination not to give my father the pleasure of my dying before he did. She got the point completely, even before I had finished expostulating it. Though Willie didn't give a bugger about what happened to the economy, or even indeed the fate of The Lady. He is far more Machiavellian than he is given credit for (and he knows that I am one of the few people in the Party who has rumbled him) and the reason he gives The Lady so much 'invaluable support' is because he feels she is bound to crash and he will have a significant part to play in the Government of All the Talents that will embellish the Great Hung Parliament. The one sector where he *cannot* make any concession is in the Home Office field as there the changes might not be so easily reversible. So, he has made himself indispensable on the broad canvas, and is allowed a free hand to implement by stealth or otherwise the progressive policies of the Home Office.

Whether or not he has a veto on junior appointments and has twice vetoed mine (Ian has more or less told me), I will make a speech praising Willie and try and get it issued by Central Office and, hopefully, published in some of the national papers. I will then be able to show this to Jopling – and to Willie himself – as evidence that I am doing my best. This won't of course convince Willie, but it will satisfy Jopling and make it more difficult for Willie to veto me in the future.

Cloisters   *Thursday, 4 February*

I heard today an account of the two meetings which the Officers of the Defence Committee have 'enjoyed'.

On Monday they went to Downing Street. Julian Critchley told me how, for weeks beforehand, Tony Buck had been getting himself into a lather, asking him to prepare a paper, text of possible questions, etc. etc., just as he used to do to me when I was his vice-chairman. Julian had produced some material but, as it turned out, Buck appeared totally unprepared. The Officers sat (as usual) in the yellow drawing room with Blaker[1] and Pattie standing deferentially in the wings.

---

[1] Peter Blaker, MP for Blackpool South since 1964; Armed Forces Minister since 1981. Geoffrey Pattie had been Parliamentary Under-Secretary for Defence Procurement since 1981 also.

Everyone was waiting for Buck to say something but he was tongue-tied. After about 35 seconds of complete silence The Lady gimletted Julian with her icy blue eyes and said, in her most hectoring tone, 'Julian, why are you looking around the room like that?' Julian, as he said, simultaneously flushing but with a *faux-rire*, 'I was looking at that gilt mirror over your mantelshelf.' Winston then laid in, threw leather rather than punches.

Of course The Lady ran rings round them, picking off each one in turn and giving them a real rasping, or basting. So demoralised were they that they 'forgot' (unbelievably) to raise their principal bone of contention which was why the Chiefs of Staff had been forbidden to address the Committee. A breathless shambles, they were evicted from Number 10 after about forty minutes.

The next day they went to see the Secretary of State. He, if you please, had the effrontery to tell them that the reason the Chiefs of Staff 'could not' come was because if they did they would have to be prepared to talk also to Labour and SDP Committees – not that there are such things anyway. Amazingly some officers went along with this. Victor Goodhew with his old Whips training nodded sagely. Little Trippier, rubberily ambitious, said nothing. For some reason even Winston (perhaps chastened by his experiences the previous day) sold up. Tony Buck, however, as an ex-Minister, likes having the Chiefs of Staff and he, Critchley and Atkins put up a heavy counter-attack. Tempers flared and, by several accounts, glass was broken.

I saw John Nott at lunch today and made some jocular reference to the meeting, at which he grinned ruefully and rolled his eyes. I think I might leak details of it to Nick Comfort of the *Telegraph* as a quid pro quo for his carrying my laudatory speech about Willie in Monday's paper.

Cloisters   *Friday, 5 February*

I put the finishing touches to the Willie speech, slavishly adulatory. In my present mood it really sticks in the throat. I rang Paddy Mayhew from my desk, pretending to ask for advice as to what to include, but in reality in order to get the word spread that I was making a 'helpful' contribution. Then I approved the text and Alison took it round to Central Office and handed it to Leslie Way. I spoke to Leslie on the phone – it was lucky for me that he was duty officer this weekend because I could explain the background.[1] This is the first time I have ever released a speech through Central Office, and we will see what happens.

The Crownhill AGM was endless. Poor old Frank Harding and Wallie Rowland, a real geriatric pair, yur-yurred their way through the agenda, halting, stammering and stuttering. The only moment of interest came when a Mrs MacDonald, who had been sitting in the front row with that special demeanour of someone who is spoiling for a fight, suddenly felt herself to be insulted by a remark, an aside almost, made by the treasurer and stomped out with a great flurry of head tossing, apparel, rustling of papers, etc. At last my moment came and I had to snap out of my 'brown study'. (All too apparent to the audience, I was told later.) I plodded my way through the text. It was the only time I have ever made a speech to my own supporters and been heckled. John Dobell was the first to interrupt, and others followed him. Never mind, it is now 'on record'.

Saltwood   *Sunday, 7 February*

To my gratification, Michael Jones of the *Sunday Times* reported my speech in depth and quite got – indeed even embellished – the point about it being coded, about Willie being in jeopardy and so on. Things are working out exactly as I had intended.

Cloisters   *Monday, 8 February*

The first thing to appear in my box was a special handwritten note from Willie, sent over by despatch rider with a purple sticker on the envelope, thanking me for my support, saying how we must discuss these things more often, etc. etc. Probably penned, I suspect, before he read the Nick Comfort article on the same subject which went a stage further and carried the rather ominous 'Whitehall briefing' that

[1] L. K. Way, the former Political Correspondent of the *Western Morning News*, now worked at Conservative Central Office.

the Prime Minister was rallying support for the Home Secretary but if his performance still did not come up to her, or the Party's, expectations, she might be 'forced' to replace him.

At this evening's meeting in the Committee Robert Atkins, whose machinations as a subversive and mouth-piece of the left are almost, but not quite, as convoluted as my own in the opposite corner, made a statement saying how much he welcomed my speech on the weekend and how he would like to express his whole-hearted support of Willie Whitelaw, etc. etc. This did not go down especially well in the Committee, the Party's antennae are sensitive and people realise that my pro-Willie speech was a far more telling indication of my hostility to him than any form of public criticism. Within about twelve hours, and with my having said nothing further, it has changed in assessment from being supportive in character to being almost Judas-like. At the officers' meeting that followed the Committee Willie looked unhappy and would not catch my eye at all.

Cloisters   *Tuesday, 9 February*

Mark Schreiber [*The Economist*] rang me at the Albany, just as I was on my fourth cup of rust-coloured PG Tips.

'I want to talk to you about yourself and Willie.'

Well, I remember Mark Schreiber. I remember him when I was a candidate, or aspirant candidate, and he was one of the people, the new wave of humane classless (although he is in fact quite grand) Tories, whom Ted Heath was grooming for high office. His lip certainly curled at the sight and sound of me in those days. But successive Associations refused to adopt him and, disappointed, he became Lobby Correspondent for the *Economist*; from which position he continues to disseminate, though without much influence and his pieces are usually unsigned, his leftish sentiments.

So, after a longish pause, I said: 'I don't understand what you mean.'

'In the past you have attacked Willie, but over the weekend you made a speech in support of him.'

'I have never attacked him. I may have criticised him; but never in public.'

After a certain amount of preliminary jockeying, I did talk to him but it was clear that he was very sympathetic to Willie so I had to tread carefully. I could not resist saying though that although I was doing my best to defend Willie from public attack, I felt that there was a widespread realisation in the Party that he was an electoral liability and would have to go before we square up for the next general election.

Cloisters   *Monday, 22 February*

The night of our annual dinner with the Home Secretary in a private room at the Garrick. Things a little stilted to begin with; we drank champagne out of silver mugs. Mellowing set in. Willie is just a tiny bit uncomfortable with his officers, particularly as Michael Mates,[1] who will always do as Willie tells him, had not turned up. John Wheeler[2] has moved away from him a little, conscious, I suspect, that Willie Whitelaw's reign is to be of finite duration and he should start a little 'distancing'. Ivor Stanbrook he loathes – and I must say, both to Stanbrook's credit and in justification of Willie's feelings, Ivor never stops attacking him at every opportunity, both public and private. Ted Gardner he is suspicious of, told John Major that he was '... too much under Alan Clark's influence.' And Alan Clark, well there *is* a very tricky relationship. I think he is a little frightened of me; he seldom catches my eye, but when he does there is sometimes a watery, pleading look in his expression. The trouble is, each regards the other as a traitor to his class.

The Home Secretary soon became jolly. He told, with much bellowing and groaning, of his experiences last week at St Aldate's Church in Oxford where, booked over a year in advance, he turned up for one of those lay preaching, question-and-answer sessions in the pulpit. To his great alarm he found that the Church was filled to bursting and the atmosphere evangelical in the highest degree. He described how the entire congregation *mimed* the words of each hymn, raising both hands to heaven at such words as 'arise', etc. A man in the congregation had turned to him and said: 'I found God here on

---

[1] Michael Mates, MP for Petersfield since October 1978.
[2] John Wheeler, MP for Paddington since 1979.

Wednesday of last week, do you think you will, today?' 'I, er, don't know,' bellowed Willie, miserably looking round.

He went on to recount how half way through they had a break and he and other distinguished visitors, clerics, etc. went up to a room above the vestry with the preacher. They knelt and various dignitaries started to recite prayers in turn. 'I suddenly realised with horror that it was moving round the circle and *I* was going to have to say a prayer.' Very splendidly, when it came to him, Willie simply mumbled, 'For what we are about to receive may the Lord make us truly thankful.'

The dinner wore on. Willie 'peaked' quite early, was interesting and sympathetic during the *prosciutto è melone*; grave during the salmon; muck-sweat and combative with the cheese; martyred and somnolent over the port. He said, interestingly, that he always asked himself where a process would end, rather than what would be the reaction when he started. This arose, apropos, when I asked why he has not sacked Gregory, the Chief Constable of the Yorkshire police who had made such a balls-up of the Ripper Case. Willie had told us that he thought Gregory was 'going', but no one must say anything in case that caused him to change his mind and fight.

Willie also said he was terribly worried about being unpopular in the Party, claimed he did not care about the Parliamentary Party, but hated losing the affection of the Party in the country.

All these observations were undertaken against a background of almost continuous and, I thought, rather ill-mannered interrogatories from Stanbrook – you're not strong enough, you have got no backbone, you're not giving a lead, you don't mean it, you are always looking for a compromise, etc. etc. At least twice I feebly said that we were assembled for a congenial and informative dinner, not as an annex to our usual post-committee meetings. Finally, and presumably inflamed by this, Willie launched into a great bellowing rampage against the *Daily Mail*. What triggered it off was that I warned him that there would be a row today when it was revealed that senior officers of the Commission for Racial Equality had had their salaries doubled in the last three years and got a £50 a day attendance allowance. Willie alternately roared on about how David English's sole purpose was to bring down the Government – no, no, surely not, we all cried – or to force him personally to resign – more likely we all thought, but said nothing.

At intervals Willie yelled that he would 'resign his seat' (the wrong phrase, he cannot really have meant this, surely?) or lapsed into melancholia, chin slumped on his waistcoat, 'I did not allow this; I did not agree to this; *why* is it happening?' and so on (about the increase in salaries for the CRE).

Promptly, however, at two minutes to eleven, he snapped out of it, rose to his feet, literally in the middle of somebody else's sentence, delivered a short farewell homily and made his way out to his armoured black XJ6.

Cloisters   *Tuesday, 23 February*

At breakfast today Tristan Garel-Jones surprised me by saying that he thought Willie should be 'moved'. I think he may even have used the word 'sacked'. As a card-carrying wet and general softy on immigration etc. I would have thought he would be one of Willie's rearguard. These tides of opinion in the Party are mysterious. There is no doubt that uneasiness about Willie has spread right across all shades of opinion. I told him to speak to his Whip.

He then told me that the real dynamo of opposition to the present Government on the backbenches was not Ian Gilmour, still less Geoffrey Rippon, etc., but . . .

'Chris,' I said.

'Yes.'

He was rather crestfallen at my having spotted this. Apparently everyone shows Chris Patten their speeches, asks him what they ought to be doing at any given moment etc. Garel-Jones had the brilliant idea that Neil Marten[1] should be sacked and Chris Patten put in his place. He could not afford to refuse; he would be out of the country for half the year; and he would be saddled with a reputable 'wet' job, but in a sector where, officially, he has reservations. G-J told me that he would ask for a meeting with Jopling at which he would argue this. Actually, it is a very tidy solution and I will mention it to IG, with whom I am having dinner tonight. I told G-J that as he was meeting Jopling privately he might just as well state his reservations about Willie at the same time.

---

[1] Neil Marten, MP for Banbury since 1959; Minister for Overseas Development since 1979.

Cloisters   *Tuesday, 9 March*

Lunched today with John Wells and Geoffrey Finsberg.[1] The meal started slowly; John Wells always poses as a buffoon – which he very emphatically is not. But after a bit of wine had flowed the conversation moved into that special level of confidentiality which one only enjoys in the Members' Dining Room (and which was very much in my mind when I posed yesterday's question).[2]

John Wells has always been aggrieved at his exclusion from the Deputy Speakership. The train of succession that leads to the Speaker's Chair is, as J W. said: 'a very stubby ladder' and there is little room for intruders. But the discussion between him and Geoffrey about possible developments was fascinating.

Apparently, the Peterborough leak that Mark Carlisle might be the next Speaker was a Whip's plant to break the news gently to Jack Weatherill that he would not succeed. Both agreed, however, that Carlisle could not do the job. Geoffrey – gloomy and ill-looking as always – produced the brilliancy that *Willie* should be made Speaker. 'He cannot stay where he is' (every evidence of how widespread is this view in the Party I find welcome). For a while, briefly, there would be Conservatives as both Speaker and Deputy Speaker. But after the next election Jack Weatherill would go to the Lords in the Dissolution Honours and Joel Barnett (another inspired suggestion of Geoffrey Finsberg) would become deputy.

We discussed the errors and omissions of the first, 1979, Cabinet. JW, who certainly does not stand on the right of the Party, said that the historic consequences of Airey's assassination could never be fully assessed. I told him that the original list was drawn up by the quartet, Atkins, Whitelaw, Thorneycroft and the PM. JW rightly said that if Airey had still been alive he would have corrected many of those original errors of judgement. I must say that he also said that if Iain Macleod had been alive in 1972 Ted would never have made such a cock-up of the Conservative Government of that period. But, of course, if he had been, then history would really have been totally different and that is now too distant from us to be hypothetical.

Now I am going to go in to hear the Chancellor make his Budget

---

[1] Geoffrey Finsberg, MP for Hampstead since 1970; Parliamentary Under-Secretary, Health and Social Security since 1981.

[2] AC asked about Members' wives being allowed into the Dining Room.

Statement which I don't doubt will be very dull as well as being
crowded and smelly (the capacity of the air conditioning system is
inadequate for a completely full chamber). I have drunk half a bottle
of white burgundy in order to induce a benign doze.

Saltwood   *Wednesday, 10 March*

AGM in prospect – always a grisly affair, with its quota of pigging
malcontents. A message from Anne: '... Mrs Easton wants to know
if Mr Clark will take questions after his speech ...' Ugh! No, of course
not, if anyone wants to ask a question they can ask me personally. I
am not going to stand up there and, in James's phrase, just let them
throw things at me.

On the way back in the train I travelled with Joe Haines[1] (whom I
had seen in a most interesting TV programme the previous night, on
Whitehall briefings, though that, too, showed how much *out* of things
one is really). JH was talking to a fat pompous man with a red face,
very pleased with himself. I intruded on this conversation, relished
letting out that I was an MP. But the whole incident brought home
to me how *naked* one would be without those initials!

Would that I had opted for Folkestone! On the walks I confided to
Jane, who said, more or less, even if one did make the wrong decision
'you're ten years too old, haven't got long to go' etc. This was
particularly unfortunate as earlier in the walk I had been saying that I
didn't feel old – apropos of my father who is very shifty and unpleasant
though in perfect health. She didn't answer.

The one thing I dread, which I had visitations of this morning on
waking is a *void* in which, purposeless and disappointed one becomes
first pre, then actually cancerous.

[1]Joe Haines, chief leader writer of the *Daily Mirror* since 1978, had been Chief Press
Secretary to Harold Wilson in opposition and as Prime Minister, 1969–76.

House of Commons Library   *Monday, 22 March*

A bunch of Argentinians are horsing around in South Georgia. The thing started as an operation to retrieve 'scrap' (by what right do they go in there and remove 'scrap' anyway?) but they have now apparently hoisted the Argentine flag. I don't like this. If we don't throw them out, preferably shedding blood at the same time, they will try their hand in the Falklands.

Before dinner we had a kind of *ad hoc* meeting of the '92' at the far end of the Smoking Room. John Farr[1] has got a Question tomorrow, which is a Defence day. Quite narrowly drawn, on maritime air surveillance in the South Atlantic, but many of the boys are lining up to get in behind him. It's all down to that fucking idiot Nott, and his spastic 'Command Paper', which is effectively running down the entire Royal Navy so as to keep the soldiers in Rhine Army happy.

So let him answer the question. We know how easily he can get rattled. Quite good sport. Because it is as a result of his compliance that the Foreign Office can't 'negotiate' at all. There is no final contingency plan.

We are all of the same mind. We are the Henty boys – 'Deeds that Built the Empire', all that. But I am not sure how much support we can mobilise in the Party. 'Defence' to most colleagues only means The Cold War. They no longer think Imperially. I was saying, surely Margaret must sympathise? Nick Budgen sliced in – 'Don't bet on that, Alan. She is governed only by what the Americans want. At heart she is just a vulgar, middle-class Reaganite.'

We broke up ahead of the ten o'clock vote, but not before it was agreed that the strength of our feeling should be conveyed to the Chief [Michael Jopling]. Patrick Wall[2] and Julian Amery are to press for a statement tomorrow afternoon, from Atkins,[3] but the betting is that, remembering what we did to Nicky he will get one of his juniors to 'field' it.

---

[1] John Farr, MP for Harborough since 1959.
[2] Sir Patrick Wall, member of the Commons Select Committee on Defence since 1980.
[3] Humphrey Atkins, Lord Privy Seal since 1981.

Yesterday went well. Notters funked the Question on air surveillance in the South Atlantic and delegated it to Jerry Wiggin, his most junior junior. And a little later we got our FCO Statement and, sure enough, Atkins dodged it and put up languid, amiable, and faintly Godwatch Richard Luce.[1] The annunciator screen conformed to the requisite minimalist note by signalling the Statement as *South Georgia (Incident)*.

Perhaps this wasn't as clever as they thought. When a Cabinet Minister is answering there are many who, conscious of the whip-on-the-bench taking notes, will not want to seem too 'unhelpful'. With a Junior, though, such deference is not expected. Indeed many of those questioning him will probably want (or may even have been ejected from) his job.

Both Jerry and Richard are Etonians. Jerry is piggy-eyed, a typical Library[2] bully; Richard is handsome and courteous. Typical *Pop.* Jerry gave the show away immediately, 'The South Atlantic is outside the NATO area'. In other words we (or at least the MoD) don't give a toss.

Half an hour later Richard was almost swamped. At least thirty people on their feet, bobbing up and down, including Jim Callaghan – a rare intruder – and Denis Healey. Richard stuck to his brief. A few slices of pure FCO-speak – 'I much regret that some of the action which has been taken has not created a helpful atmosphere ...', and he repeated the Argentine claim that the whole operation was 'commercial', although having to admit that the ship which carried the 'scrap-dealers' was a naval one!

I could see the whips fussing, leaning down the bench and whispering to Ministers. John Farr raised the usual Point of Order after an unsatisfactory answer and signalled his intention to raise the subject in an Adjournment Debate. We've got the whole thing opened now. Clearly the Labour Party are also indignant, and if she [Mrs Thatcher] doesn't get the Argentines out by next week there will be a major disturbance.

But no sign of Ian Gow. He should be trawling the corridors, 'taking the temperature'.

---

[1] Richard Luce, MP for Shoreham since 1974 (Arundel and Shoreham, 1971–74), Minister of State at the Foreign and Commonwealth Office since 1981.

[2] 'Library' is Etonian parlance for Prefect.

On this topic I am disillusioned, as I believe are many, with The Lady.

Cloisters   *Thursday, 25 March*

Today I went on *Question Time*. I was meant to sparkle. But, as I said
to Jane when I drove her to Waterloo after we had lunched with Julian
Amery and the Turkish Ambassador, I felt like King Harold who was
forced to march south and fight the Battle of Hastings immediately
after Stamford Bridge. Because Julian, as always, had supplied one
with the most wonderful food and drink (Jane only just caught the
4.30 p.m. train) and by 5 p.m. I was feeling acid and sleepy. My
original plan had been to 'bant' and then rest, taking a quick slug of
vodka half-an-hour before going on the air.

As it was, by the time I arrived at the Greenwood Theatre Hospitality Room, I was sombre and withdrawn. I sat hunched in my
place and ate nothing. A full glass of *appellation controlé* 'claret' sat in
front of me. Robin Day radiated bonhomie; little Arthur Scargill, so
soft spokenly amiable as to be almost feline; John Alderson, returning
the clichés with a straight bat; and Patricia Rothwell, a handsome
blonde in blue who shed at least fifteen years under transmission
(unless you watched her neck). All shimmered and contributed in
their different ways at the dinner. Poor Barbara and Liz[1] became
increasingly concerned. Was I egg-bound with nerves, they must have
been thinking. They had made a defective choice. The other panellists
were going to have to 'carry' me.

As the hour approached people came back into the room at shorter
and shorter intervals, announced that the audience was being suitably
warmed up, etc. Eight minutes before we were due to go on my hand
shot out and I drained the glass of *appellation controlé*. I looked round
the room frantically like the Charles Addams boy.[2] 'Do you want

---

[1] Barbara Maxwell and Liz Elton, producers of *Question Time*.
[2] AC frequently refers to the famous strip cartoon by Charles Addams, which depicts an
innocent little boy playing with his chemistry set. Accidentally he stumbles on some
overpowering and magical potion that transforms him into a ravening and hirsute
monster. By about the eighth frame, completely transformed, he is looking round
desperately for the glass containing the remainder of the magic fluid. He finds it, drains
it and has in some curious way exceeded the critical dose, reverting to being a polite
and charming child. In the last frame the nursemaid, having heard a terrible commotion
as he rampaged round the room, looks round the door and finds him sitting inoffen-
sively, as she left him, with the chemistry set strewn on the floor.

something?' asked Liz. 'Yes, another glass of claret.' She rushed to the sideboard and opened a new bottle. Minutes later we were seated at the table and of course it really went quite all right, although the audience was a bit piggy. Within a few minutes I was completely at ease (although on seeing myself later I thought I was still too facially disturbed when emphasising a point; this is a fault of mine which I have noticed on previous occasions. I must somehow correct it).

Afterwards we walked through the audience and I was lionised by cuties who were very pretty and shy and done up to the nines (in case the camera should alight on them for an instant, of course). But I was glad that I was appreciated, as I had made one or two remarks to which ardent feminists might have taken exception. Barbara Maxwell made a special point of being nice and said how good I had been. It was nice to have a bit of Tory wit, she said. But she meant 'class' as Jane said when I repeated her comment.

Saltwood   *Friday, 26 March*

I was in the train to Plymouth when Neil Macfarlane[1] walked past. For some reason I did not recognise him instantly, but he patted me on the shoulder and said, though not with any sincerity: 'You were very good last night.' He then went on through to the buffet car. I don't (or didn't) especially like Neil Macfarlane and I was offensive to him on the floor of the House about two months ago when I questioned him about the subject of the World Cup team logo. On the way back he again tapped my shoulder and said: 'No, no, you were very good.' We exchanged a few pleasantries and he went back to his place.

Earlier, I had seen some reserved cards for four nearby, where I had left my luggage. When I returned after breakfast there sat Macfarlane, his rather common (but painted up) personal secretary and a bearded civil servant – who presumably keeps him straight, i.e. progressive, on such matters as apartheid in sport. Within a few minutes Macfarlane was again at my side and sat down. 'What do you make of Hillhead'

---

[1] Neil Macfarlane, MP for Sutton and Cheam since February 1974; Minister for Sport since 1981.

etc., etc. We soon got on to the subject of (what else?) the next reshuffle. He showed himself to have a much higher level of political intelligence than I had suspected and made some interesting suggestions.

Saltwood   *Saturday, 27 March*

It's blissful. Next week we have the Easter Adjournment Debates. Vote free, and the House is winding down for the short recess. I have been cutting the Bailey lawn and the greens are so yellowy-fresh. When the air is still, as all day it has been, every scent of spring claims ascendancy. The birds are busy, and fly low as they pop to their nest with building materials, or food for the sitting mate.

Cloisters   *Wednesday, 31 March*

Today I asked an offensive question about Jews. It is always thought to be rude to refer to 'Jews', isn't it? I remember that slightly triste occasion, watched from the gallery, of my father being inaugurated into the Lords and my rage at Sidney Bernstein, who was being ennobled on the same afternoon and would not take the Christian oath. As loudly as I could I muttered and mumbled about 'Jews' in order to discomfort his relations who were also clustered in the gallery. Unhappily, Col kept trying to correct me: 'No, no, old boy, you say Jew*ish*.'

I had hung it round the Foreign Secretary's visit to Israel and the issue of stamps depicting Irgun terrorists who shot Lord Moyne in 1948. The House took it quite well, a few guffaws. It is always fun to see just how far you can go with taboo subjects and titillate the House without actually shocking it.

I did some dictation with Alison and on our way upstairs I saw that the Prime Minister was giving a statement on the European Council Meeting. I wondered if I should go in and support her and, hearing a great deal of noise as I passed the doors into the Chamber, decided to do so. Again the Speaker called me, this time with an effective question, which I suspect pleased her, drawing attention to the effect of socialist policies in France, with the interest rate over 20 per cent, etc. etc. Perhaps my rage at not being called in the Trident Debate has somehow percolated back to the Speaker and he is trying to make amends before he gets my letter.

Roy Jenkins made his debut.[1] He speaks from the second row back and, of course, the moment he rose to his feet Dennis Skinner started firing abuse with the intention of disrupting him in the same way as he does with David Steel, as they share the same microphone. There was also a great deal of booing from our side, although quite a few toads were shushing because they wanted to listen to him.

'ORDER,' bellowed the Speaker. He then delivered a personal warning to the Member for Bolsover [Dennis Skinner], saying that he would not tolerate interruptions from his position.

Thereafter, Jenkins, with excessive and almost unbearable gravitas, asked three heavy statesman-like non-party-political questions of the PM. I suppose he is very formidable, but he was so portentous and long-winded that he started to lose the sympathy of the House about half way through and the barracking resumed. The Lady replied quite brightly and freshly, as if she did not particularly know who he was, or care.

Saltwood   *Friday, 2 April*

I was due to go down to Plymouth this morning. But when I looked in at Dean's Yard to collect correspondence for signing in the train the whole room seemed to know that the Falkland Islands had been invaded. Delighted to cancel, I made my way over to the Chamber; but somewhat apprehensive as Atkins was due to make a statement at 11 a.m.

No point in hanging about. I got back to Sandling at six o'clock. 'We've lost the Falklands,' I told Jane. 'It's all over. We're a Third World country, no good for anything.'

She is used to my suddenly taking the *apocalyptic* view. Didn't say much. I ate some brown toast and crab apple jelly and, it being such

---

[1] As Leader of the Social Democratic Party; he had just won the Glasgow Hillhead by-election, to return to the Commons after a break of six years.

a lovely evening, went for a meander down the valley. I am so depressed
by what I heard today – the shuffling and fudging, the overpowering
impression of timidity and incompetence. Can it have felt like this in
the Thirties, from time to time, on those fine weekends when the
dictators, Hitler and Musso, decided to help themselves to something –
Durazzo, Memel, Prague – and all we could do was wring our hands
and talk about 'bad faith'? I have a terrible feeling that this is a step
change, down, for England. Humiliation for sure and, not impossible,
military defeat. An apparition that must have been stalking us, since
we were so dreadfully weakened at Passchendaele I suppose, for the
last sixty-five years.

Cloisters   *Saturday, 3 April*

I had hardly got home last night when I realised that the House would
be so crowded that I would have to be there to book my place before
8 a.m. So I rose early – it was another glorious day with a thick heat
haze – and took the 6.17 a.m. train. By 8.30 a.m. the Chamber was
a snow storm of cards, like Budget Day.

I had spent the previous evening trying to convene a joint meeting
of the Defence and Foreign Affairs Committees to discuss the question. For reasons of protocol I had advised Bob Boscawen and he,
predictably, tried to talk me out of it, said it would be better to have
a meeting 'after Margaret had sat down.' I knew very well what this
meant. It was an attempt to shift all the most pugnacious Tory MPs
out of the Chamber up into Room 10.

I would have none of it. Buck was unobtainable, presumably
out drinking somewhere. Little Winston, following his new appointment of what must be the tinkiest job in the whole Government –
that of 'presenting' Government defence policy under the aegis of
Central Office – was somewhat spaced out in his response.
However, I managed to get hold of a few like-minded colleagues
and we had agreed to assemble in Committee Room 10 at 10.15
a.m.

Later, Bob Boscawen had rung back and said that he had arranged
for Victor Goodhew (an old whip and very 'reliable' in crises) to chair
the meeting. In fact when I got up to Committee Room 10 this
morning I was gratified to find it extremely full and the panic that my

moves had set in train was reflected in the fact that no lesser than the
Chief Whip had been brought in to 'listen'.

Jopling led off by making a soft-sell appeal for (need one say) loyalty,
absence of recrimination and so forth. This did not go down very
well. Speaker after speaker expressed their indignation at the way the
Foreign Office had handled things. Many were critical of John Nott.
Much the best speech, and the only one that elicited the banging of
desks, was by Robert Cranborne. Expressionless, Michael Jopling
took notes. Then, fortified by our mutual expressions of empathy, we
trooped down to the Chamber for Prayers.

The place was absolutely packed. Julian Amery, who very seldom
puts a card in, had to sit on the stairs in the gangway between the
Government bench and the lower block.

First, Humphrey Atkins made a clear, short, but unsatisfactory
statement explaining why he had misled (unintentionally, of course)
the House about the timing of various announcements yesterday. This
certainly did not make The Lady's task any easier as it set the tone,
giving further corroboration, as it were, to the general impression of
almost total Government incompetence which was to pervade the
debate.

The Lady led off. At first she spoke very slowly but didactically,
not really saying much. But then, when she got to a passage, 'we sent
a telegram . . .', the whole Opposition started laughing and sneering.
She changed gear and gabbled. Far too fast she rattled off what was
clearly a Foreign Office brief, without any reclamatory, or even
punitive action.

This was depressing for the Conservative benches who were already
in a grumpy and apprehensive mood. Michael Foot followed with an
excellent performance. Fortunately, for those of us who wished to
thump the Argentine, the fact that they are a fascist Junta makes it
very much easier to get Labour support – and my God we are going
to need this over the ensuing weeks as, apparently, it will take twenty-
one days for the flotilla to arrive on station.

I was tense and had written an excellent speech, provocative and
moving. But as the debate wore on I realised that it might, curiously,
have been inappropriate and was glad not to have been called.
Although I did intervene when provoked beyond endurance by Ray
Whitney's toadying defence of the Foreign Office, the weasel words
in which he still and most ill-judgedly plugged the sell-out argument
which we used to hear all the time from Ridley.

The debate wore on with Bernard Braine[1] turning in a robustious performance. One of his great ham displays of indignation. So splutteringly bombastic that in a curious kind of way he makes the House, that most cynical of audiences, pay attention.

Poor old Notters on the other hand was a disaster. He stammered and stuttered and gabbled. He faltered and fluttered and fumbled. He refused to give way; he gave way; he changed his mind; he stood up again; he sat down again. All this against a constant roaring of disapproval and contempt. I have seen the House do this so often in the past. Like the pack that they are they always smell the blood of a wounded animal and turn on it. I saw them last do it to Nicky Fairbairn in January, and once this mood is abroad it requires a superhuman display of courage and fortitude to overcome it.

The coup de grâce was delivered by David Owen, who had spoken earlier. He forced Nott to give way and he told him that if he could not appreciate the need to back negotiations with force he did not deserve to remain one minute as Secretary of State.

After the debate we all trailed, yet again, up to Committee Room 10. This time Carrington and Nott were both present. Thirty-three Members asked questions and, with the exception of three heavy-weight duds (Patten, Kershaw and van Straubenzee), every single person was critical. I asked a long, sneering question about the failure of our intelligence.[2] I made a point of addressing it to Peter Carrington whom, with my very long memory, I had not forgiven for snubbing me at a meeting on Afghanistan in December 1980, in the Grand Committee Room. As my irony developed, people in the Committee Room started sniggering, but poor Notters was still so rattled and blubbery that he leant across and answered it, while Carrington sat staring at me in haughty silence.

---

[1] Sir Bernard Braine, MP for SE Essex since 1955 (Billericay, 1950–55).

[2] After saying that he was not alone in the Committee in feeling deep dissatisfaction with the answer given about our intelligence reports, AC went on: 'The questions I would like to put to the Foreign Secretary are these: First, do we maintain a diplomatic mission in Buenos Aires? Secondly, if we do maintain such a mission is there anyone charged with collating and verifying intelligence material? Third, if there is such a person does he not have a duty to transmit this material to London? Finally, if he could find no material that was, in his judgement, worth repeating, could he not at least operate a press clipping service and send us extracts from the Argentine newspapers?'

This meeting finally broke up just before 4 p.m. I still had had no early morning tea, no breakfast, no coffee and no lunch, but felt wonderful, full of adrenalin. What an exciting and historic day. I could not go home as I was booked to appear on *Newsnight* at 10 p.m. Ravenously hungry I went to the curry restaurant, but it was closed. I was lucky to find a plastic carton on the back seat of the Chevrolet in which there were some old sandwiches and an orange which Jane had given me for a train journey to Plymouth. I drove into St James's Park and ate them and fell asleep.

Cloisters   *Monday, 5 April*

I am certain that there has been collusion between the Foreign Office and the Argentine over this whole affair. Why were there no casualties among the Royal Marines? Seventy-five determined men, as the Battle of Arnhem demonstrated (to take but one example), can hold off greatly superior numbers just using small arms and bazookas from drains and cellars in territory that they know. I have started the rumour that last night I rang Enoch, Julian Amery, and the *Guardian* – that there were sealed orders to the Governor to be opened when the invasion started, and that these orders were for him to declare an immediate cease fire. I believe this to be true. I also believe that unofficial representations were made by the Foreign Office to the Argentine indicating that all would be well provided no British blood were shed. And what is more, I believe that these unofficial contacts may still be taking place.

Accordingly, when I arrived in the House this morning at 9.30 a.m. I tabled three priority written questions on these three issues and sent copies to *The Times*, the *Telegraph* and the P.A. I then went along to James Callaghan, who had asked to see me privately in his room. I have a rapport with Jim. Nick Budgen says that he is an intellectual admirer of mine and, quite by chance, he has been in the Chamber when I have made three of my best speeches – on Blunt, on Bobby Sands and on the NATO commitment. I also sent him a copy of my Fortress Britain lecture, to which he replied at length. He was, as always, compos, amiable and clear-headed (it is in one's 60s, isn't it, that one starts to draw dividends from not consuming alcohol in middle age). But there is a certain detachment, impersonality, behind those powerful spectacles. I suppose this may be something that comes with the recollection of absolute authority – although of course little Wislon does not possess this at all.

Callaghan talked interestingly about the Falklands. He said it was the most frightful situation and fraught with danger, that it was important to find a way out, short of a full scale amphibious assault with all the casualties that might accompany it. He was gloomy about the long-term prospects about defending the Islands.

I tried to correct him about this and said that the Labour Party would rapidly back away totally from its position of support on Saturday. But he did agree that it was essential to punish the Argentines, and to sink some of their ships before negotiations restarted. He was very critical of the way the Foreign Office had handled the whole affair, said the whole administration was riddled with incompetence; the MOD was a mess, nobody there could think creatively.

He said that when he was Prime Minister, every week he had a briefing at which, on a Mercator projection, every major ship in the Royal Navy was shown, and every tanker. Apparently, this was an old practice dating back from Victorian times so that the Government would know at any moment the level of naval flexibility that they commanded. But the Civil Service finally got rid of it with the 'European commitment'.

After a bit Callaghan asked me to advise him on what he should say in his speech in the debate on Wednesday. This could be very important as he will be making a speech on a subject of which he has clear knowledge and a proven record of success, but from a position of objectivity as a senior statesman. Plainly he has to counsel against too bellicose an attitude, but I have got to make sure that his nerve holds and he includes a strong recommendation for a punitive strike to establish a grounding of strength on which to base negotiations. I will give this some thought and draft a memorandum for him. I will see him on Wednesday.

When I got down to the Members' Lobby from Callaghan's room there was a rumour running wild that Carrington had been sacked and sure enough it was confirmed a couple of minutes later. Carrington *and* Atkins and Richard Luce! A clean sweep. God knows what the consequences of this will be, but they cannot be all bad as Carrington's influence was grossly appeasing and the collusive element in the Foreign Office (see above) has now been decapitated. Party feeling seems to indicate that Francis Pym will become Foreign Secretary, but there are thrills – and spills – in store.

Little Patrick Cormack is chubbily rolling around the place, very pleased with himself and thinking he has done it all single-handed. As a matter of fact, I think it was the leader in *The Times* that finally tipped the scales, or was that, in fact, prompted by an inspired leak? These days, when intrigue and treachery are positively Neronian in their dimension, it is not always easy to put events in causative sequence.

The wets, of course, are livid and discomforted, they are taking it out on poor old Notters, saying he should be sacked, that it was intolerable that he should have survived, etc. etc. But Notters, I fear, comes later. His turn will be after the failure, or abortion, of the naval strike.

After lunch I went to 'Rab's' memorial service. Stuffed with politicians. Guess who was down to read the lesson – Peter Carrington. Listed, of course, as Her Majesty's most honourable Secretary of State ... etc. To do him credit he read the text with great aplomb. He, too, has large and impenetrable spectacles that conceal the emotions of the soul.

Very much less sleek was poor Richard Luce, who sat immediately in front of me in the stalls, grey and dishevelled, with a glazed look and deep eye ditches. Cancroid indeed, like the wretched Notters on television yesterday and, as Jane rightly spotted, as having auto-activated an instantaneous malignant condition.

After Questions there was a Statement about commandeering vessels and the trade embargo. Already the first odours of appeasement began to waft round the Chamber. Members on both sides were muttering and shuffling about commercial contracts, deliveries, banks, etc. etc.

On the way up to the Committee Corridor I was caught by Norman St John-Stevas, who could hardly contain himself with glee. 'Have you ever seen such a Government? So many nonentities. It is really pathetic, it would be farcical if it were not tragic ...'

He, too, was heavily anti-Nott, said it was extremely dangerous to have a Secretary of State for Defence, someone whose whole career depended on a successful assertion of martial vigour. I said it was not only the Secretary of State whose career depended on such a showing, but the whole existence of the Government, and indeed of the Party. St J-S said not necessarily so.

Well, he would say that wouldn't he?

Cloisters   *Tuesday, 6 April*

At the Foreign Affairs Committee today. Feeling in the Party is still very strong, but already one or two predictable weasels are poking their snouts out of the undergrowth. That sanctimonious creep, van Straubenzee, made a long and unctuous speech – I think he actually 'wrung' his hands as he regretted 'a certain jingoistic tendency.'

Cloisters   *Wednesday, 7 April*

People who should know better are striding up and down the Smoking Room Corridor telling anyone whom they can apprehend that the *Invincible* is sailing without her radar operative; that many of her weapons systems have already been moved; that the Sea Harrier cannot land on deck in a rough sea; that many of the ships in the Task Force have defective power trains, etc. etc.

It is monstrous that senior Tories should be behaving in this way. It is only on occasions such as this that the implacable hatred in which certain established figures hold the Prime Minister can be detected. They oppose Government policy whatever it is – they would oppose free campari-sodas for the middle classes if they thought The Lady was in favour. They are within an ace, they think, of bringing her Government down. If by some miracle the expedition succeeds they know, and dread, that she will be established for ever as a national hero.

So, regardless of the country's interest they are determined that the expedition will not succeed. The greater the humiliation of its failure, the more certain will be the downfall of The Lady's Government, the greater the likelihood of a lash-up coalition, *without* a general election, to fudge things through for the last eighteen months of this Parliament.

At the moment the House of Commons is very determined. One angle from which that determination can be attacked is via the so-called 'expert' opinion, which is that we just do not have the equipment to launch and sustain an expedition of this magnitude.

Some others are openly going round making the comparison with the Sicilian Expedition that led to the downfall of the Athenian City State. Sometimes, I must admit, this analogy occurs to me also, although I keep my thoughts to myself. If we are going to go, I feel, let us go out in a blaze – then we can all sit back and comfortably become a nation of pimps and ponces, a sort of Macao to the European continent.

Saltwood   *Good Friday, 9 April*

Pleasantly tired after mowing the *whole* Inner Bailey in one swoop – four hours dead. Daffodils out, but cold – though Saltwood just starting to 'smile'.

As I said on the walks to Jane: 'It's even a fudge; two to one a disaster and The Lady resigning from the despatch box; three to one a naval victory and the bunting round Nelson column.'

Cloisters   *Wednesday, 14 April*

Yet another Falklands Debate today.

I took the 07.19 train from Sandling – how lovely it is in the early morning. *Why* don't we, in the spring and summer, follow the birds turning in at dusk and rise with the ever-recurring beauty of the dawn? Train late, taxi to House, and wrote out note of encouragement to The Lady (Jane's idea, and a very good one). I had to do a second draft as I spelt Britannia with two t's, spastically. I walked with the envelope up to Downing Street and handed it to the policeman outside Number 10. A few mangy photographers with heavy beards and leather bum-freezer jackets hung around the other side of the barriers, but very few members of the public.

Then back to St Stephen's Gate, where I met the TSW crew.

Slightly unsatisfactory, as they were making a programme about the
'impact' (standard W. Morning Gasp word) of the Falklands crisis on
the defence cuts. But it was not going to be screened until 29th, so
much of what one was going to say could be overtaken by the march
of events.

I did not take to the pasty, weasel-eyed, cortisone-cheeked 'interviewer'. He had a clipboard under his arm with various hand-written
notes on it. 'What are those?' I asked. 'They were my questions to
David Owen.' But when I started reading them he went pouty, said:
'I never allow politicians to see my questions.' 'But you said these
were questions for David Owen, not for me.' Stupid pompous little
prick. Anyone who uses the word 'politician', not themselves being
one, means it as an insult.

The interview was held in the Lords' Gardens. Passers-by peered
curiously and some hung about. He was a very unskilful interrogator
and kept clumsily trying to 'trap' me into making critical remarks
about the Government's defence policy. Naturally, I was quite equal
to this and I fear some of my answers may have been tinged with
irony, or, worse, sarcasm. On and on it dragged. Plainly it was going
to be cut to pieces before it was shown to the public and I am afraid
my replies will appear mulish and inconsequential.

Immediately, on returning to St Stephen's I was picked up by the
Swiss Television crew. A much nicer lot, although the bearded guru
who conducted the interview did put a number of awkward questions,
such as about The Lady's future if things go wrong, and so on, which
are not easy to answer. He winced a bit when I asked about a fee, but
said he would telephone Andrew at the Chalet so that our friends in
Zermatt could watch it.

After this I dictated answers to letters about the crisis, with one
exception *universally* supportive, and went up for an early lunch in the
Members' Dining Room. Beaumont-Dark, Steen, John Spence[1] and
Ian Laing, the trite Scottish Whip (whom Michael Ancram asked me
to sign for at Pratt's and whom I subsequently saw had accumulated
very few additional names).

Colleagues were kind about my performance on *Newsnight* on
Monday. I mentioned in the most cautious way David Howell's
appearance on *Question Time* the previous week, which had – rightly –
annoyed Jane so much. The effect was instantaneous; 'absolutely

---

[1] John Spence, MP for Thirsk and Malton since 1974 (Sheffield Heeley 1970–74).

disgraceful,' 'monstrous,' 'that man is useless', 'ought to be sacked'.

Beaumont-Dark, who had finished his meal, rose with a flourish saying that Howell had made a mess of the pit closures, a balls-up of the heavy lorries, and was so ineffective as to be unfit to hold any official position in the Party.

Who should then soft-spokenly materialise, but instantly, and take the empty chair but David Howell! There was an uneasy silence. Poor David. What very thin wrists and stooping gait and pale – but not clear – skin he has. Suddenly he turned to me and said: 'I ran into a branch of the Alan Clark fan club the other night . . .'. He was talking, of course, about Barbara Maxwell and Liz Elton who had told him that I was the best Tory backbencher they had found for ages, etc.

I left the Dining Room early. Anglia Television want me to do an hour long debate with Tam Dalyell on Friday night. Every single day has been busted to pieces by 'appearances' on the media. But I have to do it. I feel passionately, really deeply, about this issue. And I am fortunate indeed that I am getting so much opportunity to express my feelings instead of just grinding my teeth in the dark.

In the Members' Cafeteria and there was Tam, gabbling and dribbling and in the most frightful state. He has actually gone slightly round the bend about the whole thing, most extraordinary. He said that the *Hermes* was suffering from mechanical trouble and her propellers were seizing. Wishful thinking, I suspect.

I could not stay very long as I had a Prayer Card in. Once again the place was a snow storm of Prayer Cards, worse than the Budget. The debate was a fairly placid business. The Lady had recovered her composure and there was a level of unanimity on all sides. This is a relief as I had feared from trends that I had perceived in last Wednesday's debate that the House might be weakening; good-boys all trying to get in on the act with their disparate compromise solutions. But, other than a dotty plea for passive resistance by poor old Anthony Meyer,[1] and a ritual vote loser by Judith Hart,[2] the House remained firm.

There was a moment towards the end of the debate when, as usual, many colleagues had not been able to get in. Ian Lloyd rose from his place next to me and delivered a 'set' speech, referring to copious notes; 'reading' in other words. He rambled on with a positive *plethora* of quotations, mostly from the classics, Aristotle, Scipio Africanus,

---

[1] Anthony Meyer, MP for West Flint since 1970.
[2] Judith Hart, MP for Lanark since 1959.

Ludicrous Sextus, etc. Frequently he both shouted and spoke at eleven times dictation speed; he stumbled over his words and, more entertainingly, transposed the authors and subjects of his learned allusions: '... as Lucius Tertius remarked when he was cornered in the Appian hills by Scipio – no, I mean as Scipio replied when Lucius Tertius confronted him ...' etc.

Immediately on my other side sat Rhodes James. How Rhodes James has diminished in stature and esteem over the last eighteen months! I suppose it dates from that absurd moment when it came out over the PA tape that he was 'considering' resigning as a PPS. Anyway, RJ also wanted to speak and was getting crosser and crosser as Ian used up all the time. On each occasion, and they were many, that the House was treated to a quotation from the classics Rhodes James groaned very loudly, and rolled his eyes.

At first Ian had completely 'lost' the House, which chattered freely to itself, cracked jokes, 'where are you having dinner?', that kind of thing. But slowly the House realised that this was in a curious way a kind of Parliamentary occasion. It was so ludicrous. The poor Lady, who had sat in throughout the debate, looked attentively down at Ian the whole time he was speaking. What can have been going through her head?

At five o'clock I went across and did a piece for Anne Perkins for BBC West. She tried to catch me out with a trick question about what would happen to The Lady if the expedition failed but, in boxing parlance, I 'got on my bicycle' and avoided it. Then at six I met Bruce Anderson of *Weekend World* and we went down to Annie's. We were meant to be having an intimate chat, but we were hailed by Simon Hoggart and two other journalists, whose names I don't know, but I am sure very important (one I think works on the *Express*). There was a good deal of general chat, some of it quite funny. In the middle *The Guardian*'s Julia Langdon came over and up to me, and I mean *up* to me, and said: 'We were having an argument about how old you were.'

'Oh, really,' I am both pleased and disconcerted by this.

'Yes, Ian (Aitken) said you looked so *ravaged* for someone in his forties. I said you were in your fifties. How old are you?'

'Sixty,' I answered. Off she went. She and Elinor Goodman (*Financial Times*) are quite decorative but really no good as political correspondents. You have to have an intuitive feel for the subject, really to be a politician *manqué*, to be any good.

Later Bruce and I repaired to one of the sofas and he gave me a great spiel about how the Cabinet was full of nonentities, how important it was for her to bring in some people 'larger-than-life'.

'For instance it is disgraceful that you have not got a job ...'

'I quite agree,' I answered.

'... and Chris Patten and Nick Budgen!'

On the whole his judgement was quite good. He really is a politician *manqué* and for all I know will become a politician *réussi*. He wants to have lunch with me next week. But what is the point? He really is further out of things than I am. There is no use in constructing castles in the sand.

After the debate I walked back, once again, to Anne Perkins' office. Fortunately, she, herself, had left but some little chappie from BBC Wales interviewed me, and Anthony Meyer.

Let us just hope that all this will have a cumulative effect of conditioning people's thoughts. I had hoped to get back to Saltwood tonight, but have been booked for the BBC World Service at 9.30 a.m. and even then I cannot get away because I am to do a CBS live broadcast at lunchtime to go by satellite all over the United States.

Cloisters   *Wednesday, 21 April*

At a meeting of the Defence Committee today Michael Mates dwelt at length on the prospects of very heavy casualties and how we ought to warn the public, etc. I notice that now it looks as if we really are going to recapture the Islands, mount a full-scale assault, the antis have shifted their ground from urging the wisdom of negotiation and are trying desperately to counter-attack increasingly enthusiastic public opinion polls, hoping that if they can get the public uneasy enough, someone, in the words of a ludicrous headline in today's *Times* filed from Washington, will cry 'stop'.

Francis Pym[1] made a very unsatisfactory Statement referring to 'arrangements' for the Argentine withdrawal; the 'interim' administration that would take its place and so forth. In answer to a question following the Statement he said that we would not shoot while negotiations were still going on. Immediately afterwards, groups of

---

[1] Appointed Foreign Secretary on 5 April.

MPs were standing about in the Lobby, grumbling and speculating about what all this meant.

I was talking to Anthony Bevins of *The Times* (who interpreted it very bearishly) when the annunciator screen announced: STATE-MENT FALKLAND ISLANDS FRANCIS PYM. We all pounded back into the Chamber, but it was already over. Apparently Francis had reappeared to make a 'correction', saying that he did *not* exclude the possibility of shooting while negotiations were still in train, and then disappeared again behind the Chair.

We dispersed again. The whole Party is very prickly and unsure of itself. I dread a sell out. I am sure we are being slowly set up for one.

There was an ad hoc meeting of the '92' in Committee Room 18 in the Upper Corridor. 'Slatted', as the Americans say (I intend going to Washington tomorrow), for 7.15 p.m. On the way up I fell into step with John Browne, the handsome, but somewhat indecisive, young right-wing MP for Winchester. He complained about Tony Kershaw, who has been weakening by the minute in his television exposures, talking about ultra-short, or nominal periods of joint administration, before sovereignty is handed over.

'Why is he a member of the "92" '? 'He is a Whip's heavy,' I said. 'A mole, reports everything.' John Browne was quite put out. The meeting was assiduous, our mutual suspicions and paranoia feeding on itself. Poor old Patrick Wall, deaf and scatty, lost control of the meeting early, as he always does, and people were arguing among themselves, cross-talking etc.

I gave my view that the old Foreign Office lobby were still live and kicking, that they had already suborned a number of Party heavies (such as Straubenzee and Mates) to state the appeasement case in its various forms and that the situation was being aggravated by a number of people who saw it as an opportunity to do down the Prime Minister. I know I said that I was not happy about the Whips' role in this, although I cannot remember the actual phrases I used.

Kershaw, who was sitting opposite me, looked expressionless. Bob Dunn, who is quite percipient and *acutely* paranoiac about the 'left' in the Party, the Whips' conspiracy to retard everyone on the right, etc., suggested that a delegation by-pass the Chief Whip and go direct to the Chairman of the Party (who is of course a member of the inner, or 'War', Cabinet).[1]

---

[1] Cecil Parkinson, MP for Hertfordshire South since 1974 (Enfield West 1970–74).

Bob is Cecil's PPS and said that he would organise it for immediately after the vote. John Browne and others suggested that I should
go with the delegation, which it was eventually agreed would also
include Bill Clark, Jill Knight, and, of course, poor old Paddy Wall.

We went up to Cecil's room after the vote. No one, including the
PPS, could make the lights work so we sat in the gloaming illuminated
only by the desk light with a heavy green shade, which added to the
sense of conspiracy.

Eventually Cecil arrived, somewhat spoiling his clean-limbed specification with a velvet dinner jacket. I spoke third and, I hope, lucidly.
Cecil, I am glad to say, was *extremely* reassuring and replied most
hawkishly. He more or less said that we would be going into South
Georgia within the next couple of days, as there was not the slightest
chance of our agreeing to any arrangement that left an Argentinian
presence on the Islands. But at the end he said, something, something,
'as an old Whip I cannot listen to criticism of the Whips ... etc,' and
I smelt trouble.

Cloisters   *Thursday, 22 April*

Having boasted a great deal to people, including Plymouth Sound,
that I am off to Washington today, '... with Francis Pym,' I cannot
get out of it, however much I dread the journey. It is the usual story.
If anyone can guarantee safe arrival and return one would spend all
one's money on air fares. But I don't just hate taking off and landing:
I loathe *going along*. And 'going along' at twice the speed of sound
must be more hazardous than 'going along' sub-sonically.

Just as I was getting into my car outside Brooks's I saw Algy Cluff,[1]
still very foppish, with a *very* thin golden and platinum watch chain,
although having seen his net worth reduced by about £18 million in
the last year. I told him I was off to Washington. He said that there
was plenty of oil around the Falklands and he had the technology to
extract it, '... if other disputes could be settled.' Good may yet come
out of this dispute, because if we can really assert our strength there
we should be able to participate in the exploitation of resources
without being threatened or disturbed.

---

[1] Algy Cluff, founder of Cluff Oil, proprietor of *The Spectator* since 1981.

I did a couple of radio shows. Unusually, Robin Day appeared to be hosting *World at One*, and then hitched a ride in a taxi to Heathrow. The Concorde lounge carried an agreeable aroma of riches, whether personal or corporate. Three little cheeky-chappies with Mediterranean accents and red coats dispensed unlimited refreshments. I drank a glass of champagne and orange juice and thought of dear dotty Alistair Londonderry, who always has this drink set down in front of him, without having to ask for it, wherever he goes.

Concorde on take-off is everything that has been claimed for it. The feeling of superabundant power is absolutely overwhelming, fields and houses became minuscule dots and patches in the space of a few minutes. The aircraft was full of pressmen and commentators.

Right up in the front, head bowed over his papers so that no one should try and 'lobby' him, sat John Louis.[1] He now looks really alarmingly like the hit-man in *Bullitt*, who furtively prowled through the hospital in his raincoat in search of a badly injured witness who had to be eliminated.

I chatted with Simon Glenarthur.[2] Although rather chinless and stereotyped in appearance, he must be quite tough as he flew in the Army Air Corps and is a helicopter pilot with British Airways. He sometimes comes to the Defence Committee and is very hard line. Due to a muddle by the PA some people, including Robin Day, had thought he was Lord Glen*amara* (poor, nasty old Ted Short, of my opposition days) and the Concorde lounge had been plastered with urgent messages asking him to get in touch with correspondents who did not bother to conceal their disappointment when they found they were talking to a Scottish aristocrat instead of a Labour life peer.

About half way through the flight I strolled down towards the tail and had a quick word with Francis. As I parted the curtains to go into his cabin I felt like Ernst Strobe, when, as Goldfinger, he bobbed out and surprised James Bond and his girl when they thought they had escaped in the last reels of the film. The Foreign Secretary must have thought that it was really *too* much that I, who had been endlessly plugging the hard line on this dispute since the day it started, should now be pursuing him across the Atlantic.

Simon Glenarthur had arranged with the captain that I should go

---

[1] John J. Louis, United States Ambassador at the Court of St James, since 1981, previously a leading American businessman (director Johnson Wax etc).

[2] Lord Glenarthur, Government Whip, House of Lords.

through and sit on the Concorde jump seat for our landing at Dulles Airport. It was with some relief that I saw that Dulles lies in flat scrubland. No special problems on over-run or, indeed, even on engine failure at take-off. Surprisingly rapidly the white runway changed in size from a laundry name tape, to a ruler, to a roller towel, to the cloth at a long banqueting table; all the time holding steady and dead centre in the 'V' shaped windscreen of the great airliner – the supersonic nose had been 'drooped' at 18,000' as we started our approach.

The captain, Massie by name, was incredibly bland and unflappable. I suspect also highly competent, as he had been given the wrong glide angle to lock into his computer and we came in 350' too high. But he overrode it manually and still managed, by using one 'g' or better on both brakes and reverse thrust, to turn the aircraft at the first runway exit. The pasty and rather common co-pilot, on the other hand, was demonstrably nervous and lip-licking throughout descent.

We had been told to look out for a 'young man' who would be holding up a notice for us. He seemed clueless, explained he was a part-time journalist, just 'helping out' the Conference while working in Washington on a project. There are as many illiterate students hanging around Washington dabbling in journalism and hoping to uncover the new Watergate as there are cuties in Hollywood seeking to make the big-time show.

Our guide drove in excess of the speed limits in a battered Honda with Kansas plates which, he said, belonged to a 'friend'. Something told me that the 'friend' did not realise that his car was being used for this purpose.

When we arrived at the Dirksen building, a sort of American Norman Shaw, full of Senators' offices, where the Conference was being held, it was twenty-past four London time and some strong Indian tea and buttered toast would have been welcome. But in Washington it was only twenty-past ten and a bright sun blazed down on the blossoms. Our guide repeated his earlier suggestion that we should go to a hotel room and relax a bit.

'I DO NOT want to "relax",' I snapped. 'I want to go to the Conference.'

Our guide wanted to get shot of us. What did we do with our cases? We humped them up the great sham marble steps and through the double portals of the Dirksen. An armed security man examined them. 'Who do you work for?' he asked suspiciously. 'The British Government,' I answered. Unexpectedly this induced respect rather than hostility.

On the sixth floor we found the Conference. Crawling with candidates, both English and American, a smattering of Senators. Two very big MPs, Mark Carlisle and Peter Emery, were booming away. Lady Emery had accompanied her husband, ludicrously airs-and-graces, looking like an ultra-tall cross between the Queen and Nanny's niece.

Saltwood   *Wednesday, 5 May*

Now nearly four weeks into the Falklands 'Crisis', and for the last three of them I have been almost ceaselessly occupied. *Every single day* I have done at least one TV or radio broadcast, sometimes as many as three. On two of the Sundays a Citroen Pallas has been sent down (*plus* a 'backup' car!) to take me up to the studio and back again, for the direct, grand, bit of Brian Walden's *Weekend World* – itself the grandest of all the current affairs programmes. Hailed as man-of-the-week in the *Daily Express*.

Westminster   *Tuesday, 11 May*

Still the Falklands crisis drags on, stimulating, but heavily demanding in time, now superimposed on the galloping pressures of openings and the unsettling, evocative, nostalgic yearnings that fine weather always induces.

Today woken very early by Angus – sun right round and low, still on the doorhandle of our bedroom. 6.05 a.m. Let him out, shuffled across in my pyjamas to pump and started it first pull; next through to Barbican walk to ensure that water was glog-gulping out into the moat. Made tea; we talked about the huge accumulating demands of openings.

Walked dogs. Grass now dry enough to walk under the railway bridge, rootling about in the shippen, and back along the railway hedgerow. Newspapers fairly non-committal – no developments though much disturbing 'informed' comment by Peter Jenkins [*The Guardian*] about pressure for a settlement being applied to The Lady.

Saltwood   *Monday, 17 May*

This is *the* crisis. I am lucky to be in the House for it. Lucky, too, to be 'recognised' and allowed to 'achieve'. When one has seen this through, *then* one will have discharged one's duty.

Saltwood   *Tuesday, 1 June*

Back in the Great Hall. How lovely, its appeal this time of year hasn't altered for me in the slightest. Today spent lounging, sploshing, swimming – pool 72°.

Last night I left Saltwood at 2 in the morning to be driven up to the ABC studios for a night chat show, coast-to-coast on the Falklands (the drive back leaving London at 4.40, getting back to Saltwood after 6 a.m.). I have long since lost count of the number of appearances I have made on the Falklands – three times on Brian Walden alone, since the 'crisis' started.

And *what* a crisis! When I think back to the state of utter depression when I got out of the train at Sandling on 2 April – on trial, complete and utter humiliation; I even contemplated emigrating. Now not only have we redeemed everything that was at stake then, but one has advanced immeasurably in self-esteem and in the status accorded to us by the whole world.

And I *did* play my part in this – whether greater or lesser than if I had been a junior minister I don't know – I suspect the former. I was almost immediately recognised by the media – the 'leader of the war party' (Alan Watkins).

Terry Coleman came down to interview me. I had been looking forward to it.[1] But the more I think of it the more of a disaster it was. Impossible to charm him. Totally humourless. Didn't ask any of the

---

[1] Coleman, whose interviews appeared in *The Guardian*, had some years before interviewed AC's father.

right questions. Kept trying to push me into a corner about 'National Socialism'. I tried to explain to him about patriotism. No good. He wasn't interested in politics. He was heavily-built, totally unforthcoming, didn't thank Jane for tea, or me for a silver mug of iced Pol Roger – or for my time, come to that.

Saltwood   *Saturday, 5 June*

Financial dream blighted by discovery that £1 is worth about 5d (or say 2p) on 1936 figures.

Saltwood   *Monday, 7 June*

I sat 'within the walls'. Tremendous burgeoning greenery, baby birds everywhere: we just failed (by what chance I don't know) to revive two baby thrushes from the nest in the crab apple tree by the openings desk – having got them through to the fifth day; there is a rather sulky successor to George (named 'Max') in a box in the kitchen, and a few minutes ago I hooked a young sparrow out of the pool.

Cloisters   *Thursday, 10 June*

I telephoned Edward Adeane[1] at Buckingham Palace and told him that there was some concern that the Recognition Committee at the MOD might be parsimonious with their awards. I urged that these be distributed in the most profligate manner – and particularly in the Parachute Regiment which has performed such prodigies. He reminded me that the Prince of Wales was Colonel-in-Chief, and I hope he took my points to heart. After a period of *froideur* following that curious leak by Willie Hamilton about my criticisms of fat, ugly, dwarflike, lecherous and revoltingly tastelessly behaved Princess Margaret, our relations have improved and are now quite good.

---

[1] Edward Adeane, Extra Equerry to the Queen since 1972.

Oh! How loathsome and draining it is to turn my footsteps westward instead of to the south on a Friday. I work very hard at Westminster and I am always *en poste* there, unlike other colleagues who scrabble around the boardrooms and come in late (if at all) for Questions, with expense-account fumes on their breath. And so, when the week is over I like best to go home and 'unwind' with the cars and the animals. And it is ghastly having to go to Plymouth and, racked with fatigue, keep silently mouthing 'brush'[1] as one moves round the faithful, and not-so-faithful.

Actually my status in Plymouth is quite high at the moment, due to all the 'exposure' that I have been getting over the Falklands. Enemies, like Speare and other malcontents, have gone quiet, they never turn up at meetings.

Although the complacent and self-centred Roy Williams came in to see me yesterday – he gets a free pass on the trains because he is a postman(!) and so likes to pop in to the House – and told me that it was very important that I should be on the Barbican (although that is not in my constituency) to talk to the fishermen (very few of whom are my constituents) at 11.30 the following morning, as he had 'arranged' for the TV cameras to be there. And, moreover, *Janet Fookes would be there.* Perhaps I was a little bit more clipped than I should have been. I mean how the hell could I possibly get to Plymouth at 11.30 the following morning at less than twenty-four hours notice?

Fortunately, Jane decided that she would come with me and this usually restricts my grosser excesses of temper. But on this occasion, having listened to some grotesque and preposterous cliché-bound bellowing – styled a 'speech' – by Sir Henry Plumb,[2] and my stomach being empty, as is habitual, I found that I snapped at some grace-and-favour female, a Mrs Randall by name, who gave me the I'm-not-certain-I'm-going-to-be-voting-for-you routine because of my failure to do something about the glasshouse industry.

God alive! I said I could not care less; that I was not in the business

---

[1] The Clarks had, early in their political life, discovered that the word 'brush', in the act of expression, draws the features into a pleasing smile; neither chilly nor leering, but authoritative and benevolent – one degree less effusive than the word 'cheese'.

[2] Sir Henry Plumb, Member of the European Assembly, former President of the National Farmers Union.

of buying votes with taxpayers' money; that I despised people who
tried to exercise pressure to secure for themselves particular tranches
of the revenue in return for electoral favours; and that she could
exercise her remedy at the next election.

'There are some Members of Parliament who might be frightened
by the sort of threats you are making, but I am not one of them.' I
have a feeling she is a friend of Joan Erskine, one of the Dunstone
carpers, who always used to complain about my lack of publicity –
although she can hardly mount that particular charge over the last
three months.

Cloisters   *Monday, 14 June*

I dined with Norman St John-Stevas, and, as always, he was delightful
company, talked obsessively about politics and what a 'dreadful'
Cabinet we have at the moment.

'There cannot ever have been a Cabinet with such a dearth of
talent,' he kept saying. He recounted how Norman Tebbit – whom
he described in a number of scatological terms – had come down to
a Conservative Club in his constituency, 'not at *my* invitation I hasten
to say,' wearing a coloured evening shirt and how, '. . . my dear, they
were all over him.'

I said that The Lady's autocracy was complete. She could make any
policy or break any individual. At the moment, I said, she is completely
fire-proof. 'Yes,' he replied, 'and will be completely combustible
shortly thereafter.'

Cloisters   *Tuesday, 15 June*

I was woken at 4.15 a.m. by a beautiful song-thrush; she rivalled,
surpassed indeed, the famous Albany blackbird, to whom I used to
listen in the spring of '76 when I would wake early in torment with
the figures going round and round in my head of accelerating interest
charges on my different overdrafts, and how was I to get the deeds of
Saltwood back out of Hoare's clutches. But this thrush sang incredibly,

never once repeating herself and with variations of infinite quality
and delight.

I could not go back to sleep, still over-excited by the events of last
night. I had got back to the House about 9.30 p.m., after dining at
Brooks's with Edward Adeane, and was reading the tape over Phil
Goodhart's shoulder when I saw something about, '. . . individual
British commanders at all levels have been authorised to negotiate
ceasefires'. 'It means they have surrendered,' he said.

The cloakroom attendant told me that there was to be a Statement
at 10 p.m., after the vote, and when I got up to the lobbies I found
the whole House, policemen, badge messengers, etc., everybody
bubbling with excitement. I rushed up to catch the news headlines
before the Division Bell rang, but for once we seemed to know more
than they did; the BBC was behind the times and fumbling.

Foolishly I lingered so, after going past the division clerk, I found
that 'my' bench was completely crowded. However, among its magic
powers, as is well known, is that of infinite expandability, and they
allowed me in lowish down – next to Alan Glyn – Peter Emery very
nobly making that ritual pivoting of the lap which actually permits
the small statutory triangle of green leather.

Hastily I scribbled some notes on the back of a card in case there
were questions – but the rumour was that it was to be on a Point of
Order. (How? Monstrous collusion by the Speaker?) And then The
Lady entered, radiant, and there was cheering – bellowing, indeed.
She made a very brief statement, but it was important in that she used
the phrase, '. . . negotiate a *surrender*' (not a ceasefire). Trust her. She
has led from the front all the way.

Again we bellowed. Order Papers were waved and, not having one,
I fluttered my little white postcard. Michael Foot fumbled gingerly
round the subject, to some heckling, but finally and generously
managed to get out his congratulations, '. . . in spite of our arguments
in the past.' Little Steel was short, and inaudible. And even David
[Owen], who has behaved so well and so enhanced his reputation,
could not be heard properly and aroused grumpy heckling, I noticed,
from the Opposition bench when he congratulated the Government.

For a few seconds we were stuck in our places by some procedural
back-and-forth; Leader of the House accepting an Adjournment of
Business, etc. I rose rapidly, pushed my way through the crowd at the
bar of the House and shot round through the 'Aye' Lobby to catch
the Prime Minister as she emerged at the back of the Speaker's Chair

to get to her room. No one else had the idea and I had a completely clear run. Not even Ian was leading her, although Willie was shuffling benignly three places behind. (What must he have been thinking?) Ignoring Willie I rushed up and said to her: 'Prime Minister, only you could have done this; you did it alone, and your place in history is assured.' She looked a little startled. Had she heard properly? She was still a little bemused by the triumph. Willie looked grumpy (maddeningly, he is not at all deaf); an unseemly display of emotion. We do not do things like that in the Tory Party.

So ends the Falklands Affair – which began in such despair and humiliation. How well I remember that first emergency debate and looking down the bench at The Lady when Enoch was speaking, at how low she held her head, how *knotted* with pain and apprehension she seemed as he pronounced his famous judgement, '. . . in the next few weeks the world, the country and she, herself, will discover of what metal she is made.'

I only hope he is generous enough to recall that moment when he speaks today.

Cloisters   *Wednesday, 16 June*

It is a great relief to me how kind people have been and how many compliments I have received concerning that Terry Coleman article. Last night I was standing in the Lobby while Jonathan Aitken was telling me what a good man I seemed in it, when David Owen came up to us and said exactly the same thing. Only a few Tory wankers are critical, they feign horror – Michael McNair-Wilson was literally speaking in whispers about it when I came in on Monday – but I suspect it is tinged with jealousy. '. . . Combination of hot sun, and fizz, was it?' said silly little John Heddle,[1] obviously delighted by my discomfiture. The only mistake I made, in my estimation, was to ask him to tone it down; although, as Andrew Roth[2] said, he should never have revealed that, as it was 'operational'.

I lunched today with my old friend John Aspinall. I had undertaken to give evidence in support of his application for a licence for his club.

[1] John Heddle, MP for Lichfield and Tamworth since 1979.
[2] Andrew Roth, editor of Parliamentary Profiles.

I can do this with a clear conscience as I am not a gambler and I enjoy the social amenities, the restaurant and the backgammon board which it provides.

Excellent food, during which Aspers declaimed much good sense about the strength of the ordinary people of the nation, how they had brushed aside the nervous and decadent caution of the establishment to assert their nationhood, etc.

After lunch we climbed five floors to his office, where a minute beady lawyer awaited to take my deposition. Young, clear-skinned, bald-pated, he was cast in the Eric Levene mould. While we talked, Aspers huffed and gasped. I thought he was meant to be fit – wrestling with bears and gorillas etc. – but my own breathing had not altered in the slightest from running up the stairs. I suppose people who puff and pant do not notice they are doing it, but it certainly makes a great deal of noise.

Back in the House I met Adam Raphael and we chatted about the political consequences of the Falklands. He told me that 'favourable mentions' about me had been coming out of Downing Street; this corroborates what Frank Johnson told me on the weekend – but what is the point? I went on up to the Defence Committee where there was much discussion about the advisability of postponing the White Paper.

I dined with Bruce-Gardyne – who really is rather awful. Too self-satisfied and assertive, and quite unrepentant about his letter to Freddy Fischer.[1] A little later we were joined, very reluctantly and having looked around the dining room for alternatives, by Michael Heseltine. On closer scrutiny I see that his face is slightly changing shape, he is becoming rather pop-eyed. Then, almost immediately afterwards, came Trevor Skeet,[2] who booms and bellows and is ineffably complacent.

I used to think he was a staunch right-winger of the old school, but he would not even sign my Motion praising the Special Patrol Group on the grounds that it might offend the ethnic minority in his constituency. And he does not even have a marginal seat as his majority is 12,413. I found it very difficult to say anything. Michael Heseltine, as

---

[1] In a private letter to the Editor of the *Financial Times* J.B-G. had said that the Falklands were not worth fighting for, that the whole enterprise was 'crazy' etc. This was much in tone with the editorial attitude of the *F.T.*, but the text of the letter, which was politically embarrassing, was leaked to the *New Statesman* by a member of the *F.T.*'s staff.

[2] Trevor Skeet, barrister, MP for Bedford since 1970.

a leading wet, made some pompous remarks about how the Northern Ireland Bill rebels were subjecting Jim Prior to a 'campaign of attrition,' and how he disapproved. Was he trying to get at me? Quite difficult, as I am not opposing the Bill, and am indeed voting for the closures. There was some long and disparate conversation about what the Argentine prisoners were going to eat. I suggested that they should eat each other.

After dinner Bob Boscawen said that John Nott wanted to see me in his room about the White Paper. Victor Goodhew and Winston Churchill had also been invited to go along, but I am glad to say that little Winston did not turn up.

While we were waiting for Victor I said to John that I was very worried about all the rumours that were circulating about his impending departure (John Connell had told me about this nearly ten days ago, accompanying it with the really awful prospect that Peter Walker would be appointed in John Nott's place. There was also an item heavily displayed in a box on page two of the *Daily Mail* this morning, and a full length editorial on the subject in tonight's *Evening Standard*). JN said that there was a conspiracy against him. About half-a-dozen Admirals, many of the naval correspondents – Desmond Wetter etc. – and a coterie of disaffected colleagues, notably Keith Speed, Michael Brotherton[1] and Freddie Burden. JN said he had no intention of resigning.

We discussed the question of the White Paper. He wants to publish it as it is, but with a loose-leaf disclaimer of intent. Crazy, I said. Bob Boscawen said we had to have five defence debates and there had to be something 'on the table' for the debates to revolve around. Why? We have not *got* to do anything, I said, except raise money for the defence estimates, and that had already been done. Far better to issue a single-side Statement reaffirming our commitment to Trident, to NATO etc. and asserting that the complex and deep-seated lessons of the Falklands Campaign will take some months to be digested.

John thrashed about on his seat, crossing and uncrossing his legs, taking his glasses on and off. Rattled, but attentive. He had started off asserting his intention to publish even though not to publish the obvious conclusion, and I had said that if he insisted I would not oppose the idea publicly, but I still thought it terribly risky. Victor

---

[1] Michael Brotherton, MP for Louth since October 1974.

Goodhew supported me and was sensible and wise. We left things that John would continue to think the matter over.

Later in the evening I saw Ian Gow, who walks about the place looking like the cat that has swallowed all the cream. In his presence I had some badinage with Jim Prior and was cheeky to him about the Northern Ireland Bill.

Ian could not get away as for formal reasons he is bound to support the Bill in the lobbies. But I had one quick word with him – 'the Prime Minister has complete freedom of action now,' I said, 'no other Leader has enjoyed such freedom since Churchill, and even with him it did not last very long.' I suppose he may have thought I was referring to freedom of choice in making appointments, but I was not, really, I meant freedom in imposing domestic, foreign and defence policies.

Cloisters   *Thursday, 17 June*

I was delighted to see that Julia Langdon had singled me out for mention in today's *Guardian* in an analysis of politicians who have emerged with credit from the Falklands affair. All the sweeter as Churchill and I were the only Tory backbenchers to be mentioned, and I was compared favourably to him. I wonder who she got this from? Perhaps Jim Lester, although I know she also talks to Norman StJS. It is useful as 'plugs' from that quarter are far more valuable than, say, the *Telegraph* (not that I have ever had one there).

The Times had an enormous centre page article, complete with caricature, stating why John Nott should resign, and the *Sun* also had an editorial, 'John Must Move On.' What a miserable business it must be to be unable to pick up the paper without reading some anonymous call for your resignation.

As for myself, it really seems as if that rather horrific business with Terry Coleman did no harm. People do not read things very closely and the majority do not appear to have realised just how awful it was. Sometimes one can be the beneficiary of inattention instead of the victim. But whatever happens, I have had an awful lot of luck in the last three months. If there is one single person to whom I owe it, I suppose it would be Barbara Maxwell, who put me on *Question Time*, and has been singing my praises to people in the media.

Saltwood   *Friday, 18 June*

I went and spoke to the Monday Club at Lympne Castle today. I really cannot bear the Monday Club. They are all mad, quite different from its heyday, when it was a right-wing pressure group at the time of Ted Heath's Government. Now they are a prickly residue in the body politic, a nasty sort of gallstone. But I could not refuse as Deirdre Margary had been so noble (it turned out) in plugging my name for Folkestone.

We trailed over to Lympne Castle and there was what is known as a good attendance. First cheese and wine was consumed and, naturally, no one was particularly interested in me, or wanted to make my acquaintance.

Then I delivered a splendid speech about how the country's mood had changed, the Jubilee, the Royal Wedding, the Falklands, etc. etc. But they are so introverted they hardly noticed. 'Questions' concentrated almost exclusively on the BBC and immigration. Groanworthily at the close of my speech cheese and wine resumed as an occupation. We could not escape as we were committed, out of noseyness, to dine with the Margarys.

In the fullness of time, Deirdre separated Jane and I, Jock Massareene and Annabelle, the local chairman of the Monday Club (heavily built and *rebarbatif*), an unsympathetic woman in late middle age who appeared to be some relation, and a young couple, and took us through into the private part of the Castle.

Nightmarishly, instead of going into dinner, Harry Margary uttered the dreaded sentence, 'I suggest we all have a drink.' I was practically dead on my feet – it was about 9.30 p.m. – and I drank orange juice. I sat, half-dozing, on the window seat, looking out over Romney Marsh, and the female half of the 'young couple' told me how she had been a girlfriend of David Owen, also something-something of Peter Carrington's daughter, but I did not pay as much attention as perhaps I should have.

Finally, we got into dinner, and I was dismayed to see from the number of knives and forks at one's place that a long sequence of different courses was in prospect. On and on the evening dragged. Almost as long as the Heddles', almost as boring as the Mitchisons'. *Never* go out locally. My boredom threshold is far too low. I should have 'sparkled', but couldn't. Gloomily I sat, my face drained and sulky. The male half of the 'young couple', seated at the centre of the long table, made from time-to-time an idiotic joke at which people laughed. Perhaps fortunately, I could not catch Jane's eye as she was shielded by flowers and table ornaments. Jock Massereene, who sat opposite me, talked good sense about animal welfare, told horror stories about deer poaching on his Scottish estates. But in all other respects the evening was purgatorial.

Fortunately, the heavily-built Area chairman of the Monday Club suffered (I assume) from an enlarged prostate gland and had to get up before the coffee and search for the 'toilet'. I took advantage of this, autogalvanised and rose also, saying that we had kept Nanny waiting far longer than we had promised, wonderful evening, everything so delicious and glorious, cannot thank you enough, etc. etc., and off we went. Ooh!

Cloisters   *Monday, 21 June*

This evening I dined with the Commandant General of the Royal Marines. A number of other officers were present at the banquet, which took place in the Stationers Hall – very collegiate, with polished oak tables on stone flags. They are all delighted about the Falklands – of course – and lobbied us (several MPs were present) for replacements to be ordered immediately, both for the Round Table class and for *Intrepid* and *Fearless*.

The officer next to me, a Major Hooper, was highly intelligent and soon showed himself to be a closet nationalist. We were in absolute sympathy over the direction of British defence policy in the '80s. He told me that the Russian attaché in Germany had said to him after the Crusader Exercise how glad he was that the British Army was so small. Hooper said the only other decent army was the German one. The US Marine Corps? The 82nd Airborne? He said they were useless. On exercise in Corsica last year, the US Marines were stoned so far that the officers in the Fire Control Unit were actually falling about and giggling for hours on end.

Cloisters   *Tuesday, 22 June*

Atkins came up to me in the Lobby and made a few oblique remarks about my 'publicity campaign', getting 'attention in the media' etc.; did this mean I might make another attempt at the Defence Chair?

Assuming that he was making the enquiry on behalf of Tony, I said (quite truthfully) that the extent to which I got attention in the media was quite outside my control. In any case, the Party had decided that it preferred Tony and I would not challenge that decision a second time. Somewhat to my surprise, he moved on into saying that he thought it would be a 'good idea', '... dear old Tony has a heart of gold,' but that the officers were so weak, etc. etc. I replied that I could only consider it if the Left 'whip' allowed a free vote in the election in order to counter-balance the various people like Pat Wall and Winston who always vote against me, even though I am on the '92' slate. He said he would think this over. But of course he is not particularly influential, although it was interesting that he should make the approach. From what he said I inferred that Cranley Onslow[1] was also in favour of the idea.

I *might* try once more I suppose, but really and truly if I do not get Minister of State at Defence in the reshuffle, or take Ian's place if he is given a portfolio, I think I will go into 'retraite'. More time for travel. Might even not be bothered to stand again in Plymouth. But I must not forget that I was turning all these things over in my mind as long ago as 1976. One has these moments of depression and futility – and if I had succumbed to temptation then, I would not have been in my place (and played such part as I did) in what was the most exciting and significant episode in our history since 1945. *What* a time to be in Parliament that was! Last night, during the Division, I stopped and had a word with the Speaker as I passed his Chair, and he agreed, telling me how he had been in his place for every moment of every debate that we had had during the crisis. He, too, played his part, subtly and welshly, obstructing the pacifists; hardly ever calling Dalyell and Faulds.[2] The basic patriotism of the working classes; far stronger than the what's-in-it-for-me motivation of the managerial class, 'Industry' and 'The City'.

---

[1] Cranley Onslow, MP for Woking since 1964.
[2] Andrew Faulds, MP for Warley East since 1974 (Smethwick, 1966–74).

Saltwood   *Friday, 2 July*

Still hanging over one is the agony of the September reshuffle. I ought, of course, to get a job: Min of State at Defence. But I know, from the Chief Whip's face as I see him in the corridors, that I'm not going to.

Saltwood   *Saturday, 10 July*

Yesterday I was hanging around by the swimming pool at Saltwood when something made me go in and ring the Message Board as I had given Alison the day off. There was a message from Alan Grundy of Plymouth Sound that I was to stand by at 6.15 p.m. on Saturday evening to fly out with the Lord Mayor to the *Canberra*. God alive! Another weekend busted; and how the hell was I to get to Plymouth? No trains, school holidays just beginning, traffic solid at all M5 interchanges etc. etc. Gah! Sadly I went back out to the garden. There is no fun in a Friday evening if you know the rest of the weekend is blighted. However I had to go.

In actual fact it was a marvellous, uplifting experience. We piled into the little Sea Otter, a sturdy twin-engined high-wing cabin plane, which gave one great confidence. After flying for about ten minutes into a grey, very South Atlantic seascape, with the horizon completely blurred, we saw the white turbulence from the double wake of a big ship with twin screws. Then seconds later her escort, a little frigate, tiny and vulnerable it seemed, with its single 4.5" gun forward. I felt very moved when I saw that little frigate and thought how she and her sister ships had sailed the whole length of the world to uphold the honour of the country and of the Royal Navy. What a truly wonderful epic event in our history was that Falkland Islands war. I have said this so many times in so many places, and on each occasion I can still feel almost tearful. There will never again be anything like that.

Then, seconds later, we saw the great ship herself. Curiously muted and solemn she seemed, there was no one on deck at all. No soldiers to wave at, no crew members unoccupied. Her bow completely rusted along the line of the prow, and frightful rust streaks and scars along the side of the hull. The complete absence of human life made her seem like a ghost ship. There was something very solemn and forbidding about it. It conveyed to one more effectively than anything else could have done how nearly she *was* a ghost. She had indeed come back from the dead, but in substance as well as in spirit.

Our pilot made many passes and lost altitude until we were only a few feet off the water and on his last two approaches he passed so close that one could have read a newspaper headline on the deck. There was something tremendously confident, detached almost, about the way that great ship, which had led a charmed life in the mortal perils of San Carlos Water, steamed on through the flat calm, monotone waters of the English Channel. It was a perfect prelude to the glorious display of abandon and rejoicing that was to break out when she finally arrived at Southampton.

While we were waiting for the plane, poor David Owen came up to me, looking ghastly. His hair is now almost completely grey, as is his complexion. He looks as if he has lost a stone-and-a-half and is obviously deeply unhappy. I had sent him a nice note of commiseration, all the easier to write because it was heartfelt. I had told him Jane's comment after watching his brief appearance on television that came at the end of a long boozy hesitant waffling by Roy Jenkins, after his victory. 'How could they?' she asked. He liked this.

He was still in an agitated state and kept asking me if I thought it all right if he refused to serve in the Shadow Cabinet. Kept saying how awful the Liberals were and so on. I tried to get him to come back and have a pasty at Bratton, which he would like to have done I know. But he claimed that he was expected home and got back into his Volvo station wagon to drive to Wiltshire.

Cloisters   *Monday, 12 July*

Willie made the most deplorable, slovenly, casual Statement today about the intruder who got into the Queen's bedroom. He treated it with no more gravity, but on a higher level of obfuscation, than he would a second-class riot, with some police injuries and a few broken shop windows, in, say, Stoke Newington. Talk about 'not rising to the occasion.'

Tactically, he succeeded in that the whole House was so flabbergasted and bewildered by the enormity of what had happened and the inconclusive routine way in which he announced it that he did manage to 'keep the temperature down'. But the press were already in a highly indignant state and by the time the Home Affairs Committee assembled some Members, notably Jack Page, were puce with anger. Usually Jack Page is never at a loss for words, but he addressed the Committee, absurdly on a Point of Order (the only other person to do this since I have been an officer, was Geoffrey Dickens). I do not think this affair is over by any means.

A little later in the proceedings I managed to make Tim Raison – whom I have disliked since we were together at Eton and whom I recognise as a closet Liberal – lose his temper. Sarcastically, I had commended the Home Office for its high-minded disregard, which it communicated to its Ministers, for the garnering of votes, citing its failure in the law and order field and its bland assumption that we could simultaneously disregard our manifesto commitments in the fields of both immigration control and animal welfare.

Tim went completely crazy. He snarled, made a dotty point about soldiers' faces terribly burned in the Falklands fighting, '. . . which we assume must concern you,' and animal research. I looked out of the window, delighted. I assume it will be reported to Willie, but it was couched in a form that makes it rather hard to relay as being openly insulting which, say, Nick Budgen and Jack Page had done.

Cloisters   *Tuesday, 13 July*

It is July in the Commons. Ugh!

Hot and balmy outside, and the Albany bedroom window, now in its fifth straight year without a sashcord, has to be propped with a block of wood and ventilates inadequately.

Inevitably, it is the Finance Bill Report Stage. A three-line whip – '. . . until this business is concluded,' which last night was at 3.50 a.m., although, naturally, the wastage was colossal, and by the end we were down to about 120. This morning I woke up and thought that *I must not take any more speaking engagements anywhere.* Indeed, I am in the mood to cancel those that I have hanging over me at the moment. Nor do I, at all, want to go to Plymouth again until – and possibly not even then – the next general election. How the hell do I get down there? The rail strike will probably last until October and the

West Country roads are totally congested except (putatively) between 2–4 a.m.

Yesterday, a typically filthy Monday morning. A dentist appointment; and correspondence scattered and not to hand; many small things (in addition to massive ones) left undone. Little Jackie Felce, who is very amiable and pleasant, came up and wanted a mine detector to look for her watch; which she had mislaid in the straw. Where the hell was the mine detector? I looked in the garden entrance (where it is always kept, but needless to say was not), the garages, the outhouses, Andrew's bedroom, Andrew's old bedroom, James's bedroom, James's dark-room, sundry other rooms and localities. Time, time slipping past. The sand *rushing* through the hour glass. Jane found it in Winifred.[1]

'Winifred's in a terrible state,' Jane said. Inwardly screeching I ran down to the garage. 'Look at this.' She pressed on Winifred's front wing. Barking my shin on some old motorbike parts, I climbed over and did the same. 'Perfectly solid, what's the matter?'

'Oh she is in such a dreadful state.'

I reeled away clutching my head, then howling at the heavens and shaking my fists in the air. Oh for time to linger on the estate, to polish and buff and mend and improve, and *unwind*.

Later, when I got up to the House of Commons, Frank Haynes[2] twinklingly, congratulated me on being the next Secretary of State for Defence. Being very vain and having a high opinion of myself I only dissimulated slightly, thinking he was referring to recent exchanges in the Commons (he kept talking about Jim Callaghan). But it turned out that Callaghan had written an article in the previous day's *Sunday Pictorial* entitled, *Why I Won't Rest Until John Nott Goes*, and had recommended me as his successor!

I rushed to the Library and made Rosanne do photocopies. It must be a treasurable compliment to be recommended by the former Prime Minister. But unlike Julia Langdon's compliment, it would not make the slightest difference in the Party. It may even be adverse. Perhaps fortunately, no Conservative ever reads the *Sunday Pictorial*.

I had a message from Mark Schreiber to ring him. I thought he was

---

[1] Winifred was the Clarks' name for a little Morris 8 two-seater which, due to its extremely short wheel-base, fitted snugly into a far corner of the long garage.

[2] Frank Haynes, MP for Ashfield since 1979; Labour Whip.

going to talk to me about the revisionist defence school and my article in *The Times*. But he asked me about what I thought of Willie's Statement.

Well, I know that Mark is congenitally pro-Willie as we talked before about the sort of pressures he has to endure from the Right, so I opened a little guardedly,

'Well I really did think it was a little inadequate ...'

Finding that he agreed and was extremely indignant, I developed the theme, told him about the noisy meeting of the Home Affairs Committee last night, Jack Page being literally apoplectic.

Mark described to me in detail the police arrangements for protecting the Palace, which are a complete shambles. There are no fewer than three police departments involved: A1 (duties in connection with royalty, under the command of a Mr Trestrail, who also has overall responsibility); A7 (crime prevention, which has an advisory role, under a man called Ashton); and A11 (diplomatic protection) *not* the Special Branch, under a man called Duffy, which is concerned with protecting the Queen's person.

All these departments overlap and, as the police are themselves conducting the enquiry, will presumably shift and shunt the blame between each other.

Mark continued to develop the theme of Willie's culpability. He pointed out that Peter Carrington had honourably tendered his resignation following what he judged to be a 'national humiliation.' Was this not a humiliation of an even higher order? I agreed, egged him on, I said I was keen on rehabilitating Peter Carrington (a total lie) and that it would do no harm as part of this process to draw the contrast between their two ways of behaving. I even suggested that they put it on the cover of the *Economist*, out tomorrow night. I doubt if he will manage this, but Mark is definitely indignant. It is very satisfactory when one can get the Left to bite each other.

Later, as I discussed this with Alison while dictating, it occurred to me to give Ian Gow a fright by warning him that I might draw this contrast myself at *Question Time*. As indeed I might. I very nearly lost my temper yesterday but on the whole probably not. It would be a classic *torschlüss*, wouldn't it?

Only last night Michael McNair-Wilson was saying to me that I had 'done enough.' All I had to do now was sit still, get through the next three weeks, and either I got a ministerial appointment in September, or I never would. Of course there is no such word as 'never' in politics, but I know what he means. It is a rather nice restful thought to have in one's mind, an excuse for not doing things, like bellowing *j'accuse* and releasing the great torrent of loathing which I feel for Willie and which, I know, is reciprocated.

Anyway, I put a call through to Ian at Downing Street. He was in with the Prime Minister. I explained the 'delicacy' of the subject matter to his secretary and she took a note in to him and put it under his nose.

A few minutes later he rang me back. I told him that some on our side, possibly even myself, might call this afternoon for Willie's resignation and contrast his behaviour with that of Peter Carrington. 'Don't do it,' he said. 'Whatever you do *you* must not do this.'

'Well some people may do it,' I said.

'Let them, but whatever you do don't you do it yourself.'

He was very intense about this. It really was a very direct message. So (needless to say) I won't do it. But I feel we are probably very near a now-or-never situation. Although whether he said don't do it because the Prime Minister has already decided to promote me (as Adam Raphael said she had), and if I had attacked the Home Secretary it would make it very difficult for her, or whether it is that Ian is hoping that it may happen, but still anticipates difficulty with Willie's veto, I really do not know. One is a strong position, the other a weak one.

My own natural inclination for cavalry tactics made me want to charge Willie head-on and hopefully get rid of him completely so the question of veto would not arise. But even if he did go, it might still be difficult for her to promote the first person on our side to call for it. Jopling would probably stop her. Ah well, we shall see.

Saltwood Great Library   *Tuesday, 20 July*

My father has had a *coup-de-vieux* and is now in unhappy decline. There is scarcely any longer a point in going over [to the Garden House] to call on him. He just sits, on his low green velvet chair by the big window. Col was very aggrieved the other day because as he approached my father smiled simperingly and said 'Ah, now, who's this?'

'It's your younger son, Colin, Papa.'

'Aha' (Of course my father knew perfectly well who it was. He just gets irritated with Col blatantly sucking up to him and talking a lot of recycled balls about art). Aha.

Of course my father would never have spoken like that to Celly. She would just have cackled, said 'You're completely ga–ga' or something equally brutal. He is frightened of her, as he is of most women. But, as far as I can make out, is still resisting pressure to set up a Trust Fund for Sammy.

Most of the time my father does not speak, or read, or really show any vitality whatever, although at intervals his face may indicate a cross expression. What is he actually thinking?

Disappointment, I would surmise, more than apprehension. And principally with his marriage. At first he started off jolly. But Nolwen is so odious, and *false*. 'Sweetie' this and 'Sweetie' that (this is, I suppose, a literal translation of *Cherie*), but he is her third husband, after all. And Papa has twice suffered 'intrusive' surgery since their wedding five years ago, once on his gall bladder, once his prostate. 'No surprises,' as Nolwen over-brightly told everyone – by which I assumed her to mean no indications of malignancy. But the operations 'took it out of' him. He is going to die. It could happen at any moment; but equally he could last for another three years.[1]

I hardly notice. Will Andrew and Jamie, if God spares them, feel like this about me? I suppose that it is inevitable. The five stages of fatherhood. First, protective. Then, love. Then, an idolised elder brother, racing at Silverstone, 'parping' blondes. Then, an old friend, giving counsel and the occasional 'treat' (or cheque). Finally the *nonno*, selfishly in the way; holding on for far too long, obstructing the natural course of inheritance.

When I said all this to Jane she said yes, but his face still lights up when you come into the room. And at once I felt terrible. If my father goes back to France this week (which I think improbable) I will write to him affectionately and just hope that Nolwen does not intercept it. She, of course, dreads him dying at the *Vieux Manoir*, knowing full well that I would seize the Garden House immediately and forbid her on her return.

---

[1] Lord Clark died in May 1983 (see *Diaries*, 1993).

The day of the Falkland Islands Service at St Paul's. I only just made the 7.19 a.m. from Sandling as the horrible little Renault, which has already broken its reverse gear, stuck in bottom and I had to transfer to the Trelawneys' car at the village green.

I walked from the Commons to Horseguards where the coaches were waiting. We surged to St Paul's, crossing red lights with the assistance of police motorcyclists, and arrived an hour before the Queen was due. So I slyly dodged round the barriers and found a coffee shop, entirely staffed by black people, where I had coffee and a sticky bun.

In spite of this I was in my seat three-quarters-of-an-hour early. Every minute was interesting as the congregation assembled. I had an excellent place, under the dome, and there in front of me, still hunched and grey, just as he had been on that Monday, 5th April, at 'Rab's' memorial service, was Richard Luce.

'What's going through your mind?' I asked him. He answered candidly: 'I am shattered, absolutely shattered.'

And sure enough, a little later, up came Peter Carrington, relegated to a row behind me with some very dud peers. Lady Carrington was *bright*, but Peter still looked a bit sulky I thought – and who can blame him, having to sit between Lord Peart and Lord De L'Isle. The first member of the Cabinet to arrive was Norman Fowler; how common he always looks. A little later up came Heseltine and I was glad to see he had been (obviously deliberately) put at the very end of the Government row so that he was blocked by pillars.

I squirmed and turned in my seat, staring shamelessly. Soon I realised that the block behind me was filling up with next of kin. Many of them were Para families and, very touchingly, they all wore something red – the red of the Red Beret – about their clothing. The girls wore ribbons or cardigans, the fathers handkerchiefs, and so on. Only two rows behind me sat three adorable winklers, two little boys and a girl, who were dressed in red jerseys with metal parachute badges, looking enormous, pinned on their chest. With the exception of the very young children, who were excited and jolly, most of the relatives looked deeply unhappy. Some of the wives, or Mums, were old NAAFI comforts and painted up to the nines, but the majority were beauties, many of them raging beauties, and none of the young ones wearing any make-up, which was probably just as well as most of them cried all the way through the service.

Willie arrived, stooping and flushed and wearing some heavy red ribbon round his neck. It looked like the Bath, what was it? He is absolutely imperméable. He now says that not only is he not going to resign, but he is going to fight the next general election.

The Royal Family arrived two by two, all in uniform I am glad to say, although the Duchess of Kent now looks very spaced-out indeed. Princess Diana looked thin as a rake and out-paced her consort with her special lanky stride. The Queen, as always, surprised one with how tiny she is; Philip consistent and splendid towers above her.

The service itself could have been worse. The most objectionable of the peaceniks' plans having been thwarted largely, I believe, following my question to the Prime Minister on 13th July. The second lesson was read by David Cooper, chaplain of 2 Para, and it was most fitting to hear that flat northern accent reading out the verses of St Mark, having last heard it coming directly from the tin church in Port Stanley on the day of the victory. Little Dr Greet,[1] with whom I have had several clashes in the last ten days, turned out to have quite a good microphone voice and his prayers were not as awful as one might have expected. And we ended with Psalm 23, but sung to Irvine's music, and there cannot have been many dry eyes in the Cathedral.

Afterwards the crocodile moved its way out very slowly down the aisle, starting from the top. I was on the civilian side, passing row after row of next of kin. Anxiously I scanned their faces, but the only emotion I could see was anguish, sheer anguish.

Cloisters   *Tuesday, 27 July*

Lunched today with Norman St John-Stevas at 34 Montpelier Square, an expensive address. It is always a good (or is it a bad?) sign when you see a house some distance away, obviously the chic-est and most painted-up in the street and, as you close the range, this turns out to be your destination. Lightheartedly, as we ascended the steps, I said, ' ... something-something fucking', to Jane and Margaret Argyll materialised at the same moment. But she is used to that kind of thing

---

[1] The Reverend Dr Kenneth Greet, Moderator, Free Church Federal Council.

and did not object. She is *unbelievably* preserved – 'preserved' being the word; but gave the show away a bit by moving very stiffly and hesitantly, being uncertain about steps, etc.[1]

The interior was gay as can be; bandbox gay, with bright paint and clashing reds and greens, and everything discreetly, but ingeniously lit by interior decorators with hidden lamps and bulbs. A smart little group, the ladies better than the men (and better looking too). Mary Roxburghe;[2] Olga Maitland, gossip columnist of the *Sunday Express*, rather scrawny and combative I thought, we did not get on. Lady something-or-other, who spoke with a strong French accent, and a young blonde cutie who had broken her leg in three places after being dropped by her boyfriend in a car park at a hunt ball and walked with a stick. At my head of the table sat Victor Matthews, just as common and nasty as *Private Eye* made him out to be, but with a very distinct vitality of his own. The ambience of power, good company.[3] I tackled him several times about the *Atlantic Conveyor* replacement. I both fluffed and slapped him. Told him that it was a question of *noblesse oblige* and that as he was now of the *noblesse* he must do what was expected of him. I told him, too, that 'Downing Street' (I had mentioned the matter to Ian Gow this morning) had said he was 'all right'. He was less susceptible to flattery than some of his breeding.

The food was very good, although the silver could have been better. We had a salmon mousse, perfectly reasonable filet of beef and then a soufflé. Indifferent white wine, an excellent claret. Does Norman have private means? There was nothing really first class in the contents, but everything was very shiny and Asprey-looking.

Maddeningly I had a summons to Ian Gow's room at 2.45pm, to be briefed on a question about the South Atlantic Fund, so we had to leave early. Goodness knows what they said about us after we had gone out. I would like to have stayed longer. Jane rightly pointed out that Norman is really a very kind person. He has a coruscating wit, but he only uses it against the hubristic and the nasty. He is never

---

[1] Margaret Argyll, around whom sexual gossip had been rampant; the third wife of 11th Duke of Argyll they divorced amidst much acrimony in 1963. At the time of this entry she was 70.

[2] First wife of the 9th Duke of Roxburghe (they divorced in 1953).

[3] Victor Matthews, created life peer in 1980, had through the Trafalgar House company owned the Cunard shipping line which in turn owned the *Atlantic Conveyor*, one of the non-RN container ships commandeered for Falklands task force, and lost in the campaign.

cruel and never – which is so easy – pots shots off the weak or the backward.

Cloisters   *Thursday, 29 July*

Peter Hordern had asked me to lunch. A rather boring terraced house in Cadogan Street, burgled four times in the last two years he told me. The other guests were Julian Amery and Nicholas Baker.[1] Hordern, who is very senior in the Public Accounts Committee, was trying to pick our brains about defence costings, concerning which he is, quite rightly, apprehensive. A very nice man, highly intelligent, but almost too fastidious for politics. It has always mystified me why he has not been made a Minister as he is extremely able. We were an ill-assorted quartet and although what Julian says is good sense, he is now a little deaf and when he is speaking himself his pauses-for-effect are so protracted that one finds oneself either interrupting or starting on one's own thesis in the assumption that Julian has finished.

The Adjournment Debate finished on time with a splendid duet by Dennis Skinner and John Biffen and we made our way to the Cavalry Club. Also present were two Whips, Carol Mather and Peter Brooke. One of the most engaging (but vulnerable) things about Ian is how *naïf* he is. Almost at once he started to complain to Peter Brooke that at an Embassy dinner party last week the Chief Whip had found himself sitting only three places away from Marcia Falkender, how tactless that was of the Embassy Social Secretary. I said that Lady Falkender wanted to join the Conservative Party and they all thought I was joking. But of course she is interested in power, she loves its ambience and misses its absence dreadfully. She is studying the Conservative Party closely at the present time and hopes to infiltrate it and become privy to many of its secrets.[2]

Over the first course, and I cannot remember how the subject

---

[1] Nicholas Baker, MP for North Devon since 1979; Parliamentary Private Secretary to the Armed Forces Minister since 1981.

[2] Marcia Falkender, created a life peer in 1974, had been private and political secretary to Harold Wilson, 1956–83, including two spells at Downing Street when he was Prime Minister. Elsewhere in his journal AC notes that she had enjoyed 'a room next to the Prime Minister's study in the Palace of Westminster and being able directly to influence affairs of state.'

originated, I said what a dreadful and dangerous fellow Robert Arm-strong[1] was. To my great surprise and delight, while Ian was getting his breath back, Carol Mather chimed in with support, said he too thought Armstrong was 'creepy'.

'It is my personal belief,' I said, 'that he is a full Colonel in the KGB.'

Nobody demurred.

Cloisters   *Friday, 30 July*

Both Government and Opposition backbenchers are longing to get away. In the Smoking Room corridor gutting my locker – the first time since 1977 – I found an enormous mass of 1977 correspondence, unsigned and neatly slotted into folded envelopes by Sue, together with a good deal of material formerly urgent, now obsolete.

Already the House has lost its vitality. Cleaners and char ladies swarmed all over the place with enormous sacks of wastepaper, empty bottles, etc. The Chamber was empty and the lights out. Those colleagues who remained were scuttling about collecting their brief-cases. Nobody wanted to talk politics; the clock had struck, and we had all changed back from footmen in powdered wigs into rats.

So ends the most enjoyable, eventful and uplifting Parliamentary session that I have ever known, or, undoubtedly, will ever experience again. I have made much impact and played a far from negligible part in bringing about policies concerning which I feel passionately. But I am afraid it was a high point. That sort of thing can never be repeated and I feel jaded now. My present mood is, what-of-it? I am no longer frightened of my constituents, do not want to be a Whip, do not really want to be a junior minister and think to myself that I could not accept anything lower than Minister of State. As the likelihood of my being put straight into that position must be rated at fractions of zero, it is hard to see what the future holds.

---

[1]Sir Robert Armstrong, Secretary to the Cabinet since 1976, joint head of the Civil Service since 1981.

Saltwood   *Monday, August 16*

Jim Prior[1] giving trouble again today. Usual stuff about a 'disgrace' having 3,000,000 unemployed, preliminary sparring in advance of (a) reshuffle, (b) Treasury 'discussions' on public spending. As to (a) I don't think there'll be one, except a few little cosmetic dibs and dabs at the lower levels including, I would guess, a painful-to-me change of junior ministry at MoD. JP's own reputation somewhat tarnished by his tinky behaviour during reshuffles *last* year, but he may have thought it prudent to stage a pre-emptive strike. There are still three wet heavies left in the Cabinet – JP, Heseltine and Walker. But owing to this ludicrous convention that Ministers measure their virility by the esteem in which they are held by their Permanent Secretaries, and as those PSs' own esteem among their colleagues is assessed on the scale of their spending budgets, each SoS, instead of considering the National Interest – still less Government policy in the strategic sense – has to 'fight his corner'. So the three heavies get the support of ponces like Younger and Edwards[2] who need funds for their wanky little principalities.

The whole distribution of Cabinet and Government posts has become absurdly distorted by what are, in the last resort, PR considerations. Minister of 'Sport', but no one for the Royal Navy. And if there really have to be Secretaries of State for Wales and Scotland in the Cabinet then they should simply be selected by the Prime Minister (like Cecil Parkinson in the 'War' Cabinet).

Also being bandied about is the succession to George Thomas.[3] Since we rose I have been meaning to talk to Norman [St John-Stevas] about this. Yesterday I finally tracked him down to his cottage. He spoke guardedly, but warmed up. Of course he would love it. I suppose he might make the Lodgings a bit *too* pink-and-apricot, but I think that his basic kindness, seriousness and constitutional sense would make him ideally suited – while coming as a bonus would be the wit and cattiness under fire. Really, if I don't get a job this autumn I don't

---

[1] James Prior, Secretary of State for N. Ireland since 1981; previously Employment Secretary.

[2] George Younger, MP for Ayr since 1964, Secretary of State for Scotland since 1979; Nicholas Edwards, MP for Pembroke since 1970, Secretary of State for Wales since 1979.

[3] George Thomas, the Speaker of the Commons since 1976 (he had been MP for Cardiff Central, 1945–50; Cardiff West since 1950).

see much point in going back at all – just using up one's time and substance – but with Norman in the chair it would still be fun to go into the Chamber. I get the feeling his constituency isn't very large.

Cloisters   *Wednesday, 1 September*

The BBC, still smarting from the criticism they attracted during the Falklands Campaign (why is it the BBC is so extraordinarily sensitive to criticism?) have set up a panel of Aunt Sallies from the MoD and have invited all and sundry to come and throw coconuts at them. The audience has been filled out with a lot of rent-a-crowd students who hated the whole operation anyway.

The only good moment came when one nameless colonel was finally goaded into telling how all the correspondents had filed copy about the attack on Mt. Longdon, ' ... preceded by the heaviest artillery barrage since Korea ...' etc., etc., and then, when the assault had successfully taken place at night, without any artillery preparation whatever, they had all scrambled to try and get their copy back from the teleprinters. That whining oaf Brian Hanrahan ('I counted them all out ...') maundered on about how journalists never tried to get scoops, never had any thought of advancing their own careers at the expense of their colleagues etc. To my private shame, when it was my turn, I omitted to make sarcastic reference to this, although I did lash out quite a bit.

Saltwood   *Wednesday, 8 September*

Telephoned to Jonathan Aitken today, to see if he could help over Andrew's expedition to the Yemen.[1] As always, he was pleasant and obliging; his wife has just given birth to a son so he was in a good mood. Just as I was ringing off he said, 'By the way I do hear, which is very good news, that there is a strong likelihood of your joining the

---

[1] AC's younger son was going to North Yemen to work with the Catholic Church at Raymah, as part of a stint of Voluntary Service Overseas, before attending the Regular Commissions Board.

Government . . .' I laughed, delighted. 'But,' (I can't remember exactly how he went on) ' . . . Gow is arguing very strongly for your inclusion, and Madam is said not to be opposed, but apparently Jopling is against it . . .' My heart sank. Jopling and Willie combined would be unstoppable, or rather *insurmountable*, if they were to veto a junior appointment. *Why?* Jane said that some remark I had made about Gail [Jopling] must have got back. But I really don't think I have made one to anybody except her. Jane rightly reminded me that indiscretion of this kind is an endemic fault of mine.

Jonathan had gone on to say that Jopling was trying to get rid of Gow himself – 'rid' of course meaning shifted to some dud ministry outside the Cabinet. J said that Jopling felt himself to have been worsted by Gow on a number of occasions – the Employment Bill, the N. Ireland Bill and was even elevating this into a test case. If that is so I *have* had it. Also I get the faintest suspicion (not that I have not had it, wrongly, in the past) that IG's influence is waning. The new accent is on the managerial – hence this ghastly, planted rumour that Heseltine is to be the new S of S at Defence. Well, what is written is written. I know I am incredibly well off and blessed, and worry far too much – about Andrew in the Yemen, about James in helicopters, about falling interest rates,[1] about my crowded desk and my (non-existent) sex-life, even about Tom crossing the road[2] – but I have got a tension-headache. Monstrous, as I said to Jane, in the middle of the recess. Also a strange weakness, muscular dystrophy in the arms, particularly the left arm. Anxiety induces hypochondria, but I have had problems with my left arm for some months. Strange.

Saltwood   *Thursday, 9 September*

This evening little Nigel Forman[3] rang. Soft-spoken in the extreme. He told me that he was having 'difficulty' with his Association and that Michael Jopling had suggested that he ask me to go down and

---

[1] AC now eschewed the stock market and kept his wealth in cash, on 28-day deposits.

[2] Tom, the Clarks' Jack Russell terrier, had no road sense, and had the habit of wandering off to the farm – which meant traversing Sandy Lane, a route frequented by heavy lorries and vans.

[3] Nigel Forman, MP for Carshalton since 1976; Parliamentary Private Secretary to the Minister of State at the Foreign Office since 1979.

make a law-and-order speech (apparently one of the accusations they are using to upset Nigel is that he is opposed to capital punishment) in which I said what a good fellow he is. I am quite ready to do this, because I quite like Nigel and he has in fact been useful in the Home Affairs Committee, stating a point of view which would normally be regarded as right wing, on such questions as the 'Supervised Release' scheme. Also I loathe constituency associations and with very few exceptions, will always back a colleague against them. I was both puzzled and encouraged that Michael Jopling had suggested I do this. I have always been at great pains to please MJ and do what he wants, and here I am doing it again. How can he possibly object to my promotion?

Bratton   *Friday, 10 September*

I arrived on the Hoe slightly late. Lots of smart Marines standing about, and the public arranged in a quadrangle with the nobs on tiered seats around a stand on which the clergy and senior commanders were located.

I had been put next to David Owen. We were surrounded by Conservative Councillors and dignatories who greeted me. No sign of Janet. The service itself was quite acceptable, heavily slanted towards 'triumphalism' with a quite flagrantly political harangue by John Watson, the Vicar of St Andrew's Church, at the end. The Royal Marines Band played a number of patriotic tunes as a mist closed in and beside me David Owen bellowed out the words, ' . . . God who made thee mighty, make thee mightier yet,' etc. When the music stopped there was a moment's hesitation before the crowds dispersed and we could see the navigation lights of a Nimrod coming towards us through the sea mist at a very low altitude. Just over the stands he lit all four after-burners and went into a steep bank. The noise was absolutely deafening, twice as loud as the fiercest peal of thunder you could hear and very dramatic. How they got the timing so split second, I don't know, but it was a fitting end to an appropriately militaristic service.

We had all been invited to partake of refreshment in the Major's Parlour, but I did not see much point in this as I had already established my presence by arriving late in full view of most of the people who would have criticised me if I had not attended. (Not that I would have missed it for anything.) And I had designs on David, who had shown himself all too ready to converse and gossip in whispers in the various periods of *attente* while the service was starting – somewhat to the surprise and irritation, I suspect, of the surrounding local politicians. I lost him in the crowd and then spotted him again. I broke off my conversation with Betty Easton, 'Why don't we go and have a curry?' He agreed.

On the way down to Mayflower Street we fell into step with an old trade union stalwart, Reg Curry, and his wife. They greeted me with the familiarity that comes from the secure knowledge of a condition of formal political hostility; but with David they were more reserved. 'You have lost weight David,' said Reg. DO brightened at the compliment. ' . . . it is because you deserted the Party that feeds you.' It quite spoilt the atmosphere and the four of us walked on in silence.

As soon as we were comfortably settled in the restaurant David launched into a great dissertation about his prospects, and that of the SDP.[1] To be beaten is agony, particularly when you thought victory was in the bag, but to be beaten by someone who you know, and everyone whose opinion you value knows, is inferior – that is really intolerable cruelty.

'I am blown,' he kept saying. 'I have had it.' He loathes the Liberals, loathes them more now than he does even his erstwhile colleagues on the extreme left of the Labour Party. At intervals he expressed his anxiety in Plymouth, admitted he was apprehensive about moving across to fight Janet, cursed himself again and again about having not fought a by-election immediately upon resigning from the Labour Party. David told me that he had been restrained by other SDP defectors who were uncertain about their own prospects if they did the same. This is of course a different tale from the excuse he gave me last year, which was that he could not afford to absent himself from the House of Commons for those critical months. David went on and on about how the Conservatives ought to have a general election this year. Volubly and persuasively he set out the plausible scenarios – the need to get public endorsement for further anti-trade union legislation; the need to avoid a pre-election blight on measures laid before Parliament next year, etc. But of course his real reasons are personal. If both the Alliance and the Labour Party are smashed, then David can play it long and rebuild the SDP independently of the Liberals,

---

[1] Owen had been defeated for the leadership of the SDP by Roy Jenkins.

but drawing heavily on the 'old' Labour Party. But if the election is put off for a year or eighteen months, the Labour Party might mend its fences in advance and the Liberals may become the dominant partner in the Alliance. David Owen will then be left with nothing, perhaps not even a seat in the House of Commons. What a nightmare for him, no wonder he looks haggard.

David talked about his immediate dilemma, which is whether to refuse to serve in the Shadow Cabinet and to refuse, perhaps, even a nominal role as a Shadow spokesman. Together we drafted letters to Roy Jenkins which would frighten him (because RJ still remains apprehensive of David), about how David would prefer to remain free to speak on any subject, how occasionally he (RJ!) might want David to deputise for him on economic subjects if RJ were away, and so forth.

At one point he started talking about me, said, 'You want to be careful though, you know Alan . . .' I thought he was reverting to his old warning of last year when he told me that I could easily lose Sutton to an Alliance candidate. But no, he dismissed that idea completely – 'of course you will be all right.' What he had meant was that I should not accept a junior post in the Government, 'with your status, and reputation, as backbencher, it would be madness for you to go in as a junior under-secretary and do a two-year apprenticeship in an obscure post. You should insist on being made a Minister of State.' David told me how he had refused to go in as under-secretary when the Labour Government of 1974 was reformed, how Barbara Castle[1] had promised to give him Minister of State status in all but name, let him sit in on all consultations and so on and how in the fullness of time Harold Wilson had kept his word when he was moved to the Foreign Office.

I was delighted by all this, but when I told Jane she shrewdly pointed out that he was only doing to me what I regularly enjoy doing to him – flattering him with mildly fantastic compliments.

---

[1] Barbara Castle, MP for Blackburn 1945–79, was at the time Secretary of State for Social Services.

Saltwood   *Monday, 13 September*

Our last day before we set off on a very short motor tour, which,
hopefully, will end in Zermatt. Still no news or mention of the
reshuffle and I could not resist telephoning Jonathan Aitken again,
bearing in mind that Michael Jopling was presently trying to get me
to do something. JA now admitted that his source was Ian Gow
himself, claimed that they had both got extremely inebriated at
Jonathan's house in early August. But, and this *was* significant, JA said
that he had recently run into Norman Lamont and asked him in
jocular terms about his (NL's) prospects in the middle rank reshuffle.
Alarmingly Norman Lamont had said, 'Apparently the whole thing
is being held up because of Alan,' ie that some wanted me, others did
not. It is really too vexing. I told Jonathan about Michael Jopling's
request and he brilliantly advised me not just to carry out the instructions, but to copy my speech both to Jopling and Willie.

After putting the phone down I decided to go one better – for all
I know this blasted reshuffle is being argued about at this very minute,
before The Lady leaves for China – and send them both *advance* copies
of what I was going to say, 'in case you want anything altered.'

Oh to be in the Citroen, wafting across France from one rosette to
the next!

Cloisters   *Monday, 27 September*

I was sitting at my desk, first day back, when Tristan Garel-Jones
walked through. He is *not* discreet. He is a good Whip because he is
independent and has a nose for information, but he cannot resist the
sound of his own voice. He said, but I think it a little simplistic, that
the reshuffle had been deferred until January because of the need to
make 'Notty' carry the can for the Falklands Enquiry. This is rather a
bore as it means one has to be a good boy for the whole winter term,
careful not to put a foot wrong, etc. Also I have got a nasty feeling
that by the time New Year comes round things may have changed a
good bit and the election may be so close that there will not be a
reshuffle after all.

Cloisters *Wednesday, 29 September*

I went today to Terry Lewin's[1] farewell party at the Admiralty building. I assumed that there would be a lot of politicians and a large crowd, but in fact there were few people in the room and practically no one I knew. Only four people spoke to me, but each in turn initiated the conversation and drew me aside from their predecessor. First, the Secretary of State, then the Chief of the General Staff (Bramall); the First Sea Lord (Leach); and finally the CDS.

It was a memorable little moment that, when the First Sea Lord, who had himself got rid of Bramall, and was complaining to me about the Secretary of State 'hanging on', was then himself similarly dismissed by the CDS, who came over, 'This looks a very naval corner . . .' and made plain his wish that Leach should leave us alone.

Terry Lewin was most interesting and indiscreet about future defence spending, the Falklands campaign, the National purpose and spoke frankly and genuinely. Not a bad bag for a backbencher, but what is the point?

Cloisters *Wednesday, 13 October*

Plymouth City Council have been bothering me about their proposals to get Cattedown classified as an Enterprise Zone. God, how boring local government matters are! Like so many other tasks, the most notable and glaringly being my tax returns, I simply cannot bring myself to take action. But today, convulsively, I did so. I have to attend the quarterly meeting of the Executive Council in Plymouth and I know that it makes good feeling, and compensates for those very long periods when Janet Fookes is daily reported for her assiduous peering at cracked pavements and bent dustbin lids and I am not mentioned at all. So I, greatly to the detriment of our motoring schedule, spoke to the City Planning Office, rang the *Western Evening Herald* (who obligingly gave me a huge headline piece that evening, so that the grumpy members of the Executive could not have avoided seeing it) and sent a letter to Heseltine formally supporting their case.

At the last moment I thought I ought to take out an insurance

[1] Admiral of the Fleet Sir Terence Lewin, Chief of the Defence Staff, 1979–1982.

policy *in case* Michael is actually made Secretary of State for Defence. I enclosed a hand note saying how much I looked forward to it, working under him, etc. etc.

Very late we got into the little Renault and fought our way down through blinding rainstorms. I made a balls-up of getting on to the M3, getting lost in Kingston, and adding three-quarters of an hour to our time. On the way through we stopped at Mackenzie's Garage and I briefly drove the old $4\frac{1}{2}$. Very jolly.

Unfortunately I was not called. Huge numbers of colleagues wanted to catch The Lady on this her first day and the Speaker took no one from our bench.

Later that evening I popped into Michael Jopling's room. Perhaps he expected me to make another grumble about the Falklands visit,[1] however it was merely to tell him that I would be sending on reports of the meeting tomorrow of the 'Tory Immigration Group' and also of the '92' Dinner (at which committee nominations would be decided) but that these reports, for obvious reasons, would be unsigned and without attribution. I am but a cork bobbing about on the storm-tossed sea.

Cloisters   *Wednesday, 20 October*

An extremely full day. Dictating in the morning, then Foreign Affairs Questions. Francis Pym made a *deplorable* performance, answers far too long and mumbly. He is simply not the man he was. Has he been broken by The Lady? She used always to live in such private dread of him, but now the tables are turned.

At the end of questions I made my way to Committee Room 8, where the Defence Select Committee was taking evidence from the Task Force Commanders about their relations with the media.

Why have we all allowed ourselves to be conned into regarding this as a major issue? Many have seized on it as the only remaining angle from which to attack the Government, and thus The Lady, over the Falklands Campaign.

Also, there is the fact that the media, having this frightfully high

---

[1] AC had been disappointed not to be included in the first Government visit to the islands since the end of the war.

opinion of themselves, which they inflame by mutual massage, get dreadfully aggrieved when not accorded the respect which they think is their due. Not having been consulted at every stage about the Operation, not having been given a right of veto, and a right also to regale the audience with their opinions and interpretations on an unrestricted scale, they were resentful.

Mind you, I get the impression that there was a certain absence of tact in the way that they were treated by the Task Force Commanders – four journalists, including Gareth Parry of the *Guardian*, were taken into Carlos Water on 'D' Day and had their billets shifted from *Canberra* to an ammunition ship, then lay at anchor fully loaded for five days under air attack. When finally their pleas to be removed from this lethal target were allowed, the helicopter pilot took them to a lonely hillside overlooking Ajax Bay, the long abandoned site of 5 Brigade Command Headquarters, dumped them and clattered off, leaving them to make their own way without proper winter equipment to wherever took their fancy.

The Task Force Commanders sat in a row, Middleton (*Hermes*), Black (*Invincible*), Sandy Woodward, Jeremy Moore and Wilson, the Commander of 5 Brigade. All seemed formidable in the highest degree, clipped and authoritative. Wilson was the least impressive. With the others one can see why we won – a very different lot from some of their predecessors in World War II.

On the way in I had a chat with Robin Day. He said Heseltine could not go to Defence – 'his hair is too long'. A very good phrase, encapsulating all the reasons why it would be inappropriate.

I stayed on at the Defence Committee as long as I dared and then went along the corridor to a meeting which Lynda Chalker had organised – with David Howell bleakly sitting in, to explain to West Country MPs about projected road improvements. Naturally, being experienced politicians, we all realised that this was some kind of soft-sell approach to try and get us to shut up about heavy lorries. Everyone was in a combative frame of mind and as Lynda is so sweet natured and it would have been pointlessly cruel to have roughed her up, we vented our rage, led off by big Peter Emery, against the senior civil servants who did the 'presentation'.

This meeting, too, I had to leave early to go down to the asbestos protest in the Grand Committee Room. Place absolutely full, packed out, people standing blocking the doorway when I arrived (two minutes late, I was meant to be on the platform) and when I tried to edge past a huge livid barrack-room lawyer with pebble lenses and a raincoat, presumably a part-time flasher, he wouldn't give way. I was within an ace of cawdorising[1] him, but restricted myself to pushing past, *very* firmly, and just reached the platform in time.

I said my piece about asbestos and then had to move on to yet another engagement. This time one with greater promise, namely, the launching of Austin Mitchell's book, *Westminster Man*.[2] I snatched the last free copy, looked myself up in the index and found that I was mentioned no less than twelve times, more than any other MP. However, the atmosphere was soon spoiled when I got into a promising chat-up with a young blonde student at the LSE who ruined everything by asking if I had been at Oxford with her father. 'Possibly,' I said. 'When was that?' '1941' she answered. As I was at Oxford in 1951 and anyone with the slightest grasp of numeracy would have seen that to have been at Oxford in 1941 would make me 63, this was lowering.

Still low I was crossing New Palace Yard on my way to the '92' Dinner when Garel-Jones asked me if we could have a discussion '... Garel-Jones/Clark terms.' He had something to confide. I said I would meet him in the Lobby at the 10 o'clock vote. Gloomily I went on to the Dinner. Arriving late I was placed in starvation corner at the end of a very long table. Bad food, tepid beer, drunken and incompetent staff bumping and banging and sploshing sauce all over one's suit.

The awful thing is I really don't like the Right Wing, and this enlightenment is, I fear, mutual. The writing on the wall was last year when so many of them welched on me in the contest for the Defence Chair. George Gardiner who is, of course, sensible, put it down to jealousy. But that is too oversimplified because there is nothing to be jealous of, unless it is that gift of nature which makes me more intelligent than say, Sir Patrick Wall, or little Winston.

However, back in the Lobby Garel-Jones beckoned to me. He said that he had a special message from Jopling. A special message in the

---

[1] Earl Cawdor, father of the Clarks' friend Hugh, Viscount Emlyn, used to open Cawdor Castle once a year in the days before the stately home industry became established. Inevitably, a queue would form on such days and once the Earl, in passing to the front, had been accosted by a visitor who tried to restrain him, shouting, "ere watch where you are going.' The Earl, without hesitation felled his visitor with a single blow to the jaw and went on through the gate without halting in his progress.

[2] AC appeared in the accompanying television series (see p. 171).

sense that it was not meant to be transmitted, but yet at the same time it was intended that I should hear of it. G-J more or less said that Jopling had undertaken to get me a job in the next reshuffle, we must do something for Alan, etc. After the vote I rang Jane and told her, but I said that I was not in the slightest degree elated by this. It is a what-of-it episode really. These undertakings are practically valueless. And if it was their intention to keep me quiet until January – well, that suits me fine as it conforms exactly with my own intentions.

Cloisters   *Tuesday, 26 October*

I was still in my flat at 11 o'clock this morning, washing up and pecking in a desultory way at housework. This always fills me with gloom – the cold empty chambers, the peeling wallpaper, the layers of dust and grease. Beautiful possessions surround one, but there is no warmth or vitality; the place is a dormitory only. I have not eaten a cooked meal there, or 'entertained', since 1974, when we gave the celebrated drinks party that is referred to in the chapters in George Gardiner's book about The Lady's accession.

Then the phone rang. I was in two minds about answering it. The telephone at Albany is nearly always bores or ill-wishers. It was the Chief Whip (the Chief Whip seems to be phoning me an awful lot at the moment). He told me that there was now a place in the Falklands delegation and would I like to go.

I could not refuse. 'When is it?' 'Tomorrow.' Christ! Apart from anything else this meant I would miss Andrew to whose return we had both been looking forward for weeks. I said I would have to talk with Jane, which I did and she said I 'must' go. I confirmed with Jopling and went straight round to the MoD where there was a briefing.

They had already started when I entered the room. Buck, who has been doing his best from the outset to keep me off the delegation, gave me what is known as an 'old-fashioned' look when I came in. They are a curious selection. Two knights, Hector Monro and John Biggs-Davison, Buck (nominally leader), myself and little Peter Viggers travelling, presumably, on a good-boy pass, and Member for Gosport. The Labour lot were somewhat more grizzled, if not actually elderly. Roy Mason (as a former Secretary of State for Defence and

Privy Councillor, he is the senior member of the delegation, though not, for Party reasons, its leader), Kevin McNamara, a shadow defence spokesman, Bruce George from the Select Committee, Dick Crawshaw from the Speaker's Panel, and a dear old boy whom I have noticed before, but to whom I have never spoken, David Young.[1]

There were three votes that evening, all quite unimportant, but the whips would not let me leave until they were over. I got away to Saltwood about 8.00 p.m. and spent the rest of the evening collecting my kit, warm clothes, etc. in a high state of excitement.

Ascension Island   *Thursday, 28 October*

We breakfasted at 7.30 a.m. and then spent about an hour looking at our beautiful eggshell white VC10 through the windows of the VIP lounge before being told that there would be another hour's delay as 'an oleo strut has collapsed' (!) I started spreading alarm and despondency, saying that it was at least a four-hour job to repair it, that there should then be proper taxi-ing trials and so on. The Air Commodore who was our temporary 'nanny' denied this.

Roy Mason and I had the two best seats, with room to stretch out our legs by the emergency door. I was benefiting, as I often do, from people muddling up my courtesy title as son of a peer of the realm with that of *Rt.* Hon. which of course denotes membership of the Privy Council and great seniority.

At intervals neat little WRAFs gave us delicious (by airline standards) meals, and at twenty to four p.m., after a very low approach, we landed at Dakar to emerge blinking on to a great white apron of concrete to the heat and glare and smells of tropical Africa.

At the top of the steps to the VIP lounge lay a beautiful cat, a perfect tiger in miniature. Not only her markings, but the very way in which she lay, was utterly different from Tabitha Twitchit in Chelsea. The MPs advanced clattering and stumbling up the steps and divided round the cat, who showed no emotion other than to bend back one ear.

---

[1] Richard Crawshaw, MP for Toxteth since 1964 (Labour 1964–81; SDP since 1981); David Young, Labour MP for Bolton E. since February 1974.

We were greeted by the Ambassador and a junior member of his staff, a serious, handsome youth, with a scar on his cheek, immaculately dressed in a pale suit. He talked intelligently about French West Africa and told me much that I didn't know. The inhabitants of Dakar are jet black but prosperous and amiable, and dress beautifully. The women wore wonderful silk headdresses and flowing robes and masses of tribal jewellery – not just crude spikes and rings through ears and noses, but elegantly in the French manner. The Ambassador said that the cooking was very good too, as is the case with all former French possessions. I would like to have spent longer there and was sorry to climb back into the VC10 and head south-west into the blue.

It was dark when we got to Ascension, after crossing the equator at 6.32 p.m. A marvellous scent, heat, sea spray and *pineti* entered our nostrils. Temperatures in the day time are in the high 80s, but every evening without fail the South-East Trades cool the Island and condense and deliver a little soft rain on the upper slopes of the Green Mountain, which dominates its centre.

An enormous airfield, and everywhere looming out of the darkness the shapes of resting aircraft – Vulcans, Victor tankers, Hercules upon Hercules, Phantoms, American C141s, that are still bringing in stores and ammunition direct from Florida. Lit from below from the orange strobe lights, the aura was one of menace and great power. Already we felt ourselves to be on the fringes of the War Zone.

Port Stanley   *Friday, 29 October*

We were woken at ten past three by an apologetic Air Marshal. I had slept badly as my bunk was immediately under the outlet of the air conditioning. Colder and colder it had got and I had spent the last hour curled in a ball with my head between my knees and shivering with a single blanket tucked in all round me.

Breakfast was delicious, beaming chefs on duty, splatting eggs into huge dishes of exploding fat. Sizzling bacon, bubbling baked beans – 'Open twenty-four hours a day,' it said. 'Last hot food for 4,000 miles.'

Then we were driving out to the Hercules, absolutely jammed with cargo up the centre of the fuselage with four ranks of side-facing seats on either side. The seats were webbing and the back bolt upright against a variety of spikes, taps, nuts and other protrusions. There was very little space, indeed, and those already established seemed not to welcome our arrival particularly, nor to be in any hurry to make room for us.

Just as we arrived on the outskirts of Port Stanley, I saw the doors of the nursery school open and out tumbled a lot of jolly fair-haired children in their anoraks, to be collected by their Mums. A completely English scene. We could not possibly have abandoned these people and packaged them up in some diplomatic deal. This has been a real war of liberation, not some dreary 'peace-keeping' effort on behalf of the UN, but a battle fought in obedience to a blood tie.

Our driver parked outside the Upland Goose and we trailed inside. The MPs, shabbily coughing and cigaretting, formed a queue outside the Reception hatch. I will never, under any circumstances, stand in a queue, so I chatted up some girls who were having tea at a table at the far end of the covered patio.

When the queue had dispersed I went to the Reception desk to claim my room. (Plainly if the reservations had been made there was no need to fuss or queue barge.) However, when I got to the desk it seemed that all the places had been allocated. Impossible, I remained calm.

I had noticed that the MPs were 'pairing off' and having to share rooms and thought perhaps that if I was the odd man I might get a room to myself. No, it was 104 I had to go to. Des King, the proprietor, guided me up to 104. Noises from within, spluttering and shufflings. We opened the door – and who should be my room mate, but Buck! Awkward, but not socially insurmountable.

Ascension Island   *Wednesday, 3 November*

From 22,000 feet the surface of the South Atlantic was rippled like the sand of a shallow tidal beach. But if I held an individual ripple in my gaze, I could watch it slowly alter shape and disintegrate into a thin white border that disappeared and blended into new patterns. With awe I realised that these were enormous waves, a giant swell that was rolling up the whole depth of the South Atlantic without interruption, the whole way from Diego Garcia, the Cape, or South Georgia itself. To have been visible to the naked eye from our altitude those rollers must have been seventy or eighty feet high. To our right were the great African cloud banks (I have never known good weather over Central Africa, invariably giant thunder heads), but Ascension Island was clear and blue.

Bleary and stubble-chinned we lurched out of the Hercules with our hand luggage. Senior RAF officers were ultra-creased and starched. Shorts, bleached stockings, chiselled tans, *they* had shaved twenty minutes earlier. In daylight I could see that the aerodrome consisted of two enormous runways in inverted 'V' formation pointing south into the alternative prevailing Trades. The centre of the 'V' was occupied by a knoll some 400 feet high of red volcanic strata – just as well that visibility was always perfect day and night – and our hosts immediately conducted us to the top of this knoll in a series of mini-buses to watch the scramble of another flight of Phantoms and their attendant tankers.

One by one the Victors lumbered down the runway. No fewer than seven were required to escort the two Phantoms to Port Stanley; three of the Victors would only be going half-way before topping up their colleagues who would give the last draft of 'motion lotion' in the latitude of the Argentine coast.

The first half of the runway is slightly uphill and the take-off of the tankers, loaded with fifteen tons of fuel, was painfully slow. Over the uphill stretch the Victors seemed hardly to be accelerating at all, then just in time, the gradient altered and at the very last moment they would rotate, and retract the undercarriage, though unable to make height until the thermals at the shoreline started to lift them. The 29 Squadron Phantoms roared down the runway side by side, showing off.

Our hosts told us with concealed – though not completely concealed – relish that our take-off had been delayed from 10.30 a.m. until 2.30 p.m., as the VC10 which was taking us back had had compass trouble on the way out and its arrival had been delayed. The statutory rest period for the crew made it impossible for us to take off until after lunch. Freezing fog was forecast for England and we might have to divert, they added.

Then to a delicious breakfast at the Ascension Chef, atmosphere very much better than the previous week when we had apprehensively toyed with our fried eggs at 3.15 a.m.

The Air Commodore then suggested that we should go on a

tour of the Island and there followed one of the most memorable experiences of the whole trip.

The mini-buses climbed away from the airfield into the foothills of the Green Mountain and the beginnings of vegetation could be detected. Dried-up, burnt-out stalks, without colour or leaf, except in little gullies where shelter from the sun had kept them green, rather like an Attenborough film of a desert awaiting the seasonal flood. But gradually, as we climbed, the vegetation became greener and thicker, brilliant and towering banks of hibiscus and bougainvillea crowded up to the edge of the roadside; dense greenery with fleshy leaves, nameless white and yellow blooms and petals and voluptuous curving ferns.

In the undergrowth one caught glimpses of Martin Johnson Heade[1] plumage. The gradient was very steep and often the mini-bus drivers had to reverse on the hairpins and hold bottom gear between swerves.

Then, quite suddenly, in this equatorial jungle, we drew up beside a perfect English vicarage of the Regency period. Everything was flawless, from the Georgian window panes, to the guttering, to the broken pediment over the arch that led into the separate kitchen garden. The lay-out of lodges and stables was precisely the same as the architect would have arranged on a hillside in Dorset in 1820. But of course the foliage that pressed around it was entirely different. And when I walked into the yard at the back to say hello to the pigs in their teak and granite sties, clouds of tropical birds flew up from the troughs.

This was the dwelling built for the Commander of the Marine Garrison that had been stationed on Ascension to help defend St Helena after Napoleon had been exiled there. All the materials and craftsmen had been brought out from Britain and the result was the most perfect country house south of the Tropic of Capricorn.

But our hosts would not allow us to linger and led us on foot through the kitchen gardens and on up the Green Mountain. Now, as in *Erewhon*, the vegetation started to change back, not to the red volcanic dust of the lower altitudes, but to a rough springy turf, gorse bushes and stunted blackthorn, a cold and penetrating mist, moisture running in rivulets everywhere. In the space of an hour we had moved

---

[1] AC knew his work well from *The Gems of Brazil* (see p. 232).

through 45° of Mercator from the tropics, the jungles to the vegetation and temperatures of the Moor around Tavistock.

The drive down the Green Mountain was a nightmare. Corporal Duffy, bandbox smart and sitting at attention, drove 'on his brakes' – and I mean *on* them. The only time he took his foot off the brake pedal (the mini-bus was loaded with an extra ton-and-a-half of humanity), was to accelerate downwards between the swerves, instead of using the gears to brake the mini-bus, and so steep was the gradient that it would overrun the rev. limit in second gear. He was actually changing up to a higher gear whenever he had the space. It was a matter of minutes before we all went over the edge. 'Don't change up,' I hissed, and actually put out my hand to hold the gear lever in second. Startled, he obeyed.

It had been suggested, and naturally welcomed by most of the delegation, that we should hang about on the balcony of the Exiles Club drinking and smoking and munching Club sandwiches, for the hour-and-a-half or so that remained before take-off. But I preferred to explore Georgetown and Kevin McNamara wanted to look at the Church, so we separated from our colleagues and drifted off on foot.

Just as I was about to turn down the hill into Georgetown quay I saw a white beach some half-mile away. I took a short cut and as I drew nearer could hear the thunder slap of those same giant rollers that I had watched from the Hercules crashing on to the sand.

'Do not whatever you do bathe,' had said the Air Marshal. 'The undertow is very dangerous and we lost quite a lot of personnel before we made it a Court Martial offence.' Court Martial offence! That made it even more irresistible.

The beach was deserted and I took off my clothes and went into the water. Perfectly incredible, the best bathe I have ever had, although the undertow *was* very very strong. It was dangerous to swim other than parallel with the beach, which meant one was rolled about and buffeted by the breakers.

I dried on my shirt and, towelled and full of white gritty sand, feeling marvellous, started back to the Exiles Club. On the way back I ran into two RAF erks who were goggle-faced. They said bathing was very dangerous and that sharks and Portuguese men-of-war came right up to the shore.

Letter to Michael Jopling   *4th November, 1982*

My dear Michael

Just a line to say how tremendously grateful I was for your including me on the Falklands visit.

It was without a doubt the most memorable and invigorating experience of my entire Parliamentary career. Within half an hour of arriving, as we came into Port Stanley, the Infants School was letting its pupils out to be collected by their Mums, and seeing all those dear little fair-haired children in their anoraks – exactly like any village in one's constituency – brought home more effectively than anything else could have done what exactly we were fighting for, and how impossible it would have been to have abandoned them to a foreign power. There is absolutely no question in my mind that this realisation is present in the minds of all personnel out there. Service morale is extremely high and practically everyone we spoke to remarked (a) on the distinction between saving our own people and 'mucking about in the Third World', and (b) on how the excitement of being in a War Zone made up for all the discomfort.

We visited and had time with RAF – flying personnel and Rapier crews – Infantry, Sappers, Artillerymen, Pioneers – and had one hectic day being transferred by Lynx from various Royal Navy ships on station, and found everyone working flat out and proud of the job they were doing (though this did not restrain their very understandable impulse to scare the shit out of us with low-flying practice firing!).

                                                    Yours etc
                                                    Alan Clark

This high point in AC's political career seems an appropriate moment to end this volume. Life and politics continues in the original published volume, Diaries: In Power, *which opens in spring 1983.*

ACKNOWLEDGEMENTS

This volume of Alan Clark's Diaries would not have been possible without the encouragement, first and foremost, of Jane Clark, to whom I am indebted.

My thanks, also, to James and Andrew Clark, who have, like their mother, answered my often ignorant questions. Following Alan's death in 1999, it was his long-time literary adviser, Michael Sissons, who first suggested that as his publisher at Weidenfeld & Nicolson for the original *Diaries* and his subsequent books, I should become the editor of this volume. I am grateful to him, and to the Clark family for their faith in me. It may be reassurance that I share the 13th as a birthdate (See Introduction, page xix, footnote 1).

Jane Clark invited me into Saltwood and gave unquestioning access to Alan's papers. She has also been a most generous host. Although the manuscript diaries are in a variety of bindings, as described in the Introduction, Alan also had a habit of jotting down entries on whatever was near to hand. This has required a diligent search. Even as this volume was about to go to press an early engagement diary surfaced and was found to contain unsuspected entries.

Jane was also an enormous help in deciphering Alan's script, particularly names of people and places, as well as in identification, not least of Alan's cars. But it was reassuring to learn that even Alan himself sometimes had trouble in reading his own handwriting.

I also particularly wish to acknowledge here my wife Sue, who put up with my absences during the transcription and editing of this volume. She, and our daughter Maria, sat at the keyboard on occasion as I deciphered an entry and dictated it to them. My thanks to each of them.

At Weidenfeld & Nicolson the forbearance of my colleagues who took the added strain when I was absent, has caused me no surprise, but I appreciate their support. I would especially single out Ben Buchan, who became my editor, Alice Chasey, our assistant, and our ace production team headed by Richard Hussey.

As that king of editors, the late Rupert Hart-Davis, once remarked, footnoting requires the arts of a detective and a network of supporters. I would like to thank:

Jonathan Aitken, Jane Birkett, Lynette Carr, James Caudle, Tim Heald, Simon Heffer, Charles Howard, Michael Howard, MP, Peter Jay, Nicholas Kent, Brian MacArthur, Douglas Matthews (and for his index), Michael Ratcliffe, Andrew Roberts, Kenneth Rose, Graham Stewart, Hugo Vickers, Lord Weatherill, Alan Williams, David Willetts, MP and the staff of the London Library.

Finally, and not least, let me thank Anthony Cheetham, chief executive of the Orion Publishing Group, who encouraged me 'to go for it'.

                                                                              IT

INDEX

NOTE: Titles and ranks are generally the highest mentioned in the text

'The best diarists, from Pepys and Boswell to "Chips" Channon and Harold Nicolson, have been the souls of indiscretion. But none so indiscreet as Mr Clark. If he is made the scapegoat for the Matrix Churchill affair, he may be written down politically as Baroness Thatcher's little loose cannon. But literature and the great British game of gossip will judge him for his diary. For its Pooterish self-assessment, for Mr Toad's enthusiasm for new things, for Byron's caddishness, for its deadly candour, it is one of the great works in the genre'   *The Times*

'Frank and vivid diaries ... Mr Clark performs the invaluable service of cheering us all up and giving us something to talk about'   *The Times*

'Unputdownable'   David Mellor, *Mail on Sunday*

'Diaries are the raw material of history and these are elegantly and pungently written'   Sir Charles Powell, *The Times*

'These amazing diaries ... a marvellous exposure of the way the Tory Party really works'
Ian Aitken, *Hampstead and Highgate Express*

'Absorbing ... staggeringly, recklessly candid ... tells the truth as he saw it without fear or favour'
Anthony Howard, *Sunday Times*

'A wonderful book ... these diaries combine the naive candour of an Adrian Mole with the imagination of a devil and an angel'
Matthew Parris, *Sunday Telegraph*

'The best political book for at least a decade. It is unlikely that Thatcher, when her autobiography is published, will provide such an entertaining and incisive account of the personalities, scandals and conflicts of her years in office'   *The Scotsman*

'The sheer fun of politics shines through ... this wonderful book'   Robert Rhodes James, *Guardian*

Alan Clark, MP for Plymouth (Sutton) 1974–1992 and Kensington and Chelsea, 1997–1999, was Minister of Trade, 1986–1989, and Minister of State, Ministry of Defence, 1989–1992. He made his reputation as a historian with *The Donkeys: A History of the BEF in 1915*, followed by *The Fall of Crete, Barbarossa: the Russian–German Conflict, 1941–1945* and *Aces High: The War in the Air Over the Western Front 1914–1918*. He also published three novels. In 1973 he edited the private diaries of Viscount Lee of Fareham, *A Good Innings*. After quitting the House of Commons in 1992 he published the first volume of his *Diaries*, the following year. His political history, *The Tories: The Conservatives and the Nation State 1922–1997* was published in 1998. Alan Clark was married with two sons. He lived until his death in 1999 at Saltwood Castle, Kent. The second volume of his *Diaries, Into Politics*, was published posthumously in 2000, and the third volume, *The Last Diaries: In and Out of the Wilderness*, was published in 2002.

DIARIES
In Power
1983–1992

ALAN CLARK

PHOENIX

A PHOENIX PAPERBACK

Originally titled *Diaries*

First published in Great Britain in 1993 by
Weidenfeld & Nicolson
This paperback edition published in 1994
by Phoenix,
an imprint of Orion Books Ltd,
Orion House, 5 Upper St Martin's Lane,
London, WC2H 9EA.

Reissued 2001 as *Diaries: In Power 1983–1992*

Twenty-ninth impression
Reissued 2003

A CIP catalogue record for this book
is available from the British Library.

ISBN 1 85799 142 7

Typeset by Selwood Systems, Midsomer Norton
Printed in Great Britain by
Clays Ltd, St Ives plc

For my beloved Jane,
around whose cool and affectionate personality
there raged this maelstrom of egocentricity
and self-indulgence

CONTENTS

ILLUSTRATIONS

A section of photographs from the author's collection
appears between pages 202 and 203

PREFACE

Diaries are so intensely personal – to publish them is a baring, if not a flaunting, of the ego. And for the author also to write a preface could be thought excessive.

Let me explain. These are not 'Memoirs'. They are not written to throw light on events in the past, or retrospectively to justify the actions of the author. They are *exactly* as they were recorded on the day; sometimes even the hour, or the minute, of a particular episode or sensation.

I wrote, in longhand, in a variety of locations; principally at Saltwood, or in my room at the House of Commons, or at my desk in the Department(s). Also in trains, embassies, hotels abroad, at the Cabinet table in Number 10 and at international conferences. When I had completed an entry I closed the notebook and seldom turned to that page again.

During the whole of this period, nearly eight years, I was a Minister in three successive Tory administrations. Politics – Party, Governmental and Constituency – dominated my life and energies. But on re-reading the entries I am struck by how small a proportion – less than half – is actually devoted to the various themes that dominated political life over the period.

So, in order to help those who want only to read selectively, I have allotted an abbreviated title to practically every entry and these can be found listed, with their separate dates, at the start of each 'Chapter' (each year in the period constituting a chapter).

Expurgation, from considerations of taste or cruelty, I have tried to keep to a minimum. My friends know me, and know that I love them, and that my private explosions of irritation or bad temper are of no import. And as for taste, it, too, is subjective. There are passages that will offend some, just as there are excerpts that I myself found embarrassing to read when I returned to them.

Much of course has been excised. But of what remains nothing has been altered since the day it was written. Is this conceit – or laziness? A bit of both, I suppose. But I found that when I attempted to alter, or moderate, or explain, the structure and rhythm of the whole entry would be disturbed.

There remain certain passages that vex me considerably. Mainly they refer to friends and colleagues with whom I have worked – or who have worked for me with loyalty and dedication: for example, Dave, my competent driver for many years; Rose, my sweet diary secretary at DTI who coped with 'harassment' with dignity and decorum; Bruce Anderson, one of my closest confidants; Tom King, Secretary of State above me in two departments, whom I still regard with affection in spite of the way in which we treated each other in the heat of our political careers. And there are many others to whom references coloured by the irritation of the moment are ill-suited.

There are also passages that, to some readers, will be unintelligible. Family joke-words, Eton slang, arcane references to events in the past, crude expletives, all these are present but I have done my best to illuminate the unfamiliar in a glossary that covers events, locations, individuals and so forth.

Sometimes lacking in charity; often trivial; occasionally lewd; cloyingly sentimental, repetitious, whingeing and imperfectly formed. For some readers the entries may seem to be all of these things.

But they are real diaries.

AC

GLOSSARY

OFFICE

Joan – AC's driver at DE
Dave – AC's driver at DTI
Pat – AC's driver at MoD
Jenny Easterbrook – Head of AC's Private Office at DE
Judith Rutherford – her successor
Matthew Cocks, Marjorie and Glyn Williams – successive Heads of
    AC's Private Office at DTI
Steve (Stephen) – Assistant Private Secretary at DTI
Julian Scopes – Head of AC's Private Office at MoD
Doug Widener – Number Two in AC's Private Office at DTI
Simon Webb – Head of Tom King's Private Office
Jane Binstead – Number Two in Tom King's Private Office

CARS

SS 100 – owned by AC since his undergraduate days
The Rolls-Royce Silver Ghost – the nicest of all to drive on a fine
    day if you are not in a hurry
The Porsche (aka the Little Silver) – used most often by AC when alone
The Citroën (aka the Chapron) – the *decapotable* belonging to Jane
    and used only for holidays
The 2CV – another Citroën, used when in de-escalation mode
The 'Bustard' – a very old $4\frac{1}{2}$ litre Bentley
The Loco – an old chain-drive racing car of 1908
The 'Wee One' – an old Land-Rover, MOT failure, used at Eriboll
The Mehari – a little plastic truck with an air-cooled engine and a
    very light footprint used for clearing grass clippings and prunings
    from the gardens because it does not mark the lawn. A kind of
    mobile wheelbarrow.
The Argocat – performs the same function at Eriboll, but will also
    go through peat bogs, and swim
The Hayter and the Osprey and the Atco – mowers designed to
    tackle the Saltwood lawns at their various stages of growth

HOUSES AND LOCATIONS

SALTWOOD

Various rooms: the Great Library; the Tower Office; the Green Room

(the Clarks' informal sitting room in the old staff wing); the
  Muniment Room
The Bailey (inner and outer) – the two courtyards (see also lawns)
The Machines – an area of a distant field where agricultural machinery
  is parked
Chittenden Stone – an old milestone reputedly dating back to the
  Pilgrims' Way from Saltwood to Canterbury
The Seeds – a large arable field at Saltwood Farm
Courtneys (aka the Secret Garden) – an enclosed lawn in the inner
  Bailey
Gossie Bank – a steep climb at the far end of Saltwood Farm
Quince, the grandest cottage on the Saltwood Estate occupied by
  Nanny (qv) until her death
Garden House – a large bungalow built by Lord Clark in 1971 when
  he moved out of the castle
Sandling – the railway station for Saltwood
Grange Farm – owned by the Simmons, next door neighbours
The 'Black Route' – a walk along the sixty foot high wall of the
  ruined chapel in the Inner Bailey

ERIBOLL

The Creaggan Road – the road that connects Loch Eriboll to Loch
  Hope by way of the Creaggan Ridge, some seven miles in length
  and climbing from sea level to 600 feet at the ridge
The Lodge – principal house on the estate
Shore Cottage – Jane's house at Eriboll, where Jane and AC always
  stay
Foulain – a shepherd's cottage at the foot of the Loch
Strathbeg, a remote croft at the head of the Polla Valley
Arnaboll and Cashel Dhu, crofts on the Loch Hope side of the estate
Ardneackie ('Anson's') – the peninsula that juts out into Loch Eriboll

ZERMATT

Chalet Caroline – the Clarks' house in the village
The Kiosk – built by the Clarks in 1985, adjoining the chalet
Trift – an inn at an early stage in the ascent to the Rothornhutte
Othmars – an inn on the Blauherd

MISCELLANEOUS

The Mews – composite name for various vintage car dealers'
    establishments in Queen's Gate
Upper Terrace – Lord Clark's house in Hampstead until 1951
Albany – Chambers shared at various times by AC, Lord Clark and
    Andrew
Seend (aka Broomhayes) – the Clarks' house in Wiltshire, which they
    now visit seldom, but retained by them after the sale of Seend
    Manor when they moved to Saltwood in 1971
Bratton – Town Farm, Bratton-Clovelly. The Clarks' first house,
    thirty-five minutes north of Plymouth

SLANG

There are a number of family sayings and shorthand expressions
    dotted about in the text. Displayed as a glossary I recognise that
    they seem both pretentious and slightly mad, but for the curious I
    annotate below.
ACHAB – (lit.) 'anything can happen at backgammon', a saying
    originally from 'the Room' at Brooks's where games can swing
    at a late stage on an unpredictable run of the dice, used often as a
    consolation in times of depression.
Cutting peat/Burning heather – activities in Scotland used as a
    general cover for the theme of escaping to the Highlands
Thompson – defecation
Satisly – arousing satisfaction, inducing complacency
Sadismoidly – virtually the same as sadistically, though less *transitive*
    in meaning; the suffix -moid, or -moidly is often attached to
    adjectives
Dutch – blustering confident though tainted with insecurity (variant
    of Dutch Courage, though without inference of alcohol)
Men's tea – elevenses in the kitchen at Saltwood where all employees
    assemble (if they wish)
The bike rule – introduced after James had a serious accident on a
    motorbike at the age of fifteen. Children out at night had always
    to check in no matter how late they returned (guaranteed to stop
    parents sleeping until this happened).
Straight to the Lords – another consolation phrase (see ACHAB)
Lala – self-regardingly overdressed or noisy (females only)

Ego – particularly assertive or insensitive (of personality or behaviour)

Tinky – diminutive, insignificant

Artists Materials – sometimes declaimed as an excuse for poor
   performance

Rest the eyeballs – sleep

Two second rule – a parable recounted in a graveyard illustrating
   finality: 'You can't put the clock back – not even by two seconds.'

Softies – casual clothes

Greywater – diaorrhea

Oopsy-la – see Lala

M. Goisot – white Burgundy (the proprietor of the small vineyard at
   St Brie from which the Clarks import their house wine)

Nonnoish – buffer-like

EMT – early morning tea

ABBREVIATIONS

NAMES

AC – Alan Clark
CP – Charles Powell
DH – Douglas Hurd
DY – David (Lord) Young
GJ – Tristan Garel-Jones
IG – Ian Gow
JM – John Major
LB – Leon Brittan
MA – Michael Alison
MH – Michael Heseltine
NL – Norman Lamont
NT – Norman Tebbit
PM – Peter Morrison
QM – The Queen Mother
RA – Robert Atkins
TK – Tom King

ACRONYMS

AAC – Army Air Corps
AF – Armed Forces
ATP – Aid and Trade Provision
BAC – British Aircraft Corporation
BAe – British Aerospace
BMATT – British Military Advice and Training Team
CAP – Common Agricultural Policy
CCO – Conservative Central Office
CFE – Conventional Forces Europe
CFS – Chief of Fleet Support

COMEX – Commodities Europe (in Chicago)
COREPER – Council of Permanent Representatives
CSA – Chief Scientific Adviser
CDS – Chief of the Defence Staff
DE – Department of Employment
DOAEH – Defence Operational Analysis Establishment
DOE – Department of the Environment
DTI – Department of Trade and Industry
ECGD – Export Guarantee Department
EFA – European Fighter Aircraft
EFTA – European Free Trade Association
EMT – Early Morning Tea
EOC – Equal Opportunities Commission
EXCO – Executive Council (Hong Kong)
FCO – Foreign and Commonwealth Office
FO – Foreign Office
GMBATU – General, Municipal, Boilermakers and Allied Trades
    Union
G-PALS – Global Protection Against Limited Strike
IEPG – European Programme Group
ISS – Institute of Strategic Studies
LegCO – Legislative Council (Hong Kong)
MEP – Member of European Parliament
MFA – Multi Fibre Agreement
MGO – Master-General of Ordnance
MOD – Ministry of Defence
MSC – Manpower Services Commission
NEDC – National Economic Development Council
OBN – Order of the Brown Nose (passim *Private Eye*)
ODA – Overseas Development Agency
OD(E) – Overseas Defence Committee of the Cabinet
OECD – Organisation for Economic Co-operation and Development
PC – Privy Councillor
PES – Public Expenditure Survey
PO – Private Office
PSA – Property Services Agency
PUSS – Parliamentary Under-Secretary of State (the lowest Ministerial
    rank)
RCB – Regular Commission Board
RFC – Royal Flying Corps

ROE – Rules of Engagement
RUSI – Royal United Services Institute
SWP – Socialist Workers' Party
UKREP – United Kingdom Representation (at European
   Commission)
UNCTAD – United Nations Commission for Trade and Development

1983

1983

A fine evening at last, with delightful and abundant birdsong. It has
been so wet that the ground squelches under foot and even the
Mehari[1] marks the lawn. The greenery is lush, bursting on every side;
so many vistas of tone across the arboretum. We visited the young
trees this afternoon and were pleased by a copper beech that Jane had
planted down in the spinney to carry the eye along from the Park.
On the way back I had a confrontation with the 'country bumpkin'
man, an inveterate trespasser. I cursed him, and he crumpled dis-
armingly.

Andrew[2] is back from Sandhurst, and looking wonderful. But my
poor father lies adying in the Hythe nursing home where, unhappily,
he receives visitors. Together we went to see him, and found him
weak and quavery. He went in for colonic lavage, to 'clear up' his
diverticulitis (which he hasn't got, of course; but the fool of a doctor
can't see, or won't accept that Nolwen[3] is poisoning him).

Then he broke a hip trying to get out of the impossibly high
hospital bed; then an operation to cure this led to (how?) a blocked
urinary tract. Now he's on a catheter as well as heavily in plaster, and
mildly doped. Before the operation he said to me, 'I am perfectly
clear, and I say this with all deliberation, that I will not be alive in a
week's time.'

I am sad, though not as sad as I used to be, that I never really made
contact with him. And, as I think about it, I suppose I'm sorry that I
reacted away from the world of 'Art', because that shut off a whole
primary subject that we could discuss together. The world of 'Civilisation'. I must have been very crude and rough in my teens and early
twenties (still am, some would say).

I am interested in Clare, the au pair whom Nolwen has just
installed at Garden House.[4] I strolled over this evening, deliberately
entered by the back door and chatted her up. She's not pretty, but is
sexual. Dairymaid. Reminded me of Portmeirion.

---

[1] The little Citroën truck used for clearing the lawns at Saltwood.
[2] AC's younger son, serving in the Life Guards.
[3] AC's stepmother, Nolwen, Comtesse de Janze, 1925–90, married Lord Clark in
   1977. AC and she did not enjoy good relations.
[4] The Dower House on the Saltwood estate, built by Lord Clark in 1972, and lived
   in by him until his death.

Tomorrow we are off to Bratton[1] for a three-week Election campaign and my journal (such as it is) – school meetings, canvassing, 'Wotya going to do for me then, guv?', walkabout, 'I say again ...' etc., etc. – will be recorded in the day diary. I intend to cut as many corners as possible. At least we'll save money, staying at Bratton.

But before closing I should record my last speech, in the last adjournment of the old House, knocking poor dear Tam[2] around as he ploughed on with his batty arguments about the *Belgrano*. So what does it matter where it was when it was hit? We could have sunk it if it'd been tied up on the quayside in a neutral port and everyone would still have been delighted. Tam is too innocent to see this.

Halfway through Tristan[3] came sidling up, sat down on the bench and offered me an even £100 that I would be in the next Government. He always knows everything, but I took the bet all the same.

I think I will be too – but as what?

Charing Cross train   *Friday, 20 May*

The Election campaign is less than halfway through, but I am returning, somewhat reluctantly and uncertainly, on account of my father's imminent (or so we are told) death.

Last night, as Jane and I approached the Hoe Conservative Club, following a successful Adoption meeting at which I spoke from the heart about the Falklands and got a standing ovation, we were accosted. Several drunk middle-aged buffers were congregated on the steps of the club, a faded Edwardian building in the grand part of the city. In the twilight – it must have been about nine o'clock – a man in 'beadle's' regalia peered at me. 'I know you', he said, breathing pungent whisky fumes.

It turned out he was the Town Crier of London, *really* was,

---

[1] Town Farm, Bratton Clovelly. The Clarks' cottage in Devon, twenty-five miles from Plymouth. AC was first elected for Plymouth Sutton, February 1974, and was about to fight his fourth Election campaign.

[2] Tam Dalyell, MP for West Lothian since 1962, was now to contest Linlithgow.

[3] Tristan Garel-Jones, MP for Watford since 1979. A close friend of AC, he had been an assistant Whip in this Parliament. His name crops up frequently in these diaries.

although at first I thought he was mobbing.[1] We had a light-hearted conversation. Then, unexpectedly, he said, 'I'm sorry to have to tell you that the police have been round. There is an urgent message for you to telephone Hythe in Kent.'

How good of him. None of the others had thought to let me know. Well-meaning and muddled, they groped their way through to an inner office (the 'Steward' had long since gone and no one could find the light switches) and showed me a telephone. I suffered a momentary *frisson* during the ringing tone in case it was something to do with the boys, and got through to Linley[2] who was calming, though shifty.

I could just have made the sleeper that night but decided against. This allowed me to attend the 'Mayor-Making', probably the most grindingly boring of all the obligatory constituency fixtures with its self-satisfied, repetitious speeches, hard chairs and defiantly bogus applause. But the MP has to be *seen* there.

At lunchtime I rang the nursing home and spoke to the floor sister. I didn't like it. She was evasive. On being pressed she admitted that there were certain 'irreversible' signs. Like what? Well, reduction, or disappearance, of a pulse at the extremities, ankle, etc. ('The King's life is drawing peacefully to a close', all that. But that announcement was signed by Dawson[3] after he had poisoned George V, wasn't it, so he really knew.)

I went straight to the station and took the 125 to Paddington, taxiing across London to Charing Cross. Eddie[4] met me at Sandling, and I dropped him at the bottom of the drive and drove directly to the nursing home.

Linley was in the car park. 'He's not too good.' (If my father were going to survive he'd have said 'his Lordship'.)

My father's door was open (a bad sign). He was sitting up, breathing rapidly but shallowly, with his eyes closed. Nolwen was bending over him, mare-eyed; Catholic peasant at a deathbed. Guillaume[5] (what the hell was *he* doing there?) stood looking out of the window.

---

[1] Etonian parlance for 'making fun'.
[2] Len Linley, Lord Clark's butler at the Garden House.
[3] Lord Dawson of Penn, physician to King George V, and generally reported to have 'eased' the monarch's passing in its closing stages.
[4] Edwin Wilson, head gardener at Saltwood.
[5] Guillaume de Rougemont, nephew of the Comtesse de Janze.

Nolwen immediately detached herself, came up to me and started talking about arrangements for the funeral! After a bit this got too much for my father and he became agitated, groaning and coughing. Nolwen was completely incapable of dealing with this. I strode over to the bed and said, 'Papa, it's Al.'

'Ah, Al. That's good, very good.' He seemed greatly relieved.

'Will you all please leave,' I said loudly. They shuffled out. Then I got hold of his wrist, very cold and clammy it was, and said, 'Papa, I think you're going to die very soon. I've come back to tell you how much I love you, and to thank you for all you did for me, and to say goodbye.' He mumbled, but his breathing calmed right down. Quite remarkable and fulfilling. I held on to his wrist for a good while, then left, kissing him on the brow.

I should have stayed longer, and I should have made him open his eyes. But I'm so glad I made it. I went back to Saltwood where Nanny gave me a thin cheese salad and the following morning Nolwen phoned to say that he had died at one in the morning.

Bratton   *Sunday, 5 June*

It looks as if we are heading for a substantial victory. A new Conservative Government. Will I be in it? We have spent the day lying on the front lawn, newspapers scattered around, just as we used to do twenty or more years ago, though now fully clothed and *white*-footed. I look at pictures of southern seas and bathing beauties. I have an awful feeling that this is my very last 'free' Sunday.

I just can't make up my mind if I want a job or not. Fool, Clark, of course you do. The House won't be much fun with nigh on 400 estate agents, merchant bankers and briefless barristers all OBN-ing. Do I provide the opposition, with a few chums? We are having a private lunch at Brooks's on 15th for the 'Shadow Cabinet'. Should be pleasing. Then I want to go to the Chalet[1] and walk out on to the verandah and touch the silver birch leaves and smell the clarity and ozone of the Alps.

---

[1] The Chalet Caroline, AC's house in Zermatt, which his family had built in 1959.

I'm madly in love with Frances Holland.[1] I suspect she's not as thin and gawky as she seems. Her hair is always lovely and shiny. Perhaps I can distract her at the count on Thursday and kiss her in one of those big janitors' cupboards off the Lower Guildhall.

The General Election on June 9:
Conservative: 397; Labour: 209; Alliance: 23.

Saltwood   *Monday, 13 June*

It was Ian Gow[2] who telephoned. I had been getting more and more irritable all day as the 'junior' appointments were leaking out on to the TV screens, and had taken refuge on the big Atco. I was practically on the last stripe when I saw Jane coming across the lawn with a grin on her face. But when she said it was Ian I thought he must be ringing to console me. Surely it's the Chief Whip who gives you the news? And even then a slight sinking feeling at his words, 'The Prime Minister wants you to join the Government.' – 'Go on.' 'It's not what you wanted.' But still a certain delight when he actually enunciated the title, 'Parliamentary Under-Secretary of State at the Department of Employment'.

I had to ring Norman Tebbit.[3] (I don't really get on with Tebbit, he always seems slightly suspicious of me. I don't net into his style of humour.) 'Hur, hur, you've drawn the short straw,' then a lot of balls about 'the rations are good . . .' but to come in the following morning at nine a.m.!

Almost immediately afterwards Jenny Easterbrook (of whom, I don't doubt, much, much more) rang and said that she was my personal private secretary and what time would I like my car?

No point in hanging about. I dressed up, grabbed a briefcase,

---

[1] Frances Holland was AC's twenty-two-year-old Labour opponent in the 1983 campaign. They had established a *rapport* doing a hospital radio show together.
[2] Ian Gow, MP for Eastbourne since February 1974. He had served Mrs Thatcher as her PPS since May 1979. AC's chief friend in the Commons.
[3] Norman Tebbit, MP for Chingford since 1974, had been Secretary of State for Employment since 1981. Created Life Peer, 1992.

straight to Sandling. In London I collected the coven[1] and off we went to Brooks's for dinner. At intervals Joei said, 'Gosh, Al, are you really a Minister, zowee.' Valerie was less forthcoming. Ali sulked and sneered. Endless well-wishers telephoned. I went in and out of the dining room like someone with prostate trouble. The only amusing call was from Morrison[2] and Goodlad[3] who were dining opposite at Whites. Peter said, 'Look, Alan, your secretary Jenny Easterbrook is very pretty. Whatever you do, don't lay a finger on her.'

Goodlad grabbed the phone, 'Especially in the lift.'

'Drunken youths,' I told them.

Driving away, we went past the Ritz and Joei said, 'Gosh, is that the Ritz? I wish we could go in there.'

'Why?'

'To go to bed, of course.'

I was thoughtful.

I have always been culpably weak in such matters.

And when I got home I thought to myself – a new life, a new leaf.

Department of Employment   *Wednesday, 15 June*

Jenny Easterbrook has a very pale skin and large violet eyes. Her blonde hair is *gamine* short, her sexuality tightly controlled. She makes plain her feelings on several counts (without expressing them): one, that I am an uncouth chauvinist lout; two, that it is a complete mystery why I have been made a Minister; three, that my tenure in this post is likely to be a matter of weeks rather than months.

I did, though, get a reaction when I asked, in all innocence, if she would take dictation. She had, after all, described herself to me only yesterday as 'a secretary'. And I wanted to clear my head by writing my own summary memo. 'Can't you do shorthand?'

'I'm an official, not a typist.'

Faster than I can digest them great wadges of documentation are

---

[1] Three girls related to each other by blood whom AC had known for many years.

[2] The Hon Peter Morrison, MP for Chester since 1974. Currently Minister of State at Department of Employment.

[3] Alastair Goodlad, MP for Northwich, 1974–83, when he became MP for Eddisbury.

whumped into my 'In' tray. The subject matter is turgid: a mass of 'schemes' whose purpose, plainly, is not so much to bring relief to those out of work as to devise excuses for removing them from the Register. Among my other responsibilities are 'statistics', so it will be me who has to tell the House each month what is the 'jobless' total.

The Enterprise Allowance Scheme, the Job Release Scheme, the Community Scheme. Convoluted and obscure even at their inception, they have since been so picked over and 'modified' by civil servants as to be incomprehensible. I ought to welcome these devices, and must try and master their intricacies. But my head is bursting. I understand Nabokov's analogy of a traveller in a foreign city, whose language he does not speak, attempting in the middle of a power strike, in the late evening, to find his hotel.

Department of Employment   *Thursday, 16 June*

This morning I woke up with a a jolt at 4.10 a.m., – the first anxiety-waking since the mid 1970s when Hoare's were holding the deeds of Saltwood and I used to worry about repaying the overdraft. Interestingly, my anxiety translated itself into a financial dream. I had asked the Manager of the UBS in Brig the state of my account and he told me that I was SwFrs. 250,000 overdrawn – but of course it is quite all right, Mr Clark, we have the security of the Chalet. In fact I'm not overdrawn at all in Brig. But the anxiety syndrome had surfaced in its old form – although in the days when I was short of money I never used to *dream* about it. I lay awake for some hour and a half, thinking how in the hell am I going to cope with this; how long is it going to take me to comprehend, to dominate this completely new field of expertise.

I made tea at about six a.m., got to the office at seven thirty a.m., unlocked the Red Box and started reading. Normally I am a slow reader, but in the last forty-eight hours I must have read more than in the previous two months.

Albany   *Friday, 17 June*

Today I hosted the 'Shadow Cabinet Lunch', in the Oval Room at Brooks's.

During the campaign, irritatedly contemplating the general dreariness of the Government, being it seems composed mainly of subservient toads or grumpy ex-Heathite heavies, I sent out a number of invitations.

Everyone accepted. We were young, and crisp (excepting possibly dear Julian Critchley[1] – but he is such a wit as always to embellish any gathering). Chris Patten[2] and I had, indeed, just put our foot on the first rung, and we hailed each other as being 'complementary' in terms of balance. Conversation waxed jollyish – but only *ish*.

I followed Ed Streator's[3] practice of, at a certain point in the meal, inviting each guest in turn to deliver a little soliloquy. The theme was, What the Government Should be Doing with Its Huge New Mandate, etc.

Some were cagey, some, notably Nick Budgen,[4] a little on the whingey side. Robert Cranborne[5] was laid back and funny. But it was curious – perhaps due to shyness or reserve – how few, if any, of the speakers saw the broad canvas, still less drew on it.

I fear that we all still suffer from a lack of confidence. Very deep-seated it is, running back as far, perhaps, as before the war and those Admiralty memoranda saying we couldn't even take on the Italian Fleet in the Mediterranean. So when we win something we can barely believe our eyes. There is no follow-through.

Entertaining is part of the fun of politics, and in the Conservative Party it used to happen every weekend, while three days a week Margesson[6] kept a table at the Mirabelle. Now we are all too busy – and too poor.

---

[1] Julian Critchley, MP for Aldershot since 1970.

[2] Chris Patten, MP for Bath since 1974. Parliamentary Under-Secretary, Northern Ireland Office.

[3] Ed Streator, American diplomat. Currently Minister at the US Embassy in London.

[4] Nick Budgen, MP for Wolverhampton South-West since 1974. An Assistant Government Whip, 1981–2.

[5] Robert Cranborne, MP for Dorset South since 1979. Heir to the Marquess of Salisbury.

[6] David Margesson (1st Viscount). Legendary Tory Chief Whip from 1931; appointed Secretary of State for War by Churchill in December 1940, but made the scapegoat after the fall of Singapore in 1942.

Saltwood   *Sunday, 19 June*

Ever since I was elected, no, adopted for the Sutton Division there
has appeared annually, or more often, in the minutes of whichever
executive council meeting I have been unable to attend, devoted to
the topic of fund-raising and social events, the flat resolution (passed
unanimously), 'Alan Clark to invite a Personality'. Invariably it annoys
me. I find it presumptuous and insulting as well as being unclear. And
so far – to their irritation – I have always been able to dodge it. But
this last weekend they had a Euro Party, to raise money for the
'EuroConstituency' (a function always enthusiastically attended, as it
is known that I am filled with distaste for all things 'Euro') and I had
resolved, in celebration of our famous victory, to produce a 'surprise'
personality.

I am ill at ease with people in show business. I prefer the company
of journalists, or other politicians, or fellow Old Etonians, or classic
car dealers, or dons. But Jane and I agreed that there was one person
who was sympathetic, and whom it would be fun to have down –
Reggie.[1]

It was soon apparent, though, that he had suffered a *coup de*
something-or-other.[2] He said nothing in the car, nothing in the train,
nothing in the Mayflower Post – whither I took him to show his
rooms and ply him with drink before we went over to the Guildhall.

In some gloom Jane and I went off to change. 'A man of few
words,' I said.

'*Few*? He's *totally* dumb.'

But once the evening got under way Reggie performed professionally. He grinned his way through the lionising, made a 'funny'
speech ending with a joke (was it blue? I didn't get it, anyway) about
Anna Ford and 'Alan Clark's hammer'. Yet the moment we were out
of the building, he reverted. Hardly said another word. Strange. I
hope he's all right.

---

[1] Reggie Bosanquet, an old friend, who was newscaster at ITN for many years.
[2] At that time (and quite unknown to the Clarks) Bosanquet was tragically suffering
from cancer of the liver from which he was to die later in the year.

Department of Employment   *Monday, 20 June*

At 8.56 a.m. I heard Jenny's phone ring in the outer office. 'Yes, he's here,' I heard her say (so Yah Boo to whoever is asking, I thought). It was Donald Derx.[1]

Jenny padded in with that special sly gait when she thinks she has caught me out with something.

'Have you read the brief on the revised conditions for the Job Splitting Scheme?'

'Yes.' (Lie.)

'Good,' she said (meaning, good I have caught you out), 'because Donald Derx would like to come round and discuss it with you.'

'When does he want to come?'

'Well, in about five minutes.'

'All right,' I said gritly. 'Have him round in five minutes.'

I calculated that I could just about read it well enough diagonally to be able to bat the ball back at least, in about five minutes. But some eighty seconds later the door opened, and Jenny showed in Donald Derx. He must have left his office immediately after he had put the phone down, as it takes roughly one minute to get from his office to mine.

He talked quite interestingly, and sagely, about certain changes that had to be made. I had *just* absorbed enough, using my Stabilo Boss illuminator, to be able to keep a discussion going, periodically taking a sly glance at the briefs which lay open in front of me.

The whole thing was a complete ambush. First, he wanted to see what time I came into my office, second, he wanted to see the extent to which I was reading the contents of the boxes. Jenny knows perfectly well that the earliest train I can get from Saltwood is the 7.19 a.m. This means that on a Monday I cannot get to the office before about 8.48 a.m. (as opposed to my usual time of eight o'clock). At best, i.e., if it had been the very first document I read on opening the box, I would have had seven minutes, maximum, in which to read it. In fact, of course, it had been hidden about a quarter of the way down the box. But I am already wise to this trick and don't take things out in the order in which they are arranged. I fillet them first, and extract

---

[1] Donald Derx, Deputy Secretary at the Department of Employment and senior civil servant under the Permanent Secretary, Michael Quinlan, who moved to the Ministry of Defence, 1988.

those little photocopied flimsies marked 'PUSS to see' and Jenny's
initials, which are the really tricky items.

Department of Employment   *Tuesday, 21 June*

I was lunching with Jerry Wiggin[1] in the House and he told me the
horror story of his sacking.

The phone rang at his home on Sunday night.

'Jerry, hello, it's Ian here . . . '

'Oh yes, hello.'

'Jerry, the Prime Minister would like to see you at Downing Street
tomorrow.'

Jerry's spirits soared, but before he could even say Yes, Ian went
on, 'I'm afraid it is not very good news . . .' and his spirits plummeted
cruelly as Ian went on, ' . . . so would you mind coming to the back
door.'

Oh, what a chilling, ghastly experience. I am very good at detecting from people's voices whether what they have to say is good or
bad and I don't think I would have been misled by Ian's presumably
sepulchral tone as he invited Jerry's attendance. What I do think I
would have said, however, is, 'Stuff your fucking door, I am not going
to bother. She can just write to me.'

And yet, as poor Jerry admitted, although he had meant to be
dignified, when he actually got into the room, he plucked and pleaded
and blubbed.

What on earth did he expect – to go in and change her mind, to
get her to go back to her desk and cross somebody else's name out?
When I told this tale to another Minister he wisely and shrewdly
observed that in the end we are all sacked and it's always awful. It is
as inevitable as death following life. If you are elevated there comes a
day when you are demoted. Even Prime Ministers.

---

[1]Jerry Wiggin, MP for Weston-Super-Mare since 1969. Parliamentary Under-
    Secretary at Ministry of Defence, 1981–3.

Department of Employment   *Thursday, 23 June*

It's not yet eight o'clock and already I've been in my office half an hour. I like to get here early, before anyone else arrives, then I can scowl at them through the communicating doorway as they take their places around the outer office. I am still so ignorant of the basic material that this is one of the few ways I can start to assert an ascendancy.

It is (naturally and heartbreakingly) a glorious summer morning, and I have drawn back to their maximum extent the sliding windows, thus buggering or – I trust – partially buggering the air conditioning system. There is a tiny *balcon*, a gutter really, with a very low parapet, below knee height. Certain death on the Victoria Street pavement eight floors below. Sometimes I get a wild urge to relieve my bladder over it, splattingly on the ant-like crowds. Would this get one the sack? Probably not. It would *have* to be hushed up. Trivial, but at the same time bizarre. Certainly it would tax the powers of Mr Bernard Ingham.[1] I might do it on my last day.

Yesterday evening I outstayed Jenny (a pang of jealousy, mild, but for the first time, when I heard her take a telephone call, presumably from an intimate). As soon as she'd gone I left and went round to the Farmers' Club, where the '92[2] were having a dinner. Dreadful food, grey beef and gravy, roast potatoes (on a hot June night) hard as Mills bombs.

Proceedings formless, totally out of control, as Paddy Wall[3] is useless. Is he gaga or just frightfully deaf? Doesn't like me for some reason, although I've never done him any harm, and so will never call me to speak. In fact this is one of those evenings when the prudent man *doesn't* speak as most of the discussion was about whether we should back Edward Du Cann[4] or Cranley Onslow[5] for chairmanship of the 1922 Committee. Whoever we back gets it. But I am in two

---

[1] Bernard Ingham, Chief Press Secretary at Number 10.

[2] The '92 Group was a 'secret' society of right-wing Tory MPs who banded together to work as a block vote in committee elections, and to influence policy.

[3] Sir Patrick Wall, MP for Beverley since 1983 after twenty-nine years representing Haltemprice, Hull.

[4] Edward Du Cann, MP for Taunton since 1956. He had been Chairman of the 1922 Committee since 1972.

[5] Cranley Onslow, MP for Woking since 1964. Succeeded Du Cann as Chairman of the 1922 the following year.

minds. Edward, I suppose, is on the way down now (less than ten years ago he was seriously, and I mean seriously – I wrote it all up at length at the time – being pushed for the Leadership). Cranley has inner reserves. Dropped from the Government once, then taken off the back benches to be Minister of State at the Foreign Office. Grand wife. Probably a better choice.

After the ten o'clock vote it was still light and I walked across Green Park. In Brooks's Jerdein and Miller were playing head on. So what? I watched for a few minutes only, then ambled down Jermyn Street. Two new 500 SLs. So what? I'm off shiny cars. I'm off just about everything. The material at DE is so turgid, so repetitious, so irrelevant to anything that real government should be about, that it requires a huge effort of intellect to comprehend it. By the end of the day my brain is completely *désseché*.

The only thing I am learning is how the Civil Service works. Perhaps this'll be useful one day.

Department of Employment   *Friday, 24 June*

Jenny continues to bait me with her indifferent stare, and flat northern vowels. Why is our relationship so difficult? If only we were lovers.

This morning she was agitated about Sir Robert Armstrong, when could she put him in the diary, etc. I was offhand. She had said something about this yesterday, that he 'wanted to see me'. I assumed that it was some kind of social call, new junior Minister, make him feel at ease, show him the ropes. I wasn't bothered.

'I don't think so.'

'He's a friend of my sister. They're both Trustees of Covent Garden. She's probably told him to be nice to me.'

'I don't think so.'

'Oh well, do as you like, put him in then.'

'Mid-day.'

'But what about Donald Derx?'

'Sir Robert is head of the Civil Service. Derx is a Dep Sec.'

---

[1] Sir Robert Armstrong, GCB, CVO, Secretary of the Cabinet since 1967.

Joan[1] drove me round to the Cabinet Office. He kept me waiting in an ante-room. When he came out, didn't invite me into his office. Rudeish. A certain amount of rather wary small talk, and I could feel our mutual dislike rising. He made tepid boasts about working for Ted, writing his speeches. (That's all the unfortunate Ted needed, I thought.)

'Who do you admire most in the Commons?'

'Dennis Skinner.'[2]

A longish pause.

Then, like a conjuror, two files appeared in his hand, one red, the other orange.

'There are certain matters that the Prime Minister has asked me to raise with you ... '

'Really? Go ahead.'

'You have been spoken of with approval ... ' he paused, and I got ready to preen myself. Then he opened the red file. ' ... by the National Front.'

'Not at my solicitation.'

'If any of them should at any time try and make contact with you, I must ask that you inform my office immediately.'

Better not make an issue of this, I thought. 'Of course. It's most unlikely, but of course.'

He put down the red file on the table between us then, seeing my hand move, pushed it out of reach.

'There are also certain matters of personal conduct ... '

I glared at him. We were on the orange file now.

' ... which could quite possibly leave you open to blackmail.'

Shit!!

'No, no. Perfectly all right. They've all married into grand Scottish families by now.'

To do him justice, a very, very faint smile – what novelists call *wintry* – crossed his features. 'How's Celly?' he asked, and a few seconds later saw me out.

'How did that go?' asked Jenny when I got back to the office.

I suppose it was my imagination, but her eyes seemed slightly slit, malevolently gleeful.

'Perfectly all right. He's a dreary old thing, isn't he?'

---

[1] AC's driver.
[2] MP for Bolsover since 1970.

She flounced out and back into her own room.

I thought about it for a little while. They *must* have been bugging my phone. There was no other explanation. And for ages.

In the evening, I told the whole story to Christopher.[1] He said he found it encouraging. 'It shows how well we are governed.'

Saltwood   *Sunday, 26 June*

Took the day off. We went to the Bentley Rally in Kensington Gardens, then to lunch with Selmes. He's looking ghastly – presumably got AIDS. He's got this new house, definitely downmarket from Lindsey[2] and it's being done up in what one might term Aggressor-Deviant mode. Mad great black painted walls; a pink Francis Bacon with a youth's demi (only) detumescent penis blotchily prominent.

'We're going to have a white spiral staircase here, this is going to be the *fun* room, I'm taking out the dividing wall the whole way along here ...' etc., etc. But it remains a rather dud Edwardian building, isolated Pont Street Dutch.

The previous owner, a German, had replaced all the window panes on the street side with black one-way-vision glass, like a cocaine addict's limousine. And why do 'active' buggers create these giant, terrifying great rococo master bedrooms in which (to me, at least) it would appear impossible to sleep, never mind perform the sex act, satisfactorily? Ian McCallum[3] – come to think of it he actually *died* of AIDS only a short while ago – had one in his house in Bath; and of course the creepiest of all is Peter Pitt Millward's bedroom at Gloria.[4]

We ate a delicious picnic in the garden, with far too much to drink. If it's Chassagne Monrachet, I always overdo it. After his fifth glass of Dom Perignon Christopher scintillated. He can still be

---

[1] Christopher Selmes, a friend of many years who had made a fortune in the City at the age of twenty-seven, but lost most of it during the 1974–5 crash.

[2] Lindsey House on the Embankment, next door to Paul and Ingrid Channon, had just been sold for £1,250,000.

[3] Ian McCallum, Curator of the American Museum at Bath.

[4] Paco da Gloria, the seventeenth-century palacio in northern Portugal, which was bequeathed to AC's brother Colin by Peter Pitt Millward.

divinely, hurtfully, witty. But his skin is scabeous, white and flaky. Poor fellow.

We travelled back by train, and by the time we arrived at Sandling I was acid and bad-tempered. But after some tea and a stroll in the arboretum, so dark and lush, I felt better.

Not for the first time I let my thoughts ramble around the many different ways that one could 'improve' the place – all, needless to say, involving vast expenditure and thus impossible. The great unexploited resource is the old lake, drained by the breach which the Parliamentarians opened in the dam in 1648 and now a lush meadow, rich in mushrooms. To close this up, contain the stream, produce a beautiful reflecting surface carrying water lilies, where one could drift in a punt and think great thoughts, with a weir and a series of waterfalls cascading through the arboretum – *Grandes Eaux* – that would be spectacular. But to what end? A beautiful private sanctuary, or a 'Stately Home' with the public trampling and soiling and scattering crisp packets?

Anyway, I can't contemplate such a scheme until I recover my liberty. I told Jane, I'm imprisoned for eighteen months, then moved to another prison – perhaps an 'open' one – or discharged. What I can't allow is for them to keep me at DE for the whole four years just so as to be 'out of the way'.

Albany   *Tuesday, 28 June*

Today is the sixty-ninth anniversary of the assassination of the Archduke Franz Ferdinand at Sarajevo, the date from which the world changed. At the time no one realised what it meant, though I often think of that prize-winning spoof headline in the *New York Daily News* in 1920: 'Archduke found alive, World War a Mistake'. Surely the two best repositories of black humour are the Bronx and the Household Division.

I am a privileged prisoner. I sit in my little cell room off the top, white, ministerial corridor, listlessly opening a *mountain* of constituency mail, 'taken into solitary confinement for his own protection'. My mental process is already torpid with *ennui*. I wake up, get up, earlier and earlier. There is about an hour, from 5.45 to 6.45, when the mind is relaxed, its muscles deknotted by sleep. Then, once the clock hands are past seven, the pressure is on, the light tension headache starts behind the eyes.

Last night I drank with Franko[1] in the Ritz. He is so clever, his wit and insight so engaging. And he is a scholar. I feel on my mettle. But he is a pessimist *au fond*. After a bit we both got depressed. Various lovelies, brown and rich, drifted about in their silk diaphanous dresses. We were gloomy voyeurs. The aura of power is an aphrodisiac, and all that. But I felt eunuch-like. It's all too bloody pasteurised. I'd like to revert to the old Ischian Al,[2] and get it raw.

Department of Employment   *Thursday, 30 June*

I still like to go to Prime Minister's Questions. I sit on the little cross bench below the bar on the Labour side, which allows me to hear a lot of what is said on their benches and also gives a good diagonal enfilade of our side.

Poor Bob Dunn,[3] one of the five back-bench promotions, made the most frightful hash of his Question Time, fumbling, stumbling and sitting down halfway through the answers until a Labour Member cruelly suggested (Bob is a junior Education Minister) that he may consider taking a course in articulacy. The Speaker, meaning kindly, attempted to defend him, but this only made matters worse. I dread my own Questions, set for 19 July; it must be absolutely terrifying. Once or twice in the last couple of weeks I have sidled into the Chamber in the mornings and held the Despatch Box and looked round. A very odd feeling.

Tony Kershaw[4] asked the Prime Minister the very question that I had in mind and would have tried to get in with had I been in my usual place – something to the effect of how she had forced the

---

[1] Frank Johnson, political correspondent and commentator. At this time writing the parliamentary sketch for *The Times*.

[2] AC often averts to his bachelor holidays in Ischia, where he would stay with John Pollock and Constance Mappin at Forio.

[3] Robert Dunn, MP for Dartford since 1979. He had just been appointed junior Education Minister.

[4] Sir Anthony Kershaw, MP for Stroud since 1955.

resignation of the SDP Leader, of the Labour Party Leader, how the successor to the Labour Leader had already lost his voice, and the Leader of the Liberal Party had retired to the country with a nervous breakdown. She was delighted and led it on by saying, ' . . . and I am happy to tell my Honourable Friend that personally I have never felt better'. For some reason this made me uneasy.

Plymouth train   *Friday, 1 July*

An absolutely glorious day; not a cloud, save the hanging vapour trails of aircraft in the Heathrow 'stack', gradually broadening into woofly white Christmas decorations. *Invariably* does it seem on such days that I am committed not to be heading south to Saltwood and sweet Jane and the gardens, but West, to the Constituency where, I am complacently told, no fewer than twenty-two people are booked for surgery. I won't even get a cup of tea there, and if there are too many life stories I won't even manage the 6.25, which is the last train that allows me to make the connection to Saltwood.

I have a stuffed box, mainly dreary PO cases[1] which will prevent me getting at this month's *Motor Sport* or, even better, resting the eyeballs. And when Joan meets me at Paddington (assuming I make it back to Paddington) there will be another box, possibly two, on the back seat.

And yet, I am enormously fortunate. I am not *compelled* to do any of these things, to endure any of these discomforts. And the boys are so lovely and strong and handsome. There was a fearful helicopter accident at Bristows yesterday.[2] No survivors. Always, unspoken in the background, Death lurks, carrying his scythe and lantern.

---

[1] Private Office cases arise where an MP refers the problem of an individual con-stituent directly to a Minister for investigation.

[2] AC's elder son, James, was working as a helicopter captain, flying AeroSpatiale Super Pumas on the North Sea oil rigs for Bristow Aviation.

Norman Tebbit is truly formidable. He radiates menace, but without being overtly aggressive. He seldom smiles, but goes straight to the heart of a subject, never gets diverted into detail, always sees the political implications.

I have just come from a meeting on 'Special Employment Measures' (these tacky schemes to get people off the Register). My own mind is a maelstrom of nit-picking detail, eligibility rules, small print of a kind that civil servants relish − not least because they can browbeat Ministers as a team, with one bespectacled *Guardian* reader in sole charge of each 'Scheme' and thus in complete command of its detailed provisions. The unfortunate Minister blunders about like a bull on sawdust with the picadors galloping round him sticking in their horrid barbed *banderillas* (if that's what they are).

'But no, Minister, ha-ha, in that case the eligibility entitlement would have lapsed . . . '

'Ah, yes, Minister, but there is no provision under the Order for . . . '

'Mmm, Minister, it would have to be discretionary and that could only be exercised in exceptional circumstances . . . '

This particular tautologous cliché always irritates me. 'I beg to enclose the enclosed enclosure,' I said.

The officials looked startled. Is the Minister going soft in the head?

But the moment Norman came in he took complete control. Admittedly, the Secretary of State is always right. Rule Number One of Whitehall. Even if he's as thick as a plank officials must rally round, and 'help' him. Norman's own position is particularly strong, as he is known to be a special favourite of the Lady, of whom they are all completely terrified. And with good reason. The wretched Donald Derx apparently became impatient with her thought processes some time ago − early in the '79 Parliament before the old *nostra* had been undermined, and these changes confirmed by the electorate; and at their first meeting was emboldened to be 'cutting' in response. She marked his card on the spot, and he is going to take early retirement, having 'had it conveyed to him' that he will never make Permanent Secretary.

So they arse-lick, massively, with Norman. Which he accepts, expressionlessly, but without letting it deflect him. At one point he turned to me. 'Well, what do you think, Alan?' I was tongue-tied. I couldn't speak the way he did, crudely but shrewdly; nor could I express myself in Whitehall, convoluted phrases, double negative conditionals. I was useless. Will I ever get any better? I've only been here three weeks, I suppose, although it feels like a lifetime. The trouble is, it's *so* boring, the material. I simply can't 'master' it. If only I was at the Foreign Office, or the MoD. Still, better get fit in the prison yard first.

Jenny is fussing about some Order I've got to put through the House on equal pay. Endless briefings she's arranging. What's the point? It's after hours, everyone will have gone home, all I have to do is stand at the Box and read a Civil Service briefing.

But I *am* a bit twitchy about 'First for Questions', now coming over the horizon. A couple of times I've been into the empty Chamber, and stood at the box on the Government side, tried to get the feel of the geography. It doesn't help. I get butterflies in my stomach.

Department of Employment   *Wednesday, 6 July*

I sat drinking late last night, after the vote (Roman hot it was at eleven p.m.), with Jonathan Aitken in the garden of his house in Lord North Street.[1] I remember thinking these houses were a bit poky, blackly crumbling, when I used to go to Sybil's 'ordinaries'.[2] I now see, of course, that they are the choicest thing you can have if you are a Tory MP. Number 8 is bigger than the others; was Brendan Bracken's in the Thirties, and he built on a long drawing room at the back. Furniture not bad, but pictures ridiculous, art dealers' junk. Not even shiny decorative Mallet pieces, but smudgy gilt on cheap frames.

Jonathan was very complimentary about my prospects. He said it was no disadvantage getting in late; said I could go 'quite remarkably high'. I knew what he meant, and dissimulated delightedly. But everything depended on one's performance at the Despatch Box. I told him about my exchanges with Sir Robert Armstrong. He was

---

[1] Jonathan Aitken, MP for Thanet East since 1974, had at the Election become the Member for Thanet South.

[2] An 'ordinary' was a party given by Lady Colefax, who, unlike Lady Cunard, another political hostess of the period, was not well off. She discreetly billed her guests a few days after the event.

sensible and wise and funny. We both agreed on how well Ian Gow
was doing. His maiden speech demolishing Kaufman[1] was a classic.
Ian is shaping up as a true heavyweight.

All this cheered me up, and I needed it, because that evening I
had been to Joei's party, and felt old and passé. *Very* handsome
young men everywhere. Joei lounged and struck attitudes; she's going
through a phase when she thinks she's Nancy Cunard. Ali, though
friendly, was for some reason tearful. Everyone beautifully turned
out; but an unsettled atmosphere, a mood of urgency suggesting
dependence on narcotics rather than on alcohol. I left early, and with
no regrets. Public life now absorbs all my energies. I can't socialise.
Politicians who try to do both can't be much good at either.

In the sleeper to Paddington   *Friday, 15 July*

What a day! On the go without let-up from the early hours. Jenny
had put in place a murderous schedule, quite deliberately, and came
along (v. rare) to make sure there was no malingering.

It came about like this. When my appointment was reported in
the *Herald*[2] I foolishly and fecklessly answered 'Yes' to the question
(semi-spastic, like all the *Herald*'s questions), 'Now you'll be able to
do something about Plymouth's unemployed, won't you. Will you
be calling in on the Unemployment offices in the city? Da, da, etc.'
Result, banner headlines on the Friday after: ALAN CLARK TO VISIT
CITY UB OFFICES. Further result, according to the local DE office (why
is there such a thing? Waste of money and personnel) who faxed
through copies of the paper to Jenny, that all the staff were keyed up
for my visit and disappointed when I didn't show up – 'Typical'.

Jenny snorted and stomped around saying 'visits' had to be organised in advance, was I going there as an MP or as a Minister, anyway
I couldn't go there as an MP if I *was* a Minister, Ministers couldn't
make impromptu visits, had to be accompanied at all times, the local
office must be informed, we'd have to bring a press officer 'in case
there were questions . . . ', *ad infinitum*.

---

[1] Gerald Kaufman now MP for Manchester, Gorton, after representing Manchester
    Ardwick from 1970; Shadow Home Secretary.
[2] *Western Evening Herald*, Plymouth newspaper.

Bleakly I heard her out. 'All right, then, lay it on.'

So there we were in the breakfast train to Exeter, the beautiful Wiltshire countryside rolling past, the fields parched and yellowing but the hedgerows and deciduous trees still heavy with foliage. Drought in a temperate climate induces pleasing, unexpected colours and vistas.

I am always nostalgic for Wiltshire, a delicious pain, where we lived so happily when the boys were tiny, and every day seemed free and golden. There is something about the train's wheel note, something in the subconscious anyway, that I always wake up, whatever I'm doing or reading when the train goes past the Lavingtons.[1] There is a lovely rambling farm there, where Jane went to a 'contents' sale; I should have bought the whole thing, lock-stock-and, moved into it and lived happily ever after. But in fact, at the time, I was restless. I wanted to get into politics, and the years were going by. I could see my friends just beginning to get old, and starting to repeat themselves. I couldn't get through a dinner party just listening to Michael Briggs asking me if I remembered what Alistair Londonderry did on the way back from Porto Ercole in the summer of 1966, or whatever.

Damnably, although I have a mountain of briefing on our visit(s), Jenny has not packed in the box(es) the folder on First for Questions, now ominously close at 2.30 on the afternoon of Tuesday of next week. Is this deliberate? Yes and no. She wants me to concentrate on it over the weekend. But that leaves hideously little time to clarify the errors and omissions in the crib. Never mind. Perhaps there'll be a *huge* IRA bomb in New Palace Yard and the whole thing will be cancelled. That's how I get to sleep at night, anyway.

All too soon Exeter came up. And there was a local big cheese, who'd come down from Bristol, to drive us about. Angela Croft, the press officer, is attractive. Smart summer suit, pretty legs. Jenny is Victorian, no, *sanatorium* pale, in her silk frock. I ought to be full of testosterone as I stride along the platform with these two cerebral cuties clip-tripping beside me. Quite the opposite. They've got me in a tungsten steel jock-strap. Within, there is nothing better than a champagne cork.

The big cheese had a new (red) Volvo. Thankfully, I made to slump in the back. But no, wouldn't you rather sit in front as it was

---

[1] From the stretch of line between West Lavington and Market Lavington could be seen the giant elms on the second escarpment where the Clarks inhabited the manor house, 1964–72.

'easier to point things out'. After about twenty minutes we arrived at our first destination, a settlement for Unfortunates.

First, a 'conference'; introduced to good-natured and worthy staff, heard their presentations. Then a Working Lunch. (As I don't take lunch, and made as much clear to my Private Office when I got to the Dept, they now get round this simply by tagging on the prefix 'working'). Small talk, rather dying away by the time we had coffee. Then a tour; the theme is 'Rehabilitation' and the inmate's tasks are simple. Conversation is far from easy.

It was a relief to get to the UBOs. Some pretty operatives. One, who I know actually was called Sharon because I asked her, let me look into her computer screen. I moved closer, she moved closer, I moved closer, etc. Jenny scowled. No one else seemed to notice.

Then the Job Centres. Another conference, another tour. Here the buzz theme was 'the Disabled'. But why? It's the *able* I want to get back into work. If civil servants think their career prospects are centred round what they can do for the disabled, that is what they will focus on. But it all causes long-term dilution. Society will become an inverted pyramid with the whole load of pensions, benefits and hand-outs for minorities being carried by a few tough and house-proud workers. This is the kind of thing I went into politics to stop. And here I am going round saying yes, yes; well done, keep up the good work.

Gloom, frustration.

Finally, I got rid of Jenny and Angela. Surgery was almost a treat. Two hours, and at the end I had a mug (I *loathe* tea in a mug) of weak tea with powdered milk.

Two lunatics. Macrae, and little Mrs Thingummy with her thirty-nine murder attempts. Fourteen 'normal' cases. One must be polite. They are so sweet, most of them. They don't whinge, really. They're just bewildered, and put upon.

It must have been well over 80° all day, more than that in the poky little constituency office. Constantly, I perspired. In the gaps between interviews I thought of the gardens of Saltwood. How many perfect days like this am I going to jettison? Will I ever have anything to show for it? I can get very sentimental and long for darling little Jane who is left alone for so long, and always so game and jolly.

It wasn't until half past eight that I was free. But then I had a treat,

supper (quite by chance) in Si Lam's[1] with David Owen.[2] He's so engaging, such good company. Like me, he despises the Liberals. Like
me, he admires the Lady. What is to become of him? I said, 'You must
be Prime Minister' and later, 'You *will* be Prime Minister.' It's extraordinary how this extravagant compliment invariably gives pleasure,
however ludicrously improbable, to whomsoever it is addressed. But in
David's case it could happen. And we could do a lot worse.

Saltwood   *Sunday, 17 July*

By the pool, before breakfast. A warm breeze, a *Föhn* it is, blows yew
needles into the water and the filter is choked. The water is 82°, its
hottest ever, but dark yellowy green. When we returned from the
Election campaign the pool was still blue, but now the algae are out
of control. We have tried drenching it with chemicals, but this simply
has the effect of making the water translucent; not transparent. You
can't see the bottom. I go down with the mask, and the floor is
covered with dark algae slime.

Yesterday, to much apprehension, we staged a musical evening for the
Historic Houses Association. In fact, and to our surprise, it was
quite delightful. Martin Muncaster recited and gave readings. The
Dolmetsch twins played most pleasingly. Many excerpts which I didn't
know, a contemporary pastiche. Moving and painful was the exchange
of letters between Henry VIII and Ann Boleyn. His first avowing his
love and torment; hers in dignity and solitude, three years later, before
the scaffold. Oh, how the human predicament endures.

   Saltwood was absolutely glorious, unique, the roses incredible.
One of the loveliest places in the whole world. This coming week is
my test and crisis. First for Questions on Tuesday; an Order to 'lay'
before the Standing Committee and, after ten p.m., before the whole
House. I wax and wane between confidence and inspiration; and

---

[1] Chinese restaurant in North Hill, Plymouth, where AC could often take late supper
    before catching the sleeper back to London.
[2] David Owen, Leader of the Social Democrat Party. MP for the neighbouring
    constituency of Plymouth Devonport since 1974 (as Labour until 1981, then
    SDP). From 1966–74 he represented AC's Plymouth Sutton seat.

sheer terror and fatigue. I can only thank God that I have this lovely place to fall back on; and, please, to spare the boys.

Saltwood   *Friday, 22 July*

Fool, Clark. Fool, fool, fool. This week I went up a stubby ladder; then down a very long snake.

Questions were fine. The first one (my very first Question on the floor of the House of Commons; how many more will I answer before I am done?) came from Cyril Smith.[1] Naturally, the crib didn't cover it, but Norman told me the gist of an answer out of the corner of his mouth as I rose to my feet. Cyril whumphed back in his seat with a sulky expression. Canavan[2] tried to give a bit of trouble but was maladroit, and I scored. Others were barely noticeable. To my great delight I read sideways in the Whip's book (it was Hamilton[3]), 'Clark dealt v. well with Canavan. He has a nice slow delivery which holds the attention of the House.' Could one ask for more? Afterwards Nigel Forman,[4] a good judge of most things, said, 'It's nice to hear a genuine toff's accent at the Box occasionally.' Many other compliments were paid.

Alas! An odious over-confidence burgeoned. Anyone can do this. Child's play. My friends encouraged me. In the dining room Tristan said, 'We're selling tickets for Al's performance tomorrow...' I resolved not to disappoint them. Looking back now, I realise I was amazingly, suicidally, over-confident.

I was booked to dine with Christopher, for a *wine-tasting*. I left the Department unusually early because I wanted to go to the Braque exhibition at the Tate. Tony Newton[5] (whom I like) was wandering round, and said something about it was nice to see Ministers broadening their minds even though they would be 'performing' in a few

---

[1] Cyril Smith, MP for Rochdale since 1972.

[2] Denis Canavan, recently elected as MP for Falkirk West, having represented West Stirlingshire from 1974.

[3] Archie Hamilton, MP for Epsom and Ewell since 1978, junior Whip. Later PPS to the Prime Minister and Minister of State, Ministry of Defence.

[4] Nigel Forman, MP for Carshalton since 1976.

[5] Tony Newton, MP for Braintree since 1974, later Secretary of State for Social Security and Leader of the House of Commons.

hours' time. Airily, I told him that I wouldn't be back in the House until ten; I was going on to a dinner.

That fucking text! I'd barely looked at it. Norman had sent for me at tea time, said good luck and all that, and 'just stick to the text'. In fairness, and presciently, he had also said, 'Don't try any jokes.' Situation not helped by the fact that officials had twice called in their original version and 'incorporated certain changes, Minister'. So I didn't really start to mark it up until I was in the back of the car going from the Tate to Christopher's house (not far). It seemed frightfully long. So long, indeed, that I would have to excise certain passages.

But which? And yet this didn't really seem very important as we 'tasted' first a bottle of '61 Palmer, then 'for comparison' a bottle of '75 Palmer then, switching back to '61, a really delicious Pichon Longueville. Geoffrey Roberts was the only other guest. By 9.40 I was muzzy. Joan had already been waiting ten minutes. I was meeting officials 'behind the Chair' before the ten o'clock vote. The text was still virtually unmarked and unexcised.

A huge Havana was produced, and I puffed it deeply while struggling with my speech under the tiny little reading light in the back of the Princess.

There were the officials, all anxious but deferential. I exhaled smoke at them. Grand seigneur. I couldn't talk, I had to pee. In the lav, that nice clean one off the Aye lobby, was Barry Jones[1], my 'shadow'.

'This shouldn't present any problems.'

'None whatever. They all want to get to bed.'

'That goes for me too.'

Nice chap. Good relations.

The Chamber was unusually full for an after-ten event. When I was called there was a ragged, undeferential cheer from the benches behind. But an awful lot of Labour people seemed to be in as well. Including, it seemed, every female in their parliamentary strength. I recognised many of the *tricoteuses* who kept us up night after night in the summer of 1976 filibustering (successfully) the committee stage of Bill Benyon's Bill to reduce the maximum age at which babies can legally be murdered from six months to three.

As I started, the sheer odiousness of the text sank in. The purpose

---

[1] Barry Jones, MP for Alyn and Deeside since the Election (Flint East, 1970–83).

of the Order, to make it more likely (I would put it no stronger than that) that women should be paid the same rate for the same task, as men, was unchallengeable. In my view, in most instances, women deserve not less but *more* than the loutish, leering, cigaretting males who control most organisations at most levels. But give a civil servant a good case and he'll wreck it with clichés, bad punctuation, double negatives and convoluted apology. Stir into this a directive from the European Community, some contrived legal precedent and a few caveats from the European Court of Justice and you have a text which is impossible to read – never mind read *out*.

I found myself dwelling on, implicitly, it could be said, sneering at, the more cumbrous and unintelligible passages. Elaine Kellet-Bowman,[1] who has a very squeaky voice, squeaked, kept squeaking, at me, 'Speed up.'

Some of the House got the point, enjoyed what I was doing, but I sensed also a certain restlessness starting to run round the Chamber. I did speed up. I gabbled. Helter-skelter I galloped through the text. Sometimes I turned over two pages at once, sometimes three. What did it matter? There was no shape to it. No linkage from one proposition to another. The very antithesis of an Aristotelian pattern.

Up bobbed a teeny little fellow, Janner[2] by name, a Labour lawyer who always wears a pink carnation in his buttonhole. He asked me what the last paragraph 'meant'.

How the hell did I know what it meant? I smoothed away. He started bobbing up and down as, it seemed, did about fifteen people on the other side, plus I couldn't see how many on my own, to my side and behind me. This had the makings of a disaster. Never mind. 'Heads down, bully, and shove.'[3]

Then, the inevitable. The one sure-fire way of breaking through a speaker who won't give way. 'Point of Order, Mr Deputy Speaker.' I sat down. A new Labour member whom I had never seen before, called Clare Short,[4] dark-haired and serious with a lovely Brummie accent, said something about she'd read that you couldn't accuse a fellow member of being drunk, but she really believed I was incapable.

---

[1] Elaine Kellet-Bowman, MP for Lancaster since 1974.
[2] Greville Janner, MP for Leicester since 1970.
[3] A slogan from the Field Game (played in the winter term at Eton).
[4] Clare Short, MP for Birmingham Ladywood since the Election.

'It is disrespectful to the House and to the office that he holds that he should come here in this condition.'

Screams, yells, shouts of 'Withdraw', counter-shouts. General uproar. On and on went the Points of Order. I sat, smiling weakly, my lips as dry as sandpaper. The Chamber began to fill up, and there were at least fifteen people standing at the bar of the House. (It is a golden rule: Points of Order on the annunciator screen for more than two minutes means a good row, so put your head round the door and enjoy it.)

On the whole, I'm pretty relaxed about rows and flare-ups. As far as Ministers go, provided they avoid taking money or money's worth from anyone except the Fees Office, even the most turbulent row will die down and soon be forgotten. But this had an ominous feel to it. On and on went the shouting. 'ORDER,' kept bellowing dear old Ernie Armstrong, the Deputy Speaker.[1] The House was alight. Soon, wearing an uneasy half-smile, definitely *not* catching my eye, appeared the figure of the Leader of the House, John Biffen,[2] to sit in his appointed place.

Now this was a bad sign. The Leader only attends business after ten o'clock when there is a *major row.* And a truly terrible threat began to seep through to me. Perhaps we were going to 'lose the business'. This is not the same as being defeated on a vote. It simply means that the whole thing has to be brought back before the House at a later date. The entire Government legislative schedule is put out of kilter – and the Whips loathe it. Indeed, as far as the Whips go, no other misdemeanour compares. I could see anxious conferrals starting up with the Chair, and behind.

Bob Wareing[3] asked if it would be in order for an honourable or right honourable Member to address the House if he were drunk. Ernie said that this was a hypothetical question, 'and now we must get on with the debate'.

Passions were (temporarily) spent and I rose to my feet. But the atmosphere was different. I had lost confidence and in its special extra-sensory way the House knew that something 'wasn't quite right'. My supporters were silent. And others on our side were emboldened to

[1] Ernie Armstrong, MP for NW Durham since 1964, Deputy Speaker since 1981.
[2] John Biffen, MP for Shropshire North since the Election (Oswestry, 1961–83), Leader of the House since 1982.
[3] Bob Wareing, MP for Liverpool, West Derby since the Election.

be portentous and, by implication, reproachful. I forced my way through to the end, another fifteen minutes or so, feeling like Lucky Jim at the award ceremony, before coming to the magic signing-off phrase, 'I commend these regulations to the House.'

Now if there's one vice in which the House really likes to indulge, it is being sanctimonious. Each speaker took his cue from the last: so sad, such an opportunity cast away, the great traditions of the Department, Walter Monckton, Ernest Bevin, Macleod (how the fuck did he come into it?), Harold Macmillan, Stockton, breadth of understanding, unpardonable levity, offensive to both sides of the argument (what argument?), after-dinner speech. And, of course, incomparably menacing, that the House should have a full opportunity to debate the issue, send for more papers, data should be placed in the Library.

I assumed gravitas. Dear Peter Morrison was sitting beside me, his face pouring sweat. Periodically I said to him, 'We must *not* lose the business.' 'I think it'll be all right. I've had a word with Ernest.'

I held my breath. It was coming up to midnight and, thank God, it had been agreed that I was not expected to 'reply' to the debate. This in fact was a trap which Labour had laid, hoping that the Speaker would then rule that the matter should be heard another day. Sure enough, with only a few minutes left, Nigel Spearing,[1] one of their best barrack-room lawyers, rose and cited Standing Order No. 3 (1) (b), which gives the Speaker a discretion to decide that the matter be adjourned. Very splendidly, Ernie said that he 'had had this provision in mind throughout the Debate'.

One more brief kerfuffle, and the Division was called. Nobody spoke to me much in the Aye lobby, although little garden gnome Peter Rost[2] sidled up and said, 'After a performance like that I almost considered voting against.'

Poxy little runt, what's he ever done?

In the car Joan asked, 'What was all that row about, Minister?' (Knowing full well, I don't doubt.)

'They were saying I was drunk. But I wasn't, was I?'

'No, Minister, of course you weren't. I've never seen you drunk.'

That's that, then.

---

[1] Nigel Spearing, MP for Newham South since 1974.
[2] Peter Rost, MP for Erewash since the Election (Derbyshire South-East, 1970–83).

Department of Employment   *Thursday, 28 July*

The House rises today, in effect. But we don't get our holiday until
September. Other Ministers will take theirs in August, and come back
fresh. It'll be, 'Where's Alan?' and when my office say 'On holiday',
it'll be, 'Clark's still on holiday'. *Les absents ont toujours tort.* Jenny is
taking hers (thank God) in mid-August, but is busy filling up the rest
of the month with dreadful draining visits to boring and inaccessible
locations.

In the dining room conversation was mainly on this topic. Our
table was joined by little Douglas Hogg, now a junior Whip.[1] I can't
decide whether he is likeable or not. (But I should say that many do
not have this difficulty.) I don't mind people being rude, provided
that they are not uncouth with it. But he is colossally self-satisfied –
or is it a chip? I suspect he has a tearful side. It is said that in the days
of their courtship he used to follow the object of his desire and her
paramour at a distance, and stalk them, peeping from shop doorways,
like a bad secret agent.

'Well,' I said, 'how are you keeping all the new boys in order?'

Without a second's hesitation he got my middle stump. 'By
offering them your job.'

Department of Employment   *Wednesday, 3 August*

I went to the NEDC meeting in the morning representing the
Department. Norman had sent his apologies. Lawson[2] chaired it,
podgy and jowelly, and there is a suspicious henna tinge to his hair. Is
he tinting, or rinsing? But he is an effective chairman.

We sat at a round table on the top floor of the CBI building and
many notables were in attendance. Five members of the Cabinet;
Keith Joseph,[3] with a permanently bored, but slightly agonised,
expression on his face combining, I-have-seen-it-all, and are-we-all-
mad? Cecil Parkinson – if ever anybody deserved the over-worked

---

[1] Douglas Hogg, Tory MP for Grantham since 1979. Elder son of Lord Hailsham
and married to Sarah, daughter of former Tory Minister, John Boyd-Carpenter.
[2] Nigel Lawson, MP for Blaby since 1974. Chancellor of the Exchequer.
[3] Keith Joseph, MP for Leeds North East since 1956. Education Secretary since 1981.

expression 'amazingly youthful', it is Cecil.[1] He is not impressive
reading from a prepared brief, but is very good when spontaneous. I
was sitting next to him and watched him keenly, as he is of course my
choice to succeed the Lady.

Peter Walker[2] was there in a country suit and spoke turgidly but
with 'oh-what-a-good-boy-am-I' overtones. 'A very impressive contribution,' I muttered to Cecil. He is a real Neddy star, he agreed discreetly.

On the other side Ian Gow was sending me irreverent notes,
'What are we all doing here, what's the point, who are all these
ridiculous highly paid people sitting at the back of the room', etc.
Robin Leigh-Pemberton[3] was unexpectedly good, crisp and clear.
Terence (or Terry, as he likes to be called) Beckett[4] was not quite as
bad as I expected, suffering, though, from a heavy tobacco cough.

Moss Evans was almost completely silent, a distinguished drawn
face, immaculately dressed like a Mafia godfather, twice as formidable
as any of the other TU heavies who were there.[5] Terry Duffy[6] was
just a dear old thing; Frank Chapple a professional rough diamond.[7]

I was nervous about having to contribute, but in fact the Chancellor *rushed* the Agenda item – absurdly, but menacingly, entitled
'Where are the Jobs Coming From' – on which there was a Departmental responsibility. I assume because he wanted to choke off monologues from the TUC end of the table. The whole thing was a
complete waste of time. No conclusions, no recommendations, no
action taken or suggested. Job creation scheme for civil servants, and
way of embarrassing Ministers.

Joan drove me round immediately to the Trustees' meeting[8] at
Christie's but the traffic was so bad that I had to bail out at the bottom
of St James's Street, ran up the little arcade past the entrance to Rhodes
and Co., the money lenders where I remember unhappily borrowing

---

[1] Cecil Parkinson, MP from 1970; for Hertsmere since the June Election, and before
    that South Hertfordshire and Enfield. Currently Trade and Industry Secretary.
[2] Peter Walker, MP for Worcester since 1971. Appointed Energy Minister after the
    Election following four years at Agriculture.
[3] Robin Leigh-Pemberton, newly appointed Governor of Bank of England. Friend
    of AC since they were at Eton.
[4] Terence Beckett, Director General, CBI since 1980.
[5] Moss Evans, Transport and General Workers Union.
[6] Terry Duffy, Amalgamated Union of Engineering Workers.
[7] Frank Chapple, Electrical, Electronic, Telecommunications and Plumbing Union,
    and the current chairman of the TUC.
[8] Of Lord Clark's settlement.

£500 in 1947. Now I was on my way to discuss carving up ten million. But nothing else seems to have altered much.

Department of Employment   *Thursday, 4 August*

Last night I dined with Ian. I asked him if he was happy and he said he was not. To my horror he told me that he had not seen the Prime Minister since 14 June, which was the day that Michael Alison[1] took over. How ruthless women can be – far worse than men. Ian was completely in love with the Prime Minister and utterly devoted to her. He must have seen more of her in the last four years than anybody else except Denis, and possibly more even than him. He was enormously influential, too. And yet now the court has sealed over the vacuum created by his departure and I doubt if he will ever recover an equivalent position. Ian said that he would gladly stop being a Minister at any moment and that he would gladly 'go back'. But you can never go back. It is the Two-second Rule. I said that he would be in the Cabinet in the next reshuffle and resume his old intimacy. But I am not so sure, and nor is he.

We both agreed that Michael Alison, although a pleasant and saintly man, could not possibly provide the Lady with the same alternating course of stimulus and relaxation. Of course MA sits in on Cabinet meetings, as a Privy Councillor, which Ian never did. But Ian told me how he used to wait in his little office at the bottom of the stairs at Number 10 and emerge to catch doubtful members of the Cabinet as they were coming in before an important meeting, haul them into his room and explain to them that a particular decision was something to which the Prime Minister attached crucial importance. I can visualise the dedication, the *intensity* – with which he used to do this. It is something which Michael, with his diffident manner, simply could not manage.

Ian told me that even the present Cabinet could only guarantee her a majority of two when the chips were really down – 'and

---

[1] Michael Alison, MP for Selby since the Election (Barkston Ash, 1964–83) was appointed Parliamentary Private Secretary to the Prime Minister in the new Government and Ian Gow was tranferred to the DoE, where he became Housing Minister.

supposing Geoffrey[1] is away?' Is that margin of one constituted by Willie?[2] I didn't ask, although his name has returned to the forefront with this ludicrous assurance that he is ' . . . standing by at his farm in Cumbria' in case the Lady goes blind and the ship of state becomes rudderless.[3]

It should have been a celebratory dinner, as last time we had dined the future was uncertain. Now we are both Ministers with a Government majority of 140 and no Opposition of any kind in sight. But there was a certain melancholy too. How often is it better to travel than to arrive.

Department of Employment   *Monday, 15 August*

An absolutely perfect morning of late summer, temperature already 66° and a light dew with mist in the valley. I walked the dogs at seven a.m. up past the dump and over the Seeds, and groaned aloud at the sheer *crucifixion* of having to go to London and visit the Brixton Remploy Office – of all places.

Ministers' Sundays are blighted by the prospect of Monday's workload. By the evening I find myself short-tempered and grimacing. Even the very minimum of correspondence and attention to pressing estate matters has been neglected. Saturday morning is wrecked by the box. Sunday morning is eyestrain headache as one trawls one's way through the ten or twelve thousand words of political commentary in the tabs and the broads. Yesterday afternoon I broke the lanyard on the Osprey on the twenty-seventh muck-sweat and cursing attempt to get it pull-started. I had to mow the whole Bailey lawn with the faithful (but tiny) Hayter as at this time of year the Atco won't cut the plantains. Up and down I went, sweating and muttering, each length a strip no wider than twelve inches.

More depressing, because more relevant to today, and indeed to

---

[1] Sir Geoffrey Howe, MP for Surrey East since 1974 (Reigate, 1970–4; Bebington, 1964–6). Foreign Secretary since 1983.

[2] William Whitelaw, MP for Penrith since 1955. Home Secretary, 1979–83. Following the Election, created 1st Viscount and appointed Lord President of the Council and Leader of the Lords.

[3] Mrs Thatcher was having an operation on her eye.

the whole Whitehall purgatory, I had spent some time in the muniment room. In a desk I had come across some of my father's old engagement diaries of the Forties and Fifties. Endless 'meetings' fill the day. Civil servants drift in and out. Lunches. Virtually indistinguishable from my own. What's the point? Nothing to show for it at all. He will be remembered only for his writings and his contribution to scholarship. His public life was a complete waste of time.

Department of Employment   *Thursday, 1 September*

I was working late at my desk, and Jenny had gone home, when the phone rang. It was Norman Tebbit. He invited me round for a 'chat'.

Norman talked interestingly. He knows where in the Party his strengths lie, and he knows, too, which of the grandees want to do him down. St John-Stevas,[1] of course; but then he's not a proper grandee, just popishly disapproving. And Willie. Sometimes Willie harrumphs menacingly about Norman, but is too shrewd not to recognise his qualities. There are others, who sneer and talk behind their hands to the pink press, but they are of little moment.

I fear Norman does have a chip, but it doesn't show – not all the time at least – and anyhow who could blame him?

We talked for a very long time. So long that the light started to fade, and as dusk entered the room so his style became more confessional.

What he really wants to do – curious how many serious politicians covet the post – is to be Chairman of the Party. Not just yet, I feel, but to keep it in his sights.

Now there was disconcerting news.

'She wants to appoint a Parly Sec.'

'*What*?' (I did not say 'who?', judging that if he wanted to identify the person he would have named him.)

'She thinks we need someone young, to counter the Steel-Owen image.'

I said the image didn't matter. In the first two years after the

---

[1] Norman St John-Stevas, MP for Chelmsford since 1964. Leader of the Commons, 1979–81.

Election the need was for organisational, not presentational skills.

Norman is of the same mind. But we agreed, the Lady does often want to 'bring forward' the very young. Reacting, I suppose, against Willie, Peter Thorneycroft,[1] Humphrey Atkins[2] – all these oldies who have been leaning on her since February 1975.

'It's a matter of having someone young and fresh to go on television the whole time and answer Owen and Steel.'

'At this stage it doesn't matter a damn. You must talk her out of it.'

He didn't answer, rose from his chair and switched on the light. I realised we had been talking for an hour or more, and went back to my own office.[3]

Saltwood   *Thursday, 8 September*

I am at my desk in the tower office, absolutely drowning in estate papers. Filing piles and Immediate piles and Pending piles are stacked haphazard on top of each other. I try to differentiate by stacking them criss-cross, like bricks, but I caught some that were sticking out with my sleeve and the whole Pisa-like tower collapsed, cascading the private and personal papers all over the floor.

So what? I haven't picked them up. I just walk on them. I will soon have plenty of time for the estate.

I am convinced that I have been allocated the black spot. To be dismissed at the earliest opportunity. Norman Tebbit doesn't address a word to me, of either welcome or farewell at the start, or finish, of meetings. Peter [Morrison] is more distant, it seems. This bloody Equal Ops Order still hangs round my neck. Albatross. Mill-stone.

---

[1] Peter Thorneycroft (Life Peer, created 1967). A former MP and Minister in the Macmillan and Douglas-Home Governments: Chancellor of the Exchequer, 1957–8; Chairman of the Conservative Party, 1975–81.

[2] Humphrey Atkins, MP for Spelthorne since 1970 (Merton and Morden 1955–70). Northern Ireland Secretary, 1979–81; Lord Privy Seal, 1981–2, when he returned to back benches.

[3] Three days later John Selwyn Gummer, MP for Suffolk Coastal since the Election (Lewisham West, 1970–4; Eye, 1979–83) and AC's co-Parliamentary Secretary in the Department of Employment, was appointed as Chairman of the Conservative Party.

Ill-wishers cite my performance as an excuse to object to the whole thing, get it 're-opened'. Tricky meeting coming up with Lady Platt (who is not an ill-wisher, but, unlike me, does understand the small print).[1]

Adrian Moorey[2] has a permanent sneer on his face. Is he being privately briefed by Ingham that I am for the chop? Often he comes into the outer office and talks in low tones with Jenny; he doesn't come on in here.

Even so, anything can happen. Norman had to 'go to the bathroom' twice during a meeting yesterday. Cecil looked *awful* on television, with sores showing on both upper and lower lips. The Lady's eye operation may go wrong.

Jenny came back from her holiday with a very very slight gold tan. Looks stunning in her oatmeal suit. At least now she allows me eye contact. I said, 'I don't expect I'll be here much longer.'

'Oh? We'll miss you.' Her stare is very direct, though limpid.

Department of Employment   *Friday, 9 September*

A lot of pointless activity in the Department, as officials start to drift back from their holidays. (We haven't had ours yet. Will we even get one, sometimes I ask myself?) Because the House isn't sitting Private Offices are having quite a little challenge to manage fulfilment of their Number One precept – *Ministers' diaries must be kept filled.* What they really like are full-scale meetings, preferably with so many in attendance that they have to be held in the small conference room. A far more economic solution would be just one intelligent civil servant guiding the Minister through the paper in his own office.

We had one of the PES[3] preliminaries today. First time I've done one of these, and I was totally out of my depth. I'm responsible for all these spastic, money-consuming Employment 'measures', so the idea

---

[1] Baroness Platt of Writtle (Life Peer). Recently appointed Chairman of the Equal Opportunities Commission.

[2] Adrian Moorey, press officer in the Department of Employment, then moved to Trade and Industry.

[3] PES: Public Expenditure Survey.

was that I should sparkle knowledgeably as a prelim to putting in higher 'bids'. I heard them out in sulky silence. Was finally goaded by Fred Bayliss, the Under Secretary, who appears to be our resident Chief Accountant. He mumbled along, '... looks as if there is going to be a shortfall as our overall provision is £408 million and at present we are going to be pushed to get expenditure over £335–360 million'.

That's not a fucking 'shortfall' I thought, or at least not my idea of one. It slowly sank in that he was rambling round for suggested ways of getting last-minute expenditure authorised so as to 'approach more closely our provision'. 'Look, Fred, Ministers in this Department are members of a Government which is dedicated to – whose *raison d'être*, you could say, is – the reduction of public expenditure. Surely it's a matter for congratulation?'

Ah no, don't you see – 'It's important to get as close as possible to last year's provision in order to have a firm base from which to argue for increases this year ... '

This was crazy. Nightmare. Kafka.

Like other officials above the rank of Principal he won't call me 'Minister'; they try and avoid calling me anything.

Is it like this with all Parly Secs, or just me? Icily I asked in what other Departments of State 'is this kind of budgetary practice prevalent'?

'All of them,' they shouted triumphantly.

General laughter, of a *tee-hee* kind.

Afterwards Jenny said, 'It's not really a good idea to get the wrong side of Fred.'

'Yeah?' I was quite pleased with myself.

Saltwood   *Saturday, 10 September*

We are host to a company of actors, who are making a children's film for television. *Tripods* is the title of the story. What a jarring name. Arthur Ransome, and (above all) Beatrix Potter knew what children really like. And adults, come to that. Myself, I am always ready to while away half an hour or so reading the tale of Squirrel Nutkin or Johnny Townmouse, and feel calmer as a result. These days authors write not so much to please the children as to earn the esteem of their own peers or, more importantly, librarians in trendy boroughs.

The team have been here for ages, it seems. But I like it. We charge a whopping location fee, and the gaiety, the costumes, the whirl of activity is all fun, and invigorates the place. They have put up a huge marquee in the car-park field where *delicious* meals (particularly breakfast) are served, and this pleases Eddie and William who have standing invitations to partake. Jane and I also stuff ourselves there, when the moods takes us.

The plot, insofar as one can follow it at all, is muddled. The story 'hops' from the eighteenth century to the late 2000s and back again. But the heroine is a pretty little thing called Charlotte Long,[1] who I know would feel exactly like Ali; same hair, colouring, bone structure. She has a really sweet nature, not at all show-business or ego. And sometimes our eyes meet across the tent, and she smiles shyly. Now come to think of it, she must be the grand, *great* grand-daughter of Walter Long[2], who was leader of the landed interest in (sic) the Conservative Party during Ll G's premiership, and was always getting in Arthur Lee's hair when he was Minister of Food in 1917[3].

Charlotte's (fictional) father, the (needless to say) 'Count' has a grey beard and wears satin breeches most of the time. He, and many others of the cast, have fallen in love with the place – which in the script has become the 'Château Ricordeau'. Charlotte wanders dreamily along the battlements to pastiche Brideshead music, murmuring about 'the loveliest place in the whole world'.

But the one I would really like to be is the Duc de Sarlat, so young and handsome and villainous, and eager to challenge a duel, with sabres.

---

[1] Tragically, Charlotte Long was killed only a few weeks later in a road accident on the M4.

[2] Walter Long, 1st Viscount Long of Wraxall, 1854–1924. Succeeded by his grandson, who in turn was succeeded by his uncle, whose son, Richard (the 4th Viscount), was appointed a Government Whip in the Lords in 1979. Charlotte was his daughter.

[3] Arthur Lee, MP for Fareham, 1900–18, when he was created 1st Baron Lee of Fareham. He had been Personal Military Secretary to Lloyd George, July–December 1916. He was made 1st Viscount in 1922.

Saltwood   *Friday, 23 September*

I sit at the long table in the Great Library. The last entry of the year
from this seat, because tomorrow we load up the Decapotable and
set off on our holiday. We won't really be back here until after the
Party Conference. By then the light will have gone, the place become
too chilly for a *reflectif*. The deep autumn will be on us – mud and
gumboots and log fires and early teas with brown toast and crab-apple
jelly.

Yesterday was forecast as the last one of this lovely Indian summer
and at lunchtime I went down to Hythe beach, being pleased to find
it deserted. High tide and clear sunlight, with an onshore breeze that
slapped the waves into friendly gusts of vertical spray. I lay on the
breakwater, and thought of times past – the golden summer of 1955
when I was running Anne, Marye and Liz, all of them living within
half a mile of each other. Another occasion, later on, when I had
jogged the whole distance from the Imperial and back, and threw off
my tracksuit, plunging naked into the November sea.

My total fitness held up for so long, with only tiny degradations,
until *Parliament* took over. It's the late nights that are shredding it. I
always hated late nights, and avoided them if ever I could, until well
into my forties. And this allowed me to bank a lot of energy. My
lymphatic system is still very low mileage.

I took off my clothes and swam for a long time. The murky salt-
tasting water was a delicious contrast to the metallic chlorine tang of
the swimming pool.

Zermatt   *Monday, 3 October*

We've been here a week, but I have neglected my diary. Glorious
weather, navy-blue skies but Alpine cold in the early evening and on
waking up. I feel rested and randy, and reassured by my performance
in the hills.

On Wednesday we went to the Schönbühlhütte, a hell of a climb,
where three years ago (was it?) I saw a wild cat just at the point where

---

[1] Jane's open Citroën DS which the Clarks habitually use for their summer holiday.

the rock track peters out and you have to rope up. Only a very few tourists. The season is over and many of the inns in the village are already closed. We took six and a half hours and by the time we got to the cable-car station at Furri the last one had left and they were closing for the night. Weary and footsore we stumbled down the hillside, the lights of Zermatt seeming to take an eternity to come within reach.

Yesterday we went across the Gornergletscher to the Monte Rosa-hutte. God, glaciers are frightening. A white maze, lifeless and implacable, so that the sight of a crushed plastic cup or, better, a fox's wispy business is reassuring beyond measure. The *patrouille* must have packed up some weeks back, because the skew poles and bright red and white tape that give early warning of the crevasses were in many places neglected or broken. Sinister and bluey-green, and *deadly* quiet (because at this season they remain frozen all day and there are no drips) these channels are interwoven for hundreds of yards, forcing detour after detour.

We must have been zig-zagging for more than an hour before we reached the moraine on the far side. I have never climbed Monte Rosa, always wanted to since, at Eton, reading Whymper's own account of the first climb which he accomplished, there and back *in a day*, alone and wearing little different than one would stalking hind in Argyll in October 1862.

Outside the hut a mound of fur moved sluggishly. 'Oh dear,' Jane said. 'It's a poor marmot who is too ill and decrepit to hibernate. He's stuck, and will die of cold.' Far from it. He was huge, massive, thrust and barged at us as we ate our sandwiches, rummaged in the rucksack, insisted on a 'tip' before we left. The 'Gondola Man',[1] we agreed.

Jane's stamina is incredible, and she is more supple than me. On the way back we both raced up the side of the Rotenboden cliff, getting to the mountain railway station in forty-three minutes from the edge of the ice, and catching the train by a whisker. It was standing only. I was bathed in sweat and my pulse rate must still have been over 120. But I looked complacently at the other passengers. The gap between athletes and spectators.

---

[1] Gondola man: a family saying denoting the man who always turns up out of nowhere just as you've found a gondola and demands 500 lire for standing beside it, like the commissionaire outside a hotel holding open the door of a taxi.

Zermatt   *Tuesday, 4 October*

Our last day. We watched Sulag's men start opening the ground for
the Kiosk foundations,[1] then climbed up to the Winkelmatten chapel,
where I always find it easy to pray.

I was low at having so soon to return to the Department, its
drudgery, sterile and repetitious. But as my head cleared I realised
how absurd, and ungrateful it was to complain. What does it matter,
the stuffed boxes and the unwashed 7.19 a.m. train from Sandling?
Tip is back safely from the Yemen, and through RCB.[2] Jamie has got
to nearly 2000 hours flying the oil rigs, and soon to be pulled out.
What good fortune attends us. Yesterday Fons[3] was chatting, up by
the Guides' Wall. He said to Jane, 'You haven't changed at all, not
one little bit in twenty years,' and walked off shaking his head. We
each lit a candle. I did Boy's, as he is a wee bit out of kilter at the
moment, and Jane did Andrew's, which was easier.

I have had a Fernandez type haircut,[4] and am looking forward to
Conference next week at Blackpool. My first as a Minister, to swagger
and ponce.

Department of Employment   *Monday, 10 October*

In the first days back after a vigorous holiday one is always full of zest.
Spitefully, although other Ministers were meant to be covering my
routine stuff, Jenny has kept a lot of it back and so there were bursting
boxes, sitting like red tombstones on my desk. But I *ripped* through
them, shouting queries and instructions through the open door. I've
got much more confidence with the Civil Service now. Most of them
are rather second-rate, with teeny vision scales. They're really quite

---

[1] The Clarks had got permission from the Commune to build a new chalet at the
bottom of their garden, which would harbour a 'kiosk' for the Sunnegga railway
station. Sulag was the building contractor.

[2] Andrew had passed the exams for the Regular Commissions Board.

[3] Alfons Franzen, the guide who gave basic skiing tuition to the family, and looked
after the Chalet Caroline for many years.

[4] A hairdresser in St Tropez favoured by AC on account of his gift for endowing a
'boyish' appearance to his customers.

glad to submit to a forceful personality, provided he knows what he wants.

Some of my colleagues are in trouble, and this always makes me calm. Poor Cecil Parkinson looks like being in what Edwardians called *hot water*, as the girl is making paternity claims.[1] But he can ride that, surely? Perhaps not. It could be that the constituencies turn nasty. They mirror, resolutely, the unhealthy combination of prurience and hypocrisy to which editors competitively pander. And Conference, where they all cluck and whisper, starts assembling today.

Then there's little Peter Rees.[2] For some reason all the commentators think he's going to be sacked. Malcolm Rutherford (*Financial Times*) today: ' . . . the most likely to become a casualty'. (No mention of me anywhere in all this, I'm glad to note.) In addition Nick Scott[3] is making a balls-up at the Northern Ireland Office, and Julian Critchley[4] has suddenly written (anonymously, thus also incurring the stigma of cowardice) an offensive piece about the Lady, referring to her as 'the great she-elephant', and in other terms of disrespect.

Albany   *Thursday, 13 October*

We drove down from Blackpool this morning, as my father's memorial service is to be held in the church of St James's in Piccadilly in the afternoon.

Poor old Cecil had a bad time. The Lady is determined to save him, but Sara Keays is equally obsessed about getting her pound of flesh. The delegates are divided, and it is not easy to tell in what proportion. Those who support Cecil are vocal of course, and give little interviews

---

[1] Sara Keays had had a long-term relationship with Cecil Parkinson whose secretary she had been 1971–9. She was now pregnant with his child.

[2] Peter Rees, MP for Dover since 1970. Minister for Trade, 1981–3, when he was moved to the Treasury as Chief Secretary.

[3] Nicholas Scott, MP for Chelsea since 1974. He survived a further four years at the Northern Ireland Office.

[4] Julian Critchley was beginning to make a reputation as a writer.

to the camera. But I have a nasty feeling that there is a silent majority who are disapproving, and shocked.

Cecil himself is handsome and fresh-faced. Seems at times almost to be the injured party. But what an ordeal! His wife, his mistress and his boss, all throwing scenes, sometimes all within the same hour.

Apparently little Gummer, who is demonstratively *churchy* and (unlike the Lady) moralistic, is making a lot of trouble.

My father's memorial service was strange. A motley collection of strays. Poetic justice, as he himself never went to anybody's.

Yehudi Menuhin played the violin, and I read the lesson in a very clear and sardonic voice, trying to convey that they were all a shower, Nolwen in particular. If you die in old age, of course, you get a completely different kind of attendance than if you are taken by the Gods.

Myself, I don't want one. Better just to disappear, like Zapata.

Plymouth train   *Thursday, 20 October*

In order to make time for a solid raft of engagements in the Constituency I crammed everything in yesterday. A really draining day.

Started at nine a.m. with Wronski (dim German Senator). Wasn't a bad egg in one of the Bond films called Wronski? Boring. Stilted. I feel ashamed, when receiving visitors from abroad, of my poky little room. There are a few things, I suppose, that might make them prick up their eyes if they are 'connoisseurs', but they never are. And the rest of the stuff – cheap desk, stained carpet – says, unmistakably, junior Minister (very).[1]

Then straight through to the Home Office for the Race Relations Advisory Council. Leon Brittan[2] really *too* drawly, sneery-drawly almost. Why? Even Etonians don't drawl that much. But he does know his stuff. No stumbling around his notes, whispering to officials, puzzled pauses. I felt rather sorry for the Blacks, who declaimed their

---

[1] AC embellished his office with an Impressionist Victor Passmore, a painting by Graham Bell and two Roman porphry urns as paperweights on his desk.

[2] Leon Brittan, MP for Richmond, Yorks, since the Election (Cleveland and Whitby, 1974–83). Home Secretary. Previously Chief Secretary to the Treasury.

woes. But it is in the blood for thousands of years, atavistic. As was said (in another context) – you might as well try and limit sexual intercourse by decree.

My own brief was excellent. But I still had to improvise, and be prompted by David Hodgkins.[1] D.H. does not have a high opinion of me, nor does he conceal it. He won't call me Minister, leans forward and says 'Excuse me' quite loudly. Bloody ridiculous and impertinent.

I walked back slowly, past that pub in Caxton Street where they have tables out on the pavement. My footsteps did *not* want to turn into the Dept. What fun to cut and run – just disappear.

As I got out of the lift Les, Jenny's new Number Two, replacing Kate, was waiting in the corridor, holding the brief for the next meeting. (I selected Les at the interview stage because he was nice and keen and smartly turned out, though only just out of a Comprehensive. But at the moment he is over-conscientious, something of a fusspot.) Straight in to a roomful of officials to talk about the Enterprise Allowance Scheme. David Hodgkins was already there, 'sat in' at the back, not at the table, superciliously. The whole encounter quite formless, without beginning, middle, or end.

I had hoped to pop across to the House, have baked beans and a nap in my office over there, with the phone pulled out. But the new S of S, Tom King[2] wanted me to sit in on his 'introductory'. He's going on TV tonight, and is clearly meant to be Mr Nice, after Tebbit's Mr Nasty. All I could get was eight minutes in the leather chair with my eyes closed.

First, he was going to meet some Union leaders. This was a bad augury. I thought we'd got rid of all that 'consultation' balls? There was much talk, comfortably in their old ways I thought, by civil servants, of 'Solomon Binding'. 'Bugger Solomon.' I said, 'It's "Binding" we want.' To Michael Quinlan I quipped, 'Solomon Gomorrah.' He laughed uneasily, and inaudibly.

The assembled Barons were led by Bill Keys, who is rumoured to have bone cancer, and looked terrible. Len Murray, fidgety, sat beside him. Ken Gill, clearly the most formidable, on Keys' left. The rest of

---

[1] David Hodgkins, an Under-Secretary at the Department of Employment.
[2] Tom King, MP for Bridgwater since 1970. Following the resignation of Cecil Parkinson, Norman Tebbit was transferred to the DTI, and Tom King took his place as Secretary of State for Employment.

the company were under a vow of silence, stirring occasionally or, in the case of Clive Jenkins, tittering.[1]

Tom King was amiable, very different from the bleak and sardonic NT. I passed a note to Jim Galbraith:[2] 'The Czarina is dead'. I didn't put 'Carlyle', which I would have done for anyone else except Quinlan, as it might have offended him. He laughed, but not in a manner that made me think he understood.

Afterwards, we repaired to Tom's room. 'Well, that went quite well.' Plainly he sees himself as a great arbitrator. But there's nothing to arbitrate *about*.

Suddenly Len Murray appeared in the doorway, breathless and furtive. Was there a basis for an intimate contact team, two on either side, to propose agenda, sort out loose points, etc? He pretended he was anxious not to be caught in there. But it looked to me like a put-up job. They were on the run. Now they want to put in place fresh 'machinery'. Yes, yes, yes, he was told, and sent on his way.

We went down to the press conference. 'Industrial' correspondents are a scruffy lot. There wasn't a member of the Lobby to be seen. Tom was amiable but not, in my view, assertive enough.

Finally back in my office for a meeting with dear Angela Croft, with her very dark, almost gipsy dark, long hair, who was worrying about the EOC Press release and Lady Platt's misgivings. I was tired, and the subject was *de minimis*. I am so weak, I am easily distracted by pretty legs and I don't expect I made much sense.

Now I am in this train with the lovely West Country fields going by, and I would rather be in the Bustard[3] thundering on 'B' roads and stopping too often for ale.

Tomorrow two boxes will meet my train at Paddington and, because it is Friday, Jenny will have arranged to keep me in the office until very late.

---

[1] Bill Keys (Society of Graphical and Allied Trades), Len Murray (TUC General Secretary since 1973), Ken Gill (Amalgamated Union of Engineering Workers), Clive Jenkins (Association of Scientific, Technical and Managerial Staff).

[2] Jim Galbraith. Under-Secretary, Department of Employment Industrial Relations Division.

[3] Family name for an old Bentley sometimes used in the summer months (also referred to in other entries as 'the $4\frac{1}{2}$').

Department of Employment   *Thursday, 27 October*

I am in low water. A lot of little things are going wrong, and are irritating me.

First, I have got 'Willie's Eye'.[1] It makes me look awful. I was at a Number 10 reception with Jane last night, and the Lady said I looked 'tired'. Blast! I have to read so much, there's no reason why it shouldn't last for months.

Then, again, Max is missing.[2] He's been gone for days, nearly two weeks. I know the 'daws all go off and scavenge the harvest fields', he's done it before. But he should easily be back by now. Max carries a lot of my good luck with him.

I'm apprehensive as my role in this sodding Committee Stage[3] approaches. I can handle it. But the sheer work*load* on top of all the other drudgery will be unbearable.

November is always a bad month for me. On Wednesday night I was playing backgammon late at Brooks's and Bartosik started to annoy me. I leaned across the table and thumped him. I must say he took it in the most gentlemanly way, even though bleeding quite badly. But Maurice Lancaster was outraged, has reported me to the Committee.

People are gloating.

Saltwood   *Saturday, 5 November*

Ghastly night. The young people are staying, guaranteed (bless them) to give bad nights. The old bike rule is still in place – rightly – which means one gets only fitful slumber until they have checked in.[4]

At dinner James had rung, soft-spoken, to say he would be 'about (sic) midnight'. At one-ish the dogs started barking and our bedroom

---

[1] A rheumy condition (named after William Whitelaw) that afflicts the whites and the iris of politicians' eyes.

[2] Max was a tame jackdaw, who had been reared by the Clarks after falling from his nest as a chick, and returned to the wild. He came very regularly to the window for tit-bits, and did in fact live to a very great age.

[3] AC was lead Minister in the Committee Stage of the Trade Union Bill.

[4] From the days when James and Andrew rode motor-bikes (James nearly lost his leg in an accident). Always check in on your return.

door opened. Andrew. Looking beautiful, though with hair too long for a subaltern, even in the Cavalry. We chatted for a while. Just after two thirty James turned up – totally bland and matter of fact – said goodnight affectionately.

I had some difficulty falling asleep and woke with a start, convinced that lights had been left on. Stumbled out on to the landing, followed a trail of blazing light bulbs to – the Green Room, where James was calmly reading a book. It must have been nearly four o'clock. What can one do? I woke with the sparrows cheeping, but was still blearily in pyjamas when Matcham[1] arrived with the weekend box.

The box took nearly three hours, then Col turned up for a walk. The only way out of this sort of hell-sequence is to torture the body. I left him at the bottom of Gossie[2] and turned in a record time of 2.50, helped by the hard ground.

Then one of The Four Worst Things happened – I LOST TOM.[3] We flayed around on Gossie for about an hour, returned to the Castle – no sign; tried the farm – no sign; went back to Gossie with Jane. She is so observant, and I am always terrified that he might get caught in one of Felce's horrible fox snares – but no sign. At last, with the light failing, Anne phoned to say he had turned up and she had him in the kitchen at the farm.[4]

Whole day gone, nothing since a boiled egg at eight thirty. Ravenously, I stuffed on carbohydrates, sloshed down Indian tea.

Now I'm sitting in the tower office, contemplating a miserable and congested week. First for Questions on Tuesday, Second Reading of the TU Bill, Plymouth on Thursday, then *back* to Plymouth on Saturday for the wreath-laying at Remembrance, so no weekend at all. Another bad night in prospect, as the boys are going out to a firework party.

It all makes me feel so old. Reading last year's entries I realise how much I have aged just these last twelve months. I remember how quickly my father went off – although in his case there was no, as it were, environmental, reason. I saw Gunther Sachs on TV last night –

---

[1] The postman.
[2] A steep cliff of downland at Saltwood.
[3] The family Jack Russell terrier.
[4] Felce and Anne: a local farmer and his mother.

totally unrecognisable from his old clips when he was courting Bardot. Men are OK from thirty to forty-five; if they're careful they can stay about the same. After that it's an increasing struggle because of jowl and neck lines, even if the waist can be restrained. And the bruising of repeated sexual rejection starts to show in the eyes.

Hotel Amigo, Brussels   *Tuesday, 22 November*

I'm here for some kind of Employment sub-committee of the Council of Ministers. Grandish hotel in the old part of the town, block booked by UKREP[1]. Jenny is with me, but I don't even know the number of her room. I share the facilities with other, nameless Europeans. Most of them, it seems, and doubtless for historic reasons, appear to be from the EFTA countries. Breakfast in sepulchral gloom, tiny pats of recycled butter in solid foil nodules.

Last night dreary sub-social dinner with a junior(ish) FCO official and his bright little Scottish wife who 'kept the meal going' à la Heddle.[2] When we got back here there was a convivial hubbub in the foyer, laughter from the bar.

'Come and have a drink,' I said to Jenny.

'Why?'

'Oh, all right, don't then.'

Earlier she had been made cross. At the airport there was one of those machines that measure your pulse through your handgrip. 'Go on, try it.' She scored 81. 'Watch this.' (I have always had a very slow pulse.) The band was graded – normal range, high normal, some hypertension, see your doctor, etc. I held on, far beyond the prescribed time. Obstinately, the needle wouldn't budge from the far green quadrant, under 55, the category – ATHLETE.

'Pah!' she said.

A succession of meetings, but no possibility whatever of getting anything changed – not at my level anyway. Everything is fixed by officials in advance. Ministers shaking hands are just window dressing. But I can see that the French are loathsome, the Germans amiable – and serious.

---

[1] The permanent UK delegation at the EC in Brussels.
[2] Neighbours of the Clarks in Kent. Practitioners of the 'extended meal' theory.

Department of Employment   *Tuesday, 29 November*

Stale air, bad diet. I have barely got the energy even to do yoga.

Anton Dolin is dead.[1] Another link with the carefree days of my flowering youth. Monte Carlo, the Beausoleil. If only one could return.

Dolin was the clipped, *un*-camp sort of homosexual. He outlasted – just – John Gilpin,[2] his golden tart and great love, who died some weeks ago after his own brief marriage to a Grimaldi bad egg. I am always sad when I think of my days with the Festival Ballet. Pam was such a dear girl, she is one of the very few I feel guilt about, along with that sweet child at the Gulf Breeze.[3] Because, in their own ways, most women are as lecherous and predatory as men, they just do it differently. It's the Thurber Sex War.

Later
Just back from a meeting with S of S, to discuss possible Government amendments to the Employment Bill at which I (a) dropped off, and (b) made one of those remarks which shows one understands nothing. Can't be good, as I am handling it 'upstairs'[4] starting next week.

I feel weary. My dilemma is, if I stay on I waste the substance; if I return to the estates can I even rebuild any longer? And even if I do, what's it in aid of?

---

[1] Anton Dolin, dancer and choreographer, who began with Diaghilev in 1923. Organised the Festival Ballet, 1950. Knighted, 1981.
[2] John Gilpin, dancer. Originally with Ballet Rambert. Festival Ballet, 1950–60.
[3] AC worked a bell-hop at the Gulf Breeze Hotel, outside Sarasota, in 1950.
[4] In Standing Committee.

Department of Employment   *Thursday, 8 December*

I have only just found time to write up my ghastly experiences last
Tuesday.

Jenny had been going on and on about the day I started in
Committee, etc., was I fully prepared, did I want further briefing, etc.

'No no, I'll be quite all right, all I have to do is read out notes
which officials pass me, yes, yes.'

But, actually, I was a little uneasy because I remember that the last
time she had fussed like this was with very good reason – before the
Equal Ops order.

'You've never *dunn* anything in Committee have you?'

'Of course not, how could I have?'

'Have you ever attended a Committee?'

'Not really.'

'Have you ever read a Hansard of Committee proceedings?'

'No, have you?'

'Yes.'

'OK then, what happens, what's it like?'

'Batty. Komm-pletely batty.'

In a way this cheered me up. But it was a bloody nuisance because
it was going to take the whole morning from ten o'clock until one,
and I had to start answering Questions in the Chamber at two thirty.
Also the sapping up time had been curtailed by Peter Morrison calling
a Ministers' meeting for 'nine-ish'. Les rang them twice, but they
were still 'getting ready'. When finally I got in they were all sitting
round, room full of cigarette smoke (i.e. Morrison must have smoked
at least one) and *coffee cups empty*. Nobody said anything.

Afterwards I made a row with Barnaby[1] and that pasty round-
shouldered maiden whom I discovered is called Di. 'Why wasn't I
told in time? I'm not a dilettante. I get here before all the other
Ministers.'

Naturally my colleagues, delighted, just thought I'd come in late.

Labour has a very tough team. Little John Smith, rotund, bespectacled, Edinburgh lawyer. Been around for ages. Their Whip is John
Evans, AEU, tough, thick. Two from the far Left; a nasty young one
called Fatchett, and a nasty (the *nastiest*) old one – Mikardo. And two

---

[1] Head of the Secretary of State's Private Office.

bright boys called Brown and Blair. Also two chunks of old heavy
metal, Frank Haynes and Mick Martin.[1]

I was on my own. Our team are under express instructions not to
open their mouths. Tom King never comes in, although, crampingly,
he had appeared in that morning to 'see me started'. Little Gummer
isn't allowed to do anything affecting 'contributions' as he's Party
Chairman. (I don't follow this rule.) And of course it's nothing to do
with Peter at all and he isn't even a member of the Committee.

Smith finished winding up, and I rose.

I had made some rough notes, intention being to be smooth,
conciliatory, just 'get the Bill through'.

Huh! I got into difficulties immediately. They were bobbing up
all over the place, asking impossible, spastic, questions of detail – most
of them, as far as I could make out, to do with the fucking *Rule Book*.
(I should have realised that this is a complete minefield. That's all the
Unions are really bothered by, lazy sods. Work-to-Rule, all that.)

The cribs were scrabblingly written out by officials, seated in an
anxious row, at right angles to us, beside the 'Chair' (in this case that
very splendid fellow John Wells, the MP for Maidstone). TK passed
them up to me, thick and fast, with a resigned expression on his face.
I couldn't read many, because they had been written out so urgently.
Anyway, if you don't understand the question, how can you understand the answer? But when I could read something I recognised
passages from the original brief that I had found so muddling or, in
Jenny's phrase 'batty', that I had avoided them. Gah!

'We've got a right one 'ere,' Mikardo kept saying in his special
plummy *artisan*'s voice.

Gummer and TK whispered unhappily to each other, 'He's not
up to it, what are we going to do?' – all that.

For two pins I'd have bolted from the room, driven down to Jane
and the hens, never left the walls again.

---

[1]John Smith (MP for Lanarkshire North since 1970), John Evans (MP for St Helens
since the 1983 Election), Derek Fatchett (MP for Leeds Central since the 1983
Election), Ian Mikardo (MP since 1945, currently for Tower Hamlets), Gordon
Brown (MP for Dunfermline East since the 1983 Election), Tony Blair (MP for
Sedgefield since the 1983 Election), Frank Haynes (MP for Ashfield since 1979)
and Mick Martin (MP for Glasgow, Springburn since 1979).

Department of Employment   *Wednesday, 14 December*

Things were slowly improving in Committee. I am managing to impose acceptance of my own style, getting (both sides) to laugh occasionally. It is a totally different ambience, and requires an adapted technique, to the floor of the Chamber.

For a start (good) there are never any press there, so gaffes and cock-ups go unreported. The Official Report is printed late, and by the time it's out nobody bothers. But there is a kind of *tenu* to the whole thing, and if one ignores this one offends the Committee's corporate *amour propre*. There's always the risk, too, of an adverse report by the Whips, although in the main they're not concerned with 'performance', only with getting the business through smoothly. As for the esteem of colleagues, they're busy doing their constituency correspondence, and it needs a pretty monumental disturbance to attract their attention.

But (bad) there is this infuriating convention that Members can get up and down as often as they want. Unlike the Chamber, where you don't *have* to give way, in a Committee there has to be a very good reason – repetitious filibustering being really the only one which is acceptable – to refuse.

This afternoon I got completely tied up, with full brain seizure. Batty subclause (6) full of lawyers' gibberish. '*Nothing* which is done ... shall affect *anything* ... , etc.' I looked round early on for Leigh[1] to help me. He wasn't there! Total panic. An unknown civil servant standing in for him supplied illegible and inadequate notes.

I can't stand much more of this. And yet I've got to do the whole of Part III (Financial Contributions), on my own, because little Gummer is barred, and TK is too 'busy' (i.e. idle) to show up.

This morning I woke at three a.m. and couldn't get back to sleep. Someone (I can't recall who) had mentioned John Davies.[2] Wasn't his brain tumour caused *entirely* by overwork? I am vulnerable. This *insupportable* load of absorption which presses. The other side now

---

[1] Leigh Lewis, a Principal at the Department of Employment, who greatly assisted AC with the Bill.

[2] John Davies had been Director-General, Confederation of British Industry, before becoming an MP in 1970. He served under both Heath (in government) and Thatcher (in opposition). He died in 1979.

realise that any amendment can catch me out, have spotted me as the weak link in the array.

Thank God there are the Christmas hols coming up before it gets too frightful. But there are so many chores to do. I must stop now, to go over before the House 'Shop' shuts and buy ten tons of whisky, port, sherry and disgusting cigarettes for my own claimants. Outgoings, outgoings, all the time outgoings.

Later

I looked in on Jonathan Aitken's party. Didn't stay long. Too crowded. Tessa Kennedy[1] was there, totally unchanged in twenty-five years, i.e. good-looking, but clipped and guttural.

A Dudley woman said, 'Whatever you do, don't sell pictures.'[2] Thanks.

Somewhat disconsolate, I strolled back to the House and ran into Cecil on the Green. We had a long talk. I said it was a disaster, the whole thing. He would have been Prime Minister. Yes, he admitted, all this he knew privately. He was the Lady's own choice, she had been grooming him, introducing him to the Royals — especially the Prince of Wales. He was going to the Foreign Office, would have really sorted it out, shifted it from 'diplomacy' to trade promotion. The switch could then have happened when the time was ripe, certainly no later than her tenth anniversary.

Was he, could he come back? Yes. Yes, if she wants me.

But he had to pine in the wilderness for some little time. Colleagues were determined to keep him out. Of course they are, I thought. 'Oh no, surely not. Who?'

Wakeham[3] was being unbelievable. The biggest leaker known to man, 'he'd even brief journalists *in the street* on the way back from Cabinet.' Cecil could never trust Gummer. Sanctimonious little creep. And Cecil suspected that Willie was against him also.

---

[1] Mrs Kennedy had for a short while been married to Dominic Elwes, an old friend of AC and Jane Clark.

[2] AC was at that time engaged in deep family consultations as to which pictures in Lord Clark's collection should be sold to pay estate duty.

[3] John Wakeham, MP for Colchester South and Maldon since the Election (Maldon 1974–83). Chief Whip.

DECEMBER 1983 57

'Plus all the mediocrities,' I said, 'like Fowler,[1] who are scared you'll show them up. But Tebbit?'

Even Norman, he wasn't so sure. (Nor am I, because with Cecil out of the way Norman *has* to be the candidate of the Right). 'He phoned me, said we were three; now we're down to two.'

Cecil said that the Prime Minister was much tougher than anyone realised. She was getting stroppy letters from Colonel Keays, all kinds of threat, never turned a hair. But once she decided to chop him, that was it.

Cecil said he could never see the child. But what, I asked, if it was a son? He didn't reply. You would have to embrace it. You would have to go down on your knees to Ann, and ask for permission.

He drew the conversation to a close and we parted.

What a waste. He is a good man, Cecil. Underrated just because he is handsome. But he has come the whole way on his own. And once he had actually *got* there, no longer had to dissimulate, I think he would have been importantly good.

Saltwood   *Friday, 16 December*

I had a meeting with Ian. He tells me that he is working his way back in with the Prime Minister. She can't do without him, and he goes round to Number 10 very late, when all her engagements are over, sometimes even when she gets back from an official dinner, and they go upstairs to the flat and drink whisky.

She has no one to confide in. Not to confide in *personally* that is, although I think she is probably pretty candid on policy matters with Willie.

Alison is useless. Saintly, but useless. You need someone with guile, patience, an easy fluent manner of concealing the truth but drawing it out from others in that job. It is extraordinary how from time to time one does get people who have been through Brigade Squad, taken their commission and served, seen all human depravity as only one can at Eton and in the Household, and yet go all naive

---

[1] Norman Fowler, MP for Sutton Coldfield since 1974 (Nottingham South 1970–4). Secretary of State for Social Services. (AC had a low opinion of Fowler (see 1 February 1991).)

and Godwatch. The Runcible[1] is another – and he actually saw action.

Apparently (but some allowance must be made for Ian's jealousy and also for his own impossibly high standards of attendance) Alison is also a wee bit neglectful of his timing, comes in around nine a.m. and tends to disappear in the evenings, only emerging for the ten o'clock vote. Does he attend the Party Committees? Apparently not regularly, except the '22.

How to correct this? Not simply by a change of incumbent. She needed something stronger, more permanent. Something on the lines of a Prime Minister's Department, with a Lord Privy Seal (or some such) sitting at Cabinet, and a couple of PPSs, the senior of whom would be a Minister of State. That's, Ian strongly implied, where I (whoopee) came into it.

The more I think this over, the more delicious it seems. Escape on magic wings, attached Mercury-like to my golden feet, from the hatefulness of Caxton House, the fire-and-water of Stage III of the Employment Bill, and to land with one bound into the very centrum, the vortex, of Power. And working closely with my oldest friend, someone who knows all my strengths (and weaknesses), who thinks alike on almost every issue.

He is seeing the Lady over Christmas at Chequers and will explore the idea further.

Saltwood   *Friday, 23 December*

Evening of the first day of the Christmas hols.

I don't seem to have done anything except get rid of a lot of cash filling all the cars with petrol. And cash is so scarce over Christmas. Again and again one goes down to the bank to draw, always the last cheque until the New Year.

At tea time I wanted pliers. I could not find pliers. Nowhere in this whole fucking place, with its seventeen outhouses, garages, sheds, eighteen vehicles. After stealing tool kits from every car I've sold on over the last twenty-five years – could I find pliers?

---

[1] Robert Runcie, Archbishop of Canterbury since 1980. Served in the Scots Guards in World War II and was awarded the MC.

I was screaming frail. I ransacked the china room, where I kept my most precious things. My new red vintage tool locker was empty, except for a lot of useless stuff for an Austin Heavy Twenty. Why? I am surrounded by unreliables.

I've done practically no shopping. How could I? When? Yet tomorrow is Christmas Eve.

As for the Dept, I never want to go through its doors again. Total shit-heap, bored blue. Strained and befuddled by all the paper work. Fuck them.

Fortunately, I'm dining with Ian on Wednesday next. I hope he gives me a boost.

Letter to Ian Gow   *Saltwood Castle*
                                                        Hythe

                                                December 27th, 1983

My Dear Ian
As always, a lovely evening. I can't tell you how much it lightens the cares, and the frustrations of our calling to be able to discuss everything so freely, and in such good humour and mutual accord.

I don't usually refer to the substance of what we talk about – but I must urge you to get the Prime Minister's dept promulgated as soon as possible, with yourself at its head and sitting at (preferably in) Cabinet. There is a long haul ahead, and these things are better done at moments of tranquillity rather than when the need urgently presses.

Complementary to this, I couldn't make out whether you were sounding me on taking MA's post. Of course I would jump at it, all the more so for having first experienced the privilege of a spell in Government. But who am I to say what I will, or will not do? To paraphrase a more sinister admonition:

La Signora comanda, il piccino va ..e fa!

Both these changes shall take place as soon as possible – certainly before the House reassembles on 16 Jan.

                                        Yours affectionately,
                                                Alan

Saltwood   *Saturday, 31 December*

New Year's Eve. I *always* go to bed early on New Year's Eve, and
sleep the better for thinking of all those silly sods compulsorily 'seeing
it in', drinking and driving.

Christmas was jolly. Jane and James had their ritual row, but got it
over quite early on. Col was here, and there was much discussion of
my father's estate, the snail's pace at which settlement with the
Revenue proceeds, 'Mr Thom' as a Double Agent.[1]

At present he (Thom) is fussing about the Maillol bust of Renoir,
why are there conflicting valuations, where is it, wouldn't it be better
if the bank held it for 'safe-keeping', etc.

'It's broken.'

'Uh?'

'Smashed.'

'The Revenue will want to see the pieces.'

'I've thrown them away.'

No, Col suggested, show Thom a broken bit of flower-pot; the
Revenue won't know the difference. Pleasing.

Last night I drank a lot of Sauvignon and had a strange dream.
The Table Office had refused one of my Questions because 'by the
time this comes up, you won't be an MP'. I realised that I had been
concentrating on the 'new possibility' (Folkestone?) and had 'missed
the nomination' for Plymouth.[2] I was crying as I explained to Jane (in
a hotel bedroom, was it Blackpool?) that I was now *out*. But twice I
woke, and realised that it wasn't true, and was delighted. What does
this portend? At dinner on Wednesday there was no doubt that Ian
was sounding me on the possibility of taking Alison's place. But I got
the impression that the 'large solution' had grown less likely.

---

[1] Mr B.D. Thom, Manager of the Clydesdale Bank Trustee Department. Lord Clark's
estate occupied the family attention for much of 1983–4.

[2] The previous year AC had been actually considering offering himself to the
Folkestone Association to take the place of the retiring MP, Albert Costain.

1984

1984

Two boxes arrived this morning, stuffed with PO cases and what officials call 'reading'. First thing, always, on top of all the folders are the grey sheets of diary pages. My heart sank as I looked at the stuffed days, the names of dreary and supercilious civil servants who will (never singly) be attending. I've got three months of this ahead of me, without a break.

At dinner the other night Peter [Morrison], who is a workaholic (not so difficult if you're an unhappy bachelor living on whisky) showed Ian and me, with great pride, his diary card for the day following. Every single minute, from 8.45 a.m. onwards, was filled with 'engagements'.

'Look,' he said. 'How's that for a diary?'

Ian, unexpectedly and greatly to his credit, said, 'If my Private Office produced a schedule like that I'd sack the whole lot, immediately.'

After Peter had gone, Ian and I returned to the subject, which is occupying a lot of my thinking time at present, of how to reconstruct the Prime Minister's Office. He *must* push the Lady a bit on this. Her natural caution will cause her to delay otherwise, and the opportunity will recede. I must write to him on the weekend with my considered thoughts.[1] How delicious if I can bring this off!

Back in the House, the Club, but immensely strengthened by experience as a Minister, and yet commanding attention wherever I am seen – tea, smoking or committee room.

Letter to Ian Gow   *Saltwood Castle*

                                                      January 15th, 1984

Dear Ian

I write with regard to the matters we have been discussing. I believe them to be urgent and I want to commit some thoughts to paper before our heads go back into the sand of our Departments (there are three boxes in the house this weekend!).

---

[1] Text of letter 15 Jan below.

I start with the premise that the Prime Minister is *everything*: what diminishes or threatens her diminishes or threatens the country – just as the country is itself enhanced by whatever does so for her authority and freedom.

She must have a department of her own. Small – as it were a floor of the Cabinet Office. The Paymaster General does not exist at the moment: he should be re-born, and much departmental paper 'copied' to him. (If necessary, some additional responsibility should be attached to him for presentational reasons.)

It is an awkward thing to say, other than to those one can trust, but policies are neither determined or evolved on a simple assessment of National, or even Party, interest. Personal motives – ambition, mischief making, a view to possible obligations and opportunities in the future, sometimes raw vindictiveness – all come into it. The Prime Minister needs someone who can provide early warning, counsel *and conduct lightning*.

One must never forget that the mob is always ready and its leaders are in the Senate. I so well recall those early very anxious days of the Falklands crisis when you could not attend a Party committee without one or other of the predictable front-men making their coded statements, whose real purpose was to prepare the way for a coup if events should lead to humiliation or disaster. To this day, I remember vividly the Chairman of the Select Committee on Defence [Timothy Kitson] hanging about the Tea Room Corridor, telling anyone he could waylay that *Hermes* had propeller shaft trouble; that *Invincible* had sailed without her electronics, etc, etc.

The question of the PPS is complementary to this. When you held that job, your knowledge of the Parliamentary Party was such that you could predict the reaction of practically every Member to any given aspect of policy. The collation of Intelligence both through social contact, committees, and Prime Minister's Questions was more subtle than the Whips' Office and its reflexes faster. But now there are over a hundred new Members, the first glow of their new status has worn off. They want recognition (in every sense) and are a prey to blandishments from many different quarters.

I cite an example of how these two requirements might interact in the next 12 to 18 months. Michael[1] will have to cut defence

---

[1] Michael Heseltine, MP for Henley since 1974 (Tavistock 1966–74). Defence Secretary since the 1983 Election.

spending by at least £2bn in the lifetime of the Parliament (as you know, I think it could be done by as much as £4bn quite safely). If he chooses to go to the stake on this and we have not made pre-emptive arrangements, he will greatly enlarge his own franchise. He picks up the Wet ticket at will. All of a sudden he will be able to bid for the Union Jack buffs also.

We can't tell what the future holds and it would be less than prudent not to do what one can to forearm against surprise.

Alan

House of Commons   *Wednesday, 18 January*

The office have found a new way of keeping me utterly exhausted. My time, already deeply curtailed by the demands of the Standing Committee, is being copiously allocated to an endless series of 'Fit for Work' presentations.

Like all Whitehall-speak, the term does not mean what first it would appear to. It is an 'Award' given, as far as I can see, to the (many) firms who 'imaginatively' overfill their statutory quota of disabled employees.

Joan drives me, accompanied by at least two officials, at breakneck speed to addresses in 'the Home Counties', or I take InterCity trains.

One mustn't be ungracious. It's a day off for many of the staff, who gather to peep and peer; there is a bad buffet, and someone who hopes that it may result at some future date in their 'recognition'. Etched with fatigue, compounded by boredom, I make the presentation, and off I go. Minimum three working hours poorer. Back at the Department in the late afternoon I read and sign till supper, then the ordeal of the Standing Committee until after midnight.

I must get out of this. I had a word with Ronnie Butt[1] about machinery-of-Govt difficulties, tried to coax him toward suggesting a 'Prime Minister's Office'. I think he took the bait. Of course I've

---

[1] Ronald Butt, political columnist on *The Times*.

got no control of the *form* in which he might put this in his article –
even supposing he does – but the importance of 'constructive leaking'
is to condition minds.

Plymouth-Paddington train   *Wednesday, 25 January*

On the way back from another of these sodding Award ceremonies.

Yesterday was one of *incredible* pressure; head-clutching. Standing
Committee all morning, and boss-eyed with fatigue as we were kept
up until well after midnight on Monday. (This for no reason at all,
pure Whips' incompetence; although just as likely it's deliberate, like
a sadistic battalion CO periodically – when the weather is bad –
ordering a compulsory five-mile run.)

I *loathe* Committee. I still get rattled even though, technically, I
know the stuff. Yet little Gummer sails along by GABBLING. He
gabbles away, and *they* don't understand *him*. While I speak slowly,
and try and give rational answers, applying my mind to questions
which are repetitious, badly constructed and ill-intentioned. It's like
bad 'discussion-therapy' in a loony-bin.

Things were going quite well this morning until I had a slight
skid, revealing that I didn't know what GMBATU[1] stood for. Dennis
Skinner (you've got to hand it to him, he's so quick on the ball) raised
it at Questions on the floor, later. I affected blandness.

In the meantime, Ronnie Butt has run his article, almost going
too far, running the whole concept of a Paymaster General, etc. Refers
to the concept coming 'from impeccably loyal sources'. This might
alarm IG. 'Al not reliable, not fully secure, better think again.' This
close, one can't tell.

Saltwood   *Saturday, 18 February*

The daylight is already getting longer.

This evening I shut up the hens, meandered around the Outer

---

[1] GMBATU: General, Municipal, Boilermakers and Allied Trades Union.

Bailey and down to the Cloisters. I sat for some little while in the 2CV, which we use so seldom now, and my mind wandered back to when we bought it in Lyons in 1964. We whirred merrily down to the Bastide,[1] and on to St Tropez, Fernandez and Cannes.

Jane flew off to see her mother in Spain. I had the hots for the red-haired telephone girl, but was so nervous for Jane's safe arrival in Malaga that I was incapable. Nostalgic evocations.

Yesterday I travelled down by train, and a plump young lady came into my compartment at Waterloo. She was not wearing a bra, and her delightful globes bounced prominently, but happily, under a rope-knitted jersey, as the new coach/old chassis train joggled its way over the many points and junctions.

I gave her a huge grin, couldn't help it. After a bit I moved over and sat beside her. She was adorable. Am I crazy? Death wish? Above us in the luggage rack the Red Box gleamed like a beacon. She works as a shop assistant in Folkestone.

Department of Employment   *Thursday, 29 March*

I was in Peter Morrison's room early. Out of the blue he told me that my suggestions for reforming the Lady's Private Office would in all probability be put into effect over Easter. But who was going to be put in charge? None other, or so he claimed, than David Young.[2]

This is appalling. I hardly know the man. But from what I've seen he's simply a rather grand H.R. Owen, the big Rolls-Royce dealers' salesman. I got to know the type well when I was working as a runner in Warren Street just after the war. Very much *not* one of the 'Club'.

Worse was to come. Peter told me that he was going to have a Red Box, Minister of State rank, and '*operate from the Lords*'. It is virtually signed up, as Peter has to find a replacement as head of MSC. The co-ordinating structure at Number 10 will be promulgated during the Easter recess. I said I was not too keen on the idea. The Party

---

[1] Home near Apt of Hiram Winterbotham, a friend of AC since his school days.

[2] David Young, property developer, director of the Centre for Policy Studies, 1979–82. Currently Chairman of the Manpower Services Commission and a Special Adviser to the Prime Minister.

never likes outsiders getting high ministerial rank without going through the mill.

This threatens to be the end of an era in more senses than one. It finally writes off Ian's chances of getting back to the epicentre of power, as well as any role for me in that scheme of things. I left early for lunch and tipped him off using one of the lobby phones. As I would have expected Ian was businesslike, showed no emotion. But he must have felt shattered. He said, as the appointment was so imminent there was nothing that could be done to alter it. That's right, I told him.

But I determine to have one try. There is only one journalist influential enough to make an effective scene about this if he minded to do so, and that is Peter Riddell of the *FT*.[1] He is well informed about all three Parties and writes with great insight.

But he might approve. Supposing he likes DY? I contemplated leaking the story to him, and made an assignment to speak to him in the Lords' corridor. Then I got cold feet; too easily traced.

Almost immediately afterwards a brilliant idea, my old friend and standby for many a dirty trick, Jonathan Aitken. I told him the problem. He was very understanding, got the point at once, and promised that he would attend to it immediately.

House of Commons   *Friday, 30 March*

The fish has taken! A critical account, on the *front page* of the *FT*, setting out the Prime Minister's intentions, her decision to appoint David Young, the rank intended for him, etc., plus a beautifully restrained piece of comment about 'reservations' in the Party concerning DY's 'controversial past' in property development, etc.

It is very late, but might just do the trick,[2] partly because it is a leak of the intention, partly because it is couched in such distinguished, though disapproving language.

---

[1] Peter Riddell, Political Editor of the *Financial Times*.
[2] David Young's appointment was, in fact, deferred until the autumn. As subsequent diary entries show, AC's initial assessment of his qualities was entirely at fault and the two did become personal friends as well as allies in politics.

Department of Employment   *Tuesday, 3 April*

Last night, at last, the closing stages of the TU Bill, Report, on the floor of the House.

I had been nervous all day as we are resisting the Labour new Clause 4, on 'Political Objects', their *chef d'oeuvre*, and I expected trouble. But when it came, it was easy. The Whips wanted my speech foreshortened (for some obscure business reason of their own) and this gave me the excuse to avoid 'giving way'.

Even so, plenty of people tried to intervene, and the House almost got restive. I am still more constrained than I ought to be by the exposed *feel* of standing at the Box, being verbally jostled. I prefer to extemporise, but was forced into reading from the brief more than I like.

For TK's speech the PM came in. She sat next to me (first time ever) and, like Chips and 'Neville', I radiated protective feelings – and, indeed, feelings of another kind(s). She has very small feet and attractive – not bony – ankles in the 1940 style. (Julian Amery[1] will nod his head sagely, and say in a gruff voice, 'There's blood there, you know, no doubt about it, there's blood.'[2] And I see what he means.)

The Prime Minister's foot twisted and turned *the entire time* although her eyes were closed, and her head nodded at intervals. The back of her hair is perfect, almost identical to previous days. It can't be a full wig, as the front is clearly her own. But I suspect it is a 'chignon'.

We engaged in desultory conversation, though without warmth on her side. At one point she rummaged in her bag and purse.

'Can I get you anything?'

'No,' she said, in tones of surprise. 'No.'

At the vote I walked with her into the lobby, and told her I was dining on Sunday with Jeane Kirkpatrick.[3] 'Oh are you? Where? She's coming to see me that evening.'

---

[1] Julian Amery, MP for Brighton Pavilion since 1969 (Preston, 1950–66). Married to Catherine, daughter of Harold Macmillan. Served in the governments of Macmillan, Douglas-Home and Heath.

[2] 'Blood'/Breeding. The upper classes at one point (before the cause became hopeless) tried to appropriate Mrs Thatcher by spreading the rumour that her mother had dallied with Christopher Cust, a notorious *coureur* on the northern Great House circuit, or more bizarrely, with the 10th Duke of Grafton.

[3] Jeane Kirkpatrick, academic, senior member of the State Department and US Ambassador to United Nations under Reagan.

She's on the ball about everything, in spite of all her worries – the miners, the 'machinery of Govt', Carol (a sad, distant piece in today's papers), Mark (must be a source of anxiety).

Yet she is *not* forthcoming to me. Distantly abandoned me in the lobby on entering, and started talking to Dykes,[1] of all people. She used to be so friendly when we were in Opposition. Does she disapprove of my 'laid-back' style (today's *Telegraph*)? Or are people making trouble?

Alison never escorts her the way Ian used to. Ian did it so beautifully, just so that she never seemed alone, abandoned that is, but always accessible. She still needs him and, let us hope, me.

House of Commons   *Monday, 9 April*

I drove up on Sunday evening in the SS 100. Should have been great fun, but the wrong side of Swanley the clutch went and I had to go the whole way through South London clutchless, which meant switching off the engine at red lights then doing Le Mans button starts in bottom gear when they changed to green. Tiring. And 'hairy'.

Joan picked me up at New Palace Yd, took me to Ed Streator's for the Kirkpatrick dinner.

I was curious to meet this Anglophobe harridan. She, and a tall, albino official at the State Department called Enders (whom Willie used to call 'the White Rabbit') were adamantly, subversively pro-Galtieri during the Falklands crisis. Even up to the end she was urging Reagan to put pressure on the Prime Minister to allow the Argentine army to leave the Islands 'bearing arms' (thus allowing a kind of 'heroically these men fought the whole British Navy to a standstill' propaganda myth to arise), which might just, I suppose, have saved the General's bacon domestically. The line is, she's so clever, she's an academic really, all that shit. But where was she? At intervals Ed would withdraw, then return looking uneasy. 'She's so tired. She's desperately tired, you know . . . '

Finally she appeared, a mixture between Irene Worth and Eleanor Roosevelt. Immediately began 'putting it away'. Halfway through the

---

[1] Hugh Dykes, stockbroker. MP for Harrow East since 1970.

meal, as is Ed's custom, general conversation ceased and the honoured guest delivered a monologue, invited (reluctantly) questions.

Odious, totally stalinist, humourless. Trotted out the Party line, consequential sentences, no rationale at all. Shades of 'Miss Newman',[1] loathsome.

Department of Employment   *Tuesday, 10 April*

I was in vile mood this morning, even on arrival. I had done a lot of washing-up, drying, wiping, etc., at Albany, and I always find this enervating. I do it so badly and so slowly. For someone as great and gifted as me it is the *most* uneconomic possible use of time.

Then, triumphantly 'marked up', a page of Mediascan[2] was pushed under my nose. *Impending sackings* (!!). Named were Arthur Cockfield,[3] David Mitchell,[4] Bob Dunn, John Butcher[5] and myself. Flushed and shocked I became.

Either way it's a bore

(a) that anyone should believe that I am a candidate

(b) it becomes self-feeding (journalists draw from each other)

(c) a plant from Ingham and Downing St

As long ago as 6 February I wrote in my Day Diary, on the space for 23 April (when we come back from the Easter break) 'Am I free today?' But now that I am actually faced with the prospect of being dropped as – allegedly – no good, I don't like it. All the gabblers are of course immune. As always, AS ALWAYS, Heseltine and that podgy life-insurance-risk Kenneth Clarke[6] are approvingly tipped. Appar-

---

[1] Miss Elizabeth Newman, the Clarks' governess during the school holidays.

[2] Mediascan: photocopied digest of all references to the Department and its personnel in the day's press.

[3] Arthur Cockfield (Life Peer, 1978). Businessman (Boots), made Chairman of the Price Commission (1973–7). Brought into Government in 1979. Trade Secretary, 1982–3, currently Chancellor of the Duchy of Lancaster.

[4] David Mitchell, MP for Hampshire North-West since 1983 (Basingstoke, 1964–83). Currently Parliamentary Under-Secretary of State at Ministry of Transport.

[5] John Butcher, MP for Coventry South-West since 1979. Currently Parliamentary Under-Secretary at Trade.

[6] Kenneth Clarke, MP for Rushcliffe since 1970. Currently Minister of State, Department of Health and Social Security.

ently (this is what makes me think there is a bit of Ingham in it) the changes will not take place at Easter, but during the Whitsun break. Or (much worse) in September, after a summer of travail and misery.

I am going on *Question Time* in a couple of days. Might gallop.

Albany   *Wednesday, 11 April*

Today has been vilely full. Went early to Leicester after a late, late vote and impossible to drowse in the train as officials were watching me beadily in case (their excuse) anything in the brief 'needed explaining'. I dropped off, as good as, several times during monologues at the various offices. Heavy-lidded, I must have looked.

There was a demo by the unemployed. Uglyish mood, they created to 'rock the car' (the one thing of which civil servants are absolutely terrified). Police useless, as always, like Hindus defending a trainload of Muslims. One puzzled constable, a 'trainee' and a pi-faced young WPC.

'I must speak to them.'

'No, no, Minister, please don't try. Minister, you must not get out of the car. Please, Minister.'

Wretched people, they were angry, but taken aback by my actually dismounting to listen. Some SWP yobs tried to get a chant going, but the others really wanted to air their grievances. One man, quite articulate, looked dreadfully thin and ill. He had a nice brindle greyhound on a leash, but it looked miserable too.

Gravely I listened. At intervals I asked *them* questions. I told them that if there was no 'demand' no one could afford to pay them to make things. They quietened down. But that's a glib point really. It's foul, such a waste.

Uncomfortable, I thought what Soames[1] and I can spend between us on a single meal at Wiltons.

---

[1] Nicholas Soames, MP for Crawley since 1983.

Later
House of Commons

I had intended to stay alcohol-free in the run-up to *Question Time* tomorrow evening. But my old friend[1] asked me along to his rooms for white wine.

I partook of very little indeed, and our talk rambled. His room has been redecorated, *un*successfully. Bathroom Pugin instead of the lovely heavy old red paper and curtains. (What happened to them, I wonder?)

He told me he was thinking of retiring (he's sixty). He'd sat in that chair for the last twenty-nine years, and was still slim and 'active', though hair thin wisps, and whitey-grey.

I had thought of bringing Soames round and looked for him in the smoking room but – fortunately, as it turned out – without success. The generations would not have mixed.

Yet I still think of myself as multi-generational. Today I saw several pretty blondes, all clones with lovely grey eyes and clear freckly skin – the BBC girl, the one on Nottingham station, the new waitress in the dining room – they could all tell I was 'interested', but smiled nonetheless.

It seems only a few years ago, say three, that the Todd Buick[2] was rumbling over the cobbles in Merton Street. Yet there are other things that seem distant by an eternity.

Albany, 7.40 a.m.   *Friday, 13 April*

A spot of turbulence.

Yesterday afternoon the car was waiting for me in New Palace Yard, to put me on the train for Bristol and *Question Time*. I just thought I'd pop up to the Chamber and listen to the Navy Missile

---

[1] A term used by AC to describe any single individual in his own close circle. In this case Euan Graham, a Clerk in the Judicial Office of the House of Lords.

[2] The Buick 'Roadmaster' owned by an American friend of AC, Burt Todd, who was up at Oxford at the same time. AC, and several others would borrow it for 'courting'.

announcement, which came up on the annunciator as I was leaving the Members' cloakroom.

The moment I saw it was being done by Geoffrey Pattie[1] I knew we (the British kit) had lost.[2] If it had been good news with a bit of Union Jack PR potential, Heseltine would have taken it. Geoffrey is good at the box. Knows his stuff and pretty unflappable. But it was bad news. One more domestic industrial capability diminished, still further reliance on the US inventory. I ran downstairs without waiting for the Opposition response and just caught the train.

Robin was *en retraite* for some reason and his place was filled by Sue Lawley.[3]

Although (perhaps because) I get on well with Barbara and Liz[4] we did not 'hit it off'. The worst possible basis for a relationship – she, an 'attractive woman', spotted at once that I have lecherous tendencies, but did not actually fancy her. She thought to put me in my place in her introduction by saying, '*He* went into politics because he thought it would make him more attractive.'

Ugh! She was paraphrasing some crack I'd made ages ago round Malcolm Muggeridge's dissertation on the aphrodisiac effect of money, 'Power is money in pasteurised form.' Embarrassment.

About halfway through came the question (must have been planted as the news only broke after the audience had started assembling) on the lines of 'does the Panel think it right that we should always be preferring American weapon systems to British ones'.

I didn't nibble at the bait. I swallowed, and most of the line, the float, the rod, the fisherman's waders, the lot. Sod it, I knew as much about this subject as anyone, a bad decision had been made – say so.

I expounded on the unwisdom of becoming more and more dependent on the Americans, the shrinkage of our own industrial capacity and (most recklessly and mischievously in answer to a supplementary) that 'it takes a very strong Secretary of State to resist

---

[1] Geoffrey Pattie, MP for Chertsey and Walton since 1974. Currently Minister for Defence Procurement.

[2] The Ministry of Defence had decided to purchase the American surface to surface anti-submarine missile 'Harpoon' in preference to 'Sea Eagle' which had been tendered by British Aerospace.

[3] Sir Robin Day, renowned interviewer and chairman of BBC TV's *Question Time*. Sue Lawley was currently a presenter of BBC TV's *Nine O'Clock News*.

[4] Barbara Maxwell and Liz Elton, BBC production team for *Question Time*.

recommendations from civil servants even though these are often quite narrowly founded'.

Sue Lawley, still bitchlike, said, 'Well, since the Minister isn't prepared to defend his own Government, is there anyone in the room who is?'

Afterwards, in the hospitality lounge, there was a slight kind of mouths-agape atmosphere. Barbara said something on the 'Gosh, that was a pretty racy answer' lines. But I thought little more of it on the return journey, being more apprehensive of the dear old boy charged with driving me back down the M4 in a hot, silent Granada. Terrible lurching swerves as, all too often, he 'nodded off'.

My first warning was from Tip who, night owl that he is, was hanging around the porter's lodge when I got back. He'd seen the programme. He's such a good mimic. But I became uneasy. 'Surely my answer on Sea Eagle was all right, wasn't it?'

He thought for a bit, then all he could manage was, 'Tricky subject, Officer.'

Oh dear.

Woken at seven thirty by the *Standard*, who read me the PA tape: 'Junior Minister disowns Govt. decision . . .' and plenty more. I just had the wits, through my sleep, to refer them to the DE Press Office. Poor dear Angela, what will she make of all this?

But FUCK, all the same.

Later
House of Commons

I got to the Dept as soon as I could. I was Dutch, blasé.

'Perfect timing,' I shouted to all and sundry. 'Sacked for Easter.'

Peter Morrison was waiting in my office (a bad sign). Mediascan was critical. 'The accident-prone Mr Clark . . .' In the *Telegraph* George Jones, who always articulates the mainstream (sic) Party viewpoint (i.e. talks to Mates,[1] the Whips, and a couple of people on the '22 Executive) refers to 'another gaffe by Mr Clark'.

---

[1] Michael Mates, MP for East Hampshire since 1983 (Petersfield, 1974–83).

Dear Peter said gravely, 'You don't really want to be sacked, do you?' and advised writing to the Chief, which I did immediately.

Then, 'The Secretary of State wants to see you, Minister.'

TK was shaken, or pretended to be. Said the Chief Whip had been on to him at midnight. Of course, he's an old sidekick of Heseltine's, isn't he? I bet H. was 'on' to him as well. 'We'll do our best to hold the line...' said rather in tones of I-don't-think-I-can-stand-much-more.

What the hell? I was almost elated. At least I would be dismissed for something that related to my own subject, a hero in my own eyes.

On the bench I ran into George Young.[1] He was very supportive, said I was quite right anyway.

By the time I got back to the Dept, the atmosphere had entirely changed. Angela reported on the Number 10 briefing: '... sees no reason why he should resign'. The latest PA tape is now headlined, 'No rebuke for Minister'.

Bernard's formula is bare-faced. He's simply issued a statement saying, 'What Mr Clark meant to say was...' and then something (*utterly* different from what in fact I said and is recorded on the video) about 'need to look carefully at all the options and give preference to British products wherever possible'.

Dear good kind sweet Lady.

Department of Employment   *Tuesday, 24 April*

The Easter recess is still on, but my 'In' tray groans and creaks. In New Palace Yard I ran into John Biffen. He told me that Heseltine had been determined that I should be sacked for 'undermining' him. Only he (Biffen) and Norman Tebbit had come out in support.

'And where it counts, of course,' he said, laughing.

---

[1] George Young (6th Bt). MP for Ealing since 1974. Parliamentary Under-Secretary at Environment since 1981.

House of Commons   *Wednesday, 25 April*

A glorious spring evening after a cloudless day. Starlings chatter in
New Palace Yard as they jostle for their night-time perches. But in
here the air is fetid. I am infinitely depressed. The passage of time, the
prospect of another beautiful summer lost. I seem, rather pointlessly
but quite pronouncedly, to have acquired a number of my father's
mannerisms. This, too, is lowering.

This morning we had a meeting in the conference room; I've
already forgotten what it was about, some MSC[1] balls. Somebody
drew the attention of Peter, who is having a war with David Sheppard,
to a quotation in this week's *Private Eye*. 'I remember dancing with
him in 1952, and thought him rather gorgeous.'

'We were all "rather gorgeous" in 1952,' I said gloomily.

'I was eight,' he said.

'In your sailor suit,' I suggested.

I've been going such a long time. Yet sometimes it seems like
yesterday. That year I was living in Netherton Grove, behind the
incinerator stack of St Stephen's Hospital, which I was only to visit
once, some twenty-five years later, to call on Joei, palely in bed after
a suicide attempt. Tanya frequented the house, together with James
Cameron, Anthony de Hoghton, both now dead. James 'rolled' by
Rough Trade in Blackheath; Anthony from drink and 'abuse' in
Dublin.

Now I am crouching in terror at the prospect of a rowdy wind-
up this evening on TU Bill Third Reading. It's too much. The House
is only back one day and I am already trembling. I'm *bound* to be
sacked in September. But I can't let the Lady down by quitting before
then.

---

[1] Manpower Services Commission, for which Peter Morrison was responsible, were
putting in place a scheme that in one of its locations involved the Diocese of
Liverpool, where the Rt Rev David Sheppard, former England cricketer, is
Bishop.

House of Commons   *Thursday, 26 April*

One backbencher who is a great success is Nicholas Soames. In the old days I used to see him roaring in the Clermont, often with annoyingly pretty girls. I thought he was just a great chinless slob. Then he began to look for a seat. One Christmas Eve I saw him at Floris buying masses of presents. Afterwards, complaining to Jane, I was put in my place when she said, 'Don't be beastly. So few of the upper classes go into politics these days, you've all got to stick together.'

In fact, since getting in here he has been a great embellishment to the place. He is always in the Chamber and very often comes to lunch in the Members' dining room, just to keep in touch, even on days when the business is dreary. He has an endless fund of funny (genuinely funny) stories and his energy is inexhaustible.

Last night we had a very late vote at 3.15 a.m. and Jill Knight[1] went through the lobby in her fur coat in order to be first in the taxi queue.

As they were waiting for the Whips to open the lobby doors I saw Nick put his arm on her shoulder and bellow, 'Now then, you're not going to wander about on your own are you?' She flinched, but did not acknowledge.

A joke made purely for his own enjoyment, as we were all dead beat, and no one who could have appreciated it was within earshot.

Brussels Airport   *Thursday, 10 May*

Flying back to Gatwick after another Eurosession.

Forty-four years ago, to the hour, the Heinkels were returning from Rotterdam and Eben Emael, the great Belgian fortress on the Albert Canal, had fallen to the *Fallschirmjäger*. It was the opening day of the German attack in the West. The first Dorniers were flying tentatively down the Channel, as we were now, to probe the English air defence.

Now it's all conferences, and interpreter-speak and protocol and 'in the interests of achieving a harmonious solution' (preamble to

---

[1] Jill Knight, MP for Edgbaston since 1966.

statement conceding whatever it is you didn't want to give away). The Germans are correct and courteous, almost apologetic. Don't any of them think, 'Hey, just a minute. We had all this completely at our feet once. What the shit went wrong?'

This time I enjoyed the conference. Got the hang of things more. It's such an advantage to speak French impeccably, and really no one on our side does. Even the officials, whose grammar and syntax are OK, speak stiltedly, with Language-School accents. Robert Cotal, who is 'close' to Pierre Bérégovoy, who is 'close' to Mitterrand said what a pleasure it was to converse with me.

I understand how one could easily become Euro-addicted. Everything done for one, so smooth and painless. Girls everywhere, cute little receptionists who chatter away to each other in *flamand*.

These visits make me realise how good I'd be at the Foreign Office. I startled an FCO official (all FCO personnel start with an ingrained suspicion and contempt for Ministers – I was going to say 'in other Departments', but of course it's true of their own as well) by interrupting a couple of Belgians who were talking to each other about a contentious passage in the communique, '*Mais les nuances sont très importantes.*' He was both awe-struck, and cross.

Now I'm going back, Cinderella-like, to the drudgery of the DE. More or less solid boredom, yet with always the possibility of an anti-personnel mine. Peter is an ally now, he leans on me more and more. Little Gummer barely puts in an appearance, even at Ministers' meetings. He's always late, and when he does turn up just 'sits in' without opening his mouth. He fidgets, though, like someone with a lot on his mind. By now it must be getting back to him how very badly everybody thinks he's doing the job of Party Chairman. S of S is unpredictable, save that if there is something disagreeable to do, he'll dodge it, if he possibly can, and stuff me with it instead.

Saltwood   *Saturday, 12 May*

Yesterday, we went to Johnny Spencer's sixtieth birthday ball at Althorp.

Just after leaving the motorway at Thame I noticed a dark red DBS V8 Aston Martin on the slip road with the bonnet open, a man unhappily bending over it. I told Jane to pull in and walked back. A DBS V8 in trouble is always good for a gloat.

'Anything I can do to help?' He said something about a banging noise. I made him start the engine and, indeed, there was an absolutely *horrendous* noise which could only come from a broken camshaft, or, at best, a timing chain. 'You mustn't drive this. Let me give you a lift.' He mumbled, got into the back of the Rolls.

There was something curiously sibilant and familiar about him. He was bending over the back seats collecting some hand luggage before locking and leaving the car, and as he turned round I couldn't resist pointing out to him that he looked very like 'an actor called Rowan Atkinson'.

Sure enough it *was* he. We drove him for some considerable distance, first to a phone box, and then to a friend's tea shop in Thame. I told him how much we enjoyed 'The Podule Sequence', a sketch in one of the *Not The Nine O'clock News* series. But actors don't appreciate being paid compliments on anything that is past, they live entirely for the present. He didn't sparkle, was rather disappointing and *chétif*.

We were staying with Nick Bonsor.[1] A nice rambling house, mainly Jacobean, in red brick with a reasonable, slightly undulating home farm surrounding it. Pot-holed drive, bent, but not totally derelict, iron railings. He walked us round outside (before changing and bar); garden a bit of a mess and very few flowers in the house.

Nick pointed out a tumbledown black-and-white 'Tudor' shed that he claimed to have sold to America for a vast sum.

Dinner guests not especially memorable, except for a cheeky chappie in 'sharp' clothes with a Eurasian wife whom nobody knew (presumably parked on the Bonsors by Raine[2]). Apparently he was mega-rich and owned some shipping line. After a few drinks his accent 'went' completely and he communicated solely by nudge-and-wink.

Francis Dashwood[3] turned up and announced at dinner that he was worth £10 million. People often say they have 'got', or are 'worth', whatever it may be, but usually arrive at the figure by counting their assets and not subtracting from the total their liabilities. Whether

---

[1] Sir Nicholas Bonsor (4th Bt), MP for Upminster since 1983 (Nantwich, 1979–83).
[2] Raine: Countess Spencer. Previously married to Gerald Legge, Earl of Dartmouth.
[3] Sir Francis Dashwood (11th Bt), owner of West Wycombe Park.

he was doing this or not I don't know. In any case, it isn't much. Over
the port there was much talk from him, Nick and myself about the
impending collapse in the value of agricultural land. This aroused the
indignation of some of the young farmers present. Jane was pleased
by the behaviour of the second Lady Dashwood, of Mediterranean
origin, who asked her how old her sons were, and on being told
snapped acidly, 'step-sons then'.

At about ten p.m. the great cortège, led by a minion of Nick's
driving a Volvo station wagon, departed. (Nick had promised Raine
that we would arrive by nine-thirty p.m. and it was a forty-minute
drive.) The order was Volvo wagon (Bonsor), Rolls Shadow (us),
Rolls Spirit (the cheeky chappie), Range Rover (young farmers) and
Mercedes 500 SEC (Dashwoods).

Fortunately the minion in the Volvo drove extremely slowly
otherwise we would never have managed the cross country journey. I
was already tight, so Jane took the wheel. Althorp itself was beautifully
floodlit and looked perfect in scale, almost tiny. The arrangements for
parking the cars – *endless* fleets of Shadows – were very efficient.

When we went into the Hall a magnificent sight presented itself:
Barbara Cartland[1] wearing an electric pink chiffon dress, with false
eyelashes, as thick as those black caterpillars that give you a rash if you
handle them, was draped on the central staircase with her dress
arranged like a caricature of the celebrated Cecil Beaton photograph
of the Countess of Jersey, at Osterly. She and Mervyn Stockwood[2]
were making stylised conversation, he complete with gaiters, waistcoat, much purple showing here and there, and various pendant
charms and crucifixes.

All very gay and glittering. Even at dinner Jane ranked no more
than equal third on the carat count, although she was wearing both
the leaf diamonds and Aunt Di's necklace. Some of the more mature
ladies at the ball itself could hardly move, so encrustulated were they.
The Princess of Wales, on the other hand, looked absolutely radiantly
beautiful and was wearing not one single piece of jewellery.

All the minor royals were there, but very few politicians. Besides
us I only spotted George Thomas,[3] Norman St John-Stevas, the

---

[1] Barbara Cartland, romantic novelist and Raine's mother.
[2] The Rt Rev Mervyn Stockwood, retired as Bishop of Southwark, 1980.
[3] George Thomas, created Viscount Tonypandy, 1983, on retirement as Speaker. MP
for Cardiff West, 1945–83.

Heseltines and little Norman Lamont.[1] NL is a social mystery, a
complete *je-suis-partout*. Why? He is quite amusing, but I don't see the
full cachet. Various other fashionable figures made their appearance,
Rupert Lowenstein, *totally* unchanged and as he used to be when we
all pennilessly frequented the Green Room in 1952. Having, as Oscar
Wilde said of Max Beerbohm, been granted the gift of perpetual old
age he now found that all his contemporaries had overtaken him,
looked older than he, and was ebullient. A smattering, too, of fashionable dons, Tony Quinton, Isaiah and, grotesquely pedantic, Professor
Asa Briggs.[2]

Jane and I detached ourselves from the throng and cased the
pictures. Everything has been restored and the effect is pretty spiffing
although, sadly, gold leaf has not been used where it should on the
frames. I see that even if all the restorers in the world had been
working simultaneously, they could not have done a proper job in
that time on the eighteenth-century paintings. So many of these look
rather hastily *scrubbed* and thin. As for the furniture, every single piece
has been covered with new leather, or new veneers, or inlays, etc.,
etc., so that although there are some magnificent pieces, the overall
effect is slightly that of the Schloss at Pontresina.[3]

Soon we had to leave, as I was due to make a speech to the
Industrial Law Society's one-day conference at ten a.m. the following
morning and they could have got the wrong impression if I had
addressed them in a dinner jacket. I drank nothing at the ball so could
drive the whole way. At two thirty a.m. the North Circular Road is
deserted and sodium-lit yellow.

---

[1] Norman Lamont, MP for Kingston-on-Thames since 1972. Currently Minister of
State, Trade and Industry.
[2] Anthony Quinton (Life Peer, 1982). Philosopher. Currently President, Trinity
College, Oxford. Sir Isaiah Berlin, Fellow of All Souls College, Oxford. The first
President of Wolfson College and latterly President of the British Academy. Asa
Briggs (Life Peer, 1976). Historian; Vice-Chancellor, University of Sussex, 1967–
76. Currently provost, Worcester College, Oxford.
[3] A beautifully furnished hotel reserved for grand German tourists.

House of Commons   *Wednesday, 23 May*

This morning the House is still sitting after a hideous night of divisions
and ill-temper on the GLC Paving Bill. Ian Gow and I had arranged
to dine and Morrison was to join us for coffee, but due to the way
the divisions fell Peter caught up with us rather sooner than I would
have liked.

IG was holding forth about Gummer's inadequacies, how everybody was complaining about him, even at Central Office. I suppose
Selwyn G. will survive because those on whom the Lady smiles can
do so indefinitely. But there is unanimity about his poor performance,
coming from CCO staff, leading Lobby correspondents, officials in
the Department here, who feel neglected, many backbenchers, and
even the Executive of the 1922 Committee. They, apparently, have
told the Prime Minister that in the interests of propriety he should
resign from one or other of his positions.[1] At present he is being paid
by the taxpayer to do both jobs though he never comes into the DE
any longer.

Ian also told me that even so loyal and devoted a person as Peter
Hordern[2] had been upset by the Lady's behaviour in snapping and
sneering at him when the '22 Executive went to see her and gave her
their views on the problems of the day. This is silly of her. She's
storing up trouble.

As always I was impressed by Ian's wisdom and feel for politics.
How lucky I am to be his friend. Certainly I owe my position in
Government to him. His is a real talent, because he is also so effective
on the floor of the House. But he has his enemies and now that he is
somewhat distanced from the Lady I fear that they will try and make
trouble for him.

We got back to the Commons about eleven p.m. and repaired to
Morrison's room where *very* substantial quantities of drink were
dispensed. I cannot bear drinking alcohol after nine p.m. as I get so
terribly disoriented, so I *conceal* slurped, raising the glass to my lips,
but not actually swallowing anything. Whisky, brandy, port and champagne were all open and being poured. Different visitors came and

---

[1] John Selwyn Gummer continued to double as Chairman of the Party and Minister
   of State at the Department of Employment.
[2] Peter Hordern, MP for Horsham since 1964.

went. At one point Stradling Thomas came in.[1] He is, I think, overrated. As a former Deputy Chief Whip he must know a lot of secrets (including a good many of mine, I suppose), but is rather dull company and makes the kind of jokes at which I find it impossible to laugh. Francis Maude was there – much the best of the PPSs, sensible and quiet, but with a good mind and sense of humour.[2] As the night wore on others came and went. Michael Spicer, Cecil's former acolyte, still somewhat bemused from his many disappointments.[3] He was made a Party Vice-Chairman at an early age and then seemed to go nowhere, although heavily tipped to be both IG's successor in the Lady's Private Office and to get a junior ministry under Cecil's whim.

About halfway through the night at one of the divisions I spotted Soames and thought to get him down and invite him to sparkle. But it was not a great success. He bellowed away assertively but didn't quite catch the mood, which was ruminative, melancholy almost. He kept asking me who I thought should be sacked from the Government. This is a question to which you cannot give an answer unless you are speaking exclusively with other members of that Government. I dodged it a few times but he persisted. Is Andrew Rowe a member of the Government? I asked in the end, rather feebly.[4]

House of Commons   *Wednesday, 6 June*

This evening I dined with Charlie Douglas-Home.[5] *Very* ascetic. Cold salad, and a bought-out 'sweet' with a bottle of Perrier water to slake one's thirst. At intervals sub-editors brought in copy, which Charlie approved, or, in some cases, altered. The great paper was 'going to

---

[1] John Stradling Thomas, MP for Monmouth since 1970. Currently Minister of State, Welsh Office.
[2] Francis Maude, MP for Warwickshire North since 1983. Currently PPS to the Minister of State, Employment. His father, a former journalist and MP, was Paymaster-General, 1979–81, and created a Life Peer in 1983.
[3] Michael Spicer, MP for South Worcestershire since 1974. Currently Conservative Party Deputy Chairman.
[4] Andrew Rowe, MP for Mid-Kent since 1983. Always a *bête noire* of AC from their days as backbenchers.
[5] Charles Douglas-Home, nephew of former Prime Minister. Editor of *The Times*. Died of cancer in 1985.

bed' round us. If you are Editor you can never get away for an evening. It's worse than a herd of dairy cows.

Charlie is very lame and gets about on two walking sticks with heavy-duty rubber grommetts at their tips. He seems to have been lame for at least ten years.

I remember him calling on us at the châlet and he was in plaster for something or other then, sat in a deckchair which collapsed and he broke (another) bone in his wrist. This evening he told me he had been 'getting better', but a stool which he was using to mount a horse at the weekend had collapsed (again) and this had caused him a setback.

I have known Charlie for a very long time. He was teeny when we were children. My mother (with characteristic, but I now see hurtful, *insouciance*) used audibly to refer to him as a 'dwarf'. I remember one summer evening we, and his brother Robin, whom I preferred and who was brilliant on the accordion and later committed suicide, were having a bicycle race. I was in the lead and ran into a strand of barbed wire which had been stretched across the road, tearing the skin on my inner forearm, which caused blood and tears. I still carry the vestiges of the scar.

In 1960 he was sent out by Max Beaverbrook to interview me in Zermatt, just before *The Donkeys*[1] was published. As a reporter he was (then) completely useless. We parted, but I had second thoughts and, stopping the car, dictated the whole article for him from a pay-phone in Martigny.

Charlie is well informed and thinks intelligently. He is a committed Conservative and a great supporter of the Lady, although he said she now drinks too much. He described an establishment dinner at Dorneywood.[2] She sat on the sofa with him and drank three Cointreaux and told him she would not bring Cecil back into the Government.

Charlie says the Prime Minister is extremely worried about the succession and that is why she intends to stay on for longer than she would have preferred. He says she is completely alone, no one to comfort her at all except Denis, and if anything happened to him she would pull out immediately.

I mumbled something about Ian. He said yes, but now she had

---

[1] *The Donkeys, A History of the BEF in 1915*, a book by AC, 1961.
[2] Dorneywood, the official residence of Lord Whitelaw.

discarded him. She never went backwards. No one was ever retrieved. We agreed that Cecil had ruled himself out now – not so much by the act of infidelity, but by the hesitations, blunderings and general aura of nerve-loss which had surrounded the episode. But who the hell was it to be? Between Tebbit and Heseltine – and of course one had to opt for Tebbit, although that was awkward and risky. Both aroused misgivings in the Party. But head to head H would probably shave it.

The subject of the Prime Minister's Inner Cabinet came up and I told Charlie of how I put the brakes on David Young.[1] That really took his breath away. He agreed it had been absolutely lethal, even though his own preference would have been for David Young to get the job.

He talked interestingly and constructively about defence. He has always been a maritimist and reminded me that he had written a paper about the ISS as long ago as 1968. I congratulated him on his leaders, which had been personally critical of Heseltine and of the [Defence] White Paper in general. He said that the answer was to put me there as Minister of State with a dry stick of an S of S, who would simply do what he was told and defend the more radical changes deadpan at the Box. Our first choice was Patrick Jenkin, but apparently he is already demoralised and wants to get out in the next couple of years, claim a peerage and pick up some compensation directorships.[2]

(How awful to be worried about one's pension! – That crumpled-faced man in the advertisements.)

Charlie finally came up with the best choice, namely, Peter Rees. Hard, beady, very good with figures and impervious to criticism from within the Party. We talked round the subject for a very long time.

When he saw me out I noticed that the ridges around the back of his jacket collar were absolutely filled with dandruff. Charlie is in bad shape. I hope he lasts out.

---

[1] See entry for 29 March 1984.
[2] Patrick Jenkin, MP for Wanstead and Woodford since 1964. Currently Environment Secretary. Created Life Peer in 1987. Became Chairman of Friends' Provident Life Office, 1988.

Department of Employment *Monday, 11 June*

Today I have been a Minister for exactly a year. Very clearly I remember Ian Gow's voice on the telephone, *just* as I was getting into a condition of total hysteria, frustration and chagrin on that hot June Monday when the 'second rankers' were being chosen.

The first two months were hideous – drowning in paper, relentlessly bullied by Jenny with her very clear blue eyes and flat northern vowels. Then, in mid-winter, the nightmare of the Trade Union Bill. Deep breathing in the little white office before going down to face the lions. Unprecedented pressures.

But now that is behind me and I am on easier terms with my officials.

The workload is really quite slight. It has been useful and instructive getting to know how Whitehall works, and I suspect that the lessons are more deeply learned when one is in a Department and coping with a subject which is uncongenial.

But I have been here long enough and I want to move on, or (equally probable) out.

I was booked to be in Plymouth today canvassing for the Euro Elections, but in fact spent the morning at Saltwood doing standard odd jobs on the estate, moving timber off-cuts. I said to Jane, 'Downhill all the way now, only one more Question Time and then the Recess and (from some indeterminate date in September) back to Saltwood for keeps' – 'Count and Conservationist'.

Today's schedule was completely upset as a large twelve-volt battery which I had been carrying about in the Chevrolet had fallen over and spilled at some point – presumably when I lent it to Andrew at the weekend and he 'threw it (the car) about'. The whole of the boot was filled with dilute sulphuric acid, which hissed and fizzed ominously and ate through carpet, rubber and paint at nightmarish speed. Everything had to come out, hoses were played on the offending liquid and bags of bicarbonate of soda spread abundantly.

Tonight I am dining with Charles Moore.[1] A sort of cult figure with the Young Fogies. Simon Hoggart[2] told me that he canvassed them as to who they wanted to lead the Tory Party. Unanimous vote

---

[1] Charles Moore, Editor of *The Spectator*.

[2] Simon Hoggart, former political correspondent on *The Guardian*; currently feature writer on *The Observer* and a political columnist for *Punch*.

was, The late Sir Hugh Fraser;[1] when told that that was not allowed, a majority vote for 'Dr Alan Clark'.

Lygrove House, Badminton   *Thursday, 14 June*

On the lawn at Christopher Selmes' new house. We've got here before him, having come from Plymouth and a tour (curtailed from ennui) of the Euro Election Committee rooms.

It is Carolingian, grey Gloucestershire stone and tiles, with the highly polished floorboards and pleasing smells of the Thirties/Forties, before 'fitted carpets' came along.

I took very much to the housekeeper, a Mrs Jenkins in her sixties, who 'came with' the house. Clearly a Treasure, although perhaps a weensy bit too genteel. Heaven knows what she will make of Christopher's guests – particularly if some of them 'scream'. After a bit, surely, she will be made uneasy by the fact that there are no young ladies?

Mrs Jenkins had been instructed to ply us with champagne, which of course we didn't want at all. A face was made when I asked for 'Indian' tea, but eventually an enormous silver pot of Darjeeling appeared, very very pale at first, but darkening up nicely with the fourth cup.

There's nothing quite like a manicured Gloucestershire lawn in high summer, with dark dark trees on the boundary, and rooks cawing. One feels a long way from the sea and, almost, from the century. It is one of the few *ambiances* where I can get carried back to the summer of 1914, or worse, the year following when the telegrams started to arrive thick and fast, pedalled up the drives of the Great Houses by sly sideways-looking postmen, and Kipling lost his only son at Loos.

---

[1] Sir Hugh Fraser, MP (died 1984) and first husband of Lady Antonia Pinter.

Albany, 6.30 a.m.   *Tuesday, 24 July*

I have slept badly.

Today I must take two groups of Government Amendments through the Standing Committee. The second session is to go through the night, i.e. until breakfast. In between there is an important Cabinet Committee (at five p.m., just when I would be eating a toasted bun in the Members' tea room and putting my feet up) at which I have to defend Tom's wet approach to deregulating small firms.

At the very point that I should sparkle, cynically but creatively, my mind will be clogged by all these hellish gobbledygook amendments.

Taking Questions next week will be almost a relief. The more I see of Government close up like this, and how difficult, cloying, time-consuming and skiddy (road surface) it is, the less I like it.

I really am *sick* of DE. I could only stay on if I were to be promoted to Minister of State and really *do* something – like winding up the whole MSC.

This would upset Peter of course, which I don't want to do. He has so many good points. He really understands the Party, a most valuable gift.

I'd think such an endowment was genetic, coming from old Lord M,[1] but look at Charlie.[2] Wet defeatist, utterly useless.

The MSC is a completely Socialist concept. Nanny State, with just a hint of Orwell. But when Peter goes to Sheffield[3] they treat him like the great Panjandrum, and he falls for it.

Saltwood   *Sunday, 29 July*

Tipped for the sack in the *D. Tel* today (by, inevitably, George Jones).

This is always out-putting. Two days ago Euan[4] rang up, concealing

---

[1] Lord Margadale. As Captain John Morrison (created Baron 1964) MP for Salisbury 1942–64. Father of Peter Morrison (third son) (see 10 Jan. 1984 and passim).

[2] Charles Morrison, second son of Lord Margadale. MP for Devizes since 1964.

[3] Headquarters of the Manpower Services Commission, for which Peter Morrison had ministerial responsibility.

[4] Euan Graham.

(but only just) his satisfaction at having heard from Perry Worsthorne[1] that I was going to 'go'.

Now I come to think of it, Perry is himself something to do with the Telegraph, isn't he?

Presumably my name was the unanimous choice at some spastic 'Editorial Conference'.

I sometimes think the only reason I want to stay on is to prove all those wankers wrong. Not that journalists ever notice – still less admit – when they've made a mistake.

They complain about this trait in politicians, but in fact they're far worse. Like share tipsters on the financial pages, they should be compelled to publish an annual audit.

Department of Employment   *Friday, 31 August*

I called in at Seend this morning, on my way back from the West Country, and said a prayer in the church – must be one of the few remaining where the vicar obligingly leaves the door open.

It's too frustrating, I can now only get this sense of peace, and of communication – something of the confessional, I suppose – in empty churches. There, in the silence, through which I can hear the whisperings of gossip and desire, the intoned devotions of two, three centuries, I feel tranquil. Strangely, I should think I have prayed here more often since we left, than in all the time that we lived in the village.

I was glad to see that the Guide, which I wrote, at Archie Kidd's insistence, with dear old 'Mr Wiltshire' (yes, I have to keep reminding myself, the sage of Wiltshire was actually *called* 'Wiltshire') is still on offer in the racks.[2]

But no proper Bible, or King James' Prayer Book. I am completely certain that this degradation of the ancient form and language is a calculated act, a deliberate subversion by a hard core whose secret purpose is to distort the beliefs and practices of the Church of England.

---

[1] Peregrine Worsthorne, columnist and associate editor of the *Sunday Telegraph*.
[2] AC had been persuaded to write a guide to Seend parish church.

Every time – usually by accident – that I attend a service where
'Series III' is used, and suffer that special jarring pain when (most
often in the Responses) a commonplace illiteracy, straight out of a
local authority circular, supplants the beautiful, numinous phrases on
which I was brought up and from which I drew comfort for thirty-
five years, my heart sinks. All too well do I understand the rage of the
Inquisitadores. I would gladly burn them, those trendy clerics, at the
stake. What fun to hear them pinkly squealing. Or perhaps, as the
faggots kindled, they would 'come out', and call on the Devil to
succour them.

The 'Secret Garden'[1] is now totally overgrown and the glasshouses
lush and tropical with unpicked grapes and fireweed. The big green
double gates still batteredly leaning, done up with baling twine, just
as we left them when, two years ago, we called by to load the Range
Rover with apples. The whole flavour of the place a little more
remote, now twelve years or more away, and through a glass darkly.
I climbed over the wall from the churchyard, trying not to put too
much weight on the rickety corrugated iron roof of the Gravedigger's
hut. A beautiful orange dogfox, as big as a setter, ran out of the potting
shed and slithered away into the undergrowth, like Sredni Vashtar. A
good sanctuary, the hounds will never find him there. The key for the
Marley store was still under its usual stone and I let myself in, prowled
about for a little while, collected some Bentley bits, yet still got to
Chippenham in time to catch the 10.08 to Paddington and the Boxes.

Last night I stayed at Lygrove. Atmosphere very subdued, conversation
(in contrast to our last visit when it had been squawky), flat. At
intervals Christopher had long telephone conversations with a man
called Suter. They would start slowly and calmly, rise in pitch and go
accusatory and loud. The only other topic was some new drug which
is being 'tried out' in New York. AZ-something-or-other. It was
working a dream, and would soon be readily available.

You can't get AIDS from bedlinen, can you? But plates and cutlery,
I'm not so sure. I was trying to drink from the glasses like a fish,
without actually letting my lips go round the rim. I'm not going there
again for a bit.

---

[1] A piece of land, an old walled garden in the village, which the Clarks retained after
selling the Manor House.

Saltwood   *Saturday, 9 September*

Got back late and tired this evening from Beaulieu. I've been meaning for ages to go to the annual Autojumble,[1] and thought shrewdly to book a stall and go as a trader. This would allow me to get rid of a lot of junk and also an advance snoop-up of what other dealers were offering on the evening before the public were let in. (Actually, there's no such thing as 'public' in the classic car business. Every single person involved fancies himself as a 'business man', i.e. all-purpose liar, cheat and conartist).

Dear Edward,[2] however, is incredibly beady. I always remember how, ages ago, he 'caught' Jane and me within seconds of our putting our noses into the walled garden, when we were just being spontaneous nosey-parkers, and insisted we came in for tea. Very sympathetically, and in the time-honoured role of stately home proprietor, he had been peeping from behind the curtains in his first floor flat, *counting the visitors*. How well I know that. It's a kind of sample polling technique. A given number at a particular locality at a given time will allow one to predict, fairly accurately, what the daily total is going to be.

Anyway, seeing our name on the list of applicants for a stall he had very nobly and generously insisted we stay the night before with him.

Naturally we were late leaving, as it took ages to collect all the stuff, which we ended by throwing, literally, into the back of the old Chevrolet, finally lumbering off with a trestle table sticking out of the boot.

Edward, as always, was kind and mischievously amusing, though *distrait* at all times. He lives in a flat in Palace House, a prisoner in his own surroundings. Very few of his (so-called) employees recognise him, or even get his name right. The youthful guard at the museum end where – mistakenly – we drew up, quackle-quackled into his portable phone, 'Mr Clark here to take tea with Mister (sic) Montagu . . .' This went uncorrected by 'Control', who clearly didn't, himself, know any better. And when Edward went to get us our

---

[1] A 'car boot sale' devoted entirely to motoring items.
[2] Lord Montagu of Beaulieu (3rd Baron) founded the Montagu Motor Museum in 1952 and created the Beaulieu Museum Trust in 1970 to administer the new National Motor Museum. Also President of Historic Houses Association.

tickets he stood meekly in the queue at the guichet. No one seemed to bother much.

I quite see why he prefers the Beach House, where we were all to meet up for dinner, and sleep. The pressures at Palace House must, during the summer 'Season', be intolerable. Edward had given us keys and later on, as we let ourselves out of his personal door, we saw three very obvious burglars, one of them a half-caste, trampling over the private lawn, laughing and sneering. The sort of thing that, at Saltwood, would have made me dash back indoors and fetch the 12-bore. But who to tell? What to do? Edward was doing his rounds; the 'guards' (if you could find one) were gormless and pasty.

Bleakly isolated amid dunes and scrub heath of the Solent shore, Beach House is a big wooden bungalow, with transom windows and thin walls through which you can hear the other occupants conversing (and, indeed, farting).

These modern (modern*ist*, I should say) houses are nearly always a failure. As we approached Jane said something about the Sainsburys[1] and, sure enough, it turned out that Hugh Casson had had a hand in this too.[2] I am doubtful if he ever brought anything off. Garden House really the best of the bunch.

A jolly children's party was in progress. The only other people at dinner were unexciting. The man had an Italian name and said he 'used to be' a barrister, now apparently something to do with concessions to sell Hamburgers – so there's a 'service' industry for you. But he gave me a bad night by saying you could go to prison for having an Anstalt.[3] But not if you declare it, surely? Yes, yes, *when* you declare it. All v. odd. But disconcerting. Like Hemingway, I am getting more and more paranoiac about 'The Revenue' as I grow older. Now that I don't owe the banks anything, the tax inspectors have taken their place.

We all parted after an early breakfast. The Autojumble was *totally* exhausting and, inevitably, I spent more than I 'took'. Many people ignored our offerings, set out on the trestle table, but tried to buy the Chevrolet itself. A Dutchman gave us some trouble. I was offering an

---

[1] John and Anya Sainsbury had commissioned a modern house near Lympne, some few miles from Saltwood, which they inhabited in the early 1960s.

[2] Hugh Casson, architect; currently advisor to Commons Services Committee and President of the Royal Academy.

[3] A Swiss bank personal trust.

old, slightly travel-stained badge of the Royal Netherlands AC; the price was £30. He didn't want to pay cash, but to swap it for a *new*, but identical badge. Presumably a post-war fake. Sorry, man, I said (repeatedly). This wasn't the answer he wanted. He hung about, muttering, rephrasing his request. Semi-threatened us with EC Regs. Dr Strabismus.

We left early, making an hour better time by going all the way back to the M25, round it, and out on the M20. At intervals the great V8 motor 'hunted', seemed on the verge of 'missing'. Perhaps, after all, I should have taken an offer. But I hate to sell faithful machinery. It's as bad as parting with horses. That's why Saltwood is completely cluttered up with wrecks and dead hulks.

Zermatt   *Saturday, 15 September*

I was determined to get away, out of reach, before the reshuffle got started. We were a day late because Nanny had to be moved to Quince[1] first. I would *not* pay a gang of piggy-eyed, nicotine-smelling removal men £300 or thereabouts simply to carry her furniture across Castle road from one cottage to another, and so did the whole thing personally, most ably and heroically assisted by Eddie. Now she can cluck away and polish things in her new nest while we are absent.

We had two wonderful days crossing France in the Citroën, meandering, almost, on the Routes Departmentales, crossing, transversely, the principal Lemming routes and watching satisly the belting straining jockeying holiday traffic and the massive dicing juggernauts. We kept the hood down for almost the entire journey. And for the first time we circled to the south of Lake Geneva, staying the night at Evian, and not linking up with familiar roads until we reached Aigle.

I fantasised, deluding myself that I might be going to go 'sideways' into Ray Whitney's job.[2] If I am going to have any future in politics I've got to get to the Foreign Office or MoD. Now that I know how to deal with officials, how the machine works, the time is ripe. I quite see how it is better to learn these tricks in a disagreeable dept, where

---

[1] A cottage on the Saltwood estate, preferred by staff as it is 'modern' (built in 1953).
[2] Ray Whitney, MP for Wycombe since 1978, had been sacked from his post as Parliamentary Under Secretary at the Foreign Office.

you have to 'keep a proper lookout'[1] at all times. But that's over now. I've served my apprenticeship, taken a Bill through its Committee stage. I'm fully fledged. I didn't say anything to Jane, fearing disappointment, but secretly hoping for wonderful news.

But it was Renton who was chosen. Renton. I was very dejected at first. Then cheered up a little, as I don't see that this necessarily rules me out in future. He was Geoffrey's PPS, had a cursory acquaintance with the FCO, was now due for a job.[2]

I am sitting at the desk in my study in the Chalet and the French windows are open on to the balcony. Fifty feet away the Wiesti foams and tumbles past, swollen by the melting glaciers. The Matterhorn is in full view, and the whole house carries that delicious aroma of high summer, pine needles and sweet geranium.

How distant, how very very distant and odious is the arid little left-right-left turn by the green fire escape sign, as I get out of the lift on the sixth floor. The messengers scuttling round with their sheaves of turgid paperwork. The unbelievable tedium of the subjects – Financial Management Initiative, Ombudsman cases (I no longer look even at the conclusions of these), anything-to-do-with-the-Disabled, the 'Measures'. This isn't politics, it's compulsory obsessional disorder.

The fact remains that there have been three vacancies now, at PUSS level, in Defence and Foreign Affairs, since I became a Minister. And I have missed out each time. Am I doomed to hang on at DE, suffering periodic humiliations, until summarily dismissed in September of next year?

I think hard of pre-empting, ' . . . at his own request', getting free to argue for Toryism *à l'outrance*, to scorn the obligations of Party discipline (so often nothing more than the convenience of the Whips' Office) and become a true Maverick. Bang would go the 'K', of course, and any chance under the ACHAB rule. But one would gain a year. And I am uneasy that my reputation in the Commons may start to fade if I have to go through another year's drudgery. It really is impossible to dazzle at the box on the Job-splitting Scheme.

One's status is embellished by 'at his own request', diminished by being sacked.

---

[1] A family phrase. (Barristers' standard 'pleading' in statements of claim in motoring litigation.)

[2] Tim Renton, MP for Mid-Sussex since 1974. PPS to John Biffen, then Geoffrey Howe, both as Chancellor of the Exchequer and as Foreign Secretary.

Zermatt   *Sunday, 16 September*

This evening I *tortured* the body by going flat out up Othmars. Took thirty-seven minutes from the doorstep, and on the downhill jog back my knees felt like water.

The bath was cold – why? The baths are never cold here – and this put me in a filthy temper.

In fading light I set off for the Winkelmatten chapel, which always calms me. I found it locked. This is unheard of. In thirty-five years that chapel has always been open for climbers before they set out for the Hornlihutte, or to give thanks for their safe return. There are never less than twenty candles burning.

Now it is surrounded by scaffolding. I peeped though the keyhole, and the interior has been stripped. The pews, altar, effigies, all have gone. Only a barely intelligible notice in German pinned to the door, advising of *Revisionen*.

First I was cross, then gloomy. Perhaps it's an omen. I returned by the back route, and saw that the dear little chestnut-wood Chalet where that Belgian cutie (how shameful to have forgotten her name) had digs in the winter of '56 – '*pourquoi que tu me prends . . .* ', all that – had been demolished and there was just a great hole in the ground in preparation for some monstrous concrete garni.

It had been one of the prettiest private chalets in the town, with a charming garden of shrubs. Quite soon the 'Caroline' (and of course the Brunmatte[1]) will be the only real private houses in the Inner Zone. That's why I am taking such pains – and expense – to make the Kariad[2] really pleasing. Two fingers to the poxy *garnis*.

Anyway, it's all too much, and we've decided to head for home on the day after tomorrow.

---

[1] The name of a beautiful Zermatt chalet belonging to the Gentinetta family.
[2] The name of the 'kiosk' chalet which the Clarks were constructing.

Saltwood   *Thursday, 20 September*

A gloomy blustery day. Low dark clouds. Saltwood is sleepy, almost as if we had been away a month instead of a week. Getting ready for its hibernation.

This afternoon, as I strolled round, I thought the one thing I am really loathing is the prospect of being back at the bloody House of C, being yerr'd at the Box by a lot of spiteful drunks, on subjects that bore and muddle me. I'd gladly chuck the whole thing in and become a Count[1] if it were not for the satisfaction this would give to others.

The nicest thing in the waiting postbag was a lovely letter from Julian Amery.

I'm amazed you survived the Reshuffle. You stick out like a red poppy in the hayfield of mediocrities surrounding you. It is very offensive to them to be original, intelligent, courageous and rich.

What a marvellous compliment, from someone who has been in public life for almost forty years. Julian has known, closely known, Tito, Winston, Anthony [Eden] and Uncle Harold [Macmillan]. The *real* times. He's entirely right. What we could do, he and I. He so nearly made Foreign Secretary when Carrington[2] legged it in '82. Loss of nerve by the Lady. She wasn't sure she was going to survive, took the Whips' advice, chose Pym[3] – with whom she quarrelled incessantly thereafter.

Or was it? Perhaps she recognised something he and I won't accept. The climate has changed.

Saltwood   *Friday, 12 October*

'At any moment I could be killed by an assassin or a lunatic.' I often quote the Führer's reflective aside to Rauschning (and indeed he

---

[1] Alternative family slang for retiring. Cf. 'Burning heather'.
[2] Lord Carrington, served every Conservative Prime Minister since appointed as Parliamentary Secretary, Ministry of Agriculture in Churchill's 1951 government. Foreign Secretary, 1979–82. Resigned following the Argentinian occupation of the Falkland Islands in April 1982.
[3] Francis Pym, MP for Cambridgeshire South-east since 1983 (Cambridgeshire, 1961–83). Foreign Secretary, 1982–3. Now returned to back benches.

himself is recorded as repeating it to Goebbels and, by Halder, to Keitel). In my case, though, I am thinking more about Estate Duty and my luckless descendants – than of Posterity.

But today a vivid illustration, followed in the late evening by a curious, almost spooky episode of imagery *foretelling*.

Yesterday at Brighton (Party Conference) the DE debate was first off in the afternoon. TK bumbustioso'd, did a pretty smudgy job of introducing his 'team'; although pleasingly I got what, for a junior Minister, was quite a good cheer from the floor (due, I assume, to the coverage in Monday's *Mail*[1]). This disconcerted TK, who faltered momentarily.

I had a few meetings and oddments to attend to after the 'Debate', and Jane went off to go round an Art Nouveau exhibition with Charles Moore before we met up for tea. Later, the American Ambassador was having a small party (but wives, oddly, were excluded).

Tea at the Metropole is always fun. So much traffic of 'notables', so much peeping, prying and listening to do. The egos flare and fade and flare again like a stubble fire. The journalists dodge about excitedly, fearful of missing something. I prefer it to the hotel lobby later on, when everyone has 'had a few' and is slower (though louder). But when we had finished, and were standing on the steps wondering whether to take a walk along the front, it being such a beautiful afternoon of late autumn, a pleasing escapist impulse came to us both simultaneously: 'Bugger the American Ambassador. Let's just go home.'

We sometimes get these urges. Notably during Elections, when we have been sent off on our own with a lot of canvass cards.

I cancelled the room, settled the account. We hopped straight into the car and were comfortably back here for supper.

But that evening an unsettling experience. The last episode of *Tripods*. Little Charlotte wandered around Saltwood, everything so beautiful and timeless. Then she was 'claimed' by the Tripods – remote, sinister, not of this world. She ascended, higher and higher (on that great lamp-engineers' lift, which made such a mess of the

---

[1] AC had been instrumental in closing off a particular kind of fraudulent claim by foreign students at benefit offices.

moat when they were shooting). Sadly she waved, and called her
farewells. On its own the scene was curiously, unexpectedly moving.
Now, with the knowledge that she had, at that time, been less than
three weeks away from death, sliced in half on the M4 by some callous
brute in a 30-ton artic, it was unbearable.

More was to come. Before breakfast, when I returned with the
dogs, Jane told me that there had been a huge bomb at Brighton, the
hotel had been all but demolished. They had 'got' Tebbit, Wakeham,
Tony Berry,[1] various dignitaries. Amazing TV coverage. The whole
façade of the hotel blown away. Keith Joseph (indestructible), wandering about in a burgundy-coloured dressing gown, bleating. The
scene was one of total confusion, people scurrying hither and thither,
barely a police 'officer' to be seen.

Mrs T had been saved by good fortune (von Stauffenberg's
briefcase!) as she was in the bathroom. Had she been in the bedroom
she would be dead.

But what a coup for the Paddys. The whole thing has a smell of
the Tet Offensive.[2] If they had just had the wit to press their advantage,
a couple of chaps with guns in the crowd, they could have got the
whole Government as they blearily emerged – and the assassins could
in all probability have made their getaway unpunished.

Saltwood   *Tuesday, 7 November*

I am somewhat underemployed at the moment.

My day-to-day work is hateful, and boring. But I have now
mastered it. It no longer holds any terrors for me. Indeed I am faster
and clearer than many of the officials who come in to 'explain' it.

Before Questions I used always to repair to the drinks cabinet in
my office in the Commons and down a teeny slug of neat vodka. No
lunch, keep the stomach empty and then, in the very last seconds
before going into the Chamber for Prayers – *Skol.*

---

[1] Anthony Berry, MP for Southgate since 1964. Younger son of Lord Kemsley, who
    had owned the *Sunday Times*, and nephew of the proprietors of the *Daily* (and
    Sunday) *Telegraph*.
[2] Tet Offensive: as part of the general offensive in South Vietnam in 1970, the
    VietCong also made a brief foray into the US Embassy.

I no longer need it. I had another good session last time, knocked everyone around including poor old Eric Heffer.[1] I used to be frightened of him but not any longer. He is suddenly ageing, quite fast. Afterwards John Stokes,[2] no mean judge, went out of his way to congratulate me, and the following day Godfrey Barker[3] gave me half his column, full of praise.

So what should I be doing? Slowly, too tentatively, I am working up a paper for the Lady. On the subject of defence, yes; but a strategic overview, a twenty-year projection. Does anyone else do this? Not as radically as I, that's for sure. And it needs to be done under a whole range of subject headings: overseas trade; industrial policy; diplomacy in the late Nineties, with whom we should be aligned, our relations with the new Pacific powers.

The FCO are sometimes said to be working on 'secret' long-term papers of this kind. But no one ever sees them. Mainly devoted, I would guess, to argument for expanding the Corps Diplomatique and the number of congenial 'postings'. I am not sure, even so, how kindly the Lady will take to my reflections, which is probably why I only turn to them intermittently. Dear creature, she is somewhat *blinkered*. (But hastily I add, as is obligatory among believers when her faults are identified, 'this of course can also be a source of strength'.)

It's a gamble. Either she'll think 'he's wasted in that hole' or 'he's crazy. For God's sake keep him where he is, indefinitely.'

Saltwood   *Saturday, 10 November*

Tristan Garel-Jones asked himself down. Odd, you could say, for a Whip to take five hours off to see someone with whom he could converse for as long as he liked the following Monday.

He is candid. At least he *seems very* candid. Slagged off most of the '22 Executive. Said there was 'absolutely no point' in discussing the Under The Bus Syndrome (then devoted some fifty minutes to doing so). 'If it happens, at any time, we – i.e. the Whips – will cope.'

---

[1] Eric Heffer, MP for Liverpool Walton since 1964. He died from cancer in 1991.

[2] John Stokes, MP for Halesowen and Stourbridge since 1974 (Oldbury and Halesowen, 1970–4).

[3] Godfrey Barker, parliamentary sketch writer in the *Daily Telegraph*.

Tristan said she would now lead us into the next Election; then we'd have to choose someone 'from your generation'. This pleased me (presumably intended to).

He agreed that Ken Clarke was a 'butter ball' (my phrase), said that Chris Patten said the same about him. Good. We gave Tristan a lot of sticky cakes, and William served tea from the Fabergé teapot, and off he went.

Department of Employment   *Thursday, 20 December*

Yesterday I attended a meeting of the Lambeth Inner City Partnership. 'Red' Ted Knight, and others.

Closed room, so no press, no posturing. Knight quite impressive. The negotiations (if that be the term) were simply about *money*.

Unspoken (because hollow) were threats by either side to 'expose' the other. Our parsimony, their profligacy.

But they are really getting in deep.

Buying votes, of course, can be very expensive. Even more costly is having to appease all the total weirdoes who clutter up the middle ranks, all of them jockeying against, and bitter about, their confrères.

Who's going to settle all these debts in the end? Not the ratepayers; it just isn't there. It will finish by falling, somehow, on the DoE, who are apprehensive.

At lunchtime we had the departmental carol service. Everyone on best behaviour, a kind of mass office party in reverse. In the choir I recognised certain pasty maidens and maddish, steel-rim bespectacled males whom I have encountered at various marginal meetings during the year. TK read the lesson, oh-so-firmly.

Boring. Tedious.

Tomorrow the holiday starts. But we only get a week. Sadistically, the Dept will be open – 'Private Offices only', on 28th.

Saltwood   *Saturday, 29 December*

A very quiet Christmas. Poor Daisy[1] came, bringing a few cases of
'61 (not, emphatically not, as a gift). He's gone to pieces really. About
six months ago he wanted to 'handle my investments', but without
telling me what he was buying and selling. To use my money, in other
words, to prime his own dodgy little deals.

OK in 1972, not any longer. I have, in John Mendelson's pleasing
phrase, 'seen the movie'.[2] Get lost, I said.

Then, partly to placate him, I asked him to get some claret. He's
always going to the sales, makes out he's an expert. What did he do?
Go out and buy a lot of '61s. He knows I'm up to here in '61s, all
bought – yes, on his advice – fifteen years ago. Now they're far too
expensive. 'You're averaging,' he said. Bah.

James and Sarah turned up, full of the pleasures and plans for Eriboll.
As a Christmas present I'd bought a Dodge Command Car – nominally for getting stalkers to the Hill, but actually as a big toy – and
we played with it.

On Friday the Gows came over to dine and stay the night. The
evening never really took off, in spite of copious, and heavily per-
mutated, wines. Nearly boring, with both of them thanking us repeatedly in supplicant, almost tearful voices. I've noticed this tendency in
Ian is becoming a little more pronounced. He *parodies* himself, 'toys
with' his audience even though he knows they are getting impatient.

Also, he is never at his (conspiratorial) best when he has Jane with
him, even though he is devoted to her.

---

[1] A nickname for Christopher Selmes.
[2] John Mendelson, at that time chief financial guru to Dean Whitter, the New York
   broking house.

1985

1985

I am not suffering quite the same degree of apprehension as I did this time last year, with the Employment Bill and, in particular, the dreaded Part III solo role overhanging. But the sheer dreariness and drudgery of the Department; the cold and miserable squalor of Albany, still (I assume) with its full sink of dirty china; the prospect of long, pointless and disagreeable night votes – all this is lowering. With something of a shock I realised that I will, this June, have been in the same Dept, and at the same rank, for two years. Guy Sajer.[1] And I have a nasty feeling that there won't be a reshuffle until September.

An article in *The Times* today by Selina Scott. She says that in two years at Breakfast TV she aged ten. I have done exactly the same in Parliament – a ratio of five to one. At this time of the year I find myself pining for white sand and lapping waters. But that, too, must be a sign of growing old. Because formerly I would want to get to the slopes, and ski divinely.

Ponting, amid much turbulence, has been acquitted.[2] There are accusations of 'lying' and insult. A set-piece Debate (inevitably it will be disappointing) is imminent, probably for Monday.

You can find people – some of them quite influential and canny people like Peter Morrison and G-J – who are saying that John Stanley[3] will have to resign.

Of course he *won't*. No one these days resigns for anything. (Perhaps, still, for direct proof of a huge bribe from a civil contractor?) But as I would greatly like his job, I am being extremely circumspect in my comments. 'No more than I myself would have done in the same circs.'

---

[1] Sajer, author of *The Forgotten Soldier*, a book to which AC often turned, served on the Russian front for three years without relief.

[2] Clive Ponting, a civil servant in the Ministry of Defence, revealed details of the sinking of the *Belgrano* during the Falklands War. He was tried for breaching the Official Secrets Act and found Not Guilty by the jury.

[3] John Stanley, MP for Tonbridge and Malling since 1974. Minister for the Armed Forces since 1983, where he remained until 1987.

This *could* be the moment, though. For although I would have loved to have gone to MoD immediately, if I do get there in the end I will be far stronger, because I have accumulated so much 'Whitehall' experience to back up my expert knowledge, hunches and prejudices. If John is sacked I must be among those with a claim to succeed him.

In the dining room last night John Wakeham shouted across from the Chief Whip's table to me that he had a special message – that I was 'loved'. And Tristan has a tale (one never quite knows with Tristan's tales, his motives are never singular) that Willie was defending me vigorously.[1]

Little Alfred Sherman[2] came to see me yesterday, at the Department, at his own request. He said that he 'wanted to discuss the Thatcherite Succession'.

Alfred said that he could 'steer me into it' using my wealth (!), that he had 'made' Keith, and then Margaret, and that he could do the same for me.

I could hardly not have been flattered, but I said little. He offered to write my speeches – but I don't like that. And anyway, time has moved on; we want not more, but less, of his medicine.

I can't decide whether Alfred would be a help or a hindrance. And anyway, have I got the oomph?

I'm not a 'hungry fighter', being too fond of my Baldwinesque leisure and hobbies.

Also, like many who have had an unhappy childhood, I am frightened of being laughed at.

Perhaps that is why I like making people laugh *with* me.

Saltwood   *Saturday, 16 February*

Before leaving London for the weekend I took time off to go to the Westminster Hospital to see my old, almost old*est* friend, John Pollock – 'Gianni' – who is dying there. He lay in 'Erskine' ward; a

---

[1] AC was getting a bad press at this time because a senior civil servant had leaked his private (but 'politically incorrect') comment about Bongo-Bongo land.
[2] Sir Alfred Sherman, journalist on the *Daily Telegraph* since 1965. He co-founded the Centre for Policy Studies in 1974 and was its Director of Studies until 1984.

miserable room, full of geriatrics, terminals and no-hopers, but where the staff were pleasant and obliging.

Gianni was frail, thin and bearded, with a sinister purple cross on his upper breast-bone where the radium gun had to be pointed.

'I've got this lump,' he said. 'Can you see this lump?' – and indeed I could.

Was it attached to the bronchial tubes? Why on earth couldn't they operate?

Gianni needed funds, presumably for cigarettes and 'miniatures'. I gave him all the cash I had in my pockets, some twenty-eight pounds in notes.

'What about the silver?' he asked. 'Aren't you carrying any silver?'

He stuffed the notes into his pyjama jacket, and the change into a box of 'Cook's Matches' on his bedside table.

Apparently the other patients, no matter how ill, crawl over and steal from those who are asleep.

I used always to visit Gianni, and his elderly patronne, Constance Mappin, on the shores of the Mediterranean during long vacation, and at other times.

Sometimes Constance was broke ('waiting for War Loan') and one evening, when 'the tables were unkind' – she was a raging gambler – I bought from her the turquoise and diamond ring which Jane still wears on occasion.

I have vivid, almost entirely pleasurable memories of Cannes, and Grasse, and Ischia. Of Don Cesare, and 'Phillipo', and Pat Hecht – one of the wildest and most exciting girls I have ever met.

Jane and I stayed with them at Positano on our honeymoon. Christina[1] turned up, and a farcical triangular sub-plot developed with Milo Cripps's[2] boy friend ('Barry') falling for her, and tears shed all round.

It all seems a very long way from Westminster. Save for one minuscule and trivial linkage – Pat had her hair cut even shorter than Jenny Easterbrook.

---

[1] Christina was living in AC's house at Rye when he became engaged to Jane.
[2] Now the 4th Baron Parmoor.

Department of Employment   *Wednesday, 24 April*

I went on a ministerial visit to Wrexham. A pretty, peaceful town, with the sun shining. How fortunate are the contented bourgeoisie in such places – or are they too racked by pressures and frustrations? They certainly didn't look it.

On the way up I saw Robert Atkins[1] in an adjoining carriage and went and had a talk with him. He told me that David Young had spoken to him for half an hour, asking RA what he should say to the Prime Minister who was always asking him for advice about personalities. I winced, as Atkins and I dislike each other quite candidly. But he is a great show-off, besides having a keen political sense of a below-stairs kind. It is not hard to extract intelligence from him.

Poor Michael Jopling[2] is going to be sacked, and Peter Rees.[3] RA also thought Quintin[4] would go, although he recognised that there was a shortage of candidates for law offices. I told him how Paddy Mayhew[5] was desperate to get back into the main stream, but RA said that although this was known, Paddy was being considered as a possible Lord Chancellor (which of course he could not refuse, even though he might not wish it). We agreed that Adam Butler[6] was to go and RA said that John Stanley would also be moved, though not, of course, dismissed, and that this would mean two vacancies of Minister of State at Defence. He paid lip service, though not very convincingly, that I should have one of these. It is notorious that I do not get on with Michael Heseltine but RA said that there was some talk of Peter Walker going there as a reward for his performance at

---

[1] Robert Atkins, MP for South Ribble since 1983 (Preston North, 1979–83). PPS to Lord Young when he was created a Life Peer in 1984 and joined the Government as Minister without Portfolio.

[2] Michael Jopling, a farmer. MP for Westmorland and Lonsdale since 1964. Minister of Agriculture since 1983. In fact he survived until 1987.

[3] Peter Rees, Chief Secretary to the Treasury since 1983.

[4] Quintin Hogg, Lord Hailsham of St Marylebone. A Minister in the Eden, Macmillan, Douglas-Home and Heath Cabinets. Now aged seventy-seven and serving his second term as Lord Chancellor (his first, 1970–4). He did not finally retire until 1987.

[5] Sir Patrick Mayhew, MP for Tunbridge Wells since 1974. Solicitor-General since 1983.

[6] Adam Butler, MP for Bosworth since 1970. The son of R. A. Butler. Minister of State, Defence Procurement, since 1984.

Energy. It might just happen, as Defence is a poison chalice until the books have been balanced, and the Lady might at present rate embarrassing Peter Walker as a higher priority than humiliating Heseltine. But the question would still remain, what then to do with MH?

All this, and more, was little more than the general semi-informed small talk that one gets when gossiping with colleagues in the lower reaches of government about changes in the autumn. It was reassuring to hear that the Lady cannot stand Kenneth Clarke, and it is for that reason that he has been so long excluded from the Cabinet, which apparently (but not in my estimation), his merits demand.

RA did then produce a stick of dynamite. He told me that it was being actively considered that the whole Department of Employment be abolished! The payment of benefit would be delegated to the DHSS. The issue of work permits to the Home Office. Health and Safety matters to the DTI. Training and special measures to a new training division that would go into a revamped Department of Education. 'Science' would be shunted from Education to DTI. I could see only too well where this idea came from (although I had only been here a week to form the same opinion).

RA said that Tom King was a prat: 'a nice chap, but a prat'. This is not entirely fair as Tom King has got a shrewd Willie-ish side, but his balls are very weak. He always loses in Cabinet and will not hold out for anything. This, and his testy manner with officials, has eroded his support in Whitehall and the long, cumbersome and never finished sentences, of which my parodies are notorious across the Civil Service, have irritated many colleagues.

Anyhow, I did not waste any time on my return in repeating this communication to Tom personally. He took it very badly. He has felt somewhat threatened of late – indeed, since David Young's appointment was hailed with only the most perfunctory disclaimer by Bernard Ingham as 'Minister for Jobs' – and there have been many similar incidents that have led TK to believe that David Young was encroaching on him. He huffed and he puffed and got more and more agitated. Indeed, he exhibited under stress those same slightly uncoordinated and disparate reactions – lateral thinking, etc., that he so often shows in discussion. He said that David Young was not a member of the club, never fought an Election, always wheedling away, the only person who had time to make this sort of trouble, and so on. I tried to calm him by suggesting that presentationally it would be impossible to abolish the one Department identified in the public eye as being responsible for the country's principal social and economic problem, and he got well *lancé* into this theme, delivering a series of unfinished, and ungrammatical, monologues. His condition deteriorated further when I revealed that the machinery of government aspect had also been looked at, with Michael Quinlan going across to Defence and Robert Armstrong getting his cards a little ahead of time, and Clive Whitmore going across to be Cabinet Secretary.[1]

We ended with TK undertaking to go to the Chief Whip and 'tweak his nose', also to Willie. Willie is not the man he was, as in the old days he would certainly have resisted this. But John Wakeham – I am not so sure.

Duke of Cornwall Hotel, Plymouth   *Thursday, 9 May*

Wasting time, and substance. Yesterday I was in the Midlands, job centres and benefit offices. I tried to be polite as well as grave. I'm good at that. People expect something different and then they're pleased.

After the vote I boarded the sleeper, uncomfortable and smelly. Walked, a lovely clear morning, from North Road station, but no breakfast served here until 7.30. Then I will walk again, saying 'brush'[2] and hoping to be widely seen and reported, from the hotel to the constituency office for my 'surgery'. There will be either twelve mendicants or three – it's impossible to predict. Let us hope three, as I have to take the 10.25 train *back* to London for an afternoon's work at the Dept. Then tomorrow back again, this time getting off the train at Exeter, motoring to Bratton where I will field a lot of phone calls from people complaining, or trying to make my flesh creep (usually both) about the SDP landslide which – by all accounts – is already

---

[1] Michael Quinlan, CB, Permanent Secretary, Department of Employment; Sir Clive Whitmore, KCB, CVO, Permanent Under-Secretary, Ministry of Defence, since 1983. This last was the only prediction that was not, in fact, fulfilled: Sir Robin Butler succeeding Armstrong (and Armstrong did in fact survive until the Civil Service retirement age of sixty).

[2] The Clarks believed that when constantly (but inaudibly) saying 'Brush' the features compose themselves in an expression of benign concern.

under way.[1] The next day, Saturday, it's the Dunstone Ward annual supper (Dunstone always choose a Saturday because Nan Howard[2] knows I prefer Fridays, so as to allow me to get back to Saltwood for the weekend) and more, this time 'live', complaints.

'The sheer hell of being an MP.'[3]

Some wanker called 'Caserly' (that just has to be a false name, probably someone on the editorial staff) has written an open letter in the *Herald*,[4] saying how arrogant and 'out of touch' (yeah) I am, will lose my seat, SDP Wave of the Future, usual balls.

Financially everything is still a mess. For the first time I am beginning to think that *I* may die before my father's estate is settled, and that Jane and the boys will have to cope with two sets of death duties simultaneously. I sometimes wonder whose side Thom is on. He rolls his 'R's with relish when, as he always does, calling them 'The Revenue'. This week he told me that they would be 'looking for' another £150,000.

In the meantime I have half agreed to sell the mask to Jerdein for $450,000, which is a whopping price really,[5] but after we had packed it up its *eye* looked reproachfully at me from where it was lying on the kitchen floor in Albany and I decided there and then to 'withdraw' it. There is so much ju-ju in that object. God knows what strange rituals it must have commanded, in steamy incense-ridden pagan temples. Blood, fertility and revenge, it carries the aura of all of these, and it is not seemly that it should be just bartered around for money in dealers' 'galleries'.

I am apprehensive, too, that once it went I might desperately want or need its return; some misfortune might be visited on me. I took it straight back to Saltwood and hung it in the strongroom where its mother-of-pearl eyes catch the light as the door opens. I am mindful, too, of that account in Ruth's diary of how Arthur[6] badgered and

---

[1] The Local Government Elections of 1985 marked the high point of SDP favour with the electorate.

[2] Mrs D. O'N Howard, Chairman of the Ward.

[3] The title of a review of a TV series about an MP entitled *The Nearly Man*.

[4] The *Western Evening Herald*, Plymouth newspaper.

[5] The Torres Strait tortoiseshell mask which belonged to Picasso. Charles Jerdein, an art dealer and friend of AC.

[6] Viscount Lee of Fareham, politician and collector. AC edited his papers, *A Good Innings*, published by John Murray, 1968. The diaries of Lady Lee (Ruth) are an integral part of the volume.

badgered an impoverished collector to sell him a little Giorgione. The man kept refusing, said he feared that once parted with it he might die. Arthur bullied and blustered, said such thoughts were 'unchristian', that he must meet his maker 'with conscience clear', pushed and nagged. Eventually the man sold. Less than two months later he was dead.

Then, yesterday, came interesting news. The client on whose behalf Jerdein was bidding, a rich Frenchman, had just had his daughter kidnapped and was in a dreadful state. Very powerful ju-jus can operate at long range. We know that.

Bratton   *Saturday, 11 May*

It's so lovely here. Slow and peaceful, buds everywhere and bright greeny-yellow leaves bursting. Jane is so pretty, her hair always gets tawny streaks in the springtime. But my balls ache, and my lower back is stiff and creaky. I have been doing the weights, but not much, surely? I will *not* give in to middle, still less old, age. Maurice[1] always said that that was what did for poor old Ian Fleming, insisting on carrying Annie's bags up and down the stairs, even when gasping.[2] But he was on forty a day and I've never smoked one cigarette in my entire life.

Now tonight we have the Dunstone supper, in the Elburton Red Triangle Hut, with everyone along to gloat and discomfit. Some stupid prick has done a 'projection' in one of the heavies showing that the SDP will have a massive overall majority in the House of Commons, we'll be down to thirty-two seats (or is it eighteen?). There is talk of mass desertions.

In fact *any* fixture after *any* year's local elections is always tricky. The councillors and canvassers are flushed with their own efforts; eager to relay stories of how 'on the doorstep' people have been complaining that they 'never see' the MP. Much talk along the lines

---

[1] Sir Maurice Bowra, Warden of Wadham College, Oxford, from 1938 to 1979.
[2] Ian Fleming, creator of James Bond, married Ann Charteris as her third husband. Her first, Lord O'Neill, was killed in action in 1944; she married Lord Rothermere in 1945. They divorced 1952 when she married Fleming, who died in 1964 aged 56.

that 'you're going to lose the seat unless you do something . . .' If I say 'Like what?' I never get any further than 'go walkabout in the Broadway on Saturday mornings' (and of course I ought to be doing that now, this minute, instead of lolling on the lawn at Bratton with milky coffee and fruitcake) or 'get more coverage in the press, Alan' (by which they mean, not what they call 'the London papers', but the bloody *Herald*). Janet Fookes,[1] whose vast arse is seldom undisplayed in the *Herald*, did in fact suffer an almost identical swing in her part of the city. But if I gently point this out it is unheard.

People have been ringing, how am I going to reply ('*respond* is the word', I say through gritted teeth) to Caserly's letter. They're so fucking stupid down here they've only got to read something in the *Herald* and they think it's true. Buttocks.

Jane cheered me up. Told how Eileen Smith had come up to her after her talk,[2] and said 'How *do* you do it?', i.e., put up with the life of being married to an MP.

Saltwood   *Sunday, 23 June*

A pleasing tale. Something of the Charley's Aunt donnée. William has always loved uniforms and panoply. For the last two years he has been 'due' a ticket to the Birthday Parade (or 'Trooping the Colour', as he calls it). Once again Lilian,[3] silly little fool, had left it too late. Or had he? At the last moment, and most covertly, he snatched or snitched one off the desk in the empty Adjutants' office at Knightsbridge. Didn't look at it too closely, stuffed it in his pocket.

I say 'ticket'. It was a beautiful embossed invitation, on stiff card.

William was delighted. Went up very splendidly in *full butler's regalia*, looking the picture of saturnine (though diminutive) elegance. Showed his ticket to a 'Greeter'.

'Aha, Excellency, how kind of you to come. Lovely. Good.'

---

[1] Miss (later Dame) Janet Fookes, MP for the Drake Division of Plymouth.

[2] Jane Clark had given a talk on 'The Stately Homes Business' to the Conservative Women's Association.

[3] 'Lilian': a family nickname for Andrew of ancient nursery standing, used when he is being unsatisfactory.

William, who is nobody's fool, drew on his long years of experience in 'service'. Kept mum, grunted only.

'I hope you'll be comfortable here. Seats can get a bit hard after a while, ha-ha. But I can offer you a cushion.' (*I* never get a bloody cushion, I told him.) 'I do hope you enjoy the Parade...'

Better and better it got. After the Anthem the Greeter reappeared. 'This way Excellency, Excellencies...'

In company with other bemedalled and exotic-uniformed dignitaries William was gently shepherded across the gravel and through the wall gate into the garden at Number 10!

At one point Mrs T. made a brief appearance and dreamily mingled. The tiny pearl-handled assassin's pistol (could have) nestled in William's breast pocket.

I don't expect the Prime Minister was concentrating very much in the company of these Corps Diplomatique medium-fry. But she would surely have sharpened up if she'd been told that among them was Al's butler from Saltwood.

Bratton   *Thursday, 8 August*

Yesterday I did something for the last time.

When you do something for the first time, you always know. Gosh, I haven't done this before. That's what it's like, is it – nice, nasty, try it again sometime, or whatever.

But when you do something for the *last* time, you very seldom know. Until, months or years later you realise – 'That was the very last time... Never again.'

This is a phenomenon that induces melancholy. It is so closely interleaved with the passage of time, the onset of infirmity. Death at one's shoulder in the market square of Samarra.

Constituency rubbish all day yesterday, and I should have left for Saltwood this morning. But at breakfast I saw in the *Western Morning News* that Mrs Barnard, the fearsome matriarch of Penhalt High Farm, had died, and the property was for sale. Something made me drive over, if only to look at the beach hut which I had coveted so long and so hard all the time we were living down here, when the boys were tiny.

Out on the Bude road, through Stratton, where a lovely and very young blonde used to stand at the crossroads in the summertime and wave. Past Widemouth sands where once Tip was almost swept away, and had to be revived, soaked, in the back of the car. And where when alone and driving the blue jeep I picked up the girl from Bray shop, and her Ma. Then over Millhook and down to Crackington Haven, and the beach hut still stood, intact.

It was in the early Sixties that we used to come here most often. And I remember one of the Barnard sons – strange and inbred they seemed at our one and only meeting in that charcoal-smelling kitchen with its long black range – baiting me by recounting how special seasoned planking from (?) the *Mauretania* had been used to build the hut.

Even in those days the paint had blistered and peeled, and the Atlantic gales were lashing the bare wood for five months in the year. But still it stood, the walls almost stripped, but without warp or rot. Several panes of glass had been broken, and the door was off its hinges. Someone had written 'Fuck Thatcher' with an aerosol spray, and there was the detritus and excrement of 'Travellers', as they style themselves. The stream was brackish, and the whole area seemed smaller and more cramped, as do often the sites of golden memories, when revisited.

I ground back up that very steep hill, with the 1 in 4 hairpin, which so often I descended, having to use bottom gear, in the [Citroën] ID 19 'Brake', loaded with children and picnic things. And for some reason, I can't tell why, my mind strayed to the possibility of 'starting again'.

I suppose it could still be done. But not while Jane is alive. I could not, would never wound her, the best human being in the entire world. And if she was taken from me I would be so shattered I couldn't do anything. All these thoughts were turning in my mind as I passed by the entrance to Penhalt High Farm and, out of curiosity, I turned in, walked some way along the track, then returned and got the car, undoing the baling twine on the gate.

It was completely deserted, not a soul. No livestock, no cat. Even the blue tits and house sparrows were in the fields.

They are handsome things, these walled Devon farmyards of the eighteenth century, with their low granite buildings, and the milking stalls floored and divided by Cyclopean fragments of slate. And there was a curious aura that hung over Penhalt, as it slept in the afternoon sun, with the seed grass everywhere overgrowing, knee-high.

I prowled about, scrambled over a wall into the little garden on the south side, terribly neglected but with two fig trees against the wall of the farmhouse, and some nice shrubs surviving. Intensely hot and still, a marvellous place for a pool.

Across the fields I could see one of those four-steepled Devon church towers, lying so perfectly in the trees in the hamlet of Tre-vinnick, and I entered the mind of others, the ghosts of former times, who must have looked upon this same view and, like me, felt wistful. Had someone, surely they must have done, served in the DCLI,[1] and looked on this for the last time on home leave from Flanders?

I was suspended; on but not of, this earth. I had detached myself from time, could move in any direction. Curious, but not in any way frightening, almost as if I had died not once but very many times.

I cannot tell how long my trance, or reverie, endured. But I became aware of a deep, heavy roaring sound, mingled with the fluttering noise of airscrews on coarse pitch. And very low, 200 feet at the most, a single Lancaster flew directly over the house, and on across towards Exmoor, being soon lost to sight.

Afterwards, of course, on the journey home, I did my best to rationalise a supernatural experience. It is true that I often transpose the loss of young lives in the World War I no-man's-land, and the repetitive sorties by Bomber Command. And there is only one Lancaster left. And the 'Battle of Britain Flight' is stationed a very long way from Penhalt. And they are precluded from flying below 1000 feet, except at displays.

But the twenty-fifth anniversary comes up in a few weeks' time. He must have been practising.

Saltwood   *Tuesday, 13 August*

I am so *bored* by my work. It spreads right across and affects everything so that I am beginning to feel stale, and déjà vu, with all aspects of public life.

At the Cavalry Club last week Ian and I had our ritual summer 'round-up' lunch. But even that was not the same. We gossiped. But

[1] Duke of Cornwall's Light Infantry.

Ian's contributions did not have that electric quality which used to run through them in the days when he had come straight from the Lady's presence. He is peevish, and fussed about Ireland.

I said, don't. Ireland is a ghastly subject. Intractable. Insoluble. For centuries it has blighted English domestic politics, wrecked the careers of good men.

Ian said the pressure to concede everything to Dublin (and thus expose the decent Loyalists in Ulster to the full force of IRA terrorism) is coming from the Foreign Office, who are themselves reacting to pressure from Washington. One must never forget that the Irish vote in America is bigger than it is in Eire. We agreed that the Foreign Office now exists solely to buy off foreign disapproval by dipping into the till marked British Interests.

There will be a reshuffle next month. 'Quite a big one.' Norman Tebbit will be made Chairman; Peter Rees and Patrick Jenkin will be 'dropped'.

On the subject of the juniors Ian was more cagey, although said that Macfarlane[1] had been a disappointment.

'If you want a change, you should tell the Chief Whip.'

'Oh, come on, Ian, everyone knows what I want.'

Once I am back here, sawing and working on the land, Whitehall and its drudgery seem remote. Only when I read something really interesting, like that article by Laurence Freedman on nuclear targeting, do I pine for what could, dare I say, 'ought' to be.

Danair, Inverness – Heathrow   *Tuesday, 3 September*

I return to London suddenly and in grumpy form.

Jane, quite rightly, said you must return *at once* as the new Ministers will be all over the place, preening themselves and bagging portfolios. You will be left with all the ullage. But what now? The holiday is buggered and I doubt if we will ever get to the Citroën for the escape.

---

[1] Neil Macfarlane, MP for Sutton and Cheam since 1974. Sports Minister (Department of the Environment) since 1981.

Am I really to be stuck for another year in that ghastly hellhole?[1]

So this morning I rose at four a.m. and took James's Saab, thrashed my way to Dalcross in blinding rain, great splashing puddles that wrench at the steering, and swirling mists. It is not possible really to exceed forty mph in many places between Eriboll and Lairg, all of fifty-two miles.

But after 'The Wee Scottish Soldier'[2] I drove at 110–115 mph wherever I could, hating every minute of it.

I keep dropping off to sleep as I write this.

Yesterday, after the junior appointments had all been announced, we set off on a walk along the shoreline, southerly towards the Viking dock and 'Grassy Knoll'.[3] Periodically I declaimed, in a rage, about the march of the greys. Practically every reshuffle there has ever been has made me angry – almost worse now I am in Government than when I was on the back benches, critical and expectant. On and on we walked, stopping at intervals to collect driftwood, which we placed in little cairns for collection by the Wee One.[4] We took supper very late, it being still light at eleven o'clock, and I cannot have had much more than three hours' sleep.

Albany   *Later*

I went straight from Heathrow to the Dept. Officials are genuinely glad I am still there – which is nice, though of little value. Peter Morrison rang from his new office at the DTI, too well-mannered to gloat[5] (not that he has much to gloat about, considering that for most of the spring and summer he was expecting to be made Chief Whip) and we went to the Ritz for lunch.

---

[1] The postings in the autumn reshuffle were finally announced. AC was chiefly affected by Tom King's appointment to the Northern Ireland Office and the arrival of David Young as Secretary of State at the Department.
[2] The war memorial at Bonar Bridge.
[3] Grassy Knoll: a promontory thus described on the Admiralty charts of Loch Eriboll.
[4] A forty-year-old Land Rover which had failed its MOT and is used for local work on the estate.
[5] Peter Morrison had been moved 'sideways' from the Department of Employment to become Minister of State for Industry.

Peter was full of how, already, he was sorting out his civil servants. They were trying to put upon him 'a female' as head of his Private Office. 'I couldn't possibly have that.'

'Really? I've had nothing but women in charge of mine. I find it rather congenial.'

'Yes, but you see, she couldn't carry my guns.'

I grumbled away disconsolately. Peter tried to cheer me up by saying that there was 'bound' to be a 'really big' shuffle next Easter. Whatever for? I thought.

But of course Peter himself wants to get closer to the Cabinet soon. He is much younger than me, could indeed be my son, but I would guess our shelf life is about the same. After lunch, very sleepy and *désoeuvré*, I sat at my desk, riffled a few dreary PO cases.

Punctually (first difference from Tom) David Young had me in at the appointed time. He is pleasant, charming almost, and fresh (as distinct from stale). He talks at twice the speed of Tom King, but listens too, cracks jokes, is full of bright ideas. I quite see why the Lady fancies him. He is utterly different from the rest of the Cabinet – yet without being caddish.

I dined at the Beefsteak with Bruce Anderson.[1] We were the only people in the room, except for Anthony Lejeune, who looked exceedingly ill.[2]

Eriboll   *Wednesday, 4 September*

I caught the 8.50 flight, and sat next to a quite pretty blonde in a white jacket. Her husband, or consort, was miniature, bearded, scruffy – but had an upper-class voice. Who the hell was he? Normally one knows every one of any consequence on that aircraft.

I headed north, at a leisurely pace, and after Altnaharra took the Loch Hope road instead of going through Tongue. It was the first sunny day for two weeks, and there were climbers' cars parked in the layby where the start of the Hope ascent is marked. To my shame I have never climbed Hope, and suddenly, irresistibly, I thought, why not?

[1] Bruce Anderson, political columnist on the *Sunday Telegraph*.
[2] Anthony Lejeune, author, reviewer of crime fiction for the *Daily Telegraph*.

There were some heavy shoes in the car, and in one of the door pockets I found a thermal belt. But I was suited, waistcoated, tie, collar stiffeners – Whymper.

A white TR 6 had parked close by, and a man was putting on a lot of gear; bright nylon windcheater, hood, gloves, special backpack. I set off immediately, nonchalant at his stare of disapproval. I was carrying nothing, not even a thumbstick. I didn't have so much as a Mars Bar in my pocket.

The ascent became a duel. He must have left a minute or so later, and made two attempts to close the distance. But on each occasion I anticipated, knowing from experience on the Trift, and other frequented climbs, that there are few things so disheartening as to make a special effort and find your quarry, mysteriously, is still at the same distance. After about an hour I sensed he was content to pace me, but I still took care whenever I was in dead ground, to accelerate to my utmost, or even to run.

The last thirty minutes to the summit are steep and debilitating, a track through scree, easy to lose in the cloud which, from about 3800 feet, was persistent. I reached the second marker cairn – there was a double summit – in under two hours, without stopping once, and was pleased with myself. For the time being it quite compensated for Whitehall and its disappointments.

But this evening I am exhausted and must have been poor company at dinner. When I recounted to Jane how relaxed and congenial David Young was she said of course – but he doesn't have to fill his mind with constituency detritus the whole time, suffer his weekends being ruined by mendicants, stay up until gone midnight voting on spastic and unnecessary measures.

Too right. The democratic overhead.

As I brood on all this, I find myself becoming crosser. I've had it. Chris Patten has been made a Minister of State; OK, he's brilliant. But so has Renton, and he isn't.[1] I can read the signs. At some point in this coming term I must seek out the Chief Whip, or possibly G-J. I want 'out' at Christmas.

---

[1] Christopher Patten had become Minister of State at Education and Science; Tim Renton, Minister of State, Foreign Office.

House of Commons   *Tuesday, 26 November*

Today my old friend made his resignation speech.[1] The House was full. And by the time I arrived my usual place behind the Prime Minister had been taken and I sat at the far end, between Carol Mather[2] and Peter Bottomley.[3] Kinnock was on his feet and, as it moved on to economic subjects, was making a hash of things and had 'lost the House'.[4] There was a general murmuration.

'When is Ian speaking?' I said to Carol.

He grunted non-committally. He is a Whip of the old school and they do not like resignations.

Last week a cruel piece by Peter Riddell in the *Financial Times* had treated Ian's resignation dismissively, for 'his career is already in decline', etc., etc., and other unwelcome truths.

Thinking it was a Whips' Office plant, I had complained to Garel-Jones, who affected horror and dismay. I remain suspicious. I believe that it was a pre-emptive plant fed to Riddell on the day of Gow's resignation in case he gave trouble. In fact, and as could have been readily predicted by anyone who knows him, he gave no trouble. But the piece was used nonetheless.

Ian was dejected and flat in tone. He spoke from the second row from the back, which is *not* a commanding position, because you fall between two banks of microphones, and this technical handicap aggravated the loss of confidence and authority in his voice. Everything that Ian said about Ulster was painfully true and although, perhaps, he over-quoted from humble correspondents in the Province it was moving and, among nationalists like myself at least, induced unease and guilt.

But the personal passage at the end was, frankly, embarrassing. He described how disagreeable resignation was; how he spoke from the bottom of his heart – 'and it is a very big heart' – (oh dear). Ian went on to say the Prime Minister might welcome the resignation of some of her colleagues more than others and he did not know (sic) into

---

[1] Ian Gow had resigned from the Government in protest at the Anglo-Irish agreement (see also entry for 13 August 1985).

[2] Carol Mather, MP for Esher since 1970; a Whip since 1975.

[3] Peter Bottomley, MP for Eltham since 1983 (Woolwich West, 1975–83). Parliamentary Under-Secretary, Employment, since 1984.

[4] Neil Kinnock, MP for Islwyn and Leader of the Opposition since 1983 (Bedwellty, 1970–83).

which category he fell. How he had enjoyed – exulted in? revelled in? – working for the Lady for four years; her great and indeed paragonesque virtues, 'the finest chief, the most resolute Leader, the kindest friend that any Member of this House could hope to serve'.

Cruel and sardonic, Peter Bottomley turned to me and said in the middle of this eulogy, 'Give him a job.'

Will he ever get a job again? I doubt it. One more example of Beaverbrook's dictum that politicians are irreparably flawed by going up to Heaven in their early forties and coming back to earth shortly thereafter. Originally said of Curzon, I can think of no one to whom it doesn't apply, with the possible exception of David Owen. But even he, although purged by passage through fire and water, may never in fact have a 'job' again.

It is this *absolute* unpredictability that makes politics so irresistible. Who in 1982, when he was rightly described as the most powerful man in the Government, could have predicted that IG would be the first of her Ministers to resign?

I think it is probably true that she was getting irritated with him in his closing months as her Secretary. Like many men who find their love unrequited, he was becoming more and more subservient and attentive. The stooping, obsequious family retainer, speaking very often in a special high-pitched tone that was almost tearful (my father, too, I have seen practising this technique).

I saw Nicholas Soames standing at the bar and afterwards he told me that during the embarrassing passage the Lady closed her eyes and went quite rigid in expression.

Much later, in the smoking room, Soames and Budgen plied me with Black Velvet and spoke indiscreetly about Ian's speech. I say indiscreetly because Ian himself was sitting only one table away with Cecil and a couple of backbenchers. On the way out Ian paused at our table and I said something gauche about not a dry eye in the House. Worryingly, he took this badly and stomped off. Poor monk![1] My only true friend in the Government. Who can I talk to now? Peter Morrison is in another Department, and too preoccupied these days. Garel-Jones is fun but unreliable, and Celtic in his motivations.

These ironic cycles and visitations of Nemesis (not that poor Ian

---

[1] Ian Gow was sometimes known as The Monk (as, indeed, but for different reasons, was Keith Joseph).

ever showed hubris in the slightest degree) occur quite frequently but do not, regrettably, usually punish the most appropriate targets. IG loathed Bottomley, whom he thought, not incorrectly, to be a closet Liberal. Out of mischief I had sent IG a cutting from Bottomley's local paper in which he said that he was, 'basically a good Liberal', and that his views 'enormously overlapped' with those of John Cartwright, his SDP neighbour. I thought no more of it until I heard later through Private Office channels that Bottomley had been carpeted by the Chairman and this made me feel uneasy.

The previous day the Chairman [of the Party] had given a pep talk to junior Ministers, telling us to be 'more political', to get around the country making speeches and generally fluff up the Associations.

I do not mind (much) fluffing up other Associations, and it usually goes quite well. Although I grudge them the time, particularly at weekends. But my own is irreparably lost. I find most of them boring, petty, malign, clumsily conspiratorial, and parochial to a degree that cannot be surpassed in any part of the United Kingdom. Once contempt and irritation passes a certain level, I am not good at concealing my feelings and I fear that it has been widely felt. My tactical energies are devoted simply to the narrow goal of beating them to the draw with the announcement of my 'standing down'.

Letter to Ian Gow   *House of Commons*
                                                                            27 November

Ian

When we spoke briefly in the smoking room last night after your speech I fear that I may have seemed a little frivolous.

Alas, it is in the nature of my (– is 'background' the right word?) upbringing to affect casualness in the face of great and unwelcome events. You will understand this.

Yes, I was embarrassed as were others in the House by the personal note that you struck at the end.

But this embarrassment was founded not in the unease with which one attends on the ritualised and the synthetic, but in that deeper unhappiness of the soul which is restrained from its natural inclination to spring up and acclaim and say,

'Yes you are right. Speak your message, speak it again. We are with you.'

Affectionately

Alan

Department of Employment   *Thursday, 28 November*

I suffer from some unease as I contemplate my time in Government, and in Parliament, drawing to a close. Because you are only a shadow, a wraith, a phantasm once you have announced your intention to 'stand down'.

I still do love the clubbable side. The swinging studded Pugin doors which exclude those unentitled; the abundance of facilities; the deeply comfortable leather chairs at the 'Silent' end of the library where one can have a sleep as deep and as refreshing as under the eaves of the Chalet Caroline. There is constant access to snacks, 'nips' and gossip. There are excellent and attentive library staff who will do all your work for you.

But all this is fully enjoyable only in winter time.

In summer and late spring it becomes oppressive and fetid. I get sudden, intermittent – like powerful twinges of pain – realisations of how *old* I am becoming. I spring in my step, look at girls, like laughs and fresh ideas. But when I was talking about this with Jane during one of those interminable telephone calls that we make most evenings, we agreed, what is my life expectancy? Fifteen years? If I spend two-thirds of that in London, or in the Constituency (actually it's more) what have I got left? Effectively – five.

At what stage does one's reserve of years change from being inexhaustible – of no concern or consequence – into a rapidly diminishing triangle of sand at the neck of the glass, which is scru-tinised obsessively?

Yesterday, at lunch time, I drove the SS 100 still, forty years on, getting that wonderful evocative thrill as I settle into the driving seat and look down the long louvred bonnet.

At the Princes Gate traffic lights out of Hyde Park I drew up beside a black BMW, driven by a blonde, registered ANY 1. I looked sideways and saw browner, thinner in the face, but still with 'something', Andy Colquhoun.

As the lights went amber the faithful SS, always unbeatable for the first fifty feet of a standing start, yelped the racing diamond tread of its 18-inch wheels, and was off – the BM was nowhere. She pursued me, *screeching* the revs to ignition cut-out, but locked brakes and overshot the right turn to the Albert Hall.

Had Andy recognised me? Or have I changed too much? Some disturbing photos have come up recently from the Press Office, showing a heavy jowel, but loose neck folds.

Department of Employment   *Tuesday, 17 December*

If I look back on the last three weeks I can see nothing of any moment whatsoever that has happened to me, save that I suffered, absorbed and phlegmily surmounted a filthy cold in the head.

I have made various 'visits', mainly it seems to workshops for the disabled, to please officials and to give the illusion of activity. But all that has happened is that I am that much older and iller, and I have been kept from the company of my loved ones. I have done nothing for my country, and I would guess that (for example) there are more people out of work today than there were a month ago.

Today we had the DE carol service. As always, ego and 'rights' to an unbelievable degree. I only can properly enjoy carol services if I am having an illicit affair with someone in the congregation. Why is this? Perhaps because they are essentially pagan, not Christian, celebrations.

Next, thoroughly disillusioned with everything, and in foul mood, I traipsed around the precincts of the Palace of Westminster looking for Alison in order to seek his advice on how I should convey to the PM that I wanted 'out'. He was nowhere to be seen. His office was sterile-tidy, deserted. I switched objectives and searched for Tristan. But he had flown. Off, already, to Spain. The House is emptying fast. It echoes, and workmen have appeared, smelling of nicotine and perspiration, and muttering to themselves.

I am frustrated, but soon I too will be in my beloved county of Sutherland, where I can torture the body, and replenish the spirit.

Eriboll   *Sunday, 29 December*

Unbroken clear skies all day, with the air quite still, and six to seven inches of snow lying. We went up the Creaggan Road to the summit, to be joined by James and the labs in the Argocat. Incredible light, with variations the whole time. The slopes of Cranstackie were rose pink from the low, low sun; but there was a great slate-coloured ridge of cloud out to sea, merging with the blues and blacks of the loch mouth. On coming down we picked up the dogs and took the road to Stra'beg, walking as far as the hirsel fence line that gives a view of the mountain hut at the top of the valley.

Got back here, thoroughly exhausted, happy and hungry after four and a half hours on the hill.

My physique is improving. As I cut logs in the little woodshed I began to think that all this talk of retiring is balls. Stay on as Minister, and do the job. ACHAB, etc. Yet this view alternates with a kind of somnolent contentment. While I love to be out of doors all day long, I do start to feel tired and escapist if I have to consider any decision relating to Saltwood, the office, the Constituency, construction plans in Zermatt, husbandry at Broomhayes, or any one of a hundred things that I carry at the back of my mind.

It is not only Whitehall that is so far away. Everything going on in the world seems remote and unimportant. We have no television, hear no wireless save the shipping forecasts. We get one newspaper, the *Aberdeen Press and Journal*, which is resolute in its parochialism, and most soothing as a result.

I have to talk to the office occasionally, although I try to do it as little as possible. Judith[1] is telling me that the Westland row, which was smouldering when we broke up, is now ablaze. 'People are saying Mr Heseltine is going to resign.'[2]

---

[1] Judith Rutherford has taken charge of AC's Private Office in the Department following the promotion of Jenny Easterbrook.

[2] The future of Westland Helicopters, which was under-capitalised, was the subject of two conflicting recommendations by the Ministry of Defence (under Michael Heseltine) and the Department of Trade and Industry (under Leon Brittan). Heseltine wanted 'a European solution' with joint venture arrangements with the European helicopter manufacturers. The DTI's preference was for an injection of capital from the US manufacturer Sikorksy, with whom Westland had often worked in the past.

I don't believe it. It's just the press stirring. Anyhow, no one resigns when the House is not sitting.

But Michael has always had this slightly scatty side. It is the only even half-endearing trait that he possesses. He is the man who pushed further out the definition of *folie de grandeur* than it has ever been hitherto.

Anyway, so what? If he does – good riddance.

1986

1986

I was on the phone gossiping to Peter Morrison at his office in the DTI when Judith tiptoed in and put a piece of paper under my nose. 'Michael Heseltine has resigned.'

I whooped, and gave him the news, but at that very moment his own Private Office had done the same. I looked demi-stupid because until that point I had been saying how I didn't see how he could, it was not in his character, he was too ambitious.

Peter said, 'Well, this could mean some interesting changes,' and we both hung up in order to take more soundings.

Shortly afterwards the Sec of State rang. Would I come along for a chat?

David recounted to me the scene. Michael appears to have done it semi-spastically, *not* the *grand geste*. When he slammed his brief shut and walked out a lot of people just thought that he'd been a bit rude, and then gone out to the loo. But the photographers were all waiting in Downing Street, so he must have tipped them off in advance. Now he was holding a 'press conference' in the big lecture hall at the MoD. What was his authority for doing that, pray? I asked. He should be emptying his desk.

David referred *veiledly* to 'accompanying changes'. Said, reassuringly, 'I know what you want.'

Secretly cheered by this, I did not like to break the spell by telling Jane when we spoke on the telephone. Perhaps this was a mistake.

Sensing 'developments' I cancelled a visit to Plymouth and came down here. At Men's Tea the Downing Street switchboard rang. 'Mr Alan Clark? The Chief Whip wants you.'

John Wakeham came on. Some pleasantries about being snowed up, and then, 'The PM's contemplating a few changes and I wanted to ask if you'd like to be asked (heart leaps) to dur-dur-dur, move *sideways* (sic with a vengeance, heart sinks) and help Nick Ridley at Transport?'[1]

---

[1] Nicholas Ridley, MP for Cirencester and Tewkesbury since 1959. Secretary of State for Transport since 1983.

I had taken the call under the stairs, and bought time by saying that I was getting it transferred to the office. Foolishly, I think, I didn't tell Jane all, only that the Chief Whip was on the phone, but my heart was pounding. I had to refuse.

'John, I don't want to seem to be difficult about this, but I have been a Parly Sec for over two and a half years. For the last eight months I have really been doing a Min of State's work as I have had to cover for Gummer since he was made Party Chairman. To be perfectly honest, I was a bit miffed at not getting Peter Morrison's rank last September when I took over all his duties.'

'Mmm. What would you like me to say to the Prime Minister?'

I put down smoke about the Channel 'Fixed Link',[1] how it was a Department of Transport responsibility but I owned a lot of the land at the mouth of the tunnel (if there was a tunnel). Could look awkward if I was a Minister in that Department. John affected to understand. He said he 'did not rule out' the possibility of an upward move later. Said the Lady had a high opinion of me 'in spite of all I tell her' (joke).

Saltwood   *Friday, 24 January*

And still the 'events' accumulate (though not yet any announcement about Lynda Chalker's job, now vacant a fortnight).[2] This week it has been all leaks and statements and counter-leaks, and fevered rumour.

On Wednesday the pressure mounted all day long for the Prime Minister to make a statement on the Purloined Letter,[3] accompanied by – source? – tales that LB[4] 'wouldn't go quietly'.

The story became current that she was tied until, in her statement, she could announce that she had accepted LB's resignation. The unhappy fall guy.

But the House might not like that. Too obvious. In the evening I

---

[1] As Eurotunnel was known at the time.

[2] Lynda Chalker, MP for Wallasey since 1974. Minister of State, Transport, since the 1983 Election, she had just been appointed Minister of State, Foreign Office.

[3] A letter from the Attorney General to Michael Heseltine rebuking him for breaking the ministerial convention, which had been leaked to the press (as it subsequently turned out) by the Press Office at the Department of Trade and Industry.

[4] LB: Leon Brittan had been Trade and Industry Secretary since 1985.

called on John Biffen in his office behind the Speaker's Chair. I said
that it was better to defuse, or rather preempt, the row by her coming
to the House and making the statement *now*, i.e., after the ten p.m.
vote. Some of her tormentors would possibly be away and, in any
case, this would allow her to outwit the morning press and to reduce
the time available for them to organise. John completely agreed.
He was cagey, but I formed the impression that he had already
recommended this very course.

However, the vote came and passed, and no sign.

We all drifted home eventually, but late and after much chattering
in the smoking room and the corridors.

This morning the lobby was ablaze. Reporters everywhere, and
the atmosphere of a bazaar (as in the East, rather than the
Constituency). Marcus Kimball[1] had turned up and was standing
about – always a sign that something is afoot. He told of dining with
Willie the previous evening, and that there had been much talk of
'too many jewboys in the Cabinet'. It appeared that the Prime Minister
had decided against a statement last night and had opted for the
'Resolute Defence' (as opposed to the 'Muzio Gambit'[2]) and would
be making a statement at the usual time this afternoon.

I wandered along to the dining room and lunched with Julian
Amery and Robert Jackson,[3] whom I like for his dry, donnish sense
of humour. I say 'with' but there was much jocularity at our end of
the room, and shouting across from one table to another. Julian had a
good bottle of Burgundy in a basket, and let me have a couple
of glasses. He told various tales, and pronounced judgment as an
experienced statesman.

Then, unexpectedly, the Chief Whip came over and sat with us.
He showed me a copy of the statement. I read a few paragraphs,
started a *faux-rire*. I couldn't help it. 'I'm sorry, John. I simply can't
keep a straight face.' The paper passed from hand to hand. Others
agreed, but were too polite to say so.

How *can* she say these things without faltering?

But she did. Kept her nerve beautifully.

I was sitting close by, and could see her riffling her notes, and

[1] Marcus Kimball, MP for Gainsborough, 1956–83. Created Life Peer, 1985.
[2] Muzio Gambit: a reckless and now little-used opening gambit in chess.
[3] Robert Jackson, MP for Wantage since 1983, had been MEP for Upper Thames,
   1980–4. At Oxford he was President of the Union and Prize Fellow of All Souls.

turning the pages of the speech. Her hand did not shake *at all*. It was almost as if the House, half horrified, half dumb with admiration, was cowed.

A few rats came out of the woodwork – mainly from the *Salon des Refusés* – Fletcher,[1] Wiggin, a couple of others. Serene and haughty, at its end she swept from the Chamber, and a little later came to a meeting of the '22. The mood was wholly supportive of her, and the Scapegoat was duly tarred.

This morning came the news. Leon Brittan has resigned.

But is that the end of it? Clearly it is intended to be; but I'm not so sure.

Saltwood   *Sunday, 26 January*

A lovely still day, clear and crisp. As I set off with the dogs before breakfast, Bob went past with a trailer of loose straw for the shippon – the pleasures of husbandry and the land. I walked over to the Machines, then round the Lake, along the valley and up to Chittenden Stone.

At intervals I stole glances at *The Observer*. We are not out of the wood, and the Lady is still terribly beleaguered. There is to be an emergency debate on Monday.

Is this the end of an era? Uneasily, I feel it may be. Perhaps they're actually going to get her, the same way the weevils got de Gaulle. Will I, alarmingly soon, be back with the books and the Heritage – but without the *cachet*?

Last night IG rang, full of gloom and portent. I discounted him, but that was before I had seen this morning's press. Ian's trouble, though, is that he is, *au fond*, a man of honour. Personally, I don't give a blow. Lie if necessary.

I have just put the phone down from Peter Morrison. Not much news, though he, too, is not optimistic. Peter said that F. Pym might vote against, with 'bad consequences' in the Lobby. Is the Conservative Party going through one of its recurrent bouts of epilepsy?

---

[1] Alex Fletcher, MP for Edinburgh Central since 1983 (Edinburgh North, 1973–83). Successively Parliamentary Under-Secretary to the Scottish Office and Trade and Industry. Returned to back benches in 1985.

House of Commons   *Monday, 27 January*

Every seat in the House had been booked with a prayer card, and they were all up the gangways.

For a few seconds Kinnock had her cornered, and you could see fear in those blue eyes. But then he had an attack of wind, gave her time to recover.

A brilliant performance, shameless and brave. We are out of the wood.

Saltwood   *Friday, 31 January*

The last day of an absolutely incredible month.

Last evening Jane met me at Sandling. I could see she was excited. 'Do you want the good news or the bad?'

'Always the bad first.'

'You've got to go back up to London.'

I groaned.

'The PM wants to see you at Number 10 tomorrow morning at nine thirty.'

Wow! I rang Judith immediately. She had received a terse message from Wicks.[1] He wouldn't enlarge. But it was Trade, Paul Channon's old job.[2] David Young had confirmed it 'in the lift', talking to one of his own staff, and the news was all over the building.

Jane and I talked incessantly. We had a complete *nuit grise* with me turning on and off the light to make notes in my little green wallet. I rose before five, and paced about, my mind ranging.

Why on earth didn't I get an earlier train, the milk train, indeed? As it was, timing was tight. The 'usual' train was (inevitably) late, and instead of a leisurely grooming and preening at Albany I had to dress in a scrabble, plopped some toothpaste on my suit, spilt the aftershave, was my parting straight? etc.

---

[1] Nigel Wicks. Since returning in 1985 from Washington as Economic Minister at the British Embassy had been Principal Private Secretary to the Prime Minister.

[2] Paul Channon, who succeeded his father, Sir Henry ('Chips'), as MP for Southend in 1959, had been promoted to Secretary of State following Leon Brittan's resignation.

I just got to Number 10 in time. Well, not really, as I was *on* time
and I should have been a deferential eight minutes early. No one
seemed to know who I was or why I was there. I hung around in the
little waiting room, repressing the urge to put my head round the
door and see what now happened in Ian's old study, where he used
to lie in wait and pull in Cabinet Ministers before a meeting and tell
them 'what the Prime Minister was hoping to achieve'.

After a bit Wicks appeared.

'Right.'

'Eh?'

I followed him up the stairs.

'She's got a cold,' he said.

A man of few words. Five, to be precise.

But there was no sign of a cold at all. The Prime Minister looked
wonderful, was effusive, genuinely friendly. Unusually, she saw me
alone, not in the Cabinet Room, but the little 'parlour'. She told me
how important the job was. I was to be Minister for Trade, *not* just a
Min of S. It was the second most important Minister outside the
Cabinet after the Financial Secretary – 'but don't shout that around'.

'Negotiation is the key. And I need someone with a *presence*,
charm, someone *different* . . . and of course with a brilliant brain.' (No,
really).

She said someone (I wonder who[1]) had said that I would be
unacceptable to, e.g., the Nigerians because of (conveyed but not said)
my remarks about Bongo-Bongo land. 'But of course you will be,
perfectly acceptable, won't you?'

Then she praised me for my work in the Department, said I was
the only person she could rely on there (uh?), how few of us there
were. At the end, when she spoke of her determination to go on, and
her blue eyes flashed, I got a full dose of personality compulsion,
something of the *Führer Kontakt*.

An agreeable vignette occurred when 'Professor' Brian Griffiths,
a courtier, came in.[2] After some small talk he said, 'No Minister for
Trade has been appointed.'

The Prime Minister indicated me, and his demeanour altered
quite markedly.

---

[1] On his own subsequent (that evening) admission, it was Douglas Hurd.

[2] Brian Griffiths, banking and economics academic, had been Head of the Prime
Minister's Policy Unit since 1985.

I returned to the Dept. Hugged the girls, and began to pack up my papers.

Department of Trade and Industry   *Monday, 3 February*

I am in my lovely new spacious office. I have rearranged the furniture so that my desk is up the far end, with a 'conference' table three windows down towards the Private Office door – and this I insist is always kept open, being the best way of asserting discipline.

It means that visitors have to cover a good distance as they approach me. Mussolini-like. And is particularly welcome in the case of the diary secretary, who is called Rose. Rose (primly she signs her notes, of which there already have been a good number, 'Rosemary') has hips, and a bust, which are almost too noticeable in someone of only (say) 5 foot $4\frac{1}{2}$ inches. She looks very coolly and directly at me when she speaks. And when she comes into the room she holds her head up and does not shuffle or stoop.

The principal Secretary, Matthew Cocks, is very good news. High IQ, pleasant sense of humour, unshockable.

I had a good press – the *FT* was particularly complimentary – and this has cheered the outer office. But I lost no time in circulating my last 'Protectionist' article from the *Daily Telegraph*, and certain Hansard extracts from way back. Matthew told me that there are still believers in the various Desks, but of course they have to stay quiet at the present time, because the vogue has altered.

We'll see about that, I said. Matthew has an engaging way of biting his lip when suppressing a giggle.

Later

I went and had a chat with Paul Channon. He is quick, and funny. His rapid style of speech may make him seem more nervous than actually he is. At one time in the past he was very cross with me, did indeed upbraid me in the library, for saying unpleasant things about Chips, his snobbish, *arriviste*, but intensely observant father.

Paul has been in the Department for ages. And for long periods – the various interregna, particularly when Norman Tebbit was recover-

ing from his wounds – acted virtually as Secretary of State. It is quite
proper that he should have been promoted.

Paul was lively and amusing about my (until last week his) job.
'It's very much an independent command.'

And his predecessors. 'I have seen three Secretaries of State sitting
in this very chair, sobbing.'

Both Leon and Cecil had, in their different ways, piccolo nervous
crises.

Paul also told me, as indeed have many others already, that every
Minister for Trade ends up in the Cabinet.

My head is swollen.

At the Council of Ministers,   *Tuesday, 18 February*
Luxembourg

I came out last night, dined and stayed the night at the Embassy. Just
before leaving Peter caught me on the DTI Ministers' landing, and
warned me against HE's wife. Apparently she likes to provoke
(argument, as distinct from advance). 'She will be wearing a tartan
skirt.'

It is a heavy, handsome building; warm and comfortable with
masses of Wilton everywhere. Big wash basins, everything well lit,
makes Saltwood really *absurdly* tatty. And a huge decanter of whisky
in my room (but not things I actually *need*, like shampoo or Redoxon).

Yes, the Ambassador's wife was wearing a tartan skirt. A big
woman, a kind of up- (but not much up)market constituency ward
chairman. She 'enlivened' the meal by making a series of ludicrous
and – even by my sceptical standards – highly eccentric remarks about
the Community, NATO, foreign policy, and so on. Cowlike, really.

'Yes, yes,' I agreed. 'Absolutely. Go on. More!'

We developed our themes while, at the far end of the table, the
Ambassador smiled benignly, though with just a touch of unease.

This morning I reported early to the Council Chamber, and was
soon closeted in the UKREP suite with officials. They were twitchy,
but curious. Totally Europhile. Sole objective, as far as I could see,
being to 'expedite business' – i.e., not make a fuss about anything,

however monstrous. Or at least, you *could* make a fuss, but only a 'show' fuss in order to get kudos from, soon after, surrendering 'in the interests of making progress'.

I took against one in particular. This female, after I had spent over an hour getting my speech notes beefed up by a few degrees, literally snatched them away five minutes before I was due to perform, and substituted a pencilled text of her own.

Earlier I had noticed her scribbling away manically, like those demented women in Lincolns Inn Hall during Bar finals. All my points had been 'toned down' out of sight. In had come or, I should say, *back* had come, great slabs of Eurospeak – total gibberish to anyone not part of the cult.

'What's all this?'

'It's the new "Line to Take"!'

'How do you mean, "New"?'

'There's just been' (plainly a lie as she wouldn't look at me) 'a telegram from Number 10.'

I was cornered. The little Portuguese (for the whole of my time as Minister for Trade I am going to find myself, at every international conference where the participating countries are identified in French – *Royaume Uni* – sitting next to a little Portuguese) was coming to his peroration.

Not, really, that it makes the slightest difference to the conclusions of a meeting what Ministers say at it. Everything is decided, horse-traded off, by officials at COREPER, the Council of Permanent Representatives. The Ministers arrive on the scene at the last minute, hot, tired, ill, or drunk (sometimes all of these together), read out their piece, and depart.

Strange, really. Because the EC constitution is quite well drawn. The Council of Ministers is sovereign, and can/could boss COREPER around. But, as always in politics everywhere, democratic or autocratic, it's the chaps on the spot who call the shot.

The civil servants beaver away, massage and congratulate each other, while the politicians treat attendance as a chore.

Now what I should have done – what every Minister should have been doing is – after the 'Conference', to call the officials in, get fully briefed on the next subjects to come before COREPER, and instruct *them* on *their* 'Line to Take'. So that, in good time, the Minister would know what was happening, what had been conceded, what was still open to play for.

But no, I was bundled off – Phew, that's him out of the way for a
bit – and took a bumpy little Fokker to Paris, to link up with an Air
France flight to Heathrow and straight back to the Department for a
bit of late pressure and a nice full 'In' tray.

At de Gaulle I forced Matthew to buy omelette and chips from
the airport *frite*, which we consumed in the company of a cross black
man and two incredible, showdykes.

Then the pleasing Airbus – always so much nicer than the baby
Boeings – but spoiled by the Air France personnel, who are odious.
Grumpy in deportment, lumpy in appearance. At the end of a flight
the BA girls always line up at the door and say 'Thank you' (and they
must get quite a quota of leers and sneers) and it *is* pleasant, although
I myself am often guilty of snubbing them if my mood is foul, or
preoccupied. The AF crew just scowl at you in silence.

Albany   *Sunday, 2 March*

I loathe London on Sunday evenings, but today Jane and I were
lunching with Willie at Dorneywood.[1] She has gone on down to
Saltwood while I stay here to blitz the boxes, and tomorrow make a
dawn raid (which, as it will be a Monday, the office will not be
expecting).

I am really *in the Government* now. A completely different status
and experience from the days of 'Parly Sec' with the officials either
patronising or incredulous; journalists and colleagues alike regarding
it as a fluke, liable to end with a bump, at any moment. Now
officials (and Ambassadors) are curious but, in their varying degrees,
deferential. All the accoutrements – attitude of the Whips, of (with
wide variations) ministerial colleagues, drivers, policemen, journalists – are enhanced. I have a huge airy office, and, at last, *interesting
boxes*.

It is deliciously enjoyable, and I feel full of adrenalin most of the
time, although conscious that I am draining the substance. My hair is,
at last, thinning and beginning to show grey.

---

[1] Dorneywood, near Burnham in Buckinghamshire, the mansion left by Lord Cour-
    tauld-Thomson for the use of a senior Government Minister, at the discretion of
    the PM.

Dorneywood is a dreary red brick house in flat country much,
and I would guess expensively, built over. Inside, though, the furniture
is good. Pictures medium only, but some amusing ('amusing' means
'erotic' doesn't it, in an auctioneers' catalogue description, and they
are only mildly that) murals by Rex Whistler. A lot of decent
porcelain – mainly Wedgwood.

Lord Courtauld-Thomson looked down from the wall upon the
lunch guests. I told Cecilia Whitelaw that his father had perished
in the R 101 at Beauvais in 1932. (Or was I mistaken? Certainly
a Secretary of State for Air at this time carried the same name.)
Curiously, she didn't seem aware of this. And that his last radio message had been on the 'just-opened-our-fourth-bottle-of-Kummel'
lines.

This made James Hanson, sitting on my right, splutter.[1] He and I
got on well, letting our hair down rapidly and using 'fuck', 'arsehole'
and 'shit' all too freely, although Cecilia gamely pretended not to
hear. Poor Swinton, opposite, who used to be fat and objectionable
is now diminished, having lost six stone (!) and is quiet-spoken and
polite.[2]

After lunch the girls separated and Willie, pretty watery-eyed,
boomed away about the Land-Rover balls-up.[3] Too extraordinary
that no one told him about it until four days before the announcement. Yet I issued a warning minute to the whole of DE on
17 September last year. And I clearly remember thinking then that
really I ought to slip a copy to Willie. I funked it as not having the
rank or responsibility, and that he might think I was up to my sneaky
ways.

But I always welcome confirmation of my infallible eye for what
is or is not *political*.

Willie was very good about the need to *help* the PM see, in some
situations, that there were other possibilities; excising her (erroneous)
belief that if she threw her personal weight behind something it would

[1] James Hanson (Life Peer, 1983). Chairman of Hanson plc since 1965.
[2] Earl of Swinton (2nd Earl). Deputy Government Whip in the Lords.
[3] There was a tentative bid on the table for the former British Motor Corporation
from Ford. AC had seen that one of the consequences would be that the
ownership of Land-Rover would fall into US hands. When the bid became
substantive this possibility gave rise to consternation among some members of
the Cabinet.

always go through. Willie said that the PM's Private Office was greatly diminished by the loss of Robin Butler.[1]

Willie said that Nigel Wicks 'will be (sic) very good ... is very good ... BUT' – a marvellous Willyism. Everyone says Wicks is useless. The great man was also extremely funny, giving imitations of the juniors in the PM's outer Private Office. Little creeps and OBN-ers.

After Hanson had clattered off in his helicopter Willie took me on one side and said that I was *always* to contact him *immediately* if there was 'anything I wanted to talk about', which pleased me greatly. Also at the lunch was Woodrow Wyatt.[2] With the exception of Macmillan (and *he* does it on purpose) Woodrow is the only person I know who seems to be more ga-ga than he is. And the dreadful Henry Plumb,[3] who Jane said was just as flatulent and pleased with himself as always.

Department of Trade and Industry   *Thursday, 6 March*

Last night Tristan called me out of the lobby and said that the FCO were already making trouble. 'Uh?' A report had gone in saying that I was 'anti-European'.

It can only have been that fucking Ambassador in Luxembourg. I said that I was trying to humour his great plain wife, whom Peter had warned me (rightly) tried to shock the dinner guests. Tristan nodded gloomily. Once a report is in, it's in. That's why, if you're *really* ambitious, you have to be cagey.

Apparently the report has also gone to UKREP, who are worried about the way I am going to chair the Internal Market Council. Cunts. Of course I will be perfectly OK.

But this bloody Presidency does hang over me.[4]

---

[1] Robin Butler, after three years as Principal Private Secretary to the Prime Minister had moved in 1985 to the Treasury as Second Permanent Secretary, Public Expenditure.

[2] Sir Woodrow Wyatt, journalist and businessman (printing) and for twenty years a Labour MP. Now a Conservative and Chairman of the Horserace Totalisator Board. Elevated to the Lords as a Life Peer in 1987.

[3] Sir Henry Plumb, farmer (President of National Farmers Union, 1970–9); MEP, Cotswolds, since 1979. Elevated to the Lords as a Life Peer in 1987.

[4] The member states of the European Community rotate through the office of President every six months. During a country's Presidency each Minister chairs the Council at Brussels that accords most closely with their domestic responsibility.

At lunchtime today in came a couple of Euro-MPs who apparently cut ice, Ben Patterson[1] and Basil de Ferranti.[2] Patterson I remember from the Westminster Candidates circus in the old days. Like many who failed the Constituency Selection process he opted (after a spell in the CCO library) to join the 'Euro Parliament'.

Ferranti looked ghastly, pale yellow. And I could not remember whether it was him staying in Mark Birley's chalet at Verbier in 1966, and drinking 'Bull-Shots', or another, blackish sheep called Sebastian. Or whether, indeed, they are not the same person?

The two of them were totally consumed with it all, and knew the jargon backwards. Tiredly I listened, thinking what irrelevant balls.

Perhaps it showed, because from time to time I could see a mischievous half smile cross Matthew's features.

British Embassy, Brussels   *Monday, 10 March*

Comfortable here; pleasant, ex-Rothschild town house. A long, curiously narrow entrance hall, then a wide staircase with important pictures of a Salvator Rosa-ish kind hanging sombrely.

There is a little time before dinner and I prowl about my bedroom looking gloomily at the heavy mahogany furniture. I open the big, cupboard-shaped windows, and look at the clear spring sky and hear the birds sing to one another as they settle for the evening, 'going to bed'.

Today I talked to other Ministers – my counterparts – and got my way with officials.

But in the long mirrors I see myself jowelly and puffed. My shoulder muscles have almost gone.

How I pine for that long, long youth that I enjoyed! To leap and stride – with every new encounter a joy of *possibility*. The 'sluice of hearing and seeing'[3] that endured for so long.

Now, I suppose, in the timescale of my life, I am in the last week

---

[1] Ben Paterson, MEP, Kent West, since 1979.
[2] Tragically Basil de Ferranti was at the time (unknown to AC) suffering from liver cancer and subsequently died. His elder brother, Sebastian Basil de Ferranti, was former Chairman of Ferranti plc; a director of GEC plc since 1982.
[3] Louis MacNeice.

of a holiday – or however the analogy should be shaped – a Sunday afternoon. By Thursday, I will have to start 'packing'.

Boy has asked for a 'Mandat' to handle the Kiosk. I can hardly refuse. I go to Zermatt less and less now. But I have never been happier than I was at the Chalet. Although I came close to it when I used to call at the Guinness pub in West Lavington after walking the beagles on Salisbury Plain. Pure happiness. Everything was so perfect then, and I will always remember it, and thank God.

Palace Hotel, Helsinki   *Saturday, 27 September*

Got here today, pointlessly, unnecessarily early. Dave had driven me to Heathrow from Saltwood on a beautiful morning of late September through that wonderful rich countryside, polo at Cowdray Park, that rolls along both banks of the M25 on the Gatwick stretch. I didn't feel nostalgic or depressed; more kind of depersonalised. What *am* I doing? Why am I going out on the weekend?

These Nordic tours are a complete fuckface, redeemed only by the girls, so blonde blonde, so clean and, at first sight, so correct. Already a clear-skinned beauty has answered my call for room service.

But, as always, I am no more than a voyeur. Officials hover outside the door. Privileged prisoner.

The little Ambassador met me. All the usual stuff about they're very punctual, you must stay to the end, you know about the custom of speaking at meals, of course, it's rude to drink without raising your glass to someone at the table (I'm not going to touch the fucking stuff, I thought grimly) and of course if anyone catches your eye and raises their glass at you you must respond.

God knows what's going to happen tomorrow. A kind of 'getting to know you' day has been laid on, with fishing on the lakes, drinking schnapps and (I don't like the sound of this *at all*) a sauna. Doesn't everyone wander about sweating, but naked? I can't even urinate if someone else comes into the gents – which, I seem to remember, is *such* a bad sign that, if admitted, it could get you a discharge from the Army as being a moral danger to your brothers in arms.

Perhaps it's something to do with Eton?

But I don't in the least mind letting girls see my penis. I suppose it is because I fear – for quite extraneous physical reasons – becoming lightly, or indeed heavily, tumescent and attracting the attention of other men, either whose curiosity or disapproval being equally unwelcome.

It's incredibly cold. I went for a walk along the Quays, and over to a great Sally Line Baltic ferry, wearing every single article of clothing that I had brought with me – cardigan, muffler, David Owen mac, Citroën cap, gloves – and still got chilled ear canals, so that I lose my balance. This condition, I know from experience, can last a couple of hours or so, and people think you are tight.

Also Jane left the hotty out of my luggage, which could be a bore when I go to bed.

All the same, I like the Finns. They are serious, and straightforward. Like Germans, but without the sinister streak.

And there is not a Club Med to be seen anywhere. Still less a 'Heavy Suntan'.

I said to the Interior Minister, 'What is your immigration policy?'
'We don't have one.'
'Can anyone come into the country, then?'
'Sure. But there's just one thing . . . '
'What's that?'
'They have to look like us. Just like Finns.'
And he burst out laughing.

British Embassy, Belgrade   *Wednesday, 15 October*

They cram my diary so tight that even *forty seconds* is precious. And this makes me ill-tempered. So that I am rude to Embassy staff (though never to the minions, who are amiable and do their best), and to 'Businessmen', especially the cocky ones. Last night there was a great big red-faced one from Davy McKee,[1] calling all the shots, being deferred to. But my feeling is that he could go belly-up at any moment, and gave him short shrift.

We had a 'day off', although even here the schedule was drum taut. The 'Jugs' (a Thirties expression, I remember my parents using it, and think it came from Oliver Lyttelton) flew me to Sarajevo. A

---

[1] A publicly quoted (at that time) engineering company.

Lear – they are always fabulous on take-off, the Lears – flown by two uniformed and identical dwarves with a young and dissolute-looking navigator. We *just* got in through a gap in the early morning fog. The approach was frightening, with a few Bosnian 'Munro's' peeping up through a flat blanket of cotton wool.

Then, standard draining session with various local dignitaries before a very fattening lunch.

But I began to enjoy myself, having insisted (and being thought eccentric, even by my own Private Office, while the Embassy did their best to put me off) that we foregather in the very hotel where the Archduke Franz Ferdinand stayed his last night, and whence he journeyed into the city. Not only that. But after lunch we ourselves had to follow his *exact* route to the very point of his assassination.

It was quite short. We followed the tram lines, still there, having been laid, I suppose, at the turn of the century. And soon I was standing on the corner where Princip[1] had waited – totally unchanged in scale and dimension; pave, granite kerbstones.

This was where the 'old coachman', gaga Czech chauffeur, had taken a wrong turning (or did he do it on purpose? A line of enquiry that has been insufficiently pursued) and gratingly engaged reverse gear. For more than a few seconds the car must have been stationary.

And then the shots, at point blank range.

I could still smell it, just as one can in a haunted room. A colossal, seismic charge of diabolic energy had been blown, released on that very spot some seventy-two years ago, and drawn its awful price.

> Not in the hands of boys, but in their eyes
> Shall shine the holy glimmer of goodbyes.[2]

Nearby was the little Princip museum, showing the youth to be exactly as I would expect. Tiresome, ego, mare-eyed, consumptive-looking. Something between Seventies CND and Baader-Meinhof.

Afterwards I was taken to the old Muslim Quartier. And I smelt here in the market for the first time that authentic Balkan tang – incense and bad fat. Sausages always frying. The women are hideous. Squat, moustachio'd and without shape.

---

[1] Gavrilo Princip, whose assassination in Sarajevo of Archduke Francis Ferdinand, heir to Emperor Francis joseph of Austria, and his morganatic wife, Countess Sophia Chotek, on 28 June 1914 precipitated the First World War.

[2] Wilfred Owen, 'Anthem for Doomed Youth'.

British Embassy, Budapest   *Friday, 17 October*

I was on the step yesterday, I can't think how. Knowing it was the last
lap perhaps – because today we are clear, with a pleasant-sounding
trip ahead of us to the great nature reserve at Lake Kiskunság.

I was forced into round after round of meetings, straight from the
aircraft. No time even to pee (always a favourite ploy of civil servants
who, as is known, have fibre-glass bladders). But I sparkled, gabbled
pressingly. Seven conclaves in succession and I was glad to see that by
about five in the evening the interpreter took every opportunity to
'rest his eyes', and his head was nodding.

At dinner I sat next to the head of the National Bank, named
Fekete. Very good company, a bankers' banker – stout, slow of speech,
heavily Hungarian-accented, deeply pessimistic and cynical.

There is a certain vocabulary, a language that outside the profession
only very rich people use: LIBOR, COMEX, the Long Bond curve.
Ministers don't get any of that stuff in Treasury briefs. But Fekete and
I were comfortable with each other. We went through the whole
world scene considering 'possibilities'. In the end, concluding that
Zurich, the good old Swiss Franc, was the only place. Perhaps a bit
of Sandoz, or Brown Boveri.

Fekete told me a wry tale of when Kádár[1] had invited him to join
the Government as Finance Minister.

'János, you ought to know that I played a part, as a boy, in the '56
uprising. There may be papers on file, photographs.'

'My dear fellow – what *does* that matter these days?'

'And also that my mother has Jewish blood . . . '

'Quite unimportant. Quite unimportant.'

Kádár paused for a little while, stroking his chin, then, 'What was
that you were telling me about the '56?'

Earlier, at the reception, I had paid too much attention to one of
the Hungarian ladies. Her skin was almost greasy, but beautiful nipples
showed through her satin blouse. She curtsied and shimmied most
pleasingly when we were introduced, and called me 'Minister' in
exhalation – always erotic.

Now the car is coming to pick us up for a day in the care of

---

[1] János Kádár. As head of the Hungarian Socialist Workers' Party he suppressed the
Hungarian Uprising of 1956 with the aid of Russian troops. Twice Prime
Minister, he remained Party General Secretary until 1988.

Dr Bánkuri, the engaging and well-informed curator of the nature reserve, who has already pleased me by revealing his knowledge of Loch Eriboll and its importance as a staging point for northerly migrants. How delicious it will be to breathe fresh air for nearly all of the day.

Saltwood   *Saturday, 18 October*

Odiously, there were three boxes in the car at Heathrow. Several e.g.s of civil servants trying to backslide while I was away.

Here, poor Jane had a tummy upset; Andrew was being prosecuted for careless driving. Brodies have lost ground in the dispute with Anson's nephew over Ardneackie, and Bird & Bird have produced a hopelessly pessimistic opinion on our proposed action against Southern Water.

I look appalling in the mirror. So puffy and pink around the eyes – plainly pre-cancerous.

House of Commons   *Tuesday, 18 November*

I have been cross and snappy all day in the office.

A tedious Businessmen's lunch at the Stafford Hotel (I suppose I am too hard on them sometimes, poor dears. Is it diffidence, or just *thickness* that makes them so dreary as company? Their French and German counterparts are keen and quick and curious, and always stimulating to talk to. Perhaps it's just another variant of always preferring other MP's constituents to one's own.)

By the afternoon I was acid-feeling, and when I was kept waiting thirty-five minutes outside a BOTB meeting I thought, and said, fuck this, and just walked off. Officials were oggly, but impressed.

So I am over here, taking refuge. I did a quick trawl, to see if there was anyone sympathetic around, but it was a bad time of the afternoon. There are a multitude of telephones scattered around the Palace, in all the nooks and crannies adjoining the corridors. Every one of them, it seemed, had an MP crouched over it, pompously pontificating. It is the hour when one must catch the deadline for the local paper.

Most of them are buffers, or demi-buffers, or *buffers-aspirant*. They amount to nothing.

I couldn't go back to being a backbencher. It's so completely artificial. What democratic overheads we carry in our system of Government!

Also, I am soft-spoken and apprehensive about going on *Question Time* this week. In addition to my inability, in practically every instance, to answer a direct question from Robin Day on 'But what is the Govt's position on ... ?' lines, I am on a hiding to nothing generally.

Whatever I do they'll get me. If I am grave and responsible, they'll say, 'Hasn't he gone off?' If I'm jaunty and reckless, it'll be, 'There he goes again, another gaffe.'

Interesting, that word 'gaffe'. Three-quarters of the journalists who use it don't, for a start, know what it means. It's monosyllabic, which is a help of course, to the Editor; and, to them, it signifies 'soundbite', or 'unpalatable truth'. A true gaffe is accidental. Mine never are. I like to shock, and I do it (though not as often as I could) deliberately.

Department of Trade and Industry   *Wednesday, 19 November*

Why is it that the coffee, quite discreetly served at Number 10, is so markedly better than the muck dished up, by defiant and oopsy-la trouts, at DE and DTI?

We were hanging around in the ante-room. The subject was to be Hong-Kong Transitional Arrangements, and the PM had circulated, through Charles Powell,[1] a scathing note about the 'flabby' suggestions that had come up from the Foreign Office.

Little Howe was padding about, lobbying. 'What we've really got to try and do is to prevent the PM discussing this whole thing *episodically.*'

She looked very *fatigué*. Her voice was flat-soft, but with a hint of impatience (further shades of B'mama).

Inevitably, her mastery of the brief is better than anyone else in

---

[1] Charles Powell, diplomat. Private Secretary to the Prime Minister since 1984.

the room, including the 'sponsoring' Department. She did let fall one aphorism – an aside, almost, but clearly from the heart.

'I've learned one thing in politics. You don't take a decision until you have to.'

Saltwood   *Friday, 26 December*

Boxing Day. We were over at the Garden House for drinks and a cold buffet. The Hubbards are staying with Celly, together with their daughter Katie, a real dish. Also in the house was Sam,[1] and Nanny came across from Quince. Col came down in his new(ish) Rolls, painted metallescent gold (or Jewish Racing Yellow, as apparently this colour is termed in the Mess at Knightsbridge). With him was Ming, and teensy weensy little Christopher.[2]

This practice of families coalescing (coagulating?) at Christmastide is OK, I suppose, but tempers can fray. The young people formed a separate group after a bit, and their laughs became loud. Then, through that big 'picture' window in the sitting room, we suddenly saw Col's Rolls, with Andrew at the wheel, James beside him wearing a silly grin, *slewing* on the lawn. The car got stuck in the big rose bed, burying itself deep, with spinning wheels.

The 'grown-ups' went for a walk, leaving the young to clear up. But when we returned their task had been discharged only imperfectly. They had drunk three-quarters of a bottle of akvavit (on top of everything else) which they had 'found' – a Christmas present from the Finnish Ambassador to me. How *do* they manage to take in so much alcohol? Both passed out in chairs in the Green Room when we got back here. But a few minutes ago, having 'come round', they were talking about going 'out', and not being back until around midnight. Oh dear.

I should be writing a résumé of the year, it is only a month off the anniversary of my appointment, but I too am muzzy and maudlin, from champagne followed by good burgundy.

[1] Sam, son of AC's sister Colette (Celly).
[2] Christopher, son of AC's brother Colin, by his third wife Helena (Ming).

I look back on a period of great and continuous pressure – travel, paperwork, schedules of a scale and complexity which I would never have regarded as tolerable if I had been warned in, say, 1971, when it was a great burden even to dress up and go over to Havant[1] for a 'function'. So many miles from those utterly carefree days when I used to take the beagles in the 2CV to Salisbury Plain, and drink a pint of Guinness in the pub at West Lavington before driving back along that flat road to Seend where Alex Moulton[2] used to test his big 'bikes, and past the Worton blondes, back to a supper of sweet Hungarian vegetables cooked by Anna Koumar. I still live off the physical capital accumulated during those middle years when my contemporaries were cooped up in fetid rooms, drinking at mid-day and going late to bed.

I am in better shape than all of them, still.

But what have I achieved, as Minister for Trade, this last year? Tightened up the MFA,[3] got a good mark for boosting the internal market. I've managed to get a few signals through to the Lady to show that I still exist.

A reasonable rapport there, although it can be dissipated in a trice.

A mildly amusing side-effect. I used to be so frightened of flying. Now, I no more notice it than I do taking the cable car to Trockener Steg[4] (come to think, I used to find that alarming until I got accustomed to it). Last year I made (including helicopters) 156 landings. Among them Brussels, Luxembourg, Paris, Bonn, Strasbourg, The Hague, Geneva, Rome, Lisbon, Budapest, Belgrade, Athens, Bahrain, Amman, Bagdhad, Singapore, Perth, Sidney, Melbourne, Canberra, Mackay (and grass strips), Auckland, Wellington, Pt Moresby, Tokyo, Hong Kong, Seoul, Oman, and Inverness.

Travel! When I was first appointed everyone said how lucky I was, being able to go to all these places. I suppose so, if you can't afford the ticket. But that's never been a problem for me. And, in any case, I haven't been a traveller – just a zombie in invisible hand-cuffs.

---

[1] In the early Seventies there was some possibility of AC being adopted as Conservative candidate for the safe seat of Havant and Waterloo.

[2] Alex Moulton, designer of the innovative Moulton bicycles, and rubber suspensions for the motor industry.

[3] The 'Multi-Fibre Arrangement', a form of treaty which protected the UK textile industry.

[4] A ski-station above Zermatt, served by a very long cable-car run.

1987

1987

The ground is dormant at present, with only a few snowdrops and early crocuses showing. For most of the day we were along the woodland walk, raking and pruning. The rake collects huge piles of dead grass, twigs and brambles, and we had several fires going.

Just after tea Peter M. rang with the news that poor Robin Cooke[1] had died. Robin was two years younger than me, and on occasion could look really quite youthful. He had been in the House for an eternity, having come in on a by-election in the first year of Macmillan's premiership. Robin overlapped even with Chips – who was himself by then bright red in the face and (as he candidly admits) feeling ghastly.

What was pleasing, and admirable, about Robin was his exceedingly blasé approach. He had a safe seat, but slowly ran the majority down from neglect, and by the Eighties his Association had got sick of him. His wife, Jenny, was bright and birdlike. And with his sardonic interrogatory style he could sometimes, on returning for the weekend, reduce her to tears. Jenny was née King and her father, a nasty old buffer who in former times had been a member of the Labour Party and a *headmaster* (it always shows), had changed sides and got elected for the safe seat of Dorset South.[2] When he retired (far too late; he was the same age as my father) it was intended that Robin should slip 'sideways', out of the clutches of the Bristol Conservatives, and start again.

But the plan went wrong – they always do – and Robert Cranborne was selected.[3] Probably better, all in all. But for Robin it was a sad blow. He had served notice on the Bristol Division, and could hardly retract. He was (ludicrous phrase, first amusingly, indeed indecently, deployed in my hearing by Archie Balfour) *between two stools*.

I am a great believer in the adage that deep disappointment can

---

[1] Sir Robert (Robin) Cooke represented Bristol West, 1957–79. At the time of his death he lived at Athelhampton near Dorchester.

[2] Evelyn King, Headmaster of Clayesmore School, 1935–50, doubling 1945–50 as Labour MP for Penryn and Falmouth. He resigned from the Labour Party the following year, joined the Conservatives and represented Dorset South, 1964–79.

[3] Robert, Viscount Cranborne, heir to the Marquess of Salisbury, succeeded Evelyn King as MP for Dorset South and would stand down at the General Election later in the year.

trigger a terminal illness. And I have no doubt that this was what happened with Robin. And worse was to come. Although he was a tremendous supporter of Mrs T. and part of her close Election team in 1983, she lost her nerve at the last moment. Robin, with all his special knowledge and feeling for the Palace of Westminster and his work for the Heritage, should have gone straight to the Lords. But he must needs console himself with a K which had, in any case, been his due for several years.

He was a great gardener, and personally used to cut the yew trees at Athelhampton every year, from tall and perilous-looking special ladders.

MPs die in batches. Just when one thinks that foul air, bad diet, unlimited alcohol and late nights ought surely to be exacting a higher toll, the Almighty springs a surprise. David Penhaligon was killed in a car smash over Christmastide.[1] And Number 10 have just been on the phone. Would I represent the Prime Minister at his memorial service in Truro Cathedral on *Saturday* (ugh) of this weekend.

What a bore. It's a long and tedious journey, that rail stretch after Plymouth. I won't even have time to dismount and make a splash on Plymouth Sound.

Still, always fun to represent the Prime Minister doing anything.

Truro-Paddington train   *Saturday, 10 January*

I have been talking with poor old Jeremy Thorpe.[2] He was sitting alone in the dining car, at one of the head-to-head double tables, being ostentatiously ignored by the Liberals who mill around, drab but noisy, and seem to have taken over the whole train. There is a hint of relief on this, the return journey, and drinks are being called for, and 'tossed off', as my mother used to say.

Jeremy has Parkinson's Disease, quite advanced, and looks gaunt, with staring eyes. He was pleased to have attention and, pathetically, tried to hold on to his right hand in order to prevent it trembling.

---

[1] David Penhaligon, Liberal MP for Truro since 1974.
[2] Jeremy Thorpe, MP for Devon North, 1959–79 and Leader of the Liberal Party, 1967–76.

I tried to get him to reminisce a little, tell a few Macmillan stories. But he did not find it easy to speak. The listener must concentrate hard. I reminded Jeremy of his peak moment of glory and, had he played his cards differently, of power, when the 'hung' results of the Election of February '74 were in, and Ted tried to do a deal, offering him the Home Office. Jeremy was barely intelligible, but his eyes were full of pain.

The Cathedral had been full to the aisles, with crowds outside in the streets and closed-circuit broadcasting. Personally I don't see what all the fuss was about. P. was an unmemorable figure really, with his (demi-bogus) West-Country vowels and *homespun* philosophy. But he personified, I suppose, a kind of soft-centre Cornish provincialism.

Come to think of it, he had something of a dud, down, down-market Jock Massareene,[1] who was at Saltwood yesterday and stood about uselessly while Jane caught and shrouded (a difficult and painful task) some peafowl that he needed, to replace casualties at Chilham.

Albany   *Tuesday, 27 January*

Sometimes there is just so much pressure at Saltwood that it is a relief to sink into the cushions, stale and dirty though they may be, of the Sandling train. For an hour and a half I am isolated, trundling along, and no one can get at me with a will-you, can-you, did-you, have-you, are-you, if-you, but-you? three bags full, query. But it's a kind of cop out, really, because I leave it all on Jane's lap, then ring in the evenings and bark at her.

I must be very near a nervous breakdown. The tower office [at Saltwood] is so bad that I dare not lift any stone there, for fear of what I may find underneath. And last night I dreamed – just before waking, always the most vivid kind – that I had hailed a taxi, then could not remember my intended destination.

This evening the Prime Minister came to the '92 dinner at the St

---

[1] John Clotworthy Talbot Foster Whyte-Melville Skeffington, Viscount Massareene and Ferrard, of Chilham Castle.

Stephen's Club. How déjà-vu it all seemed. Backbenchers bobbing
up and down, trying to be goodboy. Same old subjects grinding round
and round. Afterwards, I told Jane, I never want to be a backbencher
again and will get out immediately I am sacked.

Even dear IG, next to whom I sat, was distrait and low. He basted
me for not having chosen a PPS. Ian said, with much truth, that no
one in any Government Department knows, or cares (except when it
causes them trouble) about the House of Commons, and a PPS would
keep me in touch.

Possibly. But I prefer to get my gossip over a bottle of wine with
Budgen, or others.

Department of Trade and Industry   *Tuesday, 10 February*

Just back from Harold Macmillan's memorial service in the Abbey.[1] I
am filled with melancholy.

The Grenadiers' Return was played, and I thought of the fife
music, and of the decimated battalion marching back in from Hulluch
on 26 September 1915, past the wounded laid out in rows on either
side of the street, groaning from their injuries. And the young classical
scholar, less than a year out of Eton, pale and shaken but heroic,
nonetheless. When Macmillan enlisted Britain was at the very height
of her power and dominion. The habitual bearing, stoicism, self-
sacrifice, sense of 'fair play'; the whole *tenu* of the English upper class
was in place and unquestioned, looked up to and copied everywhere.
Now look at us – and them!

Julian Amery read the second lesson. His voice, which still can
command the attention even of a crowded House (for the very reason,
I think, because it is so genuinely cast in the tones of the olden
days, without self-parody and unlike, for example, the embarrassing
plumminess of Derek Walker-Smith) has lost a little of its timbre. I
nostalgicised for government by the upper class; which is what I
thought it would be – the whole thing really run by the OE mafia –
when first I wanted to get in in 1964, and Julian and I had a long
conversation at the Chalet and he said I was too old. I did just, *just*, I

---

[1] Harold Macmillan, 1st Earl of Stockton, had died aged ninety-two.

suppose overlap. But by the time that Ted had got rid of Alec he was determined to keep all the others out if he could.

And who is to blame him? Profumo exposed their essential rottenness.[1] The few who remain – Gilmour, Whitelaw, Carrington – are impossibly defeatist. With the exception, I think the *sole* exception, of Robert Cranborne the real toffs have opted out. A few garden openings like Charlie Shelburne,[2] otherwise they're just into tax avoidance and gossip columns. I looked up at the great circular window, to which I have raised my eyes at so many services, and thought, I must – *when* will I – write my great work, *Tories and the Nation State 1922–74*. Perhaps it is for this that I will be remembered? If I am spared.

Department of Trade and Industry   *Tuesday, 24 March*

Last night Heseltine, a bit flushed-looking, came up to me when we were going through the Aye lobby, and leered.

'Have I lost you your seat?'[3]

'Could be,' I shrugged. 'Could be.'

'Never mind. I'll write you a letter of apology.'

Odd. Unlike him. Many others would have found such behaviour disagreeable.

Saltwood   *Sunday, 5 April*

Had a bad, overhot night, which can often happen if one goes to bed too early. Two strange dreams, with which, I would guess, a soothsayer could have little difficulty. First, something muddled about the delib-

---

[1] In the closing phase of the 1959–63 Macmillan premiership, the War Minister, Jack Profumo, who was married to the actress Valerie Hobson, had become involved with a young lady who was also enjoying the attentions of the Soviet Military attaché.

[2] Charles Maurice Petty-Fitzmaurice, Earl of Shelburne, heir to the Marquess of Lansdowne, of Bowood House, Calne.

[3] Michael Heseltine had just announced his plans to 'privatise' the Royal Naval Dockyards in Plymouth.

erate infection of surgical instruments by 'sufferers'. Woke, muck-sweat, walked about. Stood at the open window.

Then, of finding a beautiful fountain pen, an old-style Parker, which wrote exquisitely. It was like a fabulous skiing sequence, when the moguls rise and fall in rhythm.

At mid-day the sun was high and we got the tortoises out of hibernation. I lay on my back on the freshly cut grass in Courtenays, looking at the sky, hearing the slow deliberate rustle as they emerged from their straw-lined boxes to a meal of tomato and sliced banana. Fortunate creatures. If humans could do this at will we, too, would live to be two hundred years old.

Department of Trade and Industry   *Tuesday, 14 April*

I am feeling sickish and tired. Is my lymphatic system packing up?

I have just returned (on foot) from a thoroughly unsatisfactory meeting with Tim Renton at the Foreign Office. Henry Keswick[1] had asked me to put in a word for British contractors, who are being edged out of various important deals in Hong Kong disgracefully, in some cases where the Crown is itself the customer.

Downstairs the desk had made a balls-up of the times, and I hung around, getting cross. Senior Ministers shouldn't be kept waiting, except in the comfort of special rooms set aside for the purpose. Was it always like this in the entrance hall, with ugly common people cackling and shouting and banging things? Probably yes.

On the first floor the rooms have very high ceilings. They must be double cubes. And the furniture is still good and heavy. Tim explained to me, effectively, that Hong Kong had 'gone'. UK influence in matters of this kind was nil. Autonomy, 'LegCo', 'ExCo', Chinese susceptibilities, all have 'to be taken very carefully into consideration'.

One more piece of wealth and real estate that has been allowed just to run through our fingers.

Through the anti-shatter lace curtains I watched some pigeons chasing each other along the balustrade.

---

[1] Henry Keswick, influential director of several Hong Kong businesses, not least Jardine, Matheson.

'It's not 1935,' I said, thinking of all these white-painted ships on the China Station which I used to memorise from the *Jane*'s of that year, the first in which I was given the book.

'No. Not even 1975.'

I lost interest in what he was saying.

Very little of the decor can have been changed in that room for many moons, and I wondered how many tricky subjects, gloomy 'meetings', unwelcome decisions had been played out there down the years.

I am blighted by the Foreign Office at present. Earlier today a creepy official, who is 'in charge' (heaven help us) of South America, came over to brief me ahead of my trip to Chile. All crap about Human Rights. Not one word about the UK interest; how we saw the balance, prospects, pitfalls, opportunities in the Hemisphere.

I'm Minister for Trade, for Christ's sake, what's the point of keeping an expensive mission in Santiago if they can't even tell me what to push? When I questioned him, he was evasive on all policy matters other than his own tenacious, *Guardian*esque obsession.

'Aha but,' soft-spokenly he gloated, 'Community policy is' we are but one in twelve, etc.

What *does* he mean? There is no exclusive 'Community Competence' in Foreign Affairs (yet!). I don't think that there is even a Foreign Affairs Commissioner, is there? This man is exactly the kind of mole who is working away, eighteen hours a day, to extinguish the British national identity.

I am depressed, and zestfree.

General Election, 11 June 1987:
Conservative, 375; Labour, 229; Alliance, 22.

Saltwood   *Wednesday, 17 June*

Tired and liverish with *reaction*. First day back at the House, and I was to rendez-vous with Soames in the smoking room for lunch.

Everyone very jolly – most had increased their majorities, although

a few seemed to know I hadn't.[1] Jopling was in splendid form, grinning
benevolently.[2] After being sacked, or 'dropped', that's really the only
way – show your face in the smoking room at once – and mix it with
the boys. (Whether I shall ever be able to do that is, I fear, extremely
doubtful.) He'd always wanted Agriculture, and of course he was
good with the farmers – the real ones anyway. But more and more
the people who call the shots on the NFU are the nasty, computer-
driven 'barons', who drench everything with nitrates and rip off the
CAP. Thus, *mutatis mutandis*, Ministers don't spend their time any
longer in tweed suits scratching pigs at county shows, but cooped up
in the Charlemagne arguing with their 'counterparts' about the Green
Pound. Hats off to him, though. Like most Chief Whips he knew
who the shits were. Memorable remark about Heseltine: 'The trouble
with Michael is that he had to buy all his furniture.' Snobby, but
cutting. He and Gail (so pretty with her red hair and lovely skin) take
their holidays in France, in leathers, on an old Honda. Now that *is*
sporting.

As for myself – was I being unduly paranoiac in detecting a frisson
of disapproval? Certainly Government colleagues – Renton, Baker,
Mitchell, Patten J. – all in their different ways radiated 'distancing'
and even John Wakeham, whose eye I had caught while we were
listening to the Queen's Commission in the Lords, seemed to be
saying, 'Phew, you really pushed it that time'.[3] That fat gossip Critchley
said something about 'rocking the boat' – rich coming from him.
Sometimes he affects the mantle of Bufton Tufton.

Soames was twitchy concerning his 'last chance', as the junior
Whips' appointments were being made at that moment.[4] And the
meal wasn't a great success as the top end of the dining room was full
and we had to sit among the Labour tables.

Atkins joined us in sour mood.[5] He's just been made a junior
Minister, at bottle-washer level, in my Department. He can't have
expected anything more, surely?

Anyhow, he slagged away at anyone who was mentioned, radiating

---

[1] AC's majority fell from 11,000 in 1983 to 4000, owing to the threat of redundancies
consequent on 'privatisation' of the dockyard (see entry for 24 March).
[2] Michael Jopling had been Minister of Agriculture for four years until the Election.
[3] A reference to an interview which AC gave during the Election campaign at which
he had poured scorn on the Channel Tunnel project.
[4] In fact Nicholas Soames became PPS to the Environment Secretary.
[5] Robert Atkins had been made Parliamentary Under-Secretary at Trade and Industry.

bitterness and frustration, while Soames fidgeted. Alternately Nicholas shouted greetings at Labour Members, most of whom were pretty crestfallen, or swivelled round, trying at long range to join in the conviviality at the other end of the room.

This was the first occasion that I had witnessed the whole ceremony, processing through to the Lords, listening to all the opening speeches, everything. It's 'theatre', I suppose, but dud theatre. Not *rep*, just dud theatre.

I drove back in the Range Rover with a few oddments from the office and a couple of Euston Road school pictures, including a Graham Bell, that I want to hang at Bratton. Very tired. The garden hasn't really recovered from our three-week absence during the campaign, and I doubt if it will now, this year. We're already halfway through. It was quite a shock when Jane reminded me that on this weekend falls the longest day.

Department of Trade and Industry   *Friday, 26 June*

Rose wanted to go to *Les Misérables*. Naturally there were no tickets. However a quick call to James Osborne and a couple of good stalls were whistled up through the show business underground, and I collected them from the major domo at Aspers' – who wouldn't take a tip.[1] I'm out of touch with these things. I suppose my humble £20 note was beneath him, like Arthur Lee refusing the Star of India for his work on the Civil Service Commission.

I haven't been inside a theatre for ages. How evocative is that smell – greasepaint, dust, scenery – that wafts out across the stalls when the curtain goes up. And how very tiresome and ego and generally oopsy-la are most of the audience (though not as bad, I must admit, at the Palace as at Covent Garden). On the way back, as we walked down Shaftesbury Avenue, everybody seemed to be staring. Women, in particular, were looking at Rose. Did they think they

---

[1] James Osborne, manager of the Curzon Club, at that time in the proprietorship of AC's old friend, John Aspinall.

'recognised' her? Or was it just prurient curiosity? Strange, and unusual.

We had a banquette at the Mirabelle. I kept looking sideways at Rose and thinking how remarkably pretty is her mouth; so cupidic, like those coquettish maidens hidden away in the upper corners of a Tintoretto ceiling. She wanted hock so I ordered a quite decent bottle of Gewürztraiminer. But just after it had been poured she sliced through whatever inanity I was saying and asked the wine waiter to bring some soda water, which she made him pour *on to* the delicious white wine. He was equal to this and didn't bat an eyelid, although I doubt if it happens very often in the Mirabelle.

'Very Byronic,' I said.

Saltwood   *Sunday, 28 June*

The first day of summer (!). We swept the Bailey of grass clippings. Probably the most back-breaking of all gardening jobs is picking them up, moistly resisting and getting into one's nose and ears; throwing them into the back of the Mehari as little puffs of breeze coming from nowhere on a completely still day blow flakes and flickings back in one's face. Then I helped Jane get a buddleia down from where it had been growing in the wall below my father's study window. Then got the pool pump working which, amazingly, it did without too much demur.

We had planned our first outside lunch, M. Goisot and a huge Brie, but forsook it to tend to a baby jackdaw who had got sump oil on his wings and (how, for God's sake?) torn off one of his legs below the knee joint. I thought he was a goner – how *could* he survive? But he had so much fight in him, and his lovely pale blue eyes were so lively that we had to try. Jane washed his wings and tail feathers, rinsing and re-rinsing the Fairy Liquid. He didn't seem to mind; positively enjoyed the warm whirrings of a hair-drier. We stuffed a couple of worms down his throat and left him to gain strength in a basket with a heat bulb glowing over. In no time he appeared to make a full recovery and later that evening, after being returned to the wild, actually *flew* from the sleeper pile to the yew tree by the long garage. Cheered by this, I started the Silver Ghost and went for a drive.

On a fine evening there are very few pleasures comparable to driving a light, open Ghost on country roads. Some will get it from waiting for salmon to take, in dark peat pools, but I am too impatient, and can't stand the midges. In a Ghost you waft along, high enough to look over people's hedges, noiseless enough (as was the original intention) to leave horses unscared. It started at once, of course, although I hadn't been near it since last November. No (*no*) modern car would have done this. Because the Rolls Royce Silver Ghost has – except for the magneto which sparks on a turn – not one single piece of electrical equipment. No battery (flat) or pumps (stuck) or solenoid (up the creek, Squire) or 'black box' (I'm afraid we're talking about a factory replacement unit, Sir, at £873 plus VAT). There are twenty-one separate actions, all of them involving beautifully crafted mechanical linkages, from turning on the gravity petrol feed to actually cranking the starting handle. And after they have been completed in the correct sequence it will – infallibly – fire on the first compression.

My car was built in an epoch when the Grand Fleet dominated the world's oceans. And under the bonnet, in the brass and the copper and the hugely overstrength componentry, there is much trace of marine influence. The factory record shows it going out to India, in Curzon's name (although I doubt he ever sat at the wheel).

Now the Grand Fleet is no more, and Lutyens's beautiful vistas in New Delhi have been overrun by shanty settlements. And yet, even when the Rolls was built brand new, 'there's something wrong with our bloody ships today'.[1]

It is the perennial problem, the need to arrest industrial decadence. At what point does the refusal of innovation overlap with the introduction of the 'black box'? – but not as an enhancement of quality, more a signpost to the soft life and 'shorter working hours'.

I drove for about forty minutes and on my return took a jug of iced lime juice and soda water to the music room where I played the piano, quite competently, until the light faded. A day filled with trivia, but *douceur de vivre* also.

---

[1] Admiral Beatty at Jutland when he lost three battlecruisers, due in part to the inferiority of their armour and the accuracy of the German fire-control systems.

Department of Trade and Industry   *Monday, 29 June*

So hot and thundery. I am feeling exceedingly tired and old. My papers suddenly seem to have got into a total mess. Fatally, I started the practice of having *two* 'In' trays, a priority, or urgent tray and a more dreary waiting-for-attention tray. The dreary one now towers massively, sometimes sliding over on to the 'Out' side which means unsigned papers go back out into Private Office. I just don't have the energy to cope with it. I am flaccid.

An East German trade delegation is in London at present. And it could largely, I suppose, be aversion to this evening's proposed happenings: a meeting with Herr Dr Reichelt, then (monstrously) following sharply on this *another* meeting with Herr Dr Reichelt with a Lancaster House reception ('I think we really must be on time, Minister') as backdrop. Then a massive formal dinner of welcome (for Herr Dr Reichelt). Interpreters. Speeches. Liqueurs? No thanks, etc.

At lunchtime I saw that randy little runt Ian Gladding trying to chat up Rose, and this made me cross.

Later I telephoned Jane and had a talk. She'd bathed.

'I'm so cross,' I said.

'You wouldn't be if you were down here.'

Too true. Ah well, only three weeks to go!

Saltwood   *Sunday, 19 July*

A social weekend at Saltwood. First to arrive (by train, naturally, I met him at Sandling Junction) was Peter Brooke,[1] in a lovely old tweed suit (ambient July temperature 70° plus) stooped and shuffling like a character from LP Hartley. He's so nice, gentle and clever. But almost too Balliol. I know Chesterfield said that one should never allow one's 'innate self' to show, but ...

Then the Worsthornes.[2] Perry not in an especially good temper;

---

[1] Peter Brooke, MP for City of London and Westminster South since 1977. Paymaster General since the Election.

[2] Peregrine Worsthorne and his first wife Claude. He had become Editor of *Sunday Telegraph* in 1986.

I had forgotten that David Young was originally meant to be coming and that I had mentioned this to Perry and I suppose he was disappointed. Andrew turned up with a couple of brother officers. One of them, surprisingly young-looking, was in fact Tara's[1] father. (She, very splendidly, on first catching sight of Jane had said, 'For God's sake watch out for my father'.) Next was dear Jonathan [Aitken] – *always* a delight in any gathering.

We were changed, drinking champagne in the music room when a commotion was audible from the hall. Dogs barking. The Parkinsons were trying to get in.[2] But William, now more and more a law unto himself, had been disconcerted by Cecil's appearance, his (very loud) change jacket, and slammed the door on him. 'Ooh, you can't come in like that, sir.' I mediated. Cecil's Private Office had failed to tell him, although I had sent many messages, that it was black tie. It's always black tie at Saltwood on Saturday evenings. This is known.

Dinner was longish, before we got the port and the ladies – reluctantly in Ann's case – went away. Then serious conversation began, punctuated at intervals by 'crude' laughs from the other end of the table where Andrew and his Life Guard friends were ensconced with their own decanter.

Perry flew his kite about where is the real opposition coming from, what are the coming ideas, that kind of thing. Cecil responded, but not really very effectively. Jonathan and I were 'ball-boys'. Peter Brooke was completely silent. Perhaps tired, perhaps just faintly disapproving.

Later in the evening I had a chat with Cecil.

She *had* intended to put him in the Foreign Office, and how he had a clear programme to 'sort it out'. He always said he wanted me to go there with him as Min of State, although had it actually came to the point, I'm not so sure. But it was not that that made me feel a great opportunity had been lost. Because all that he said rang so true; all his criticisms of their misplaced – but extravagant – effort are so valid. Cecil also told me that she had clearly planned to groom him as her successor, arranged little private meetings with the Prince of Wales, that kind of thing. Will he ever be able to build it back? I doubt it. She's in love with David Young at the moment. But even

---

[1] A girl friend of Andrew.
[2] Cecil and Ann Parkinson.

there I get the feeling that it could already be waning. *La Donna é mobilè.*

After everyone had gone to bed Jonathan and I talked. I said that I had finally blown it for the Cabinet. He, somewhat tenuously, I thought, advanced the theory that I might be brought in as they were all so *boring.* We both dread the Lady's health cracking up. 'No one can stand this pace,' he said.

Very late that night I tiptoed across the lawn to the Great Library and turned off the tapestry lights. It's spooky over there after midnight, and I was not strong enough to go through to the little lobby where I have positioned that beautiful erotic marble, Boucher's *Captive,* which I bought last week at Sotheby's for double its estimate. (I wonder who the underbidder was?)

On Sunday everyone, thank God, left promptly. Perry had to go to Chequers, and was not sure of the way.[1] We paced on the lawn for a little while. He was disappointed in Cecil, 'He's not a philosopher king. I don't know who could play that role. Perhaps you could?' I'm a sucker for any compliment, and this cheered me up.

There is no doubt that Cecil is better *à deux* than in a general, High Table kind of conversation. He was quite funny about the Lady's health and holidays. 'She *won't* relax, *won't* go to bed.' (I have heard Willie say exactly the same thing.) 'That's why Ian Gow was so bad for her. He *encouraged* her to stay up, later and later. They would sit up in her flat above Number 10, and have just another "last" whisky.' Quite. I can see (but did not say) a number of reasons why Cecil might object to this.

They're expensive, these hospitalities. In drink alone I'm down three bottles of Dom Perignon, three Talbot blanc, four '78 Morgon, one Cockburn '60, and a lot of brandy.

---

[1] In fact the Worsthornes, notwithstanding the clearest instructions from AC, turned right instead of left at the M25, and were nearly two hours late at Chequers.

Charing Cross   *Friday, 24 July*

A muggy, late July Friday, and I am sitting in a first-class compartment of the Sandling train, odorous and untidy, which, for reasons as yet undisclosed, and probably never to *be* disclosed, has not yet left Charing Cross. 'Operating Difficulties', I assume, which is BR-speak for some ASLEF slob, having drunk fourteen pints of beer the previous evening, now gone 'sick' and failed to turn up.

'Term' is over. I will not need to go to the Department more than three days a week – the rest can be done by phone, fax and Dave bringing down boxes. I must now make sure that the hols are not frittered away. Yoga, filing and paperwork backlog, *moderation in all things*.

I am not feeling particularly energetic or constructive. Last night we had the end-of-term binge, organised by Gow, and this year in the Macmillan Room of the Carlton Club. Not a wild success, as poor Ian had a setback at the outset. It came about like this. We had arranged to meet in my room, and go over to the Carlton together. But on the way, I wanted to drop in my little note to Charles about my conversation with the Governor.[1] Half mischievously I showed it to Ian.

He took a long time to read it, although it was only one side of one page. 'But this is addressed to a (sic) Mr Charles Powell.'

'That's right.'

'But he is a civil servant, is he not?'

'Yes.'

'And you are a Minister in the Government, a Minister of State, indeed, the Minister for Trade?'

'Yes.'

'And you, a Minister of State, are communicating directly with a civil servant – and a very junior ranking civil servant – in another Department?'

'Oh come on, Ian, you know Charles's position . . . '

Ian sighed. I mean he Cone Ripman School of Acting sighed, and said no more. But as soon as we got to the Carlton and after

---

[1] The Governor of the Bank of England. On the Monday of that week AC had sat at dinner next to Robin Leigh-Pemberton. The Governor had taken some time to enlarge on his views that the Community would in the end be moving towards a single currency (which was at that time anathema to the Prime Minister).

sinking his first White Lady, he announced that he felt 'ill', and didn't (*most* unlike him) 'want to stay late'.

Poor fellow. He so misses Number 10. I don't really know how much she sees of him now. But those days when he controlled and monitored *everything* are gone − I suppose for ever. He was so good at it. But her problems are no longer (or not at present, anyway) political. Intelligence relating to the parliamentary Party, gentle massaging of their various egos, is less important. Her problems are machinery-of-government problems − both national, and international. And at coping with these Charles is brilliant. Workaholic, but cool.

Star turn at the dinner was (or was meant to be) Nicky Ridley.[1] But he was *désseché* and, as often these days, aggressive even to his friends. He said the 'Old Guard', by which (he made clear) he also included me, were finished. No new ideas. 'Where are the new, young radicals?' The same sort of crap I'd been getting from Perry last weekend.

'We don't want any fucking new ideas,' I said. 'We've got plenty of problems as it is.' I tried to play Baldwin. Consolidate. Stay calm. I told the story of my grandfather advising 'garaging' whenever one starts to get ahead. (Not everybody understood this, but Soames and Hesketh[2] did. Very much a café society litmus test).

Richard Ryder[3] sparkled gravely and intelligently. I used to think he was a bit of a creep, confusing him − because he is of that generation − with the Blue Chip[4] mutual admirationists. But he is far better than any of them. He knows his history, which is important. That's what makes Alastair Goodlad[5] (another example) so much more interesting than he first appears.

---

[1] Nicholas Ridley, Environment Secretary.

[2] Lord Hesketh (3rd Baron). A Government Whip.

[3] Richard Ryder, MP for Mid-Norfolk since 1983. Mrs Thatcher's Political Secretary, 1975–81. At this time an Assistant Government Whip.

[4] Blue Chip: A dining club, self-selected, of ambitious young fellows who entered Parliament in 1979. They met at 13 Catherine Place, the home of Tristan Garel-Jones. Their group portrait, in oils, hangs in the dining room.

[5] Alastair Goodlad, Parliamentary Under-Secretary, Energy.

UK Mission, Geneva   *Wednesday, 29 July*

I am out here for the UNCTAD meeting. Ulterior motives, of course, but they look like being thwarted.

It seemed safe enough, because of all the United Nations quangos this has to be the dreariest and least consequential. Nothing of substance is discussed, no decisions are ever reached, the political impact at home is nil.

My plan, to put in an appearance, shake a few hands, 'Excellency, how very agreeable to see you again; how well you are looking; I would so greatly value your opinion on . . . ; let us get our staff to arrange a short bilateral meeting; such pleasure, such pleasure.' And all that. A set speech to the assembly (not deviating by one iota from the turgid DTI text). And then, hand over to officials, take the train to Visp – one of my three favourite train journeys in the world – and up on the V-Z Bahn to Zermatt in time for a delicious meal in the station restaurant. And the following day a Whymper scramble. I gave them the Chalet phone number. 'I can be back in Geneva at two hours' notice' (lie).

I had reckoned without (how can I still be underestimating this?) the absolute determination of civil servants never to let a Minister out of their sight if they can possibly avoid it, and how they put this objective above all others.

Also, there is a heavy FCO input here, as indeed there is at every international gathering. The Ambassador fusses and clucks; actually offered his own brief of what I should say and do, on a kind of spot-the-difference basis from the DTI brief. He appears to be sending a totally separate set of telegrams to the Foreign Office while at the same time processing our set, which Tony Hutton[1] is writing each evening, to the DTI. And for what? Absolutely nothing.

What a bore for the desk clerk.

Everybody knows the FCO is crazily overstaffed and treasures these sort of conferences as its own private job creation scheme, but there are limits, one would think.

So it was no surprise to be woken by Marjorie this morning at seven fifteen or thereabouts (the taxi to take me to Geneve Gare was ordered for eight thirty) on my jangling bedside telephone and be

---

[1] Anthony Hutton, civil servant in Trade and Industry, then dealing with external European policy.

told, breathlessly – she always gets slight asthma when she knows I'm going to be cross – that things had got rather 'difficult'.

'Meaning?'

'It looks, Minister, as if the UK is going to be *isolated*' (FCO dread-word, she lowered her voice reverently, almost as if she was saying *buggered*) 'on the Common Fund, both in the Community, and in Group "B".'

'So?'

'Well, Minister, I've been talking to Christopher Roberts – '[1]

'Already?'

'Well no, Minister, I spoke to him last night' (once she mentioned Christopher, I knew I'd had it as she's more frightened of him than she is even of me) 'and he feels it would be unwise of you to be away today, Minister.'

I thought it over. It was no good, I couldn't go. There would be too much *angst*, I wouldn't really be able to enjoy the high Alps. And it was the sort of tedious mini-dispute that might just get referred across to Number 10 by the FCO – they certainly would sneak if they could – and then there'd be a 'Where's Alan?' crisis. Blast, though. I was thoroughly dejected.

Sadly I went for an early morning stroll along the corniche. Very very faint evocations did I feel of earlier, unblighted strolls, distant in time. Water slapping against the hulls of launches after a speedboat had gone by. A man slaloming on water skis, and the burble of Riva exhausts; a girl getting out of her red swim suit and laughing. It was not yet eight o'clock and there was already the promise of great heat, with haze over to the Evian side of the lake.

Saltwood   *Sunday, 4 October*

Vilely depressed after a bad night. (Tom kept us awake fidgeting and flapping his ears and when finally I staggered down to the yard with him at two a.m. he disappeared for three-quarters of an hour ratting, and at intervals barking shrilly, behind the log pile.) This morning a

---

[1] Christopher Roberts, civil servant. Deputy Secretary, Trade and Industry, since 1983.

scotch mist, and everything soaked. You can hardly see across the Bailey.

The papers are full of Heseltine, 'to be the star of the Conference', etc. How can he be, if he hasn't got a perch? He'll have to speak from the rostrum, with a time limit – although even as I write I realise there isn't a Chairman of the National Union made who would cut off that man's sound. Four-fifths of Central Office are closet subversives anyway, always have been. He's got a word-of-mouth going, which is why Bruce,[1] who is a terrific Vicar of Bray, was all 'cor' at lunch yesterday. But *what a bore*.

Yesterday evening at dinner I said, 'I'm even tireder at the end of the holiday than I was at the beginning' (little knowing that I was going to suffer a *nuit cassée*), and this morning I'm just sick and fatigued thinking of it all. I've barely got the energy even to be indignant. Why is it always the bad eggs who seem to get to the top in politics? The only other character given heavy billing today is that ambitious creep War(sic)grave.[2]

I went down to the long garage and sheeted the SS 100, some, very little, of whose brightwork I had lethargically and incompetently cleaned in fading light yesterday.

Later that morning I tiptoed across the soaking lawn to the Great Library. Dehumidifier stopped, naturally, full to the brim. I emptied it, collected my notebook, and meandered round the room, drawing all the curtains to prevent fading.[3]

When will I next be over there? To look for a book perhaps, but to work? Not until next May.

---

[1] Bruce Anderson, columnist on the *Sunday Telegraph*.
[2] William Waldegrave, MP for Bristol West since 1979, actually a friend of AC, irritated him by affecting a 'correct' pronunciation of his name that omitted the 'de'.
[3] Centrally heating the Great Library was discontinued by AC when he moved into Saltwood in 1971. It is shut down from November until March.

HS 125, Luxembourg-Northolt   *Monday, 5 October*

A totally wasted day at the Council of Ministers. No conclusions, no nothing. I can't remember what we were discussing although the meeting only broke up an hour ago and the Line to Take from the Foreign Office was 'prepared for any eventuality' and some six pages long. The background brief weighed about four kilos.

Sorghum, I should think. It's always sorghum, sometimes sorghum and maize.

Only mini-recordable event was the appearance of the French Minister,[1] oh-so-fashionably dressed, and wafting a most terribly expensive *parfum*. Wasn't there something that used to be advertised in old copies of the *New Yorker*, 'Tabu' with an illustration of the (implicitly latin) violinist passionately embracing his young singer? This must be it.

I spotted her as soon as I came in, on the opposite side of the table being all lala with her officials. Our eyes met, but my expression was – or was intended to be – *disdainful*. The meeting was late starting, as always. Years, *years*, must have been wasted in aggregate by no Community Ministers' meeting ever starting less than three-quarters of an hour late. I was standing in a little huddle with the UKREP officials just behind my chair, when along came Madame, swinging her hips most outrageously, and all 'get me'. She quite flagrantly (and with great style, I must admit) swept between us, then paused and posed. Poor old David Elliott[2] somewhat gauchely made the introductions.

The whole thing was so outrageous that I had to grin. She immediately froze up, went all don't-think-I'm-that-easy. High horse. Yes, I suppose she is 'attractive' (in quotes), a kind of up-market Irene Worth. But alas (and indeed, as Irene herself found on the *Queen Mary* in 1951) I am not in the slightest degree aroused by 'the older woman'. They are fun to sit next to at dinner, but I don't want to get any closer. For me, girls have to be succulent, and that really means under twenty-five.

As I write these words I look across at dear Rose demurely stuffing

---

[1] Mme Edith Cresson, Internal Market Minister in the French Government (and later Prime Minister).

[2] David Elliott, deputy head of UKREP under Sir David Hannay, Ambassador and UK Permanent Representative to the European Community.

on RAF biscuits. I *insisted* she came, I *challenged* her to come, and
dutifully she did. But like all (or many) of my most devious plans, it
got snagged. There is an air controllers' strike, so I thought there
would be a good chance of being able to show her the old city, etc.
But in fact we've got this nice little RAF HS for the whole DTI party
and can whizz in and out on our own route. So now we're all heading
back to London and it's only five o'clock.

I feel stale and out of condition. All morning I dozed and hallucinated.
The Greek soliloquies are particularly good at sending me to sleep as
the interpreters alternate, and one of them translates it 'through'
French first, which makes it Kafka unintelligible – as it were a foreign
female voice reciting a *Private Eye* parody of John Cole.[1]
    I revived, briefly, walking across the tarmac to board for the flight
home. The dense *Ardennois* woods press almost up to the main runway,
and I felt a great urge to plunge in, never mind the Minister's suit and
Gucci slippers, walk for four hours, absorb the smells of the wet
countryside and watch for the foxtracks.
    A few minutes ago there was a break in the clouds, a long sunset
strip to the north, reminder of the beckoning wistful call of the Ben
Loyal range when we were driving back from Pait Lodge[2] – was it
only two weeks ago? Perhaps that was why I dreamed of Pait Lodge
last night.

Transit lounge, Bogota Airport   *Wednesday, 28 October*

Totally Kafka at present. An air-conditioning unit *roars* nearby, hate-
fully lowering an already uncomfortable temperature. It would be
intolerably cold were we not at present 'centrally' heated by the bodies
and bloodstreams of some three hundred or so fellow passengers. The
noise makes conversation, still less comprehension of the gabbled
Spanish PA system, impossible.
    Outside a motley scrapyard of cannibalised aircraft, mostly DC 3s,
lie about forlornly. My first and (so far) only ride in a 707 has consisted

---

[1] John Cole, BBC Political Editor, born and brought up in Belfast.
[2] Pait, the stalking lodge of Colin Stroyan in Argyll, a personal friend of AC, and a
    family trustee.

in taxiing, trundling rather, to the end of the runway, 'spooling up' unconvincingly, and then returning for *Cosa tecnica*. Now we're two hours late leaving and no one seems to be specially bothered.

Is God trying to do something for me? The programme is that we take off, overloaded – if we're lucky we'll be on maximum load for sea level, and Bogota airport is altitude 6000 ft, more likely they haven't done a weight calculation at all – and then fly over 3000 miles due south with the Pacific Ocean under our starboard wing, and the Andes under our port wing in a very old aeroplane that has done service first with (say) Pan-American, then with a US regional airline, then to Europe – a dodgy carrier – then three or four years doing *cargo* in the Caribbean until finally, thirty years after leaving Seattle, it has ended up here, with Air-Colombia.

But being stuck in Bogota is almost equally dangerous. Haven't I read somewhere that it has the highest homicide rate in the entire world? Nigeria would be nastier I suppose, but at least a British Minister would cut more ice. What about Carlos something-or-other Esteban?[1] Perhaps he could get us out. Where is he?

This morning I rose very early indeed. The call was for 4.45 a.m. As usual I started twitching and turning and putting on and off the light from 1.10. At 4.17 (8.17 in London) I called to Charles,[2] got him out of a meeting with the Foreign Secretary, and told him the 'views' (largely spurious, *my* views would be more like it) of the Venezuelan Oil Industry on the BP share placing, and how we must not be browbeaten by Salomons,[3] just tell them to say Thank you, ma'am, and sod off. It was an open line, and Charles was discreet: 'I've noted carefully what you have said . . .' etc.

We drove to the Caracas protocol lounge. Empty except for a couple of guards, gun-toting, who chewed. And a big fellow in a rumpled suit who turned out to be a King's Messenger, George Courtauld by name, dozing intermittently on one of the sofas. Had he been there all night?

The Embassy party came to see us off, including that *beauty* whom I spotted going round the Consular section yesterday and to whom

---

[1] The notorious 'Cocaine Baron'.
[2] Powell, at Number 10 Private Office.
[3] Due to the stock market crash BP shares had fallen below the underwritten price, and Salomons, the principal underwriters in the US, were trying to get out of the deal.

nobody would introduce me. A true phew-wotta-scorcher blonde with a lovely figure and lots of sparkle and confidence. Erica. We conversed far too much, I suppose. At intervals other Embassy staff tried to interpose. George Courtauld very splendidly (because he must fly hundreds of thousands of miles a year) said that he never could allow himself to fall asleep on aircraft because he had this private superstition that it was only his will-power that kept them aloft, and if he should doze off they might fall out of the sky.

So now what? I could see this South American trip months away as being potentially odious. But it's still fun staying 'buoyant', and making black jokes while round me the officials become pasty and apprehensive. They, too, are worried about Carlos tarumptico Esteban.

Later

Back in the aircraft. Suspended reality. Jane was the first to spot this; one is halfway to God, or rather, between God and earth. There is a residual fear, and doubtless a great lake of terror to burst its banks if some really nasty symptom should manifest itself ('manifest itself' – what awful solecisms one perpetrates when speed jotting), but I no longer try to hold my breath when flying long distances. Even in this elderly aeroplane I am quite serene. Adrenalin synthesises pleasingly with the detachment that accompanies great distance from home and normality.

Yesterday evening I strolled in Caracas to 'shop'. I bought some shoes, slightly caddish beige brogues, and a couple of nice belts. But I was a zombie, something from *Orphée*.[1] Girls with clean hair in summer frocks, shabby touts, cheeky salesmen, cabdrivers, I am not of your world. I am from the nether regions, and to there, when I am summoned, I will return. I recall this feeling first one fine afternoon of late summer, driving back across Green Park by the back route from Lancaster House. Felt it again very strongly at the Frankfurt Motor Show. Tired, *drained*. A privileged prisoner with officials dogging one's every move, trying constantly to stuff empty corners of one's schedule.

I undress and look at myself in the glass, noting the subtle alterations of shape, the loss of muscle tone first remarked on by Beth[2]

---

[1] The film, scripted 1948 by Jean Cocteau.

[2] Mrs Evans Smith, his physiotherapist, when AC had put out his back in a fall on a difficult ski run in Zermatt.

when she treated me for my second back injury in 1978. Always on such occasions do I remember Moran's[1] words to Churchill, 'Physically, you inherited a fortune, but now you've spent it, nearly all.' We'll see.

The night before I left I had a dream, which only came back to me on waking from a nap in the 747 that afternoon. I dreamed that the old Al, the Al of the sheepskin coat photo and who could swing without stopping twenty-two times from the iron flagstaff bar on the roof at Saltwood, escaped. In the middle of the night he stole away from his bed and went on to the lawn, which was lit by the full moon so brightly that you could almost (although you never really can, in fact) notice the colours of grass and stone – then later, after quite a short while, having to creep back to his enfeebled body, still lying between the sheets, with its many degradations.

I still ponder the significance of this. I had the potential even then. But to release it, get into public life, past all the mistakes and mis(mine)understandings, defeat all those – Ted, Central Office, the Eastons[2] – who were determined to obstruct me, involved an enormous expenditure of the physical capital that I had built up over twenty years, from 1945 to 1965.

I look at my contemporaries. They have sagging waistlines and little broken veins on nose and cheek. The hair on their head is wispy. They drink 'convivially'.

Sometimes I feel certain that I would rather die than become a buffer. But when faced with it, I'm not so sure. I suppose I would settle for becoming a sage, a kind of up-market Anson.[3]

---

[1] Lord Moran, for many years Churchill's doctor.
[2] Rodney and Betty Easton, City Councillors in Plymouth who were opposed to AC's nomination in 1972.
[3] Anson MacKay, ferryman at Eriboll, at that time eighty-nine years old. He died in October 1992.

British Embassy, Santiago   *Friday, 30 October*

And still I expend (physical) capital. It is impossible to get time to relax or reflect. This morning, by gulping my breakfast, I 'made' forty minutes and 'disappeared' upstairs. But no, bloody officials who had (I can only assume) been furtively clustered in the corridor outside my room, promptly alerted by the sploshing sound of a freshly flushed *toilet*, knocked authoritatively on the door before I was even back out of the bathroom and had 'adjusted my clothing'.

'Yes,' I shouted, half snarl, half bellow.

'Minister, we just need to fill in a few details concerning the Miami trip . . . '

'*Miami*? What *are* you talking about? This is Chile, isn't it, I thought we were going back to the Department before we go to Miami, when do we go to Miami, am I wrong, what is this . . . ?' etc., etc.

'Yes, yes Minister, of course but no, but . . .' (Civil servants are the only human beings beside my mother who can say 'yes' and 'no but' in the same unpunctuated sentence.) 'Post want to get some details settled. You see you're attending the Pan-American Trade Conference, the exhibition *and* the dinner (what a treat), there'll be a bit of a gap in the first afternoon, Post have one or two suggestions for filling it . . . '

I bet they have, I thought. Brusquely I shooed them out of the room. I am so exhausted and resentful that I don't think I will be able to speak to them again on this trip, not socially anyway.

Now I have barely got ten minutes left before the Ambassador[1] will start fussing in the hall and the day – visits to Ministers, a lunch at the Ministry of Foreign Affairs (HE and other officials are for some reason very nervous about this – perhaps they think I will 'come out') then a presentation of the Escondida project (I gather this involves a film show so I might get a nap) and then – Caramba! the centre-piece of the trip (at least in FCO eyes) the dinner for 'leading figures in the Opposition'. Guests 'to start (sic) arriving at 8.30 p.m.', so I suppose we may be sitting down by half eleven.

Actually little White himself isn't so bad. A bit guarded, but that's probably down to the secret FCO biog which precedes me at all destinations. I am not (*not*) getting on with his wife, though. There is

---

[1] Alan White, British Ambassador in Santiago.

this certain type of woman who simultaneously demands that you make a pass (or at least flirt) and then gets show-outraged, demonstratively outraged if you do. I want to say fat chance, dear, calm down. Perhaps this shows. I remember one summer in Florence Dido and Clio[1] used to amuse themselves riding the trams in very tight sawn-off jeans and clingy T-shirts and seeing how many men's faces they could slap – and they slapped really hard – before lunch. But they were aged fifteen and seventeen.

Later (much)

We've finally got rid of the dinner guests. A strange occasion. First a drinks party. As I don't touch the stuff when on duty it meant standing, exhausted, with the same warm glass in my hand for two hours while various locals were produced to say their piece. Only value (in every sense) was a regional director of Rothschilds who spoke interestingly about the world economy. He has his own vineyard, and had the calm, crease-free café-au-lait complexion of the international rich. He asked me to come and stay with him. I must ask Marjorie his name which I, drainedly, have forgotten.

The actual meal was a shambles; Mad Hatter's tea party. The so-called Opposition is variously fragmented and, as is usual in such cases, the various fragments are barely on speaking terms. Those that are in the running to help form a government can hardly believe their luck, and chatter recklessly. One who is tipped as a possibility for President, a chap called Aylwin,[2] got drunk immediately and monologued persistently; although at one point he got into a spat with a couple of others about who 'denounced' whose sister during the period of military rule.

Frankly, I'd have put them all under arrest as they left the building. I might say that to Pinochet, if I get to see him on Friday.

Well, it's nearly one a.m. and I have an early call tomorrow for seven thirty breakfast – or is it seven – to go into the desert and expose myself to sunlight, blinding sunlight, for two days. I haven't packed. I'm cross, fatigue and acids, and I will sleep badly, if at all.

During the 'presentation' of the Escondida Project this afternoon I got a fright. I was thinking – a totally wasted day; then with a start,

---

[1] Daughters of Edward Goldsmith and his first wife Gill (née Pretty).

[2] In fact elected President in 1989.

how many more days have I got left? Two thousand? Three thousand at the most. Each one is more significant, and more important, than its predecessor. Sad, and frightening. I compensated by fantasising on the rumour that George[1] is to be made Chairman of the Party and I could take his place at the MoD.

The VIP lodge, Chuquicamata   *Saturday, 31 October*

Rich, rich experiences today. We had flown up here in a little De Havilland Otter, a high-wing aircraft, with Lycoming propeller engines; quite reassuring, you feel it could put down almost anywhere – unlike a 737 which had overshot the airstrip only a matter of days earlier, broken up in the rock-strewn hinterland and caught fire. Its blackened dinosaur carcase was all too visible.

'Everyone all right, I assume?' lip-lickingly enquired one of the officials.

But no, far from it. They were all dead!

Clean and comfortable, but *icy* cold – though still the air conditioning pours out its refrigerated vapours. We must be at about 7000 feet. The Andes lie to the west, but the belt of foothills and desert plateau is quite wide here. It is unnaturally dry, and the sun shines with an implacable strength that makes Trockener Steg[2] like April in Aldeburgh. Last night a reasonable meal, I stuffed on olives and a coarse brown bread. A grand piano beckoned, and I would happily have strummed from my repertoire. But I have long learned the lesson that it is discreet first to ask if anyone in the party 'plays', because the trained ear is uncomfortable with my renderings of 'Smoke Gets in Your Eyes', or 'Stormy Weather'. And sure enough Kester[3] timidly volunteered. After we had all gone to bed I could hear some quite pretty Chopin for a little while, ending with a sombre passage of Liszt – probably from the 'Années de pèlerinage'.

We left early in two FWDs, a Land-Rover and a (surprisingly nasty) Chevrolet minibus, our destination a village, San Pedro del Acurama, which had prehistoric remains and a folk museum. Hot, glare-dry

---

[1] Younger, Secretary of State for Defence.
[2] A very high ski-run on the glacier behind the Clarks' chalet in Zermatt.
[3] George Kester, Assistant Secretary on the South American desk at DTI.

gravellidos rattled and spat against the bodywork. A 'rest stop' (I am an inveterate pee-er but in this climate the kidneys need every drop, the bladder calls only twice a day) in the Vala da Luna, a terrible place of bleached and twisted rock formations. No vegetation; no soil even, not one scrap of living substance within sight or reach.

San Pedro is an oasis on the banks of a river which spates just often enough to irrigate its immediate environs and even when trickling, as today, offers clean and reliable water from the distant Andean snows. Not unlike Forio[1] in the old days, with a plaza and crumbling shops; house doors opening directly on to the street, bead curtains. Searing mid-day heat and white dust on the trees.

We went round the geological museum. Brand new, the building more interesting than the exhibits. The Curator, prematurely grey, but lean, spoke little English and showed his impatience. That suited me, and so there was time to kill before lunch.

In the 'prehistoric village' (indistinguishable from the *Alt Broch* settlements at Eriboll except that the walls are of mud instead of dry stone) I suggested that we go to the summit on which an ancient lookout tower brooded. HE and the officials were unenthusiastic. Sadismoidly I said, Yes, Yes.

The lean Curator led the way. Within minutes we had outdistanced the main group. It was quite difficult keeping up with him (plainly he was trying to shake me off, or get me to cry 'Pare'). HE, although I suspect younger than I, had, after a perfunctory sprint, settled for 'Guide's Pace'. The official party faded, first from earshot, then sight. I took strength in the last *diréttissima* from Alpine recollections, the Rothorn, the Metalhorn and, of course, that last heart-pounding sprint through the gorse on Gossie Bank.

Incredible view from the tower. I reflected on those ancient civilisations, and the pleasing early maturity of the young in the southern hemisphere. I spoke drawlingly, to show I was not out of breath. The Curator could barely acknowledge. He, too, was controlling his breathing. I've noticed this before with Spaniards. They never salute their adversary. A German, even a Frenchman, would have made a joking aside; some kind of acknowledgment of sporting rivalry that had ended in an honourable draw.

---

[1] Forio d'Ischia, where AC spent many happy summers in the late Fifties.

Westward-bound 747, 2 hrs out of   *Monday, 16 November*
Vancouver

How very *dry* and flushed one becomes on these great long-distance
flights. My Harold Acton death spots gleam reproachfully in the lights
of the silent, stainless steel lavabos. Round me, my fellow travellers
who, some eight hours ago, boarded groomed and confident with
their Etienne Aigner luggage, are now pinched and watery-eyed. We
have sat through two full-length films, one quite good, watchable,
about double and treble agents in the CIA; the other total rubbish. By
spastics for spastics. *The Stakeout*, a particular – always embarrassing –
Hollywood genre, the 'comedy thriller'. A *Private Eye* parody could
not have been more ludicrous or more trite.

Below, the Canadian tundra slips past. Many lakes. Skirting the
Northern Ice-cap was deeply frightening – more so even than the
Andean Desert. So *utterly* lifeless and bleak. In the desert there would
at least be foxes and insects and little roots waiting to be nurtured by
the rain. But the Polar route is all ice cliffs, and pale chasms of depth
unknown.

Oh, these hateful flights! I look at the map, and there on the UK
is marked 'Ben Hope 927m'. And the two stretches of water, Eriboll
and Hope, are clearly set out. Within these bounds is my beloved
property; the gimmers and the peregrine falcons and the pine martens;
the great tawny badgers, the stags, the little musquat deer and the sly
peat foxes. I think fondly, sadly, of them all.

If one is nurturing cancer, pre-cancerous, which I often think I
am, these hideous great flights must be the very worst thing.

I long, I physically long for a great walk, to breathe deep gulps,
and to stretch the spine. We have been in the air eight and a half
hours, yet the clock has advanced less than twenty minutes since take-
off.

We are almost keeping pace with the sun.

And what am I going to do when I get there? No real objectives –
just hang around as a ritual dummy being polite to people, HE's
Reception.

San Francisco   *Thursday, 19 November*

I was principal guest at a lunch given by Barclays Bank. Conversation was lively. More so, at least, than it would have been at an equivalent function at home. And an absolutely delicious Mondavi white burgundy. The location was a low-ceilinged dining room in the Bohemia Club. No women present, although there was much talk about their now having to be admitted.

But I was most alarmed by the appearance of the *waiter*. He was exceedingly, unnaturally, thin. And his eyes were shiny and overbright. Why was he perspiring? He had the most dreadful blotchy sores on his arms which, far from concealing, he *flaunted* by rolling up his sleeves.

Oh dear. Were we in a district called Haight Ashbury? I read recently that ninety per cent of the population there is a 'victim'. I didn't touch the salad.

Afterwards Steve[1] said to me, 'How about that waiter, Minister?'

I groaned. I am trying not to think about it.

Saltwood   *Saturday, 19 December*

On Thursday Ian and I had a very jolly dinner at the Savoy, indulged ourselves. Also present (at my suggestion) were Francis Maude,[2] and David Heathcoat-Amory.[3] Both the youngsters were good, and sparkled sensibly. Fine wines were ordered, and consumed. I really think that the Savoy River Room has the most *reliably* good food in London. Not the absolute best, perhaps, but I've never been disappointed there.

Ian talked about the next reshuffle, and we pricked up our ears. (But is he actually as close to things as he used to be? I would say not.) He started off circumlocutory, became more specific as Puligny-Montrachet gave way to Beaune. She intends to make Geoffrey leader in the Lords, and Nigel Foreign Secretary; John MacGregor[4] Chancellor.

[1] Stephen Phillips, Number Two in AC's Private Office.
[2] Francis Maude, now Parliamentary Under-Secretary at the DTI.
[3] David Heathcoat-Amory, MP for Wells since 1983.
[4] John MacGregor, MP for South Norfolk since 1974. Minister of Agriculture.

This seems a pretty tall order to me. Maude, supported by David H-A, said Lawson couldn't be Foreign Sec as a Jew. This made Ian very indignant. 'Do you mean to tell me that today, this very day, in this the Conservative Party – I take it that we are all members of the Conservative Party? – you are seriously suggesting, no asserting...' and so on.

Ian then switched to 'he's not a practising Jew, anyway'. But we couldn't quite swallow it. I said something – something Hurd, and Ian snapped, 'She can't bear him. Can't *bear* him.'

I thought, it's all very well for he and she to swop these sort of ideas over the third or fourth whisky after midnight but come the morning and she's usually more circumspect.

But it's nice to have the Christmas hols, which is always an agreeable time, spiced up by speculation about changes of this weight. I must ring Peter Riddell on Monday, although I expect his scepticism will match my own.

There were three late votes; then Francis and I went to the DTI basement, where the Christmas party was being staged. Matthew was there, having lost so much weight that he is now quite *markedly* handsome. As always full of sense, as well as fun. He told me that Lynda was going to take Arthur Cockfield's place on the Commission – or so the Brussels inner rumour mill claimed. If that happens it could mean Parkinson going to the FCO instead of Lawson (plus A.N. Other!). All greatly preferable to the version we had been getting from Ian at dinner.[1]

As I stood somewhat stiltedly making conversation with Matthew and Marjorie I could see Rose out of the corner of my eye. After a bit she braved their joint presence and came up to me: 'You're terribly late getting here.' I kissed the back of her hand and she stood in *very* close proximity. I could feel my veins raging. She pouted, and nobody pouts like Rose. Nobody has such (I suppose the Barbara Cartland word is *full*) lips. 'It's too hot.'

'Come for a drive,' I said.

Later, when I got home I thought – I've been behaving like this, absolutely unaltered, for forty years. Crazy. Scrawny old time-warp.

---

[1] But equally ill-founded in substance.

Saltwood   *Monday, 21 December*

It's too boring. This lovely holiday break is upon us, James and Sally
are coming down, and Jane always does Christmas so well, it's pure
pleasure.

But I am now convinced I have got cancer of the jaw. Those
symptoms that I have been carefully monitoring ever since that triple-
view shaving mirror in my bathroom in the Embassy in Santiago, are
gradually amplifying (is that the word?). Will I be able even to 'smile
bravely' throughout the festivities?

I am going in shortly to drop in some of the local Christmas cards
in Folkestone. Julian[1] is such a dear, I think I'll just ask him for a quick
check-up.

Afternoon

Julian was marvellous; saw me immediately; didn't turn a hair when
I told him. He said it was 'pretty rare', he'd only seen three cases in
the teaching hospital. He made a thorough examination. Glands
totally normal. No sign whatever of local swelling or ulceration.
'Pain?'

'Well, er, no.'

'Happy Christmas.'

Phew.

Saltwood   *Thursday, 24 December*

Christmas Eve. I've got £700,000 in my Abbey National Crazy-
High-Interest account. But what's the use? Ash, ash, all is ash. Lay
not up for thyself treasures on earth. The cars are all getting streaked
and rust spotted, the books foxed, the furniture dusty. The window
panes, all 52,000 of them are *revolting*, so greasily blotched. Translucent
only. And there is moth everywhere. My grandfather's great Rothschild coat, bought in Wien in 1906, is terminally degraded ... The
whole thing is out of control.

And why? I know why. Because I'm not rich enough to have

---

[1] Julian Smith, FRCDS, the Clark family dentist.

servants. We have to do everything ourselves, and we just haven't got the time, and things get neglected. This morning, rummaging up in the archive room I found the old Wages Book for 1960. That was the year James was born, and we bought our first new car, a dear little red Mini. It was the cheapo model with cloth seats, and we saved a further three pounds and ten shillings by hand painting the registration numbers ourselves. Total cost 'on the road' was £460.

The total wage bill, per week, for the seven servants who worked at the Castle, was thirty-two pounds and five shillings. MacTaggart, a clumsy fellow who had such ugly hands that my mother always made him wear white gloves when he was waiting at table, and who crashed my father's Bentley in circs that will never wholly be explained, in Lee Green, got £12 per week and occupancy of the Lodge.

Everything has decimal points – to the right – or worse. I'm bust, virtually.

Saltwood   *Tuesday, 29 December*

Yesterday we went to lunch at Chequers. I was excited. Some of the lunches over Christmas are very *réclamé*. One is for 'family and close friends'; one is for Cabinet intimates; one is for Court favourites and so on. I hoped, naturally, that it was this third category. But Jane, flier, said no such luck, it'll be Captains of Industry. All too true. They were amiable, quiet-spoken, on good behaviour. Except for her son Mark (is he a 'businessman'?) who kept muscling in on conversations, saying 'something-something *two million* dollars' in Cor! tones. After a bit I got sick of this and said, 'That's not much' (which it isn't) but people affected not to hear.

Sometimes on these occasions she draws me into another room for a little intimate chat. But not this time. Although I must still be in favour as she kept introducing me as 'My wonderful frightfully good Trade Minister', and she had read that book on the Japanese threat which I had sent her via Charles, and had marked passages.

As we left I caught Aunt Ruth's eye,[1] as I always do. 'See you again,' I said. 'Often.'

On the way back, on the last bit of the M25, Dave drove slower and slower, and slower. 'What's up?' He'd forgotten to check the petrol before leaving and was trying to 'conserve' what was left. After we'd filled up he felt 'kind of faint'. Usual story. None of the Government Car Service drivers is capable of driving outside the Metropolitan area. I took over and drove the rest of the way to Saltwood.

---

[1] Viscountess Lee of Fareham, the wife of Arthur Lee, whose papers AC edited. The Lees gave Chequers to the nation in order that the Prime Minister of the day should always have at his disposal a country house for entertaining. One of the provisions of the Chequers Trust is that Lady Lee's portrait by Sargent should always hang in the entrance hall over the visitor's book.

1988

1988

The House has not yet returned but officials, who can't bear it when Ministers are out of the building, they don't quite know where, and they themselves are all in there, shuffling papers around, had arranged for me to meet the '2000 Group', some kind of conclave to assist Japanese 'Inward Investment'. Poor old Patrick Jenkin[1] was 'leading' it. He who had once been Secretary of State, now soft-spokenly hanging about in the waiting area. The democratic cycle. David Young, on the other hand, into whose presence he was finally ushered, was bronzed and silvery-sleek.

Much time is wasted with these sorts of meetings. The delegation believe themselves (I suppose) to be getting 'access'; the 'leader' is earning his fee by 'delivering' access, and the civil servants, who fidget and fuss and make notes, justify themselves and, of course, find such occasions useful in attaining their principal objective, which is always to stuff a Minister's day diary so full that he can't breathe – still less think. I can't think of many occasions when a Minister's mind has actually been altered during a discussion – although it can happen, most notably with the Lynx delegation.[2]

As soon as I got back to my office I asked to see my own 'long term' diary. This threw them, and a long delay ensued. Through the open door I could hear mutterings, heavy rustling of paper, subdued internal phoning. 'Where is it?' I shouted at intervals. When, finally, it was produced I growled at every entry. I must admit, though, it was really quite light. Only two overseas trips, to the Balkans and, possibly, the Maghreb.

This, I suppose, is a bit of a swizz on the outer office. The great perk attaching to the Minister for Trade's staff is the ability to accompany him abroad. As I can buy my own airticket anywhere, compulsory overseas trips aren't so much a privilege, more a bore. Paul went everywhere his officials pointed him at. I know better. '*Les absents ont toujours tort.*'

[1] Patrick (now Lord) Jenkin (Life Peer, 1987). Between 1979–85 was successively Secretary of State for Social Services, for Industry and for the Environment.

[2] Lynx was a charity staffed by young volunteers who had visited AC on his appointment as Minister of Trade, and had found in him a kindred spirit. Single-handed, against massive opposition from civil servants in several Departments of State, AC had drawn up an Order which would force fur traders to label garments made of the skins of animals that had been caught in leg-hold traps.

This is the last stretch, isn't it? Or is it? I *should* be made a PC in June, which will allow me to stagger on until the end of the summer hols, 'Government Changes' in September. And then what?

I never want to see Plymouth again. Sometimes I think that all I want is to stay in office here long enough to get my fur legislation on to the statute book. I was looking through some more papers which have come in this morning.

Horrific illustrations. Worst was a great circular crater, some 16-foot in diameter, dug out of the frozen earth (for all around was snow) by a poor badger, just using one hand, as he went round and round and round; caught by a steel jaw on the other leg, chained to a post in the centre, trying (for how long must it have taken him?) to escape, he dug that great pit. Until, finally, he just lay down and died.

There's stacks of stuff about the Inuits, who make their money out of these barbarities and among whom 'the incidence of alcoholism has risen sharply in recent years' (so what?), the likelihood of the fur trade applying for judicial review, the (inevitable) probability of the Foreign Office fussing, Ambassadors (lazy sods, nothing to do) filing whingeing telegrams and so on. Good. Makes me feel I'm doing something really worth while. Fuck them.

Department of Trade and Industry   *Monday, 11 January*

Back fully in harness this morning (fine and crisp – naturally – after a week of wet, moist oozing) and went first to Albany. I turned on fires and radiators, unpacked shirts and meagre provisions. As I rounded the corner into the 'B' staircase I was filled with gloom. Now for months of confinement. The Lent term (as it used to be at Eton) is always the longest of the House sessions. There are no public holidays to break it up; and it gets dark so early that there is no escape home at times of light whipping.

The Christmas break was lovely, but only in the last couple of days did I start to 'feel a little better'. Recovery very limited. I still get tired, overpoweringly tired. I haven't done Gossie at all, it's too muddy and slippery. And twice I've felt rather awful for a little while. It may be psychosomatic, I suppose, it often is. But I've noted myself just sitting glazedly; too short of energy to do a lot of things that need doing, and are quite interesting.

I shouldn't be like this at the end of the hols.

Department of Trade and Industry   *Tuesday, 12 January*

I sit wearily in the office. My 'In' tray is high to twice its own depth. In the mornings, when I am fresh and fast, officials bring me very little paper. But after five p.m. and a day of 'meetings' and outside engagements, the folders flow thick and insistent. I must also finish the *Spectator* review of Terry Coleman's book.[1] Even so, I am sticking to my record of never taking boxes home. I will not leave this desk until the tray is empty; and there is nothing so pleasing as 'I think I'll lock up now, Minister...' and off goes the last one. But it's never Rose. Why? She could easily stay late if she wanted to. Perhaps the others prevent her. Most officials are fearful spoilsports.

On Sunday evening I was prowling about in the Long Garage. I thought I must change the seats round off the Loco[2] and take the Ghost staff car[3] in hand. Great fun, but needs a few days' undivided attention. No chance of that until Easter; and by Easter, God knows, a hundred other pressing tasks will have once again displaced it.

The civil servants have all left. My room is in darkness, save for the desk light, and I am sipping Malvern water. If I was at Saltwood now I would be on my fourth cup of PG Tips, eating hot buttered brown toast and jam.

House of Commons   *Thursday, 14 January*

In and out of the House all day. Now it's back in session I feel better, it's such fun; such a pleasing ambiance. But there are an alarming number of people I simply don't recognise at all. I became irritated with a total stranger who was somehow blockingly, *disrespectfully* reading the ticker-tape in the smoking-room corridor. 'Who's that?' I asked John Taylor, a Whip. Didn't know. Asked a badge messenger,

---

[1] *Thatcher's Britain* by Terry Coleman. In accordance with an understanding between AC and the Cabinet Office the text was shown to Sir Robin Butler, who advised against publication.
[2] A 1908 Locomobile racing car.
[3] A Rolls Royce Silver Ghost.

pointing at the now retreating figure. Didn't know. I pursued him along the corridors. He had a start on me, and a long stride. I had to travel fast, but with dignity. As he turned into the press gallery staircase, 'Excuse me, who are you?' 'John Lloyd, an officer of the House.' What did he think I was? A loony? Or just a busybody? Or was it a case of mistaken identity? Actually he looked not unlike Charles Powell.

I lunched in the Members' dining room with G-J and Rhodes James.[1] RJ relatively amiable; not drunk, though cigaretting mightily. Talk was mainly of Willie.[2] Rhodes James claimed already to have written his obituary, 'not entirely friendly' (I can't imagine Robert writing an *entirely* friendly piece about anyone). We swopped anecdotes. Richard[3] joined us for coffee and told the most pleasing. He had approached Willie, late at night, but early in the Parliament and before it's full horror was apparent, and asked him what he 'thought of' the Poll Tax.

The great man stopped in his tracks, and glared. His shoulders heaved, went into *rigor*; his face became empurpled and sweat poured down his forehead, cheeks and the end of his nose. He wrestled with some deep impediment of speech; finally burst, spluttering out the single word – 'TROUBLE'. Then he turned on his heel.

Department of Trade and Industry   *Friday, 15 January*

I get on well with the Labour Party. The MPs, that is, not the functionaries who hang about in the corridors, still less those crazy hyped-up 'researchers'. There's that dreadful little tick with curly hair and glasses, four foot six or thereabouts, I've never seen him smile.[4]

Frank Dobson[5] and I swop stories. His are *so* filthy that really

---

[1] Robert Rhodes James, historian and biographer. MP for Cambridge since 1976.
[2] Lord Whitelaw had suffered a slight stroke attending the carol service in the Guards Chapel, but was now 'on the mend'.
[3] At this time Ryder was Under-Secretary at the Ministry of Agriculture.
[4] Dave Hill, Director of Communications, Labour Party.
[5] Frank Dobson, MP for Holborn and St Pancras since 1979, and shadow Leader of the House.

they're unusable, even at a Rugger Club dinner. At the moment we're into 'fuck' e.g.s. Question: who said, 'What the fuck was that?' Answer, 'The Mayor of Hiroshima.' Who said, 'Talk about scattered fucking showers'? Answer, Noah, and so on. The fun is to pass notes across the Table during debates. Juvenile. I know who wouldn't like it if he knew – Sir Robert Armstrong.

Last night, while waiting for a division I had a word with Bob Cryer.[1] Speaking as an historian as well as an old mate, I told him Prescott *must* stand.[2] He became very enthused, said Prescott was checking with his Exec Committee, and certainly would. Bob agreed completely with my analogy with the Tory Party in 1976, and how we recovered our confidence when Mrs T. gave us a bit of conviction. The Labour Party is full of 'idealists' (sic.), it depended on ideals. 'That's right,' I said. Stirring.

While we were talking Frank Haynes[3] came over. He and Bob personify the two main strands in the Labour Party. The 'activists' (Bob is really an elected activist), most of whom are subject to a destructive envy; and the Trade Unionists (Frank is old-school NUM), whose convictions are more traditionally rooted. They just want to do as little as possible, and be paid as much as possible for doing it. And who can blame them? Very little different from the standard chinless riff-raff who hang around Smith's Lawn.

Frank said to me, 'You're a very good Minister' and meant it. Like all traditionalist Labour he believes trade policy should be founded on protection. Look after Number One. So he approves of my running battle to keep the MFA in place. But how are these two, and tens of thousands like them, going to tolerate all this natty suiting and buttonholes? Compulsory role fulfilment as local government officials who've taken a correspondence course in glad-handing. They've had it. It won't fool anyone.

---

[1] Bob Cryer, MP for Bradford South since 1987 (Keithley 1974–83).

[2] The Labour Party had changed the terms of its leadership selection, and it was being considered whether Neil Kinnock should be challenged. John Prescott, MP for Hull East since 1970, was eventually a candidate as Labour Leader when Kinnock relinquished the role in 1992.

[3] Frank Haynes, MP for Ashfield since 1979.

Department of Trade and Industry   *Tuesday, 19 January*

Little John Moore is in trouble.[1] It's the NHS debate today and the
whole House will turn out, hoping for blood. The poor fellow has
been in bad health (Health Secretary, bad health, etc., etc.) and has
been 'on the sick list', i.e. not around.

At one of the long tables in the tea room people were gloating,
his own colleagues particularly: 'Are you aglow with excitement at
the prospect of actually setting eyes on this legendary figure?' said Eric
Forth.[2] Titters. Someone else, cruelly, 'You may set eyes on him, but
you'll have difficulty hearing him.' The wretched man has had throat
trouble for ages, goes terribly hoarse a couple of minutes into his
speech.

Why is everyone so beastly? John was literally golden. Although
in his forties he has golden kiss-curls like a babyfood ad. He is athletic,
and 'trains'. He did time in the States on some election trail or other
and has an American wife in PR. What-a-team, etc., etc. Last year,
Number 10 were 'letting it be known that' he was the chosen
successor, and his speech (not at all bad really) to Conference was
billed on that basis. I can see that this can arouse envy and, not that
he is scrabbling, *Schadenfreude*. But John has always been perfectly
pleasant to me. Shallow, but amiable. Not like some of those wankers
who are so ambitious they won't even tell you the time when you
ask.

Of course he is mildly of the Right, and has attached himself to
Her. I am told that in Cabinet he echoes her views and then later (or
even on the same morning) if she alters her view, echoes that too.
This irritates. But if I ask myself why Tristan, and Patten, get so cross
about him; why it is said that John Major[3] (outwardly the mildest of
men) is reputed to have sworn to 'get' him, I must suppose it is
because he is the only possible contender for the leadership of the
Party who is outside the 'Blue Chip' club.

That tight little masonic group, so ably managed and convened by

---

[1] John Moore, MP for Croydon Central since 1974. Secretary of State for Social
 Security since 1986, after spells at Transport and Social Services.
[2] Eric Forth, MP for Mid-Worcestershire since 1983. Parliamentary Under-Secretary,
 Trade and Industry, since 1986.
[3] John Major, MP for Huntingdon since 1979. Chief Secretary to the Treasury since
 1987.

Tristan, is determined to monopolise the allocation of higher office, to the exclusion of the Right.

Hounslow Suite, Heathrow   *Friday, 29 January*

I sit here, acid from wine at lunch and weary in my bones and joints. I have been in attendance all day at the French Summit meeting at Lancaster House and then tried, through wet Friday evening traffic, to get to Heathrow in a half hour. I don't think even Joan could have managed it (although I must admit that with her I never actually missed anything). Now I have to wait for nearly two more hours until the next Zurich flight.

These VIP suites are windowless, and heavily sound-insulated, so that nervous travellers are not made anxious by the sound of Boeing turbines on take-off, shrieking at their point of maximum thrust. There is bad coffee, and 'assorted centre' biscuits on offer, and masses of neatly folded newsprint. Gently we are drawn into the nether world of deep jetlag.

I had been looking forward to Davos,[1] and planned that Rose should be 'asked' to accompany me. Predictably, the office thwarted this, although she had coyly agreed. So now I am on my own, flushed and hypochondriacal.

The Summit was interesting, although more for the opportunity that it gave to make personal observations than for any outcome of policy. At the start, the Lady was to greet Mitterrand as he came up the steps into the central hall (*not* at the entrance, I was glad to note), and lesser acolytes hung around in the background. I fell into conversation with Douglas. His is a split personality. *A deux* he is delightful; clever, funny, observant, drily cynical. But get him any-where near 'display mode', particularly if there are officials around, and he might as well have a corncob up his arse. Pompous, trite, high-sounding, cautiously guarded.

Douglas said to me how he used to be so excited before these Summits – history in the making, all that – now no longer. I said it

---

[1] The World Economic Forum, a conference of 'world leaders and opinion formers' convened every year at Davos.

was a bad sign. We were getting jaded. Perhaps we ought to get out? I said that I wanted to get out every Monday morning, as I got dressed and shaved. Rather splendidly, he agreed.

Before the Plenary started I had a few words with Michel Noir. As always, attractive, intelligent. A true Gaullist. I agree with him on practically every issue.

Punctually we were seated. Opposite me, [Jacques] Chirac yawned and cigaretted. He is in his prime. Handsome in a fifty-five-ish sort of way, smelling beautiful, but ill-at-ease with *Le Président*. Mitterrand himself is seventy-one, a pale elderly sage, a BB[1] with balls. And plainly determined to hang on. Winston and Anthony must sometimes have seemed like this, although in Chirac's case the succession is far from assured. But at least he looks fit, while poor Anthony was already sickening in 1952. I did notice, too, that whatever he may think of her Mitterrand's manner with the PM was courteous, and grave. Chirac, on the other hand, lounged and fidgeted and doodled and smirked at his own thoughts.

A faintly absurd 'structural' device had been introduced, at the behest of God knows who, whereby Ministers in Attendance (i.e., myself and Noir, Lynda [Chalker] and some little runt from the Sûreté who smelt of garlic and hadn't shaved) should 'present papers' before the summing up.

Naturally, this was a great bore for all concerned. But it did offer scope for the Lady to give one of her little mini-displays of bitchiness and mischief. The order was to be Lynda (as 'Deputy' Foreign Secretary), then the runt from the Sûreté who was going to talk about border control; then Noir, then me. ('I don't think anyone is expecting you to talk for very long, Minister,' i.e., the Foreign Office have asked us to keep it snappy.)

But when the moment came for our contributions the Prime Minister, who was of course in the Chair, said, 'Minister for Trade.'

Buoyantly I sparkled, noticing high indignation among Lynda's officials. Then came the little Sûreté man, then Michel. All the time Lynda rustled with her notes and made kind of 'ahem' noises. Finally, with every indication of reluctance and distaste, the Prime Minister just said, 'Mrs Chalker.'

How I love her for that kind of reason!

---

[1] Bernard Berenson, art historian, connoisseur and sage, lived in Florence until well into his nineties. Always known as BB.

Albany   *Monday, 22 February*

We are just back from a dinner at Number 10 for Cap Weinberger.[1]

Sixty-four guests – but only four Ministers – Howe, Parkinson, Younger and myself. I was high up the table, and this disconcerted a grand lady on my immediate left.

'Why are you here?'

'Because I have been invited.'

'Yes, but why were you invited?'

'That, surely, is a question better addressed to our hostess.'

'Well, I don't see what you are doing here.'

'If you find my presence offensive, then I suggest that you restrict your conversation to the person on your left.'

I turned, ostentatiously, and began to speak to the woman on my right who, fortunately, was 'open'. Nobody pulls rank on me, least of all the dried-up wife of a Permanent Secretary (if that be what she was). We were a mixed bunch. Themes, if one could detect any, were the Falklands, and Anglo-American camaraderie in war. Willie was there, and with him any conversation, however brief, is always a pleasure. I had a word with Charlie Sweeney – now must be the ugliest man in London, bright pink and hairless, though pale eyes still glinting with residual lechery at age seventy-five. I also saw Rowse,[2] A.L., shy and benign but with an *appalling* melanoma on his temple.

The Prince of Wales had (apparently) suffered a *mauvais placement*, being put on Cap's right whereas he should, or so the clucksters maintained, have sat at the right hand of the Prime Minister. Lady de Lisle,[3] who is very splendid in many ways but is not, I suspect, a raging fan of the PM, stirred this incipient row primly but firmly.

Charles [Powell], however, was adamant. Tetchily so.

'Of course we checked with his office. I wasn't born yesterday.'

On Monday Charles had asked me to provide some 'possible headings' for the PM's speech of welcome. In fact I wrote the whole thing, from beginning to end, and was delighted that she used most of it. It was the first time that I have heard my own words and phrases from the mouth of another. Cap responded excellently. Started out

---

[1] Caspar Weinberger, American Secretary for Defense 1981–7.

[2] A.L. Rowse, Shakespearean scholar and Fellow of All Souls.

[3] Lady de Lisle, second wife of the former Conservative Secretary of State for Air and herself the widow of the 3rd Baron Glanusk.

funny, then moving. I recall the first time I heard him, at a Congressional Committee in Washington in April of 1982, just after the Falklands War began. He was flat, and colourless – though he did let go that most excellent remark, deprecatory and engaging, which I have often myself used since, on inviting questions, 'because then there is a reasonable chance that what I have to say should be of interest to at least one person in the room'.

I was pleased to learn afterwards that he had been touched by what the Lady had said 'and the beautiful language', and had asked for a copy of the text.

Sandling - Charing Cross train   *Wednesday, 24 February*

This morning I was out very early with Tom. A completely blue sky without a single trace of cloud and the grass blades all crisp and frosty. We went as far as the lake, which was iced over, but treacherous.

On our return I saw Tom alert and bristling, hackles up, at something in the corner of the 'peppercorn' field where the fence crosses the dyke. Fearing a dead or wounded fox (John often sets a snare at that point, as the fence wire is taut across the water and animals can use the bank to squirm underneath), I walked over with a sinking heart.

It was a badger, still with some life in it. I bellowed at Tom, and he reluctantly followed me, running, back to the house where I telephoned angrily to the farm.

John appeared prompt, but sulky, with one of the Apps boys, and then another. He was carrying a pitchfork with which he tried to pinion the unfortunate creature's neck and head. But the badger was strong still, and dangerous.

'Get some sacks,' I told the boys.

I muffled the badger and he went quiet, knowing I was a friend, while John worked with the wire-cutters.

Once he was released the little Brock squared up to us, bravely and aggressively. Then, when we made no move, bumbled off at a very fair pace toward the old railway line. I hope and believe that he was saved by his rib cage. What is awful is when they worm their way down the noose by exhaling (as foxes, being more intelligent, do) and then tighten it against the lower gut in a final effort to break free.

In spite of my early start this diversion caused me to miss my train, and thus the first of the morning's dreary Meetings with Officials. Good! What are they beside the saving of a beautiful and independent creature of the wild?

Hotel Insulberg, Konstanz   *Saturday, 19 March*

I write this at the conference table – always a good spot for an entry. People think that, assiduously, you are making notes. And the setting is conducive. Universal boredom and a sense of futility make the atmosphere *piano*, sepulchral, almost. This is a *World* (not just EC) Trade Ministers Conference so my next-door neighbour is a little Thai instead of the usual Portuguese mouse. We have been sitting for an hour and a half, and he has smoked seven cigarettes.

Slow and repetitious as are our proceedings in the chamber, they are as nothing to the longeurs of the 'cocktails' and the Reception. I dodged the morning coffee break (far too long) and walked along the Lake front, saying hullo to some feathered friends who quacked and jostled amiably beside the water's edge.

On Thursday evening Bruce [Anderson] told me that he had been in conversations with Wakeham,[1] who had told him, 'She'll have him in the Cabinet if she can.'

And it is true that I am in good favour at the moment. Perhaps because I send her a multitude of little notes and reports, but always through Charles, and I never ask for anything.

But my status is precarious, and I fear that I may be heading for an unwelcome passage of arms, because I have now cleared every single hurdle, even the assent of the Secretary of State himself, for my Fur Order. But the Prime Minister watches everything. She has a lot of furriers in Finchley. And she, herself, has I fear very little empathy indeed with the animal kingdom.

---

[1] John Wakeham, now Lord President of the Council, chairman of many Cabinet committees and believed to be highly influential within Government.

Words of welcome at Brize Norton 1987. (Gorbachev's interpreter is speaking).

Althorp. 'I rallied the Ministers present and, with much chivvying, got them to a room on the first floor where a tame photographer took our picture.'

'Straight in from the hover James stood the little Gazelle on its tail and went into a vertical climbing torque turn directly over the great sycamores.' 21 July 90

Once in each summer by tradition AC braves Weils Disease and swims the length of the moat and back.

'Charlotte wanders dreamily along the battlements to pastiche Brideshead music, murmur

spring. The first cut of the lawn.

at "the loveliest place in the
ie world".' 10 September 83

'This morning I swam very early, before seven,
and the view *from the water* was unbelievable
because the eastern light is on the towers – which
happens only for a couple of weeks in high
summer'. 14 July 90

Above centre: Ben Hope (alt 3,080 ft) from the Creaggan Road (eastern side).

Tom guards the game bag.

Left: Panorama from the Creaggan Road (western side). Left to right: The small byre; Postie's Cottage; the boathouse; Shore Cottage; LochanDhu; the chapel; Ardneackie peninsula.

DTI ministers at Saltwood 1988. Back row (includes) From left: Francis Maude, John Butcher, Geoffrey Sterling, AC, Robert Atkins, Maxwell Beaverbrook, John Taylor, Nick Baker. Front row: Kenneth Clarke, Jane, David Young.

Alfresco lunch at Saltwood. Jane, Richard Ryder, Frank Johnson, Tristan Garel-Jones, William Waldegrave.

Ian Gow drinks brandy in the garden at Saltwood. ...

... and so does Bruce Anderson.

CARS

The Jaguars: 'SS100',
C-Type, 'XK'.

The 'Ghost'.

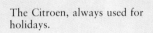

The Citroen, always used for
holidays.

The Chalet Caroline in Zermatt, winter and summer. The lower picture also shows the new kiosk (unpainted).

Bratton, Devon.

British Embassy, Sofia   *Wednesday, 13 April*

Far too many people seem to know that today is my birthday, which of course I don't like at all as it makes it more difficult for me to ignore the fact that I am sixty. I *refuse* to be sixty. 'Mirror, mirror, on the wall...' etc. And the Bulgarians are threatening to sing 'Happy Birthday'.

In point of fact, the mirrors here are kind. And yesterday afternoon on arrival, I seemed glossy and confident. But this morning my face is swollen, and from some angles I could be an *ill* sixty.

I *must* not drink on these tours. Foolishly and youthfully I had two glasses of Fendant and then two of Dole on the Swissair flight from Zurich. I felt cocky at the time, but very tired when I finally got here from the airport, having made smalltalk to HE all the way in the back of the Jaguar. I had to go and lie on my bed and rest the eyeballs before the evening meetings got under way instead of, as I would have preferred, writing up this journal.

At dinner, in the not unacceptable Sheraton Balkan, I drank a glass of vodka with the (vast) shrimp cocktail, and then at least two glasses of Bulgarian white. Christov, my host, three years younger than I but unarguably more crumpled and jowelly, drank copiously as obedient waiters – slow in discharging other functions – refilled his glass.

Conversation did *not* sparkle. Hardly surprising as we had had a meeting at the airport; a formal meeting in his Department; followed by two hours, plus, sitting next to each other at dinner.

Christov asked me what hours I worked.

'Eight thirty in the morning until about seven, seven fifteen. Some days until midnight. Average twelve.'

'I thought it was only Socialist Ministers who had to work that hard.'

'All Ministers,' I said. 'Except perhaps in Italy where, anyway, they don't count.'

HE is quiet, and does not 'keep the ball rolling'. He is hosting a big dinner for me tomorrow, so I hope he perks up. In his last year, so probably free-wheeling a bit. But I have known worse; both more idle, and more beadily intrusive.

Ginev, my other mentor, is heavily built but in good condition the way some overweight men (Strauss another example) can be. He travelled back with me on the Varig flight from Punta del Este, and knows I like girls. So whenever I catch his eye he seems to be twinkling conspiratorially which is, potentially, a bore.

At the end of the meal (which went on *far* too long) Christov walked me over to an adjoining table, and introduced a friend of his, a 'heart surgeon'(!). Also sitting there were a kind of brigand with villainous features, and a very pretty young girl with long red hair below her shoulders.

The Embassy is a fine building. Assertively Edwardian, and with its original nickel-plated plumbing. But HE's wife is *demonstratively* colourless. She seems pleasant and intelligent enough, but apparently has Parkinson's disease. Why is it that only innocent people, never nasty ones, are visited by these disagreeable diseases?

Now I can hear officials padding about in the corridor, preparing for a draining and meaningless day of meetings and protocol. Last night Christov asked me about my hobbies.

'Walking,' I said, and thought of the Creaggan Road.

Velikiye Tournovo   *Thursday, 14 April*

Today should have been quite agreeable – a motor drive across Bulgaria, some pleasantries on arrival with the Mayor, and a more or less private dinner in a tavern with the rest of the party. But nothing (nothing good, anyway) is as we expect it.

I had gone to bed vilely late as the amiable, but useless, buffer of an Ambassador (how freely I now used the word buffer of people who are younger than me) kept us up until gone midnight at a dinner in the Balkan Sheraton, *plying* me with drink, most of which I managed to avoid. Conversation, such as it was, of absolutely minimal value other than a brief passage when, emboldened, HE admitted/boasted that he had twice tried for adoption as a Liberal candidate (not surely the most demanding of ordeals?) and that he was strongly opposed to Trident. I couldn't really be rude, so kept quiet. But long silences, most definitely *not* filled by attentive staff bringing a succession of courses, dragged out the meal interminably.

So I hardly felt a thousand per cent this morning, sinking rather frailly sick into the front seat of the Jaguar and lowering my eyelids. The interpreter, or rather -trix, couldn't quite see, but could sense, that I wasn't paying full attention. Unrelentingly she jarred me. She was of the same school as yesterday, i.e., big greasy gypsy stock. She spoke English well, understood it poorly. 'Freed from the Ottoman yoke' and 'a self-taught master builder' were two phrases which, Kafka-like, recurred a great deal.

Once we were in the countryside I tried feigning sleep, though snapping 'awake' at one point on hearing that 'workers and peasants had united in an anti-fascist uprising in 1923'. Surely fascism hadn't existed in 1923, I growled. It came in with Mussolini. Ah no, though. It was the *concept* of Fascism that they had risen against.

En route, there was the Thracian tomb. (Pillaged in times past, so hardly worth looking at, but I disconcerted one and all by asking for a lavatory – it was nearly three hours since yoghourt and black coffee, four cups; am I the only human being who has to relieve his bladder at these intervals?)

Then, a tour of the Hydraulica factory and a formal lunch. Two set speeches from the Mayor and, obligatorily, two (off-the-cuff) responses from me. The Mayor was beautifully turned out and groomed in the way that only the lower classes manage when they are really trying, bless them. He was not unlike Cradduck[1] (good head of hair, carriage, Pisanello medal, all that balls) and spoke in inflexible paragraphs about the charms of his region. He said that at University he had been President of the Temperance League, and of the anti-tobacco society.

As I could hardly fail to notice that he was 'nipping' freely, and smelt of cigarettes, I asked, 'And then what happened?'

At this he appeared non-plussed, although the company laughed.

In the early part of the afternoon we drove through acres and acres of rose plantations, not yet in bloom, and they told me that it took three tons of rose petals (Heliogabulus)[2] to make a litre of oil. The interpretrix said that 14 February was St Tristan's day, the patron saint of pruners.

In Britain, I said, you send a card, with a message of endearment, to your loved one, but without signing it. And I reflected on how often I have missed this date, with a particular subject in mind. Why,

---

[1] Head gardener at Saltwood for twenty-nine years, from 1951 to 1980.
[2] *The Roses of Heliogabulus* by Alma Tadema, a famous Victorian painting depicting the Roman Emperor being smothered by, and wallowing in, rose petals.

for example, did I not send one to Rose this year – or last, come to that?

British Embassy, Bucharest   *Friday, 15 April*

We changed Jaguars at the Danube bridge and set off through flat, wet country; many horse-drawn vehicles. I saw a sad, friendly dog, like a rather shorter 'Ding'[1] standing with her ears back, lost?, in a truckers' layby. Just before the frontier a wonderfully ramshackle peasant lorry had rendezvoused with us and the occupants had 'shown' the cane garden furniture which, impetuously, I had ordered in Sofia. I issued a cheque for 270 US dollars – a bargain, if I ever see it again.[2]

Bucharest is *incredibly* grotty and rundown. Giant, flooded pot-holes; battered rusty trolley buses looking as if they had done service as roadblocks in the first battle of Rostov, disgorging crowds of sullen, shabby (but overweight) lumpenproletariat. Ceauşescu is bulldozing great swathes of the old town in order to impose a Haussmann-like pattern of squares and boulevards. Partly megalomania but largely, I would suspect, the same motives as Napoleon III's own instructions to Haussmann – in order better to enfilade the mob with cannon.[3]

HE is grey haired and bearded – 'active don', with a U-accent.[4] Slightly *distrait* style, but could be likeable. To my great satisfaction I found that we are in Tilea's[5] old villa. Still with some traces of his decor, or even Syrie Maugham, wrought-iron grilles and open plan in 1930s Florida style. Upstairs, though, the proportions are rather more *Torquay*. The carpets in the living room are exactly the same colour and design as the chaise-longue in the Chalet Caroline, which must have been covered at about the same time.

---

[1] A little mongrel bitch from the farm at Saltwood which AC always coveted as a pet.

[2] The cane furniture was punctiliously delivered in a Bulgarian lorry to the gates of Saltwood and is installed in the Garden House.

[3] Baron Haussmann replanned medieval Paris between 1853 and 1870, replacing narrow streets with wide boulevards to make the constructions of revolutionary barricades more difficult.

[4] Hugh Arbuthnott, British Ambassador to Rumania since 1986.

[5] The Rumanian Ambassador in London in the Thirties. A great socialite and scaremonger, *vide* Cadogan's diaries, etc.

Mrs Arbuthnott is rather attractive, and knows it, with the faintest undertone of mocking curiosity. Reminds me a little of the Dunne girls.

Blast. I've been lying not on but in my bed (the room is freezing) while, as I thought comfortingly, the bath ran. Now I find that the hot tap is lukewarm and the cold has diluted it beyond the acceptance limit. I must make do with a quick Pirbright scrub.[1] Then it's blue suit, white silk shirt, and off. Another formal dinner in prospect.

On the Danube   *Saturday, 16 April*

This is the river trip to Calstock[2] in spades, with diamond and oakleaves cluster. Rule of life, learned far too late, most recently at Konstanz is – never 'put in for' boat trips. The tiny, ill-built, thrumming *Riubeni* is conveying us down the Danube canal to the hotel at Sulina at the mouth of the delta. The return journey, tomorrow, will be against the current and slated (sic) to take over eight hours. It is really quite exceptionally cold – long grey overcast clouds, driving rain and the great river flooding and over its banks everywhere.

A teeny 'sandwich' (cold) has been served, and an 'orange juice' – the thinnest of wartime 'Jacks'[3] orangeade. In an adjoining cabin, the 'lounge', I can hear the Ambassador valiantly holding his own with the heavily made-up *Romantourist* lady who communicates in bad French. So, all in all, it's a dodgy prospect; pyjamas *and* underclothes in bed tonight, I should think, and an early start, curtailing the possibility of a thompson,[4] at 5.45 a.m.

Yesterday evening, however, was more fun. Dinner at the Athenee-Palace in a lovely 1907 dining room with fine-quality Tiffany glass lights set into the ceiling and a (too modest) Orpen maiden in a blue dress and an oval frame over the fireplace. *Musica* interrupted my desultory conversation, in (on his part, at least) poor French, with Mr

---

[1] The Household Division depot, where all recruits are subject to an especially arduous infantry training course.

[2] A habitual Constituency engagement on the River Tamar which AC used to find particularly irksome.

[3] A tuckshop adjoining the fives courts at Eton.

[4] Family slang for defecation.

Vadura, the State Trade Secretary. The violinist and his band played every tune from the big musical box at Saltwood.

Then some 'local' dancers came bouncing on and performed very merrily in national costume. I 'fixed' the best female, a nicely built blonde. Later, in a 'tableau' of four cloggie-type performers, I spotted that the one in a dog's mask was really a girl – from her slightly smaller size and quicker, neater movements. And sure enough, at the end she threw off the mask and a lovely mane of copper red hair fell out. A good round of applause and Mr Vadura said that he had thought she was a man. I said no, and the old interpreter smiled and nodded knowingly.

Later, I may have disconcerted Mr Vadura by trying to explain what I meant when I said Brisbane was the ice-cream capital of the world. He was making Ceaușescu's excuses; the President was 'touring Australia'. But when I talked about young blondes he became uneasy.

Not so the plump and corrupt 'manager' of the hotel who suddenly whipped out a medal and sash, of a *chevalier de fromage* kind, and hung it round my neck. 'Now follow me.' He took me down a narrow spiral staircase directly into the lobby of a *Hullo* nightclub, barking at a couple of (quite good-looking) whores who were sitting on the banquette. HE and the rest of the party were following, I was sorry to see, sheepishly and at a distance.

Live band. Very sympathetic saxophonist in glasses, jacket, open-neck cricket shirt who conscientiously studied his score throughout. And a pleasing floor show. The cuties, sinuous and blonde-skinned, shimmered and bounced with ostrich feathers and other, slender, accoutrements. The vocalists were talented and loud, 'Pasadena', etc. From time to time HE would lean over (he was about four places away at our table). 'You don't really need to stay, Minister'; and 'They won't be at all offended if you leave, you know'; and (desperate now) 'We've got a very early start tomorrow morning...'

Unusually for me, I had accepted a huge delicious Cuban cigar from the commercial attaché, and wouldn't move until it was finished. But the night was not so comfortable. Very cold indeed and I had to pee twice, once after a nasty dream about Tom being burned in a train.

Aboard the Riubeni   *Sunday, 17 April*

After breakfast (egg swimming in grease, coarse ham, wet brown rolls, erzatz coffee – which I quite like but HE wouldn't touch – and good natural cherry jam) I found a nice *warm* little cabin which I have designated my own. Outside the rain belts down and the waves (unusual for a river to have waves, surely?) slosh against the side of the hull. The engines throb reassuringly. This is the only heated cabin, but I am not entirely at ease as upright, and waiting for a thompson to announce itself.

The delta is vast. Two hundred thousand square miles or so we are told. Reed and willow trees and huge brackish lakes. Not much bird-life in evidence which is hardly surprising as the boat gives noisy advance warning of our approach. From one island a poor thin dog on a chain barked at us. When was he last fed?

Last night, as I foresaw, it was again '*quarante minutes entre chaque plat*'. And I lost patience at course 4, a nasty-looking steak, and asked for a jug of boiling water. Somewhere in my night case I had a 'portion' package of delicious Swiss *cacao*, pinched from the hotel in Konstanz for just this emergency, and my plan was to retire immediately, drink it, and have a (relatively) good night. But even this took fifteen minutes to arrive and to my – first pleasure, then annoyance – the task of taking it up to my room, with me, was entrusted to the sweeter of the two little waitresses who, in spite of poor complexion – unmade-up, poor little dear – definitely 'had something'; notably a large bust. But she was, we were, escorted most clumpingly up the wooden staircase by the huge and powerful manager and also by the police spy. So she wouldn't even catch my eye when I thanked her and said goodnight.

Later

The Captain, in spite of having four rings on his sleeve, has made a succession of balls-ups, twice ramming the bank, getting entangled with floating tree-trunks, throwing the little craft into 'hard astern', etc. Revving belchingly, he broke off a lot of willow (destroying, incidentally, our aerial so we are now completely incommunicado). I saved two sprigs in case they could be transplanted at Saltwood. I will put them straight into the basin in my bedroom at the Embassy, but I

fear they will die before I can get them home.[1] I did manage a 'formal'
thompson, one ranking for the *extremis* star along with the all time
winner – under the trucks at Ascension Island, Wideawake airport.
There was no lock on either outer or inner door, and the 'toilet' itself
so narrow that, say, Cyril Smith could not have fitted in, much less
.on, it.

I caught sight of myself in the shaving mirror. Very heavy and
jowelly I look. I must get out soon, and was cheered by the thought
of the Privy Council list.[2] But of course there's always 'And yet . . .'
This trip illustrates it in microcosm. *What* a bore it is having to meet
the local Party Chairman (the same all over the world), listen to
his wooden exposé of the district's 'technical, social and economic
achievements in the co-operative sphere'. Yet how agreeable to have
instant access and treatment.

And so in my life. Lovely to have the time, now I know what to
do with it; sad to discard the trappings.

Department of Trade and Industry   *Wednesday, 27 April*

David Young and I dined together last night at Brooks's. He was very
friendly and confiding. 'You're the only person I can talk to . . . '

I asked about his little grand–daughter, a few pleasantries, then
moved in.

'David, it's rather earlier in the meal than I had intended, but I
must speak frankly as I have something to say which you may not find
welcome.'

'No, no. Far better speak frankly. I'd much prefer it.'

(I suspect David was thinking that some rebuke might be on the
way. In yesterday's papers he was criticised for not being in the Lords
enough – an obvious plant by Bertie Denham,[3] who does *not* find
David congenial.)

---

[1] One survived, and is growing on the south bank of the stream flowing through the
arboretum at Saltwood.

[2] A recurrent theme of AC's. In fact he was not appointed to the Privy Council until
the 1991 New Year list. See the closing entry in this volume for an account of
his induction.

[3] Lord Denham, Government Chief Whip, House of Lords, since 1979.

'Well, the point is approaching when you must start seriously to turn your mind to the question of whether you should enter the Commons.'

I could see at once that he was delighted. 'I'm not talking about the mechanics of it at present. They are not insuperable, if the will is there.'

We discussed the alternatives. His own 'scenario' had him moving in September, to take Health out of DHSS (the present Dept is to be split into two), sort that out, and become Chairman of the Party to win (eh?) the next Election.

His reward – to be Foreign Secretary.

At some point in the *next* Parliament a by-election would be arranged, with the PM's assent. David would then be poised to contest the succession.

I shot this down. Full of flaws. Time-scale too long (at mercy of the unpredictable); uncertainties too prolific – would she consent? Would his 'record' sustain it? Wouldn't it be too obvious that the move was simply in order to pitch at the succession?

I told David that if he was really serious he *had* to have a period in the House of Commons behind him, and experience of one of the great Offices that are open only to Commoners. (Naturally he would like best to be Chancellor.) I said that the very latest he could do it would be at the General Election, swim in on the tide. But he should be prepared to move fast if/when Bufton Tufton keels over in this Parliament.

'How long would a one-clause Bill take?'

'Two hours.'

'Would it have to go to the Lords?' (I didn't know the answer to this, but thought it significant that he should have asked.)

Plainly David is taken by the idea. I know from talking to Robert Atkins that sometimes it is mentioned 'jokingly'. David suggested that I sound out the PM, when next an opportunity offered. And at one point, I seem to remember, there was wild talk of standing at a by-election regardless, like Tony Benn, and daring the Commons to do its worst.[1]

---

[1] Tony Benn, MP for Chesterfield since 1983, who successfully instigated an Act of Parliament that allowed heirs to relinquish hereditary peerages. On the death of his father, the 1st Viscount Stansgate, Benn had been forced to resign his seat (then Bristol South East).

I advised against this. I reminded David that Benn was already in the Commons, having been endorsed by the electorate, when old Stansgate died and the problem arose. David admitted that many – he gave Kenneth Baker as an example – would turn against him once he had discarded the fleece (my analogy) and was running with the pack. I thought of, but didn't mention, Willie.

'That's why it mustn't be too obvious.'

I told David that he must get in, sweat out the initial phase of uncomplimentary profiles, malicious and wounding 'Diary' entries, trials of strength at the Despatch Box – get all this over before the 'Contest' actually starts. The analogy was with Alec [Home], I said. Someone whom nobody saw coming, but once it was settled 'the boys all breathed a sigh of relief'. (But of course Alec *had* done a stint in the Commons, when he was Neville's PPS.)

David began to run through the key personalities. He was voluble, but spoke shrewdly.

John Moore, totally destroyed, finished. Could even be dropped without trace in September. Ken Clarke, lazy, flawed, though 'quite good'. (Irritatingly, when he said 'Ken' I had thought he was referring to Baker, and I rejoined 'very' good.)

I compensated by saying, 'I couldn't work with him.'

'Oh quite. Quite.'

Nigel Lawson and Ridley were both washed out. But I queried this in Lawson's case. I said there was no such condition as 'not wanting' the top job – 'it's like a person's sex drive; there is always *something* there that can be kindled'.

John Wakeham no longer a contender, but wants as always to be the kingmaker. In some situations his conduct will reflect this.

Norman Tebbit was schizophrenic. (I heard various tales of his incompetence at CCO. David said that the book *Campaign*[1] was entirely accurate as regards chit-chat.) Interestingly, David said that Norman was behind all the stories and leaks about Peter Morrison – 'whose career is now at an end'.

David said that Michael [Heseltine] was really dangerous. The front runner. I calmed him. That's what they all say. I made the point that the Leader of the Tory Party has never been seen coming, that the way Michael was going round the place telling everyone he will

---

[1] *Campaign!* – 1987 Election book by Rodney Tyler.

get it, preening himself at Conference and so on, he couldn't keep it up for another two years. I told David that I was the author of those various remarks in Graham Turner's profile, comparing Michael to Lord Stokes, 'what he thinks – if his mental processes can actually be dignified by the word "thought"', etc., and he laughed, spontaneously.

David asked me where I would like to 'go' in September. I emulated Lord Halifax, indicated, but did not say, that I was reluctant to move 'sideways'; Trade was the best of the Min of State jobs, and so on. But equally, of course, I had done it long enough. (Foolishly, as I now realise, I did not say that I had to be made a Privy Councillor in June.) I said that I didn't really care, would just as soon go out.

'Oh no. You mustn't do that.' He asked me about Defence.

'I really feel that unless I were made Secretary of State I would find it so frustrating, I couldn't bear it.'

David made various tangential remarks about George Younger,[1] his father dying, wouldn't be able to hold his seat in Ayr, and so forth.

I didn't get the point until David said that if I was *in situ* when this happened (as Procurement Minister of State) it would be easier for me to slide upwards.

I tried to backtrack. Earlier, when I had said that I would like Paul's job[2] he had nodded, perhaps *overfast*. But he did say, 'She's got to have you in the Cabinet. She *must*. She's so short of supporters.'

Department of Trade and Industry   *Tuesday, 14 June*

We are now poised to put in place my personal *chef d'oeuvre*, the Fur Labelling Order. It has to lie on the table for a month, and then a brief debate in the House, after ten, and if necessary a perfunctory whipped vote on a two-liner. I have devoted enormous energy and time to this measure, and it is a purely personal triumph – over lawyers, Ambassadors, senior civil servants in several Departments including my own; eskimos, furriers, 'small shopkeepers' – they have all been in and alternately (sometime simultaneously) threatened and cajoled.

But yesterday, sinisterly, Charles rang from Number 10 to say that

---

[1] George Younger, MP for Ayr since 1964. Defence Secretary since 1986.
[2] Paul Channon had been Transport Secretary since 1987.

the PM 'would like a word' on the subject, could I come to her room in the House after Questions?

H'm. Could be bad.

Later
House of Commons
Charles was waiting behind the Chair, to catch me before I went in, a bad sign. He tried to soften me up.

'The Prime Minister really wants to drop the whole thing.'

'Not a chance, I'm afraid.'

'She's very worried about the effect on these local native communities of their livelihood being destroyed.'

'That's all balls.'

'Apparently Carol has just come back from there with heartrending stories.'

'She's just been conned.'

'The Prime Minister would like you first to go out to Canada and see for yourself.'

'Sure, I can do that. But it won't make the slightest difference.'

'No, but the Prime Minister's idea is that this would allow you to come back and say that you had seen for yourself and that you were not going to proceed.'

'Forget it.'

'You know that she herself is visiting Canada shortly?'

Of course! She could probably have resisted the Finchley furriers. But that blasted High Commissioner in Ottawa was winding her up with predictions of demos, placards, bad atmosphere, 'attention diverted from principal objectives of the visit', I could see it all.

'Let's go in.'

Hamilton[1] was there, on an upright chair. The PM and I sat opposite each other on those yellow damask sofas in the 'L' of the room.

'Alan, how are you?'

I ignored this. 'I'm so sorry that you should be getting all this trouble from the Canadians.'

'Oh it's not really *trouble*. I think there's more to it.'

This was going to be very difficult. She had a letter from Mulroney;

---

[1] Archie Hamilton succeeded Michael Alison as PPS to the Prime Minister in 1987.

from Resource International (I remember being warned about the clout they carried); she was going to address the Canadian Parliament. As the Prime Minister developed her case she, as it were, auto-fed her own indignation. It was a prototypical example of an argument with a woman – no rational sequence, associative, lateral thinking, jumping rails the whole time.

'Why not labelling of battery hens, of veal who never see daylight, of fish which had a hook in their mouth – what about foxes? Do you hunt?'

'Certainly not. Nor do I allow it on my land. And as for veal, I'm a vegetarian.'

'What about your shoes?'

I ignored this the first time. The second time I said, 'I don't think you would want your Ministers to wear plastic shoes.'

CP and Hamilton smiled. She did *not*.

Too far gone in indignation now, she just said something about the feet breathing better in leather.

'It's not you, Alan. It's so unlike you to respond to pressure.'

'I'm not "responding" to pressure. I'm *generating* it. I believe in it.'

Off we went again. Her sheer energy, and the speed with which she moves around the ring, make her a very difficult opponent. There was talk of wolves around the house.

'How would you like that?'

'I'd love it.'

Her argument, if such a confused, inconsequential but ardent gabbling can be dignified by that Aristotelian term, was 'it's-all-very-well-for-suburban-bourgeoisie-to-inflict-this-legislation-but-what-about-the-noble-savage?' I was prepared to respond on a philosophical plane. I said something-something about it being 'the first step'.

This was a mistake. She gritily repeated the phrase to herself several times, half under her breath, '–the first step?'

'In enlarging man's sense of responsibility towards the animal kingdom.'

She shifted ground again. Didn't like labelling orders, weren't we trying to move away from all that?

After four and a half minutes of this I realised I'd lost.

The meeting, scheduled for fifteen minutes, went on for fifty-five.

About three-quarters of the way through I said, 'Well, if that's what you want, I will obey you.'

Later I said, 'When you go to Canada, don't have anything to do with that "Humane Trapping Committee". It's a put-up job, you'll just make a fool of yourself. They'll think they've conned you.'

She grunted assent.

'I hate quarrelling with you, Alan.'

I snarled, 'I wouldn't do it for anyone else', and went out of the door.

Later
Department of Trade and Industry
A few minutes ago Charles rang. The PM was anxious to try and help me 'out' of this. No note had been taken of the meeting. (All that means, of course, is that the note which *was* taken will not be circulated.)

'I won't land her in it' (thinking of all those nice sincere young people in Lynx whom I was letting down).

No no, of course not, it wasn't that, she just wanted to see if she/we could help at all. Charles suggested that the order did still go on up to OD (E)[1] and that he would put up the Attorney and the Foreign Secretary to co-ordinate a very strong expression of legal opinion that would stop it in its tracks.

I like Charles. But *au fond* he is an apparatchik, although one of superlative quality. But my relations with the Lady are damaged – perhaps beyond repair.

Should I preempt? It would be the first time that a Minister will ever have resigned on an issue concerning the welfare of creatures that don't have a vote.

I rang Jane and she was wise and calming, though sad. Said, don't do anything hasty.

Albany   *Wednesday, 15 June*

I rose at four a.m. and made tea. The House has been sitting all night and, I am assured, will 'lose' today's business. A small stroke of luck

---

[1] OD (E): The Cabinet committee whose responsibility it would be to consider this topic.

as I am First for Questions this afternoon. A delicious sense of benefice – an unused day! I think I will go down to Saltwood, take breakfast there, and tackle estate papers.

But the oppression of yesterday's defeat is unresolved. I woke just after two, lay unhappily thrashing until four. Why had I woken so early? What was that waiting to come through the subconscious? The brain scans for seconds (it seems longer) then all the weight of those as yet unanswered letters, hundreds of them, of praise and encouragement; the thought that at this very moment animals are being caught in the wild; all the pain and despair on which their exploitation depends, I felt utterly dejected. I felt rage, too, at the PM having so totally swallowed the commercial lobby's case. Who has been feeding her all that stuff?

When the cock blackbird started up, on the dot of four, I put my head out of the window, the better to listen to him. So clear and beautiful, as he went through his whole repertoire, he passed to me a lovely message of Nature's strength, her powers of continuity and renewal.

And I drew some small consolation from this.

Nature's timescale is so different from ours.

House of Commons Terrace, evening   *Tuesday, 28 June*

It is humid. Warm but with a very light drizzle. I haven't sat out here to make a diary note for many years. The river boats going back and forth, always with some drunks, who jeer; the smells and breezes still, after forty-three years, evocative of 'Rafts'.[1] It is so hateful being stuck in the House during the summer months. (I must have written this a hundred, two hundred, times.)

As I left Saltwood this morning I said to Jane, the days are getting shorter again. One barely notices it at first but I believe myself at this point to start getting older and stiffer and sleepier, like the peacocks loosing their tail feathers. Whereas in the happy months of April and May, as the light lengthens, I am goat-like, and scrawnily boyish.

---

[1] The rafts and sheds on the Thames at Windsor used by the Eton rowing teams, or 'wet bobs'.

My Private Office are hopelessly incompetent. I had a bad brief for the ECGD[1] meeting. And they themselves are being timid and useless over the text of the press release. This should be hyping the extra billion which I have finally secured for special 'national interest' cover in defence equipment contracts. But there comes a point when officials suddenly lose their balls, become nervous of the Public Accounts Committee, or the National Audit Office.

However dear John Major very nobly allowed me to appeal directly to him, and overruled his own officials who had forbidden me (through *my* officials) to use the word 'extra'. This would of course have robbed the announcement of any impact at all, thus achieving what the civil servants wanted, as they can't bear Ministers making announcements on any topic unless the idea originated with them. I often think that in their ideal world the 'Line to Take' is prepared before the policy concept itself. No programme, but *none* is so true to life as *Yes, Minister*.

At eleven o'clock I left the Department for Aldershot, where the MoD has sponsored an arms sales 'exhibition'. I travelled down by car. Beside me on the back seat (I never like this but could hardly say 'sit in front, please', as I had never set eyes on him before) slumped a totally useless senior official who didn't know the name of any weapon, the calibre of any gun, the size or specification of *anything*, it seemed. Said he'd 'only been in the job six months'. Really! Six *hours* should have been enough for him to answer some of my queries.

I did a tour of the stands with the official following at my heels muttering to himself. I made all the running. Weapons are one of our best exports, and unlike most of the manufacturing sector there are still some bright young people around – though the boffins are better than the 'managers'. If I ever get to the MoD I'd be able to do a lot more. But the whole subject is blighted, in policy terms, by input from three separate Departments, DTI, MoD and Foreign Office. Friction is caused – as much by the *amour propre* of officials whose tenacious defence of their own (frequently illogical and outdated) position generates paper and delay.

At lunch I sat between Prince Michael of Kent and Frank Cooper,[2] the Prince in his ludicrous high collar and 'stock' like a cravat. He

---

[1] ECGD: Export Credit Guarantee Department.
[2] Sir Frank Cooper, retired civil servant. Permanent Under-Secretary, Ministry of Defence, 1976–82.

warmed to my talking about the Mille Miglia.[1] Anyone who has driven a DBR 1 in that ordeal can't be wholly without interest.

Frank was fascinating. He told me that at some conference in 1977, when she was still only (just) leader of the Opposition, the PM had turned to him and said, 'Must I do all this international stuff?' 'You can't avoid it,' was his reply, and she pulled a face. Frank says she remains a Little Englander through and through. I'm not so sure. I think she now relishes the role of statesman. Who wouldn't, after all, prefer the motorcade to being shouted at twice a week by little Kinnock. Frank said that during that period she and he had met Reagan and Carter, and she was *astonished* at how stupid they were. 'Can they really dispose of all that power?' etc.

Some interesting vignettes about the Falklands. That first Friday evening FC was dining with John Clark and Alistair Frame.[2] The phone rang before they could sit down, and he was called at once to the Prime Minister's room in the Commons. Henry Leach[3] (*not* in uniform, incidentally, that story is a myth) was the only Chief of Staff available.

Leach made a quiet, confident, measured presentation of how he could deploy the fleet. No one, curiously (and in retrospect fortunately) mentioned air cover at that time. Foreign Office officials cowered in a corner, sulky and apprehensive, but quiet. The Army were 'useless, couldn't take it seriously'. The RAF were slow to wake up, then panicked at the idea that the Navy would get all the credit, started moving on flight refuelling, insisted on deploying *their* Harriers for ground attack, etc.

Frank said that at one point there was a school recommending that *all* the Commanders be changed, including Woodward![4]

---

[1] A race over public roads in Italy, restricted since 1958 to 'Classic' cars.
[2] Sir John Clark, Chairman of Plessey, and Sir Alistair Frame, Chairman of RTZ.
[3] Admiral of the Fleet Sir Henry Leach, Chief of the Naval Staff and First Sea Lord.
[4] Admiral Sir John (Sandy) Woodward was Senior Task Group Commander, South Atlantic, during the Falklands Campaign, April-July 1982.

House of Commons   *Monday, 18 July*

The three-quarters of July syndrome. Everything stale and fetid. I
walked through the Members' lobby this afternoon, then to the library
and down Speaker's corridor. People – many of whom I hardly knew –
scuttled and bustled self-importantly. I thought, if and when I 'stand
down', not one single person, except possibly Ian and Tristan, will
even notice or miss me for thirty seconds. Julian Amery, perhaps.

That fat creep Bruce Anderson[1] again wrote about the reshuffle
and *again* left me out (probably prompted by John Whittingdale[2] who
has always been doubtful, spelt j.e.a.l.o.u.s.). I have no future. Why
should I go on stressing and straining and destroying the substance?
'Go out while they are still calling for more', etc. I suppose there is
an off-chance of an upheaval if Walters[3] comes back, Lawson goes
completely pouty and things fall apart. But in fact the next major
reshuffle 'to take us into the Nineties' (ugh) is scheduled for 1989.
And that actually will be the signal for me to be exited. Why hang
around until then?

Department of Trade and Industry   *Tuesday, 19 July*

Tedious day. To the Arab-British Chamber of Commerce exhibition.
Like an old cavalry horse, I dozed on the hoof as I went round the
stands. The Prince of Wales 'opened' it. He has a strong handshake,
like all polo players, but is pretty useless, I judge. Trite, tinky sentiments, prissily delivered. During his speech I dropped off into a
mildly erotic dream. I am tired and nonno-ish, and my stubble is
going grey – *why*?

---

[1] But see other mentions.
[2] A member of the Number 10 Policy group, later head of Mrs Thatcher's Cabinet
in exile.
[3] Sir Alan Walters, personal Economics Adviser to the Prime Minister, 1981–4, now
back at the World Bank as economics adviser.

Department of Trade and Industry   *Tuesday, 21 July*

I was in today before eight. By six I was completely exhausted, but still thought I might look in on Stephen's goodbye party, on the off-chance of setting eyes on any of the girls I fancy. At the door I ran into dear Judith, sweet and correct as always but looking, I thought, a tiny bit washed out. There was a fattish blonde whose name I don't know but she once said, or sang, 'there's someone following me . . .' when I was behind her, and admiring her dimensions, in the lift lobby – but no favourites.

However S of S was present and in ebullient form. We left together and he asked me back to his room. He said he'd had a 'good talk' with the Lady that very afternoon, and recommended me for Defence (at what rank? I didn't have the courage to ask). He said she had 'not reacted badly'. I was elated. David then said that I should try and get to see her in August 'when there is nothing much going on'. I said, 'But one should never argue one's own case. It's always counter-productive.' Oops! He wanted me to argue *his* case (!). He wants to go to Health, zap it before he becomes Chairman.

So I'm none the wiser. I don't know whether he *really* pushed my case, or whether she *really* reacted favourably, or whether he was saying all this in order to get me to boost *him*. Gossip and tittle-tattle in our game is only very rarely pure invention. The skill lies in objective interpretation.

Back in the House I ran into Chris Patten, told him that things were getting a bit 'closer'. He said that the Defence Dept was totally out of control. 'You'll be the most unpopular man in the Party.' 'I couldn't care. It's got to be faced.' Chris said that 'more and more intelligent people are saying this'.

Only two hours earlier I had been feeling appalling. Now, effervescent with glee and anticipation, I shot round to Brooks's and my dice sparkled. I took £500 off Nick Blackwell and we all crossed the road to dine at Boodles. Delicious claret, and Michael Stoop told several good stories – poignant was his recollection of a beautiful Belgian lady, a Madame Charlier, forty-two years old when as a subaltern in Rhine Army, he loved her after the war. Her body, 'and what we used to do' he recalled perfectly. Forty years later, eighty-two and unrecognisable, she hailed him at a restaurant in Brussels. 'She,' I said, 'who was once the helmet-makers' beautiful wife.'[1]

---

[1] The title of a sculpture of a very old woman by Auguste Rodin.

Department of Trade and Industry   *Monday, 25 July*

This morning I was tranquil. Little work pressing, and my office is full of flowers which Jane has sent up from Saltwood and which, queanly old sommelier, I took time and pleasure arranging.

I thought I might get G-J to dine with me at the Beefsteak (in the summer that long table with the bay window at the end is so much more congenial than Pratts. Pratts is more of a winter burrow.)

'Yes,' he said. 'And we can talk about the reshuffle.'

Got the point a bit too obviously, I thought, but never mind.

Some twenty minutes later I wandered into the outer office – Rose is looking so gorgeous in her yellow dress that, on one excuse or another, I have put my head round the door about six times already – and there on her desk was the early edition of the *Standard* – RESHUFFLE IN PROGRESS. 20 CHANGES.

I knew, of course that I was safe, but I was annoyed at its suddenness and disappointed at being passed over. I sat brooding for a few minutes, and was then interrupted by a summons to go round to the Secretary of State immediately.

David was a *husk*. Hadn't been consulted, hadn't even been warned. Wicks (as always somewhat off-hand) had simply rung to say that 'the name' was Newton.[1] I said that John Nott[2] told me he had absolutely no choice in who his junior Ministers were, and it was very unusual for a Secretary of State to be consulted.

But David was shattered – 'not even the courtesy of . . . ', then stopped himself. His hands shook, his blue eyes were watery. He sees the writing on the wall – a drastic diminution of his own influence.

Clutching at straws I said that 'the big one' (i.e. affecting the Cabinet) could be later. But no, Wicks had squashed that too. Nothing until 1989. Just another year to go through while we all grow older and the young Turks, Patten J., Patten C., Waldegrave, glint and glister.

I tried to extract some comfort from the situation by saying, 'The Nigel thing isn't finished yet . . . '

David agreed. And it is true. But what use will that be? And who

---

[1] Tony Newton, Minister for Health, had been made Chancellor of Duchy of Lancaster and a Minister of State in Trade and Industry.

[2] John Nott, former MP, who as Defence Secretary resigned in 1983, left Parliament and became Chairman of the merchant bankers, Lazard Brothers.

is she talking to? Not Wakeham; not Cecil; not repeat not, DY. Waddington?[1] But that's mechanistic only. Willie? Possibly. He was in London last night.

I drifted over to the House. Francis Maude was already there and we sat at the stationery table in the Aye lobby. Francis was tearful.

'I thought that at least I might have some recognition for all my work in the Financial Services field.'

He looks terrible. Appearance quite altered from the narrow-faced, fresh youngster who used to whip Employment. So puffy around the eyes that they are almost closed. His vision must be affected. Francis said that he had a brief meeting with David immediately after me. That he told David to remind Newton that he was only a Minister of State who happened to have a place at the Cabinet table.

DY, apparently, said that he would. But of course he won't, he's too shell-shocked. *Meni Meni Tekel Upharsin*.

Anyway, Newton is quite harmless, not a threat to anybody.

Tristan turned up at the Beefsteak. I thought it more tactful to talk about him – why had he not accepted (sic) a ministerial post? He had to work in Government in order to qualify as Chief Whip in the next Parliament, surely?

Tristan waffled around. Not particularly subtle. I got the impression that he, too, had been somewhat taken by surprise.

He was not optimistic, in the wider sense. Tristan is over-poweringly Europhile, and (as with his opponents in the Party) the subject becomes obsessive, and towers above all others. Great bore. The subject of 'Europe' is almost, though not quite, as bad as Ireland must have been at the turn of the century – and still is for some poor souls, like dear IG. Tristan said that 'confrontation' in Cabinet (what did this mean?) was inevitable 'one way or another'.

But when I ask him what he means he just bites his lip and nods his head, makes elliptic remarks like 'You'll see' and 'Just you wait'. In the end, he said, the Prime Minister will find herself isolated by her three 'heavies' – Howe, Hurd and Lawson – and in a crisis Brittan would go native at once, and add to her troubles.

I changed the subject, and urged that Nick Soames be appointed

---

[1] David Waddington, MP for Ribble Valley since 1983 (Clitheroe 1979–83). Chief Whip.

to one of the vacancies at the Whips' Office.[1] Tristan said that Nicholas didn't want it. His life was very complicated at the moment. Great mistake.

After dinner I told Jane and she said no, no, you must get hold of Nick and tell him not to be an ass.

I had to speak to him that evening, which wasn't easy. He was 'with the Prince of Wales'. But the Downing Street switchboard were magnificent, as always, and located him *via* Clarence House at the US Residence in Regent's Park, and got him away from the Ambassador's dining table.

Nick was sweet, effusive – but adamant. I told him that it's very difficult to make progress as a Minister unless (thinking ruefully of myself) you have done a stint as a Whip. He simply must grit his teeth. But he is worried about looking after his baby son. A good fellow.

Albany   *Monday, 12 September*

I have come from dinner with Richard Ryder[2] at Pratts. He's such fun. So intelligent, and has the right views on practically every topic. But he does repeat himself which, in someone his age, is a bad sign. Or at least it is if he doesn't know he's doing it. Yet some of his stories are so stylised that, Homeric, they depend on and are embellished by repetition. I've lost count of the number of times I've been told the story of Julian Amery on the (recent) parliamentary delegation to Rumania asking about Count Dracula and, after some inter-consultation between the guides, being told that 'Count Dracula is being reassessed'.

But of all Richard's stories I think my favourite, and one he tells with great panache, is a Battle of Britain folk epic which delights me however often I hear it. He and Douglas Bader were debating on opposite sides at a classy girls' school. Somehow, Bader got involved

---

[1] Nicholas Soames, PPS to the Secretary of State of Environment since 1987. He had been equerry to the Prince of Wales, 1970–2.

[2] Richard Ryder, an Assistant Whip since 1986, he was briefly to become Parliamentary Under-Secretary at Agriculture, and in 1989 Economic Secretary to the Treasury.

in telling of one of the occasions when he was shot down over the Channel:

'... And my engine was on fire, I had two of the fuckers on my tail, one fucker was coming up at me from the left, and there were two more fuckers about a hundred feet above me waiting for...' (At this the headmistress panicked and interrupted. 'Girls, as of course you all know, there was a type of German aeroplane called the FOKKER.') But Bader: 'I don't know about that. All I can tell you is these chaps were flying Messerschmitts.'

Department of Trade and Industry   *Wednesday, 14 September*

Last night I walked back from the 'Kundan'.[1] The previous evening I had walked from the Department to Albany. Tiny little saunters – about the same, I suppose, as from Shore Cottage to the Long Byre at Eriboll farm. There was a mass of starlings in St James's Park, chattering and jostling as they turned in for the night. I always like going past Clive Steps, especially in the evening when there are few people around, and I conjure up images from 1938; the great Foreign Office crises, Halifax and Cadogan walking anxiously in the Park. Chamberlain, and Horace Wilson[2] also, used it as an escape route.

As my legs stretched I still had an appetite for more. But how long will this last – five days or so? All too soon one is back in the debilitating routine, slumping on the back seat of the Jaguar even to make the journey from the Department to the House of Commons.

I have a bundle of interesting papers to read this evening. The Lady is going to make a speech at Bruges on the occasion of some Euro-anniversary or other. The Eurocreeps have written for her a really loathsome text, *wallowing* in rejection of our own national identity, which has come up to me for comment in the trade context. They even managed to delete a ritual obeisance to Churchill, his ideals, all that and substituted the name of *Schuman*. Really!

---

[1] Kundan, the curry restaurant in Horseferry Road.
[2] Sir Horace Wilson, chief industrial adviser to the Government, 1930–9, was seconded to the Treasury for service with the Prime Minister, 1935. Permanent Head of the Treasury and Head of the Civil Service, 1939–42.

I hardly know where to start in pulling it to pieces, but Charles, too, is having a go. We must win this one.

Saltwood   *Friday, 16 September*

Yesterday morning I felt vaguely, non-specifically ill; but cheered up when Jane arrived and we went over to Lancaster House for a lunch for the Prime Minister of Malta.

The PM made a *point* of seeking me out in the pre-drinks throng before the meal. She thanked me for my help, said she was going to press ahead with the Bruges notes virtually unchanged, in spite of FCO complaints. (I had earlier seen the revised, third version, and was glad to note that it hadn't altered, at all, from the second). 'You and I agree on this, but Douglas Hurd is completely committed.'

'Bugger Douglas Hurd,' I said. 'He's only the Home Secretary.'

She looked away with that lovely, distant smile she puts on when I 'go too far'.

A pleasing encounter. Fortified, I told a fabulous little blonde waitress, whom I have never seen before at Lancaster House, 'You're incredibly good-looking' as I went into the dining room, and took pleasure from watching to see how long it took for her blush (or flush) to die away.

I sat next to the Maltese High Commissioner, Manduca. A good Anglophile. I hope he's being properly treated. On my right was Carla Powell, and on *her* right sat Rocco Forte. Carla is always so full of life: 'Look at me, what fun to be sitting between two such handsome men, da da da, etc.' But as far as Rocco was concerned she somewhat spoilt the effect by pronouncing 'Rrrocco' repeatedly in an accent that my dear Mama would have categorised as *proprio siciliano*. This had the effect of making Rocco *chétif* and ill-at-ease, as clearly he would prefer to be considered, in this setting at any rate, as an English gentleman. He spoke in beautifully clear and modulated tones, rather like the Prince of Wales (on whom, for all I know, he models himself).

Carla told me that Charles was *not* leaving immediately, but they were terribly short of money, having to borrow against the little house in the *Laghi* which had been left to her by her father. He didn't want an Embassy, not unless a real cracker (by which I inferred Paris or

Washington), would really rather go straight into the City. I will try and talk to Hanson, or David Alliance.[1] Some weeks ago, when I mentioned this problem to Jimmy,[2] he said, 'That man is so important he really ought to be paid £200,000 a year just to stay where he is.' Yes, of course. But Jimmy is not always reliable, although his judgments are seldom wrong.

As the lunch broke up I had a quick word with Charles. Practically every suggestion that the Foreign Office have made[3] has been rejected. They were foolish, because by their interference and provocation they have turned a relatively minor ceremonial chore into what could now well be a milestone in redefining our policy toward the Community. Charles is in a difficult position personally, I can see that. But he is resisting his own Mandarinate without flinching.

Department of Trade and Industry   *Monday, 19 September*

An incredible autumn morning, still and hazy. At seven or thereabouts, before going to the station, I walked the dogs over the Seeds.[4] All the fields are yellow with corn stubble, but in the valley the trees are dark, dark green; in that last cycle before they start to shed their leaves.

I am filled with gloom at the thought of having to go through it all again for yet another year. I am often mindful of that passage in the Moran diaries when Churchill is complaining of certain degenerative symptoms – 'Why can't you do something about them?' and Moran tells him, 'You were born with the most wonderful physical endowment. But now you have spent it, every last penny.'

By next autumn I feel that I will be down to my very last reserves of physical, I should say phys*iqu*al, capital. I read a long article in *The Times* on the train, through massive, prolonged, shunting at Tonbridge (even so-called Third World railways can't be this bad, the driver presumably was one of their statutory quota of 'disabled' employees and having an epileptic fit) about *cancer*. I really ought to avoid these blasted A–Doctor–Writes pieces. They're always unsettling. It 'can be

---

[1] Sir David Alliance, Chairman of Coats Patons.
[2] Sir James Goldsmith, founder and proprietor of a number of commercial enterprises.
[3] For the text of the Bruges Speech.
[4] A forty-acre field at Saltwood home farm.

undetected – and undetectable for *a long time* before striking'. Really!
I thought the whole point was that it grew at colossal speed and, as
poor Annie Fleming told Celly, one had to 'run, not walk, to the
nearest doctor'?

I have appointed a new secretary, as Peta is leaving to get married.
Tedious. Her name is Alison Young. She was not Peta's preferred
candidate, but at the interview she showed spirit. I noted that her hair
was wet, for some reason, although it was a fine day.

Saltwood   *Sunday, 2 October*

The place is full of Phillips' employees, doing an inventory. They
shuffle about amiably, opening cupboards and chests, peeping and
poking. I'm amazed at how ignorant they are. I mean some of
them have specialised knowledge, of course, which I can't match on
porcelain or silver or 'gems'. But most of them give the impression of
learning as they go along. There's that mysterious greenish picture
that hangs over the fireplace in the red study; the man from the Getty
(I can't remember his name and he's been sacked since coming here)
said it was a Bellini; v. unlikely, I feel, but it is important. The
'paintings expert' looked at it for a bit, literally scratching his head,
finally said to Jane, 'Did Lord Clark ever meet Bernard Berenson?'[1]

So different from real enthusiasts like Peter Wilson, or Byam Shaw.
Something would catch their eye and they would look at it for ages,
and really love it. What was it worth? Oh nothing really, two or three
hundred pounds, but that didn't matter, the point is they *loved* it.
Christie's are the worst. What I really object to is the way that they *sneer*
at the stuff as they go round: we don't mind slumming occasionally, but
tee-hee, look at this, how quaint, nothing like the one in the Frick,
etc, etc. Sothebys are jollier but they charge. And anyway, I don't
want them to know what I've got here. No one's got into the keep
before, and I'm only doing this at the behest of the Revenue. With a
bit of luck some of Phillips's definitions will be sufficiently imprecise
as to be untraceable.

---

[1] Lord Clark worked under Berenson in Florence for three years after leaving Oxford.
They remained close friends and colleagues for the next fifty years.

Another thing that irritates me is that they are all *men*. Why no birds? I know that the atmosphere at Saltwood, creepy passages and little chambers and casement windows, can have a mildly aphrodisiac effect on female visitors. Once I've separated the girl from her group she gets alarmed, which is fun. They breathe faster, talk nineteen to the dozen, keep changing the subject. (I fear that if I'd come from 'an underprivileged background' I'd probably by now have done time for GBH, or assault, or even what Nanny calls *the other*.)

Damn. Bruce is coming down for a chat over lunch. There are a few dreary papers on my desk relating to the MFA which I haven't looked at yet and if the train was on time he'll already have been waiting, owlishly puzzled, on the platform at Sandling.

Sunday evening

We opened a bottle of Palmer '61. Bruce laid down the law on personalities, and *ratings*. My own shares are badly down after that slip on the Channel Tunnel. She was not going to keep Paul on. Bernard had the briefing to hand. Then at the last minute Paul was reprieved. At the time, and since, I felt that that was my last real chance to get into the Cabinet. And at lunch Bruce made things worse by telling me that the next Transport Minister would be Lynda.[1] How does he know? He can't know. And yet I still believe him.

Bruce was dismissive about Tristan: 'not up to it'; and Gow 'can't get a grip on things'. I don't like this. These are my friends, I mean my close friends. Then he made matters worse by saying that he had had a talk with Michael. 'He is formidable. He' – pause – 'is' – pause – 'formidable.'

I got him back to the station at four thirty, smelling powerfully of brandy. Seeing I was a bit dejected, Bruce said he would plug me with John Major and David Y, with whom he is having lunch at Conference next week. But do I really want it?

These lovely autumn days... Dear God, please spare me for at least one complete season on my own, enjoying freedom, The Philosopher Prince, adding to the store of human knowledge.

---

[1] Chalker. In fact it was to be Cecil Parkinson.

Albany   *Monday, 17 October*

Today the Anglo-Italian Summit, in Maggiore.

I rose early and confident. But Dave *lost the way* in light fog. We had to enter Heathrow by a special security gate on the north side of the perimeter that gave direct access onto the tarmac. Like all the lower classes, he went to pieces quickly and sat rigid at the wheel, slightly leaning forward, squinting into the fog, being overtaken by vans on either side. Too flush-faced to admit that he'd 'done wrong', he would neither turn round, nor even stop to get his bearings.

I was fidgety. I am only too well aware that as a Minister of State I attend these summits only at the Lady's whim. As far as Hurd, Howe, Lawson, *et al* are concerned it's very much on sufferance: 'We seem to be waiting for Alan...' From time to time I uttered peremptory instructions and we would backtrack through sleepy suburban crescents distant, it seemed, from the airport. Paperboys with orange *Guardian* satchels.

Finally, with only seven minutes to spare, we found ourselves at the familiar Spelthorne entrance. I leaped out and asked for directions. Naturally, it was a gate some distance along the perimeter which I had already suggested. It was apparent that we were only milliseconds ahead of the PM. Frantic policemen holding Uzi's[1] waved us on, on... Air Marshals covered in gilt and stripes saluted. Whumpf! I alighted in my seat. Hurd and Younger were opposite in the adjoining foursome bay. Before I could fasten my belt – for the Lady had followed directly on my heels – the engines screamed and we were off. No nonsense about waiting for the tower.

At Malpensa a large, but somewhat scruffy, guard of honour was lined up. Would they play God Save the Queen? Always a source of mischievous pleasure. And yes, they played it. I put on my raybans and walked over to where the helicopters were waiting. Douglas Hurd and I boarded a Bell 212. The Home Secretary, next to me, was nervous and thrummed his fingers. Sadismoidly I drew his attention to an adhesive notice in red just above my window: '*Sling load not to exceed 400 lbs until next* (sic) *overhaul*'. 'It's the word 'next' I don't like,' I said. The Home Secretary licked his lips but didn't answer.

We flew over the lake, and did two circuits of the beautiful Isola

---

[1] The 7.62 mm short-barrelled submachine-gun favoured by 'personal protection squads'.

Bella, home of the Boroneos who had asked the party to call on them and I don't doubt had prepared a wonderful reception. But it had been blocked by the tiresome little HE, officious and bespectacled (who was to materialise later). God, the amount of cumulative damage done to the British image by small-minded gauche and insensitive Ambassadors – *daily* around the globe – must be incalculable.

I remember the Boroneos at Elba[1] in 1966, when they made their entry into the dining room of the Pineti, the Count in a rumpled flannel cricket shirt and tweedy long trousers. At the time we thought they were muddled bourgeoisie out of their depth. Now I know that only the very rich behave like that. I succumbed to a sentimental fantasy of carnal desire for their young daughter. (Shamefully, I can't recall her name.) There was talk of an exchange visit, but it petered out. *Ancora tempo perso.*

Bumboy drivers in nasty little Alfa Romeo sedans took us from the heli-pad to the Villa Taranto. Totally spastic fast-driving with a police escort. So much so that at the villa gates they slid past on locked brakes and had to reverse back over their own skid marks before turning in.

I first had a bilateral meeting with Renato.[2] What a nice, thoughtful, civilised man he is. It's always a pleasure, and I always learn something. But the Italians are useless, the country is a mess – corrupt and unreliable – what earthly point is there in having a 'summit'? The Lady is short of friends in Europe and the Foreign Office have sold her the idea of starting the rapprochement here. But even if we did a deal the Italians wouldn't stick to it. Or the government would change before they had time to deliver.

Anyhow, whatever the Prime Ministers were doing they 'ran over' and the plenary meeting was (thank God) cancelled. We hung about in the garden waiting for the group photo. A policeman tried to keep me out of it – '*Solo Ministri, non funzionari*' – was this a compliment?

At lunch I sat next to Andreotti, old but not gaga. He ate well, though is lean and stooped. He told me the story of the villa's owner, a man named McEachan: before the war McE gave the property to Mussolini in order that the Duce should have a residence by the Lakes. This allowed his janitor to protect it both against the Partisans (it

---

[1] The Albergo Pineti in Elba, where the Clarks took their children for the summer holidays.

[2] Sr Renato Ruggiero the Italian Trade Minister, and AC's opposite number.

belongs to an English milord) and the Germans and Fascisti (it was a gift to the Duce). McEachan married an Italian girl. Having had a premonition, he forbade her ever to take their son in a car. She disobeyed him and the little boy, then aged five, was killed in a crash. McEachan divorced her on the spot. Later he married for a second time, but had no children.

How he recovered the villa after the war I don't know, but he was still comfortably installed there in the Fifties, employing (according to Andreotti), over forty gardeners. He died at the age of ninety and left his furniture and pictures – he had a good collection of Australian art – to the janitor and the house, again, to be a residence for the Prime Minister of Italy. Sadly, but predictably, the Italians have ruined it inside, lowering the ceilings and lining the walls with asbestos panels in order to help the air conditioning in much the same way as the French have wrecked the Chateau de la Muette, by covering part of the boiserie in the dining room.[1]

On the return flight in the VC 10 the PM invited me to sit at her table with Hurd and Geoffrey Howe. She was fussed about Barlow Clowes.[2] Should we bail out the 'investors'? Yes, I said. They were greedy, but small. It's the *big* greedy ones who should be punished, like that slob Clowes himself. I took the opportunity to warn her about Jaguar[3] being in jeopardy, which she didn't like. But what can we do? We just don't have the industrial or financial firepower any longer. But I was interested and gratified to hear her pass a comment showing that she had read *The Audit of War*.[4] She only drank orange juice.

After a bit Geoffrey Howe started getting restive. No one had addressed a word to him. He heaved himself past me, saying that he was going to change into a black tie. 'Good,' I said. 'Then you can serve us all drinks.' He pretended not to have heard, but when he came back, 'Two large gins and tonics, please, and Prime Minister, the maître d'hôtel is here and wants to know what you're going to have?' She didn't say anything, but grinned engagingly.

---

[1] The location of the ministerial lunch on the occasion of the annual OECD meetings.

[2] A financial 'bucket shop' offering very high rates of interest that had just gone bust, stranding hundreds of depositors.

[3] Sir John Egan, Managing Director of Jaguar Cars, had told AC that Ford of America were buying Jaguar shares systematically and threatening a takeover.

[4] *The Audit of War*, by Correlli Barnett.

Luxembourg   *Wednesday, 26 October*

I have been in the Foreign Affairs Council all day. Quite extraordinarily draining and repetitious. It is the representatives of the
smaller countries (particularly Denmark) who – presumably for their
own domestic political reasons – like to 'come in' several times,
hashing and rehashing the same subject into finer and finer mince.
The European Community must surely be the centre of that great
hobby/cult (is it twentieth century, or is it ageless?) which thrives on
the creation of problems; the minting of a special language or jargon –
itself a *part* of the problem – in which it is expressed, and the
long ritual Morris dances by which, very tentatively, a 'solution' is
approached.

We rattled – a relative term, mind – through the morning's
business, then had a good lunch and prospects seemed bright for the
early afternoon plane (the next one doesn't leave until seven p.m.).
But over lunch we ran into a Saragossa Sea of indecision on the
form which the – pretty tenuous – South African sanctions should
follow.

Should they take effect by a Community Instrument? Or by
individual States' legislation? Or (a real pedant's picnic, this) by a
reference to *Vu le Traité*?

Some delegates wished for one, others feared another which might
be domestically 'difficult'.

'How do you get observation of a voluntary ban?' Geoffrey was
asked. 'What mechanism do you have for enforcing (sic) it?'

'The Honours system,' I said, half under my breath.

This was my sole contribution to the whole morning's discussion.
Those who heard it, laughed.

But that was four hours ago. Now we are up in *petit comité*, after
two fifteen-minute adjournments, and have got stuck on Syria. The
French, shits as always, have gone back on the assurances given before
we sat down.

The *huissiers* clear the baize tables, empty the ashtrays, distribute
more mineral water. The air-conditioning is turned up. It is remi-
niscent of afternoon gambling, and this reinforces the painful sense of
waste and unnatural exhaustion.

I used to gamble many years ago. Most notably in the Winter
Casino in Cannes, where once I was cleaned out by red coming up
nine times in succession. I had to borrow money for the journey

home from 'Major Frank', Jimmy Goldsmith's benign old father, who owned a chunk of the Carlton.

Department of Trade and Industry   *Tuesday, 20 December*

Last night I went down to Highgrove.

Late, of course, and the position not helped by Dave getting into one of his M-way trances and slowly, oh-so-slowly (sic), slowing down – from 80 to 75 to 70 to 68 to 62 – then I say, 'Why are we going so slowly? The road's completely clear.' And he lurches forward and attaches himself to the tail (to the *tail*) of whatever is the next vehicle, preferably a TIR lorry, which he catches up.

As we covered the A429 from Malmesbury to Tetbury, past the house where little Sir John Rothenstein[1] took refuge in the early months of the war, and then the corner where I abandoned the Ford V8 drophead, as a child terrified of fire when Newy had left the cigarette lighter stuck in (a good early example of *cigaretters' dyslexia*) and it was smouldering – I thought, that *was* a long time ago, fifty years.[2] And now I'm a Minister of State, going to a private dinner with the Prince of Wales. George VI was on the throne then, and Charles didn't exist. It was 'the little princesses'.

I was the last to arrive, and the Prince had already 'joined the other guests' (in spite of the pretended informality we had all been issued with a meticulously timed programme. Guests were advised to arrive between 7.45 and 8 p.m. From 8 to 8.15 they would talk quietly among themselves; at 8.15 they were to be joined by the Prince, etc., etc., all the way through the evening.)

The sitting room door was shut. Through it I could hear a subdued respectful humming noise. As I entered the 'businessmen' (who else?) stopped talking and looked at me. Some feigned indignation. Most were complacent: 'Hur, hur, he's already blotted his copybook.' The Prince, on the other hand, did not stop talking. The minute and anxious equerry bobbed about trying – in my view gauchely – to interrupt.

---

[1] At that time director of the Tate Gallery.
[2] During the early years of the war the Clarks were living at Upton House, Tetbury.

The Prince – in my view rightly – paid no attention.

I looked about. Chintzes, Edwardian furniture of good quality, masses of photographs of 'The Firm', as they somewhat affectedly style themselves. A few big maritime water colours of a Wyllie-ish kind, and some washier ones that may have been by the Royal hand. No ivories, snuff-boxes, miniatures, objets d'art of any significance. Why not? Royalty have amassed these huge collections, by presentation and acquisitiveness, over the last two hundred years. Where is it all? In vaults, I suppose. Sometimes shown under glass to a dullard public procession. 'The Queen's treasures on view', all that. But this bourgeois unease is only two generations old. Edward VII had a kind of Farouk-like taste, and George V, as I know from my father, had a good knowledge of his drawings, and where they all were.

I had a few words with the Prince. Banal subjects. At one point a pleasing pup materialised, smooth-coated and self-assured, and with a Coster tail[1] and HRH told me that it was a Jack Russell that hadn't been 'docked'.

The purpose of the dinner was to bring together a few favoured 'Captains of Industry', the Secretary of State for Education and Science (Kenneth Baker was in the room, with his Cheshire-cat grin, glinting glossily) and the Minister for Trade, and discuss what could be done to remedy the almost universal inability of British managers effectively to communicate in any language other than English (and not very well even in that).

An important subject. And certainly worth a high-level committee, *provided* it had the power to see its recommendations through. But the trouble that affects all attempts by Royalty to 'inform' themselves is that the other participants are mainly, no, solely interested in scoring goodboy points and ingratiating themselves with the Royal Chair. Whatever for, one is tempted to ask. They certainly wouldn't bother if they knew how the Honours system actually operates.

Prince Charles has a nice voice, as I have often noted in the past. Distinctive, and every word beautifully clear. But he has a certain unhappy searching style of manner and expression, rather like his father, though less aggressive. At one point during the meal he hit the table, not authoritatively, but petulantly, '*Why* can't something be done? . . . We've got to do something . . . '

---

[1] The name of a dog belonging to Juliet Frossard, one of AC's personal secretaries, whose tail curled round like a whiting.

I was a long way off. As far, indeed, as I could be. At the opposite end of the table, facing the Prince but heavily covered by a row of cut-glass vases containing (quite prettily arranged) flowers or blooms. Very little drink. Nameless uniformed minions did not refill guests' glasses. Periodically they tried to deflect the Royal Russell and shoo him back through the baize door. But he was equal to this, and weaved his way around under the table. Furtively I fed him titbits.

With the (unbelievably minuscule glasses of) port, the main subject was addressed. Each visitor in turn was invited to make a contribution. In the main, it was auditioning for the All England Local Government Officials' Triteness (Bronze Star) Award. I came late. I tried to sparkle.

'Japan is already the most powerful country in the world. In 1943 she had learned the lesson that military power is a function of industrial power, and vowed to overcome this. Now already she has. Don't be misled by the fact that Japan doesn't make weapons. She could go on to a war footing in six months, produce missiles that would make the US versions look like muzzle-loaders.

'In thirty years' time, although English will be the *lingua franca*, Japan's dominance will mean that English will be no more than the language of the global peasantry. The tongue – *and the calligraphy* – of the Elite will be Japanese.'

The businessmen glowered at me through the cigar smoke. HRH looked uneasy. Only dear Kenneth's smile remained benignly in place.

And the Prince was distant to me when he bade me farewell. But I was glad to see toys and general disorder in the porch.

As we drove off I asked myself why we had all to go down, dressed up, in the middle of the busy week, to Gloucestershire, like unhappy winter Glyndebourners, in black ties in the five thirty rush hour?

On the way back Dave (inevitably) 'came over queer' and I had to take the wheel. When I told Cranley [Onslow], he said next time I should simply accelerate away and leave him on the verge.

All I got out of the whole experience was a pleasing demonstration of what happens when you don't dock a Russell puppy's tail.

1989

1989

Department of Trade and Industry   *Tuesday, 17 January, 1989*

A perfect cold clear winter's day. I have watched the sun move through its parabola, unshielded by cloud, from eight thirty this morning until now, gone two o'clock, when it is sinking. What have I got to show for this? Nothing. Shuffled papers about. I could have been in the Park at Saltwood, or on the Creaggan Road. All that has happened is that I am nine hours older.

I've had it. The Lady no longer knows my name. David pinches all the good 'initiatives' and I'm left with nothing. Who am I?

Other Ministers of State are high-profile. Waldegrave, Patten (both) Mellor (although everyone loathes him), Portillo.[1]

It has been conveyed to me that, after being so prominent a period of obscurity and 'good behaviour' would be prudent and beneficial, show I was 'serious', etc. All that has happened is that I have become obscure and passé. I should have realised that my enemies, who are numerous (why?) will be able, and will do their best, to exploit either condition equally effectively.

Department of Trade and Industry   *Wednesday, 25 January*

I long for July. Today I flagged the last week of that month in my engagement diary with a yellow marker, *Enfin la clef des champs*.[2]

But before I get there I have to traverse hateful deserts, mountain ridges. A trip to Bahrain; night flights to and from Yemen. Austria. The Maghreb. Madrid, Brazil, Mexico. In the very middle of the lovely cherishable Spring Bank Holiday week, when the peat is dry at Eriboll and the bracken starts to uncurl, there is an OECD conference in Paris.

Little MacGregor had a 'collapse' in Brussels. He felt ill, left the

---

[1] William Waldegrave, Minister of State at Foreign Office since 1988. Chris Patten, Minister for Overseas Development since 1986. John Patten, MP for Oxford West since 1983 (City of Oxford, 1979–83). Minister of State, Home Office, since 1987. David Mellor, MP for Putney since 1979. Minister of State, Department of Health since 1988. Michael Portillo, MP for Enfield, Southgate, since 1984. Minister of State, Transport since 1988.

[2] Verlaine.

room, slid to the floor in that long corridor leading from the *salle d'écoute*, and lay there with his mouth open. They took him to hospital for 'tests'.

He had been in continuous session in Council for six hours, and he was due back to lead in the Agriculture debate, with a full day before the Select Committee tomorrow.

The pressures on a Minister. Most of it unnecessary, and all of it gleefully and sadistically co-ordinated by officials with expressionless faces who stand by waiting for the Minister to 'break', and a new one to be delivered.

I am visiting Plymouth a lot at present. Alison comes with me, and we do the constituency correspondence on the train. She is more efficient than Peta, and more fun to be with. Her eyes are blue-grey.

Saltwood   *Saturday, 4 March*

Tristan has been trying to get hold of me.

He told me that Bruce Anderson had come in the previous evening, slumped down in a chair, and said, 'I think Clark is a sell.' Elaborated.

Earlier – not much earlier – BA had in fact telephoned to me, said he was depressed about my prospects but 'the shares are down, but they are undervalued. A buy at this level.'

Politics. How I adore it.

                                    ★   ★   ★

On the early morning of 13 March, AC left for an unofficial visit to the Maghreb. Some of the luggage including the case containing his notebook, was mislaid and his first entry for the period is subsumed in a letter to Jane dated that evening.

Monday, 13 March   *British Embassy (the Villa Dar al*
                                                     Ayoum), Tunis

Hello Lovey!

   This is the most interesting building, quite grandly laid out – like
a Moorish Gloria, with all the walls tiled (as well as the floors) and
many old-fashioned fixtures-and-fittings. Given to Queen Victoria
by the Bey in 1850, it was Alexander's HQ after the German surrender
in 1943 and Macmillan lived, as resident Minister, in the annexe. I am
occupying his actual bedroom.

   We had tea on the patio where they spread their maps (a little
round jug like the one we use[1] squinted at me reproachfully). HE a
good man – wrote a thesis praising 'football supporters' for his Foreign
Office promotion exam; now that *is* courage!

   He told me, prompted by his wife (who is an 'invalid') the story
of the resident donkey. This creature was tied to a tree, all the year
round, suffering terribly from heat and flies in the summer, for
seventeen years. Towards the end of his life he was so downcast that
the staff didn't even bother to tie him up. He just stood, cowed and
stooping, among the thorns. His plight came to the attention of two
maiden ladies who run the Distressed Arab Donkey Society (or
whatever it's called) and they reproached HE for setting a bad example.
Rightly, in my view. So HE issued directions for its welfare and
instructed his staff to get another donkey to keep it company. They,
corruptly, bought a broken-down mare actually from *within* the abat-
toir (and, presumably, kept the change). The mare, covered with sores
and her rib-cage showing, nonetheless showed some spirit. She bit
the guard at the gate on arrival, lashed out with her hind legs at all
and sundry, sank her teeth into the shoulder of the – presumably
startled – elderly local resident and chased him round the paddock. In
the end the vet had to be called to sedate her (thus, as so often, costing
more than the amount 'saved' on the 'bargain'). However (that was a
year ago) things settled down. The elderly resident 'picked up'; the
mare put on weight and her sores healed; and now, most pleasingly, is
pregnant!

   She has a beautiful dark coat, like Eva (I insisted on meeting

---

[1] At one point in his career AC most disreputably pouched or pinched from Government hospitality a tiny white milk jug with a crown on it, and the Clarks
   frequently make use of it on their early morning tea tray.

them); while the buffer though still notably venerable, is handsome and silver. So 'what-do-you-think-of-that, then?'

As you can tell from the length of this letter I have a short period to myself only because, I fear, dinner starts so late. But it was nice to arrive in daylight and get wafts of the hot Pineti smell. Now for a bath (always a risk) and into blue suit for formalities and – inevitably and loathsomely – 'a few words in response' at the end of the meal.

Lots and lots of love
Al

British Embassy, Rabat   *Wednesday, 15 March*

A wonderful long day when refreshing incident balanced, almost, boredom and sense of waste.

We visited a carpet factory. British machinery, and more to come, with a chunk of ATP[1] money. I don't know how defensible it is to subsidise foreigners to buy machines which they will use to put British factories out of work. I suppose that they would get the machines from someone else if we didn't supply them. It is all part of 'restructuring'. But it still makes me uneasy.

Then we drove south, past Enfidaville where the 8th Army linked with the Americans in May of 1943, and Rommel knew the game was up, legging it back to Germany and leaving the scene to von Arnim and Kesselring.

A meeting with the Mayor of Sousse – identical in form and substance with that (almost exactly a year ago) with the Mayor of Velikiye Tournovo in Bulgaria. The district, its charms and attractions, its achievements, ambitions, much statistical jumble. He was a gloomy, though youthful, Levantine with that heavy shading around the circumference of the eye that is a special mark of the Lebanese – the only race that has a completely circular 'ditch'.

In the museum there are marvellous Roman mosaics, particularly those of the sea, and fishes. An elaborate depiction of a courtship/rape in six scenes, including a pleasing one of the girl *viciously* scratching

---

[1] ATP: Aid and Trade Provision, part of aid budget administered by Foreign Office.

the man's face, depicted him – I was surprised to see – detumescent throughout, although naked.

Had they been bowdlerised during 'restoration'? I was also suspicious of the 'Sea-God's' face. Neptune, they said. But it was not Roman at all, or remarkable and unique if really so. I suspect 'forged' in the Renaissance.

Next, I had to take lunch with, and address an assembly of dignitaries at the new, brand-new resort complex of Port El Kantouri. As our cortege, four black Mercedes plus HE's armoured Jaguar, drew up, sirens wailing, a crowd of pink and unshapely tourists gawped. We must, in our suits and dark glasses, have looked like a posse of Mafiosi as we dismounted and strode authoritatively about.

It is an all-white replica of Port Grimaud. The party were conducted into a 'show' apartment, price £80,000 (too much). Directly on the beach, but so what? On the way over I had made a black joke about skin cancer and HE told me, with some gravity, about his sister-in-law who had had to have whole areas of skin 'literally peeled away'. Oh dear, I didn't like the sound of that at *all*.

'It finished her, really.' Worse and worse.

'How old was she?'

'Thirty nine.'

Gah!

Sonorously, I read my speech. My accent, as Glyn[1] told me afterwards, better than that of the (Tunisian) chairman himself. But after a time sheer muscular exhaustion sets in, and one cannot get one's tongue properly around the syllables even though the brain continues to transmit the correct orders. But the audience were pleased by my performance, and flattered.

HE is very good company. On our return we looped inland. The countryside is bleak, but not destitute. And the Ambassador spoke interestingly and informatively. Bedouin tents showed at intervals, like black marquees. The tribesmen are allowed to come in off the desert and graze certain areas, with their goats and camels, at this time of year.

We stopped at a section of the great aqueduct to Carthage. 200 BC. How the Romans did build! Most of the huge sandstone blocks had been removed for local use, but the arches still hung on the rubble and mud-cement that had infilled the pillars.

---

[1] Glyn Williams, head of AC's Private Office.

I detached myself from the party (I expect they thought I was urinating) and found what looked like a route up the vertical face of one pier. I kicked off my shoes – the faithful 'Co-respondents' – and started up, heart in mouth, using even my fingernails. If I got stuck I could hardly call for help.

After about six minutes I was standing in the watercourse itself. A beautiful perspective of the arched duct, lit by inspection holes every thirty metres or so. I hauled myself out through one of these and, standing on the roof, hailed the party (who by now must have thought I was thompsoning, or had suffered a tiny coronary).

They were not pleased, responded with little warmth. Rather as did the 'official' party in San Pedro di Chuquicamata when I had my little duel with the Spanish museum curator.[1]

The flight to Rabat was overlong, and not particularly comfortable. And the drive from the airport was almost entirely occupied with listening to, and reassuring my hosts' complaints about 'Suleiman Rushdi'.

Not difficult for me. Can't we swop him for Terry Waite? I didn't suggest this, however.

Mamounia Hotel, Marrakesh   *Friday, 17 March*

Arrived here 'for a complete rest', *'se reposer'*, entirely at my own (I judge likely to be considerable) expense. I am curious, yellow, as Winston was here before the Casablanca Conference; and down the years other louche figures. It was a *wet* trip – it's still raining now – in M. Benani-Smires' new model Mercedes. His chauffeur seemed uncertain of his metier, hooting at very long range, though somewhat hesitant (due, I assume, to defective vision) about actually overtaking. Except in towns, that is, where he invariably drove too fast, and heedlessly.

Alas, it is my impression that the hotel is now little different from any other heavy clip-joint; i.e., barely civil staff, crowds of objectionable and riff – rather than raff – clients. Much chattering and slummy dress. The assistant manager is pressing me to come to a

---

[1] See entry for 31 October 1987.

'cocktails' this evening, but in truth I feel little more attracted to this than I am by the prospect of the Western Area cocktail party when I am changing in my hotel room at Blackpool.

Have I become unadventurous? Perhaps it is just exhaustion. Monsieur Calouri, who has been deputed to – at long range – exercise custody, titillates me all the time '*vous n'avez que desirer quelque chose...*'

Later
After a bath I felt better, went down to the Reception. But it all looked terribly dull, waste of time. I veered off and made for the dining room.

M. Calouri materialised. I not going to the 'party'? Clearly he was disappointed.

I'm pretty sure M. Calouri would procure for me, but I haven't got the nerve to couch (sic) my requirements. And anyway, think of the *boredom* potentially. They'd be bound to take photographs, tape, video everything. For all I know, my bedroom has got a two-way mirror. So embarrassing for the dear PM – 'I'm afraid it, er, looks as if Alan has been behaving, er, badly...'

The food was excellent, though 'nouvelle', which means tiny helpings. A number of agreeably low and coarse English blondes tottered past my table as I guzzled. I don't think they were whores – just tight, randy (several of them said 'Good Evening' as they went by) wives. Their husbands were ludicrous. Pink, as-it-were Simpsons dinner jackets and blue bow ties, yet balding and specs. Something of the Midlands fruit Mafia.

The restaurant management had tactfully surrounded their table with portable glass screens, from behind which coach-tour cackling and shrieks could soon be heard.

British Embassy, Warsaw   *Monday, 17 July*

I am now on what must be my very last trip as Minister for Trade. When I get back to London the reshuffle will be in full swing – perhaps over – and I will be at either the Ministry of Defence or the Foreign Office. So what's the point, one might ask. I have some businessmen in tow. But neither I nor any of the Ministers I am going to meet have (it seems in their case, I know in my own) any sort of tenure at all.

I read in the papers that the Defence Secretary after this weekend is going to be Tom *King* (for God's sake). Any idea that I will do Defence Procurement under that man is OUT. And I will give the Lady my reasons.[1] I'd really rather be back on the estate.

Now a boring three days in prospect. Bilateral meetings, prompt cards, interpreters, 'hospitality', *return* hospitality with identical personages. Then, the secret purpose of the visit unfolds – a visit to the Masurian Lakes and on 20 July (anniversary of the *Attentat*) to Rastenburg.

I am tortured by impotence – that utterly negative feeling, a void; zero between the loins. I must look up when I last suffered from it. Also, I am bored blue by the company of businessmen. I have absolutely nothing in common with them. I don't like sitting around with a glass in my hand. I don't understand references to Chelsea FC. I couldn't hit a golf ball to save my life. I like only the heavy movers, people like Arnold[2] or Jimmy [Goldsmith].

I must suspend this entry as it's HE's reception in half an hour and I have neither had a bath nor read the brief.

Masuria   *Wednesday, 19 July*

We drove for some two and a half hours out of Warsaw in a northerly direction, before crossing the old East Prussian border and bearing eastwards into the very heartland of the Masurian Lakes. Mile upon mile of forest – hardly surprising that Samsonov[3] got himself into such a mess – mixed pine and silver birch with a good sprinkling of ash and sycamore. Wooden railed deer fences (so much nicer than the horrid wire and galvanised skimpies in Scotland) and few dwellings. Turning off the 'B' road we went through a No Entry sign and motored for about 150 yards on an unmade surface that lost itself in the trees. The track then smoothed out into newly laid, but little used tarmac that wound and dipped through the woods for some six or

---

[1] But see in fact entry for 24 July, below.
[2] Lord Weinstock, Chairman of GEC.
[3] Commander of the Russian Army at Tannenberg in 1914.

seven miles. I could only judge this by comparing it with the distance from Ardneackie to, say, Foulain[1] (but all the time in dark forest).

We came upon a metal gate, militarily painted in red and white diagonal stripes, guarded by a sentry. He saluted and we passed through. Another mile, another gate, the sentry armed. Some five minutes later we came upon the 'Guest House'. We were greeted, unhappily, by the 'manager'. Like most Poles he is big, but with a tired, ill face. It is a modern two-storey building, right on the water's edge. The only other vehicle in the residents' car park is a khaki coloured police Pobieda.

My room has sliding glass doors opening directly on to a balcony that overlooks the Lake. Below, pleasingly, swallows fly in and out of their nests. Water flat calm, no breeze, great silence. Just a few bird calls. Something, not the smell, evokes Scotland. I suppose we are at the same latitude. Perhaps it is just the enveloping silence. But we are privileged prisoners. Escape from here would be truly impossible.

It is lovely, at my age, still to be experiencing new sensations. Charging the batteries from new terminals. The food isn't bad, and I eat a lot of rye bread and butter. But I am hungry at the moment, and thus irritable.

David Young's message duly arrived, in code (that he 'wanted to meet me on Monday') to say that I was remaining in the Govt. But I have almost decided not to accept anything except S of S Defence. Procurement would be impossible and FCO only acceptable if I was quite clearly Number 2, and *recognised as such*. I will talk it all over with Jane. But it is fun to have the option and to be able to toy, over the weekend at least, with the idea of 'cutting peat'.[2]

Masuria   *Thursday, 20 July*

I woke at four o'clock and the room was quite light. Thinking it was the moon shining, I rose and went on to the balcony to catch the light on the water. But it is already dawn, and the swallows are chirruping excitedly. We are very far north here, deep in the Runic

---

[1] Hirsels on the Eriboll Estate.
[2] A family phrase for escaping to the Highlands.

lands. A long long way from the Judaeo-Christian ethic.

I got dressed and strolled out to the wooden jetty that adjoins the lodge. The forest comes right down to the water's edge, turning immediately into reed-swamp that forms a belt about sixty to a hundred feet deep around the rim of the lake. Here, seventy-five years ago almost to the day, the wretched Russian infantry sought refuge and were cut down, for hour after hour, by the German machine-gun teams, and the waters were stained dark red for a hundred metres out from the shore.

Today we are driving to the *Wolfschanze*.[1] Stauffenberg's bomb exploded, forty-four years ago, just after two o'clock. I hope we get there in time. No one will know what is going through my mind – except possibly Glyn. And he will only know half.

House of Commons   *Monday, 24 July*

I have been hanging around all morning. It is foully hot, and I keep the windows open on to Star Court, which makes the room noisy. There are wild rumours. Maddest of all is that Geoffrey Howe is to be sacked. Apparently he has already been twice to Number 10, and emerged without a statement.[2]

So who would be Foreign Secretary?

I see all this from my own aspect. There are only two jobs that I could be offered (or would consider). One, that Chris Patten mentioned when I made an official call on him a couple of weeks ago, is to be 'Mister Europe', keep an eye on the Commission. Tristan has also hinted at this, and David too – 'as a joke'.

But would it actually be Lynda's job? Could I really work with Geoffrey and, more to the point, could he tolerate it? (Although if rumour is correct this won't actually arise.) It would be lovely to try the FO – but I would have to keep my nerve and insist on the continuity of Lynda's title there, and be *Deputy* Foreign Secretary.

I still think Defence is more likely. So many people have said that

---

[1] Hitler's headquarters at Rastenburg.
[2] Howe, who had been Foreign Secretary since 1983, became Lord President of the Council, Leader of the House of Commons and Deputy Prime Minister. John Major was appointed Foreign Secretary.

I am to go there first as M of S in order to be poised to slither upstairs if George [Younger] inherits, or goes somewhere grander. And it would be bound to be Procurement. Partly because I know all the weapons system specs off the top of my head, partly because the Army brass won't have me in AF because of *The Donkeys*.

Other junior Ministers have been drifting in and out of here all morning. Most are fretful. Peter Morrison doesn't know anything. A couple of years ago he was always first with the news.

Later

The phone rang. It was the harsh-voiced telephone operator from Number 10. I don't know any of their names, but there are two with lovely friendly voices and manners and one, this one, who is like Goneril in *Pinfold*.

'Mr Alan Clark?'

'Yes.'

'Hold the line for the Prime Minister.'

I held on, for an eternity. Then the operator came back, snarled, 'Are you still there?'

'Yes.'

'She [sic] is tied up at the moment. Will you be remaining at this number?'

'Of course.'

Over an hour passed. Nervously I fantasised. Could some miracle be taking place? There was another false start.

Then, finally, it was the Prime Minister.

'Alan, I want you to go to Defence.'

I said nothing.

Her voice flattened in tone. 'As Minister of State.'

'Who is going to be Secretary of State?'

'Well, don't tell anyone, because it hasn't been released yet, but Tom is coming back from Ireland to do it.'

Christ alive! Not only was this an appalling prospect, but it also put paid to my secret scheme/hope of slipping into George's shoes when he moved on.

'I'm sorry, Prime Minister, but I can't work with Tom. I went through all that when I was at DE, I can't do it again. He's too ghastly.'

'I know what you mean, but he is much better now.'

'I just can't do it, I'm afraid.'

'Alan, you've always wanted to go to Defence. I've stood out to get you this job (uh?). You can't let me down by refusing.'

'Oh all right, Prime Minister, thank you very much.'

'Right then, that's settled.'[1]

Oh dear! *What* a feeble resistance. Just a few shots in the air.

It is up to me what I make of this, I suppose. But it will be difficult. In that Department, of all Departments, seniority is everything.

I feel more than a little down. I have always wanted this. But it has not quite come in the form that I would have liked. I see trouble ahead.

And it was all so rushed and terse. Quite different from that lovely private encounter when she made me Minister for Trade.

Garden House   *Saturday, 29 July*

Is it really only five days since the reshuffle? It seems an eternity. I have had tension headache most of the day. There is *so* much to do here – cars, papers and estate. And what should be the very best weekend of the year, the weekend of the *clef* is already warped and occluded by the curtailing, *yet again*, of the holiday summer.

I am having to come to terms with a new set of officials, and they with me. So far I detect two clear divisions. There are polishedly respectful, or rather formally courteous seniors, who probably don't give a toss for a Minister of State *'en passage'*. And an almost openly sceptical Private Office who radiate their unease at my dilettante style. I read Notes for Incoming Ministers in an hour and a half (meekly and subserviently this should have taken me three days or, preferably a weekend).

I had called them in immediately: 'The first thing I want to make clear is that the 'Friday box' comes up on Thursday. Right? I'm not having everyone clearing their own desks at three p.m. on Friday and sending it up here to sod up my weekends.'

'But Minister, what about the weekend box, Minister?'

'There isn't one.'

They shuffled off into the outer office. I have the communicating door open at all times so that I can bellow and this curtails their own conversation.

After a little while Julian[1] came back in. 'What would you like me to do with Friday's material, Minister?'

'I will read it on the train to Plymouth.'

'But what about material that comes in after you've left?'

'I will see it on Monday.'

'But what about urgent material, Minister, what about weekends when you are Duty Minister?'

'I have a portable telephone and there is a land line to the office in Plymouth.'

'But what if it is too highly classified . . . ?'

'That is a problem to which, I do not doubt, a solution will be apparent when it arises.'

They load my In-tray with papers of widely varying importance and density, stacked haphazardly – the oldest, corniest trick in the Civil Service. I insisted on colour-coded folders (it is perfectly incredible that in this vast and brontosaurian Department so simple an aid to efficiency should be unheard of). I rang dear Rose at DTI and she sent round immediately a batch – Blue, letters for signing; Yellow, key information; Orange, useless information; Red, action.

It was apparently impossible to get a paginated notebook in which I could make my *own* notes of meetings (another thing civil servants don't like) and ideas. Very difficult even to raise a pencil. When I asked if Ministers could, ever did, circulate each other with notes the concept was greeted with startlement, if not consternation.

I want to send off two notes straight away. One on the importance of retaining the Armilla Patrol;[2] the second on the idiocy of overriding a planning authority refusal to extend the nuclear store at Devonport.

---

[1] Julian Scopes, Private Secretary. Within a few weeks (see later entries) he and AC had become firm friends and confidants, and co-operated closely in the gestation period of 'Options for Change'.

[2] Since the Iraq-Iran conflict at least one destroyer or frigate was permanently on station at Jebel Ali for emergency response.

Both issues show the Admiralty at its worst. They don't like Armilla because it 'strains resources'. What are 'resources' *for*, for fuck's sake? And they want to extend a dump for radioactive waste that abuts on an infants' school at Weston Mill.

I got the little Admiral round. People tried not to tell me his name, just referred to him as CFS[1] (every one, or thing, here is denoted by their acronym. All part of a conspiracy to befuddle in-comers.) I told him that nuclear power was essential to the security of this country in two fields, and two only: warheads, and maritime propulsion. If we were to retain public support, or at least assent, for these we must lean over backwards in assuaging their environmental concerns. What he was proposing to do wasn't just bad PR, it amounted to wilful sabotage.

He bounced about in his chair crossly. Conveyed he thought I was half Red spy, half do-gooder academic. Card marked.[2]

At present my game plan is to stay in for six months, until Christmas, see my way around the Dept, what's happening exactly, particularly *where the money is going*, and let the Lady have a considered three-quarter-page report for reading over the Chequers Christmas weekend.

But the first thing to do is get Private Office in on Monday and sort a few things out. They've picked me off with a series of papers about weapons, and the attendant procurement 'problems'. But how can I pronounce judgment unless I know the background, the kind of war we are expecting to fight? Or even against who we are expected to fight? I see that everyone's career is predicated on the horrendous Soviet 'threat'. But that's all balls. My problem is that as far as 'top management' is concerned I appear to be both a Red agent *and* the man who's going to wreck their careers.

I think I'll also give them a fright about the gauche and spastic way in which their muttered enquiries and complaints about me are getting straight back, after hours. Rhodes James tells me what his secretary, Polly, reports to him. But Julian is married to Polly's daughter and Polly is the doyenne of the secretarie's room in Deans Yard where

---

[1] Chief of Fleet Support, Admiral (later Sir) Jock Slater.
[2] From the outset of his tenure at the Ministry of Defence AC found that the Admiralty Press Office in Plymouth was always ready to brief local reporters about his failings.

everything is repeated. The Westminster hothouse. Doug[1] himself even said to Alison, 'Does he realise how hard he has to work?' which she repeated back to me, at dinner in the Kundan that same evening.

Tom King, meanwhile, is true to the form which I remember so well from DE. Kept me waiting for an hour on Friday afternoon by the phone, then left the building. Much later his office 'stood me down'. Loathsome puffball. Archie Hamilton[2] is something of a *faux bonhomme* and already suspicious of my 'encroachments'. (Just wait until I get started!) Michael Neubert[3] is serious and hardworking but (according to Julian) did not want to be switched across from Armed Forces and be my subordinate instead of the amiable, but somewhat *unversed* Tommy Arran.[4] All rather fun, but draining also.

I must not lose *élan*.

Michael Quinlan[5] is benign. Always hard to tell what he's really thinking. Which is as it should be with Permament Secretaries. The Chesterfieldian masque should be discarded only at times of acute crisis.

Saltwood   *Sunday, 30 July*

Bruce Anderson had asked himself down for a general gossip. I always said I'd open a bottle of 1916 Latour when I got to MoD so we split that as an *apéritif*. He's in my good books as he wrote percipiently about the Government changes, 'Mixing Alan Clark and Tom King could be the only mistake of the reshuffle.' He said he was interviewing David Owen first. 'Why don't you bring him down?' Bruce said he would try. Sure enough, they both turned up.

In strictly social terms David is oddly *un*sophisticated. Almost ill at ease, he said he didn't 'know much' about wine. Gently, I *tâtai le terrain* on the political scene. David said that 'she' had tried really hard

---

[1] Douglas Wiedner, Assistant Private Secretary.

[2] Archie Hamilton had been Minister of State (Armed Forces) since 1988.

[3] Michael Neubert, MP for Romford since 1974. As Parliamentary Under-Secretary newly moved across from Armed Forces to Defence Procurement.

[4] 9th Earl of Arran. Parliamentary Under-Secretary for the Armed Forces, 1989–92.

[5] Sir Michael Quinlan, Permament Secretary at the Ministry of Defence. Both AC and Tom King had worked as Ministers with him when he was Secretary at the Department of Employment 1983–5.

recently, got hold of Debbie at a Number 10 reception and really turned it on. But he couldn't. How could he switch a third time? 'Winston did,' I said. How could he disappoint yet another group of followers? (What he meant, I suspect, was how could he get re-elected.)

David has this lovely grin – the most engaging grin in politics – and a good sardonic expression at other times. He commented freely and without inhibition. But he is a realist, and he *doesn't see his way*. Ll G, Enoch, now him. Great men, of massive authority and vision, find themselves disqualified by chance of circumstances and their own transient misjudgments. It seems to have nothing to do with quality. But I see no future for him.

While I was out of the room both he and Bruce said to Jane that I could 'quite easily' now get into the Cabinet.

Eriboll   *Thursday, 17 August*

This morning I bathed, before breakfast, in the loch just opposite the targets. I don't know what the temperature is; a tiny trace of Gulf Stream perhaps, but not much. One feels incredible afterwards – like an instant double whisky, but clear-headed. Perhaps a 'line' of coke does this also. Lithe, vigorous, energetic. Anything seems possible.

It was a still, mild day, high cirrus cloud, and I was half minded to attempt the great walk to Loch Stack.[1] But I did not leave enough time, and had to settle for a reconnaissance. I pressed right on beyond the oakwoods at the top of the Stra'beg valley, and started to ascend steeply, past the first of the two big waterfalls there. The second I could only reach by balancing on a succession of huge slippery boulders. Below me the black peat water flowed in that fast and silent manner that denotes great depth. I splashed my face and drank from one of the pools.

Then I left the watercourse and traversed the upper Polla valley – strewn with rowan trees, all carrying their bright orange fruit – and

[1] From the shore of Loch Eriboll (north Atlantic) to the shore of Loch Stack (running into the Irish Sea) a distance of some twenty-three miles with the ascent of two ridges over 2,000 feet, eluded AC until May 1991. He and Jane repeated the expedition in July 1992.

began the assault on the An Lean Charn Ridge. This is very steep, both hands are needed. But there is a profusion of heather, and foliage of stunted holm-oak and silver birch – rather like the opening passages of *Erewhon*. Near the col the treeline stops abruptly, and one must negotiate a series of dried peat water-courses, storm channels I suppose they are, which must be terrifying when in spate, with banks six to eight foot high. On the crest of the ridge there is a track (shown on the Ordnance Survey) for the stalkers' ponies and, indeed, hoof marks could be seen. I contemplated following it, but this would have slowly wound me down to Dionard – one of the bleakest and most remote of all the Highland lochs, a kind of landlocked Coruisk – then to God knows where.

I trailed down the hill on the SW side for a little while being unable, for some reason, to bring Foinavon into view, then swung back and down to the Polla valley.

By the time I was back at the Land-Rover I had been on the hill for more than seven hours. The walk *is* feasible, but one would have to allow up to ten, and pray for good visibility.

Yesterday we went to the Lairg Sale.[1] Poor Michael Wigan had the transporter with all his sheep on board in collision (fatally) with the district nurse in her Metro on a corner of the road between Boroboll and Rogart. The great truck turned over and about 100 lambs perished.

In the meantime little Moncreiffe was strutting about in his new plus fours, as pleased as punch with having sold Ribigill for three million or, rumour has it, thereabouts. I couldn't remember his Christian name (he was at Eton with me, but it was thought 'unhealthy' there to know other boys' Christian names) and when I whispered to James 'What's little Moncreiffe's Christian name?' he very splendidly answered, 'Little'.

Moncreiffe made a short, not very good, pompous speech about '... the farm will carry on', 'thankyou for buying my sheep', that kind of balls.

He was listened to quite attentively (most unusual in the Ring at Lairg) because everyone wanted to know who had bought Ribigill.

---

[1] A great annual event in north-west Sutherland combining social and economic activity. It is considered obligatory for all the landowners to attend.

Naturally, he didn't say. All it boiled down to was, 'Well, I've trousered a couple of million, and I'm off.'

Royal Navy Equipment Exhibition,   *Tuesday, 26 September*
Portsmouth

Last night I travelled down to Portsmouth for the Royal Navy Equipment Exhibition. I was booked into the Lady Hamilton (sic) suite at the Holiday Inn. A vast room, panoramic windows which, thank God, could be slid open and fresh air sucked in. Far below on the flat roof I could see the air-conditioning plants humming away; puzzled, possibly, by having to cope with this irregularity on the eighth floor. Vast bed, batty bath in the centre of the room, to get into it you had to go up a flight of stairs; sumptuous lounge en suite. But the detail was neglected. The fridge was empty, a bottle of still mineral water on the table had the seal broken and the level was about three inches down, and the telephones were completely congested. It was impossible to get an outside line for thirty minutes, nearly as bad as Warsaw.

Later that evening I hosted a dinner at Admiralty House for the more important foreign delegates. Admiral Jeremy Black[1] received me. Quite impressive (most senior sailors at the present time strike me as hopeless). For some reason – perhaps for that reason he is unpopular with his peers. This may relate to his period in command of *Invincible* during the Falklands. I remember at that time his colleagues were briefing journalists about how bad tempered and obstinate he was. He was not particularly friendly but to my gratification said, 'Didn't you come to the EFA meeting?[2]

'Yes.'

'I thought it strange that the Minister for Trade should be opposing

---

[1] Admiral Sir Jeremy Black, Deputy Chief of the Defence Staff, 1986–9, recently appointed C-in-C, Naval Home Command.

[2] When Minister for Trade, it was arranged by Number 10 that AC should attend a special briefing for Treasury Ministers at the Ministry of Defence where the case for the European Fighter Aircraft was to be argued. At the time Mrs Thatcher was doubtful about the wisdom of so large a programme and hoped that AC's technical expertise would be of use in attenuating the RAF case.

this project. I thought it would have the support of the DTI.'

Maddeningly, I cannot remember who else of the various officials tried to keep me out of that meeting and all of whom spoke at once in order to refute the arguments I was putting, I now see, in the course of my business at the Dept. Of course we could have blocked the whole project if the Lady hadn't changed her mind halfway through. Whether she was right or wrong I simply don't know at present, although I am inclined to think that the best solution is to maintain design and research teams and keep giving them more and more advanced projects to work on. But defer going into production for as long as one can. The moment something goes into production it is obsolescent and all the in-service problems start crowding in.

Surprise of the evening was the US Admiral Peter Hekman. After a slow start he showed himself to be an original thinker, well read in economics and philosophy. We discussed the great formative seminal works. Both agreed that Paul Kennedy demanded a place – to my surprise he had read all Kennedy's learned treatises in historic and foreign affairs. I suggested Keynes's *Economic Consequences of the Peace* but Hekman said although it had had tremendous influence this would be seen as short-lived.

Keynes had formulated the poison but not the antidote.

We touched on the evolution of power, alignments and interests over the next twenty years. Hekman asked which would be least acceptable to European opinion, a standing army of United (i.e., West and East) Germans or a revival of the Japanese carrier fleet. For me, and I suspect for the Anglo-Saxons, it would be the latter. Hekman told me that the Japanese were already 'feeling' for permission to build a carrier, which is presently forbidden under the peace treaty.

Saltwood   *Saturday, 30 September*

I have just returned, exhausted but triumphant, from the Chequers CFE Seminar.[1]

Although we left early Dave got in a muddle after leaving the

---

[1] The Conventional Forces (Europe) Treaty, under which mutually agreed Force reductions were to be tied to a timetable. From having been obstructive the 'new' Soviet regime under Glasnost was actually leading the way.

M40, and more time was lost because I, starting nervous, soon developed hyper-anxiety and forced him to stop twice in order that I could relieve myself. Just in time (were we the last? I expect so) we turned down the back drive and into the roadblock of merciless-looking police sharpshooters.

I stayed quiet for most of the first half – although an awful lot of balls was talked, mainly by the heavyweight military men present, and by Michael Alexander, our Ambassador to NATO, whose higher intelligence has made him see that the writing is on the wall.[1] 'The Threat' (that always slightly ludicrous term) has now become a personal one – to their careers.

After an hour or so the discussion moved on to the kind of equipment that was going to be needed in 'the new scenario'. Lawson, who knows that I will be able to save him money, said, 'Prime Minister, could we hear on this subject from the Minister of State?'

I set out my stall, named and costed a number of programmes which could be eliminated without any risk. This induced *show* intakes of breath from the military men, but I could see Lawson and Lamont[2] beaming with approval. Martin Farndale[3] tried to come back at me, but the PM cut him off and she started on a quite well informed (Charles's hand clearly in evidence) summary of the approach to equipment problems, and the need for 'inter-operability' across NATO.

When the Prime Minister said that 'further work was needed' I jumped in. It was now or never.

'Prime Minister, may I have your instructions to draw up a schedule of our equipment requirements over the next five years, in the light of anticipated progress in the CFE negotiations?'

It simply is not allowed to interrupt the Prime Minister when she is summing up at the conclusion of a discussion. Everyone at the table turned and looked at me. I could see TK, some few places away on the other side, jaw dropped open, saucer-eyed. I could guess what *he* was thinking.

'Yes. We must be able to make some savings now. But ... (going

---

[1] Sir Michael Alexander, diplomat. Former Assistant Private Secretary to Sir Alec Douglas-Home and James Callaghan, and Private Secretary (Overseas Affairs) to Margaret Thatcher, 1979–81. Ambassador, Vienna, 1982–6.

[2] Norman Lamont was at that time Chief Secretary at the Treasury.

[3] General Sir Martin Farndale, outgoing Commander-in-Chief of BAOR.

dreamy-voiced — I know this — it is a defensive tack)... I want particular attention payed to inter-operability.'

What a coup! The meeting ended, and there was no scope for anyone else to get in.

I was ebullient, foolishly so.

'Well done, Alan,' said Lawson, as we drifted down to lunch, but he said it *sotto voce*.

'Do you realise what this means? This is the Defence Review. I've got a free hand to write it.'

'Yes, if you play your cards right. I wouldn't shout it from the rooftops.'

I came up behind Quinlan. 'How about that, then, Michael? This is the Defence Review. We're off.'

'Well, don't call it that, whatever you do.' He didn't seem too happy.

Once in the car I telephoned to Julian at his home.

'We've made it! Single-handed you and I are going to write the Review.'

He couldn't really believe it. I took him through the whole thing stage by stage.

Julian said, 'Minister, you *must* be identified in the Meetings note, otherwise S of S's office, or the Permament Secretary, or both, will take the whole thing over and smother it.'

'Don't you worry. Leave it to me.'

I was exultant, convinced it was the ox's hide.[1]

As soon as I got back here I started trying to reach Charles. I *had* to speak to him before he finalises the note, which he will be doing this very weekend. Finally I got him at Number 10.

He started friendly. 'I think that went rather well.' (All civil servants use this expression unless there has been a complete disaster.) I explained the problem.

'Oh no. I couldn't do that. It would be most unusual. I can really only name the heads of Departments.'

---

[1] From the legend of the Baron who asked his King for 'only so much land as can be encompassed by an ox's hide' and, getting permission, slew the largest ox he could find. He then cut its hide into a long leather lace, within whose circumference the Baron constructed a powerful castle which soon dominated the surrounding country, and from which he came to challenge the King himself.

'If you don't identify me, the whole thing will be stillborn.'

'Oh, surely not. Tom was there. He heard what the Prime Minister said.'

'Come on, Charles, ha bloody ha.'

'Well, I don't really see how I can.'

'Will you please ask the Prime Minister? Will you please tell her of this conversation?'

'If you insist. But I must warn you of my opinion that she will take the same view.'

'Even if she does, I'm no worse off. Please tell her.'

'All right.'

Fingers crossed!

Ministry of Defence   *Wednesday, 4 October*

Yesterday there was still no paper on the 'Conclusions' of the Chequers meeting. Strange. Number 10 are usually so efficient. But I did not dare ring Charles, it would have seemed importunate. There's nothing that I could do now. Every time Julian enquired of S of S's office the answer came that they had not yet been received.

But I was in the cafeteria at lunch, and saw Norman Lamont. He started talking about it. When did he get his copy? Monday. Again I tried Julian, again a blank wall from down the corridor.

In the evening I rang Number 10. Charles was away but his secretary said yes, they had gone over to MoD on Monday. 'Actually, you got the first batch.'

I explained that I hadn't received mine, must be stuck somewhere in the pipeline, could I come over for a copy?

'I don't have any spare copies, they are all restricted circulation.'

But she very sweetly agreed to make a copy of my copy (i.e., of the copy I should have had). I was to collect it first thing this morning.

And, sure enough, at the end of the instruction were the magic words, *Minister, Defence Procurement, to take the Lead* (!)

I showed it to Julian. He could barely believe his eyes. Yet Tom's office will not release our copy, which was sent to them by Number 10 for onward transmission. The most we can get from them, late this afternoon, is that S of S 'is considering how best this can be tackled'.

Ministry of Defence   *Thursday, 5 October*

Ministers was cancelled today, which is highly unusual. At ten o'clock word came for me to go along (subject of discussion not disclosed, again unusual).

Tom was standing behind his desk, motioned to me to sit at a small chair facing him. Simon[1] padded out and shut the door.

'I just want to get one thing straight.'

'Uh?'

'I'm in charge.'

'Well, yes.'

'I've talked to her. I've talked to Charles. I'm handling this.'

'Quite.'

'If we're going to work amicably together, which I'm sure we are, we've got to trust each other.'

'Quite.'

'I cannot have you passing notes to the Prime Minister down the chimney.'

'No.'

When I got back to my office they were all peering at me; what for? Contusions?

'Fear God, and stay calm,' I said. 'No man's way leadeth to harm.'

They don't know that aphorism. Perhaps sometimes they think that I am going off my head.

Plymouth Train   *Friday, 10 November*

I am on my way down to a series of dreary Constituency functions, including a massive surgery list.

I am staying the whole weekend at Bratton, as already (the last one seems only months ago) it is Remembrance Sunday, and the Hoe

---

[1] Simon Webb, head of Tom King's Private Office.

Ceremony. But before I get out there I have to make a speech at Peter Whiteley's house where a rally to raise funds is being held.

In fact I don't mind this part as he is a good chap, a former Commandant of the Royal Marines, and the IRA are always trying to kill him. Pretty wife, too. Peter is of a certain type, whose *heart* (as in 'hearts and minds') is in the right place, but he is undemonstrative. They are valuable, these men.

My days in the Department are very full at present. Because in addition to my routine ministerial duties I am covertly preparing the secret draft of the Defence Review – of *my* Defence Review, I should say.

Alison and I have really done the whole thing together, on the word processor in my Commons Office. The only 'trace elements' have been the periodic requests for facts and figures which Julian has sent down to various desks within the Dept.

Julian is being wonderful. Helpful, tactful, assiduous; he warns me when he thinks that I am going too far. Though sometimes even he can be made to look slightly pop-eyed and startled. We were working late the other evening and when he brought some papers to my desk I smelt whisky.

'Julian, you've been drinking!'

'Yes, Minister, I have had a small whisky, yes Minister.'

I am a spoilsport really. All Ministers have a huge drink allowance, administered by Private Office, and a vast store of bottles for 'entertaining'. It is common practice for Private Office to help themselves in times of need. I never touch it. But many colleagues are convivial, and do a 'sun's-over-the-yardarm' act most evenings.

I am in despair about the Navy or, rather, the sailors. This is the Service which has to be the centre-piece of my plan – swift, flexible, hard-hitting. Yet the only thing they want is to be the forward ASW screen for the United States Navy in northern waters.

That's all over, I say. Forget it. The Soviet 'threat' no longer exists. Raise your eyes. Have not any of them read Mahan? Or Arthur Marder? I suppose the whole thing started to go to pieces when (effectively) we abolished Dartmouth. The soldiers are little better. The careers structure of the British Army is and for the last forty years has been anchored on 'Rhine Army'. They simply cannot come to terms with the change that has occurred. They won't even *train* differently – I suppose because to do so would involve admitting that there may, conceivably, be other enemies, other 'theatres'.

On the whole, though, I am getting on well with the civil servants. They are clever, of high calibre, most of them and not irredeemably set in their ways. And I am lucky that the Permanent Secretary immediately answerable to me, Peter Levene,[1] is thoroughly congenial. A quick mind and – so important – a sense of humour.

Ministry of Defence   *Thursday, 21 December*

It's all a bit awkward. I live dangerously.

But the key thing is, I have finished my paper, boldly entitled it 'The 1990 Defence Review', and lodged it with Charles at Number 10. Afterwards, Alison and I went up to the Pugin Room, split half a bottle of champagne; then another.

My paper is succinct and radical. And I have followed the two guiding principles in such matters – keep it short, (5 pages and an annexe) and get it in first, ahead of any other(s) that may compete for attention. (One thing I have learned in Whitehall is the need to be first 'on the table' and take pole position against which all else is judged.)

I just – *just* – beat the great 'official' departmental paper which Quinlan has been preparing for months, ever since he had that nasty shock at Chequers.

But Quinlan's is a Motherhood paper. All in all, the possibility cannot be excluded, it seems likely that; existing uncertainties, need to consult closely with Allies at every stage, must be careful not to drop or, as important, *seem* (or is it 'seen'?) to be dropping our guard; real savings a considerable distance in the future, need for absolute secrecy, discussion confined to a very small group.

The first meeting, to discuss the Dept's own paper, is scheduled for this evening, at which the Permament Secretary is to distribute draft 'Headings', and explain how he is proposing to 'draw the threads together'.

Julian rightly and shrewdly said that I must get my paper to Tom, and to Quinlan himself, before (but of course only just before) this

---

[1] Sir Peter Levene, Chief of Defence Procurement since 1985.

meeting is convened. Deftly I altered the first page so that of the four copies they appeared to be getting Numbers One and Three.

Unusually, the meeting started in time (Tom is driving down to Wiltshire tonight, immediately the meeting is over, for the Christmas hols). When I got in everyone was reading, avidly and urgently.

Quinlan had his head bent right over my text, lips moving occasionally – like my father's description of Picasso when first confronted with a portfolio of Moore drawings.

No one bothered about the Dept's paper, indeed it was hardly referred to throughout.

Tom waved mine in the air. 'This is pretty drastic stuff.'

He launched into a rambling dissertation on the unwisdom of reducing our strength in Germany, followed by a (clearly) prepared passage on a 'scenario' that involved starving Poles storming a Red Army food train. Bizarre.

'Could put NATO in a very difficult position.'

But he is not a fool, Tom, in matters such as this; and he was eyeing me closely.

'What we have all got to ensure is that this does not get into the hands of the Prime Minister.'

Silence, except for a grunt from Hamilton, who was looking very bad-tempered.

'She'd get hold of completely the wrong end of the stick.'

I said nothing.

'Not straight away, anyway, Alan? Huh?'

'I find myself in a very difficult position.'

'Why?'

'She knows that I am writing it.'

'How does she know that?'

'Because I am doing it at her request. You recall the note of the Chequers meeting?'

'Well, not until we've cleaned it up a bit. It'd be very bad for morale here if this got out in its present form.'

'I don't think it would for a minute.'

'Oh yes, indeed, I'm afraid it would. At least, we must hold on to it until after Christmas.'

Then, poor Tom, he said – was it plucking, or was it sinister? – in front of four other people it was certainly odd: 'You promised that you would not send her any notes without showing them to me at the same time.'

'I am showing it to you.'

'Well, that's agreed, then. We'll all keep tight hold of this until after Christmas.'

'Yeah.'

I was on ultra-thin ice. I could *just* say that, I pretended, because I hadn't handed it to her, but to Charles.

The breathing space didn't last five minutes. Back in my office I used my direct line to dial Charles direct. Engaged. I redialled half a minute later. Still engaged. Then I heard the phone in the outer office.

Julian came in, white-faced.

It was Simon. He had rung Charles to excuse the delay in submitting the departmental paper, which had been promised *for* Christmas, and said that the 'Min DP has also written something to which we are giving consideration'.

'So am I,' Charles had answered. 'It's on my desk now.'

I could feel myself break into an instant sweat. *So* embarrassing.

'Christ. What do I do?'

Julian was thoughtful.

I just wanted to leap into the car, drive down to Saltwood, hide for a week or so. Time, the great healer.

'I wouldn't do that, Minister. I think that you'll have to go round straight away and apologise.'

'Impossible. Anyway, he will have left by now.'

'Just let me see.' He rang Simon again.

'The Secretary of State is still there. He can see you now.'

Tom was seated at his desk in I'm-in-charge mode. And the chair stood directly in front, ready for a pre-caning homily.

'I'm most frightfully sorry. I just couldn't own up in front of all those people.'

He waved my explanation aside, said something about you should always feel free to let me see everything, it makes it so much easier for both of us.

'Anyhow, I've had a word with Charles, whom I know well. He agrees that the Prime Minister should not see this paper before Christmas – otherwise, ha-ha, she'll be making all our lives a misery over the holiday . . . '

'Very good of you to take this line '

'No, no. Yes, yes. It's just one of those things. Anyway, have a good holiday. Going skiing?'

I felt a bit of a shit. But how else could I play it? Good old Tom, though. Magnanimus Sextus.

1990

1990

Here come the Nineties! It's impossible to write anything contemplative without sounding demi-E.J. Thribb.

But am I, for a start, going to achieve my life's ambition? Auguries
at the moment – poor.

Total silence from Chequers. Nothing indeed since Charles, rather
gruffly, acknowledged in the Cabinet Room at Number 10, the
personal delivery, by me, of The Paper before Christmas.

I look back on the start of previous decades.

1970 was miserable. I had been rejected in the selection process
for Weston-super-Mare[1] and believed that my last chance to get into
the next (or any) House of Commons had gone. We were in Zermatt
for Christmas, but James had broken his leg badly, was wan and in
plaster.

1980 was little better. The 'new' Conservative Government wasn't
getting anywhere. The Lady had surrounded herself with Heathites
and was too timid to embrace me. While we were in opposition
Humphrey Atkins[2] had been a most objectionable Chief Whip, and
had marked my card. Looking at old journals I see it was about now
that he gave me a spastic 'dressing down' for smashing one of the
House telephones. Just like Jacques at Eton,[3] 'We don't do that sort
of thing.' Stupid cunt. Also Peter Thorneycroft, who didn't just
censor, he vetoed a complete article that I was commissioned to write
for *Conservative Weekly*. I was beyond the pale.

Now, though, my zest for life is stronger than it has ever been.
My energy is excellent; the *width* of my appreciation continues to
expand, and there is no sign of fading intellectual powers. This is
going to be my year. Or...

In fairness, I should say that I really love my job (being racked
only by the pains of not being Secretary of State). For the first time
in Government I actually look forward to the end of the holiday,

---

[1] For a by-election in 1969 the local constituency selected Jerry Wiggin, who had
previously stood as Conservative candidate for Montgomeryshire in 1964 and
1966.

[2] Humphrey Atkins, Northern Ireland Secretary, 1979–81. He was created a life peer
in 1987 and took the title Baron Colnbrook.

[3] L. H. Jacques was AC's House Tutor (housemaster) at Eton and they were not in
sympathy with each other.

getting back to my desk, where all the papers are so interesting. Before Christmas I was dropping with fatigue and nervous tension, but already I have fully recovered.

First to be decided though, is will I get to the next Chequers meeting? I had hoped, secretly, for a phone call over Christmas. But no contact.

I put my all into that Report. Truly it was the apotheosis of my whole career both as a historian and in public life. But it has turned out, it seems, an embarrassing non-event. Not to be alluded to.

If I am excluded from the meeting TK will be cock-a-hoop. He will no longer be fearful of me, as I will have played my big card, and been ignored. Also I will have lost face with my own Private Office. All Julian's doubts will be confirmed just as, by sheer intellectual vigour, I was converting him. Sad, because he has been splendidly loyal over these last difficult weeks.

Have I overreached? Did I gallop too soon and too recklessly? It's impossibly difficult to set great reforms in train from a middle-ranking position. But I *know* I'm right. Mine is the only way we can keep military clout and not go bust. I couldn't just sit back and duck it in exchange for a comfortable life signing documents and having little exclusives in the HS 125.

This is my last job, isn't it?

Be realistic, Clark. If you're going to make S of S you won't do it just by sitting still and being a goodboy. And we are at one of those critical moments in defence policy that occur only once every fifty years.

Always remember, 'At times of acute crisis in the course of human affairs, a man will emerge. If he does not, it means that the time is not yet ripe' (*Wolf*).[1] A curious inversion of conventional thought. But even if true, not especially comforting.

---

[1] AC sometimes refers to Hitler by this cognomen, which was used only by his 'Bayreuth' circle, Elizabeth Wagner, etc.

Saltwood   *Sunday, 14 January*

I've made it! The Chequers meeting (Mark II) is fixed for 27 Jan – to be *utterly* secret, 'The Prime Minister has asked me to emphasise that if any . . . ,' etc.

I am invited, listed at Number 4, below Hurd, Chancellor and T.K. (How maddening for TK. Hee-hee.)

My paper is, it is clear, *the* lead document. How shrewd and good I was to get it in first! The FCO papers are bulkier, came later, and carry the imprimatur of a committee of officials.

Willie Waldegrave, whose task it is to co-ordinate the material, was not friendly when I saw him in the dining room. Reddish with drink, and small-eyed, he said it was 'very petty' not to circulate the Annexes (which contain the financial provisions).

'Not my idea,' I said.

'Anyway, the Treasury have got hold of a copy.'

Too right they have, I thought, I sent them one.

On the day, everything will depend on (a) her mood, and the level of counter-distraction (b) my own confidence and sparkleability.

Word has spread through the Department, and I am buoyed up by the now open tendency of senior officials to defer to me, quote my views with approval even when (normally unheard of) Tom is present. I retoy with the idea of supplanting him, and promptly.

Of *course* I should be in charge, handling the whole thing at international level also, Washington, Brussels.

My present solution is to move TK to Health, where he could be pinkly affable and repair some of the damage caused by my 'abrasive' namesake. But that could only happen if Clarke has a nervous breakdown – unlikely in one so fat – or – perfectly possible at any time, he must make the Norwich Union wince – something 'happens to' him. One mustn't be uncharitable (why not?) but this after all is the roughest game, at the biggest table.

On Thursday afternoon Soames, who was sitting just behind me, occupied a lot of Agriculture Questions (and I don't doubt a lot of TV footage, so it's as well the audience couldn't hear) telling me about an incredibly powerful new aphrodisiac he had discovered.

I liked the sound of this, and after Prime Minister's Questions I drove him back to his flat and he brought down a 'phial'. It has to be kept in the fridge.

Ministry of Defence   *Wednesday, 17 January*

Tom is frantic. He is harrying and pestering officials all over the building to get 'his', i.e., *The Official MOD Position* paper(s), prepared.

He won't let me see it in draft. I doubt if I'll get a sight of it before I walk into the room – if then.

But not only was my paper first in, it was only five pages long. All this stuff they're sending up now is ten, twenty pages per memo. On-the-one-hand, on-the-other-hand balls. No one will bother, and in any case all will be read in the context of my argument.

Julian told me that the Treasury had commented that mine was 'the first decently written paper they had seen for thirty years'.

Ministry of Defence   *Friday, 19 January*

Today I *dominated* the Dept. Repeatedly I sent for Quinlan, Spiers,[1] John Colston.[2] Periodically I talked to Arnold Weinstock. By sheer energy and clarity of thought I put together the deal that saved Ferranti, and its Radar, and thus EFA[3] in time for us to outface Stoltenberg[4] on Monday when the German delegation come over.

John Colston took notes, and tried to keep TK (*baffledly* at the end of a 'bad line' outside his house in Wiltshire) in touch.

I ran the whole thing at a break-neck pace, and afterwards Donald Spiers said, 'It's a wonderful feeling, to get hard decisions and clear instructions.'

But the sweetest moment of all came at the end of the day, after our third meeting, when Quinlan materialised, Jeeves-like, beside me: 'Fingers crossed, but well done!'

---

[1] Donald Spiers, Controller Aircraft, and Head of Profession, Defence Science and Engineering, Ministry of Defence, since 1989.

[2] John Colston, an Assistant Secretary at Defence.

[3] The Germans were already voicing their misgivings about the European Fighter Aircraft (EFA) project. At this time their excuse was that Ferranti (stipulated as the radar contractor) were commercially unviable and this put the project at risk. AC encouraged Lord Weinstock to take Ferranti's radar enterprise into GEC, thus totally altering its commercial status.

[4] Gerhard Stoltenberg, German Defence Minister since 1989.

Ministry of Defence   *Friday, 26 January*

Yesterday a great gale swept through London in the afternoon, tearing at roofs and scaffolding. The police, as usual, overreacted and closed off streets and by-ways at random, blocking motorists and shouting at pedestrians through loud-hailers. The whole of Westminster and the West End went into 'gridlock' from tea-time until about nine p.m., with angry and resentful drivers lurching and clutch-slipping up on to the pavement and abandoning their cars.

I cancelled my trip to Plymouth and, seeing Archie Hamilton in the library corridor, fell into conversation.

I am in the ascendant at the moment, with my place at the Chequers summit assured, and drawing much deference from officials. On Wednesday night there was a big dinner at the RAF College at Bracknell. Moray Stewart,[1] very slightly in his cups it must be admitted, said to me, 'Why don't you take the helm?'

Not bad, from a Deputy Secretary. But I must be careful not to have a tumble. And I wanted to find out a little more about the PM's attitude (her real attitude as distinct from her public posture) to German reunification.

Archie Hamilton and I went into the smoking room – to be alone. Strange, the decline of the smoking room, even in my time. In former days there was spirited discussion, conviviality. Friends and colleagues spoke ill or, very occasionally when they hoped it would get repeated, good, of those who were absent. But now it is frequented only by soaks, traditionalists, and Memory-Lane buffers.

I suppose that the implication was that I would try and conform with whatever her own line was – although this has never been my style.

But Archie was interesting. He claimed not to know what she really thought, just said, 'She's against it, ho-ho.' (You'd think that, having worked as her PPS, he'd know a bit more but I never, I suppose, make enough allowance for the actions of people who want to set me back a few pips.)

Archie said that was the mistake John Moore[2] had made. During

---

[1] Moray Stewart, Deputy Under-Secretary of State, Defence Procurement, since 1988. He would become Second Permanent Under-Secretary, Defence, later in the year.

[2] John Moore had been dropped from the Government in 1989, after three years as Social Security Secretary.

the high months of his status as her chosen successor he framed the Health Service reforms exactly on the basis of what he thought she wanted. But she kept changing her mind. One minute she wanted to go further, the next she got an attack of the doubts, wanted to trim a bit. Each time the unfortunate John agreed, made the adjustments, came back for approval. The result was a total hotchpotch and 'she ended up thinking he was a wanker, and got rid of him'.

Saltwood   *Sunday, 28 January*

I am flat and reactive after Chequers.

Last night on my return I was still on a high... Percy Cradock[1] had made a point of telling me 'how much the Prime Minister admired your paper', and going into lunch – although we had had quite an argument during the morning – she had said how good it was, 'so full of original thought'. But perhaps I overplayed my hand? Did I trespass too aggressively into the field of Foreign Affairs?

But surely defence policy can only be considered in the context of our foreign commitments?

I suppose, on reflection, that I did not make enough allowance for the fact that every colleague (except the Treasury) and every official (except Charles and Percy) is hostile to me. The Prime Minister herself is friendly, but implacable. I argued cogently for accepting, and exploiting, German reunification while they still needed our support.

No good. She is determined not to.

'You're wrong,' I said. 'You're just wrong.'

Everyone at the table smirked at each other. Now he's really torn it; fucking little show-off, etc.

During the coffee-break I cornered her.

'These are just a re-run of the old Appeasement arguments of 1938.'

'Yes,' she said, eyes flashing (she's in incredible form at the moment), 'and I'm not an appeaser.'

---

[1] Sir Percy Cradock, distinguished diplomat, who had been British Ambassador to Beijing before leading the UK team in negotiations over the future of Hong Kong in 1983. Adviser to the Prime Minister on Foreign Affairs since 1984.

John Major,[1] whom I like more and more, said to me *sotto voce*, 'You're a military strategist. Oughtn't you to be sending your tanks round the flank, rather than attacking head on?'

Saltwood   *Wednesday, 31 January*

I am skiving. Second day of 'flu'. But having been rather awful and restlessly dry-hot yesterday (I took to my bed) I am now over it; and sitting around in the Green Room eating sundry delicacies that Jane sweetly prepares (*not* in *nouvelle cuisine* portion size).

Two 'crises' preoccupy the Department. Neither anything to do with me whatever. Complacently I can spectate. The first is something to do with a 'dirty tricks campaign'. These are always a bore. As far as I'm concerned 'dirty tricks' are part and parcel of effective government. But apparently Number 10 were misinformed by us – or so they claim.

More serious, news is about to break concerning the trouser-leg (sic) fractures in Warspite's cooling system. This could affect every nuclear-powered submarine. The whatever-it-is Authority have already given their advice that we should 'cease to operate' them until the condition is 'rectified'.

The result would be over twenty submarines tied up in UK ports, crews with nothing to do, local papers making inquiries, general trouble.

TK, quite rightly in my view, is continuing to keep the newer ones on station (although whether this is really his decision or was forced on him by the Lady I simply don't know). I suspect the latter because when, sadistically, I rattled him at a meeting, 'If – *if* there is an accident, it's not just you who resigns; the Government falls,' he didn't blench.

In a calm frame of mind I was eating chicken livers on toast when the phone rang. Jane answered. It was Julian.

'Julian at seven p.m.?'

As always looking on the bright side, she suggested, 'Perhaps TK's had an accident?'

---

[1] John Major, briefly Foreign Secretary, 1989, before becoming Chancellor of the Exchequer following the resignation of Nigel Lawson.

'He hasn't. You have,' could well have been Julian's answer.

A leak about the Chequers meeting is to be in tomorrow's *Times*. It is said that it comes from me.

'We *know* it's him,' according to the S of S office, passim 'Number 10' – in other words, Charles himself.

Julian was grave. Very, very grave.

'As you remember, Minister, the PM reminded everyone of the need for total secrecy.'

This has to be a frame-up. It just has to be. Because I know to whom I have spoken, and it's no one. Not just no journalist, no one. Except Julian himself and, very obliquely, Peter Levene.

I padded off, sweating profusely in my dressing-gown and having suffered a total regression, to the tower office, and rang Charles at Number 10. He was bland, diplomatic, but said it was 'regrettable'. Too bloody right. This sort of stain hangs with one a long time. And *completely* without reason.

On reflection, though, as I write this, my suspicions are aroused. Apparently it is to be carried in an article by Michael Evans.[1] Now I've never met Michael Evans. I wouldn't know what he looked like if he came into the room, still less am I on terms to 'leak' him something.

But when I said, both to Julian and to Charles, 'I'm going to find Michael Evans and have it out with him' they both counselled strongly against.[2]

---

[1] Michael Evans, Defence Correspondent on *The Times*.

[2] On Julian's advice AC raised the matter with the Permament Secretary. On 8 February came Michael Quinlan's graceful and elliptic response:

'As promised, I caused Hugh Colver to make some enquiries on Tuesday about the piece in *The Times*. He spoke to Bernard Ingham.

'Bernard said he knew nothing about the idea that Evans had "owned up" to a source, and he found it strange. His assumption was that anything Charles Powell believed about sourcing could only be inference from the piece's contents. Hugh took the opportunity of conveying to Bernard, on my instructions, that I was wholly satisfied that the content did not come from you. Bernard (who is often at odds with Charles) has his own suspicions.

'The only way of taking this any further, it seems to me, would be for you to tax Charles Powell directly. I think it has to be for your judgment whether that would be a useful operation.'

Ministry of Defence   *Thursday, 1 February*

One should not take pleasure from the discomfiture of colleagues, I suppose. But without question it is one of the more agreeable bonuses of the *sport* of politics. So unpredictable, and so random it seems, in those it afflicts.

This morning there is a really *lethal* piece in the *Daily Mail* – a full-scale article on the leader page – about poor old Stradling Thomas, 'Stradders' as he is known; 'Is this the laziest man in the House of Commons?'

It is clear that he took a lot of drinks off the reporter, they were in the Strangers' Bar for hours. But when the unfortunate Stradders came back from voting and the reporter asked him what he had been voting 'on', Stradders didn't know. Great indignation. But we seldom ever know what we are voting 'on'. Apparently the public like to find this shocking.

Anyway, there was poor old Stradders alone at a table in the dining room. Thinking he might be a bit low, nice old stick in the Whips' Office, all that, I joined him.

He was disagreeable. Didn't make sense, started up a totally Kafka-like quarrel (attributing remarks or, at least, thoughts to me and then demolishing them) about pronunciation. 'A Hotel'; '*an* Hotel'; '*an* apple', etc.

Batty. He looked completely degenerate in the way that real alcoholics do; details of personal appearance so neglected as to make a really off-putting, smelly whole. Cardboard City. Serve me right for trying to do a good deed.

During the afternoon Peter Levene came in. He is concerned, like me and practically everyone else in the building, at the pace of progress on the Review. Tom muffles everything, sits on it for weeks. Even his Private Office admit that he is driving them mad. Yet in a way I understand. The buck stops with him. He's racking his brain for catches. He knows there will be a lot of opposition from within the Party.

Let's face it, though. His real problem is he doesn't understand what's going on.

Peter was frustrated and (unusually for him) gloomy. Then *he* said to me, 'Why don't you take the helm?'

That's two Dep Secs in less than a week!

'But how?'

Peter had an ingenious solution. To set up a 'Review Con-
trollerate' with him in charge; three Young Turks from the three
Services; *reporting to me*. Mouth-watering. If the original September
Chequers remit was the ox's hide then this surely (to pursue the
analogy of medieval politics) would be a permit for my own chivalric
Order. But Tom would see it a mile off. The Review is the only real
activity in the Dept at present. If I'm put in charge, effectively I'm
running the whole shoot.

There's only one person who can ordain this. We'll have to see.
At least it wouldn't be so brazen as the time I asked her to take ODA
away from Geoffrey and put it into Trade.[1]

Albany   *Tuesday, 20 February*

I dined at the Cavalry Club with Ian Gow.

He is deeply apprehensive of the future, said that no Government
had ever been consistently (over six months) behind in the polls at
this level, and at this stage – halfway he said – in the electoral cycle,
and gone on to win.

'We aren't halfway, we're three-quarters. The Election would
normally be in '91.'

Ian said that all the indicators were bad for this year, and that
inflation would still be at 8.5 per cent in November. (He's a terrible
old Jeremiah about the inflation rate.)

'Personally I wonder if it matters all that much. It's a million per
cent, or whatever, in Brazil and you can still get taxis and delicious
meals. Sex doesn't stop.'

Usually when I make remarks of this kind, which are Boswellian,
to draw him out, Ian smiles with what is called 'a faraway look'. But
he was serious, earnest.

'Evidently you do not appreciate the significance of the month of
November?'

Of course! The leadership election.

Ian elaborated. There is a real risk of a challenge, and this time a
serious one. He said that even when Meyer was standing last year he
had a hard time persuading many colleagues to vote for the PM –

---

[1] Recorded in July 1986, but not included in this edition.

although then most of them were minded to abstain.[1] He had told them that if they really were still discontented, felt that there has been no improvement, 'You will have another chance next year.'

'Are there many?'

'Yes. I am sorry to say there are. Very many.'

I didn't like to ask. Not out of tact but because I didn't want to hear the answer.

Ian said that Heseltine's disclaimer, 'I can think of no circumstances in which I would challenge Margaret Thatcher', is susceptible to any number of let-outs. Acute crisis, Party's fortunes, irresistible pressure, etc., etc.

'It'd be all or bust for him. I don't think he'll dare,' I tried.

Ian replied, but without much conviction, that Heseltine would lose anyway.

I'm not so sure. He might win the contest, but lose the General Election. Then where would we all be?

We are off this afternoon to Scotland. The IEPG conference[2] is booked at Gleneagles. It's a freebie really, and wives are invited.

But first I must prepare some more notes for the PM on 'Bruges II'.[3] Am I helping her to dig deeper her own political grave?

Later

A note on the subject came over from Charles, marked SECRET, PRIVATE and PERSONAL.

'A good way of drawing attention to something,' I said to Private Office. It enhances my status in the Dept. But it's in total breach of Civil Service convention, there may even be rules of procedure.

If a civil servant at Number 10 wants to get a message to a Minister in another Department the correct way to do so is to communicate with the Private Office of the Secretary of State of that Department – and if it is a junior Minister (itself an unusual enough contingency) then it is for the S of S's office to pass it on down to the head of the office of the junior Minister concerned. Good old Charles.

---

[1] Sir Anthony Meyer, MP for Clwyd North West since 1983 (West Flint, 1970–83) had challenged Margaret Thatcher as Leader of the Conservative Party. The result: Thatcher, 314; Meyer, 33; Abstentions, 24.

[2] Annual meeting of European Programme Groups (a euphemism for those senior civil servants who had oversight of weapons procurement).

[3] At that time the Prime Minister was minded to deliver a sequel to her celebrated speech at Bruges the previous year.

Gleneagles   *Wednesday, 21 February*

At dinner last night I sat next to the wife of the Turkish Minister. Not one word of English could she speak. She took a chance, said she spoke French '*un petit peu*'. No problem, I gabbled to her in French. Not one word could she understand, or speak. She was fat, and squat. And wore a black dress with very little jewellery.

Earlier, at the reception, I had my first sighting of Chevenement.[1] Odious. Rude, uncouth, objectionable. TK thinks he has established a 'relationship' with Chevenement, and boasts about it.

Dear Tom, sometimes I feel quite protective towards him. How could he possibly think that little Frenchman would do anything but cut his throat if he could get even fifty francs out of it?

This morning, before the session, I went for a constitutional with Peter Levene, and we walked down to the lake, looked at all the manic golfers milling around the club house. Righteous and crazy-faced, they glared back.

Peter is restless. His time at MoD is drawing to an end. He is tempted by Industry, and Arnold Weinstock teases him constantly with chimeric offers.

But Peter fancies also the possibility of remaining, advancing indeed, in the public sector. He would like to be Permanent Secretary at the DTI.

Tricky, I said. The Dept is starved of cash these days and anyway, haven't they just appointed Gregson?[2]

He toyed also with the idea of becoming (sic) a diplomat. Really? Yes, what he'd like best is Washington.

I don't often gulp but, privately, I gulped.

'Well, Peter Jay[3] got it,' I said. 'It's one of the posts that does occasionally go to an outsider.'

I suppose that I am just the same. All vigorous and ambitious men live by considering that anything is within their capability.

---

[1] Jean-Pierre Chevenement, French Defence Minister. Sacked by Mitterand in February 1991.

[2] Sir Peter Gregson had moved from Energy (Permanent Under-Secretary) to Trade and Industry (Permanent Secretary) in 1989.

[3] Peter Jay was Economics Editor of *The Times* when the Prime Minister, James Callaghan (and coincidentally Peter Jay's father-in-law) appointed him British Ambassador to Washington in 1977.

Saltwood   *Sunday, 25 February*

I remain in depression. I might give up drink for Lent. A good start in Arabia next week, as I always enjoy refusing it from an Ambassador – they are so loathsomely *arch* when they produce the whisky bottle, 'I expect you'd welcome some of this, eh? Ho-ho' – and the orange juice at all those meetings is the best in the world.

I thought I would play on the piano. But when I got to the music room there was water pouring in and down the east wall.

Last year I spent £11,000 replacing the lead just on this one roof. What's the point? The Aubusson can really no longer take any more punishment.

Bugger it, I thought, anyway. It can't stop me playing.

Melodiously I strummed. 'Sentimental Journey'; 'Smoke Gets in Your Eyes'; 'My Guy's Come Back'; 'Stormy Weather'.

Always I think of that Pole who played in the NAAFI at the Army Mountain Warfare Training School at Llanberis, in 1945. For hours on end he played – Chopin, Rachmaninov, Liszt, anything from ENSA naturally – preferring when the hall was empty, and it echoed. Was he thinking of home, and his dead children? Of his horse, shot from under him in the last September battles on the Vistula?

I have done, seen and experienced an awful lot of things. And I like in these tall Gothic rooms, with all these beautiful possessions around me, accumulated by my father and by my grandfather, to nostalgicise.

Why am I still, in the main, so zestful?

I know, but I don't like to say.

In case the gods take it away.

Saltwood   *Saturday, 3 March*

Yesterday went on too long.

I left Paddington by the early train to speak at a Party lunch in Truro. Low key, upper-class candidate, a few bright(ish) sparks. I thought these old Etonians were extinct by now – they certainly are in 'safe' seats – Central Office toad/clones have seen to that. Clearly the Association have reverted to the Piers[1] mould.

---

[1] Piers Dixon had been MP for Truro, winning the seat in 1970 and again in February 1974, only to lose to the Liberal David Penhaligon in October 1974. Following

In any case it's ridiculous that Truro should not be a Tory seat. All these rentiers, a few landowners, some contented farmers and a lot of holiday-dependent shopkeepers and boarding house landladies.

The trouble is, once the Libs get stuck in, really stuck in, they are devilish hard to dislodge. Their trick is to *degrade* the whole standard of political debate. The nation, wide policy issues, the sweep of history – forget it. They can't even manage to discuss broad economic questions, as they don't understand the problems – never mind the answers.

The Liberal technique is to force people to lower their sights, teeny little provincial problems about bus timetables, and street lighting and the grant for a new community hall. They compensate by giving the electorate uplift with constant plugging of an identity concept – no matter how minuscule – to which they try to attach a confrontational flavour: 'Newton Ferrers Mums outface Whitehall' and a really bouncy commonplace little turd (or big turd in the case of Penhaligon) as candidate, and they're in.

So I am rather pessimistic concerning the prospects for this pleasant, diffident young man, even though I firmly, and repetitiously, referred to him as the next Member of Parliament for Truro.

I just caught the train back. A long journey.

The box didn't take long and I fidgeted, did a trawl of the seats for discarded reading material, bought and consumed two Mars bars, which gave me a headache.

I couldn't get home as there was a little dinner at Lyall Street.[1] Just Aspers, Jimmy Goldsmith and Charles Powell. The 'guest' was Conrad Black,[2] the purpose to see to what extent he was amenable to being leant on, in the gentlest manner of course, to steer Max[3] away from plugging Heseltine so much. The answer, it soon became clear, was – not at all.

Black is young, quite attractive looking, very clever and widely read. If I look back over the newspaper tycoons I've known it is only Beaverbrook with whom he compares. Some, like Vere, are just thick,

---

Penhaligon's death the resulting by-election in 1987 saw Matthew Taylor retain the seat for the Liberals. In the 1987 General Election he had a majority over the Conservative candidate of 4753; in 1992 this increased to 7570.

[1] Number 1, Lyall Street, town house of John Aspinall.

[2] Conrad Black, Canadian newspaper proprietor, born 1944, who had come to London and bought the *Daily Telegraph* in 1987.

[3] Max Hastings, Editor of the *Daily Telegraph* since 1986.

others like Roy Thomson bluff away and you don't know, but they're boring. Cap'n Bob is the most entertaining, I suppose, but you never quite feel he's giving you his full *attention* – and this for reasons, let's say, unrelated to the setting in which the conversation is taking place.

The subject had to be approached delicately. Charles was diplomatic, Jimmy blunt. But Black simply couldn't care. He made a competent, almost dismissive defence. It's my paper, I do what I think right, anyway he (Heseltine) is an interesting chap, we look like we're in a mess, heading for a bigger one, etc.

Black's preference seemed to be for talking about Washington. He's knowledgeable and interesting here too. But as to its principal objective, the dinner was a failure.

Saltwood   *Sunday, 4 March*

A beautiful day of early spring, quite perfect in light, colour, the shadow and tone of stone and lawn and blossom. We have started to mow with the sit-down mowers that roll and stripe. No more rotaries until September when the plantains grow.

I was resigned to settling back 'with the Heritage' when I had a long call from Tristan which electrified me.[1]

We're 28 points behind in the polls, and the leadership is in a panic. The Lady has rocky moments of self doubt. (This has happened before, I told him, Carol used to tell me how dejected she became in 1985 when all the economic indicators were looking good but people still wouldn't respond.) The Cabinet are all over the place. Most of them are 'pretty doubtful about' (read *loathe*) her but don't know what to do. G. Howe is behaving 'poorly', *chétif* and unsupportive. The Government have got to find a billion, at once, to buy off the Poll Tax complainants.

'That won't be enough,' I sniggered.

No, wait, he said, I told them 'the only person who can give this to you is Alan Clark'.

John Major, somewhat ruefully, agreed.

Exultant, I waxed on how I could square things in Washington,

---

[1] Tristan Garel-Jones had been Deputy Chief Whip since 1989.

fix it with our various collaborative partners that we got out of these fearful projects, kick ass in the Army Council. I ended, for the first time, actually *asking*. I said the only thing for it – and to be done promptly, Whitsun at the latest – was to make TK leader of the House and me S of S Def.

'Thank you very much,' he said. 'This conversation has been very useful.' Then added the usual disclaimer that there was nothing he could do . . . etc. I feel that I am closer to my ambition than I am ever likely to get again.

Saltwood   *Sunday, 25 March*

On Friday I was in Plymouth for the Constituency AGM. The atmosphere was not good. Personally the activists, or 'voluntary workers' as they prefer being called, were friendly. But there was much muttering.

Jane thought it went better than I did, yes, but to balance my own paranoia should be set the fact that everyone likes her. So it's easier for them to respond to her happy personality.

They all (except dear Romaine Palmer) complained, in different ways, sometimes directly, sometimes in code, about Mrs T. But I'm used to that. We had it in 1981, in 1985. It's cyclical. The trough is always two years away from the next Election date.

It's these fucking Councillors, that's what people really like listening to. Their own kind; petty, inarticulate, short-sighted, mildly venal.

Ralph Morrell, who rarely attends the AGM in good times, had got himself (for some technical reason connected with the vote for Treasurer) into the Chair. Ralph is Dean of the Tory local government machine, and 'respected'. He spoke after me. Every time he mentioned the doings of the Councillors he got applause, bigger than anything granted to my own somewhat ritualised performance. A ripple of approval whenever he criticised the Government. This he did mainly on grounds which I simply don't understand, have indeed made no attempt to understand, as the subject bores me.

It's all to do with this spastic concept of 'capping', as it's called. This is itself bound up with the Poll Tax (as one must NOT call it), which has got everyone into a rage. The only objection to the tax, as far as I can see (and as I did in fact point out, to the manifest irritation of the Lady and all eleven other Ministers present[1] except the Chancellor), is that no one will pay. It'll be like jay-walking.

And by 'no one' I mean all the slobs, yobs, drifters, junkies, free-loaders, claimants, and criminals on day-release, who make their living by exploitation of the benefit system and overload local authority expenditure. As usual the burden will fall on the thrifty, the prudent, the responsible, those 'of fixed address', who patiently support society and the follies of the chattering class.

I walked around the town, in very cold winds. I did not want to be recognised, still less accosted, and kept my head down, looking at the pavements.

My surgery was huge, with many time-wasters. Many came in to have a grumble and, in spite of my going into Emergency-Unctuous mode, did not leave satisfied.

Yesterday we lost Mid-Stafford, poor little Heddle's seat, on a swing of 23 per cent.[2] In Plymouth I'd be obliterated. Just as well I'm not standing again.

And yet ... Jane told me that on the drive down she had been held up by some motor-cycle police for a Jaguar which swept into the Intelligence HQ at Ashford. Suddenly she had a taste of what it was like 'on the outside'.

I think what saddens me most is the so near and yet so far experience at MoD. I have written the Defence Review. It has, to all intents and purposes, been accepted by Number 10. But no one is getting on with it. It's all being screwed by this absurd 'Options' exercise, which muffles everything.

On Friday I had to circulate a rebuttal of some batty recommendation that we should – effectively – *annexe* East Germany, run exercises there, defend the air space. Simply crazy. A transparent power-play by those in the Dept who are determined to keep the Central Front alive as a magnet/concept for their own careers. But that's all I could do – circulate a paper. It's miles outside the Procurement responsibilities. However taut you stretch the Ox's hide it won't cover straight AF matters, and Hamilton's office (not, to do

---

[1] On the sole occasion which AC attended a meeting of E(LF), the Cabinet Committee which considered the tax.

[2] John Heddle, MP since 1983, had committed suicide in December 1989. At the 1987 General Election he had a majority of 14000.

him justice, Archie himself; or at least he doesn't allow it to show) get angry, make trouble with Julian.

This happens the whole time. It's not just the slow balls-up of the 'Options' project, it's a hundred examples a week of waste, blinkers, vested interest, idleness and failure to put the country before narrow personal, regimental or sectarian considerations. Unless or until I'm Secretary of State I just have to watch them go rolling past, make a private note to chase it if I ever get the chance. Julian, though, is sympathetic, and does what he can.

A long letter today from beloved Tip. He says that the whole of Rhine Army is completely demoralised. There's a 'freeze' on spares, so if vehicles break on exercise they're just towed back to Sennelager and abandoned. The great Panzer workshops that featured in Hitler's exchange with Jodl after the fall of the Remagen bridge are now a scrapyard for broken Land-Rovers. The 'chaps' are good, still, and keen. *They* want to get out into the Empire, sort out the 'trouble spots'. But he says some of the new recruits are almost illiterate. They can't even do sports because these are banned at school as being too competitive.

It's all so depressing. Especially when you think we've had a Tory Government for the last ten years.

House of Commons   *Wednesday, 28 March*

The Lady is under deep pressure now. It just won't go away. As soon as one paper goes quiet another one, or two at a time, start up.

As far as I can make out practically every member of the Cabinet is quietly and unattributably briefing different Editors or members of the Lobby about how awful she is. This makes it easier for people like Peter Jenkins[1] to say that 'she has virtually lost all support in Cabinet'. Malcolm Rifkind[2] is actually quoted today as saying, 'I'll be here after she's gone.'

There is even talk of a coup in July. Heseltine is quite openly spoken about as the heir-presumptive, and preens himself in public.

---

[1] Political columnist on *The Independent*.
[2] Malcolm Rifkind, MP for Edinburgh Pentlands since 1974. Secretary of State for Scotland since 1986.

How has all this been allowed to come about? The Community Charge has got on everyone's nerves of course, and generated the most oppressive volume of correspondence. Persistent deficits in the polls of a nearly insuperable order rattle people. But I am inclined to think that the Party in the House has just got sick of her. She hasn't promoted her 'own' people much. Her 'constituency' in this place depends solely on her proven ability to win General Elections. But now this is in jeopardy she has no real Praetorian Guard to fall back on. There's been a lot of talk about 'one of us', all that, but most of them are still left to moulder at the '92 dinner table. When's the Revolution? In the meantime, all the wets and Blue Chips and general Heathite wankers, who seem ineradicable in this bloody Party, stew around and pine for her to drop dead.

Most critics move, in the open, under (pretty transparent) camouflage. A number of 'heavy' backbenchers of the 'Centre' (i.e. Left) of the Party have let it be known that her 'Decision-making Circle' should be widened, that they are uneasy about the 'privileged access' enjoyed by 'certain key and unelected advisors'.

This of course is a shot across the bows for Charles and Bernard. But without them she really would be lost, as the Chief Whip, Tim Renton, is Howe's creature; Peter Morrison is of little use as a PPS under these conditions; Gow is neutered and doesn't cut ice any longer and Garel-Jones, who would relish the task of rescuing her as Victor Ludorum in the Whips' Challenge Trophy, is tied up in the Foreign Office, and on overseas visits half the time.

My own position is affected in a number of ways – all unwelcome. My special *access* is less potent because, with the rest of the Cabinet more or less openly plotting their own positions, and jockeying, her disapproval counts for little. We're almost getting to the point where they are no longer afraid of her. And indeed, her sponsorship could actually be damaging. Second, it disturbs my own plans for smooth and easy withdrawal, booking a 'K' at once and a Lords ticket in the next Parliament. Will I even get my PC in May? Finally, I could be faced with the ultimate hideosity of being stuck at MoD during a Heseltine 'reconstruction'. Should I leave immediately, or hang on for certain humiliation forty-eight hours later?

Oh dear. How quickly everything can change.

House of Commons   *Monday, 2 April*

Last night there were riots in Central London – just like 1981. All the anarchist scum, class-war, random drop-outs and trouble-seekers had infiltrated the march and started beating up the police.[1]

There is this strain in most Western countries (except, curiously, the United States) but it is particularly prevalent in Britain, where this rabble have – confirming their middle-class social origins – their own press in *The Grauniad* and *The Independent*. Far from having their capers cut by the revolution in Russia, the removal of a distant but supportive ideological menace, they are flourishing in that very curtailment of discipline and order which the fall of the ancient Soviet autocracy has brought about.

But it is bad. *Civil Disorder.* Could cut either way, but I fear will scare people into wanting a compromise – just as did Saltley Colliery and the three-day week in 1972/3. In the corridors and the tea room people are now talking openly of ditching the Lady to save their skins. This is the first time I've heard it *en clair* since a bad patch (1977?) when we were in opposition. Some of the Lobby, Tony Bevins[2] in particular, hang around outside the Members' post office and fly kites.

There is a wild rumour going round that she may be 'deputised' at the end of July. 'Uh? Deputised?'

'Yes, you know, receive a deputation, the Chief Whip, the '22 Executive, Willie, that kind of thing. Told to throw in the towel.'

Contemptible.

Ministry of Defence   *Tuesday, 3 April*

For months I have been resisting expenditure (some hundreds of millions) on a completely unnecessary new piece of Army Equipment known by its acronym as ACEATM.

It is a 'sideways firing mine' – itself an unlikely, indeed contradictory concept, surely? The idea is that you position one of these incredibly expensive and 'intelligent' devices in the window of a house and when a tank goes past it shoots out at it, 'sideways'.

---

[1] An anti-poll tax demonstration in central London.
[2] Anthony Bevins, Political Editor of *The Independent*. His father, Reginald, had been an MP, and Postmaster-General, 1959–64.

From the first moment I saw the papers it was clear that this was a complete waste of money, conceived at the height of the Cold War, and now totally unnecessary. Trouble is, I'm not really meant to question 'Operational Requirements'. I'm meant to 'seek' and then, by implication, follow advice on anything about which I have doubts. In the nature of things, the advice comes from the same people who drafted the 'Requirement' in the first place.

Finally, after much deferment, a full-scale 'Meeting' was called.

'You leave them behind, you see, to slow up the enemy's advance.'

'What advance?'

'Well, er, his advance, Minister.'

'What enemy?'

'The Warsaw Pact, Minister.'

'The Warsaw Pact no longer exists. It's disintegrated.'

'In villages, in built-up areas,' shouted somebody else, also in uniform. Why the fuck are all these people in uniform? It's not allowed. Just so as to intimidate me, they think.

'I thought the first rule in deploying armour was to avoid built-up areas?'

'Roads, Minister. Choke-points.'

'What happens if a truck goes past? That would be a waste, wouldn't it. How does it know not to shoot?'

'Well it knows, Minister. It's programmed with all the Warsaw Pact silhouettes.'

'Warsaw Pact?'

'There's a lot of Russian stuff Out of Area now, you know.'

'I do know.'

'It's Next Generation, Minister. A very intelligent sensor.'

'Better programme it to recognise all the French stuff, then.'

'Ha-ha, Minister. Oh, ha-ha.'

What can one do? Nothing. I can block this spastic weapon, and make them cross, and complaining. But about *them* I can do nothing.

I want to fire the whole lot. Instantly. Out, out. No 'District' commands, no golden bowlers, nothing. Out. There are so many good, tough keen young officers who aren't full of shit. How can we bring them on, before they get disillusioned, or conventionalised by the system? If I could, I'd do what Stalin did to Tukhachevsky.[1]

---

[1] The purges of the Red Army in 1938–9 when three-quarters of all officers of field rank and above were put to the firing squads.

Ministry of Defence   *Thursday, 5 April*

The Lady scowled startledly at me on Tuesday when she came in for
Questions. Although she is completely absorbed in her own brief,
hyped to the nines for her ordeal against little Kinnock, and pays no
attention to her surroundings whatever, her presence beside one on
the bench is always a little constraining.

My own last Question was reached, and my performance was
not as relaxed and dominating as it should have been. Is my voice
losing timbre?

She spat at me again during a somewhat *ponderoso* question
from Nick Soames about Rhodesia. I reminded her about BMATT
and our training detachment out there, but she didn't use it.[1]
Pre-programmed.

Somehow this little experience brought home to me how utterly
unrealistic is any idea that she might make me S of S. How? Why?
Lucky even to get PC next month.[2]

Our position continues to worsen. I urge for blood, and still more
blood.

The Last Days[3] and the Whips are divided among themselves.
Some want blood. Some, covertly, want 'a change'. G-J's own position
is equivocal and he probably thinks, may even have been told, that
Heseltine would make him Chief. Renton, the existing Chief, doesn't
think strategically – or even tactically. He is amiable, social; but
never did his groundwork as a junior in 'the office'. In any case,
my suspicion has always been that his loyalties incline towards
Geoffrey Howe.

Gow, Ryder, Aitken and I dined at 'Greens' the 'new' restaurant
on Locketts' old site, set up under the aegis of Simon Parker Bowles
(*relation*, I assume). Confirmed the bad impression when Alison and I
tried it out last week. Waiters either *completely* incapable of understanding English – or French, or Italian. Are they Rumanians from an

---

[1] BMATT: British Military Assistant Training Team. AC's younger son, Andrew, had
done a year of duty with the unit attached to the Zimbabwean Army.

[2] AC was thinking of the Queen's Birthday Honours when the names of new
members of the Privy Council would be announced.

[3] *The Last Days of Hitler* by Hugh Trevor-Roper, AC's tutor at Oxford, now Lord
Dacre.

AIDS hostel? – or chinless youths, spaced-outly smiling and chatting to each other in upper-class accents, waiting to get on the waiting list (sic) for Cirencester.

The boys were gloomy. We none of us see our way. Quite difficult to approach the Lady at the moment, as Ian is finding. And what advice do we give her? Shed blood, I said. We are planning to take revenge on Mates. Jonathan undertook to contact Tam and prime him with a question about Singer Link Miles (who pay Mates) who are in contractual relationship with us.

When I fell asleep I had a curious dream; gently ascending the hill behind Sandling station, having resigned, and being at peace with the world. Bernard Braine[1] came into it somehow – perhaps because Jonathan had been telling me that he was determined to stay on, in order to block Ted from becoming 'Father of the House'.

Ministry of Defence   *Wednesday, 11 April*

Last night I won £1,000 off John Sterling at backgammon. This always makes me wake up in a good mood. But today, the last of the 'Lent' term, is just too full. I woke at 5-ish, had made tea and enjoyed Cadogan's memoirs by 7, collected the boxes from the Lodge and read the brief for the DOAE[2] visit by the time the car arrived at 8.15. With luck I will be through in time to catch the 7 p.m. train to Ashford.

I'm looking forward to five lovely days at Saltwood, and mustn't fritter them. Last weekend we drew up a little daily schedule.

As I went along the Rope Walk this morning I worried about the blackbird. No sign this spring. Sometimes, at first light, I can hear one a very long way away. But surely, even if he/she is dead there should be some offspring here? I suppose the *same one* can't still be alive as it has been causing me pleasure since 1975. But to have none is sad.

There is a thrush in Speaker's Court who sings goodnight so

---

[1] Sir Bernard Braine, MP for various Essex constituencies since 1950 and Father of the House since 1983. When he finally retired at the 1992 Election, Edward Heath (also elected in 1950) gained the Father of the House soubriquet.

[2] DOAE – Defence Operational Analysis Establishment.

beautifully each evening. When I can, if I'm in my Commons office, I come upstairs and listen.

How could anyone shoot a song-bird?

Saltwood   *Friday, 20 April*

A date which usually marks a period of good fortune, and the transition from spring to early summer. But it is cold and blowy, and there has been a fall of snow on Hampstead Heath. Only at Eriboll is it shirtsleeve hot, with the loch like glass. James rang and said that he had ferried fourteen tups across to their summer quarters on Eilean Chorain.

Yesterday evening Tristan and I repaired to Wiltons, and took a pullman.

I told him (uneasily aware that somewhere the cock would be crowing) that very reluctantly, and with great sadness and not a little apprehension I had come to a certain conclusion. Tristan said that he was glad I had admitted to this. Some weeks ago he had written a paper in his own hand; circulated it to the Chief Whip, Ingham (?!), Andrew Turnbull,[1] John Major and Mark Lennox-Boyd.[2]

Not, I noted, to Charles. No point, he said, CP 'too fanatically committed'.

Each of the recipients had 'tried to push him through her door' (i.e. to say it in person).

'Well, why don't you?'

Yes, he was going to supper at the Number 10 flat on Sunday – just him and X-B[3] – and told me how he proposed to play it. The Party was 'lazy, sullen, and frightened'. Unless there was a marked improvement by early to mid-October *over* 100 votes would be cast against her at the leadership contest, which was inevitable, in the

---

[1] Andrew Turnbull, Principal Private Secretary to the Prime Minister since 1988.

[2] Mark Lennox-Boyd, MP for Morecambe since 1979. Parliamentary Private Secretary to the Prime Minister since 1988.

[3] X-B: AC here uses the abbreviation employed by Jim Lees-Milne when referring to Mark's father, Alan (later 1st Viscount Boyd of Merton), Colonial Secretary, 1954–9.

month following. Tristan's view was that over 100 against would mean
that she would have to stand down.

I couldn't help grinning. 'Try telling her that.'

Tristan named a number of individuals (ranging from Phil Goodhart[1] to Marlow[2]) who were totally disillusioned, didn't bother to
vote any longer. Party discipline was breaking up. All this he would
say if necessary.

It is clear, although he didn't say as much, that he has a low
opinion of Renton, who has not got a grip on things. In any case,
Renton is Geoffrey's nominee, has no feelings towards the Lady.

I said that 'Mid October' was balls. The time scale was far shorter.
It had to be settled before the Party Conference and that meant,
effectively, in *this* parliamentary term – which in turn means before
15 July, because for those last two weeks of the Summer Term we
are all in a limbo of rumour, lassitude and low motivation. Proper
consideration cannot be given until after the May local election results
have been analysed, so that means that the *band* stretches from mid-
May until mid-July, no more.

At this exact point in our conversation I spotted Heseltine coming
up the steps from the bar! And with Mates! He was shown, not to a
nearby, but to the *adjoining* table. This was ludicrous. He and Mates
sat down, got up again immediately, were spirited away.

A nearby group of 'businessmen' were oggly. 'Didn't take long to
get rid of *him*,' I said, without reverence.

But I bet Michael was thinking, 'They won't treat me like that
when I'm Prime Minister.' One more score to settle with Clark. A
little later I signalled to Albert[3] and said would he please give Mr
Heseltine my compliments and apologies for spoiling his evening. I
would be very glad if he would allow me to settle his bill.

But whether Albert did so or not, I don't know. If he did, the
offer was not accepted.

---

[1] Philip Goodhart, MP for Beckenham since 1957.
[2] Tony Marlow, MP for Northampton North since 1979.
[3] Head waiter at Wilton's.

House of Commons   *Tuesday, 1 May*

I had a conversation with IG in the smoking room. Aitken joined us. What could we do to succour the Lady? Do we even want to? We were stuck with the same inflation rate as when we came into power in 1979. Ten, eleven years of endeavour (or however we call all those deprivations to life and family) and nothing to show for it but the passage of time and the intrusion of age.

We had moved into the chess room for privacy, but it was dinner time, and posses of MPs moved past on their way through to the dining room, and made mocking comments. Atkins, in particular, is cocky and hostile now, as he watches the decline of the Praetorians.

We came to no conclusions, but aggravated each other's dejection. After about a half hour I lied about a dinner engagement and made for the Kundan, but it was closed for a reception. I went to Brooks's, lost £150 and my appetite waned. Returned here and ate a toasted bun, first food since a banana at 1.30.

In the tea room I had a chat with Fallon, a nice cool Whip.[1] I complained to him about all this rotten, irrelevant, unnecessary legislation which clogs our time. Firearms; Football Supporters; War Crimes; *Supermarket Trollies (local Authority Recovery Powers) Restricted Amendment* ... etc., *ad nauseam*. Compounded with the abject failure to sort out the rioters at Strangeways prison it was all accumulating evidence of a government in decline. To my considerable pleasure, he was in complete agreement, citing, additionally, the Iraqi supergun. 'We should be making them, and selling them to everyone.'

'Good God,' he said. 'All this stuff about a decline in our manufacturing capability, but they had to come here to get the barrels made, didn't they? We should put it in a Trade Fair.' Splendid fellow.

Of course, in the nineteenth century this is what *would* have happened. And this morning I was on the roof of the old War Office building, looking around at Whitehall. The Admiralty opposite, the Cabinet office, the Treasury, the Foreign Office. How well it was all planned, how *confident*. We ran the Empire, and the world with the same number of civil servants as presently exist in one Department. Instead of spending no more than ten per cent of our Social Security budget on the Royal Navy, the proportion was exactly reversed.

---

[1] Michael Fallon, MP for Darlington since 1983. Shortly to become Parliamentary Under-Secretary at Education and Science.

I had wandered through the building, empty for years, but destined to be the nerve-centre of the intelligence services. The PSA[1] have a giant job-creation scheme running here. Dust, bare cabling, little transistor radios blare.

Magnificent rooms; heavy Edwardian panelling; oak plank floors one and a half inches thick; all being torn up to take the giant computers and their wiring. I stood in the central hall, grimy but forbidding, still. 'Only Major-Generals and above could use the main door on Whitehall.' (Who thought that one up, I wonder?) I tiptoed into Jack Profumo's private bathroom, still bearing traces of Valerie Hobson's redecoration, and telepathised for him; those moments of anguished realisation, when he must have known the Keeler affair was breaking.

Particularly, too, as I meandered along those gloomy corridors, still untouched, I reflected on past characters, long dead, who had paced excitedly there during those difficult months of the Great War when 'The Big Push' – and then again 'The Big Push' – was being planned. How many hundreds of thousands of Death Warrants were stamped in these rooms?

Albany   *Wednesday, 2 May*

I woke too early for *The Times*, even here, where Herbie delivers it at 6.15, and turned to Chips for solace with my EMT. I became absorbed by some of the very late entries:

Arturo Lopez-Wilshaw at 18, Rue du Centre, and Neuilly. Alexis de Rede, 'the Eugene de Rastignac of modern Paris' (who he?) at the Hotel Lambert. 'Eighteen, semi-gratin and very grand . . . Footmen and candelabra on the stairs; gold plate . . . the Palazzo Colonna *en petite*.'

'I was particularly glad to see the Etienne de Beaumonts again; They are so intelligent, so *fin*, so decadent, so old, so painted and so civilised.'

This was only forty-five years ago. Now we live in a squalid scrabble. It's nonsense to say we're better off. We're catastrophically

---

[1] Property Services Agency.

poorer due to (a) death duties and (b) 'levelling up' of standards and expectations in the lower classes so that it is completely impossible to find, even if one could afford, domestic servants.

Poor darling Jane drained and cleaned the pool *herself* yesterday. Of course she felt utterly exhausted. Saltwood slowly disintegrates round one, sector by sector (presently the Great Library and my father's study) as poor William – *aet* 70, and *cum* some 370,000 Virginian cigarettes, is terminally ill – gets 'out of reach' and needs a major blitz, up to two full days, to get it back 'up'.

We're too exhausted, and time is too precious, to 'entertain' – although we have the perfect setting. Anyway, it's so expensive, with good claret at £100 – minimum – per bottle.

Albany   *Thursday, 10 May*

Today is the fiftieth anniversary of the German attack in the West. The day that Valentine Lawford, the 'rather second Empire' secretary, omitted to tell Halifax that Rab Butler was waiting in the outer office with a message (that Labour would serve in a coalition under him). Halifax slipped out of the other door – to go to the dentist (!). By the evening it was too late, and Winston was Prime Minister.

I really don't know, I still can't judge, whether that was a good, or a bad, thing for the Britain that I love and cherish, and whose friendly, stubborn, dignified and sensible people have so often been let down by their rulers.

House of Commons   *Monday, 14 May*

The whole Department is in a state of frustration. What *is* happening to the Review?

'Options for Change' – I ask you!

Spastic title. There shouldn't be any fucking 'options'. It should be – 'It's like this. Now get on with it.' As it is, we're just haemorrhaging away on needless expenditure, and morale is plummeting with the uncertainty.

I have 'leaked' the situation. I chose Andy Marr[1] because he is young and clear-headed, and politically acute. We met, clandestinely, on the terrace, at the far end by the Lords fence. He will run something in the next issue, probably on Monday.

House of Commons   *Tuesday, 15 May*

I am in tremendous form at the moment.

This afternoon I pleased the House at Questions. It is a triumph if you can make *both* sides laugh good-humouredly, as I first discovered, memorably, questioning Merlyn Rees in 1977.[2]

Dale Campbell-Savours[3] came in with an ill-natured supplementary – 'Will the Minister ensure that his Department . . . does not get into bed with any of the companies from which the Member for Petersfield is drawing a retainer . . . '

Mates sat staring straight ahead, face as black as thunder.

Much uproar, 'show' indignation, points of order.

When it settled down I was expected to make a pompous rebuttal; at the very least a reference to the Committee on Members' Interests, every confidence, etc., etc.

But I don't like Mates; the House doesn't like Mates.

I said, 'One thing I have learned, Mr Speaker, is that it is never the slightest use telling people who they shouldn't go to bed with.'

Everyone was delighted – except, of course, Mates.

---

[1] Andrew Marr, parliamentary correspondent of *The Economist*.
[2] A smash-and-grab burglar had been given a very light sentence. Many on the Labour side were generating a synthetic row with Merlyn Rees, the Home Secretary, claiming that it was because the miscreant was an Old Etonian (which he was). AC said, 'Perhaps it was because, as an Old Etonian, the Bench took the view that he had already served the equivalent of five years in gaol.' Merlyn Rees, MP for Morley and Leeds South since 1983 (South Leeds, 1963–83), who had not long moved to the Home Office after two years as Northern Ireland Secretary, responded: 'There is one difference – in prison they learn to read and write.' See *Diaries: Into Politics*, 21 June 1977.
[3] Dale Campbell-Savours, MP for Workington since 1979.

House of Commons   *Thursday, 31 May*

I am getting a marvellous press.

The Economist article was just right, all the more so because Andy
had sought, and quoted, corroboration from senior officials in the
Dept.

Last week I had lunch, privately, at the *FT*, and sparkled. A highly
complimentary piece followed on the Saturday – 'one of the most
attractive (Hullo!) as well as one of the cleverest of Mrs Thatcher's
Ministers'.

'Profiles' everywhere, none of them too embarrassing. I got off
the sleeper this morning to find a full leader-page article in the *Mail*
by Gordon Greig: 'Could this be the moment when one politician
finally gets a grip on the Cold War warriors after 50 years of meekly
obeying orders?'

TK is putting a brave face on it. The message from along the
corridor is that 'he is keeping his own counsel' (i.e., wondering how
the hell he can get even).

Saltwood   *Friday, 8 June*

Yesterday evening I got involved with some kind of 'decision-makers'
groupette at the LSE. Brainy people on the up-and-up, with a few
heavies to pour cold water.

On my left the scatty (American) boffin in whose honour the
meal was being held; on my right, David Sainsbury the (now reluctant)
funder of the SDP.[1] Actually, if you didn't know he was so rich you
would just think he was just a dreary little Jewish accountant.

The discussion, if that be the term, was quite ably chaired by the
School's chairman, but pretty empty for all that. Just another approach
to saying if you don't have a strong economy, you're not strong. So?
What's new?

I made some provocative remarks about 'The Nation State', and

---

[1] David Sainsbury, Deputy Chairman of the grocers since 1988, had been a Trustee
and major contributor to the Social Democratic Party since its inception in 1982.

Sam Brittan,[1] who has disapproved of me for a very long time, shifted uneasily on his (not unmassive) haunches, and mutter-heckled. Finally he came out with it.

'What *is* "The Nation State"?'

'If you don't *know* what The Nation State is,' I said, 'you're decadent.'

John Moore was also there. Oh so golden and youthful looking. But a husk, a husk. Cut down so young.

Albany   *Monday, 11 June*

We went to the Gilmours' garden party, at Syon.[2]

The weather was fearfully cold and, as we wandered the gardens, elderly dowagers were complaining of 'frostbite'. Mollie Buccleuch, with a stick (who was it in the Thirties who referred to her and Mary Roxburghe as being 'randy as schoolgirls'?) One of Ian's sons offered to (re)introduce me, and enjoyed it when I said 'no', she disapproved. I told him the story of the Blenheim raid by Loders, in 1950. He was, of course far too young to remember Miss Ball.[3]

People were keen to talk to me, and admiringly curious. I am still in the backwash of the 'Defence Review' publicity.

Young – *policeman* young – Victor Smart[4] came up, after bobbing round a group, and introduced himself. Light-heartedly I protested about his piece: 'There is now considerable doubt as to whether the two Ministers can continue to exist in the same Department', etc.

Then Adam Raphael[5] came up, all ingratiating: 'We're running a

---

[1] Sam Brittan, principal economics commentator of the *Financial Times* since 1966 and elder brother of Sir Leon Brittan, a Vice President of the Commission of the European Communities.

[2] Sir Ian Gilmour, 3rd Bt. MP for Chesham since 1974 (Norfolk Central, 1962–74). Former owner of *The Spectator*. Married to Lady Caroline Margaret Montagu-Douglas-Scott, younger daughter of the 8th Duke of Buccleuch.

[3] Miss Ball was a fashionable beautician who had a client list of rich ladies of a certain age, including AC's mother, among whom she used with considerable relish to spread gossip.

[4] Victor Smart, political correspondent, *The Observer*.

[5] Adam Raphael, Executive Editor, *The Observer*, since 1988.

Profile of you in the next paper.' After he'd gone Smart said, '*He* was the one who insisted on the 'Two Ministers' bit.'

Willie Whitelaw I also talked to. He was nice, and on the ball and – I was delighted to see – still rheumy-eyed and *repeatedly* calling for his glass to be refilled. He told me I was 'quite right; absolutely right . . . to do what you are doing' at MoD. It had to be done. 'A lot of people will try and block you. But you must press on.'

I was hugely cheered by this. If only Willie were still 'around'.

But Willie was deeply gloomy, in the traditional High Tory way, about electoral prospects. There was a bit of 'does anyone tell her anything?' and 'No good getting mobbed in America, and thinking that's going to work here.'

The fact that Willie no longer has a proper consultative role (in which he was so immensely valuable) is an indictment of our present system of government. He was worked off his feet as Lord President in order, nominally, to 'justify' his position in Cabinet. He chaired a lot of bloody stupid committees that easily could have been steered by any number of different nonentities. In the evenings he had stuffy dinners, on weekends Party functions.

As a result he got a stroke.

Much better to have been four days a week in Penrith, and just coming up for Cabinet, and critical meetings.

We brought Ian and Caroline a tiny present. Their parties are so congenial – pretty girls, children in party clothes excitedly running hither and thither, bishops, Whig heavies, clever journalists, *Refusés* – and I never write a bread-and-butter letter.

It was a bottle of '67 Yquem. I stood it on the dining-room table (we had arrived late and our hosts were already mingling). When we said goodbye it had gone. I hope the staff didn't drink it.

Ministry of Defence   *Thursday, 14 June*

I was host at the NATO Defence College lunch at Lancaster House. Made a routine Darling-you-were-Wonderful speech. The Italian General thought (according to David[1]) that I was Secretary of State and TK was 'just another Minister'.

Kenneth Baker is a clever fellow. When I went to see him at

---

[1] David Hatcher, APS in AC's Private Office.

Central Office[1] – to clear my slate in 'Party' terms – he was effusive. 'You're doing brilliantly well. A textbook. You have my fullest admiration.'

But to TK he had said, 'You must find it very difficult working with Alan.'

I like this. If you are a serious player, it's no good being 'straight'. You just won't last.

Saltwood   *Sunday, 17 June*

This morning I killed the heron.

He has been raiding the moat, starting in the early hours, then getting bolder and bolder, taking eight or nine fish, carp, nishikoi, exotica, every day.

I had risen very early, before five, with the intention of getting a magpie who has been pillaging all the nests along the beech hedge. But returned empty handed. They are clever birds, and sense one's presence.

Suddenly Jane spotted the heron from the casement window in my bathroom.

I ran down and took the 4.10 off the slab, cocked the hammer. He was just opposite the steps, took off clumsily and I fired, being sickened to see him fall back in the water, struggle vainly to get up the bank, one wing useless.

I reloaded, went round to the opposite bank. Tom beat me to it and gamely made at him, but the great bird, head feathers bristling and eyes aglare, made a curious high-pitched menacing sound, his great beak jabbing fiercely at the Jack Russell.

'Get Tom out of the way,' I screamed.

I closed the range to about twenty feet and took aim. I did not want to mutilate that beautiful head, so drew a bead on his shoulder.

The execution. For a split second he seemed simply to have absorbed the shot; then very slowly his head arched round and took refuge inside his wing, half under water. He was motionless, dead.

---

[1] Kenneth Baker, MP for Mole Valley since 1983 (Acton 1968–70, St Marylebone, 1970–83). Chairman of the Conservative Party since 1989 after three years as Education Secretary.

I was already sobbing as I went back up the steps: 'Sodding fish, why should I kill that beautiful creature just for the sodding fish...'

I cursed and blubbed up in my bedroom, as I changed into jeans and a T-shirt. I was near a nervous breakdown. Yet if it had been a burglar or a vandal I wouldn't have given a toss. It's human beings that are the vermin.

At breakfast I had a handsome photograph on the front page of *The Observer*. There was a heavy and tendentious piece about 'Service chiefs have lost confidence in Ministers'. Three columns wide, lead item. 'The Deputy is making all the running'.

Too bloody right he is. But will he bring off the *coup royal*?

Ministry of Defence   *Wednesday, 20 June*

I went to Sothebys to look at some sculpture. There was a pretty alabaster frieze of a hunting scene by William Haydn, which photographed well in the catalogue, shown as 72 inches. But in fact it had been broken, and a piece was missing. The joined-up fragments jarred, and it was in some curious packing-case type frame.

I spotted Nico Henderson, and hailed him. 'My God, Alan!' He turned to an elegant blonde lady *d'une certaine age*. 'You must meet this man. He's the most important man in the Government. He's producing the peace dividend.'

She looked at me through (as it were) her lorgnette. Demi-dreamy, and spaced out. (All these rich old former beauties are *on* something, as Jane said.)

'I knew you as a child.'

It was Marietta, Ronnie Tree's young and (then) nubile second wife. A name to conjure with in NY. Still alive.

---

[1] Sir Nicholas Henderson. Having retired after spells as British Ambassador to Warsaw, Bonn and Paris, was persuaded out of retirement and served as Ambassador to Washington, 1979–82.

Glasgow-Inverness train   *Friday, 22 June*

The closing entry for this volume. The second half of the year will overlap with 1991, in a new notebook which, crisply expectant, sits in the drawer of my desk at MoD. What will it record? A continuing ascendancy – for verily I am in the stratosphere at the moment? Stagnation? Or decline? Or perhaps, most romantic of all, the sudden stop. When the lunatic or the assassin do their work or, simply, the gods lose patience.

How I do enjoy my job! And how full of vitality I feel – mind racing, gifts of expression, spoken and written, better than at any time. My self-confidence is complete. I don't even use the folder at Questions any more, just lounge on the Bench and answer off the top of my head.

'For the second day running,' said the BBC *Yesterday in Parliament*, the star of the Defence debate was Alan Clark, the laid-back but cerebral Minister of State.'

Two more Profiles, both laudatory, are due out on the weekend.

So where do I go from here? The objective must be now – and I mean now, very shortly, July at the latest – to displace the Secretary of State.

Tom remains affable, but wary. He sees Hugh Colver, the Press Officer *for an hour* every day. (I shouldn't think I've had more than five minutes with a press officer since walking into the building last summer.) Tom's office have 'let it be known' that I am 'getting more publicity than is desirable'. 'Desired' by who, pray?

But what can happen to the Secretary of State? Where can he go? Leader of the House is really the only practical possibility now.

But I don't plot. I sleepwalk. My timings are rarely calculated, more often luck and intuition. I cannot predict what will happen, I have no feel for it at all.

Now I am in my beloved Scotland. Past the window glide all those delightful halts, with their tidy white-gabled granite station masters' offices – Dunblane, Gleneagles, Dunkeld, Pitlochry, Blair Atholl, Dalwhinnie, Newtonmore, Kingussie. A list for me as evocative, in its different way, as the route of the Orient Express; which the girl with the golden voice used to recite before the departure from the Gare du Lyon.

I will have a day at Shore, and try walking, The Prince of the

Captivity, in isolation in the hills and coires, and think through my prospect.

Ministry of Defence   *Wednesday, 27 June*

This morning I went out to Greenwich – *what* incredible buildings, better than Versailles, really we ought to be doing something more important with them.

The traffic was heavy, and I had time, on the back seat, to embellish the dreary little text – 'user friendly' – which officials had given me to utter as an 'introduction' to the morning's proceedings.

I am impatient with the sluggish pace, the caution and derivativeness of our warship design. There are many clever and original naval architects, in our ancient tradition, still around – at Vosper, at Swans, at consultants like Yard. But they are feared and disliked by the huge overstaffed troglodyte Admiralty settlement at Bath. Why the fuck isn't *that* place privatised? How can the private sector ever compete with an organisation so closely linked, in terms of career advancement, with its own main customer?

So I added in a good bit about changing needs, different theatres, the need to allow ships the capability to fulfil their new roles. You get pirates in the straits of Malacca, terrorising and robbing civilian traffic. A corvette answers a distress call. Then what? The pirates will have armour piercing 0.5 in Brownings in rubber boats, Republican Guard stuff. What do you use against that, an Exocet?

This was received in pretty piggy silence by my audience, whose 'mix' I couldn't quite, through the footlights, determine. The Admiral, Kenneth Eaton,[1] who was on the platform with me, remained expressionless throughout. But as he neither applauded nor, when others nervously did, laugh, his view was plain enough.

There were high-ranking uniforms scattered about, but the majority were suits, 'industrialists'.

I stayed on for the first 'real' speaker, a Professor of Industrial Trends (I must tell John[2] about this new 'chair'), and he made a few

---

[1] Sir Kenneth Eaton, Controller of the Navy since 1989.
[2] John Sparrow, Warden of All Souls, 1952–77 and a fastidious critic of fashionable trends in higher education.

mildly critical remarks about the government, which were clapped.

I thought if any of those sodding sailors was clapping I'll have him cashiered. As for 'industrialists', they're almost (but nothing, no one, not even 'Claimants' Unions' can be) *as* bad as farmers. If I said to them, 'Look an "exciting" (correct usage at last) new Initiative: In order to cut down on bureaucratic form-filling red tape, etc., I've arranged for you to go next door and my assistant will hand over a cheque on the Bank of England, pre-endorsed. All *you* have to do is fill in the amount' ... 'Wha'?' ... 'according to your needs' – they'd still grumble.

Directly after lunch I went to E (CP). Chaired as always, soft-spokenly, but firmly, by the Chancellor. Little Gummer[1] made a most halting and turgid presentation of his paper, on *retaining* (for God's sake) the Milk Marketing Board. 'Is he always as bad as this?' I said in a note to John Patten, on my left.

Later we moved on to the de-regulation of motorway restaurants. Roger Freeman,[2] not a man to get into trouble, you'd think, ran into heavy flak, led by Nick Ridley.[3] 'Why can't they be totally free of regulation?' No restriction on hours, area, alcohol. Pure Adam Smith Institute. Then Francis Maude (how does the Foreign Office have an interest in this, pray?) joined in and added to the hard-line free market declamation. Poor Roger tried to remain calm, but was losing. Uncomfortable for him.

I tiptoed out and went to Brooks's, where I had a tryst with Peter Jenkins. He was already there, pouring the tea. He doesn't smile much – at all, you could say. And like many charmless people, he is immune, even when it is being deployed towards him. The only thing he respects is power, or access to power. So I am gratified that he should have invited me. I have come some distance since he used to describe me as a zealot on the far Right, then more recently as a 'loose cannon'.

Now, it's 'the highly intelligent Mr Alan Clark'.

Peter does recognise that I am trying to do something at MoD that it is logical, but difficult. He warned me that the Party would turn against me, if it has not already started to do so. Yes, I said, but not if I was Secretary of State, because I could explain and persuade.

---

[1] John Selwyn Gummer was now Minister of Agriculture.
[2] Roger Freeman, MP for Kettering since 1983. Minister of State, Transport.
[3] Nicholas Ridley, Trade and Industry Secretary since 1989.

As it is, I am tongue-tied, and the vested interests in the Department leak against me.

One of the anomalies is that 'Defence Correspondents' practically never talk to Politicians. They have no sympathy with or understanding of politics. They get all their briefing, and their leaks, from soldiers.

I explained that I was doing my best. But I had to balance Party, Treasury, the PM's own periodic bouts of cold feet and waverings.

Whether any good will come of this meeting time alone will tell. But a certain mending of fences. Of all the Lobby he has the least gossip, and the least small-talk. Admirable, but no fun.

Albany   *Thursday, 28 June*

Last night we spectated at the Queen Mother's special ninetieth birthday parade from the big window at Admiralty House. Chiefs of Staff and their wives, Hamilton, a few minor Royals and the Prince, tetchy and inattentive. TK was beside the QM on her dais for 'taking the salute'. The concept was pleasing. Instead of a lot of bands and soldiers, there was a little detachment, all puffed up and spick and span with pride and pleasure, from each of the organisations of which she was Patron.

Actually, you don't really get a very good view from these windows, especially if you have to be 'polite'. But some participants I did notice, and was cheered by. The pleasing Jack Russell, who confidently led one section; and the jolly beige hens – *Orpington Yellows*, apparently they are called – in their wicker cage. Two fine bulls in trailers also drew applause – was I the only person to reflect on their fate, all too soon? The squalor and terror of the stockyard corridors, the mishandled 'stunning', the mechanical guillotine?

Jane sat in the centre front, with Princess Margaret on her right. The Princess smoked resolutely throughout, at one point reprimanding her nephew who had moved *out* of her line of sight, thus exposing her to a telephoto lens.

Afterwards we repaired to a huge reception at the RUSI. The Queen Mother herself was perfectly incredible. In spite of having stood for at least half the time on the saluting dais, she moved among the guests for nearly two hours, radiating a deep personal happiness and concern for all to whom she was introduced.

Somewhat reluctantly TK finally produced us. 'This is Alan Clark, he must be a neighbour of yours in Scot...'

She sliced through the booming and asked me, 'How is the library at Saltwood?'

We had a nice little chat. She said that Saltwood had one of the loveliest atmospheres of any place she had ever visited.

TK, out of things, got restive and tried to move her on. She showed her reluctance.

What a marvellous performance. I could never have managed it, and I'm thirty years younger.

Albany   *Wednesday, 4 July*

I was reading Cadogan's diaries with EMT. Something made me look up Oran, and I found that this very day is the anniversary of our destruction of the French Fleet at Mers-el-Kebir. Winston Churchill's greatest stroke (not least because it must have been so hurtful for him). But that action, more than any other, showed that we were going to fight, and fight rough. From then on we were undefeated – Battle of Britain, Sidi Barrani, Tobruk, Benghazi. We could have made peace at the time of the Hess mission and the world would have been completely different.

Spontaneously, I wrote a note to the PM reminding her, and of the Foreign Office memo pleading that it would make 'all the difference' (yeah) to our relations with Vichy if we allowed the French battleships to return to Toulon. Pat dropped it off at Number 10 on our way to the Dept, and I hope she enjoyed it.

Later, when I was in the Commons, I was caught on the stairs to the committee room corridor by Don McIntyre[1] thoughtfully, as is his wont, attentively strained and agonising. He told me that the Chiefs of Staff, who were seeing the Prime Minister next week, were going to 'complain' about me. Exceeding my authority, doing 'damage', who's in charge? etc. This is lowering. Of course she'll

---

[1] Don McIntyre, political correspondent of *The Independent on Sunday*.

resist it. But it may shake her faith; make her think it's impossible to promote me there. And this, presumably is what they want, a pre-emptive strike.

Plymouth train   *Friday, 13 July*

My father's birthday. He would be eighty-seven today, if Nolwen hadn't poisoned him, pottering about and probably something of a nuisance. After all, Uncles Colin, Russell and Alan are all in fine health, and in their nineties.

I am in good spirits. Last night at the seven o'clock vote the talk was all of poor Nicky.[1] I said to Iain Lang,[2] so tiredly drawn and handsome, 'There's nothing so improves the mood of the Party as the imminent execution of a senior colleague.'

Robin Maxwell-Hyslop[3] told me that on behalf of the Trade and Industry Committee he had passed a message that I would be their preference as Secretary of State to succeed Nicky (unlikely to swing it, but can't do much harm); and going out through the vote doors Paul Channon[4] fell in beside me, 'Well, I hear you're going to be Secretary of State for Trade and Industry.' Now Paul has very good antennae. Secretly thrilled, I dissimulated.

'Seems obvious to me,' he said. 'Would solve a lot of problems simultaneously.'

Thoroughly delighted with myself I held court in the Lobby. Around me I had John Cole, Colin Brown,[5] a swarthy little fellow from the *FT* and a *very* short cheeky chappie from one of the comics.

---

[1] Nicholas Ridley was under pressure to resign following an interview in *The Spectator*. Ridley claimed that Dominic Lawson, the editor, had kept the tape running after the interview had ended, and then revealed the full text. Certain forthright remarks by Ridley had caused offence in Germany.

[2] Iain Lang, MP for Galloway since 1979. Minister of State, Scottish Office, since 1987.

[3] Robin Maxwell-Hyslop, MP for Tiverton since 1960, had been a member of the Trade and Industry Select Committee since 1971.

[4] Paul Channon had returned to back benches in 1989.

[5] Colin Brown, a political correspondent on *The Independent*.

George Jones[1] hovered; but as he has a low opinion of me – he only talks to Mates and the Left – didn't approach.

I said that Nick's performance was a welcome return to the old doings of the nineteenth century, when major figures in the Govt could digress giftedly and constructively on the issues of the day, without constantly being hauled over the coals by some wanker in the FCO Press Office.

'But in those days it took three weeks for the papers to get to Berlin,' said John Cole, not without reason.

All evening the tide continued to run. Jane and I were at a dinner at the French Embassy – little tables – and as we drifted into the drawing room for coffee the Chief Secretary[2] made a point of coming over: 'By Monday you could well find yourself Secretary of State for Trade and Industry.'

Jane, bless her, is secretly delighted. *Into the big frame at last*! But we dare not say anything, even to each other. And in this morning's papers I am tipped as Number One probability by Gordon Greig in the *Mail*, and as a likely contender in *The Independent*.

At intervals I stop writing, and fantasise. The Prince's Return. To occupy that very office to which formerly I was summoned by Norman, by Paul and by David. To get Matthew to run my Office, with Rose as the Diary queen; sort out a few of those officials who 'took against' me and bring forward the loyal ones.

We'll know soon.

Saltwood   *Saturday, 14 July*

This morning I swam very early, before seven, and the view *from the water* was unbelievable because the sun is on the towers:

> And Lo! The Hunter of the East has caught
> The Sultan's turret in a noose of light.[3]

– which happens only for a couple of weeks in high summer, and

---

[1] George Jones (*Daily Telegraph*).
[2] Norman Lamont.
[3] *The Rubaiyat of Omar Khayyam*, Edward Fitzgerald.

the tobacco plants are in flower. The rays are too flat, still, to touch the poolside and the Morning Glory flares purple. The whole pool area is wonderfully overgrown this year, and enchanted.

I was pleased to find myself tipped this morning in *The Times*, the *Telegraph* and *The Independent*. How fickle and derivative the press are. In many cases these are the same people who regularly predict my dismissal whenever there is talk of a reshuffle.

I spent most of the morning out of doors, though fretting (for the first time in my career) that the phone might be ringing. Why was I so unsettled this time? Realising subconsciously, I suppose, that the chance was good, but it was the last.

I remember saying to Jane, 'Actually none of this really matters compared with whether James will beget a son.'

I took calls from Wastell, B. Anderson, Sherman (time-wasting) and *W. Evening Herald*.

This last, naturally, wanted to talk at length about the Plympton Water Works. Not a word about Ridley or my prospects in Government, although I don't doubt there would have been plenty if I was being criticised, however oblique, remote or irrelevant the source.

(As I write this I am reminded of an exemplary occasion, which I don't think I recorded at the time, when a *Herald* [female] reporter rang me, all of a state, and said, 'You've been black-listed by the Esperanto Society. What have you got to say about that?')

Bruce was his usual slightly dampening self – and nothing from Tristan, a bad sign. Did BA mention Lilley?[1] I think he may have done. He is usually pretty well informed about undercurrents.

By mid-afternoon my private hopes had waned. Then, at tea, the news came through. Nick had resigned, 'and his successor will be announced in about a half hour' – then back to some prat standing outside Number 10.

We sat in silence, rustling stale newsprint, and clinking cups as we poured and repoured.

Some fifteen minutes later the announcement that it was Peter Lilley, 'at forty-six the youngest member of the Cabinet'.

Flatly we sat, reading and grumbling.

Then the phone rang. I made Jane answer, in case it was a reporter or a colleague calling for a concealed gloat. But it was Sally. And I

---

[1] Peter Lilley, MP for St Albans since 1983. Financial Secretary at the Treasury.

could tell from Jane's sudden squeal of pleasure, and the nature of her questions, that she was giving news of a confirmed pregnancy.[1]

How wonderful! And so magically soon after my remark that very morning! With tears in my eyes, I congratulated her. Everything seemed to fall into place now, all the careful structuring of the Trusts, the interlocking provisions and possessions.

I took out the SS 100 and drove down to St Leonard's, prayed and gave thanks in that same pew where I had sat at my father's funeral, immediately behind Nolwen.

I had forgotten his birthday, but now I realise that it must have been confirmed on that day – and is due in February![2]

Ministry of Defence   *Thursday, 19 July*

Still hot, scorching sun. A very end-of-term feeling. The House is tetchy, and mock-playful. Endless votes last night – none of them of the slightest importance, but all subject to 'heavy' two-liners.

Poor old Alan Glyn[3], 'had a turn' in an excessively *ego* location, the library main doorway, at the junction of tea room, smoking room and Speaker's corridors. He was attempting a few shuffling, stompy steps, as very old people do (he's not old at all, but caricatures himself), with Beaumont-Dark[4] and A.N. Other supporting him by holding his elbows. His jaw hung open, slackly. Hours later I saw him sitting, completely glazed over, in the 'porter's chair' by the library entrance.

I catnapped on the sofa in my office, staggering up for the last Division at 1.20 a.m. Seeing Ian Gow I said, 'See you tomorrow.'

'No,' he replied. 'Today.'

Ugh.

---

[1] Sadly the child was later miscarried and Sally divorced James in the following year.
[2] Both AC's own sons were born in February.
[3] Sir Alan Glyn, MP for Windsor since 1970.
[4] Sir Anthony Beaumont-Dark, MP for Birmingham, Selly Oak, since 1979.

Albany   *Friday, 20 July*

The last day of 'term', effectively. There is some patchy business next
week, an Opposition supply day on Tuesday, but nothing to speak
of – ending with the Buck House garden party and a reception at
Number 10.

This morning I woke very early, and with that special late July
tranquillity, before even the buses start in Regent St, and the sky is
still pale grey from heat haze. No shadows as yet, and the promise of
another very hot day.

There are few things more delicious than anticipation of the
imminent long summer holiday – particularly while we still have to
taste the picquancy of the 'Junior Reshuffle'.

Last evening we had the 'End-of-Term Dinner'. Not quite a
dining club, as we only meet on the Thursday before the Long Recess.
There is no actual election process. Membership (and discardment)
are osmotic. Ian 'convenes', though Soames and Ryder are each active
in organisation. Class is undeniably a factor.

The oval room at White's. Boring food – smoked salmon, roast
beef. Who the hell did this, in *July*?

In attendance were Gow, Heathcoat-Amory, Bertie Denham,
Jonathan Aitken, Hamilton, Garel-Jones (a 'first' for him!), Alexander
Hesketh and Cranborne.[1] Fun to see Robert, and a tribute to IG's
discernment as in theory he is out, until 'Harare'[2] dies. But Robert
keeps his finger on the pulse, and is knowledgeable.

An uncomfortable atmosphere. We don't like what we see, and
we don't like admitting, even to each other, that our beloved leader
may be fallible. Not in front of Ian, anyway. But because we don't see
our way, substantial political discussion was at a discount. Gossip was
stale, and people fell back on dirty stories. Pure dirt, I mean, the
Dorm.

I had Soames on my left. 'You'll be in the Cabinet by Monday.
Oh no. This is what I hear ... ', etc. He is shameless ('Straight to the
Lords.'[3])

---

[1] David Heathcoat-Amory, Parliamentary Under-Secretary, Environment, since
    1989; Lord Hesketh, now Minister of State, Trade and Industry. Robert, Viscount
    Cranborne, heir to the Marquess of Salisbury, had stood down as MP for Dorset
    South at the 1987 General Election.
[2] 6th Marquess of Salisbury.
[3] A phrase in the Clark family signifying a glorious finale.

A propos of the Lords, was Bertie Denham sounding me out when he kept asking 'what I wanted'? Was he trying to lead me into hinting at the Lords as a working Min of S? Perhaps I muffed it by saying I wanted to be S of S for Defence. He looked disappointed. He seemed pretty tight, but the Upper Classes *remember* what they (and you) say when they were tight.

At the end of the meal, significantly and in contrast to earlier years, instead of a *tour-de-table* and monologues on the topics of the day, a colleague's failings, or whatever, each person gave a little 'performance'.

Ian, *very* boringly, gave us 'Albert and the Lion'. Waste of time. Bertie was the bluest, Richard the funniest – still – with the Bader at Roedean story. I did 'Frankie and Johnnie'. Most people know the first few verses, but the punch line is in the last:

> Sheriff came over in the mornin',
> said it was all for the best.
> He said her lover Johnnie
> was nothin' but a doggone pest.

We don't *need* to have an Election for two years, we kept telling each other. Technically true, but balls as well.

I thought there would be more talk of a possible 'challenge' in the autumn but, ominously, there was none. The prospect, though, is implacably in the middle distance. A towering thunderhead of Alto-Cumulus, precursor of change not just in the weather, but in the Climate.

That evening, at Saltwood
This must have been the hottest day of the year. Everything is so full, and overripe, and pale yellow.

It is a quarter to nine, and I am sitting out in shirtsleeves by the pool. It is the day of the *Attentat*. A year ago, exactly, I visited the monastery at Rastenburg and strolled around the *Wolfschanze*.

I am worried about growing old. After I had been swimming I went to the top of the towers and hung on the bar. I couldn't do *one* pull-up. In the summer of 1955, my last at Saltwood before I went to Rye, the summer of Marye thirty-five years ago (and yet it seems like six or seven) I could easily do four. And over twenty swings of ankles above my head.

Eight o'clock in the evening, and still overpoweringly hot. I sit out by the pool, which is yellowy-green, and touching eighty degrees.

Today I went to the helicopter show at Middle Wallop. Lunchtime in the VIP tent was a furnace, worse even than the IFA in Madrid,[1] or the BAe tent at the LaserFire demo in Dubai.

Interesting discussions. The two units on which I would most like to spend money freely are the Army Air Corps and (to provide them with a quota of medium-heavy weapons) the Parachute Regt.

But the AAC are guarded in their approach to the 'Air Cavalry' concept. We have a number of good ancient Cavalry regiments which, because of the shrinkage in armoured deployment on the 'Central Front', will have to amalgamate or even disappear altogether. The need to expand the AAC is obvious (or obvious to me, anyhow). These regts have been already – as they saw it – traumatised once when they lost their horses and went into tanks. Would not a reversion to helicopters be symbolic, and welcome? But the officers here (I've noticed this with the SAS at Hereford too) like to keep it small and cliquey, where you know everyone, NCOs and men as well, by their Christian names.

James came and collected me this early morning with a Gazelle. His co-pilot was a Staff Sgt Pengelley, whom I remember for his enthusiasm in the AAC mess at Stanley when I visited the Falklands with the Defence Committee in October of 1982. Like all who have flown in combat conditions he is adamant on the urgent need for *fighter* helicopters, to intercept enemy transport and ground attack, and to defend our own.

As we arrived at Wallop James was at the controls, and too insouciant for Pengelley, who got anxious.

'These lose speed very quickly on approach.'

'That's OK.'

'You can get caught by surprise.'

'I have control.'[2]

I was proud of him. Even more so on the return, when he made a beautiful, totally accurate landing opposite the Garden Entrance

---

[1] IFA: a hotel in Madrid where AC was once marooned with his family after their car broke down.

[2] The phrase indicating – from the captain – that he does not need assistance.

after taking the neater (but more difficult and funked by many visitors) approach from behind Thorpe's Tower.

When they left James was still at the controls and performed a salute on the east side. Going straight in from the hover he stood the little Gazelle on its tail and went straight into a vertical climbing torque turn directly over the great sycamores.

It was spectacular. But in the midst of Life we are in Death. A tiny malfunction of the gearbox, a hesitation in the tail rotor, and the frail little machine would have crashed – before my very gate – and burned to a cinder. I draw strength from reflections such as this. Because if God wants to plunge in the knife, then He can do so – at any time.

The Garden House   *Sunday, 22 July*

I think this is my first entry from over here. It is very warm and silent, well separated from the cares and pressures of the castle. A true *Pavillon* in which to work or contemplate, and extravagantly accoutred to 'self-catering' status. We have cleaned it up, painted the weatherboarding, spent money, 'got it very nice'. Now the easiest part, and the most fun – furnishing and arranging. Few traces of my parents. Of Colette, none whatever. Save for some missing electric light bulbs, she might never have set foot in the place.

I wonder what its fate will be?

This afternoon we went to Bethersden to pick up Jane's Citroën. On the way over we found ourselves drawn to explore the overgrown drive of a concealed manor house.

The façade was dark and had an abandoned air. But the back quarters were a delight. Heavy vegetation had encroached on the yard, and there were saplings everywhere pushing through the brick pave. A half-hearted attempt had been made to cut the very long grass with an Allen which stood, well-maintained looking, but inoperative. Just adjacent was a (still) working oast house.

Formerly there had been HONEY signs fixed to the gate, but not today and Jane needed some persuading to reconnoitre. But our reward was this beautiful friendly home, with low-roofed intercommunicating rooms, comfortable and sheltering. Hens talked inquiringly, and walked in and out of the kitchen. A fine fluffed tawny tabby strolled by assertively with his tail up.

The owner appeared, pleasant, elderly. He could almost have been ex RFC. Most courteously he did produce honey, and passed the time of day.

I felt overcome by a wistful nostalgia for starting again. As Jane said, an utterly perfect place to live as young marrieds, and bring up children.

But you can't put the clock back by two seconds – never mind twenty-five years.

Jane set off alone in the Citroën and I made a detour for Tom Mason's garage, where I got involved in a very long ritualised ceremony to buy a few sidelights, and get some old leather seats 'thrown in' because I had paid him £1000 for a new Silver Ghost hand pressure pump.

On the return journey I cut across to the old A20, passing the sign for Hothfield where in the nurses' quarters on a summer's evening in 1955 I experienced the most perfect physical sensation, never before or since, with Marye. Jealous and inquisitive colleagues tried and rattled her door, departing in the end to get Matron. She, stout woman, portentously interrogated Marye through the keyhole, but the sweet girl (who looked, now I come to think about it, not unlike a bustier version of Jenny on HRT) kept her superior at bay for some precious minutes while I got dressed and climbed out of the window, to stumble across unlit lawns and rose bushes.

Ministry of Defence   *Monday, 30 July*

I must record a curious phenomenon. If something is happening, or has happened, that affects one adversely, is upsetting – 'bad news' – one feels very tired (over that time) even though one still doesn't know. I remember Jane telling me that she had experienced this on the afternoon we were driving back from Hawtreys and Jason was run over.[1] And this morning I felt dreadful in the Sandling train. It's not

---

[1] A sad episode in family history when a favourite labrador puppy was killed.

just feeling a bit sleepy; it's feeling absolutely shattered, as if one was getting polio, only without the fever.

When I got to the barrier Julian was waiting, looking anxious.

'Minister, I have some very, very bad news.'

For a split second I feared it must be Andrew. But something in his eyes was missing (the look of fear, I suppose, and embarrassment that I might actually *break down*). 'Ian Gow has been killed by a car bomb.'

'How spiteful of them', was all I could say. But I thought particularly of the poor Lady. She wept at the first casualties in the Falklands. I wonder if she did today? Because Ian loved her, actually loved, I mean, in every sense but the physical. And then in the end, as lovers do (particularly that kind), he got on her nerves, and she was off-hand with him. He played his last beseeching card: 'I will have to resign.' 'Go ahead, then.' (I foreshorten the exchange, of course) – and that was it.

We talked briefly by the newsagents, and I cautioned Julian to hold his tongue in the car as I did not want Bob 'horning in' and trying to curdle our blood.

Even a silence would have been 'pregnant', so I outmanoeuvred Bob by talking in matter-of-fact tones throughout the journey about the Options Statement, and kindred subjects.

Once ensconced here, I became thoughtful. My old friend. Ian got me into Government, surmounting much opposition and, even from her, misgiving. Very few people had so clear and cogent an understanding of how Whitehall, and the Cabinet Office building worked. Although in recent years Ian had become a little saddened and, indeed, irritated by the way in which the Court had changed and Charles Powell had got the whole thing in his grip. And this, together with his increasing distance from the reality of office, had led him to indulge in *manneristics*. He practised, sometimes beyond the bounds of tolerance, the always tricky *jeu* of self-parody. But Ian remained always witty, clever, industrious, affectionate and almost *painfully* honourable.

My closest friend, by far, in politics.

He was *insouciant* about death. In the garden of his tiny little house, south of the river, he would point up at the tower blocks which loomed to the east.

'The Paddys are up there,' he would say, in good humour, 'with their telescopes.'

Now they've got her two closest confidants, Airey[1] and Ian. I suppose I should be apprehensive that they might come for me. But, strangely (because I am in many circumstances cowardly) I'm not. Just as well, because 'The Police' down here, as in Sussex, are completely useless, if not actually hostile. It was those same Sussex police, wasn't it, who 'cleared' the Grand Hotel in Brighton before the bomb went off?[2] And whose constable didn't like using dogs, 'in case it upset the miners'?

I've only seen the local police twice in the last ten years. Once when a spotty constable threatened to arrest me for using 'insulting language' on the (fat) wife of a parish councillor who had been stealing firewood; once when, very reluctantly, a red-faced coming-up-for-retirement constable 'took particulars' from two youths caught by me red-handed, and detained, while vandalising and trying to steal valuable stained glass from the south guard-room. Naturally, they were never prosecuted. And Jane was once visited by a couple of CID men who wanted to look at some cannabis plants which hippies had planted far over in the woodland, and they suggested (because no one must be beastly to or about hippies) that it was 'probably one of your children'.

I fear that the police have abandoned their old class allegiances. Indeed many of them seem to carry monstrous chips, and actually to enjoy harassing soft targets. And where has it got them? Simply widened the circle of those who resent and mistrust the police. Two or three stabbed every day and the assailants usually discharged by the Magistrates.

There *are* good ones, young, tough and dedicated – just as there are in MoD – but it's the devil's job bringing them forward; because of that customary (and very English) repressive conspiracy of the incompetent.

So, I'm not particularly frightened. I just feel 'What is written, is written'. Although I wish my affairs were in better order, and I could

---

[1] Airey Neave, MP for Abingdon. Opposition spokesman on Northern Ireland after Margaret Thatcher became party leader in 1975, he was murdered when an IRA bomb destroyed his car at Westminster in 1979.

[2] Of course it was in fact the Security Services who had responsibility for checking the hotel. Allowance must be made for the grief and indignation from which AC was suffering at the time of making this entry.

have passed on more to Jane. The tax authorities would love it. A sudden death allows them to really sink their teeth in.

A huge fine, for doing one's duty.

Saltwood   *Sunday, 5 August*

It's crazy hot. The shade temperature today in the yard was 95°. In and out of the pool all day long. But, perhaps because of this, we are listless, and out of condition.

We can neither afford the time nor the money to go to 'Champneys', and detox. But Jane had a brilliant idea – we'll go there 'in all but name'.

As from this evening, no alcohol (naturally); no fats, practically no carbohydrates; no eggs, no nothing. Fruits and astringent. Mineral water. Sluice the kidneys. Torture the body. Lissomly we will emerge, and purified.

Saltwood   *Tuesday, 7 August*

Yesterday I was in MoD all day. The Iraqis are starting to throw their weight around. I wouldn't have believed it possible, not on this scale. For nearly two years the FCO section of Cabinet minutes was a long moan about how the Iraqi Army was on its last legs, and the Iranians were going to break through. Now it turns out there are more Soviet tanks there than in Poland, Hungary and Czechoslovakia combined.

The only consolation is that sooner than expected the Clark *Bahrein* yardstick[1] has its credentials confirmed. But there is no credit in being proved right, here or anywhere else (except, occasionally the Futures market).

I felt ghastly all day long. Persistent headache, stiff joints, 'lassitude', generally out of sorts. Returned by train and cursed and mumbled at

----

[1] In developing his original 'Options' thesis, AC discarded the traditional NATO requirements and asked instead, 'How effective will it (or they) be in holding the end of the Bahrein Causeway?'

all the holiday-makers, so carefree and (some of them) fetching, in
their summer frocks.

But at the station Jane admitted that she had been feeling exactly
the same. Of course! 'Champneys!'

As fast as we could we prepared, and then stuffed on, an enormous
meal; poulet l'estragon with rice and lots of little vegetables cooked
in butter and (baby carrots) sugar; fresh home-baked bread and butter
(again); six or seven – each – lemon curd tartlets and gobbets of heavy
Jersey cream. I drank half a bottle of good Burgundy. We slept like
tops and felt incredible this morning.

Saltwood   *Wednesday, 8 August*

We drove over to Ian Gow's funeral service in St Saviours, Eastbourne.
An ugly Victorian building selected by Ian – I assume – because of
its inordinately *High* practices.

The heat was oppressive and we set off in casual clothes, intending
to change *en route*. Some little distance from Pevensey we diverted and
found a wooded glade just nearby to the canal, and started to undress.
This aroused the disapproval of two people, fat and ugly, who were
slumped in deckchairs by the canal bank and who clearly thought we
were going to make love. To tell the truth I would have liked that.
The proximity of death always makes me feel sexual. But our timing
was tight. Guests were enjoined to be in their places at least forty-five
minutes before the service started.

I cannot adequately record how ugly those people were. The man
squat, paunchy, resentful in his horn rims; the woman *gross*, runkled-
up nylon skirt, varicose veins, eating from a paper bag. At intervals
each drew on a cigarette. Beside them glistened two luckless baby
bream which the man had caught with his line.

Jane had a brilliant idea. That, once impeccably dressed in our
funeral weeds, we should reverse back to their site and kill them,
leaving the wreath which we were taking over for Ian. And removing
instead, a fish, to lay beside the open grave. Lovely and black, that
humour. Pure Buñuel.

On and on went the service. The PM read the first lesson beautifully. But there was *too much* jingling, and scattering of incense, and
High longueurs. Afterwards (about one and three-quarter hours) we

gatecrashed the tea party at the Dog House.[1] Uninvited, and thus not on the police list – whether by intention or accident I know not – we were nonetheless hailed at the door by Peter Hordern and our presence accepted as quite natural.

I spoke with the PM at some length, and to Cecil's evident irritation as he had (literally) cornered her against a hedge in the garden. He kept interrupting and trying to edge between us. She was ultra gung-ho on Saddam Hussein, wanted to send a CVS,[2] etc. But I am a little uneasy. Where will it all end?

Jane Gow had quite consciously and admirably left the – very disagreeable – crater in their yard where the bomb had detonated, and there were flowers strewn around. I went through and stood there alone, in meditation, for a while. Jane told us a macabre little tale. After she had returned to the house, following some forty-eight hours of continuous and intensive forensic scrutiny and searches, one of the dogs wandered. When it returned it brought in its mouth a garter of Ian's, blackened by the explosion, though fortunately without any of his body adhering to it, that he had been wearing that morning, retrieved by the wuffler from a nearby paddock or hedge. Further testimony to (let us say) 'overstretch' in the Sussex Constabulary.

Not many members of the Government had bothered to turn up. From the Cabinet only Howe, Brooke, Waddington, Cecil Parkinson. Of junior Ministers just myself, Ryder and, bizarrely, the Bottomleys.[3] She has lost her looks almost as fast as I did when I first went into the House. And her husband is so *odd* that it grates. Even watching him, and that curious little half-giggling smile and 'scamp' haircut, brings out the worst in me.

---

[1] The Gows' house at Hankham.

[2] An 'Invincible' class aircraft-carrier.

[3] Since the 1989 reshuffle Peter Brooke had been made Northern Ireland Secretary; David Waddington Home Secretary, Richard Ryder Economic Secretary at the Treasury, Peter Bottomley, Parliamentary Under-Secretary, Northern Ireland, and Virginia Bottomley Minister of State, Department of Health.

Saltwood   *Thursday, 9 August*

The great heat has subsided. But we still throw ourselves into the pool at 7.15, and take EMT on the heavy oak seat beside the top border.

This morning I was calm, and enlarged on the prospects for an ideal autumn.

Delicious diversions. First Zermatt, the chalet verandah, some nosey-parkering, the climb to Trift, the wild flowers. Then, in late September steal another week before Conference. Eriboll, with the northern light getting thinner and more brittle; and the air colder. The portents of winter and solitude, with the deer beginning to 'come down' and the road traffic non-existent.

But, as I have often found, and endlessly predicted, if you look forward to something keenly it won't happen. The markets are crashing, the price of oil is shooting sky high and the Iraqis are recalcitrant.[1]

In a few minutes I am off up to blitz my desk at MoD, and call on an expensive dentist who has been recommended by John Sterling.

Saltwood   *Monday, 13 August*

It's very late, and Pat has just left, bearing a secret note for Charles at Number 10.

The day started slowly, and tiresomely.

Officials, who relish – and award themselves points for – getting Ministers back from holidays, preferably on a Monday, had insisted I come up in order to approve a response to something that had come over from Number 10.

TK is in Scotland and they couldn't get hold of him. Grimly certain that he would have surfaced by the time I got to the building (I've been caught like this so many times in the past), I set off.

But no, he was still incommunicado – the moors, come on – and I was in charge. Charles's queries were all perfectly valid, points about Rules of Engagement, Command Structures, relation to US Command, Air Traffic Control, etc.

---

[1] Saddam Hussein had shown every indication of resisting by force a UN resolution requiring him to evacuate Kuwait.

Unfortunately Simon is away and those in charge of the office are simply not in the same class. Their limp, partially illiterate (as all too easily happens when fusion is attempted of advice from three separate Desks) response would have irritated Charles and infuriated the PM. I sent for the officials.

Robin Hatfield (not bad, but not used to my 'ways') came up immediately, but there were others whom I found less impressive. They muddled up the various Tornado designations, ADV, GR5, etc., and cross-permed them with Harriers.

I spent some time tautening the response, making sure my name was prominent at the start and at points in the text; made it plain that TK was on holiday and (unlike the PM who is also on holiday in Cornwall but *manically* in touch) ungetattable. While they were working it up I had a good meeting with the US chargé, and his younger, gung-ho aide, who nodded when I was speaking. We *must* get uniformity of ROE. It's humiliating, and dangerous, that the RAF should be subject to a legally binding process of hesitation when the Americans and the Saudis can shoot on assumed hostile intent. But officials, and Peter Harding,[1] were cooperative, and pleased with the result. I dashed for the train, confident that the note would be shortly over with Charles.

Negligent boy. You *can't* be too careful, or too suspicious, in this game. I should have made Pat drive me, so as to be on the phone. But the roads are dreadful with holiday traffic at the moment and the train faster. In fact, I shouldn't have left the building at all until the note had gone over. S of S's office, rightly anticipating his wrath, wouldn't transmit until they had succeeded in contacting him, in spite of frequent promptings at my behest.

At lunchtime TK finally surfaced, on a very bad line (as I have already discovered at Eriboll our special high-power secret-agent type portables are defeated by the Scottish Highlands and don't work north of Inverness).

He took, or rather snatched, the helm. Anything to stop AC getting prominence, currying favour. All references to me were deleted and the text watered back down again to conform with Douglas's (i.e., FCO wankers' line) preference.

Immediately I sat down in the office here and drafted a com-

---

[1] Air Marshal Sir Peter Harding, Chief of the Air Staff.

mentary note, based on my original text, for circulation within the Dept. But the real point, of course, was to get it over to Number 10, show that there is someone here with balls, and it's AC.

Then, an unpredictable stumbling block. Again showing that one should (in Mr Gulbenkian's invaluable – but too often disregarded – phrase) *never leave the Bridge*. Isn't that what had landed TK in it? Instead of indulging myself down here I should be camped in the bloody place, with a sleeping bag, interfering in all and sundry.

David Hatcher said that he 'couldn't' deliver it to Number 10.

'Why not, for God's sake? It's only across the road.'

Well, it wasn't appropriate. He couldn't be party to communication with CP 'behind the back of' the Sec of State's office. Sodbollocks. Am I always to be thwarted? Surrounded by nincompoops and inadequates?

Shortly afterwards TK's 'agreed' draft, characteristically turgid and evasive, came through. Jane fortified me. She said Mrs T. *must* see the stronger version. So out I retyped it, on the old Swedish machine in the summer office here, and gave it to Pat who, very loyally and inscrutably, has guaranteed to put it through the door of Number 10 tonight.

She'll have it when she starts – usually five-ish – tomorrow.

Ministry of Defence   *Tuesday, 14 August*

At twenty past eight this morning the phone rang. It was the Downing Street switchboard. 'Mr Clark? Charles Powell wants a word.'

I assumed that it was about the note, but he brushed that aside, though clearly grateful for it.

'The Prime Minister is anxious that a Minister of State should go out to the Gulf immediately, and the fickle finger of fate seems to be pointing at you.'

I was exultant. 'Bugger the fickle finger. I want to be told that I am the PM's personal choice.'

Ass, Clark. Of course he couldn't possibly say that. Just as at the Chequers seminars, I was being extended over and above my actual rank. Charles was tactful.

'It's probably better to aim (sic) to leave tomorrow.'

I rushed back into the kitchen and hugged Jane; I could feel the adrenalin coursing. Was I to be Resident Minister in the Middle East? Macmillan at the Dar al Ayoun?[1]

I had to have a VC 10, ideally *the* VC 10 which the PM uses. I rang him back. And the press statement had to say that I was the Prime Minister's personal emissary.

Yes, I could have *a* VC 10, but for obvious reasons the wording of the statement would have to be carefully drawn.

'If I'm to have the authority I need it must at least say that I am travelling on her instructions.'

Well, yes, that could probably be included. A 'small pool' of reporters should go along, as well.

I telephoned at once to the Private Office, who were pleased and excited thinking, rightly or wrongly, that it was consequent on yesterday's note about which they are now more than a little shame-faced.

I believed that everything was in hand and, having done a lot of shouting, to staff and to civil servants, I took tranquillising therapy. I polished the top of the tallboy in my bathroom, then tidied and arranged the objects that sit there. When I return, they will greet and smile at me. A last rushed bathe while Jane packed my tropical suits and aertex, then back to the station.

In the meantime, however, a drama had been unfolding. TK, finally contacted on the moors, had taken the idea badly.

'I'm not going to have Charles Powell giving orders to my Department without going through me ... What? Hullo? This is a very bad line', etc., etc.

Jane Binstead was in a bit of a jam, unfortunate female.

Finally:

'I order you to stop these arrangements. I myself am going out there very shortly. I will bring the dates of my departure forward. This is something *I* handle, it's my area. Nothing to do with Procurement. I order you ...'

'Wha–?'

'I ORDER you to stop all arrangements concerning this proposal.' Bellowing.

---

[1] See AC's letter, 13 March 1989.

Jane unhappily came along the corridor and gave an account of her predicament. After she had returned David, quite making up for his attack of nerves last evening, adroitly and stealthily rang Charles at Number 10, who at once contacted the PM in Cornwall.

What was then actually said to TK, I don't know. But he climbed down.

A little later another note came over, this time direct (a 'top' at last!) to my office, reaffirming the PM's intention.

And still later TK phoned me, all bland. 'I was a bit doubtful, but I've thought it over . . . Good luck.'

He went on – inaudibly as well as unintelligibly – to express reservations about the press, and 'Publicity'!

I went over to a meeting at the Foreign Office. Nothing that ever happens anywhere must take place without the Foreign Office claiming (at least) foster-parenthood. Tiny room. Diffident officials. W. Waldegrave chairing. All hunka-munka food. No real info. Dominic Asquith, William's Private Secretary, is irritatingly handsome in a very pale suit, pale tie, etc. But already putting on a little too much around the waist. In five years he'll look like Bruce Anderson.

By the time I got back to the office TK had again 'thought it over' (that's one of the advantages of Scotland, I said, it's a wonderful place to think) and said 'NO PRESS'.

Uh? But CP had said he/she had wanted reporters to go along. Once again we had to refer back, and once again he was overruled.

One might think all this would impair my relations with Tom. But he's so rubbery that it just bounces off. He's a true professional. Whatever our feelings may have been during a duel, we are always genial in each other's company. Or am I being too complacent? Is he harbouring terrible resentments?

Who cares? I am off tomorrow on a wonderful adventure.

VC 10 en route   *Sunday, 15 August*

We are all rather congested in the front portion of a *tanker* VC 10 (storage tanks empty, I trust. I can't believe that we are actually flying fuel out to this so fuel-rich region). Every seat, and they are none too comfortable, is taken and 'facilities' are at a level between 'Business' and 'Standard' classes on a civilian flight.

Alas! All our efforts to get the famous 'White' aircraft with its drawing rooms and beautiful linen were to no avail. But we do have tables, rather like the Plymouth train, on which I am writing this note.

Opposite me is VCDS, Vincent,[1] and his two acolytes. He is a very good man. Clear-headed. I first encountered him at Chequers, where he impressed. Beside me David, and a rather congenial man from the FCO, with hooded lids, who is in charge of subversion and 'dirty tricks'.

On the other side of the bay some pressmen – 'Diplomatic Correspondents' (ludicrous title), of whom the *Times* chap, McEwen, seems amiable; and dear Bruce, beaming benignly. I hope that they don't get disappointed. I have given instructions that they be plied with drink at all times.

When first charged with this I wanted to be more contemplative, solitary, classicist. There may still come an opportunity, although the schedule looks ninny-tight. Maddeningly, I couldn't find my Doughty[2], and I now feel myself becoming a little rattled. This could be due to loss of sexuality (or could be causing it). Travel jitters can sometimes have exactly the opposite effect, and I need to jump on the nearest WAAF. But in any case all the cabin staff on this trip are male.

Abu Dhabi   *Saturday, 18 August*

The palace of the Amir is surely the most extravagant building in which I have ever trod. The whiteness of the Carrara marble (I was reminded of Jim Lees-Milne's anecdote of the rich American lady who, noticing a mousey governess's necklace and inquiring of what it was made (malachite), said, 'Yeah? At home we've got a staircase made of that stuff') the richness and depth of the Savonnerie, the newness and cleanness of all the silks and stuffs, the glistering of the gold, is dazzling.

In Europe, or in the East, palaces have grown over the centuries,

---

[1] Vice Chief of Defence Staff, General Sir Richard Vincent.
[2] *Arabia Deserta* by C. M. Doughty.

acquired their contents at the behest of many different tastes and proprietors. But in the Gulf the palaces of the Sheikhs are *instant*. One huge cheque was written, wham, and there you are.

The only flaw, but in this instance it is an intrusive one, is the weak and hesitant proportion of the staircase. I see that it is ornamental only, as everyone uses the lifts, but it is central to the hall, and the scale is wrong. Better suited to the 1929 Florida villa from which, I would guess, it was copied.

They are cool, these buildings, and I am comfortable in any one of my identical Lesley and Roberts blue suits. Much more of a uniform, in every way more appropriate than the pale 'summer' fabrics, already at 11 a.m. rumpled and sweat-stained, of my entourage.

And I am welcome. The Sheikhs are glad to see an English Minister, especially one who smoothly opens the courtesies by saying, 'The Prime Minister has charged me personally with conveying to you, Your Majesty, her very highest expressions of personal regard.'

These old Sheikhs are very wise. And of them all my own preference is, I think, for Sheikh Isa of Bahrain. Such beautiful manners. Such cool and practical judgment. Only very occasionally does he become agitated, shifts in his robes and worry beads appear in his hand. He has a little of Woodie[1] about him (come to think about it, they must be around the same age).

They have come from the desert, these old men, and their fathers fought with Lawrence, with their rag-tag cavalry and camels, against the Turks. I quite see that their new wealth is so abundant, so vastly prolific that they cannot keep a really close eye. What is wealth for, but to improve the quality of life? If hours every day are to be consumed with checking 'books', complaints, rival claims of scheming accountants, then what's the point?

But one or two tiers down lies a whole stratum of parasites, competing, dealing, cutting each other's throats. Everywhere a pudgy 'Crown Prince', café-au-lait smooth, will sit in on conferences, puzzled and fidgety, sometimes in military uniform. He will be his father's favourite. But lurking, too, and occasionally glimpsed, are the lean and hawk-eyed 'nephews'. Expressions burning with ambition and lust.

When we get down to business, it is soon plain that these 'Ruling

---

[1] Ian Woodner: see entry for 12 November, 1990.

Families' are more than a little apprehensive. Iraq, more than any other, is the country of the mob. And was not Baghdad the city where the mob, it seems like yesterday, burst into the Royal Palace and dragged the regent Nuri es Said into the street, cutting out his entrails and pulling him along the gutter, still alive, behind the royal limousine?

So the assistance they hope for is of a specialist kind. Each, in their different way, has asked for a strong detachment, preferably with light armour as well, to protect *them*, personally. Because of course if things really start to disintegrate they couldn't trust even their own bodyguard.

The request is never put so crudely as this. The danger of 'raids' by Iraqi 'Special Forces' is usually the closest they approach to an admission of their real fears. But I understood immediately, and as soon as I did and began to expound on the kind of mix needed they would become excited and pleased.

Free water, of course, open facilities of every kind, special provision for RAF aircrew – and much else. There is no problem with any of these. But it is their own skins that concern them most.

Nor is this a request that should be treated lightly. If the ruling families start to pack up, emigrate to their lodges at Newmarket or Longchamps or, worse, patch up some 'Arab Solution' deal individually with Saddam, as that oily little runt Hussein, the King of Jordan, is openly recommending, then we've had it.

Midnight:
We have landed at Riyadh to take on fuel.

Tom has specifically 'barred' me from going to Saudi, claiming it as 'his' area. But the Ambassador, Alan Monro, a very good man indeed, keen and clever, came out to meet me.

The airfield is half blacked out and we walked, he and I, in the heavy night heat – it must still have been over 85°. I could sense, and occasionally hear, junior officials searching for us. Periodically we stopped, tacit co-conspirators, in the deep dark shadow of a C 140 wing, or took cover behind an undercarriage leg. We were joined by Sandy Wilson,[1] another very good man. Both of them told me that the Americans were going to attack, no doubt about it – but when?

There are F 16s here wingtip to wingtip, and more transport

---

[1] Sandy Wilson: Air Vice-Marshal Sir Andrew Wilson, at that time Commander, British Forces, Arabian Peninsula.

aircraft than I have seen since Wideawake on Ascension Island in 1982. Once a military build-up passes a certain stage battle becomes almost inevitable.

It is the railway timetables of 1914, and the Guns of August.

Albany   *Sunday, 19 August*

I got in to Brize at 3.40 this morning, and drove directly to Saltwood, alternating between Red Boxes (three) and all the Sunday papers. After two hours the back of the Jaguar was a giant rat's-nest of mussed-up newsprint, 'supplements', and official folders.

Home at last! And, again, unscathed.

I changed into softies, ate a big scrambled egg breakfast, lots of coffee, bread and honey; and wandered over to the Garden House to look at the new 'summer' furniture which had been delivered while I was away.

After a very long flight I like always to *oxygenate* by taking a really strenuous walk, expelling the toxins of recycled air and 'petit fours'. But something (thank God) made me first ring the Duty Clerk at Number 10, to check in.

The clerk was crisp, unready to be generous. Sunday was no different from any other day. Worse, in this particular instance, because Mrs Thatcher was due to return from her 'holiday' this evening. He left me in little doubt that she would be expecting my report at the top of her first box.

'But I haven't even typed it out, my handwriting is illegible, there's no secretarial staff at MoD . . . '

'The office facilities here are at your disposal' (*not* calling me 'Minister').

Groan! I thought I'd gorge some of the caviar, take the 2.40. Then realised – providentially, as it turned out – that this would be too tight, so skipped lunch entirely and just made the 1.40. No driver, so walked in warm humid rain from Waterloo to the House where confused and faltering 'Security' men reluctantly emerged to fumble and mutter with bunches of keys. (The police all seem to take Sunday off.) It took me about fifteen minutes actually to get installed in my room.

David had kept the folder, and all my 'green' notes.[1] The whole report
had to be written, from scratch, in my hand. *Then* – but was there
time? – transposed into a clear typed text. I was much interrupted by
reporters and radio who jangled me at the desk.

Round, finally, at 5.35 in the faithful little Porsche, to Number
10. There I dictated solidly, for over two hours to Sally, leading Garden
Girl and brilliant typist and screen operator.

By that time the PM was almost due back from Cornwall. I did
not want to be caught by her in 'half-change', with the Porsche
lending a somewhat frivolous tone to the Downing St car rank, so
accelerated away straight after signing the fair copy – except having
first rather cruelly but deliberately booked a call to TK through the
Downing St switchboard, though not staying to take it. ('What the
hell's Alan doing at Number 10 on a Sunday evening?')

Now it is late, and I have been 'on the go' for nineteen hours, or
longer if you include the flight. Tomorrow I am to attend a meeting
at Number 10 at 9.30; just Hurd and TK besides the PM. The inner,
inner group. Anything could happen. But I must thank God. He
could have lifted his protection a hundred times in the last eight days.

Ministry of Defence   *Monday, 20 August*

My report was 'On the table'. Both the Lady and Charles congratulated me. But Hurd put in the standard courtesy put-down,
'looking forward to reading it'.

Unless a document has been written by a FCO Minister or, better,
filed by one of those useless resident 'diplomats' it's not a real 'report'.

Tipped off that I was attending by, I would guess, Len Appleyard, a
former ambassador and now No. Two in the Cabinet Office, Douglas
had insisted that Waldegrave also came along. If Tom has a Minister of
State with him then the Foreign Office should also field two Ministers.
When William appeared there was a certain amount of agitation
of a 'the Prime Minister wants to keep this to a very small group' kind.
And, at intervals during the meeting, she snarled and spat at him

---

[1] When writing in his own hand on Government papers AC always affected a green
pen.

which, in his rather splendid nonchalant way (Etonian education, of course, because I happen to know he actually feels quite rattled), he took in his stride.

At lunchtime I was on the news both going into, and emerging from, Number 10! I do hope Jane saw it at Saltwood.

Ministry of Defence   *Tuesday, 21 August*

I was caught today, had to say 'No, Prime Minister' at the morning's meeting.

The whole thing was a complete set-up. The Foreign Office control the telegram traffic. There was an important telegram referring to a new Resolution of the United Nations, governing our powers of interception on the high seas. Hurd's office kept it until the very last minute, then sent it over to Simon just as (it transpired) we were on the verge of setting out. Naturally nothing came near me.

Consequently when the Lady said, to me, 'Have you seen it?' and I said, 'No', she will have assumed that it was just idleness on my part. Al not doing his homework properly.

One of the oldest tricks in the Civil Service.

Ministry of Defence   *Thursday, 23 August*

Early this morning Tom sent for me. He was bumbustious. Archie should go to these meetings. Of course quite often there was no need for a Minister of State, but if there should be, then obviously it ought to be Archie.

'Quite.'

Tom then, shamelessly, picked my brains for three-quarters of an hour. He's going through one of his terrifically good-form phases, which usually coincide with his having got the better of me.

As soon as I got back to my room I rang Charles. But he had a lot on his mind. 'It's a bit hard to justify giving the Procurement Minister a higher access rating than the Armed Forces Minister at a meeting of this kind.'

Shafted.

Saltwood   *Wednesday, 29 August*

I have been in a vile mood all day, and beastly to Jane.

This fucking Saddam thing has given the AF side of the Dept a renewed *raison d'être*. A war to fight! Whee-ee. As a result everything has gone on hold, the Consolidated Fund 'tap' is unlocked – buy anything, order anything. All great fun, but I sense that those who are opposed to me and what I am trying to do are in the ascendant.

I am 'back in my kennel'. I have a lot of extra approving to do, of emergency procurement. But I am completely excluded from policy meetings (although TK often picks my brains ahead of them). The irony lies in the fact that this is exactly the kind of conflict which my Chequers paper anticipated – but before we are ready for it.

Even my weapons effectiveness test, 'how quickly can it get to, and how able will it be to protect, The Bahrain Causeway?' is eerily prescient.

Saltwood   *Friday, 31 August*

A long day yesterday. I was up at six, took an early train to Cannon St, then drove to Plymouth via Bristol. The picture restorer in Bristol is helping with the huge Duncan [Grant] centrepiece; the enormous canvas of the youth (Present it to the Terence Higgins Trust, Jane said) and the two only slightly less big ones of the ladies playing their lutes. They are good craftsmen but the whole operation now looks like costing more than £20,000 – good money after bad?

I got to Addison Road about three-quarters of an hour late for my surgery and gaga-ly went into the wrong house via the back door, interrupting a solicitor's conference.

'Can I help you?' said a lady, pretty icily.

'No thanks,' I said. 'Oh well, yes. You could move that white BMW that's stopping me putting my car there.'

At the Conservative offices Roy Williams was in charge as Anne is taking her holiday.

'How are you then, Alan, all right?' He always says that, like that. Quite a few times. Is it paranoia, or do I detect a hint of (non-specific) reproach? How very *black* his hair is, and how yellowish-ill his skin seems through the cigarette smoke.

A journalist took a picture of me behind my desk with Roy sitting in as a 'patient', and I thought ruefully of that photo, posed with Veronica (a more fetching 'patient' than dear Roy) that I used in my 1979 Election Address. My hair was glossy brown and I was still wearing those giant halter collars now only sported by Prince Michael of Kent, and Algy Cluff.

'Alan Clark takes a few hours off from the Crisis to deal with constituents' problems . . . '

'Each person has their own crisis with their own problem – it's important for them,' I fed in.

That should be OK.

Then I went down to the Council Chamber to a specially convened 'Policy' committee, where I was somewhat startled at being suddenly told to 'stand' for Ron King who had, it seemed, died in the night.

I recall him as comparing favourably with his Tory counterparts. Genial and shrewd – though always with that somewhat *tight*, suffused bodily appearance that predicates the sudden X.

The meeting was wholly pointless, as far as I could see. Simply an ego trip for the deputy leader while Tom Savery, the titular Tory boss, was away. Mike Lees (how muddlingly ludicrous, infuriating and utterly Plymouthian that the Association Treasurer and active wheel, a very *short* man, should be called Mike *Leaves*, and the chairman of Plymouth's largest private employer, another very short man, should be called Mike *Lees*) read out the text of an internal letter which had already been leaked. Neither of the two committee members, who are also Tory councillors in Sutton, made any attempt to speak to, or to acknowledge me. They get cross when I turn up at these sort of events as it interferes with their dossier of malfeasance.

Their problem is, they don't see how they can quite get rid of me while I'm still a Minister. Their immediate concern is of course the local elections next year when, if they are trounced, they will blame the Government; if they are returned they will delight in recounting how 'on the doorstep' people are saying we'll vote for you, but we're not going to vote Conservative in a General Election.

It was gone six o'clock when I got away. Ravenous, I turned off the motorway, to stop in the Johnnie Crow lay-by[1] where, exhausted, we sometimes took a snack during the campaigns. As I wolfed my Marmite sandwiches I thought, Well, I *am* glad not to be going through all that again.

I know, and they *don't* know. As I think about it I realise I could have only a year left. Relief at last! But I fear that I will be sad to leave the 'tawny male paradise'.

The House is being recalled next week, which will be fun. An occasion. But unlikely, I feel, to compare with 2 April 1982 – the most electric moment that I have ever experienced in that place; or it for many years I suspect, perhaps since 8 May 1940. There is something about the atmosphere, the clarity of purpose, that will be absent.

Because the whole Gulf affair has sunk back into a kind of stalemate, with the wily Saddam paying out the hostages like a salmon line and – God knows how he fixed it – the ghastly Branson 'standing by' with an airliner for his 'mercy mission'. It's been a bad day for those who wish ill of slobs because Ronson and Parnes have *already* (twenty-four hours) been moved to Ford Open where they can loll about making phone calls, playing the market, and sending out to Fortnums for food and drink.

Saltwood   *Saturday, 8 September*

I've done, it seems, what I have managed to bring about in quite a few years since entering politics: just *lose* my summer holiday.

Exceptional circs, of course. But when it happens it's always exceptional circs, of some dimension.

Trouble is, I always fall for the beguiling notion that if you let everyone else go in August you have an easy time while they're away, and are then due a pleasing free period when they all start work.

But it never goes like this, although admittedly I stole a march on

---

[1] Johnnie Crow lay-by: so called after a large and benevolent crow who would perch on driving mirrors and ask for sandwich crusts.

TK with the Gulf trip. The departmental diary is filling up – and with things which I miss at my peril. I am tired, with that late August staleness that only the Alps can remedy. Even as I write this, I am determined to get to the Chalet – if only for forty-eight hrs.

The martins have gathered, chattering urgently, and gone. The swallows are diminishing in number – just a few fussed parents and their second broods. It is grey and breezy. Dead hollyhock leaves lie on the surface of the pool, and the water temperature is below 70°. It won't go back through that band until next May.

Ministry of Defence   *Thursday, 13 September*

There were two boxes in the car, lots of interesting stuff. Pat drove me directly to the Dept and I had to go straight in to a meeting which TK had convened to discuss publicity – his favourite subject – for tomorrow's announcement.[1]

It went on for one and three-quarter hours. I was dry and sardonic. A palpable chill of embarrassment spread across the room when Tom said that he would like a huge montage of a tank behind him, a photo blow-up. The soldiers weren't too keen. But 'I suppose you could wear a flak jacket,' I said.

Laughter, in which, good naturedly, he joined.

I recommended against having an FCO presence. Waldegrave wants to sit on the platform.

'At least make sure he doesn't bring a child.'

Smirks only. Officials aren't meant to laugh (except in Private Office) when one Minister makes a joke about another one.

I am scratchy and ill-tempered. TK consults and asks my advice the *entire* time. On technical questions. And also on strategic and political ones. Before meetings with Generals, before going to Number 10. But in truth, deftly and effectively, he's sidelined me.

If I was really a clever politician I'd lay a trap for him, suddenly and critically give him *bad* advice, watch him get in a twist. But I just can't. It would offend against the Socratic concept.

---

[1] Conveying our participation in the Gulf Force.

Saltwood   *Wednesday, 19 September*

A good example today of how mulishly vindictive is the Tory Party.

David Young's book is out. A kind of memoir, not very well written, which he has called, innocently, *The Enterprise Years*. His publishers staged a party, and took the ballroom at the Savile. But no one – *no one* of his former colleagues turned up except Patrick McLoughlin, who is a nice man but not a card of very high value, having served only a short time under David and in a very junior position.[1]

What are they all so cross about? The book doesn't seem to me to be so very indiscreet, save only for that enjoyable and all too obviously true account of the great panic at Number 10 on 'Wobbly Thursday' when David gripped Norman Tebbit by the lapels and said, 'We're going to lose this fucking Election.'

That, and the attendant whisperings and scamperings on the staircase at Number 10, was all a very good read. This extract was serialised in the *Sunday Times*. But after, I would assume, the guest acceptance list had been published, because they all stayed away.

Of course they were jealous of David, and frightened also, because of his special powers of access to the Prime Minister. Unlike most Peers in the Cabinet, he had never served an apprenticeship in the Commons, with all the hateful and long drawn-out initiation rituals of late votes and constituency pressures. David had not even served as a *junior* Minister. And so once he was down, they kicked him.

But David was very pleasant to work with; clever, and possessing of a quick mind. He had fresh ideas, though was a little too ready to 'devolve' to the private sector; not seeing that this can cheapen the responsibilities of Government in more than one sense.

If David had a fault, a weakness rather, it was that he could become a little nervous when in the company of his superiors in a small room. He would become *over* affable, crack too many jokes, and laugh at them himself, when it would have been better to be icy, and ruthless.

David had set his heart on becoming Chairman of the Party, and indeed when his bandwagon was really rolling anything seemed possible.

---

[1] Patrick McLoughlin, MP for West Derbyshire since 1986 who had been Lord Young's PPS, Trade and Industry, 1988–9. Now Parliamentary Under-Secretary, Transport.

Willie, though, was always doubtful, and stories were spread of
'poor attendance' and 'disrespect' in the Lords. Bertie Denham would
brief shamelessly to the Lobby.

What finally brought David down was his picking a quarrel with
the Brewers. I had no idea how many Tory MPs are on that payroll
until I saw how widespread was the opposition within our own Party.
Even big Jim Couchman,[1] a PPS in the DTI, would raise his voice at
closed ministerial meetings. It coincided of course, with falling out of
favour with her. She was already beginning to transfer her affections
(*La Donna é mobilè*) to John Major.

But if you were a sociologist you could say that David was brought
down by two traditional strains in the Conservative Party: anti-
semitism, and the brewers' lobby.

Saltwood   *Sunday, 21 October*

Bloomsbury evening at Saltwood. We entertained the 'Friends of
Charleston'.[2] I don't know what they charged for tickets, but I hope
they made money.

I had the brilliant idea of stuffing the Garden House, which has
been standing more or less empty since Colette moved out, with all
our Bloomsbury 'items'. We hung and distributed everything, thirty-
seven in all, plus a good few ceramics, save only the giant Queen
Mary Duncans. The whole made a pleasing, and entirely private
exhibition.

I made a little speech of welcome, fraudulently and bogusly
referring to my father's death 'from a falling tree'. What mischievous
impulse made me do this?

Pure Roger Irrelevant. I did just manage to keep a straight face,

---

[1] James Couchman, MP for Gillingham since 1983. His entry in the 1990 Register
of Members' Interests included under 'Employment or Office' – Chiswick
Caterers Ltd, Adviser to the Gin Rectifiers and Distillers Association. The post
of PPS is unsalaried and does not require Members of Parliament to relinquish
their outside interests.

[2] A charitable body dedicated to the maintenance of the farmhouse where Duncan
Grant and Vanessa Bell had their studio, where Keynes wrote *The Economic
Consequences of the Peace*, and Lytton Strachey and others were habitués.

although William, from the far end of the room, gave me an odd look.

We then processed over to the Great Library, rich and enclosing as always on such an occasion, for the performance by Eileen Atkins of Virginia Woolf's essay, 'A Room of One's Own'. How well she did it! And what a beautiful, moving and dignified text it is. The audience listened in a rapt silence and at the end I had tears in my eyes.

Olivier Popham materialised; benign and knowledgeable. I remember her, just, at Portland Place. Very sleek and dark like a young seal. She asked to see Graham's pictures, and chided me gently for selling her portrait which he had painted in 1939, in the great Death Duties sale.[1] I could hardly say, 'I thought you were dead.'

Her big, deliberately common-voiced daughter Cressida, who is famous for 'fabrics', accompanied her. Both showed a true Bloomsbury mocking spirit when confronted by the great Nurnburg 1490 iron safe in the lower hall.

'Is it a Coca-Cola machine? Or a coffee dispenser?'

Another character, gently on the way down, was a blonde, attractively composed, and underdressed, who was in tow behind Professor Skidelsky. She was Victoria Heber-Percy, Robert's daughter and in her day (would it have been the late Sixties?) a great society beauty. She got married to batty, cross, erratic Peter Zinoviev but later, I suppose, got rid of him. The League of Helmet-Makers, Beautiful Wives.

Saltwood   *Sunday, 4 November*

The papers are all very bad. Tory Party falling apart, the death blow,[2] that kind of thing. Something in it, I fear, unless we can get a grip on events. The only person who can restore order in the parliamentary ranks is Tristan. He can do it short-term (like many intelligent people

---

[1] Olivier Popham was the mistress of Graham Bell, who was killed in the RAF in 1943.

[2] Sir Geoffrey Howe had resigned from the Government the previous Thursday, and his resignation speech was awaited with some trepidation.

T. can only see things very long or very short) but that's enough. Get us past November.[1]

After breakfast I telephoned Chequers.

'The Prime Minister is speechwriting.'

'Who with?'

'Charles Powell.'

'When will she be free?'

'There might be a minute before lunch.'

'When's that?'

'One o'clock sharp.'

I was being kept at bay. Unusual. The Number 10 switchboard girls are always helpful. With Chequers I've had this problem before.

'Oh well, please pass her my name, in case she wants to take a call then.'

It was a lovely crisp day of late autumn. I had said I'd join Jane in the garden. Now I was going to be stuck indoors waiting for a call. But I had barely got to the doorway to give her a shout when the phone started ringing.

'Alan . . . '

I tried to cheer her up: 'There's an awful lot of wind about', 'Hold tight and it'll all blow away', 'Geoffrey was past it by now, anyway.'

I said, with suitable preface, that I would never seek to tell her who she should employ or why; but that if she could find something for 'Tim' to do . . .

'Tim who?' (thinking, I suppose, that I wanted her to bring someone called Tim into the Cabinet. Blast, blast. Too oblique. Never works with her.)

'Renton. You really ought to make Tristan your Chief Whip.'

A very long silence. I almost said 'hullo', but didn't.

'Oh but he's enjoying his present job so much . . . '

I don't think she realises what a jam she's in. It's the Bunker syndrome. Everyone round you is clicking their heels. The saluting sentries have highly polished boots and beautifully creased uniforms. But out there at the Front it's all disintegrating. The soldiers are

---

[1] November was the month when under the Leadership Rules, a challenger was permitted to offer himself. Once the month has passed there would be no further opportunity until the new parliamentary session.

starving in tatters and makeshift bandages. Whole units are mutinous and in flight.

Saltwood   *Sunday, 11 November*

Back from Plymouth with what is, by tradition, the nastiest weekend of the year behind me. The Constituency engagements are dense and unyielding. The surgery is always particularly crowded and irksome. I invariably have a cold, often flu, and the Remembrance ceremonies on the Hoe drag and chill. New, and unwelcome, ecumenical balls caused the service to grate. Some nameless mystic read out words, unintelligible, from an unknown text. Drenching rain.

But at the civilian Memorial a magnificent Grenadier in a bearskin handed me my wreath, and (as I always do) I *hammed* the role, stiffly bowing and clicking. From a corner of the crowd I could see Vera and Tom oggling crazily, but I acknowledged them only with my eyelids.

At last I was free. I climbed into the valiant Little Silver, and drove exhilaratingly fast. A lot of the time I was running up to 120 mph, and the very last home straight on the M20 at a continuous 140. Average speed for the whole journey from the Hoe car park to Saltwood Lodge gates, including fuel stops, contraflow, caravans in Langport, roadwork lights, was 77.8 mph. One of the best ever.

I had no time even to open a newspaper. But now I see that they are all packed with Heseltinia. Plugs of one kind or another. Some, like the *Mail on Sunday* (who had a heavy flirtation with David Owen at one point, I seem to recall), have quite openly changed sides. Every editor is uneasy. In the woodwork stir all those who have lived for the day when they could emerge and have a gloat without fear of retribution.

It looks to me as if Michael is going to get forced into a position, whether he likes it or not, when he'll have to stand. He's cunning and single-minded, yes. But he's also a bit, well, *dyslexic*. Galvanised, jerky movements. On the only two occasions when I have had anything to do with him on matters of policy, I recollect him getting into a great state.

When I was at Employment the question arose of whether a second frigate should be built at Cammell Laird, or at Swan Hunter.

Michael has this infatuation with Liverpool, Merseyside, and it was all bound up with him showing his mettle to the crowd. He gabbled over the phone, was wild-eyed in the lobbies. Apparently threatened to resign. Why not? Get lost, she should have said, *then* give the contract to Cammells.

The second time was, of course, Westlands. I only spoke to him twice, something to do with Bristow's new fleet, quite marginal really, and found him almost off his head with rage and – to my mind – persecution mania.

Ministry of Defence   *Monday, 12 November*

I lunched today with Charlie Allsopp[1] at Christies. He's unsquashable really. 'Sharp' but engaging. He told me that Ian Woodner had died.

Good old Woodie, the auctioneer's friend. He will have been sad not to have outlasted Armand Hammer who was (a lot) richer and (only a little) older.

He loved drawings, and he bought and bought in the closing years of his life, almost as if to prolong his expectancy. He went to prison for a while, as rich people in America sometimes do but, like Eddie Gilbert, was revered by the convicts, whom he helped in those tiny ways which make uneducated people grateful.

I have two clear memories of him. Bidding, implacably, at the Chatsworth sale in the summer of 1984. Some of the stuff was wonderful, worth every penny. Not all, though.

Once Col brought him down to Saltwood and made me set out a lot of drawings, normally kept in the safe, for his edification. Woodie was silent in the main, and stroked his moustaches. He made a half-hearted show of interest in the Renoir Circus girls; but the only piece that really excited him was the Quail and Lute. In the Catalogue Raisonée[2] I showed him the entry *Locativa Incognita*, and he became agitated.

Not only did Woodie have taste, but he was an accomplished artist in his own right, modelling himself on, and being obsessed by, Odilon

---

[1] Charles Allsopp, Chairman of Christie's since 1986.
[2] Of the work of Giovanni da Udine.

Redon. He once threw a huge dinner party at Claridges, taking the entire dining room and, at the end of the meal, he delivered one of the most moving personal testaments of the meaning of art, and draughtsmanship, to which I have ever listened.

On the way out Charlie showed me into the room where the English furniture for the next 'important' sale was accumulating. A *quite* nice cabinet, bow-fronted, was offered up, faded walnut and marquetry.

'Did you know Billy Wallace? It came from his widow.'

Poor Liz! So pretty and bejewelled as a smart-set groupie when we were all at Oxford. She must be in her mid-fifties, and childless. And Billy, too. Whom I remember meeting and half hero-worshipping at Lavington in 1945 when he had an old SS 1 with a blown exhaust, and drove about at night. Two years ago he died from cancer of the mouth. What a lot of people I've seen 'out'. And still I prance.

I came back here, but couldn't concentrate, and strolled over to the House. We are on the verge of great events. Wild rumours are circulating about the leadership 'contest' for which nominations close on Thursday. Today's favourite is that there just won't *be* a contest this year.

'Too close to the Election, old boy. Frozen.'

This has to be balls.

The Whips have totally clammed up. A bad sign. Already they have gone into 'neutral' mode. Secret policemen burning the old files, ready to serve.

The ballot would, should, be on Tuesday of next week. Only eight days to go and I have a dreadful feeling – not all the time, but in waves – that Heseltine will stand, and that he will win. I haven't communicated this to anyone. No one at all. But I wish Ian was alive.

House of Commons   *Tuesday, 13 November*

The Party is virtually out of control. Mutinous. People are not turning up for divisions. Dissidents get bolder and bolder with their little off-the-cuff TV slotettes. Code is abandoned. Discipline is breaking up. Geoffrey will make his resignation speech this afternoon, and apparently the entire text is the work of Elspeth. Received wisdom is that this will finally tear the whole thing wide open.

But why should it? Who gives a toss for the old dormouse? Yet I suppose on the Berkeleian principle, if everyone thinks something is important, then it is important.

After Ministers this morning I signalled Andrew MacKay[1] to come into my room. He is so shrewd, he really knows the Party as well as any Whip. Why has he twice refused an invitation to join the Office?

We agreed that the situation is serious, very serious. It's the arithmetic that looks so nasty. There is this *bolus* of wankers, mainly in the North, who are fearful of losing their seats, and will try anything. Elizabeth Peacock:[2] 'We can't be any worse off than what (sic) we are.' Add this to Michael's own claque, itself at least fifty because adhering to it is the whole *Salon des Refusés*, plus all those like Charlie Morrison who have always loathed her, and before you know where you are you're dam' close to 150. Then, there is the considerable body of the soft optioneers, the abstentions. 'An honourable protest.' Crap on every side.

What a lot of people don't realise is that if we get a bad result, closeish figures, she will be hamstrung.

One can write Hugo Young, Peter Jenkins, Robin Oakley,[3] all those who've been waiting for this moment, off the top of one's head. Broaden the Government; must think very long and hard about policy; Heseltine must enter the Cabinet; 'effectively Number Two'; the death-knell of Thatcherism – the clichés, leavened by spite, will roll.

At mid-day I had a meeting with Peter Levene. He told me that at the Lord Mayor's banquet last night she was greeted with virtually complete silence. She started punchily, then got flatter and flatter. I've seen her do this in the past. If the punchy bits don't get them going she reverts to text, and only rarely (Conference being one of the exceptions) are her texts any good.

We are at present in a state where any news, however slight and tenuous, spreads like wildfire if it is damaging. The effect is cumulative, and reinforces doubters, sceptics who need an excuse for transferring loyalties. 'She's virtually lost all support outside, you know . . . '

I change my own mind by the hour. In some ways it would be better for her to go completely than to hang on mutilated, forced to

---

[1] Andrew MacKay, MP for Berkshire East since 1983. PPS to Tom King.
[2] Elizabeth Peacock, MP for Batley and Spen since 1983.
[3] Columnists Hugo Young (*Guardian*) and Peter Jenkins (*Independent*); Robin Oakley (Political Editor, *The Times*).

take in a Trojan Horse. But she has not got the nature to make a withdrawal to Colombey, and for that course it is now really too late. We're down to ensuring that Heseltine doesn't win in a stampede. And Douglas, who could play a role here, is deeply reluctant.

Later
I forced my way along the Minister of State's bench, stopping two places short of Janet [Fookes], who always sits, massively, in the camera-hogging spot just behind the PM. The House was very full indeed, with much chattering and giggling from recusants. The loyalists are glum, and apprehensive.

From the moment he rose to his feet Geoffrey got into it. He was personally wounding – to a far greater extent than mere policy differences would justify. Elspeth's hand in every line.

All those Cabinets (seven *hundred* he said) when the Lady had lashed and basted him (there too, it must be admitted, more savagely than could be explained by nuances of attitude. But it was to a smaller audience and did not, I think, start until about three years ago). In his mind he will also have been carrying the brutal briefing on the 'non-existent' role of Deputy Prime Minister, the messing-around over the houses. It all seethed and bubbled in the cauldron.

The Labour benches loved it. Grinning from ear to ear they 'Oooh'd' and 'Aaah'd' dead on cue. At one point he illustrated his sense of betrayal with some cricketing analogy, being 'sent in to bat for Britain ... only to find that before the game the bats have been broken by the team captain'. Everyone gasped and I looked round to catch Jonathan's eye. He had that special incredulous look he occasionally gets, mouth open.

Geoffrey ended his speech with an ominous, and strange, sentence: 'I have done what I believe to be right for my Party and for my Country.' (They all say that.) 'The time has come for others to consider *their own response* to the tragic conflict of loyalties with which I myself have wrestled for perhaps too long.'

Afterwards a lot of people, semi-traumatised, didn't want to talk about it. The atmosphere was light-headed, almost.

I spoke with Norman Lamont. He very naively ('I can see *you* weren't at Eton,' I said) questioned whether any member of the Government – not Cabinet, *Government* – could vote against her on the first ballot. 'Quite monstrously disloyal,' etc.

Afterwards I thought maybe it was a plant. You can't trust anyone at present.

We were joined by Tebbit. Wildish and gaunt he seemed. He mouthed a bit about a special role he was going to play; he had been in close touch with Peter M., and so on. Interestingly, he said we must *not* go for a compromise candidate. We must fight all the way, to the death.

This appeals to me. Leonidas at Thermopylae. But we don't win. It's the end of me. I came in with her. I go out with her.

House of Commons   *Wednesday, 14 November*

A curious state of limbo. Briefly, and unaccountably, the House has gone quiet. Many are leaving early for their constituencies to take the temperature.

The papers are terrible. The Lady is said to be 'foundering'; 'holed below the waterline'; 'stabbed'; 'bowled middle stump', and similar far from original metaphors. Much worse than Westland. There are even rumours (in the press, I can find no trace of them in the corridors so it may be a plant by Mates or Hampson[1]) that Cranley Onslow is going to advise her not even to *contest* the election.

Perfectly ridiculous. No one seems to have given a thought to the constitutional implications, still less the international. How can a narrow caucus in a singular political party unseat a Prime Minister just because it calculates that it may improve its election prospects thereby?

Tristan rang from his car. He's driving in from Heathrow, just back from some pointless and diverting voyage when he should be tirelessly cigaretting at the very centre of things here. Counting and calculating and ordering our deployment. Naturally he was *very* against NT's idea of a 'last stand'. He thinks he can fudge up a solution that will keep H out.

'Of course,' I said. 'If it works.'

'It's got to fucking work,' he answered.

Exciting, but unnerving, times.

---

[1] Dr Keith Hampson, MP for Leeds North-West since 1983 (Ripon 1974–83). PPS to Michael Heseltine, 1979–84. Before becoming an MP he was a personal assistant to Edward Heath in the 1966 and 1970 General Elections.

Saltwood   *Saturday, 17 November*

I have been listless and depressed most of the day, with ill-at-ease tummy. Perhaps I drank too much in Denmark.[1] But it was mainly Schnapps. Poisoned on the aircraft, more likely. The papers are terrible. Only exceptions being the leader of the *Daily Telegraph*, and Paul Johnson.

Everything else is tipping Heseltine. Bandwagon. And the five o'clock news was even worse. Heseltine doing this, doing that; going down (or up) escalators; leaving (or arriving at) his house. And all the time with that uneasy, almost Wilsonian smirk. But among Conservatives *in the country* she still has majority support. Alison, who is sensible, remains a fervent fan. 'What *are* you all doing?'

The Lady herself is away, out of the country. It's absolute madness. There is no Party mileage whatever in being at the Paris summit. It just makes her seem snooty and remote. And who's running the campaign? Who's doing the canvassing? Who's putting the pressure on?

I became more and more dejected, decided to telephone Tristan. He attempted to calm me, said that Peter Morrison was in charge of collating the votes, that he was calmly confident. But when pressed Tristan shared my scepticism as to whether this was really the true picture.

He launched into some dissertation as to how Douglas (who will be in Paris with the PM, about to go into a Banquet − shades of Potsdam) and John Major (who will − for God's sake − be in *hospital*, having just had four teeth taken out) will speak to each other in that first critical hour between 6 and 7 p.m. on Tuesday and, it is to be hoped, settle what should happen next.

I don't like the sound of this. It will be Halifax, Churchill and George VI, and they may decide who runs. In which case, *passim* Halifax, Douglas will probably stand aside. We're then left with John Major who, being calm and sensible, is infinitely preferable to that dreadful charlatan, H. But John is virtually unknown, too vulnerable to the subtle charge of 'not yet ready for it'.

He has personal handicaps, not of his own making. The product, indeed of his virtues. He's not at all *flash*, and a lot of colleagues think

---

[1] AC had been in Copenhagen for an IEPG meeting.

it's flash that we need at the moment. And he's not classy, which doesn't worry me in the slightest, but worse, he doesn't (like Mrs T.) even *aspire* to be classy.

Pinkish toffs like Ian [Gilmour] and Charlie [Morrison], having suffered, for ten years, submission to their social inferior see in Michael an arriviste, certainly, who can't shoot straight and in Jopling's damning phrase 'bought all his own furniture', but one who at any rate seeks the cachet. While all the nouves in the Party think he (Michael) is the real thing.

'Look,' I said. 'All these arguments are being tossed around on the assumption that we have to go to a second ballot.'

'That's right, Baby.' (A strange affectation of Tristan's, calling me 'Baby'. I don't mind, but I do know from experience that it usually presages some piece of news which I am not going to like.)

An appalling thought struck me. Michael couldn't actually *win* first time round, could he? I put the question convolutedly. 'Do you think it more likely than not that he won't get a majority in the first ballot?'

'Yes.'

'Do you put the odds on this happening at worse than (longish pause) sixty per cent?'

'No.'

This is terrible. He's barely worse than evens.

Did I start gabbling? I don't remember. Tristan cut through it saying if there was any 'uncertainty' (good neutral word for the tapes) a group of us are to meet at Catherine Place after the 10 p.m. vote that evening.

I remain deeply anxious that The Establishment simply hasn't got the machinery, or the people, in place to operate effectively in that very narrow timescale.

I went down to the Winter Office, and drew up a little table showing the three alternatives. There are only three, none of them other than bad, though in varying degree, for me.

1) The PM survives, but maimed. The wind-down period, perhaps to a Gentlemen's Coup in the spring. This is the best one can hope for, and would at least give me time to make some plans. I suppose it is just possible, by a combination of luck and circumstance such as she has enjoyed in the past, for her to make a gargantuan effort of 'projection', dump the Poll Tax, win the war, call a khaki election at once (it'd be nearly four years, after all) and once again be mother of

her people. Certainly that is what I would advise. But good though she is, she's not in the shape of 1983, or even 1986 when she routed them over Westland.

2) It's A.N. Other, after a messy second ballot. Either Douglas or John Major would keep me, I'm pretty sure. Fun to watch a new administration getting the feel of things, but I would no longer be on the inner loop.

3) MH wins. Sudden Death. He might even have time to strike me off the PC list. Would anyone else refuse to serve? Cecil, I would think. Micky Forsyth[1] and Eric Forth[2] certainly ought to. Peter Lilley and the rest would just cower until he sacked them.

That's Politics (Baby).

House of Commons   *Monday, 19 November*

The whole house is in ferment. Little groups, conclaves everywhere. Only in the dining room does some convention seem to have grown up (I presume because no one trusts their dining companions) that we don't talk 'shop'.

'Made your Christmas plans yet?' All that balls. God, the dining room is boring these days, even worse than Pratts'. Big, slow, buffers 'measuring their words' oh-so-firmly; or creepy little narks talking straight out of *Conservative News*.

But in the corridors it is all furtive whispering and glancing over shoulders. The institutional confidence (seen at its most obvious in those who have served a prison term, and which I first noticed in my early days on Warren Street[3]), that special grimacing style of speech out of the corner of the mouth, eyes focusing in another direction, is now it seems the only way of communicating.

Most people are interested – not so much in the result, as in knowing what the result will be in advance, in order to make their

---

[1] Michael Forsyth, MP for Stirling since 1983. Minister of State, Scottish Office, since 1990.

[2] Eric Forth, MP for Mid-Worcestershire since 1983. Parliamentary Under-Secretary, Employment.

[3] AC worked as a dealer's runner in Warren Street (at that time the focus of the trade market in used cars) for several months after coming down from Oxford.

own 'dispositions'. To ingratiate oneself with the new regime – *a* new regime, I should say, because the outcome is by no means certain – even as little as a week before it is installed, looks better than joining the stampede afterwards. The issue, which can be discussed semi-respectably, is who is most likely to deliver victory at the General Election? But it is packaging, conceals a great basket of bitterness, thwarted personal ambition, and vindictive glee. Talk of country, or loyalty, is dismissed as 'histrionics'.

And there is a strange feeling abroad. Even if the Lady wins – and here I am writing 'even if', pull yourself together Clark, say 'even after she's won' – there will be no escaping the fact that at least one hundred and fifty of her parliamentary colleagues will have rejected her leadership. That's a big chunk. Some people, particularly those who pose as Party Elders, like Tony Grant,[1] are intimating that it might be 'better' if, faced with so blatant a show of No Confidence, she decided to 'heal' the Party by announcing her intention to stand down at a given date (i.e., become a lame duck which the Labour Party could taunt and torment on every occasion, and a busted flush internationally).

And as the savour of a Heseltine victory starts to pervade the crannies and cupboards and committee rooms, so more and more people are 'coming out'. 'Oh, I don't think he'd be so bad, really . . .' 'He's got such a wide *appeal*.' 'My people just love him, I must say . . .' 'I know what you mean, but he'd be so good at dealing with . . .' (fill in particular problem as appropriate).

Most conspicuous in canvassing are Hampson (loonily) Mates (gruffly) and Bill Powell[2] (persuasively). Michael himself is quite shameless in offering all and sundry what they have always wanted. For example, he would probably have got Paul's support anyway, but 'sealed' it with an assurance that Paul would be Speaker in the next House; Soames fell straight away for the 'your talents are long overdue for recognition' line, as did little Nelson[3] and Rhodes James ('you've been treated abominably').

Michael stands in the centre of the Members' lobby, virtually challenging people to wish him good luck. He gives snap 'updates' to

---

[1] Sir Anthony Grant, MP for Cambridgeshire South-West since 1983 (Harrow Central, 1964–83).
[2] William Powell, MP for Corby since 1983.
[3] Anthony Nelson, MP for Chichester since 1974.

journalists, and greets suppliants who are brought along for a short audience by his team. The heavier targets he sees in his room. The Cabinet play their cards close to the chest, although Mellor,[1] apparently, speaks to Michael twice a day on the telephone. Some, like Kenneth Clarke, want her out so badly that they don't need even to blink. And I would guess that there are a fair coterie of Ministers of State and Parly Secs like Sainsbury[2] and Trippier[3] who feel uneasy with the Lady and like the idea of a change.

At the top of the ministerial staircase I ran into G-J. He was bubbling with suppressed excitement. I don't think he actually wants 'Hezzy' as he (spastically) calls him, to win. It would be disruptive of the Blue Chip long-term plan. But he's high on the whole thing.

Tristan said, 'Of course every member of the Cabinet will vote for the Prime Minister in the first round.' Like hell they will.

I said to him, hoping he'd deny it, 'One cannot actually exclude the possibility that Heseltine will score more votes than her on the first ballot.'

'No, I'm afraid one can't.'

'Can one, even, be completely sure that he will not get both the largest total and the necessary margin to win without a second ballot?'

'No, I'm afraid one can't.'

This was really chilling. Apocalypse. Because time is horrendously tight if we have to organise an alternative candidate. Four working days and a weekend. But if Michael scoops it in one gulp then that is the end of everything.

Maddeningly, I had to return to the Department. Meetings, and an official lunch. Scandinavians.

'I assume that there is no likelihood of Mrs Thatcher being defeated for the position of Prime Minister?'

'Oh no. None whatever. It's just one of these quaint traditions we have in the Conservative Party.'

But the encounter made me realise the enormity of what we're doing – *changing the Prime Minister* – but without any electoral

---

[1] David Mellor, Minister of State, Home Office, since 1989.
[2] Tim Sainsbury, MP for Hove since 1973, at that time a Parliamentary Secretary at the Foreign Office.
[3] David Trippier, MP for Rossendale since 1979. Minister of State, Department of Environment, since 1989.

authority so to do. I thought I'd have a talk to Peter,[1] although he doesn't encourage it, and I cancelled my early afternoon engagements and went back over to the House.

I listened outside the door. Silence. I knocked softly, then tried the handle. He was asleep, snoring lightly, in the leather armchair, with his feet resting on the desk.

Drake playing bowls before the Armada and all that, but I didn't like it. This was ten minutes past three in the afternoon of the most critical day of the whole election. I spoke sharply to him. 'Peter.'

He was bleary.

'I'm sorry to butt in, but I'm really getting a bit worried about the way things are going.'

'Quite all right, old boy, relax.'

'I'm just hearing bad reactions around the place from people where I wouldn't expect it.'

'Look, do you think I'd be like this if I wasn't entirely confident?'

'What's the arithmetic look like?'

'Tight-ish, but OK.'

'Well, what?'

'I've got Michael on 115. It could be 124, at the worst.'

'Look, Peter, I don't think people are being straight with you.'

'I have my ways of checking.'

'Paul?'

'I know about Paul.'

'The Wintertons?'[2]

'The Wintertons, funnily enough, I've got down as "Don't Know's".'

'What the fuck do you mean, "*Don't Know*"? This isn't a fucking street canvas. It's a two-horse race, and each vote affects the relative score by two, unless it's an abstention.'

'Actually, I think there could be quite a few abstentions.'

'Don't you think we should be out there twisting arms?'

'No point. In fact it could be counter-productive. I've got a theory about this. I think some people may abstain on the first ballot in order to give Margaret a fright, then rally to her on the second.' (Balls, I thought, but didn't say.)

---

[1] Peter Morrison was in charge of Mrs Thatcher's campaign.
[2] Nick Winterton, MP for Macclesfield since 1971, and his wife Ann, MP for Congleton since 1983.

'What about the '92? They're completely rotten. They've got a meeting at six. Are you going?'

'No point. But I think *you* should.'

In deep gloom I walked back down Speaker's corridor. It can't really be as bad as this can it? I mean there is absolutely no oomph in her campaign *whatsoever*. Peter is useless, far worse than I thought. When he was pairing Whip he was unpopular, but at least he was crisp. Now he's sozzled. There isn't a single person working for her who cuts any ice at all. I know it's better to be feared than loved. But these people aren't either. And she's in Paris. '*Où est la masse de manoeuvre? -Aucune.*'

I went into the members' tea room. The long table was crowded with Margaret supporters, all nonentities except for Tebbit who was cheering people up. Much shouting and laughter. Blustering reassurance. Norman was saying how unthinkable it was to consider dismissing a Prime Minister during a critical international conference. 'Like Potsdam in 1945,' I said. No one paid any attention. If they heard they didn't, or affected not to, understand the allusion.

The crowd thinned out a little and when he got up Norman said that he wanted a word. We went into the Aye lobby and sat at that round table in the centre with all the stationery on it.

'Well . . . ?'

'It's filthy,' I said.

'It could be close. Very close.'

I agreed, '*Fucking* close.'

'If it's like that do you think she should stand in the second ballot?'

I simply don't know the answer to this. Governing would be very difficult with half the Party against her. She might have to make 'concessions' to the left. I asked Norman if he thought she would have to bring Heseltine into the Cabinet?

'She'd certainly be under a lot of pressure to do so.'

'Renton.'

'Yeah.'

I said that the key tactic was to get Chris Patten to stand, and draw off the left vote. At least the hard left vote, Charlie Morrison, Bob Hicks,[1] all the wankers. Norman said, 'And Ken Clarke.' I told him no, if you have too many candidates people just get in a muddle and

---

[1] Robert Hicks, MP for Cornwall South-East since 1983 (Bodmin, 1970-March 1974; October 1974–83).

Heseltine walks through them, just as she did in 1975. Norman said that a lot of people now regarded Michael as a *right*-wing candidate anyway.

'Well, we know different.'

'Too true.'

Norman said, 'If it's open season, I'm dam' well going to put my name in. The right must have a candidate they can vote for.'

'You'd lose.'

'It's likely I would, but at least we'd know our strength. That could be useful in a changed situation.'

'Look, Norman, we want to put additional names in to reduce *his* total, not ours. I don't think Heseltine has that big a personal vote. It's just an anti-Margaret coalition.'

I could see he was thoughtful. But he didn't want to prolong the conversation, which we were conducting in tones just above a whisper, though still arousing the curious attention of passers-by.

Raising his voice Norman said, 'Well, this time tomorrow everything will be settled,' and gave one of his graveyard cackles.

The '92 meeting was in one of those low-ceilinged rooms on the upper committee room corridor. The mood was tetchy, and apprehensive. There was a kind of fiction running from several (Jill Knight, for example, shockingly), just as Norman had foreseen, that 'Michael' – as defectors call him (supporters of the Prime Minister always refer to him as 'Heseltine'; and this is quite a useful subliminal indicator of how the speaker is going to vote when he or she is being deliberately or defensively opaque) – was 'really' on the right.

The trouble with this club, to which I was elected almost as soon as I arrived here, but with which I have never really felt comfortable, is that it personifies in extreme form two characteristics found in the majority of MPs – stupidity and egomania. It is only the shrewd and subtle guidance of George Gardiner[1] that has prevented them becoming a laughing stock in recent years. But such integrity as they might originally have possessed has been eroded by the inclusion of many from marginal seats. None are quite as awful as Elizabeth

---

[1] Sir George Gardiner, MP for Reigate since 1974. Secretary of '92.

Peacock, who spoke squatly and fatly against Margaret – why bother, she won't be here in the next Parliament anyway[1] – but most are concerned solely with saving their own skins. I spoke loyally and, should have been movingly, of our debt of loyalty to the PM. But there was a hint of what's-she-ever-done-for-us from the audience and with some justification, so few ministerial appointments having come out of the '92. I tried to make their flesh creep with what Michael would do, got only a subdued ritual cheer when I said Margaret is undefeated, and never will be defeated either in the Country or in this House of Commons. I'm not particularly popular with that lot. They think I'm 'snooty'. Perhaps my boredom threshold shows. But in the ballot tomorrow I'd say they will divide no better than 60/40.

After dinner I had a word with Norman Lamont. He'd just come back from somewhere-or-other. 'I don't like the smell,' he kept saying. 'There's a bad smell to the whole place.' He's right, of course. It's the smell of decay. It's affecting everything, the badge messengers, the police, the drivers. Something nasty is going to happen.

I write this very late, and I am very tired. Perhaps I'm just needlessly depressed. I'd ring the Lady if I could, but she's at a banquet. She's not even coming back for the ballot. Lovely and haughty.

Albany   *Tuesday, 20 November*

I was at my desk in MoD early, but spent most of the first hour scanning the newspapers. At nine o'clock Carla Powell rang. 'We must do something about poor Bruce.[2] Couldn't you ring Conrad Black, and get him to give Bruce back his job?'

I told her that we were all in limbo. No one, not even Mrs T. herself could today cut any ice at all with anyone.

'Poor Bruce. It's so unfair.'

Yes, yes. I quite agree, it's awful. Everything's awful. It was a little

---

[1] In fact the prediction by AC was in the result shown to be defective. In the 1992 General Election she retained her seat by a margin of 1408.

[2] Bruce Anderson, columnist on the *Sunday Telegraph*, had been fired following an alleged breach of confidential information.

foretaste, the first one, of how diminished how deprived of influence and access we are all soon to become.

Of course I write this very late on the night, in the full knowledge and shock of what has happened. But I think that even this morning we, those of us who can *feel* these things, were despondent, fatalistic.

I worked for most of the morning and had lunch, a long-standing engagement with Robert Campling.[1] Hard to get further away from politics than that. Alison brought him down to the Strangers' tearoom, and the three of us talked about his ideas for Bratton, about Charleston, and Bloomsbury matters in general.

The afternoon hung interminably. Labour MPs were everywhere, ghoulish and heavy-handed with their jokes. Our fellows seemed all to be in hiding.

As is my style at all 'counts' I went up to the committee floor very late. A huge crowd in the corridor. The entire lobby, TV teams from all over the world. (How did they get in, pray – all part of the general breakdown of order and discipline which is licking, like stubble fire, at everything in the Palace these last two days.)

There was, inevitably, a balls-up over the figures. We, the Tory MPs, packed tight and hot and jumpily joking to each other in the committee room, did not (a monstrous error by Cranley Onslow, for which he will pay at the next election[2]) get the figures first. We heard a loud noise, something between a gasp and a cheer, from outside the door, as the journalists digested first the closeness of the result, then the killer element – that there had under the rules to be a second ballot.

Four votes, that was all there was in it. I get so cross when I remember Peter Morrison asleep in his office. For want of a nail a kingdom was lost.

I dined with Jonathan Aitken and Nick Budgen. Bruce was at the table. To my amazement they were all confident. 'She'll wipe the floor with him next time round.' 'The abstainers will all come in.' 'You don't understand, Alan, all those people who wanted to give her a fright, they'll support her now she's up against it.'

---

[1] Robert Campling, a young artist who paints in the Bloomsbury style and whom AC had commissioned to redecorate certain rooms at Bratton.
[2] The error was to give the voting figures to the press first. At the next election for the chairmanship of the 1922 Committee Onslow was defeated by Sir Marcus Fox.

How can people get things so wrong?

Perhaps there was a lot of this kind of muddled thinking around before the ballot. But that's historic. She's a loser, now. Doomed.

I hardly bothered to argue with them. I suppose my dejection was infectious because, by the coffee, we were all silent. Save Bruce who, although jobless, is going to shut himself away and do a Randolph,[1] an instant book on the leadership campaign.

At the ten o'clock vote Tristan found me in the lobby, pulled me into the window bay by the writing table. 'We're meeting at my house, straight after this.'

'Who's "we"?'

'Oh just a few mates; *Chris* and people. We need to talk through the next steps.'

'How do you mean?'

'Ways of supporting the Prime Minister.'

But he wouldn't accede to any of my suggestions; Aitken, Maude, David Davis[2] or Lilley, in that order. Even Andrew MacKay (not obviously of the right, as were the others) caused Tristan to pull a long face.

'We're all friends. It's a very small gathering, we all know each other and can speak freely . . . '

As soon as I walked into the room it was apparent why no one else from the right had been allowed in. 'Blue-Chips' wall-to-wall. Five Cabinet Ministers. Rifkind, who was the most dominant, and effective; C. Patten, also good but (relatively) taciturn; Newton, and Waldegrave.

Waldegrave was sympathetic, in a relaxed, jokey way. The only person to say what a personal tragedy it was for her, how she was still of a different dimension to all the others. Lamont was there, stood throughout, Mephistophelean in his black tie. He shocked me by saying at the outset that he could conceive of Michael as being quite an 'effective', *tolerable* (sic) Prime Minister.

Patten said, 'Well, he's not mad, is he? I mean after you've had a

---

[1] In 1963 Randolph Churchill wrote *The Fight for the Tory Leadership: A Contemporary Chronicle* (Heinemann) an account of the way in which the Conservative Party selected Lord Home as leader following the resignation of Harold Macmillan.

[2] David Davis, MP for Boothferry since 1987. PPS to Eric Forth, Parliamentary Under-Secretary, DTI.

meal with him you don't get up from the table and think, that fellow
was mad, do you?'

There were three Ministers of State in the room, besides myself,
Hogg and John Patten. Tim Yeo[1] was there 'representing' Hurd,
whose PPS he is, but stayed silent.

Douglas Hogg piped up, 'I think any one of us could serve under
him [Michael].' And there was a sort of cautious mumble of assent.
What I assume he meant, of course, was, 'I don't think any one in
this room is likely to be sacked – so we can all enjoy ourselves.' Mutual
preening took place.

I said it wasn't quite as easy as that. What we had to ensure was
that the person who replaces her is the one most likely to win the
Election.

'All right, then, Al; what do you think?'

Michael was unreliable, I argued. Any electoral capital he brought
would soon be expended. What we needed now was a Baldwin,
someone to reassure rather than stimulate. I expanded, people were
nodding. But when I said Tom King, Chris Patten laughed aloud.
And John P., taking his cue, said, 'I presume you're joking.'

Tristan said, 'Come on, Al, you'll have to do better than that.'

Only Douglas Hogg, surprisingly, admitted that he saw the point.

I had one more go. I did *not* say that Tom was Willie's choice as
well as mine. That might have generated a class backlash. But I dwelt
on his overall departmental experience in Northern Ireland, how
good he was on the stump, as I had often seen.

Yet as I was speaking it dawned on me that winning the Election
was not uppermost in all their minds. They were, most of them,
twenty years younger than me, carving out their own career prospects
and wanting to identify with the new winner.

Not only was there no one of my generation, there was no one
(although Richard, who is a Norfolk Squire, came in very much later)
of my background. There was no one, except possibly Tris, who
understands and loves the Tory Party for all its faults, knows it as an
old whore that has been around for 400 years.

Young Turks. And Young Turks are bad news, unless there is some
dilution. They all poke fun at Tom now. But if he became Prime
Minister, assumed the authority, he could metamorphose and

---

[1] Tim Yeo, MP for Suffolk South since 1983. He had been PPS to the Foreign
Secretary since 1989.

put them all in irons. The old Postman in Remarque's *All Quiet . . .*

Although I had been expecting Tristan to try and rig it for John Major, the concensus did in fact build up quite rapidly for Douglas. I remained doubtful. He is *too* much of an Establishment candidate.

Of course, this is a crisis for the Establishment, and they have left it horrendously late to organise. But DH looks, speaks, moves, articulates as prototypical Establishment. I'm not sure the Party wants that. It's very risky, unless there is another candidate from the left who will peel off a tranche of Heseltine's total.

It is difficult. If we confine the contest to two candidates, the issues are starker. If there are more than two there will be some cross-transferring, but there remains a danger that Michael's core vote will be strong enough – just as she herself (opposed by the Establishment) was in 1975. Never mind the abstruse calculations according to the 'Rules', the third ballot is a foregone conclusion. Whoever gets the highest total next time, wins.

It was only when I got back here, at ten minutes to one a.m. that it dawned on me: at least five of the people in that room fancied themselves as 'New Generation' candidates, in the nearish future. They want Douglas, but *as a caretaker.* They're not quite ready, themselves. As we were breaking up one – it could have been William – actually said, 'If we put John in, he'll be there for twenty-five years.'

The really sickening thing, though, was the urgent and unanimous abandonment of the Lady. Except for William's little opening tribute, she was never mentioned again.

Albany   *Wednesday, 21 November*

This is going to be – politically – The Longest Day. I woke very early, in spite of having gone to bed at twenty past one, and with a restless energy matched only by that on the February morning in 1986 when I knew that at last I had escaped from the DE and was to be appointed Minister for Trade. Yet today it is the exact reverse. Not only my own prospects, but the whole edifice which we have constructed around the Lady, are in ruins.

It's quite extraordinary. Fifteen years have gone by and yet those very same people – Dykes, Charlie Morrison, Tony Grant, Barney Hayhoe[1] – who have always hated her and the values she stood for, are still around in the lobbies, barely looking any different, grinning all over their faces – 'At last we've got her.'

I can't think of a single anti-Thatcherite who has died or receded throughout that entire period.

By 6.30 my tea was cold and I had read the papers. Still an assumption, in some columns, that Michael will be defeated in the second ballot – but by whom?

Always remember what she did in '75; all that shit about now its 'really' going to be Willie, or Jim Prior,[2] or you name it. The Party may be just entering on one of its periodic bouts of epilepsy.

I put a call through to Paris. They're one hour ahead, and I wanted to interrupt the pre-breakfast conference. Peter came on the line. I said I must have two minutes with her. Charles would have always put me through. So would Bernard. He gave me the usual runaround. Frightfully tied up just at this minute, try and fit it in before we go down to breakfast . . .

'Go *down* to? Don't you have it in the room?'

'There's a Working Breakfast.'

'With a lot of fucking foreigners, I suppose. I want to talk to her about last night.' I gave him a (selective) résumé of events at Catherine Place.

'I'll try and call you back.'

'When?'

'Well, within half an hour.'

'Peter, you will tell her I rang, won't you?'

'Yes, yes. Yes.'

'Because if you tell her, she will call me. And if she doesn't call me, I'll know it's because you haven't told her.'

High-pitched giggle. 'Don't worry. I'll tell her.' He won't though. Cunt.

---

[1] Sir Barney Hayhoe, MP for Brentford since 1970.
[2] Jim Prior (Life Peer 1987). MP for Lowestoft, 1959–83 (Waveney 1983–7). A former Leader of the Commons, Secretary of State for Employment and Northern Ireland Secretary.

Later
Ministry of Defence

No work is being done in Whitehall today, whatsoever. My 'In'-tray is about an inch deep. I don't think a single Minister in the Govt will be at his desk; or if he is, it will be only so as to telephone to a colleague or to a journalist. The civil servants (all of whom, down to Principal level, I suspect, were terrified of the Lady) just can not believe their eyes.

Yet still she won't return. There is talk of a 'fighting statement' later. But this wastage of time in Paris is sheer lunacy. Harold at Stamford Bridge.

It is the general sense of disintegration now affecting everything, that is so damaging to her. Unless MH is slaughtered in the final ballot – impossibly unlikely – she herself is going to find it highly difficult to reassert her authority, even if eventually she emerges as the victor. Short, that is, of giving them the full coup-loser's treatment – arrest, manacles, beaten up in the interrogation room, shot while trying to escape. Real blood, in other words. Fun, but a bit *Angolan*.

Before walking over to the House I called Andrew MacKay into my room and we had a long talk about Tom. Earlier, we had both lingered after Ministers and sounded him.

Tom likes the idea, preened himself, straightened his jacket; but he is cautious. He would need to be sure of at least thirty votes to even 'put down a marker'. And in any case, convention obliges that no member of the Cabinet puts his name forward while she is still standing. (I hear rumours that that pudgy puff-ball Kenneth Clarke is considering breaching this, but am keeping that in reserve.)

'Look,' I told him. 'If the Lady is doomed, our Number One priority is to find, and instal a leader who will win the next General Election. And we haven't got long. Who is best suited to do this?'

I told him that Heseltine would burn out very quickly. His rhetoric pleased Party Conference, but was less reliable in the national context. Anyway people are sick of passion, they want reassurance.

The only two figures who can do this are Tom and John Major. Douglas is now past it; is thought rightly or wrongly to be a buffer and a bureaucrat. John is more engaging than Tom in some ways, with a lovely grin, but seems really too youthful. There is no time to project him. Even in the House he is barely known, has never been seen under fire. Tom, on the other hand, does have gravitas. Also he's good on the stump, in small groups, canteens and so on.

Andrew was in broad agreement. But:

'Tom won't make a move while she's still in the field.'

'So what do we do?'

'I tell you what I'm doing, if she stands second time round – voting for Michael.'

I was appalled. Here was this good, intelligent man, tough and (in so far as it still means anything) right wing... More than any other experience this conversation has made me realise that she will lose, finally, head-to-head against Heseltine. But if she does stand again we are in a log-jam; the only people who will join in the contest are wankers like Clarke who are not worth twenty-five votes.

Andrew said that he would, very quietly, take soundings for Tom. The immediate priority is to find a way, tactfully and skilfully, to talk her out of standing a second time.

Now I must close this entry and walk over to the House.

House of Commons

I was greeted with the news that there had been an announcement. 'I fight, and I fight to win.' God alive!

Tebbit is holding an impromptu press conference in the Members' lobby.

Fifty feet away, down the tea-room corridor that mad ninny Hampson is dancing around on his tippy-toes calling out to passers-by, 'Tee-hee, she's standing. We've made it. We can't lose now, etc.'

I came back here, to my room. I kept the door open and an endless succession of visitors trooped in and out. No one seems to have any idea of what we should do. Her 'Campaign' is a shambles now. John Moore (who he?) is running around with bits of paper – 'draft statements' – asking people what they think. He seems to have a temporary HQ in Portillo's room, which is next door to mine. First I heard that Norman Fowler was going to take charge; then John Wakeham. Or was it the other way round? Gamelin's been sacked, Weygand is on the way out; Pétain's in the wings. '*Où est la masse de manoeuvre? – Aucune.*'

Every time I trawl the corridors I run into another batch of chaps who say they're going to switch, or abstain, or when-are-there-going-to-be-some-more-candidates-to-choose-from? The only visitor who has made any real sense is Francis Maude. He claims, forcefully, that John Major has a better chance than we all realise. But John won't make a move while the Lady remains in the field. 'I must get to see her. Can you help?' Apparently Peter stands sentinel, and is outside her door the whole time.

I have closed the door. These random conversations are too discursive. Tomorrow is the last day for nominations. I must clear my head.

1) If she fights head on, she loses.

2) Therefore, the opposition vote has got to be diluted by a candidate from the left – preferably Patten, making it triangular. Besides dilution, this has the advantage that it will crack Cabinet 'solidarity' open and others may lose their scruples. Therefore:

3) Try and talk Patten into standing. QED.

Archie Hamilton's just been in. Didn't make any sense. One minute he says she 'could still' win; the next that we've all 'had it'. I'm off now, upstairs.

Later
Kundan Restaurant
It is very late, and finally I have withdrawn here for a vegetable curry, and to write up the traumatic happenings of this evening.

I made first for Chris's room. On the way I passed her outer door and said to Peter that I must have a minute or so. He looked anxious, almost rattled, which he never does normally. 'I'll do my best. She's seeing every member of the Cabinet in turn ... '

'Francis wants to see her too.'

'I'm doing my best.'

Chris wasn't in his room. The Secretary of State's corridor was deserted. Hushed, but you could feel the static.

The policeman by the lift said he was 'in with Mr Rifkind'.

I knocked and went in without waiting for an answer. Also in there, loathesomely conspiring, was little Kenneth Clarke. Her three great ill-wishers! Clarke wasn't friendly at all. If he'd said anything to me, I'd have answered 'Fuck you', so just as well.

Chris was quite amiable.

'How many votes she got at the moment?'

'It's a rout. She's down to ninety.'

'*Ninety?*'

'You've got to stand. You can't let Michael corner the left.'

He was diplomatic. A discussion was impossible. God knows what they were talking about, but it stank. Never mind, I have sowed the seed; or watered what was already there.

I went down the stairs and rejoined the group outside her door. After a bit Peter said, 'I can just fit you in now – but only for a split second, mind.'

She looked calm, almost beautiful. 'Ah, Alan...'

'You're in a jam.'

'I know that.'

'They're all telling you not to stand, aren't they?'

'I'm going to stand. I have issued a statement.'

'That's wonderful. That's heroic. But the Party will let you down.'

'I am a fighter.'

'Fight, then. Fight right to the end, a third ballot if you need to. But you lose.'

There was quite a little pause.

'It'd be so terrible if Michael won. He would undo everything I have fought for.'

'But what a way to go! Unbeaten in three elections, never rejected by the people. Brought down by nonentities!'

'But Michael... as *Prime Minister.*'

'Who the fuck's Michael? No one. Nothing. He won't last six months. I doubt if he'd even win the Election. Your place in history is towering...'

Outside, people were doing that maddening trick of opening and shutting the door, at shorter and shorter intervals.

'Alan, it's been so good of you to come in and see me...'

Afterwards I felt empty. And cross. I had failed, but I didn't really know what I wanted, except for her still to be Prime Minister, and it wasn't going to work out.

I sat on the bench immediately behind the Speaker's chair, watching the coming and going. After a bit Tristan came and sat beside me. But he had little to say. What is there to say? She's still seeing visitors. Then, along came Edwina.

'Hullo, aren't you Edwina Currie?'[1]

'Now then, Alan, there's no need to be objectionable.'

'If that is who you are, I must congratulate you on the combination

---

[1] Edwina Currie, MP for Derbyshire South since 1983.

of loyalty and restraint that you have shown in going on television to announce your intention to vote against the Prime Minister in the Leadership Election.'

'Alan, I'm perfectly prepared to argue this through with you, if you'll listen.'

'Piss off.'

Which she did.

Tristan said, 'She's not a bad girl really.'

At half past eight I left to come over here. The archway exit from Speaker's Court was blocked by the PM's Jaguar. She had just taken her seat, and as the detective's door slammed the interior light went out and the car slid away. I realised with a shock that this was in all probability her last night as Prime Minister. I came in with her. I go out with her, and a terrible sadness envelops me – of unfinished duties and preoccupations; of dangers and injustices remaining, of the greed, timidity and short-sightedness of so many in public life.

Albany   *Thursday, 22 November*

Very early this morning the phone rang. It was Tristan.

'She's going.'

There will be an official announcement immediately after a short Cabinet, first thing. Then the race will be on. Apparently Douglas *and* John Major are going to stand. I said I thought it was crazy, Heseltine will go through between them. I could sense him shrugging. 'There you go.'

Anyway, would I come over to his room at the Foreign Office and watch it from there?

Afterwards, very *triste* and silent, I walked back to the MoD and sat in on a late (and unnecessary) Ministers' meeting. Tom told us that it had been 'awful'. She started to read a prepared statement to them, then broke down, and the text had to be finished by the Lord Chancellor.

Listless, I drifted over to the House. I had a word with Charles, drafted a couple of valedictory passages for her speech[1] this afternoon, did I don't know how many impromptu TV bites.

---

[1] Not in fact used. Mrs Thatcher told AC that if she had, she would have broken down again.

Heseltine is meant to be coming to Plymouth tomorrow, for a fundraising dinner. I rang Judith,[1] told her we couldn't possibly allow him to use us as a platform to plug his own candidature. She only half agreed, so I immediately telephoned to the *Western Morning News* and told them that I had 'instructed' that the invitation be withdrawn. (Not unrich, considering I was not the host, and had long ago told everyone that I wanted nothing to do with it.)

I didn't think I could bear it, but curiosity drew me into the Chamber for the Lady's last performance. It would have been too macabre to have sat in my habitual place, next to her PPS, so I watched and listened first from behind the Chair, then from the Bar of the House. She was brilliant. Humorous, self-deprecating, swift and deadly in her argument and in her riposte. Even Dennis Skinner, her oldest adversary was feeding her lines; and at one point Michael Carttiss[2] shouted, 'You could wipe the floor with the lot of 'em.'

Too bloody true. What is to become of her? Aclimatisation will be agony, because she is not of that philosophic turn of mind that would welcome a spell at Colombey. Can she just remain on the back benches? It will be hard. What happens when she starts to be 'missed', and the rose-tinted spectacles are found in everyone's breast pocket?

This evening I had a strange, possibly a significant experience. There is a semi permanent prefab studio on College Green, where endless conclaves of MPs record their comments on the respective vices and virtues of the second-round candidates. Around it are many secondary groupings, each with a shoulder-held video and a very bright light, recording any, yes any, it seems, comment by any, yes, any one who is going past.

Emerging from this brilliantly lit pool into the darkness at its edge, I was accosted by a familiar figure who, being dazzled, I did not at first recognise.

'Hey, Alan, take a look at this.'

It was Bob Worcester.[3] He showed me a poll, the first to be run, asking how respondents would vote if (names) were leading the Tory Party. One of Michael's great hidden strengths has always been the huge margin which he had over Mrs Thatcher in this very context.

---

[1] Judith Roberts, Chairman of the Sutton Division.
[2] Michael Carttiss, MP for Great Yarmouth since 1983.
[3] Robert Worcester. Head of MORI, the opinion polls organisation.

To my amazement, I saw that John Major had already drawn level! And in one case was actually ahead, actually preferred – notwithstanding the *continuous* exposure which Michael has had these last two weeks.

'Christ, Bob, these have to be rogue figures.'

Bob took umbrage. 'Look, Alan, we're MORI. We don't have "rogue" figures.'

This could be critically important. If John can break through here, he's won.

Not so many in the Party really want to vote Heseltine, for himself. Some do, and will, just to spite her. But the bulk of Michael's support comes from his so-called Election winning powers. People have guilt about condoning what he did to Her. Once they have a real reason to do so, they'll abandon him.

Tomorrow's papers will tell us more. I am taking an early train to Plymouth to 'sound out' feeling (i.e., get cover for the way I cast my vote). But even if I can't get a single person in the town to tell me to vote for John Major, that's what I'm going to do.

In the Ruler of Oman's DC9   *Wednesday, 28 November*

I am winging my way out to the Gulf.[1] I am *not* a Minister, as Private Office were (unhealthily) eager to explain to me. So there will be no HE to greet me with his Union Jack bedecked Jaguar. I will have no status with dignitaries or administrators (like hell, I thought, just watch me). This is because, with a new PM, all ministerial appointments lapse, revert to his gift, and have to be 'confirmed'.

Immediately in front of me is the bald pate, surrounded tonsure-like by a wreath of wispy white hair, of my old friend the distinguished historian Alistair Horne. He wrote *The Price of Glory*, that brilliant and harrowing study of the battle of Verdun; still, I believe, the best of non-contemporary accounts of the Great War. But after that he went a bit soft, and got heavily involved with Macmillan who I still think would have been better done by Robert Rhodes J. I remember once in the Fifties when Alistair and his wife at the time, Renira,

---

[1] The *Cercle*, an Atlanticist Society of right-wing dignitaries, largely compered by Julian Amery and Herr Franz-Joseph Bach, staged one or two conferences a year and this one was travelling to Oman at the hospitality of the Ruler.

came to stay at the Chalet, a very handsome couple, tall and athletic, and skied with us. Why do I make these little obituary-like notes when I run into friends from former times? They always look older than me, sometimes at death's door. But there is a *Recherche du Temps Perdu* aspect as well. My other life.

Now we are all on our way to Muscat, as guests of the Ruler, the whole thing most ably arranged by dear Julian Amery, so that one can be confident that it will be smooth, interesting, and subject to much deference. There is a distinguished attendance list, and Jonathan Aitken, who knows absolutely everybody in the world has, amusingly and indiscreetly, guided me through it.

It is pleasing to be at 35,000 feet, carving our route to the warm waters of the Arabian Gulf, while behind in Britain colleagues lick their wounds, or feel stale with anti-climax. Was it only last night that Jane and I watched Cranley, on the TV screen in Needham's office,[1] bellowing the figures, and then very shortly after, Michael conceded?

There was one strange, unscripted episode. Very late in the evening, after I had seen Jane off in the car, I was coming up that back staircase which leads from the transport office and comes out in the Members' lobby. At the last turn in the landing I heard the top door open in a rush and there, quite alone, wild-eyed and head to head stood Heseltine.

'Hullo Michael,' I said.

He made no answer, rushed past. He could say he had 'cut' me. But he was a zombie, shattered.

It was Mates who brought him the numbers. Must it not at that moment have been:

> A Great Hope fell.
> You heard no noise
> The Ruin was Within.[2]

Later
Eighth floor at the Al Bustan
I have a vast suite here. Bedroom, master bedroom, bodyguard's bedroom. Sitting room, dining room, conference room, ante-room (for the bodyguard).

---

[1] Richard Needham (Earl of Kilmorey, but does not use the title). MP for Wiltshire North since 1983 (Chippenham, 1979–83).
[2] Emily Dickinson.

With all my traveller's experience, I still think this is the best hotel in the world, with its incredible hall, like the new Mosque in Islamabad, and a thousand minions to bring room service at any time of the day or night. There is a French restaurant, an Italian restaurant, and an Arabic restaurant, and always the sound of wavelets caressing the soft sand of the beach.

Andrew[1] appeared, tall and beautiful as ever. He moves among the delegates with a very faint smile on his face, but his eyes are always watching. What experience in childhood, what gene, makes him instinctively so observant, and from which side of the family does this gene come?

There was the sound of water sloshing, and the head of the Dutch Secret Service emerged through a swing door, looking haggard, but relieved.

'Greywater after the flight,' said Andrew. 'Airline food.'

I detached myself from the group and we had supper together. Andrew told me of his tales, and of the mood among the Military. Oman is a long way from Iraq, and their traditional apprehension is of Iranian muscle, their principal irritant is South Yemen. But the men, many of them, think privately of Saddam as a hero, who is leading the West a dance.

A certain undercurrent against the 'white-eyes'.

Can it have felt like this in Cawnpore, in 1857?

Al Bustan, Muscat   *Friday, 30 November*

I sit at my balcony. It is not yet 6 a.m. and all is still, save for the soft-soled attendants who are cleaning, bleaching, arranging the towels, chairs and surroundings of the vast swimming pool, a hundred feet below.

Last night our delegation had dinner with the Ruler, Sheikh Qaboos, at the Barakha Palace. The drive was nearly a mile long, and every palm tree was floodlit. On either side of the entrance there were great braziers of smouldering frankincense, and the odour was all pervading.

---

[1] AC's younger son Andrew, a Major in the Life Guards, was serving as 2 i/c of the Sultan's Armoured Force.

It was a buffet, but one a very long way, in every sense, from the second floor of the Guildhall in Plymouth. The boards groaned; superlative and exotic dishes that one could eat with confidence. I could have stuffed for hours, and become bloated. But there appeared to be some convention governing the courses (was my gluttony leading me into solecisms?), because at intervals the whole dining tent went still, and the Ruler would suddenly click his fingers, rise and sweep over to lead a new assault on the tables.

Qaboos had put me on his left, with Julian in the place of honour on the Ruler's right hand. He is intelligent, quick, almost feline in his responses, and commands the most perfect English – a mixture of Sandringham and Miss Newman.

In contrast to the other Ruling Families on whom I had called in August, he is not frightened of Saddam. And his contempt for the oily little King of Jordan, who is, was palpable. Qaboos said that Saddam was, at this moment, scared, but that he was a 'slippery fellow' and had a reputation in the bazaars, which he cultivates, for getting out of scrapes.

'He's going to need an awful lot of MiG's to get out of this one,' I said.

But Qaboos was thoughtful. Arab coalitions are fragile creatures, he told me. If it should be thought that Saddam may survive there are many who would like to 'take insurance'.

Qaboos is delightful company. Wholly royal in manner and deportment, but never *remote*. He engages with you. Detached yes, but so different from the Windsors (except the dear QM) who are all of them remote – and obtuse.

At lunch I had sat next to General Schwarzkopf,[1] and formed a high opinion of him. At West Point he was an amateur wrestler, and looks it. But he has a keen brain and an infectious humour. Earlier he had given us a most competent and interesting 'presentation'.

Schwarzkopf was in Vietnam, first as an Adviser, then in command of a battalion, and has no illusions as to the military prowess of Third World countries. He told me his one dread was to find his spearhead still stuck in the 'berms' and wadis of the enemy line at first light after a night attack, and then to be drenched with chemicals. Gas is of little

---

[1] General Norman Schwarzkopf, Commander of the US forces in the Gulf, who would gain celebrity during the Gulf War.

value in the mobile battle, but can be seriously nasty against fixed positions.

Already this morning I have swum. The sea temperature must be about 85°. I walked the length of the beach, barefooted on the volcanic sand, in a state of reflective melancholy, brooding on the sadness of affairs of the heart, and unrequited prospects.

'Behold a gift, designed to kill.'[1] Whenever I am in the desert I think always of that brilliant, worrying poem and its strange imagery.

My own career is now on a descending parabola. The events of last week have inserted a new generation and, episode by episode, the effects will make themselves felt.

Both Jonathan [Aitken] and Paul [Channon] are teasing me mercilessly, and with not a little secret spite, about how probable it is that ('sadly') I will be left out of John Major's new administration.

'You've lost your protector,' Paul kept saying.

Rude, because it implies that I have no individual merit, just held the job(s) down for seven years because I was a favourite. There are no true friends in politics.

We are all sharks circling, and waiting, for traces of blood to appear in the water.

Now I am going to start work on the script of my lecture. I am lying low this morning, in order to get it polished, although I fear it will not be widely welcomed. This entire outing is a right-wing think (or rather thought) tank, funded by the CIA, which churns Cold War concepts around. I am going to tell them that the Cold War is over and NATO is washed up, unnecessary, a waste of time and money and (as is the 'streetwise' expression) space.

Al Bustan   *Saturday, 1 December*

I had a good meeting with Erik Bennett.[2] He is a courtier of the very highest class. What are the characteristics? The voice, the intonation, the clarity of diction. The superficial speaking well of all and everyone.

---

[1] Keith Douglas.

[2] Air Marshal Sir Erik Bennett, Commander, Sultan of Oman's Air Force since 1974.

The way all communication occurs by the lightest of implied comment. Smooth, unwrinkled skin, and limitless endurance through ceremonial tedium. Also, in Erik's case, intelligence and wit.

He has set up a draft letter 'from' HM inquiring about surplus military equipment sales after (EB said) 'rapprochement with Iraq'. I substituted 'a clearer determination of unpredictability in the region', which he admitted was preferable.

Last night another huge dinner, given by the distinguished Doctor Omar. In contrast to the previous evening the pleasures of the flesh were much in evidence. Lashings of alcohol – the claret was all '85, and there were some wonderful white Burgundies. Sinuous and scented lovelies shimmered about.

At the end of the meal a belly dancer performed. On and on she went with graceful, but ever more suggestive, rhythms. Her stamina was unbelievable and never once did she repeat herself. From time to time she 'fixed' particular guests in their places, a special treat.

But she was defeated by Anthony Cavendish, who had early on become tired and was fast asleep, head on his chest.

There was a French Admiral sitting next to me, his face expressionless. I said, it helps one to understand how women can experience ten or eleven orgasms in one night. Myself, three render me *complètement, totalement épuisé*. Ruefully, he agreed.

Albany   *Thursday, 6 December*

There was a rumour running round the Lobby that Tom, who had gone to Brussels to attend some idiotic NATO meeting, had been taken ill with 'flu' (covers everything) and come back prone, on a stretcher.

I kept my ears pricked, and at the ten o'clock vote Andrew MacKay *pulled* me from the chamber and recounted that Tom had been 'taken straight to' St Thomas's and operated on immediately for a quite minor 'blockage' (uh?) in his 'back passage'.

'Quite,' I said, and, 'What bad luck', thinking I hope that never happens to me.

I went back to Brooks's, where I was playing in the backgammon tournament, in high spirits. Room here for some fantasising.

When finally I left the Club Bruce Anderson was standing on the pavement with a pretty willowy blonde in a black coat. 'What's happened? What's the matter? What's he got?'

I was in good form and treated it lightly. 'I don't know, I wasn't in the theatre.'

She giggled. Are, suddenly, the stars running?

Albany   *Monday, 10 December*

This evening I gave the Liddell Hart Memorial lecture at King's. My text was a cleaned up version of the 'NATO today – a bureaucracy in search of a pension' theme, with which I had teased the Cercle at the Muscat seminar.

It went well, and afterwards Laurie Freedman[1] and Frank Cooper (both good judges) were appreciative.

But for me, it was symbolic. Basil was my tutor in Military History, and in much about life, as well. He was godfather to James, and nurtured me when I was young and obstreperous and made mistakes. But he always had faith in me, told people like Michael Howard[2] who (quite understandably) disapproved, that I would go far.

Many of Basil's aphorisms are essential in politics. 'When questioning the validity of a piece of information ask always who was the original source', and, 'On every occasion that a particular recommendation is made, ask yourself first in what way the author's career may be affected.'

I stood at the rostrum, and I knew that he would be beaming.

It was a close-run thing, though. I had to get *some* cover because what I was saying was very contentious. Shamelessly I 'bounced' dear Peter and an unfortunate junior in 'Policy' who, unable to master – or perhaps to believe – the subversive conclusions that were implied,

---

[1] Professor Laurence Freedman, Professor of War Studies, King's College, since 1982.
[2] Sir Michael Howard, former Regius Professor of Modern History at Oxford and a noted military historian.

reluctantly 'passed' it. I was meant to be at King's for tea and small talk at 4.15. Like the Review, it had to be done 'privately', and it was not until 4.30 that Alison took the last sheet out of the printer. We got there, helter skelter at 4.58 to deliver a lecture billed for 5 p.m.

Thirty years ago, when I was writing *The Donkeys* at Bratton, I would have thought this evening the very pinnacle of attainment and recognition.

But now, alas, having 'arrived' I know that soon I am about to depart.

Ministry of Defence   *Tuesday, 11 December*

Tom occupied most of Ministers this morning telling everyone how his 'complaint' was very common, happens to practically everyone at some time, and so on.

As we dispersed he indicated that he wanted me to stay behind. The 'pupil's chair' was drawn up facing his desk, and he told Simon to leave – always a bad sign.

'How are you?' I drawled.

'I'm perfectly all right. It's you I want to talk about.'

He gave me a heavy basting. 'If you want to criticise Government policy, then you must do it from outside the Government.'

'I wasn't criticising Government policy.'

'Well, that certainly isn't the impression held by the Prime Minister. Or Douglas. Or the Chief Whip.'

Suspected balls, I thought.

'I can't go on defending you, you know. I think you'll have to look on this as your last chance.'

Back here I thought about it. If I am sacked (which I don't think I will be) then it is for saying what I believe, and what is manifestly true. How much consolation is that? Some, I suppose. But there's poor old Keith Speed, sacked for 'speaking out' nearly ten years ago, and still no 'K'.[1]

---

[1] Keith Speed, MP for Ashford since 1974. Parliamentary Under-Secretary (Navy) who resigned in protest at the reduction of frigate numbers set out in the 1981 Defence White Paper (Cmnd. 8288).

Ministry of Defence   *Wednesday, 12 December*

Last night I dined with Franko and Perry at Wiltons.[1] We had a 'pullman', but I noticed Paul and Ingrid Channon at that dud little on-the-edge table on the right, at the junction of the L.

Perry, *vu grand, comme toujours*. He spoke of the sweep of the Thatcherite legend, how we all had a duty to propagate it. Both were plainly getting ready to be 'disillusioned' with the unfortunate John – whom I personally believe to be tougher and more clear-headed than they realise.

I took the whole thing as a bit much coming from Perry who, in his day, has written the most flesh-crawling stuff about the dear Lady not having the 'class' that you need in adversity, deploring the absence of Gentlemen, all that sort of demi-balls. Frank, at least, has shown real affection and loyalty, only pulled her leg from time to time.

There was some talk about who would do *The Book*, how important it was. I must say my spirits fell when they said John O'Sullivan was going to 'ghost' it.

Ghost! Good God! The greatest political story of the century, and they're looking for a 'ghost'.

During the night I thought, why shouldn't I write it? She would trust me, I'm sure, with the papers. As a Privy Councillor I can get access to Cabinet Office records. I am trained as a historian, and she has often said (in public) how much she admires *Barbarossa*.

Early this morning I caught Peter on the ministerial floor, and expounded. He was enthusiastic. Said the present situation was 'a mess', 'too many cooks'. He promised to speak with her, and this time I think he is going to.

Ministry of Defence   *Thursday, 20 December*

Tom is looking strained and lined, still. He cut his leg on the weekend with a sickle and now, being full of every kind of antibiotic, finds it going 'septic', and has to keep it propped up on a chair.

---

[1] Frank Johnson (political columnist on *Daily Telegraph*) and Peregrine Worsthorne (Editor and columnist of the *Sunday Telegraph*).

All due to Al, Jane said, who is harrying him while he is run down. An article by Peter McKay, always fresh and amusing, in yesterday's *Evening Standard* – 'Top Dogs, Wrong Collars' – suggested that we should simply change places. Harmful to me, but fun none-theless.

I was having a chat with David Davis, and he told me an interesting footnote to the leadership affair.

After they received the figures of the second ballot Heseltine's claque – notably Mates, Hampson and Macfarlane – were frantic that he should hang in there, contest the third 'in order to strengthen his position'. H. ignored this, immediately conceding. (Presumably calculating that his total could well go down, and reduce still further his bargaining strength.)

However, when he met with John Major Heseltine made no attempt whatever to get places for his acolytes, being concerned only for himself, and cut the painter immediately. Later Mates threw a tantrum, and has apparently been promised something (unspecified) 'in the next Government'.

Saltwood   *Friday, 21 December*

The shortest day. Darkness and depression.

Bruce Anderson came to lunch, arriving terribly late. We didn't sit down until 3 p.m. Although he had asked to come and talk about his book on the leadership he hardly mentioned the subject. A general and rather repetitive gossip about where we're at, who's in, who's out.

He left me in little doubt that my shares are a listless market. I am the oldest member of the administration. My chances of getting into the Cabinet are nil. There was some (I thought slightly bizarre) talk of my being John's PPS in the next Parliament. I'd have done it straight away, but I won't do anything in the next Parliament unless it's from the Lords.

I have OD'd this last month, on politics. I have a huge backlog – for the first time – of work in the Dept, most of it turgid. But after I had seen Bruce on to a train I felt limp, and sated. Even my PC, to which I am greatly looking forward, is somewhat blighted by having acquired, it seems, the status of the *Medaille militaire* in the Charennes hospital at Verdun.[1] (The Lady's list, out today, contains little of interest or importance, although a K for poor Peter M, and a KCMG for Charles Powell – the latter most signally deserved.) Bruce told me of a comment on Derek Lord, the gay, intelligent, ludicrously self-assured black companion to Michael Brown, who was active in the Gayfrere Street bunker. From a rough Derbyshire farmer, a constituent of Michael's; 'Eee that twat's dad moost've eaten a posh missionary.'

Saltwood   *Christmas Day, 1990*

A lovely blustery day, cold driving rain and the glass falling fast.

We went to Communion. Not many people, but immediately behind us an *incredibly* tiresome woman, whom I've never seen in the village before, who thought she had a classy voice. She RADA'd up the responses – though at all times with a hint of reproach in her tone that, I came rapidly to believe, was directed at me personally.

Her buffer of a husband – pink face, watery eyes – blundered in occasionally, nicotine tones, and always out of time, so that momentarily he came to be 'leading' some of the prayers.

Now it's lovely to be here on our own. Snug, pressure-free, with presents to open, a huge meal, and a bottle of Giscours '61.

Leafing through a bound copy of *The Car* of 1906 I came across a delicious piece of useless information. Byron (no less) once rhymed 'intellectual' – troublesome, admittedly – with 'hen-pecked you all'.

I must contrive an opportunity to use this, 'spontaneously', in the House.

---

[1] Awarded to those dying of their wounds.

1991

1991

Just as obituary pages nearly always cause satisfaction – if not *Schadenfreude* – so do Honours Lists invariably irritate. Like Parliamentary Selection, they seem always to be bestowed on the wrong people.

I have tried very seldom to secure 'recognition' for anyone – although I did get an OBE for Betty.[1] So by now my two particular nominations – Phil Drabble for all he has done to enlarge our knowledge and enjoyment of nature and the countryside and the relations between man and beast; and Alex Moulton, for being a brilliant inventor, who has always risked his own money in putting his ideas into practical effect – are overdue to come up. But no. Who got the 'Industry' K's? A couple who personify all that is wrong with British 'businessmen'. Morton[2] – aggressive, nasty and stupid. And Sheehy[3] – self-indulgent, nasty and stupid. It's a practically infallible rule (though, most fortunately, vitiated in our recent leadership election), that the bad guy always wins. I can barely think of a single 'businessman' who has ever deserved a K except Ian MacLaurin[4] and Colin Chandler.[5]

I was with the Lady today. A strange menage. The tiny little house, lent her by Alistair McAlpine,[6] on College Green, still carries the faintest whiff of Number 10. Sloaneish secretaries bustle about on the ground floor, where telephones ring; handsome, though slightly effete young men slide in and out of her sitting room, bend over her ear, carrying sheaves of papers.

'I detect a distinct aura of Elba,' I said.

'Elba? Elba?'

'Where Napoleon was exiled before his return.'

'Yes yes I know *that*, I mean – how interesting.'

We talked for a little about the events of last November, and Peter Morrison sat in, lobbing her the occasional softball. Her sense of

---

[1] Cllr Mrs Betty Easton, OBE, Chairman of the Sutton Division for many years.

[2] Sir Alastair Morton, British Chairman of Eurotunnel since 1987.

[3] Sir Patrick Sheehy, Chairman, BAT (formerly British American Tobacco) Industries since 1982.

[4] Sir Ian MacLaurin, Chairman of Tesco, knighted in 1989.

[5] Sir Colin Chandler, Managing Director, Vickers plc, since 1990.

[6] Lord McAlpine of West Green (Life Peer, 1984). Honorary Treasurer, the Conservative Party, 1975–90.

betrayal is absolute, overrides everything. Lamont had been scheming; Patten plotted the whole thing; Kenneth Clarke had led the rout from the Cabinet Room. Rifkind was a weasel. Even John Major (who announced yesterday that some benefit was to be uprated, depicted in this morning's press, gleefully, as a 'Reversal of Thatcherite Policies') is by no means cloudfree.

I remembered a remark I had once heard Norman Tebbit address to her in private. 'Prime Minister, it is you who chooses your Cabinet', but said nothing. What was the point?

Gently, I brought the subject round to the book.

'I want *you* to do it, Alan, because you are a believer.'

'It shouldn't be "a believer's" book. It doesn't need to be.'

'How can you say that?'

'The facts speak for themselves. They illustrate the scale of your achievement.'

'But look how it ended. The treachery . . . '

'Margaret, these aren't Memoirs. You don't want to get into that game. This is your *Biography*. Where you came from, how you got there, what you did for the Conservative Party, and for Britain. A major work of political history. It will go into every university library in the World.'

As our conversation developed I could see she was having second thoughts. I told her that I would pay proper attention to the strange and disreputable circumstances of her ousting. That I could see the symmetry between what happened to her, and the way Grantham Council treated Alderman Roberts (being a subject to which she adverted several times).

But the standpoint *had* to be objective. A tract, even a great big thick tract, would be a wasted opportunity.

She didn't much like all this. I changed the subject to that of money. Michael Sissons[1] had told me that he could envisage a total take of about eight million (sterling). I said I didn't want any royalty. I would write it for a fee, but it would take me three years . . .

'Three *years*?'

'Minimum. This is a major book, six hundred pages. It has got to be impeccable. I'll have to pay an assistant.'

I have often found that once sums of money under discussion pass

---

[1] Michael Sissons, Chairman and Managing Director of the literary agency, Peters, Fraser and Dunlop.

beyond a certain level – no more than a couple of million usually – reality tends to be discarded, 'quotes' get wilder and wilder. It's all Monopoly.

Apparently Mark had been winding her up: ' ... Could be as much as twenty.'

Who's going to 'handle' it, anyway? There was talk of a hot lawyer in New York. Mark's favourite was apparently someone called McCormack, who plugs Sports 'Personalities', where the sums are enormous.[1]

I'm doubtful about all this. It's tempting, I can see, to allow yourself to be regarded as a 'property'. But slightly demeaning for the premier politician of the Western world. Better by far to keep the whole thing on an astringent, almost academic level. In the long run the yield will probably be little different.

Feeling the whole thing to be slipping away, I thought I ought to make one point absolutely clear. 'I am the author, not the Ghost. It's the Official Biography *by* Alan Clark. Not "as told to", or anything of that kind.'

I think that tore it. Perhaps just as well. I don't want another round of 'negotiation' in which she makes some concessions, and is then taken aback by my request – and I appear 'unreasonable'. But what she wants, I fear, is *Margaret Thatcher. My Story.*

It's all rather sad, particularly for future generations. Dilks[2] could do it. But he'd take an eternity. Possibly John Charmley.[3] But a 'ghost' hack will spoil the tale. Hard to say of course, as it depends who they choose, but could be even worse than if she tries to write it herself.

Winston did, why shouldn't she? she may be thinking. But consider for example that wonderful passage in Moran when Churchill explains the difference between scansion and resonance in a text.[4] I don't think she would be aware of that, bless her.

---

[1] Mark McCormack, chairman of International Management Group.

[2] David Dilks, Professor of International History, University of Leeds, since 1970. Edited *The Diaries of Alexander Cadogan.*

[3] John Charmley, historian, lecturer in English History at University of East Anglia. Author of *Duff Cooper, Chamberlain and the Lost Peace* and *Churchill: The End of Glory.*

[4] After his death Lord Moran, for many years Churchill's doctor, published *Winston Churchill: the Struggle for Survival.*

Saltwood   *Sunday, 6 January*

First dinner of the year. David Davis and his wife (good strong chap, very much our sense of humour. Did the 'black' route without turning a hair, then retraced his footsteps, hands in pockets – first time *that's* ever been done!). Richard Ryder and Caroline,[1] the Deedes,[2] the Michael Howards. We were eleven and the table and the food were terrific. But the meal somehow lacked *Stimmung*.

Tristan, a last-minute addition, performed sparklingly. But Bill Deedes, though splendid, and still a minter of delicious unfinished sentences is going deaf and 'misses' things. Even so, he remains one of the great ingredients in any grouping. He is wise, politically shrewd, still; and has a vast, archival fund of historic experience. Bill told Jane that he used to play golf with Philip Sassoon[3] before the war and Philip was so impatient that he employed two extra caddies who were sent ahead to see where the balls landed, so that Philip and his partner wouldn't waste time looking for them. (I know nothing about golf, but thought that 'looking for the ball' was one of the secondary ritualised pleasures?)

Lady Deedes, whom I called 'Evelyn' but Michael Howard (I don't doubt correctly) addressed as 'Hilary', was a pool of tranquil, though amiable *longueurs*.

When the ladies exited, I started the conversation on the lines of what are we to do about Margaret?

Following my meeting with her on Thursday, and the very bitter feelings of betrayal which she so evidently holds, my feeling is that she, her behaviour, could present the Party with one of its most vexatious problems over the coming months. There was some desultory talk about 'the book' (I gave nothing away. Only Richard knows that she and I are talking). Agreement on the general 'problem' of Mark. We couldn't really get into a good gossip, as Tristan would have done, left to himself.

---

[1] Caroline Ryder, MBE, the daughter of a former Clerk to the House of Commons, was a secretary to Margaret Thatcher.

[2] Lord Deedes (Life Peer, 1986). Journalist (Editor of the *Daily Telegraph*, 1974–86), who was MP for Ashford, 1950–74 and Minister without Portfolio, 1962–4. Allegedly the 'Dear Bill' to whom *Private Eye*'s Denis Thatcher letters have continued to be addressed (Thatcher and Deedes have long been golfing partners).

[3] Sir Philip Sassoon, 3rd Bt. Unionist MP. Private Secretary to Sir Douglas Haig, 1915–18. Under-Secretary for Air in the National Government in the 1930s.

Bill to some extent inhibits this – the Old School. And Richard was totally, *owlishly* silent. So much so that I thought he must be terribly tired, half asleep (he had been shooting in Norfolk all day). But on the few occasions that he uttered, monosyllabically, it was slicingly to correct errors of fact made by the participants. As a personality he is deeply pleasing – intelligent and '*aimable*' in the French sense.

DD also impressed. The concept of having clever, tough, *congenial* people in the Whips' Office is relatively new. In former times they were just fieldsport enthusiasts whose last and only fulfilment-period had been bullying (and in some cases buggering) Lower Boys at Eton. Now it is recognised as a nursery for junior Ministers. (I remember Nigel,[1] when I reproached him for going there, saying that the experience was essential – how Parlt works, how 'Business' is arranged, if one is to do a ministerial job properly.) As for myself, although I like to boast of having been blackballed – 'both to have been proposed, and to have been blackballed is equally complimentary' – I am sad not to have done a stint there.

At present we are all a little constrained. I first noticed this at the End of Term dinner last July.[2] The polls are implacable. The date of the Election approaches. I think we will win, but I can't tell how. And behind everything lurks this tedious, unnecessary but debilitating 'question' of Europe. We are all (except for dear Tristan) true Tories. But we cannot give expression to our true feelings.

Ministry of Defence   *Monday, 7 January*

I have been 'on call' all day, i.e., can't leave the building, because TK 'may' want to see me urgently.

The UN deadline[3] expires in a week's time and the place hums. But it has been conveyed to me, *via* the Private Office network, that I am not to take any part in the TV coverage of the war. The Press Office have been instructed to refuse all 'bids', and I am to refer those that are made to me personally. Where? Back to the Press Office.

---

[1] Nigel Lawson had been an Opposition Whip, 1976–7.
[2] End of Term dinner: see 20 July 1990.
[3] The ultimatum requiring Saddam Hussein to withdraw his forces from Kuwait.

Catch 22. 'Must make sure we all speak with the same tongue.' But of course it's not that at all. They recognise that I am more glamorous, and have a quicker mind, than the other Ministers, who mustn't be 'outshone'. It's like a trendy Local Authority banning competitive sports.

Ah! Peter has just come in; it's coming up to 7 p.m. and S of S office have rung to say I can 'stand down'. I assume that he was intending to huff-locute this instruction to me personally, then either lost his nerve or got involved with some other topic.

I have been whiling away the time reading through a bundle of congratulatory letters.[1] Those from officials please me most, and of them Charles wrote much the nicest. A document to be treasured. But do officials write in much the same way to every Minister who gets a PC? Perhaps. With very slight variations.

It is an important, but highly specialised form of recognition. The *Herald* came on, but couldn't understand it at all. 'Does this mean you'll be able to do more for Plymouth?'

Plymouth train   *Friday, 11 January*

I have already finished the box. Very little for me these days. The whole Dept is concentrating on the war and, at all costs, Archie and TK have to keep me away from that.

Reading through *Classic Car* I saw a photograph of Jack Fairman. I suppose he must be about seventy now, but he looked at death's door. He was the first of what we now call 'The Mews'[2] whom I ever met, when I went over to Horley (while still at Eton, and risking the sack) to look at the cars in 'Speedsters' garage.

Fairman was clipped and authoritative, with a black moustache and experience (he implied) of war in the desert. He took care to distance himself from E.W. Gillette, who was the proprietor of 'Speedsters', claimed (as far as I can recall) to be his landlord, the proprietor of the huge bus garage in Redhill where the stock of cars,

---

[1] On the announcement of AC being appointed a Privy Councillor.
[2] A family expression for the Classic Car 'movement', the majority of whose emporia are located in South Kensington Mews.

even then very glorious and glamorous – 'the cream of pre-war sporting machinery' – and today, I should think, worth getting on for £100 million, was housed.

No. Fairman was 'not in the dealing line'. But I do remember him on several occasions in the Fifties and Sixties as an indifferent competitive driver with a curiously inflated reputation. Did he ever win a race? Even I have won a race, after all. But he was a player on the scene, memorable for the defiant 'I spun the car' quote during the Nurburgring 1000 km race in 1959, to which Jane and I went with Desmond O'Brien and Noel Cunningham Reid. Stirling Moss[1] won, against very strong opposition, in a DB 3S, in one of the most epic drives I have ever witnessed.

Anyway, there he is now, gaunt and old. And further on, pictures of Fangio[2] (now eighty) *crashing* a Mercedes 'W' Grand Prix car on a 'demonstration lap' in Australia. The great man then took Sir Jack Brabham[3] (another golden oldie) round in a Princess-Diana-model 500 SL to 'open' the track, and crashed *that* too.

It's age, I fear, pure age. When's going to be the first time I do it? I haven't had a crash for twenty-five years, since silly little Juliet led me into an ambush in the $3\frac{1}{2}$-litre Bentley, in Wiltshire, and old Lord Margadale suddenly turned up on the Bench as visiting Lord bloody Lieutenant and, odiously, fined me £450.

James is already making mischief by saying he has followed me in the Porsche in Scotland and that I drive dangerously. And Alison flinches whenever we drive in traffic.

Yesterday in Brooks's I heard that Julian Earle (age sixty-two) had died 'suddenly' of a heart attack. Bland, keen golfer, not many grey hairs. What's going on?

Coming out of the gents I ran into Jim Slater,[4] who repeated the news.

'You're next,' I said, then realised that the humour may have been a bit *too* black as he looked alarmingly blotchy, and his suit hung loosely. Cancer, I suppose.

---

[1] Stirling Moss, racing motorist, 1947–62. Competed in 494 races, rallies, sprints, land speed records and endurance runs and won 222, including 33 Formula One Grand Prix.

[2] Juan Fangio, Argentinian racing driver. Five times Formula One World Champion.

[3] Sir Jack Brabham, racing driver. Three times Formula One World Champion, retired 1970.

[4] Jim Slater, former Chairman, Slater Walker Securities.

Ministry of Defence   *Tuesday, 15 January*

The UN deadline runs out today, and the air attacks could start any time. TK is relatively benign, now he's fixed my PR for me, very kindly. And he goes through the *motions* of being hyperactive. But he hasn't really got control over the place, or what's going on. Increasingly the Military are taking first slight, then medium, soon major decisions and then 'advising' Ministers afterwards. I sense it is with relief that TK settles back into more mundane, but congenial topics like photocalls and the briefing of foreign correspondents.

Yes, I am bitching. But I have been completely sidelined. Nothing of any interest comes into my box, nor is my opinion sought on any issue. I am being treated like a middle-rank executive in a large corporation who is going to be forced out by having his desk moved around the whole time.

It makes me cross and frustrated; but it's also bad luck on Private Office who are supportive and loyal and can remember the days when Charles used to phone and send stuff over from Number 10 all the time, for info or 'suggestions'.

1990 was such a wonderful year, almost until the end. I have a terrible feeling that 1991 is not going to be happy.

Ministry of Defence   *Tuesday, 22 January*

TK is bumbustious this morning. His press conferences are being carried live in the US! Heaven help us.

Ministerial meetings are a complete waste of time now. Jokes and small talk. They were all in good form, though keeping straight faces, this morning.

There had been a heavy headline in the *Sunday Express*: REVENGE IS SWEET AT THE MoD.

A biggish picture of me, entitled – *Disliked*: Alan Clark. If I'd been in stronger form I might have enjoyed it. 'Deeply disliked by both Civil Servants and Ministers . . . ', went on to talk of one of the most prestigious posts in the Government in coming weeks, 'the front men will be King and Hamilton. Clark will be kept entirely [sic] out of the limelight.'

Buttocks. The whole piece is long, and prominent. I know how the press works. This isn't just a sliver of overheard gossip. It has to be a specific plant from the Press Office, with the tacit concurrence of Tom or Archie. Quite unnecessary, as I had already agreed to this arrangement. No one at all mentioned it at Ministers, which is a clear (though gauche) indicator of a guilty conscience.

Ministry of Defence   *Wednesday, 23 January*

We're five days into the air war, but I am unhappy about the strategy. Attacking missile sites is always wasteful, has very little tactical effect and occurs mainly in response (as most obviously now) to political demands.

We lost another Tornado last night. That's now *five*. I can't help noticing that traditions (ancient and revered) of Bomber Command are reasserting themselves. From the Tabuk mission last night, out of ten sorties six either aborted for technical reasons, or 'jettisoned ordnance while manoeuvering to avoid (sic) SAMs', or took targets of opportunity. (Uh? At night?)

The sad thing is that it's always the brave ones, the true grit, who press on regardless (the contravening tradition) and get killed. Of the Italian flight of six *five* turned back and only one brave boy went ahead. They got him. It's the difference between James and Andrew. But I want James to survive, don't I?

MGO[1] has been here for an hour and a half. There's a potential ammunition crisis in some calibres. Unbelievably our NATO 'partners' are being most reluctant to pool their stockpiles, even though we're paying cash. The smelly little Belgians, who would never fire a shot at anyone and never have, and who did their best to shaft the BEF in 1940, have actually refused to let us have anything, except 'humanitarian supplies' – bandages and general past-its-sell-by-date detritus we don't need.

We talked about the Battle Plan. It's good news, at least, that we have been moved out now to the 'left hook', on the desert flank. But

---

[1] Master-General of the Ordnance. Sir John Stibbon, the senior General under AC.

I was apprehensive that our Sappers, 'because they are so good', were going to have to lead the breaching operation. There shouldn't *be* a breaching operation at all. We should go to the Euphrates, Basra if necessary, and draw the Republican Guard out in the open to attack us. Alam Halfa.[1] Not bother to go near Kuwait until it just falls off the tree.

Time lies on my hands. I spend much of it with Alison, and we do the *Guardian* crossword in the cafetaria. I am glum, and must be poor company.

Saltwood   *Saturday, 26 January*

It's a Saturday, but I've got a splitting tension headache.

I was doing a regional broadcast from Bristol on Thursday night, fairly routine stuff, when the commentator suddenly asked me how well our NATO allies were helping.

Just as one can sometimes be less on one's guard abroad, or in a foreign studio (foolishly and recklessly ignoring the fact that news can be flash-faxed to Whitehall before one has even got out of the door) so one can easily think that regional radio is a bit *hick* – particularly in the W. Country.

Hick! They had a teeny television camera concealed in the sound room and gleefully sold the whole interview as a TV performance (which of course I have been 'banned' from doing). I was cross, and feckless. I made some rude remarks, 'more concerned with heading for their cellars', totally unreliable in a real crisis, etc.

Afterwards, as always, a certain remorse. There was a lull. Was it all a strange dream?

But after a day's lull it has exploded, first in the *FT,* quite small, then everywhere.

I am under siege, refusing all requests for comment or interviews. Could still go either way. It had to be said. People *in the street* are very supportive.

---

[1] The classic 'drawing on' armoured battle fought by Montgomery before Alamein.

Ministry of Defence   *Monday, 28 January*

I loathe being in London on Sunday evenings, and last night I had to come up so as to be in time this morning for another of these useless ministerial conferences, scheduled for 8.30, never start until after 9.

The flat is bleak and shabby, and takes a couple of hours to heat up. There is dust and grime, and crumbs in – not on, *in* – the carpet. The great damask curtains, that originally hung between the Partridge pagodas at Upper Terrace, are torn and fragile, so that the soft white felt lining bulges through the fabric. I hear of 'Sets' no different from mine changing hands for seven, eight hundred thousand. But B5 is squalid – almost, the straitened quarters of an Edwardian bachelor on his uppers.

The 'Conference' follows its usual pattern. Beforehand, at about 8 a.m., one is shown, with much flaring of feathers, a folder marked SECRET, an 'Operational Sitrep' consisting mainly of items little different, it seems, from those to be found on page 2 of that morning's *Daily Telegraph*. Then (always late, although TK has only to walk across the street from Admiralty HO) we sit round for a monologue. On and on goes the droning, round and round come the (same) subjects. As we dispersed this morning Tom indicated that he wanted me to stay behind.

'Well, you're not exactly flavour of the month, again.'

'Oh really?'

'John isn't at all pleased.'

'Oh dear.'

'You go and do this just at the moment Douglas is trying to get Kohl to stump up some cash towards our costs in the war.'

'I'd have thought it might help. Shame them.'

'The fact that you can say something like that, shows, *if I may say so*, that you're really not quite *au fait* with things. It's all a bit tricky.'

Actually, the old thing wasn't unamiable. He knows I'm not a threat to him any more and he can draw mild satisfaction from my digging deeper into my own hole.

I'm dreadfully tired. I hardly slept last night and the adrenalin that would pump if I had any role whatever in this place at present just isn't flowing. I'm indifferent about resignation – were it not for the fact that I want to put certain *concepts* in place before I go. And particularly to order the new tank. There's a lot of pressure building up there – in the wrong direction.

CSA[1] came in to see me. A routine call, but our conversation took flight of fancy. He is a nice man, and clever also. Furthermore, he always searches for the best solution *for Britain*; none of your fucking 'in the interests of reaching an acceptable compromise' balls.

The need for an intermediate nuclear weapon. The danger implicit in the American development of G-PALS[2] (a good litmus test of the Nationalist, this. I see it as most unwelcome that the US should have implied power of veto over our ballistic systems, still further concentration of power in the Washington dung-heap). The advisability of getting back into the (satellite) launch business. (*I* had to suggest using up the old Polaris rockets, constructing a makeshift base area at Ascension.) We agreed on the need for extending the range of EFA. Adapting Tomahawk to SSN 20 tubes. The total untrustworthiness of the French, in any co-operative context whatever. All in all, the US our only reliable friends – and even there the limits may start to encroach as the Pentagon-Congressional Committee axis loses weight.

All rather depressing, and the only effect to make me wish, or re-wish, that I was Secretary of State.

A little later came a message via Private Office that Quinlan had been 'very impressed' with my contributions at the Steering Group meetings. Butter. I expect he wants to restrain me from being too radical. You never know with Clark. He's underemployed at the moment. He may be writing some tiresome paper.

To cap it all, I believe myself to be 'fighting' flu. In my experience, 'fighting' flu is like 'fighting' cancer. You always lose.

And I have run out of fizzy Redoxon.

Albany, 11.40 p.m.
Just got in from the House. At the ten o'clock vote I was 'lionised'. Colleagues from all sides coming up and saying how they agreed, endless 'well-done's from people I hardly knew. The press has been kind, and I hear that even *Time* magazine is going to run a favourable para.

My cup runneth over; with a typical performance by that creep Hugh Dykes who told the TV cameras I should be sacked at once.

---

[1] Professor Ronald Oxburgh, Chief Scientific Adviser, Ministry of Defence, since 1988.
[2] The US developed anti-ballistic missile system, Global Protection Against Limited Strike.

Albany   *Wednesday, 30 January*

Today I visited Shorts in Belfast. Interesting weapons, the 'Streak' family. Very much the next generation, light, accurate, crazy-fast. And conforming with my long-held view, which I expressed in the Sopwith Memorial Lecture last year, that missiles should be *multi-elemental*. One close-range type should be adaptable to sea, infantry and helicopter use. It's always the Navy who resist this, isn't it? They love to spend millions and millions on 'systems' that only sailors can use.

Northern Ireland is unbelievably nasty. Grey, damp, cold. Big puddles just lying; blackthorn hedges; low standard of life. I saw one pretty girl, in a crowd that had been evacuated from a building on account of a '200 lb bomb scare'. They were all standing, patient but dejected, on the pavement. White police tape everywhere. On her own, she was jumping about excitedly, *very* nice legs.

But the general atmosphere is bleak; overlaid with the oppression of terror; deep and perpetual feuds, suspicion and callousness.

I am confirmed in my opinion that it is hopeless here. All we can do is arm the Orangemen – to the teeth – and get out. This would give also the not slight advantage that, at a stroke, Infantry 'overstretch' is eliminated.

Constituency Office, Plymouth   *Friday, 1 February*

I got off the sleeper this morning and picked my way along deserted streets to the Duke of Cornwall, which opens for breakfast ahead of the other hotels in the City. 'Picked' I say, because it was *black ice*, and I was carrying a heavy box and an overnight bag and wearing *tutti* town slippers. If one had been on form, showing off and laughing, the gradient outside Sainsburys was schussable.

I ate my international traveller's breakfast – a double cornflakes and natural yoghourt – which I have consumed all around the world from Sydney to Bogota to Anchorage, often the only swallowable food offered all day, and read the local paper. It must be over a year since I called here, and I doubt if I will ever do so again, as I have no intention of getting into that sleeper train any more if I can possibly avoid it.

The place is redolent of memories, particularly of the early days.

The downstairs 'Conveniences' were always unpleasant, wiped rather than cleaned, and smelling of beer and ablutions. But I could find, still intact and unchanged, now nearly twenty years and no one has yet thought to put a hook on the back of the door for your coat, the little private thompson loo on the first floor, and used it well.

To get there I had to traverse the corridor – not just looking but smelling – identical to that climacteric evening when Norman Fowler and I were waiting, on two separate settees, for the outcome of the parliamentary selection.

Fowler, the Central Office choice, shovee you could say, had by now got an uneasy impression that things were 'going wrong'. And sure enough when finally Tom Bridges[1] emerged he walked past the unhappy MP (as he then already was, but for a seat that was going to be Labour next time), did no more than grunt at him, and came over to me, hand outstretched.

Now all I have left, at the very most, is a year. I am trying to steel myself to the great transition. What are my objectives? Limited, I suppose, by comparison. Full and proper attention to my papers and to the Heritage. A dilettante man of letters? A (old Etonian) Guru? A more attentive husband? Freedom to travel at will, and EARLY NIGHTS. The deferral of old age, I suppose. But this is in itself rather wet and feeble, and invites Nemesis.

The sheer scale of the enforced change, the fact that I will be *excluded* from the Commons, from the beloved, magical electric aura of the Chamber, and by my own hand, has yet to sink in. Although periodically, as now, I try and face it. But I would not wish to grow old in the House. Rumpled. Dandruff. The young ones pushing past.

Will I get a peerage? Claimants always say they want it for their wife, but I would so like to present it to Jane while she is still young and pretty. Sometimes I have been foul to her. Why? Hormones, I suppose.

But they'll do their best to stop me. I have lots of enemies at middle rank, perhaps even in the Cabinet Office – although not, I hope, Robin whom personally I like (although it is easy to make the mistake of thinking that those one likes reciprocate the feeling). I doubt if I have a single friend in the whole Foreign Office, not a male one anyway.

---

[1] Chairman of the Sutton Division, 1972–5.

Then there are the two heavies. Hurd has always been against me, told the Lady not to make me Minister for Trade – which she very splendidly repeated to me on the evening of my appointment. Arsehole. He's looking more and more like Aldridge Prior.[1]

And of course Michael. Michael *knows* – just as when one has had some frightful bout of food-poisoning one always by instinct knows which particular dish caused it – he knows that it was me who tipped the scales in the two days immediately after the coup, by winding up the Constituency Associations. And my podgy namesake.[2] He's always been suspicious of me, and actually *sued* the manufacturers of Trivial Pursuits because they had muddled us up.

None of these people can face the idea of me in the Lords because instead of treating it as a Garden of Remembrance I might actually say something. *Unpredictable.*

Only dear Richard [Ryder], who is intelligent and sweet, would be my advocate, though not, I fear, as resolutely as Ian did in finally persuading the Lady to 'try' me in Government some eight years gone by. And Chris (Patten), I don't think would mind. I hope not, at least, as he is a good guy.

If they could, my enemies would block a 'K' as well, although this is more difficult unless the subject has actually been corrupt (practically the only failing, I suppose, that I never have had).

But in any case, I wouldn't want to rank myself with Buck and Emery.[3] Perhaps better to compose myself always to being 'Mister'. Like John Wilkes.

House of Commons   *Tuesday, 5 February*

Today I was inducted into the Privy Council. A rehearsal of the ceremony had been fixed twenty minutes before at the PC office in Whitehall. I changed – in the dark little lobby outside the bathroom which I share with the Chief of the General Staff – into my new navy

---

[1] Aldridge Prior – The Hopeless Liar, a character in a strip in *Viz*.
[2] Kenneth Clarke, the Health Minister.
[3] Sir Antony Buck (Kt, 1983), MP for Colchester since 1961, and Sir Peter Emery (Kt, 1982), MP for Honiton since 1967 (Reading, 1959–66).

suit, which still carries O'Brien's[1] 'delivery' creases and which I don
only very sparingly. I thought my shoes looked scruffy. No one in the
outer office (why not? Julian always had a pack) had any shoe polish.
So I had to go via the Commons. I bickered briefly with Alison, got
my fingers black-streaked with the Kiwi. Had to go into the drivers'
loo and continuously scrub under the (boiling) tap. All water, everywhere, in the House of Commons is *always* screeching hot, especially
in July. I was now late.

Just as we drew up outside the Cabinet Office the carphone rang.
Private Office. Where was I? etc., etc. All right, all right, I'm at the
door. I could feel my bladder contracting and remembered I'd forgotten to pee. Blast.

A discreet attendant in spectacles was waiting for me. He conducted me into the presence of the Privy Council Secretary, a dear
old thing not unlike Farky[2] at Kings in 1943. He and, more particularly,
his secretary sized me up at once as being 'difficult', i.e., not sufficiently
overawed and softspoken. 'We've just got time, I think,' he quavered.

'*Just*,' snarl/sneered the assistant secretary.

They 'took me through' the ceremony. Quite long drawn-out
and, because of its repetitive quality, easy (as I was to discover) to
skip a stage.

'I think we'd better go to the Palace now.'

'I'll follow you.'

'I'm afraid we may get separated. I've got a special ivory pass that
lets me through Horse Guards Arch.'

'So've I.'

Taken aback somewhat he told me a put-down story about when
he was a Dep Sec at the Home Office he had tried very hard to limit
the issue of the ivory passes. I retaliated with the tale of the occasion
when Andrew refused to let Geoffrey Howe through. Deuce.

At Buck House I was indeed the last to arrive (I should nervously
and respectfully, have been the first). MacGregor,[3] the Lord President,
Bertie Denham, Paddy Mayhew,[4] Nick Scott, Wakeham. We hung

---

[1] Mr O'Brien, head cutter of Lesley and Roberts in Savile Row.
[2] Warden of the college, 1929–43. AC was taken over to visit him by John Sparrow
  from Eton in 1943.
[3] John MacGregor, Education Secretary since 1989.
[4] Sir Patrick Mayhew, Attorney General since 1987.

about in the hall through which one processes on Garden Party days. Small, very small, talk.

We were joined by two Palace functionaries – handsome, nicely dressed, middle-aged; both of them with that shallow courtesy, smooth complexion and careful coiffure of the Establishment homosexual.

Tactlessly, I interrupted a lot of cant about cold-weather allowances for the aged – poor people, what a good idea, etc., etc. – with a crack about the opening that very day at the QE II Centre of a World Conference on Global Warming.

Conversation petered out.

Then, jarringly, a 'household' electric bell rang and little Mac-Gregor sloped off for a preliminary audience. About eight minutes later it rang again. The Councillors trooped in, me last. Stop at the door. Bow. Approach the Monarch, bow again. Take the Hand, *ultra* lightly. Walk backwards or rather crabwise, into the line-up.

A smallish room, much Savonnerie, indifferent pictures. The Queen sat at, or rather adjacent to, a *secretaire* copiously encrustulated with boule. A vase of blueish flowers, conventionally arranged. Moyses Stevens.

The business of the Council was announced. First item 'to receive into the Council', etc. (they gave me my courtesy title). I stepped forward, knelt awkwardly on the stool (bloody difficult), held up the Testament in my right hand and the dear old boy read out the oath. 'I do,' I said, firmly. I rose, advanced about ten feet diagonally to *another* stool, bowed, knelt, took the Monarch's hand and 'brushed it with my lips'; rose, bowed, back into line.

A pause ensued. Why? I made to go forward, down the line, shake hands with the Lord President as forewarned and instructed. No. Blast, fuck, etc. There was *another* oath. The old Clerk, secretly delighted, rolled his eyes in mock resignation and signalled me to raise, again, the Testament in my right hand. He then read out a very long passage the substance of which, as far as I could make out, was that I undertook to maintain total secrecy even, particularly indeed, about colleagues concerning whom I might hear unsatisfactory things. (The more I think about this the odder it seems.)

This time, when I said 'I do' I looked directly at the Queen. I bet many don't. But I was glad to see that she was looking directly at me. I then did the handshaking act, Lord President, Attorney General, the rest, and returned to my place at the end of the line. At which the Queen got up from her chair and moved over, *regally*, to initiate a painfully, grotesquely, banal conversation, loosely devoted to the various other Orders in Council that were on the business list. Inevitably, these were all concerned with Euro-legislation. Most of them, today, seemed to be concerned with lifts, or *ascenseurs*. Some light banter was attempted, notably by Paddy Mayhew. Splendid fellow, totally unsquashable. And when there were a couple of hesitant jokes about continental lifts 'that don't have sides' I nearly told one about the Ganymede lift at St Thomas's that goes round and round and can invert the passengers. But I was just too far down the line to guarantee getting it across.

This last phase was somewhat drawn out. Not for the first time I wondered about the Queen. Is she really rather dull and stupid? Or is she thinking, 'How do people as dull and stupid as this ever get to be Ministers?' Or is, for her, the whole thing so stale and *déjà vu* after forty years that she'd really rather be going round the stables at Highclere, patting racehorses on the nose? I suppose it might feel different if she had real power. And yet she *does* have the power. It's all there in the Constitution, all she has to do is renounce the Civil List for her ill-favoured siblings, pay taxes on her private wealth, and get on with it.

I drove back to the House, and had a boring, overcooked lunch in the Members' dining room.

EPILOGUE

And all my endeavours are unlucky explorers
come back, abandoning the expedition;
the specimens, the lilies of ambition
still spring in their climate, still unpicked;
to find them, as the great collectors before me.[1]

---

[1] Keith Douglas, 1944.

INDEX

All Orion/Phoenix titles are available at your local bookshop or from the following address:

Mail Order Department
Littlehampton Book Services
FREEPOST BR535
Worthing, West Sussex, BNI3 3BR
telephone 01903 828503, *facsimile* 01903 828802
e-mail MailOrders@lbsltd.co.uk
(Please ensure that you include full postal address details)

Payment can be made either by credit/debit card (Visa, Mastercard, Access and Switch accepted) or by sending a £ Sterling cheque or postal order made payable to *Littlehampton Book Services*.
DO NOT SEND CASH OR CURRENCY.

Please add the following to cover postage and packing

UK and BFPO:
£1.50 for the first book, and 50p for each additional book to a maximum of £3.50

Overseas and Eire:
£2.50 for the first book plus £1.00 for the second book and 50p for each additional book ordered

---

BLOCK CAPITALS PLEASE

name of cardholder .... | *delivery address*
.... | *(if different from cardholder)*
address of cardholder .... |
.... | ....
.... | ....
.... | ....
postcode .... | *postcode* ....

☐ I enclose my remittance for £..

☐ please debit my Mastercard/Visa/Access/Switch (delete as appropriate)

card number ☐☐☐☐☐☐☐☐☐☐☐☐☐☐☐☐

expiry date ☐☐☐☐   Switch issue no. ☐☐

signature ....

prices and availability are subject to change without notice

'This book is as necessary to read and absorb as the two that preceded it, not for a better understanding of the milieu in which Clark was writing, but for a better understanding of the human condition ... the last pages are incredibly moving and compound the sheer, Technicolor humanity of what we have read before'   Simon Heffer, *Literary Review*

'The skill in the diaries and memoirs of most politicians lies in the delicate airbrushing out of their faults and weaknesses. Alan Clark's self-portrait, on the other hand, is defiantly warts-and-all ... His three volumes of diaries will ensure his immortality'
                              Craig Brown, *Mail on Sunday*

'Ever present in this volume is his preoccupation with the illness that finally claimed him. It is more sombre, infinitely more fore-boding than his other work ... The last entries, by Jane recording Alan's final days, are hugely moving ... This is simply the best book I have read since – well, since the last Clark oeuvre'   Steven Norris, *The Times*

'A rare record of what it is like to be dying by a master of the English language'   Bevis Hillier, *Spectator* (Books of the Year)

'This volume of Clark is better on small details of an indulged life, of Eccles cakes and stilton, the vanity of his timed runs up flights of stairs, his befriending of jackdaws whose pellets he takes abroad for good luck'   Quentin Letts, *Daily Mail*

'The last diaries are a muted version of the others, full of sten-gun judgments, scorn, candour and opinion – also ambition recollected in imperfect tranquillity'
                              Edward Pearce, *Tribune Magazine*

'Alan Clark's relationship with God in these diaries is both funny and moving ... These diaries do not stalk the corridors of power. There is very little high-level gossip, but some of our favourite characters from the early diaries make appearances ... As his hypochondria gives way to real sickness, his moral gambling to terror, his selfish and equivocal attitude towards his wife to absolute love and gratitude, the diaries assume an immense sadness and profundity ... Alan Clark was not a good man, but he was a dazzling diarist. He writes, self-pityingly: "I suppose I will be remembered for the Diaries." He will, and for this one most of all. A grand love story eclipses a political career'

Sarah Sands, *Daily Telegraph*

'A long way from the acerbic knockabout looked for by Clark's admirers ... The latter part of the book is darkened by the diarist's recognition that [those] frissons of demise are no illusion: he has brain cancer ... the journal of a disappointed man becomes that of a mind at the end of its tether. At the same time the heartless, even caddish, candour gives way to impassioned avowals of devotion to a sorely tried wife. When he finally abandons his pen, Jane Clark adds her own brief log, in which reciprocated devotion sits uneasily with sick-room grue. "I love God," she writes, "but this is such a cruel way to demolish such a brilliant brain"' E.S. Turner, *TLS*

'Pure pleasure ... there ought to be a constant supply of Alan Clarks' Sue Townsend, *Mail on Sunday* (Books of the Year)

Alan Clark, MP for Plymouth (Sutton) 1974–1992 and Kensington and Chelsea, 1997–1999, was Minister of Trade, 1986–1989, and Minister of State, Ministry of Defence, 1989–1992. He was married with two sons and lived at Saltwood Castle, Kent. Following his death in 1999, a second volume of his journals – *Diaries: Into Politics* – was published in 2000. A collection of his motoring journalism followed in 2001 under the title *Back Fire: A passion for cars and motoring*.

Ion Trewin, the editor of *The Last Diaries*, is Editor-in-Chief of a London publisher. He was previously Literary Editor of *The Times*. He also edited Alan Clark's *Diaries: Into Politics*.

By Alan Clark

FICTION

Bargains at Special Prices

Summer Season

The Lion Heart: a tale of the war in Vietnam

NON-FICTION

The Donkeys: A History of the BEF in 1915

The Fall of Crete

Barbarossa: The Russian–German
Conflict, 1941–1945

Aces High: the War in the Air
over the Western Front 1914–1918

A Good Innings: the private papers
of Viscount Lee of Fareham (*edited*)

Suicide of the Empires:
The Eastern Front, 1914–1918

Diaries: In Power, 1983–1992

The Tories: Conservatives and the
Nation State, 1922–1997

Diaries: Into Politics, 1972–1982 (*edited by Ion Trewin*)

Back Fire: A passion for cars and motoring
(*edited by Robert Coucher*)

The Last Diaries: In and Out of the
Wilderness (*edited by Ion Trewin*)

THE LAST
DIARIES

In and Out of the Wilderness

ALAN CLARK

Transcribed and Edited,
with Introduction and Notes,
by Ion Trewin

PHOENIX

A PHOENIX PAPERBACK

First published in Great Britain in 2002
by Weidenfeld & Nicolson
This paperback edition published in 2003
by Phoenix,
an imprint of Orion Books Ltd,
Orion House, 5 Upper St Martin's Lane,
London WC2H 9EA

ISBN 0 75381 695 4

Typeset by Selwood Systems, Midsomer Norton
Printed and bound in Great Britain by
Clays Ltd, St Ives plc

'Diaries are so intensely personal – to publish them is a baring, if not a flaunting, of the ego … These are not "Memoirs". They are not written to throw light on events in the past, or retrospectively to justify the actions of the author. They are *exactly* as they were recorded on the day; sometimes even the hour, or the minute, of a particular episode or sensation.'

Introduction, *Diaries*, 1993

'God this is a filthy pen, I'm going to change it.'

Qatar, 12 May, 1991

'How delicious is "the quiet hour". There are few more agreeable (intellectual) conditions than a pot of Indian tea, a nice pen (earlier I was fussed because I could only find a biro) and a blank page.'

11 February, 1995

CONTENTS

ILLUSTRATIONS

The photographs in *The Last Diaries* are a
selection from the Clark family albums.

GLOSSARY

Eva ('E') – Rottweiler
Hannah and Lëhni – Rottweiler sisters
KK – James's labrador
Bok – Bokassa, labrador, successor to KK
Max, George, 2Boy, Bromley, TC – jackdaws

WESTMINSTER

Sue Line – secretary at the House of Commons
Alison Young – secretary at the House of Commons
Pat – driver at the Ministry of Defence
Patricia (Trish) Sill Johnston – secretary at the House of Commons

CONSTITUENCIES

Barbara Lord – Conservative agent, Kensington and Chelsea
1a – Chelsea Manor Street, SW3, the Kensington and Chelsea
   Conservative Association headquarters

HOUSES AND LOCATIONS
SALTWOOD

The Mains – another name for Saltwood Castle
The Castle: various rooms including the Great Library; the
   Tower offices (winter and summer); the Red Library; the
   badge room (glory hole of mainly car parts); the archive
   room; Peggy's pantry; the Green Room (the Clarks' informal
   sitting room in the old staff wing); the asthma rail (by the back
   door); Rabies Room; the Knights Hall
Pavillon – summerhouse by the swimming pool, which the
   Clarks gave themselves as an anniversary present
Lady Conway's Bridge – across the moat and linking Garden
   House to the Castle; widened during Lady Conway's
   ownership of Saltwood
MFS GH and MFS GL/Gt Hall – 'My Father's Study'. There are
   two, one in the Garden House, the other in the Great Hall,

behind the Great Library.

Garden House (GH) – a large bungalow, designed by John King in the old kitchen garden in the grounds of Saltwood, for Lord and Lady Clark, when they moved out of the castle in 1971

Sandling – the railway station for Saltwood

Gossie Bank – a steep climb at the far end of Grange Farm, Saltwood; AC often refers to the time he takes to ascend it

The Seeds – a large arable field at Grange Farm, Saltwood

The Bailey (inner and outer) – the two courtyards (see also lawns)

Courtneys (aka 'the Secret Garden')

ALBANY

B5 Lower/Upper – Piccadilly chambers which AC inherited from his mother. The Upper, more an attic, had once been servants' quarters

ERIBOLL

The Lodge – principal house on the estate

Shore Cottage – Jane's croft at Eriboll, where Jane and AC always stay

The Creaggan Road – connects Loch Eriboll to Loch Hope by way of the Creaggan Ridge, some seven miles in length and climbing from sea level to 600 feet at the ridge

Foulain – a shepherd's cottage at the foot of the loch

Strathbeg (sometimes Stra'beg) – a remote croft at the head of the Polla Valley

Arnaboll and Cashel Dhu – crofts on the Loch Hope side of the estate

Ardneackie – the peninsula that juts out into Loch Eriboll

Birkett Foster – rocks that reminded AC of a seascape by the Victorian painter, Myles Birkett Foster

ZERMATT

Châlet Caroline – the Clarks' house in the village, which they
    built in the early 1960s
The Kiosk – built by the Clarks in 1985, adjoining the châlet
Trift – an inn at an early stage in the ascent to the Rothornhutte
Othmars – an inn on the Blauherd

BRATTON–CLOVELLY

Town Farm – an early home; in west Devon, near Okehampton
    and about three-quarters of an hour's drive north of
    Plymouth

SEEND MANOR

Broomhayes – near Devizes in Wiltshire; retained by the Clarks
    when they moved to Saltwood. Latterly the home of Andrew
    and Sarah Clark

RYE

Watchbell Street – including No 11, where the Clarks lived after
    they married

HOUSE OF COMMONS

House Library – House of Commons, a favourite spot for
    writing
Dean's Yard – an office, mainly for secretaries, by Westminster
    Abbey
1 Parliament Street – where AC had an office after his return to
    the Commons in 1997
White Office – ministerial office in the Commons during AC's
    time at the Ministry of Defence

SOME CARS AND RELATED MATTERS

(where cars mentioned in this volume are transitory purchases,
   they are sometimes identified within the text)

The Mews – composite name for various vintage car dealers'
   establishments in Queen's Gate, London
Coys – dealers in classic cars
Macrae & Dick (Derek Presley) –   Land Rover dealers at
   Inverness
P. & A. Wood (Andy Wood) – specialists in Rolls-Royce and
   Bentley
Scott Moncrieff – purveyors and restorers of classic cars
The Discovery – Land Rover
Big Red – S-type Bentley Continental, number plate AC1800
Hen 3-litre – Bentley
New Bing – Bentley Continental S1 manual
KGV – Rolls-Royce Silver Ghost
R Cont – Green Bentley manual
Toyota – Truck used for wooding
Bustard – Bentley 4¼-litre
Bang Bang – R Cont manual with Bradley Brothers body
Barnato – Bentley 4¼ made for Wolf Barnato
C-Type – Jaguar XC13
XK 120 – owned by AC since his undergraduate days
Little Silver – Porsche 911 Carrera Cabriolet
Chapron – the Citroën, the decapotable, the very last of the DS
   cabriolets, built in 1978 to special order; belonging to Jane
THEBUS – 'the bus' – Transit van, at Eriboll
VDP – Vanden Plas
Winter Car – 1967 Chevrolet
Summer Car – 1967 Chevrolet
Buick – Straight 8
Old Ministerial – Jaguar bought by AC when at MoD
Citroën Mehari – a little plastic truck with an air-cooled engine
   and a very light footprint used for clearing grass. A kind of
   mobile wheelbarrow

Argocat – at Eriboll, performs the same function as the Mehari, but will also go through peat bogs, and swim

Hymac – mechanical digger at Eriboll

Countax – successor to the Westwood ride-on mower

Atco – cylinder mower for inner Bailey

SLANG

ACHAB – (lit.) 'anything can happen at backgammon', a saying originally from 'the Room' at Brooks's where games can swing at a late stage on an unpredictable run of the dice, used often as a consolation in times of depression. Adaptable in other circumstances, substituting 'politics' for 'backgammon'

AF – what AC called aortic fibrillations, not literally, but circumstances that set the heart racing

Dave-at-eight – getting up in time for the arrival of the official car, driven by Dave (or whoever the driver was)

Greywater – diarrhoea

Grunge – country clothes

Cutting peat – sometimes literally at Eriboll, but also getting away from it all

Lenin Stadium – anxiety so extreme it induces physical symptoms

Longies – long johns

Norwegian Embassy – weak at the knees

Piccolo – minor, but telling, as in 'piccolo triumph'

Sadismoid – as sadistically, though less *transitive* in meaning; the suffix -moid, or moidly, is often attached to adjectives

Satisly – arousing satisfaction, inducing complacency

Softies – recreational clothes

Thompson/plopson – defecation

too-hot-Henry – a phrase used by an actor during filming on location at Saltwood

Venice train – completely asleep on a journey

'w' – walk, as in going for a walk

white screen – computer

ABBREVIATIONS

NAMES

AC	– Alan Clark
AH	– Archie Hamilton MP
'ASPERS'	– John Aspinall
BLJ	– Beloved little Jane
CH	– Charles, Charles Howard
CS	– Christopher (aka 'Daisy') Selmes
DD	– David Davis MP
EG/EDG	– Euan Graham
'FRANCO'	– Frank Johnson
JM	– John Major MP
GJ	– Tristan Garel-Jones MP
LPF	– L.P. Fassbender, accountant
MH	– Michael Howard MP
MRDH	– Michael Heseltine MP
TK	– Tom King MP
'WOLF'	– Adolf Hitler

ACRONYMS

BB	– Big Book, otherwise *The Tories: Conservatives and the Nation State 1922–1997* (published 1998)
CGT	– Capital Gains Tax
CCO	– Conservative Central Office
CUCA	– Cambridge University Conservative Association
DE	– Department of Employment

EDM	– early day motion
EMT	– early morning tea
FP	– famous person
K&C	– Kensington and Chelsea constituency; Kent and Canterbury Hospital
KTH	– Kensington Town Hall
LCA	– love, care and attention
LLG	– loch like glass
MOS	– *Mail on Sunday*
MFT	– Minister for Trade
MOD	– Ministry of Defence
NOW	– *News of the World*
O/D	– overdraft
OECD	– Organisation for European Co-operation and Development
OUCA	– Oxford University Conservative Association
PC	– Privy Counsellor
PFD	– Peters, Fraser & Dunlop, literary agents
PQ	– Parliamentary Question
RREC	– Rolls-Royce Enthusiasts' Club
RUSI	– Royal United Services Institute
SE	– Stock Exchange
SEDOC	– out-of-hours doctor service in Kent
SOS	– Secretary of State
UBS	– Union Bank Suisse
UCH	– University College Hospital, London
VGL	– very good looking
WD	– 'wet' dream

INTRODUCTION

Alan Clark started keeping a regular diary in 1955 when he was still in his twenties. On quitting the House of Commons in 1992 he edited and published a selection from his decade as a junior minister in the Thatcher and Major governments and called quite simply *Diaries*. First published in 1993 to enormous success,[1] they were the start of his becoming, what he called, an FP, famous person. He did not demur; indeed subsequent entries often go on to rebound to the phrase, 'I was lionised ...', or at the very least, 'demi-lionised'.

In historical terms his account of Mrs Thatcher's downfall as Prime Minister is now seen as definitive. On a personal level his frankness caused little surprise to his friends, whether in how he came to make a ministerial statement in the Commons after indulging too liberally at a wine tasting or in recounting the attractions of a pretty face. Fool, Clark, fool! he would say. His diaries (sometimes he called them his journals, at others his memoirs) show a man who delights in writing, not least about pastoral events at his homes in Kent, Scotland, Switzerland and even in London (the Albany blackbird). Ask an admirer of the Clark diaries to name a favourite passage and it is odds on that the day he came to shoot a heron will figure high.

Before his death in 1999, and six years after the first publication of *Diaries*, Clark was persuaded (not least by financial considerations) that it was time, at last, to raid his past diaries for two further volumes: the 'prequel' to begin when he entered

---

[1] In paperback it is now titled *Diaries: In Power*.

politics in the early 1970s, and finally, to complete the trilogy, a
sequel to the original, what happened in the 1990s after he first
quit the House of Commons only to be elected again five years
later for one of the Conservatives' most prized and copper-
bottomed constituencies, the newly merged Kensington and
Chelsea.

When he became ill in the late spring of 1999, with what
turned out to be a brain tumour, he had done some preliminary
work on the next volume.[2] The question of the third – and now
final volume – was a matter for Clark's widow Jane. In deciding
that it should go ahead she was mindful that it would not prove
wholly pleasant reading for her, and that the 1999 entries would
revive for her memories of her husband's final illness and death.
However she also appreciated that her husband's standing would
be incomplete without it. In fact Clark was writing until five
weeks before he died. His script, rarely easy to read, became
often shaky, increasingly minuscule. But despite the cancer his
mental and intellectual powers were undimmed. Deciphering it,
as ever with Clark's variable handwriting, was often laborious,
but with Jane Clark's inestimable help I was defeated only rarely.

The original *Diaries* ended in February 1991. In his final
entry he recounted being made a Privy Counsellor and walking
back to Westminster, where he 'had a boring, overcooked lunch
in the Members' dining room'. The new volume opens two days
later with an intense affair, and ends in August 1999 with his
love for Jane renewed and restated, but his own life coming to
an end. Alan and Jane were married for 41 years. As Clark himself admits he was guilty at times of treating his wife appallingly,
and even at one point in these diaries he thought of leaving her
for someone else. But that thought never became a deed. These
diaries, however, reveal an occasion when Jane's patience snapped,
and she left him a note (see 14 December 1997). But of a more
serious marital breach, in 1992, AC has left no comment, except
evidence of pages torn from his diary.

---

[2] It was finally published a year after his death, as *Diaries: Into Politics*

Like his father Kenneth Clark, who in the early 1970s gave him Saltwood Castle in Kent, Alan was a hypochondriac. In this final volume the borderline between hypochondria and his own self-diagnosis of the ill health that is to come is tantalising for the reader. We know that Alan will die from brain cancer. He, however, does not, even though two years before his death he is writing increasingly of headaches, of an inability to defocus, of a weakness in one arm, of a spot on his lip, of changes in taste, appetite and sense of smell. He is capable of thinking the worst, but at this distance readers will share with his editor a surprise that despite test after test, no one in the medical profession identified the cause of his illness until it was far too late.

Politics remain a driving force. His decision to quit at the 1992 election was mostly to do with his exasperation at representing Plymouth Sutton. Clark and his Conservative association (as readers of *Diaries: Into Politics*, in particular, will recall) were often at daggers drawn. Clark found constituency surgeries particularly irksome. Even when he returned to Westminster five years later as MP for Kensington & Chelsea (could there have been a constituency more ideally matched to his talents and his personality?) there are rumblings about his lack of attention to detail. What he loved most about being a politician was Westminster itself, political gossip and debate. Shame about the constituents, he once joked in my hearing.

These last diaries are drawn in the main from eight A4 HMSO or 'Banner' hardback volumes of numbered lined pages (some pages are missing, as mentioned above, but there are no obvious gaps in the narrative). The paper quality is variable, and Clark's choice of pens often relies on whatever was available. He rarely writes in ballpoint; green ink is, as he says at one point, usually, but not exclusively reserved for holidays at Eriboll and Zermatt. These though were not the only diaries. At Shore Cottage, Eriboll, the far north of Scotland estate the Clarks acquired following the death of his father, he kept a diary to which photographs were added, and from this I have transcribed his account of the 'great walk' undertaken in 1991. The record of the 1993 Alpine rally in which he drove his Rolls-Royce Silver Ghost comes partly from an intermittent motoring diary. But there are also entries on single sheets, often House of Commons notepaper and not always slipped into the appropriate place. I do wonder what other treasures may yet be found.

I am, though, surprised that he does not write more about some of the key events in which he was involved during the 1990s, among them the Matrix Churchill trial (and the Scott enquiry which followed), his legal action against the London *Evening Standard* over their spoof 'Not the Alan Clark Diary', the court case against one of the Clarks' Rottweilers after an incident involving a BBC cameraman. He does not appear to have written about either of his sons' weddings, although he delights in recording the christening of grandchildren. But on whether he was accepted into the Catholic Church shortly before his death, as Father Michael Seed has claimed, the evidence points firmly to the status quo. If Alan Clark had taken this momentous decision while on his deathbed one can be certain he would have written about it. God is never far from his thoughts, or from his diary, and, nightly, he said his prayers.

With the best part of nine years of journals to draw from I have had to be selective. As a writer, sometimes with crowded days between entries, he is repetitious. He has a habit of announcing what he will be doing the following week, and then a week later giving an account of what happened. I have only occasionally included both. With events described more recent than in either of the two published volumes I have also disguised three of the cast list.

Reliving his life through his diaries has been a rewarding experience. He has an eye for what is important in politics. He is good at spotting talent that will emerge later: both William Hague and Iain Duncan Smith are mentioned well before their leadership ambitions are tested. He is widely read: these diaries contain references as varied as Chips Channon's diaries, Evelyn Waugh's *Brideshead Revisited*, the *Faber Book of War Poetry* (edited by his former parliamentary colleague, Kenneth Baker), A.W.

Kinglake's *Eothen*, Sapper's Bulldog Drummond novel *The Final Count* and, perhaps less surprising given its setting, John Buchan's *John Macnab*. But above all it is the richness of the life he leads and enjoys, despite frequent protestations of being depressed.

The question arose at a late stage as to how to end the volume. What I did not know when I began transcribing AC's journals was that Jane Clark had herself started a diary during the final weeks of her husband's life. It seemed appropriate therefore to describe what happened through her account. Jane at one point asked Al, who had by this time stopped writing, if he would like to continue by dictating entries to her. No, he said, it would be 'too melancholy'. Jane Clark's account, which I have edited, is by its very nature sad to read, and inevitably for someone bedridden at the end contains reports of bodily functions that some readers may feel are in excess, but that was a fact of Alan's last days. Yet it also has its moments of tenderness, of exasperation, even of humour. Jane Clark has showed herself to be a worthy fellow diarist as well as a devoted wife.

Ion Trewin
July 2002

EDITOR'S NOTE

Footnotes give the present and sometimes past – but rarely future – positions of individuals, usually at their first appearance. Nor is an MP's political allegiance shown except where this may be unclear from the text.

AC's occasional inconsistencies in style, dates, capitalisation and even English grammar, have sometimes been left as written. I have followed his own practice and, where appropriate, silently edited passages.

In the matter of financial dealings, AC often left out the final '000'. Thus the value of a picture given as, say, £300 is actually worth £300,000. I have not altered his way of expressing figures as the sums involved are usually obvious from the context.

In the case of a clearly intense affair, which was not revealed publicly at the time, I have felt it necessary to protect the name of the woman involved by referring to her throughout as 'x'.

IT

1991

Despite my resolve to keep 'x' out of this volume I find it practically impossible to concentrate effectively on anything else. She is in my thoughts the entire time, sometimes exclusively, some of the time in parallel, as it were, with whatever else one is meant to be doing.

The journey down to Reading University in the snow.[1] I was so dejected. She was quite perky. Very cold on arrival; no one to meet us. We sat at 'the bar', drank half a pint, G&T. I said 'all I really want to do is to kiss you …' She bridled. Enjoys it, but doesn't want to seem timid. After meeting up we were guided to the Common Room, then the Hall. They had totally balls'd it up, turned it into a *public* meeting packed with SWP [Socialist Worker Party] and anti-war groupies. I acquitted myself well and she was 'encouraged', and alone among the audience asked a helpful question. In the train back I felt immensely weary. When I leaned forward and put my elbows on the table she leaned back; but when I slumped back – and stayed back for the whole journey – she leant forward to counter this.

She looked incredible in her Russian hat, totally Zhivago. I hold this image in my mind at the moment; it gives me a nodule headache on the left side now, and a sort of despair really. How *is* this going to end? It's such agony. I haven't the nerve to cut it off.

It's preposterous. I'm actually *ill*, have been for a month, lovesick it's called. A long and nasty course of chemotherapy – but with periodic bouts of addiction therapy when I delude myself that I may be cured without 'damage'.

---

[1] AC, Minister for Defence Procurement, was speaking at a Reading University meeting in the midst of the Gulf War.

White Office   *Tuesday, 12 February*

Still regrettably obsessive. After Ministers TK[1] 'held me back';
he's nervous of me, still needs to pick my brain – in this case just
before going to Washington. But *won't* let me 'in on' anything,
TV, Radio (Archie [Hamilton][2] is on every day) or even
meetings with PUS and Mottram, CDS, Vincent,[3] etc etc,
because I will show him up in front of them.

Lunched with Dilks[4] at Brooks's. His first words as we sat down
were 'How's the delightful "x"?' He was quite interesting about
Mrs T's 'Memoirs', said they could easily be ghosted – but it was
critically important that the 'ghost' should have access to all her
papers. It was something that ought to be spoken now with
Robin Butler, certainly ahead of the next General Election.[5]

Saltwood   *Sunday, 17 February*

On the way out to Bratton[6] yesterday (was it really only
yesterday?) we stopped at Brentor and I had a long, long prayer.[7]

---

[1] Tom King, MP for Bridgwater since March 1970; Defence Secretary since 1989.

[2] Archie Hamilton, MP for Epsom and Ewell since April 1978 and Armed Forces
Minister since 1988.

[3] Permanent Under-Secretary at Defence: Sir Michael Quinlan since 1988; Richard
Mottram, Deputy Under-Secretary since 1989; Chief of the Defence Staff,
Marshal of the RAF Sir David Craig since 1988; Field Marshal Sir Richard
Vincent, Vice CDS since 1987 and about to succeed as CDS.

[4] David Dilks, academic, newly appointed vice-chancellor, University of Hull; had
been research assistant, successively, to Anthony Eden, Lord Tedder and Harold
Macmillan; editor of *The Diaries of Alexander Cadogan* (1971).

[5] AC had discussed with Mrs Thatcher the writing of her biography (see *Diaries*, 4
January 1991). She was appalled at his estimate that it would take him a minimum
of three years. Sir Robin Butler had been Secretary of the Cabinet since 1988,
having been Mrs Thatcher's Principal Private Secretary, 1982–85.

[6] Town Farm, Bratton-Clovelly, Devon.

[7] Approached from the main Okehampton Road at Mary Tavy, this twelfth-century
Dartmoor church at the summit of Brentor stands all alone. Although it is a steep
walk, many thousands of visitors annually are attracted to it.

Should make me serene. And it does while I'm talking to God. But as soon as I stop doing so it comes seeping in. Because like all addicts I can vividly remember the incredible rush of vitality and well being that comes from a good 'fix'.

Then talk of an Election in May–June. Less than three months to go, it would seem or could be. And at that my life really will turn. A major crossroads – but I refuse to accept that thereafter it's all downhill to the grave. I just will not. ACHAB.[1]

I suppose it's better, perhaps, to put 'x' out of the way *now*. Honestly, I'm almost too weary to 'get involved'. The ache not quite as bad, lots of scar tissue there now. But, curiously, my principal concern is to find a way of starting with Jane. We had a horrible passage on Saturday night. Poor little darling – why should *she* be punished because I am being? [AC's question mark]

Last Friday I woke at 6-ish, took some EMT and 3 dry biscuits, boarded the 7.30 train at Charing Cross which didn't *leave* until it was 30 minutes late. BR now totally 3rd-world performer, no middle management in sight (too early) and periodic gabbled illiteration by a – plainly – platelayer drafted in to glottally 'try his hand at' the intercom. Got to Saltwood and loaded up Discovery. Set off at once in snow/fog/drizzle conditions and ground along M25, M3, A303 – many, many roadworks with piggy tailbacks – M4, got to Plymouth just after 4 p.m. feeling distinctly *dry* with exhaustion; just time to get a cup of tea and a scone and cream (I had no appetite – why?); then to surgery, people already making heads visible in a row through the looking glass of the outer office. A tall, strangely classy and distrait policeman who was my guard for the evening. A message from Alison[2] to ring her 'quite urgent', but naturally, she was engaged and NR [no reply] from the main switchboard so couldn't break in.

---

[1] AC was contemplating 'standing down' from the Plymouth Sutton constituency to which he was first elected in February 1974.

[2] Alison Young, AC's secretary since September 1988.

I started dealing with the mendicants, mainly complaining about their solicitors not being responsive enough. (What on earth am *I* meant to do about *that*?) Finally got through to Alison; she found me a number for Andrew Neil[1] who wished to speak 'before the deadline'. I had to spell WEDELN[2] for her. Then found I hadn't got a black tie – I was changing, as so often, into a dinner jacket in the upstairs lav. of the constituency office. Just got Jane at the hotel,[3] could she ask the manager? etc etc. Drove out to Crownhill; Nick Bennett, not a bad chap, some wives and relations at the Family Centre. Admiral Grose[4] turned up (without his wife). They are nice people – the families – though probably as wracked by trauma, infidelities or incest as any other grouping. I made a short speech – poll tax exemption – and then we moved on back into Plymouth.

The arrangements for Cecil[5] were characteristically gauche and irritating. The 'nobs', i.e. top table of about ten people had a room to themselves, with masses of drink ... untouched (but probably charged for) bottles. Then very late – doubtless blamed on me – we moved through increasingly resentful hoi polloi to the dining room. Cecil performed, just adequately, was good with questions – mainly hostile, and about interest rates. Most of the body of the room were characteristically Plymothian and 'rights'-type indignant. I escaped after dinner to our room – we had providentially booked into the Duke of Cornwall – but Jane valiantly remained downstairs chatting. At that same bar, indeed, and in that same dreary-decor room, where my adoption meeting had taken place in September 1972, nineteen years earlier.

---

[1] Andrew Neil, editor of the *Sunday Times* since 1983, executive chairman, Sky TV since 1988.
[2] 'Skiing. A technique using a swaying movement of the hips to make a series of short parallel turns.' (*The New Shorter Oxford English Dictionary*)
[3] The Clarks were staying at the Duke of Cornwall Hotel on Plymouth Hoe.
[4] Admiral Sir Alan Grose, Flag Officer Plymouth since 1990.
[5] Cecil Parkinson, MP for Hertsmere since 1983, a long-serving Minister under Mrs Thatcher, and former Conservative Party chairman; returned to the back benches in 1990.

MoD   *Thursday, 21 February*

Let's face it, I'm not really enjoying myself at all at the moment.
I am distracted, more or less constantly, by the pain of my
maladie and I can't concentrate on the really major points of
strategic policy (I must write a 'Cosint Paper' on 'Geostrategic
Policy 2000').

The Lady has now decided *against* my doing her biography –
going for the big mechanistic technique of researchers and
capable hacks. She's got no sense of art or scholarship at all,
really. And has always been unreliable, loses her nerve and goes
conventional.

Tuesday, 26 February

I have a tension headache. I'm eating very little (overnight down
to 11.2 (+)[1]) not drinking at all. I do the [MoD] stairs to the
6th floor, one minute dead at a 'normal' swinging pace, 45
seconds *prancingly*.

There are so many things going to come to a head this year
– but I can barely see things in perspective at all. Even quite
calming things like sorting through my briefcase I can't 'face'. I
suppose I'm in a pre-nervous breakdown condition.

MoD   *Thursday, 28 February*

The Gulf War is over. Too soon, I think. Bush[2] has ordered a
ceasefire. Now a long and messy interlude with Saddam[3] stalling

---

[1] AC used imperial measures, thus weight was expressed in stones and pounds.
[2] George Bush, US president since 1989.
[3] Saddam Hussein, Iraqi president since 1979.

and dodging and quite likely to start shooting again. The
Foreign Office has no idea what it wants. Never seems to have
given any thought to the post-war pattern, the western military
presence, commitments – OBJECTIVES. I could write a
scintillating paper on this, but I'm exhausted and my morale is
at zero. Last night Mrs Thatcher (as she must now be called)[1]
chided me for being asleep on the bench when Tom was making
his statement.

An article in *The Times* by Oakley[2] – a man who always
ignores me – about the leaderless Right. No one mentions my
name. How quickly this can happen! There is now talk of a
General Election in June. Just time to claim, massively, some
allowances out of 91–92! Interviewed by Melanie Phillips[3] last
evening and she asked me about the adrenalin of power how it
keeps one going through this hellish existence; I said, 'But look
what happens when people retire or get flung out – they shrivel
up and get cancer immediately.'

MoD   *Monday, 4 March*

Darling Jane is looking a wee bit strained. She knows something
is up, and is quiet a lot of the time. But she doesn't question me
at all – just makes the occasional scathing reference. I do want
to make her happy – she's such a *good* person.[4]

And what of my medium-term plans? I must get rid now
of 'x'. What then? I *very* much wish an early Election. I

---

[1] Margaret Thatcher, usually referred to by AC as The Lady, although no longer
  Prime Minister was still MP for Finchley; she was not created a life peer until 1992.
[2] Robin Oakley, political editor of *The Times* since 1986.
[3] Melanie Phillips, journalist with an influential column on the *Guardian* before
  moving to the *Observer*.
[4] A few days later AC confesses: 'I fear I am as bad as I have ever been. No progress
  at all. And darling Jane somehow knows. She was cross, just a little sad and puzzled
  and listless. I would love to do something to really make her happy.'

popped over and spoke to Richard Ryder[1] this morning.
He was in agony from a recently (18 hours) ricked back –
playing tennis. But benign and delightful as always, said wait
until 20 April – but of course it doesn't matter giving late
notice to the constituency.[2] Registered my bid for a 'working
peerage' with a smile, but indicated approval. Also nodded
sagely when I said what a fool and how objectionable, was
TK.

Saltwood   *Sunday, 10 March*

God, is it already *10th* March? A quarter of the year gone by,
and I have done nothing, not answered a single letter, paid
a bill – still less 'played' with cars or other hobbies. I *must*
break out of the cycle, but I can only really effectively do
so by giving 'notice' in the next three weeks. The sheer
administrative complication that this entails compounds it.
This morning, woken up from a deep muck–sweat slumber by
Jane at 2.30 a.m. I lay awake for about 1½ hours, thought
among other things – I really would just as soon pack it in
now, just not go back to London *at all*. She rightly pointed out
I must see through Options,[3] the tank etc – leave my mark.
Then again, I suppose, the Cabinet changes at Easter – if there
is to be no General Election – but even Secretary of State
would almost have to ask – because of how it might have
been.

---

[1] Richard Ryder, MP for Mid-Norfolk since 1983 and government Chief Whip
since 1990.
[2] AC was subject to conflicting advice. Over lunch, three days before, Tony
Fanshawe (formerly Anthony Royle, MP for Richmond, 1959–83 and now a life
peer), told AC not to 'antagonise people' by leaving his 'standing down'
announcement until too late.
[3] The Ministry of Defence was, like other government departments, looking into
the future, in this case the role of the British armed forces into the twenty-first
century. AC concentrated on equipment.

Finances are now in a total mess – Coats at 160 + .[1] Vast new
out-goings of Mains in prospect, lead roof, moat leaking. I fear
it will have to be the Degas[2] because we will save the CGT by
doing it through Andrew. Might yet scrape by as stock markets
are recovering. But how do I see my future? Get the diary into
shape as soon as you can, then really become a recluse, naturalist,
pinpoint feats. Loch Shiel to Loch Eriboll.[3] A kind of upmarket
Albert (if he was called Albert) Wainwright. With a hint, perhaps,
of Poucher (and a touch of class, as Jane said, with Robin
Fedden).[4]

But right at the moment, I am in really bad shape – shaking,
inability to concentrate. The knowledge of this makes me
medically apprehensive.

Winter office, a.m.   *Tuesday, 19 March*

In a state of abject depression – cross-streaked with apprehension so that my hands and forearms shake and feel watery.
Poor old Archie H came into my office yesterday afternoon and
stayed for ¾ hour whingeing on about end-of-an-era, all over,
etc etc. The pretext was on being 'boxed-in' on Options,
Treasury squeeze all that and I made some tangential slagging
off of TK, his indecisiveness, inability to make any judgement

---

[1] Coats had amalgamated with the Clark cotton thread business, J. & J. Clark of
Paisley, in 1896. AC's great-great grandfather had invented the wooden spool or
bobbin. The decline (25½p in 1997) in the price of the Coats shares is never far
from his mind.

[2] Edgar Degas's *Femme s'épongeant le dos*, left to AC by his father.

[3] AC's grandfather owned the whole of the Ardnamurchan peninsula, on the west
coast of Scotland, to the south-west of Eriboll.

[4] *Alfred* Wainwright and W. A. Poucher, two indefatigable guides and proselytisers
for the Lake District; today Poucher is the less well known. A chemist by training,
who worked for thirty years with Yardley's, the cosmetics company, he climbed
and photographed the uplands of Britain. He wrote more than thirty books and
died in 1988. Robin Fedden, former deputy Director-General and Historic
Buildings Secretary of the National Trust, author of *The National Trust Guide*.

save that of short-term political 'impact', 'how will it go in the house' etc. We are back to the old Conservative Government days, Eden at best. I said at least we broke the unions in the last decade, you won't hear much from *them* in the future. He agreed, but was still doleful. There's the general feeling that the baddies are getting away with it again – most apparent as Jane said at the weekend with all that fuss about the 'Birmingham Six',[1] yet one more excuse to slag off the police, wretched fellows. Jury wouldn't even convict an IRA gunrunner with their Kalashnikovs in the car and hands smelling of Semtex!

In the evening I went (with Alison) to Kensington Conservatives. *Very* clued up and intelligent and good company they were with many aspirant candidates. My address not *quite* up to standard, but questions sparkled. Dudley Fishburn[2] (whom I had warned Alison was a 'non-event') said nice things about me. His majority at a by-election I must admit is only 800.

Saltwood   *Saturday, 23 March*

Bruce Anderson rang,[3] and we gossiped around a bit. He is of the *agnostic* school concerning JM's private life.[4] But admitted that Norma had told him 'John's not nearly as much fun now; doesn't seem to have the energy … always into the boxes, etc'. Bruce said that Richard [Ryder] now 'pro' me, and there was some talk they might both come down for dinner and the night

---

[1] The 'Birmingham Six', six men who spent 16 years in prison after being wrongfully convicted of the 1974 Birmingham pub bombings.

[2] Dudley Fishburn, MP for Kensington since July 1988 when he succeeded the late Sir Brandon Rhys Williams. Kensington's merger as a constituency with Chelsea would not take place until 1997.

[3] Bruce Anderson, political journalist, currently with *Sunday Express*.

[4] The press had been full of concern at John Major's state of health. He had been PM for little more than 100 days, and was suffering from intermittent ear and throat infections. His wife Norma was quoted as saying, 'He's awfully tired and not getting enough sleep.'

at Easter. But he said my enemies were rampant, Douglas in particular.[1]

Charles P[2] had told him, 'Under no other Prime Minister would Alan have been either given office or promoted; and under any other Prime Minister he would long since have been sacked.' So I felt rather awful about already disowning the old Thatcherite rump the way I do. But actually, they're just a lot of old has-beens – all leaving public life. Who's going to lead them? Bruce said 'Michael Spicer'.[3] Well, *really*! Apparently John M made a long flat speech at Southport where the [Conservative] Central Council meeting (a fatiguing and probably somewhat disapproving body which I have never attended) is being held. TK, irritatingly, got a standing ovation – too easy after the Gulf – but MRDH [Heseltine][4] was greeted 'stonily'. I don't quite know what the Party is doing at the moment. It's a limbo year, which will, I suppose, suffer the planning blight for most of its course. For the first time ever, I believe, I watch the approaching springtime with gloom and apprehension. There is no way out of total agony on the w/e of 10 May[5] (cruelly and paradoxically the very solstice of physical delight and renewal).

Sunday's papers show the Party in considerable disarray – now likely to be aggravated by the six-point deficit shown in MORI. Although actually, it would be slightly more tolerable to be out under Labour than under a *new wave* Tory administration.

---

[1] Almost certainly a reference to Douglas Hurd, MP for Witney since 1983 (Mid-Oxon February 1974–83); Foreign Secretary since 1989. He and AC were on opposing sides of the Conservative Party.

[2] Sir Charles Powell, Private Secretary to the Prime Minister, 1984–91.

[3] Michael Spicer, MP for South Worcestershire and, like AC, elected in February 1974. Junior minister under Mrs Thatcher (Department of the Environment, 1990).

[4] Michael Heseltine, MP for Henley since 1974 (Tavistock, 1966–74), Cabinet minister in Thatcher governments, beaten in the 1990 Tory leadership election when John Major succeeded Mrs Thatcher; currently Environment Secretary, something of a poisoned chalice.

[5] An official visit, as Minister for Defence Procurement, to the Gulf States, following the end of the war.

I have no idea what the future holds this year. How, when, do I break it to Alison that I'm not standing, for example?

Saltwood   *31 March, Easter Sunday*

The special moisture in the spring air – if not the foggy inland – with the sun lightly obscured, but a luminous promise. We went to Communion this morning. I enjoy it now because of the opening prayer, whose significance (as with so much until now) I never before appreciated. '… to whom all hearts are open, all desires known, and from whom no secrets are hid …'

Ashford Station (50 feet out!)   *Sunday, 14 April*

A great series in the *Sunday Telegraph* on 'the Mid-Life Crisis' today. It's going to be hard to come to terms with this – particularly in the knowledge that it's my 'fault'. Eleven years left, I suppose. If I'm lucky. I'm anxious about my nose (left side); my diabolic pressure must be sky-high; I tried to hold my breathing within the chest limits and got – at great cost – to 1¾ minutes (should be 2-2½) but on subsequent shots could only get it to 1.

This whole experience could take hold of as pre-cancerous.

Only good moment: I watched John Major[1] on *Walden*. He took it very well. I thought I'd ring Richard R and tell him; couldn't get through so switched to No 10. Yes he was there, could 'they' ring me back? Came through very quickly (though not as quickly as the Lady in crisis) and was *pathetically* glad to hear praise. 'Bless you, couldn't have come at a better moment'

---

[1] John Major was being criticised by, among others, Sir Alan Walters, former economic adviser to Margaret Thatcher, for his economic policies.

etc. I made reassuring crack about we all loved the Lady and her style 'none more than me ...' etc. But things more difficult now, people wanted it different. 'But have you seen today's papers?' *The Observer* – I couldn't remember anything *particularly* objectionable in *The Observer*, but looking at it afterwards, I suppose he must have meant Nick Wapshott's bitchy repetition of Mrs T's crack about 'the B-team'.[1] Fortunately I'd read the leader, which was broadly laudatory, in yesterday's *Times*, and quoted that. I think he was pleased. But where it's all going to end – like absolutely every other 'problem' which lies on us – God knows.

And talking of God – I went down to St Leonard's last evening to pray. Norman Woods[2] was there, pleasant and serious as always, counselling a handsome and classy couple about their Christening. I knelt and reflected on 'it' all. I almost asked Norman to hear my confession, but didn't/couldn't, though afterwards Jane said he would have. I was rather shocked to find how I prayed so selfishly. It was quite an effort to *focus* on the real purpose and to release darling Jane of her pain and sense of betrayal. She's going through exactly what I did in February – and I know what it's like – total hell (and in my own case all too likely to recur in slightly different form any minute). Only feebly did I give thanks for this wonderful life and all my blessings. Disgraceful.

White Office   *Thursday, 18 April*

Even allowing for the fact that it was mainly written in the train the standard of writing in the last entry is perfectly awful and indicates the level of mental disturbance from which I am presently suffering.

---

[1] Nicholas Wapshott, political editor of *The Observer* since 1988.
[2] The Rev. Canon Norman Woods, vicar of St Leonard's Church, Hythe.

Plymouth–Paddington train   *Saturday, 20 April*

I think, probably, I'm worse than at any previous point this year. The real problem is the *total* uncertainty hanging on prospects. I can't seem even to pray properly. Even last evening when I climbed to Brentor church. I could think things through, but make no real contact because, I suppose, what I really want to do is cruel and disreputable. My personal and political anxieties overlap inextricably. I had a rough meeting with the councillors (brilliantly thought up by Alison and organised by her). Some reasonable noises from Mount Gould and Efford, with some grumbling by (inevitably) Plympton St Mary and Erle, 'it's too late ...' etc; then a whole list of what should be done tomorrow much of it impossible, a crash visit from Douglas Hurd (?!) etc. 'Well, if it's too late', I said, 'what's the point of doing these things?' Then (was it Campbell?) suggested that Michael Heseltine 'would go down very well' if he came here. 'Well, that's a good suggestion,' I said, 'because he's a bit short of places where he would go down well at the moment, and I expect he'd be glad of the invitation.'[1] More titters from loyalists.

   All right, so I'm not standing again.

   And 'x'? I've had so many breaks with her, but the day of the death sentence approaches. May, the magic month. At the end a solitary trip to Scotland. June and July the last months in public life. Will the obsession then be extinct − or at least diminishing?

Later − Tuesday
I just can't focus − the summer, the autumn, plans for the recess or 'leave'. Doesn't anyone go *abroad* at all? Will the Porsche or the ID decap [Jane's Citroën] be used? I sit at my desk in the

---

[1] As Environment Secretary Heseltine was unpopular, having to cope with the aftermath of the poll tax, one of the most hated measures of Mrs Thatcher's period as Prime Minister.

White Office getting impatient, watching the red phone light –
which has been on for 35 minutes.[1]

Albany   *Tuesday, 30 April*

An awful night, little more than three hours' fragmented sleep.
This morning Valerie[2] rang, claimed to be coming over in May
– so what?

Only good thing. Jane is better. Quite cured you could say. I
try and tell myself that this is what is really important. But (more
than) half of me says no it isn't – what counts is the incredible
joie de vivre, the physical and mental delight of being in love
and in the company of your adored. God alive! This confusion
has been going on for nearly five months. At least I do the stairs
in MoD, now weigh 11.6 and did Gossie last Sunday evening in
an incredible 2'28". All for what?

Later

In the White Office, with a batch of nasty questions (7 out of
top 13) all potentially awkward, and TK got me in to 'make sure'
that I was not going (presumably) to commit a 'gaffe'. First
impressions endure, and I suppose he is still conditioned by our
experience together when I was his junior minister in DE. And
all against a background of horrid (really horrid) personal
deprivation – which keeps recurring in a hundred different
ways, which affects my concentration.

---

[1] AC added his own footnote: 'turned out to be Keith Simpson'. Simpson, Special
  Adviser to the Defence Secretary 1988–90, and a former lecturer in war studies
  at Sandhurst, became Tory MP for Mid-Norfolk in 1997.
[2] Valerie Harkess, one of three women, a mother and two daughters, described by
  AC as 'the coven' (see *Diaries: Into Politics* and *Diaries*).

Saltwood   *Bank Monday, 6 May*

Really vile weather. It's been like this for three weeks, blowing
so hard we can't even have a fire in the Green Room, rain, lawns
a mess, so cold that one naturally puts on longies. The Grahams[1]
came last night. EG looking incredible (though hair *very* white
in the centre and surprisingly old person soft and fluffy to the
touch). Funny and intelligent about medical matters, friends
who are dead. An excellent venison dinner, but the wine made
little difference to me. I am depressed, aimless. I see no future,
no objectives, no 'satisfaction' except possibly the traditional one
of 'getting things in order', a gift more to darling Jane than
anything else. Even when I went out in the Buick, this barely
registered, drove it badly, had forgotten how to change gear. I
never really want to see the Buick again, whereas I do sometimes pine for the Black Caddy. I am in bad shape, apprehensive
of my Gulf trip, ability to stay 'strong' this week and next. Max
[jackdaw] and his wife, appeared at the window this morning.
He *very* clearly and characteristically left me a pellet on the
windowsill, which I will take on my travels.

Saltwood   *Tuesday, 7 May*

Spent most of the day clearing the nettles of Lady Conway's
Bridge. Yet more capital expenditure threatening – to get
Barwick (presently doing the café wall) to make up the bridge
and then to get the roadman to 'dress' it when he does the drive.
But at tea I felt really gloomy. Recurrent pangs of 'x' all the time
I pulled, or *eradicated*, the nettles. But I know I shall have contact
with her this week. Once I acknowledge her loss, and it really is
'gone for good' how empty the whole thing will be? What will

---

[1] Euan Graham, long-standing friend. He had retired in 1984 as Principal Clerk of
Private Bills, House of Lords. He and his first wife, Pauline, were divorced in 1972.
By his second wife Caroline he had two daughters.

be my purpose in life? Just to stave off old age, I suppose, stay (outwardly) boyish for as long as I can watch people dying around me.

But not knowing where she is and what she is doing will be agony. Even worse than (as now) knowing what she *is* doing.

HE's residence, Qatar [1]   *Sunday, 12 May*

Out to Shaafa today and then to see Tip[2] who was magnificent, handsome, clear-headed and hugely popular with his brother officers. In great heat (43°) was shown round the 'sheds'. Impressive installations, promising recruits, grotty equipment (CVRT[3] and Chieftains and M60s). Our helicopter, a shabby Bell Huey, wouldn't start and we switched to another, even shabbier one. Our pilot – slightly James-like, young, blond. On the return journey he said we'd make a detour on the Jebel Akhdar. At the time I thought this sounded a bit dodgy, said nothing. Drank some camel's milk (quite delicious) in the mess, felt pretty good. But in fact he lined up a gorge with 3000 ft sides – less than 40-80 ft wide in places, climbed up to over 9000 ft looking at little villages, mud hut settlements etc. One of the most obviously dangerous things I have done for ages, and not enough lateral margin for side draughts or gusts ('whoops!' he said at one point). After it was over, and were all in the HS125, I, and the others, felt a real *high*. The beginning, it seemed, of 'feeling better'.

---

[1] For his official visit to the Gulf, AC flew on an HS 125 via RAF Akrotiri (Cyprus), and moved on to Oman before reaching Qatar.

[2] Andrew Clark was attached to the Sultan of Oman Armoured Brigade.

[3] Combat Vehicle Reconnaissance Track.

Saltwood (Long Garage)   *Sunday, 19 May*

I wouldn't have thought I could get lower, more depressed and
unsettled. Partly, I suppose, because Jane is getting worse all the
time, not eating anything (her weight is down to 8 stone, mine
to 11.4 (*net*) I have lost 10½ lbs – nearly a stone). She has got a
lot of confessions out of me, along the lines of what-do-you-do?
when-did-you-do-it? type interrogation. I almost relish the
admissions as of giving a dimension, a reminder of what occurred
and has now ceased.

This continues to have a frightful effect on my routine,
output, concentration. It's been running now for six months and
no sign whatever of a diminishing of its intensity, quite the reverse
in fact. Practically nothing gives me enjoyment any longer: cars,
cleaning nickel with wire wool and Bluebell; the Heritage – that
lovely May vision of the arboretum with its yellowy greens;
politics – the 'comment' in the Sundays is total dross, I'm barely
interested although vaguely *constater* that the Conservatives'
fourth term is now in serious jeopardy in which case my title
and even 'k' are now down the drain; Brooks's, the Mews, the
company of 'friends' or journalists means very little. I said to
Jane, the only things left that I like are seeing and talking to the
boys (I had had a good conversation with James and Eriboll is
ok, because Wimpey's[1] are going to step forward, also Tip was so
fabulous in Oman with his lovely tidy quarters) and driving the
Porsche. Yesterday we came back to Bratton in 3hr 24 minutes
– Jane was very patient and good.

But she is *devastated* by what is happening. She knows,
inevitably, that I still pine for 'x'. Yesterday she was so sweet to
me on arrival, tried to seduce me on the lower end of the
asthma rail. I would have loved to, but terrified over one more
failure and disappointment. Sometimes she says, 'I love you so
much, I really feel I ought to let you do whatever you want.' At
other times she says I have destroyed so much there's no point,

---

[1] To extract gravel.

she won't even pray. What really hurts me is the knowledge of
my own affliction. If I were younger I could hold both these
women without trouble.

I'm not wholly wiped out, and I get little waves of hope that
something might happen. God might dispense a favour. But he
has given one so much. I've really had my quota already. I
wonder how Scotland will be. Will that, too be a failure? Somehow, I think not, although the Whit weekend will be painful.

Eriboll: the great walk   *Saturday, 25 May*

Today I completed the great walk that has been on my mind
almost since seeing it on the map some six or seven years ago.

Left the croft about 9 a.m. (later than I had hoped) and parked
the Volvo at the end of the Stra'beg track at 9.18. I went via the
bothy – unusually unoccupied although it is a holiday weekend
– and made a short entry of my intention in their log, allowing
a time of seven hours. Started the 'approach march' up the valley
at 9.37.

Just within the hour, at 10.35, I crossed the fence into the
Westminster [estate] territory having forded the Polla, and
almost immediately began a very steep climb through birch and
mossy peat gulleys, much riven by natural storm channels. Once
above the tree line the gradient slackened, although great cliffs
and cornices of peat showed the effect of flash flooding with
water pouring off the Cranstackie ridge.

At twenty minutes past eleven I reached the stalkers track that
runs up from Loch Dionard to the summit of Creag Staonsaid
and on over to Glen Golly.

The cloud line was at about 1600 feet, and I had some
difficulty in orienting myself on the descent to Dionard. My
intention was to follow Alt an Essain Ghill up to the ford shown
at the sortie from An Dubh Loch, then pick up the track that
skirted the Creaggan Meall Horn. There are two burns – both

quite difficult in spate – that run down here from the southern
slopes of Creag Staonsaid, fordable today, but pretty foamy and
dangerous I would judge in the autumn. As I worked my way
down I saw very clearly the lines of the track (not shown on the
O.S. 1:50 'Cape Wrath', but just delineated on the 1:25
Pathfinder of 'Arkle') that climbs up from Dionard on the w.
side of the Alt an Essain Ghill. I searched for a ford (or 'leap')
and just made it, losing my stalking stick, which I immediately
pursued down stream. It got stuck between rocks a couple of
times then freed as I approached and tumbled on. Finally I
caught up with it and scrambled up the bank to the track. This
is in reasonable repair, would carry an Argocat over this stretch
though deteriorates to little more than a firm grassy spine
higher up. Quite soon after, it seemed, at 12.30, I reached Coir
an Dubh Loch, sinister and dark jade green, being fed by waters
from Lolhan Ulbha above it. Cold drizzle, poor visibility. I ate
my pack lunch and restarted at 12.32 getting on the steep early
phase 'aortic fibrillation' – *passim* President Bush – but just
thought sod it, and pressed on.

There is a burn (unmarked) that feeds Dubh Loch from
Creaggan Meall Horn and the track plays with it sometimes
skirting, sometimes deviating, but the actual turn to cross is very
obvious and marked by good stepping stones. Within one hour,
at 1.32, I reached the cairn where there is a junction with
another track (not shown on the Pathfinder) and a gradual
descent, increasingly grassy, follows the line of the Alt Horn,
though well above it to the NW. The 'worst' of the traverse was
now over and, exultant, I ran most of the way, feeling now that
I had a 'record' time within my grasp. At half-past two I emerged
from the Glen with Loch Stack visible on the right and a steep
downward track – not unlike the first approach to the Trift
ascent in Zermatt – leading into a Westminster pine plantation,
now mature. Exited from this between two huge rocks, fifteen,
sixteen feet high that framed the iron gateway. It took me nearly
another hour's walking along the flat to follow the vehicle track
around the eastern edge of the loch to the causeway, which

joined the main road to Laxford Bridge. Here I slouched on the
bank and ate the remains of my picnic, then walked westerly for
another hour and a bit before sighting Jane and the 'Discovery'
just past Stack Lodge. Whole time, well under seven hours, so
that five, really, to the deserted croft at 'Lone' that marks the end
of the walk. I saw no one, until the last point on the flat where
I called to some 'serious' folk, well kitted out with nylon back
packs and new climbing equipment. At first rebarbatif they may
have thought that I was a scruffy laird questioning their rights.
They became more amiable, but were, I judge, uneasy tyros.
They didn't know where Eriboll was, even, and proclaimed their
intention of climbing Foinaven and Arkle (different objectives
surely?). Had the cloud line lifted the walk would have been
even more fulfilling, and alarming. But there is no doubt that
one is helped immeasurably by the tracks on the Westminster
side. Natural judgement would have probably taken a different
route skirting Creaggan Meall Horn earlier and following the
burn in the Alt Horn much lower down.

A wonderful taste of the remote glens, and now whets the
appetite for some of the crueller and steeper corries.[1]

Saltwood   *Sunday, 2 June*

Half-way through the year, and no let-up *whatsoever* in the
misery factor. Quite the reverse in fact. Yesterday I had a raging
temper tantrum after catching some 'pinks' with the Countax
under the library windows. Bellowed and roared, threw my
clothes around, cursed, cried etc. We were a tiny bit better at
supper, but Jane had a bad night and this morning at breakfast
staged a *duet* of wailing and recrimination in the course of
which she threw and smashed a coffee cup, at the news that 'x'
was in contact with the contractors about putting in a bathroom

---

[1] Elsewhere, AC summed up the great walk: 'as good as a "medical".'

at B5. After we'd calmed down went over to the Hardys at
Sandling Park and strolled, for a little too long, among the
rhodies and azaleas. When we got back I 'striped' the Bailey (first
time this year). 'Tea' was at 6.45, and now I'm over in my father's
study to record – what? That I still have no taste for anything –
cars, heritage, politics, papers, paperwork, tidying, wine,
company of friends – the endless variety of lovely May vistas is
dross for me, all this for the very first time in my entire life.
'Nineteen ninety-one, the end of all the fun.'

I say, how is it all going to end? I don't know, I mean I
suppose it *isn't* going to end, although the intensity of the pain,
its obsessive and all-excluding nature may ease off. I'm in an
impossible situation, impossible, that is, to conceive of any happy
outcome. 'x' isn't really attracted to me any more; it's waning all
the time. I *did* have one more chance, but I flunked it, and now
I'm just the 'preferred escort'. But in any case, how *could* I run
away from Jane? Thinking of her, and what *she* was doing and
thinking will be just as painful and disturbing as, at present, is
thinking (ditto) of 'x'. 'x' wants, half wants me to take her away
for a little while. How the hell do I arrange this? And whose
were those initials I saw in her diary for Friday lunch?

White Office   *Tuesday, 4 June*

Yesterday I went to see 'Dr' Page, Rowntree's successor.[1]

Young, absurdly so it seemed, but probably a contemporary of
Tom Bates.[2] I told him my tale and he seemed concerned, asked
a few faintly conventional questions about 'stress' and so on.
Subjected me to an examination; blood pressure high ('it always
is'), but he looked most piercingly into my eyes using a tiny, but
powerful light and said that the blood vessels were normal. Took

---

[1] Dr Nick Page, who had taken over from the Clarks' long-time doctor, Dr Rowntree.
[2] Tom Bates, private consultant in Kent.

blood for 'tests', talked of giving hormones or whatever, asked about diabetes (urine sample), did nervous reactions (left side not so good). Said, disconcertingly, that testicles were 'atrophic', 'shrivelled' (in that case why do I still get WDs?). He seemed dismissive about my claim of good general health. I had climbed the MoD stairs in 42 seconds and the Eriboll/Stack walk, said that this was probably the way that stress was finding its impact on my good (i.e. normal) health pattern. Certainly it's true that it has been worse since I got to MoD. I can't bear to look at the records since then – so many lost opportunities.

My spirits were high when I left his surgery. But since then I have become depressed. My relationship with 'x' has altered – I fear irreparably, although we went through all this in February – and in any case it all poses such complexities.

Uncertainty, total uncertainty, and apprehension wreak their damage.

Sunday, 9 June

I am still miserable. I have been all year (with the exception of the long three weeks which I was recovering ground in end March early April). I just can't go on like this. I am being beastly to Jane; one had another awful night yesterday after I collapsed on hearing that Andrew had been sent a letter saying 'I am crying as I write this.' But really this incident, it's my way, I suppose, of venting my own despair. For once in my life I'm going to stick to the plan. *Nothing*, I'll try not even to see her until Thursday evening, and just see if she turns up from the train.

Yesterday I had a conversation with Richard R[yder] and he told me that the House would go on sitting into August. I can only get through August if I anaesthetise, a tourniquet, or whatever it is in July

A pretty awful day. We had planned to go into the arboretum

and clear wood. But for some reason the Toyota battery – perfectly all right when we put it away – had a dud cell and wouldn't start. There followed frequent battery changes; R Cont to Toyota, New Bing to R Cont, Mehari to Bang Bang in order to make place for hiding R Cont as peacocks were vandalising, I mean crazy scratching and leaping at their reflection in everything from the Shadow to S16.

Finally getting to the arboretum I made a balls of pruning the rowan tree,[1] didn't really get much done although Jane was incredible, staking and planting. I have a latent sore throat (yesterday also) and 'lost' my voice. It has no power, like an old person. So needed to shout for Tom[2] (and Jane). More impotence.

MoD   *Thursday, 13 June*

I'm really now quite thin and gaunt. I slept well – continuously indeed – but only for six-and-a-bit hours. Today I'm going *into the care of doctors* in that rather more indicative mode that one does, I suppose, in one's sixties; probably that most creepy of all specialities, the endocrinologist, glands etc. My hormone count was right down, and so will presumably want to take a lot more tests etc etc. Page, when he told me the reason, was slightly guarded. Similarly, I am clearly suffering from a resurgence of the nose place, slightly back and to one side.

Saltwood   *Saturday, 15 June*

A bad day. We had really been looking forward to a 'free' weekend, particularly the open Saturday. But James is here

---

[1] AC believed in the magical properties of the rowan.
[2] Tom, the Clarks' Jack Russell terrier, also known as T.O.

having run away from Sally.[1] *Désoeuvré* as always, standing around
or going out to get cigarettes. So what the hell's going to happen
here? I think they're irreconcilable – or is it irreconsilable? We
drove over, having nothing better to do, to Mike Stallwood's[2] and
I questioned him lightly about his arrangements and finances.
The Eriboll account is o/d £20,000 and the same again next
year I suppose as he's employing 2½ shepherds and the grant has
been cut, the sheep sales don't cover the expenditure (the worst
possible background for 'explaining' that we can't go ahead with
Wimpey's; although my conversation with Colin Stroyan[3] disclosed that we *could* get out of it – at a cost of course. I still think
we'll have to, because it will smash the estate, the endless sound
of the crusher, breaking that special peace of the loch etc etc.) I
will have nowhere to go on my retirement – hadn't I resolved to
die on the Creaggan Road? Then again he's got all these 'military
vehicles', quite unsaleable I suspect. He asked for a release (loan)
of £20,000 from the Trust for 'investment' (i.e. speculation),
which he wouldn't disclose as it always brought 'bad luck'. The
idea is that he's going to Eriboll for a trial separation. But he
can't live there alone indefinitely, and anyway half admits that he's
drinking too much. And what does he do to occupy himself? So
there we go – *worrying about James*, just as my parents, or mother
particularly, worried about Col on and off all his life.

Then another setback. I don't think those bloody hormones
are making the slightest difference. No night or morning erections
– an initially, mildly heightened sexuality, I suppose. But this
morning at breakfast Jane suddenly said – I think when I was
trying to fluff her, on my knees – 'Having your skin-cancer
tests?' (Having slyly seen, but not commented on, the bill for the
path lab in the bathroom at Albany). I had to explain what it is
for – unhappily cancer, but I needed, also, a path lab for my nose
spot. Started whingeing, then went off to do the henhouses.

---

[1] Sally, James's second wife.
[2] Mike Stallwood, a dealer in militaria.
[3] Colin Stroyan, a friend of the Clarks, and a trustee of the Eriboll estate.

Jane and I finally had a short walk, snapping at each other. I said, 'this is going to be a very bad year, I know somehow that it is ...'

'I wish you wouldn't keep on saying that, I really dislike it.'

So health, sex, money, politics (Labour now settled at 10 points ahead and *Mail on Sunday* openly plugging Heseltine again) all bad – and with a long run ahead.

Monday, 1 July

These entries are so few and far between. Testifying to the fact that 'x' and the anxiety she generates fill every waking hour that I'm not working. I don't concentrate on my work – particularly Saltwood paper work – although I can still garden manically, sit on mowers etc. I'm also terribly bad tempered and snappy.

Wednesday, 3 July

Yesterday in *The Times* I saw that they were 'looking for' a new chairman of English Heritage. I toyed with the idea. Could keep me in public life and, with House of Lords, and – fantasising now – would offer an attachment/platform for 'x' ('Oh she's mistress/lives with the Chairman of English Heritage').

As I write this, inevitably, I can get a heavy blood flow. It's too boring, the whole thing is controlled by the brain. (One minor plus is the virtual disappearance – after three scabbings each slighter than its predecessor – of the 'nose place'. Could this be the result of the hormone boost? More and more I think that the interaction of brain and blood is everything. Page wants me to go for another test on the 20th.)

Saltwood   *Sunday, 7 July*

A lovely fine day, really hot – so much so that I bathed (three
times) in *last year's* black water (at 72°!) and felt wonderful. As
we brought Saltwood to life, and looked at all the lovely vistas
and possibilities (in Garden House too) I thought there is so
much to do here. I must get a book, a couple of Saltwood
ledgers and write them up, so that the boys have something to
refer to – contents, vistas, possibilities. They or my grandchildren
would be interested.

King's Cross train   *Sunday, 14 July*

Last night we went to *The Magic Flute* at Glyndebourne. Frightful naff, pretentious audience, longueurs etc – but in fact it was
rather fun. David (Young)[1] had invited us, and he's always fun to
meet and talk to – though still with that slight hesitance,
deference almost, that was his undoing in the upper reaches of
the Party. He asked me (depressing) about my plans, implying I
would not be in the next Government. But as Jane and I agreed
this morning at EMT *at present* the Home Secretary[2] (also there)
went out of his way to chat; the Employment Secretary[3] made a
point of asking for a drink and a private meeting; 'Sir' Geoffrey
Leigh[4] was gravely courteous and I 'stung' him for an iced coffee

---

[1] Lord Young of Graffham (life peer 1984), brought into government (from the
Manpower Services Commission, where he was chairman) by Mrs Thatcher, and
successively Employment and Trade & Industry Secretary (1985–89); now
executive chairman, Cable & Wireless.

[2] Kenneth Baker had been Home Secretary since 1990. MP for Mole Valley since
1983 (Acton, March 1968–70; St Marylebone, October 1970–83).

[3] Michael Howard, Employment Secretary since 1990; MP for Folkestone and
Hythe since 1983, thus Saltwood was in his constituency. MH and AC also found
that they shared many political views.

[4] Sir Geoffrey Leigh, property magnate with strong arts interests; founded Margaret
Thatcher Centre, Somerville College, Oxford.

and a Dundee cake. All this will evaporate when we become penniless hermits.

The performance itself was 'jolly'. New wave director (Sellars) and librettist (some American poetess)[1] with huge photo back-drop of California, captions and text in flash red dot writing. Some, but fortunately very few obvious but pretentious 'in' jokes. The whole thing redolent of sex, from a slightly feminist style – which depressed me more. Is everyone now enjoying it? One good moment at supper when Lita [Young] squawked when Jane told her how old I was.

Bratton   *Saturday 20 July*

A nice free day here, until the 'frolic' (ugh) this evening. The place slowly coming round to shape up; the empathy and 'studio' giving it a new dimension and Campling's unfinished work[2] making the *link*. Tiny touches (some bare pelmets saved from being thrown out by the couple in the cottage) remind one of how untouched it has been since the days of our penury in the very early sixties – curtain rails in the dairy dining-room, e.g. This year we should get it really comfortable, and acceptably (though not by 'x's' standards) clean and tidy.

Then there is the restoring of the place. *Massive* expenditure (Jane has now very sensibly acceded to a total overhaul of Albany). The cars are unsaleable – except, possibly, the SS, my 'folly' (although I like it very much) and the R-type Continental. But if I'd kept the 8-litre money on deposit I could have bought the Napier for nothing (i.e. inclusive of profit of 225) we'd all be millionaires.

More uncertain is the career prospect. There could well be a

---

[1] Peter Sellars had revived his 1990 production with libretto by Alice Goodman.
[2] Robert Campling, painter of all things Bloomsbury, had partially painted a door at Bratton.

'standing start' reshuffle now, or in September. Albany just done up in time to entertain, but, as Jane said, 'no one will want to know us!'

MoD   *Tuesday, 23 July*

I parked the Porsche in the members' garage and walked along the cloisters and through the tunnel. A badge messenger acknowledged me deferentially. Not for the first time I reflected that all this will be over next year. This is my very last *chef des champs* summer. And I have *no* idea where or what I will be in July 1992. It is still less than a year ago that Ian[1] was murdered; his funeral and the start of the Gulf War with all its unhappy memories of Pavlovian alternatives. These twelve months have been sad for me. I've lost my love, seem to have become much poorer, and find my career becalmed (at lunch last week Bruce Anderson said, 'I don't quite know the Extel rating on Clark at present.' He meant – no dealings. It's over).

Are my relations with Jane set to improve? That would be some consolation.

MoD   *Wednesday, 24 July*

Incredibly tired. I drop off during meetings. It's muggy and humidly showery. Jane came up for the 'end-of-term lunch'. Soames was host, at the Cranbornes'.[2] I found it disparate and

---

[1] Ian Gow, MP Eastbourne, February 1974–30 July 1990, when murdered by an IRA car bomb. He became Mrs Thatcher's PPS in 1979. AC's chief friend in the Commons, he resigned from the government in November 1985 in protest at the Anglo-Irish Agreement.

[2] Nicholas Soames, MP for Crawley since 1983; Lord Cranborne, heir to the 6th Marquess of Salisbury, MP for Dorset South, 1979–87.

rather pointless. Too many guests – so a buffet. No butter
(why?). I missed supper last night and breakfast this morning,
but wasn't particularly hungry. Jane had had greywater yesterday
and looked terribly thin, poor darling.

But the real point is … it is the end of the parliamentary
summer – FOR EVER. This time next year I have *no* idea what
I'll be doing or where. But I do know that I will no longer be
a member of the House of Commons. No more chauffeur cars
or solitary policemen. No more passes to flash. (But no more, I
trust, wrecked Sunday evenings and Monday morning rushes.)

This, and my affliction, and the departure of my love, presently
at her most blithe and feckless, make me very depressed, but with
a 'nasty temper' lurking.

Saltwood   *Saturday, 10 August*

I don't really know what happened to last week. Not really very
happy. This morning I said I was more unhappy than at any time
since I could remember – Jane, too, she's terribly standoffish and
cries at intervals. She is confronting me with things that I've
done in the past which have been 'out' many times before and
were 'kissed and made up' since, but still I'm basted. We had
dreadful row coming back from Bratton. A journey which I drove
continuously in the Discovery using m-way the whole way and
with my foot absolutely flat down 95–100 in pretty thick traffic,
under four hours, but small thanks I got etc etc. I've promised
(a) not to whinge (b) not to swear (c) not to 'drive fast'. It's all
part of the castrating syndrome.

There is a certain type of woman of which Jane is one and
Valerie (to take an obvious and most emphatic example) is not
who would rather have their man a eunuch than have him
'chasing around'.

Zermatt   *Monday, 19 August*

Arrived here after a long – but not disagreeable train journey
from Zurich Flughaven. Dead tired and 'unwound' as one is in
the train to Zermatt after a flight, we dozed intermittently and
lolled in the heat. No picnic to stuff, Jane says she will never
make me a picnic again, or clean my shoes. She looks 'a beauty',
but very thin and washed out.

I am irreparably (short of a miracle) low, I simply do not see
my way. How bitterly odious that I should have lost my sex
drive at the very moment (sic) but all kinds of possibilities of
liberation are, or were, open. Normally, indeed always in the
past, it has revived in Zermatt.

On the way walking dreamily to the chalet from the station a
group of young people approached. I felt a huge jealous rage.
You can't pick up a paper without reading about how much
everyone else is getting and how much they enjoy it. I used to
think this was simply bluff and balls but now, after talking often
with 'x', I know it isn't. There have been changes in attitudes and
practices. I look at every couple, every man indeed with prurient
curiosity and envy. And the effect it has on me is disastrous. My
psyche totally blocks me.

I've been depressed before, of course, and recovered. We'll
see …

Zermatt   *Saturday, 24 August*

Yet again the Zermatt magic has worked. Blissful in the chalet;[1]
fine, dry, clear weather. Pleasant routine of late breakfast, picnic,
expeditions. We're still too exhausted to read, or write or think.
Sexual powers completely returned, back almost to the sixties

---

[1] Seven years later AC contemplated retiring to Châlet Caroline – 'a beach hut as
Jane quite properly calls it'.

and later seventies. Jane 3 times in last four days, each one more pleasing than the last.

Saturday, 14 September

Arrived at Cromlix,[1] very sleepy, but relaxed and philosophic.

It took exactly 8 hours (including an hour stop south of Stoke at the Welcome Break) to do the 522 miles from Saltwood to Gleneagles, a total average of 65mph and cruising of 75mph. We left at 6 a.m. We ate a huge tea at Gleneagles, sent a few PCs ('horse-riding' for 'x'). Jane mentions 'x' periodically, but the atmosphere is much better – more flirty – even though she claims she will leave me if I do anything (*anything* as far as I can make out). Although I am quite open, joking, 'I want to fuck "x"…' I hope we will have a quiet, satisly week at Shore. It certainly should be better than in May. Then return at the weekend to face basic problems.

Shore   *Saturday, 21 September*

Very lethargic and depressed. The wind blows in squalls; Jane is silent and reproachful. (Why? Thinks I'm 'starting up again' with 'x' I suppose). Time seems to have foreshortened morning (sic) and Saltwood looms (we leave for Inverness this afternoon, and a particularly long sleeper journey that doesn't get in until 9.30 a.m.) with its mountains of uncleared paper and unordered 'statements'. Too soon – I am 'undecided', and fearful, about whether to go on the Brittany Rally – comes Party Conference and then … a vacuum. Either a kind of limbo period in Parlt and the Dept in which nothing much happens and we wait for

---

[1] Cromlix House, a favourite hotel of the Clarks, near Stirling, Perthshire.

events that will cause the 'Polls' to fluctuate – or the dissolution
and the End, in every sense, of an Era. Even so my preference
would be for this last (sic) as I feel I would sort of lose ground,
become obscure, in those last months. Or would I? Anything
can happen at backgammon.

I have never been in a condition of such total uncertainty –
not at least since I was trying to get a job in San Francisco in
1957. Yet at least we both have good *health*.

Blackpool train   *Wednesday, 9 October*

And so to the very last conference. One's written this before of
course, but this time it's got to be the last one. I've got, at most,
six months left in the House of Commons. I whinged a bit to
Jane in the train on the way up, and she quite rightly said 'you
could do *another* four years going down to Plymouth, stuck in
the House of Commons, what, who, etc, are your …' True. But
my chance of actually going to the Lords is 3–1 *at best*. Every
diarist (except possibly Jim Lees-Milne[1]) toys reflectively with
this idea. None of them made it. I've been sort of promised it
by Chief Whip, Tristan, Tony R. etc. But doesn't really amount
to anything.

I just don't see my way. I've lost so much ground – it's really
only habit anyhow – with 'x'.

We had quite a nice room at the back of the hotel, changed,
ran Alison through the ladies' cocktail party – providing her
with some good 'contacts',[2] and then tagged on, just – Jane and
I were on the point of going off to dinner on our own – to

---

[1] Whereas three of AC's favourite diarists, Sir Henry (better known as 'Chips')
Channon, Leo Amery and Sir Harold Nicolson, were MPs, much of the career of
James Lees-Milne centred around the National Trust (*Ancestral Voices* and
Prophesying Peace).
[2] Alison was seriously considering going into politics, did in fact speak in the
debate.

Bruce Anderson party which went on to the Victoria (including Tom Strathclyde, Sophy McEwan, Angie Bray, David Davis, the Needhams).[1] Drank too much. Randy in the night. Illish in the morning.

We listened to Heseltine's 'come-back'. Quite accomplished, though as always symbolic and vulgar. We steadfastly sat throughout the 'ovation'. Yet today (Friday) the camera showed him during John Major's speech looking spaced out, almost gaga. What was he thinking? This is the speech, the occasion, which I so narrowly missed, perhaps for ever? Or had he just had a little too much wine with journalists at lunch, before coming on the platform? John M is so lucid, and decent, and genuine. What a lucky escape we had.

As always I get depressed (*more* depressed I should say) watching the Cabinet move around congratulating each other on the platform. At dinner the weekend before, when I was telling how I had been twice proposed and twice blackballed for the Whips Office, David Davis said – 'if you'd been a whip I have no doubt that you'd have been in the Cabinet by now …' I don't know, one mustn't be ungrateful for what has happened and all the good fortune that has come my way.

Plymouth train   *Thursday, 17 October*

I have got into a very good sexual relationship with Jane, so now have 'confidence'. She, incredibly, is insatiable. Would gladly do it 3 times every 24 hours! So this is a very great improvement on our relationship in the spring. It also changes a lot of parameters. I certainly don't want her to leave; it dulls the pining and the

---

[1] Lord Strathclyde, junior Minister in the Lords; Angie Bray, press secretary to the Conservative Party chairman (Chris Patten) since 1991; Sophy McEwan, a special adviser; David Davis, MP for Boothferry since 1987; Richard Needham, junior Minister in the N. Ireland Office, MP for Wilts North since 1983 (Chippenham, 1979–83) and his wife Sigrid.

dottiness of yearning for 'x'; it will ease the transition to 'civilian' life. I called for a miracle by the rowan tree, and the more I reflect on it the more I resolve it delivered.

I 'opened' on the second day of the Defence debate. I had been headache-light preparing the speech all morning. But by sylphless cutting (of Civil Service balls, on-the-record stuff) and adlibbing on Julian Amery,[1] regiments and Labour problems, a put down of 'Captain Browne'[2] much acclaim – whips, Godfrey Barker the next day.[3] This may well be the last speech I ever make in the House of Commons.

Yesterday I dined with Bruce Anderson at Greens. There is no longer any balls of my getting into the Cabinet – even the H of L project has diminished; a certain amount of 'you'll miss the House of Commons ...' Well I don't think I *will* much. As I trod the Pugin patterned carpets yesterday, popping up to the Members Tearoom to get some fruit cake to bring down to the cafeteria, I thought 'really I've had quite enough of this ...' Stale and fetid, etc. I know I can't go back, and I may regret it. The real problem is: I'm still active; bags of energy, keen mind, good health and appetite (now with an 's'), sleeping, stamina. It will be depressing feeling this atrophy – reading Ann Fleming letters,[4] she (and practically everyone else) seems continually to be ill – terminally ill in the sense that they were degenerative conditions that left you older and weaker and nearer the grave

---

[1] Julian Amery, served Conservative Prime Ministers from Churchill to Margaret Thatcher.

[2] John Browne, MP for Winchester since 1979, had previously risen to the rank of Captain in the Grenadier Guards.

[3] Godfrey Barker, *Daily Telegraph* parliamentary sketch writer, wrote that AC 'gave a lesson in how to cope with trouble from all sides. After a speech which was vivid, thoughtful, historical, witty and ad rem, Mr Clark complained that he was "amazed at the docility with which the Labour party has received my remarks ... a caricature of what happens to a party when it has absolutely no policy, just a great gulp of crocodile tears" over any changes that had to be made. And to attempted trouble behind him from Mr John Browne: "I can't give way to everyone".'

[4] *The Letters of Ann Fleming* edited by Mark Amory and just published. Ann Fleming was the widow of Ian Fleming (creator of James Bond) and had been twice married previously, to Lord O'Neill and the second Lord Rothermere, proprietor of *Daily Mail*.

even when 'cured'. Only Nico Henderson[1] has emerged unscathed from the *Galere*, still preening and striding.

Yesterday I committed a massive solecism going into the Lords and sitting down on the steps before prayers. I then sat through Craig's introduction[2] (inflection of the voice-print still the surest guide to class). Haven't seen one of these since my father – how cross I was on that day, being reminded of it again by the objectionable 'for life' peerages.[3]

VC10 to Akrotiri   *Wednesday, 6 November*

For the first time am on an abroad journey in a state of pleasurable exploration. The VIP VC10, lots of space, food, service, crew of five in the cockpit, as far as I can make out. First stop Akrotiri, then on to Dubai for the air show, then to Diego Garcia (nature notes), then Malaysia. The kind of trip that would have had me out in boils ten years ago, but now is an adventure, a comfortable adventure.

All this year I have been neglectful of my papers, have been unable – it seems – even to find time to concentrate my thoughts, think strategically (as the P.M. would need to do, now, I suspect, over his successor). I will be sad and depressed to be out of office. I ought to be S o S, but only a miracle can bring that about, and 'that's enough miracles' – Ed.

Poor little Alison is longing to fight the next election as my 'Campaign Director'; I dread breaking the news to her. I can't face it, so just hope something 'turns up' (Another miracle!).

I feel that 'x' and I may be approaching a consummation. But

---

[1] Sir Nicholas Henderson, former British Ambassador in Warsaw, Bonn, Paris and Washington, had been seriously ill.

[2] Former Chief of the Defence Staff, Marshal of the RAF, Sir David Craig, had been made a life peer following his retirement.

[3] By 1969 (the year of Kenneth Clark's barony) life peerages had become the norm. There would be very few exceptions in the years to come.

how the hell is this handled? When? And then what? I can't actually leave Jane now, although I must admit there were times when I did contemplate it. Could I risk it for a couple of weeks, ten days? Could I get my wish – a double life? Again, it's a miracle that's needed.

But I must record, I'm happier than for ages. It's hope that counts, always.

Diego Garcia[1]   *Sunday, 10 November*

This morning I was determined to bathe *privately*. Much of the charm of this place is spoiled by the constant surveillance of officials (the Commission is about as bad as Peter Watkins[2] who is adhesive in his silent quality), yesterday at the old plantation manager's home, a Somerset Maugham setup on East Island, I realised what Royalty must feel like. But this morning I rose slyly and stealthily, let myself out – yes, there was the Commissioner moving across the grass quadrangle. He said something to the very pretty (dark, lovely bones, ultra discreet/shy) WRAC whom I noted, and scored by calling, 'Doreen'.

I was aware of the fact that the Commissioner wanted to follow me, or call out, but couldn't quite. I walked in light, delicious humid rain to the edge of the beach. Low tide, lovely pale green ripples slapping the sand. The water was delicious, like silk. To Ascension and the Al Bustan I have now added Diego Garcia. My morale uncertain now, though not as bad as when I bathed at the Al Bustan in May. On my return I saw a little polished crab claw on the sand and pouched it. I don't know what power it will have, but it will be a reminder of a curious voyage when pain is still around, uncertainty is everywhere and the terrible incurable infatuation has one in its grasp afresh.

---

[1] British Indian Ocean Territory and a military base with access only to military or civilian contractors, and the occasional visiting British Minister.
[2] Peter Watkins, Head of AC's Private Office at the Ministry of Defence.

Saltwood   *Sunday evening, 15 December*

I was cheered by a letter from Charlie Allsopp saying the Gainsborough was 3–400,[1] which eases my mind about the pending arrival of the C-type.[2]

Poor Jane has had a 'blip' from Tom Bates this time, sending something along to be analysed: 'my secretary will be in touch in a week's time …' – what bad luck!

I feel myself continuing to lose standing and attention in politics. Work in the department has wound right down – I seem to spend much of my time shopping for, or tidying B5 in its new 'naff' form. This is going to be 'very successful'. It had to be done, and the boys will be pleased, although I don't want them using my bed. But ironic that it should be complete, and a place for people to come back for drinks – or even eat – at the very moment when I am about to retire and don't need it. Because I now feel increasingly that the likelihood of my going to the Lords is *very* small. Or, at least, going immediately, which would give the continuity that I want.

This morning at EMT Jane and I discussed her anxieties and finality of 'standing down'. I *dread*, of course, telling Alison, the admission, that for both of us, our professional relationship is over. A certain cowardliness, too, in telling the [constituency] Association. But we both agreed that you have to go out while they are still calling for more and anyway (my own dread) I might *lose* – worst of both worlds.

Will I then get very 'slow' and change my appearance? We'll see. Christmas first, and Andrew's young lady, and most important of all, the result of Jane's test.

Never seem to have done any shopping this year.

---

[1] Gainsborough's *Going to Market*. Charles Allsopp, chairman of Christie's since 1986.
[2] AC paid £360,000; it arrived in time for Christmas.

Saltwood   *Boxing Day, 26 December*

I'm very depressed – not from hangover, as had drunk little, though Christmas lunch was always lovely and I consumed (sic) three glasses of Stolichnaya with the caviar, then more Roodeburg than Andrew with the turkey and pudding. (His young lady Sarah, was a success.)

I'm concerned, somewhat profoundly, at the recandescence of my nose place; my sexuality seems to be diminishing again. I'm dust off the dial in terms of political insignificance – Bruce Anderson no longer makes contact, but he wouldn't 'chuck' like this if he thought I rated. Also, of course, I'm miserable about dear little 'x', away in some French ski resort while I mope around here trying to get old cars to start and splitting firewood. That's something else that is going to come to a head this year (if it hasn't done so already).

Well it's no good moping.

I must pull myself together … I will 'hold the line' at the Department – might even get in a couple more jolly trips. Then it's cutting peat in the Highlands and the fallow period of editing the diaries[1] and inventorising the contents and dispositions.

I wonder how long I've got? I have this nasty feeling that things are going to go so badly this year that I will be 'on the way out' next Christmas. My hair is white in certain back lighting. When I'm 65, sadly, I will actually look 65. Shopping for Jane on Christmas Eve I 'happened on' a ski shop in Folkestone's main street, thought to buy her an anorak and also found myself buying a ski suit for myself. It made me feel ten years younger. Oh if only I could really regenerate!

---

[1] Rather than memoirs, AC had now decided to see if he might emulate Chips Channon, Harold Nicolson *et al* and publish extracts from the diaries he kept while an MP and Minister.

1992

Saltwood *Monday, 6 January*

I've been 'lying up' here since Dai Davies[1] on Thursday. An expensive affair since I had it 'in theatre' in order that the path lab could pronounce it 'clear' (sic) on the (nose) spot – which they duly did. I don't know how long any disfigurement will last. Sometimes, these last days, I've got frissons of impending ill health and demise.

Wednesday, 19 February

I am in limbo at present. The major hurdle – telling Alison that I am not fighting the election – is over.[2]

Thursday, 20 February

Yesterday I had a great 'triumph' on my last occasion at the despatch box, pleasing the House and teasing the Labour Party. I had forced Jane to come up, and sit in the Gallery. 'A "last" is always important,' I told her, 'and you can compare it with the Lords.'

Whether I will 'make it' there or not, I don't know. Of course that is fundamental to the success of the scheme. 'x' and I wrote out the 'best' and 'worst' case scenarios on a napkin. She is so game, she's really trying now to see the bright side. Is it going to mark that episode which she identified in her letter of 'final' separation? Although I pretend that I wouldn't mind

---

[1] London-based consultant, who removed AC's 'nose place'.
[2] Nearly four years later AC reflects (17 December 1995): 'How well I remember being parked outside the entrance to the General Post Office in Plymouth with the letters of resignation in my hand. Alison begging me not to – as she had in the train coming up.'

that much I know that there would be the most awful period
to get through. It could last for months, it might diminish me
for ever.

For periods I can become 'serene'. I would, indeed be entirely
reprehensibly serene if I wasn't worrying about 'x'. Even last
night she was out dining with some friends I started fretting
after 11.15, because she hadn't phoned me. When she did – after
midnight – we talked for 3¼ hours.

MoD   *Wednesday, 26 February*

Left out the traumas of the 'Final decision'. The 'statement'. The
deceptions and hesitations. Got a *very* good press. A nice piece
in the *Mail* followed up by a 'commission' to write four articles
during the election.[1] Fun! I sent a reproachful *handschüd* to
Simon Jenkins[2] and he responded with a glowing leader in
today's *Times* trailing oh so subtly the idea that I might 'continue
my ministerial career in the Lords …'

There lurks, of course, the pang of a final parting with 'x' –
how ironic that it should be Chile again, which signals this.
But she is being so vile at the moment, interrupting with
pointless and offensive remarks about my conduct, family etc,
that in a way it makes it less painful. This time, for the first
time, I am strong enough and determined enough not to
plead.

---

[1] Gordon Greig, the *Mail*'s political editor, wrote that AC 'who has amused and
shocked his party over the years, leaves it just three weeks to find a replacement
candidate.' 'Personal reasons' for his departure were mentioned by the Sutton
agent, to which AC riposted: 'I never said that. "Personal reasons" usually means
there has been a scandal, and I can assure you there is nothing of that. It's just time
to go.'
[2] Simon Jenkins, editor of *The Times* since 1990.

Tristar. Bermuda-Panama   *Wednesday, 4 March*

A short stay in Bermuda.[1] Lovely colours pleasing architecture,
winding streets and friendly black servitors. But hunka-munka
food. Everyone, it seems, so old, and certain things like driving
fast, and dogs, effectively banned. The food is disgusting. US
muck. The interim discards of a Brixton tenement. Couldn't
even get yoghurt, or pasta. We did fit in a bathe though – to add
to Ascension and Diego. Quite chilly. St Austell in July.

VC10K to Santiago   *Friday, 6 March*

Last leg of our flight with the RAF. The trip great fun, and Jane
played the part to perfection, and really enjoyed it. We had a
'loose' day in Ecuador, because a special battery change (would
you believe it) was needed for one of the Tornados which was
stuck at Bermuda and wouldn't start. Really! So the Nimrod
flew back from Panama where we offloaded it from the Tristar,
and we then went on to Guyacil, Ecuador with the Harriers.
   Dirt, rats, rotting refuse, puddles, sewage open, incredible
battered pick-ups and buses – but great vitality and a sort of
contentment. The Hotel Oro Verde, owned by a Swiss company,
a little oasis. But the last day I was sulky and tired and avoided
food at the *longueurs* dinner. The Air Attaché, a common little
man, attitudinised me much as the chairman of a strong ward in
the Association might – knowing I didn't live in the constituency and didn't come down enough and held certain
'extreme' opinions. The Consul, however, was impressive. A
caricature of an Englishman, like someone out of *White Mischief* [2]
– tall, brylcreamed hair, moustache, caricatured manners. But
had made a great success of his business, which he started as a

---

[1] AC's final ministerial trip, flying the flag on behalf of defence exports to South
   America.
[2] James Fox's 1982 account of the notorious Erroll murder in Kenya.

breakaway salesman from ICI and I felt guilty at not sparkling. I would have liked to talk more with him.

The next day (yesterday) we went for a drive 'up-country' in the Embassy Range Rover. A military road, new and wide, that took us to 'Chimbo' in 3–4 hours. But in *Cholera* time (and Guyacil had much of *Cholera*[1] about it) this would have been the great pilgrimage of Fermina Deza after her father had sent her away following his discovery of Florentino Ariza's letters. The township was pleasing. More than a little of *Black Rock* (as in bad day[2]) but sans menace. A memorial in the centre of the square, very much Highgate Cemetery school dated 1899. How remote it must have been in those times! On the way, through terrible slums and swamps. Children bathing quite literally in sewage pools. But much colour and much greenery.

Ferme Hotel   *Saturday, 7 March*

Arrived at this very peculiar, somewhat sinister place for a late (2.30 p.m.) plein lunch. A long drive, ending with about six miles of unmade yellowish gravel road and an antiquated iron bridge. The room, at ground level is dark, cool, and (in my opinion) cancer fetid. A bad night is in prospect plagued – I expect – by insects. I tried to Venice train after lunch, but wasps and marsh mosquitoes.

It's a strange clientele. Children – largely unattractive – and very elderly people hobbling about. Oh old age is so awful. How can I avoid it? Can I choose my moment as deftly as I did my exit from the Commons? I'd like to outlive Pin and Colette,[3] though. A fine parrot, or macaw (another link with cholera) sits in a giant green cage in the centre of the grass-covered patio.

---

[1] AC, encouraged by Jane, had read Gabriel Garcia Marquez's *Love in the Time of Cholera*.

[2] *Bad Day in Black Rock*, classic American film (1955) with Spencer Tracy.

[3] Colin (known as Pin, Col) and Colette (Celly), AC's twin siblings.

The following morning
We had a good night, after a long, but not objectionable 'banquet' at which I drank slightly too much and was giftedly 'amusing' to Richard (attaché) and Andy. We made love this morning, then drowsed, then had a long carbohydrate breakfast. I am much calmer. My God what a dance 'x' has led me! I think I must just relaxedly let go, resign myself to its ending or, at least, going into abeyance, because as far as I'm concerned it can never really end. When I'm strong enough I can write up all the nice episodes, like the piano duet. But right now I'm detached, serenely sated, philosophic. (Even so I must admit, I wonder if/what she should suddenly walk through here and across the patio and come up to my table where I am writing this.)

Well now the 'holiday' part of the jaunt is nearly over. HE is demi-hovering to 'go through points' for tomorrow's meeting. Pasta this evening. Air show all day tomorrow. Tuesday more meetings. Jane has really enjoyed it; been lionised by the RAF crew as well as doing nice characteristic things like collecting seed pods. God has really been kind to us. And she is really so good and sweet. That's what makes the situation so impossible. I mean what do I want? Certainly not to leave her and cause her pain. And yet as she herself admits 'x's appearance has revived our sexual tension by all the jealous cross-currents it arouses.

Lord Clark's Study, Saltwood   *Wednesday, 18 March*

Immensely serene. I must record that I am settling down very calmly to a pleasant detached existence with so much to hand in the way of diversions and accoutrements.

Just talked to Alison who is going down to Henry Bellingham[1] for the 'campaign'. Gosh, I'm glad to be out of it![2] It's delicious

---

[1] Henry Bellingham, MP for North West Norfolk since 1983.
[2] The general election had been called for 9 April

speculating, with just the right amount of access through the *Daily Mail*. But the polls this morning are bad, *very* bad, each showing 5% Labour lead. I don't particularly mind, even a touch of schadenfreude if it weren't for my lost peerage, even my lost 'K'. Although, intriguingly (sic) the lunch yesterday with Alastair Campbell[1] opened, just by a chink, the possibility of a semi-alignment with Kinnock – 'the other side'. Whew!

Saltwood   *Wednesday, 25 March*

Appetite and sleep perfect. I dozed between 6.30 and 7 and dreamed that I was squinting through the internal window into the Chamber. David Wilshire[2] was going in *in a shirt*; Robin Corbett came out and said something to me, like 'you can't go in there any more'. I thought, 'silly ass, it's only a dream, of course I can'; then woke up and the dream was reality – I never can again. I was sad and thought I should have been in for the Dissolution, heard all that mumbo, bowed to the Speaker and so forth. In a sort of dotty way I think I might still go back, a crash adoption for a safe by-election. ACHAB

Friday, 27 March

Last night we dined at the French embassy. My last Ministerial. Beatty's old house in Regent's Park, a pleasing dwelling with, unusually, Nash getting the proportions just right. Jane looked pretty in her turquoises, and slimline black dress, well holding her own over the French ladies. On the way back Pat[3] drove

---

[1] Alastair Campbell, political editor of the *Daily Mirror* since 1989.
[2] David Wilshire, MP (C) for Spelthorne since 1987; Robin Corbett, MP (L) for Birmingham Erdington since 1983.
[3] Pat, Ministry of Defence driver.

sepulchrally. Earlier he had agitatedly told me the MoD was investigating his 'prudent' overtime claims.

Car (M20)   *Tuesday, 31 March*

This my last (or last but one) trip up to London in the official car, with Pat driving. My appearance seems to have altered, my nose nob won't go down any more. I am feeble and drowsy after an interrupted night (stumbled down and took two Redoxons). Eva[1] is poorly, though sweet-natured, and the vet yesterday could find nothing (though stopped me bidding for the 'Bentley Box' at Sotheby's[2]). Jane shellacked me at tea for ringing 'x' 'behind her back'. Said I am 'not a minister, even an MP, nothing any more'. Bruce Anderson just chucked me – said 'Once you're out of Election politics, you're dead ...' I'm not so sure. If I was in the Lords at least I could say, 'I fought five elections, and never lost one of them.' So what's my vote?

Paddington train   *Wednesday, 8 April*

Well, now the era has ended. I am in the Paddington train; warm, comfortable, porridge breakfast; so evocative of jolly journeys with sexual tension high, and delight at being in the loved one's company. I will never be able to afford this again. £38 one-way from Exeter, and that with an OAP reduction card. Briefly back to MoD for farewell calls. Then load up carpet and clock and sundries and leave Whitehall – for ever, as it now looks.

We were in Plymouth yesterday. Practically no posters at *all*.

---

[1] Eva, the Clarks' dog, a Rottweiler.
[2] AC remarked in his day diary that he was 'livid' not to acquire it.

A strange, dead feel to it. Jane said canvassing would be 'very heavy going'. Damn right it would. I simply wouldn't know what to say. A very disagreeable protracted experience, with no certainty as to the result – a nasty count, etc. And even then – what? If I was defeated I'd just disappear; none of the accolades of early March. If I scraped back it would be to a low and miserable House (although the whisperings would be fun); a hideous prospect of being permanently unpaired; a certainty of being 'eased out' by the constituency before the October election. The whole summer fraught and ruined for nothing. No I think I 'Houdinied' it as well as could possibly have been expected.

On the way back to Bratton I stopped and climbed to Brentor. It seems a long time since polling day in '87 when I asked for help after my 'gaffe' on the Channel Tunnel.[1] Periodically since, when in torment, I thanked God for a wonderful additional grant and all that incredible life-enhancement. Even if the total dream – the sword in the lake – has gone, I still feel that there is quite a bit to unfold. Although not, I fear, in my personal life. The wonderful, excruciating, highly dangerous 'x' 'affair' has burned itself out and, to my utter nostalgic depression we are now only, and I fear never again can be more than 'good friends'.

That charming sheepdog appeared the moment we arrived at Bratton last night. Jane brilliantly remembered the basket in the pump room and we lined it with felt and he settled down in the back porch after a fine meal. This morning he wanted to come back with us, and jumped bravely into the Discovery. He was so good and intelligent when I said 'stay' in the front garden. I do hope no ill befalls him.

---

[1] A reference to an interview which AC gave during the election campaign at which he had poured scorn on the Channel Tunnel project.

Garden House   *General Election, Polling Day, Thursday, 9 April*

Lovely and fine. Yesterday very weary and creaky (both Jane and
I have got the 'Office Virus' – an exceptionally tenacious head
cold). I got out of the car, last journey with Pat, having sadly and
foot-draggingly left the MoD after 'farewell calls' from Moray
Stewart[1] and Quinlan, and Saltwood was benign. The first day of
spring.

Last night an early one. But before going up I saw the 9 p.m.
news – the gap has closed to 1%. Tristan[2] rang this morning –
always a good sign – and said we could just shave it. So today is
one of total limbo like – though not as disagreeable – awaiting
the result of *tests*.

*General Election result: Conservative 336 seats; Labour 271 seats;
Liberal Democrats 20 seats; others 24 seats. In Plymouth Sutton,
AC's successor as the Conservative candidate had a majority of
11,950.*

Friday, 10 April

Up all last night, bed at 3.40, and then up at 6.10 to 'catch up'.
A 'private' car to TV Centre with George Younger and Nicky
Ridley,[3] gossip with (inter alia) John Cole and Barbara Maxwell[4]
and several times nearly dropped off in the Porsche on the

---

[1] Moray Stewart, Second Permanent Under-Secretary of State, MoD, since 1990.

[2] With Tristan Garel-Jones, MP for Watford since 1979, AC had an equivocal
relationship.

[3] George Younger had retired from the Commons at the general election after
representing Ayr since 1964. He had been Defence Secretary (1986–89); a
hereditary peer (4th Viscount Younger), he was made a life peer in 1992; Nicholas
Ridley, MP for Cirencester & Tewkesbury, 1959–92; one of Margaret Thatcher's
keenest supporters.

[4] John Cole, political editor of the BBC since 1981; Barbara Maxwell, sometime
producer of BBC's *Question Time*.

return journey. Much pain on the screens – Kinnock and Glenys; Patten and Lavender.[1]

GJ [Tristan] very loyally at teatime said nothing in particular. Are there any lost days in (even) the outer circle? We always knew it would be painful, watching the new appointments. I reported briefly to the MoD on my way in. The place completely stripped and 'sanitised'. 'Notes for incoming Ministers,' I said glumly.

Sunday, 12 April

The days are lengthening rapidly now. It's 8 p.m. and quite light. Jane is still planting trees down in the 'new woodland' along the iron fence. I am very flat and *désoeuvré*, brought on by contemplating the year – the whole year in which there is nothing, but *nothing*, to tie the structure to. I make various noises about when we go away to Scotland, to M Goisot,[2] to Zermatt etc etc. The whole thing curiously in vacuo. I always wanted time, even a day, three hours was priceless. Now it is limited only by my death or infirmity.

Another boring thing. Income will be much lower. No facilities. I will miss particularly the Library at the House. I thought I'd save the £30–50 a week in petty cash from 'going to London' but there are so many other new demands. Even, as Jane said, having to buy your own *New Statesman*. There was a good few hours today of weak fantasy. TK was sacked (along with Baker, Waddington; Waldegrave lucky to survive).[3] And this

---

[1] Neil Kinnock, Labour Leader since 1983, had now lost two elections; MP for Islwyn since 1983 (Bedwelty, 1970–83); Chris Patten, Chairman of the Conservative Party, had lost his Bath seat (which he had represented since 1979) to the Liberal Democrats: majority of 2,009.

[2] From whom AC bought wine in France.

[3] Kenneth Baker (Home Secretary); Lord Waddington (Leader of the House of Lords, life peer 1990, MP for Nelson & Colne 1968–September 1974, Clitheroe March 1979–1983, Ribble Valley 1983–1990); William Waldegrave (MP for Bristol West since 1979), who had been Health Secretary, became Chancellor of the Duchy of Lancaster.

made me hope briefly that Hamilton would also be chopped, and for the sake of continuity, they'd keep me on – but from the Lords – my original scheme. I even went so far as to visualise the Black Turbo B from P. & A. Wood[1] for Pat; the Minister's room with red leathers and the computer; Alison back as my PA while she also doubles at another job at Westminster. A reunion dinner at Wilton's; in the Smoking Room – for the first time really since 1974. Wouldn't it be luvverly ...[2] As it is I suppose I will have to subliminate into asceticism, restoring order and the journals.

I drove the C-type last night and ended up at St Leonard's. It was locked, and I got the key from the Rev Wood. In almost complete darkness I tried to pray a bit, to little avail. The whole 'x'/Jane affair made a block last year of course. Now I am worried that by standing down from the Commons I have *wasted* the advantages He offered me.

Tuesday, 14 April

Here I am, in my office at the Garden House – how very nice, warm, bright and silently welcoming it is when one owns the key and even at 9.30 in the morning – *en retraite* at the age of 64 (exactly). There were two mini-moments yesterday – at MoD when Carol returned to me the portable '... in case No 10 want to get in touch with you', heightened by rumours in the drivers' room that 'Lord Arran's office were shitting themselves ...'[3] Then called by Peter Watkins, strangely distant in the morning, almost calling me 'Mr Clark', and later ringing with a message that 'there will be a ministers' meeting in the (tomorrow/today) morning: you are of course entitled to attend,

---

[1] P. & A. Wood, Rolls-Royce and Bentley specialists favoured by AC.

[2] AC's own footnote is in the form of musical notes (*My Fair Lady*).

[3] Lord Arran had been Parliamentary Under-Secretary of State for the Armed Forces, MoD, since 1989. In the post-election reshuffle he had been moved to the Northern Ireland Office.

but there is no expectation that you will …' Then particularly, briefly, rallied by dear Tristan ringing at about 8 p.m. and saying '… any news?' *Why?*

I am doomed now to the wilderness, to awaiting 'tidings of men and events …' It's difficult to keep one's hand in. I find to my surprise that my hunger for politics now causes me to buy *more* newspapers. I am going to ask Tristan to send me Hansard. On second thoughts I think I shall subscribe myself. (I paused for a second and thought that 'if nothing happens' I will wait a month or so and then write to Richard [Ryder] saying how awful I feel.) But things were put into scale, in a most alarming way this morning at EMT when Jane told me that Andrew had said that James had said, phoning from Eriboll, that he was so depressed. Made me feel very spoilt and grumpy. I am going to write him a long letter this morning.

Many full and lovely days lie ahead. But curiously, directly I shy away from 'holiday' planning – the magic months of June to September – I only notice how triste and dejected I have become when I taste, very briefly, the exhilaration of thinking it might still 'happen'. Because I still think – perversely for one usually so realistic and cynical – that if I were there as Minister of State I would inevitably get S of S – *even though a peer.*

Ah well, although we are nearly half way through this year it still seems only to have started. *So far* it hasn't been as painful as the past four months of last year were. But the future is a blank – and not a specially reassuring one.

Sandling train (!)   *Tuesday, 28 April*

A fortnight since the last entry. Withdrawal symptoms only flare periodically, but a lot of suppression is going on. So in subconscious it festers. I dream of reviving Commons privileges, tearoom, reference library and so on which I wake and realise are closed to me for ever. In the daytime I have to close my mind to the full extent of my depression. I am 'put out' by my friends ignoring me. Especially wounded by Richard. I did think that he was a friend, and I a confidant of his. I am filled too with distaste and resentment at all the new Conservative MPs and some of the new Ministerial choices. But there's no point in dodging it, when you're out you're out. The people who are *in* simply don't have time to waste on someone who, however 'amusing', is not au fait with the daily round of gossip, of 'men and events'. I suppose, if I were to get my peerage promptly I could still 'catch up', swoop into the tearoom, mob around. But notification for the Dissolution Honours has passed, and so – almost – has that for the Birthday. I guess it will be like the PC and take at least two years longer than postulated (sic).

As for life at Saltwood – well it is pleasing, more so in some ways than I had anticipated. Delicious food (too much indeed, I'm putting on weight, am 11.7+ and at intervals get it at 12 even when dry).

Friday, 8 May

Very low and 'muddled'. Yesterday had nasty blows (3 if you count Bertie Arbeid[1] saying that my 'historic' *lippen* spot 'we should keep an eye on it'(!)).[2] A dramatic pathetic encounter with 'x' and a hopeless parting; followed by an extremely disturbing, and unsettling phone call from Tony Fanshawe which interrupted my scrambled egg high tea, telling me Tristan G-J had been instrumental in the Robert Cranborne transition;[3]

[1] Bertie Arbeid, the Clarks' dentist.
[2] A spot in the form of a blood blister on AC's lower lip.
[3] No wonder AC was upset; any remaining hopes he might have entertained about speaking for the government on Defence matters from the Lords were dashed by the transition of Robert [Viscount] Cranborne, heir to the Marquess of Salisbury, who had been 'summoned to the Upper House, as Baron Cecil of Essendon in the County of Rutland'. He became Parliamentary Under-Secretary of State at MoD, in effect government Defence spokesman in the Lords.

then, even more alarmingly, that 'a few peers' were complaining that my 'abrasive' style, while fine in the Commons, might not go down too well in the Lords, put people off a bit, and so on.

When I phoned him, 'people like who ... Francis?'[1]

'Kimball'.[2]

Yes that figures totally. He has always been deeply antipathetic to me since we were on the same corridor at 'Waynflete'. Said no chance of being on either of the two coming lists (Dissolution and Birthday); must aim for January 93; don't bother to see Richard *now*, wait till they come back 'in September', i.e. October 'have it out' with him then.

All very depressing, only redeemed by a nice note from Soames.

Saltwood   *Saturday, 9 May*

I have been wrestling with the lawn in the Inner Bailey. We bought a new ATCO and it cuts crazily well so that even a half stripe needs its large plastic basket emptying. But the lawn remains obstinate – resistant to striping and with ridged 'bare marks'. The garden is relentless in its demands on time. Not only is the lawn like the Forth Bridge, it needs restarting as soon as you finish, but there is scything of nettles and use of the tractor in the arboretum and the wood, and a few 'artist's touches' in the Garden House.

I have a mountain of paper. The far end of the Green Room seems to have about four running white boxes in it, while the Summer Office has simply been evacuated, like the old battlefields of the Somme, and about 300 separate filing items lie around.

---

[1] Possibly Francis Pym, MP for Cambridgeshire 1961–83; Cambridgeshire SE, 1983–87; Foreign Secretary 1982–83, a life peer since 1987.
[2] Marcus Kimball, MP for Gainsborough, February 1956–1983. AC's Eton contemporary; a life peer since 1985. Part of their mutual antagonism stemmed from Kimball's devotion to fox-hunting whereas AC was totally against.

The cars – far too many of them – have overflowed the accommodation, they need drastic culling, but I seem not even to have time to write up a favoured culling scheme. Jane has a good amount of spare cash, and I want to work out an investment scheme for her – but that, too, needs time and care. Perhaps even more importantly, I cannot get *in* to the diaries, although many (namely Michael Sissons and George Weidenfeld are pressing me for them).[1] Never mind, today is foul; wet and gusty, and I may get some preliminary order. I am taking a year's sabbatical – slightly under – and hope that this will leave me next summer 'off' before the die is finally cast at the July or September reshaping of the Government. It is a huge waste of my talents that I am not in. Partly self-inflicted, I admit. At least I jumped, *really* jumped I mean, off the deck, before people even got round to thinking about it. But we dined at Aspers[2] the night before last, and I sat next to Barbara Amiel – attractive, intelligent but not (as I said to Jane) 'my cup of tea'. Conrad Black's mistress,[3] but writes well. I tried to sparkle – perhaps did a bit – but was conscious throughout of my diminished status. Today I read in the papers that the Government is going to bail out Olympia and York by taking a huge amount of office space at Canary Wharf. How I wish I was in the House to ask the Chancellor:

'Does he share my distaste at the proposal to bail out the property developer Olympia & York? Does he recognise that this – if he allows it – will be just the precursor of a giant "demand" from "Sir" Alastair Morton[4] – surely now the

---

[1] Michael Sissons, AC's long-time literary agent (Peters, Fraser & Dunlop); George Weidenfeld, who had published one previous book of AC's (*Aces High*), but also AC's favourite diarist, Chips Channon.

[2] John Aspinall founded a series of London clubs beginning with the Clermont in Berkeley Square. AC and Aspinall had first met at Oxford. In these diaries he is usually referred to as 'Aspers'.

[3] Conrad Black, Canadian-born newspaper proprietor (including the *Daily* and *Sunday Telegraph*, *The Spectator*) and Barbara Amiel, noted journalist, were soon to marry.

[4] Sir Alastair Morton, chief executive of Eurotunnel since 1987.

President Emeritus of the Delorean Club for a huge cash injection into Eurotunnel which never has and never will make a profit?'

There. Quite fun composing that, though sad.

Tristan rang yesterday. He was reassuring, but non-committal. Said he would try and have a word with Richard soon; with the PM in the summer when he stayed with the G-Js in Spain. Agreed that there was plenty for me to *do*, but I needed a 'perch'.

Tuesday, 12 May

I am having my 'quiet' hour and slight (nervous) indigestion/ wind and mild AF wondering if the phone will ring. PMQs on television. I watched them all sitting on the front bench and thought – barring a most unusual and improbable miracle – I can never again sit there. All made me a bit depressed. Progress here is *so* slow, haven't even mock approached the diaries extracts yet. The 'white boxes' have taken over all the top shelf space in the Green Room. I seem to be terribly stiff and creaky; I suspect I'm quite a few pounds overweight, and I have a weak prostatic trickle if I pee in the night (which I don't often do, I must say, and it's normal in the morning). I don't even partic- ularly want to go to Scotland this weekend, as there is so much to do here. Yet last year, when I was a Minister, one recharged over Whitsun. We are totally victims of Parkinson's Law. If you look at the wall-chart May–June are now full. And July and August fill me with some apprehension, because I believe they [James and Sally] are going to make a trial separation. Never mind. I must keep up my letter writing.

Wednesday, 13 May

First day of the 'heat wave'. I get waves of terrible depression, but not as bad, really as last year this time. Last year, I know, I would have been phoning in. And I must say when I think of the House of Commons in June, Finance Bill Committee stage, long whipping, even the beloved access to the Terrace doesn't outweigh the preference for being down here. Now that there appears to be a severance with 'x' I don't really see any reason why I should go to London at *all*.

Garden House   *Wednesday, 20 May*

The whole place burgeoning beautifully, and the last thing I want to do is go to London and on to Oxford to make a speech at the Union. Started filling the pool yesterday and I had a p.m. splosh in two feet of water. The wall-chart is totally blocked out, it seems, for June; worse than the DTI already. So we're back to 'observe' Parliamentary recesses. Altnaharra for sale for £7m. Can Marcus [Kimball] really have got in that deep? It was an idyll for me, even at Eton when he talked about this, and his blue Chevrolet. I wrote him a (guarded) letter of commiseration.

Garden House   *Monday, 25 May*

I am very tired. We made love in Courtneys in the afternoon. It always leaves me with nostalgia and wistfulness. A strange punishment, so packed with irony. The total melancholy of my relationship with 'x' is itself almost an attraction.

Eriboll   *Saturday, 6 June*

Very hot day, and I have 'caught' the sun. Delial is the *only* thing
that really protects and I left it behind. There is a tiny, spreading
mark under my nose nob, and I'm mildly concerned about the
'poached egg' on my shoulder – although admittedly this has
scared me on and off for years. For the last four nights (with the
exception of Cromlix, 10.15) I have been in bed after midnight;
so sunlight and bathing (Hope and Eriboll today, immersion
only) have made me feel – and look – very weary.

Yesterday we came up via Hope and I forded the river and
walked from Cashel Dhu up and over the Creaggan. Two hours.
And was quite delighted to see my little brown pup terrier
waiting and expectantly peeping for me so went and had a little
chat with her. The real *treat* of being in Scotland in June,
without obligations or commitments. Jane is being slightly
distant and not looking particularly attractive, as can sometimes
happen when her hair has been badly 'done'. The place is
terribly dry, dust (the first time I have seen clouds of dust at
Eriboll) and I am worried that many of those expensive little
trees will die. Also, there is so much to do here. One could fill
the day just as usefully as at Saltwood. On my way over the
Creaggan yesterday I thought a lot – about 'x'. And the more I
thought, the more insoluble it became. Perhaps the simple fact
is that I'm just too old and getting older. But certain key dates
do approach and give me a light AF *grippe*. Notably the summer
holidays. I am now so frightened of Jane. I can't do anything at
all with 'x'.

Reading yesterday about the man (an Army Captain, needless
to say) whose girlfriend killed his wife. They had sexual intercourse under water; and also about Charles and Diana: 'their
separate marriage'. How odious the Palace is. Nearly 30 peers in
the next two lists, including, apparently, six new 'working peers'.
Richard has not kept to his part of the bargain.

Saltwood   *Sunday, 14 June*

It's ridiculous, really. I sit here, on a hot Sunday, cloudless but hazy, and round me the Bailey is, *passim* Bruce Anderson (now never heard from), 'one of the loveliest places in the world'. The cistus are out along the border, and many of the roses. The honeysuckle by the pool, and a particularly fine 'French' geranium fills the 'plinth'. Tomorrow is *not* 'Dave at eight', although we may be going up for the Gilmours' garden party,[1] so I ought to be relaxed, creative. In fact I'm not so much depressed as oppressed. I've been out since mid-March, and made no impression on files, or cars. No order in day-to-day affairs (except start of ledger); barely keeping pace with day-to-day correspondence. Will just hold the garden in check, and make some nice potential development in the wood.

But my 'sabbatical' has really got nothing to show for it, except, perhaps, the beginnings of a familiarity with the word processor. And the DTI wall chart is now full. Every day seems to have something on it – and one 'thing' will actively blight and distort a whole day. But what has really depressed me is the list of 'working' peers. I mean Hayhoe! How ghastly and mediocre – the archetypal safe Tory politician – can you get? Stewart, little Stewart and dear old Bill Clark (which will cause problems if I ever get there) and they were all knights, so my exclusion from the 'K' list doesn't mean anything.[2]

---

[1] Lord [Ian] Gilmour, former MP (Norfolk C and then Chesham and Amersham), Minister, editor of *The Spectator*, and his wife Caroline; at their home by the Thames at Isleworth.

[2] Barney Hayhoe, MP for Brentford & Isleworth 1974–92 (Heston & Isleworth, 1970–74); Bernard Stewart (who took the title Lord Stewartby) MP N Herts 1983–92 (Hitchin February 1974–83) and William Clark, MP for Croydon S 1974–92 (E Surrey, 1970–74; Nottingham S 1959–66).

Saltwood   *Tuesday, 23 June*

We went up to London for Enoch's 80th birthday.[1] A ragbag of a
dinner, ill assorted – wives and husbands sitting (as I had predicted
to Jane) together, and so on. There were some eminent people –
George Thomas,[2] Robin Day,[3] Mrs T etc and a lot of strays. This
mix never works very well, although I was glad to have a word
with Portillo.[4] Jane was in a good cache of politicians, said little
Budgen[5] was very chippy, 'I've only got two friends ...' he said
maudlinly at one point. 'I'm not surprised,' she said.

    Speeches were *de profundis* in seniority terms – old Salisbury,[6]
George Thomas, Enoch, combined ages 243. All rather lowering, particularly the number of people who sort of accepted the
fact that I was now 'out'. 'Write a letter to *The Times*,' said John
Biffen.[7] On the way back in the car I complained to Jane about
this, but she wisely said, 'No. You're still ahead.' Budgen, typically,
had said that there wasn't the slightest reason why I should get
a peerage, reckoned it highly unlikely, and Robin Day, who was
listening, didn't demur.

    We had run into Andrew and Sarah on arrival and were having
tea in the Albany sitting room when the phone rang. I went
through to answer it in the bedroom and it was 'x'; she always
sounds specially sweet and hesitant when *she* is initiating the

---

1 Enoch Powell and AC had known each other for more than 25 years. In December
   1972 Powell made what AC called the 'prophet's visit' to Saltwood. They shared
   many of the same views, particularly on immigration.
2 George Thomas, Labour MP for various Cardiff seats from 1945, a celebrated
   Speaker, 1976–83, when he was created Viscount Tonypandy.
3 Sir Robin Day, broadcaster and author, a noted political interviewer.
4 Michael Portillo, a rising star in the Conservative Party. MP for Enfield Southgate
   since December 1984; Chief Secretary to the Treasury since 1992.
5 Nicholas Budgen, MP for Wolverhampton SW since 1974. Powell had been a
   Wolverhampton MP.
6 The 6th Marquess of Salisbury had been president of the Monday Club, which,
   as Simon Heffer, Powell's biographer, has pointed out, was in the 1960s 'self-
   appointed Praetorian Guard of Powell and the Powellite interest.'
7 John Biffen, MP for Shropshire North since 1983 (Oswestry November
   1961–83); Leader of the Commons, 1983–87.

call. I had to dissimulate, and afterwards, and all evening, I felt
that I had betrayed her. How many times am I having to do this
sort of thing, how often can she stand it?

Saltwood   *Friday, 26 June*

Yesterday a sort of horror day. James (who else?) played a major
role. Full depths of horror never plumbed without a James
intervention. Wanted to talk about Sally; tried to put him off,
and he broke down. I had to ring Sally, who was cool and wary
etc etc, anyway her little dog was dying. All this against a background of Gay and Nigel Harris, Sarah's parents, arriving and
being fluffed, and to whom I had to pay attention.

   When, finally, I disentangled myself to go to bed I got upstairs
to find the bed 'stripped', and had to 'make' it, the biggest bed
in the house, at midnight.

Garden House, p.m.

Very melancholy and fatigued. I wish it wasn't so fine. All the
plants and baby trees need water. I got all the cars (except Loco
and XK) out of the Long Garage this afternoon and the Ghost
was incredible 'for' Nigel – started on five cranks of a quarter
turn! But *all* the cars need LCA. I seem to have no time at all;
the Green Room is as usual a mad jungle of paper on flat
surfaces, and I have three speeches to write while James's visit
overhangs us. This is the only place where there is any tranquillity. But even here reflections can induce melancholy. I
dreamed, again, of the House last night. I was in flying kit, the
Secretary of State was somewhere around, but I couldn't gain
access, and Jane was keeping me waiting.

Garden House   *Saturday, 27 June*

Gloomy this morning. Still terribly hot and dry. I worked a little nearby and thought how pleasing to have a pace of life when one can do this, and two hours at the word processor in the evenings, and play with the cars a little, inventorise, propose. There is a *sort* of fallow period opening up in the [late] autumn, I suppose. I was pleasurably anticipating the rest of this year, and its uncertainties. Now I'm not so sure.

Garden House   *Sunday, 28 June*

Went on to Aspers, very late, and had a good solitary dinner (Conrad Black and Barbara Amiel had chucked). He is now wise and majestic, in his old age. Though like so many he's been very ill – typhus (?), rheumatic fever, cortisone, chronic leukaemic condition. I'm lucky to have evaded that sort of general ill health. But whether I shall continue to do so now that both political and sexual adrenalin have been withdrawn must be doubtful.

Perhaps just as well I'm not in the House, although I feel it could in fact get tremendously interesting. JM now putting it about that he will resign if doesn't get Maastricht through.[1] Then could in fact be a very interesting period of 'factionalisation', just as I predicted. Will I get there in January? (*passim* Harold Nicolson).

---

[1] What became known as Maastricht began as an idea of Jacques Delors, President of the European Commission since 1989, for an International Governmental Conference on European political and monetary union. It was swiftly to act as a lightning rod, polarising the pro-Europeans and the Eurosceptics. The key issues became the ERM – exchange rate mechanism – and EMU – European Monetary Union. The conference led to a Treaty, which had to be ratified by each EU member.

Monday, 29 June

Private Office came down yesterday evening and gave me a tree.
Very sweet of them. Perhaps gifts should have been 'exchanged'?
Carol told Jane that it was an endless 3-line whip and Jonathan[1]
was never allowed away. 'AC couldn't stand it.' But as I sit here,
in oppressive heat, too-hot-Henry condition, almost the only
thing I can do is 'amend' the dictionary on the word processor.
But I wish, in spite of it all, I was in the Commons, stirring all
this 'M' stuff, using the underground car park. Oh dear. I'm very
low at present.

Tuesday, 30 June

Yesterday, after writing that entry, I trained up in the great heat to
London (2 hours – dozing off and waking with a start – only
Marden and Headcorn). I had Indian tea, having gone through the
usual cycle (vide) of total dejection, rising towards paradise, then
being disappointed. I set off for Chris Patten's Durbar Court
farewell party[2] parking my car – actually Andrew's Audi – in that
side street beside DE. I walked to FCO, Clive Steps, passing St
Stephens Tavern where officials hang out. *Very* hot, dreamlike
almost. I was in a suit, still a perfect Minister, but ethereal. Orphée.
I could do nothing, give no instructions, penetrate no sancta. The
Party was the following day, a lone custodian informed me. And I
walked back – like a masque – and set course for Saltwood.

---

[1] Jonathan Aitken (MP for Thanet South since 1983; Thanet East February 1974–83)
   had succeeded AC at Defence as Minister for Defence Procurement.
[2] Patten was leaving UK politics to become the last Governor of Hong Kong.

Garden House   *Sunday, 5 July*

Tristan had rung Jane with a rumour that I was to be the next
editor of *The Spectator*. That might be quite fun, too. Let rip!

Garden House   *Monday, 13 July*

A grey day. A time for planning. We really should operate to a
timetable. Things that must have black lines set aside for them
(not necessarily every day) are:

(a) house work in Garden House – cleaning kitchen, hanging
    pictures, plugs on lights etc
(b) word processor – already 7.30-8.30, provided this is
    working after KK. 7.45–8.45?
(c) Filing in summer office – *at least* one hour per day
(d) Cleaning cars
(e) Scything and forking? } possibly alternate?
(f) SUNDAY FREE

I must look up old timetables.

Thursday, 16 July

I gave the 'RAF' lecture at the RUSI yesterday. Quality good
audience – but I suffered from not having a typed-up text.
Afterwards I ducked out of a dinner at the House. I just did not
want to go into the Strangers Dining Room until I'm a Peer.
People ask me if I miss it. 'Yes, dreadfully,' I say.

Garden House   *Wednesday, 22 July*

So little to actually *show* for the last 12 days. I am low, and *serene* – almost Lenin Stadium with a feeling of total emptiness at the groin, as if I was a man of eighty. Page yesterday, and casually he said he'd send my blood for the Prostate Cancer Test as well as a testosterone count. I said surely if I had it I'd know? He said oh no, 80 per cent of postmortems show 80% of people over 80 (that's enough 80s! – Ed) or more do have it. 'It can be dealt with quite effectively.' But I know how I'd deal with – by chemical castration. There are worse things, I suppose, like going blind. But it's bad luck on little Jane, after this lovely year – for which eternal thanks. Would it have to be 'allied' with chemotherapy so that all my hair falls out? The effect has been to devastate me utterly – combined of course with the fact that it's now nearly six weeks since the last injection. And so much to do. The diaries, the inventory, the files, the 'dispositions'. I've been aware that my looks and general stamina (I seldom want to do weights and press-ups) are much less than last summer. What a long 'Indian' summer that was!

Saturday, 25 July

We bought the huge Sidney Cooper for £110,000[1] – which makes things very tight. I will have to sell a little modern art, but what? The 'chair' perhaps?[2]

---

[1] Nineteenth-century painting of Saltwood Castle.
[2] By Cézanne – but not sold.

Garden House   *Sunday, 26 July*

I was so depressed and hopeless. Almost I feel as if my life is over
now. Just a few months to establish order; lay down some
'guidelines' which my successor can follow. It's such a wrench
being out of the Commons. The papers are full of articles
exculpating Mellor ('the mood has changed', all that)[1] and
saying how wonderful and powerful and reclamé MPs are. On
Wednesday it's the Quintons's[2] party on Lords Terrace and I
hardly know if I dare go to it, the nostalgia will be so acute; and
after that a 'farewell' from the Chief of Staff. I suppose, if my
'tests' are ok, I can just chat and get through. If not, well that *is*
it, and this entry is just a preface. My symptoms are not
imaginary. I am very low on energy – for instance in the old
days, however hypochondriacally I felt, I would take a terrific
walk after tea. Now I just enjoy a drive and the nostalgic
thoughtfulness it brings (today the DS Chapron). I have an
intermittent sore throat – traces of – and I break out into sweats
from time to time. In the morning I don't wake 'refreshed'.

I feel the biggest mistake I ever made was to 'walk away' from
the Commons.

Garden House   *Tuesday, 28 July*

Yesterday, no more than 50/50 confident of good 'tests', I don't
see my way out of it. If I have to submit to treatment – strange
tubes and probes and chemotherapy, well, I won't. I'll accept my
sentence – of a few weeks or months, then go in my prime, as
from the House. At that decision, I felt much better and stronger.

---

[1] David Mellor, MP for Putney since 1979 and Heritage Secretary since the general
election had resigned following saucy tabloid newspaper revelations about a sexual
affair.

[2] Anthony Quinton (life peer, 1982) and his wife Marcelle. A philosopher, he was
not long retired as chairman of the British Library.

Then, when I got to Albany, there was Page's letter marked on the front: <u>Personal, Medical and Confidential</u> – an invitation to snoop if ever there was one! 'No trace whatever' of PreCan, testosterone right down, everything else ok – he sent me print out – except for cholesterol, about which I could not care. Can now revert to thinking demi-clearly about the summer and autumn. I must organise a proper car cull.

Last night at the Chief of Staff dinner at the Tower I was demi-lionised. Only person to be mentioned in Dick Vincent's speech, both he and Moray Stewart talked to me at length. Ken Carlisle[1] said 'we miss you dreadfully. You are a real H of Commons man. You could always make the House do what you wanted ...' More nostalgic thinking.

At one point Lady Arran said – well what do you want? I said 'to be a Member of the House of Commons and a Minister in the Government.' 'Would you swap with Tommy?' If, well, that was another matter, and I didn't give a proper answer.

Garden House   *Monday, 3 August*

I'm depressed, and slightly rattled today.

My interview with Graham Turner – although it read very well (for a connoisseur) – contained objectionable, i.e. that to which objection could legitimately be taken, research about poor old TK, and also about 'The Royals'.[2] It has been taken up, and *distilled*, in the *Express* today and will, I suspect, disqualify me from any 'perch'. BLAST. The photos that accompanied the Turner article were unflattering, particularly the one with Jane. Even she said I looked 'cortisoned'. I have become a little bit too

---

[1] Kenneth Carlisle, MP for Lincoln since 1979; Parliamentary Under-Secretary, MoD 1990–92.

[2] In the *Sunday Telegraph*. The piece began with AC on Tom King: 'He was ghastly, an awful person to work with – indecisive, blustering, bullying, stupid and cunningly cautious, even when he didn't need to be.'

heavy, off the old dial and standing at 12 stone. So I am stiff in the joints and a bit lethargic (But if I don't eat lunch I get sleepy and faint). I'm my most *en retraite* at the moment, as I often get with 'unfortunate' publicity. Just want to hide.

Shore Cottage   *Sunday, 16 August*

Watery August sun directly through the sitting room windows at 8.30 a.m. I am a little uncertain. Curiously, now that I can spend as much time (figuratively) at Shore as I want, I feel myself to be less keen on it.

I had an indifferent night (not a total submersion) peeing 4 times – but not at all prostatically. My first worry was dear little Meg, who greeted me specially. I won't be able to get her back this time as we are in the Jaguar and Jane is dropping me off in London, but I will reassure her; and next time we are up will prepare her kennels here, so she can live with us for a little while before the trekking south.

James, though, touch wood does seem much better. He's back in charge of Saltwood and got 'Ruby' going. Incredible!

Garden House   *Thursday, 20 August*

Exactly a year ago we set off for Zermatt. Private Office got me, literally at the airport gates and said Gorbachev has been overthrown. So what? We went on, and had a lovely week.

Then I came back, and made a balls-up of a lot of things.

Now I'm weary, creaky, 6lbs overweight, back pain.

I can't sell any of my cars and seem to have used up all my money. I'm 'out' of things, although I have a short 'flash' life in prospect until the diaries are out.

What I really need is a holiday, a proper one.

I said to Jane – a hut by the beach, Club Med type. White sand that gets between your toes, lapping water, a deckchair *in the shade* with six or seven books (*passim* Richard Ryder to whom I spoke on Thursday and is off to Corfu) and delicious meals available at a central dining room. She said, 'If anyone took a tape of you, they'd think what a really *awful* man.'

Garden House   *Monday, 24 August*

I walked into the Garden House this morning. The light is fading earlier and earlier and we have got a fire in the Green Room. I thought, when there was last a fire in this grate the election was on, and I was in high hopes for 'value' and (at least) administrative achievement this year. But nothing. Just 40 pages of diaries and a lot of unanswered trivialities. James's arrival has imposed some strain – but he has been incredible with the machinery; 'mending' the Westwood, the XK120, 'Ruby'. But I am the weak link. Selfish, moody, de-energised.

Monday, 31 August

David Owen has got the Euro-rep at Yugoslav Peace Conference job. So he's back in the stream.[1] Julian Critchley[2] writes in the *Observer* that I was the kind of MP (person in – sic – politics) who had style. I am pleased by this. But I don't see my role. I am OUT not IN and I notice the difference more and more.

---

[1] David Owen, MP (Labour 1966–81, SDP 1981–92; Plymouth Sutton 1966–74, Plymouth Devonport 1974–92) had been appointed European Union Co-Chairman, International Conference on Former Yugoslavia.
[2] Julian Critchley, MP for Aldershot since 1970 (Rochester & Chatham 1959–64) and author, was commenting on the *Sunday Telegraph* interview with AC.

Garden House   *Tuesday, 8 September*

I was a *mauvais relations* with Jane yesterday. She made me cross
by questioning me about *why* I was going up to London. I
thought I'd been so 'good' for four months that I might be
allowed a day off. But no, it was you haven't been to London for
ages and now you suddenly want to go to London. I want to
know why. Was clearly thinking/said, either I am going to meet
'x', or lunch with some tittles of a journalist, or have a hormone
(sic) injection. Sex, actually, is all women think about when they
don't know an answer. This made me cross. And it was unfair. I
had twice admired and complimented her on her appearance
and all she said was that I was like Frank Bough (whom I had
always thought ghastly, long before he got caught in a 'sex den'
– or whatever it was). I really do *not* resemble Frank Bough.[1] It's
most unfair.

But actually, I suppose, there is no reason why I still go to
London at all – ever, really.

B5 Albany   *Thursday, 17 September*

A very bad night. I woke at 1.20 – rather less than an hour after
putting the light out, with complete insomnia. Could have
made tea (*did*, in fact, after padding down to a night porter and
collecting some milk) and driven the Little Silver anywhere.

I dined with Jonathan, Ryder was there, Tristan came in later
(I'm glad to say, because he wasn't as much fun as the other two;
showed his limitations). Jonathan told me that Conrad Black had
told Moore to pay *anything* to ensure that he collared the diaries,
and Richard said that Jonathan Holborow[2] was a great fan of

---

[1] Frank Bough, television broadcaster, who specialised in sports reporting, had had
his sex-life exposed in a tabloid newspaper.
[2] Two newly-appointed editors, Charles Moore, of the *Sunday Telegraph*; Jonathan
Holborow, of the *Mail on Sunday*.

mine (seemed surprised, *why?*). But I felt *out* particularly when they started talking about the new MPs, and their disorderly behaviour, 'the hunger for the soundbite', as I put it.

Shore Cottage   *Sunday, 20 September*

Yesterday evening I spoke to Max Hastings.[1] We talked about the Government turmoil and how *bad* they all were (including the P.M.).[2] Max said he had threatened Norman Lamont[3] with implacable liability if he didn't resign. Max had lunch with Ken Clarke[4] (it's really too awful that the choice of alternatives should be Michael Heseltine – still – and Ken Clarke) who had ruefully said that, in Thursday's emergency debate, the Government couldn't admit that it had neither an Economic nor a Foreign policy.

I drove very slowly back down Eriboll Street in the (nasty) Range Rover in the dark and realised, almost with panic, just what I had thrown away by 'standing down'. I suppose I should have continued to trust in God, that He would give one the opportunity for the sword in the lake. Essentially it was selfish, opting for a quiet and comfortable life; sidestepping humiliation. God has given us self-determination, too, and of course if we are determined we can reject his gift.

---

[1] Max Hastings, journalist and military historian, editor of the *Daily Telegraph* since 1986.

[2] The twin causes of the turmoil were the Maastricht Treaty, which had caused twenty-two Conservative MPs to vote against the government, and Britain's membership of the European exchange rate mechanism (ERM). Sterling had crashed, and on 16 September, swiftly dubbed 'Black Wednesday', interest rates were raised temporarily to 15 per cent and British membership of the ERM was suspended. In short, the government's economic policy was on the ropes.

[3] Norman Lamont, MP for Kingston-on-Thames since May 1972; Chancellor of the Exchequer since 1990. At this point he did not resign.

[4] Kenneth Clarke, MP for Rushcliffe since 1970; Home Secretary since the general election and a rising star in Conservative circles, even though AC would immortalise him as a 'pudgy puffball' when *Diaries* came to be published.

Garden House   *Wednesday, 30 September*

Adrian Lithgow down this morning to 'help' one with a second
draft of a 'conference' article for the *Mail on Sunday*. Neat,
saturnine, 'slight' and cigaretting. An easy way of earning £2k,
you could say. I don't know how it will look, but I remain
restless and discomforted at being *out* of the House. Pat
Kavanagh has failed to improve on the *Mail on Sunday*'s offer of
£200k for the serial rights.[1] But half paid now and half on
publication so let that sort a few things out (but not, I fear the
Turbo R Cont). Then next week, agreeably, all those hardback
contenders of £150k are going to make 'presentations' to
ingratiate themselves.

Brighton   *Wednesday, 7 October*

On the way over here I parked the car, got out in the moon-
light, and walked along the Downs to a 5-bar gate. I spoke to
God. I apologised for having avoided Him for so long. The
muddle of guilt and lust over 'x' had blighted our contact for over
a year. Now I had to make penance – first for hurting sweet Jane
over 'x', and for still harbouring sinful, muddled thoughts there;
second for having discarded the special advantages He had given
me, to *get* me into Plymouth Sutton so late and so old, without
consulting Him or taking his permission.[2] Now the moment
had come, at last, when I could do something. But how could
He give me another chance? If He did, of course, our relationship would be impregnable. But could He? Everything is
possible of course. But nothing works out so easily.

---

[1] For the 'Diaries of a Junior Minister' as they were provisionally titled; Patricia
Kavanagh, director Peters, Fraser & Dunlop, AC's literary agents.
[2] See *Diaries: Into Politics*.

Garden House   *Sunday, 11 October*

It's drizzling and the long Park Ward 4¼ [Bentley], almost my
favourite car, is getting spoiled as it sits outside the towers,
where it has been since the grey 4½ arrived, waiting for 'Barry'
(classic car transport driver). The contract people are roaring and
thrashing in the level-crossing field, even though it is a Sunday,
which is always unsettling. Poor dear Eva is in ever-sleeping
decline. I don't think she'll last another fortnight. And yet so
sweet-natured still. Jane will be shattered. I am a long way
behind with my page schedule for Weidenfeld,[1] and 'one' for
The Times, a review of the Schwarzkopf book.[2] I must quickly
draft out, also, an article on how 'social policy' is catching us up.

　　Oh to be back in! (and *not* as a peer).

Garden House   *Monday, 12 October*

Poor 'E' is now in terminal decline. I had to carry her off the bed
and down the second flight front stairs today. I could never have
done that in the great days of the 'room fighting'. For the first
time she is herself really low, and hangs her head as in the last
minutes in the bullring. Thank God for the long break in
Scotland, where we have a lovely picture of her, beautiful in the
heather.

Garden House   *Sunday, 25 October*

I'm so depressed. Sunday papers go on and on about how awful

---

[1] Following the 'viva' of the hardback contenders to publish his diaries AC had
chosen Weidenfeld & Nicolson. His editor would be Ion Trewin.
[2] The memoirs of the US Gulf War general, Norman Schwarzkopf, *It Doesn't Take
a Hero*.

the Government is. But there is no leader on the right – like me
all having left the House. *I* could be doing it. Of course there
are endless imponderables. It was only after I left that I realised
how much I had been appreciated; but would I still have been
in the government? Probably yes. And if I were – would I have
had the guts to resign before the parity debate? (I broke off for
quite a while, composing and reciting a marvellous speech in
the House of Commons that would have called on John Major
– yes, there is work here for two Parliamentary terms – to think
radically.)

The Old Bailey   *Wednesday, 4 November*

Testifying in the 'Matrix Churchill' trial.[1] Day wasted, though I
get £70 for an ITN interview at lunchtime on 'John Major
leadership' (Maastricht vote today, but the dignitaries have sold
the pass – George Gardiner, Rhodes Boyson etc – presumably
because they realise there's no one to take his place).[2]

Yesterday I met VH [Valerie Harkess] for a drink, not looking
bad, really. Well-preserved. V good 'bust', and *very* restrainedly
dressed. She said I would have been leader, 'got the leadership'
if I'd still been in. It didn't need saying. I said 'it was the most
catastrophically bad decision'. We walked up Piccadilly and
parted outside the Park Lane Hotel, past two clubs where – in
bedrooms, in the Ladies, etc we'd coupled. I said to her (which

---

[1] During his period as Minister of Trade (1986–89) AC had a meeting with machine
tool exporters who as a result thought that the British government would turn a
blind eye if they declared that exports to Iraq had general engineering rather than
specifically military applications. The trial of the Matrix Churchill directors
accused of selling weapons to Iraq, what became known as the 'arms-to-Iraq'
affair, had begun on 12 October.

[2] Sir George Gardiner, MP for Reigate since February 1974, a council member of
the Conservative Way Forward group, and seen by the party hierarchy as a key
rebel where Europe was concerned; Sir Rhodes Boyson, MP for Brent North
since February 1974.

is true) 'I have never felt the same degree of sheer physical desire as I did with you with any other human being.' She was pleased. She said I'd never given her any (sic) money. '£10,000', I said. 'Do you think I'm worth £10,000?' 'Well,' I paused, 'if you *can* quantify it, I'd say you were ... "worth" £450,000.'

Went back to Albany. Curiously desexualated. Left a message on 'x's phone, did the flowers. Left, saying I'm going to Brooks's. But no sooner had I got to the Club than the Porter said she'd rung. Must have done so immediately she got it. I was delighted by this.

Garden House   *Tuesday, 8 December*

And what about testifying to Scott?[1] Last night Detective Inspector Lawrence phoned, asked for an appointment 'after Christmas' (brain washing to wreck in the holiday) for a meeting 'with my solicitor' and a 'statement'.

'I have nothing to say,' I said. Well could I put him in touch with my solicitor ... etc.

'I don't see why I even need to pay a solicitor.' He was puzzled.

'Come and arrest me.'

'It's not an arrestable offence.'

My only choice is to 'clear my name' with Scott.

---

[1] The Matrix Churchill trial had folded on 10 November, following AC's answer to Geoffrey Robertson, defence counsel, who had remarked that a statement attributed to AC – 'that the Iraqis will be using the current order for general engineering purposes' could not be correct 'to your knowledge'.

AC: Well, it's our old friend being economical, isn't it?

GR: With the truth?

AC: With the *actualité*. There was nothing misleading or dishonest to make a formal or introductory comment that the Iraqis would be using the current orders for general engineering purposes. All I didn't say was 'and for making munitions'. Sir Richard Scott, a Lord Justice of Appeal since 1991, had been appointed to chair an inquiry

Garden House   *Friday, 11 December*

We buried dear 'E' today. She looked lovely, literally asleep with
all the tension gone out of her body; and we put in 'Squeaky',
an American bone, and some other mementoes and Jane's
headscarf.

Last night she was so collapsed and intermittently crying in
pain, even when I picked her up she couldn't stand. I went
down to fetch Carlile (nearly missed him, not at Sandgate etc).
A massive (x 4) overdose of anaesthetic and her head dropped
into Jane's hand immediately. Jane could feel her last breaths.
That morning, Jane said, she had gone out into the yard, the
Bailey, just looked around – for the last time – and turned back.
Thinking to the past I recall her doing 'last' journeys to so many
familiar staging points – Lord Clark's Gate, the Long Garage, the
car park field gate – separately, on different occasions. Right to
the end she smelt beautiful, and had a lovely expression and
smooth head.

Garden House   *Saturday, 12 December*

I had a tiny stroll with Jane. She said what an annus horribilis it
had been for everyone. Only want to escape. Saltwood is such a
mess, so distressing, absolutely nothing 'to hand'. I would like to
be minimalist. A south sea island, a Club Med hut, some decent
books and a 2CV. Perhaps, after the 'publication' [of the diaries]
I can escape, totally?

I am lucky, surely, still to have my health and energy. 'No
warnings'. But how long have I still this dispensation?

Garden House   *Monday, 14 December*

I have just finished transposing the entry for 20 September 1984.[1] Should have been much less cliquey, widened my circle of friends, never let my boredom threshold show. I should have entertained, in cycle, members of the 92, little dinners. Pressed on. I didn't realise, until too late, the prestige I commanded. I thought that they would think I wanted something. I should really have had a dinner every fortnight.

Now, in this dead and dingy and aimless parliament everyone would be talking about me.

I SHOULD NEVER HAVE LEFT THE HOUSE OF COMMONS.

---

[1] In which AC describes a letter from Julian Amery ('you stick out like a red poppy in the hayfield of mediocrities surrounding you …') after surviving the reshuffle (*Diaries*).

1993

Never[1] have I contemplated the end of the holiday with such gloom, and headhung pressure. I am under *such* pressure with these *Diaries*, and my eyes are going red-rimmed. Piccolo row yesterday after my (very well-written) piece in *The Times* on 'Winston'.[2] No more writing now, until the end of the *Diaries* (whatever I write people will always look for the ooh! 'controversial' bit).

At EMT we agreed first half of the year *choked* (up to 'The Wedding'[3]) then blank. Keep it that way.

Monday, 4 January

Did a broadcast at 1 o'clock [Radio 4's *World at One*]. Quite good-natured, with Andrew Roberts and Jim Naughtie.[4] But 'Charleston' of *Western Morning News* rang and said W Country MPs (none of whom liked me) said my article 'sour grapes' because I was out of things; and Bruce [Anderson] rang, congratulating, to tell me of a piece – very chippy – 'social misfit' etc by Cameron Watt in the *Standard*. *Guardian* wants to do an interview/profile; bound to be hostile, but must do my best to be bland. But *think* (as I said to Jane) what will happen when the *Diaries* come out! There's so much jealousy about. 'People' will

---

[1] AC's own footnote: 'not for a long while anyway; since European Bill Committee'.
[2] Inspired by John Charmley's about-to-be published biography, *Churchill: the End of Glory*, 'the most important "revisionist" text to be published since the war', said *The Times* on its front page. AC's thesis, which would even be called 'ludicrous' in the pell-mell that followed, was that Churchill by refusing to make peace with Hitler in 1940-41 betrayed the Commonwealth, lost the Far Eastern empire and shattered the British social order.
[3] Andrew Clark would be marrying Sarah Harris later in the year.
[4] Andrew Roberts, historian, whose first book, *The Holy Fox* (a life of Lord Halifax, 1991) had been highly praised, was at work on a series of essays that would be published as *Eminent Churchillians*; Jim Naughtie, former *Guardian* political editor, had recently transferred to radio.

really have something to fasten on to then. I will (ideally) be in the Alps, wrestling at the wheel of our Silver Ghost.[1]

Ups and downs. But one just takes consolation from the fact that the intensity of reaction is usually a good yardstick to the effectiveness of a particular quest.

Sunday, 24 January

Crazy spastic headline in today's *Sunday Express* – 'Yard moves in on ex-Minister'. Really! I am dutch, though slightly put out.

Sunday, 31 January

Only a month left to finish the *D*. I am lack-lustre and particularly depressed. Without hope, now, of 'x'. I'm in purdah for the next four weeks.

Wednesday, 10 February

I am back from London, desperately tired and low, having been 'lionised' at lunch with Jonathan Holborow, Dobbie, Angus McPherson and the definitely attractive Caroline Michel.[2] Why oh why (sic) did I leave the Commons? They more or less agreed that I could be leading the Right. I fantasise, sometimes,

---

[1] The Rolls-Royce Enthusiasts' Club Alpine 93 (hereafter called the 'Alpine' by AC) in June in which AC would drive his Silver Ghost, to mark the twentieth anniversary of the previous RREC Alpine, in which Alan and Jane had taken part in 1973.

[2] The *Mail on Sunday*'s bid to serialise the *Diaries* had been accepted; Peter Dobbie (long-time political writer), Angus McPherson, members of Holborow's team; Caroline Michel, marketing director of Weidenfeld & Nicolson.

that I could be *called* back into the Commons … But I need so many miracles. I fear my potency is waning.

Garden House   *Saturday, 20 February*

I am very unhappy. None of the old standbys that used to calm me are working. The Garden House – so warm and enveloping; so many little touches. The badge-room, the 'workshop', to fiddle with the cars, the archive room. I now see, of course, that they were only delicious when one had the position to fall back on. Now they are just 'hobbies in retirement'. I don't *want* to retire. I don't feel like retirement at all. My mind races, I am hungry for news and gossip, resentful at John Major, Richard Ryder (shameful), Aitken – how *could* they? Although, of course, the cruelty of politics is its attraction

I have come over here to write and to pray, for my 'game plan'. Could God give me just this one more chance? Since my last entry Judith Chaplin has died suddenly at Newbury (a very bad seat).[1] It would have to be ACHAB – as never before or since.

Is the sword still there, though now at the bottom of the lake?

Monday, 22 February

It was good. Clear, assured, moving. I looked compos and in my 'prime'. Many people saw it. All were enthusiastic. Today acres of coverage in *The Times*.[2] Particularly valuable was a compliment

---

[1] To call it a 'very bad seat' seems on the face of it surprising as Judith Chaplin, former political secretary to John Major, became MP for Newbury in 1992 with a majority of 11,057. But it marked a crucial electoral test for the government following sterling's ejection from the ERM the previous September.

[2] This first extract from AC's contribution to Channel 4's Opinions series of lectures, was spread across two pages under the heading 'Bold surgery needed to cure our once-great nation.'

from Bob Worcester.[1] He said I (not a CCO template twerp) *could* win Newbury. Hugely excited, I rang Peter Stothard at *The Times*.[2] He made a good point when I asked if I could 'enlist his help' – said the candidate would really be chosen by Major and Fowler.[3] They would have the choice of winning with me, and losing with a centrist – they'd probably prefer the latter. But how smoothly everything seems to be running at present. Almost creepy, down to the little note in *The Times* Diary (where from?) that I may be 'standing' at Newbury. Shades of 1968.[4] Later this afternoon Michael Cockerell rang, very appreciative, professionally.[5] *Deo volente* at present.

Tuesday, 23 February

Complete and utter dejection now. Everything gone. Nothing in *The Times* except a kind of play-safe piece by Peter Riddell.[6] No one has really noticed. So my 'game plan' has failed. But, at least, I said my piece – *and I said it well.* I poured out my heart to Jamie last night and he was encouraging. But I am blighted too, horrendously so, by the fickleness of my minx.

[1] Robert Worcester, founder of MORI, a leading political pollster.

[2] Peter Stothard, who had not long been appointed editor of *The Times*.

[3] Sir Norman Fowler (MP for Sutton Coldfield since February 1974, Nottingham S 1970–74) had succeeded Chris Patten as chairman of the Conservative Party.

[4] *The Times* Diary had run early stories about AC's political ambitions (*Diaries: Into Politics*, 14 June, 1972).

[5] Michael Cockerell, BBC political journalist, was making a television profile of AC, called *Love Tory*.

[6] *The Times*'s political analyst.

Thursday, 25 February

I am in limbo. Ten days to complete delivery of *Diaries*.[1]

But everything is overshadowed, made slightly *unreal* by Jane/
Bates, need for slides and tests. I can't believe it. But hope the
ju-ju hasn't gone wrong somehow. I feel slightly depersonalised,
almost demob happy by all this.

Would almost have forgotten about politics, were it not for a
call from Jonathan Holborow and a full political fix. Apparently
Richard R[yder] is going to be eased out to be Minister of
Agriculture, and David D is to be chief [whip].[2] Which will be
good. But where do I fit in?

Garden House   *Sunday, 28 February*

A series of little extra pieces fall into place. On Friday evening
Dobbie rang me and asked if I would do a piece backing Paul
Keating's attitude to the Royals.[3] 'Look, if I'm going to fight the
Newbury by-election, the last thing I want is an anti-Royal
article.' 'Cor, Alan, you're having me on …' etc. This just covered
me, as it turned out, because the very next morning, in *The
Times* leader 'Newbury die' I was named twice!

So this morning good friendly coverage in Black Dog (top),[4] and
v reasonable in *Sunday Express*, thanks to dear Bruce who is coming
down for lunch, and wants to be my campaign manager.[5] Perhaps
more importantly and *complimentarily*, my verdict on JM in Graham
Turner's *Sunday Telegraph* piece 'I have a high opinion of him …'

---

[1] As they had finally been titled.
[2] Turned out not to be so.
[3] Paul Keating, Prime Minister of Australia since 1991, had, typically, been making
some provocative remarks about the Queen.
[4] *Mail on Sunday* political diary.
[5] Bruce Anderson had suggested AC to Richard Ryder as the candidate who would
do least badly. Norman Fowler, apparently, thought it a crazy idea.

It all has a strange, magical quality. Almost as if I, and other forces, was willing it. Could I really bring it off? A year's sabbatical to assuage Jane, get the *Diaries* done. And then back to the second serious phase. And the lights of AC1800 in the garage, and the big party in the Jubilee Room, 'to celebrate the result of the Newbury by-election'.

Garden House   *Thursday, 4 March*

Still the accumulation of events. Yesterday Jane's 'tests' proved *negative*, and thus a fresh boost as the overshadowing lifts. Then Matrix, DPP 'cleared' me, good TV coverage – 'vindicates' etc.[1] Spoke to Gill Shephard[2] – she very indiscreet, said, 'You must put in' and (without telling Jane) I now intend to 'take things one stage further' today. Then, after Ch 3 [lunchtime ITN] news, phone rang and, rather quiet and sorry for himself, Richard !! It's all so impeccable, the timing. Polling just before the book comes out; and also the lawyers suggested excisions [to the *Diaries*] made it much easier to sanitise without upsetting the publishers.

Am I really contemplating the humiliation of a selection process, and then the Campaign and the bad polls, and then the count – and then ... I can get wild AF, yes. But until I am *stopped* it would be a derogation of responsibility and doubt 'to pull back'. The sword is on the surface of the lake floor.

---

[1] AC had feared he might be charged in connection with the Matrix Churchill case.
[2] Gillian Shephard, MP for South West Norfolk since 1987, Employment Secretary.

Saturday, 13 March

What I will never know is whether in fact I had any chance of being 'seen' at Newbury or not *before* little Sarah Sands' interview in the *Standard* yesterday.[1]

I suppose it was a mistake – led astray by a pretty girl, as usual.

Terrible row with Jane followed. All I wanted to do was step into a hole.

Trouble is this was really my last 'window'. Because once the book is out – with its crazy indiscretions and element of romping – I will no longer be taken seriously.

I am *not* released. A bit apprehensive of bad publicity. Heard from *Daily Express* (typically) that 'down to 18' and not on list. Very flat and depressed. I slept after tea on the floor of the Green Room. I am tired and aimless. I must also try and restore the body a bit more. I have been drinking too regularly, taking very little exercise. I am creaky and fatigued ('ravaged' in appearance – Sarah Sands). Strange though for three miraculous weeks it all seemed to fit in such a pre-ordained way, climaxing with the Matrix Churchill acquittal.

Garden House   *Monday, 15 March*

It is a beautiful spring day, and the lawn looms. One needs really a *continuous* week to get the lawn 'under'; at the moment it seems always to be 'getting on top of one'.

Last night I was doing the Runes – *very* pessimistic, started with the Ice Rune – nothing; then 'prediction' – but reversed, then the Black Rune – death.

Nobody in the papers rang at all. I am a non-person. Just that

---

[1] Sarah Sands, feature writer, on London *Evening Standard*, had interviewed AC at Saltwood, where he was indiscreet about the forthcoming *Diaries*, about affairs and much else.

last spluttering of the candle. Nick Budgen rang and said would I stand as the Referendum candidate at Newbury. Talked for ½ hour. Then rang again in the evening. But Jane got the perfect word – 'floundering'. You can't really stand against your own party.

Garden House   *Thursday, 18 March*

I have a very heavy heart. Took in the last pages of the *Diaries* today, and a long session (the 3rd) sorting out editorial queries. Now it is out of control, and the date approaches when 'serialisation publicity' starts. Jonathan Holborow is going to spend £½ million – and God knows what they will be saying. I will have to go 'into hiding'. Any idea that I can sign books and 'show' myself is ridiculous; I will be a figure of fun, like Mellor. It signals, too, the end of my career in serious politics; and the end of any hope of, even, a 'K' (the only thing I thought I might have 'hooked').

Sunday, 28 March

Walking down to the Long Garage this evening I felt some-thing on my nose, right-hand side. Asked Jane, she said it was a 'little melanoma'. That's how the last nodel began, a little black dot. But in the mirror it's more of a line. Strange and depressing.

Garden House   *Friday, 2 April*

First of the galleys – to 1985 – arrived today

I'm not so sure about the book. Is it really very *slight* indeed? I am nervous and apprehensive. I have been going through a phase of hypochondria about my melanoma and my right shoulder. It is certainly a worrying shape, a configuration rather, but not large. But my real problem is that there is this huge void – between policies and frivolities.

Zermatt   *Wednesday, 14 April*

I have arrived here, now an OAP, and my hair is really quite white on my left side. I have a headache and my eyes aren't working very well. I feel completely desexualated. On my bed in the dressing room a PLO scarf was spread out, and a note of 'present' for 'the Minister' from Andrew. I thanked him, then expressed quite a little shock when he said he had left it there last year. It's eighteen months since we had our 'momentous' summer hiking stay. I've made mistakes in the period. Bad ones.

Suddenly, Zermatt like, I have had the most wonderful sign. I opened the drawer of Mme Piper, and in the violet shirt were my *candidate links*[1] This opens many doors.

---

[1] AC's speech at the Plymouth Sutton selection in 1972; 'Mme Piper' was a chest of drawers; the cufflinks, of lapis lazuli, had been given by Jane to AC, who wore them the night he was selected at Plymouth.

Garden House   *Saturday, 24 April*

At last the 'filming' is over.[1]

In the last days I became quite tetchy with them all – too much repetition 'if you could just do that again, Alan' etc. Much hanging about, intrusion on meals etc.

But now that is past, and the galleys are delivered. Nothing to do except dodge (or under direction accept) interviews until the serialisation starts. Time is incredibly congested. I am in a state of acute dejection and find it difficult to concentrate. Instead, I just come over here and mope, and relive agonies from the past.

What is my role? Christopher Silvester interviewed me today. Not specially sympathetic, somehow. He asked me who were my friends in politics. I mentioned Rhodes James, Garel-Jones, Soames.[2] 'But aren't they all much younger than you?' Yes, I said, thinking that my contemporaries are all buffers.

But audiences, as raised by Nick Wapshott and the Greenwich Defence 'students', all kind of expect one to 'go back' into politics.

It's not really possible, is it?

But ACHAB.

The second half of the year is a void. I fear the worst. I have to get over May 10 (*always* bad sexually for some reason), then, a Knight for the Tamar estuary and – Keith Douglas again –

The next month, then, is a window

and with a crash I'll split the glass.

Behind it stands one I must kiss.

Person of love, or death

A person, or a wraith?

I fear what I shall find.[3]

---

[1] Michael Cockerell and his camera crew had been filming AC (and Jane) for his BBC *Love Tory* documentary.

[2] Sir Robert Rhodes James, historian who edited the Chips Channon diaries (1967); MP for Cambridge (December 1976-92). He and AC were (friendly) rivals.

[3] Keith Douglas, who died in Normandy in 1944, was a favourite poet of AC's. These lines are from 'On a Return from Egypt'. He also quotes him at the close of *Diaries*.

Garden House   *Monday, 26 April*

A dreadful day. Jane is ill, and I sent her to bed (freesias and Ribena, fluffing the pillows). I was got off the loo today to be asked 'Nick[1] wants to know how long it takes to get here from Gatwick' (!). I've had to scrape, scrape the barrel to pay for Andrew's house. Jonathan Holborow will not now even restore me the balance. And 'US rights', if there is such a thing, I will not sell to Harry Evans.[2]

I really wanted to escape today – just go with books and a deckchair to the sand – or perhaps to the châlet. But I finished cutting the Bailey, and I thought how beautiful Saltwood looked. I sang *Die Soldaten* and wondered what all might have been and what (if anything) is in store.

Garden House   *Tuesday, 27 April*

Walked from Sandling [station], darling Jane had made a balls-up of the arrival times and gone to Folkestone. London had been blocked solid. And now I return to find Jane is being bullied by Bates again and he's taken *twelve* slides. Uncertainty, complete, prevails.

Saltwood   *Sunday, 9 May*

A week, much filled, but little achieved.

The flat surfaces in the Green Room are choked and towering; 'key' letters like RREC Alpine and LPF[3] are still unattended

---

[1] Nick Beuttler, Jane's brother.
[2] Harold Evans, former editor of the *Sunday Times*, now President of Random House, the New York publishers.
[3] L. P. Fassbender, the Clarks' accountant.

to; the yard and workshops are a shambles and the lawn is never quite fully under control.

Jane was forced by Bates to undergo an operation – a 'lumpectomy'. We were in silent abjection (I will always remember, though not as vividly as if it had marked the end of an era, answering his phone call to say it was a bit 'suspicious' after I had (demi-randily) my first after-lunch rest for ages, a Bank Monday – which had to be bad). But it turned out, on Friday, to be 'all right'. He splendidly rang me at supper. So I feel free to restart again, so soon after making or implying all those promises in St Leonard's where I had repaired after reading the interview which made me feel so sad and proud of her. But her being away is appalling. The pups[1] are a delight, but needlessly demanding: the weather is foul, with a high wind blowing all the time. I get up at 5.30, but still have only just got the kitchen in order, pups fed and walked by 7.

I am faced with difficult times. My instinct is to hide. Not even read the papers, just baste them nimbly.

But that was a lucky break at Newbury![2]

Garden House   *Tuesday, 18 May*

Today the first day of the hols. For I don't know *how* long, we came back from taking Pam[3] to Gatwick and just collapsed by the pool. Exhausted in our bones.

Saltwood is so lovely in May, each year one forgets how high

---

[1] Two Rottweilers, sisters, to whom the Clarks gave names with German association: Hannah (Jane's, after Hannah Reich, Hitler's test pilot) and Lëhni (AC's, after Hitler's favourite film director, Leni Riefenstahl).

[2] AC was indeed fortunate: the Conservatives were mauled at the by-election held on 6 May, with the Liberal Democrat candidate, Old Etonian David Rendel, overturning the Tories' general election 11,000 majority to achieve a LD victory by over 12,000 votes. As for the referendum/anti-Maastricht candidates, together they polled fewer than 700 votes.

[3] Pam Beuttler, Jane's mother, who was returning home to Benalmadena in Spain.

and sensuous enveloping is the Queen Anne Lace and the yellow-green foliage.

Garden House   *Wednesday, 26 May*

I feel very tired. The 'pressure' of all those interviews, publicity, serialisation, never anticipation of *disappointing* sales, plus need to really do quite a lot of paperwork before leaving. I pine for Eriboll, the long May light, where James is enjoying wonderful weather and no one can badger me.

Albany   *Friday, 4 June*

I feel I have now reached a point in my life when certain directional signals can no longer be ignored. (And by me not welcome.) I am up here alone and unsettled. I hate sleeping the night in Albany, being badly affected by nostalgia and a sadness, vestigial recollection of earlier torments.

Today a signing in Hatchards. Then lunch with Diane.[1] As I noted at our first meeting she is *very* sexy, legs and figure. Had the face, but not unattractive with blonde hair and specs. But just not interested. Slightly embarrassed if anything. The *Daily Telegraph* man rang with silly questions about Frankie Holland,[2] said she said I was 'avuncular' in my interest. Then an article I read about HRT for men, 'poor performance' etc has actually *made* me impotent.

Tip has finally failed Staff College, poor darling. He's such a good soldier. Fucking stupid system. I just spoke to James in Eriboll. He's not as close as he used to be. But if he is content that's something.

---

[1] Diane Rowley, publicity director, Weidenfeld & Nicolson.
[2] 'I'm madly in love with Frances Holland ...' wrote AC (*Diaries*, 5 June 1983). She was his 22-year-old Labour opponent in Plymouth Sutton at the general election.

Garden House   *Sunday, 13 June*

The last Sunday here for some while.

When I am back the days will be shortening, and the peacock feathers will be all over the grass. I am relatively tranquil. The 'worst' seems to be over on the *Diaries*, thanks to Michael Cockerell's film and Jane's attractive performance (relegating me to 'best supporting actor'). I don't yet feel quite as I should. My energy is down and the special thrill of plunging into the pool seems less this summer. I suppose each year now I will get a little older.

But the 'Antique' is a joy now it's back from Scott Moncrieff, and I am kitting it out for a (sedatory now) *Randonée Alpin*. I just hope it holds together, and I have time to brood and philosophise, as well.

B5, Albany   *Tuesday, 15 June*

Up for a 'round-up'. A 'long' envelope at Brooks's; and I know what that means. I am desexualated, too. No night E's any more, only very feeble half ones on waking. But I shouldn't really complain − I have had such a wonderful life; and all the bad decisions have been my own.

I woke too early for *The Times*, and read Chips. So interesting on Nazi Germany,[1] his trip there in 1936 (the best year for everything from Miro to the 4¼ Bentley). Chips will be remembered for his diary, and so will I. But I have one already over Chips − I'm still alive! − so ACHAB.

---

[1] 'Hitler was coming and he looked exactly like his caricature − brown uniform, but not grim look … I was more excited than when I met Mussolini in 1926 in Perugia, and more stimulated, I am sorry to say, than when I was blessed by the Pope in 1920.' − *Chips*, 6 August 1936.

*AC achieved his ambition and drove his Silver Ghost S1914 Ch 59
TW, otherwise known as 'The Antique', in the second (possibly harder,
he thought) Alpine Commemorative twenty years on, organised by the
Rolls-Royce Enthusiasts' Club.*

Schönbrunn Palace Hotel   *Saturday, 19 June*

Goodness knows what will happen.[1] A challenge, of man and
machine. Is this my last solo adventure? I hope my dear
'Antique' holds up. Strange, a bit of catharsis, almost. It's not that
I can't believe I will from July onwards, be a 'buffer'.

Vienna to Salzburg   *Sunday, 20 June*
Solo. 257 miles. 7 a.m.–7.45 p.m.

The Antique was parked in the Schönbrunn gardens. Looking
very 'macho' (as 'Dan' Meyer said) beside all the shiny show-offs.
But I was secretly uneasy about the clanking or *clonking* noise.
Alan, who was scrutineering, seemed dismissive of it, however.
In colonial, thundery heat I blundered about unpacking and
reloading. Duncan Dickinson and 'Tony' stood about helpfully.
I had a great dish of venison and noodles and retired, to wake
just before the 4.50 (3.50 UK) alarm call. I virtually missed
breakfast due to 'losing' things in the bedroom – particularly
RayBans which seem to have gone irrevocably – and dashed
swearing and carrying four pieces of luggage to load up.
    Typically, and an ominous precursor – I would guess – of
what was to follow, we stood thummingly in line outside the

---

[1] Part of this account – taken from AC's motoring journal – appeared in *Back Fire*,
a collection of his motoring journalism (2001), but only when transcribing his
1993 journal did the editor of this volume discover additional entries. Here AC's
complete account of the Alpine is reproduced for the first time.

Palace for some forty-five minutes before moving off. I soon
became impatient, and by double-parking and out-accelerating
people (not difficult as I weigh 35 cwt only) I soon caught up
with John Kennedy in Radley's old blue 'Eagle' R587 and a
nameless in a red Ghost (also quite quick). Quite soon we
started to misfire, or rather *hesitate*, which deteriorated into a full
misfire. My spirits sank. Was it ignition?

At one point it seemed to recover when I jiggled with the
Adjust-Retard lever. She was unhappy, though just firing on all
six on the long straight out, where the Austro-Daimler cars used
to be tested, and the hobgoblin in the red Ghost – slowly drew
ahead. In a moment of recovery, at the start of the scrutineering,
I surged past them exiting a hairpin; then she stuttered
hideously and audibly as the cut-out was open. I was thoroughly
out-of-sorts. But I filled the tank and (over)filled the radiator.
Thereafter, fingers crossed, she gave no trouble and behaved
beautifully, triumphantly when I swung out and passed Radley,
at the very outset, and had the satisfaction of him getting smaller
and smaller in the mirror. As I overtook him he did *not*
acknowledge, but muttered to himself as we swept ahead.

Was in buoyant form as far as [Wels?] (arrived in rain) en fête.
But reasonable lunch in marquee – ruthlessly barging to get
ahead of queue. But after lunch rained very disagreeably and continuously. I stopped to put on more and more clothing. Got to
Salzburg by the back route (unchanged) refuelling at the auto-
bahn junction and getting angst about her restarting. Dodged an
obviously pointless civic reception, and arrived by luck at the
hotel to park in underground garage with all the other Ghosts.
Triumphant at the high mileage, and glad of a rest day tomorrow.

In Salzburg   *Monday, 21 June*

Fiddled with the car a bit. Drove (late) to a boring reception
outside the Civic Centre, peasants gawping. Car was leaking

water massively and afterwards I found 'Alan' who greased the water pump hugely – and cured it. Early start tomorrow. The engine 'clanks' objectionably, but Alan is calm. The car is really lovely to drive.

Salzburg to Toblach (Tirol)   *Tuesday, 22 June*

Left, in drizzle. Some difficulty and hesitation stops getting out of Salzburg. It's very hard navigating solo, and several times I overshot, had to reverse, left the indicator going on restarting, etc etc. I know that if we could do the Tavern (long and steep) then she would do the Katschberg (even steeper, but shorter). Refreshed in Mauterndorf, poured in a lot of oil, but no water needed, thanks to Alan. Timed start, and she swooped off going splendidly though baulked by that slightly suspect Irish group going spastically slowly.

Palace Hotel, Merano   *Thursday, 24 June*

A most incredible day today. Comparable to the final four hours of the 1955 Le Mans or the closing laps of the 1959 Nurburgring 1000km when Moss overtook the Maseratis after the delay caused by Fairman 'I spun the car'. John Kennedy (with whom I now have better relations) offered me a seat in the back of his beautiful Alpine Eagle (although I noticed that the gearbox was rougher than the Antique) to ascend the Stelvio. Christ! What a pass! 9,500 feet. An endless series of Ghosts gamely ploughed on, sometimes having to reverse on the lacets (a 'K' turn big fat Dan Meyer called it).

Quite spectacular and exciting – although I was rebuffed by the little BBC 'Top Gear' girl, whom Johnny H had tipped me off about, and got fearfully *chilled* – after getting *soaked* yesterday for the third day running – and am now unhappily drinking *thé limone* with a lumpy sore throat, blazing cheeks and pulse of 84 (just taken it) and a temp of 99°. I do hope I'm not going to be thrashed, as I really would love to complete the Alpine now, best of all meeting Jane in Venice.

Saturday, 26 June

Was a little better yesterday; but this morning *stress* mark on forehead (perhaps due to the slow deterioration of Antique's performance and reliability factor – now hates starting from hot).

Sitting in gardens in shade of cypress trees by the pool, but blazing cheeks, tight chest, pulse 81 (fluctuating) temp 98. No appetite. Periodic nose blowing. Voice seriously diminished. I was ?heavily nostalgic driving here.

I talk to Jane and she is tired and fussed. I'm not apologising enough. I'm worried, too, that the pups will have forgotten me.

Jane told me that it was terrible watching Heseltine[1] getting out of his wheelchair to get into the helicopter, white-coated attendants still carrying the drip. The old lion in decay. Five days in a Venice hospital, and no boxes. Yet lean, didn't drink or smoke. And Hughbugh[2] has gone – from lung cancer. We've got his very last letter.

Wien [Vienna]   *Tuesday, 6 July*

Back at the Schönbrunn. I can hardly believe it. The Alpine went *incredibly* – after a catharsis in … when Andy Wood[3] changed the coil, and Alan cleared the switch points at the bottom of the steering column.

---

[1] Michael Heseltine had had a heart attack in Venice.
[2] The 6th Earl of Cawdor, Hugh John Vaughan Campbell, an Old Etonian, but four years younger than AC.
[3] Andy Wood, of P. & A. Wood.

A rest day, after a desperate drive yesterday in great heat to get 'first over the line' accolade. Tonight the ceremonial dinner – *longueurs* but I'm used to that. I'm going through a *lippen* scare (the blood blister of many years standing that Bertie Arbeid suddenly 'worried' me about).

Now for the final trial (who knows, perhaps the most arduous of all?) of the long drive home. A great thunderstorm is building up. I do hope we don't have to drive through blinding rain tomorrow. But what a triumph to drive home back through the Barbican gates! At least, we have done the great rally – and acquitted ourselves brilliantly. Jane has had a lovely three days, too, and a 'break', and a feeling of being needed.

Saltwood   *Wednesday, 21 July*

A dreadful cold wet July, intermittently 'muggy'. I bathed, one length, this morning and cleared a headache (almost a hangover headache caused, I would stress, by that 'Lido Hotel' wine which tasted good, but is clearly full of antifreeze), but the water is the same colour as the moat, and smells of vegetation.

Yesterday we went to the [Buckingham Palace] Garden Party, calling first at Andrew's dear little house in Farnell Mews. He was grave, though beautifully handsome. I felt tired, and lost interest. Opposite was the ideal mews flat and garage, 'under offer' at £210,000. But I no longer have the liquidity, and anyway I have too much *on* to take on more commitments. At this rate I will be dead before I've done the basics here; but my major works priority must be to open the moat and arch of the Barbican bridge. No one else has the vision to do this.

I had interviews with two high cards at once. First Mrs Thatcher, rather unmade up, blonde hair not usual etc. Denis looking ghastly, thin, grey, though cigaretting massively. As always she doesn't actually engage in conversation, but states propositions and concepts. But no ill-will there, in spite of all the innuendo and interpretation in the hype. Then bumped into (literally) Geoffrey Howe[1] in the cake queue, and mobbed him. He came and sat with us, talked about Scott, and the Commons. As I said to Jane the mafia band of politicians in the same party is such that we really can't bear grudges, it's not worth it.

A cheery little fellow, ludicrously badly dressed in a pale grey morning suit came over and sucked up to Geoffrey; knew my name and introduced his wife. The new MP for Blackpool.[2] A mild pang; as also when talking to Tony Grant[3] who looked very fit and fresh (must have a mistress).

Garden House   *Friday, 30 July*

The opening of a new volume, in which events are likely to be lower-key – a gradually declining trajectory.

I am remarkably creaky and de-energised. My morale is down and I am more than a little scared of the *lippen* operation on Monday. At the back of my mind, I suppose, lurk fears of image mutilation. 'I think perhaps we better return to this under a "general", radiotherapy etc.'

Last night I slept from 10.40 to 7.10 without waking at all – 8½ hours. I had been incredibly tired yesterday after Soames's end of term, when we stayed up drinking until 1.30. Soames looked ill, sweated a lot and at one point very splendidly *took his temperature* (it was 98, having been 102 earlier in the day). He's had his gall bladder removed and I remember from my tonsil operation that one does suffer afterwards from violent

---

[1] Lord [Geoffrey] Howe, former Chancellor of the Exchequer and Foreign Secretary during Margaret Thatcher's government.

[2] Harold Elletson, MP for Blackpool North since 1992, and his wife Fiona. Elletson was forty years AC's junior, but also an Old Etonian. He held the seat for only one parliament.

[3] Sir Anthony Grant, MP for SW Cambs since 1983 (Harrow Central, 1964–83).

fluctuations in fever and depression. The boys were genuinely
friendly, and tired; but I sensed, as I wrote afterwards to Richard,
the 'gossamer curtain' between those in power and those who
are OUT. Jonathan, so thoughtful and wise, asked me what I
would say if Faust offered me a miraculous translation straight
back into the Commons – Government or back benches as you
wish – at the price of surrendering the *Diaries*. Initially, I suppose,
one says 'no'. But always there is the heavenly recollection of the
sword, now on the floor of the lake's bottom.

However, all that seems much more remote than it used to at,
say, the time of the Newbury selection. I no longer fret, the way
I used to, about going into the Government again (although a
pang yesterday talking to Peter Watkins – on how I did enjoy
myself drafting a response to Scott's 'discussion' paper and zapping
Muttukumaru[1] and talking to Robin Butler).

This morning we went to Ashford market, the Hobbs Parker
sale of agricultural oddments. A lovely atmosphere of de-
escalation, and I bid for some of the old tractors, none made
more than £500, all were running and the little Ferguson Diesel
with spindly wheels made £320! Much of the stuff 'on offer'
was really just scrapings from Bob's Room. The 'Poet' (I can't
recall his name at the moment) appeared and talked knowledgeably. He is a habitué of such functions. He told me that the
Channel Tunnel people had acquired the site – why? With what
powers? To build a supermarket and the auction was going to be
moved to a 'green field site'.

I have been very nostalgic and homesick for Scotland these
last weeks and days. And I privately pine for a de-escalated
existence, playing with old machinery, no pressures.

---

[1] Christopher Muttukumaru, lawyer, secretary to the Scott inquiry.

Garden House   *Monday, 2 August*

A delicious 'cleared' from the youthful, but impressive locum at 55 Harley Street, took 11 seconds to say 'no, no' (as opposed to Whitby's 'oh ho!'[1]).

I must work on my speaking schedules and topics for the autumn, and how I am going to phase that in with an image build. I really don't know how I am going to evolve (because I *must* still evolve, even if it is only into de-escalation) this next year.

'Diarist, a Political Savant' I have been saying. But Jonathan said 'book a safe seat, get back in' (to the Commons); flattered that he should still think me youthful enough to do this. In a way it is lovely to be free and independent, and (semi) sought after. But I must try and improve my fitness.

Shore Cottage   *Wednesday, 17 August*

Was it only yesterday that I welched on the Los Angeles trip?[2]

It seems like weeks. I think it has done me considerable damage, the inner ache of *another* bad decision. The young had 'booked' Jane in to dine with Heather Gow [owner of the adjoining estate] last night. If I'd known that it would just have tipped the scales and I would now be expectantly waiting on delicious room service breakfast in the Biltmore [LA hotel] before going out with Charles and Uta for a good tyre-kick and a deep 'taking of the temperature'.

As it is, I'm only slightly what-of-it? here; thinking of the mass of paperwork, and already 'tentatively' planning a date for

---

[1] Whitby, doctor in Hythe.
[2] Charles Howard, friend and dealer in classic cars, had suggested the trip to hunt out interesting classic cars, but Jane had countered: 'All you've been saying is how much you want to get away to Eriboll; now the moment you get here all you want to do is leave.'

our return to Saltwood. Yesterday I hung around while James
very slowly (it is a nightmare of complication and trial and error
needing a forklift with 1 ton capacity *and* a hydraulic crane)
adding a section to his RAF shed – which is very nice quality
and beautifully made of Oregon pine from Canada, part of the
RAF expansion programme of 1938/9. Then in the afternoon
we met for a 'stumble' in the new plantation at Arnaboll turning
back before the rowan grove; and after that I went to Whales
Corner and brought back three loads, a 'caulk' (which I had to
trim with the saw) and two heavy 2" planks. Slept continuously
until woken by the dogs at 6.20 or so.

   The trouble is, this kind of idealised EARTH existence is only
truly enjoyable (just as open peaceful days at Saltwood for which
I used to long when in Parliament) if the other life is there ready
to be embraced, grasping at one almost.

   I need BOTH. Said to Jane I was going to LA because I was
'bored'. I wish I was there, talking to one and all, spotting new
self-styled experts in the 'movement' and filling my reservoirs.
Then, on return, I could savour the low pace and the cleanliness
of the Highland tempo. I am still more restless than I thought,
I suppose. Or is it the consciousness of the days left reducing
all the time in number? So that one which goes by without
anything to fill it is a waste? Unless of course it is occupied by
rehabilitation and recovery.

   I hardly think of 'x' any longer.

Green Room   *Thursday, 16 September*

Yesterday evening I finished putting on tape the *extracts* from the
book [for an audio cassette] and came to the passage (penultimate on the tape) when I contemplate my exit – February
1991. There was over a year to go before I announced it. And
indeed I had been just as decisive in 1985. But of course then it
was to leave the Government, not the House. Yet, I think if I had

left the Government then Plymouth would have got rid of me in 1987. They would have struck as soon as I stopped being a Minister.

If I am really honest with myself I dreaded the General Election because I thought I *and* we were going to lose. I was very unhappy torn between 'x' and Jane; and I suppose Richard must take some of the blame for half-encouraging me. But oh, how I miss it. It was all right during the summer as the great benefice – the wonderful utterly memorable Alpine rally – would not have been possible.

Yet now the hour is gathering 'Conference' first, then the temperature rises. This is the second conference I've missed. I will be forgotten by the rank-and-file. Yet I remain active, interested, consulted ('a natter', *passim* Michael Howard).

B5, Albany   *Tuesday, 21 September*

I have been walking about London, somewhat *désoeuvré*. Tomorrow a snoop on 'Scott'.[1] Poor JM under screeching pressure – in Tokyo, of all places – and in Brooks's, extempore, I drafted a note to send him.[2]

---

[1] AC's only comment afterwards was that he 'quite liked Presiley Baxendale', counsel to the inquiry.

[2] Major was leading a party of senior UK businessmen to Japan, but before leaving Britain there had been leadership speculation, possible stalking horses for a contest in November; Norman Lamont, now the ex-Chancellor of the Exchequer, writing on the first anniversary of Black Wednesday, had criticised the Prime Minister; and on the flight to Tokyo Major had been indiscreet to the press party on his attitude to the Eurosceptics. AC eventually sent his note to Major, 'trying both to cheer him up and ingratiate myself.'

Garden House   *Tuesday, 5 October*

I should be calmer. The 'new' Ghost, 20UB, has arrived and is ultra pleasing. I really want it here so that I can play with it. And this morning I had a nice letter (a poignant letter, you could say) from JM, which made me feel calmer in myself.

I hang around the Garden House thinking how lovely it is, how peaceful and enveloping. It's a great tribute to my father's good sense. Would he have been better, or less effective, if he hadn't been rattled so much? I used to think it was my mother who rattled him, now I realise it was guilt.

Saltwood   *Sunday, 24 October*

I had sat down to write a passage, a couple of days ago, in the Garden House, but was interrupted by the urge to write a note to Richard Ryder (following my lunch with Willie Whitelaw) at Mrs T's Foyle[1]). I asked him to set up a Defence Commission with me as Chairman.[2] Naturally he didn't reply ('Alan goes mad every so often and wants to get back in, last time it was a week before the Matrix trial'). It was strange that lunch. Sweepings really. Is that really all she could manage in terms of distinction, being between the Indian and the Hungarian ambassadors?

But I still want to be a *player*. Thing is – on *Question Time* I had a heavy time. Peter Mandelson said, 'you're still so young.' Peter Sissons [chairman] talked sensibly and confidentially to me about broad trends and JM's PR men, and so on.

---

[1] Foyle's, the booksellers, had as their guest of honour at a lunch Margaret Thatcher, whose memoirs, *The Downing Street Years*, were published the previous week.

[2] On the opposite page to this entry are a series of rough notes under the heading 'to RR'. The main thrust is 'the security of the UK' with participants to include Lord Lewin (former CDS), the historian Sir Michael Howard and John Keegan, defence editor of the *Daily Telegraph* and historian. AC added a sub-heading, 'Social points' – where the commission should meet – 'the dining room at Saltwood is out of commission' and suggested for a final dinner 'the oval room at Brooks's'.

I can't quite settle down. Although the lure of de-escalation is delicious I am under heavy financial pressure. Can't see prospect of fresh earnings ('new money'). I am going to have to cull both cars and pictures.

In the meantime I am copying out (opposite) the great list of (pre)occupations from an envelope in the kitchen, together with the objectives for the next six months.

<u>Jane and Alan Clark</u>   <u>September 1993</u>

Stately home owners
Classic car connoisseurs and enthusiasts
Public speakers
Essayist and author
Keen gardeners
Shrewd investors
Collectors of paintings and other pleasing artefacts
Alpinists
Nature lovers and crofters
Political consultees
Television personalities
'Famous persons'
Artists – and much, much more.

<u>The Struggle for Order</u>   <u>Late in October 1993</u>

Bank statements
Car files
Resurrect ledger
Summer Office
Press cuttings (headings)
Photos and albums
Garden House (motor mags; shape up)
Archives and the archive room (to be plastered?)
Winter Office
Headings for, and subsequent entry on, computer

Saltwood   *Friday, 29 October*

When I got home I pottered in the Long Garage, realised I didn't actually want to sell *anything*. Earnings won't cover everything owing – anyway near – so will have to do it from Art. Why not? The cars are a collection – bit of 'Applied' rather than 'Fine' – Art. It is the full moon, Halloween tomorrow. Unusual combination.

Of course, £350 for the Mask[1] would do very nicely thank you, but I'm glad I resisted that. It must work spells for me, because I saved it, will have to make other sacrifices.

Saltwood   *Sunday morning, 31 October*

Woke, and shrank instantaneously with thought of pressures – financial and paper. But we went for the 'w' and the trees were so beautiful, a perfectly still morning of late autumn so early that no one was about, and vistas and colours that you get only once every three or four years. I was worried about the bark on the great oak – it must be done next month. But the walk – the dry leaves were so lovely and calming, that we both felt better.

When we got in, Jane said, 'we've got everything, and yet we don't enjoy it.' So true, so very, very true. But she said it in good humour.

If I could get significant liquidity then I could plan out a schedule for *The Struggle for Order*.

Later, p.m.
I am so old and creaky in the afternoons, and generally.

I like just to sit in my chair by the bookcase, not always even listlessly turning the pages of an old mag, a car directory.

---

[1] The Torres Strait tortoiseshell mask, bought by Kenneth Clark, once owned by Picasso. Charles Jerdein, a dealer and friend of AC's, had offered $450,000 for it ten years before (*Diaries*, 9 May 1985).

And yet, if I look at the schedule etc of barely a year ago there, at midday, was Gossie. I seem to have aged at too fast a rate. My face looks more crumpled on TV, and when I run my hands over it I can feel folds of skin around the eyes and the dewlaps.

Of course, in London, I barely ever drank at lunch. Today I had two glasses of Sauvignon, two of '70 Palmer, and two of '83 Palmer. I know it's meant to stop heart attacks, and in the evenings (less so) I will still do it. But from now on I am going to drink at lunch only on Saturdays and Sundays.

Monday, 8 November

A strange dream last night. I was looking after Tom, and he had lost his lead, but I was making do with bailing twine. In a kind of way he was muddled with the dreadful, harrowing story, dribbling out day-by-day in the courts, of the cruel 'walk to death' of Jamie Bulger. After he got demi-lost a few times we ended up in College Green. I realised that I could not cross the street to get into the Palace of Westminster. I reflected that my life in Parliament really divided into three phases (1) as a backbencher, much boredom, relieved by backgammon. Time wasted, in the main, like early years at Oxford. (2) As a Minister before, and (3) after 'running into' 'x'. The further stage I eschewed – the 'respected backbencher'. But I think best of all the factor that forced me into this, it was my bad relations in Plymouth that was the principal one – just as it was they who cramped my style in the very early stages.

Garden House   *Thursday, 11 November*

A lovely fine still day. At the eleventh hour, of the eleventh day, of the eleventh month we walked, almost by chance, to Lord C's

Gate and were seated there when the Western Front fell silent. A good moment to put things 'in perspective'.

I started the morning (after an intermittent night, waking and rewaking with those damned sums going round in my head) by walking to the dump on the Seeds. I thought how I longed to back off, have just two weeks before we go to Scotland grubbing about here, tidying and adjusting. I have taken on far too many engagements – usual feature of the autumn; one fills up the diary during the summer doldrums. Yet each one is income, of course. I have written two articles this week, each at £1000, and tonight go (unpaid) to the Cambridge Union to debate – press impartiality – I'm in favour of it – with Max Clifford (!) and Simon Jenkins.

I would feel myself, just, capable of handling this – even the boredom, but this morning managed to get a hand-mirror to illuminate this strange spot at the top of my head which looked sinisterly dark pink, if not red. Special hypochondria cramp set in. Now I have to go and collect my things for a drive to Cambridge via Andy Wood, for the Union debate.

Garden House   *Monday, 29 November*

A very cold, clear day. Our undulant 'virus' is still around, and Jane coughed continuously for the latter half of the night. Our sex life is somewhat dormant at present. *That* was the true miracle – and to think that at the time I couldn't really recognise it! Last night, watched the second half of *To Play the King*. Ian Richardson so good[1] … the scenes in the Commons made me wistful and nostalgic. 'You can never go back,' Jane said. But how wonderful just to walk into the Chamber after Christmas. Can *anything* happen? Yes it can. My energy *is* down. And I am

---

[1] Ian Richardson had earlier played in *House of Cards*, also by Michael Dobbs and also with a Westminster background.

creaky. But nowhere near 'par' for my age yet of course. There is still enough potential to respond to a boost.

This coming year I had planned on, virtually, a sabbatical. I don't know if I would just get fossilised. But such a relief to move away from deadlines and 'engagements'.

But in the familiar phrase, 'I can't afford it.' It's not just the pressure of tax demands, but it is simply grossly irresponsible to pass up £300,000+.[1]

Just down here it's a full-time occupation, never going to London at all, to keep my cars reasonable; 'polishing' them one at a time (at present I am working on the Buick); and the garden – especially over here – reasonably under control.

So next year we must keep sections 'blocked-off'. It will be the only way. So as to accommodate both 'work' and 'recharging'. It is a bore, the Jimmy expedition,[2] as it blights the start of the year, but it is necessary I fear.

Saltwood   *Tuesday, 30 November*

I went over after tea to shut the drive gates of Garden House, and on the way back I looked at the dark outline of the Mains, the Santé wall. My open prison. I am not ready to stand back yet. But I am nervous of *using up time* – even when, e.g., 'polishing' the Buick – because I dread that suddenly, I may 'go'.

Saltwood   *Saturday, 4 December*

Blustery and soaking. When I woke up the first thing that came in was the failure of the 25/30 to sell at Brooks's. Cars are just unsaleable – quite soon they are going to be unsaleable at *any*

---

[1] He had been offered this sum for the book and newspaper serial rights to a second volume of *Diaries*.

[2] Sir James Goldsmith, 'founder of industrial, commercial and financial enterprises', had invited the Clarks for a holiday on his Mexican estate at Cuixmala.

price, like 'yachts' (scope for an article here, tying in with 'buying value' for restoration that will never be undertaken again). Yesterday I went round Sotheby's giant Christmas sale – a large Turkey farm, I said.[1] Really the only nice car there was the 12/50 Alvis 2-seater. Some incredible black Mercedes 7-series – you could visualise them sweeping up the foothills of Berchtesgaden – but totally 'what's the point?' unless you are buying 'input'. But a certain nostalgia emanated from the great planes: the Lancaster, of course; and the Lightning. Did I see a TSR2 there? (Never forget what he did, Denis Healey, posing as affable and bluff, actually a nasty old thing.[2]) And of course the V-bombers Victor and Vulcan. I watched, by chance, the film of the Vulcans taking off. We seem to have come down an awful long way since then. Another quarter step downward from the heyday of the Spithead Review.

And last night with news of the Princess of Wales, so enchanting and clean and emblematic, 'standing down'.[3] Forced out by the rival and relentless pressure and undermining of 'the Prince's Party'. I put a call through to Andrew Neil – he was abroad, didn't respond. Then spoke to Jonathan Holborow – he totally agreed with my line – it's the end of monarchy. The Queen Mother will be dead in five years' time – who will we be left with?

Shore Cottage   *Wednesday, 22 December*

Christmas marks the end, and the beginning of 'our' year, and already since getting here I have been 'unwound' and contemplative.

[1] Taking place at the RAF Museum, Hendon, north London.
[2] Cancelled in the April 1965 Budget, when Denis Healey was Defence Secretary in Harold Wilson's government. AC considered the TSR2 a British warplane that was in advance of anything else in the West. Two prototypes survive, but not at Hendon.
[3] Princess Diana, her marriage to the Prince of Wales in tatters, announced that she wanted a break from the stress of public life.

A pleasing journey, with just the right amount of 'challenge'. I ended up in the ditch just out of Altnaharra pine woods on the Tongue road. How? Most odd. I took my eyes off for one second, laughing and joking with Jane and next thing I know we were bouncing about on the verge, snow going in all directions. Jane screaming.

A kindly fisherman (*most* providentially) soon put in an appearance in a Japanese 4WD and pulled me out backwards (with, thank God, a very slight gradient) and I was none the worse except for a broken or bent o/s wheel trim. We still managed, just, to get to Eriboll before the light faded.

The first part of our journey was mainly, to all intents and purposes, *under water*, and we were one hour behind schedule at the 'Welcome Break'. But held to the old times thereafter and v pleasing at Gleneagles (now preferable to Cromlix) with room 302, a black pianist at dinner who played 'Stormy Weather', 'Smoke …' etc.

Boxing Day

Very cold, all the roads have frozen hard, in to its ridges and the puddles are solid translucent grey. We went beachcombing from Whales Corner and, unbelievably, bathed in the glass-like loch, in the low sun (we have bathed from there before in the summer).

I have now been here five days and each day have taken two hours on the hill – in one form or another – and then one fine evening meal, an early night and 10 hours' sleep.

Something cautions me away from *Diaries II – Towering Inferno II* etc. Also I'm not quite ready to get locked into the Great Work[1] preferring to pick, still, and read round it (greatly enjoying *Beaverbrook* by A.J.P. Taylor at present). So my considered

---

[1] What would become *The Tories: Conservatives and the Nation State, 1922–77.*

favourite, at present, is to take up Jonathan Holborow's offer and try and make something of it.[1]

It will be hard work; discuss Tuesday morning; lunch every Tuesday at the Beefsteak, to get the atmosphere. Reading all the papers. First draft Wednesday morning. More Thursday and usually Friday (are faxes portable, by the way?). Allow six weeks' hols – two at Christmas, two at Whitsun, three in August. To some extent I will be on call, which I don't like.

Tuesday, 28 December

Sleety and gales in the night.

I set off up the Creaggan at lunch. I thought briefly, I can't tell why, of 'x' and sadly – though philosophically, not achingly as on previous visits. It is over. And I became sentimental and composed a letter, which I doubt that I will ever send.

Then I said a prayer to God. How rare it is to do this nowadays! I thanked him for 'seeing' me through; said that I was still ready, if it was possible, to make one more try to fetch the sword from the lake's bed. I prayed for him to keep me fit – as so manifestly I still am – and also for a tiny heir, before I am too old for the 'generation gap' to be happily bridged in their early childhood when I can impart wisdom. I must face the fact that I will be seventy now, at least, before I can really start talking and playing; and that I may die while they are still at school.

On the way back I stopped and spoke to James – somewhat *désoeuvré* around all his great machines. We talked of weapons and the incredible concession for the very big guns, and tank armour. His knowledge is so extensive, his recall so immediate. It makes me sad that, really, we did so little together while I was at Procurement. One more sadness at being excluded from the House as it reassembles, warm and enclosing in the great interior of the Palace of Westminster, which 'never sleeps'.

---

[1] A weekly political column in the *Mail on Sunday*.

Shore Cottage   *Thursday, 30 December*

For the first time this holiday I am not tired out in the evenings.
In spite of fiddling around with wooding in the Jeep etc most
of the day and ending with 1 hour helping shovel out the gravel
into the trenches around 'Jane's shed'. Ready now to move back
to the Mains and start tackling things. (Peggy's 'envelope' arrived
this afternoon, so thin that one thought it had been sent empty.
Only the faxes enclosed as 'too many cards to decide which to
send'. – *Really*!! The epitome of primitiveness. Pure domestic
servant 'left in charge'.)

I am reasonably calm about the year in prospect. But yet a
little uneasy when, flicking over the pages of the green diary I
come upon August. Supposing things are 'no better' then. Will I
just be that much older, that much further removed from the
centre of things?

One of my great preoccupations remains to put off old age. It
has started to show – very slightly – in my hands. The cross vein
remains in place, and several pale death spots are appearing. My
neck is sometimes really quite embarrassingly thick – even
between the video of the Alpine and the start of the books-of-
the-year interview with Jack and Jill.[1]

Up here, at least, I drink very little. Nor do I want or need to.

Shore Cottage   *New Year's Eve*

I am now fully 'programmed' to return on Sunday. My mind is
rambling round tasks and preoccupations and objectives and I
am neither so sleepy (in spite of walking the Arnaboll round
today, starting by going over the ridge) nor so easily relaxed/

---

[1] AC means John McCarthy – held hostage in Beirut – and Jill Morrell. Their joint
memoir was called *Some Other Rainbow*. The three of them appeared together on
the Sky book programme.

comatose. We have been here ten days, and much fabric has been repaired. But if we stay longer we will no longer be on holiday, not even 'crofting' so much as 'in residence' with all the cares and duties that then start to close in on one.

Some things make me sad – I've always felt sadness at Eriboll, though really nothing like the dreadful Highland melancholy of '85, '86, '87. Julie, Jane and I were standing round the church, talking of how to protect and refurbish it; there was mention of a christening. That evening, helping James with his 'bucket' for the Hymac [digger] he said he would be 34 next year (in two months). Sadly I realise I will never (unless God is exceptionally kind) live to see my grandchildren marry. Will I ever have any? We have this slightly unnatural existence at the moment, Jane and I. The boys grown-up and (in theory) settled, but no Grandparental duties.

1994

A day spent with chores and various, before heading south on a great drive tomorrow. There is always so much to do at Eriboll. Some things have been left undone for six, seven years. And the *Maid of Morven* still lies on her side, her entrails slowly rotting.

Just as the light faded I walked with Jamie, to Birkett Foster.[1] He is much, much better. And sensible. He might get married this year, to Julie. Laughed when I said, 'breed, anyway'. He was realistic about the onset of old age, concurred with my analogy of the hourglass triangle.

I have been less affected by depression than ever before on this sojourn. But tonight I am low.

Thursday, 20 January

Today, in contrast, I woke fresh and felt reflectively confident on Indian tea in the kitchen. Why? Nothing has really changed except one's mood. What has caused this? A good night, I suppose, and waking with an erection.

Everything seemed to come to a head today.

I'm completely impotent – *why*? I'm sitting in my 'romper' suit; all I've had is Indian tea and a piece of shortbread. I don't seem to have done anything at all and it's already 12.30+. I took calls from Dobbie and a very long one from the BBC about a programme on the Windsors.

---

[1] AC owned a small seascape by the Victorian painter Myles Birkett Foster, with rocks like those at Eriboll.

This piece for the *Mail on Sunday* hangs over me; it is a permanent blight, from which there is no relief (except, I assume, in August when everyone else is 'off' and the weather is hot and foul and muggy and one becomes strangely ill). I am so short of time; and yet I do nothing, it seems with what I have got. The endless pressure of paperwork – now totally out of control again, as I 'cleared' the Green Room table and dispersed the various piles into either/or the dining room or Green Room.

Accounts, Taxation and VAT, i.e. the very core of paperwork, are in total confusion. I appear to be in an identical situation to that prevailing (say) ten years ago when Jane and I would have great convulsive sort-outs – grading things by year, all the Kafkaesque brainwashing of 92–93 is *called* 93–94 (or is it 91–92?). Pile after pile after pile. On top of this, and having no secretary or even will have a secretary, I have to do all the other stuff about *Diaries*, speeches, toadies writing about how much they admired my father etc etc. Only interesting thing that still surfaces and, I suppose I must admit, gratifies me, is that I don't get any 'hate' mail.

Small wonder that I am strained to shrieking point. Jane said I was being really awful, never been worse. As for income, typically, it never matches outgoings. Yes there is a new contract for *Diaries* II, but for some reason Sissons has negotiated only a £25 on signature instead of £50,000 as last time.

I'm still owed driblets and droplets from past contracts and welchers, but it's an endless labour 'chasing' them.

Yesterday I had lunch with a 'tittles', Julia Llewellyn-Smith.[1] Really rather nice, long clean fair hair, *no* eye make-up (is this the new thing?). I was greeted – without giving my name – by the maître at the Savoy Grill (as last time with Jonathan and Dobbie), which is good for one's ego. I've no idea what 'tittles' thought, although she conversed giftedly. But I was irritated by the way she seemed to have had lots of boy-friends (her age 17). Just like 'x'. I've had it.

---

[1] Julia Llewellyn-Smith, feature writer on *The Times*.

The previous evening as I drove over Westminster Bridge and saw the Palace I felt so depressed. So utterly abandoned. Like when I see TV shots of a crowded chamber.

Only mildly cheering thing was David Dudley speaking about RREC matters; said he'd been given my *Diaries* by his son – familiar pattern – and was angry at my continued preoccupation with growing old – 'someone as fit and athletic as you ...' This sort of remark gives me encouragement.

Saltwood   *Friday, 28 January*

A clear cold day, with the high winds dying down. The great sheds are going up. At last we are getting enough *covered space*. I am brushing them down inside and cleaning the window panes. Wood is the only material for sheds and these have wooden floors also.

I am depressed at being excluded. You only really know what's going on if you are inside the Commons. Although I suppose as a peer I would have access. I miss it dreadfully. When I was there living on physical reserves, I spent these, all but, but accumulated a huge intellectual bank. This is slipping through my fingers fast and in a year's time I will be left with nothing. If 'Scott' clears me, and if JM survives I suppose there is a faint chance of New Year '95. But after that I'd have to wait for the next Conservative government even for the offer of a 'K' – at the age of 76.

Saltwood   *Sunday, 30 January*

The wretched JM is under appalling pressure still. Right across the front page of the *Sunday Times* a terrible photo of him at the Leeds dinner, hands clasped behind his head held over the

plate.[1] Could have been doing a Bush in Japan. And the usual
row – extended now to include total non-starters like
Redwood[2] – of leadership contestants. What *did* I do? Why did
I not consult and reflect? Jane did give me a let-out when she
said it's really almost too late … (to serve notice). My
calculations were entirely justifiable – not included in
Government, boredom of being in opposition, funking losing
seat, drainingness of hung parliament. Could be last chance to
'book' peerage. But if I had really got away, walked, talked with
my voices I suppose that the sword in the lake would/might
have held me.

Saltwood   *Thursday, 3 February*

And now Pin[3] has got cancer. Of the prostate. Perfectly ghastly.
How long have I got? It's hard to know what is right – straight
into the hands of surgeons or hold out – and when it comes just
GO. Force yourself over the edge on the Creaggan. I fear the
latter is probably right – but would one have the courage? It
would be like turning the gas on, or pipe from the exhaust; it's
no good changing your mind when you get drowsy. Then it's
too late.

---

[1] John Major was speaking to the Leeds Chamber of Commerce. Whatever the
photograph *appeared* to show, Major was particularly relaxed that evening. Anthony
Seldon, in his study of the Major government, wrote, 'The audience appreciated his
spontaneity and his wit, and he spoke well … at one point later in the evening he
doubled up and was photographed head in hands, an image to be endlessly recycled
in the press thereafter as evidence of a man at the end of his tether.'
[2] John Redwood, MP for Wokingham since 1987; Welsh Secretary since 1993.
[3] Colin Clark, AC's younger brother, also known as Col.

Saltwood   *Friday, 4 February*

I was slouching in my chair, suffering from toothache. Both my back wisdom teeth have disintegrated into blackened stumps or stalagmites, they hurt at intervals, but Bertie Arbeid is always within reach. But in Mexico ... I dread some agonisingly expensive, strange dentist, AIDS-infected needle, the pressure of a long return flight. Ergo, I must contact Bertie on Monday. The phone rang, and it was Dobbie dissatisfied – inevitably – with lack of 'impact' in article about Special Relationship. The money is wonderful, but their demands. The 'jar' in journalist is going to make it impossible. We'll see.

Then I thought I ought to help Jane clear out her studio, the old sewing room. We came across a cache of photographs, everything seemed so much fresher in those days and we all looked young and vital. Max/George [jackdaws] was teeny, Tom was teeny (I am worried for Tom; he is slow and down on energy and sleeps an awful lot. Then, too, the Mexican trip hangs ...). There are photos of the Yeos, and Mrs Cloake, and Peggy looking so smart at 'Teas', and Christopher and Geoffrey[1] coming down in the Cloud III. Also my first, and I think, only 'letter to my constituents' between elections in 1974 with a photo on the cover taken from election night that February when I must have had the highest quotient of adrenalin ever running through my veins.

I suppose I will be remembered for the *Diaries* (*still* at No 2 in the *Evening Standard*).

Jimmy Goldsmith's, Cuixmala, Mexico   *Wednesday, 16 February*

In the swimming pool pavilion, with its straw roof, by Jimmy's pool, itself drained and refilled with salt water every day.

---

[1] Christopher (aka 'Daisy') Selmes, a friend of many years standing, who had made a fortune in the City, and his boyfriend Geoffrey; both were to die of AIDS.

Everything is oversize, mattresses, deckchairs, urns, parasols. Lovely chevron clay tiling on the pool floor. The staircase down is pure Alma-Tadema, out of Port Lympne, with many a coign of vantage and beautiful pots of blooms so bright and vulgar that, as Jane says, you need acrylic to do them justice and the delicate box of water-colours is inadequate. The whole level of sumptuocity is magnif-icent – separate 'villas' for the guests cunningly sited within the flower and jungle hillside of the condominium. Makes Jeffrey Archer's 'apartment' look like a journalistic bolthole.[1]

Jimmy is magnificent, a philosopher-king. Eloquently he expounds on the devilish dangers of the GATT, the indignities of Maastricht. Also staying are Ed Epstein (writer and critic)[2]; Nancy Kissinger (beautiful and attractive style); Toby (Jimmy's keen young gofer in Hong Kong), Michel (?), president of the Bradley Foundation and his *much* younger wife Mary-Jo. He is just a little hunted-and-shunted in manner; she is a sporty young gymnast/swimmer.

Last night hit it off again with Kissinger[3] – but a sad moment. He was talking about my 'getting back in'.

'How old are you?'

'65.'

Incredulous. Spluttered. '55?'

'No, 65.'

Just stared, in silence. I am always delighted when I impress, and K made it clear that he thought I should be active in the Conservative Party, 'which is so short of strong men'.

But of course for most people 'age 65', it isn't just difficult, it's unthinkable.

Ah well, we'll see.

---

[1] Jeffrey Archer, author, former MP (Louth) and deputy chairman of the Conservative Party, had a high-level flat with panoramic views across the Thames to Westminster.

[2] Edward Jay Epstein, who made his name for himself with a study of Lee Harvey Oswald; currently at work on a life of Armand Hammer, the oil millionaire.

[3] Henry Kissinger, US Secretary of State, 1973–77 (under Nixon and Ford); and Nancy, his second wife.

On Friday evening young people turned up, with a coal-black band imported from New Orleans. They were *so* chic they were virtually incredible. 'Chamber music,' I said – which for some reason went down badly.

An attractive young American blonde was seated beside me. She was intense, so politically correct it wasn't true. Got into a 'state' about Bosnia etc, especially the way Muslim women had been raped.

I had a great scare the following day when (after taking off from the grass strip in the Merlin, just, JUST, our flight attendant frequently consulted not only the map, but the manual (!)). At the BA desk in Mexico City a stylish rather classier version of 'x' materialised 'to look after us'. We hit it off immediately, and she started to 'audition'. Jane, naturally, was livid, and put on the special strained expression she wears when she knows I fancy someone nearby.

Saltwood   *Sunday, 27 February*

Just put the phone down talking to Pin.

Poor Pin! It's too awful, the slow Chinese torture of the big cancer operation – like Lloyd's, but with your life, not just your fortune at stake. He says the surgeons are 'so good'.

'How do you know?' I asked.

'They are so confident.'

'Well Ronny Cornwell[1] was confident, when he was selling insurance, doesn't mean a thing,' I said.

There is so much to do. I shone the torch over the SS100 (moved up into the new shed today) and got a quick evocation of Oxford, the Morris Garages where the cars were lined up on opposite sides of that great shed, and I used to go and wax it

---

[1] The father of David Cornwell (the writer John le Carré) had been revealed as a confidence trickster by his son in the novel *A Perfect Spy* (1986).

most evenings, and a canny Irishman with black curly hair
offered to drive it in the TT for me. And I thought then I had
absolutely nothing to do or read or watch over. I was waiting for
the next edition of the *Autocar*. Now I really don't think I will
finish it all before I die. It's part of getting old, is it, accumulating
more and more pressing memories?

Garden House   *Friday, 4 March*

Fine and bright, though cold wind. Spring now due to arrive
any moment, with all its demands out of doors, and no progress
whatever in interior management. First task in less than three
weeks, which means dining room, top landing (Jane's 'studio') all
cleared, Great Hall spruced and garden – or Bailey at least –
reasonably orderly.

I am demi-listless. Last night the 'paperback' publication
dinner at the Groucho – itself low-ceilinged and dirty-carpeted
– and I was sub-lionised. I sat next to the manager of W.H.
Smith. Pleasant, intelligent, spoke sensibly about books, my
book indeed, and why le Carré was so much more 'the real
thing' than Jeffrey Archer. He was luke-warm though about
Diaries II (as indeed was Roger at Waterstone's). Said, 'Don't do
it. Go back in, instead.' When people say things like that it makes
me really wistful. Driving up last week I had a nostalgia/fantasy.
Get adopted; fight a really wild campaign, just win! 'If he can
win a by-election, then he will win a General Election.' The
point being, there is *no one* with my charisma and intelligence
whatsoever in the House of Commons at present. I have all the
experience I need; I am good, now, at the bar. Confident and
level-headed. In 18 months it could be mine.

On Tuesday there was a letter from 'x' at Brooks's. Began 'Dear
Alan'. Not friendly, but long. She's made a real study of *Sir
Gawain*, and how apposite it was!

Saltwood   *Monday, 7 March*

Incredibly tired after a whole day consumed ('wasted' one could almost say) by Walden.[1] Car came at 10.20, didn't get back here until 4.40 – nearly six hours.

I sparkled. They got rid of Tom Clarke and Alec Carlile[2] and we gossiped, Brian, the editor and the producer and I in the upstairs corner 'Hospitality Suite'. Brian is still, of course, a manqué politician. He knows the real thing. And once again I thought 'if only' and 'I wonder'. 'Well, who can lead them? Who *is* there?' Jane kept saying at breakfast. I nearly said 'Me', but didn't. A little later, in the correspondence section was a note saying 'Alan Clark should be Prime Minister'. This evening I thought really my only chance, I suppose, is for Michael Howard to die, and for me to *force* them to let me take his place. ACHAB.

Garden House   *Tuesday, 15 March*

I am not in good shape. I am sleepy and my bones – joints ache. Poor old Peter Harding has resigned, just walked into it and Bienvenida Buck setting things up.[3] Every week a 'scandal'. But it, and the comments, and the letters all remind me of a time that is past. I will never again have a mistress. I could have had a huge rapport (which we both knew and Jane did also) with the 'hostess' at BA at Mexico. But I will never have the opportunity now. Ministers' room in the Lords, directors' ante-room in

---

[1] Brian Walden, TV presenter and journalist (*Weekend World* and *Walden*), previously a Labour MP for two Birmingham seats 1964–77.

[2] Tom Clarke, MP (Labour) Monklands West since 1983 (Coatbridge & Airdrie, June 1982–83); Alex Carlile, Labour MP 1983–88; Liberal Democrat since 1988 (Montgomery).

[3] Marshal of the Royal Air Force, Sir Peter Harding, Chief of the Air Staff since 1988. Bienvenida Perez-Blanco had briefly married (as his second wife in 1990, marriage dissolved 1993) Sir Antony Buck (MP for Colchester, 1961–83; Colchester North 1983–92).

Lloyds PLC (*that* was a short-lived fantasy). Archer living on his own, with secretaries, just doesn't get 'around'. And if it means you have a frightful nemesis at about 82–84 *so what*? Better really to 'go out' than become a figure of pity.

Then all my 'friends' have abandoned me. Only dear Soames was on the answering machine this morning, and still keeps in touch. Jonathan [Aitken] is having me at his dinner for Richard Nixon on Thursday, but is correct on other topics.[1] Richard – silent; the PM – silent; 'Tristan' quite openly trying to shift the Scott blame on to me as the 'direction of the Inquiry's finding starts to emerge', and winding up toadies like Bruce Anderson to say as much.

Politically, I'm now really a non-person. And at least half of me wants to go North – for good. 'Care and maintenance only.'

I've been driving different cars, and enjoying them. The 1914 Ghost – so lovely; how incredible it would be with the 'Nicholosi' body on it! And then the Buick Roadmaster – the Todd Buick. Quite extraordinary and unworn. The only new car I've got except the Continental Turbo R. But I can't do this until the place is orderly, and inventorised. So that when I (or anyone else) come back I have only to stretch out my hand and find it/pick it up.

Finally there is the problem of dear Tip. He is determined to leave the Army, which formerly he loved so much. Got down by the new tendency – the bookkeeping and being wankily career conscious, sneaking a 'late luncheon', going 'classless' etc. He's no idea what he's going to do … 'travel'. Won't get a pension or a golden handshake. But his face is a little crumpled, and unhappy. Today Malcolm Rifkind is going round – with David Hart (strange ménage).[2] They are looking at it[3] to see about selling it

---

[1] Jonathan Aitken had published a well-received biography of former US President Nixon.

[2] Malcolm Rifkind, MP for Edinburgh Pentlands since 1974; Defence Secretary since 1992; David Hart had been an *éminence grise* among special advisers, originally to Margaret Thatcher, now to John Major and soon to Michael Portillo.

[3] The headquarters of the Household Cavalry.

off, to Jews, to make into offices. Andrew, partly because he is
marginalised and out of favour, is deputed to show them the
men's bedrooms. Don't despair, I said, that's all politicians are
interested in.

I asked, what about the horses? How can you move out of
those lovely stables? Ah no, a 'report' is being prepared at the
moment (by a *sailor*) on possible 'options' for reducing the
cavalry strength – or even getting rid of it altogether.

This, as so many things at present; the toadying to Delors, the
impossibility of getting offences against the person punished, the
politic and contemptible appeasement of Ireland. With each
fresh atrocity they get up and bleat about '... will not alter our
determination to ...' (now 'search for peace'; formerly 'crush
terrorism').

It is an extraordinary interlude, the Thatcher decade. Now we
are back with Mr Wilson, or worse. The moment will come
when I have to say this (so to that extent I am fortunate still to
have the column in which to say it) – but not just quite yet.

Having been loyal through thick and thin, all the scapegoating
etc, what will finally cause me to turn is that they are leading
the Party into a barren defile where it is going to be *annihilated*.

Saltwood   *Tuesday, 29 March*

Jane has gone on a 'massive' shopping round – Glass Co,
Geerings, possibly Canterbury map shop. It's really rather
pleasant and relaxing being left in the empty home.

I would like to get out and play out-of-doors. But here I am
two years out of retirement and chained to the paper, and the
desks, more than ever. (Just reread an interview with Robin Day
who has said on the difference between capital and income –
'with high capital you are a free man; with high earnings you are
a slave'.) And tomorrow the Coutts team are coming down –
like tea for the IMF.

Garden House   *Thursday, 31 March*

I am low, and feel that things are slipping away from me.

A re-run of November '90, but without, of course, the platform or perch.

The week's papers have been blazing – Major finished, end is nigh, not a friend left, sooner he goes the better. Sterling crisis – you name it.

Jonathan H talked for an hour on Tuesday. He'd had lunch with Jeremy[1] who gave him 'the whole thing is over' spiel; then that afternoon JM did poorly in the Commons and Marlow bagged a headline with his you-must-go declamation. Dobbie got more and more apocalyptic – finally calling at 9-ish p.m.

I booked a meeting with Richard – 'the Chief Whip will come and have tea at Albany at 3.30 p.m.'

Later in the evening Soames phoned – part II – and said it was a shambles, Baker was taking people on one side and saying 'JM was dead in the water' etc. I asked him if he wanted to be chairman of the Party and he said yes. Why anyone wants that job beats me, but anything can happen … if I could afford it myself I'd grab it.

But (later) when I put this to Richard he said 'Nick who?' 'Oh, give him a director-general to pay the wages,' I said, and got the only real chuckle of the afternoon. RR was reasonably communicative. Admitted that the only real danger would be a Cabinet welching; a 'difficult' meeting at which one or more people expressed reservations.

Quite.

Richard was amiable, almost Gow-voiced in his insistence on a 'dinner' soon after Easter. But of what clout does he actually dispose? At one point I said, 'You must find something for me to do.' Did he even acknowledge? I will return to this next time.

---

[1] Jeremy Hanley (MP for Richmond & Barnes since 1983), currently Armed Forces Minister, but in the summer Cabinet reshuffle would succeed Norman Fowler as chairman of the Conservative Party.

But this morning I have been trying desperately to keep Jonathan Holborow from 'plunging in'. Apparently M. Heseltine was imploring Dobbie last night to take his side – 'on his knees'. Perhaps mistakenly, I said to Jonathan, *you* see him; make your own mind up. You're in the strongest position of the Sundays, not in anyone's 'camp', not concerned with personalities.

They put the whole thing in place immediately. So that while I was talking to M Howard (he, too, took my call immediately!) – also very splendidly said, 'tape the interview and run that.' It may have been a miscalculation; Jonathan H could be overcome as he is still, in one sense, politically *naïf*. At present I've got calls in to Bob Worcester (the polls are crucial in this) and David Davis. Tristan is no longer friendly, and I see no point in showing my hand.

My handwriting is terribly disturbed.

Garden House   *Sunday, 3 April*

The papers are full of Heseltine – ludicrous, this, nearly four years on. No mention of me anywhere except at No 2 in the paperback lists. I'm not interested in the book, in writing, at the moment. I don't 'return calls' from Orion. I am desperate, though, for peace. I came over here, and it's not bad, but too many cabinets and dog-earedness and dust. The great rug, which I had on my floor in MoD and which David Franzes[1] charged £700 (I seem to recall) to clean is fading fast.

While it is true that I can't bear being OUT, it's also true that I seem to be wasting my time so much here so that if I *did* 'get' anything there would be a mountainous backlog. If I can just establish the infrastructure then I can leave a framework of instruction – a recommendation to my successors, a note for my

---

[1] London dealer.

literary executors. How old was Papa when he was fussing about this – 74, 75?

Now too late to book the Buick in at a discount to train up to Eriboll. *Why* is May so dreadfully congested? Poor Col sitting in a chair with a rug on his knees. Was quite funny about the Prince of Wales whose Aston broke down in the Brompton Road – 'this kind of thing always happens to me ...' and 'just my luck'.

'He's a prince, for God's sake, married to one of the world's most beautiful women, with two lovely boys, what's all the whingeing about?'

Garden House   *Easter Monday, 4 April*

Today, I think for the first time, I actually found myself accepting the reality of defeat.

The old analogy – with the Reich in 1943–5 – is less valid than Vichy France in 1940. I have now to go through a Pétainist period. Really quite hard to see what will extricate me. No one rings any more – except people who want to pick my brains on the cheap, or also want to put me on their programme and lift its status – for £35.

Anyway I am going to get everything in order – and then I will be free. I can walk out – but without going to 'another woman' (although, of course, it will be suspected that I have). Where do I go to? I would really prefer Scotland, but I suppose it has to be Bratton, as that's the only place, absurdly enough, that belongs to me. I might start in Zermatt, in fact.

During the night there were *five* interruptions: Tom (urinated twice on the white carpet); then Lëhni urinated in my bathroom, went out re-Thompsoned; then Tom had to go out Thompsoned; then Hannah met me on the stairs, took her down – she Thompsoned. Finally Tom hyper-ventilated, looked into the Yard briefly, settled for the Green Room.

Jane, I may say, made absolutely no effort whatever to cope with any of these episodes except the first when she ably removed most of the stain using rubber gloves and Jif.

So this morning I am utterly exhausted. Had to come straight over here after EMT to type some letters. Now I'm back here, very depressed, nothing on the machine, and will spend 40 minutes or so 'Windolening' the plate glass before shuffling back across to the Mains.

Garden House   *Tuesday, 5 April*

I was over in the Great Hall study with Jane, looking for some of my father's articles which I need for 'Michael Delon' (sounds quite scholarly in his approach). I came across some tiny pocket engagement books of my grandfather,[1] *very* sparingly entered: 'out', 'shooting', 'Inverary', 'Mrs MacArthur to lunch'. Some are clearly future engagements, clear (if the word can be considered applicable) records.

In August of 1914, the week of the great seismic tilt, when the earth plates buckled, they were sailing off the west coast of Scotland – 'Oban', 'Poolewe'. About the 14th, they took the train to Euston, spent the night in their London house (visited v rarely) in Berkeley Square (come to think of it, all the satinwood stuff must have been bought for this, from Malletts – just round the corner) the next day took the train to Sudbourne.[2] Stayed there (shooting) all through the Battle of the Marne. What a style! Three large and expensive houses (plus the lodge at Poolewe and the villa at Cap Ferrat), the yacht, hordes and hordes of domestics.

My own structure still shadows it – but with no support whatever. Like the Royal Navy in the 1970s, compared with the Grand Fleet.

---

[1] Kenneth McKenzie Clark, who inherited wealth and enjoyed it to the full.
[2] The Clark estate in Suffolk.

Garden House   *Sunday, 10 April*

This is, as it were, the birthday-boy entry – next week is 'a horrible' and I won't be back here Thursday morning.

Recently I have been thinking about an escape plan. It goes like this:

Put Saltwood on 'care and maintenance' ('it is already on care and maintenance', Jane says.)

Reduce the contents virtually to modern museum level – bare, clear walls – except for the Red Library and the dining room (in mothballs for 'crash' meeting). Garden House ticking over warmly for a visit when necessary.

Look for a low 18th-century stone house with nicely proportioned rooms in Perthshire – 200 acres for wintering the Eriboll flock, a good chunk of hill and a nice black-spate salmon river for Jane to fish in. Plenty of outbuildings. I even fantasise about getting Bill Holdings to put up one of his sheds there. That way we would be near enough to James and Julie, especially as they are now talking of 'winklers'. It would mean selling Seend for Tip.

I've always said I'll never move, and probably won't. Lord Astor sold up Hever, went to Scotland and died of cancer very soon afterwards. It would mark the transition into an old man I suppose from (*passim* today's *Sunday Times*) 'much-missed in the corridors of power'. A final abandonment of the sword and helmet. Even as I write that I realise I can't do it. But pleasant to fantasise.

Albany   *Monday, 11 April*

Although cold at Saltwood it is warm and springlike here; St James's Park burgeoning with yellowy-green buds. Why does this always make me so nostalgic? In recent years, of course, because I have associated it with 'x' 'going off' somewhere (I think no agony compared with the agony while I was on my second trip to Oman in May of '91). Also because I have habitually likened it to the preference of *not* being able to enjoy the countryside. Now, although free, I seem to have completely filled May, again. This must never be allowed to happen in the future.

As I crossed Westminster Bridge I felt the usual agonies of being banned from the precincts. Then I walked into Wiltons – in 'Grunge' – and there was Franko[1] sitting on the bankette. I lunched with him and we gossiped. In came Heseltine (!) and a PA who was *all over him*. He was in a brand new dark grey suit, white silk shirt, hair coiffed (I mean Teasy-Weasy coiffed) from behind. Loathsome.

Frank is intelligent and, doubtless for that reason, we depressed ourselves. Then walking out to go to Chatham House library I ran into Bruce Anderson! He was fluent and radical. Make David Owen Foreign Secretary etc etc. He doesn't give Major much chance. But it emerges Tristan is still 'seeing' him (and giving bad advice).

Saltwood   *Wednesday, 20 April*

Fearfully beleagured by pressures – which have 'got to me' that I feel extremely tired and don't see any sunlit uplands. I sit at the table in the Green Room – absurdly laden, now, with the various trays. Behind me several Pisa towers of sundry news-print, car sale catalogues, important incoming letters interleaved (I don't doubt) and every kind of unexpected document I've beside my chair and on the bookcase.

The speaking engagements are disorderly. Some acceptances lurk, unrecorded on the chart. Fresh-faced undergraduates

---

[1] Frank Johnson, deputy editor of the *Sunday Telegraph* and former parliamentary sketch-writer.

telephone 'to confirm'; what's the use of that? I appear to be simultaneously double-booked (sic) for CUCA and OUCA, just as tomorrow I am double-booked for Simon Heffer and David Evans.[1] Tonight I allowed myself to be booked for a 'Five Alive' show that I ran a pilot for Alastair Campbell.[2] At the time I thought I was to be booked on to a panel (say alternate weeks). Boring, because from the hours of 12 to 2 a.m., but maybe £4000 for 6 weeks? But it has already degenerated into a *chat* show (without even Alastair chairing it), which I have vowed not to do.

I had a bad night, or at least woke early, worrying about funds as much as anything. 'Where are the jobs coming from?' I hung around in the Lodge for the youths on bicycles who have been emptying the milk bottles. Caught some and photographed them, though was not cool enough. Now I feel sickish, terribly congested, and for some reason my toothache in lower left has returned.

Yesterday evening, after [dog] training (which did not go well; I was distracted by a pretty young woman with a nervous Alsatian), I walked down the valley in fading light, which I used to when I was living here and before going away to Rye. I thought: I suppose to a detached observer at least, my life in terms of potential, is over. But instead of pleasing open days I have in front of me a Matto Grosso of paperwork and filing which I must try and get in order before I depart.

Nixon had a stroke today. 81. He can understand, but he can't talk. The worst of all, because so soon they start talking about you in the room, in *audio oblique*. The days are lovely now, longer daylight than in August. It would be so lovely to be meandering about outside, like one used to at Seend. Will one ever be free of *will we ever*?

---

[1] Simon Heffer, deputy editor *The Spectator* since 1991, about to rejoin the *Daily Telegraph* as deputy editor (he had been a political and leader writer there previously); David Evans, businessman and former chairman of Luton Town football club, MP for Welwyn Hatfield since 1987.

[2] AC recorded at the time (February 1994) that the panel included Tessa Jowell, 'who is apparently a Labour MP [Dulwich, since 1992] but I thought was a "liberal" Conservative'.

Monday, 9 May

Absolutely blind with tension pressures. These last two weeks I
haven't even filled in the day diary – never mind the journal.
And all against a background of *The Heseltine Assumption*. Poor
JM getting in more and more difficulties.

My own schedules are even tighter than in the halcyon days
of being a Minister of State at DTI (MDef blighted of course by
the angst of my 'double' life). Flailing with the earnings – but no
more than a treadmill, just keeping the 'limits' at bay.

Tomorrow up by train to see [Charles] Jerdein at 3 p.m. about
selling the Mask (his *client* is raising his bid), which I can't really
do.

Sunday, 15 May

I just dare not accept Jerdein's offer for the Mask: $100, plus
£265. Would solve all debts. But if I keep it, it will go on
generating its protection, I believe.

Albany   *Monday, 16 May*

I had to stop the car (Big Red) in the lay-by just as the M20
ends and nap for 15 minutes, and when I got here I thought –
I'm emerging now from my pining for public life. It took a very
long time, just as it did to emerge from 'x' with each trough
followed by a blip, then slightly lower still until – almost – the
yearning is extinct. Helped, I suppose, by thinking that perhaps
after all Labour (Blair) will now be the next government. I will,
finally, be relegated into the older generation, which I have for
so long avoided. Do a full switch, into historian, and do the Tory
Party book.

Ritz dining room, Paris[1]   *Sunday, 29 May*

Just drank a delicious glass of orange juice. A very good hotel (except no tutti slippers in the bathroom). Staff – unusually for French – courteous and obliging and I had a lovely room on the 6th floor with double windows and balconies looking out over the roofs.

Oy! What cramped and nifty writing … A bit apprehensive, I suppose, though basically dutch, at the Harkess 'story' which has broken – manically – in the *News of the World* and been, gleefully, I don't doubt, picked up by the *Sunday Express*. Jane is gamely meeting me at Manston and I may have to ride from Sandling to Saltwood in the boot of Big Red.[2] It's really too boring. I don't enjoy this kind of 'publicity' at all and it has been running on and off now for a year really. I suppose it may sell some more books, but expect Orion won't be able to provide demand, just use the 'subject' to clear their stocks.

A *very* painless way of getting around. About as effortless as being minister (and without the *longueurs*). Jimmy's plane from Farnborough; met by a fleet of 'stretched' Mercedes and drove to the Ritz with Annabel[3] (still great fun, and voluptuous) and their incredibly bright little son Ben-Ben.

Saltwood   *Tuesday, 14 June*

A lovely evening of high summer – longest day (how quickly it comes up on one) next weekend. Then it's shedding tail-feathers and quieter all round.

---

[1] AC was in Paris for Jimmy Goldsmith's 'L'autre Europe' party.
[2] AC arrived in the Goldsmith private jet at Manston. Jane had forced her way through journalists outside the Saltwood gates, saying she was just going off to do some shopping. She returned, with AC indeed in the capacious boot of Big Red, drove straight to the Long Garage; AC did not emerge until they were safely inside.
[3] Lady Annabel Goldsmith, third wife of Sir James Goldsmith.

A certain sense of peace – 'at last'. But there is much talk of a reshuffle after the disasters – but not *that* disastrous – Euro elections.[1]

This is my first *contemplatif* for over two weeks. I was under some pressure – all those journalists and questions [over Harkess]: '… are you going to answer the charges (sic)?' actually assume one's guilt. I couldn't even fill out the Green Diary day-by-day.

I suppose the tide actually turned on 'the' Wednesday. Tristan rang that evening (welchly late, as I said to Jane, but an indication that we had made 'if not port then the lee of the shore').

If there were turning points I would say, Richard Littlejohn aside, *The Times* leader,[2] the *Daily Mirror* dope on Joei and finally the Judy Finnegan show which showed them – thanks to Judy and her husband – *in a poor light*, culminating in a vote when the score was 72–28.

I may even have 'come out ahead' having sold at least another 20,000 paperbacks and, ludicrously, been approached to go into a 'National' Police advertisement scheme (I'm still doubtful about this) with an appearance fee of £25,000 plus (!).

In my present form all really I want to do, though, is to stand back and become a guru-sage.

Wednesday, 22 June

The seat by the moat after EMT. Mid-summer, the anniversary of Barbarossa. This time, fifty-three years ago the whole Eastern Front was ablaze and the YAKs were smouldering carcases,

---

[1] 'Disaster', in hindsight, is too strong a word: the Conservatives held eighteen seats, more than even the most optimistic had forecast. However the Tory share of the vote was the lowest achieved by a major party in a national election in the twentieth century, and in five constituencies Tory majorities were less than 1 per cent.

[2] 'With his *Diaries*, he has written himself into the life of our times with a panache and candour that ranks him next to Boswell or Pepys.' (*The Times*, 10 June 1994).

wing-tip to wing-tip, on the Soviet airfields. But only three
years later it was the collapse of Army Group Centre (always one
of the strangest failures of nerve of the magnificent German
army) and the 'rush' into Poland.

Things have taken a turn for the better for us. So far this week
I have been a 'triumph' (*passim* Paul Channon[1]) on *Frost*;[2] then
a call from Cdr Aylard[3] saying how interesting the Prince of
Wales had found my piece in the *Mail on Sunday*. Selina Scott
wants to include me in her next series with Clinton, Murdoch,
Pavarotti etc – 'from a woman's point of view'.

We went up to Jimmy's great party. Lovely fun. Everyone was
there. And Princess Diana turned up 'for the coffee', looking
incredible as always. Isobel Goldsmith sat on my left wearing the
most beautiful necklace. 'Do you deal with the Nortons?' I
asked. Of course she did. It had come from Nicholas.[4] Opposite
me, on Conrad Black's right, sat Jane Wrightsman[5] gone from
being blonde to being gypsy black; with tiny birdlike movements of vain, elderly women who are trying to conceal their
age.

My 'approval' rating remains high ('four times that of the PM,'
as Charles Moore giggled) and people as varied as William
Shawcross (who he?[6]) and the doorman – who was a Serb,
wonderful people – came up to 'shake my hand'.

Jane drove me back in the Big Red and I lollingly dozed.
Slept like a top. Strangely, I don't think I have been happier, or
more fulfilled since Seend – and perhaps first being made MFT.
And I thank God.

---

[1] Paul Channon, MP for Southend W since January 1959, succeeding his father, Sir
Henry ('Chips') Channon.

[2] Sir David Frost's Sunday morning 'sofa' show, as AC called it, was required viewing
for politicians. Frost had come a long way since satire shows of 1960s.

[3] Cdr Richard Aylard, private secretary to the Prince of Wales since 1991.

[4] Nicholas Norton of S. J. Phillips, jewellers in Bond Street.

[5] Jane Wrightsman, widow of Charles Wrightsman, American oil billionaire.

[6] William Shawcross, journalist, author, married to Olga Polizzi, daughter of Charles
Forte.

Sunday, 26 June

A lovely hot still day and we rose early and sat breakfasting by the pool, then afterwards in the long chairs by the fig tree reading the Sundays. Publicity – I get it. Absurd really. Only cloud is little Page who came in when I was having an injection, said I should have a check-up. Wouldn't have minded so much if it hadn't been Col's doctor who said, 'Your brother should have a PSA test.'[1] So this hangs over me. But I am much calmer now, and seem none the worse (dare I say it, slightly better for the whole experience).

Great Hall Study, Saltwood   *Sunday, 10 July*

Last night we went over to Sissinghurst, arriving early for dinner and walked round the gardens. Lovely, and no public, and very redolent of Harold and Vita and 'Miss Niggeman'.[2] 'Cleaned up' as NT properties always are, but one could still imagine the old boy driving back from Tunbridge Wells station (old Austin taxi, of course) and thinking about the countryside during the Battle of Britain and then, much later, shuffling out of his study in the tower, and collapsing. 'Is this where he collapsed?' I rehearsed in the car going over, and Jane had a *fou rire*. At dinner I was lionised. Marvellous to be compared to Byron, Shelley and Pepys in one's lifetime – and by such good judges. Stephen Spender and Elizabeth Longford[3] quite effusive, Natasha Spender, whom I remember as being dark and voluptuous and rather frightening still very attractive, at 70+, with short blonde-dyed hair and lovely eye ditches.

---

[1] Protein Sequence Analysis for early detection of prostate cancer.
[2] Kent home of Nigel Nicolson, author, former Conservative MP, son of Harold Nicolson and his wife Vita Sackville-West, who restored the house and its gardens, now in the hands of the National Trust; Elvira Niggeman, Harold Nicolson's secretary, 1938–65.
[3] Sir Stephen Spender, poet; Lady Longford, biographer.

I sat next to Rebecca Nicolson[1] and she and some ambassador[2] gave me a bit of 'when are you going to take the helm?' treatment. All v gratifying, but frustrating also. Phone and fax silent all day.

Next week the result of the 'test'. Will I be 'cleared'?

Talking of which, little Archer[3] again in trouble over 'insider trading'. Every week a new scandal.

Saltwood   *Wednesday, 13 July*

We have had two days of very great heat – 86° and more in London. On the Monday we drove (in the Jaguar, as Big Red has gone away for part exchange[4]) to Highgrove. HRH very magnetic – greatly to my surprise. I took a liking to Paul McCartney, saw a few other notables (little Gummer[5] notably unfriendly). A slightly bizarre grouping. But at the close we were escorted to the car park by Richard Aylard, to whom I talked giftedly and recklessly.

Highgrove is terribly nice, really organic. But the place was incomplete, without a woman.

Saltwood   *Saturday, 16 July*

As I walked back from the Garden House, having finished my *Mail on S* 'column', I saw the mother hen and the little black baby bantams under the beech hedge and went over to talk to

---

[1] AC 'tried to get off with' Rebecca Nicolson. She was flattered, but refused.
[2] Michael Pakenham, British ambassador to Luxembourg; son of Elizabeth Longford.
[3] Archer had been accused over Anglia TV, where his wife was a director.
[4] AC was exchanging his present Bentley for a new one, identical in colour, also called Big Red.
[5] John Selwyn Gummer, MP for Suffolk Central since 1983 (Eye, 1979–83, Lewisham W 1970–February 1974), Environment Secretary since 1993.

them. On the other side of the moat one of the moorhens was busying itself. I was deliciously at ease, not having drunk anything at midday, felt marvellous. In the late afternoon drove with Jane in the KGV car to collect some of her framed pictures from the Evegate Art Shop and then on to get petrol at Tesco. Tea with black bread and pepper salami (only a croissant so far today) and then I wandered up to the top of the house to open the tower playroom door for the swifts. I found an old, very old Bartholomew cloth-backed Ordnance Survey map of Sutherland (Tongue and Cape Wrath, sheet 26) possibly even Victorian as it showed the Creaggan as fully driveable, two ferries across the Loch, one going to 'Port Eriboll'. Then I hung on the bar without ill-effect. On the way down through the upper floors I fantasised about ways of 'doing them up' and realised what lovely things there still are here. A day of real contentment and tranquillity, unchronicled for a very long time, and thanks be to God.

In the Volvo at the Creaggan peat workings   *Wednesday, 10 August*

The ninth day here, but – unusually and sinisterly – I am very much not 'a thousand per cent'. That little spot on the tip of my scar has turned into a basal, I'm sure of it. Irrevocably it enlarges and hardens. My rear lower wisdom is aching intermittently – and for longer at a time. How can it? If the nerve has been taken out, how can it hurt? Everyone away (naturally) until September has prescribed antibiotics. But why/how should/could there be an infection there at all? Jaw cancer is always one of my great horrors.

I am really fit – do a lot of scrambling and walking, out practically all day. But I am not unwound. I dread the journey back – I suppose we'd better grit our teeth and try and do it in a day.

I am unsettled by all the boring things I have to do in

Sept/Oct/Nov. I cancelled poor Selina. She was so sweet. But would it have worked? I think not; it would have been *Love Tory* II. We have cancelled *Diaries* II, because that wouldn't have worked 'out' either.

I still contemplate cancelling everything, and just concentrating on my book, TNS[1] and periodic reviews, but if I am to keep up the column then I suppose I need periodic nourishment. What do I actually want? Soames replied to my letter of congratulations immediately; Cranborne after three weeks; Aitken not at all.[2] But I'm not *inside*. My burning determination to get back in and scare them is slowly dying down. I'm sublimating it, I suppose, in the great work. But I am not yet at ease with myself.

Looking back I think the only *really* happy day I've had, quite perfect and utterly memorable was the day in July of last year when Jane had just joined me and we drove along some lovely Slovena valley, bathing naked in the river pool while the other Ghosts wafted by above us, and got to our hotel, made love and walked in the town listening to a wedding choir and then praying in the Catholic church (or have I compressed two days? No matter).

Although to be fair last Saturday here was lovely, also. But I am so unprogrammed.

Shore Cottage   *Saturday, 13 August*

I have massively overdone it physically. Must have shifted 2–300 bales of hay – but not as decrepit as I might be. No time to walk *long* (I had wanted to go to Whiten Head – might make a recce

---

[1] Also referred to in these diaries as 'Big Book'; what AC saw as his magnum opus, *The Tories: Conservatives and the Nation State, 1922–1997*, eventually published in 1998.

[2] In the summer reshuffle, Nicholas Soames had been made PPS at Department of Employment, Lord Cranborne Leader of the House of Lords, Jonathan Aitken Chief Secretary to the Treasury (the latter two joining the Cabinet for the first time).

tomorrow), still have to write – although ideas for the Tory book ferment pleasingly. I am a bit apprehensive at intervals, occasionally almost Lenin Stadium and indirectly about the congestion of the nose-place op, and all those bloody speaking engagements.

As Jane said last night – 'We're going to head south for a complete rest.'

Actually for the first time today I can contemplate the going home. As always at Eriboll we've banked a lot of stamina.

Garden House   *Sunday, 28 August*

It was sensible of me to go on to 'Mr Page's rooms' as I had suffered a setback and Dai Davies[1] who had settled for 'a cyst' (it wasn't, having a tiny core of basal cells) etc etc. Then on to Page for blood tests and a discussion about whether this is affected by men on HRT. Page says don't know.

Saturday, 3 September

It is fifty-five years since Chamberlain broadcast the declaration of war, and we were staying at the Hare and Hounds Hotel at Westonbirt (oh so near to Highgrove) and that afternoon (or the next day) rummaging in some stables/shed looking for a 'secret package' when Mr Ashmore (or Ashmole) appeared, surprisingly, and said that the *Courageous* had been lost and to my private dismay I could not remember what class of boat it was.[2]

Now I sit at my desk in the Garden House, very depressed. I have so little time left. It is so precious. There is little enough until I actually die – even less before my 'powers' fail.

---

[1] Dai Davies, specialist.
[2] An aircraft carrier, actually sunk by a U-boat in the Bristol Channel on 17 September.

Saltwood   *Thursday, 15 September*

This morning I read a little of Julian Critchley's book.[1] So light
and pleasing a touch. A charming and witty fellow looking
(until very recently) younger than his years and most unsuitable
for a whole range of reasons (some of which he shared with me)
as a backbench Conservative MP. But when he writes about the
22,[2] and personalities in earlier times, I felt so wistful. It took me
almost to the day when I first wanted to go in, under 'Uncle
Harold'. Like sex, I wasted an awful lot of time, yet, as it were,
'finding my way'.

I wish to goodness I hadn't taken all those speaking engagements for the autumn. I suppose I thought that could I still
ingratiate myself with a constituency? ACHAB. And you could
say it keeps me 'in touch'.

Monday, 19 September

It has been very wet and cold – almost underwater conditions
all day today, and dark. We are due to fly from Gatwick
tomorrow for the Hamilton rally. It seemed a good idea at the
time – lots of expensive sports racing cars hustling along D-
roads in the Lot region driven by rich spoilt amateurs. But as the
weather faded and faltered we decided (I think brilliantly) to
quickly commission and despatch (also) in the truck the Citroën
('always used on holiday' – qv). Prospect, ideally, of idling, one
hand on the wheel, as the Chapron effortlessly keeps up with a
lot of expensive trash, some of it pre-war like all those 2.3 Alfas,
in swishing rain and *nids-de-poule*. It may not work out like that,
though.

I think it *very* unlikely I'll be doing the column again next

---

[1] The memoirs of Julian Critchley, *A Bag of Bottled Sweets*.
[2] The Conservative 1922 Committee of backbench MPs.

year (I may not even be invited to do so) unless offered pointless extra. I suppose for 120 I would have to say yes, but I would really rather be free (it was delicious last weekend being at Saltwood yet not having to concentrate on Friday evenings/ Saturday mornings and just do the odd TV and book review).

On Saturday night we went to dine with the Howards. The Lamonts, MH and Sandra, Jane and I, Aitken and Lol. One passé, one in jeopardy, one OUT, and one in ascendant. Aitken was again disagreeable – said something on the lines of '... for those of us in the front line ...'(i.e., not you). I thought he was rather giggly and high-pitched. 'My goodness, you're dark,' I thought as we were introduced. Jane said he must be dyeing his hair and sure enough there were discreet henna 'lights', up market *PropinoMilanese*.

On getting home that evening, I was depressed.

Rosemary L (rather likeable now) said was I looking for a seat, and got excitedly inquisitive when I said 'yes'. But I know better. Only *just* tolerated at Uckfield; interest more prurient than approbatory.

How long have I got? I'd settle for another ten years – but can't realistically expect this. Fair? I would be wise (as I am) to get the books done, be a granpapa, and a semi Howard Hughes. I think it is this knowledge that there isn't all that time left that makes me so irritable when a day is being wasted.

Thursday, 29 September

As I pottered about Garden House this morning I thought how lovely to have a whole year – see the seasons round – without a single engagement. But can I afford to chuck the *Mail on Sunday*? And can I resist invitations? My problem is that I can't really relax unless there is a *clear run* ahead. But if there is a clear run, however short, I fill it up (like paying off an o/d, and then 'taking advantage of the facility' again).

Thursday, 13 October

My very last Party Conference – short of a miracle. It must be all of 20 years – could have been '69 or '70 when I went to Blackpool nervous about being, as it were, *visually probed*, been keen (how little I knew then) to find and suck up to chairmen. Now most of the cheeky-chappies, 5' 8" high and with 'waisted' jackets and exact templates/candidates of the kind that were all over the place then, and saying the same things. CCO standard issue.

I comment[1] shrewdly and drawlingly at the start and end of sessions. But glimpsing myself in the monitor at the end of the day's session with Huw (Edwards, I think?) I thought how old I looked. Earlier in the day the sweet little make-up blonde was getting friendlier and friendlier; expressed sympathy at the idea of 'going for a walk on the beach'. But when I asked her, she said, 'You mean take off our shoes and walk barefoot in the sand?'

'Yes, yes.'

'I don't get a lunch hour.'

Was she mocking? She didn't turn up all afternoon.

I walked along the beach alone …

Portillo and Heseltine 'clashed'. Portillo got the better ovation. The first time anyone has beaten MH for years (except, of course, and by rote, the PM).

MH, also, looked old at times. Almost 'Mr Chips' in his half-moons. And last night as I worked the conference hall it was so clear that people were unhappy, and longing for a lead. They cheered Hanley,[2] but only a kind of knee-jerk – because basically he was *low*. You can get laughs, and 'affection' that way, but it's not leadership. (I must say, though, that I did get a pang

---

[1] The BBC had employed AC for interpretation and summing-up.

[2] John Major had made Jeremy Hanley party chairman in his summer reshuffle, believing that Hanley with his easy manner might do for the Conservatives in the mid-1990s what Cecil Parkinson had done for the party early in Margaret Thatcher's time as Prime Minister.

when Malcolm Rifkind, introducing his front bench, pointed out that the entire previous line-up – Aitken, Hanley and Cranborne – had all gone into Cabinet.)

I went to two fringe meetings. Little Lamont, making the intellectual case for complete withdrawal from the EC; and less publicised, but colossally crowded, the Goldsmith-Tebbit meeting. A lot of Cuixmalan freeloaders there – Aspers, Taki, Ed Epstein, Greville Howard[1] – playing at politics. Brian Hitchen – first time I've seen him in the flesh – bright red and taut with over-weightedness.[2]

On the way back I was waylaid by the *News of the World* gang and had an open-air negotiating session with Piers Morgan. Quite engaging (high flown, aet. 29). Offered him a clear run for £25,000 – including my costs. Very generous.[3]

Garden House   *Monday, 24 October*

I took a train up to lunch with Ion at the Garrick. 'Have you seen anything of "x?" I said to George thingummy in the bar. 'Yes, I went to the wedding.' It was like some terrible surgery on flesh-wound administered through a huge local anaesthetic. I can feel the knife entering, but only barely the pain. I suppose that the real blow will be when I hear of her child. Strange, but in a curious way half encouraging (or do I mean comforting) that she couldn't tell me.

I explained to Ion that I am going to take a sabbatical – a real sabbatical – starting on (effectively) 18 December. Eschewing

---

[1] Lord [Norman] Tebbit, a mainstay of Margaret Thatcher's Cabinets, later Conservative Party chairman; Taki Theodoracopoulos, Greek-born social columnist; Greville Howard, Norfolk gentry, chairman of Fortress Holdings and a member of the council of the 'Europe Yes; Euro No' Campaign.

[2] Brian Hitchen, editor of the *Sunday Express*; AC added a later note – 'at last a crazy illustration of the medical term "hypertension".'

[3] Following the *News of the World*'s serialisation of the Harkess' story, AC was threatening legal action; Piers Morgan, the *N of W*'s editor.

the column? Speaking? Occasional journalism? 'Yes – all of
them.' It will cost me £200,000 minimum.

Replete with a kind of melancholic loathing.

I am almost revelling in the idea. 'Alan Clark is dead.'

'No he isn't.'

'Yes he is … I'm sure he is.' etc.

Saltwood   *Monday, 12 December*

I am back now in the Tower Office, having been driven out by
the sheer height of the piles of paper in the Green Room. I am
quite out of kilter and made extremely thoughtful by poor
Eddie having had, a couple of days ago, a mini-stroke.[1]

He is 'muddled', and frail and – I fear – a write-off. I called
on him this morning and felt moved by how sweet-natured and
loyal he was – 'I'll be back shortly, just do a few odd jobs, get
some wood in …' etc. But apparently when Peggy came back
from the farm he told her that he had fed Pepper. She found that
he had taken the back off the wireless and put the batteries in
the dog's dish (a quite dream-like surreal sequence). And there
is an unhappy look of fear, almost of panic, in his eyes.

The ramifications of this are enormous, and uniformly unwelcome. We can't go away together, and leave the dogs. How
can we leave the dogs? So no Zermatt together, no rallying, no
(unless we can persuade Andrew and Sarah down) Mexico. Even
when we go to Scotland for Christmas and take the dogs we
will have to lock up the whole house, take potluck over (a) a
burglary (b) a fire (c) an appalling leak.

Then there are so many odd jobs he did – already a leak that
needs bitumising in the workshop; a Yale lock on the back door
of the wooden shed. The top border. Oh dear. I suppose we
must take consolation that it will force our hand into searching

---

[1] Edwin Wilson, groundsman and gardener of long standing at Saltwood.

for a 'Treasure' or couple.

Also a timely reminder of how suddenly 'it can happen'. I have high blood pressure myself, this is known. 'At any moment I can be eliminated by an assassin or a lunatic'(Wolf). But how awful not to be eliminated, but just drastically crippled. And you always get another within three years of a stroke – often less.

Shore Cottage   *Tuesday, 20 December*

Arrived in the afternoon, very wet lying, but light beautiful and Julie had got the croft in shipshape order. James had made a really beautiful strong bench for me and sweetly had stuck a red ribbon on it – my Christmas present.

Shore is simply divine – needing only a porch, a little decorating, a deep freeze in the cold larder and a double bed (new) and oak bookcase in my 'study' and I could 'work' here for weeks on end. Even now it is a most wonderful refuge – completely away from the telephone, rentaquote, newspapers, howling peacocks, M-way roar, calling out, engine noise, television etc etc.

Yesterday we came up the Great North Road, leaving two minutes later than 'bogey' time and alighting in Gleneagles car park at *exactly* the same time (2.46 p.m.) as on the previous visit. Heavily laden (with the – quite cheering – cockatiels[1]) in the new Discovery which is quieter, even more economical, slightly better handling, but quite a little slower than the old one. I must say that at Gleneagles dining and after tea (I was too exhausted even to read) I did get a most wonderful sense of relief.

An 'open' – relatively – year stretches ahead. And, absurdly, like the last weeks before a reshuffle the anticipation is agreeable.

---

[1] As at Saltwood the cockatiels took up residence in their cage in the 'warmer kitchen'.

Shore Cottage   *Wednesday, 21 December*

Detached myself at midday and went up the Creaggan, low
sunlight, but the air quite still. Thought of many things, and
quite content really, although I have not got long enough to live
for all that I need.

I returned and joined Jane in a meander along the shoreline
and on the way back saw 'the young' and I upbraided Andrew
for having chosen the 'wrong' Range Rover (the diesel instead
of the V8). Jane said his face crumpled as I shouted and sneered.
Why do I do this to those I love? Almost immediately after it
emerges that it was the BMW diesel – a most interesting
comparison. I tried hard to make it up. I do so adore Tip, and
hate to wound him.

Shore Cottage   *Friday, 23 December*

First entry at my desk in the panelled room. Eddie's tubular
heater makes it incomparably more congenial than the 'sitting
room'. Right height. I look out at the shed and the bank, hear
the stream running. Yesterday I fiddled with the cars (James
came down in the evening and got them all going in one
burst!). Meandered along the foreshore, spotted driftwood. In
the evening the young all came down for supper which we held
in the kitchen at Meecee's table – v successful, except for dear
Tip who is a bit quiet and overshadowed by (a) James and (b)
Sarah. Sarah said, quite insouciantly, that 'everyone in Zermatt
says what a bad influence I am on Andrew: he used to be such
fun …' etc etc. Poor dears. I do hope things work out all right
for them.

I am heavier than in previous years with a 'pot' that needs
controlling. But I sleep, eat and Thompson satisly and my cock
is fine. Senescence is indicated by getting sleepy and passing out
at moments during the day, and by poor recall (having said to

Andrew: 'Did you hear what Tom did – locked himself in the car – ?' 'Yes, I was there'). But my mind still runs freely and actively around the future.

Shore Cottage   *Saturday, 24 December*

It is a truism that any holiday only lasts three – or possibly four – days before some jarring episode or reminder changes the atmosphere and arrests the process of unwinding.

At EMT Jane and I were sitting this morning, still utterly comatose and uncoordinated. She was dressed, and after a bit decided to take the dogs, starting ahead of me while I Thompsoned and dressed. Quietly, ruminating on the loo with *Three Years of War in E Africa* (first time this hol)[1] I thought I heard shouting, rather Saltwood-like. Thought no more of it, then unmistakably Jane SCREAMING hysterically. Rushed out naked, barefoot in wellingtons with only a Jaeger dressing gown on. The dogs had attacked a sheep, forcing it in and out of the stream. Poor darling, she was white and gasping; hit Hannah fiercely with my stalking stick. This made me deeply gloomy – can we never let the dogs off the lead – much less free range – again? It's hard enough to get her to come to Eriboll, still less to stay here for any length of time …

Later I went to gather driftwood in the jeep and Andrew got it at a really dangerous angle above long beach. It then suffered fuel starvation and I went back on foot to the byre, noting at the same time how very fluently and fast the young walk (rather like the Charles Moores).

---

[1] By Captain Angus Buchanan; another Eriboll favourite.

Shore Cottage   *Monday (Boxing Day)*

We went to midnight carol service in Tongue. As always, ahead
of a 'function' felt comatose and reluctant. But it was pleasing.
All the good tunes, and perfectly sensible message of reassurance
about the resurrection, a good audience (including some in
crew cuts and bomber jackets) and not one mention, from start
to finish, of the Third World or the need to 'combat' racism or
homelessness or poverty or any of that crap.

Now it is hailing and with a cold wind and I sit at my delightful
study window and at the Seend gratis desk and ponder.

Saltwood   *Thursday, 29 December*

Back here and in a high state of nervous readiness (quite the
reverse of nervous randiness). We 'did' the post (nothing from
John Major or the PoW), caught up with a few cards and I sent
off £5800-odd worth of cheques.

Our journey back was comfortable. Incredible, surpassingly
beautiful light as we drove over the Moyne, and across Crask.
Several times we stopped the car and looked over the snow-
covered moors to the peaks of Loyal, Klibreck, and Hope from
the eastern side.

More and more I incline to the view that in art it is the
representation of light that ranks above all else. 'Form' is a poor
second, cubism all that. Cézanne is colour, that and light – just
a mess, really, of splodgings vaguely evocative of sans illumina-
tion. Monet, Heade, Church, the 'luminists'. And what about the
distant horizon in, e.g., the little Rousseau of the Becs[1] before
'cleaning' away, for ever, the pale lemon dividing streak between
sea and sky.

One has only to write these all down to see that it is not

---

[1] A picture owned by the Clarks.

simply a matter of going back refreshed and tackling things with vigour. The whole day, like the flat surfaces indoors, is impossibly congested. 'Discipline,' Jane says. Yes, that would help. But the sheer scale of the task may force, in the end, 'its own modification'.

1995 – so hard we must strive. (Followed, perhaps, by 1996 picking up sticks.)

Am I also going to be able to concentrate enough on the problem so as not to make 'a bad decision' of cutting back? I do have too many cars. I really can only manage three (H) classics. And while I get great pleasure from going into 'the smart part' at Saltwood will it ever really be used again? There is masses and masses of wealth scattered here. There, too, one can draw up a retrenchment plan, a *cuvée privée*. But, of course, once the Mains is stripped, or demi–stripped, it could never really be filled again.

Later

This had come to me very forcibly the previous day. Quite late in the afternoon I took the old Volvo to Whales Corner and walked along the shoreline and past Grassy Knoll. Jane I left on the long strand searching for seashells and watched slate blues and blacks and pinkish backlighting; as the storm clouds changed, by the minute, I did reflect a little. I am excluded now, I suppose, from political prospect (though, endearingly, James told us on the last night that, demi–in–his cups, Tip-book said that he wanted to go into politics). While I am in Scotland I wanted to stay there, to go *en retraite* after this year, last 'stint' with the *Mail on Sunday*. Timing just about right, I suppose, as by then either we will be 'picking up' or the Tories will be doomed for ever. This year, too, I should be cleared by Scott, and so will, in the autumn, demand my dues (or perhaps better leave it until November/ January though this could be tricky as JM could be ousted in November). But once I am back here, read my mail – all favourable – the papers, talk to Dobbie and Soames, I feel I still have a lot of activity left.

Saltwood   *New Year's Eve*

More and more I am convinced that the most precious com-
modity in the world is TIME (was it not the clip of my father
comparing himself to the White Rabbit perpetually looking at
his watch that moved me to tears in Michael Cockerell's film?).

Today I just squandered it. The 'piece' for the *M on S* (written
yesterday and looking quite good on galley, although I had my
doubts about it) was done, and I repaired to the Garden House
to do my correspondence. Only managed three letters – one of
them completely unnecessary and will make bad feeling, on
Jeffrey Archer's personal number plate to the *Guardian*,[1] and still
not typed up the new setup for BB. Was in a vile mood, no food
except a digestive biscuit and two cups of Darjeeling at 7.30.
Rotten post, and the Honours list.

It really is too much, Hosker (Treasury solicitor who 'allowed'
– sic – certain documents for the Matrix trial – admitted it to
Scott) got a knighthood.[2] Also Rocco F[orte].[3] The line-up of
the 'businessmen' looked even lower, scruffier and more venal
than the politicians. I have simply been bypassed. And once
'bypassed' it is virtually impossible to get 'streamed' again. Why?
Scott the excuse, of course, but when I am 'cleared' (a nice
Christmas card from C Muttukumaru cheered me up) it will be
too late. The excuse will be my 'private life' – even though that
was known to the Cabinet Secretary and the PM before I was
appointed to the Government.[4]

[1] The *Guardian* diary ran a competition when Archer crashed his car. The number
plate was blanked out in the photograph and readers were asked for suggestions.
AC produced a cutting, from the *Glasgow Herald*, with the original number plate
clearly visible. He also disclosed a second Archer number plate, a 'low-digit Exeter
registration … at present (one assumes) on a retention certificate'. The *Guardian*
diarist made AC runner-up.

[2] Gerald Hosker, Solicitor to the Department of Trade and Industry (hence his involvement over the Matrix Churchill matter) 1987–92; then Procurator General, Treasury
Solicitor and Queen's Proctor.

[3] Rocco Forte had risen in the eponymous restaurant and hotel chain founded by
his father, Lord (Charles) Forte, whom he succeeded as chairman in 1992.

[4] See *Diaries*, 24 June 1983.

I didn't get back here until 1.30 and then ravenously ate some
macaroni cheese and chutney. Slept (for 15 minutes) in my chair
then collected the battery charger thinking I would try and start
the Porsche. Went to the archive room to collect some boxes –
the '95 boxes for categorised paper – and was diverted by some
material on Upper Terrace.[1] God! What wonderful rich stuff
there was in that house! Practically nothing left, it seems except
the Renoir jugglers (which I would sell if I could) and the great
painted Blenheim bed.

Next I went over to 'Woolletts Garage'. Totally predictably the
Porsche battery was undetachable; the spanner did not have the
room, due to the curvature of the front wing, to attach to the
terminal nut. I fiddled and fumbled for hours, it seemed, sometimes just resting with my elbows on the wing looking at it
dejectedly. Then moved sideways to try and start the Barnato
car. Pump trouble (naturally). I forgot that when I put it away
there had been some problem with the Mitsubas getting choked.
Got back here again just in time for a not very comfortable tea
perched on the edge of my chair and the fire in the Green
Room starting to smoke viciously. The photos of Christmas at
Eriboll are dreadfully revealing of me. Red-faced, thick necked,
something almost of Evelyn Waugh ('all right then, Grandad?'
Jane said). Something of Tom King and Marcus Kimball – who
was portrayed stoutly *Jorrocks* in the saddle in *The Times* yesterday. He's hung up his riding gear, poor Marcus, for ever. One
thing after another closing in on him.[2]

So it has been a very frustrating day. And this pen, which
seemed so nice, is actually foul and making my already disturbed
writing disagreeably – as opposed to codedly – illegible. I can't
remember a New Year's Eve when I have been more tense, and
frustrated and restless. What it boils down to, I suppose, is that I
am afraid of dying before I have done the things I want/need

---

[1] Upper Terrace House, Hampstead overlooking the West Heath, a post-war home
   of the Clark family.
[2] Marcus Kimball had been joint master, at varying times, of the Fitzwilliam and the
   Cottesmore Hounds.

to. Irrevocably the mathematics illustrates this. Divide the time it takes into the time left, and it 'won't go'.

Supplementary note

I've resolved not to answer the phone – at all. Just listen first to the message.

No more 'quotes'. Don't get caught by journalists.

I must get stuck into Big Book.

Last year I had the prospect of enormous tax demands, but was calm. Somehow, they were 'coped with'. This year there are the huge Lloyds-like calls on Big Red. Again I am calm, although it is only two weeks away. Why? How?

Sometimes I get so cross about the cars, the way I can never get at them. It always seems (and always will seem) as if I am 'playing' when I should be doing something more virtuous – like, today, cleaning the greenhouse windows.

But every car I think of (even the green Buick, which I am now contemplating using for the Polish rally) has a reason. Even though, if *force majeure* were to supervene I would be quite content to be left with 3 (+1).

1995

Dined with Richard Ryder at the Berkeley. He told me Churchill wanted Tommy Dugdale to succeed Margesson as Chief Whip,[1] but was 'talked out of it' – who by? It's a colossal task, to complete Big Book in the two years left. January has got off completely 'on the wrong foot' with all three 'pieces' and book reviews. Will pull in about £1500, plus £3000 from TV. But today I signed the first of the cheques for Big Red (looking identical – what's the point?) and then funked ringing Hoare's to tell them. I went back with Richard for the 10 p.m. vote so that his driver (Janet) could take me home. A strange, sad evocation as we passed all those cars double-parked on a wet night, for the first 3-liner of the New Year. First time I have seen them like that for over two years, must be nearer three. I feel older and sadder, and somewhat more convinced of the impossibility of return.

I think I have only a very short time left to live. I am desperately worried about finishing Big Book, which could/will be so good. A possible 'researcher', Graham Stewart, came down this morning.[2] I took to him almost at once; good mind, sympathetic attitude, we think alike on the main subject. Oh so lucidly and giftedly I took the entire drive from Sellindge to Albany expounding, got quite hoarse. But made a convert I suspect.

---

[1] Captain David Margesson, very much Neville Chamberlain's man; Churchill did not trust him. Dugdale had been Stanley Baldwin's PPS.

[2] AC was looking for a researcher to help him on *The Tories*. Graham Stewart, who studied Modern History at St Andrews University before going up to St John's College, Cambridge, was at work on his first book, eventually published as *Burying Caesar: Churchill, Chamberlain and the Battle for the Tory Party*.

Saltwood kitchen   *Saturday, 11 February*

How delicious is 'the quiet hour'. There are few more agreeable
(intellectual) conditions than a pot of Indian tea, a nice pen
(earlier I was fussed because I could only find a biro) and a blank
page. I find it impossible to do this if first I sometimes glance at
a newspaper, so it is critical to start before the papers can have
arrived (and that is why the entries are so much smoother, and
better written, in Scotland).

I had lunched with Alastair G[oodlad].[1] Something especially
pleasing about entering Sibyl's house at lunch-time − although
of course while remembering the geography I never (or did I
once?) came as a guest in my own right.[2]

I thought the lunch went, on the whole, 'well'. Clockwise
from my left: Soames − lovely as always and jollily responsive
though fussed about his diabetes so that he dieted spastically and
ascetically (though without, it seemed, any effect on his weight).
Magnus, nice quiet intelligent son of Alastair. Charles Moore,
came in late, not much to say for himself − but of course never
good at mixing it in a shouting chorus. Richard R[yder], looking amazingly young ('on work experience', as Jane says), Jonathan
A[itken] whom stupidly I allowed to half cut me upstairs and
with whom there is now a clear froideur. Paul Johnson, now
senior, and permanently cross.[3] Alastair benign and alert. Robert
C[ranborne] − also unchanged, lovely company. Then between
me and Robert, Tristan [Garel-Jones].

What is it about Tristan that now makes him something of a
bore? I suppose that once he was removed from the epicentre of
power and intrigue his *raison d'être* disappeared and all that was

---

[1] Alastair Goodlad, MP for Eddisbury since 1983 (Northwich February 1974–83);
a former Whip, he had been a Foreign Office Minister since 1992.

[2] Sibyl Colefax had lived at Argyll House, King's Road, Chelsea until the death of
her husband, Sir Arthur Colefax. She moved to 19 Lord North Street, off Smith
Square, Westminster, where she entertained famously. Given its location, it was a
particularly desirable London home for a Member of Parliament.

[3] Paul Johnson, historian (*The Birth of the Modern: World Society 1815–30*) and
former editor of the *New Statesman*, whose political views had moved to the right.

left was the camouflage. So he's now simply a kind of raconteur, almost down to the '… and do you remember when …?' level. T said he never went into the House, except to vote, now. 'You'd hate the tearoom Al, not a single person you'd want to sit down with.' (Misunderstanding completely, of course, why I want to get back in – which is to motivate and galvanise those boys who are leaderless and unsettled.)

That evening T rang me at my desk in GH. Earlier, talking to Jane, he had said, 'Al's his own worst enemy; people say "how can you like that awful man?"; there never was any chance of him getting to the Lords.'

Speaking to me he said he was going to have 'that' luck himself – it was 'magic', etc etc (a crash gymkhana). But then, rather irritatingly went on to try and commiserate – 'don't repine', all that. Made it pretty clear that I had no hope of getting into the Lords – or anything else (quite different from talk of 'condign recognition' and 'we must find a perch for Al' in 1992).

When I got up to leave no one followed me out (the 'journalists' had already gone; much later I began to suspect that they had been discussing me/real stuff '… now that the journalists had gone').

Continued Sunday, 12 February
This was confirmed by today's *Sunday Telegraph*, which led off with a spastic item 'Alan Clark to "mourn" Jill Phipps', clearly 'placed' at behest of Aitken/ G-J (or was Moore acting on his own behalf?).[1] Frightfully depressing, somehow. This endless search for the *disreputable* angle. I just want to hide. A *Daily Express* reporter rang, and I tried to give her reasonable and measured answers. I could sense her getting impatient. 'Haven't

---

[1] Jill Phipps, a 31-year-old mother, was a member of the campaign protesting against what she – and many others – saw as the cruelty of the export from Britain of live veal calves to the Continent, a campaign AC actively supported. A fortnight before she had died after being run over by a cattle truck that she and other demonstrators were trying to prevent from entering Coventry airport. Many in the Conservative Party disapproved. In May AC reports a call from Tristan Garel-Jones saying he was being considered a 'loony' for his animal rights activities.

you left it rather late to talk to Jill Phipps's mother?' etc. So I am very tired, very depressed, very beset by 'engagements' and demands – and by shortage of money, too; I can't settle the car cull. I caught sight of myself in the window of Andrew's jeep this afternoon. I am puffy and lined. Last empty week coming up and I will show discipline, by (a) not drinking, (b) taking a walk (Gossie or M-way) each day.

I wish I didn't even have to do the column. I'd rather pay back my advance to Weidenfeld,[1] clear the debts and be a recluse (I wish, too, that I could get even with my 'friends'. What debt do I have (sic) from them, anyway? No recognition – companionship of any kind – just kicked out).

Tuesday, 14 February

Back from a long day (though the journey was smooth) to Coventry to Jill Phipps's funeral. I had hoped for a pilgrimage, a Mecca, a mullah's funeral. But although the Cathedral was respectfully full, it was nothing like at capacity. The Sutherland altarpiece is incredible, magnificent, and one of the most impressive works of art I have ever seen. The size of Saltwood towers inner façade, perhaps even a bit under. The lady priest (deaconess?) was lovely, attractive and with a lovely clear voice, looked not unlike Presiley Baxendale. The service, with some nice blessings, none too awful in even the new English – and then an address, quite an ordeal for him, I suppose, by 'Justin' thingummy. (Jill, who clearly was attractive, was hop-picking in Kent four years ago!)

---

[1] AC was annoyed that his agents, Peters, Fraser & Dunlop, were representing his brother Colin for his diary, *The Prince, the Showgirl and Me*, and that to compound matters Weidenfeld & Nicolson had offered to publish. In the end it was published by HarperCollins.

Wednesday, 15 February

Splitting headache and paralysed by paper pressure.

When it gets to a certain level you can't start, dread starting on account of what it may disclose. An example, the KGV garage doors ('workshop') were left open about a week ago. Since then it has rained every single day and blows viciously. I've just left them open. Why not shut them? Why not, indeed?

I woke this morning and realised that at my next birthday I will be 67. Now that figure, actually, is OLD. 62 (say) seems quite cheeky and youthful. Not only is time running out, but I am not using what I've got left properly.

I *must* clear the decks for Big Book.

Finance and Trusts need attention (money-raising and cars selling).

On the way downstairs teeny Tom, so game and bonny, foolishly fell on the corner flight and squeaked. He just crouched there paralysed, like a praying mantis. I had to carry him into the yard, where he could pee (because couldn't balance), later he slunk back into the 'kennel' cubby in the kitchen. Later he climbed out of it (while we were dressing) and rallied and then sat by the Aga.

I carried him down for the 'w' and he just managed two Thompson blobbets on the first bunch of snowdrops.

Sunday, 19 February

On Friday the little yellow cockatiel died. Poisoned by that sprouting seed-corn which I had brought in from the silage dump by the level crossing and put in their cage. She was so bonny and curious and alive. I felt awful. The grey one is going to die tonight, I know. He is just a few days behind her, being more cautious and discreet. I talked to him, softly. Told him that he was going to the rainforests where there would be sunlight and warm and shoots and leaves and roots that would keep him

well and happy. I am, to my surprise, even sadder about him –
because it was he who found us; was frightened by the dogs and
then returned, of his own accord, to the yard. Had a miserable
time in a tiny cage, then came into his own in the big cage,
spread his wings so beautifully at breakfast time and particularly
enjoyed the apple stump with its many perches.

My tongue is sore on one side and I am tired and low.

Saltwood   *Wednesday, 22 February*

In London yesterday. We went to the *Guardian* party for Richard
Norton-Taylor's book on Scott,[1] then to the National Gallery
to see our little Zurbaran[2] hanging extremely well besides the
other Zurbaran which was very shiny and restored. The
following morning I found myself having a kind of catharsis.
The Conservative Party is doomed unless it really pulls itself
together. This faffing around, making jokes at Party audiences
saying it's all going to be all right when the economy picks up
etc, is not on any longer. I'm going to switch my tack to we have
to face facts, take risks. The Party can no longer delude itself.

By chance that lunchtime Roger Scruton[3] came round – in
complete agreement, wants to start a 'group' to meet regularly. I
was mildly irritated about an article by Henry Porter (I'm still
waiting to get even with him) about the 'young historians' – also
'the group' – Andrew Roberts, d'Ancona[4] etc. Nucleus of the
'Resurgent right'. But all these people are waiting for the defeat
revamp afterwards. Useless. We must try and do it now.

---

[1] *Knee Deep in Dishonour: the Scott Report and Its Aftermath* by Richard Norton-
Taylor, Mark Lloyd and Stephen Cook.
[2] A still life, *A Cup of Water and a Rose on a Silver Plate* by the Spanish Baroque
painter Francisco de Zurbarán, 1598–1664.
[3] Roger Scruton, writer and philosopher, Professor of Philosophy at Boston University,
Mass., since 1992; a tenant of the Clarks, using the attic above B5, Albany.
[4] Matthew D'Ancona, assistant editor, *The Times*.

Henrietta Royle rang. Lately I have – I just don't know why – been thinking about Chelsea as being the ideal constituency.[1] Albany resident, garden parties at Saltwood, safest seat in the country, etc. She told me that they had booked the meeting for Chelsea HQ and were advertising it in the Chelsea newsletter! Suddenly I thought – could this be a sign? I know Chelsea are considering their vacancy, how far have they got? I don't want to know. All I do know is that – for all my fatigue and listlessness at intervals when surrounded (as now) by paper I am still driven. I just feel that something may happen. After speaking to Henrietta I popped over to the Great Hall and said a prayer at the long table where I composed my speech for the Sutton selection twenty-three years ago.

Senator Dole, I'm glad to see, is the leading character for the Presidential Election in two years' time and he is already 71.[2]

Albany   *Friday, 24 February*

Woke at 3 a.m., figures going through my head. My debts are £350,000 (Lloyds[3]), this, after a bit, made me tinkle. Couldn't get back to sleep and waiting for alarm, set for 5 a.m., so as to allow me to 'beat the traffic', get to Christie's viewing of the 'model' sale (James wanted me to go) and then Bertrand (sic) Arbeid. Thrashed, and 'took cover' for a bit, but no use (why am I going to a sale when I can't even write a cheque for the Heal's repairs to the mattress?). 'It's the giant sell-off,' I said to darling

---

[1] Following boundary revisions Chelsea (MP – Nicholas Scott) and Kensington (MP – Dudley Fishburn) were merging to become Kensington and Chelsea. A safe Conservative seat by any standards, the selection of its new candidate guaranteed a seat in the Commons at the next general election.

[2] Senator Robert Dole, Republican Senator (Kansas) since 1968, had just become Leader of the United States Senate, as well as a contender for the Republican presidential nomination.

[3] AC was not a Lloyd's 'name', but often used the analogy when discussing his financial situation.

Jane. She doesn't worry about debt any longer (or at least doesn't mention it), she doesn't do the correspondence. Yesterday Mrs Frowd[1] told her she had potential 'heart' trouble. So unlikely, but her grandmother, father and mother all did.

Went into the larder to get some organic digestives for my coffee and saw all those lovely entries on the doors. So happy and tranquil: 'Sir Sydney Cockerell[2] died peacefully in his house' etc. Might transfer them to the great ledger and notes with inventory.

Albany   *Thursday, 2 March*

(One of the few advances in recent months is that I have at last got into the habit of writing my 'a's' more legibly.[3])

I am still extremely rattledly congested with tasks. I ought, for example, to be presenting a beautifully polished, balanced paper to the Staff College this morning. But I only started it on Tuesday night – set it out in skeletal form, will have to infill verbally. Partly, I suppose, it is an aversion. Why was I not Secretary of State? Partly because the subject is uncomfortable, at least in its conclusions, but largely because I have so much to do that the system has become less efficient. I glaze over, can't prepare, defer until the blinding urgency of 'the last minute'.

I'm lunching with Portillo on Monday (every day next week is pre-empted). I'm slightly getting cold feet about the address to Chelsea.

---

[1] Mrs Cindy Frowd, Hythe reflexologist.
[2] All the Saltwood cockerels were named after Sir Sydney Cockerell (1867–1962), museum director and bibliophile.
[3] Sadly for his editor, it didn't last.

Saltwood kitchen a.m.   *Saturday, 4 March*

I've been waking early; this morning 4.30-ish and nagged –
though not nearly as much as (perhaps) the situation warrants –
by total exhaustion now of liquidity. Wasn't even able to pay the
quarterly interest charges on the various overdrafts – all, at their
different banks, at the limit. I was a success at Camberley. Almost
at the point of frivolity, but not.

Saltwood   *EMT, Friday, 10 March*

Last night dined with Andrew Roberts. Expensive flat in Cadogan
Gardens, quite nicely fitted out with lovely library shelves. The
Hamiltons (Neil)[1] – he a little pinched and nervous; she very bossy
and almost Miss Newman[2] disapproving. That evening a somewhat unguarded interview by Rory Knight-Bruce in the *Standard*
in which they said they were 'dining with Alan and Jane Clark'
(demi-boring for Andrew and Camilla) and Christine H then
went on to say, 'I do wish Jane Clark would do a bit more to stick
up for herself.' Andrew's neat little fiancée [Camilla] is Welsh
(it turns out) and her mother also. Attractive, both of them.
Conversation didn't quite mesh, somehow, at dinner. Disparate,
and too many guffaws. But I had a pleasing pic with Andrew in
the library afterwards. Much journalistic gossip. Not many people
seem to get more than £100 a year. A.A.Gill was mentioned.
Apparently I am being considered as literary editor of the *Sunday
Times*. Would I like this? Yes, for a five-year contract I suppose. But
Big Book must not suffer any longer.
    The night before I had been to Eton. Distorted, at least in its

---

[1] Neil Hamilton, MP for Tatton since 1983, a junior Trade Minister, 1992–94, and
   his wife Christine. Hamilton had issued a writ against the *Guardian*, who in
   October 1994 had alleged that he (and a second Tory junior Minister, Tim Smith)
   had taken money to ask questions on behalf of a lobbying company.
[2] Miss Newman, a Clark family governess.

approaches, by traffic. And seeming much smaller, everything
closer together. The Provost, Acland,[1] was his usual diplomatic
self, benign, but reserved. The boys polite and effete. 'Thank you
for being so entertaining' said one of the wives. I was tired, and
couldn't drink. Just adequate, I hope. The names preceding me
in the book were Aitken and Jeffrey Archer! Earlier I had done
a teeny home movie on 'Eton during the war', masterminded
by a boy/beak team. And was disconcerted at how thin were my
memory and recollections.

Saltwood   *Sunday, 12 March*

The sunshine hot on one's face for the first time this year.
'Edward' came down from Danny [Mews], and the Ferrari 340
Mexico started at once. We all drove it, and later pitted it against
the C-type. Pleasing, and a hint of the *douceur de vivre* of the old
Lartigue album. It went magnificently, handled uncomfortably
(transverse-leaf front suspension). When really pressed, over 5.8
or so, it belched smoke, and this also came into the cabin. But
when I went in the dear 'C' – so smooth, flexible and balanced
– I realise how dangerous 340 actually is.

Tip and Sarah went off, having bought some tropical finches
at the garden centre. Next week Sarah is going to Thailand and
Oman on her own. She is a character. They are a modern
couple. While James and Julie, really, are old-fashioned. Much
more like Jane and me.

It all reminds me of what is to happen to Saltwood, and the
family Trust. We are in limbo, until the grandchildren are born. I
still feel ok, in some ways. But moving about this morning at
midday I felt rather old and feeble. Was I 'dying' for a drink? I
certainly feel much better with the first two glasses of M. Goisot.

---

[1] Sir Antony Acland, diplomat (Head of the Diplomatic Service 1982–86; Ambassador
to Washington, 1986–91) before becoming Provost of Eton in 1991.

It's strange this condition I'm in. It is almost as if I am sedated. Five years like this (72), eight with the grandchildren (80) and five or whatever God gives me I'm a sage. Just feasible.

I am almost drinking too much at the moment. Not quite, but almost. But we have given up sweets for Lent.

Saltwood   *Tuesday, 21 March*

Occupied myself with an exchange of correspondence with Max Hastings over Scott (useful to have heard from him that the Prime Minister was trying to persuade people to accept me as a 'burnt offering'). I tried my hand at composing a letter to the PM which combined grievance of not getting any 'recognition' with veiled menace at what Max had told me of any role I might play in the coming leadership and General Election. All may be altered of course as there is talk – yet again – of Heseltine taking over in a snap poll. But when? Unless JM stands down voluntarily it would mean calling it in December, which just not likely.

This morning a row with Jane at breakfast as the tablecloth had been laid over crumbs. The one thing I can't bear are 'previous' crumbs on a table when you sit down to a meal, even in Zermatt this upsets me.

Looking at how teeny this writing is – and compare it with the clear, balanced hand when I was at Shore Cottage.

Albany   *Tuesday, 28 March*

Drove up in the Old Ministerial, very flat and quiet.

Walked along Whitehall, noting the new smart gates outside the MoD, past the 'new' building entrance, an official car was coming out of New Palace Yard.

At St Stephen's entrance I 'shot' the queue and a policeman called out, then recognised me and was amiable. The pretty policewoman ditto, and asked me to take my cap off. I walked up, past the benches noting that the tiles have degenerated even more, like the hall at Chenonceau; the first time I was in that corridor, I suppose, was with Malcolm McCorquodale[1] – thought it all so boring. It was agony. I wanted to tinkle, thought how easy it would be to dodge left into the one at the end of the Members' cloakroom – MEMBERS ONLY. Standing in the Central Lobby I watched MPs scuttling across to meet 'delegates' whom they had kept waiting – 'so sorry', 'hul-lo' etc etc. Before I turned into the gate I had briefly fantasised about slyly going in that way after winning the by-election. I was half in a dream, half awake.

Met up with Frank Pakenham, lunched with him and Fr. Seed.[2] I don't wholly dismiss all that, and will read Newman over Good Friday.

I still cannot wholly surrender. ACHAB – and I know if I really asked, *really* asked, it would happen. Is it that I am afraid of the price?

Saltwood   *EMT, Sunday, 2 April*

I can't really face the idea of turning back the clock, 'nursing a constituency' etc etc. Yet, curiously, I don't pine for the Lords now. It's the death sentence (deferred), the nailing down of the coffin lid. From then the next step really is the grave.

---

[1] Malcolm McCorquodale (1901–1971), created Baron 1955, later chairman of McCorquodale & Co., printers, a National Conservative MP pre-war and MP for Epsom, 1947–55.
[2] Frank Pakenham, former Labour Minister, in his ninetieth year, who succeeded his brother as 7th Earl of Longford in 1961. Father Michael Seed, Roman Catholic priest, credited with a number of high-profile conversions to the Catholic faith.

Garden House   *Tuesday, 11 April*

Yesterday I was frantic with frustration and pressure and then, on top of it all (sic) I was phoned to ask if I would do a leader-page piece.

'How much?' – 'Pound a word.'

I laughed. 'Not nearly enough.'

'How much do you want?' – 'Two.'

'Done.'

So all afternoon I was locked into the little white computer room. Not sure I got the tone quite right, and *eleven* phone calls of different kinds including a lady (Jane Gordon (?)) doing an article on mid-life crisis ('I've been enjoying one for the last 40 years,' I said) and then, portentously, Graham Stewart, to talk about his installation in June. So I was an hour late filing, and walked out of here leaving the French windows open all night.

All based on my brief crack on the *Today* programme. *Today* is like *Breakfast with Frost* – everyone listens to it. I said that whether a government of celibates and train-spotters would be any different from what we've got ... I didn't know.

In the meantime Jonathan Aitken went demi-bonkers and staged a press conference in Central Office.[1] Certain fatal (*Hello*-type) cliché 'the fight-back starts here ...' etc.

On the 'early evening news' I saw that Senator Dole had got the Republican nomination – at the age of 71. This cheered me up immensely. A classic example of ACHAB. All (sic) I need is, somehow, to get back into the Commons. The Lords I'm no longer really bothered about.

I walked down to the Long Garage; too late to go for a drive,

---

[1] Jonathan Aitken was yet another Conservative involved in 'sleaze' allegations. He was suing the *Guardian* for defamation over their allegations of improper commercial relationships while Minister for Defence Procurement. His statement included a phrase which would enter modern dictionaries of quotations: 'If it falls to me to start a fight to cut out the cancer of bent and twisted journalism in our country with the simple sword of truth and the trusty shield of British fair play, so be it. I am ready for the fight. The fight against falsehood and those who peddle it. My fight begins today.'

something drew me to look on the side towards the rowan and I wondered if – *if* – I could call on God for a miracle. The moon was almost obscured but I waited, it got virtually invisible, then quite rapidly cleared and shone metallically bright. Strange, how mercurial my miracle can be, still.

Easter Monday, 17 April

How I long for solitude and tranquillity! This must be one of the most pressured Easters ever – and yet I am 67 and 'retired'.

We did the whole lawn yesterday. Tomorrow night I set off for Eriboll with sundries in the Discovery (sit-down mower, enamel sign, iron chandeliers for the chapel, etc) on probably the last Motorail journey ever.[1]

Monday, 24 April

How am I ever going to get out of this?

I can buy 'space' I suppose, by letting the Degas[2] go. But as I said to Jane late afternoon it's really Saltwood – the whole ethos of the great curtained room almost unchanged into which I can wander, and reflect, go back 20-30-40 years and play the piano. I have never left the Music Room without feeling stronger. And I remember the pain of selling the bronze (so fortunately recaptured).[3]

But time roars past, an absolute mill-race. There is far more to do; I am far more behind than when I was a Minister. Yesterday evening I had a full attack of Sunday evening blues. Something

---

[1] The Motorail service from London to Inverness was being withdrawn.

[2] *Femme s'épongeant le dos* (see March 1991).

[3] The dancer bronze (also by Degas) was sold and then bought back.

I swore I would never get again once I had 'stood down'. This great block of paperwork I have to tackle before I can 'stand back'.

EMT, Tuesday, 25 April

Many entries at the moment – indicating unsettlement.

I am most heavy-hearted at losing the Degas. Go up and look at her often, at different times of the day – and last evening sat there, on the facing sofa for quite a while talking to Jane. Jane is 'definitely uneasy' about it. But is it not the practical solution? We can't really 'freeze' everything – Mask, Zurbaran, Moores[1] (cars, 'C' and Big Red etc etc). That would be so unbalanced. And to make up the cash from lesser items would involve 'stripping' (which both boys have objected to and warned against) to a far greater degree. But now, just as I notice and remember the hip of the dancer only in Crowe's office, I notice so many extra colours in the whole picture, that reddish around the basin; shadow on towel?

Sunday, 30 April

Yesterday it was pressure, pressure. Finishing the 'piece' (not a very successful one on Ashdown) and clearing up for the Americans (coming today) and 'Little' and – 'Littler' – his partner.[2] They'd hardly been in the place five minutes before I wanted to say to Jane 'these guys are just a couple of bull-shitters'. 'Little' probed me about the Degas, which I had originally mentioned no more than in passing as the reason for

---

[1] Kenneth Clark and Henry Moore were friends, and the Clarks had a number of Moore's works.

[2] Two London dealers.

trying to sell the 'Coptic stuff'.[1] He said he could get his 'big client' straight on to the case, wouldn't hesitate. Lyingly said I had been guaranteed £800, wouldn't, couldn't deal under 1.5. They prowled about, 'Littler' peering at everything – Burne-Jones Angel, 'torchères' in the Great Hall (known fakes) up a ladder to look at the Alexander the Great tapestry etc. Afterwards there was a long courtesy recital of travellers tales ('3-card trick', as Jane pleasingly called them), half Jewish, half just straight Mews.

Saffria, 'Charles Cates' (who he?), Lord Wimborne, of getting … 'my big client' Saffria again (who strangely put 'Little's' back up by walking into the showroom and saying to 'Littler', 'I like you, we can work together'). 'I can think of worse things he might have said,' I suggested and Jane giggled, but they didn't. This went on for too long and was too circular. A cursory look at the carpets, clearly they didn't want them. 'A rug like this, Alan, would be 70-90-100 if it was in good condition.' 'Surely in this condition it would be 35 then?' I wanted to say, but didn't. Off they drove. Later the phone started ringing. We had been working all afternoon in the Great Hall and were exhaustedly lying low in the Green Room, left it to the machine. Hung up a few times then finally 'Little' soft-spoken with a message to ring a number (which I had already checked out on 1471). His 'client' – I can't believe this – is ready to buy the picture unseen. But was it in the book? Jane and I had a long, but unsuccessful time, rooting about in the library and various sources of books including the package I removed from the Garden House. Never mind, an 'Art Critic' called Sylvester (never heard of him)[2] was coming down *today* at 2 p.m. – naturally coinciding with the US visit – to look at it. Nothing will come of this, because he will spot the two worm holes, and all rich people bother about is 'condition'. But all quite fun.

---

[1] Framed tapestry fragments.
[2] The art interests of AC and David Sylvester obviously didn't coincide. Sylvester's expertise included Moore, Magritte, Bacon, Spencer and Giacometti.

Saltwood   *EMT Friday, 5 May*

During the day I had been constantly recognised and hailed as I walked about London; sat in café in Marylebone Road waiting for the GLR programme and a blonde appeared, smiled, walked on; a 'gay' got into a 'boo-hoo-I've-had-the-sack, too' conversation (sat while they waited, at my table). An American woman came up and said 'you don't know how much we admire you…'; going back up the street a Rasta, a Brian Classic lookalike, AN Other etc all acknowledge me. Earlier a mulatto lady in jeans.

I walked to the Beefsteak, sat next to little Hague.[1] Cagey, like all people who have a great future ahead of them … Mark Lennox-Boyd[2] came round at the end of the meal and said that 'Alison Young' was working for him.

I sit here, on a lovely fine still May morning; but I funk ringing Henrietta Royle and asking if Chelsea has yet 'chosen'.

The carpetsellers, after much phoned bull-shitting put in a pointless demand – for the Christie's guarantee – the 'client' obviously thrashing around for a way out. I said piss off and Christie's, a week later, are collecting it. But at least we are through the psychological hurdle of selling it and Jane has made that incredible, inspired copy.[3] I will now attempt to force the pace and continue with cash-raising: Broomhayes, R Cont, SS100, possibly Zurbaran for $1m with Feigin.[4]

---

[1] William Hague, MP for Richmond, Yorks, since February 1989; Social Security and Disabled People Minister since 1994.

[2] Sir Mark Lennox-Boyd, MP for Morecambe and Lunesdale since 1983 (Morecambe and Lonsdale 1979–83).

[3] Jane Clark, an accomplished painter, had never previously worked in pastels. She measured the picture, studied what she thought it might have been painted on, the nearest (some brown laundry paper), and set to work. Looking back she says she was inspired. Her reproduction has fooled experts. She did though refuse to replicate Degas's signature. AC marvelled at what Jane had done: 'her brilliant, spooky translation' (27 May 1995); 'Jane's miraculous substitution' (19 September 1995).

[4] An American art dealer and friend, Richard Feigin.

Garden House   *Monday, 8 May*

Frightfully tired and glazed. Almost last engagement this
evening – colossal longueurs at the Savoy for the AT&T book
award. That £5000 fee, which looked so tempting has actually
worked out at about £20 per hour – less than a 'daily' in a posh
bit of Hampstead what with reading 150 books, four judges'
meetings, general hassle and a 5-hour award ceremony.[1]

Yesterday in absolute despair. Randyish, so sexual frustration
and self-pity mingled as I talked to myself a great deal –
whingeingly. Fiddled with the 'Webb' [mower] in the morning.
But really no achievement until interrupted by the answer-
phone p.m. and a Count (nearly – a Duc in fact – de Magenta)
(which I thought a bogus, or trade name) to deliver the wine I
had ordered. He was handsome, distinguished, beautiful manners
as only the very grand French have, but tottery. His wife, I
couldn't at first believe it was his wife, was at least 45 years
younger. English, but quite attractive. He expressed deferential
curiosity, hovered around the Barbican gates. The dogs, demi-
baleful, impeded progress. 'Go round behind me,' I said, legs
astride them both and holding their neck scruffs.

Jane arrived and called the dogs and I put-putted (it's on one
cylinder at the moment) them both sitting on the Mehari with
all the wine; she hesitated on the slope up to the Bailey gates.
Showed them the Great Library. At very end he produced his
own 'brochure'. The moated Château de Sully, with the largest
Renaissance courtyard in Europe! For some reason this cheered
me up, and I drank some of his wine at supper – quite delicious
– Montrachet-ish, and I was drinking from the chef's bottle.

We went up to the battlements for the VE-day service, and I
cast my mind back, thinking that 50 years ago I did assume that
I would be the Prime Minister. Expected it.

---

[1] The £25,000 award went to Mark Hudson for *Coming Back Brockens*.

Saltwood   *Friday, 26 May*

Will the Tories lose? Now it really feels as if they might be going to; I would still like to be there, if only to play a part in the succession. An elder statesman in the corridors (but *not* in the Shadow Cabinet). But has the opportunity finally gone for 'this is the way that Britain can recover her former greatness; and I am the person to do it'? Read this morning at EMT for the first time for many years Rauschning, and where I marked it.[1] Germany was perfectly structured for Hitler, of course, who simply used the old Freikorps cadre to impose compliance on an essentially capitalist structure. Quite different from Russia where communism depended on a huge urban/agricultural proletariat and all its latent waste and incompetence.

All v lonely the thought of these dreadful Islingtonians getting in. (I was more put out than I care to admit by little Juliet Stevenson[2] being nasty about me and my book, in that special implacably humourless way that the PC adopt.)

But what do we offer as an alternative? Mawhinney?[3] And a vast army (soon rapidly to disintegrate) of template PR specialisation and 'researchers' without substance and conviction of any kind; or commitment save to their own self-advancement.

Can anything happen? I need to retreat, and think uninterruptedly for a little.[4]

---

[1] Herman Rauschning, author of *Hitler Speaks*.

[2] Juliet Stevenson, actress (*Les Liaisons Dangereuses, Death and the Maiden* etc).

[3] Brian Mawhinney, MP for Peterborough since 1979, Conservative Party chairman since 1995.

[4] On the next page AC has started a draft of a letter to John Major, which begins: 'Dear PM: I haven't written for ages, and I feel you must need this explanation of the access to which Privy Counsellors are allowed. I am now, for the first time, just a little bit worried about your safety …'

Thursday, 1 June

Ted Heath[1] spoke in the Bosnia debate last night. His voice now rich (I said). Jane: 'no, it's gone.' Voice timbre is so indicative. My own is at its peak; will decline, I suppose in my seventies. Seventy-five is when it goes off, the last thing really except for sight.

MFS, Great Hall   *Wednesday, 7 June*

On 27 May (less than two weeks ago) I said that I needed a sign. Three days later, or so, Nick Scott 'crushed' a pushchair when reversing his car after a 'party' in his constituency, then shambled off 'to a friend's house', but was pursued, breathalysed positive, and arrested.[2]

Well, of course, for some reason (I forget its origins), perhaps the Henrietta Royle initiative, the agent's own invitation to speak next Monday at their 'garden party', I have had my eye on Chelsea for these last months.

Took a cab, to Chelsea, ostensibly (sic) to talk to the agent about arrangements for Monday. On the way the cabman – who had shown no sign of recognition – chatted.

Self: 'Fucking King's Road always blocked; half these fucking people ought to be at work' etc.

He got going on the Tory Party: 'John Major all right, but what he wants is a bit of panache (pronounced 'panarsh'). No style, too apologetic' etc etc.

---

[1] Sir Edward Heath, Father of the House, MP for variously titled Bexley constituencies since 1950, Prime Minister 1970–74. He and AC had not always been on the best of terms.

[2] Nicholas Scott had been MP for Chelsea since October 1974 (Paddington South 1966–February 1974); his career in government had culminated in seven years as Minister of State at DHSS (latterly Social Services). The episode AC refers to led to a series of cliff-hanging reselection and selection processes over the next eighteen months.

'Well,' I said, 'who do you fancy?'

'Do you really want me to tell you?'

'Yes.'

'I'm a bit embarrassed ...'

'Oh, really? Go on.'

'You.'

It was a real sign. He was serious and I was serious.

I spoke to Tip on the phone this morning.[1] He was serious, said huge numbers wanted me, 'scaffolders etc, as well as upper classes'.[2] I went for a walk and my fantasy developed, even down to choosing the government, the first night in Scotland: 'You've a PM and a Chancellor who are Scots – I doubt if you'd get better than that even with full independence.'[3]

As I walked around the huge rape-oil field opposite to Hobbs's farm, I noticed this very difficult wadi that protected Summerhouse Hill. If the entire Luft Jagl Division, all their Ju52s, had regrouped after Eban Emael, landed on the dunes behind Folkestone *as Dietrich promised*, we'd have gone. Illustrated how quick a roll will work if you take every opportunity as it comes up.

But (I explained the whole thing in a backgammon illustration to Tip) I must throw 4×4 to get any pair 'free'; then $3 + 1$ to imprison his sole straggler; then 5×5 twice to get ahead on the runner.

But I almost half know that, if I allow myself to become possessed, submit, it can't work. Exhilarating, really. I took out Wolf's portrait,[4] and put it back in its place. First time since leaving Parliament.

---

[1] Andrew and Sarah Clark were living in the constituency.

[2] Elsewhere AC recorded a constituency big-wig asking, 'where is the Wellington?' AC mused, 'Something in his manner made me think he wanted me to say, "it's me"; or he wanted to say, "why don't you do it?" I didn't answer.'

[3] On the opposite page of the journal, in very faint pencil, AC picked his government: 'OUT – Hurd, Clarke, Howard. IN – Owen, Rifkind, Mayhew ... Eric Forth, S of S Scotland.'

[4] AC kept a signed portrait of Adolf Hitler (Wolf) in the Saltwood safe.

MFS GH   *Thursday, 8 June*

Yesterday was fantasy, euphoria. Today plunged into gloom, apprehension and accidie. At EMT Jane drew attention to a lesion on my left shin, and lower leg, about 23 mm across, brownish, circular and sandpapery rough and v slightly raised. Not 'angry', no 'rolled-up' edge. Not (yet) a melanoma as too pale. Could it be a squamous. Very depressed and drained over this. 'Needs watching' was the verdict, so I watched it the entire time.

Reading the papers later, Andrew Neil *again* on the demoralisation of the whole Tory Party – 'Michael Heseltine will be in No 10 by Christmas.'

Then the little duck, which had done so well, and is so composed and amiable, was again terrorised by the dogs – which deliberately turned round and went back while we were fitting the handle (not wholly satisfactorily repaired) to the KGV car. I thrashed them both with Hannah's collar. But I fear it can't take two goes of this. Terribly depressing. We failed with the baby blackbird, then with the duck, next with a baby jackdaw that is hanging around outside the kitchen, signalling that he 'needs help'.

Then a phone call from David Leppard of the *Sunday Times* to whom I was offensive – but discursive. God knows what he will print.

I am low, rattled and apprehensive. How things can change! But can change upwards, too, of course.

MFS GH   *Tuesday, 13 June*

Yesterday we went up to the Chelsea Garden Party. I was apprehensive; I was not fully prepared and did not like the idea of speaking out of doors in a garden off the King's Road. As we passed over Westminster Bridge I saw that canopies were out, and felt a terrible pang. I am driven, which is why I am so unsettled.

In fact the meeting was a success. The chairman introduced me as 'the most interesting politician since Lloyd George …' – to some titters (because, presumably, of Ll G's goat-like tendencies), but I was delighted. People were friendly, and appreciative (except for that strange, handsome, groomed man whom one often sees at Party conferences – is he something to do with Central Office?). A young bearded, in company with a pretty girl with bad chin – acne – and a chinless boyfriend – said to me, 'I'm not into politics at all, but that was a really good speech. It meant something to me.' Then, in spite of the intense cold there followed a number of amiable and interesting questions. Dear old Nick Scott *was* there – looking quite fit I was sorry to see – and we put on a show of camaraderie. Also that berk who was on the Swinton course with me and held up all the traffic on the M1 on the way up. 'Do you want to go back into the Commons?' he asked as were leaving. 'Yes,' I replied; and the agent – Barbara Lord, with whom we – thanks to Jane too – are by now on better terms, pricked up her ears, and sought to confirm.[1] So I need a/*the* vacancy. I know I can do it. Because if the vacancy occurs it means I am meant to do it.

Bet for a by-election in September. A blazing Conference speech, and then back in the House 'introduced' on the first day back. After that ACHAB. Half of me actually sees it as inevitable. So strange.

It blights everything else. I still write well (a good piece in today's *Independent* about Mrs T) and was calm and handsome on the *Frost* programme on Sunday (this helped to give me 'confidence' for Chelsea).

But I am totally becalmed in paperwork.

---

[1] Barbara Lord, agent to the Chelsea (and later Kensington and Chelsea) Conservatives.

MFS Gt Hall   *Wednesday, 21 June*

It is midsummer's day, and the year half gone, with nothing, really, to show for it. Except earnings just keeping pace with expenditure – the treadmill.

Last night my programme on *Myths*. Good I thought, voice excellent, particularly the VO. It clashed with fresh turbulence over the Scott leak. First the substance of the leak itself – which I rode blandly. Then it degenerated into a rumour (presumably Tristan had something to do with it) that *I* was the source of the leak. This panicked me briefly as I have lost some of the papers and anyway hadn't read them properly. However, after a lot of phoning to Mike Brunson,[1] the Tribunal staff, etc etc, I was cleared. Might even, as can sometimes be the case, have come out 'stronger'.

I am still so restless politically. Something must be going to happen, I feel. Some sign will manifest itself. So everything is still secondary to that. As a result paper worse than ever. The whole system has broken down. Will the Degas sell? I hardly care. All I want to know – PM's Questions on TV drives me frantic – is how do I get back into the Chamber?

The pool is only now filling up – but heating rapidly (already over 66°). Even the swallows, so sadly few this year, have perked up and begun to chase each other; although their dawn chatter is restless and curtailed.

MFS, GL   *Saturday, 24 June*

How I love Saltwood – for all its pressures and 'claims'. After EMT I went into the front part to wind the clocks. It is peaceful there and still quite timeless. I wonder how long the boys will

---

[1] Michael Brunson, political editor, ITN, had gained a draft extract from Sir Richard Scott's report, which appeared to implicate several ministers including AC.

maintain it, and felt a pang (I am getting these more often lately) at not being able to see my grandchildren. The Degas is coming up next week – but I am resigned to it not making its reserve (which I will come under pressure to reduce, and won't). But if it sells I will *just* be able to set up another Trust, and slip 'sideways'.

Big Book has been totally neglected since (I suppose) February.

Here I am using, in my father's old study, the far side of the Great Library, the only remotely clear flat surface in the entire complex, and the great Adam long-case clock ticks readily (one per second) as the jackdaws chatter busily and unbeknownst outside the windows.

Really my diary is my only true solace.

I am wrecked, *wrecked* by my impotence at the turn of events.

John Major has offered himself for re-election,[1] and the television shows the blue door (another blue door this time in Cowley Street) of his headquarters, people scuttling in and out. But somehow, transposed 1939 to an old 1918 shot.

Yesterday I went to Gordon Greig's funeral.[2] Sensibly choosing Big Red at the last moment so that I was 'on the phone'. Jane rang to say Douglas Hurd had resigned![3] Correspondents hanging about outside the doorway. As I arrived, though, slit-eyed David Hunt[4] said, 'You should still be in the House, Alan. Then you could put your hat "in the ring".'

---

[1] John Major resigned the leadership of the Conservative Party, immediately offering himself for re-election. This was his offensive against what he called 'a small minority in our Party' who opposed him, undermining the government and damaging the Conservative Party. 'I am not prepared to see the Party I care for laid out on the rack like this any longer.' John Redwood immediately resigned from the government and announced that he would also be a candidate.

[2] Gordon Greig, long-time political editor of the *Daily Mail*.

[3] Douglas Hurd, Foreign Secretary since 1989, had told John Major some time before of his intention to retire at the next reshuffle; he had turned 65 in March.

[4] David Hunt, MP for Wirral West since 1983 (Wirral, March 1976–83), successively Welsh and Employment Secretary, then Chancellor of the Duchy of Lancaster, 1994–95.

Earlier a man in the car park had approached me, said how much he enjoyed the TV programme. Simon Heffer said, 'you should put in for the leadership – you don't have to be an MP – just a member of the Party.' Paul Dacre[1] said, 'We'd use him, but he belongs to another paper.'

A little later Alastair Campbell said, 'Why don't you come over?' I said I might leave the Tory Party if they put in Heseltine. On the way back I stopped for petrol in the Tesco car park and a big man – demi-loony, or was he drunk? – started shouting. Unintelligibly, but on the lines of 'give you thirty bob for your car, must use a lot of petrol etc etc'. After filling my tank I walked over to him in my what-the-fuck-are-you-on-about? mode. 'I'm so sorry I can't hear what you're saying.' He shook my hand, 'You are the only Tory with any balls' etc.

Is it any wonder that I can concentrate on nothing? Over here this morning I was on the point of making my appeal. I spoke out loud to God, apologised for my frailty and hesitation, always making excuses. Soon I will. Very soon.

MFS GH   *Tuesday, 27 June*

That pleasant feeling after a giant tour (50 NADFAS from East Sussex) when Saltwood breathes easily again and everything is so hot and tranquil and summery; and the leaves and the greens are so magical.

I swam a couple of lengths in the pool now only one week full but 67°. At such a time, and in this season, the pool at Saltwood is 'one of the loveliest places in the whole world'.

But this year, perhaps, there is a pervasive nostalgia, a certain mild *courant d'air* that trails a sea change. Normally, as in previous years, it is the pre-reshuffle time. Except for my first years at DE I was not apprehensive, but anticipatory. It will be better for me

---

[1] Paul Dacre, editor of the *Daily Mail* since 1992.

than for some, and the hols lie ahead. Now there is a reshuffle
with a capital 'R' under way – and I have no part in it – except
as an extra.

Very early this morning I was on College Green, and behind
me the House so bandbox clean in its yellow sandstone – but
terra prohibita. All those other MPs, Irvine Patnick,[1] little dapper
'boyish' Alan Duncan,[2] could just walk straight in. And yet – I
am demi-lionised in the Millbank office, and a dark girl in a
tight white suit greets me. When I parked the Porsche at 7 a.m.
there in Great College Street was a stooping white-haired old
gentleman walking his dog, with a peevish expression on his
face. It was Peter Walker,[3] younger than me, the Great Hope
and Rising Star – thwarted and done down by Margaret (one
of her – not few – personal mini-achievements). 'Good day,
Peter,' I shouted. He mumbled. 'Enjoying it all?' He didn't
respond.

The previous night I had dined with Gill Shephard at
Wilton's. To my surprise she had accepted at three hours notice
on a phone call from Saltwood. I was worried about the whole
party going into meltdown. I can't believe that Heseltine
would get it by default – but to be sure of that there must be
someone from the centre-right to come through. And, as I
have often said (including to her) I think Gill is that person.
She is keen, did some – but not too much – personal boosting.
Expressed her irritation with the chaps' atmosphere at Major's
headquarters and when I raised the question of who might
inherit his organisation if it went to a second round said she
thought it could be Ian Lang.[4] She is a tiny bit too short. Has
lots in reserve and I think would be good against Blair in an
election.

---

[1] Irvine Patnick, MP for Sheffield Hallam since 1987. Knighted 1994.
[2] Alan Duncan, MP for Rutland & Melton since 1992.
[3] Peter Walker, Lord Walker of Worcester (MP for Worcester 1961–92), member of
Heath and Thatcher cabinets.
[4] Ian Lang, Scottish Secretary since 1990, MP for Galloway and Upper Nithsdale
since 1983 (Galloway 1979–83).

Saltwood Tower office   *Sunday, 2 July*

A great psychological cloud lifted by letting the Degas go at 515 so can now (a) keep Big Red, which Jane really likes, and (b) set about Trusts.

By the pool, Saltwood   *Sunday, 6 August*

A great sense of well-being pervades me. The dinner party (15 people as Mary Archer asked herself *en supplement* at the last minute) was an enormous success. There are no functions left this summer, and an 'awayday' next Wednesday 9th when we go up to Bisley to see the Howards (Charles having had another heart attack, his 3rd – or so I was told by Bartosik[1] in the room at Brooks's, while actually *at the board*!).

Picking systematically at paper and files before heading north at an early hour on Thursday, 17 August. Confident-in-the-knowledge that there is precisely 500 on deposit in Coutts money market.

As to the autumn – a friendly letter from Angela Rumbold;[2] made me realise how incredible if I could pull that one off. Graham Stewart is more amiable and discreet than I had anticipated. And I am at peace with my cars. The only one I feel I ought to let go is the SS100 (but there was little Mrs Ben How coming up to me on the Albany/Royal Academy traffic island majestically and saying 'How's my car?') Probably also the R type Cont and the Todd Buick? Would raise 85, 60, 16 (XK 140) and 24, so not far off 200 (and what's the difference?).

A note about the dinner: we worked – myself intermittently, Jane continuously – for nearly a week; 'Duke of Norfolk' getting the whole 'ceremony' so that it went through flawlessly.

---

[1] Sam Bartosik, backgammon player (see *Diaries*, 27 October 1983).
[2] Angela Rumbold, MP for Mitcham and Morden since 1982; DBE 1992; writing in her role as Deputy Chairman of the Conservative Party.

Shore Cottage   *Wednesday, 23 August*

On Sunday we had left Saltwood at 3.30 a.m. – bathing before, on Jane's initiative, and I had (*for the first time*) a wonderful and perhaps never-to-be-repeated experience – swimming on my back, frog-legged, and looking up at the stars. We made good time to Scotch Corner in very light traffic, then headed on through the Border country and the Buccleuch estates – simply beautiful. Jane did most of the driving as I was comatose and she triumphantly delivered me to Gleneagles (where, as always, the dining-room staff were efficient and the food delicious, but the bedroom was poky, an old staff bedroom classed as '1st class' and costing £400).

The next day after the massive and nourishingly delicious breakfast – sitting somewhat apprehensively at Mrs McTavish's table – we cruised along the A9, took the Hope Road and, on impulse, and fully loaded – three dogs, and the old 'yellow' Hermes computer and screen as well as some lead for James's weights plus God knows what else, and two crates of drinking water – took the ford at Cashel Dhu!!

Slept again for eleven hours; woke with slight sinus headache, still v feeble.

I suppose if one did this for 2½ weeks – no alcohol and 'rest' alternated with writing and physical – one should show results. 'Feeling' better though comes before improvement in appearance. It takes longer – three months rather than three weeks – to reduce sacs of fluid and build up muscle tone. I should be encouraged by Tom, who is now 115 and his back legs cause him to stumble quite a bit – he fell into the burn yesterday after failing to recover from rolling in something – then he goes up and down the banks sorting out the burrows and led the way along the shoreline to the 'Great Burrows' before turning and separating from me to return to the croft. This morning he did a most wonderful prancing leap over a broken rung in the foot-bridge. As so often in the first days here I simply let my mind stray, I don't look at the papers, we have no radio and I don't rootle in my briefcase. It is all I can do to send postcards.

Shore Cottage   *Monday, 28 August*

Back this afternoon from a 'break' at Pait Lodge.[1] Practically everything was as one had anticipated – but nicer.

The people were old, but not as old as we expected; boring, but in a congenial way, not-yer-herr-herringly so.

The Lord-Lieutenant, Burton, a stooping man with white hair and the mien (deceptive it would appear as a tale was told of his 'short' temper, and slamming the car bonnet down on the fingers of some individual who was trying to effect repairs at the bottom of the drive – dodgy behaviour, surely, for the Queen's representative?) of geniality. On thinking it over, he looked something of a mix between Maurice and Jo Grimond,[2] having the 'old school' high table style.

Perhaps it was this (although neither he nor his strangely fey wife, a former demi-beauty *en deuxième noce*, now dressed unaccountably from head to foot in black, stayed the night) that induced in me an overpowering access of nostalgia. In the late afternoon Jane and I took a walk up the glen, it was intended to last an hour or so, but we were out for more than two and a half hours.

We were escorted by young Richard Hamilton, a charming lad, immensely athletic, who had *run* up several of the Munros,[3] and disconcerted me on our return – there was only just time to take a bath – by saying that he was going to 'fit in' his press-ups. 'How many do you do?' 'A hundred'.

But the whole experience was steeped in Buchan – as Richard's innocence (it is curious how this can be combined, as it was in Buchan's time, with witnessing the most dreadful scenes – he had seen a man beaten to death on a train in China)

---

[1] Pait Lodge, the home of the Clarks' friends, the Stroyans.

[2] Sir Maurice Bowra, Warden of Wadham College, Oxford; and Jo Grimond, Liberal MP for Orkney & Shetland 1950–83 and leader of the Liberal Party, 1956–67, May–July 1976.

[3] The Munros, the highest of Scotland's mountains, 284 mountain tops named after the man who first catalogued them, the Victorian mountaineer, Sir Hugh Munro.

and his asceticism. And the furnishings of the lodge ('Sapper's' *The Final Count*[1] was by my bed) all bought en bloc from old Lady Stirling who used to knock her pipe out in the butter dish, in the early sixties. Tongued and grooved pine, and enormous jug-and-basin washstands.

John Macnab.[2] And the Royal Navy on station around the globe. In Belgrave Square the great town houses are August-silent and dust-sheets over the furniture.

As the boat took us back down the loch I underwent a strange inducement of feeling. Those great Munro's falling into the water, utterly remote and free of human imprint. Far glens and slow curves and the shoulder of distant Coires. At the time I was absorbed and brooded on my own destiny. But now I wonder if I shall ever see it again?

At the pier on the Monar side two stalkers' ponies were waiting, fully saddled-up, with a ghillie leading them.

Saltwood   *Wednesday, 27 September*

What should have been a delicious *désoeuvré* day, free of obligation, and with choice, soon evaporated. On came that tricky little prick Sebastian Shakespeare.[3]

'Always a pleasure to talk to you.'

'You may not think so this time ...'

Asked me about putting in for Chelsea; I referred him to the agent. 'People are saying you wrote your CV on House of Commons notepaper' (Gaaah!). I explain I'd paid to print it myself. But what a lesson in how everyone is just waiting to fault-find. Whispering he mentioned something about the 'Matrix Churchill scandal'. Silly little runt.

---

[1] The last of Bulldog Drummond's four rounds with arch-enemy Carl Peterson.
[2] The eponymous gentleman poacher of Buchan's novel.
[3] Sebastian Shakespeare, editor of Londoner's Diary in *Evening Standard*.

Saltwood kitchen   *Friday, 29 September*

Still very unsettled. My jaws ache (both sides) and I have split a
back molar on the right due to avoiding (funking) Bertie Arbeid
for the last three weeks. Naturally he's away until next week.

Quite a friendly piece in today's *Independent*: '... allowed his
name to go forward.' That's more like it – just the phrase. So far
I'm managing to keep this out of Jane's notice, as it's still 50:50
that nothing at all will come of it. Alastair Stewart[1] wants me on
Sky TV – but I'm not so sure that's wise at the moment.

What is really irritating – but totally 'serves-you-right, Alan'
– is that – muddled and fatigued – I refused Carla's[2] dinner for
Jimmy [Goldsmith] last night; all she could say is that Redwood
and Jonathan A were going to be there. I didn't specially want
to see Redwood who I think slightly loopy.

But now it turns out to have been a really interesting
conclave. Conrad Black, David Frost, Alexander Hesketh, John
Patten, Evelyn de Rothschild[3] and many others (including
Jonathan A). I could have made a real contribution. Then today,
p.m. Jonathan H[olborow] rang softspoken. Stewart Steven has
resigned from the *Standard* and Max (of all people)[4] has taken
over. Key question, therefore, who is going to get the *Telegraph*?
Jonathan wanted me to approach Conrad. I couldn't, left a
message, but hasn't called back. If I'd been at the dinner last
night it would have been so much easier. Why did I duck it?[5]

---

[1] Alastair Stewart, newscaster and TV presenter previously with ITN.
[2] Carla Powell, wife of Charles Powell, private secretary to the Prime Minister
1983–91.
[3] 3rd Baron Hesketh (various ministerial appointments in the Lords, also a Whip);
John Patten, MP for Oxford W and Abingdon since 1983 (City of Oxford 1979–83),
Education Secretary, 1992–94); Evelyn de Rothschild, chairman N. M. Rothschild
& Sons Ltd.
[4] Stewart Steven, editor of the *Evening Standard* since 1992, *Mail on Sunday*,
1982–92; Max Hastings, editor of the *Daily Telegraph* since 1986.
[5] Charles Moore (*Sunday Telegraph*) succeeded Hastings; Dominic Lawson, editor of
The Spectator since 1990, succeeded Moore.

Saltwood   *Saturday, 30 September*

Very heavy-hearted now that I know I'm (barring a *total* miracle) finished. I think all my 'public speaking', TV, column, phoning, lunching and dining with colleagues – Portillo, Gill Shephard, M Howard, the rest – has been in the context of assuming/hoping/fantasising that somewhere somehow I would be offered the choice of a constituency and a return.

Up through the members' cloakroom, the big staircase (or the little front one by the loo) along the corridor, past the big octagonal writing table in a bay window and into the Members' Lobby – through the door that only Members can use, so that as they swish open any waiting journalist will know that only an MP can be coming through. Then a glance at the telephone message board (perhaps a 'badge-messenger' handsome in their white ties and tailcoats) will spot me and shout 'Mr Clark' and bring a letter from the message board on the other side. Perhaps look into the Chamber, see what's up, how full it is; stand 'at the bar' for a minute or so. Then down the tearoom corridor look-ing in there, or on into the library; drift up past colleagues busy at the various desks – Nick Budgen, Enoch always in his tradi-tional place (last time I was there) and on to the No-Smoking and the Silence room (where if people talk too loudly you can call out 'ORDER') and slump in a chair there to read the *Spectator*, or something more esoteric.

Yes, all that still mesmerises me and for three years I used to dream about it, half certain that I would return. But now that Chelsea (which, somehow, so much seemed pre-ordained – the speaking invite, Nick's accident, the audience reaction etc) won't even see me, I realise that, in fact, it is hopeless.

So I might as well pack everything in. No more columns (I'm just starting to get a wee bit stale and repetitious); no more appearances, public speaking and soundbites. If I'm around (but see below) perhaps the occasional nicely crafted review to help pay for 'petrol'. In theory I become bookish, concentrate on Big Book.

But this afternoon I begged Jane to come on a long walk with me and help me think things through. It was a failure. We started by bickering; she just didn't comment at all on my dilemma except to say things like 'you've had your chance'; 'you (by implication) failed, flunked it ...' or whatever. Never far below the surface the 'you've been undone by women' accusation. A good deal of stuff about how absolutely impossible I am to live with. I suppose I am only making her unhappy (still). Then on my return from Patel in the Bustard I left the Barbican gates open – only for such time as it took to put the car in the garage, come in and phone Patel. Although the dogs don't, in fact, wander she was concerned I had let them out, got into a fearful state. I drove off in S16 in case they were loose in the street. Naturally they were not, and when I got back (having been buttonholed by a nice lady who wanted me to revisit Dover docks which I must do next week) they emerged from the undercroft. But yet more damage had been done, and we sat in total silence all through tea.

I really feel I must get away. Really away, I mean – *Eothen*. Just do a Stephen Fry.[1] I can't, of course, until I have got some order so that, at least, she doesn't have debts to banks or other unfinished business. This can only be done by selling cars – but which?

My solace at the present time is to drink even more deeply from the Buchan nostalgia. That way of life '...and the Grand Fleet was stationed around the globe'.

Saltwood   *Tuesday, 3 October*

Went over to Garden House. My phone had twelve messages on it – goodness knows when it was last cleared. Among them a

---

[1] Alexander William Kinglake's *Eothen*, or *Traces of Travel Brought Home from the East*, first published anonymously in 1844, ten years after the journey it describes had been undertaken. Kinglake (1809–91) was an Old Etonian, who went on to Trinity, Cambridge. Stephen Fry, the actor, had recently disappeared after opening in a play in the West End. On his return he admitted to having suffered a breakdown.

perky-sounding Barbara Lord. With thudding heart I returned
the call (perhaps mistakenly starting by saying '…I assume it's
bad'). But no, she was just apologising for the piece in the
Standard. We had an amiable conversation getting down to twenty
before Conference – interviews afterwards. I felt wonderful –
lifted. But now as I write this I fear it means that 'notices' will
go out before Conference and so if I'm not in the twenty I will
be thoroughly out of sorts (again). I went to the Great Hall (by
chance as I left the light on there) and sat at the long table. God
told me to ask for serenity and balance. If I didn't make it – well,
decks are clear. Because contemplating being back in, delightful
though it is, consider the implication of enchainment until old
age or death. In spite of everything I said, I will become a buffer
– or quasi-buffer – in harness. Easier to commute to Saltwood,
of course. And I know how to 'swing the lead'. But I would be
turning my back on will-we-ever?

MFS GH   *Thursday, 5 October*

I was all day at P. & A. Wood having the new steering wheel
fitted to 'Big Red'. What a luxury! Raises it to the level, almost,
of 'the ultimate driving experience.'

   This evening I pottered over here because the Executive is
sitting in Chelsea deliberating the twenty. Am I, actually, a 'front
runner' – *passim The Independent* – or is the whole thing
ridiculous? I prayed at the long table. And drew some strength
from the fact that it may not have been a bad idea to 'stand
down' in '92. Because in the last three years I have become a FP
– my status may work in my favour; may not. But it helps me to
become philosophical. If I lose at Chelsea then I will become a
sage.

Zermatt   *Thursday, 12 October*

Arrived here to find the whole place unchanged, undisturbed as usual. The new block of flats behind really quite tasteful – very little sense of oppression, though one needs some kind of *blocken* trellis to protect the back wall along the terrace going up to the house and the backgammon-room chimney.

We came in the Discovery (having earlier wavered between the Citroën or 'Big Red'), recording extraordinary fuel consumption figures and enjoying James's green *Ausweis* on the windscreen which – inestimably convenient – allows one to drive the whole way to the 'Parking'. En route, quite late in the afternoon when we were looking carefully at the signs on the autoroute, Jane spotted the name Colombey-les-deux-Eglises. For a second I thought no; no time to make a detour; but then *of course*. Because what-is-written-is-written we drove through ineluctably French countryside and villages. First (due to unnecessary diversion) coming by way of the memorial – an extraordinarily powerful erection; a croix de Lorraine about 120 feet high in granite bits, pinkish in colour with a very slightly parabolic contour and against the lower wall just the letters (in forged bronze) GENERAL DE GAULLE.

No one about at all. I spent a little time there, went to the shop – noting the General's Quinze ('Big Six') Citroën which he had used until 1958 – bought and sent postcards to, inter alia, Soames, Ryder and Goodlad.[1] We then went down to the Boiserie. A 'homely' low-built house covered in Virginia creeper, heavy white gravel, garden rather contrived, rather Ascot-like. But the beautiful view of distant forest-covered hills so unforgettably mentioned in his memoirs. The interior also quite confined: the dining room intimate, you could not have sat down more than eight. The salon also, and the General's library and bureau in the ground floor of the turret and his desk

---

[1] Alastair Goodlad, newly appointed government Chief Whip in succession to Richard Ryder, who returned to the back benches.

looking out over the countryside. There, too, was the leather armchair, nicely stuffed, where he had died. 'So important to die at home,' Jane said.

I fantasised a little, nice to absorb atmosphere, but not very successfully. I am too wound up with the last charge of the Royal Guard of Charlemagne – as it is. But I am glad to have visited the place; and like almost everything else in this extraordinary saga the timing is uncanny.

Because at the weekend after the short list had been chosen I was on the *Today* programme with my 'essay', and *Breakfast with Frost*, where I drew the extraordinary compliment from Michael Foot. 'I always think Alan Clark articulates what both on the left and the right wing of the Conservative party feel better than they do themselves.' We'd hardly been here an hour before Sheila Gunn was on the phone saying how (truthfully or otherwise) the Chelsea constituents at conference had 'enjoyed' my CV.[1]

Monday, 16 October

Yesterday, another bullish signal. I rang the Kensington-Chelsea paper to find out about back issues, giving my name. 'Oh, uh, Alan Clark? ... You're going to be the next MP for Kensington and Chelsea.' This from the News Editor herself! Greatly boosted I started putting my speech into shape, and running it through the tape recorder. A useful trial – as seemed far too slow at first. I can't decide whether to use the jokey opening or not. But there is no doubt that the Scott extract works.

---

[1] In *The Times*, Sheila Gunn, one of its political staff, wrote, 'Not many rate his chances ahead of less colourful figures.'

Sunday, 22 October

After return from the selection committee.

A curious experience – seemed to go well; almost too well? Barbara Lord said to me, on the way out, 'you were marvellous.' But then went on to say, 'I think … [hesitation] what will tell against you is your age … If they do decide to replace Nick it will be with someone much younger …' I was bland and understanding, though hiding it. 'But …who can tell?' she added. Did she mean *on the night*, or 'today'? The nice fat girl who gave me a map of the constituency said the calls would go out 'about 5.30' which is what it is now.

I ought to welcome release. Three and a half years later. But I am really tense (this morning in Albany mirror I had 'stress stripes') which mean the let-down will be dreadful. So many signs were good, all the way through.[1] *Waiting for the phone.* One of the great ordeals of modern politics.

Great Hall, Saltwood   *Monday, 23 October*

I suppose that I knew last night by 7 o'clock that it was over – for certain by 8 p.m. when I went sadly through to the kitchen. Nothing this morning save some probing gloats from the *Standard* and the *Independent*.

I set off for a great walk, it being such a lovely autumn day. As I rounded the corner, looking across to Saltwood church nestling in the fields, I felt a dreadful pang. No longer the profound, paternalist, nostalgia of 'this is the country I am defending; for which I am responsible'. Because I am no longer responsible, and never can be again; for if age was the cause of my rejection that is a condition that worsens every day.

---

[1] In a brief diary note on 19 August following 'a trail in Black Dog (*Mail on Sunday*)' about the Kensington & Chelsea selection process, AC remarked, 'all the angst, tension and (probably in the end) humiliation.'

I walked up the Down to the great cattle grid looking down on Beechborough. Sat for a minute and tried to pray. I search for a formula for some kind of serenity. Reflect utterly is the best; lie low while 'transitionalising into a sage'. Financial penalties, of course, but a certain guarded self-containedness. Practically never leave the walls, more and more eccentric, saveable now only by a miracle.

Can the mind overcome this reversal? The mind can do anything, even reverse a malignancy, if it is properly programmed.

Only consolation is that Franko is back as Editor of the *Spectator*.[1]

Saltwood   *Wednesday, 1 November*

Dinner at Bucks where (ludicrously) I was 'guest-of-honour'. Poor old Robin Day was crotchety, parodied himself to the point, almost, of discourtesy. Ronnie Millar[2] also, very frail and queer. Could almost be 'sickening' or 'fighting', but softspokenly asked for my phone no, a lunch at Brooks's soon. (No thanks, I think, for a bit.)

Donald McIntyre[3] walked me back to the Albany shutters. He is curious, but supportive I think, about both Scott and my search for a seat. We talked for some time about the former. As to seats, when I said I was also putting in for Mole Valley, Horsham, Arundel, 'Oh, so you really are serious ...'

This made me feel better, and I still thought about it when I woke just before my alarm call at 5 a.m.

---

[1] Frank Johnson succeeded Dominic Lawson, who had been editor of *The Spectator* since 1990, with Lawson becoming editor of the *Sunday Telegraph* where Johnson had been deputy editor.

[2] Ronald Millar, playwright, but best known latterly as speechwriter to Margaret Thatcher and John Major.

[3] Donald McIntyre, political writer on *The Independent*.

Saturday, 4 November

Very depressed. Ticky little agent at Mole Valley wrote with 2nd-class stamp saying 'applications closed' on 26 October.

I went for a walk, to get out of the place, as Jane in foul mood. (Although as well as doing my piece, I also lit fire, laid breakfast coffee, rolls etc, she was black as thunder, didn't comment.)

Came back, said a prayer in a dimly lit Great Hall. 'Do something' – swimming pool or House Colours, though not so intense of course. The message was stay calm, await the moment. It may yet come if you don't give up.

But then, during tea, Soames rang from his car. Bellowed away – quite funny, he told the Mole Valley dinner, 'You owe it to the nation to choose Alan Clark ...' I gathered, though, that this didn't go *all* that well. I slumped and brooded. Later, found myself a glass of Dôle from the Migros bottle I brought back. And as I walked in the moonlit outer Bailey I thought back to the buffet at the Bahnhof in Brig. The blind beggar playing his accordion and my early, as I often did in those days, tête de veau vinaigrette. And the Simplon pass which I knew well in those days, not much used as people preferred to take the tunnel. I always intended to do it once in the Bang Bang (now parked outside the Long Garage, dead, perhaps it is that which subliminally triggered it). That was all of thirty or more years ago. Before even my first rejection at Weston-super-Mare.

But, strangely, I am not yet finished. An interesting lunch with Phil Hall.[1] Pleasant, but *naïf*. Needs me on the paper to advise and consult about politics, write leaders at intervals ... Rupert[2] himself is putting the pressure on. Jane is totally opposed (but I have fixed her reward). Alastair said 'grab it'. Jonathan Holborow I am dining with on Tuesday. I hope he doesn't offer a lot more money (Phil has already gone to 125) as I think I am better 'standing back' from that anyway. But he won't be pleased.

---

[1] Phil Hall, newly-appointed editor of *News of the World*.
[2] Rupert Murdoch, the owner of *News of the World* through his company News International.

Wednesday, 8 November

Dined (modest dinner) with Jonathan Holborow at Wilton's. He is keen for me to stay at *M o S*, is 'reorganising the paper round you, Alan …' Has said he will be faxing his 'offer' today. We got on well; my only slip-up, when setting out the 'generous' terms which Rupert (alias Phil H) was offering, was when J said, 'He's not offering you a seat on the main board …?' 'Oh, no, I wouldn't want that.' Perhaps that was what J was going to work up to?

It is a difficult decision. Associated are (marginally) more congenial to work with – but I don't see how they can match Phil's 125 (+25).

EMT   *Friday, 10 November*

Last night was the Chelsea selection. Am I strong enough to recognise that this has to mean the '… end of that particular road' – *passim* Ted Heath at the Party Conference?

Albany   *Wednesday, 15 November*

I was at the Garrick, in the bar, prior to lunching with Ion and (asked himself) Sissons. On the way up in the train I had found among my mail a very pleasant acknowledgement from Nick Scott of my 'a thousand congratulations, good luck with the Rozzers', etc note. And there he was at a table with a dignitary of the Kensington and Chelsea Association ('you are such a success that the chairman let it run over by popular acclaim') and an Iranian 'businessman'. Point being, just a whiff of Tammany there – and good luck to him – lots of people had an interest, in the Nelson sense, in helping Nick *en poste*. Plus the old biddies of course.

Even so as I walked back, though, that phrase of Nick's, 'you still hear the drum' haunted me.

Then, somewhat unenthusiastically, I went across to Wilton's to meet Bob Balchin.[1] Just as David Davis had predicted – almost high camp. But we got on better and better. He was not discreet (although we both drank water), tipped me off about seats; told me to redraft my CV; said, 'no, no, get on with it' with *N o W*. So the whole day, the little Charles Addams boy, and the medicine.

Saltwood, EMT   *Tuesday, 28 November*

Still very mild, and this morning a (somewhat faltering) dawn chorus. At least one blackbird, or a thrush singing prettily. I found myself touched by a wistful nostalgia. The dawn chorus in late autumn. A year gone. While in May, of course, it holds all the promise of a major summer – sunlight and well being.

A false dawn with Chelsea (I genuinely thought it was *written*). Now it has to be a miracle. Tunbridge Wells at the last moment. I must stay in there, and bet. But what I hope, quite firmly now, is that the Tory Party is smashed to pieces and a huge number of people lose their seats. Then, at last perhaps, my particular brand of radicalism can grow.

Saltwood, EMT   *Wednesday, 29 November*

Jane lay awake last night for two hours (she told me this morning) in a mood of depression so black she could have killed herself. My fault, I suppose, because I had 'bitten her head off'

---

[1] Bob Balchin who via David Davis had offered to meet AC and, if he approved, to introduce him to constituency party chairmen in search of the right candidate.

yesterday morning when she brought photocopies of the typescript of my piece on Scottish independence when what I wanted was the copy of the piece in the paper itself – the cutting. And at dinner last night after being compelled to apologise, which I did – I don't doubt it seemed – with my usual ill grace I set out my own grievances.

Saltwood   *Saturday, 16 December*

The tail end of flu hangs on, and makes me depressed and lassitudinous. This afternoon I just stood in the Long Garage, defeated by the fact that the Bustard battery lugs had screw attachments not 'female' post sockets.

Had a sardine tea, but with the orange cake I got 'dyspepsia'. Cancer scare again as I had a sudden aversion to bacon this morning at breakfast. May be an element of 'nervous stomach' as I now realise that my Christmas holiday is also going to be 'filled out'; because James-Julie are here until 30th and KK [labrador] for a month after that. My first column for *News of the World* not until 21 January and I was hoping to use the vacant period for a last assault on the paper. We waste so much time looking for things. If that could be aggregated into tidying time we'd be so much better off.

So all in all, I'm in (8 days ahead of normal) standard pre-Christmas depression; and frustration, too. Jane is happily whistling and singing in the hall doing Christmas greenery. She really loves Christmas; and I am such an old Scrooge and wet blanket. Twice in the last two days to Canterbury, and everyone so busily bustling and rich. Coats' are going down which always puts me out of sorts.

The vein across my hand (particularly left hand) is permanently bluely raised – as I used when a child to notice in people of '60' (i.e. old people). My face has become so crumpled and jowly that it is irreparably downgraded. Still more muscle tone lost. Only eight days in Cuixmala can cure this. And as I write I realise that of course the presence of KK makes this impossible in the only free period we've got. Oh dear. No wonder I have a slight tension headache, and wind.

My recuperative powers are, or need to be, excellent. But they do need a 'kick start'. I somehow feel if I don't get on in the first two months of '96 I will suffer a downward step.

Saltwood   *Sunday, 17 December*

Helped Jane erect the (lovely and big) tree on an empty stomach. I had felt awful on waking – stiff, tired, de-energised – and was in the 'siren suit' over my pyjamas. Then I drove off in the green Continental to post some last-minute cards and collect a *N o W*. Tom had escaped (through a gap in the 'Roman' wall, involving a long glissade the other side – how's that for activity at age 17, '119 human'?). Walked over to the farm, collected him from Ann.[1]

Darling Jane was decorating the tree. The lights were fixed and I – 'watchman', most ceremoniously – lit them. Lovely. But the whole thing so *hollow* somehow. How many are we going to be? Four; five with Julie's mother. Later we looked through the window and it looked so lovely. 'Why aren't there children scampering about?' I asked sadly. I will never live to see my grandchildren marry. And what worries me is that I will now be old; shaky and selfish, when they have difficult passages between the ages of 9 and 18. Sex, drugs, shocks and bikes. Later we watched that (excellent) film on the Labour Party. Poor Kinnock – too much himself. Fatal in politics. Lessons, most of them melancholy, for the Tory Party in its present condition.

---

[1] Ann Felce, a friend and owner of Grange Farm.

Saltwood   *Saturday, 23 December*

One pleasing thing has happened. The Yeats 'Rose in a Basin' has actually come back here (cum expenditure of some £21,000 in legal and sundry expenses).[1] I never really thought that would happen. Now, of course, I look at it more closely just as I did those Yeatses in the room at the National Gallery in Dublin (incredible, so strong). Interesting, and satis because yah-hoo to 'McCann' (the thief) and his solicitors Stephens Innocent (sic).

Otherwise – not good. The Zurbaran is still in the USA with Feigin. Next year my own earnings will plummet catastrophically. I can't really live in present style and level of activity without £1.2m in the money market. So cars will have to be sold – but which? Even the SS100, which I feel rather warmly towards. Really the whole lot, I suppose, should go, leaving just the Alpine Ghost, the XK and the New Bing, plus one other (summer car or 'little Black').

---

[1] The picture, by Jack Yeats, had been stolen from AC's stepmother, and turned up in Ireland.

1996

It is only a week since I started on the Winstons.[1] But the
tendrils had been moving below the surface for so long ... (no,
a poor analogy; I should say the material was all tinder-dry in
my brain so the fire spread at colossal speed). And have done
sixteen pages plus, in spite of being up in London on Thursday.

Big Red up and down. What a magnificent vehicle it is.
Virtually no fatigue factor. Every mile a pleasure, and
comfortable-in-the-knowledge-that ... but cars are going to
have to be sold. It's very sad, but at least 300-worth needed
really.

I have one more year of this high earnings – from which no
savings will be makeable, all directed to debt and taxes.

I must try and get Zermatt sorted out this year, too – and that
requires a substantial sum (preferably in US $) on deposit and a
kind of treuhand [trust].

James reported that Andrew – who has already claimed
Broomhayes much to the indignation of the other couple – is
complaining about my affairs in disorder. What happens when
Daddy dies? ... etc. (This must be the first time the young adults
are starting to worry along the same lines as I used to.)

I was planning really to devote myself to the Winston this
year. A long haul. Fired by progress I talked to Ion about length.
We agreed at 450pp. That's 40 pages a month (allowing for
holidays and wastage) or 10 per week. At this rate I'm ok, just.
But plainly it is unsustainable. The timing is going to be perfect
– for Tory conference 1997. But I'm sure others will be doing
the same thing. 'Spoiler' operations.

Last night I had a talk with Tony Benn.[2] He was the only
person even half-right on the subject of North Sea oil. And how

---

[1] One of AC's many names for what will become *The Tories*.
[2] Tony Benn, devoted MP for Chesterfield since March 1984 (Bristol SE, November
1950–60; August 1963–83), a radical, a parliamentarian, a diarist, and a minister in
the Wilson and Callaghan Labour governments (including Postmaster-General,
Industry and Energy).

fascinating he is to talk to! His mind so quick and versatile – but
the loony prejudice (and this of course the motivation that
keeps him active) never far below the surface. 'We want an Asia
economy so as to be like Singapore – with its penal code' etc.

Politics still consumes and fascinates me. But I am conscious
of being a little slower (at last). Somehow I can't always remember a name. And I am too tired/lazy to master policies in detail.
This matters less than many think, but – *passim* E. du Cann and
Jane's comment twenty years ago – you need it a bit or its
absence shows. Watched John Major on *Frost* this morning v
compos – greatly superior to Blair. But lined and strained and
his bad English handicaps him.

And am I still capable of returning? The Thurber moth of
course, but I just feel a tiny bit less alert than earlier in the period
(even the last year). John Preece [from Plymouth], whom I have
always liked, rang a couple of nights ago: 'you'll make it. Just keep
trying. A lot of people down here have a lot to say for you' etc.

Do I still *burn* enough to do it? I have aged, quite suddenly
and noticeably.

Kundan   *Thursday, 11 January*

Up in London – goodness knows I did not want to leave the
Mains this morning – for two TV 'shows' and tomorrow a BBC
Kaleidoscope. On a (virtually) empty stomach spent 2½ hours
with mustard keen Mark Fulbrooks of Parliamentary Services,
preparing my CV.[1] And my gosh he knows his onions.

And although I thought for the first time, I am too old for
this, I've lost it. I don't want to get on a constituency interview
list. The last time I have really experienced this sensation, all at
once anyway.

---

[1] AC felt that a professionally massaged CV would help in his quest for a
parliamentary seat.

But after Jon Snow – Channel 4 News (watching the Lady's 'domestic' speech) then being door-stepped by the little untidy-haired but lively BBC *Breakfast News* interviewer *I smelt powder and flint.* The special exultation, a version of which I felt after the first friendly/apologetic call from Barbara Lord at Chelsea. I am good on TV. So important. Who knows?

Saltwood   *Friday, 12 January*

Got back this morning, picking up a thin and unappetising-looking mail. Opened a letter stating something-something Sevenoaks Conservative Association. Almost before I got to the end of the paragraph I skimmed ahead, as it were, simulta-neously to an invitation to 'put my name forward' (!!!). And from a vice-president association treasurer for five years: 'I write in my personal capacity, but feel I am confident I have the support of many of my colleagues.'

So in a state of total euphoria. Second, really, only to Chelsea from the point of view of convenience.

A new roll has started. How lovely life is, and thanks be to God.

EMT   *Wednesday, 24 January*

I feel terribly tired today. And over the last 2–3 days I have suffered very brief spasms of 'Norwegian Embassy' – which I haven't suffered for several years, plus a very tight lower back. It's all too silly, the way I am still at SD (Standing Down) plus four years hemmed in by pressures and obligations.

This morning, briefly on the back doorstep by the asthma rail I smelt the crisp air from grass and water as the sun gets up on a winter's morning when the light has started to lengthen. Why was I not just pottering about out of doors – wooding or polishing? Then meandered in here and cast my eye over Big Book fragments – just scholarship. Again, tranquil and tempting.

Various clouds on the horizon. Scott: ought to be all right and am steadfastly refusing to comment, but occasionally wake in the night and think of the ultimate nightmare – Henderson (and all the other Matrix C directors) suing me under the direction of little Gilbert Gray.[1]

Saltwood   *Sunday, 28 January*

Bitterly cold. Yesterday I came back from Grantham, where I had been to deliver the Ernest Bevin memorial lecture to some trade unionists. The place got snowed-up and I had to take a cab from Grantham to Peterborough. The A1 was unrecognisable; a hesitant black-ish streak wound, down one lane, with barely a vehicle in sight as we crept round the double roundabout at Blyth so crowded and busy in the summer when we are heading north (or, return, south).

At Bertie Arbeid on Thursday to have a fantastic 'bridge' fitted (v successful; laughingly in the mirror I answer difficult questions at a press conference).

Saltwood   *Wednesday, 31 January*

After cup of tea at Albany went round to No 10. JM came to fetch me from the little reading room – so boyish and jokey. Really immensely attractive and in good form. He has had a

---

[1] AC worried that if he were criticised in Sir Richard Scott's report he might in some way be open to legal action from the Matrix Churchill directors represented by a QC of the stature, say, of Gilbert Gray, a Recorder of the Crown Court since 1972.

magnificent weekend[1] and is buoyed up by it. 'I'm beginning to think you might make it,' I said. Delighted, he agreed.

Saltwood   *Friday, 9 February*

Nothing like the peace of mind after 'filing'. I have now really got into the hang of the *N o W* column. Although this evening, just as I was talking to Bob Warren[2] – very surprising cultivated 'suit' – he said a huge bomb had gone off in Canary Wharf.[3] And now the IRA has declared an end to the ceasefire. (So I have to rewrite something for it.)

Do I really want to 'put in a bid' (*passim* the Italian newsagent at Sevenoaks) for the various seats, Guildford, Arundel? It really is going backwards – and Simon Hoggart's interesting article – on the barrenness of the chamber was off-putting and sad. No more F. E. Smith and Baldwin.

Wednesday, 14 February

New cares, literally countless, weigh me down. Is it (light) alcohol poisoning? Oh-so-foolishly I told a reporter last night (ridiculously I don't even know who it was) that I was going to Mexico 'on behalf of *the* PM'. Extraordinary, this weakness of mine – and just as I thought I had it under control.

---

[1] The PM had given an upbeat interview to the *Sunday Telegraph* that weekend, which concluded, 'I like elections, and clearly we are within fifteen months of an election, so I am beginning to sniff the wind and feeling much happier about it.' AC had an audience with the Prime Minister to mark the start of his column in the *News of the World*.

[2] Bob Warren, of the *News of the World*.

[3] The IRA ended eighteen months' ceasefire by trying to destroy the new symbol of a resurgent Docklands; two people were killed.

EMT   *Thursday, 15 February*

Two punches landed yesterday. Clydesdale suddenly wanted
their money back – 45 – all of it, at once. And Coutts wrote to
say o/d is just over 60 (how *can* it be? I nearly always keep rough
tallies in my head and thought it was about 35-40 at most).
Rattled by Scott build-up[1] (some stupid Scotch wanker rang last
night about the Al Habobi missile 'when you were defence
minister'. 'When was that?' 'In 1986.' 'I didn't go to MoD until
1989.' Curiously rang off at once).

Later

Strange how one can feel better – more confident, ready for
adversity and exploitation (should read 'opportunity', but
exploitation sounds better, no double '-ty') after three cups of
EMT. Caffeine is a stimulant, alcohol a depressant, isn't it?

Le Bourget   *Friday, 16 February*

In the (chocolate and cream painted) 757.[2] Not very
imaginatively fitted out. Rather Arab with the seating arranged
in grouplets – no private snuggery, but the loos are sumptuous.
A taxi-driver had, or so he claimed, waited for three hours, took
me to Le Bourget. Still cost £20. Now a long flight in prospect.
Fellow passengers not v appealing; a mature lady in black –
'groomed'. A little Italian professore-type, muddled and anxious
to please (*later*: actually the cook). Jimmy skulks unhappily in his
bedroom in the tail – Howard Hughes!

---

[1] Sir Richard Scott's report due to be published that day.
[2] The private jet owned by James Goldsmith. AC joined a house party put together
by Goldsmith for a few days at Cuixmala, his estate in Mexico.

Later

A v rich, but ill-looking Jew in young middle age with a pretty unbleached blonde wife. A French 'gentleman' ('not comfortably off' – Jimmy's phrase, but 'keeping up appearances' with chateau outside Paris). The illish-looking passenger is No 2 in, and heir to, the whole of Lazards, £200m+. But what's the point? Manners – simultaneously insecure and un(successfully) assertive. Jimmy is being charming to me. Speaks brilliantly on USA (high opinion of Pat Buchanan,[1] naturally) and French campaign of Michel Noir[2] now finally in total trouble – 'a write-off'. I wish BLJ was with me.

Cuixmala   *Saturday, 17 February*

4.0 p.m. English time. It is 9.10 a.m. here? I'm muddled. But slept well and had a delicious Cuximala breakfast. Spoilt only by the fact that my return here, Thompson pressing, the tiny maids (amiable, but 4 ft high) are encamped. And I know from experience that they will be here for at least another hour. Oh for three years of war in East Africa.

I just so wish Janey was here. The blooms and trees have grown vastly since we were here exactly two years ago. There is cloud, patchy, and the sea is less angry. A breeze, humid and gentle refreshes. I am in Ed Epstein villino and contemplate the rough, almost Cornish, coastline of the eastern Pacific seaboard; with reddish rock outcrops sparsely covered in vegetation and breakers foamily dousing them.

I am already feeling better. Although still worried-ish about sexual mechanism, problems building up in UK (are papers

---

[1] Pat Buchanan, right-wing Republican, aiming to get his party's nomination for the next US presidential election.
[2] Michel Noir, former Mayor of Lyon, who had been supported by Goldsmith in his attempt to become French president.

bothering Jane?[1]) and certain sign of age – particularly random memory failure.

We talked about Aspers (has got leukaemia, but 'under control'. Had a dreadful abscess in his mouth necessitating a double operation as 'they left some tools in' – eh? Uh?). Politics: Jimmy told me, most relevantly to the work I am reading up at present on the two '74 elections, that Heath had sent him out to Brussels to inquire of Christopher Soames what he wanted as price of desisting – apparently he was in cahoots with Peter Carrington – from furthering their plot to deseat Ted (illustrating, but I must look this up in Campbell's biography,[2] Ted's obsession with 'heavyweights' – just like JM's notorious phrase 'we've had a very good Cabinet' – and ignoring the electorate, in this case the parliamentary party). Soames said he would lay off if he got the Foreign Office in the next government. But there wasn't going to be (this was between the two elections) 'a next government'. Presumably he was talking about the 'Cabinet of distinguished people of good will outside party politics'. When I pointed this out to Jimmy he said – old Mexican political adage – 'in politics assurances only bind those who receive them'.[3]

In the night I was gloomy. I thought, what, at all, has been achieved in the two years since we were last here? A high profile, but even that seems to be going off a bit. How right I was not to do or say anything pre- or post-Scott. Apparently it

---

[1] Huge row over the Government's handling of the Scott report, but AC was exonerated.

[2] John Campbell, *Edward Heath: A Biography*, 1992.

[3] AC researched this account further. It was not quite as Goldsmith related in Cuixmala. In 1974, Jimmy, whose father had been a Tory MP, was already rich and wishing to make 'rapid ascent within the Conservative Party', he joined, on an unpaid basis, the Conservative Research Department, where he came to Heath's notice. Heath used him as his emissary to Soames.

As AC relates in *The Tories*, 'Yes, Soames would endorse Heath, align himself firmly if a squall blew up. His price? The Foreign Office. Heath knew that Soames still fancied himself as a possible Leader of the Party. He had been exerting massive pressure in Central Office to "find" him a parliamentary seat. "He'll ask for the Foreign Office," Heath told Jimmy. "Tell him 'Yes'."'

is still being puffed in Britain. But they'll have to do it without me.

Bernard [a French guest] said — when Jimmy was trying to explain the 'scandal' — 'I hope you made a lot of *monnaie* …'

Jimmy, like me, sometimes looks like my father in his stooping movements and expression. Last night he escorted us to the villino, and I was worried by how old and shuffly he looked.

At breakfast he said he kept no papers — none. Because anyone in the USA can sue you, and hard disks are impossible to wipe.

Cuixmala   *Wednesday, 21 February*

Happy to be going back. I have missed BLJ so many times. Not specially worried about the flight — only it is always disagreeable suddenly waking from a catnap and realising one is over the Pole. Also I don't like all those people in the back of the plane spewing germs into the system.

I am returning (barring major and specific crises) to press attacks,[1] financial pressures, correspondence (even five days) backlog. Funny about James, Andrew, why no grandchildren? Humiliation at Sevenoaks. Days just being frittered, however good one's intentions may be. Breakdown of discipline. And until one masters discipline nothing will ever happen.

Jimmy meanwhile is recovered from his brief malaise (he is congenitally manic). He bubbled with enthusiasm. I note that he does sometimes forget the place in mid sentence, almost Hiram-like.[2] On Monday, just before lunch and down by the pool he suddenly said, 'What's the time?' 'Five to one.' 'I must go and have an insulin injection.' He walked round to the car park, went up in one of the FWDs; I'm lucky not to be *on* anything.

---

[1] The aftermath of the Scott report.
[2] Hiram Winterbotham, a mentor of AC and taught him to drive. A specialist in Georgian domestic architecture, he was a friend of Kenneth Clark and responsible for AC becoming a Governor of St Thomas's Hospital in 1969.

EMT   *Tuesday, 27 February*

Walked out into the Bailey this morning with T.O. and pink sunlight on the Great Library wall, through traces of mist. The grass white with frost and 6–8 ducks waddling about on the far lawn.

These last two days I have managed to get out for an hour or so, perhaps more, in the middle of the day and 'pull' brambles. I am working on 'The Bank' (corner of) below GH.

Jane said she is still stressed, couldn't get to her studio. I pointed out that at least the Webbs[1] were now installed and the dogs had taken to them. She said it was because I wasn't working on Big Book. Quite right. I did eleven letters yesterday, all ullage, and easy for any competent secretary. Another sixty to do.

Later

I am in strange, if not 'poor' shape. I walked the Giorgione,[2] half draped in a suit bag, half wrapped in bubble-plastic, to Emily Black at Sotheby's. She is very pretty, with grey eyes. Unimpressed, 'too badly damaged', N. Italian, 'Putto with apples.' 'Really not worth very much at all.'

'It's a matter of complete indifference to me what valuation you put on it,' I smiled.

'£4–600.'

When I told her, she (actually claiming to know Jaynie Anderson[3]) held her ground. 'How do you know?' etc.

Next I went to Christie's. Here it looked better propped up on a chair. Unfortunately the atmosphere was slightly rarefied

---

[1] Lynn Webb, who became housekeeper at Saltwood, and her husband Ken.

[2] *Cupid in the Guise of an Angel*, a fresco fragment acquired by Kenneth Clark from the Ruskin picture collection in 1931. He identified it as by the Renaissance artist, Giorgione, from the Fondaco dei Tedeschi, the German customs house in Venice. AC had even attempted some restoration on it in 1972, and, as a result, his father observed in a letter, 'a certain amount of it has come away. But there is still enough to be of considerable interest.'

[3] Jaynie Anderson, art historian, who was writing the *catalogue raisonnée* on Giorgione (not published until 1997).

by the receptionist recognising me and calling me 'Lord Clark'. So when Ben whatisname looked at it he realised 'there is something important here'. Thrashed about, though getting that it was a fresco transferred to canvas, and declared it at £2000. I tried to get Charlie H[1] down to look at it, but he was tied up in a mega-deal.

I came back to Albany. Drank five cups of tea, etc, Danish pastry and fell (deeply) asleep. Woke up not knowing where I was, hyper-chesty and with a pulse-rate of 82. Found a thermometer, but only 97°. Strange. I cancelled any thought of going to Pratt's.

EMT   *Saturday, 2 March*

I sit here and, after a few pages of Jim Lees-Milne (I am dabbling in *Caves of Ice*[2] at the moment) I felt calmer and more reflective.

But in fact I am showing classic signs of diarrhoea. Last experienced on this scale in September in Zermatt; Jane said it was nervous-stomach ahead of the Chelsea selection. Now the timing (ahead of the Sevenoaks selection) is almost identical.

Let this, at any rate, be catharsis. The agent (Ann Barrow) is pleasant. I am to see her on Tuesday. My 'contact', Kenneth Miller, is probably less doddery than he seems. He has asked me to lunch at the Carlton on Wednesday week '… assuming you get through the interview …' (uh?). If we can't bring it off here then I will have 'done my best', and will settle for being an academic. Three months will have been lost. But with Graham's [Stewart] help this is still reparable.

---

[1] Charles Allsopp, chairman of Christie's since 1986, had become the 6th Lord Hindlip in 1993.

[2] *Caves of Ice* was the third published volume of James Lees-Milne's diaries.

EMT   *Wednesday, 6 March*

When I wake I groan with the sheer – self-inflicted – pain of how I am expending my time.

Yesterday I went over to Sevenoaks. The agent Ann Barrow dark, pale, unmade-up, in black, was pleasant, mildly cynical sense of humour, seen-it-all.

There were two members of the selection committee there fussing about with papers. Each, outwardly amiable (-ish), plainly were working their own schemes. She took me through the set questions. All matters of policy – concerning which, of course, I am completely ignorant. Also a good, not very encouraging and hard to memorise rundown of the wards. After a bit I just felt terribly tired and hopeless. Thoughtfully I drove back to Saltwood (after contemplating going straight on up to Smith Square to collect the briefings).

I rang the Research Department of CCO. A pleasant-voiced, but coolish young secretary would make no promises. I faxed a set of headings. I will drive up (in the Discovery of course) this morning to get to CCO at 11, then down to Sevenoaks to talk to the chief reporter of the *Chronicle*. This individual, like all provincial journalists, totally clueless about politics, very hack – asked what I was 'doing' now and then, 'I hope you don't mind my asking this – how old are you?'

As I said 67 it kind of came through to me how ludicrous this whole thing is. And yet Bob Dole (now doing well), Ross Perot, and the 'entire Chinese Cabinet'.

So I forced the pace, not knowing what the result will be; or even if it is favourable how much operational time I have left to me. I concentrate single-mindedly on this – to the neglect of urgent things like signing contracts (i.e. raising cash) for Nick K[1] and Ion. This Friday, ungetoutableof – I tried – my 'Stamford Bridge Before Hastings', the Macleod Society in Winchester.

---

[1] Nicholas Kent, head of Oxford Films, for whom AC would make a television version of *The Tories*.

Usual thing – M25 – on a Friday night. Exhausted all day Saturday zapping up. Sunday up previous in order to be at Sevenoaks (sinisterly Ann Barrow said I was to be greeted by Maj-Gen Pellerew who, so Kenneth Miller told me, thought I was too 'me-me'). Apparently I had also called Mark Lawson David until Ann Barrow tactfully corrected me. Also wrote down 'nursing', in list of policy headings. Had said, at the end, 'what does that mean?' 'Nursing the constituency', she said. Of course. We had discussed that at length. Then, that evening the coup de grace, or, conceivably, the stay-of-execution. If the latter, up to Ampleforth to pray, or to give me a lever with Father Seed to mobilise support in the seat. Executive reception, with Jane, plus speech on Tuesday. Final catharsis on Thursday. Then – more or less open skies except for 'police bail' – 4 April, fatuously the day before Easter.[1]

Saltwood   *Saturday/Sunday, 9/10 March*

Usual rejection syndrome. Very, very sad, but I must show resilience and 'class' even though now the lake is far, far distant. It's now 1.30 (I must have woken at about 1, and furtively took the clock *under the bedclothes* upon pressing the little button).

I looked out of the window, and saw a half/three-quarter moon over the woodland. God gave me the news/hope of a grandchild yesterday.[2] And just now I said that I would strive for constancy, and youth. That is to say I must retain my *tenu*. Not flag (*Spectator* articles etc). Take more exercise and drink sparingly.

I can now 'clear my diary'. I suppose I ought to have a blood test; particularly as I am now completely impotent, I need a heavy boost.

---

[1] Following a bomb scare close to the Albany entrance, parts of Piccadilly had been closed off. AC, who had the Giorgione with him, had driven the Discovery within a few feet of a suspect package that bomb squad officers were about to destroy in the aftermath of the IRA ending its ceasefire.

[2] Sarah, Andrew's wife, announced that she was pregnant.

EMT   *Wednesday, 13 March*

A 'full' day yesterday, but not wholly satisfying. Up to London by
train (incredibly cold, knife-like, wind) and walked along the
Strand – very much against the tide of pinched bustling office
workers – to the Temple to hear Richard Scott on Matrix
Churchill.[1] He is a splendid man – cool, clear-headed and witty.
He was interesting – it was by and for lawyers – on case law.
Lambasted discreetly Tristan Garel-Jones[2] and the whole deception
of the 'response' document in the House of Commons Library.

(On the way back I glanced at the doorway of the chambers
where I crammed successfully for the Bar Finals in 1955, a good
discipline.)

MFS GH   *Sunday, 17 March*

I went up, somewhat against my inclination, but at Jane's
prompting ('V-sign them') to Frostie. For some reason the
camera stayed on me practically the whole time so when I
wasn't speaking I could seem to be wanting-to-sit-on-my-
tinkle-face and fidgeting. Also a weenie bit more mature now.
Some shots good, some not so good.

John Redwood was there. More authoritative than formerly,
less ready to smirk deferentially. Said JM's only skill was staying
in office.[3] I wonder what he feels? There is a lot of talk now
about a 'long' parliament, or a small Labour majority. I'm not so
sure. I still think it could be very, very bad. (And of course
finally, if I don't get back – which now seems virtually

---

[1] After his report was published, Scott gave a number of talks to lawyers and at
universities.
[2] On the evidence of Tristan Garel-Jones, who had been a Foreign Office minister
at the time, Scott called it 'risible'.
[3] John Redwood had stood against John Major the previous July in the leadership
contest.

impossible – would prefer this. All those second-rate Tories just
threshing around getting nowhere.)

On the walk we released a woodcock, which had got stuck
between the two fence lines – always satisfying. But earlier I had
been caused heartache by 'Cross Bencher' [*Sunday Express*]
relating to the Sevenoaks shortlist – Stephen (ghastly), Fallon,
Johnson[1] and thought of that note: 'You were in the frame until
quite [sic] late'.

I suppose I really ought to concentrate on the BB. But it is
the lure of the sword that agonises me. Will anything happen?

Tuesday, 2 April

As I write this date realise this is the 14th anniversary of the start
of the Falklands war. When Jane met me at Sandling and I was
making my plans to go lock-stock-and-barrel to New Zealand![2]
(very odd). Later, though, I got into my stride. (Occasionally)
wonder if I might have aimed at the premiership had I been
made Navy Minister when Keith Speed resigned, been *en poste*
when Notters had eased him out.[3] I would have been in rivalry
with Cecil, of course. But at that time I was blacklisted on the
computer.[4]

When am I going to get into Big Book properly?

---

[1] Michael Stephen, MP for Shoreham since 1992; Michael Fallon, MP for Darlington, 1983–92, who was ultimately selected as Sevenoaks candidate and won the seat in the 1997 election; Boris Johnson, *Daily Telegraph* journalist (whose route to the House turned out to be at Henley, where he succeeded Michael Heseltine in 2001).

[2] *Diaries*, 2 April 1982: 'We've lost the Falklands,' I told Jane. 'It's all over. We're a Third World country, no good for anything.'

[3] Keith Speed, MP for Ashford since October 1974 (Meriden, March 1968–February 1974), had resigned as PUS, Defence (Navy) in the early days of the Falklands imbroglio; Sir John Nott, MP for St Ives, Cornwall, 1966–83, Defence Secretary 1981–83.

[4] Elsewhere AC recorded '*spilling the beans* to an Inspector what's-his-name' after learning that a mistress was threatening to get some Italian Mafioso ('I've forgotten his name') to shoot him. 'A fine example of premature and ill-thought-out panicking.'

I simply don't know what to do about the cars. Am going over to P. & A. Wood this morning taking some nice stuff to be plated. Why? KGV car unsaleable. Ditto the Bustard; if I make an exception then why not x? or y?

MFS GH   *Easter Saturday, 6 April*

Foolishly and semi-drunkenly I broke the great terracotta pot by the swimming pool with the tractor. Jane was very cross and upset. On the walk she marched several paces ahead of me all the way. This morning I thought of the châlet – for the first time since 1960 no one has been there all through the whole winter-sports season. I'd like to get away – but I can't. Big Book is terrifyingly demanding now. I haven't any feeling of relaxation at all, [slight] workaholism. James rang to say that 'it's 78° at Eriboll', LLG and T-shirts. But here it is grey-cold, featurelessly light, and I must finish mowing the Bailey.

Easter Sunday, 7 April

I am getting intermittent toothache from lower-right. Why? The nerve is meant to have been removed and it's capped with a powerful gold–ceramic bridge.

Last night and again this morning we talked about a total Saltwood overhaul – lights, wiring, plumbing, decoration, the lot – £2 million? Need the Giorgione (or the Lottery?). Would have to be photographed first, then we move over to Garden House, precious stuff to Bank/Great Hall or GH. No longer feasible to contemplate for my 70th birthday.

Perhaps, too, fate would intrude, ficklely, and have me 'claimed'; just as the packing cases are full and the work started?

But the concept, now it's been given shape, homes in ...

MFS GH   *Saturday, 13 April*

Already Birthday Boy; the year one-third gone and this note-book coming up to half distance. Rather more melancholy than on previous birthdays. But oppressed, too, with the need for BB to do its stuff, because 'its timing' will be spot on. SE Staffordshire by-election and swing of 22%;[1] I don't see how we can win the General this time so in autumn of next year the Party will be 'trying to find itself'.

I have a perfect vantage point *in the wilderness* – but with just this horrid dissatisfaction – I have no seat. Odious, every prospect of being an elder, a senior knight of the shire. Only a miracle can solve this.

I bought myself a birthday present (self-indulgently). A huge royalty cheque came in, £78,000,[2] abolishing at a stroke the Coutts overdraft. Almost within 12 hours I spent 40 on Core's 3-litre. On the way back from looking at it today I recherché-du-temps-perdu at Hurstbourne Tarrant;[3] looked at the old rectory, smaller than one remembered – as is everything when one revisits. A planning application notice for converting old stables (looked to me as if they had already *been* converted).

My mind wandered back, nostalgically. We were golden then. Short of money, living at Rye/Bratton and envious of the Grahams'.

I would like to write a where-do-we-go-from-here piece. Must be over further to the 'right' – you cannot have two competing centre parties. But never forget that Mrs T, who was, suffered endless criticisms and ridicule for telling us where we ought to be going up to '79. To leave the EC and simply to anticipate its natural – and inevitable – implosion.

This ought to go in *The Times* – but can't (I will offer it to

---

[1] Sir David Lightbown, MP since 1983, had died. In the by-election Labour turned a Tory majority of 7,192 into a Labour majority of 13,762.

[2] In particular sales of the paperback edition of *Diaries*, but also the ongoing success of two of AC's campaign histories, *The Donkeys* and *Barbarossa*.

[3] Where Euan Graham lived.

them, though) because all they do is put Libby Purves, Bernard
Levin in the prime place.

But first it must be written – when?

Right now I am going to work in the evening light, and pick
at the badge room for goodies to fit on the 3-litre.

EMT   *Monday, 15 April*

I suppose that, technically speaking, I am in a pre-nervous
breakdown state. I got up at 5.30; driven by pressing bladder
(although had feebly urinated at 1.20 a.m.). But an hour and 20
minutes have gone past – and I can't do anything (just written
these four lines). Look at my teeny crabbed writing. The last
time I wrote even half legibly I was in Cuixmala. I have read
Woodrow Wyatt – not much there really; they're better off with
Al; M. Winner pretty cheap; the whole paper[1] is *so* tacky. But
that's what people want?

Did fifteen letters, including a cross one to Clara[2] about the
programme going to pieces – her idea to get Mellor and Edwina
Currie (for God's sake) – and only just caught the post. As
always, didn't quite have time to start up and go off in a classic.

Then went to start the mower. But although Ken had
sharpened the blades beautifully – he had not re-tightened the
belt, so the cutter drive shaft just rotated impotently. I went across
to wash the Little Silver. Superficially an easy job, it is actually very
time-consuming to do it properly. And, as frustratedly I worked,
so did I get myself into a rage about the police stopping me
yesterday on the M20 (where else?). Sure, the car was not taxed.
But what caused them to check out the number? They couldn't
have seen it. Sheer spite and aggression. You're worse off in a silver

---

[1] Lord (Woodrow) Wyatt, former Labour MP, chairman of the Tote since 1976;
Michael Winner, film director – both fellow columnists in the *News of the World*.
[2] Clara Glynn, AC's director on the TV series based on *The Tories*.

Porsche than a black youth with dreadlocks in a BMW. In the latter case some of them, at least will be put off by the thought that they might get stopped.

Later the Webbs turned up and Ken tightened the blades. I cut the lawn until a late, late tea – 6.15 – as all we had at lunchtime, 2-ish, was some delicious smoked salmon and toast followed by *too much* of the unbelievable Doney's-like chocolate cake.

Thus it was already almost too late to go out in the Bustard, which, for some reason, fluffed a bit (very unusual) and backfired. But is still a beautiful example. No play in steering and springs at all. Wandered about in the gloaming, full of maudlinesque self-pity.

I am so rattled by pressure on time. I've been edged out of my office (early entries shows how important as a refuge) by Graham – which I knew would happen. And now Clara pre-empts the first of the week while the column forecloses Thursday and Friday. Saturday is always a particular scramble for the incredibly early (but useless, as it does not catch a Monday delivery) 11.45 post.

My time overdraft is even bigger than my financial one. This is real stress. It will be interesting to see how my blood pressure is when I have my tests (which I am funking).

Albany, EMT   *Tuesday, 16 April*

Mrs Frowd, sinisterly, asked me if I had any 'indigestion' – '*is the colon all right?*' This made me feel terribly low.

Once again, a lovely open evening – and it is 'to London', the night at Albany. Dined with David D (he has taken the place of Richard R as my principal *fix*). He said 'something-something your seat'; 'we did want to talk about ...' I am dismissive and he didn't press the point.

He made some good remarks: 'MPs are different these days, socially and economically. They are a levy. And what happens when a levy is put under pressure? It runs.'

'Twentieth-century politics is the medieval warfare. The leaders are in the front line and the standard is what is important for rallying. The standard must be high, and it must be visible.'

And 'in' politics the natural (Darwinian) selection process for the larvae is quite different than that for the survival and advancement of the adult/leader ...

These are real aphorisms.

He was late arriving and while down at the end using his mobile phone to check with his office, Annabel Goldsmith came in plus Jimmy and Ben Ben (he now looking sinisterly terribly like Desmond Guinness at Eton with dark eyebrows and (as it were) striking bleached hair).[1] I had already drunk two glasses of the Wilton Puligny Montrachet and was 'silly'.

I ate six oysters, pâté de foie and toast, grilled turbot, and delicious crème brulée and raspberries, at least two-thirds of the bottle plus a glass of claret with the pâté.

In the night (2 a.m.) woke, felt uncomfortable. If I'd turned, or even moved, I 'could' (sic) have been sick. This morning I rose at 5.50 and again (finally) at 7.20. Looked dreadful – jowls sagged right down – and felt so old and creaky. In particular and looking back at the dinner I feel that I no longer have anything left in real politics. I must make my way with BB. But have I got the time?

MFS GH   *Sunday, 21 April*

To record a lovely day. These last two or three I have been low – concerned that I may have cancer of the colon ('any change in bowel habits should be investigated immediately'). And since Mrs Frowd – most sinisterly – had asked one about indigestion, and the 'colon' it seemed to deteriorate – so that I was convinced that I was not evacuating properly.

---

[1] Ben Goldsmith, James and Annabel G's youngest child.

However the sun shone and the air was lovely, still and clean.

I rose very early and looked at some texts for Big Book over EMT. Later I said to Jane ¾ of my stress derives from not properly addressing Big Book; I can feel the level easing off as I get near it. So much twist (or 'spin' as it is called) to put on this subject.

After breakfast we loaded the Discovery with stuff for the dump. Had our boilies early and only collected the papers on our way out. Dabbled our toes in the water at Hythe beach (Jane rightly pointing out a film of dilute sewage which lay on the surface of the LLG water). I finished cutting the Bailey and we had a pasta and salad, followed by mangoes and Belgian chocolates, which the young had given us.

No time for a zizz, but did a formal 'w' along the woodland (a fox by the stream bank now sojourns the day at the edge of his earth by the bottom tree).

Graham brought over an immensely polite undergraduate who is doing a PhD on the Manchurian crisis and I showed them round. A cup or two of Indian tea, and out for a drive in the Bustard.

Still light, and I'm over here to record 12 hours of almost continuous euphoria.

On days such as this I think – am I not fortunate to be an active academic (self-styled), living with a pretty and affectionate wife in 'one of the loveliest places in England', charged with a most fulfilling task and with two lovely sons and the prospect of a grandchild. How could I complain, or fret. And thanks be to God.

EMT   *Friday, 26 April*

The Party yet again in trauma. If you have no sense of direction ('no compass' in the current code) you don't know where you are going. This makes you vulnerable to attacks of panic and, particularly, mutual recrimination.

Of course it all makes me regret so sadly not being in the House. Not just for the gossip; but because I believe that I *could*, just possibly (certainly I could now with the acquired experience of knowing what to do), have been urged to take the helm myself. Anyway for the fourth, or is it the fifth, time in this Parliament the Party is in turmoil – this time over Jimmy.[1]

It starts with the feeling that seats are threatened – threatened more than is usual that is – then a feeling spreads – why not? There is talk of major figures (*passim* Redwood and Lamont) insisting on a referendum now, declaring a splinter Conservative Party and forcing an early election with all the Goldsmith money and campaigning zeal getting behind them. It could be valhalla of course.

But if between now and the local election results, JG gets serious, plans a campaign and this means saying what he will do in power, there could be a creditable freshness for the second stage. This means getting in professional campaign managers, a chief of staff, and an analyst (all, I know, uncongenial to Jimmy who likes to be a solitary buccaneer).

Yesterday at tea I was looking at the atlas and my eye wandered over a later page that showed the Western and Central Highlands. I said to Jane that there is a will-I-ever scenario that has been plaguing (sic) me since Portland Place,[2] almost. When will I/why can't I load my tent into the old Buick and meander about, climbing ridges and photography? W. A. Poucher constituency at last. I could, I suppose, still do it at 70.

---

[1] Sir James Goldsmith had announced the formation, and funding, of a Referendum Party, which would put up candidates against Tory MPs who were pro-Europe.
[2] A Clark family home in central London close to Broadcasting House before both Upper Terrace, Hampstead, and Saltwood Castle.

MFS GH   *Wednesday, 1 May*

Over here in some trepidation. Is this my very last free weekend
at Saltwood? Several times in the past I have thought this, I
admit. Yesterday while talking to Jaynie Anderson about the
Giorgione – a slow-moving saga – with my feet up, as usual, on
the jamb of the 'Tinker' door, I felt a strange lump on the
tendon of my left knee. An unusual place, surely, to have a
malignant growth? Whitby away, so booked into Nick Page for
a grand slam on Tuesday next; will also be bringing up the
Zurbaran and going to Rosemary for 'oral hygiene'.

Later
I don't object to current affairs taking so much time; except that
– like trying to keep fit – what's it all for? The death knell finally
sounded at the Sevenoaks rejection. DD more or less said 'it was
my reputation, and they felt they couldn't run the risk'. Now I
no longer do the *Mail on Sunday* (Mr Crocket, the boiler man,
one of today's many time consumers, reproached me for this).
I'm scrawny; my weight is back at 11.3½, 3 lbs down. So really
(if God spares me) I'm doing little more now than 'working out
my notice'. But if Big Book works out, then I will be satisfied.

EMT   *Friday, 3 May*

The local election results. Has the tide turned? Or is it perhaps
'*on* the turn'? A 2–3 point recovery, no more.[1]
    I suppose for both selfish and nostalgic reasons I would
welcome utter defeat. I don't want to see all those colleagues
who no longer court my attentions preening themselves.

---

[1] With only 27 per cent of the vote, the Conservatives lost 567 seats, but CCO's
worst estimates approached 700. This allowed the Party spokesman to say that the
results were less bad than in the 1991 local election, which was followed a year
later by a Conservative general election victory. Would the same happen in 1997?

Quietly back to 'where we came in' – a Labour government and a long period in which to foster nostalgia and in which my book (oh the book, how good it will be – and how difficult it is to 'put it together') will be a guiding light. But the vox-pop session for Basildon made me uneasy. No one offered a reason for voting Labour – only about voting against Tory. I feel in my bones that there might be enough of a rally to produce an 'almost-hung' parliament. And what wheeling and dealing this would give rise to!

Last night I spoke on the phone with Francis Maude;[1] clipped and authoritative, not unlike Redwood in his own way.

Lovely in a way, like pining in love, this sadness that I can induce about here, going down the wide corridor from the members' staircase to the Lobby, past the bay window where Clay Freud[2] used to sit and work out his bets before diving into an adjacent telephone booth to ring his bookie.

Bank Monday, 6 May

Very low today. I should have gone to Duxford[3] for the anniversary rally of the Spitfires. But slept in, intermittently, 30 minutes at a time, and was/would clearly be late leaving. Wanted to hear the Merlins,[4] see Alex Henshaw and get him if possible to sign the Mew Gull para in Jane's [*All the World's Aircraft*]; tell him how I saw him win the King's Cup air race at Lympne when he dived under the little blue Pobjoy monoplane.[5] I felt a tremendous pull to this, and hated myself and my intentions for

---

[1] Francis Maude, MP Warwicks N., 1983–92, Financial Secretary to the Treasury 1990–92.

[2] Clement ('Clay') Freud, journalist and droll broadcaster; MP (Liberal) for Ely, July 1973–83; Cambridgeshire NE, 1983–87.

[3] Former Second World War RAF station in Cambridgeshire, now an outpost of the Imperial War Museum.

[4] The Merlin, Rolls-Royce engine that powered the Spitfire and many other aircraft of the period.

[5] In 1938, when AC was ten years old, Alex Henshaw, a distinguished air racer of the 1930s, was piloting a Percival Mew Gull monoplane.

shirking it. Totally frittered the day. Mainly spent helping Tip wash and clean S16 (which responded beautifully, I must say).

I just hope the Zurbaran which I am taking up tomorrow can be placed. Really one needs £1 million in the Trust to yield income, relying on remaining contents to 'protect against inflation'. I absolutely refuse to sell, but perhaps the grandchildren will thank me.

B5   *Wednesday, 8 May*

At the flat phone ringing – would I take a call from the Chief Whip? Paraphrasing Chips I said – 'I can never resist a Chief Whip', Alastair [Goodlad] – worried about David D. 'He's going to chuck it in …'(?) Had seen the P.M. on Thursday, was going to talk again to him that afternoon. What had he been like at the weekend, etc?[1]

That's my third call from a political notable in 24 hours.

I took the Zurbaran back to Christie's. Then I drove slowly home in Big Red as I tried to ring David D and counsel him to ask for what he wanted. Finally he came back, as I knew conciliation-wise he would – while I was filling the tank at the M20 BP station.

Somehow I got the feeling that the tide had turned. I got back, ate scrambled eggs and finished polishing S16.

Shore Cottage, Eriboll   *Monday, 20 May*

Slept last night from 10 p.m. until 5 – can't even remember turning over. Yesterday we were drowsing on-and-off during the

---

[1] Now a FO minister, David Davis was said to be disenchanted by the government's handling of the EC's ban on British beef following the outbreak of 'mad cow' disease, and by not being promoted in Cabinet.

day – usually this ends on our first or second day – and now at
last beginning to feel better. Need at least another week. Could
consolidate tonight, but promised to take the young out to the
Creaggan.

On Saturday we went to look at the great Arnaboll Forest
project. Could be incredible. Already the game are back in
copious (*passim* Jane) quantities. Strange and unknown vitality
in plant life, secret and long dormant mosses and lichens. From
a rocky outcrop James showed us the contoured lines of the
plantings that leave plenty of glade and open areas for the
wildlife to congregate. As far as the eye could see, some seven or
eight miles on and over to Cashel Dhu. In ten years' time it will
be noticeable. I hope to come as a buffer, in my plus fours, with
a stalking stick and stompily survey it, but even James will be
dead in seventy years, when it comes to full fruition.

On the way back we looked at some of the foundations, some
of them even pre-Christian of the original Arnaboll settlement.
At the graveyard the children's headstones were in the main still
standing. But some vandal had – most recently as a fresh apple-
core was nearby – levered out the lead lettering, scratching the
marble with his knife, of little Jane Mackay who had died aged
5½ in 1867 and had such a pretty gothic stone. Loathsome
scrounger. I hope some ill fortune befalls him.

Shore Cottage   *Tuesday, 21 May*

Our last day. Bright sunlight, bit windy. And there are two
swallows back in the long shed – though none, yet, in the boathouse. I am hating the prospects of getting back. Almost as bad
as leaving Portmeirion for school in 1942. Speaking engagements, Clara, mail, police proceedings (unspecified); always the
relentless pressure of the Mains, at the centre of whole vortices
of claims.

Like the Wehrmacht, and the Waffen SS in 1944-5 winter, just enlisting any old riff-raff into the fight. I can't/daren't work out how little time there is until have yet more 'under my belt'.

Always when I come up here I think of emigrating. Saltwood in care and maintenance. Everything in trust. This is such a lovely little study. And it, too, will become outdated shortly after the General Election, when BB is delivered.

Saltwood   *Sunday, 26 May*

Jane's birthday, and she has been absolutely sweet all day since we had EMT upstairs and talked about things – children, car-culling,[1] possessions generally.

I did my ten letters, and we then attacked the 'slab' – dispersing the dust of 13 years – since, I would think, last public openings as a tiny packet of 'Cadet' cigarettes stuffed with butts smoked down to the filter was found in the old shell-case that holds the walking sticks.

But for much of the day I have been uneasy, almost to the point of AF. *The Sunday Times* was loathsome – page 3, and huge colour mock poster plus – needless to say pictures of Valerie and Joei, various actors – 'Clark gets cold feet' etc. Thank God, and due largely to Jane, I'm out of that. Phew! But of course 'damaging' like being summoned 'Minister faces jail sentence' just in time to wreck Reigate.[2]

Then at tea, Jane – unerring eye – chanced on a long article about someone who had appalling metastasised cancer starting with a melanoma. Like seeing a bad motor accident, it makes it

---

[1] 'Yet again we return to the car cull,' writes AC opposite this entry, and then lists, with his estimated prices in £(thousands): 4½ litre Bentley (100); SS 100 (110); New Bing (40); XK140 (15); Loco (45); Big Red (120); B'Bang (18); plus in US $ Buick (45).

[2] AC was having second thoughts about a dramatisation of the *Diaries*; AC's court appearance was imminent; Reigate Conservatives were looking for a successor to George Gardiner, Eurosceptic rebel.

practically impossible to drive/look at one's shin. I am willing
myself to have this condition; like giving your opponent good
dice at a crucial point in a backgammon game.

Just as I was going to join Jane on the 'w' Jimmy Goldsmith
rang. Rightly said that 'Beef war' was the wrong battle. He
should have been fighting on fish. Will see what happens – but
outcome looks like peace-in-our-time over gelatin. Then ...
'will have to see what we do.'

JG quite interesting on world financial markets. Wall Street
crazily over bought; prices have no relation to earnings. Pure
tulip bulbs. 'Social conditions and unemployment etc likely to
worsen in EC as Free Trade continues to bite in.' What should
one be in? Government bond, gold, Swiss francs; US $? Even if
the Zurbaran sells (most unlikely) will it be in time? Already, as
I suddenly realised and pointed out to Jane, as we walked around
in the dripping mist of the 'wettest Whitsun on record', we are
already only three weeks away from the longest day. How
infinitely melancholy.

MFS GH   *Monday, 3 June*

Still apprehensive, Jane this morning said, 'I'm frightened for
you.' But the likelihood of imprisonment (slight, surely?) for
obstruction ('they always go mad on anything to do with
bombs', she rightly said) is not what is rattling me, but the
strange silence on the Harkess book front.[1] Just behave with
dignity, like Charles I.

---

[1] AC's court appearance, for driving through a police cordon in Piccadilly, took
place at Bow Street; AC pleaded guilty, apologised, and was fined £650 plus £50
costs. But next morning headlines and photographs concentrated on the fact that
he gave a homeless man (also due in court that day on a begging charge) £5
towards his fine rather than face a jail sentence. Meanwhile a Harkess memoir had
been announced to the press in South Africa, Valerie Harkess's domicile. In fact
nothing more was heard of it.

MFS GH   *Friday, 7 June*

A lasting feeling of complete disengagement.

A hot, hot June evening and because the shadows are so long and the light so persistent with all the full green foliage and wild flowers we could be in north Italy.

We went over today to Bromley – the 'Kentish Gadabouts' all over 70, it seemed. And I talked for 40 minutes without notes. Asked, of course, if I want to return to Parliament and gave a reasoned reply. Jane came, fluffed them impeccably and looked sweet in the white silk dress and pearls.

On our return I took a call from Mike White. We chatted. It wasn't either Redwood or Portillo. The AN Other should be me. I know that. History knows that. Apart from anything else I 'so good on television' *passim* Clara.

But for this to work only the very last combination of fortune will do. Reigate *and the by-election?* I went into the Great Hall and prayed, aloud.

Dear God

You have given me so much. A lovely family, wonderful possessions, this incredible place, and now, even, the promise of a grandchild.

So I don't like to ask you for things. Because if you give then you can take away. Which is demanding of one really, I suppose. But I want to go back to the House of Commons, because I want to save my Party. And only you can so order this. Because of course you can do anything.

I funked Sevenoaks, which you offered me. Have I learned from that? Whatever happens, I need you to save me from myself.

It is lovely to communicate. Please stay with me.

Saltwood, EMT   *Thursday, 27 June*

It is 7.10 a.m., and I have just read a little Chips to get in the mood to write.

Little Tom came in a second ago. He wagged his tail at me so pleasantly, and I let him out at once where he quickly did a giant tinkle. Alas, and for the first time, real old age seems to be troubling him. He is (rightly) cautious about 'ball-play' and uneasy beside the pool.

He stumbles when he walks (how he still goes up, and even more dangerously, down stairs I just don't know) and didn't quite get on net with 'Keegan' and the ball at the England-Germany semi-final last night. I couldn't bear to put him down so hope he passes away suddenly.

Albany   *Wednesday, 3 July*

Up today for Jimmy's Press Gallery lunch.

Greatly to my delight I was 'lionised' – might never have been away. George Jones said, '… and I see Alan Clark there,' or something of the kind; 'Thank you, George, and thank you for singling me out …' Hugh Pym spirited me away to some 'clips' on MPs' pay, the Somme, and the Referendum Party.[1] Julian Brazier[2] talked to me about the great homes row at MoD. Yesterday, after the sad news from N. Dorset,[3] I was even more determined to return. And at David Frost's party on Thursday dear Gill Shephard was specially encouraging.

---

[1] Two political correspondents, George Jones (*Daily Telegraph*) and Hugh Pym (ITN).

[2] Julian Brazier, MP for Canterbury since 1987.

[3] N Dorset, yet another possible seat in which AC showed an interest, chose Robert Walter, who had contested the Labour stronghold of Bedwelty in south Wales, 1979.

MFS GH   *Thursday, 11 July*

Flat and rattled. Trying to stay off drink. Took too much with
Dobbie yesterday at the Savoy Grill (recognised by the waiter
when I went back to and tipped £10); cut by Mawhinney who
was lunching with Peter Oborne.[1]

Dobbie offered me – I genuinely thought he was an emissary
– 400 for the serial rights [of *The Tories*] as 'pre-emptive'. This
really did 'make it all worthwhile'. This morning, naturally, it
turns out, or he claims, that he had no status at all.

Then, I cannot get rid of this dreary-sounding compulsion to
'put in for' seats. Angela R[umbold] told me that David Simpson,
the regional director [of the Conservative Party] was against me
(ageism). I thought of ringing and bawling him out. Don't do
that, I was advised, ask him to lunch. I got him on his mobile
(he was on his way to meet Mawhinney!). Was he not the person
who came over when the two maidens from Blandford came to
interview me?

But it's all such a drag. Nothing will come of it, I know. It's
absurd, I'm 68. But I can't stop.

GH   *Saturday, 3 August*

One thing I must note – both welcome and unwelcome. I am
almost an alcoholic. I 'have' to have my half (a generous half,
often) bottle of wine, usually Burgundy red or white, in the
evening. If I don't get it by about 7 p.m. I feel irritable and
(similar to) hungry.

But, when I don't drink I feel much better waking-up in the
morning (we never go to lights/bed before 11 p.m. now it
seems). And, particularly, if I don't drink at lunch I feel much
better at tea-time and in the evenings. Today, for example

---

[1] Peter Oborne, political writer on the *Evening Standard*.

although we had late salami-cheese lunch by the pool and it is a Saturday, I still would not slurp. Nor do I intend to drink tonight, although I would love, if I think about it, to drain a glass of the Marquise's Chasagne Montrachet. Champneys in August? It is only the second day. But not only do I feel better, but I feel more sexual. And my prostatic symptoms have completely disappeared. Strange.

GH   *Saturday, 10 August*

The cockatiels escaped. Jane brilliantly – how? – recaptured the little grey. But the yellow (maiden) is flighty – literally – and calls at intervals from different points around the Mains; venturing this afternoon bravely to the giant sycamore over the Long Garage.

Shore Cottage   *Wednesday, 21 August*

V low cloud, and fine, though penetrating rain. Doesn't worry me at all, though depressing for James as we noticed lovely piles of turned hay in the half-light as we approached yesterday evening.

   We did the whole journey in one gulp and, I must say, it makes one incredibly tired (though very slightly less so, I must admit, after deferring to the Grampian police and driving at only 60 mph on the A9. Last night I could barely manage to get to the boat house. Jane and the girls streaked away from me. I slept round until 8.15 (having been briefly woken and licked by Lëhni scratching at the door at 4-ish).

Shore Cottage   *Saturday, 24 August*

Woke this morning both of us absolutely knackered, still, in spite of 10½ hours. Thought we would never recover. But in the early afternoon we went out in the little Pioneer with James to clear the lobster pots. Absolutely divine – the loch was like glass and the silent little Yamaha outboard throbbed reassuringly on tick over. An absolutely perfect hour of tranquillity.

Shore Cottage   *Saturday, 31 August*

We found our gravestone the other day – sent by God, just off the Birkett Foster bank. I will go out and look for it in a second or two.

Saltwood, EMT   *Friday, 13 September*

Short of miracles, this is the last charge. I went over there [Tunbridge Wells] on a recce on Wednesday. Recognised almost immediately by a charming man who accosted me and said how glad he was that I am to be 'the next MP'. The agent, Steve Owen, not just grumpy and rebarbatief, but slob-like; with shoulder-length hair and a beer belly. A dreadful ward official in his late sixties – the kind of organisation that illustrates the tenacity of the human body when exposed to carcinogenic factors – and common-voicedly talking to the agent. Ignored me; then at the end said, 'Hello, young man.' 'Hello,' I simpered.

Archie Norman[1] is the favourite. 'I hope he trips himself up,'

---

[1] Archie Norman, chief executive of the Asda Group since 1991, who had political ambitions.

indiscreetly said the agent. Mrs (sic) Fookes[1] is the dark horse, according to my contact, Kenneth Miller. I'm not so sure about him, either, now. He talks almost loonily – 'I seethed for an hour' when people said I was being interviewed for 'entertainment'; and is very keen on telling me people's objections.

As I walked about I got a somewhat Cheltenham impression. Could go in any direction. Then sure enough Bob Worcester's poll results came through. We are in a minority. 'New Labour' are second and a still very substantial Liberal vote.

The whole thing is too ridiculous. I am telling myself to fight a seat that is worse than Plymouth in 1992. Once this is out of the way then I really can revert. I think the odds against me must be in double figures. But it is possible – if I am inspired. Will K-C inspiration come?

By 'The Boy' [statue by pool]   *Saturday, 14 September*

A simply beautiful, still September morning. I drove over to Bob Worcester to get the (very expensive, £7+) MORI printout for Tunbridge Wells. He briefed me – on the inevitable Tory defeat. Even T-W, 42 last night is now down to 40! He has this theory that the Lib-Dems will actually benefit as a stop-over from switching Tories. I'm not so sure. Could be that all these SE seats split 40-30-30 for us.

But I still don't see how we can do anything but deteriorate. At present our majority is ONE. Are we actually going to *win* seats?

I said to Jane over croissant cheese and figs, which we ate deliciously by the Barbican, 'In 24 hours I will be free.' Almost like 1992. And yet, inwardly, of course, I want to win. And go on

---

[1] In boundary changes Janet Fookes's seat – she had been the constituency neighbour of AC as MP for Plymouth Drake since 1974 (Merton and Morden, 1970–74) – was disappearing.

being 'good on TV' and a 'personality'. It's just that my compensation mechanism is working hard.

I am leaving my *revision* dangerously late. I know nothing about Education, Hospitals etc. *But this is it, Alan …!*

MFS GH   *Sunday, 15 September*

An absolutely beautiful still autumn day.

As the swallows, the remaining ones, dart about and feed their fledgling babies I wonder, in some gloom, what state I will be in when they return.

We will have a new government. Privately, I hope, of course, that it will be Labour. Sort those party toadies out. Eight years as 'shadows' is no fun. Agony, of course, if it is a 'hung' Parliament with Conservatives holding a balancing chunk. Jimmy is blank, incidentally. Quavering his voice on the phone 'just wanting a chat, nothing special'. Personally and unpleasantly attacked by Mellor in the *Mail on Sunday* yesterday. But it is, I fear, a rag-tag army, and he may well lose heart, and abandon the field.

Then, how will my own health be? Will I be a grandfather? Almost certainly yes. Will my affairs be more orderly? Will I have culled some cars, inventorised some structures?

Ahead of my disappointment at T-W I began to fantasise on the Venetian nobleman: he insisted on going up to the villa even though they had long closed it down; only the old man-servant, Mercurio, was evocatively in place. He plunged into the greeny semi-stagnant swimming pool – and had a seizure.

At tea yesterday I philosophised to Jane (who didn't pay much attention) cited the example of those old Venetian families who hang on to their crumbling palazzi, with their wonderful contents, and their archives.

I just want to be sure that Saltwood stays as an entity, even though the foci may exist separately – Eriboll, Broomhayes, Garden House etc. Just to walk through the rooms, with the lovely things, in the low summer light. Silent, and redolent of earlier regimes and generations.

This morning was so beautiful that I left Jane and the dogs. I walked over and back along the valley. So full the leaf on the deciduous trees. It could have been like nineteenth-century France. But it wasn't. It was England, my beloved England of *Our Island Story*, which due very largely to my own selfishness and impotence I am drifting away from.

Saltwood   *Friday, 20 September*

V convincingly Archie Norman 'walked' Tunbridge Wells. Same age as I was when chosen at Plymouth Sutton – a generation ahead I ought now to be calm and free – 'relaxed'.

EMT   *Tuesday, 8 October*

Drove early to Gatwick and at Geneva Airport lashed out at Caviar House, bought a medium-sized tin of Beluga, bottle of Fondant and sundries. Delicious picnic in Geneva train and took the supplement old-style coach on the Glacier Express (restored and not very comfortable – should have had period prints). The châlet at first seemed a little shabby and dated, but soon we are happily ensconced. Gamely we walked up to Ried – raising heartbeat to 140+ and fibrillations – and to a high tea and early night. The next day a lovely Zermatt meander in the morning, up to the Winkelmatten Chapel where I said a real prayer of thanks and back via the watch shops.

The day after our return we drove in Big Red to Broomhayes and found Andrew and Sarah had really settled in happily. After tea across the fields to the church and over the wall by the grave-digger's hut and found the Marley shed still with its

Above and left AC on his last Ministerial trip, flying in an RAF Tristar via Bermuda, Panama and Ecuador to Chile, where on seeing 'Children – largely unattractive – and very elderly people hobbling about', he muses in front of a medical centre, 'Oh old age is so awful. How can I avoid it? Can I choose my moment as deftly as I did my exit from the Commons?' (17 March 1992.)

Below The 1992 election photograph that was never used. AC had for a year contem-plated retiring from the Commons, but only told his constituency three weeks before the deadline for nominations. Tom, the Clarks' Jack Russell, who was now nineteen, had been a feature of the Plymouth election campaigns since the beginning.

Above After the Gulf War in 1991 AC, as Minister for Defence Procurement, was despatched to the Gulf. At Oman he met Andrew (right), on attachment to the Sultan of Oman Armoured Brigade, 'magnificent, handsome, clear-headed and hugely popular with his brother officers'. (12 May 1991.)

SALTWOOD

'When we got back I "striped" the Bailey.' (2 June 1991.) But not as beautifully as mown by Brian the gardener in this photograph.

Weeding by the pool, with the statue of the boy, during a heat-wave in 1995.

'Private Office came down yesterday evening and gave me a tree. Very sweet of them.' (29 June 1992.)

'This afternoon the christening of tiny Albert.
Afterwards we posed, the three males in line,
beside my father's gravestone.' (8 March 1997.)

'The endless pressure of paperwork –
now totally out of control again, as
I "cleared" the Green Room table.'
(26 January 1994.) Only purple teddy
survived this particular onslaught.
Left AC has moved to the dining
room, watched over by TC, one of
several jackdaws that became part of
the Saltwood family.

'A great sense of well-being pervades me. The dinner party (15 people as Mary Archer asked herself *en supplement* at the last minute) was an enormous success.' (6 August 1995.) Jane surveys the table in the Great Hall the morning after. The other guests: Jeffrey Archer, Algy and Blondel Cluff, Jonathan and Vivien Holborow, Selina Scott, Nigel Nicolson, Fr Michael Seed, Sandra and Michael Howard, Sarah and Andrew Clark.

'Rang Andrew Roberts [right], said "come down" and he suggested bringing Dean Godson. Just what I like. We sparkled and enjoyed ourselves with a rosé and two Bourgogne Aligoté in their "sleeves". Jane adapted brilliantly with heavy-duty canapés.' (27 September 1997.)

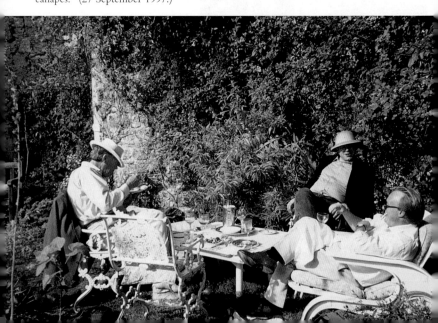

Shore Cottage, with the new porch ("the wheelhouse") at Eriboll. 'One of the best-value expenditures ever, it is commodious – even room for the two Bulgarian straw chairs plus the "Army" work table, plus length for gumboots, heater, Julie's (return reluctantly offered) Canadian pew. Coat hooks banned. It really is a most congenial spot.' (Easter Sunday, 1997.)

'The Christening – so pleasing in the little candle-lit church and the Catholic ceremony – Fr John Maguire – much more significant. Afterwards we did pile into the jeep for the Christmas-card photo. The last occasion for some while, I fear, when we will all be under one roof. (28 October 1998.) With Jane sitting next to AC at the wheel, back row: James (with Angus), Sarah (with Albert); middle row: Julie, Andrew (with Archie).

Left AC on what proved to be his last visit to Eriboll in July 1999, with James and Julie's son Angus.

Middle 'Today a great walk all around the forestry plantation.' (30 August 1997.)

Below 'I see always the beautiful view of the shoreline from boat house beach and hear the slap of the wavelets.' AC swimming with Lëhni and Hannah at Eriboll. (5 July 1999.)

Top 'There is always so much to do at Eriboll. Some things have been left undone for six, seven years. And the *Maid of Morven* still lies on her side, her entrails slowly rotting.' (New Year's Day, 1994.)

Above 'In the early afternoon we went out in the little Pioneer with James to clear the lobster pots. Absolutely divine – the loch was like glass and the silent little Yamaha outboard throbbed reassuringly on tick over. An absolutely perfect hour of tranquillity.' (24 August, 1996.)

Left James with Angus in an Orkney fishing boat named Katoomba after one of the Clark family's yachts

Relaxing at the Schönbuhl Hut in 1996, but to reach it – one of AC's favourite walks – required iron nerves as the path has vertiginous stretches. (8 October 1996.)

His grandfather's estate in Suffolk. 'Detoured to Sudbourne. The great house demolished ... I posed for a photograph, got on some disintegrating stone steps with a large cedar growing nearby. The whole garden now a wilderness and the lake grown over.' (13 October 1996.)

'En route, quite late in the afternoon when we were looking carefully at the signs on the autoroute, Jane spotted the name Colombey-les-deux-Eglises', synonymous with Charles de Gaulle. AC stands in front of his '"homely" low-built house covered in Virginia creeper, heavy white gravel, garden rather contrived, rather Ascot-like'. (12 October 1995.)

With Andrew and Albert, just six months and the youngest member of the Kensington & Chelsea Conservative Association.

'The Bailey in July at 1 p.m. was full traditional Saltwood. Beautiful, sunny, warm, hollyhocks burgeoning.' (28 July 1999.)

'We then did the "w", woodland as always. It always can make me sad, will I be doing this next year?' (22 May 1999.)

At Eriboll. 'How I wish that I could stay up here and just cure myself by God helping me to regenerate (as he has done so brilliantly up until now).' (3 July 1999.)

In the Knight's Hall before AC's funeral on 7 September 1999. 'A white damask tablecloth of Great Granpa's with Albany gold curtain over and then the shroud on its wooden base. Did the flowers, 2 large bowls. The white urns inside the blue pots – full of chrysanths, lilies, bay, rosemary, old man's beard and Russian vine and hops. We put our individual posies on Al – peace lilies from Hannah and Lëhni, mixed little bunches from all of us. Very pretty it looked.' (Jane's journal.)

'Felt very shaky, but hope I looked ok for Al, black plain linen dress, black stockings, black shoes, hair clean and loose. Only jewellery my diamond cross Al had given me, and my sapphire rings.' (Jane's journal.) From left, behind Jane: Julie, Col, James, Graham Stewart, Andrew and Sarah.

Lëhni sits on the stone that marks AC's final resting place at Saltwood.

windows intact, but besieged and entangled by brambles of wire rope.

On the way back via Seend Street ran into Peter Rogers now looking like a mildly corrupt senator from Oklahoma with a fine head of white hair, 'chiselled' features and dark eyebrows. Mrs Rogers amiably attractive still. And Wiltshire seemed very much as if (almost) one had never been away and delighted to have Andrew and a new generation there.

Saltwood, EMT   *Thursday, 10 October*

Back late last night, having driven the Little Silver *without glasses* from Bournemouth in 2¾ hours on 3 gallons of petrol (it seems). Slept like a top.

Conference, as always, left no time for anything. Lionised, still, but selectively. Middle-rank colleagues (except, interestingly those on the Right, like Townend,[1] Gardiner etc) are suspicious, don't want intercourse. Old mates – Ancram,[2] Goodlad ('love thy neighbour' was his elliptical parting shot) just as if I'd been speaking to them yesterday. Nellies, some of them up-market, are always friendly, and I am universally recognised by policemen. Some tough young 'graduates' (the best). Most of my time I seemed to spend in the company of ladies, Clara, of course, Jackie Ashley,[3] Sue Tinson[4] started me off on Tuesday evening. She saying 'you must see Major, he loves you ... etc' (shades of 'she'll have him in the Cabinet if she can'). Bruce

[1] John Townend, MP for Bridlington since 1979.
[2] Michael Ancram, Minister, Northern Ireland Office since 1994, MP for Devizes since 1992 (Berwick & E Lothian, February–September 1974, Edinburgh S, 1979–87).
[3] Jackie Ashley, *New Statesman* political writer, married to Andrew Marr (former political editor, the *Economist*, editor *The Independent*), the daughter of former Labour MP, Lord [Jack] Ashley.
[4] Sue Tinson, DBE, associate editor of ITN since 1989 and its link with Number Ten.

Anderson also told me that 'it was JM who had said "put in for Luton".' Then at the dinner I sat between two fat ladies – both amiable and intelligent. Although I had thought it would be low-key, a second XI and was wary of Gary Streeter[1] and his hostile wife (who Jane told me had widely said to the ladies at a Plymouth function – 'If he's so exhausted why doesn't he just stand down and make way for somebody else?'). Actually, fortified by a late, giant gin and tonic with Sue Tinson and some champagne and red wine I deftly whizzed over and sat next to and mobbed/flirted most indiscreetly with Rebekah Wade[2] (!) who I was interested to see was a flame-haired lovely (and must in 1993 have been even more luscious).

To some extent my whole performance was bogus. I have no standing. Am I famous, or infamous? Sarah Baxter, looking very attractive, wanted me to be 'interviewed' for the *Sunday Times*. I was in two minds, but finally assented, mindful of the risk, but thinking it was quite funny that I should be the post-conference profile in the *ST*. Will see what happens.

MFS GH   *Sunday, 13 October*

I sit here in the gloaming (about 6.30 p.m.) The porphyry desk set, the faded leather and veneers of the giant 'partners' desk'. The John Adamson long-case clock ticks slowly, a giant tapestry covers the north wall. Everything over here is shabby, but romantic still and with a latent glow, awaiting burnishment.

I was pleased by Sarah Baxter's article – 'busy reinventing himself', a perfect formula. On the way back from Aldeburgh we detoured to Sudbourne.[3] The great house demolished, but wonderful stablings, and outbuildings still, although the glass

[1] AC's successor at Plymouth Sutton, a Whip since 1995; his wife Janet.
[2] Rebekah Wade, deputy editor of the *News of the World* since 1989.
[3] The Suffolk estate of AC's grandfather, Kenneth McKenzie Clark.

canopies for resting the cars and carriages are gone, like the huge greenhouses – although the walled garden perimeter is still intact. What a huge property! All the cottage ornée are untouched – almost vulgar, but my goodness they were well built. We wandered about. It is sad not knowing more about inventories and schedules and how many staff there were and so forth. I posed for a photograph, got on some disintegrating stone steps with a large cedar growing nearby. The whole garden now a wilderness and the lake grown over.

When we returned I got out the albums – everything so spick and span. But a vast undertaking. My grandfather went there quite a lot; taking trout in May, pheasants in October and November. In between to Scotland – on the yacht – and sometimes just for a night on passage to 25 Berkeley Square (!). Yet Sudbourne could never really have been kept on – which Shielbridge [at Ardnamurchan] could. Though both estates so vast that without perpetual supervision you were going to get ripped off. When we got back to Saltwood I wondered if, in ninety years time, my grandson would still be here and to what extent the estate/property would have been forced to yield.

Saturday, 19 October

A curious 'turn-up' on – as so often can happen – several different fronts at once. On 16 October at 6.31 little baby Albert McKenzie was born. 'King George VII' I call him mindful of the signature 'Bertie' in the Port Lympne visitor's book (though even as I write I realise that this would have been Lord Bertie – a courtier of some kind – as it also contains the signature in a round, juvenile hand – 'Albert').

We went to see him the next day at the very pleasing and brand new Chelsea-Kensington Hospital, built on the site of that gloomy St Stephens (was it?) next to Netherton Grove. Even as I write this I am reminded, one of those ineradicable memories, of that summer night (it would have been the summer of 1954, I should think) when I heard a child crying, crying, crying in an upper room in one of the houses – which one? – that backed on to the gardens from a parallel street. It was so deeply and entirely distressed that alarm woke, and a little knot of concerned people gathered in the street. But what could we do? Knowing now what one has learned about child abuse, and the like, I suppose we should have been more assertive. But we dispersed and, after many hours, from exhaustion I judge he (for it was male) fell silent.

I felt sad, curiously so, when I looked at the tiny baby. 'A page turns', I said, only half-jokingly, 'on to a new chapter of anxiety and heartache ...' Curiously I found that birth gives one a sharper sense of one's own mortality than death. How seminal was that film *2001*![1] What a strange sensation and experience, to open one's eyes for the *very first time* ('He's nought', Jane said) in one's life, and take in the surroundings of a maternity ward.

I did privately notice that Nick Scott had barely improved his position by being 'found' collapsing face-down in a side-street in Bournemouth, and saw he had been summoned to his Executive Council on 4 November. Last night Soames rang, claimed to have been told that people in Chelsea who had voted for him once now going to vote for me. 'But don't do *anything*, Alan. Promise me you will say *NOTHING*' etc.

Largely fantasy of course, but fun. I mustn't think about it. But no doubt I am on a roll at the moment.

Garden House   *Sunday, 3 November*

Just took time off from BB to record how immensely happy I am. I must thank God, and do something for him – but I don't know how or what.

---

[1] Subtitled 'A Space Odyssey', and directed by Stanley Kubrick, 1968.

Albert is sweet and healthy; Andrew and Sarah are 'excellent parents'.

All is as well as can be expected at Saltwood.

Jane has 'passed' with Tom Bates just as I did a couple of weeks ago.

The Bustard has been sold for £125 (and they also want the Loco for 60/5 and the SS100 at 98).

The Zurbaran is plodding on, and will consolidate Zermatt and possibly start a treuhand.

The Giorgione is full of promise, and we may go to Venice on 23 November – think of that!

BB is potentially terrific. I am devoting more and more hours on it, and recovering confidence (and shape). A difficult passage, the Churchill-Eden government to Suez has turned out very readable.

And Nick Scott comes up (*again*) for de-selection tomorrow.

Garden House   *Sunday, 17 November*

I'm glad I made the last entry, recording how deliciously happy I was – because now I am rattled and disconsolate. All (or nearly all) a matter of mood, I suppose – but none the less real for that.

In the last six weeks I have become conscious of being much older. I am now so still and wobbly when I carry Tom downstairs in the mornings and I (excusing myself by 'stiff back') can no longer bound up the stairs.

Really resigned to the fact that even if there's now a vacancy I probably won't even be *seen* (re) by Chelsea. Also (perhaps because of this) it is all much more through-a-glass darkly now. That last draft of nostalgia. Now it seems remote, being desirable. A new miracle needed.

This is reflected in my standing. Many fewer approaches now. No Christmas party invitations. I wrote to JM suggesting a supper with myself and Simon Jenkins and Sue Tinson – no answer. Soames' own voice print kind of gives it away.

I must just concentrate on BB. But last night, v 'frail' and jumpy (I am lividly jarred when Jane bangs saucepan lids in the kitchen), I came over here to do a couple of pages on Ted. For some reason the machine went shifty and I kept getting 'You may not leave Winword' in a large oval white box after doing 'exit windows – ok'. In the end, livid, I switched it off and lost a whole evening's work. Ha!

Summer Bedroom   *Saturday, 23 November*

That delicious sense of relief and calmness that comes as one emerges from a filthy flu-cold. Yesterday I just lay here, eyes streaming, incapable, listlessly plucking at *Hello* or an Audi catalogue.[1] Ate nothing till the evening, then had a mini-craving for a piece of white bread and butter and a raw onion and knew that 'the crisis was past'.

Down at the gates this morning (the interior of the Mains is shabby with neglect – will it outlast us?) and thought how long have I got? Usual answer – '20 years'. But this is unrealistic. Ten, then? But I will/would be the same age as my father when he became doddery and feeble-voiced. And anyway, *ten isn't enough*. How can I say this? I am so fortunate, so much for which to thank God. It just is I would like three completely free, but still with some vigour, to enjoy myself with Jane.

---

[1] Jane Clark says AC never read *Hello*; much more likely to have been *The Field*.

Tower Office   *Monday, 2 December*

Nick Scott is clearly going to win his public meeting tonight (his *third* in tenure) – but in any case, no one remembers me any more. I've suddenly become, and look, 'too old'.

Saltwood   *Tuesday, 3 December*

Back from Julian Amery's memorial service at St Margaret's.

Little Winston's address quite good – don't know who wrote it – and reminded one of how long and rich Julian's life had been – though never with complete fulfilment. Mrs T let him down; just as she did today by not attending. And last night Nick Soames said, quite true, that he was weak at the base – though wonderful on his feet as a back-bencher.

St Margaret's was less than two-thirds full. Jonathan [Aitken] very splendidly intercepted us and conducted us to the centre aisle. I sat next to Lolicia [Aitken] and we were later joined by Richard R[yder] (now, as Jane observed, just a little accountant. Quiet, deafish and chetif). On the way out he scuttled away through a side door. Spotted little Budgen (unaltered and as chippy as ever); Pirrie Norrie[1] benign, but seeming to have put on most of Lawson's shed fat; Paul Channon – looked quickly away when he caught my eye – like so many of us had added to his jowl.

As Jane said in the car everyone seemed a good deal older (has it all happened in the last two years?), and she meant people like Richard Shepherd[2] and Mark Lennox-Boyd – but they/we are from a generation after Julian, he was our father. His death marks the passing, finally, of an era. We, too, have been shunted up a tier, and are now obsolete.

---

[1] Norman Lamont, as he was known by the Clarks.
[2] Richard (Rick) Shepherd, MP for Aldridge-Brownhills since 1979.

No one spoke to me much. Afterwards I did a quick bite for the *World at One* in the Millbank studio with a sweet dark Welsh girl with a slightly sideways face/jaw, as if she had had an accident some time. But absolutely no approaches or overture from Chelsea – which must be seething now.[1] Immediately after the (surprising) vote Nick Soames rang; some talk that four out of the six people he was dining with said they would vote for me etc etc. He wound me up – and we had a very bad night. I lay there unable to de-focus and mindful of the fact that yet again an empty period now looks like being filled and fraught.

Almost where we left off/opened the volume.

But as this last entry closes I must record I have personally had some setbacks. Blood in the urethra, attack of 'distorted vision', heavy eyestrain (glaucoma). No longer race up stairs, some strange AF attacks in middle of night, pulse rate 140 plus. Appearance rather cross and alarmed or apprehensive, with hair white and receding. Sexuality declined almost out of sight. Even so – lucky to be around, to have so much, sweet Jane and the little baby grandson.

Saltwood   *EMT, Tuesday, 10 December*

I am depressed. I am worried simultaneously about my health, my book (BB) and the state of the party/politics. My entire morale seems to have suffered, and it is only on the great Beechborough walk (slightly over two hours) that I feel better and freer (I can't remember when I last did Gossie – was it a true 'last'?).

On Sunday, having got a lot of logs in and pleasingly exhausted, I phoned the PM. after his broadcast. He was pleased

---

[1] In the latest round of a roller-coaster selection process, Sir Nicholas Scott, who had been MP for Chelsea since October 1974, found himself rejected by the new Kensington and Chelsea Conservative constituency association set up as part of the boundary reorganisation that would come into force at the general election.

and friendly, though seemed a little unhappy. What is happening to the Party? They are now a medieval army in the reign of King Stephen – pre Ironside – each one concerned to preserve their individual estates (constituencies) fragmenting into even smaller Margravates around dignitaries who may, or may not, be in a position to distribute favours and booty. Discipline has completely broken down, and they loot the countryside as they march and counter-march. It is the warlord syndrome. Harold and Stamford Bridge; Afghanistan, Mozambique. Am I half pre-empting disappointment at being rejected by Chelsea? Do I want to be back at the House – right back – in opposition and in smaller numbers, I would judge, than in even October 1974-79?

Sandling train   *Monday, 16 December*

Daily the assumption grows that we will be routed at the election. And there is the strange smell of 1938 in the air – of a massive, ill-disposed accumulation of power on the European continent. It can be appeased, concessions made – each one at a higher cost; or it can be resisted – almost an act of desperation and with consequences wholly unpredictable. And again, as in 1938, it is hard to find any leadership that exudes complete confidence. Major's intuition (like Neville's) was sound, but he is hampered by party political constraints.

Saltwood   *EMT, Saturday, 21 December*

Decks clear for Christmas! (Whatever that means.)

I am still somewhat blighted by my head (eye) ache. I have sat here at the kitchen table for nearly 40 minutes pressing my temples with fingers and trying – very occasionally succeeding – to defocus. Yesterday I forced myself to do one page of 'Heath

II' (BB) at the white computer. A brain tumour would be moving faster than this, surely?

K-C remains a mirage. I get little bursts of enthusiasm, but have suffered too many disappointments (I mean I really did think I was a shoe-in for Sevenoaks). But at Max Hastings' party (he had raging flu and a high temperature) I spoke with David Heathcoat-Amory.[1] Always an interesting, clever man. He said the whole course of history both of the Party and the country would be decided in conclave after the Election by who backed whom for the leadership.

Pirrie Norrie's party the previous day was a total frost. As Jane said coming up the stairs we realised there was no buzz. I was glowered at by some (as it were) Area Chairmen on the landing.

MFS Garden House   *Monday, 30 December*

I must set out a résumé – both 'where am I', and what has been.

Jane excelled (even) herself over Christmas; the whole house so beautifully, and tastefully decorated. Greenery everywhere, quite pagan, a calling out almost. But this time, first occasion for thirty years or more there was a *pram in the hall*! Nanny's great grey, which pushes and rides like a silver ghost, was wheeled down from the Rabies Room and, somewhat, admittedly under HE's-Reception conditions I Autosolvol'd the wheels and the dumb-irons, Simonizing the 'coach-built' body. Little Albert was lovely, changing each day. We all went to Canterbury for the carol service and he was a little starfish in his blue ski-suit, and quite placid. I carried him (v heavy) a little way in the aisle when we left – to approving glances. But how much of him, or of any brothers or sisters (or cousins) will I live to see? I am multi-hypochondriacal at present – after a sign of prolonged

---

[1] David Heathcoat-Amory, MP for Wells since 1983, Paymaster-General 1994–96 and before that Deputy Government Whip.

gestation. My memory has quite rapidly become atrocious. Can collect it up to a point, but now almost pre-Alzheimer. But my appetite is fine, weight 11.4½ (+) or so. I drink third of a bottle of wine every day.

Sunday Times Magazine did its usual gallery of people who died last year, aged 73-77. I can't believe that I have only about five years left, preferring to think that like Bill Deedes I will still be scrawnily around aet.88.[1] But I must admit that the likelihood of my going back to the House, even being interviewed for Chelsea does seem quite remote. It no longer seems realistic. A colossal effort of inspiration would be required although there are of course reserves which I can draw on if they will allow me to.

Paradoxically, if I were back in the House there would be more free time. I suspect because life is more orderly and compartmentalised, and much is done for you. I have been my own secretary now for nearly five years – and it shows.

If I could just get BB (and the TV show) out of the way this year perhaps in '98 we can choose.

1997 – could go back to Heaven

1998 – a lot less/more on his plate

So I simply don't know. I don't know if my health will hold up, or the book get finished, or I am finally excluded from public life. Or if by some strange and miraculous concatenation I return as a big player.

Garden House   *New Year's Eve*

The handwriting recently has been abominable. Is this poor vision, or 'nerves'? I went down to Hythe P.O. (long queue) to record the letter and CVs to K&C. Everybody slouching up and down the street absolutely flush, each person holding a plastic

---

[1] Lord Deedes was actually 83 at the time of this entry.

bag bulging hideously with merchandise. I called back here to make a note, of how it is HE's reception the entire time at the moment. I don't seem to see a clear run ahead (the best, actually was five years ago when I first 'holed up' here for the G. Election) – a switch-off fortnight as driven by the tyranny of the column.

1997

A little calmer, which is surprising, because the entire morning was spent 'doing' the top of the tallboy in my bathroom. But fortunately I 'forced the pace' and went through to the end – i.e. polish and rearrange the tortoise-shell objects, so that tiny sector is now 'clear'. But, as I said to Jane, Walcheron Island. Consumed the entire Canadian Corps from Sept '44 to March '45 and when it was over, and the Scheldt clear, so what? My eyes are better today. Last night I wrote a my-patience-is-exhausted letter to Goodlad. Eleven lists since I stood down, and no recognition of any kind.

Monday, 6 January

David D rang last night. Said that Heseltine most likely to succeed in the post-election contest – between him and Michael Howard; at first round there will be seven or eight candidates. But whoever has their nose in front will win the second head-onner. Dorrell[1] probably won't stand. Ken Clarke might not, not wanting to get a tiny total (I don't believe this – Gillian [Mrs Clarke] will make him, anyway); and would probably let it be known that he was supporting Hes, having been promised Foreign Secretary. The Right, on the other hand will be a shambles. Portillo, Redwood, Shephard, Rifkind (dark horse – 52 votes)[2] and Howard himself. In between the two ballots Heseltine's supporters will say (a) a bandwagon is rolling; (b) 'he's really on your side, you know.' Not much fun leading in opposition – but Labour may 'get into trouble' early on – particularly over Euro-vote.

What an exciting House it is going to be! If I go back in there

---

[1] Stephen Dorrell, MP for Loughborough since 1979, Health Secretary since 1995.
[2] Malcolm Rifkind, Foreign Secretary since 1995.

I will die, or at least become impossibly infirm in harness. If I
don't I will be a recluse; not at Colombey, not even at Elba, but
at St Helena. How very melancholy. I am sad, and so apprehensive
that sometimes my hands are improperly co-ordinated.

Dean Godson rang last night. He was grave, but, considering
he wanted me to go to Hull[1] on his behalf (something which
earlier I have refused) not optimistic.

EMT   *Thursday, 9 January*

At his invitation I drove over to Michael Howard last night.
'Congratulations on your part in ... helping the Chancellor to
concentrate his mind on aspects of the single currency at
Cabinet before Christmas,' I said – showing that I was well-
informed (but *how* well?).

He launched straight in. Without telling JM Michael raised at
November 30 Cabinet the need for a debate, said Ken Clarke
should prepare a paper for the pre-Christmas Cabinet. Ken C
blustered, said he didn't see any need for a new paper, but would
'of course' provide any Treasury documents, that 'colleagues'
might want to look at. Somewhat disingenuously (more likely
hyper-shrewdly) Michael claimed that he had not warned the
PM so that he (PM) could say to Ken and Hes afterwards, 'I had
no idea that this was going to happen'; also, of course, because
five or six people in Cabinet who 'take PM's orders' (Lang,
Newton, Freeman,[2] Dorrell, ?Goodlad, ?Cranborne, ?Gummer
[AC's question marks]) would, if alerted, have talked it down.

The mood, expressed thus, was for a 'paper'. This didn't please

---

[1] Dean Godson, deputy chairman of Kensington and Chelsea Conservative Association
1995–98, was also Tory candidate for Great Grimsby. In his mid-thirties, he had
been chief leader writer, *Daily Telegraph*, since 1996.

[2] Tony Newton, MP for Braintree since February 1974, Leader of the House of
Commons; Roger Freeman, MP for Kettering since 1983, Chancellor of the
Duchy of Lancaster since 1995.

Clarke at all, and a good deal of leak and counter-leaking began. By the time the 'paper' arrived JM had of course worked on his own placemen. But (in order not to give early warning) had not made approaches of any kind to the sceptics. So at the debate, very narrowly, lost 9-11.

The No 10 machine, however, did not leak a 'sceptics routed' story. Instead it indicated that Clarke had been told to go back and take another look at it all.[1]

Saltwood   *Sunday, 12 January*

Lovely and enclosed by snow/fog. The M-way is silent, and one is reminded how peaceful, magical Saltwood could be transferred to a position in, say, Herefordshire, or the Welsh marches.

David D down – talk at breakfast, then dinner. A clever boy, but like Major a little chippy still. Neither he nor Michael Howard says anything of the 'you're needed' type, and Soames hasn't rung for weeks. A quiet recognition that my time has passed. Well, that's all right if what is written is written – though I am still haunted by the fact that it is *my fault*.

Later

Jane pointed out that at least a gallon of water had leaked/ seeped from the Hen 3-litre. Did Guppy not put anti-freeze in? A 3-litre block would cost – at a guess – £4,000, water pumps and things still more.

Reading at the moment Thatcher account of the coup[2] against the background of the Gulf War. TK gets a favourable mention. I am too sharp/clever for Mrs T. Like Ian Gilmour, but without the polish. That was six years ago. Sometimes it seems

---

[1] AC adds a note: 'continued in BB'; indeed the story of the internal battle within the Conservative Party over Europe as related by AC has a definite insider feel about it.

[2] In the first volume of Margaret Thatcher's memoirs, *The Downing Street Years*.

like 18 months. Then followed by the miracle. Zermatt in 1991, and a lovely three years. Now the quality of my life has deteriorated. But it remains within my capacity to recover (most of) it.

EMT   *Thursday, 16 January*

On Monday, sitting quietly at the 'white' screen in Garden House, at 8 p.m. I felt so overcome by depression, sense of waste of being out *due to my own idiocies and weak character*. I love the history, the participation, the minutiae. But at the back lurks, too, the sword. And yet the *machine*, the pigginess of the Party, will not allow me ever to be seen.

The hour has come, and passed, when the call should have come through.

So I prayed – properly, but shortly. Thought little more of it. Patrick Hennessy for the *Standard* on the answering machine – presumably for a gloat. I was out-of-sorts. Doing paperwork with Jane in the Tower Office (she is so good at that, quadruples over rate). Then on came Barbara Lord. I was to be interviewed – I gave her the works; she very sweetly said she preferred me. I have got quite a good vote ('which surprised her' – compliment?) set out rules of secrecy. A huge wash of adrenalin *surged* through me. I went straight to Beechborough. What *is* written?

The next day she rang again – purposely to apologise for the leaking (as they had the whole list it couldn't have been me), but significantly said that Trish Sill Johnston[1] wanted to talk to me, tell me of a few local points. Now this (I thought) was significant. An overture from the Nick camp as well …! For the first time it seemed to be realistic. Sitting on the Green Room floor I got flu symptoms alternating with AF. Could it really be feasible? Jane, as always, was brilliant, though drily unimpressed. I had a baddish night, semi near the surface most of the time.

---

[1] Patricia (Trish) Sill Johnston, Secretary to Nicholas Scott.

Up in Big Red this morning to lunch at Marks (lost the way
and arrived late) with Dean [Godson]. Intense, indefatigable,
something of a young Isaiah (Berlin) about him. I thought he
was a teensy bit guarded – but we have agreed to dine on
Saturday and he will 'tell me the questions' (shades of Graham
Butland).[1] I've got to come up on Saturday morning, that's quite
clear, to 'walk the Borough', get to know local issues etc. And so
there we are – the last offensive, April 1918, on the Ardennes.

EMT   *Monday, 20 January*

I must record the developments in this big eerily, crazy, half-
tragic, almost incredible and possibly calamitous final charge. I
had a *nuit cassé* on Saturday night. Went to bed with the speech
unformed; a reasonable end paragraph, an opening formed on
my long adrenalin-dispersing trek that afternoon before getting
a cab back to B5 tea, and out to dine with Dean Godson (or
Dean Whitter,[2] as Jane amusingly calls him) – but no third link
passage about the majority party and social events. These sort of
formed into shape in a two-hour half-sleepy period from about
4 a.m. But it was still far from solid. And untimed. Soft-spoken
I 'rehearsed' after losing the place. Then parked, beautifully
timed, on corner of Flood Street. Mini panic and demi-
breathless arrival at '1a' (as it is now called) and ushered more or
less straight in. Atmosphere very pleasant. Andrew Dalton hyper-
smooth. They did, I must say, 'put me at ease.' Speech just got
past; a couple of good passages. The first question from 'Big'
Barry Phelps:[3]

---

[1] Graham Butland – at Plymouth Sutton in 1972 (see *Diaries: Into Politics*, 31 January
  1982). Godson backed AC in the initial, but not in the latter stages of his K & C
  candidacy.
[2] Dean Whitter, as in the bankers Morgan Stanley Dean Whitter sometimes used by
  AC.
[3] Barry Phelps, local councillor.

'Mr Clark, last time you appeared before this committee and I asked you a question you delivered a prepared answer that had no relation to it whatever. This time would you like to give the answer first, or second?'

'Well, Barry, the committee should know that with your customary sensitivity to the feelings of others you have always told my younger son and daughter-in-law who are constituents of yours, that there was no point in my putting in for the candidacy as I didn't have a chance and I was just wasting everyone's time ...'

Great applause and laughter (in which he chiefly joined). Got me off to a good start. After that, not too difficult, could be statesman – giving my 'single-currency' answer.

Interrupted at this point: I was going to write about all those people on the committee who had rung last night 'taking out insurance' as I said; but Lynn spotted the fact that I sounded 'coldy'. I am snuffly, runny nose, eye-ache and pulse 84 (it only goes to 72–76 if just 'agitated'). Spoke to Barbara Lord and she said that every single person on the committee had voted for me! But what's the use? – flu for the final – I cannot believe it – McEnroe.

EMT   *Tuesday, 21 January*

Today the most tiresome bit. The 'Executive'. But 150 (!) of them so had to include a number who are opposed, and a mike necessary, which I hate and am unused (*Brideshead*) to.[1]

When I woke I thought so fondly of darling little Jane. I am putting her through this ordeal. She is so loyal. Doesn't, of course, want me to get through. And she is right, but I am driven by the sword. My stars are incredible. Everything seems to be

---

[1] AC adds his own note: 'Marquess's son unused to wine'.

falling into place. Is it to be 'all my life seemed but a preparation
for this hour …'? Or back here, having 'lost' 10 days which I can
ill-afford, to be an academic?

I thought, too, that if I win I will immediately write Jane a
long letter, not just telling her of my love, and my gratitude; but
setting out my commitment to her and to regulating (at last) our
life so that we can be 'Mama Paça' as well as FPs.

I am on this fantastic roll at the moment. What a let-down
when it evaporates. But of all the meetings this somehow is the
one about which I am most uneasy.

EMT, Albany   *Tuesday, 28 January*

I should have made an entry earlier; at once, indeed on the
Friday morning. But instead went for a full Beechborough.
Jane let me out of the conker-tree gate where a single agency-
photographer who 'knew the area' was lying in wait. Stumblingly
he walked backwards down the rough and muddy path from the
iron bridge; his red light glowed at intervals but like all cameras
malfunctioned, and seldom flashed.

Soon I was on my own – utterly, ineradicably euphoric. Then,
one last, magical sign. I was walking along the bank above the
dyke before the valley curves round and a huge fox, lovely and
orange like the one living in the tyre-shed at Broomhayes church.
Loped very casually in front of me. For a second he stopped; and
turned round, looked at me and then disappeared. I don't mean
he ran off. He simply disappeared. Magic. I know what he was
saying – 'we helped. And we understood what you had to do.'

As I crossed the bridge on the M20 I sang. A prayer of thanks,
of total happiness. I don't honestly think I have been so utterly
happy in my entire life as on that Friday morning. And I
climbed on up to the cattle-grid where I have so often sat sometimes in disappointment, sometimes in search of inspiration or
to contemplate and speak to God.

This, though, anticipates the happenings, the agonies, the dry-mouthed soft-spoken, foodless, sleepless hours that ran on from the previous Tuesday. The Executive, as I had anticipated, the most difficult audience. Preceded by a 'cocktail' party (the glass of white wine most welcome) at which Jane was lovely and made 'a conquest' of the initially un-twinkly battleaxe who had been allocated as our 'minder'.

But I underperformed. I was carried away by my supporters. So although I came out top. It was done not by conviction, but by allegiance. Even the voice print of Andrew Dalton's[1] message carried the faintest nuance of uncertainty when, having slept exhausted but fitfully, I staggered down in the morning with Tom to switch it on.

So now we are committed. The last great offensive. In the afternoon of Thursday the reconnaissance. The Kensington Town Hall so red and soulless. The hall, and the gallery. At 6.40 p.m. we parked Big Red in some nameless, expensive street and made our way to the doors where a mass of hateful paparazzi and brutal reporters with mikes mobbed us.

'Why do you think K&C will choose you?' 'Aren't you even worse than Sir Nicholas Scott?' 'What do you think your chances?' etc.

'Well they can't be worse than 3 to 1,' I said bleakly. The press (literally) was frightening and hostile. I got separated from Jane – literally manhandled by Central Office officials through the doors to where a huge crowd of disapproving members were queuing for ballot papers. Most of them avoided my eye. 'Like the polling station at Leigham,' I said to Jane.

We were all confined to an underground 'green room', windowless, tableless with four bottles of mineral water (three of them fizzy, so liable to induce a burp when answering questions).

The other candidates all had something. Trish Morris – nice-looking, long copper-curled hair, vivacious, had wowed

---

[1] Andrew Dalton, chairman of Kensington and Chelsea Conservative Association.

conference earlier on the ERM.[1] Daniel Moylan outrageously camp, but a former president of the Union and with a high-profile record in local government; and Martin Howe, 'the Eurosceptic QC' with a pretty wife and a portentous manner. I was last. I found a make-up room with a flat-surface in front of a mirror and rehearsed, timing three lines through – being interrupted only once by a tiny, tubby Asian man who came in to urinate – what was he doing in the Ladies anyway? I was demi-transcendant, the space-craft was on course – collision, burn out, or triumph. Jane quite rightly came and fetched me out, knowing that I would be unsettling myself. Daniel had returned – frightfully funny and quacky about Elspeth Rhys Williams' intervention – and the atmosphere lightened. We all started to talk among ourselves, agreeing, naturally, how awful they all were. Daniel smoked eleven Camels. Longer and longer we waited. What on earth had happened? Then suddenly, Andrew Dalton re-appeared – I think he was actually doing what my mother called *priest*, dry hand-washing. 'Well, the contest is over …' making across to me, '… and Alan has won. Alan has won.'

I was incredibly happy. But also got a hint of 'all my life has been but a preparation for this hour …' Now almost at once, it seemed generally preordained. (It turned out that they had been counting all three ballots without telling us.) We went up the stairs to a loud cheer. I made a few anodyne remarks of gratitude; then congratulations, including lovely ones from Sarah and Tip[2] – and out to a battalion of flash bulbs and that most incredible sense of euphoria. Finally we were hauled away, followed Barbara to Jeanie Craig's house (all I wanted, desperately, was a pint of beer. I couldn't/didn't drink the champagne). Took calls, immediately, from David Davis in the car – *he* saw the point! – and then home at 2.30 a.m.

---

[1] Exchange rate mechanism, which at the time was rarely out of the headlines when the European single currency issue was being discussed.

[2] Andrew and Sarah Clark, and their 15-week-old son – 'the association's youngest member' according to *The Times*.

Albany   *Wednesday, 5 February*

Pam Churchill[1] has had a stroke in the Paris Ritz. Now they're trying to 'save' her. Why? What is the point of preserving the beautiful and vivacious courtesan as an old crone in paralysis?

As well as the sheer bliss of having the safest, nicest and most convenient seat in the country – and as a result of total victory in an outright, full-scale contest – there is the prospect of Big Book. Now I can dabble in this with real participating (ugh, oy! Etc) enjoyment.

EMT   *Sunday, 9 February*

I am sitting at the kitchen table; outside is dark and misty. Around me are spread all the constituency engagements, and the active election planning ... the old warhorse smells powder! Bogus of course, because hard to lose this one. In the night I worried if I might be assassinated during the campaign? I don't want to be paralysed, as politicians often seem to be after such attempts.

Albany   *Monday, 10 February*

Almost a fairy tale come true. This morning William Rees-Mogg in *The Times* – across four columns – 'Who will be the next Conservative leader? I suppose Alan Clark is too much to hope for.'

---

[1] Pamela Digby was the first wife of Randolph Churchill, Winston's son, and went on to marry the American theatre producer Leland Hayward and the diplomat Averell Harriman. She was sometime US ambassador to France. Her son, also Winston, had been MP for Davyhulme since 1983 (Stretford, 1970–83).

B5   *Thursday, 13 February (James's birthday)*

I am looking ghastly in the glass. Scrawny, jowls all too easily
hanging. In the night I woke at 3.40. I had sweated (nothing
new about this) and my faint, disparate, oculo-related headache
'came in'. I worry about my health and when it will perceptibly
disintegrate. The headaches are related to inability to defocus/
relax.

Bruce [Anderson] at Pratt's last night said as choice for chairing
the 22 committee I would be 'bigame', then the same word to
describe my selection at K&C. 'You don't seem entirely at home',
I said, 'with the Anglicised usage of what is, in origin, a French
adjective.' I am lowered by the prospect of black, unproductive
opposition. What I really don't know, and sometimes can't get to
grips with, is the pace at which I should move. A pleasing remark
last night from Bruce. 'Once they spot the skull-and-crossbones
on your masthead they'll all be on to you ...' Jane said, though,
that same evening, 'You must push yourself.'

Saltwood   *Tuesday, 25 February*

Returned this evening to find, and instantly, enter into, a state of
deep depression. Lëhni's jeopardy is clearly not over.[1] Our
advice is that she is protected by not falling into either of the
two categories in the Dangerous Dogs Act – Designated Breed,
or Out-of-control-in-a-public place. The moment I saw the text
I spotted – but did not tell Jane – the catch-all clause, 'or being
in a place, not being a public place, where it should not be' (i.e.,
on the other side of the asthma gates).

---

[1] The day after AC's selection at Kensington and Chelsea, Saltwood was besieged
by the press. A BBC camera crew set up opposite the back door waiting for AC's
return. Lëhni jumped up and grabbed the arm of a technician, tore his jersey and
drew blood. The technician seemed unconcerned, declined an offer to come
inside, said he would finish the interview and then use his own first aid box.

I've just refaxed Birt,[1] having basted his secretary earlier in the afternoon. BBC complete shambles; no one in charge, no one able to locate still less override 'line managers'. All they can say is 'Oh, I'm sure they don't want to destroy the dog ...' Fat lot of use that is. A totally worthless assurance.

The whole thing incredibly upsetting and distracting, which is sad really, because I had a most interesting lunch with Soames (35 minutes late, as I had to walk from Albany, got as far as Wilton Road – clearly not the place. Backtracked – still on foot and carrying my cases – to Wilton Street. Had intercourse with a policeman of the Special Protection Group (the only good ones left) outside a house – 'is this a restaurant?' (it had exterior carriage lights full on at 1.20 p.m.). 'No.' He laughed. Turned out it was Ted Heath's London abode. 'I'd better clear off then. He's not too keen on me'.

Finally caught up with the great man. And he is great, real Churchill genes, as he talked with such intensity and understanding. Full F. E. Smith, and streets ahead of dreamers like Budgen, or other has-beens or *déseché* remittance (of ideas) men. He was good advising me. Most sensible.

MFS GH   *Saturday, 8 March*

I am serene and contented. This afternoon the christening of tiny Albert. In the kitchen last night, horrified by the 'alternative' form, printed on a cling-film-coated card which 'Reg'[2] had handed the young, I went upstairs and fetched the little white parchment-bound prayerbook, inscribed by my father for Jane at the time of our wedding, and read to them the true form of service. I don't know what Andrew did, but most pleasingly Reg intoned the age-old phrases while the little

---

[1] John Birt, director-general of the BBC.
[2] The Rev. Canon Reg Humphriss, rector of Saltwood.

prince was humped and jigged by me, fretting just a little, on and off, but easily distracted by the stained glass. Afterwards we posed, the three males in line, beside my father's gravestone.

Thursday, 13 March

I had lunch in the 'Churchill' room [at the Commons] with Jonathan Aitken and Alastair Goodlad. It is glorious being back in the Commons. Everywhere I went I was hailed by staff; no one questioned my right of access (I put my luggage in a locker in the dining-room corridor). Dawn Primarolo[1] held a door open for me – or was it Tessa Jowell?

Saltwood, EMT   *Sunday, 16 March*

Depressed and out of sorts. Fatigue comes into it, of course, plus the oppression of every day filled with engagements. (Not all of those, I suspect, on the chart – like I had totally forgotten meeting the pensioners in Kensington Town Hall tomorrow – the first meeting I went to, on the wrong day last month.)

Last night at 3 a.m. precisely poor T.O. had, or rather started, a very long fit. He convulsed into walking movements, though lying down, defecated. I thought he was going to die – but he's so tough. We carried him outside, legs completely paralysed it seems, his ear cocked, but he slowly picked up. Back indoors he walked round and round incessantly, would not settle. We went back to bed and after two hours' sleep I went down – he was still pacing up the corridor through the top Green Room door, then back and round. He must have walked to Ashford. This

---

[1] Dawn Primarolo, MP (Lab) for Bristol South since 1987.

morning he is still muddled, but drank his saucer, went out as in routine. He's 18 years old.

So many people have come up to me to wish me well. Nellies in the street, the loony man from Wensdyke with his Cumberland accent; a sweet shy boy who stuttered slightly who walked all the way across the forecourt at Ashford Tesco. And yet, just as I knew I was going to get it – from way back, when Henrietta Royle first said, 'a lot of people from Chelsea may be there' (to the speaking engagement, my first entry to 1a) – so I also have the terrible feeling that I am never actually going to 'take my seat'. Ill health, crisis, personal anti-vote … My despondency increased by a very poor performance on Jonathan Dimbleby's show this morning. The whole of Sunday demolished, and I was old, hunched, and out manoeuvred. 'You must be aggressive (sic),' as Jane said. TV finds you out, and I was slow and stooping.

Just occasionally I ask myself – especially when threatened or worsted, what's the point? There are all those brambles in the woodland; and the Hen-Bustard hood-irons still to be blacked, and the early spring surge in the Garden approaching … 'Are we all mad?' (Chips).

Summer Office   *Tuesday, 18 March*

Last night we dined with Daniel Moylan – and a cocktail party first. The smartness, and the sophistication! 'You'd never get *one* of these people in a normal constituency,' I said to Jane, ' – never mind a roomful.' But is it all doomed to ash? Personally, I mean. Nationally, indeed, we are on the verge of annihilation it seems. Polls this morning show Labour 26 points ahead and the *Sun* has turned.

I haven't had a normal pulse for ten days.

Sandling train   *Thursday, 20 March*

David Davis interesting – cool as always. Said Cranborne and co
were 'a cloud of parasites looking for a host on which to settle ...'
Wanted to fix everything first; 22 Executive elections etc.
Suggested that they would probably prefer Tom King as 22
chairman. Key thing is to get Major to make a statement
immediately that he will ask 22 chairman to convene an
election before the summer recess – doubting that we could
extend it to November. JM himself may anyway not stand; but
would have time to test the water and recover.

MFS GH   *Saturday, 22 March*

I hate elections. This one hasn't yet started; but already I want to
fast forward. I have had bad experiences already – Jonathan
Dimbleby; and the pensioners (most notably reported in the
Kensington Times), the Lympne postmistress said to me, 'There
are a lot of discontented people about ...' I am always
susceptible to hostile press comment (as must be everyone who
habitually enjoys being preened). Complete meltdown is
possible. My own majority is far from secure because of a
personal anti vote which is solid (the lady with a spaniel and
head scarf from Swan Court) and my fan vote is fickle.

MFS GL   *Tuesday, 25 March*

Poor old Allan Stewart[1] forced to resign – instantly – today as
PPC because of his 'association' with a woman he met at an
alcohol-dependency clinic, even though his wife is 'standing by'

---

[1] Allan Stewart, MP for Eastwood since 1983 (E Renfrewshire 1979–83).

him. It is really preposterous, this kind of witch-hunt. There is now a total blurring of the lines between personal (sexual) conduct and personal (financial) conduct.

And I know, I can't say why or how, but I just know that something awful is going to happen to me and I get AF thinking about it.

Shore   *Easter Sunday, 30 March*

Really, with the possible exception of the balcony at the villino at Cuixmala I don't think there can be any more pleasing site for EMT – particularly, and most inexplicably, on a 'rough' day – than the new porch at Shore. We can't go past without popping in. One of the best-value expenditures ever, it is commodious – even room for the two Bulgarian straw chairs plus the 'Army' work table, plus length for gumboots, heater, Julie's (return reluctantly offered) Canadian pew. Coat hooks banned. It really is a most congenial spot; the wheelhouse of the *Hebridean Princess* with views down the Loch and up Eriboll Street to the Lodge and the Creaggan, opposite the Long Shed and the 'Gossie' bank. Truly panoramic.

The dignitaries in the Party are going down like nine-pins. Since we came up here Allan Stewart, Piers Merchant, and now poor Mickey Hirst – on the point of getting (Stewart's) seat – has 'crash'-resigned in the face of 'charges' of a relationship with a (male) researcher.[1] As Jane said, 'are the Labour Party made up of 200 virgins?'

---

1 Piers Merchant, MP for Beckenham since 1992 (Newcastle-upon-Tyne Central 1983–87); Sir Michael Hirst, Scottish Conservative and Unionist Party chairman since 1998.

Shore   *Easter Monday*

Am I relaxed, confident, beautifully turned out, one of the few
'real' Conservatives, historian, authoritative, high-profile media
figure: to be returned smoothly to the new 'difficult',
'interesting', etc House of Commons?

Or am I shaky, nervous of crowds, with incipient prostate,
bowel and basal cancers; demi deaf in one (right) ear, completely
non-functionally impotent with a limited lifespan and an
enormous crowd of ill-wishers waiting for me to fall over?

The next month is critical. But it is April; my 'lucky' month.

MFS GL   *Saturday, 5 April*

More apprehensive and ill-at-ease than I should be. Was it
only yesterday that the *Evening Standard* came out showing
that I had a 6-point advantage over the Party average in
London(!). I am really chuffed. The hottest currency in
politics. Then (in all probability) blew it by telling stupid little
Michelle Stephens, who was trying to set up an 'open' debate
between me and Robert Atkinson[1] − fired by his 'triumph'
with the pensioners he thinks he can parade local issues
around which is, of course, all a 'local' paper wants. Were they
interested in my 6 points? − not at all. Foolishly, in explaining
it, I lost my temper and said the 'Royal Borough is bloody
lucky to have me as a candidate.' What a headline! Fool, Clark,
fool, etc.

---

[1] Robert Atkinson, Labour candidate at Kensington and Chelsea.

B5   *Sunday, 6 April*

I wrote this with a ball-pen (which I dislike) that has cost me
£233 – the price, including tip, of a two-bottle lunch at the
Berkeley with Soames (splendid, but illish-looking) and Ancram
– grinning and compos. Jonathan A, somewhat diminished as
Soames and I – not for the first time – agreed, had given us
champagne at Lord North Street, but was depressed, almost
chetif.[1] We had come from the Candidates Conference in that
very low-ceilinged room with its strange overhead pipes, like
the ward-room of an escort carrier. Some pleasant young boys,
friendly and fresh-faced, who were going to be cut to pieces by
the *jagdstaffel*; some old warhorses (everyone looking quite a bit
older, I must say) and some sharp and indeed Semitic-looking
template figures who presumably had taken the best seats.

Mrs T spoke fantastically. Turned to the man on my right –
'she could still win the election', and her charisma, vitality and
blue-flashing eyes, still could. John M was competent, better
than adequate. I was filled with gloom at my manifest inability
to answer questions on any topic. Came back here and
wrestled with my Election Address text. Completed it about
7.30, very much 'in my own write', but on the phone Jane
liked it. I stopped the car in St Leonard's Terrace, walking back
to snoop on what looked to be a street-corner meeting, but it
turned out merely to be a group of late-evening tourists with
a guide.

Ancram repeated the Cranborne line, that we must all get
together more promptly – the Friday if possible – to stop JM
resigning if defeated badly. Norma [Major], apparently, is sick of
the whole thing and urging him to do that.

---

[1] Jonathan Aitken, despite his ongoing legal action involving the *Guardian*, was
standing as the Conservative candidate at Thanet South, which he had represented
since 1983.

Tuesday, 15 April

Almost completely soft-spoken and AF because Carol Midgley, of *The Times*, said 'Max Clifford keeps telling us of something really big – but he won't tell us what it is.'[1] Luckily, for my crumbling morale, we scored seven bull's-eyes as we went along the street. She and the photographer 'had to admit it'. A little later as I said, 'I hope you will agree that I am not encountering a very high level of personal hostility,' Carol had to admit, said something about 'everybody likes you'. And we had a boost from a TV wife who said Parliament should contain people like me and Tony Benn. In the *Standard* tonight MORI showed 20 points deficit. Intractable. Could be interesting.

Garden House							*Saturday, 19 April*

My hair has perceptibly whitened and I have lost ½ stone since 11 April adoption meeting. I don't know what is going to happen. Whether we will be routed (197 seats) or Parliament hung. Soames last night bellowing that 'we will win, Alan. We-are-going-to-win!' Apparently canvass returns are not bad.

MFS GH							*Sunday, 20 April*

Last night we did sleep well. The worst point, about 8 p.m. when comment from the Sundays would be sought. And I could feel that wonderful sensation of anxiety lifting – as in a benign diagnosis. One more period of jeopardy tonight – for Mondays.

---

[1] AC had been told that James Harkess, husband of Valerie Harkess, was flying from South Africa to campaign for Robert Atkinson, on the grounds that AC was 'not deserving of becoming an MP'. The Max Clifford 'threat' haunted him for the rest of the campaign.

Then, during the week we will be at Albany. I would have to address them from the steps, like General Gordon and the Mahdi. The very last Sunday would be too tricky for them to leave it so late.

Albany, EMT   *Tuesday, 29 April*

The news is dreadful. 'The Tory Party gives up' – headline in *Independent* (Anthony Bevins, naturally, he's not a reporter at all, but a Labour Party activist). The gap is intractable, widening indeed. Can this really be the case? Yesterday we decided to watch Major's last, and only, 'soapbox' performance on (ironically) College Green. A 'papered house' and only got to hear of it because CCO rang Barbara and asked for 20 activists to be bussed round and applaud. As we walked to and from the site, the streets of Whitehall seemed curiously empty. A sense – though not to the same degree – of the atmosphere in the Palace of Westminster just before the Lady fell. Not so far distant T34s were again at the fortifications on the Oder. I was calm. 'I have arrangements for my family to travel to the Argentine.' Even though as I composed this I was conscious of lapsing into 'parody' as Peter Bradshaw (whose last entry, after a miss the previous week, was very funny).[1]

Poor Major looked exhausted, his voice flat – and Jane said Norma looked absolutely shattered. I must speak to Robert Cranborne, perhaps today, to discuss a *petit comité*[2] at Saltwood on Saturday evening to talk through next steps.

---

[1] Peter Bradshaw, author of 'Not the Alan Clark Diary' in the *Evening Standard*, over which AC would later sue for 'passing off'.

[2] On 13 February 1992 AC had noted the following as possible members, complete with partial annotation: 'Heathcoat-Amory√, Derek Conway?, G Johnson Smith√, Andrew Mitchell√, David Caneva, William Hague, Peter Brooke, Jonathan Aitken, Soames, ?Cranborne, David D, Piers Merchant.'

EMT   *Thursday, 1 May*

I walked in very fragile sunlight to the paper seller in Piccadilly Circus underground and bought the whole lot. Robert Cranborne with whom I had a very interesting talk in his delightful comfy house at Swan Walk last evening, Robert was grave, but admirable in his sense of scholarship. First we must brush Redwood out of the way. Then keep Major in long enough for Heseltine's faults (of which we are all aware) to become apparent. Much depends on timing, and how to manoeuvre. In particular, the 'structure' of the 22 committee and its executive and chair.

(On the way back a plain young lady, alone in the street, said to me, 'I hope you lose – philanderer', which quite set me back after Buck House lights where I grumbled to Jane about a young yuppie lolling back in the taxi next to us, and then he wound down the window, 'I'm voting for you Alan' – and shook my hand!)

It was apparent as the first results came in that, as the polls predicted, Labour had a landslide victory. Labour 417 seats; Conservative 165 seats; Liberals 46 seats; others 28 seats. At Kensington and Chelsea, AC had 19,887 votes; Robert Atkinson (Labour) 10,368; Robert Woodthorpe Browne (Liberal Democrat) 5,668; others just over 1,000. AC's majority 9,519.

Saltwood, p.m.   *Friday, 2 May*

Down here after two hours' sleep and looking like death. Saltwood is beautiful; a completely still day and the greens yellowy-springlike. Doves, jackdaws and swallows go about their business in the Bailey. I am so exhausted I cannot bear to look at a press cutting or a newspaper or even talk to David D, or whoever. Already Jane is quite rightly making me 'take calls'.

People in London appear to be more shell-shocked than 'in the constituencies'. Archie Hamilton was far the most compos. Asked me straight out if I wanted the 22; some stuff about Butterfill[1] had beaten him for vice and Townend[2] was going to go for it, but yes he did want it for himself. Geoffrey Johnson Smith is the Whips' candidate.[3] Alastair Goodlad was so taciturn as almost (no, delete) to be unfriendly. Perhaps because of my 'anti-European' stance. Actually he was rather unpleasant.

Monday, 5 May

Most of yesterday seems to have been spent on the phone. The candidates are a mouldy lot. Portillo, probably the strongest, out.[4] Ken [Clarke], supposedly the most genial and experienced – won't get past the hard right. Little Hague – my aphorism about 'the guy's a golf ball' has already got currency, I'm glad to say. Redwood is fluent in today's *Times* – but I don't like him. Lilley is cerebral – should be the leader, but hasn't got the oomph – white rabbit in the teapot at the Mad Hatter's tea party.[5] Michael [Howard] presents me with a problem. I ought to support him, but I'm hesitating.

---

[1] John Butterfill, MP for Bournemouth West since 1983. He served as vice-chairman of the 1922 Committee until 2001.

[2] John Townend, MP for E Yorks. since 1997 (Bridlington 1979–97).

[3] Sir Geoffrey Johnson Smith, MP for Wealden since 1983 (E Grinstead, February 1965–1983; Holborn and St Pancras South, 1959–64).

[4] Michael Portillo had lost Enfield Southgate seat, which he had represented since December 1984.

[5] Peter Lilley, newly elected as MP for Hitchin and Harpenden (St Albans 1983–97), Trade and then Social Security Secretary in John Major's Cabinet.

EMT   *Thursday, 8 May*

Yesterday I was up in the Commons. The whole thing should
have been too delicious for words – but I was haunted by apprehension, and also a curious sense of hostility from colleagues,
even Tebbit, whereas staff, and Labour MPs – Skinner (walking
back from Church House, 'I thought the idea was to take power,
not to give it away'), Mark Fisher,[1] Tony Benn – brilliant speech
at the swearing-in.

Saltwood Garden   *Friday, 16 May*

Woke at 4 a.m. this morning in a panic that I wouldn't get
anyone to sponsor me for the 22 chair. Got up, wrote composite
letter to Peter Brooke[2] who was cool and abrupt to me in the
'Aye' lobby last night – leading to the fantasy nightmare that
Peter Lloyd[3] had said, 'I gather you've put up Alan for the 22?'
'What?' etc etc. Also doubled up in seeking sponsorship from
Francis Maude, David Heathcoat-Amory. *The Times* arrived, and
I saw I was at 2% – same as Dorrell and only one point behind
Lilley (!) – but drawing support equally from Labour and Con
– so wrote also to Gill Shephard.

After EMT and one biscuit drove to House, just in time for
prayers. Sent a note to Peter Brooke (*to which he did not reply*
though perfectly affable). Listened to start of Devolution Debate,
then urgent message from Soames. I knew what it would be
about. 'You can't do this. You're mad. You'll be slaughtered' etc.

This came at exactly the wrong moment. No reply from P.
Brooke; nothing on board from the others; feeling of *guarded*

---

[1] Dennis Skinner, MP for Bolsover since 1970; Mark Fisher, MP for Stoke-on-Trent
Central since 1983.
[2] Peter Brooke, newly elected MP for Cities of London and Westminster (City of
London and Westminster South, February 1977–97).
[3] Sir Peter Lloyd, MP for Fareham since 1979.

suspicion right across Party. I went out and drafted statement to Press Association. Told Jane on the answering machine, rather sadly went over to Trishy. Ann Perkins appeared almost at once, told me that John Macgregor wasn't now standing (!). Thought Geoffrey Johnson Smith was. Blast! Who dares wins.

Then when finally dead tired and stressed I got down here. Andrew Dalton very reproachful and disappointed ('wimpish'). As, although she was too sweet to show it, was Jane.

My line, I'm sticking to, 'don't want to split the vote' ('for the things I think need to be done'). We'll see how it is taken. My star was heavily in the ascendant. A lovely piece by Don McIntyre today in *The Independent* and yesterday in the tunnel Peter Oborne[1] was ruefully laudatory – said 'a great recalculation might have to be made'. Something though tells me I wouldn't have got it. Might next year *if* (and even that is not certain) I get on the Executive. Memories soon heal over in the House – provided I perform. But I must get my speech for Tuesday spruced up.

Tearoom frontage   *Saturday, 17 May*

An absolutely perfect morning of mid-May. Still wood pigeons cooing, whole place heavy with the sweet cloying odour of the Queen Anne's Lace. But I am not relaxed. Mrs Frowd this morning and we'll see what she says. Partly I am tormented by having bogged the 22 election. Lost my nerve under Soames's blustery. If only I had got Jane and not the answering machine, she would have said, 'Balls, go for it, lead from the front.' Soames rang again – said 'you *must* be more serious. If you're always on TV you're like Beaumont-Dark'.[2] Well, yes; but as Jane said someone must speak for Conservatives. In any case I'm minded to think that the old, stuffy rank of Tory MPs are different now.

---

[1] Peter Oborne, now political columnist with the *Sunday Express*.
[2] Sir Anthony Beaumont-Dark, MP for Birmingham Selly Oak, 1979–92.

They don't think like that any longer ... What put me in a panic was that nobody would 'sponsor' me. But I still should have waited until Monday – or even the very last minute.

I must speak, and question, and sit in on debates (and send congratulatory notes). I think the Party will slowly destroy itself, actually. So the tactic is to come out at an individual position.

H o C Library   *Wednesday, 21 May*

Last night at Conrad Black's dinner. Drank a tiny bit too much, and may have shouted. Influential people said why aren't you standing as chairman of the 22 committee. On the way up in the train the stars (Jonathan Cainer) had said go for it – too late. Even the 'conventional' excuse – 'better let it go a year' etc – is a cop-out. Next time could be in the context of having tried to rush it – then 'accepted colleagues' verdict' at waiting for a year.

I was in the position of the 3rd Army, and should have remembered Patton's aphorism – 'we ... don't worry about our flanks; it's for the enemy to worry about his.'

This absurd and embarrassing 'leadership contest' rambles on. In fact, as I was saying to young, intense Bernard Jenkin[1] in the aye lobby this morning, they may have 'thrown their hats in the ring', but the election campaign can't formally open until the nomination papers are filed with the (as yet unconstituted) 22 committee. The Left has now decided to make a showing for Ken, then switch en bloc to Hague (Dorrell is an irrelevance). Soames, a baleful though pleasing *éminence énorme* was going to vote for Ken, 'one's got to make sure he gets a good initial vote' – on Monday; then switch, 'it's got to be Hague'. Garel-Jones is running the Hague campaign. Let's hope he doesn't get a peerage.

---

[1] Bernard Jenkin, newly elected MP for Essex N since the election (Colchester N, 1992–97); his father Lord [Patrick] Jenkin had been an MP and Minister in the early 1980s.

Garden House   *Tuesday, 27 May*

Went over to Lympne. Michael (H) alert, and full of life-force, although he knows he's 'up against it'. Also there, particularly thoughtful, was Norman Lamont, and Rosemary. Norman was grave, but mock-statesman. Told how at 5.45 on election day he had set out for a last leaflet drop (an admission of pressure, and bad auguries, if ever there was one). Some slob of a councillor had refused to get up, but said 'would they drop in his leaflets as well …?' Then at 9 a.m. a champagne breakfast for 40 people, paid for personally by NL. Hung-over all day, and through to the humiliation of the count. What ordeals everyone suffered![1]

Refuge is taken in the assumption that Labour will hang themselves and people will say, 'this business of Government not as easy as being claimed …' Possibly. But will they then turn to the Tories? I think not. If only because they want not to admit so soon that they were wrong/conned? What part do I play? I'm guilt-free.

Friday, 30 May

The meeting of the [K&C] Executive at 1a was intensely depressing and I drove back, after 2 hours, very slowly and sadly. Not quite down to Plymothian standards, but they bickered and autogrumbled away. All the Kensington creepos were there, including that ghastly tall man who marched in front of us on walkabout bellowing at people in Kensington High Street, 'Would you like to meet the prospective parliamentary candidate?' One of them harangued the meeting about not having 'right-wing policies' in an American accent ('a Jewish accent,' Barbara said); another that we should wait for 'the

---

[1] Norman Lamont had lost his Harrogate seat to the Lib-Dems, majority 6,236.

Governor of Hong Kong'.[1] When they voted it was: KC 35; Hague 28; Lilley 14; Dorrell 2; Redwood 1. Poor Michael got zero! But an overwhelming vote for the Left. How lucky I am, to get selected there! Or at least what additional proof this offers of divine intervention.

As for myself, already I could feel my popularity slipping. And I have a suspicion that the book, and the TV series will annoy.

I spoke to Michael (he rang me at 9 a.m.) this morning. Explained I couldn't now 'come out' in the Sundays. He took it very well.

I don't actually know which candidate, *for me*, will be best. I had driven in the C-type and put £200 on Ken Clarke (now only evens).

GH   *Saturday, 31 May*

I am excruciatingly, unhealthily fatigued. Missed lunch entirely, but had a cream-scone tea – a private opening. Then trailed round with James's new little compressor and blew up tyres on the Hen (which we pushed out and it started at once, though pouring water) and the black Chev. At one point dear sweet Jane told me that she had been intermittently bleeding poor darling, and ought to see Ursell. Poor little pet. If she actually fell ill, my life would be effectively over. I would be a total recluse and try all the time to talk to her. I would close down Saltwood, I think – 'care and maintenance' – and live here half the time. But for long periods 'Ansoning' at Shore.

Perhaps it was this that has made me so utterly de-energised. I can't do Gossie – still less the Downs. Perhaps I ought to try this tomorrow.

---

[1] Chris Patten, former Tory MP (Bath 1979–92), Minister, and chairman of Conservative Party, was in his final weeks as last Governor of Hong Kong before its return to China. Aged 53, his future was much speculated upon.

Friday, 6 June

My confidence had earlier been raised by a meeting of the '92'. The good ones – Duncan Smith, Shephard etc – interrogatingly having an audition of candidates. Clarke, cleaned up in appearance, but not especially friendly; Hague, shifty little bureaucrat (voice jarring, like Wilson); Howard white as a sheet, but still impressive. Dorrell has now dropped out, but is dutch in the tearoom (*also* white as a sheet, and looking ghastly). At one point in the 'discussion' I bellowing dominated the room. Half-serious Iain Duncan Smith[1] said come round here, give us a talk, take some questions, 'throw your hat in the ring'.

Oh! But what bliss this all is. The sheer ecstasy of having walked out of a dream, and found it to be real ...

EMT   *Monday, 9 June*

Today Bill Cash[2] having a *petit comité* for a hard right grouping after the ballot. And I will give my spiel. By sheer force of personality I am in fact the epicentre of the 'Right'. And with two delicious corollaries (i) I am completely independent (of constituency pressure), (ii) whatever the solution – except possibly a Michael Howard victory – it will be explainable.

Barbican seat   *Sunday, 15 June*

The 'leadership' contest continues. Both Lilley and Howard welched on Redwood most odiously. I shall be voting for

---

[1] Iain Duncan Smith, MP for Chingford and Woodford Green since 1997 (Chingford 1992–97).
[2] William Cash, MP for Stone since the election (Stafford 1984–97), founder and chairman of the European Foundation.

Redwood in the 2nd ballot in order to maximise the recognisable numbers of the Right; then for Clarke in the final on the basis that he is the weaker; least likely to last the term, easiest to attack.

1 Parliament Street   *Thursday, 19 June*

The last vote in the leadership 'contest' today. Last night I broached, at the S. Stanley garden party, my notion of a spoilt ballot paper. Didn't go all that well. Andrew Dalton sneakily opposed. I 'hid my face' while the vote was counted 14–8. Typical constituency. The hard core of party spastics who don't like a 'loose cannon'. I was originally going to write BUTTOCKS on the voting slip. A bit tricky to 'live with', although not as dangerous as at first it seems as it would be what is 'expected' of me.

The dignity of abstention must, though, be reinforced by a mellifluous and persuasive think piece written this weekend. What I can't quite make out is do I say anything at this stage – probably not.[1] I still judge, tactically, it is better for me if Ken wins, then fluffs it. It's the old '72 Heathites, against the young 'Thatcher's children' plus a shower of failed Ministers cut off in mid-career, but without an idea in their head.

The phone rang, and it was Kirsty Wark wanting an interview on *Newsnight*.[2] But I'm not sure if the timing is ripe. It's 'don't rush it' versus 'grab the opportunity' on Tuesday night, after the second ballot.

Sat in the smoking room drinking (iced ginger beer in my case; scotch and g. ale in his) with David D. Shaun Woodward[3]

---

[1] AC was still considering putting himself forward as party leader, conceivably in November 1997 ('by popular demand if our poll figures have really plummeted'), but more likely 'a long haul to 1998'.
[2] Kirsty Wark, presenter on BBC2 *Newsnight* since 1992.
[3] Shaun Woodward, MP for Witney since 1997.

hovered. Pure bliss. Was I really lounging in the smoking room, talking of politics from the inside track less than a year after I had been, in desperation, seriously considering doing a Churchill at N. Dorset?

Earlier in the afternoon, while walking along the pavement outside New Palace Yard, a voice behind me said, 'That's a very smart car of yours which slid past me this morning.'

'I love it,' I said.

'But every police force in the country must have the number?'

Thinking he was 'trying to be nice' I said, 'I never thought I'd find myself saying this: but I wish you were in the running ...'

MH [Michael Heseltine] replied by going into a long thing about 'I never could understand, you were taking the wrong briefs, we could have worked together' etc etc. I reminded him of the message I sent through Peter Levene from MoD.[1] He tried to push it aside.

When I told David D he made an interesting reply, 'you're opium now, he had to have some. He's aching with withdrawal. No, worse, you were a still smoking stub on the pavement which he picked up for a last drag.'

The delicious irony of it all. Now I'm going over to hear the count.[2]

EMT (Albany)   *Thursday, 10 July*

A year ago if you had said to me, etc etc. Last night I was elected (by a very good vote, as Patrick McLoughlin[3] said) to the 22 Executive. Most notable that there is real attendance at 22

---

[1] Lord Levene had a long association with Michael Heseltine, being his personal adviser at Defence, Environment and the Board of Trade, 1992. He had also been Chief of Defence Procurement, MoD, during AC's time as a Minister there.

[2] In the final ballot of Tory MPs, William Hague had a 22 majority over Kenneth Clarke.

[3] Patrick McLoughlin, MP for West Derbyshire since May 1986; a Whip.

elections; not like those somewhat spare grouplets that contest the Party committees.

Felt immediately an elevation of status. David D, who always keeps a lot of himself to himself, but was loyal in my wilderness years, had a chat in the smoking room afterwards. 'Get a group of the new "good" ones down to Saltwood,' he advised me, an end-of-term picnic.

Strange, his 'sponsorship'. What is going on at the back of his mind? Could it be the same sort of thing that lies in mine? (Although today I read Peter Riddell – one of the small-print merchants – complaining of 'GDP' deflation. How can a Prime Minister, unless he be exceptionally boring like Wilson, be expected to 'brief' himself on these arcane matters?)

Saltwood   *Sunday, 13 July*

My father's birthday. He would be 94, just – I think – older than Bernard Berenson was when he died.[1] Now the Great Reaper moves without disguise among my own generation. There is poor Jimmy [Goldsmith], in agony for the last 30 days at (Burgundy) where his new 'Indian' doctor is curing him (yeah) by 'withdrawing' painkilling drugs. French doctors are good at keeping you going right up until the end, Pompidou, Mitterrand, by ruthless use of steroids and others. Then, finally, the body collapses. After all it was only 1 May that Jimmy was chanting in triumph at the odious Mellor (who now, or so we are told, is to go 'straight to the Lords'[2]).

I am seated on the front step, with the door wide open, on the Coronation chair. My grandfather's diary for 1909 shows

---

[1] Kenneth Clark studied under Berenson in the 1920s.
[2] Although David Mellor had lost his Putney seat at the general election after 20 years as MP, AC was unnecessarily pessimistic: he was not elevated to the Lords.

that they were at Poolewe (with, I assume, that almost brand-new 'Katoomba'[1] riding in Loch Ewe) and that week he caught a 16 lb salmon. Just one very brief time I was there, aged 3-4, I suppose. But I can recall the smell of peat water, and the newly caught fish; and that stayed with me all my life until fulfilment with the return to Eriboll.[2]

My weight is 12 stone 4. I've put on a stone since emerging from the General Election. I am under huge pressure with Big Book. I am also looking forward to the first meeting of the 22 Executive, and 'take the temperature' of that. The cars, and practically everything else, being hopelessly neglected.

Great Hall   *Friday, 18 July*

I have this equivocal position in the Party. Many expect great things of me. I was 'lionised' at the Conservative Way Forward group meeting on Wednesday. Lots of young people. And, as I ran for a Division, a very young boy with crew cut and large single ear-ring, shouted across the street, 'That's Alan Clark, man.' I waved, and he made a finger & thumb sign – 'Top boy ...' Who else could get that, aged 69? But I am not quite clear how to capitalise.

I have to consider how to handle the Party Conference. If the TV series has already started – my line has to be 'yes, there is history' and one can learn from history; but our real task is how we re-form, and how in future we relate to the electorate.

---

[1] Katoomba was the name given by AC's grandfather to his yachts. The word came from Australia's Blue Mountains.
[2] The Clarks purchased Eriboll following the death of Lord Clark in 1983.

Wednesday, 23 July

Absolutely ideal conditions. I sit at the table in the window of the no-talking annexe. River sounds. I have turned off the air conditioning and opened the window and a gentle summer breeze comes in. Already I have been here since 8 a.m. when I arrived (every single light from Albany to Parliament Square was (just) green) in the Little Silver, put in a prayer card and had a gossipy breakfast with the boys.

EMT   *Friday, 25 July*

Yesterday we went to the end-of-term party at Buck House. One had been 'placed' (I suspect by a resentful Lord Chamberlain) on the duds day. Not a single member of the governing classes up at the top corner of the tea-tent, where, naturally, one gathers; just as the domestics separate themselves at a grand wedding and congregate around the great circular tree seat by the lavatories. I drank four of the delicious iced coffees. The iced coffee at Buck House is the most delicious in the world.

Saturday, 2 August

Blair created 57 new peers today. The Upper House is being turned into a sort of Senate (by appointment) and JM gave a peerage to Tristan!

EMT, Saltwood   *Saturday, 9 August*

In the night (4.30) 'wind-Thompsoned' – thought 'change in
bowel movement' (now a year old). The evening before coming
back over for supper I had 'field of vision' restriction (plus
'jagged' not intense halo) lasted about 18 minutes. I went on
working through it. In the afternoon I got relaxed voice ('easily
tired' – Dr Thomas Stuttaford, first sign of throat cancer) driving
back from Allington.[1] And during the night I had to tinkle at
4.10, 5.30 and 6.30 – copiously. The only frightening symptom
is return of the glaucoma. My eyes are taking such a beating at
present from the 'white screen'.

EMT   *Saturday, 16 August*

Yesterday afternoon for 3½ hours Clara and Nick[2] and I sat in
the hall of the Garden House and agreed the 'mods' necessary
to programme four, the Thatcher-Major section. So the TV will
'go out' on 14 September for 4 weeks. I think it is rather good
and glossy, though quintessentially superficial, because that is the
medium.

As for my state – I am unfit, saggy, scrawny, bags under my
eyes. I am using up my margin fast between being 70 and looking
70. (Yet I still can't visualise myself as 70.)

A little later
Went for a 'w' with Tom. The full, dark colours on every side.
Each year this time of the seasons makes me nostalgic. The great
house starts its autumn siesta. I walk in the keep while the
House of Commons awaits. Continuity. But what new

---

[1] Allington, like Saltwood, also originally restored by Lady Conway; now the home
   of Bob Worcester and his wife.
[2] Nick Kent, producer, and Clara Glynn, director, of *Alan Clark's History of the Tories*,
   as the TV series was now titled.

generation will appreciate it, and maintain, even skeletally, this old Venetian, faded grandeur. So important as a reservoir from which to draw strength.

Shore   *Friday, 29 August*

Our last 'real' day here. I am deeply apprehensive. So often in my life, school/Upper Terrace, Portmeirion etc, I have felt this mixture of gloom and foreboding before return. As always I think to myself – why can't one 'see the seasons round' or at least dig in for a meaningful session? Surely next year BB will be 'behind me'.

In the night I had some kind of muddled dream that James and Julie's child was going to be a little girl. Poor little darling, a rich, brainy, beautiful blonde, but what awaits her? James would be secretly disappointed, I know. He would be such a wonderful father for a little male-bairn.

This evening at 8 p.m. I strolled down to the loch and caught the high tide. Quite still, the water was, and so far in that I could use the Katoomba trailer as a pier. The sky was slate grey with wonderful passages of lemon and pink behind the clouds. I swam, more freely and longer than at any other time. Just wonderful, and I strolled back in philosophic mood. Of one thing there is no doubt. Two weeks at Eriboll does repair the physique.

Shore   *Sunday, 31 August*

We went to the island, although the breeze was getting up. Lovely, although my mind was on the return. Jane found a cowrie, and we looked at the site of the island house. As we were pulling the dinghy ashore Julie arrived at the boathouse in the Range Rover.

'Have you heard the news?'

'I don't want news. Just don't tell me.'

'Diana and Dodi have been killed in a car crash pursued by paparazzi'. So soon after my article! [in *The Spectator*]

We felt a great rage. Nothing will change, except that a lovely icon has been destroyed. Most fortuitously it was the Eriboll service that afternoon – in the Gaelic – and Donny[1] adapted beautifully. (Unlike, I was horrified to note that evening, the service at Craithie.[2])

EMT   *Friday, 5 September*

Went for a tiny drive in the R-Cont yesterday afternoon to collect my accumulated OAP (over £300) and thought how lovely it is – especially at low, vintage, speeds. That change from 2nd to 3rd, perfect in feel and unity of b.m.e.p. and engine revs.

We are off this morning to park the car in the Commons, camp in the office at 1 Parliament Street for the cortège tomorrow. In the evening, a service at St Mary Abbots, with the Mayor, dignitaries. Rather fun, in its way. And pleasing to note the discomfiture of 'the Royals' as they struggle to cope with this great outpouring of love for someone they were trying (and succeeded) to destroy – from jealousy and incomprehension. Also, can't get away from the here-I-am syndrome. It could scarcely be more convenient/privileged, than to park in both senses on the very corner of Parliament Square.

---

[1] The Rev. Donny McSween.

[2] The church for Balmoral, where the Queen and many of her family were on holiday.

EMT   *Sunday, 7 September*

Back yesterday for Diana's funeral. Very slowly and sadly one drove along in Big Red – twice yellow 'high' bikes trailed their coat at me, but I had no will to respond, and 'proceeded' at, mainly 58–65 mph (this using, by comparison, practically no fuel at all).

The day before we had been to the service at Kensington Church, a nice formal duty. And heard at the outset while waiting in the pews, the Queen's broadcast – clipped, formal, utterly without warmth and affection. Then we walked in Kensington High Street and along to the memorial – an exciting atmosphere of happening, of unity of purpose. A crowd entirely friendly, each recognising one another in this common purpose.

A quiet curry at the Kundan – we neither of us wanted to read – and then strolled back through the crowds mainly now with candles, and little make-shift shelters. We slept, not badly, in the office; Jane on the tried and proven camp bed used at Netherton Grove and even on the Le Mans 24 hours, in the fifties. I on the armchair and snoof. A rattling on the door at 5.20, and I called out 'we're in here' thinking it to be the waste-paper lady. But the voice which answered was (surely?) Trish's. I put on my trousers and staggered out blearily in the Cuixmala T-shirt. There was Trish, immaculate in a white trouser suit. I reeled off to the gents to sluice my face and she bossily moved in, rustled papers and without so much a by-your-leave to Jane, turned on the television! This, and Stewart's [Cill-Johnson] presence – triumphantly with his walking stick – in the most comfortable chair did somewhat cramp the atmosphere in the room. But the combination of cortège, TV, crowds, and the service itself was overpowering. My only wish is that I could, for the service, have been transposed to Hyde Park, watched there on the enormous screen, and applauded with the crowd at Charles Spencer's brave utterances.[1]

---

[1] In an interview in the *Guardian* (15 July 2002) Spencer said: 'Alan Clark wrote me … and said I agree with every word you said but just watch now. The press and the royal family are two of the most powerful institutions in the country and they will make sure your name is dragged through the dirt.'

EMT   *Wednesday, 17 September*

A bad night. Jane is stressed, predominantly over the dogs. But once awake – she sleeps for about 1¼ hours, from 11.45 to either side of 1 a.m. we can't hug and console each other because we both get hot (temperature rise). Was it only two years ago that we could lie wrapped in each other's arms for most of the night after making love and then enjoying shortbread ('complacently') with early morning tea?

Last night I tried to coax her into a breathing therapy and she wouldn't even try – said she was *holding* her breath, was 'too stressed' to let it out. I got out of bed in despair. It's all my fault, I suppose, Lëhni certainly is. And this bloody lawsuit with the *Standard*. Denton Hall insisting on coming down on Thursday morning,[1] while the whole of Saturday afternoon is occupied by Terry Lambert[2] going over evidence for the 31 October. The untidiness everywhere. If this clears up – but can it, ever? We both went to tinkle and Jane said 'we have no time'.

Saltwood Pavillon   *Saturday, 27 September*

A pleasant Saturday. Did 15 letters, demi-mechanically, while Jane was at the hairdresser. Rang Andrew Roberts, said 'come down' and he suggested bringing Dean Godson. Just what I like. We sparkled and enjoyed ourselves with a rosé and two Bourgogne Aligoté in their 'sleeves'. Jane adapted brilliantly with heavy-duty canapés.

This morning the news (leaked) that Hague was going to dispense with hereditary peerages (i.e. adopted Blair's 'reforms'). For me this is the last straw – already. Coming on top of message

---

[1] AC had decided to go ahead and sue the *Evening Standard* for its *Not the Alan Clark Diaries* column. His solicitors were now called Denton Wilde Sapte.

[2] Terry Lambert, partner at Mowll & Mowll, the solicitors acting for the Clarks in Lëhni's case.

to Gay Pride, Notting Hill carnival (aren't there any worthwhile causes he could send a message to?). It's got him marked. Give him a good bit more rope, though. We have the advantage that whatever he does he can't pick up any points this year.

Pavillon   *Sunday, 28 September*

I think the Party has had it. Our grip was ephemeral while Labour, even in the low, low times post-1983, had its hard core of TU and urban support. Now the hard core remains – 'it has nowhere else to go' – but the whole sticky-crap consumerist ad-speak culture has seduced our centre.

Saturday, 4 October

Today our 'last' bathe at Hythe beach.

Each afternoon we have been going down there; Jane always 'mock' reluctantly, but with her bathing dress under. It is quite delicious, the water now clean and the great long arc of the shingle like the Chesil Bank – or even Biarritz. The pleasure of swimming 'over-arm' with lots of space (too frightening, as well as too chilly, to 'let oneself go' at Eriboll) make them real bathes and put me in mind of 42 years ago.

Now I am somewhat debilitated, but still happy and well, and my shape not unrecognisable, and I thank God.

Garden House   *Wednesday, 15 October*

I came over here to browse, look at notes in general. I am still emerging from flu/cold – so feel placid and philosophic (most oddly, for the period of convalescence, i.e. after the Saturday, which was foul, my eye seemed much better, and yesterday would defocus better than for ages).

When I am in these rooms, particularly when – as today – Graham [Stewart] is absent, I feel quite 'a different order' of calmness. I look ahead to being 'domiciled' here, distancing myself from the Mains, though always ready to prowl in the historic environs and absorb the combination of nostalicism and uncertain continuity. And indeed to 'rest' it for periods.

Working here, academically but at a lower pace, advising the trustees accordingly. Only in the South for a proportion of the year; then North and serenely in the Highlands – 'still climbing Munros well into his seventies'. And, of course, in the late autumn, cutting south to the Alps, drinking wine as we cross France.

Idyllic – if there are mildly uncomfortable overtones they are there: one evocative of my father (he, too, made over Saltwood when he was 68 – I'm a year later). The moving sideways from the sword in the lake. It was almost within my grasp before Blackpool. Oh! That silly, show off (as always) aside.[1]

EMT   *Thursday, 16 October*

Jane slept badly (how many good nights does she get per year? Three maybe). Poor little soul, she carried all the problems of my (ir)responsibility. She never goes to the studio now, simply sits reading newsprint. This ought to be redundant now with the agency; but actually she finds quite interesting general things. On 19 September we had a fraught discussion about her going to her mother – and we must find time for that.[2]

---

[1] At the party conference AC had said (apropos the continuing N Ireland stalemate): 'The only solution is to kill 600 people in one night. Let the UN and Bill Clinton and everyone else make a scene – and it is over for 20 years.'
[2] Mrs Beuttler had lived in Spain for many years.

Summer Office   *Friday, 17 October*

The Sotheby's 'team' wander about for the 'Trust' inventory. The deed box has yielded its usual crop of missing, or obsolete, and unintelligible documents. I am feeble, and have ocular head-aches again, my weight is now 11.2 – alert level. I am in the evening of my life – although it is still daylight.

EMT   *Sunday, 26 October*

Yet another beautiful late autumn day. I thought, said to Jane, 'Will we ever?' now widened to 'will we ever relaxedly be able to say to each other – "what shall we do today?"'

And yet … tomorrow I won't even be able to come to Mowll and Mowll[1] because I need to get up to put in a prayer card in order to get called for 'my place' to question the Chancellor and this first day back. The pleasure and the price.

Yesterday the all-day CPC conference and I hung in there fortified by a delicious mouthful of fish pie in the 1a kitchen. Jeffrey Archer underperformed; read, stumblingly, a speech text on 'the future of London'.[2] The future of *me*, I had warned the audience in advance, bitchily. He gave me a lift back to New Palace Yard in his Mercedes drophead – incredibly cheapo finish interior, most disappointing. I drove home in Big Red, discreetly, except unable to resist a last gallop on the Ashford concrete. Jane was in happy form and we set about, at 7 p.m., a magnificent repast: started with fresh orange juice instead of gin and tonic; ½ bottle Bourgogne '93; chicken liver pâté and toast, slice of red pepper tart; two helpings delicious venison from Eriboll and red cabbage, Anna Koumar carrots, mashed potatoes,

---

[1] Solicitors representing the Clarks in the forthcoming hearing over Lëhni, their Rottweiler.

[2] Archer wanted to be the first new mayor of London, as constituted by the Labour government.

horseradish. Then fresh apple puree, double cream and meringues. We staggered up to bed, didn't stir for over ten hours.

Thank you, God, quite literally, for my good luck.

Parliament Street   *Monday, 27 October*

A little sad. Disappointed at not being called to question Gordon Brown. And the context of what he was saying. The slow 'count-down', all the nuts and bolts of the infrastructure being put in place, for EMU at the next election. I had a good place guaranteed to speak in the Defence debate. But it barely matters now. I can't revisit it, because if I had been Secretary of State it would all be so different. Now our nationhood is being taken/given away. Along with the BA tailfins, the handguns, the sale of Rolls-Royce, the Queen, fresh from her insults in India, submitting as usual to any humiliation. There is practically nothing left of the Nation-State except the bravery of the football fans who stood up to the armed and armoured Italian police in Rome.

On top of all this is the strange sadistic ordeal of the case against Hannah/Lëhni. This is ravaging Jane, who has been warned that she might have to be in the dock for AN HOUR, and the whole case to last all day.

B5, EMT   *Thursday, 30 October*

I am so rattled and pressurised that I have lost concentrative powers. I don't know what's in my diary – even for today – and dare not look at it. A new and most unsettling phenomenon is the lesion, which I now look at every three minutes or so, on my forearm. A new basal, presumably.

I am really apprehensive about the case. (It's not that it's paranoia, I just know that they are out to get me.) Slept intermittently being woken by the certain knowledge that I will be cross-examined about my pressure on Birt, BBC, perverting the course of justice etc and even if we get a good verdict, *arrested on the steps of the court.* That's why they are pressing on with the case, so as to get certain admissions on record.[1]

Now I feel a tiny bit better. I have just seen the Albany blackbird.

EMT   *Monday, 10 November*

Yesterday we went to the memorial service and I laid the wreath at St Mary Abbots. We are WW1-minded at present. Jane has done her beautiful Passchendaele series, so upsetting. What a remarkable artist she is.

MFS Saltwood   *Saturday, 15 November*

A wonderful feeling of tranquillity as the volume ends surpassing, I believe, any other.

Yesterday we walked across wind-blown pavements and over the River Tay to Inverness Cathedral where we knelt in church (what a cold building) for the birth of baby Angus (George McKenzie). The consummation of that wonderful moment (on par with Andrew Dalton in the basement of Kensington TH) when 'Boy' was on the answering machine at the flat – just read out his names. James was ebullient last night as we waited in the (far from unsympathetic) lounge of the Station Hotel at

---

[1] The magistrates, at Folkstone, found for the Clarks, who were awarded costs. But it was an ordeal, nevertheless, AC recording in his day diary that Jane 'almost fainted'.

Inverness. And then I enjoyed what must almost be the recognitory apotheosis of my political career – a complimentary ticket for the Scottish TUC cealídh on Friday night.

EMT   *Monday, 17 November*

Yesterday I went for a good two hour walk – Beechborough and back up Kick Hill. Then strolled in the woodland, thinking of my glass of wine. Overdid it with 'Wiltshire Plait', then ate far too many old Belgium white chocolates – SLUMPED. Dozed fitfully. Woke feeling sinister – worried about brain tumour, Thompsoned hugely and slumped back feeling 'far from right'. Jane said, 'If only we could have a complete week here …' And now, even writing this, my glaucoma headache has returned.

1 Parliament Street   *Thursday, 27 November*

Spectator Politician of the Year lunch at the Savoy yesterday. Sat next to Ian Gilmour – as always funny (such an infectious giggle) and slyly mocking. Tristan Garel-J – I took at least half the meal to warm to him – told me that on the Friday after the '92 election he went straight to Major, told him to *instruct* Chris Patten to stand for Kensington & Chelsea. Neither would play (although I suspect CP would – 'if pressed'). The episode shows T.G-J's limitations.[1] So consumed by his addiction to whispered intrigue, and so infatuated with Patten that he was unable to see it from JM's aspect. Why on earth should Major, who had just won an election, want to ease the path of his most conspicuous rival? *Out*, Patten would be invaluable as friend and counsellor. In – it would be only a matter of time.

---

[1] AC had long been equivocal about Garel-Jones.

G-J remains unlikeable, and deceitful in the extreme. It is a weakness of mine that I succumbed to his blandishments dictated, I assume, by a feeling that I was one of Margaret's 'favourites'. He started to walk back across Savoy Gardens with me, then turning back, feeling, I assume, his attention and company would be better expended on others.

Yesterday the great (Friday) Hunting Debate. I wore my (brand new) O'Brien suit of faintly grey checked flannel, waistcoat and white silk shirt. A 'Parliamentary occasion' and the Speaker very nobly arranged for me to be called early (at No 3 on our side after Heseltine – himself stopped in his tracks and demolished by Denis MacShane[1] – and TK). I revelled in it; congratulating a preceding member, '… what an ordeal to have to do it before so crowded a chamber'; and fortuitously slapping down Paul Flynn.[2] And as I think about it my mind, as often, goes back to those exclusion dreams – particularly when I was *behind the chair* and couldn't go back in. Which, itself, I think must go back to the time Hugh Rossi[3] says what a pity I am retiring, and I suddenly realise the Chamber was locked and with the House dissolved I was no longer an MP. Nor ever would be.

Saltwood, EMT   *Monday, 8 December*

Early on Friday morning, before it was fully light, I walked from Albany to the House, carrying three pieces of luggage, but dressed in softies. I passed by Clive Steps – always a mixture of evocations, from Chips: 'The Chief Whip's car is waiting …' to the feeling of absolute exclusion at the seat tryst (April 1992) and 'best-attended memorial service since Aircraftsman Shaw' as

---

[1] Denis MacShane, MP (Lab) for Rotherham since May 1994.
[2] Paul Flynn, MP (Lab) for Newport W since 1987.
[3] Sir Hugh Rossi, MP (Con) for Hornsey and Wood Green 1983–92 (Hornsey 1966–83).

I said to Chris Patten when he staged his great party in the Durbar Court. And this time I really revelled, wallowed in the pleasures of my condition. Here I was, having voluntarily selected the wilderness and then (been) returned to a position of huge strength. The previous night, at Norland ward, people had again been saying how awful Hague was and why didn't I …? etc etc. Now I am going to enter the sleepy House of Commons which I love so much to collect my Little Silver and whizz down (more likely creep down as it's bad light and I'm low on fuel) to Saltwood for scrambled eggs. So, except for my eyes, and approaching old age, and guilt/withdrawal symptoms about BB, I would be extraordinarily happy. Absence of sexual activity I barely notice. I welcome it almost; and prostatic symptoms totally dormant. Have abated, indeed, virtually since Tom Bates a year ago.

But the future, the future of the sword is opaque. The Conservative Party is utterly shattered. Our total in the opinion polls is 22% and the Liberals at 17%. On Wednesday the 22 Committee met for 1½ hours to talk about 'the Party reforms' and when they came out into the corridor there was not a single journalist waiting. We have become irrelevant. And quite soon after our return from Christmas recess, I predict, the Liberals will be at 22 and we will be at 17%. Part of the problem, I have no doubt whatever, is the hopeless, exhausted and repetitious quality of our 'Shadow' front bench. Dorrell, Lilley, Mawhinney, Howard, Redwood, I can't think of the others, the Electorate has already said 'No thanks' in the biggest possible way. Why on earth, since most of them are saying the same things as they did in April 1997, should the public listen at all? They owe their place, in any case, not to merit, but to a series of deals patched up and traded off during the whole ludicrous 'Leadership' contest. At present, I do not see the way forward. Soames rang last night, talked for hours. Said we must rebuild around 'householders, farmers, small businesses'. I must read a lot of that new stuff from the residual Left. But will this actually be enough to fuel a party resurgence? Careful thought on the holidays required.

Anyway, after bellowing like this for 15 minutes, Soames then said he 'wanted out'. Asked me to ask Alastair [Campbell] to get Blair to make him ambassador in Paris – 'it's mine by descent … etc'.[1] Shades slightly of Christopher's [Soames] dinner at White's. He's running away. Driven out by Oborne, and Black Dog ('foul-mouthed Tory toff …' etc)

House Library   *Wednesday, 10 December*

Up early, and waistcoat for an interesting day.

I plan to stir the 22 Exec on our supporting the government to reject a Liberal amendment on Single Mothers. 'I was not sent here by my constituents to go through the same lobby as Blair, Prescott and Harman.'

Still apprehensive about my eyes and panicked last evening that they might seize up before or during my reading at the Sloane Street church carol service. But it passed off ok – after last-minute scramble to get a King James text. Earlier, in a very busy day, I had spoken to the (mature) students; and won their approval and spontaneous chat and answers. One (long face, long hair, still attractive and classy) said 'do you want to be Prime Minister?' 'Of course,' I answered, and she was delighted.

The night before (Monday) I went to the Privy Council dinner – Royal Gallery, and overflow in the Robing Chamber presided by Prince of Wales and including various – Cranborne, Ancram, TK and – God alive, how did he get one? – Atkins, R.[2] Copious and excellent wines.

The Queen is transformed, no longer the wicked stepmother with her frumpish and ill-natured features that have been permanently in place since Mrs T rescued the 1992 election. As

---

[1] Nicholas Soames' father Christopher (son-in-law of Winston Churchill, former MP and Minister) had been British Ambassador in France, 1968–72.

[2] Robert Atkins, MP South Ribble 1983–97 (Preston N 1979–83) and a junior Minister in Major government; made a Privy Counsellor 1995.

I said at the time, the whole Royal Family delighted at the elimination of Diana, and now has settled back comfortably into their favourite role – preservation of their own perks and privileges at the expense, whenever necessary, of other individuals and institutions. The Empire, the Church, the Law, the hereditary principle, the Lords, even a yacht, and now there are faithful servants who are being dismissed in droves as they modernise Sandringham and Balmoral.

MFS GH   *Friday, 12 December*

I seem to remember this is always a baddish time.

My eyes are really causing me concern – thirteen months since the opthalmicist in Hythe told me to go to hospital. I now have had a slight frontal headache and inability to 'defocus' for over 24 hours. And was advised yesterday to make an appointment (via Nick Page) with 'Spender'(?)[1] in Harley Street. Don't mind glaucoma so much – unless it stops me getting a driving licence – but am terrified of cancer of the optic nerve. 'Very rare,' Nick said, 'only in infancy and the elderly.' But that day I have read of poor old Walter Matthau (aet. 77) 'going blind' for this reason.

Then, 'on top of it all he was diagnosed as HIV positive'; i.e. the INLA man[2] is over here with the intention (according to sources) of levelling scores. Can only take it demi-seriously, but … *Plus* Denton Hall all next week; I worried that my witnesses will fold. *Plus* how *do* we get to Eriboll, with a 3-line whip on Monday? Physically impossible; and lovely to dwell here in our burrow, but fearfully bad luck on dear 'Boy'.

I must record, though, a tiny incident last week when I was hurrying to Kensington in the Porsche. Circumventing again I

[1] Actually David Spalton.
[2] A representative of the Irish National Liberation Army.

accelerated across Cadogan Gardens and quickly had to pull out across Pont Street ahead of the oncoming traffic. I very nearly was hit by a motorcyclist. It would have been terrible. God still protects me. Whether or not he continues to do so, may he look after dear sweet Janey, the boys and the lovely bairns.

MFSH   *Sunday, 14 December*

Extraordinary mood-swings. On Friday I was hyper-buoyant. Filled with confidence (head-ache lifted as soon as I had finished 'filing' the *Classic Cars* column[1]), now contemplate 'trading up' from Big Red to a 'T', and sent (foolishly and youthfully) the 'we-owe-it-to-each-other' Christmas card (which I must try and retrieve).

Yesterday was lovely; on our own and pottering and in the evening *hammering* at the Green Room table. Even visually ok. But T.O. woke us by Thompsoning at 4.30. I was still deeply asleep. Afterwards we slept very lightly in contact until nearly 9 a.m., but didn't feel rested. Intermittently I thought how sweet and dear Jane is to hold on to me like this. Is it because, consciously or sub-consciously, she is aware of the INLA man? I will write her a love letter. I ought to do one to each boy also, but that is itself headache-inducing as it requires administrative recommendations. I am now entering the last decade of my life. If I pass through this I will have outlived my father;[2] but (presumably) I will be shuffly and my voice lost timbre. I did speak last night to EDG and his voice was perfectly ok. He has the most incredible genes and his liver has not registered *at all* to the alcohol washing through it, and both his parents died at 90-something. But he did speak of joints, and balance is in

---

[1] AC had been writing a monthly column under the heading 'Back Fire' for *Classic Cars* magazine since 1995.
[2] Kenneth Clark died in 1983 aged 79.

decline. Quite frankly I will never ski again. The last time was at the Davos (1991) conference where the feeling afterwards was almost like being reborn. But I do hope scrawnily to stride in the Highlands.

The point is, though, when? It is perfectly glorious – almost the early spring – but in fact before the iron discipline of winter asserts itself.

On the Green Room table we found this card ...

6 August 1996
What <u>are</u> you
doing – London today
when you have no time
to spare or so you tell me.
Well I've gone too –
don't know when I'll be
back – to feed dogs, water
things, iron things, tidy things
cook things, find things –
the 'things' wives do –
we have so much and yet we
don't have time for each other.
Well make it, or lose it you
selfish genius. It's been
one moan all these past
weeks. If it is my fault say so.[1]

I suppose at that time I was ghastly to live with. I was consumed by the search, not for the sword, but at least the path, through rocks and undergrowths, to arrive at the lake. Yesterday evening I said, 'I could step down now, I suppose, because I proved, to everyone, that I could come back and get adopted for the safest seat in Britain.' I still half believe that my moment may come. I cannot predict its shape. A possible coup last week – the Social

---

[1] AC had stapled Jane's actual message into the diary.

Security Bill vote (I was the only Tory to abstain on a 3-line) was thwarted, and now the whips are cool to me. The first three months of this ('98) year will be spent assiduously voting, and working out certain policy stand points (sic). If the local elections are bad, and the polls still against us I might try something in the early summer.

Although rather than attack one's own side it is probably better to state alternatives, avoid personalities.

House Library   *Monday, 15 December*

Very tired and low. I haven't eaten anything except two digestives and a small slice of camembert 'in the conference room at Denton Hall'. And yet I am not hungry. I am apprehensive about my eyes, which ache dully and resist 'defocusing'. Print vision poor. I barely think about the 'INLA man', though will lock the back door tonight. I listened to 'proceedings' all day in Court and was wearied by their repetitious quality and treadmill feel. The Judge – 'Lightman' – was beady, but I sensed hostile (perhaps having heard on the grapevine that I am 'anti-Semitic').[1] When Peter Prescott[2] recited, ad nauseam, extracts from the 'Diaries' I loathed it. I went back and read a nasty piece in the *Independent on Sunday* with 'a Westminster source' quoting unpleasantly and maliciously. Had Tristan fingerprints on it.

Everyone loathes me, or dismisses me: *The Times Diary* entry on Friday emphasising my age, if not senility. All people really want is to write *ill* of their subject.

I will dine here alone, and early, and probably without wine unless I can find a companion.

---

[1] AC was over-sensitive. Mr Justice Lightman, QC 1980, had been an admired High Court judge since 1994.

[2] Counsel for *Evening Standard*. QC, co-author of *The Modern Law of Copyright*.

Thursday, 18 December

Sitting in Albany kitchen – still in dressing-gown at 11.05; and the delightful, and unusual pleasure of the two clocks striking simultaneously 'across' each other. Very Edwardian, or early twenties. I am hugely calmer and more contented – although of course anxiety in new form will always flow into the vacuum created by the extinction of a real one, and I am apprehensive. The trial has not gone badly and the judge seemed sympathetic, although Prescott was odious at every stage. If I lose, of course, I will be open season. But my real consolation, fresh boost, is Spalton.[1] Stuttery, amiable and bespectacled (naturally) oculist. He tested me, I told him all my symptoms [here AC draws on the page the edge of a spot]. He was unphased. Said the optic nerve ok etc. And I really haven't had a headache of any kind since …! Defocusing, and periodic lights and 'flooders' of no consequence. This is such a relief; I clap my hands in prayer of thanks a lot of the time and when I wake up at night.

Just in time. As I need to think long and hard about the next three months. The real damage and threat to Parliament. The cogent conspiracy between Blair and Hague. We are actually going along with what Blair is doing.

B5   *Sunday evening, 21 December*

Travelled back from Stansted by the aero-train and changed at Tottenham Hale to Victoria Line tube to Green Park. Swift and painless. I am alone at the flat instead of, as I should be, 'thundering' with Janey and the dogs to the north. I rang Gleneagles at 6 – she still wasn't there. I'm sure she will be all right, but I did say a prayer of thanks and protection for the sweetest, goodest person in the entire world, the only one

---

[1] David Spalton, Harley Street eye specialist.

whom I believe to have not one vestigial streak of cruelty or deceit in her character. Yes, the 'what-if-died' scenario (I am always particular, see the extreme in any situation) crosses my mind at intervals. Of the smash, at the dogs being gleefully 'put down' by police marksmen as impeding, or 'likely to impede' the emergency services.

Tomorrow paperwork and the two 22 meetings. We are on the run, we MPs. The tacit conspiring of the 'New leaders'. This is worth an article in itself. But the great 'Must the Conservative Party Die?' piece slowly matures. I will put some more flesh on it on the Hermes [typewriter] at Shore.

Station Hotel, Inverness   *Monday, 22 December*

Flew up today, a joining seat taken at a very late stage by Caroline – never did get her surname. Plastered, she was, and odd. 'Ah a McKenzie tartan,' she said, spotting my scarf. I started off thinking no, oy, etc. She was completely shameless first in her verbal inquisition, then in her physical attentions. Suddenly, she started to admire and then handle my hands. I feigned sleep, but she kept pushing up close. She was a classic Norse red-head – 31? – plumpish with blue eyes and pale skin. Looking sideways I saw pleasing cleavage, with a lace-bordered low-cut T-shirt. Pushed her head on my shoulder and she held first my arm, then put her hand on my chest. What the attendants thought I can't imagine. She kept struggling and fidgeting, trying to get closer. Amazing. Quite salutary and encouraging. Derek Presley[1] met me in the not-at-all-nice Freelander and by the time I was on the concourse she had disappeared. I have barely the face to record all her compliments.

Christmas is in prospect, and my only anxiety is that James has still not turned up yet (it's 12.20 p.m.).

---

[1] Friend and manager of Inverness Land Rover agent, Macrae & Dick.

Shore Cottage, 8 p.m.   *Wednesday, 24 December*

An anxious Christmas Eve. Not since Andrew had bad asthma
at Zermatt in 1965 and Gentinetta wanted to put him on
steroids. I slept like a top – uninterrupted from 9.10 to 6.10.
Janey not so well, complained of a 'sore tummy', and said she felt
sick(-ish). I didn't put too much to this until, at EMT, she said
she didn't even want to finish her ½ cup (we were in the
kitchen; it must have been about 7.30). She was leaning against
the wall, just by the window, suddenly said 'God' or something
like that and her legs buckled, she went down with a terrible
crack (like my father's description of my mother having her
stroke at Albany in 1973). I rushed over to her, called out,
begged her to move a hand or an eyelid, could she hear me? etc.
I kept telling her I loved her. Her head, utterly limp, was at a
curious angle when she first fell, and I wondered if Nanny had
looked like that when Jane found her at Garden House. After an
age, she came round. She hadn't even felt my putting a pillow
under her head, or moving all the dogs into the wheelhouse etc.
Then she 'came to'. 'What happened?' I wanted to move her to
the sofa. She said she felt sick again. Would she like me to help
her to the loo? I picked her up, was holding on to her elbow
and her knees buckled totally. She collapsed with a terrible unconscious groaning. She vomited, but not properly. Some of it
must have caught in the windpipe and she made dreadful draining coughs. I really thought she was going to die. She recovered
a little. Still couldn't remember anything. I settled her, drove up
to the Lodge and Julie rang Dr Belbin who said he would come
straight over to examine her in the kitchen; then the ambulance
and the paramedics. Now she's in Raigmore [hospital] and
(naturally) the floor sister is guarded. She is 'tired' and all wired
up to a heart machine etc. X-rays. Blood tests. Would I be able
to take her away tomorrow? Unlikely.

Poor, sweet, sweet Janey who was game and pleasant even in
this tearful adversity.

I took the dogs along the shoreline; back over the top. I

thought of how catastrophic if she died. I had to see it in personal terms. I would withdraw utterly. 'In mourning.' Instantly become a recluse (and a pretty scrawny one. All I have eaten today is bread and butter!).

But even so. Things are cyclical. The hubris (partially intended) of that card. The extraordinary good fortune that has blessed us this year. There had to be a downturn. I'm off up to the Lodge for dinner.

Shore Cottage   *Sunday, 28 December* [1]

Immensely contented and at ease

We have been sleeping 9½-10½ hours per night. Jane not yet 'quite right', and Tom is ill-at-ease, now definitely in his closing months and wanders around the house making little wheezy noises. How unhappy is he? Head of the house until the end. Nineteen years old next month (Feb).

I am reading simultaneously Rhodes James's *Lord Randolph Churchill* and WSC on the same subject. Hugely enjoyable to read of:

> 'The announcement in *The Times* this morning immediately and sensationally terminated the Christmas calm in political circles. Holiday plans were abruptly cancelled …' etc. [2]

and the calm in the knowledge that I can myself now go back, wreathed in fantasy yes, but *potent*, and push through the doors marked 'Members Only'. Who (save me) a year ago would have conceived of this as in any way feasible, still less likely?

Now I am going upstairs to write letters to RRJ and David

---

[1] AC has written above this entry: 'Poor handwriting for being written on knee in wheelhouse as Jane's artist's materials over table.'

[2] This is how Robert Rhodes James, in only his first book, wrote of Lord Randolph's resignation. Winston Churchill's life of his father was published in two volumes.

D. Later I will be on the hill and will go to the little church and pray thanks and a hope for protection – particularly of that tiny baby who kicked and chatted so merrily and conversationally as Julie was changing him yesterday.

Shore Cottage   *Tuesday, 30 December*

Tremendous gales today. For the first time since arriving I have taken no long walk in the daylight hours. Last night I worked on BB, some correction in green pen of bound (red) Book I. Thought how good, how melodious it is. Much – or perhaps not so much – to do. But it ought (personal anti-prejudice apart) be a prize-winner. Worked also on the Intro, and showed a page to Jane which she liked – 'reads so well'. (I had woken in the night and worked on it for an hour; so easy to potter across the landing and into the little stripped-pine, pent-roof study.)

The routine at the little croft is snug and restorative. I rise around 7 (or whatever time it may be that has given 9½-10 hours sleep). I let out T.O. who hates the wind and always heads for the grass bank along the stream where habitually, in former times, he would Thompson. But now he is so unsteady on his pins that I have to head him away. Quite shivery in my dressing-gown and slippers/mules, 'damn you, Tom', I can be heard saying. But T.O., bless him, is always regular.

Perhaps because I am impatient to get back to it. Perhaps because intermittently I think I am 'starting' a head cold, my temper degenerated (wind always makes me rattled).

Cursingly I amassed quantities of fuel for the Tyrolia, with staged back-up piles in the little store, the big store, and (Jane's idea) a 'flu stack' right next to the stove.[1]

---

[1] Elsewhere AC notes: '… set to at the Tyrolia stove, which nearly always picks up with newspaper and kindling, i.e. seldom needs even a match … I can sit with the little door open at the wood crackling merrily with an orange flame.'

Up at the Lodge I collected some old *Telegraphs* and getting back here was made uneasy by news of an INLA assassination inside the Maze prison and a tit-for-tat murder on IRA men by the UVF. I hid this so that Jane wouldn't see it. She is very sweet and uncomplaining, but her voice timbre is down, as is her life force. As I thought she has done some perfectly beautiful Dürer-like pictures of feathers and seashore *trouvées*. I hope she recovers enough while we are here to enjoy it.

I fear that when the gales abate the snow will start. I do not want to be cut off here, and already, very slightly, I have at 7 days (effectively 5) got 'wandering feet' and think of the Mains, and the piles of correspondence, and the 'white' computer. Am I like this because I feel I have little time left? Can't effectively be much more than 5 years surely – which isn't much. Like my father standing impatiently about in the hall of the châlet in 1977.[1] Or is it that my energy still comes back fast? A bit of both.

Jim Lees-Milne died at the weekend. 89. Suits me. But there were references in his diaries to 'recurrent bouts of cancer' (uh?).

---

[1] Lord Clark visited Châlet Caroline only once; it was not a success.

1998

We're not sleeping well. Last night I was convinced that I had jaw rot (for want of a better word) under Bertie's [Arbeid] great bridge. For some reason I am getting a pulse, off-and-on, in the upper palate. I can feel it (rot, not pulse) now; and wonder if it is related to my occasional shooting headache on the R. side. I had been put out by how *old* I looked (Reagan – but with his heavy polish) in the 60-minutes CBS film.[1] And Jane, of course, had been upset by some references. The whole day has been completely frittered. I had hoovered out the Discovery. The 'side' in the kitchen is cluttered. I went over to GH briefly and was alarmed at how slow I was getting the green ink corrections into the machine. Ion now wants to 'set in stone' a delivery schedule, which both depresses me and makes me feel cramped.

Also, Chris Patten (Phil Patten I call him, a 'wishee-washee', the Chinese laundryman, as *Private Eye* do) has surfaced increasingly and everyone is saying how he has huge political career ahead of him. (What about D. Owen, by the way?[2]) I don't know what I have to do to be taken seriously. Win the *E Standard* case, for a start. I am too busy now even to open Romeike.[3] Everyone is out to get me. Radio silence from Denton Hall.

Still most unfit. Much of my listlessness explained, perhaps, by the fact that the scene, the Commons etc, really is changing. Politics has become different. I am old now, also. In my last decade before a true sage. I don't want to die, but if I do, let it be on the Creaggan Road and my last sight being of little Jane's face.

---

[1] The American CBS TV channel had included AC in a 60-minute documentary, filmed after the Kensington and Chelsea selection.

[2] The fortunes of the Social Democratic Party, of which David Owen had been leader since 1988, were in steep decline.

[3] Romeike & Curtice – cuttings service to which AC subscribed.

EMT, Saltwood   *Saturday, 24 January*

Last night DD rang. We did one of those long tours d'horizon
that I once so much, yet so wistfully, used to enjoy during the
period I was out. How delicious and nourishing it is now to
conduct the conversation as an equal. We talked through and
round Hague's clumsy attempt to interfere on the 22. He takes
a more extreme view of the Exec's situation than I. 'Why didn't
you speak?' he asked. It wasn't because I funked it; more because
I don't think the time is ripe, but it is ripening. Each of us is
approaching our goal stealthily. Leadership for him; chair of 22
(probably come first) for me.

   That is why a low profile – except in the House – is important
for me at this stage as my book moves into preparation.

   DD rightly said that half the Party don't come in to the
Chamber any longer. The running is done by the 'new intake',
and the 'four horsemen of the apocalypse' (who they? – Forth,
me, DD and Maclean[1]).

EMT, Saltwood   *Friday, 30 January*

Yesterday the unpleasant experience of being sacked (over
lunch) by Phil Hall[2] – who seemed, as his words ended, to
change from an enthusiastic *naïf* into a ruthless and beady 'senior
executive' in steel-rimmed spectacles. Went back to B5 feeling
immensely tired. Couldn't, just had the sense not to, go to bed
and zizz, as Tip came round with some pheasants. Lovely and

---

[1] Eric Forth, MP for Bromley and Chislehurst since 1997 (Mid Worcestershire,
1983–97); David Maclean, MP for Penrith and the Border since July 1983.

[2] Phil Hall, editor *News of the World* since 1995. A week later, though, AC noted: 'Am
cheered by the fact that my 'departure from the *N of W* coincided with their dis-
closure' that a fellow Conservative MP's daughter was "a hooker". He added: 'So
cruel and irrelevant an attack on a colleague would make it impossible for me to
write for the paper anyway.'

giggly as always. Went off on his little bzzip scooter – in which I fear he does the most horrifying dangerous things. He crisply cornered out of Albany courtyard.

Saturday, 31 January

Just a note, I should have done one long ago, an appreciation rather than an obituary of dear little T.O. Still, and unshakeably, 'head of the house'.

Now he's in his twentieth year, the toughest and most indefatigable of all terriers. Keegan, at ball-play in the pool, and incredible football performances – 'a dog against ten boys' with the Essen school.

Very, very slowly, his faculties and performance have declined. Today, quite a good morning, he briefly did seahorse still, but in the last 6-8 months he has slowly withdrawn, even from scampering down the drive to get the papers and waiting at the Barbican gate to go off like a rocket to the 'black' postbox. He has gradually lost his sense of smell, can't even pick up cheese on the floor until it is literally under his nose. Sometimes he is very blind, and is almost totally deaf. As a result he often looks unhappy. But he is still in routine. Up 7ish, excellent Thompson, in kitchen for EMT in his 'saucer'. Sleeps a lot during the day, but will enjoy a car drive. I now carry him up the stairs and 'throw' the 'markie' for him on his bed.

But he can still, and did until a week ago, manage the back steps. He is still the all-knowing puppy, and I will never let him down. But oh for the elixir! I see my own decline – if I avoid cancer or stroke – following this pattern.

House Library   *Thursday, 5 February*

An EMT note, really. But the (even) more congenial atmosphere
of the House Library I now prefer [to 1 Parliament Street].
Yesterday was very full indeed. There is something about
Wednesdays – because rather than in spite of the early start –
that causes it to be filled to the brim.[1]

So, blearily and creakily staggering to get dressed (yesterday's
shirt – why?) went without EMT to the Members Lobby where
Tapsell[2] was already crouching in the messenger's chair at 7.28
p.m. Exceedingly rich (or so one must suppose – 'I don't deal
for individuals, only for countries'; 'I'm not a stockbroker' etc
etc).

There were three of those interesting morning adjournments.
House totally empty on our side except for Anthony Steen[3].
Libs everywhere; many 'New' Labour members who had ousted
our own people in May. I had quickly to bodge together some
remarks about organic farming, Scottish communities, 'afford-
able' housing etc etc. It is really too depressing. There is our great
Party, its historic roots dependent on rural dwellers and walkers
in the countryside – and we don't even turn up, still less
illuminate the Debate.

Later Soames performed massively, and statesmanlikely on the
Middle East peace process. His father would have been
delighted.

Then came a total shambles. Little Letwin,[4] cheekily with his
detailed sequences etc etc tried to do to 'Cookie' (as Labour call
him[5]) what David Maclean had two weeks ago so brilliantly

---

[1] AC adds, if irrelevantly to the matter in hand: '"causes it-always-to-be-full" –
second half of a pentameter.'

[2] Sir Peter Tapsell (Kt 1985), MP for East Lindsey since 1983 (Nottingham West
1959–64; Horncastle, 1966–83).

[3] Anthony Steen, MP for Totnes since 1997 (South Hams 1983–97, Liverpool
Wavertree 1974–83).

[4] Oliver Letwin, MP for West Dorset since 1997.

[5] Robin Cook, MP for Livingston since 1983 (Edinburgh C February 1974–83),
Foreign Secretary since 1997

done to the Paymaster [Geoffrey Robinson]. Walked into a firestorm. Stuttered and stalled. Michael Howard[1] speaking from the backbenches (why?) equally useless. Fatchett[2] (reading a text clearly written by Robin C) said:

> 'The Right Honourable Gentleman, since 1 January, has tabled no written questions on the EU Presidency, the Middle East peace process; the crisis with Iraq; the Dependent Territories; or China ... He seems to regard the position of Shadow Foreign Secretary as a sabbatical between his period in the Home Office and his rumoured high-paid job in the City.'

Poor Michael! Ever since the Ann Widdecombe assault (could so easily have gone 'either way')[3] and then the nil score among the voluntary workers, he has been losing ground. What on earth can he do next? He's not even, like John Moore, boyish-looking.[4]

House Library   *Wednesday, 18 February*

I went to Enoch's [Powell] funeral. A beautiful, perfectly chosen service. Not one word out of place – which is hardly surprising as he wrote it all himself bar (sic) John Biffen's address which was even better. In the congregation outside Ronnie (I had a

---

[1] Michael Howard, MP for Folkestone (Saltwood in the constituency), Home Secretary 1993–97, had been shadow foreign secretary since the election.

[2] Derek Fatchett, MP for Leeds Central since 1983, Foreign Office Minister.

[3] Ann Widdecombe, MP for Maidstone since 1987, had, as Minister of State at the Home Office (1995–97), criticised Michael Howard, the Home Secretary ('he has something of the night about him') over his sacking of Derek Lewis, head of the prison service.

[4] John Moore, MP Croydon Central February 1974–1992, Transport and Social Services Secretary in the mid–1980s, had for a time been seen by Margaret Thatcher as her successor. Later, in his early fifties, he went into financial management.

mental block, as always, on his name until someone came up to us – 'Ronnie') Grierson[1] he said 'have you written yours yet?' or perhaps it was 'I assume you've written yours?'. 'I'm not 70,' I answered, hearing that EP had written his in 1983 when he was, in fact, just 70.

1 Parliament Street   *Friday, 27 February*

Why is it that I do not find this office particularly sympathetic? Greatly preferring the House Library, where I now have established 'my' table, recognised by staff and messengers alike being the first small one on the right by the window as you come into the *silence* room.

On Wednesday of last week we [22] had a meeting with little Hague. (Still terrified of me, I was glad to note; caught his throat and swallowed when he had to say 'Alan Clark'.) Pretty disparate. Some, but not total, brown-nosing. Hague in his usual stuff about our being 'arrogant and out-of-touch', said the polls were 'just turning now'. I said my bit, that I was 'arrogant and out-of-touch' and proud of it, and still got large audiences – cited Kent University, overflow room etc.[2]

The following day Norman (Archie)[3] was in the tearoom and talking a lot of rot about Euro-MP selection and how we would now be putting the 'good' ones at the top of the list. 'What *is* a good Euro-MP?' I asked. He scowled, blackly.

---

[1] Sir Ronald Grierson, vice-chairman, GEC, 1968–91.
[2] Three weeks earlier AC had noted, 'Hague is slowly emerging from his "right wing" carapace (as I predicted to the '92, within a week of getting back, that he would – "Hague is *of the Left*.").'
[3] Archie Norman, MP for Tunbridge Wells since 1997.

EMT (kitchen)   *Thursday, 5 March*

Came back last night having 'not eaten all week'. *Delicious*
2-egger, demi-braised venison and rhubarb and clotted with
remaining ½ bottle of Palmer '88.

Exeter Station   *Monday, 9 March*

Been down to Bratton, leaving Saltwood at 5.35 in the Porsche,
which I dropped at Carrs for its big service; borrow a Golf again
(v nice – and no problems at all).

The whole place very scruffy indeed. Only the 'studio' is
pleasing with Campling's door,[1] and the giant (and, as it now
turns out, not invaluable) Duncans for the Queen Mary.[2]

It's strange, for ages I was sad and calm and nostalgic about
Bratton. Now I see that we never really got it right, should have
planted dense shrubs etc. It was monstrous of my father to keep
us so short of money that I had to sell the fields – 'the cream of
Bratton' for £500. I did write (most of) *Barbarossa*[3] there, and I
recall walking up the 'dump' road, looking over 'Bennett's' gate
and feeling immensely content. Not much later came 'Jollyboy'
and 'more run' in the white pushchair.[4] Also pining for Tilfy and
the magic afternoon with the girl from Bray Shop. But I only
developed into real living at Seend – Anna Koumar[5] and the
banks of sweet peas in the 'secret garden', which we 'dedicate to

---

[1] Robert Campling's painted door is now on one of the Saltwood tower office
walls.
[2] Duncan Grant, Bloomsbury artist, had, on the recommendation of Kenneth Clark,
received a commission to paint huge pictures for the *Queen Mary* liner in the
1930s. They were rejected. Jane and AC bought them in the 1970s.
[3] *Barbarossa*, AC's third volume of military history, following *The Donkeys and The
Fall of Crete*.
[4] 'Jollyboy', yet another name for the Clarks' elder son James, who so enjoyed being
pushed at speed in his pushchair that he invariably asked for more.
[5] The Clarks' cook.

the church'. So it seems perfectly natural and proper that Seend
survives (and the garden and workshop too) and is now 'dedicated'
to the Amazings.[1]

In the second drawer down of the 'Rye' desk I found a lot of
old diaries, of the early 60s. Somewhat mannered writing.
Written, indeed, more 'for publication' than subsequently. There
are a few lines worth saving. But in the main it is a time-warp,
and of a time when we were pushed for cash, and made-do-
and-mend. Even when I was 'local MP' I never really got it *up*,
although a lot of '2nd house' allowance money went on it, to
hold my position in my last Parliament.

'My last Parliament.' Hm. Everything seems to be collapsing.
The Tory Party really doesn't *make any sense* at present. Just
running behind, fetid, panting. Now I read that the Queen is
cutting down as fast as possible – on ceremony, while the dear
House of Commons is going to change for ever if PR is
brought in. How crazy to get rid of the coach and uniforms! I
remember watching the Birthday Parade in 1982 and thinking
– yes, all this finery and ceremonial. But these chaps can shoot,
and fight. Undoubtedly the display that 'only we can do', that is
what should be impressive, and unique.

There must be few things so tediously misleading as the
'focus group', a lot of total strangers sitting round in a room
trying either to show off or recycle the fashionable clichés
of the moment. Yet they are dominating the 'forming of
policy'.

So all in all, I am pretty low. Of course I can say fuck them,
fuck-you-all. But I am sent back to have one more try at the
sword. At present I am lost in the undergrowth. I say, keep calm
and concentrate on BB.

---

[1] 'The Amazings' – Andrew and his wife Sarah, who had a habit of using the word
'amazing' to describe everything.

EMT   *Monday, 23 March*

My 70th birthday approaches. Hard to believe, in some ways, when I sit at the table in the tearoom. What do colleagues think? There is a man of 70? Yesterday I tried to avoid Garel-Jones, but as everyone else went up to the new compulsory arse-lick at 5.15 on Mondays – the 'Forward Look' meeting – I was stuck. He boasted a lot about money – but unconvincingly – retold a story about UBS securities relating to a cousin of his who (very) allegedly had 'a billion dollars'; then got into his soft-sell approach on EMU. Did get through three cigarettes though, I was glad to see.

But I am creaky in my joints. Erection is a total loss – except for the one curious and reassuring experience on the Inverness flight. My arms are weak now (and look it).

I have arrived in Parliament at the very point when it is being 'marginalised'. Neither leader wants to have more to do with it than is possible. Blair because it's a nuisance, interferes with news 'management' by the exploitation of 'focus groups'. Hague because it raises issues about majority support – particularly of the 22 Executive.

Patience, but not *too much* patience. Let us see how the local elections go, and what is our rating when the summer winds down.

Harrogate   *Sunday, 29 March*

On Friday evening we set off for Harrogate Central Council. V jolly as we had the eight centre-seats on the train. Jane and I had bought pleasingly at Fortnums and I went off and got a 'bottle' (of Australian Chardonnay). How lovely and friendly and uninhibited K&C are compared to any other constituency I have ever visited. We were at the conference hotel (the Moat House) and I had hoped to be lionised a bit more than I was.

That evening the atmosphere was sceptical. To a journalist (*not* quoted, I'm sorry to say): 'There's a limit to the number of times he (Hague) can say "you're a lot of obsolete anomalies who ought to be ashamed of yourselves".'

The next day, though after a somewhat jaded opening by Cecil [Parkinson] (how many more times is he going to do this?) along came Hague. Tory audiences are far more conformist than Labour; they are utterly undiscerning. Hague's performance, though illuminated by some good lines and showing stamina (he went on for over an hour), was strangely flawed and insubstantial. He had clearly watched my pro-grammes, the way he went into *history*, and talked about 'one nation' (which shows (a) why he is so scared of me, and (b) how/why he never talked to me about it or anything else).

Poor old Archie H[amilton][1] was there totally on his own, both at breakfast and walking about the street. He came on and did his speech of support and penitence – deliberately forced on to show there was no 'breach', a stooping figure broken, all conformist after the KGB interrogations, at a show trial. He's finished. But will I be able to take his place?

In the train coming back Michael Spicer said, 'Thought they can get rid of us (the 22 Exec) at the next elections, of course.' Could be all or bust, though David D ought to be a great help here.

Theresa May[2] is the upcoming bête noir as I spotted some months ago. Yet she is the No 1 conventional plug at the moment. Even John Bercow[3] in whose Buckingham constituency I spoke on Thursday, was fulsome (though not as fulsome as he was about me in his vote of thanks). A strange and long drive that was, in his F reg Ford Sierra leap-frogging along the M-way. When we arrived an unmistakable smell of burning brake-pad which I had thought, hoped, might be coming from HGVs

---

[1] Sir Archibald (Archie) Hamilton, chairman of the 1922 Executive since 1997.

[2] Theresa May, MP for Maidenhead since 1997.

[3] John Bercow, MP for Buckingham since 1997.

adjoining us in traffic jams. And on the way back John's view of high-beam was bizarre. So much so that some big lorries were reduced to putting on their reversing lights.

EMT   *Friday, 17 April*

Two things have depressed me lately; dear little T.O. steadily in decline. Periods of 'remission' are now so short. He was, miraculously, 'seahorse' just for a few feet the other day after his morning Thompson. But he now doesn't run expectantly to the Barbican gate and wait while it is unlatched, never will again. He is terribly muddled and almost blind so bumps into things quite hard. Night before last he had a 'turn'; not one of his worst, but wouldn't come out of it properly. So last night we gave him a one-third child's aspirin and he slept better.

The photos of me with the babies (Albert and Archibald) show an old, maddish man, scrawny and streaked, aet. 73 – first time I have ever looked *more* than my age. I wake at 6 a.m. with ringing in my ears. I dread getting a stroke, like my mama.

Garden House   *Sunday, 26 April*

I was on *Frost* today. Unhappily scabious he looked, and *distrait*. His hand shook when he passed me the butter at breakfast; and at 8.50 a.m. he took out and offered me one of 3 huge Havana cigars. Jack Straw, Home Secretary, controlled and capable, 'a man of power'. Ten years or a little more ago I remember 'slapping him down' when I was junior employment minister and he was a backbench socialist 'trying to find his way'.

I am 70, and feel much weaker. I am really sad that I can't make love to Jane any more. It's different from last time when for years I didn't really notice her. Now I look at her and think how sweet and attractive she is.

Garden House   *Saturday, 2 May*

On the way back from the post I saw an amiable, though rumpled figure hammering in 'Garden Open Today' signs. It turned out to be Harland, whom I have not ever consciously met. 'Last year nobody came,' he said. I took Jane up there at teatime. Absolutely lovely. The age of the rhododendrons and azaleas – some going back to 1820. A lovely boggy valley of a garden with endless glades and dells and sudden *aperçus* and vistas. That's why it is called 'The Garden House' (hitherto I always thought because of his fruit farm).

The house itself, long and low, must have been sensational in its heyday (could have been 1911, or 1922). Now needed a lick of paint all round – but sympathetic. The little summerhouse where we had an excellent scone tea (though served in paper cups) was cottage *ornée* 1860 or earlier and presumably attached to an earlier building which was pulled, or burned, down. The green tennis court was spongy and ill-maintained, indeed the whole place bore signs of one-man maintenance, with the marks of tractor tyres on the fairway. But the more magical for that very reason. There appeared to be four generations around. Old Harland (aet. 95, or so he looked) had parchment skin and needed to be helped. Liquidity is clearly a problem, as with so many valuable (as this so clearly is) properties. I felt nostalgic there, and at tea thought of the tennis parties, and their personal desires and tensions.

Why is it that good manners and the domination of the world's oceans by the Royal Navy did coincide? Now both have vanished. I'm sure there is a linkage.

MFS GH   *Saturday, 9 May*

On Thursday evening I collapsed from a very late tea at B5 and we went to dine at Brooks's. Collapsed in bed. But around midnight I knew I had to go to the count at KTH. Expensive

taxis as I was *cum* a ½ decanter of claret. A little tension at the
Earls Court and Pembridge tables, but the Rolls-Royce
machine had performed. Barry [Phelps] strutted and paced, like
an archduke in his dinner jacket. His Labour opponent came up
and said how he had wanted to meet me, and how when he was
canvassing people would say how much they admired me.

House Library   *Wednesday, 13 May*

I did two TV clips, spoke in the Drugs debate – deliberately, so
as to take revenge on George Howarth;[1] admired Blair at
PMQs; sparkled at the Defence Committee. It is bland, 'perfect'
summer weather 68°–73° I would guess and the breeze flows in
from the river. Yesterday I was so exhausted. My limbs are stiff,
and weak in all the joints so that I can barely walk properly (a
symptom since walking back from Sandling one night a couple
of months ago). I am utterly desexualated. I drink, I suppose, just
a tiny bit more than I ought, with wine every day. And yesterday
I was melancholy all day long, because of something concerning
which I had long fantasised – the Ecosse Rallye actually coming
to Eriboll, and stopping at Ardneakie; it was taking place and I
was not there. Where's the C-type? What's happening to it?

I must write about something which I have long avoided.
Dear, game, lion-hearted little T.O. is now in his last stage. He
can't even 'seahorse' again; even when he tries he stumbles
suddenly and falls on his chin, so now only walks about bandy-
legged and his spine a little twisted. He sleeps a great deal,
sometimes he bleeds from his scrotum. Often he is very 'bad' and
bumps into things. But still he will eat, and he is not incontinent
and only two or three days ago caught his 'markie' at night-
night with that same old satisfactory clunk of the jaws. He is

[1] George Howarth, MP Knowsley North and Sefton East since 1997 (Knowsley
North 1986–97), had been Parliamentary Under-Secretary, Home Office, since
the general election.

19½ years old. It's fifteen years since we had him on our election address in Plymouth, and an item in the *Western Morning News*. Watching his decline is depressing; not just for its depiction of a game little soul slowly being dragged down, but also for its implications for me, at 70. And my suspicion that recovery will be more difficult, as decline steepens over the next five years. And then old age will supervene.

Saltwood, EMT   *Saturday, 23 May*

The day in 1940 (is it the actual day? I know it is the date, but am finding it often difficult in my writings to clarify the day of the week, but this is so important for atmospherics) of the Cabinet meeting when Halifax argued for a 'settlement'. We could not do it then. We had to fight to a point when we had proved our mettle, which we did on 15 September, and a few weeks later in the desert.

Are we better or worse off now?

House Library   *Thursday, 9 June*

A fortnight since the last entry, but seems a month at least. I 'mislaid' the brown, 'Scilla Hotel' gift briefcase containing the journal and so missed recounting a lot of incidents – most pleasing of which probably being Jeffrey Archer's 'fine wine dinner', and the cast and conversation. Last night Rocco Forte, good(-ish), but house too *Italianate* in its decoration, stuffs and drapes and curtains – though lovely Burne-Jones drawings in the hall; sketches, or so Rocco told me, for the figures in the Berlin museum.

As it is, I am depressed. I am *so* oppressed by work. This evening I have five, simultaneous [constituency] invitations, plus

there are two votes at 6.45 and pre-10 p.m. I wanted to do
Transport Qs, but had to go up to Sue's[1] where there was a stack
– I mean a stack, 10″ high or so, of signing.

In the morning I went out to Aubrey Finsberg. Even worse
than I suspected. A shed, open, corrugated iron flapping. A youth
bashing panel deafeningly the moment one got involved in
conversation. The poor C-type stripped of its body panel at
back, looking like a write off, dirt and discarded wires and pieces
everywhere. The mystery of the 'crankshaft pulley' – how? and
when? I just felt terribly tired and sad. Something told me she
had gone. A lot of braggadocio about 'doing our best, Alan'. Sort
of balls, but not the slightest chance of getting it ready for 26
June or 26 July or August, September or even 26 October. I was
really furious. I have a hate thing with mechanics and just like
builders (workmen). Only P. & A. Wood are orderly and compos
(worth every penny).

Saltwood, tearoom terrace   *Friday, 12 June*

First entry this year from a favoured spot. Brian has started to
scythe the sycamore slope and we are near to the longest day
(by which, I hope and trust, BB will be delivered and I will be
quietly awaiting my first tranche of £50). I am calm. Fax from
Knight Frank saying that Bratton sold for 186. I had hoped to get
200. This will just restore our liquidity ration, and allow me to
use the royalty payments and BB to produce (at last!) 'solvency'.
Very nearly dislocated everything today by buying the ever-so-
nice 'lightweight' VDP 3-litre tourer at Goodwood (Brooks's).
Authorised John Leyland to go to 41. Fortunately it made 49.
Would have been huge fun to clean and activate, but came back,
looked at the Hen and was reasonably content. My cross remains
91MX, but we had a lovely outing. Jane brilliant at the

---

[1] Sue Line, AC's secretary.

autojumble stalls. And v splendidly dismissed the Barn VDP by saying that it looked 'teeny bit Wolseley'.

I spoke last night at the dinner; just about ok, I suppose, but goodness knows what I looked like under the lights. Sat next to the v attractive Mrs Jane Major. Paid £2000 so can't complain.

Parliament Street office   *Thursday, 18 June*

In that slightly rattled, dry-mouthed condition one gets into following a 'gaffe'.[1] I don't in the least regret speaking out on behalf of the 'fans'. Part, as Charles Moore said, of my *weltanschauung*. But usual correspondence of cor-there-he-goes-again type. And Conservative Central Office – predictably – got in the act 'condemning' me.

Great Hall   *Saturday, 20 June*

This is midsummer weekend. And, as usual, I make an entry from the prayer seat on the long table in the Great Library where, at 7 p.m., the sun is still high.

The ramblers were down all day. I was somewhat (sic) dreading them, when we met them at 10.07 at Sandling. I walked with them as far as Acrise. When I first 'offered the booking' I said to Jane 'this will be the hottest day of the year'. And sure enough, after weeks of thunderstorms and winds this is what it has turned out to be. I turned at Postling Road and walked back to Sandling; waiting by the station my pulse was erratic, at 130+. But as soon as I had swum it was back to 78

---

[1] On BBC's *Today* AC had praised the 'martial spirit' of English football fans in Marseilles involved in fighting French riot police. 'Football matches are now the modern equivalents of medieval tournaments.'

(some doctors might have said 'don't go in the cold water might risk a stroke'). They came back for tea and the atmosphere improved, with the groups fantasising.

Poor Aspers is dying. What will happen to the animals? Do they know their protector is in travail?

I got the better of everybody over the football-supporters 'gaffe'. Central office are briefing against me, as always. 'Tough on dinosaurs; and tough on the causes of dinosaurs.' Hague is ill, with flu.

Saltwood, EMT   *Monday, 22 June*

Big Book is finished. At 8.50 p.m. last night I put the very last sentence onto the computer.

Thursday, 25 June

I dropped a tart note to Sebastian Coe[1] off at 32 Smith Square with copies of all my fan letters.

On the way over I had been striding along, saw cross-faced Roy Jenkins[2] in his little purple car turning into the Lords car park. Returning I looked up at the Palace and inhaled great lungful of air, I took pleasure in its appearance like some lovely ridge in the Highlands, and knowing that I have climbed it.

---

[1] Sebastian Coe, former athlete, MP for Falmouth and Camborne, 1992–1997; Private Secretary to William Hague as Tory Leader since 1997.
[2] Lord [Roy] Jenkins, former Labour Minister, one of the 'gang of four' that broke away from the Labour Party to found the SDP, which he later led.

House Library, 11.40 p.m.   *Thursday, 2 July*

I felt rather dreadful before 'turning in', at intervals in the night, and even on waking (though recovering now, on Indian tea and grapefruit juice). Dinner at Wilton's with Soames and Woodward. S crocodile, so occasionally shrewd; but unfocused, too easily distracted in conversation. W is good, but of the left of course; and makes mistakes of judgement – like plugging 'the Governor'. All agreed that Hague must go. But not, naturally, this minute. He's now been 'staying out' for over ten days. Quite ridiculous with medical science in its advanced state – look at Mitterrand (or Yeltsin) not to mention Mrs T, Winston, Anthony etc. The Party can just about carry him. But it simply means he can never be ill again, like Michael Heseltine being allowed only one heart attack. The boys want, of course, to replace him with Clarke. Almost as difficult, I would think, to get the Party to swallow K as to swallow A!

I hope this weekend to do some thinking – for the first time almost since Scotland. But at the Carlton Club finance meeting yesterday evening all the men in the room were glowering. What a dreadful, seedy mediocre bunch the party apparatchiks are! There were some Nellies in the doorway and I 'gave' one a kiss for the photographer – which caused a huge coach-tour whoop to echo round the crowded room, to everyone's disapproval, except for dear Michael Ancram, who was speaking.

EMT   *Monday, 13 July*

Last night we went to bed at eight – slept shallowly until it became dark, then deeply. This morning at 6-ish I said something to Jane and she answered 'ye-es' in a very sleepy drawl that reminded me of when (twice) I have visited her in hospital and she has still been under anaesthetic. In a curious way her very sweet nature comes through. And very briefly I had a sad projection forward – which of us will die first? Me, I hope. But then would dear sweet Janey be nicely looked after once I was gone? Who would spend 'quality time' (new *in* phrase) with her; what about her pets? She is so patient and kind.

Sunday, 19 July

A lovely hot day, almost the first of this summer. I am sitting out by the tearoom (not in use this year). I drank the delicious new Riesling and could be at a café table beside a *place* in Normandy, 'putting the world to rights'. If I was also sexual I would be completely happy. With this one exception, my good fortune is so TOTAL that it makes me apprehensive – both as to possible reverse, and also regarding my debt to 'put something back in'.

After all, the three little grandsons; BB delivered; the safest and most pleasing of all seats – to which I am perfectly suited; the nicest part of the summer ahead. It is gone 8 p.m. and very still, with exceptional golden light in the left-hand sycamore. Swallows, jolly now, still swoop and chatter excitedly although they, and all the birds, are about to retire.

Bratton   *Thursday, 23 July*

Yesterday I was absolutely depressed. The sad, final news that Tom – missing since 8 p.m. yesterday – had been found dead or drowned at the Towers end of the moat; its many sad reminders of – in slow motion – my own steady decline. Then an inconclusive (as nearly always) meeting of the 22 Executive followed by 'the Leader's address'. Hague really awful. Trite, insecure, verbal disconnection. Worse, I think, even than Ted. Certainly Major was incomparably better. What is to happen to the Tory Party?

Last week DD, who is proprietorial for me, suggested I give a lecture on the constitution in our history, preferably at Conference with Robert Blake somewhere around. Just right, if it weren't for the fact that if BB 'flunks', which clearly is going to, my reputation (always partially spurious) as a 'historian' goes with it.

Now this afternoon, after getting up at 5 a.m. we are at Bratton for the last time.[1] It is smiling, and I sit in the front garden after a lovely tea. I have practically no pangs (though disappointed at the price of £180,000). It took us 5½ hours to drive here from Saltwood. The West Country is inaccessible in the summer months, and much here has changed, with the death of Mrs Lintern and David's sulkiness, and the unpleasant publican. It is peaceful, on a sunny July afternoon, because there is no background noise, no 'M-way roar'. But the house looks dreadful from outside now, paint peeling off all the windows, and a generally neglected air.

I bought it in a rush, driving down to Okehampton on the Bank Holiday in the Olds 88 after we saw it when cruising through to look at a National Trust property in the north, where we might have been tenants. In fact we did not live here very long. Under pressure from Nanny [Greenwood] we went back, after the birth of Andrew in 1962, to Rye, first to No 30 (an awkward, vertical house at the corner of Watchbell Street and Church Square); then with some Trust money to the Wades (No 12), bought, heart-stoppingly – for £9800. We still used Bratton as a summer place. I remember particularly the lovely Whitsun of 1963 with the Grahams staying, using the [Citroën] ID Safari to go to Bude. In winter we were at Zermatt (though interrupted that year by the typhoid scare, being only saved by Taugwalder's [lawyer] greed from closing the sale of the châlet at 120,000 francs. This we continued until 1964-ish and bought Seend Manor, living first in the Manor, then at the Park, and as

---

[1] In a note three days later AC recalls how he and Jane were 'absolutely knackered' after the double drive – Saltwood/Bratton/Bratton (Broomhayes)/Saltwood.

I often write in many ways the most physically fulfilling period of my life and long walks with EDG on the plain with the Beagles and the 2CV.

Then, captivated by Enoch, and courted by Alan Warner and his crew at Langstone (Havant) I approached politics.

My father moved out of Saltwood in 1971 and 'new readers join here'.[1] Bratton remained intermittently while I was Plymouth MP kept going by periodic grants from our 'second-house allowance'. But now we haven't visited (much less lived) here for seven years. 'More Run' has surfaced – my *Rosebud*. The furnishings will be dispersed around the family.

House Library   *Tuesday, 28 July*

Last night I was so exhausted. I could barely drag myself to 'Pembridge' [ward] party – the last of the social round. Did *not* sparkle. Had come straight from Hague talking about 'the State and the Community' at Carlton House Terrace (being *not* recognised by the tittle on the desk when I arrived). 'What a lot of waffle,' said the elderly man on my right.

I went to Pratt's, drank a glass of white wine, felt too tired to remain and returned to B5. Ate an Eccles cake bought at the tearoom counter, tried to ring Saltwood – engaged. Dialled Eriboll – engaged. Talking to each other (again). Read a long passage about German strategic policy in winter 1940.

Outside Long Garage, Saltwood   *Saturday, 1 August*

Yesterday was our wedding anniversary. Forty years. Janey still looks incredible; I have deteriorated since last summer when the famous Christmas card photo was 'snapped' by Caroline Stroyan.

---

[1] See *Diaries: Into Politics* which begins in 1972.

In the early mornings I am so stiff and weak that I almost fall over (as, presumably, like my father – and grandfather – I will at some point in the next decade). I am hypochondriac about my jaw – is it rotting slowly under Bertie's great carapace? What does one do when the teeth go? Like the king elephant in *Babar*, it is the end. No more photocalls either.

BB is going to cause me damage. I will not be the Party's historian and (as I had intended) its sage; still less its Maxime Weygand.[1]

Wednesday, 12 August

Although we have been sitting by the pool (the last 4–5 days have been incredibly hot) saying that we wished we need not move, now suddenly the pull of Scotland is felt. As at the House (catalpa trees in flower) so at Saltwood where the hollyhocks have more than half lost their petals then the season has changed gear. We must assert ourselves and when we return the air, and the colours, will be different. So tomorrow, up the A1 with the customary 5.50 a.m. 'through the gates'. For the first time ever, though, without T.O. on his 'jump seat' – although his hairs are, as Jane would say, copious on the seats and carpets.

I am fractionally better, and would have improved more if in fact had been to bed earlier, as one had intended. Down on energy and zest, though. No press-ups by the pool this year, or weights, or Gossie in the evenings.[2] I had a nasty frisson walking in the old family garden this evening. How many more times will I see it, in its August fullness? Two or three (with luck) in my present condition; then perhaps another four or five as a buffer, or demi-buffer.

---

[1] Maxime Weygand, who was recalled in June 1940 to take on the crumbling French Army.

[2] By October he is noting, 'I have only done about three sets of two press-ups this whole year.'

Shore, Wheelhouse   *Tuesday, 18 August*

Last night I slept – without interruption of any kind, barely even
'surfacing' – from 10 p.m. until 7.10 a.m. Opened my eyes, said
a few words, then slept again until 8.20. After lunch I slept in the
deckchair in the wheelhouse until woken by Hannah for the
'w'. Each time we are in Eriboll I sleep like this ('too much') for
the first week. I remember Peter Morrison[1] when I asked him
what he 'did' at Islay just answered – 'sleep'. That is what
Scotland is for.

At tea in the wheelhouse I looked across and thought – 'if
two years ago I had been told that I would be sitting here, and
beside me a beautiful little baby boy in a high chair being fed
by Julie with chunks of fruit salad, I would have thought, "there
is nothing more I can ask for …" Two roots of the generation
tree now started in the soil. But continuity is now as much in
God's hands as in mine.

What an incredible two years it has been! Was it only that
long ago that Sarah Baxter interviewed me at Bournemouth –
'reinventing himself'. But of course in that time I have become
much older. My limbs are feeble and achy in the joints. So much
so that at this rate I will be bufferish at 73; while I want to be a
mixture of Bill Deedes and (as it were) Paul Johnson.

What of poor old Aspers, I wonder? He must now be at
death's door. Or rather, Death be at his. I watch the obituary
columns quite eagerly; each contemporary down is a private
score. This is the counterpoint of getting much-sweat and
bladder compression in the night thinking of how much I have
yet to do to assert order.

---

[1] Peter Morrison, former MP for Chester, junior Minister and Mrs Thatcher's
campaign manager when she lost the Party leadership.

Shore Cottage   *Saturday, 29 August*

The holiday is over. Two lovely last days; yesterday we went out
in Katoomba (I felt queasy, but 'held on') and dined up at the
Lodge. Today a great walk all around the forestry plantation
taking 'Bok' as well as the girls. I bathed twice, and Jane very
gamely joined me for the last one this p.m.

The recall of Parliament.[1] Yes, it is a chore, cuts into other
'options' for departure day. But just think of it! What would I in
1992, 3, 4, 5, or 6 have given to be recalled from Eriboll to an
emergency sitting of the House of Commons! And at the same
time to be leaving behind James and Julie and the tiny baby
Angus! How can I even for half of one minute start to whinge
or question my unbelievable good fortune?

EMT, Saltwood   *Saturday, 5 September*

Demi-serene. I performed in the emergency session. I
stumbled – why? Slightly alarming in retrospect – calling
Madame *Deputy*-Speaker, then my honourable *members*, but
got professionally into my stride. 'I am fortified ... ('all too
true', chuckled that bearded nameless who bothers me from
the other side; v unfair as I hadn't drunk anything all day, but
no one would believe it) ... by fact that deputy leader of the
Liberal party has just withdrawn his name from a motion
signed by his own chief whip' (this thanks to injunction from
Mackay[2] and Michael Howard).

It was a most classic example of the House of Commons
coming alight while the two front benches sat mute, looking at

---

[1] Parliament was reconvened to pass emergency anti-terrorist legislation in the
wake of the Omagh bombing by the 'Real' IRA.
[2] Andrew Mackay, MP for Bracknell since 1997 (Berkshire East, 1983–97); deputy
chief whip 1996–97. Opposition spokesman on Northern Ireland since 1997.

the floor. A quite brilliant speech by Richard Shepherd, almost on the verge of a breakdown, inspired people to argue.[1]

Ashford train   *Wednesday, 9 September*

The time seems to be galloping past now we are back. This year the September second half of holiday is blighted by the launch of BB. I feel lethargic and passed over; and just lately I am reading a lot about Chris Patten (his book is just out) and his impending 'return' to politics.[2] I can get sad if I think of being finally 'out'. But am I to die in harness? When I am over at the Garden House I think of my retirement there. And when I walk through the rooms at Saltwood now I can half feel my own death. Almost an Orphée-like revisitation.

And yet the 'practicalities' oppress. Three days ago we thought that we might clear one piece, delivered from Bratton, from the Hall, and decided to move a small chest of drawers up to Andrew's room … Like everything at Saltwood tampering with the mud and wattle dam released first a dribble, then a jet, then a cascade. The chest seemed better in the bathroom. And that in my bathroom beside Jane's (summer) bed. Thus 'releasing' the ludicrous wooden washstand, which has been her bedside table for the last 25 years into the passage. This involved a total re-organising and cleaning of the original (Rye) chest in my bathroom, polishing the Herman box, the glass desk-top, rearranging the photos etc.

One minor point of interest in the back lid flap of the inlaid writing case we found a letter beautifully written in copperplate complaining about his 'posting' to Ireland, the 'brigands', the delays to the stage [coach] and so on. 'While writing this I have

---

[1] Richard Shepherd had been the *Spectator* Backbencher of the Year in 1987 and *Spectator* Parliamentarian of the Year in 1995.
[2] Titled *East and West* it proved a bestseller. But would Patten return as a saviour of the Conservative Party? Patten, shrewdly, did not rise to the bait.

a sword at my side and a pistol, cocked and loaded, on the table before me.' For 150 years or more this has been the 'norm'. How then, about the Peace Process?

Thursday, 17 September

I wrote an article defending Bill Clinton and – unbelievably – on being asked for a quote Hague's office said, 'Mr Clark periodically makes a spectacle of himself, but most people know his views are not those of the Conservative Party.'

Sunday evening, 20 September

All depends, really, on the Book and how it is received. Robert Blake reviewing it for the *Sunday Times* – this could be critical.[1]

A lovely still late autumn, with the barometer rising. How delicious to live on here, just daily tasks. The Mains, the Garden House, the Woodland (both sides), the cars.

But I've tried this; withdrawal symptom too strong (because, of course, I know that the next big 'event' is death).

So what is to become of me?

Rebecca Salt[2] has fitted up the whole week, like an official. Doesn't leave a single gap in the diary, not even to tinkle, still less eat.

---

[1] Lord Blake, who had himself written an earlier history of the Conservative Party, was good-tempered.
[2] Rebecca Salt, publicity director, Weidenfeld & Nicolson.

House Library   *Wednesday, 23 September*

An absolutely beautiful still September day, the barometer rising
all week. A special agony at leaving Saltwood (at least I did
bathe, briefly to stimulate the system out of its abject and listless
depression) because of a feeling that there really are so few left
– ones when I can still stride, if not prance.

'Don't go, *don't* go. Why are you leaving? How can you leave
us? Always you do this, and always it makes you unhappy; and
always you have the same excuse – "must" do this or that
(utterly transient; ephemeral and draining task) and, at the back
of your mind, "next time, next year I really won't." But that's not
true. You think we will always be here, and that because you love
us we will always love you and protect you. But in the end, we
will be gone. *Please* give us a little time ...'

Thus I felt the call from the trees and the corn-stubble and
the songbirds.

Zermatt   *Tuesday, 29 September*

This is the time to come here. And now that the silver birch and
the larch are so grand their leaves filter and dapple the sunlight.
The house is set back from the street, blocked on the southern
side by the Kariad, and its screen of trees in leaf protect it most
pleasingly.

We started off as on a meander but, as nearly always in the
Alps, it turned into a quite stiff (for the first day) expedition. A
nice young man, beautifully dressed in a navy overcoat with his
lady (in a black fur) smiled and took my photograph in the old
inn; they were on their honeymoon as we were just exactly
forty years ago.

Last night I had difficulty getting to sleep. I tinkled five, finally
six times quite copiously. In the morning Jane found blood on
my pidgy bottoms. How? Why? Unsettling. I am absolutely

desexualated. A nullity. Up until only two years ago I would always wake with a sleepy erection at 5.30. Seven years ago we started again out here. Absolutely delicious, never been sexually happier with Jane.

Saltwood   *Thursday, 15 October*

Conference – AC1800 parked 'modestly' bang outside the very Blackpool-like (we were of course in Bournemouth) 'Trouville' Hotel. Then Eastbourne for the 'bonding'. I turned up in a 3-piece (sic) suit with a pink shirt – tight collar, accidently chose a size 15 instead of 15½ – and OE tie. Surrounded by reporters as I got out of the cab. 'It's a statement,' I told them.[1]

Later

'Do you want to be Mayor?' Jane asked.[2]

I just don't know. Or rather I do know and the answer is, by a narrow margin, 'yes'. But what I do not want is a campaign for the mayorality. Yes, the ideal scenario remains, as Moira Stewart[3] put it, 'become Mayor, then after two years strike for the Leadership of the Tory Party.' And certainly the odds on this are no higher than, two years ago, they must have been for a 67-year-old animal rights activist with a lurid private life and a record for colossal indiscretion, plus falling foul of the Police, HM Customs, and the Scott Inquiry to get selected for the safest Tory seat in the country.

Or the Speaker, conceivably?

A nice lead piece in Cross-Bencher [*Sunday Express*] to which – interestingly – NO ONE referred the following day at

---

[1] A Central Office spokesman had said: 'we don't want people turning up in suits.'

[2] The Labour government had decided London should have an elected Mayor. Candidates were beginning to jostle along party lines.

[3] Moira Stewart, BBC newscaster, in conversation with AC at a literary lunch in Kensington Town Hall.

Eastbourne, except DD slyly in his cups at supper. I did say to Jane – here we are discussing these marvellous possibilities and here I am with three lovely little grandsons and a safe seat – surely some catastrophe is due to strike? I try and avoid hubris, but do, of course 'show off' (*épater*). Not quite the same thing, but invites Nemesis none the less.

House Library   *Tuesday, 20 October*

Last night the first meeting of the Sybil club. The unlikely duet of Bill Cash and Shaun Woodward have invited twelve 'interesting' colleagues (ten MPs, two peers) to meet on a monthly basis and talk things through.[1] No factional lines. Ruffley (clockwise), Simon Burns (an unexpected figure – but pleasant), Bercow, Cash, Tapsell, Q. Davies, Gowrie, Woodward, self etc.[2] Robert Blake talked, or rather read in very poor light at a slow pace a quite nicely composed text – the plot of the novel, its lessons etc.

All of the contributions were worth listening to. An enormous amount of drink was consumed. Quite suddenly at the end of the meal after port and Sauternes a selection of new, and delicious, clarets were proffered. I smoked, most rarely, a Havana cigar. We 'broke up' at 12.55 and completely stupefied I left the Porsche in the street asking Shaun's butler to feed the meter from 8.30 a.m.

In spite of walking back at a fine pace and reading at some length from my own published *Diaries* I woke up quite quickly

---

[1] Political dining club named after Disraeli's landmark novel, *Sybil: or the Two Nations*. AC sometimes misspells it 'Sibyl' (after the hostess Sibyl Colefax?). The Woodward-Cash 'Sibyl' met at Woodward's Queen Anne's Gate home. Like Bill Cash, Woodward was wealthy, but politically they were on opposite sides of the Conservative Party. One black-ball excluded.

[2] David Ruffley (Bury St Edmunds since 1997), Simon Burns (Chemsford W since 1997; Chelmsford, 1987–97), Quentin Davies (Grantham and Stamford since 1997; Stamford and Spalding, 1987–97); Lord Gowrie (chairman of the Arts Council since 1994).

– bitter vomit in the upper throat. Should have got rid of it at once, but this would have meant losing a lot of quite good food as well. Dropped back off, woke again – cold. Tinkled and immediately and strongly came over Norwegian Embassy. Only just got back to bed; a bit worried about cerebral haemorrhage. This symptom is now definitely linked to (far) too much drink.

Shaun showed me two little pencil sketches done by a woman of Winston on his very last day [in the Commons].The last one, of him making his way out of the Chamber with his stick, achingly moving.[1]

House Library   *Wednesday, 21 October*

I walked this morning across Star Court, wet and exhausted, and was reminded of that strong, upsetting, and never wholly eradicable relationship – my last, indeed my entire, two years at MoD. A long time now; next year it will be ten years. I get a kind of satisfaction now, looking back at passages when I felt bitterly unhappy, but now think – 'well, I got through that …' Many, many times I think of 'x' and would love a 'chat'. But I don't make contact not wanting to let down Jane.

Parliament Street   *Wednesday, 28 October*

This, to all intents and purposes, is the final entry.[1] I should have started it at Shore, where we were last weekend for the christening of the bairn. So lovely Shore, 'the little house', as Jane calls it, with the light changing and the husbandry and the panelled 'work-station' and, of course, the wheelhouse.

---

[1] The artist, Juliet Pannett, worked for the *Illustrated London News*, which is why she had a ticket for the Commons' press gallery.

As so often (and I expect that I will return to this) I turned my mind to shifting the centre of gravity: Saltwood on care-and-maintenance with only the Red Study and a semi-stripped Music Room intact. The most symbolic of all transfers the hens to the sleeper-shed taken place. Would I then get on 'Boy's' nerves. Quite probably, certainly on Julie's. An ironic mirror image of my father at Garden House in the closing years. We could be at Saltwood for periods only; probably mid-June to end July. Zermatt in October; conceivably, and again in end March early April. Christmas would alternate.

At the moment, though, it is not feasible. The House consumes me still, I love it. I want to come home early on Thursday, but must wait and speak in the Quarantine Debate because I always promised myself that whatever else happened to me if I should ever 'get back' I would speak for the animals.

I still haven't described the Christening – so pleasing in the little candle-lit church (Mary's iron candelabra) and the Catholic ceremony – Fr John Maguire – much more significant. Afterwards we did pile into the jeep for the Christmas-card photo. The last occasion for some while, I fear, when we will all be under one roof.

Saltwood, in bed, Summer Bedroom   *Monday, 2 November*

Third day of a cold. Saturday night was dreadful, 100.5° at 3.30, I lay diagonally restive – 'simply on the floor at Mother Teresa's, nothing to be done' etc. Hannah occupied most of the space. Jane carrying forward the analogy saw her as a cow, also ushered in to lie among the sick and dying. To complete the image, there was no water.

Yesterday I was mainly in bed, though did totter down to 'run up' the C-type. I'm reluctant to part with the C-type; but have gone right off cars. That bloody 91 MX – a bill for £20. And

what, incidentally, of Bratton? It's just a write-off. A nil amount.[1]
Had a 'Lem-sip' last night so slept round from 11 to 7 a.m.

EMT   *Tuesday, 10 November*

A very long 'cold', now in its twelfth day and still bright green,
chestily and my voice tenuous in the extreme which worries me.

After the Remembrance Service on Sunday I spoke to little
Dr Jonathan Munday our new Mayor of the Royal Borough,
said I'd been feeling shaky for eight days and had lost my voice.

'Feeling ghastly for ten days, eh?' Vomiting, diarrhoea? No.
Shortness of breath, chest pains? No aches in the joints? No.
Waterworks, digestion? OK.

Hm. I trailed the idea of getting throat cancer from 'straining'
the voice. He spluttered. Spoke reassuringly about the vocal
chords.

We drove back in Big Red. But I am far from right.

Saltwood   *Saturday, 14 November*

I refuse to close this volume until I am 'feeling better'.

Saltwood   *Tuesday, 17 November*

'November is always a bad month for you, isn't it?' said Jane at
EMT.

'Yes,' I answered. 'I know that I will die at ten minutes to three
on a date in November – probably between the 4th and the 10th.'

---

[1] Although the buyer had, as AC notes elsewhere, 'welched' on the deal, we 'very
clever to have pouched deposit'.

1 Parliament Street   *Thursday, 19 November*

My first entry[1] and I am low, uncertain, and 'not myself'.

Now (tomorrow) coming up to three weeks with my 'cold' and, pace Mrs Frowd, 'spot' on the trachea. No longer green, but voice tremulous and with a low endurance. *Only very slowly* recovering energy. Is this Eric Forth's (many colleagues have had the germ), 'you think you're getting better and then it comes back at you'? Or more sinister?

I am gloomy that it is a step-change. Will never quite recover off the back. Last night, eating solo and lightly in Wilton's, a *very* old buffer next door asked me how old I was. '70'. 'I'm 70' he said ('you look and sound – he was v quavery – 80'). 'You'll have a stroke this year' he said. Hm. On inquiry turned out to be a rather dim 'explorer'.

B5   *Monday, 20 November*

Going to give myself a fresh treat and looking at a C-type which Gregor Fiskin is offering at £475,000 (!)

House Library   *Thursday, 24 November*

I drove up this afternoon in typical November afternoon weather. Poor light, moisture, mist, heavy rain that could almost be snow. I felt listless, and exhausted. Already I had cleared out the hen houses, and put in fresh straw, then over to Garden House to clean up my *New Statesmen* 'Diary' which last night most perversely went *off-margin* in the biggest possible way. Once more I am condemned to stay all day Friday and then

---

[1] In what would prove the final manuscript volume of AC's journal.

a mock speaking engagement – but it is in John Hayes's[1] constituency and he is a good guy.

Am I pre-cancerous, or even cancerous? Certainly I get sudden fluctuations in body temperature. Last night Jane woke me. When she is hardly awake she speaks in absolutely normal, conventional tones, which I don't like in the middle of the night. Worrying about Bratton, which *is* a bore of course. I don't mind (much) 'taking a bath', but don't want there to be no bids at all.

Surgery for two hours, switching on the lights for 'ML Welss',[2] followed by a book signing. I drain myself. And tomorrow early for the Savoy and a Hague breakfast.

Tower Office, Saltwood   *Saturday, 28 November*

This week I put 100,000 Coats into the Eriboll Trust. All too easily they might have been (in the mid eighties/early nineties, when I was jobbing in them at 200-ish) the balancing element against the *Times* dollar portfolio. It is less than fifteen years since I identified the asset objective as 'a million Swiss francs, a million dollars, and a million Coats'. Now they are 25½p! So on a negative basis I suppose that is 'phew!'. 'Shows what can happen' etc and just as well, as Bratton clearly isn't going to sell and we will be down £180,000.

I am a lot calmer. I feel myself to have recovered, and today pulling some 'fruiting bodies'[3] and pottered pleasingly in 'classic-car' weather standard for November with moist road surfaces and condensatory precipitation.

I just took a few moments off to go through and be told that it was pheasant this evening. So opened a bottle of Lynch '62

---

[1] John Hayes, MP for South Holland and The Deepings since 1997.
[2] Chelsea and Kensington food shop.
[3] AC's name for brambles.

(the best claret of all time, *I* think) from the case which Jane found among a full case of Yquem '67 and Margaux '61 in Peggy's pantry, under the Great Library, of all places. I think a lot about the Party and my mission – conceived last January. I will, I hope, draw a dividend on my many speaking engagements, my appearances at the top of the fund-raisers league table.

Later (Monday)

I was inspired to write draft notes for a speech to the AGM telling of how I felt I needed to 'break out'. Went up to the bath, there noticed the ulcer on my shin which has been there on and off for quite a time (originally thought to have been hit while walking through metal parts in, as it were, the workshop).

How long has it been there? Certainly not changing as now, but often a little red scab. At once deep gloom, a full onset of hypochondria so soon after finally emerging from the viral 3½ weeks.

Now it is a lovely, fine gusty morning, but I am low and feel my leg. As soon as one realises oneself to be afflicted it's 'what's the point?'.

Tuesday, 1 December

Have done a couple of medias today; the (potentially hateful) Leasehold Reform Lobby; then 3.15 Pinochet[1] on 'Westminster Live'. Last night I heckled – demi – Hague on the 'Forward Look' Committee on the Lords and PR which has got me on to *Today* on Wednesday. Most people in the room (even, e.g., Ainsworth[2]) agreed with me.

As I walked back this morning from Millbank I passed under

---

[1] Britain was refusing extradition demands from Spain over General Augusto Pinochet, former Chilean dictator, who was living under house arrest in a house in Surrey.

[2] Peter Ainsworth, MP for Surrey E since 1992, opposition deputy chief whip, 1997–98.

the windows of the office of my old friend EDG from which sometimes he used to hail me. It was fun in those days popping in there every Tuesday before lunch for white wine. But I was far more frustrated then than I am now. My constituency was in a mess, intense dislike and unease. My political prospects nil. My private life uncertain, as my finances.

Now I am happy and fortunate. Last night sat at my desk, rang Jane, didn't know what to do. Aimless Beefsteak or House dining room? Chose House, ran into Ancram, dined with him and joined by Goodlad who was a little uneasy about being nominated Commissioner. A bad press and Patten has announced that *he* would like it. 'You'll get it,' I told him.[1] Later he said that 'once your radar shuts down even a bit (we were talking about Tom King being deaf) you're finished. You're out.'

Goodlad told me that my radar was always at 360° fucking even when I was out of Parliament.

Leaving the dining room I was taken in by little Duncan.[2] Beautiful, but a weenily bit tiddly, and we sat in the Savoy Room to be joined by Ainsworth and then – TED.[3] Mellow and pleasing and a white dinner jacket. His eyes are still alive, very.

Quite like old times.

Ashford train   *Friday, 4 December*

A couple of days ago I was depressed and flaccid. I came across some 'poor' reviews of my book – which has unquestionably proved a 'disappointment' (and, in its reception, to me). I seemed

---

[1] AC was wrong: Patten became a member of the European Commission in 1999.
[2] Alan Duncan, MP for Rutland and Melton since 1992; PPS to Health Minister 1993–94.
[3] Sir Edward Heath, aged 82, Father of the House, having first been elected for Bexley in 1950.

to be pointless in the House. Perhaps even the 22 Exec[1] would be taken away ...

Then, at the Wednesday PMQs, Hague walked into an ambush which (as it turned out) he had set up for himself. He started asking Blair about 'a deal' to include hereditaries in the reformed House of Lords. No one – either side – had the slightest idea what he/they were talking about. Soon it became apparent from Blair's responses that Hague himself didn't either. Robert Cranborne[2] had done a private deal to save the Cecils' skin and give the hereditaries a toehold in the 'new' House (because of course there never will be a 'stage 2'; there never is). At first sight it was monstrous. The corridors were buzzing and little Liam Fox[3] caught up with David D and me in the Library corridor as soon as we left the tearoom and said it was 'the greatest act of betrayal in the history of the Tory Party'. There was uncertainty, bewilderment and resentment abroad. Most colleagues were low. Another filthy setback (although there was little blaming of Hague's handling).

At the Executive there was much complaint. Everyone agreed it was a miserable affair and the *balance of resentment* seemed to be against Robert. Suddenly there was an agitated tapping at the door. Lidington[4] burst in, white as a sheet and wild-eyed. 'William has just sacked Cranborne and wants to come and address the full Committee in 20 minutes' time.'

Hague himself was 'grimfaced'. Quite clear, but how his voice does *grate*! He's quite like Harold Wilson minus only the bogus and infuriating penchant to suck on a pipe. Wilson, though, would never have got into this jam. The next morning I was woken (one had 13 votes the previous night after 10 p.m.) by *Today* programme and croakily and (when I saw the transcript)

---

[1] AC had been elected to the executive of the Conservative backbench 1922 Committee earlier in 1998.

[2] Lord Cranborne had been Leader of the Opposition in the Lords since 1997.

[3] Dr Liam Fox, MP for Woodspring since 1992, Opposition spokesman on constitutional affairs.

[4] David Lidington, MP for Aylesbury since 1992, Hague's PPS since 1992.

incoherently said we were in a 'double-sided mess'. All day, clips
and bites. I judged it right to be 'loyal'. But the fact of Hague
afterwards accepting the 100 exceptions does seem to show that
in fact he's all over the place. And in Sunday's (today) morning
papers he had briefed that he intends to reform the Upper
House 'root and branch'.

As Jane remarked, 'one's instinct is to support Robert; but
from the Party point-of-view I suppose that one must stay with
Hague – for the time being at least.'

Gratifyingly, Alastair C[ampbell] came on the phone for 35
minutes on Friday night (twice offered me a peerage, incidentally).
In the end we were cut off. I assume that the Downing Street
switchboard were changing the tape. So when it immediately re-
rang I said, 'Are you at No 10?' It was Soames! He gulped and
moaned. A little later I phoned Cranborne. Hannah answered,
coolish. 'Robert will ring you back, maybe tomorrow.' R came to
the phone at once. Spoke for another half hour. Two sides to this
tale. Funny about the 'epicene young men' who forced their way
into the Peers meeting *with* Hague (quite discourteous and
improper). Told of how when he said, 'I can resign now; or later, or
you can sack me', Peter Carrington[1] stepped forward, venerably, 'As
someone who, so to speak, has experience of resignation, hah-
hah, could I suggest …'

'*NO*.' Hague pushed him aside. 'Yah sacked.' It is an indescrib-
able mess. I wrote roughly the same piece for the *Mail* (rejected);
then for the *Mail on Sunday* (rejected), each time being paid for.
There is the usual talk of the succession. Ken [Clarke] crazily in
the wings; Maude hovering. Neither is realistic.

But 'the front *is* collapsing' – as I predicted.

At least it is a lovely winter's day, and crisp underfoot. We are log-
splitting and stacking. I have my Mains, and my old-timers. I am
content. (My 'ulcerly leg' is healing itself.) The little boys, Albert,
Archie, were here yesterday en route for Broomhayes and divine.

---

[1] Lord Carrington, Margaret Thatcher's first Foreign Secretary, had resigned in 1982
at the time of Argentina's invasion of the Falklands.

But there is just this void. I can only barely see the lake. Over Christmas I must think very carefully.

House Library   *Tuesday, 8 December*

Oh-so-low driving up (in mist and rain). Last night Lëhni suddenly got *full-blown* ear flapping (as in 'full blown' AIDS). On and on she paw jabbed it, yelping and whimpering all the while. We rose, blundered about; Jane found Miss Bett's Powder – stored in a Colman's Mustard tin.[1] Later she paw-licked oh-so-jarringly. 'An *early night* always involves an interruption.' Old and true saying. Perhaps it was depression induced by recalling how we would start leaving Tom down there after he had one of his fits and sometimes he used to bark, and we pulled the blankets over our heads. In the morning we would go down half almost hoping that he would have 'died in his sleep'. I am still nostalgic for Tom and miss him when I come round the corner for tea at the end of the day and the log fire is burning merrily.

I am lowered more than I care to admit by Max Hastings' unpleasant introduction to Bradshaw's *Not*.[2] 'Many Conservatives loathe him', etc. Realised, of course, that the 'Chairman of the 22' who was quoted as saying that 'Don't people understand that Alan's not *pretending* to be a shit? He really *is* one,' would, can only, have been Hamilton. Read over the weekend account in *Grauniad* of man of 73 getting, and dying from, cancer (written by his daughter). If I am rejected … General gloom.

Fear God, and stay calm …

But why, incidentally, won't Jane pray? Too frightened of it working, I suspect.

---

[1] 'Thornit', a patent medicine from Miss P Bett, Thornham, Norfolk.

[2] Selected columns from Peter Bradshaw's pastiche Diary as they appeared in the *Evening Standard*, now published as a paperback.

EMT   *Monday, 14 December*

Heading now into pre-Christmas week with the election to the 22 Executive and the 'Clarkson' show behind me.[1]

Elections ok, so much so that I would like the results, the numbers that is beside the names, published. As I said to John Bercow these are the only (beside Parliamentary committee scrutinies) posts in the Party that have true democratic legitimacy. The whips have woken up to this and now try and get their men in, as a matter of routine, to guard against 'truth' in the coming year (this year particularly). So we have to put up with Jacqui Lait[2] whose matronly good living-ness got her through.

Wednesday, 16 December

Left Big Red slightly 'skew-whiff' (spelling?) in Piccadilly as the [Albany] courtyard was full up with loathsome, idle-rich up for Christmas shopping, discreet 'office parties' etc. So this morning my own internal alarm clock woke me at 4.50 and I dressed in softies over the pidgys and went down; as I started it I was aware of a strange, youthful, walker-of-the-night leaning on the pedestrian railing and attempting to catch, or rather pinion my eye. Plainly he thought I was stealing it and wished to 'bond' rapidly before going off to a squat.

Now it is an hour later and I am enjoyably on my third cup of Irish Breakfast tea (the best since the great Pakistani package of 1987).

These last days have been somewhat muddled, with much 'exposure'. I have been uneasy (lightly so) about health matters.

---

[1] AC had appeared on a 'sofa' show hosted by Jeremy Clarkson, the motoring writer.
[2] Jacqui Lait, MP for Beckenham since November 1997 (Hastings and Rye, 1992–97).

Intermittently throaten to the extent of being gravely plus upper-respiratory early symptoms. Almost a head cold being 'dealt with' by immunisation established after the great three-weeker. For a good deal of the time this makes me depressed, or worse, and I think of my shrinking life expectancy. The approach of the end of my 'leave period' and back to the Scarpe when I go through Purgatory before d.o.w. in base hospital and being reborn – as what? Please not as an orphan, or 'pet' animal. (Talking of which, I took time off to go and cheer up a tiny group last night who were standing by Barry Horne placards astride New Palace Yard entrance.[1] I'm afraid they were un-attractive, not to say dysfunctional. And yet the animals are so important. I am prepared to take risks for them.) More cheer-fully, did a book programme last night with Pat Hollis – still pretensions of attractiveness – and Philip Gould.[2] I was prepared to be objectionable to PG but he won my heart in the Green Room by saying 'why don't you take charge? You should take over …' of the Tory shambles.

Earlier the 22 had assembled to hear Hague. Still pretty dread-ful. Baroness Elles,[3] who was opposite me, looked at him the entire time with a strange expression of distaste and contempt that reminded me of Mama. At the end there was *spastic* desk-banging.

At the start that old trouble-maker Keith Simpson[4] tried to criticise my 'naughty' teasing on Clarkson. 'It's not a current affairs programme', I said, 'but a Sunday evening chat show.' He

---

[1] Barry Horne, animal rights campaigner, who had just ended 84 days' hunger strike while serving an 18-year sentence for arson.

[2] Baroness [Patricia] Hollis of Heigham, the government's social security spokesman in the Lords since 1997, author of a biography of Jennie Lee, one of the creators of the Open University and wife of Aneurin Bevan; Philip Gould, strategic and polling adviser to Labour Party. His book, *The Unfinished Revolution: How the Modernisers Saved the Labour Party* had been published in October.

[3] Baroness Elles (life peer 1972), former Conservative foreign affairs spokesman in the Lords, MEP Thames Valley, 1979–89.

[4] Keith Simpson, MP for Mid-Norfolk since 1997, Special Adviser to the Secretary of State for Defence 1988–90, and a former lecturer in war studies at Sandhurst.

changed the subject. How many other Tory MPs would be asked on? And would they not be wet blankets, or embarrassing? Ann Widdecombe is now taking bookings for March 2000. This made me feel terribly tired when we talked about it. She and I (Hague excepting, for particular reasons) are the only two Tories who can fill rooms. So over Christmas I must *think*, and plan how to advance. At least two walks to Beechborough?

First thing must be a proper Question schedule. Phased speaking engagements. Briefing journalists. Am I doing this a year late? I suppose so; like (and because) delivery of BB was a year late so for the first six months of this year I was frantic, immersed in the Library. 'I have my friends' (Neville). Cheered by the 22 Exec I must be graver also. Papers and lectures. A Pamphlet? I've a feeling that 'western man is superficially content, but oppressed by forces of which he is aware, but cannot easily identify'.

It's wonderful, as I write this I feel full of energy, intellectual vigour. It's 6.37 and I have been up for an hour and a half. Just thought of a sly device. I will wear a dinner jacket to Dr Munday's [reception]; this making it look as if we 'have to go on' which I did on Monday when I took Jane to Archer party. He really rather sweet and plucking as he showed his most recent acquisition – a Tenniel drawing of Dizzy slumped on the bench. He does have taste, Jeffrey. And it is elusive. Alas his status sinks. The room was 'B' list as Jane immediately noted. We went up in the lift with Basil Feldman,[1] ran into Geoffrey Howe as were leaving. 'Going on to somewhere smarter,' he observed.

EMT kitchen   *Friday, 18 December*

Rose early, pleased at the approaching hols. But could do no more, once tea made, than sit glazedly. A mile of tasks. Yesterday, exhausted after being 'on the go' continuously. Should have

---

[1] Lord [Basil] Feldman, holder of many senior posts in Conservative Party.

asked PM 'so one bombs Iraq for three days … then what happens?' But didn't quite have the *go*. [Douglas] Hogg,[1] on my right, called; then Soames pompous, but incoherent.

Scooped up a mass of folders and signing ullage and took the 8 p.m. train signing most of the way.

Saturday, 19 December

Bratton sold at auction yesterday. Jane was crossing the bridge, just by the Bratton 'box' implant when a message – quite calm and jolly – reached her. So that chapter is now closed. I was apprehensive that the room (the Red Lion at Okehampton) would be empty. But it was sold to a man from North Lew who hadn't even been inside (saw it that morning) for £167,000. Almost forty years ago that I went there in the blue Olds '88' on a bank holiday Monday in order to exchange contracts – yes, in Okehampton. Estate of Leroy Fielding for £2,500.

The whole Bratton sequence is so filled with *ifs*. If we hadn't been so hard-up that we had to sell the field ('Cream of Bratton') to Hortop, I was ready to buy the connecting vicarage strip, possibly later bits of Eversfield. Fortunately we did always have the châlet and wintered there. *If* Jane hadn't miscarried/had to work so hard when still drained by having Lilian. I remember coming back in the blue 220 after being in Germany (when I first met 'D'[2]) and thinking I must have cancer of the gum (in fact an abscess). And, particularly, first 'calling' the little boys in their blue cot.

Now I have just enough liquidity to 'carry' me (DV) until the Giorgione millennium exhibition – if it ever takes place. In all probability I will set up a 'small' sale to try and pull another 100 or so.

[1] Douglas Hogg, MP for Sleaford and North Hykeham since 1997 (Grantham 1979–97).
[2] David Cornwell (aka John le Carré).

My plan would be to:

£90 – Coutts MM (60)

£30 – Barclays Classic (30)

£30 – adding to the family holding of Coats – at present going down again. And, incredibly unhealthy chart.

My leg 'ulcer' has very slowly healed to a tiny pink spot, half the size of the original 'lesion'. I remain 'throaten' – now seven weeks intermittently. Especially in a.m. and when voice is 'tired' in the evening. I must say, though, that practically everyone in the House of Commons is mildly, or totally, throaten at the moment. We are, though, getting into 'see your doctor' territory.

Now I must stop to restore some order in the dining room as Christmas is approaching and the whole house is full of lovely greenery and decorations.

Saltwood Tower Office   *Boxing Day*

The Amazings left this morning, squeezing most deftly all their belongings plus two 'show' baby box trees, plus all manner of presents and groceries into their 4-door Golf sedan – with the two little boys confidently strapped into their 'space-tracker' safety seats.

When first they arrived my heart did sink a little – 'how the hell are we going to get through this?' – three nights etc, and I am getting worried about little Albert, the princeling, who seemed peaky and chesty and easy to tears. In fact it was fine, and Albert 'recovered' amazingly (sic) and ran about and climbed things while Archibald was benignly *Winston* at all times. Now a delicious sense of relaxation – a couple of non-dies (tomorrow and Bank Holiday) then a week 'off'. Then a firm, but engaging week of 'duties', but no movement outside the walls. I won't at present, think of scheduling, or look at my orange PFD[1] diary.

---

[1] Peters, Fraser and Dunlop, AC's literary agents, who had for more years than he could recall provided him with his annual office engagement diary.

But I would like this mini-cloud to lift so that I can think of the *grand perspectif*, how to be 'un homme serieux'. Last night a nice (though somewhat croaky) late night talk in the red study after Jane had gone up to bed − she has a dreadful throat and dry cough at present. The Amazings were alert about politics and the state of the Party. But at no time did they say, as an adjunct to 'who is there?' − 'why don't you do it?' or 'Do you think you have got a chance?'

If I can clear up my health (and I'm afraid this means going to Nick Page for a blood count) then I can establish my schedule of tabling, asking, working up my thesis: 'western man is everywhere threatened by forces of which he is aware, but cannot identify'. This is most easily done with a couple of glasses of Lynch 62 in the hand. Slowly start to incorporate into speeches.

Boxing Monday, 28 December

Soames rang last night. We talked and I felt better because together we have time-warped. Could have been Oliver Lyttelton[1] and Julian [Amery]. Lovely to do this from inside. But the Tory party has in fact changed out of recognition. We're not 'new Tories', we are the remains of a beaten, scattered rabble which has in large part discarded its weapons. What we need is a revived guerrilla army that will start a long march and live on the captured equipment of its enemies.

---

[1] Oliver Lyttelton, later Viscount Chandos, served in Churchill's War Cabinet.

Saltwood Green Room   *New Year's Eve*

Full-blown head cold. Most unusual so soon after (four-fifths) recovery from upper-respiratory throaten that went on for eight weeks. I sit here gasping and blowing my nose. It damages eyes, and diminishes concentration and energy. Naturally I would feel that I have still got time to recover before return before, even, the TV crew come down on Thursday. So, just a little uneasy at this calendine turning point. Now I have to go and print/compose (on the grey machine which I loathe) letters to Brodie's (for James) and Sotheby's (for Jane).

1999

The first time I have written 99. Low water; heavily upper-respiratory and uro-genitary – often quite insistent and then back pain. This has affected work output of course. Slowly, oh-so-slowly, I am eroding the cliff of paper on the Green Room table – but after trying the device of recategorising into 'file' and 'urgent attention'. Many boxes are extraordinarily and bizarrely mixed and muddled, and occasional nuggets surface. A clear and orderly breakthrough by Monday evening – but is this feasible? We promised ourselves not to 'work' on Sunday. All too clearly I see the approach of that familiar situation – 'Anything for one more day ...'

Particularly important this week is to work up my pamphlet, but this means going to the Garden House, ideally with a glass of good claret.

And then there are these basic headings where I must make progress – Trust structure (I have an insurance demand for £16,000 for Jane, but haven't really any idea how it all works); insurance, household and cars; and the car folder itself.

For the first time this morning I have the pages of the orange PFD book to look forward. Hold it. And we both agreed that we are not yet strong enough to put up and fill in the new '99 chart.

We had a two week 'holiday' in prospect, a lovely open unencumbered stretch holed up in the Mains. Now, just past the half-way point we should be full of enthusiasm and returning vigour. Of course this was the Monday when the holiday actually ended, it was simply that we had intended to stay at Saltwood, 'receive engagements' here instead of travelling. Now, though, it's arrived, and we are, arguably, in worse shape than

when we settled back – that delicious moment when the
Amazings had packed up and left and we sat by the Green
Room fire on Boxing Day, joined by the dogs who had been
excluded for three days. For a start, we have both of us remained
chesty throughout. I ran through full-blown head cold, now in
its tertiary, phlegmy-cough phase. I would sleep nine hours plus
(quite often unbroken), but we're exhausted still. During the day
I can get sweats and also 'go' genito-urethrine. Final blow –
sweet Janey put her back 'out' last night, this morning could
hardly move at all. She's so sweet-natured, never really grumbles
– but has been looking decidedly pale and drawn of late. 'Still,'
I said, 'we could either or both of us be coming back in an
ambulance from an accident on the M25.'

DV.

EMT   *Tuesday, 5 January*

Still wet and close. I am chesty and unhealthily on-the-step. This
morning to Jane's astonishment I dressed before EMT. Semi-
conditioned to 'Dave-at-eight' although we have in fact got the
whole of this week.

Last night my usual one-hour conversation with DD, burgundy
balloon in the hand. The Labour Party are being buffeted. Whelan
has gone – but under odd circumstances. To Alastair [Campbell]
earlier I had said, 'praise him, don't fire him.' That's three quite
important ships sunk in a week[1] – all while Blair himself is on
holiday still.

What can one make of all this? We can't claim credit for it;

---

[1] Peter Mandelson, MP for Hartlepool since 1992, and New Labour's 'master of
spin', had been forced to resign as Trade and Industry Secretary, following
revelations of a loan (to purchase a house) made to him by Geoffrey Robinson,
who had also had to resign his position as Paymaster General. Charlie Whelan,
press secretary to Gordon Brown, the Chancellor of the Exchequer, was blamed
for leaking documents relating to the loan.

there's no credit around, anyway. We mustn't gloat, and I prefer the line that it diminishes the whole of Public Life and is to be deplored. It is/should be cowardly Labour while we (should) seem to be political and crisp. Some hope! The Party can only think in terms of wankers like Willetts[1] coming forward with ideas for clipping the benefit and education policies 'at the margin'. I am not applying, enough, though to what I should be myself doing.

I turned off the lights on the tree for the last time yesterday; what a beautiful tall specimen, short of the height of the lower hall by 2-3 metres only, and like Wolf [the Führer] was filled with sadness and foreboding also.

EMT   *Thursday, 7 January*

A *nuit cassé*. Awake from 11.45 till past 3 on and off. After I came back from tinkling second time (2.30-ish) Jane said, 'are you ok?' 'Not really,' I said. I felt illish and sub-prostatic. I sweat hugely at night. During the day I am feeling incredibly tired. Yesterday we went out to the Garden House and while Jane and Eddie were wrestling (from time-to-time literally) with a tap in the kitchen I sat at the desk feeling utterly exhausted. I read parts of Graham's book on Churchill – very good, almost excellent.[2] Made me feel sad for my own. Jane, when I said I felt illish, said again, and rightly, you're trying to do too much. One coined:

1997 – 'A ticket back to heaven.'
1998 – 'You may be too late.'
1999 – 'All he does is whine.'

---

[1] David Willetts, MP for Havant since 1992, opposition front bench spokesman on education and employment since 1998.

[2] Graham Stewart's *Burying Caesar: Churchill, Chamberlain and the Battle for the Tory Party*. Stewart, AC's researcher on *The Tories*, had been given the use of the Garden House at weekends.

Sandling train   *Monday, 10 January*

Was in excited form; hair wash, looking 'beautiful', clean shirt, pressed suit, etc. 'First day back at school.' Then Big Red totally flat battery, plus strange grey TV-tuner lying 'prominently' on the boot floor close to the little Lucas charger. Caught by Penny Newell (wife of former Lord Mayor and daughter of Paddy Ridsdale[1]) for unanswered – I've never heard of it – invitation for 10 February. Black tie. Greatly crowded by all these invitations/functions.

I do hope this isn't the year of setbacks, when (at last) I still not get to feel, but to show my age.

Later
London seemed almost deserted; traffic light, an icy wind scouring the streets. In deep gloom I walked to Parliament Street. I felt tired and old and barely yesterday it seemed I had been in high spirits (though exhausted) at the prospect of the Christmas hols. The frightful constricting feeling that comes from a blocked-out chart (with more waiting 'to fill in the corners') plus an uneasy feeing that when actually I do get a release ticket I won't quite be myself any more, to put it lightly.

My prostatic-urethric symptoms are now more or less constant, which is quite an acceleration from, say, December when they were intermittent. A fairly constant strain always in the groin after peeing, plus a hard to define feeling that is not quite right. I fear I must ring Nick Page and have a blood and significantly PSA test. Then it comes out. 'Oh dear' – what do I do? I certainly don't want to be cut up and mucked about. I dread the leaked (as it is bound to be) publicity signifying the end of the old Al – the Clarkson Show prancer. Can't do it. Can't do it quietly because (a) an MP, and (b) the constituency. Have I got time to be still compos while I consolidate the wills,

---

[1] Lady Ridsdale, DBE 1991, chairman, Conservative Wives Association, 1978–91, married to Sir Julian Ridsdale, MP for Harwich February 1954–1992.

and get everything in order (ugh!). (Just rang Nick Page – on holiday, pity, but am booked in for 10 a.m. on Thursday).

Yesterday I went to the Forward Look committee at 5.15 – a bore this function, at a slightly awkward time. Mainly fantasy strangely coloured by 'we're-still-in-government-really' aura. People trying to score good-boy points, but the whole thing decidedly tactical – if that is not putting it too high. It's Hague, who now uneasily sits in, hears every suggestion, or invitation to pronounce policy, or even attitude, who just swallows and looks away – e.g. Angela Browning[1] made a very important point about Iraq, the unfinished business etc. Presumably Hague is entrapped by some Privy Council deal so that in return for snippets of info he doesn't make Party criticisms? Old trick. I raised the question of the EU Parliament. Surely we should at least address the question of whether we want to 'call for' (six) individual Commissioners to be accountable/sackable? Do we want the EU Parliament to be more effective, or not? Possibly 'not'. But we must be clear.

Later the Sybil. Simon Heffer.[2] People shouting. Shaun W said Hague should not have been away while the Labour Party was getting into all those messes. Shaun is the most resolute critic of Hague in the room, always. David Howell,[3] as often, was impressive. David Davis had a ghastly cold and I found myself sitting next to him. Damn, Damn!

House Library   *Wednesday a.m., 13 January*

A lovely crisp day, I cursed and muttered as I dressed – could have taken another two hours in bed (slept without waking

---

[1] Angela Browning, MP for Tiverton and Honiton since 1992.

[2] Simon Heffer, now political columnist on the *Daily Mail*; his official biography of Enoch Powell had been well received.

[3] Lord [David] Howell, life peer 1997, MP for Guildford 1966–97. Energy and Transport Secretary in Margaret Thatcher's first government.

from 11.5 to 7, but none the better for it). An extraordinary free
run in the Porsche, got from Albany to Norman Shaw lights [at
Parliament Square] in under three minutes (!). Yesterday I felt
dreadful. Doom-panicked in the morning and rang Nick Page
– back from holiday, so when I see him tomorrow he will be
(his first appointment) bronzed and youthful …

A condemned man, I trailed out to Fulham Broadway to
'attend', or re-attend the Chelsea village inquiry. In the council
chamber I sweated at intervals, took my pulse, felt flushes. My
rate would not go below 78 – sometimes hovered above. I am
still harbouring germs.

But when I got back here how lovely and enclosing the
Palace is! I took a piece of cake, cheese and a pot of tea and
settled behind the screen (Janet Fookes' position) in the tea
room and started to reread Routledge for the extra work the
Observer want.[1] Last night I saw Mandelson in the corridor.
He was white and shiny and distrait. Had lost weight. Ah,
politics!

Saltwood   *Saturday, 16 January*

In limbo. But after Nick Page's consultation I slept eight hours
for the first time since Scotland.

Bratton money in and earnings building, no o/d (except
Barclays), calm about cars, still getting media attention, looking
forward to *Observer* tomorrow. If PSA okay must really devote
myself to a strategic plan, then talking to Anji Hunter[2] and
Alastair. DV. Before the consultation I whispered to God that if
it can be done this will be the *year of dedication*. If it fails then
spectator, or buffer.

---

[1] In the light of Peter Mandelson's resignation, AC had been asked to revise his
review of *Mandy: the Unauthorised Biography* by Paul Routledge. He called it, 'that
most tedious of all literary phenomena, the virtual biography'. .
[2] Anji Hunter, the Prime Minister's personal assistant.

I do like life, and am eternally grateful even if it stops
tomorrow – or today.

House Library   *Monday, 18 January*

A draining morning with the Aon man (Moffat). Jane out to
Tom Bates and was told she needed a mammogram. Poor
darling! This made her low, but very sweet and quiet.

I drove up oh-so-unassertively in the Porsche. Went straight
(in softies) to Parliament Street and cleared/signed complete
folder. 'Withdrawn' but – therapeutically – in bare feet. The task
done, and preparing to go across to the House, I suddenly
realised that I felt terribly homesick. I miss Janey at these times,
and am sad that effectively we only get one holiday a year – a
long period when we can plan things and go on the wing. And
only two days, if we are lucky, out of each week. Which means
that each year out of 365 we only have 130-ish to each other.
So how many days have we got left – a thousand? Perhaps far
fewer. I hardly dare write the PSA, for myself:

   Under 3 – irrepressible
   Under 4 – confident
   4.2 – 6 – worst of all – DECISIONS
   Over 6 – so what? Just plot what happens; but played, of
              course, into gloom and apprehension.

And yet must always remember these last two fabulous years
– it's now exactly two years.

House Library   *Tuesday, 19 January*

(Still) no letters so had to ring Nick P using the little door-
phone in the Library corridor and, briefly, thinking that I might

faint if the news was really bad. In fact it was ludicrous: nought-point-five. My health *in the clear*; the sheer, total delight of daffodils and birdsong and lengthening days; the relaxed enjoyment of planning jaunts and trips and going 'on the wing'.

But there is the obverse. I have now got a clear two years to make my mark. Perhaps practically too late starting, although BB was useful to have 'behind' me. A heavier handicap is all this ludicrous boxed paper that eats into one at Saltwood when I should be philosophising on my screen. Just at present I am totally exultant, and dreamy. Must somehow get away to pray at the weekend, and Beechborough, too.

Saltwood   *Saturday, 23 January*

I have been upper-respirating for nearly three months on and (v occasionally) off. So although I should be *relancé* by the astounding clearance from Nick Page – actually set the dial back further than when first measured – I am very creaky, and enervated. I glaze over and shirk and flinch from obvious tasks. This morning incredibly frustrated trying to make cars respond. Batteries, carburettor needle sticking and petrol flood, damp terminals, etc etc. Quietly I went into the family garden and attacked fruiting bodies. A slightly petty piece in *The Times* by Matthew Parris attacking me for my 'love' of animals. This is the third time he has been unpleasant about me since I came back. Triggered, I suppose, by my – much acclaimed – Mandelson review. Essentially, all Parris is interested in is homosexual politics; the emancipation of homosexuals. Hey, just a minute, I thought they were emancipated? No, no, I mean really emancipated; so that unpleasant, overt heteros like Alan Clark are seen in a minority, and a slightly disgusting one to be racially discriminated against. Anyhow, I doubt it will have done me any harm. But this year I must attack. Opening say, 'This can't go on.' I attribute no blame, I do not seek to personalise the problem, but the Party is in mortal danger. If we went into a general election now could lose another eighteen seats. And that, actually, would be the end of the Conservative Party.

House Library   *Wednesday, 27 January*

I am wretched – why – it's so unfair.

Still going upper-respiratory (*again*) on Thursday as I got home. Held it off during the weekend, but deteriorated on Monday with *Willie's eye* – so postponed 'Blakeway'.[1] Slept poorly that night – though not as poorly as last night – and weeping so profusely on Tuesday morning that walked, 9-ish, to Spalton. Diverted, at some distance in time to F[oculist] in Wimpole Street. He amiable, if anything preferable to Sp., almost too laid back. Gave me chlorophormical drops which I got from a nearby Pakistani chemist who gravely showed a picture of himself with Omar Sharif (now somewhat portly and cum a triple bypass).[2] I seem to have deteriorated during that day. Voice went at the Courtfield and Earls Court AGM. People are *definitely* less friendly now. 'Where's the bright, ebullient Alan Clark?' asked John Major at dinner. I announced my 'flu' and was pleased to note that both he and Tom King moved away to more distantly laid places.

Slept intermittently, woke feeling cold (but not shivery) almost replay of that last afflicton. Made a little 'Ceylon' tea, inhaled from Vick and boiling water in the eggtimer saucepan. This morning temp 99.8°, pulse 89+, gobbets of green. No voice at all (it had gone speaking to Jane the previous evening). Left eye now also inevitably Willie so popped chlorophormical into that one, also.

---

[1] 'Willie's eye', named after the rheumy eyes of William Whitelaw, former MP, Minister and Margaret Thatcher's deputy; Blakeway, an independent TV production company.
[2] Omar Sharif, Egyptian-born actor, whose films include *Lawrence of Arabia* and *Funny Girl*.

Tower Office   *Saturday a.m., 30 January*

And still this strange virus shifts its territory. Last night, fourth
in a row, 'chesty' and phlegm-bound. At 3.30 found difficulty
tinkling, thought that the 'germs' had shifted location to the
waterworks (as in May '75) v depressed and muck sweat. Then
remembered that Nick's letter had said urine test (last week)
'... had shown no indication of possibility.' Tinkled splashingly,
more or less at once.

Expectations disappointed. ... Matthew Parris brilliant,
but highly unsettling piece the previous day.[1] I've let a whole
year go past.[2] BB, which should have given me status, hasn't
really.

In the meantime the Party is in total dumps. People are
simply losing interest – period. The climate, and the scenery, is
shifting. For some reason I don't have the energy really to
tackle this. Most colleagues (like most constituents) 'don't
want to know'.

It is 11.30 a.m. on a grey January day. On the morning walk
I looked up at the Mains (we walk around the moat now, in
order to avoid contact between the dogs and the public), said to
Jane, 'For four years all I wanted to do was get back through the
bulkhead door that has no handle; now what I would like best
is to settle at Saltwood, order my affairs, restore the Great
Library and study, travel and drink good wine.'

---

[1] *The Times*, 28 January, headed 'It's time to panic: I don't know what the Tories are
about. And neither, it seems, do they.'
[2] A few days before, AC had asked, 'And when am I going to get started?' Mike
White [*Guardian* political editor] said, 'Look at Ann Widdecombe. She just kicked
the door in ...' As a further alternative AC confided to his diary (10 January 1999),
'My game plan, if I don't break out in some way in the next 18 months, is to get
Alastair to fix my being Speaker in the next House.'

House Library   *Tuesday p.m., 2 February*

Last night we went to the Christie's dinner for the Monet Exhibition. All the paintings beautiful, dazzling you could say and all cleaned (save the beautiful fog-bound view of the Palace of Westminster and the seagulls) to the same sanitation standard. The two of the Contarini Palazzo in Venice, some of the water-lilies, particularly those with the willow branches reflecting, were incredible.

On the way up I had started to develop a sore throat. How could I be getting a sore throat now, at three weeks plus intermittent 'upper respiratory condition'. And to think that when it started I just thought it was the ordinary flu-cold, had my day 'on the floor of Mother Teresa's waiting room' and expected the recovery pattern to set in thereafter.

However, this morning I read the accounts of SAD [seasonal affective disorder], and cheered up a bit. Sparkled in the tearoom. And today a wonderful Parliamentary occasion, the House of Lords debate[1] with speeches from Ted, John Major, Robert Marshall-Andrews[2] and Rick Shepherd. Ted spoke, personified gravitas. Good voice still, carried well, miles ahead of Enoch who started in his seventies to go 'piping'. Yes, I should have spoken too, but had no time to collect my theme, nor energy to sustain it.

Tuesday, 9 February

I am always quiet and melancholic-reflective after Shaun's dinners. Bed at midnight and half woke several times with v slight feeling that something was 'physically wrong' (like being

---

[1] To debate the government Bill to reform the Lords, bringing to an end the hereditary peerage's right to sit in the House.

[2] Robert Marshall-Andrews, a QC, Labour MP for Medway since 1997.

precursor of flu). Oh-so-gloomy on waking. What is the point? The Conservative Party is a husk, its place has been taken. I am old now, and my enthusiasm wanes easily.

Dinner was the usual shouting match. Willie Rees-Mogg just the limit, bit deaf now with intellectual hair cut.

Before going in Tapsell had shouted: 'I want Alan Clark to lead the Conservative Party' and on the way out Willie said: 'You could be a kind of Reagan, really,' and I reminded him of his favourable article after I was selected.

Drove back (risk-takingly[1]) in the Little Silver. I had Positano steps coming down the B staircase [Albany], just controlled it, then halted and spat at the 4 St James's Street Island and realised I had to go to Brooks's and essay a vomit.

I am not myself the morning after Shaun's dinners.

Saltwood   *Friday, 12 February*

Memorial service today for Alan Hardy.[2] Saltwood Church absolutely overflowing. Robin Leigh-Pemberton through to Ann and Bob [Felce] – although no sign of Eddy Rothschild.[3] Reg [Humphriss] uttered a pleasing biography of Alan, who was a big man with an *enormous* stomach, one of the largest I have ever seen. He was exceptionally rich, owning much land (a small part of which he recently sold) and having inherited from his old father, 'Skinflint' Hardy, his beautiful and exclusive gardens. He married Carolyn, a beautiful and lively student of Wye Agricultural College who rode a 250cc BSA 'Bantam' motorbike.

Afterwards, walking in the woodland, Jane asked what I wanted 'in' my own memorial service. The first time the subject has come up. Originally I said (post *Diaries*) I just want to

---

[1] At some later date AC has added an alternative in green ink: 'oh-so-ill-advisedly'.

[2] Alan Hardy, local landowner with exceptional collection of rhododendrons and azaleas.

[3] Edmund Rothschild, a senior member of the banking family and a keen gardener.

disappear, like *Zapata*.[1]

I suppose if I am in Parliament still I will have to have one at St Margaret's, W[estminster]. Must have a choir, I said, to sing the hymns and 'God be in my head ... and at my departing' (probably at end). Also the hymn 'Guide me, O thou great Redeemer' and 'He leadeth me' (psalm 23 sung as a hymn). All prayers and lessons in the Old Form. Lesson: *Genesis* – 'In the Beginning ...' New Testament: 'the star on the edge of Galilee'. Reading: the Housman lament from Enoch's, with an introduction by me to be read by James. Who shall do the address? Then it all disperses.

EMT, B5   *Tuesday, 16 February*

Returning to the House I was desperately hungry.[2] Cranborne was in the Gallery and I tried to persuade him to come out to dinner at once. He couldn't. Soames, always ready for a nosh, agreed to get a taxi for 7.10 and we went to Wilton's where he paid for the food and I the wine (bott Montrachet, not v good at £65; a Volnay for £55). Usual discourse; grumbling. Party absolutely no idea what it's doing or where it is going. At the end Nicholas was Churchillian. As David Davis said, when a short time ago I told him 'I'm on the verge of making a declaration ...', 'Who's going over the top with you?'

This morning I felt odd when I rose. It is a lovely crisp day. But I don't throw back the bedclothes any more and spring up as I used to for twenty years in here. I'm 70 of course, and this morning I had mild alcoholic poisoning. Yes, I'm *ok*. Low testosterone is a tiny price to pay (when occurring naturally) for a PSA reading of 0.5.

---

[1] Zapata, the early 20th-century Mexican revolutionary, was shot dead, but his ghost was said to return. AC at one point in the early 1970s affected a Zapata-like moustache (see photograph *Diaries: Into Politics*).

[2] AC had been in a TV studio.

This is an easy week except for the absurd and ludicrous 'Listening to Britain' session on Wednesday evening (contrived of course to clash with the 1922 committee). Papers in order, none. A nice long weekend at Saltwood. I must go for a week rebuilding the fabric a little. But really I need three weeks for that – Zermatt or the Highlands. And that is impossible. This year I will know whether or not I 'miss the bus' and just concentrate on the heritage. Trusts, maintenance and inventories. A dear old patriarch.

I read Chips a little. Exactly 61 years ago Anthony Eden resigned and Chips, to his huge delight, was made PPS to Rab. He was 41 and for him it was, I suppose, the equivalent of being Minister for Trade.[1] Whitehall in those days being smaller, and the Magic Circle far, far tighter. This was the moment when Chamberlain made his bad decision – to go for the 'friendship' of Italy. He should have seen things globally, but (comparably to John Major) he simply did not have the confidence to set up a great carve-up conference plus backing it with selective rearmament.

Tower Office, Saltwood   *Saturday, 27 February*

Yesterday I was nearly killed – nearly killed myself, rather – accelerating hard on a greasy road in Big Red in (as it were) Bilsington. The great vehicle slewed and skidded. I found myself going head-on at a truck sixty feet away, lifted off, thank God did not panic or brake, skidded past. The whole incident over in 3-4 seconds. It would have been a pure accident. Dead. But a 'mystery'. Dead straight road, head on crash, etc. Spared. Like being spared to go back to H of C. But am I anyway now doing

---

[1] Chips on 2 March 1938: 'Of course I cannot believe it, I, Chips at the Foreign Office.' Rab Butler had been made Under-Secretary of State for Foreign Affairs, with Lord Halifax as the new Foreign Secretary. AC was appointed Minister for Trade in 1986.

enough? Jane cautioned me against 'creep-back' on Thursday.
Plus, for the first time in our lives we found ourselves talking
seriously about accounts. Jane rather sadly said what does she
do, how does she see Saltwood after I've died and my earning
power has gone?

EMT, B5   *Tuesday, 2 March*

For some time I have been shirking a full considerative entry –
one that faces the fact that I am not *doing* enough, or my profile
is sinking. Last night Tony Bevins[1] cautioned me against 'shooting'
until the Euro-elections are out of the way ('otherwise you will
do yourself damage – perhaps irreparable'). A bore, and only four
weeks of summer left then. *But ...*

Then, at dinner, Michael Spicer[2] came in with the news that
automatic reselection is now in the rules for everyone. Full
meeting, all members eligible, secret ballot etc. What a draining
prospect! Another giant tour de force in KTH. Also a cramping
of my style (for the remaining two years) as a rebel standard-
bearer. Back in Easton territory[3] after all (as of course is the
CCO 'intention').

House Library   *Wednesday, 3 March*

Yesterday I had my AGM in Chelsea Old Town Hall.
A straight victory. Virtually no opposition. I am dominant, ran

---

[1] Anthony Bevins, the son of Reg Bevins, working-class Postmaster General in
Harold Macmillan's government, had been twice political editor of *The
Independent* (1986–93 and 1996–98); he then moved to the *Express*.
[2] Michael Spicer had been on the 22 Executive since 1997.
[3] AC is remembering his clashes with the party organisation at Plymouth Sutton,
where a leading light was Mrs R. M. (Betty) Easton.

a joke combining wind-power and Jeffrey Archer through an oh-what-a-good-boy-was-I recital to a fine peroration.

At the 'President's Party' afterwards people congratulated me. One man said he 'nearly' (sic) said 'why don't you take the helm?'(as it were). I drank a glass of delicious iced white wine in the kitchen and was effusive. Janey drove me back to the House to vote, then to Albany. A hint of 'that's that, then'.

I have really no excuse now not to achieve this year. Health, wealth, seemingly. But was exhausted, listless.

At lunch today in the Members Dining Room John M[ajor] said how uncharacteristic of Blair to chuck PM's Questions twice a week. How they used to hog our time. Every Saturday was blighted by Tuesday. The middle of the week blasted out. Thursday practically the only 'free time'.

EMT   *Friday, 5 March*

Last night on *Question Time*,[1] which I have been trying to avoid for months, in Maidstone. Probably went as well as could be expected. Asked about sex on TV I said 'They're only actors. It's simulated sex, isn't it ... Myself I prefer the real thing.' A charming, civilised black man said how sex should be pinnacle and when I responded and deplored the yob culture, said how footballers and pop stars were 'role models'. Dimbleby got agitated and said 'Role models etc ... Do you consider yourself a political role model?' 'That's for others to judge,' I said – and the entire audience clapped delightedly!

I was buoyed up by my 'triumph'. I haven't seen the tape yet, and may have been *too oggly*.

Last night, after lights, I hopped out of bed again and prayed – just pure thanks, for the fact that now I am an MP again, and

---

[1] *Question Time*, BBC 1 equivalent of Radio 4's *Any Questions?*; David Dimbleby (b. 1938) had been presenting it since 1994.

for the safest seat in the country. While last time I was on to him I was wilful and pluckingly defiant.

I had a long talk with Dimbleby at dinner. Usual beef about BBC management. He would like to have been Director-General, now says he is too old (!). But a pleasant man really.

Saturday, 6 March

A lovely Saltwood day. The wind is unpleasant, cold rain that is almost liquid snowflake. Yesterday I spent polishing a hostile review of George Walden's 'memoir'[1] (and my instinct instantly proved right, because just at the end I caught a most typical, and (designed to be) unpleasant passage about myself). Yes, I do very vaguely recall doing a *Today* programme with him. Apparently I didn't 'speak' while we were waiting. Sounds typical, listening, as I have always thought him an ill-mannered waste.

We spent most of the day in Papa's study in the Library block, Jane painting the wall, I 'sorting' books and Liberoning the leather surface of the great desk. That's a marvellous room, such lovely things. I have hung the 'Babars' behind the big Bratton sideboard which has now displaced the big, old, ill portrait of my father taken in 1978.

As (per) usual, all I want to do is stay down here. Just a few lightning forays. The weekend gone by so fast and at present I am very tired in the mornings and sleep on after Jane has got out of bed.

---

[1] George Walden, former diplomat, MP for Buckingham 1983–97. He called his memoir, *Lucky George*. AC in his review in *The Times* wrote: 'part memoir, part autobiography, part half-baked docu-fiction novelette.'

EMT   *Monday, 8 March*

Lovely fine morning, and fall in atmospheric temperature so
that you can see your breath, which hangs in the air. I thought
of little T.O. and gloomily half worried that I am getting more
like him. Sometimes just standing, unable to remember what I
am going to do. One of the dogs' towels is white with black
blobs on it, and when it lies on the floor by the Aga it could,
out of the corner of the eye, be Tom.

Tower Office   *Thursday, 11 March*

Today I screeched with pain and frustration at being unable to
find the insurance certificate for Big Red, so can't tax it. Everywhere I rummaged I found *needy paperwork*. Had meant to come
down last night but was – as usual between 5 and 7 p.m.
Connex'd[1] at Charing Cross; unhappy travellers ('customers') on
the concourse; inaudible, but bellowing high speech-rate
announcements; unhappy and unrecognisable trains appearing
one-at-a-time at unfamiliar platforms.

   Why do I do all these speaking engagements (still)? Plus endless sundry appearances and journalism. Partly for the money,
yes; the odd monkey and grand accumulate at almost the rate
they were doing in '92–3. Partly also to 'keep my name forward'.
In the tearoom queue yesterday afternoon I said to Gerald
Kaufman,[2] 'Thank you for your article bolstering my leadership
bid, which will be irresistible once the Conservative Party is
down to a dozen seats (there being only seven which we hold
by a majority of more than 50%).' He turned and looked at me

---

[1] Connex South East won the franchise to run train services out of Charing Cross
  including the Dover line. It quickly gained a reputation for unreliability, perhaps
  no worse than its British Rail Network South-East predecessor.
[2] Gerald Kaufman, MP (Labour) for Manchester Gorton since 1983 (Manchester
  Ardwick 1970–83).

very seriously, 'Alan, I honestly believe that a successful leadership by you would be the only way left for the Conservative party to survive.'

I am pleased by this. And by MacShane, who said, 'Why don't you become Shadow FCO Sec?' Also by Barbara [Lord], when I raised the question of re-selection, shall I write a letter, etc etc, said, 'Oh no, I don't think there is any feeling like that. There may have been when you were selected, but not now.'

But in the train today I read Heffer, who said, 'Bring back John Major.' Heffer of all people. With the exception of Alan Clark I think he has by now plugged every single senior member of the Tory Party.

Saltwood   *Sunday, 14 March*

A really happy day. Fine. First day of spring, and we released the tortoises. This morning I was on GMTV 'sofa' with Alastair Stewart,[1] and tried (not unsuccessfully) to be *statesman*. Ancram also there. And I (Chips) 'made a conquest of James Landale'.[2] Then back down in time for 'boilies' and collected some lilac from the railway line after Jane brilliantly forced the pace in getting the Mehari to belch merrily into summer life.

Finished cutting the Bailey and drank (unusually) some of the Marquie's red Puligny Montrachet. Before that went for a drive in the blue Chev (block almost dry, as it turned out!). Then Julie and baby Angus turned up. I feel intensely at ease and optimistic.

---

[1] Alastair Stewart, news presenter, originally with ITN.
[2] James Landale, political journalist on *The Times*.

Tower Office, Saltwood   *Sunday, 4 April*

It is Easter Sunday. I have changed my 'work station', first from
Garden House, then to the dining room here, now to the
original Summer Office.

My eyes are giving me a bit of trouble – blurry, intermittent
inability to defocus leading to periodic headache. I have an
antipathy to the crabbed scrawl in the blue Banner notebook.
And mindful of the pre-booked (I already have one of the
contracts, but not signed it) £450,000 for 'The Early Years',[1]
think that with posterity in mind I can now type a bit. The
'Mouse' makes it so much easier to tune and correct as you go
along, apart from anything else. Harold Nicolson typed (most
evenings); so, I think, did Dick Crossman. Tony Benn dictated
into a machine. Chips wrote in longhand. (Or did he? Robert
[Rhodes James] in his introduction does not confirm this. I will
telephone to Robert this evening; have been looking for an
excuse for some time. He will like to be asked his opinion on
Kosovo, but I must also ask him *how he is*, as there is news in the
tearoom that he has had a 'successful' (yeah) operation on his
colon.)[2]

Of course a pre-printed is less secretive. If only because it can
be read by any nosy parker who finds it. And if it is in a hiding
place it will be read – even 'pirated' – still more avidly. It might
be possible to get a ring binder with a lock on it; even to have
one made, I will ask at Smythsons.

It is a fine day, and our priority must be the yard and the
badge room before the swallows come back (according to *The
Times* they have already arrived in Dorset). Last year we never
did the yard, or the workshop at all.

On Thursday morning I felt absolutely happy, relaxed and

---

[1] AC had agreed to make a selection of his early diaries, as a 'prequel' and had pre-
sold the serial rights to *The Times*.
[2] Since his retirement as an MP in 1992 Rhodes James had returned to writing and
was currently at work on a sequel to his study of the later Churchill (to be called *A
Study in Triumph*), but became ill with what was later diagnosed as cancer in 1998.

independent. A Bank Holiday weekend, and the week following ahead. That was a working day, with 'Bill', the Atco delivered. Chris the PSA carpenter, Alan-from-the-garage, and others making their claims. But after that we would be claim free. Yesterday most of the morning went on cleaning – really cleaning – out the hen houses. I was muck-sweat and 'adversarial' in the Chinese dungarees. V exhausting, but after tea I felt traditional enough to walk the Seeds and the valley. Then shunted all the cars round so that the line-up is not jarring (l to r) Cont 'S'; R–Cont; Buick RM; New Bing; Summer Car; Ghost. All on the button except the Buick whose battery is on slow charge up at the village. An American is being brought over on Monday week by Robert Coucher[1] who has a very 'hot' R–Cont. Could be fun, provided that Saltwood does not scowl and drizzle.

But one of the reasons I am typing is that a full-scale *résumé* of position-and-prospects is overdue and can be properly set out.

I am hugely depressed about Kosovo. Those loathsome, verminous gypsies; and the poor brave Serbs. The whole crisis is media-driven. Editors have no idea of, or respect for, the truth. They are concerned simply with *scooping* their rivals, and/or pre-empting counter-scoops. But an orthodoxy of public indignation is built up, stoked up, you could say, and the politicians have to respond. Each editorial conference is concerned with how still further to raise the 'temperature'; each political session with how best to be seen as 'seizing the initiative'. I have spoken in the Commons debate, written in the *Observer*, been several times on television – but no one is interested. I doubt that I shall get another invitation.

And this also throws into uncomfortable relief my own *lange pause* since returning to the Ho. I have got good relations with the constituents – as good as can be expected anyway – still. I

---

[1] Robert Coucher, editor of *Classic Cars*, for whom AC wrote his monthly column, 'Back Fire'.

can command media attention – Frost, Alastair Stewart – and often I refuse bids. I have an enormous backlog of speaking engagements, and turn down many, often, culpably, from universities and young people. 'One of the few people who brings a bit of colour to the Conservative Party' etc.

But (with the exception of Oborne) I am never tipped to be 'brought forward'. 'Friends' like Bruce Anderson will never do so. Never have, indeed. Even during Mrs T's reign it was always regarded as a mixture of joke and accident – except during the immediate aftermath of the Def Review paper to Andy Marr. I suppose my high peak in this Parlt has been when Jonathan Holborow rang from the Lab Party Conf in 1997 to say that I was the tip for 'stalking horse' that autumn (this was before the Party electoral system changed) and just a few weeks later I blew it (and a lot else besides) with my reckless and intemperate comment on the 'solution' for dealing with the IRA.

Now a huge change of mood infects society and politics. I must contact April whatever-she-was-called whom I met at that PR party in Kensington. What have I done with her scrawled address? It has extended out of touchy-feely, Diana-caring into a *correctness* that has become an orthodoxy. So that 'human rights' can override all considerations of national sovereignty, even of UN Articles and the authority which depends on them. The 'democratic right of protest' now extends its immunities from prosecution or even restraint to demonstrations here in London, and other cities whose governments are not in any degree to blame for the 'plight' of the demonstrators.

I suppose the first intimations of this were those ludicrous Moluccans who used periodically to make life intolerable for everyone, whether tourist or inhabitant, in the Netherlands. Once a group exceeds critical mass in a situation of disorder, be they gypsies, 'new age' travellers, asylum seekers, squatters, they acquire both immunity and access to the media; who will aggrandise their cause of complaint and seek to find, or to concoct, various 'human interest' angles from which to illuminate it. I heard a

ghastly story from Keith Simpson about an (Italian) TIR driver
who noticed that his truck appeared to be full of 'refugees'.
Virtually incapable of speaking English, he telephoned on the
lorry phone to his employer in Milan. 'Go straight to the police,'
he was told. The unfortunate driver saw a sign off the main road
to an RAF station, with sub-headings one of which was 'RAF
Police'. At the perimeter gates the puzzled redcap phoned for
instructions, was told to contact the local station. Needless to say
the local police (it was in Norfolk) wanted nothing to do with
the situation, said it was for Immigration. 'Immigration' said the
same, as the 'subjects' had already passed through the cordon.
Finally, after a pretty crisp harangue from the station commandant
a couple of police trainees and a squad car did turn up and took
the miscreants off to a 'hostel'.

Saltwood   *Wednesday, 7 April*

Skip day. We have been out of doors most of the time loading
junk, total detritus accumulated over God knows how long into
a skip.

My health not yet right. I felt terribly sleepy, almost Shore-
like at 7 a.m. Jane gets up and goes down. I follow about 25
minutes later. An exact reversal of the 'quiet hour' routine
which prevailed for so long. About half an hour into loading
the skip I began to feel really tired again and useless. It wore
off, then Ann Felce arrived to talk me into lowering her rent.
Subtly fault-finding as usual. She said that I should high-
pressure hose down all the garden seats. Fucking cheek. None
of her business.

She muttered something about her horse, Northern Starlight,
running at Ascot this afternoon. I thought I'd put something on
it, partly so as she wouldn't be able to gloat if it went well, and
popped down to the bookies, gave them a couple of new red

boys, plus two purps on Skip'n Time which Lynn had ably spotted on the card later in the afternoon.[1]

Have I been *herniac* these last few days? What a bore. It felt unhappy when I was humping on to the Mehari great sacks of wet grass from mowing the Bailey. But I think it is Christopher's Revenge – having been 'triggered' by desperate twisted straining to get a box of Lynch '61 on to its side in Peggy's pantry in order to read the label. Solicited by Christie's I am contemplating the sale of a very few cases of (really) 'fine wine'. Apparently Palmer '61 is worth more than Yquem '67, being £6000 per case.

EMT, Saltwood   *Thursday, 8 April*

A manuscript entry (much disturbed by 'TC' who either pulls at my pen or, from my shoulder excruciatingly, at individual hairs on my scalp). I woke in the night with the knowledge that something unpleasant had happened. First time, really, since heard of the Sevenoaks rejection from 'Ann Barrow'. James has lost his seat on the council in Durness.

Saltwood   *Friday, 9 April*

I woke this morning after a good night, but realised that I was a little sad, almost unhappy, tho' that is too strong a word, and ungrateful to God and the Fates. I just don't feel any sense of either freedom or excitement, or anticipation aka Rho J and Lord Randolph Churchill – '... all clubland was agog' etc etc.

---

[1] Northern Starlight came in 2nd, but Skip 'n Time romped home first at 6 to 4.

Saltwood   *Saturday, 10 April*

Just watched myself on GMTV – *too* pouchy, 106 years old, so puffy and eye-bagged. I must not let crews come down here with their own lighting. I look too awful – though still all right in the studio. Jane and I had a lovely evening in the Gt Library. Such potential, but slightly shaming in that we have neglected it for 30 years.

Saltwood   *Sunday, 11 April*

Now the holiday is over. Never been near the Green Room table, or done more than lightly scratch the KGV workshop, the yard, or the badge room. Or, more seriously, written more than one page of 'The Early Years'. But we have worked ourselves to exhaustion practically every day. Jane has been brilliant, everything from the swimming-pool loo revived, the skip loaded, the yew pruned down by the Long Garage.

Little oh-so-meek George Ramsden was here, yet again, on Saturday. We finally 'dealt' and I exchanged some more of the Wharton books for a selection of my father's 'personal' library (sold by Celly for £20,000 en bloc in 1986 to Zwemmer, or was it Maggs?) and a cheque for £2000. I would have settled for less; he might have paid more. In the end I found him quite sympathetic. He said that suiting books, bindings and 'runs' to shelves was 'like arranging flowers'.

Jane agreed to the terms, and thoroughly joined in as we explored the Gt Library and laid our plans. An incredible room, but many of the books are not in a good state, greatly to our discredit as we have barely touched them, or the furnishings, for 25 years. My father's study on the other hand, has been thoroughly done over and is quite perfect.

How is my health? I am at least half sure that my l/h hernia has re-torn, although Mrs Frowd (only last Friday) said not. Last night I was woken by 'pointing' pain inside the left hip. At one point I had such a sweating attack it was almost like a hot tap running over one. And I am still v down on energy, though not as much as during the 'viruses'. It is probably something to do with SAD as one does feel better when the sun comes out. But I have done no yoga, nor even walked to Beechborough Down.

Later

I talked briefly to poor Robert. The cancer had spread out of his colon, and he had been on chemo. But was calm. The Cambridge oncologist was 'satisfied'.

Brave he was, and calm-sounding though just a little weak of voice.

Later we watched the Jimmy [Goldsmith] film. And a huge pang at the shots of Cuixmala. Not enough of Jimmy, but what there was conveyed his incredible magnetism.

Very typically the script closed with a sneer ('right to the end he was a bad loser ...'). Of course the media have never forgiven Jimmy for hating them, and never quite worked out how to get even – not unlike their relationship to Jonathan Aitken.

B5, EMT   *Wednesday, 14 April*

I am 71, and listening to the Albany blackbird doing his repertoire. Outside it is cloudless, but cold.

Saltwood   *Sunday, 18 April*

I am low. Last night a tittles from the *Mail* had left a message asking me to comment on 'Cardinal Hume's cancer'. Uh? I did not return her call. But on the nine o'clock news we were told that he was 'carrying on' though with 'inoperable cancer' – at the age of 76. I don't understand this. You don't have cancer at that age surely without any warning? 'Cancer is the last barrier before Old Age' etc. And at 76 you have arrived at old age.

I am down on energy and depression is in the bones. Literally, almost, as when I go and tinkle at 3.30 a.m. all my joints are so stiff. Last night Lëhni had not come up so I left the bathroom door open. I wondered if possibly I might meet myself, now dead and wandering about, not wholly at rest, to monitor things. I am not particularly frightened of death, but I do not want to die as I am enjoying life. I don't want to be reduced to ash – obviously; nor do I like the idea of being buried – not, at least in a coffin or a stone-lidded vault. Best, perhaps to *swim* and meet God, falling like a giant leaf into the undersea garden.

I never get at the cars; I'm more concerned, in truth, to conserve the fabric and inventorise the contents. I can get back into wistful mode, enjoying the garden and *an easy routine*. This is the eternal tension, between the sword in the lake or standing down.

I think if my health picked up back I would still go for the sword. But I do love Saltwood, and am so lucky to be here.

House Library   *Wednesday, 21 April*

Yesterday I networked. The Southend expedition was a success. Teddy Taylor[1] drove fast, but not well, in his blue Ford (I later found out that it was a Cosworth, and had done 173,000 miles). I gave the lunch all four barrels. Went well, and questions also, although the return journey, in light drizzle, took longer than coming in from Saltwood. We slowed down past 'City Airport', through a pointlessly long tunnel, then crossed Tower Bridge, but didn't turn right until far too late. I was glad to be the passenger.

---

[1] Sir Teddy Taylor, MP for Southend East since March 1980 (Glasgow Cathcart 1964–79).

A hint of HE's reception getting ready for the great Margaret Thatcher anniversary dinner at the Hilton. 'Why have you come here?' asked a reporter. 'To hear Ted heckle,' I answered.

But at my table I was demi-lionised by David Young, Basil Feldman and particularly and interestingly, Phil Harris.[1] Lita Young gave me some good lines – she is firm and bouncy, like a *diva*. Then who should come over, but Michael Ashcroft! Talked about setting up the lunch. 'Alan, these are all women you are suggesting,' he said.[2] Earlier Victoria Borwick had embraced me, also raising her leg tango style. Several men, youngish, had sought me out and expressed admiration. A move-on from the sort of function I used to go to as a nervous aspiring candidate in Monday Club days – or even later as an obscure MP. But main personnel hardly changed.

Saltwood   *Saturday, 24 April*

Jane left for Spain today. I drove her to Gatwick, and now I am *en garçon*, with fish cakes in the fridge which I never really seem to be very good at cooking, they break up in the pan.

It is wet, and I am extraordinarily tired, keep wanting to drop off, like when prowling about the House of Commons after a ten o'clock division. This is because we drove back down last night after the Association dinner, not getting to bed until gone 1 a.m. Soames spoke. He was big, and *mixed*. Good, very good, and moving on Churchill as an artist, his sense of colour; and a pleasant, funny style with his *racontes*. But Soames was abrupt with questioners, told one 'trouble-maker' that he should 'change his Party'. They don't go for that much in K & C.

On the Thursday I had been most terribly depressed by a

---

[1] Lord [Philip] Harris, carpet entrepreneur and contributor of considerable funds to the Conservative Party.

[2] Michael Ashcroft, controversial Conservative Party treasurer; AC had earlier sent a list, noting that Ashcroft, 'wants lunch, which is good of him considering how rude I was in my reply to one of his demi-reproachful money-raising letters.'

quite brilliant op-ed piece in *The Times* by John Laughland, whom I had never before heard of, but I rang Andrew Roberts who said he was very good and emboldened I took his number and entered into a brief conversation on the telephone. Laughland illustrated by ruthless logic the inner meaning of NATO's persecution of the Serbs.[1]

Garden House   *Sunday, 25 April*

Little Hague continues to make a complete hash of things. Why is it that journalists cannot work out a bum steer and one with intelligence? There is talk of a reshuffle and whose face is prominent? Why Theresa May, of course.[2] This is because there is nothing they like more than an internal row which translates into 'left' (good) versus 'right' (bad).

Whoof! The Sandling Train!   *Monday, 26 April*

I have had a dreadful two days. A paltry supper of four tiny fishcakes, and lights at 10.50. Woken by *paws on board* – TWICE. Walked alone (dogs bolshie and puzzled), and very nice and fulfilling it was. I noticed a thread of dead grass on the 'family' camellia, went to pull it away and to my great delight saw a beautiful new nest! No eggs yet, so hope that 'everything turns out all right'. Made some scrambled eggs (quite incredibly, my only culinary attainment over the entire period, as it turned out)

---

[1] 'The war is being fought to destroy the very principles which constitute the West. This is not moral, it is megalomaniac' – *The Times* heading to Laughland's piece.
[2] The MP for Maidenhead was 'spectacularly promoted', said the *Daily Telegraph*, to education and employment spokesman, 'a phenomenal promotion that has surprised many, for while she is clearly competent she has done little that obviously merits so swift an ascent.'

and Douwe Egbert instant coffee. Sunday papers all garbage. My hernia seemed to be pointing uncomfortably, but I decided to clean off and black the hinge iron on the Great Library door, wanting something to show Janey when she returns. First I tidied and reorganised the Red Study.

The hinge blacking v arduous and time-consuming with its many stages of wire-brushing, rubbing, painting and brush polishing. Dogs came on the walk this time, but were bored, would not attend on the getting of 'layer pellets'. An egregious tea (not 'high') at 5 p.m. with a little camembert, then to the 'work station' to continue on the Stephen Glover piece.[1] I sipped some chilled wine James came on the line; pleased and calm, but fussing about the (old) safe-deposit book key. Took 35 minutes. On and on went round the clock hands. No point in preparing dinner. I tiptoed through about 10 p.m., opened TC's cage door, took an old slice of Jane's sultana cake (all that was left) and up to bed, where dear, dear 'H' had already pitched her tent. This morning up v previous. Neither dog interested so went down to the site with a camera.[2] Predictably, it 22-window-clicked, had only one exposure. Went back: fed hens with stray bits of old bread found in a green Fortnum bag. Then made some instant coffee (no EMT) and two slices of brown toast. Then to print letter to Colin Paine of Shepway [council] and *Mail on Sunday*. Then back down to finish Glover piece. 'Colin Paine' rang and wanted an instant site meeting. Next down there and heard his 'compromise' suggestion. The unpleasant, hard-faced engineer was in evidence. Just back to Saltwood in time to put on a suit, gallop down, muck sweat, to get into Bill's (he wearing a sleeveless vest) red Vauxhall. Slept exhaustedly and intermittently in the carriage. On arrival a solitary, badly served lunch in the Commons. Then to Sue, masses of supportive letters, and across to Statement. Not called.

---

[1] Published under the title 'Why I Hold Journalists in Low Regard', in *Secrets of the Press: Journalists on Journalism* edited by Stephen Glover (1999).
[2] Shepway Council were at work on anti-flood measures.

Walked back to Charing X with incredibly heavy briefcase that
I was not at all looking forward to carrying from Sandling. This
is not a comfortable period.

House Library   *Tuesday, 27 April*

Keith Simpson, yesterday in the tearoom said to me '... and Alan
what do you make of all this?' ... (the ludicrous Hague, Lilley
row).[1]

'I find it profoundly depressing.'

'But you don't really, do you, Alan? This kind of confusion
and reverse should be giving you pleasure. As, I suspect, it is to
not a few of our colleagues.'

I sometimes get irritated with Keith. He is mischievous, in
general and often towards me personally (*passim* his spastic
'mock' letter of invitation to the Garden Party). But I enjoy his
company. And he was after all the first to spot the personal
analogy between me and Maxime Weygand. Recalled at the age
of seventy-something to take command of the shattered French
Armies – but with the private remit of keeping them intact so
as to maintain 'order'; to defeat, that is to say the battalions of
'workers', who had taken advantage of the political situation in
both 1848 and 1870. DD encourages this and sometimes refers
to it. Anything is possible, that I do know.

Delightedly, I fell back into this fantasy. 'Yes. I think of the
atmosphere in the C-in-C's dining room (not 'mess') in Damascus.
On, say, the 27 May 1940.'

Because this was not a simple colonial outpost. Surrounding
them are the names – Saone, Krak des Chevaliers, Chastel
Rouge, of the great crusader fortresses, so redolent of French

---

[1] Peter Lilley, in his role as Conservative Deputy Leader, had been accused by
William Hague of speaking out of turn in ruling out big private-funding solutions
for health and education.

chivalry and military prowess. And also, occasionally or so they had been conditioned to believe, of English perfidy and cowardice. In the presence of great art – in the case of the crusader castles the absolute apotheosis of medieval architecture both ecclesiastical and military – one is entitled to feel contempt for the *little worms*, their mediocrity and plodding quest for everything that is banal.

1 Parliament Street   *Wednesday, 28 April*

Last night a dinner at Shaun W. Michael Portillo came and, somewhat to my surprise, *was* impressive. Towards the end he said that if we were going to talk about the leadership he would have to leave the room (pompous and guardedly shifty).

This morning bad headlines – 'Tory Party in mutiny' etc. Breakfast in tearoom subdued by presence of Jacqui Lait, big frumpish ex-whip who disapproves of me and everyone like me. But afterwards a pleasing little conclave with Eric [Forth] and DD in the 'Aye' Lobby as Hague apparently insists on coming to the 22 this evening. Bloody cheek, I say, it's not us who needs the pep talk. Are we or are we not, do we rate above, or below, a focus group?

So I really do look forward to this evening's Executive; and I am enjoying being an MP. Even Peter Luff,[1] waiting for a taxi, said he ought to fit *you* in …

1 Parliament Street   *Thursday, 29 April*

A day of considerable turmoil. Dreadful (for Hague) headlines; MORI figures still further collapsed.[2] At about 11-ish were told

---

[1] Peter Luff, MP for Mid Worcestershire since 1997 (Worcester 1992–97).

[2] 'Hague fights to save his political life'; MORI showed 56% for Labour, 25% for Tories; Hague's personal rating dropped from −26 to −31, meaning that twice as many disapproved of his leadership than approved.

that there would be a meeting of the Executive on Tuesday (as soon as we return from Whit recess) and Hague would address us. The Lobby was in considerable turmoil, and I spoke to several – though not all – journalists. By 6 p.m., though, he had 'bottled out' and the meeting was cancelled. Order, counter-order, disorder. I left and drove to Gatwick where, at 10.15 p.m., I picked up Janey, sweet and refreshed from a week at Benalmadena.

MFS   *Saturday, 1 May*

Yesterday was stressful. Too much going on and 'things' against one, like the Discovery battery giving trouble. I had to drive over to Dover, but even the New Bing seemed to have a 'flat spot' and some fault with slow running. I'm really off cars by now. The place is full of catalogues – Brooks's, Christie's, Coys etc. I 'couldn't care ...' Quite fancy Nick's [Beuttler] 2CV, of which he sent me photos; alternative – so what?

Today, though, has been lovely. We sat on the 'summer seat' at the end of the moat for salami salad and 'Max' attended on us, while other birds flitted about busily. I am more tranquil, I don't (it seems) have glaucoma after all. Spalton wrote today. My hernia less obtrusive; my weight back to 11.4 (+) and reasonable ½ erection in the morning.

But how do I get *noticed*? Do I make a speech, or give a lecture, or arrange a TV news conference, say? The great test, the 'New Paternalism' and the glowing reviews. I would talk to DD, natch; also Michael Gove.[1] I had a call through to Alastair, but he was still away. What is lovely is the sunlight, which does just slightly raise the vitality quotient.

I do thank God, though, everything is so lovely.

---

[1] Michael Gove, opinion page editor on *The Times*.

Sunday, 2 May

Really hot sun, and the comfortable knowledge that tomorrow it is not 'Dave-at-eight', but a free day.

But, a potential setback this morning. I had cleared out the hen house, then dashed off a letter to Stewart Steven[1] and rushed up to the post. Around lunchtime I was busy at Bill Holding's[2] shed when I started to feel *odd*. Almost like dropping off (before 'lights') when different reasons and evocations move across the consciousness. I had been contemplating a glass of Puligny Montrachet, but thought first to go down to the Long Garage. But by the time I got there I was feeling peculiar. Headache by side of skull, v livid. Half 'Hungarian embassy', almost sickish. Sat on the seat by the VW axle and started a sub-panic sweat. I worried about a possible stroke. Just about pulled out of it. But had no appetite for a salad of prosciutto-melone, which Jane concocted. Felt, and continue to feel, incredibly sleepy, almost as if v late last night (which we weren't) and/or jet-lag. May be linked with o/d-ing of sunlight which is affecting my blood count. I daren't (although Jane urges me to) put up my feet and drop off for fear of how I may find myself when I awake. Boring, and rather frightening also.

Summer Office, Saltwood   *Tuesday, 4 May*

I seem to have virtually no appetite, and I no longer like alcohol, not that it makes much/any difference. Am I heading for cancer? And if so, where?

A nice bath and hairwash from Jane before getting dressed,

---

[1] Stewart Steven, now a columnist with *Mail on Sunday*, had remarked on the quality of *The Tories*.
[2] Bill Holding's, the Saltwood garden shed, not only for tools and powers, but also, sometimes, the Mehari and other cars.

but doing my nails I saw in her mirror that the bags under my eyes are very pouchy.

Later in the day I felt stree-ange; almost light, as with a high fever – indicating some body out-of-balance factor. I am being eaten by stress.

I drove up v slowly in the little 911, then had three cups of tea, an Eccles cake and a slice of Stilton; calmed down at the prospect of a calm week.

Thursday, 6 May

I sit now in the Library, and I am ill-at-ease and *light*. It is a strange condition, a Lenin-Stadium variant, but in that case I could take refuge in a secret sexuality. But I am not myself; and particularly *put out* by the non-performance of alcohol. Last night a pint of beer in Pratt's[1] – made no impact whatsoever. I seem to remember Cindy [Frowd] saying that this is an incredibly bad sign. At one point (middle of January) I said, 'something-something-cancer-of-the-spleen'. Nick did, I think, hear it. But made no attempt to 'pick it up'.

How do I get out of this? Saltwood is no fun without sex or wine. Calm discipline and thought. But my self-confidence (due to its link to testosterone, perhaps) is down. Do I see my way?

That evening, Great Library (study)
A very sad blow. TC died (was killed) at Lëhni's hand. He/she had popped out on my return, had a drink and a good meal from his dish. I had a pleasing double poached egg (having come down on the 3 p.m. – excellent – train). We decided to stroll down and look at the workings, and putting my shoes on at the asthma rail I suddenly heard Jane shouting – knew at once what it was. Lëhni had clamped him *on the nest*.

---

[1] Pratt's – club owned by Duke of Devonshire, at Park Place, SW1.

We are absolutely shattered. We stood together looking at him on his tablecloth on the kitchen table. So warm and plump, he seemed. I hate the sudden invasion of death – 'in the midst of life we are in death', and was unhappily reminded of the vulnerability of the sweet young. Happily, as soon as we got back from our short and melancholy stroll, the phone rang and I said that may be the young; and it was Boy – very compos and lovable.

When Jane met me at Sandling I was 'Depressed Prince Enters Clinic' and she said how 'good' I was looking. Fun to be home – 'for three days of prayer and contemplation' I said (little knowing of the setback ahead and unhappily aware of inner lippen which seem to die down but quickly revive after 'eating'; or being 'caught'. From the day diary I see it is only 5–6 days old.

It is very great loss to lose a jackdaw, because they are magic birds, and carry reincarnationary powers. Last night (was it a portent?) I am almost in tears as I remembered the little dog – mentioned here earlier – whom I used to wave at and occasionally bring milk for at the top kennel by Eriboll byre; and how I had let her down; and is she, I assume, now dead? Not dying, I trust, too unexpectedly but I hope to meet her – greet her – in Heaven.

Sadly I thought about it all as we walked back up the path from the workings. Just to die, or induce death – not so likely to be treated. Like, almost, being sick. It may make you feel better, but actually *doing* it is horrible.

Jane produced some photos including one tiny almost unrecognisable shot of 'x'.[1] I have that of her a couple of times. Could she have been reincarnated? All mysteries.

Little Alan Duncan, sitting on the Front Bench while I was waiting to speak in the London health service debate. Said (after

---

[1] A few months before AC remarked about meeting 'x' – 'that extraordinary, obsessional and almost ruinous affair (out of which, indeed, my marriage to Jane emerged so much stronger, "miracle" and all).'

I had praised him on his article in the *H.S.N.*), 'Lining yourself up for the impending vacancy.'

'We don't want a vacancy.'

Self: 'You do if you've got a good chance of filling it.'

He was delighted: 'Only if you are my campaign manager.'

'Ditto,' I said.

Saltwood, EMT   *Friday, 7 May*

We buried TC today at noon, in the *Pavillon*.

He was laid in the little portable hamper, with a host of personal 'belongings' selected from his diverse and conscientious 'nest' assembled over so long and with such Herculean effort. That special silk scarf (which he used to keep purloining even after it was 'reclaimed') also his/her tiny, miraculous eggs; her 'tin'; a biro, a clothes-peg, a silver spoon and the little horse-brass of Jane's which she had carried (although heavy) all the way along the passage from the back stairs windowsill. 'Money-for-the-journey', an 1868 Victorian sovereign which had for several years been lost on the floor of the Winter Office and which I knew his magic would lead me to immediately, and I put my hand straight on it, beneath the desk. Brilliantly, Jane made me snip off with the kitchen scissors a ¾ length of the grey marker ribbon from the orange PDF day diary, which he would always try and remove at EMT, and this was about his person.

It was a sad, a very sad, little ceremony. Last night in bed a sad couplet from the childhood nursery rhyme kept going through my head:

'All the birds of the air fell a sighing and a sobbing ...

– as they learned of the death of poor cock Robin.'

We are very very low, at losing someone who had so much magic. Did I betray his trust? Accidentally – yes. But perhaps it is this which makes me so dejected (and Jane, also, I suspect). I did say, aloud, a short prayer for him/her. 'I don't want to say it aloud,' I said. (Jane and Lynn were both in the Pavillon.) 'It'll make me cry.' 'Cry, then,' Jane said. And quite right too.

For the rest of the day I was completely dejected. I had no energy at all. And a recurrence of toothache in the right lower wisdom (which is, of course, 'false', i.e. made by Bertie Arbeid, or whatever that root specialist was called). This must be sinister. I was also made lower by inner lippen which seemed to be expanding.

I feel now as if I may be about to die, possibly quite soon, 'nearing the end of my life.' A huge sadness, as if I am/may be looking at so many things for the last time. Somehow I am going to be cheated of my chance to get hold of the Tory Party, and this realisation, coming on top of the accumulated stress, will do me in.

After lunch dozed off in the Pavillon, deeply. Then wrestled with fruiting bodies on the GH bank. In its own way even this was depressing because of the sense of neglect, and the way they have been killing the azaleas. Tea, and we decided to go for a walk, along the front. Almost empty, mild, and tried to take in lungfuls. Some nostalgia for the great days. We returned along the shingle, and could almost have plunged in the sea, which felt inviting. A clinical regime, as in 'Depressed Prince Enters Clinic'. Then a nice bath, and into pidgys. Trying to calm down and de-stress. Now going in to dinner, but afflicted by a particularly unwelcome symptom – the absolute non-effect of alcohol. Normally this is a time when wine inspires the mind. Not at the moment. There has been (on our TV screen) little Hague, in his 'Bruce Willis' haircut (whatever that is) and his dreadful flat northern voice. I find it just awful, skin-curdling, that the Party – our great Party – formerly led by Disraeli, Balfour, Churchill, Macmillan, Thatcher (even) could be in the hands of this dreadful little man who has absolutely no sense whatever of history, or pageantry or *noblesse oblige*. The whole enterprise to be conducted on the basis of a Management Consultancy exam tick-box, and the 'findings' of a 'focus group' 'Is not the 1922 Committee a valid "focus group"?' as Eric Forth, justifiably, complained.

Saltwood   *Saturday, 8 May*

The date (although not, of course, the *day*) of the Norway
Debate in 1940.

I woke this morning so depressed. The pile of *germane* – or is
it mundane? – tasks. Terry [Lambert] wants a copy of the Trust
Deed. Where are the Wills? I am fairly certain that I will be
dead, or at least *hors-de-combat* in 6–8 months. Weight now
11.4lbs (+).

The message light on and it was Keith Simpson wanting 'a
word' about little Duncan. This, + two cups of Indian made me
feel better. Today we are going over to Lynx (by Land Rover) to
collect (one of) the XKs. Why bother? My taste for the cars is
gone. The white XK is an icon, but the rest ... The minimum
stable (so often attempted in the Dealing Book): Discovery, S16,
'little black (?)', SG, XK120, prob 4¼. I am quite minded to go
out in 9AKC, now the Chev Summer Car. And there is also the
Chapron.

Later, My Father's Study
It's 5.30 p.m. and back to an almost habitual, or usual condition
of feeling slightly better after a full (Indian) tea (in this case
backed by fish cakes and Heinz ketchup) except for anxiety
about rear r/h wisdom toothache. But 'hernia' has virtually
disappeared. We went to get the 'noisy car'.[1] Also an enormous
bill for the grey 140. Quite nostalgic, almost upsetting, going
through Rye – oh the pining to 'start again'. But I did 'start
again' it must not be forgotten, in Parliament. I do worry and
get 'depressed' very easily, that I have so much to do before I can
die at peace – for sweet little Jane for whom I am feeling very
loving at present – and for my descendants. Trusts and
inventories.

Sometimes, as now, I feel pretty ok, but I am not looking very
young.

---

[1] 'noisy car' – the XK20.

Saltwood   *Sunday, 9 May*

Just in from the walk, a lovely mild spring/May morning. Felt so tired and listless on waking, I barely wanted to get out of bed (at 7.20 a.m.) and go down to EMT. In many ways this 'Depression' is extending out into a 'Nervous Breakdown'. But I am not frightened of dying; just scared of packing up. Dirk Bogarde has gone, at 78 (same age, almost, as my father and still seemingly a long way off).

How do I ensure that I stay in command of the Mains, but with everything clear and composed for Janey? I really love her. And I love James when I hear his voice on the phone, so clear and compos.

I am almost near-to-tears. Not at all as programmed. Where is *FE*?[1]

Later, p.m.

In the afternoon, quite hot, I went for a walk to Beechborough. I have for long been fascinated by this property, often remembering in its first heyday the girl (owner's wife, presumably – much, much later after my Jaguar article in the *Telegraph* – she wrote to me) quite nice-looking with long hair who drove a faded metallic blue 120, nearly always with the hood up, and I used to see her on the A20. They were a young couple, I assume, trying to make a go of it with bed and breakfast.

Of course in those days I was living mainly at Saltwood, 1955-ish I should think. I often think that I should have bought the whole place, lock-stock-and, which I could probably have managed then; painted it all white, and filled it with pre-Raphaelite paintings, Alma-Tadema, Leighton etc. But as Jane points out had I done so she and I would never have met. Because then I was getting restless, and quickly bought Watchbell St, and first started to see her and Pat at 'The Lookout'.[2]

---

[1] The 2nd Lord Birkenhead's two-volume biography of his father, F. E. Smith.
[2] At the end of Watchbell Street; one can see across to Camber.

This afternoon I made a point of climbing over the battered iron railing fence to the 'lake' (in reality a freshwater reservoir). A strange and romantic mystery pervades this location, with the overgrown reeds and water lilies, the occasional wild moorhen. Something, perhaps, of Leslie Hartley, *The Go-Between*.[1] But, less happily, I found out only a couple of months or so ago that the main house had been a convalescent hospital for the Canadian Division in the Great War. Eighty-four years ago, give a week or so, fell the anniversary of the very first use of poison gas in the attack (on the Canadians) in the Ypres salient on 28 April 1915 when those poor brave soldiers stood on the parapet to raise their heads above the cloud and continue firing. Their only mask was a handkerchief soaked in bicarbonate of soda. How many of them must have been hospitalised afterward to Beechborough, with their lungs terribly damaged.

I was rattled because time passed and I had agreed to return in time to take Jane to the Rhodi and Azalea walk up in the American garden, plus I ought really to write a piece (at their solicitation) for the *Mail*, on Kosovo. Got back too late, so we had tea in the Pavillon. Then went for a run in the White Car, first time out for years, to try and capture some Jaguar music, but too much stuff (as usual) in the way.

Saltwood   *Monday, 10 May*

I am really 'poorly'. I wake utterly demoralised and so low that I want only to drop back asleep. I don't want to do anything in particular, no zest. Not even a delicious anticipation at going up to the House to see what 'unfolds'.

On the walk with the dogs I no longer brighten at the thought of coffee and a fried egg and bacon.

---

[1] 'A *Go-Between* trysting place in a hot hot July,' as AC described it in November 1995.

Later, House Library

Driving up this morning in Big Red I felt incredibly sleepy and de-energised and zest-free. Had hardly got the other side of Ashford, and was doing 75-ish, unassertively and being over-taken – almost as if in a big old American. I thought to myself, I actually *am* having a nervous breakdown.

I think what was wrenching at my heart was a little con-versation I had last night on the telephone with James at Eriboll. I suppose at one point I may have said '… got to go now; I'm in a rush.'

Very very sweetly, not at all cross, he said, 'Almost from my earliest childhood, when I wanted to talk to you, I can remember you saying, "I haven't got time just now." But now you are still saying it to me. You still very, very often say it. But I am your son and heir. There is so much I need to talk about. It is to the others that you should say this …'

I really love 'Boy'. He has got a lot of greatness in him. I told him that we had now decided to come up over Whitsun, he and I would have a really good 'w', and look at the plantings together. But he wanted to talk *then*.

How awful it will be if I were to die (or still worse he) without our ever really having *taken time together*.

My hernia has cleared. And my 'inner lippen' is not notice-able. But I do seem to have jawline aches. It may be just because I clench, or grind, my teeth, including the giant 'bridge', in frustration when, notionally, sleeping.

What am I meant to be doing now – 'with myself'?

Not only have I lost my palate for cars, and to some little degree for the heritage; but also for politics, at present; even for political gossip. It is a Sibyl tonight, but holds out no promise. Douglas Hurd is g. of h. Even more boring and self-regardingly pompous than TK, who still bogusly pom-posticates from the backbenches when called (which happens far too often).

I did get into the Kosovo statement, and forced Robin Cook to exculpate the RAF from the destruction of the Chinese

Embassy in Belgrade. Then up to the 'Forward Look' Committee in room 21, right up on the top floor. Hague jarringly ghastly, as always. I could feel no tremors of inside track, even. Into a black tie for the Sybil, signed a few oddments. I have got rid of a couple of unpromising speaking engagements. One at the Oxford & Cambridge Club, where Commodore something-or-other had the cheek to 'suggest' that it might be more 'tactful' if I did not mention Kosovo; also one for Nick Winterton[1] that had all the makings of an ordeal: return fare £155 − monstrous that I should have to pay this; and totally impossible to return from Macclesfield without changing trains at Stafford, and anyway they only go to Euston. Saltwood weekend ruined.

Anyway, on the Thursday I want to use the occasion of a quite promising Liberal Opposition Day with an amendment to cut Hague's salary because he is so useless, making my own cerebral speech about what the Conservative Party is/should be. Plus masses of overdue sorting of paper.

This actually *raises* stress, although it ought to abate it. There is little Derek Fatchett,[2] a clear victim of the Ministerial destruction-test − the classic 'HE's Reception syndrome having to be revived' (they failed) − 'while fighting for his life on the floor of the pub'. Heart attack; dead. I could almost, almost, retire to the croft; leaving Saltwood care-and-maintenance. But what about the constituency? What's he up to? Etc. ('Doctor's orders.') But that really would be the end − of me; in every sense.

The only way I can recover real freedom is by getting Wills and Trusts into concrete. Then, 'Come-and-get-me, Larsen'.[3]

---

[1] Nicholas Winterton, MP for Macclesfield since 1971.
[2] Derek Fatchett, Foreign Office Minister, died suddenly aged 53.
[3] A phrase from a 1950s American television series.

House Library   *Tuesday, 11 May*

Sybil no fun really. I was between Bill (Cash) and Oliver Letwin, to whom I am now warming a little more. Hurd, predictably, was largely Position-Paper balls. When dear Bill C finally weighed in about Europe/generally I rose and left. Drove (!) back having discarded my black tie and boyishly donned the grey cashmere pullover. As I said to my fellow diners, 'I am utterly demoralised.' Shaun told me that Gordon Reece[1] was in hospital in Houston *waiting to have his tongue taken out* (would it be called a *labiectomy*? Oh dear). Cancer. 'Started with a cough.' No it didn't, I thought. Can't have. He had a bad cough, I would think, went to the doctor who said 'let's just take a look, open wide', etc etc, and then … 'Hey, what's this?' How awful for Gordon. The great John Diamond saga excruciatingly continues.[2] How fortunate one is. I can't let my mind roam over that dilemma.

One part of my depression, as I sense my palate dulling for so many things is that it may in the end *go* for my real reservoir of strength and inspiration – Nature and greenery or, worse, 'At peace in the Highlands'. Then, actually, I see how those in Deep Depression can at that point suffer acute despair – John Webb from Devizes church tower.[3] One pleasing development to record. Stirrings this morning. And in the tearoom I suddenly realised that I was enjoying *looking at* that waitress, what's her name? (who I have long in the abstract – in her striped blouse she is *exactly* like the cutie in a 'Careless Talk Costs Lives' poster of the 1940s – fancied) and I still get testicular writhings, tho' mild. Perhaps another next week before Whitsun in the Highlands.

---

[1] Sir Gordon Reece, influential public relations adviser to Margaret Thatcher.
[2] John Diamond, a journalist and married to Nigella Lawson (daughter of Nigel, sister of Dominic) was writing regularly about his experience of throat cancer.
[3] John Webb (d. 1991), a clerk at the House of Lords and a friend of AC and Euan Graham, who committed suicide by jumping from the rampart at the top of Devizes Church.

Later

It's 6 p.m. and Sue has made a mess of my going on TV at Millbank. They've 'got someone else'. Adds to the general 'what's-the-point?' syndrome.

I am so demotivated. I ought to write a great speech for Thursday. Don't at present know if I am going to succeed in getting out of Nick W at Macclesfield.

But this afternoon I started to feel ill. Just very slow and sleepy and uninterested. My mind went back to little T.O. Sometimes Tom just *stood*, wherever he was, and often he would get (deliberately, as I believed, and unthinkingly allowed it to irritate me) 'caught up' with bits of furniture, fireguards, the cross-bar of a kitchen chair, or whatever. I rang Andrew about my will. Did he want anything in particular?[1] Poor little Albert has dreadful chickenpox. He came to the phone and spoke so beautifully; clear, and with perfect diction.

I am so down on energy. This has always been my most precious asset. How is the whole thing going to end? I am apprehensive – undoubtedly an anxiety derivative. Classic Lenin-Stadium. So that I can't even look forward to the Scottish May-week jaunt; or the summer hols – *enfin le clef* – the Palace, and Public Life, closed off. Before then, though, certain vicious *hurdles*. Most daunting, the Saltwood Garden Party. Invitations, lists, coach reservation, crockery, cheap (huh!) champagne.

Followed disagreeably soon by the XKs. It's strange, now about the XKs.

I'm not even in the mood to clean up my own two, plus the 'C'. Also the *retraite* of P & A Wood. 91MX is there, but nothing happening (not even a bill) and no response. In theory we are doing the BDC Europe Rally next year, and the Rolls Jordan ('Crusader Castles') rally in September.

Not interested, old boy.

I would gladly *write my own chit* and stand down, as a crusty

---

[1] Andrew replied with a 'hope to get' list – 'a hard choice as one looks to the future, and with it goes the terrible sadness that accompanies it'.

heritage-man. But just a minute! We've had this before. The
tortured withdrawal symptoms, the pining – part 'x', part FE etc,
all inflamed by the material for BB as it accumulated; and the
intermittent flow of letters from people saying why don't you
go back, take the helm … and all the delusory temptations of
articles and TV shows.

But if I did, again, 'step down' I'd break the White Office vow,
and would deserve anything. Perhaps I should pray again, this
weekend. Talk to God. He is understanding, and helpful.

Wednesday, 12 May

I am seated in the doorkeeper's chair by the chamber entrance,
having come in early in order to write a place-card. There is an
account in *Chips* of Winston Churchill sitting in one or other
of these chairs (when actually Leader of the Opposition) before
a late-night Division and making jokes with, and waving at,
passers-by, while puffing at his cigar.[1] All sounds a bit gaga to me.

I still feel awful. Too many times have I made this comment,
in the last seven months. I suppose it all (the destruction of my
immune system) goes back to October, while suffering from the
onset of that strange upper-respiratory virus that shattered, and
reshattered us both over many weeks and did, I believe, inflict
great damage. Long for relief – and the melancholia of having
passed away pre the sword, on the reeds at the water's edge,
would be almost welcome.

---

[1] 'Winston smilingly made his way towards one of the Porter's chairs and asked for
snuff, which the attendant handed him in a silver box. Then, surprisingly, Winston
looked at the chair (which he must have known for 40 years) as if he had never
seen it before in his life, got into it, and sat there for fully five minutes, bowing
and beaming at other Members who looked at him through the little window. A
boyish prank. How endearing he is, sometimes. A few minutes later, however, he
was making what was to be one of his very greatest speeches … to a crowded and
anxious house …' *Chips*, 28 September 1949.

Later, House Library

Pull-yourself-together, Clark! If I were told, 'yes, you can go back *IN*. The price is a colossal and draining change on your paper load, and your "Diary". But the condition of this is that you "disperse the load, and get stuck in to a regularisation of your own fiscal structures".' Of course I would have assented. Now these latter two conditions – draining though they are – have got to be 'addressed'.

There is one rather disturbing psychic phenomenon to which I am minded to refer. Often in my bedroom I will, have for many years, suddenly get out of bed and pray for a little boy who is being terribly and mercilessly bullied and/or abused. Now this has slipped into the kind of WWI image – the Scarpe, Arras, all that – which is sort of out of *real* into *virtual* time. And the 'little boy' is of course Albert, or Angus. And I may be watching in agony as a disembodied spirit, and unable to act.

The wills are a total mess I must get them redone properly – everything to each other, and no legal gobbledegook. I must also, though, write to darling Janey – a real text of love, and commiseration at all the frightful things, paper-mess, 'How-do-I?', 'Where-is?' etc that I bequeath to her. Investing and private values. Car values and historian. All something of 'a note to my literary executors'.

Soon I am going up to the 22 Exec – full meeting.

House Library   *Thursday, 13 May*

I've (almost) had it. Don't really see my way to make the 'Great Speech'[1] this afternoon. My energy quotient is almost nil.

---

[1] In a draft note, dated Wed 12 May, AC had written, of the debate, '*make an impact*'. And later, 'Impact is certainly what it would have made. I could have got it in, but semi-peaked because that awful little git Hague had already *sold the pass* at the start with his "support" or, as I now realize I should have described them – "plaudits". A perfect high-profile background to the speech I want to make in the debate tomorrow.'

Intermittent jaw-like aches, seem to have lost weight again. I feel, and am almost certain, that soon I am going to die ('Tom' just standing). Before my heart actually stops, I must get the Trust docs out so as to be absolutely clear where we are. This is itself a major undertaking because of boundaries (sic) of 'Private Apartments'.

For the first time in my life I see no recovery scenario; nothing to kick-start (*passim* Nick Page) and 'put a spring in my step'.

Saltwood   *Saturday, 15 May*

Last night I had a useful mental catharsis, and slowly began to feel a little 'improved'. I couldn't raise Eriboll, though left a couple of messages on their answering machine. Andrew I did speak to, and apparently he is considering changing his job to become a City 'trader' (!) a 'flipper' they're called, apparently; I must ask Keith Pinker what that is. We chatted a bit. I explained how 'low' I felt. I asked him to promise me always to look after sweet Albert, the 'Prince' who might be in jeopardy of some kind one day. Also that if I died before Jane he would always ring her every Sunday. Also ahead of Christmas, just to talk through 'arrangements'. It is so lovely for old people to have very young children scampering around at Christmas. They must never be allowed to feel left out. He said he would.

If I get my affairs – Trusts, inventories, bequests – in order then I *can* take the risk of dying, or inducing death (on, say, the Creaggan or the Schonbulweg) in order to evade misery. I don't really know how ill I am. If I look back over recent scares – 'urethric' (but PSA 0.5, it turned out); 'herniac' (lifted immediately); failing vision (passed glaucoma test) – I should derive some reassurance. In the late 70s I used to worry dreadfully at the prospect of financial obliteration – at the hands of the tax 'authorities' and C. Hoare & Co who held the deeds of this place. I had this analogy of the last days of the Reich – how should one play it, how good will the V-weapons be? Sometimes this was useful in getting to sleep. Now I am falling back on my ramparts, the siege of Acre, is the Keep secure? If I am convinced that it is I will be more at peace.

Now I am stopping to type out a new (real) Will.

THIS IS THE LAST WILL AND TESTAMENT of me ALAN KENNETH MACKENZIE CLARK of Saltwood Castle Kent CT21 4QU

1. I hereby revoke all former wills and testamentary dispositions made by me.

2. I APPOINT my wife Caroline Jane Clark, and my two sons James Alasdair and Andrew McKenzie to be the Executors and Trustees of this my Will.

3. My Trustees shall be empowered to make and retain investments in the name of any nominee or nominees reasonably deemed by them to be reputable, and to seek advice concerning matters of Administration from Mr Graham Camps of Bird & Bird, Solicitors, of 90 Fetter Lane or, failing him, from Mr Terry Lambert of Mowll and Mowll, solicitors of Castle Street Dover, and to pay any reasonable charges for such services.

4. I HEREBY BEQUEATH unto such of my two sons JAMES and ANDREW as shall be living at my death and if more than one in equal shares absolutely a cash sum of an amount equal to the upper limit of the nil percentage rate band (at the time of my death) in the table in Schedule 1 of the Inheritance Tax Act 1984 (or any statutory modification or re-enactment thereof).

5. I GIVE all my possessions and property, both real and personal (to include cash and equities and chattels within the meaning of section 55 (i) (x) of the Administration of Estates Act 1925) to my wife CAROLINE JANE absolutely. And this I do in the knowledge and expectation that she will make

such later distribution by way either of gift or bequest as I would myself have done, were I alive, and in consultation with JAMES and ANDREW, and carrying always in the forefront of her mind the interests of our grandsons Albert, Angus and Archibald

6. (mss additions) I have hereunto set my hand etc etc plus witnesses Lynn Webb and Edwin Wilson, Housekeeper and groundsman, and their addresses.

Saltwood, Tower Office   *Sunday, 16 May*

We went over to dinner at Allington yesterday. Just before leaving, in the Pavillon, I started to feel decidedly odd. Full Lenin-Stadium. This did not abate in the car, was aggravated, indeed, by being unable to find the place on the road map, where-do-you-leave-the-motorway etc. Jane, though, brilliantly sleepwalked on to both the exit and the route. On arrival I remained uneasy, though. Felt that I might have to absent myself at some point to go and sit in the car. Was some kind of cerebral occlusion building up? Something had told me to get page 1 of my new will signed and witnessed, or perhaps even bring it so that, gaspingly, I could have signed at the scene – drama! The fact that I hadn't added to my anxiety.

The Worcesters have done a good job on Allington. It is cleaner and tidier than when Jane and I first 'viewed' it. But I certainly wouldn't want to live there instead of Saltwood (or Shore, or Broomhayes, come to that). Jane rightly loved Margaret's long, modern kitchen; an example of what we ought to do here with the Green Room and Embersons. But that wing is very well built, and would entail major demolition reconstruction, RSJs, dust and disturbance.

When I came down this morning the little grey cockatiel was dead on the floor of his cage. He has been a bit withdrawn and huddled lately, and we were concerned, although he has been like this before and recovered. I was very sad and depressed by this, the second intrusion of Death in two successive weeks. Bad-things-come-in-threes, all that. I don't like to think about it. In fact I was not so traumatically moved by his death as I had been at the loss of TC. My great regret is that I never managed to get him out, and have him walking around on the kitchen table. But I really did love the way he would greet me when he heard the back door, or even the telephone door. And how to get attention he would do the whole Benny Hill repertoire (this would amaze strangers, particularly workmen). He and his female consort once escaped and flew over the Knights Hall to the woodland. How well I remember walking across the moat and up along the woodland desperately whistling their tunes. It was the grey one who returned and Jane, with amazing speed and skill, nipped and pouched him (that same morning) off the Laurestinus by the garden entrance. We agreed that that is where he should be buried (discreetly in a linen napkin as a winding sheet) and he will be able to hear the telephone, and listen to conversations.

Stress builds up in me. Quite a lot of the time I can feel sickish, and at night I have these strange dream sequences, not exactly bad or even narrative (as in the 'Saltwood Dream'), in which some non-specific but apparently insoluble problem occurs; recurs, indeed, every time I go back (not always easy) to sleep.

This condition is not going to lift until I have created the kind of relative order that would allow me to 'step down' not just from politics but from Life itself.

Curious; I always used to be certain that a time would come when I withdrew from Public Life and simply concentrated on finance, and establishing durable structures. We tried that once, in 1992; but then came the lure of the will o' the wisp, and the great triumph of 23 January 1997. After that anything seemed possible, but now my political career seems to have hit the buffers (sic); being loathed by the Leader, and undermined by his courtiers. From the Constituency itself unease is reported back at my 'disloyalty' (aka the Eastons and Latimer in Plymouth in 1974[1]).

So if I can just get my will completed and valid, and the Trust structures settled and properly filed with boundaries etc. Also the contents inventory and private history and putative values ('the map of the oilfields') then serenity might be in sight.

Later

Just got in from the interment of the little grey cockatiel. It is too depressing, almost an RFC mess in 1917. Jane found a perfect spot just under the Laurestinus and we carried over from the Knights Hall a huge XIXc terracotta chimney liner which just serves to protect the grave mound and into which we scattered a lot of wild bird seeds from his dish. It will be humid in there and they may grow, exotically.

I am unsettled by a story which Margaret had recounted to Jane. One evening, with Bob away, she had encountered a couple of intruders carrying beer cans (worst possible sign). On inquiry they, objectionably, shouted that they were 'ramblers'. Later she found that they had cut their way through the chain-link fence with long-handled metal shears.

If I get to have a 'w' with Boy in Scotland, or Andrew also, how do I explain to them our plight? We are menaced, almost, as the law is structured; at the mercy of the rabble, and their yob nominees. Vandalism, road rage, casual larceny. There is a huge tide of scum rising, motivated by vulgar preference, *schadenfreude*, envy and class loathing. There is nothing we can do as they and their modish sympathisers have monopoly control over the whole legal process. But we are the counter-revolutionaries. Like XVIc recusants we must lie low, drawing strength from our own certainties. And we must be patient, and prepared for when our day may come, and by the action we then take we will stand to earn the gratitude of all our people.

This afternoon we drove over to Harland's in the Discovery,

---

[1] See Alan Clark *Diaries: Into Politics.*

and wandered around. Part of the idea was to get tea, which arrangement I had ballsed up last week by being out too long. In fact it was a swizz – 'tea and biscuits'; and in polystyrene cups. Jane was so sweet and loved the shrubs and blooms and made plans in her head. My love for her, and a premonition of parting soon, made me terribly sad and I thought that I ought to write her a proper letter. I thought that I ought to 'go into' the question of how and where I am buried. It has got to be by the fig tree. Better in a winding sheet, against the earth, than a cold vault. But I would so like to have her beside me, when the moment comes; the stretching out of the hand, or the foot. I am sure it is right for us to dig our grave there. Afterwards we can always 'go to Scotland' when the usual time comes round, and our spirits will frequent the many haunts there, from the place where once, nude-bathing, we saw a seal very close in. And, of course, the Birkett Foster rocks and also, for Tom's sake, the burrows.

On our return we took the dogs into the woodland and wandered back from the Old Family Garden along the stream. A delightful stretch; all Jane's vision and doing, and I well remember at the time she was envisaging it and giving instructions to Holliday's men I was lukewarm, and limp. On the telephone I spoke briefly to Tip, who asked me what was the matter? The more I talked about it the more 'anxious' I found myself becoming. I have a very steady jawline ache which frightens me, plus nervous about going to bed and trying to sleep. I am having a bad time at the moment. Tip, very splendidly, could hardly understand. Looking back I don't think I would ever have envisaged it being 'like' this. Or indeed 'it' taking place at all. What a waste …

House Library   *Tuesday, 18 May*

Today I hope to speak in the Kosovo debate; and I have a slight, 'half-pointing' headache on the right side of the skull. Had this before, something linked to the eyes and the need to 'defocus'.

Sandling Train – Ashford   *Wednesday, 19 May*

I am so utterly down – on the verge of tears, because everything is so lovely – the morning sunshine, the birdsong, the scents and sounds. And sweet Janey so adorable, such lovely *company* as well as being so attractive-looking. I hated saying goodbye, even though 'formally' until the weekend.

I really dread, dread (almost as a child must) dread being parted from her. I write these dreadful entries, partly as a kind of exorcism, partly for the fun (can tell myself) of turning back to them when I am 'better'. One of the things that most depresses me is the loss of *joie de vivre* so that (as I have repetitiously noted) I no longer spring from the bed in May and autumn full of eager anticipation at what the day may bring. Nor do I feel lance after the morning Thompson.

One thing to look forward to, it's not *too* bad a week. Will give Terry's dinner the Press[1] piece and on Thursday back lovely and early (I have just, this minute, satisly filled out the warrant for a return ticket). On Friday, Cindy Frowd who might, ought, to *therapise* me. If I can get 'better', next week is the Flower Show, and the drive north. Providing no more setbacks. I must talk to God.

Later, House Library

Illish-feeling and utterly disillusioned. Self completely unreported in today's press (as Jane rightly cautioned me, 'Matthew Parris will never mention you …'). Out of the Members Entrance Porch and across New Palace Yard and thought – I'm absolutely sick of all this. Nothing left to go for – it's all draining and/or aggro. I want out.'

A measure of my decline into this strange condition. Walking back from Charing Cross I would, in earlier years, have been jaunty, confident, pleased at – almost *inviting* – visual recognition in the street. An MP striding towards the House of Commons!

---

[1] AC's piece for Stephen Glover's collection, *Secrets of the Press*.

A condition, a *mise-en-scène* I have been pining for ever since I first used to hang around the TV crews on College Green while OUT (in '93-ish, I'd guess) and said to Nick Budgen 'who's that buffer over there in a hat?' and he reproachfully told me that, '… if I may say so that is just the kind of mistake you can make when you are no longer one of the Parliamentary Party'. (It was, in fact, Iain Duncan Smith.) Now, this afternoon, I am back into a state of raging anxiety. As soon as I got to the office I could feel it getting aggravated as I redid the Engagement Diary with Sue. The dreaded great green book first introduced by Trish. The secretary's battering-ram. Speaking engagements and social (the Norland 'Summer Party' etc etc) I could feel myself getting 'unhappy'.

Once back here I got to thinking – 'how do I get out of this?' Perhaps the really haunting spectre is that I would have to turn my back on the lake, and the prospect of the sword. This would mean (a) announcing that I would not contest the next Election or (b) arrive at the same position by openly applying to be readopted (the Muzio gambit, or the *Coup Royale*). Once done, either result would make me secure. Would lift the have-you, could-you pressures, the correspondence, and the sense of obligation and possible lurking ambush.

At the same time, and in parallel I must confirm the Trusts in existence, the validity of the wills, and such insurance cover as there may be. (Some little runt of a 'Loss-assessor' turned up at 10 a.m. to 'look at the wiring, and the security' and wasted my time. Any insurer will turn to the most convenient (for them) excuse to keep taking the premiums but dodge the claim.)

How feasible is this scheme (or 'game-plan'?). Well, of course *c'est possible parce que tous est possible*. But we've sort of been here before, have we not (like, say, in 1991-92)? I will pray, perhaps with Janey, at St Leonard's (maybe on Thursday) and then we will talk it over *viciously*.

I love Janey so much now. It is terrible how I miss her. I long for contact – it is almost like a child, waking in the dark in fear and calling out. I need the mummy to come in. It is a physical reassurance, and she is so reassuring and willing in the things she says and her lovely giggle. It was partly grounded, of course, this melancholy, in reminder of how horridly I treated her; it is ironic indeed that now I *really* can't do without her, even for a little while, and salutary also that I should be punished for my callousness in former times. Additionally, and 'at the margins' I suppose that I have been made uneasy by the antics of that nasty dark-haired 'student' who is *rights-ly* turning on J.D. Salinger,[1] and selling his letters. I can't bear to think of something happening and hurting Janey again. One is never safe, I suppose. But she should really be able, her position is so strong, just to laugh it off. I suppose that's why I keep repeating to myself how uniquely special she is and has always been.

Pavillon   *Friday, 21 May*

Talked this morning to 'Dr Thomas Stuttaford' (no, actually, I did) whom Jane brilliantly spotted as writing on depression. He v splendid, quick and almost reassuring. Said I could be dosed (there is a school of doctors who think in these terms) remedially with Serotonin. 'Replenishes' (sic) the brain. I don't hugely like the sound of this.

Max[2] is around, flies down benignly; a very different kind of presence. I give him didgys from the EMT tin.

---

[1] J. D. Salinger, author of *Catcher in the Rye*, became a recluse and used any means that the US courts could provide to avoid biographical material from becoming public.

[2] Max, one of Saltwood's jackdaws.

Pavillon   *Saturday, 22 May*

I am relaxed here – quite therapeutic – and let the mind run
over the sad death of my old friend and in today's obituaries.[1]
Too many deaths at the moment. Are we going to be able to
atone for TC after Jane briskly and competently scooped up a
(*very*) baby jackdaw and has been nurturing him on the Aga?

Felt awful this morning. A *nuit-demi-cassé*, Guderian on the
Meuse in 1940 (exactly this time in May). Woke with an awful
headache. Artery muscles in the skull just above the collar-line.
Then suddenly *caught unawares* while dressing and retch-
vomited tea and biscuits into the wooden loo. Still only 11.3 (+)
on the weighing machine. Went down to Cindy Frowd, who
was far from reassuring. Said I still had a retentive virus (possibly
on chest). But that my *liver* is right up the creek, which may
explain loss of appetite and indifference to wine. A bore and
sinister. Fats banned (like Janey). I could barely eat my delayed
breakfast. Scrambled egg decidedly what was not wanted. I've
noticed that I've been off egg yolk, in its various forms for some
time recently. Sinister. Liver cancer always starts with jaundice,
doesn't it? Looked up the symptoms: 'extreme lethargy, weight
loss, loss of appetite'.

This pretty well finished me. Jane very splendidly saw this, and
said 'Go to Bed' (in the Summer Bedroom). But I was afraid of
doing that; too much of an admission; so came over here and put
my feet up wrapped in the 2-tone brown cashmere rug. Mrs F
had told me that we must go abroad for two and a half (!)
months. No. Not Scotland. *Abroad*. Would that we could. Well, it
would be lovely, and probably therapeutic, to go to the châlet. I
wouldn't mind going via Colombey, either. But if we do go to
Shore sitting in the wheelhouse, or walking the Creaggan
should be pleasing. Although the Highland melancholy is never
far away. We'll see.

But I am not 'right'. No, not by any means. I feel so tired and

---

[1] Robert Rhodes James had died on Thursday, 20 May.

listless. Duty/projects tower over me. Not just the Trust Deeds, returns, and inventories, but do-we? how-can-we? is-there? jarrings connected with the Garden Party. Ultimately the apotheosis of falling-in-a-dream beckons – *'told by his doctors to rest for two and a half months'*. Would de facto signal my not standing, or being selected to stand at the next election, but what about the White Office vow? Awareness of this certainly heightens my stress level, as also receiving encouraging notes like that yesterday from Dr (sic) Morgan of Trinity Coll, Dublin, '… it is not impossible that you may find yourself at the head of the Conservative Party'.

As I became drowsy I found (as one can) a formula. Michael Heseltine! Doctors' orders, etc; of course – Al and Heseltine! In no time I dropped off into a perfectly acceptable zizz.

Later, that evening
We then went over to Garden House to collect a plant. It is really nice over there, always. And, as often happens I felt a sort of wistfulness for the early days working on BB, which had so much promise – and was very good, but late getting completely finished and always bound to be panned. I wanted to find something on the shelves on the Battle of France 1940 (the Meuse crossings etc) but couldn't, though left with Leo Amery's diary,[1] always one of the very best reads.

We then did the 'w', woodland as always. It can make me sad, will I be doing this next year? etc.

Back at my desk I decided to phone Mrs Frowd: 'If I had liver cancer would you have picked it up?'

'I didn't pick up cancer anywhere … You are still carrying a virus around.' (Hey, just a minute, I thought I was suffering from deep depression?) She wants to see me as soon as we are back, clearly expecting an 'improvement'. But I am not looking forward to the trip as much as I would be normally. No point

---

[1] Another diary much read and re-read by AC: *The Empire at Bay: the Leo Amery Diaries 1929–1945*, edited by John Barnes and David Nicholson (1988).

in going to Gleneagles, and the treat of eating in the conservatory, and their excellent *carte de vins* – if you can't *consume*. Must try not to be too much of a wet blanket for Janey.

Pavillon   *Sunday, 23 May*

I sit here (ironic how often I seem to find myself getting like my father, with cashmere rug, writing pad/text on the knee) and am feeling awful and apprehensive, having woken with a headache, then uncontrollably retch-vomit on the 'w', just at Lynn's Bank. Now wonder that I may be getting jaundice (was it vaguely like this at Eton, when it started, in 1942?). Utterly without appetite, have indeed an aversion to food (couldn't even eat a didgy with EMT). Just thinking about releasing PA statement – 'Alan Clark to "rest". The MP, 71, suffering from strain, has been advised by his doctors to "take a complete rest" and has cancelled all public engagements.' This will obviously affect my position in the constituency, and also in the House, itself.

Summer Bedroom, 12.30 p.m.
It is early afternoon, in May, and I am frightened. Jane, perfectly sensibly made me come up here – the full sickroom, pad on, teddy [hotwater bottle] warmly dutiful.

I feel very weak, I doze intermittently, and can't 'keep anything down', not even half a tumbler of water. I'm just convinced I'm getting jaundice and have (or am just about to contract) liver cancer. I feel as if I am dying, as indeed I have for several months. There doesn't seem to be any escape from it – except to 'pass away'.

I don't want to leave Janey, and Saltwood which [I] love and the birdsong. There is evidence of one of TC's little messes on the duvet. Sadly I remember how he used to come up and find me here in the early spring when it was a 'sickroom' and once fell out of the window and into the rose.

I am fussed about the impending (tomorrow) flower show. Billy Wallace's famous intelligence of sitting next to the QM and feeling sick ... Am I going to have to dash from the tent – that special, unmistakable and stooping dash into a giant handkerchief?

I will, I suppose, tell the boys. I would like to have them with me when I die, as I have always said, like the squire in *Tom Jones*. Just to hold all their hands and tell them – what?

I have not felt so ill, or been so low – a mixture of fear and gloom – for a very long time.

I see, incidentally, that it is exactly three weeks to the day that I had my little turn in Bill Holding's shed and walked down to the Long Garage wondering if 'anything' was going to happen.

Later

A symptoms note. I feel viral. Very much 'the floor of Mother Teresa's waiting room'. No sense of improvement of any kind, however slight. How do I get out of this? It is, literally, incurable. Jane, with some truth, said, 'I couldn't drive north in this condition.' And of course it is so true that driving on the A1 adds to the strain. Don't want to miss the trip. Train or plane? I need the hills, but I am very, very weak now, like Tom? My little simple 'tea' hasn't come up yet; but already I am feeling sinister.

Summer Bedroom   *Monday, 24 May*

I spoke to Angela Rhodes James. Made me worse because Robert, it seems (after coming back from Australia and another 'go' of chemo), walked into his house and simply went upstairs to bed (he was feeling terribly weary, 'because I think his liver was packing up') and just lay down – and died. 'It can happen, you know, sometimes', i.e., exactly what I half want to do, half think quite soon is going to overtake me. It is strange up here, and creepy, as the wind blows the rose branches against the

window. The blackbirds, though, sing 'goodnight' enthusiastically.
I am more depressed, I think, than I have ever been.

Summer Bedroom   *Tuesday, 25 May*

I am still in the Summer Bedroom. It is a fine Tuesday in May.
I am behaving exceedingly like (because, I fear, I am) someone
'with' cancer in the '20s or '30s. Yesterday started better; we
drove to Barton Court for the Chelsea Flower Show. I took a
taxi to Nick Page. Then I walked round to Dr Muncie, who is
attractive. She ran the ultra-sonic scanner over my abdomen.
Images linked to a screen nearby. At the conclusion she claimed
to have noticed that 'everything was all right'. This cheered me
massively and I made a triumphant entry to Simon Hornby's
lunch tent.[1] Shook little Nick Brown[2] by the hand, then flirted
with the red-haired married lady on my right. Disconcertingly,
though, a glass of Sancerre had only an adverse effect.

It is very, very busy as the Royals have to be greeted at 4.50
and said goodbye to at 7.15. I was typing at my desk on Monday
morning just longing for an excuse (for Jane, possibly), an
instruction to abandon it. If anyone at that time had said 'you
are going to have to sit next to the Queen at tea' I would have
protested quite literally that it would have 'made me ill'.

The whole thing amazing (sic) confirmation of the status of
Chelsea as an utterly incredible constituency. At the gate fell into
conversation with the Bernsteins (David and Anne) when a figure
half attached himself – it was Heseltine (!) – 'in the papers' this
morning, Henley are thinking (sic) of de-selecting him. He looked
a bit wildish.

---

[1] Simon Hornby, President of both Royal Horticultural Society and Chelsea Society
since 1994. A former chairman of W. H. Smith, he had also twice been a Conservative
parliamentary candidate.
[2] Nick Brown, MP, Minister of Agriculture since 1998; (Labour) for Newcastle-
upon-Tyne East and Wallsend since 1997 (Newcastle E, 1983–97).

Jane – darling sweet Jane, she does so much – drove all the way home. Ate a small amount of curry and naan.

Later
Janey was sitting on the bed. 'Are you going to blub?' She nodded. 'Come over here.' The poor sweetheart, her lovely grey eyes were full of tears. This is my real sadness. I just can't bear to be away from her – for so long.

Summer Bedroom   *Wednesday, 26 May*

I forgot Jane's birthday – how could I? Only remembered when Sarah rang this morning. Last night quite soon in I was woken by her pretty face against mine, she was distinctly wet with tears. I am so sleepy I suppose I just dropped back off; but was soon rewoken by her touching my cheek, and hair and face. Jackie Kennedy and Jack in the Dallas infirmary. Poor little love. 'I don't want to lose you,' she kept saying. I am so exhausted I couldn't respond properly. What made her wake up to do this? For us both this is a deeply unhappy time.

Before supper I had made a start on a Saltwood note for the boys. However, at the end James and Julie rang and were compos and cheered us up – have now definitely decided to provisionally (sic) drive north.

Later I prayed. 'God; I am frightened. You have given me so much, everything really; and particularly my little love, whom I betrayed. How I wish I hadn't done so! The thing I fear most is leaving her. She is so good, so important. Please, please will you care for her also …'

We went up (1.27 train) to the 'mayor-making.' First looked in on Graham Camps.[1] He is reasonably reassuring, and Jane agreed. Then to House, taking tea except I risked a slice of apple

---

[1] Graham Camps, partner of Bird & Bird, solicitors, Fetter Lane, London.

strudel. I went up to the 22 Exec, felt illish when I repicked Jane up at the Family Room, but just got to KTH, where cheery black attendant thanked us for our Christmas cards. Improvised my way through both the ceremony and the reception (I see Barry Phelps looking at me fishily these days). [Andrew] Dalton hanging about, but not effusive at all. We cut the dinner, then drove back in Big Red. I had most recklessly eaten a canapé. It had the miraculous effect of making me hungry! So on getting back I had a tiny Jane-2-egger cooked in oil. Slept pretty well.

At one point yesterday Nick Page rang about the results – he was talking about a coloscopy. 'Cancer of the colon is the 2nd biggest killer of men after lung and (I would assume) prostate.' And I thought of Robert Rho J.

I must not go on whingeing. It is fearful-making just being in the Summer Bedroom at the end of May and so feeble. Don't quite know how we're going to get to Scotland, or what I will do when I get there.

As for the medium term. I agreed talking to Jane that what I really want is to *cancel engagements*.

Now with some trepidation am going to speak to Nick Page and hope he doesn't say anything unsettling.

'There is no evidence of any liver, kidney, pancreas or heart disease; and the second blood tests are all normal.

'This tends to confirm the clinical impression that there is no disease here and I suspect it may be the psychological factor that lies behind all this ...'

This *has* calmed me, and made me feel hungry. I'd like a yoghurt and cereal.

Pavillon   *Thursday, 27 May*

So hot this May morning. Adding to my misery, in a curious way, because I love the month of May. I went over to the Great Library. I thank God for everything. He has given me so much since I wrote the Plymouth selection speeches at the head of this long table in June of 1972. And then of course, supremely, helping me at K&C. I asked him to help stabilise me and me to stabilise myself. I could not forgo the long march (to the reeds by the lake's edge). But I am so down on energy that everything seems to accumulate and get me down!

Today Lynn made a brilliantly perceptive suggestion. Jane was shopping, but 'Bill the gardener' had sort of made a balls-up of the Atco. The clutch had started to slip again and he had taken off some of the shields. Wanted to take off clutch, but 'could only be done by bending it.' Certainly not, I said. I cannot bear employees who abuse machinery – as they all love to do, and it irritates me every time I hear the Mehari going.

'Nothing for it,' Lynn said. 'You'll have to retire and take a job as a gardener.'

What bliss! But how totally illustrative of the sort of dilemma which, probably more than anything, is 'stressing me out'.

Summer Bedroom   *Friday, 28 May*

I am suffering from *apprehension*, triggered by an initial attack of panic (brought on by what?). Last night, e.g., couldn't raise Eriboll though left several messages and got this awful child-in-the-dark panic – of which I had had an attack earlier on at Garden House when Jane suddenly disappeared and wouldn't respond to my coo-ees.

Now I am really low. Everything seems so ephemeral.

By the evening AC had deteriorated – feeling awful, headaches and wanting to be sick. Jane recalled sitting up in bed in the middle of the night saying 'I think you've got a brain tumour. I'm going to call a doctor.' That morning he was examined by Chandrakumar (the Clarks' local GP) who said he wanted him to have a brain scan. Despite AC's protests Jane drove him to the William Harvey Hospital at Ashford. By the time they arrived he was so dehydrated he could no longer stand and had to be admitted in a wheelchair. The scan revealed a massive tumour and despite it being the Whit weekend it was arranged for him to be taken to King's College Hospital, London, by ambulance – Jane recalls someone apologising that it was not 'as comfortable as one of your Bentley's'.

Jane drove up to see him on Sunday. No longer dehydrated he was in typical AC form, ordering everyone about. The surgeon, Nick Thomas, had arranged for AC to undergo surgery the following day. AC takes up the story:

King's College, SE5   *Whit Monday, 31May (pre Op)*

Just woken and (a bad sign) thought I was in France. Actually in King's College, SE5 – quite nice private room.

Jollier last night; boosted by talking to both boys, doctors and Jane. Watching TV. Fell asleep instantly 11pm. But head filling with putative engagements for today ...

Woken, panicking, by drip alarm. V sleepy. In came nurse and changed reservoir.

Slept totally till 6-ish. Then started looking at clock. Could easily have depressed you (no!). Is this a function of the tumour itself? Heaven knows what it will be like when coming 'round' (sic) from the anaesthetic.

Yet last night the Registrar was charming, said I was the only person who could rival Blair's combination of charisma and authority.

Saltwood Summer Bedroom   *Friday, 4 June*

Green ink! Originally reserved for holidays (Z or E).

I am back from (in a sense) the dead. I nearly – sic, etc – died last week. Tried to get through to Father Michael [Seed] etc.

That second operation ... 'to stop the bleeding' ... on Monday (!).
My physique (Nick Thomas, surgeon, very splendidly said to
Jane, 'biologically, he's young') has taken a real battering. Last
night Janey, quite brilliantly drove me back in the Discovery in
the dark to get here at 2-ish. (For five hours she had devotedly
sat in my room at King's College while we both watched the
three blood-transfusion sacs drain down.)

Yow! Did I creep – first real slip-change down into old
age/infirmity with the walking stick – through the Garden
Entrance, up the front stairs, line of route in reverse etc. And the
previous two days in hospital I could hardly straighten the legs
out without setting the heartbeat knocking, the blood coursing.

But today, physically, I am doing more and more. It's the mental
work, any kind of analysis which is what I am really trying to
avoid. It particularly does/did affect the brain. But quickly leads
me into unwelcome little naps with observationalist dreams
involving my father, which make me a little frightened.

This morning I woke, thought myself to be a little short of
psyche. In spite of reassurance from Nick and Chandrakumar I
know it could quite well be George VI valet.[1] Certainly the best
(least 'controversial') way to go. Pin just been on the answer-
phone. 'I shall be so cross if you go ahead of him,' Jane said.

But to some extent the whole episode has 'cleared the air'. At
least outline parameters will have been set, and I have been able
to talk seriously to the boys. Also (sadly) I have withdrawn,
effectively, from public life. This at least should reduce the
number of neuro-toxins circulating in the skull (if I stick to it,
and try not to strain the mechanism).

But the only way for real peace of mind is to wind the whole
thing down.

As a start I should ask – if I had died in a collision last
weekend and then reappeared, what would Jane have wanted to
ask me?

---

[1] George VI was found dead by his valet in the morning at Sandringham; he had
died peacefully in the night.

Sunday, a.m.

Less batteredly pensive. But feeling so empty. I must be terrifyingly anaemic, ½ panicky about the haemoglobin and awful green, vile-smelling colonic cancer Thompson.

I seem to be wasting.

But yesterday went out, really needed the stick, to Tom[1] and back. Turned at the garden entrance and went to the well. Then on to the sun-dial in the rose garden.

In the evening a personal handwritten letter from Blair. 'Come back and give me a hard time.' Utterly delighted and moved.

Baddish night. Awoke and apprehensive from about 1.30 round past 3.15.

Jane, though, snuggled up and was quite incredibly lovey and reassuring.

Summer Bedroom   *Sunday, 6 June*

Helped Jane start C-type (which she did brilliantly). She also coaxed the white duck and her brood out of the conker-tree door.

But I am really worried about constipation (I think this is partly responsible for a recurrence – sic – of headache). Appetite ok-ish. Not sick. But it is all impacting.

I am catastrophically depressed. How is this all going to end?

Much fiction being generated about 'recovery'. 'You'll be back' etc etc. But my objective simply to 'get comfortable'. Tie up ends that need it, and then calm down for George VI valet.

I'm very, very weak. But at least I'm getting (bounding, almost) out of bed a good deal.

I don't, though, want to read anything about myself.

Also, am fully dreading 'next stage'. How do they get the stitches out?

I never want to go into a hospital again.

---

[1] The grave in the Bailey of Tom, the Clarks' Jack Russell.

Monday, 7 June

7 *a.m.*

Another fine day. I would have been prepared to go up to
King's College, but am dreading it. Now Nick T will himself
come down this p.m. I still wake feeling ghastly at 2.50–3.10
(incredibly bad luck on Jane). Rewoke 5-ish and my plight came
crashing in. Almost couldn't quite believe it. But mini-step. At
8-ish heard duck and ducklings under pressure. Leaped from bed
and out into Bailey in pidgys and bare feet.

Sad that, what a way to go; if I have to. Thanks be to God and
Janey in particular.

Tuesday, 8 June

8 *a.m.*

Nick came down yesterday p.m. and took out the clips. Forty in
number. First 'reasonable' night. (Unexpected, strangely, after
being told, indirectly, that you've 'got' cancer.) 2.50 a.m.–3.10
a.m. not so bad. This morning quite hungry and ready for
action. Even went down, and 'did' the padlock. This is the first
morning that I haven't felt absolutely ghastly. At present, watching brief. Must not get involved in office paperwork (neuro
toxins etc). James may be here tomorrow, which I'm looking
forward to. I am over-active. General frustration compounded
by 'big' Bill who (after ego-ly asking for a 'manual' for the
compressor) oafishly using the Countax and then blocking out
the Bailey for most of the day, I would think.

My special worry, is, of course, colon blockage, if not cancer.
But I would think the anaesthetic is now 'out', almost, of the
system. I leap from my bed the whole time and am quite ready
to 'take over' the Countax, e.g. from 'big' Bill. I am still quite
composed about George VI valet (but today I am not – so far –
glazing over into, and then resisting, mini-coma).

But when it happens the transition must be smooth. There is a
hell of a lot of heavy-duty paperwork still to be put in place (the

worst sort of situation). I have now wound up a notch in imagery. It's reconstructing Vichy after the fall of Paris. But I am doing too much admin – the sort of thing I ought to be avoiding.

A nice round. Did Roman Tower, then Welsh, then round the half moon and Jane drove me back from Towers in Discovery. Dear Hannah still pawing me. I can progress forward, ready to force the pace. Chandrakumar coming (jarringly) at 7.30. But will not ever (DV) go into a hospital again. That's why I am so worried about a blockage. Then went to have first bath in the Cork [bathroom]. I have lost weight, a stone, and look like a thin old man. I recalled a lovely high spot of physicality and natural delight when Jane and I bathed naked at the slipway round Eriboll shore towards the sheep fence and a seal came up and said hello and we waved at him.

Wednesday, 9 June

Really frightened at about 1.30 a.m. I must not sleep until I have seen 'Boy'. Sweet Janey blipped (the first time) at EMT.

1. I am really ill.
2. Never going into 'hospital' again. I am now the chieftain at the Mains.
3. So it may be George VI valet.
4. Or I may go, doing something. Nothing anyone can do about it.
5. So diminishing I have got to force the pace a bit.
6. Potter about. Make free with the place. Reacquaint yourself with the Long Garage, the Great Library.

Long talk with James, before I got deafer and deafer and my arms weaker and weaker. Walked in the Bailey a little, smoked salmon 'snack'. Sleep one hour after lunch. I am weak. Arms tired. Frightened of being sick.

Thursday, 10 June

First 'good' night. Plopson at 4 a.m. and again at 10.30 a.m. after breakfast. Arm fatigue diminished. Lovely talking to James about Eriboll, Burrs,[1] lots of things. Jane still incredibly pretty and fresh-faced.

I'm still a tiny bit worried about visual co-ordination and have had a brief left foot-toe panic. But more energy, less fearful (spelt also with a 't') though still hate falling asleep ('naps') in bed. More energy. I must try not to look too far forward. I'm alive. I feel better. If I do a Simon Fraser[2] the situation is more clear for my successors.

Whether or not I will be spared gradually to consolidate my position as a Renaissance Count is still to be seen. But even if not, better King George VI valet now than cardiac in the ambulance on Monday p.m. when I wanted to fetch Father Michael.

At 8 p.m. drove and turned XK140!

Friday, 11 June

'Not quite right' (?mark, eyes, throat, toes etc etc) – frightened of falling asleep – strange dream patterns. But found that achieving is the most therapeutic. Did the gate and just came back now from winding and setting the stairs clocks.

Lilian due at 10.15. Will bugger (sic) my plan for a supplementary Thompson. But long to see him too. Then it's just me and Janey after today (which is looming with cars, mowers, etc.). Her wonderful remark – 'now' (i.e. post-King's) 'it's all bonus'.

---

[1] Burrs, shop and property at Tongue.
[2] Simon Fraser, Master of Lovat, had died suddenly in 1994, in his mid-fifties a year before his father, the 17th Baron.

Later on Friday, 11 June
I just list what God has given me today (lunchtime):

1. A long talk with Andrew.
2. A general feeling of being energetic 'on the case'.
3. The will and impulse to go down and phone DD.
4. A strange feeling of fulfilment (much reduced glazed 'napping').

Later
Been ruthlessly stirring myself. Bast'd *Express*. Rang *Classic Cars* etc.

Almost 'normal' over in Bill Holding's with James. Putting compressor on Countax; trying to start Mehari, etc. Appetite normal.

Two black spots. Thompson still y. Funking suppository in case it doesn't work. Eyes a bit out of focus. Dread 'consultation' looming next week on 'Radio Therapy'. Nasty decisions.

Also livid with 'Bill' who has broken every machine. Want to break him. But 2 days now with Janey at peace.

Saturday, 12 June

A nasty night – usual panic time.

Arm weak, sight awkward, difficulty in defocusing. Suppository/ Thompson while Jane in Hythe. Morale rose. Had a nice lunch (smoked salmon and macaroni cheese). Series of cat-naps and deliberated. Seem much *livelier* today.

Went to join Jane in the woodland, I drove Countax back (!) – What a way to go, etc etc. I am much tireder today, and looking awful.

Sunday, 13 June

V good night. Arms less feeble. (Suppository Thompson at 11 p.m.)

Get stressed talking to Jane about 'Big' Bill. I'm more worried about stressing her – she's so brilliant. Even Countaxed the woodland yesterday.

But I feel that God has given me additional strength. I am hungry and have written a checklist.

Later

Best day physically. Worst day morale – blood in (utterly inadequate) stool 11.10 a.m.

Arm weak on and off all day. But blissful afternoon. Starting Chev, Big Red, Barnato (to reverse) and Jane gets Mehari going. I thank God for such happy times.

Monday, 14 June

V good night.

Unbelievably manic this morning. Plopsons. Had started 3 letters and dictated EMAP to Sue.[1] Jane has brilliantly put Bill on notice. Irritatingly the garden is full of schoolchildren. Soon the Amazings, including Albert, arrive. If it wasn't for eye trouble (defocusing v difficult) I'd be *in the lead* at still not quite two weeks. God is being marvellous to me.

Tuesday, 15 June

A bad night. Indeterminable. Jane didn't sleep well either.

But semi-redeemed by double plopson at 5 a.m. and 7.30.

---

[1] AC's monthly column, 'Back Fire', for *Classic Cars* magazine.

Weight exactly 11 stone. Eyes (left now too long-sighted) only remaining worry – radiotherapy 'consultancy' (will talk to Nick first).

Calmly concentrating on getting Estate in order, so the transition (sic) can be smooth ('seamless').

I really love being out-of-doors. But decided to 'overdo' things. Yesterday was apotheosis with the blonde babies crawling about on the grass while Saltwood 'shop' was run by Lynn, Andrew and Jane.

Later that evening I walked the upper woodland.

11 a.m. I continue to be amazed at my recuperative powers, grateful to God. Spoke C. Hoare & Co on Jane's behalf. Cut verges a little and spoke to Bill in the Bailey. Spoke about arrangements generally. Then Sue.

Now I must lie still for a bit. Outside a girls' school is on a visit. But all temptation is lifted. Particularly, and most liberatingly the whole congested diary; 'speaking engagements' etc.

I can plan with a calm mind. As Jane said, 'it's all bonus'.

Wednesday, 16 June

a.m. I can scarcely believe that I am where I am. 2 plopsons this morning (without aid). Coping with Coutts, Eriboll Trust, Bill's letter of dismissal (although this 'fussed' me at breakfast). Feeling full of energy. Eye-focusing only remaining symptom.

God has been incredible to me. It's 2 weeks and 1 day.

I shook hands with Eddie in the kitchen. Is this 'my best day'? There must be a reaction ... (or, DV, not).

Friday, 18 June

Just back from 'w' to machines! Tired – but v good plopson at 7 a.m. (they are so much better in the old wooden[1]).

Talked things through with Jane at EMT. Whole affair is in many ways perfectly timed.

I look at my engagement diary. Sunday, Church Service in Chelsea. Rest of week, and the next, impossibly demanding, each weekend eaten into.

For what? 'Image projection.' For what? '… if you shall find yourself …'

But actually whole strategic position had altered with Tory 'triumph' in Euro elections.[2] 'Hague walks tall' etc etc. Stuffing Shadow Cabinet with 'young Turks'. My position would have been greatly weakened, but the 'engagements' would remain.

As it is I can devote myself, with a clear conscience, to Saltwood and the family. Every day is a day gained, and being put to good, satisfy, or constructive use.

Will I succeed in being the Renaissance Count, but still holding myself ready to do God's command?

Monday, 21 June

Yesterday was my best day. Felt energetic, grappled paperwork, moved cars around (SI Cont turned round to face out; XK140 moved to Bill Holding's etc) and striped – most of – Bailey. Cindy Frowd came and also did good. A lovely cheese and cauliflower dinner. I slept excellently – best yet.

But this morning we were up early, and ready at 9 a.m. with John Williams with pump and hoses for pool. Initially I was amazing.

---

[1] A Saltwood lavatory with wooden seat.
[2] With only a 24 per cent turnout, Labour's poor showing was soon discounted.

But later Chandrakumar arrived to take some blood. Checked on haemoglobin (what's the point?) accompanied by a *nurse*.

He let fall the dreaded word oncologist about Coulthard (or whatever he's called)[1] and his radiotherapy. Actually this depressed me dreadfully and today I feel weak in the arms, tired, and at intervals cold. I 'overdid' it striping on the tractor and I seem no longer to have the almost manic level of energy for proper work. Almost a hint of back to square one. It's strange, because I am feeling better and my weight has now crept up again to over 11 stone. I now realise that the great benefice of Nick's operation (excision) was the return of enthusiasm, almost of *joie de vivre*, so that last evening, e.g., I classified all the Coutts, C. Hoare statements.

Now I am listless and my morale low. I feel somehow as if I am already undergoing radio therapy. The VCC visit and even the XKs[2] on 18 July hang over me, because I so love the blank time with Janey.

I must go to Eriboll and see Angus and the Birkett Foster rocks before a decline sets in. That week, just for a few days on the sleeper seems the best bet for a little 'pic'. I somehow can't realistically envisage myself, certainly not at yesterday's peak form, being there for long in August. I am sad today, the first, almost, since the operation three weeks ago.

Tuesday, 22 June

Woke depressed. Weight still 11. Talked to Jane at EMT, mainly about after my death; how my spirits will always find her at 'Tom and Eva'.

---

[1] AC thought he was related to the racing driver, David Coulthard. In fact the oncologist spelt his name Stewart Coltart.

[2] The Veteran Car Club and the XK Jaguar-owners' club, who had arranged days out for members at Saltwood.

She made a remark that really chilled me. I will be so vulnerable on my own, 'just an old lady with a couple of dogs'. The moment my death is announced all the crooks will converge on the place.

This morning I am low and frightened. God please deliver me a little (last night Nick T very good on the phone, said 'no contra-indication' for glass of red wine!).

Far my worst day from the point of view of morale and apprehension. When I rang Canterbury the woman on the extension said 'oncology'.

My physical symptoms are ok. I do things, like being outside, I'm 'getting better' if it were not for this awful overhang – Chandrakumar blood test and the 'oncology'. Only God can get me out of this.

Wednesday, 23 June

Another stage to make, I fear, a reversal of both fortune and direction. I have been getting steadily better each day, since the operation and since (especially) my sortie to Saltwood. Last night I was incredible, and even this morning 'normal'. But from today I will be in a morale-based decline. The oncologist appeared at 12.30 and I did *not* take to him. Quite clear (as I have all along both suspected and know) that radiotherapy is both disagreeable and useless. 'No cure, so don't expect one' etc. The word cancer was freely mentioned a lot.

Almost at once I decided to go on a sortie to Eriboll. We sat in gloomy silence at lunch. Then I went for a walk in the woodland. Now I am very sleepy and going to risk a nap. It's so sad, as I was really 'making medical history'.

Friday, 25 June

A good night. I always sleep well after Cindy Frowd has been.

Yesterday evening I mowed the *wanderweg*.[1] Had spoken to
Nick who said 'ok' to go to Scotland and he would write the
prescription for boost steroids which John the chemist has very
gamely agreed to provide. Am I up to the journey? Tinkling
and Thompson, Macrae & Dick[2] on arrival etc. Jane is very preoccupied at the moment. How very ironic that our plateaux of
serenity should be disturbed by these two car events, VCC and
XK.

Saturday, 26 June

I am writing this in my father's study in the Great Hall. I am
low, more depressed than I have been for a very long time.

A bad night. Headache, eye-tension derivative. My head felt
so hot. Poor Janey, so long-suffering. I was near to panic; all these
horrid little malignant tendrils starting up again. There is
absolutely nothing that anyone can do – except possibly the
very last stages of cortisone/steroid dosage.

I am made apprehensive immediately by this bloody VCC
coming tomorrow. But more so by the imminence of the
Scottish trip. I want to go to Eriboll asap; there are certain sites
– Birkett Foster, the Creaggan and summit, Tom's game bank,
some of the beaches and coves where we used to nude-bathe –
into which I have got to lock my spirit before the body gives
up. Why am I so feeble? I seem to be worse than for a couple
of days. I dislike the bright, hot June sun. I hate the bluebottles
which buzz round me whenever I settle. Just back from Cindy
Frowd. Jane drove me down and I felt slightly carsick. She

---

[1] The mown grass path from outside the towers.
[2] Land Rover dealers at Inverness. The Clarks always bought their Land Rovers there.

didn't seem to do much for the eyes – unlike on Thursday. I wonder about my blood test. Chandrakumar is keeping himself to himself. Perhaps my haemoglobin is still down – but so what?

Later back in MFS GH
I seem to have done an awful lot today, but feel knackered. I swam (!) – in the ¼ full pool. Delicious. Should have done two circuits, and funked it. Then on the walk in the woodland at 6 p.m. I felt so exhausted I thought I might have to lie down. Read my grandfather's diary for 1912 this time. At Poolewe, fishing, what a lifestyle! Why drink yourself to death?

I napped after lunch under the fig tree, and sweet Hannah came over to see if I was all right as I didn't come on the 'w'. I love that dog, she is so quiet and devoted. I felt awful again. So weak, and this is new. Arranging, etc, a lot of chairs, tables etc for tomorrow.

I don't want to die until I have seen Eriboll and there I may be able to contrive it.

What I particularly don't want is to lose some faculties, vision especially. This is a bad time. What I don't understand or like is why I am not so strong as I was 3–4 days ago.

MFS GH   *Sunday, 27 June*

I must record a wonderful day (against all expectations).

I rose early, moved things, fussed. When the visitors and their rather boring brass-age cars, were assembled I mingled, spoke to them (shades of Robin Tavistock in *Country House*), felt pretty amazing. Jane was pleased with the way everything went. Saltwood 'putting on a show'. Then I slept, went on the 'w'. But I still feel as if I am 'getting better'. Quite remarkable. If I didn't have radiotherapy and Chandrakumar's silent blood tests hanging over me I would be over-confident. Came over here after tea and said a prayer of thanks. It's lovely this kind of demo that God can do anything.

Brian Moore came in his red Ghost with 'Alpine' tourer. I remember how fast the car was the first straight out of Vienna and told him so.

Later I reminded Jane how lovely and romantic was our meeting at the Monaco landing stage in Venice, then going on to Trieste, making love in the hotel room before dinner; and then the rest of the magical [Alpine] rally.

I have this divine serenity at present. I do hope it lasts.

Eriboll Wheelhouse   *Thursday, 1 July*

It's incredible. At 8 p.m. I sit in the wheelhouse. Troubled only by a full colon (blocked, presumably, by a(nother) tumour). But what an achievement to be here! Came up on the day train yesterday from King's Cross. A lovely journey with attentive staff, although I became adversarial with the passengers including a man of my age who sat on the other side of the aisle and seemed to be observing us and listening to our conversation. He did not, irritatingly, appear to have prostate trouble. (Nor did I come to that.)

Derek Presley[1] met us with the latest Discovery — very pleasing indeed. Jane drove and stopped at 9.15 p.m. at the new curry restaurant in Bonar Bridge. Amiably they produced a beautifully packed and labelled take-away and as we drove along to Lairg we ate one of the most delicious meals I have ever consumed. It was dusk and drizzling when we arrived, but still I walked in my raincoat alone and with the big stalking stick to the boathouse. On the shoreline I thanked God for getting us here 30 days after Room 17. Then a cup of Ovaltine and slept like a log, as did Jane.

---

[1] Derek Presley, managing director of Macrae & Dick.

JULY 1999

Today I have done a lot. Incredibly walked around the walled garden, going to Birkett-Foster, sawing some logs. Almost like old Eriboll crofting days.

But one little additional bonus. Yesterday morning we arrived in good time at New Palace Yard and while a cab was being summoned and loaded I went up to the tearoom – alas almost empty except for Cheryl Gillan.[1] She was nice. Did not as I should have done tip-toed round and stand briefly at the Bar of the House. It would have been my very last time; just as, too late, it would have been in April 1992 when the badge messenger said, 'You can't go in, sir, you're not an MP any longer.' The Speaker had just announced the Dissolution.

I was lionised by many, especially by the policeman; and the taxi driver who took us to King's Cross. But it made me not in the slightest bit nostalgic. Because, with Hague consolidating there is absolutely nothing I could do.

Wheelhouse, Eriboll   *Saturday, 3 July*

This morning, for practically the very first time since the 'illness' struck I felt a certain anticipatory elation when getting dressed after a good plopson and prior to walking with Jane to the boathouse.

The Eriboll magic. Yesterday I went to the Creaggan, lifts [by car] for some of the distance, but walked the last bit to the summit of the col and then across to the little knoll (which featured in *Love Tory*[2]) and round it. This made me very tired. I couldn't dine or linger at the Lodge, but I ate five of Angela's oysters and slept virtually without interruption for ten hours!

Today we went to Arnabol in the new Discovery. I felt very

---

[1] Cheryl Gillan, MP (Con) for Chesham and Amersham since 1992.
[2] *Love Tory* – Michael Cockerell's 1993 BBC film, made at the time of the publication of *Diaries*.

tired on and off, but the pluses are unavoidable – especially no more weakness in the arms or muddled obsessionalist dreams.

How I wish that I could stay up here and just cure myself by God helping me to regenerate (as he has done so brilliantly up until now). But tomorrow we return, for me to be slowly and systematically destroyed. But how wonderful to have come up here, and tasted its strengths and touched all the beacons.

Monday, 5 July

We got back last night after Jane had driven heroically from Eriboll-Inverness (Scotch mist started on the Moine) and London, H of C car park, to Saltwood.

Didn't have a very good night. Worried about the little pea-chick which had drowned accidentally.

But this morning after an excellent plopson I am serene, having been to all those lovely places where God could at any time take my spirit if he chose. I am now back at the Mains and must look to him for strength.

Later

Soon I got lower and lower. All those bloody chits from Dept of Oncological Radiology etc. I am homesick for Eriboll. The sweet oystercatchers all came in a flock, full strength, to say goodbye to us yesterday morning at 6 a.m., when we were loading the Discovery. I see always the beautiful view of the shoreline from boat house beach and hear the slap of the wavelets. That is heaven for me. But today I seem to be an awful long way from it; and it's very inaccessible. There I would gladly lie down and die. But the gulls and the hoodies [crows] would take out my eyes, which would be upsetting for Jane.

Later still
I bathed today, one length. The first this year. Thank you, God

MFS GH   *Tuesday, 6 July*

I'm very tired. But today I went to Canterbury for 'planning' –
i.e. fitting the mask.[1] All quite encouraging

Then I did a lot of mowing, also swam two lengths – just like
the old times with Lëhni waiting aggressively on the steps.

I don't have much of an appetite, and after my 'nap' was
muzzily headachy. But it cleared with the tea. And here I am in
these lovely rooms, still acquiring strength and confidence. My
blood test, haemoglobin etc totally ok (as Chandrakumar was
forced to admit).

Looking back at the PFD diary, and the period 4–6 June, my
progress is really incredible. I dare not even write down what
God could do if he chose so to do. I am happier now than I was
in those days. Partly I suppose my recuperative powers. Partly,
also the impact of the wonderful Eriboll memories, especially
the Creaggan knoll, the boat house and the oystercatchers.

Pavillon   *Wednesday, 7 July*

I have been coping with Stuart J. Dawes and the repaired Atco
and Countax. I am feeling really tired and feeble. Back a notch;
and this makes me depressed and apprehensive. I woke, and felt
utterly exhausted and shattered, like in the early days here (6
June etc). I am not eating enough. My appetite is on a hairline,
and am losing weight visibly. But God can get me out of this as
he has every gloomy situation …

---

[1] A clear plastic face mask used when undergoing radiotherapy of the head.

Later, Garden House

I am in my father's study. I have eye-headache coupled with some dizziness. No great appetite.

I virtually finished the Bailey with the repaired Atco. A delicious machine, but fills its green box in 1½ stripes. Felt very tired, but swam one length. I remain depressed and apprehensive. Just like May, I fear.

I think about when I may 'take my leave'. Once I get to Eriboll to the boat house, I am so close to heaven. But to get there is so difficult.

Whereas here, with all those lovely things around me, it could always be '*Suddenly at Saltwood*'. My eyes are not good today. They ache. But I am not as bad as I was in the first week in June, when I was almost frightened of falling asleep.

The Catholics are coming. 'Guild of the Divine Sacrament' on Saturday. I hope I'm up to it.

Pavillon   *Thursday, 8 July*

This, so far, is my very lowest day. I am so de-energised, almost like May, and have an unpleasant, eye-related frontal headache.

Napped after lunch, but couldn't even (literally) take the plunge. Resorted to splashing my face, which did no good.

Before lunch I was standing in the Great Library with Jane and Lynn. A month ago I used to go over there on my own just for the fun of arranging books. This time I had to sit down, couldn't do anything.

I dread the inference that there must be another tumour lurking in there. X-rayed today in Canterbury. But then what? I feel that I am cut off especially from Eriboll. All I want to do at present is 'rest'. My eyes complain if I do any kind of paperwork, like, e.g., even writing this note.

Progress has come to a halt.

Later

After tea (always the best time) I got a good adrenalin fix. Rang Anji Hunter to inquire if Blair would like to come to the Mass on Saturday. Long chat. Felt 'tons better' at once. The combination of female admiration and political inner loop.

Friday, 9 July

A(nother) very hot day. I am de-energised, utterly, almost like I was in May; and I have horrible eye/headache. Cindy Frowd said that I was much better than when she first started which cheered me up. But after my 'nap' I am filled with gloom. Prayed in the Summer Bedroom before going to join Jane in the woodland.

It all seems unending. But how does it end with cancer of the brain? Mark Boxer and Jock Bruce-Gardyne.[1] Do you lose your faculties, vision, speech, balance? I wish I could conceive of an escape route. It is just so difficult to get to Eriboll. And anyway I must, I suppose, give the treatment a chance. I fear, though, that now I am degenerating into an invalid ...

MFS, Great Hall   *Saturday, 10 July*

The Guild of the Blessed Sacrament have just left. A wonderful hot afternoon and by 4 p.m. the Inner Bailey had the appearance of a garden party. After my 'nap' I felt ill. No energy, no appetite, and those filthy headaches.

Last night Jane gave me a little reflexology on my thumb to

---

[1] Mark Boxer, cartoonist ('Marc'), journalist, editor of *The Tatler*, died 1988; Jock Bruce-Gardyne, journalist and politician (C, South Angus 1964–Oct 74; Knutsford, March 1979–83), died 1990.

ease the head pain; and amazingly it worked – I dropped off almost at once. But today is *so* fine and lovely it's terrible to be captive on a hot July afternoon in the Summer Bedroom. One should have serenity, be laughing, and with a feeling that there is still a lot in reserve.

Father Michael came up trumps. He produced the Marchmain case out of *Brideshead*, gave me sacrament for the sick, oil, holy bread etc.[1] For a few minutes I felt cured. But it soon reverted. No appetite, or energy, headache. At periods I am back to May – which is particularly lowering.

Summer Bedroom   *Sunday morning, 11 July*

I am ill today. Headaches, no appetite, weight implacably stuck at 11 stone. It is really hot and fine, but I am exhausted and sleepy. This is strange and rather unnerving. Even in the early stages of my recovery I was full of bounce.

Howard Flight[2] has just made some rather splendid remark (about leaving the EU) from the Treasury (Opposition) front bench. And been 'reprimanded'.

Later
Feeling really ill, still. I collected all Jane's share certificates and brought them up here to see how they should be consolidated. 'Quite a nice little list …' But feel eye-related sea-sick. I know I am exhausted, but surely food is as important as sleep?

---

[1] AC often quotes from Evelyn Waugh's *Brideshead Revisited*. If he saw life imitating art one wonders if he knew that in Waugh's novel art was imitating life? As Waugh explains in his diary (13 October 1943) he drew inspiration from the death of his friend Hubert Duggan, and the priest saying: 'Look all I shall do is just to put oil on his forehead and say a prayer. Look the oil is in this little box. It is nothing to be frightened of.'

[2] Howard Flight, MP for Arundel and South Downs since 1997.

Monday, 12 July

Continued to deteriorate during the day. Sweet Janey cried, heart-rendingly, after 'lights'. 'I don't want to lose you …' The laughing, the chatting, the strength. I went down and rang Nick Thomas who (as always) returned the call immediately. He was unwelcomingly grave. Authorised 2mg of D/M[1] per day. But spoke of 'new' cyst. Could be removed surgically. I am so depressed. The stagehands are now fiddling about with the curtain(s). I took a D/M, and slept pretty well; though immediately on waking unease and pain starts to come through the eyes. I remain very, very exhausted and sleepy. I don't see how this can end now, except with my dying. I do not look forward to the gravediggers clumping about. God, please help to keep Janey's morale up.

Later

After breakfast (of which I did not partake) Jane went down to a 'site meeting' at the Workings (stream). After a bit I came into the Green Room and just started to get things 'in order' when I had a 'little turn'. Quite frightening. I could have fainted, or just sat down and passed out; or perhaps be sick? I felt ill, and see how Robert Rhodes James (and others come to that) can just give up the ghost. I panicked and appealed to God. Reading the past, marvellous, entries, He has given me so much strength, and favour. At the moment my sights are set on 'clearing' the XK visit.

After lunch

I don't think I have ever felt so terminally ill, headache on both sides. Weight won't even now read at 11 stone.

---

[1] AC's shorthand for Dexamethadone, one of the drugs he was prescribed.

Summer Bedroom   *Tuesday, 13 July*

I sat on the bed here, feeling feeble (just had a bath because I, and the pidgys, have become poofy).

It turned into rather a sad little morning.

Jane and I had an argument about the size of the D/M dose (not easy to calculate owing to the confusion of the milligrams and micrograms). Lynn was in the kitchen and Jane ran out crying. I swallowed all eight, told Lynn to find her in the green-house and tell her I had done so. I read a piece in *The Times* about a new cure, but with a poor prognosis.

I then retreated to dictate the review of Graham's book[1] to Sue on 6212. This took quite a while. No sign of Jane. So I left a note and went out to walk in the − her − woodland; lower path and twice I missed my footing and fell. I was quite frightened. Only God can give me strength now. I don't really want to die now, or here. Back to the old conundrum. How do I get to Eriboll and the oystercatchers? I suspect that Jane will thwart this. She does not want me to die in the north, probably for administrative reasons.

So I am low. The D/M has banished the headache, but the eyes can still induce nausea and dizziness. What is my *raison d'être*? If there is ever going to be an *être*?

Bonjour Tristesse; comment tu vas − ou vas tu?

Green Room   *Wednesday, 14 July*

Very, very low and depressed. I feel sick (again, it is the breakfast). Couldn't even manage EMT (a new low). We talked about my present arrangements. Poor Janey is going to be under *so* much pressure.

---

[1] *Burying Caesar*, Graham Stewart's first book. AC was by no means alone in praising it.

Later (back to bed)

The most depressing of all conditions, when you can measure your regress. I now have no energy to do anything. And all the escape routes to Eriboll seem to have been closed off mainly by logistic difficulties – distance, Lynn's hols, the dogs. The fact must be faced. I'm weaker than I was on 30 June – with the triumphant return to the tearoom, and the Station Hotel in Inverness later that day.

Back in Summer Bedroom   *Thursday, 15 July*

a.m. Eyes really ache. So no appetite at all. How do I emerge from this? Dreading the XKs.

Wrote Jane a letter for our wedding anniversary [31 July] and gave it to Lynn.

We went to Canterbury. Not much encouragement. After the skimpiest lunch I had ever consumed, tried a nap, but disagreeable, blighted by a non-obsessional dream sequence. On waking up – where am I? What's going on? What's next?

7 p.m. Now – 'sick headaches', accentuated by where is the hat?[1] Jane has finished mowing the Inner Bailey. Started to sort – not a good idea – some of our Eriboll photos. Made me so homesick. Surely there can be no location better suited to taking leave of one's earthly body. How to bring this about?

Saturday, 17 July

Feeling simply dreadful. Is this how Death approaches? This morning I could eat no breakfast to speak of. The smell of bread

---

[1] The Clarks' name for a cardboard receptacle in case AC needed to vomit.

frying made me nauseous, as I was going out of the kitchen, Jane snapped 'why?' at me. I tried to explain, but was, I recognise, soft-spoken in the extreme.

'Your problem is', Jane said, 'that you want to die; but are frightened of dying.' Too true. It is the journey that scares me. Partly, I suppose, due to those unpleasant dreams that recur. It is only a few weeks ago that I was buoyed, in the Great Hall, etc. etc.

The Amazings are coming in this afternoon to help with the XK rally. Poor Jane is so exhausted. Can one wonder? She does so much. (Jane has just brought me a glass of cool sorrel tea.)

Garden Entrance, Terrace   *Sunday, 18 July*

The XKs parked all over the place. Andrew extremely competent in coping. The blue, the white and the grey cars all 'won' awards. (So there!) I said to James on the phone. Fitting, somehow, that my impending departure should be attended by this huge retinue of XKs. 'You must think positively,' was all he could say. Useless advice, although well meant.

Monday, 19 July

This morning I am in absolute despair, though can still be talked out of it by Janey.

I remain low, and frightened. What is my objective? Just to get through this, I suppose, and return to good health – or at least to feeling like I did a month or so ago. My brain seems to operate on two halves. The second one is muddled and potentially obsessional. I have been quite wary of it for some weeks. It seems to subsist on creating bogus problems and then attaching spurious solutions to them.

I am very unsettled, and more than a little frightened.

Tuesday, 20 July

Yesterday in mid-afternoon I felt so ill I wrote Jane a note.

Darling
I think I'm going …
    The divide between giving up life and *being sick* is a narrow one.
    You must not forget how much I love you, and regret having caused all this 'aggro'. Talk to Fr Michael. He knows.
    Also get a message to the oystercatchers. And to Tom, also.
    I will always be *for you*.

                                                              A x x x x

When I was writing the note Jane was crossing the bridge, and heard me calling … we are very psychic, and she particularly.

Saltwood, Summer Bedroom   *Thursday, 22 July*

Woke this morning after a 'good' night and suddenly realised that my mood had altered. I thought that I was 'feeling better'. Alas, soon back into whirlpool. Tried to contact Macrae & Dick, via Julie; this infuriated Jane (for whom I must be a hopelessly trying companion).[1]
    Only redeeming feature on the horizon (sic) is the arrival in September of that same *Discovery* from Macrae & Dick. If it coincides − as I think it will − with the end of my treatment, then it does open up the possibility of getting to Shore Cottage for nice contemplative period. At the moment the day does not seem quite to have acquired a finite shape. And I am not quite happy that I am using the time properly.

---

[1] Jane had given the number to AC, who must have misdialled it; hence his call to Eriboll.

Earlier this p.m.

I have been doing a certain amount of contract note work to clear the decks for Janey, and all. I was thinking well at least I'm still living. But the actual end is very nasty to contemplate. Just going downstairs and Nick Thomas on the line. Looked at the scans: 'There is really nothing more that surgery can do ...'

I really don't know what I should do next. I am scared at losing my faculties and dying without dignity. How I wish that I could hand on K&C to Tip. He would be so good there.

I still don't feel very well, but what is really horrible is the knowledge that you can't 'get better'. God could help, but why should he? Still, I might, I suppose, have died already like JFK.

Saturday, 24 July

A good night – 9 hours. However, at EMT, when I turned to Janey and said, 'you know what worries me about the difficulty of getting to Eriboll?' 'Hello, here we go again', she answered in good humour.

I had just re-read my note to her of Monday ('I think I'm going'). Feeling so dreadful telling the XK Rally etc and asking her how she could get a message to the oystercatchers, which would have to be 'his body is somewhere else. But in spirit will always linger here and seek your consolation ...'

Yesterday, I'm glad to say, we did quite a bit of work in consolidating her investment list.

Later p.m.

Over in my father's study for cool and shade from 'the glare'. Dreadful eye-ache, of the kind one used to be able to relieve by D/Ms. Once again (as last Monday) I am absolutely miserable. Feeling trapped almost to the point of panic. How to get independence back? That wonderful feeling when we stopped the little demonstration Discovery beside the stream on the evening of 30 June after that incredible curry en route from Inverness. I was unsteady on my feet. But the oystercatchers guided me. Slept perfectly, because I knew I was safe. 'Don't thank me,' God said, 'thank BLJ. She brought it about.'

Saltwood Summer Bedroom   *Monday, 26 July*

A lot of hustling and bustling with different doctors. My treatment starts tomorrow and in some apprehension I look at the tube of Biafine Emulsion[1] which is meant to protect the skin from burns and (can it?) disfigurement. Last night felt ghastly. At one point it could have been 'Suddenly at Saltwood'.

Green Room   *Tuesday, 27 July*

Jane drove me back today from the first day of treatment at Kent and Canterbury Hospital. My vision has gone and I am most worried about it; now see double images, particularly vehicles coming towards me, which quite underlines Nick Thomas's early caveat.[2]

I am very very in despair. Where do I turn? Something told me, again and again, 'don't come back from Eriboll.'

A little later I rang Broomhayes and spoke to Lilian. As I said later to Jane I do love the way they have all settled in, after a fashion, on to the Seend scene. One of Seend's premier families. After all, the little boys can't be much less aged than when we were there in the sixties and we were making waves at (say Ned Whiting's) and forging memories. A lovely, friendly, beautiful

---

[1] Nick Beuttler, AC's brother-in-law, sent the cream, available over the counter in France.

[2] AC had been told not to drive for three months after his operation.

place in Wiltshire. I will always remember the first time I saw Broomhayes, when we were looking over 'Miss Usher's', as it came to be called, and thought – 'gosh, there is a plum'. So neat and pi – 'building society advertisement'.

Blast, as I wrote this I am finding it more and more difficult to focus, and to alter focus.

Now it is Wednesday, 28 July

The very favourite date in a Parliamentarian's diary. All over. The great long recess is finally under way. For me the delicious feeling of relief is irrecoverable. And the prospect of the Pait weekend.

This realisation ought to be coupled with a feeling almost of triumph. Aha! I've given them the slip etc when it first seeped through the anaesthetic in June. Now I'm trying to escape something nasty. No sooner back from Canterbury than a headache, usual mussy kind linked to the optic nerves began to creep back. The Bailey in July at 1 p.m. was full traditional Saltwood. Beautiful, sunny, warm, hollyhocks burgeoning. I suppose that I should just have stripped and plunged in. The shock of the cold water … what a way to go! A nice irony after all my earlier physical exultations there.

I look at a 'piece' in the *Sunday Times* – 'stars (sic) all home in on Scotland'.[1] A map and illustrations. This made me very sad, the knowledge that I am not physically in shape to enjoy it, because of bad vision, headache, and extinction of appetite. Also, let's be fair, loss of *status*; tied in with impending loss of life itself.

---

1 The Clarks and Eriboll were included.

Green Room, Saltwood   *Wednesday, 28 July*

Oh dear, I am down! Actually I do not think that I have ever
been worse. Came back this morning from Canterbury ('radio').
A man with an unattractively shaved head in the waiting room.
Now I see, piecing together what is on the label of the cream,
'*ne pas appliquer sur des brûlures infectées*.' Oh dear! Those awful
close-ups in articles about cancer of huge scabeous sores,
blackish and overtly malignant.

At present there is a huge vacuum around my life. What am
I actually waiting for (that is of course itself exceedingly
carcinogenic)? No more comradeship drinking, shared and
competing ambitions, gossip, taste.

These are all the things I love in (and about) life. Perhaps that
is why at present I am getting so many nostalgic evocations –
the N7,[1] the café at Kalpetran,[2] even, Jane remembered, the
great expedition down to Zinal when she and (I think) both
boys met me in the Porsche.

Well, weather it as best I can.

At some point, as the news gets worse, I find myself resolving
to take a bolt. Head for the highlands and put my body at God's
mercy.

Saltwood Summer Bedroom   *Thursday, 29 July*

Talked with Boy on topic of Zermatt. Did I imagine it or when
he rang off I thought the word Treuhand was mentioned?
Suddenly realised this might be the answer to everything. Stuff
(sell) a lot of the Sotheby's inventory, which I have got 'forward'
into the AG!! Slept more calmly after a nice vol-au-vent supper.
Must talk to Janey today, or asap.

---

[1] The old route to the south of France.
[2] A halt on the way up to Zermatt.

Just back from Canterbury – yes, it makes one so tired it's unbelievable. I'm up here now and ill, but don't even want to sleep, daren't would be truer. I'm in a dead end at the moment; both physically and morale-ly.

I've got this nasty headache – literally a 'sick' headache – and am really scared of losing my vision, possibly totally. Jane didn't deny this possibility, but did say 'think of the sounds …' (at the water's edge). Then I couldn't induce a coronary; I'd just have to drown myself and be buried off the 'machine' or thereabouts, but how do I get there? It is all so miserable.

AC's wedding anniversary letter, to be opened on 31 July, but written on Thursday, 15 July

Just back from a visit to Kent & Canterbury, not a very good day …

Hello, my sweet Janey!

I am reminded that only 41 years ago I was somewhat apprehensively sharing digs with Celly and Caryl in Victoria Road Westminster – a short distance from Grey-Coat Gardens.

At that time I was already bonded, and would soon formally be *pledged*, to the sweetest, kindest, most percipiently intelligent human-being I would ever encounter. What a union that would prove to be!

Those lovely 'fair-heads', of every generation! And all the sympathy and knowledge for *plants* and *animals* that has radiated out from you and transformed the whole ambience of the family seat. (Am I getting a bit illegible? If so, damn, and apologies.)

For every minute of the day you have worked for me, us and the family. Worked *too hard* (Henry). A hundred times I ask myself how I could have been so cruel to you. Fool Clark,

ool. *Nasty* fool, also! What's the use of my saying you are, will
always remain, the only true love of my life? If you should
ever need me, I will, I hope, be possibly at certain known
localities in the grounds (of each property, even Zermatt).

Love, love, love from

A xxx

Saltwood   *Sunday, 1 August*

Fact is, I've got brain cancer. And it is fairly disagreeable.

My body realises that there is no hope. I mean what is the
next stage? The next (local) demon with which to wrestle?

My wrist shakes – why? Shades of little T.O. I could not eat,
even put into my mouth, any of the delicacies prepared at lunch
time today. Or even the 'accompanying medication' which
hourly makes Jane very depressed.

I am afflicted by a kind of despair, also.

The Amazings coming in tomorrow. What can I say to them?

The house is like an oven now, excepting the rooms on the
north side.

JANE

Although AC did not know it as he wrote, his entry on 1 August would be a true 'last', as he would say, the final entry in a journal that he first began writing almost forty-five years before. His eyes troubled him; he stopped reading and writing and often found the glare even from a clouded sky too much to bear and asked for the curtains to be kept closed. He may have lost his own will to record his decline, but Jane now took up her pen. In a spiral-bound A4, green, soft-covered notebook she started recording the events of each day. What follows are extracts:

Day 5 of radiotherapy[1]   *Monday, 2 August*

Al got dressed and so wobbly – came downstairs on his bottom, me placing his feet on each step. He is really bad.

Day 8 of radiotherapy   *Thursday, 5 August*

Took ¾ of an hour for the pill saga and 1 minute piece of toast to be completed. I long for a meal that I don't have to get up every few minutes for some whim. I long for Al to take the pills without having to yet again explain what each one is for (more than twice, it's 4 or 5 times).

He is now off dried fruit – the sight, the smell etc. Lunch soup (spud garlic parsley) and tomatoes, slice ¾ of apple. But he radiated such depression I felt completely drained by its silence.

10.25 came to bed – Al had eaten *no* food nor had he even taken his pills.

---

[1] AC had started a course of radiotherapy at the Kent and Canterbury Hospital, with Jane driving him there and back daily from Saltwood.

Day 9 of radiotherapy   *Friday, 6 August*

It's 7.20 a.m. Have bathed and made breakfast. EMT in bed writing this with Al sitting on the edge of the bed trying to be sick and soft-spoken. I feel ill with the struggle ahead – long for a dark, warm place that is silent, snug and I can sleep.

Car luckily in Bailey which was easier. Do not think he could have done back steps and slope. Late leaving which I hate as it's so rushed, but in spite of 3 traffic lights made Canterbury by 9.10, time to offload Al into a chair and for me to put car in car-park and to run back. Collected pills for sickness on return. Into Pavillon – lunched there and Al rested – I made him go under the willow for this as Pavillon too hot. Had got from Rabies Room wheelchair of Bonny mama. Tyres pumped up well and Lynn gave it a good wash. It is jolly good.

In and upstairs via chair – had to walk from Huega tiles as chair would not go through gap. Upstairs on hands and knees.

Bed 10-ish – tired, but no early start tomorrow.[1]

Rest day   *Saturday, 7 August*

Rained in the night hard, but cleared up and now fine. Woke at normal times, but Al slept well – and only tinkled once at 5.30-ish. Lovely lie-in. Didn't move until 8, swam and made EMT, gave Al his sick pill – he didn't have a biscuit – but did drink a cup of tea.

In bed all day dozing on and off. Peed again at lunch. He ate *so* little – 3 teaspoons of spud, a scrape of cheese – then a curtain rest, tea v poor – I had walked dogs etc and went up with tea to find him on the floor in the passage by the banisters. Got him up and back to bed – he has bruised quite badly and small abrasions on his elbow/arm R.

---

[1] The radiotherapy department at K&C Hospital did not operate over weekends.

It seems to have had the effect of completely unhinging his mind. He mumble rambled – did not really notice anything. Seemed far away – on about a PhD and being on water. Quite frightening and he was so good in a.m.

Supper 1 banana whisked in milk (½ cup), he had 2 spoonfuls v reluctantly and then pushed it away saying it was going all round his head. Told him he was a b fool and of course it wasn't. Couldn't, so he drank some more, almost ¾ of it, which was good.

Rest day 2   *Sunday, 8 August*

Bad night. He woke for a tinkle at 1-ish, but could not get back to sleep, so nor did I – at 4-ish or bit before he decided he had a headache so I had to fetch dry biscuit so he had something in his stomach before pills.

Raining – swam, made tea and porridge for Al, which he did eat (small yellow bowl used). Al in bed all day – peed not in pot so changed pyjamas. Have got wheelchair upstairs to take him to loo.

Just been upstairs. He just lies there making bizarre zany muddled sentences or mostly just saying nothing, but lying looking miserable. I find myself so demoralised now being in the room, so deeply depressed by it all.

Decided to run a bath and give him a wash and hair wash, too. Back in chair and left him in it by window (curtains closed as bright sunlight), made tea, and only into bed after tea – just left him. He has been sick. Damn, damn. Not a lot, says it is the vitamin pill so *they're* out.

Cut his toenails and filed rough skin. He looks so much better. Wish he would read a little or take an interest in things.

Day 10 of radiotherapy – only 10 to go   *Monday, 9 August*

So rushed didn't even do hens today – oh dear, oh dear.

Mrs Frowd came 4 – was pleased with Al's progress.

Over to GH to collect other chair – back with Eddie pushing it – he stayed for tea,

I mowed Tom's grass – and potted up aloe vera in greenhouse. Lots of tomatoes now.

Came in from the Pavillon about 8 as Al wanted to go to the loo. I had a breakdown as first couldn't negotiate the small rise by yard door, then hit a lot of things in outer lobby, and ended by kicking everything to right and left hurling boxes of papers, chairs etc. Shouting at poor dog (Lëhni) whose paws were slightly in the way. Broke down in tears in Cork bathroom with Al on loo.

It's 9.40, I still haven't had a proper meal and am desperately tired. Al would not eat *anything* tonight just lying there hiccuping, retching.

This whole thing is a ghastly nightmare. I do not know how it will end.

Day 11 of radiotherapy   *Tuesday, 10 August*

At 20 to 12 woken by movement, but Al still lying down – then the noise of a pee. I can't believe it. He is peeing in the bed, just peeing. I confess I freak out somewhat – it's through the sheet, underblanket and saved from mattress by electric blanket and New Zealand wool underblanket – pyjamas naturally sopping. I take them off him and hurl them out of the window; all the while he tells me he hasn't peed. Change entire bedding, put sheet into machine, feel sick. Poor darling Al. Both take long time to fall asleep. Up 6.45 – swam, did hens, breakfast, porridge, tea, coffee for A which he didn't drink today and ate not all porridge. Into car in good time, but oh dear I had left it

switched on. Battery *totally* flat. All change into dear S16[1] and
into K&C. Saw Stewart Coltart afterwards and he gave me the
shattering news that it was pointless to go on with R – unkind
to Al and the family. He shouldn't be like he is after 11 doses,
bladder going, no balance, lack of appetite etc. Very bad sign. I
was in tears – Al had gone out of the room for a blood test. In
my heart I *knew* it wasn't right although trying to look positive.
We went to find Al, me with tears pouring down my face past
all those people waiting – Al didn't really seem to have taken it
in – has he? I don't know – although I was in tears he made no
sign of compassion which isn't him at all. A gloomy drive home
in suitably torrential rain, which stopped at M20.

Into Pavillon as usual and in to Lynn for a good cry.
Lunching, he ate a very small amount of spinach and spud the
size of acorn which produced retching – and half a pear. I am
to cut down on Dexamethadone – only 2 a.m., 2 lunch, not the
tea or supper ones any more.

It's strange I feel numbed by this news – waves of tears when
I sat in Pavillon for tea – he didn't notice at all. Earlier I had
come back from hens and walk to find he had an accident with
water bottle so had to change every stitch of clothing. Dressing
him quite difficult as he is limp, but if you say move this way or
that he can't seem to work out how to.

I love God, but this is such a cruel way to demolish such a
brilliant brain – I dread to think what lies in store.

Talked to Andrew, Sarah, James and Julie. They are equally
shattered. Amazings will be here Thursday and James as well.
How long we have got only God knows – but miracles sometimes happen. It is the eclipse tomorrow. For us it was going to
be a turning point – but now the beginning of the end.

---

[1] An old Volkswagen Golf, used as a runabout.

Eclipse today, 11.20 for us   *Wednesday, 11 August*

Sister Angela Rourke (Irish?) district nurse came 11.30 to
'assess' Al and offer me advice and what have you. Got v cold
during eclipse and quite dark – v cloudy, could just see a
crescent of sun. Light amazing as it came out so beautiful and
bright – '… and let there be light.'

Walked dogs – saw Eddie who was terribly upset at the news.

Back – Al tried to pee, but failed – he won't drink or eat.
Noticed spots on his chest and back. Tried to make him drink
water – he was terribly sick after 3 sips – oh God, why? He
looks so desperately unhappy and knows only too well what is
happening.

9.15 Rang Mummy – she poor darling is v ill too. I should be
there as well as here.

Crisper and fine day   *Thursday, 12 August*

Spots are worse now.

I didn't bathe, thought I saw worm in pool. Threw in
remaining chlorine tablets. Have a headache and feel sickish. No
breakfast for Al. Helen Blake from hospice team came, stayed for
hours, Sister Rourke also came. They discussed anti-sickness pills
etc, etc and saw Al. Thought the spots needed something. Dr
Mohr coming later to see them. Andrew, Sarah and boys turned
up, Cindy Frowd turned up. It was awful – *so* many people –
meaning well I know, but I'm not so sure they don't make you
worse – *counsellors* – not for me. I need them for making Al's life
unpainful, painfree and for access to commodes, sheets,
waterproof etc.

Tup brilliantly mowed Bailey and dealt with battery problem
– it was totally flat, wouldn't take a jumpstart at all. He also
shaved Al and helped move him from Cork to bed, while I ate

lunch. Came with me to find depot to collect mattress etc etc. Would *never* have found it if he hadn't come with me.

Went and sat with Al in bed. He did eat a tiny sandwich and sipped tea. Then a bath – will it be the last? He is so vulnerable and frail. I dread him falling. The Zimmer is brilliant, very light, but strong and good for confidence.

Overcast, but dry and windy   *Friday, 13 August*

No night disturbances, but I slept badly waiting to leap out of bed. The dogs were intolerable, scratching and panting on and off all night. Must deflea. Up at 6.15 as Al wanted to pee – got in commode, which he thought ok and used. Thompson and tinkle so v good. I think Al *better*. Just a little bit – the pills against sickness seem to be working so he kept down breakfast. Made damson purée. He had two 2 tea-spoons.

Very fine and windy after wet night   *Saturday, 14 August*

Al has not spent a penny now since 3 p.m. yesterday. I do hope James will come before it is too late. I am tearful. Al has just drunk a ¾ cup of tea! More muddled today. Have asked him if he wants to say anything – he likes the idea, but fears it would be too melancholy – his journals through my pen.

Asked Al what he thinks when he looks out of the window.

AC: a path through a jungle really and I suppose the … I am being consulted about it.

JC: Carry on, turn back?

AC: you can sort of divert.

James arrived as I was putting him back to bed just in time as he is now difficult to move. My back is going – I get on the bed and pull him on and up if alone.

Feel I rather abandoned dear Al as he was in and out with
James, but James had some nice talks and shaved him, which was
good for Al's morale. He was also quite tough about drinking
and breathing.

If this is a game of snakes and ladders we have met the biggest
snake – a veritable pit of them.

Still, crisp and sunny   *Sunday, 15 August*

8.30 I must get up. We are lying side by side. Al completely silent
and looking so vulnerable and *young*. Not an old person at all.
Tup saw him, said how much he had lost weight from
Thursday's visit. It's lovely having everyone about, but I feel I am
more with them and *cooking* than with Al. We had a Sunday
lunch of roast venison, Yorkshire pudding, spinach, beans and
spuds. V good for me as I ate well! I took my tea up and lay in
the bed with him for 2 hours talking and weeping. It is so hard,
he does not really respond as if a river was between us, and he
can't/won't hear and can't/won't respond. But I know he hears
as when I queried God's role in this he stopped me and said I
mustn't blame God. I don't, but why does God think *I* need
proof of his powers – what is he trying to say to me, to us both?

Monday, 16 August

Al turned as I put the [EMT] tray down and said, 'Is that all the
ships?' I affirmed it was.

Al seems to be slipping away from us. No breakfast (or EMT)
– only sips of water.

Dr Chandrakumar and Gail (District Nurse) came 12.20. Dr
C briefly saw Al and the rash, and agreed it was caused by drugs
– why don't they say *medication*? He then took me and Gail into

the Red Study – I called in James and Andrew and he told us it would not be very long now. It is inevitable and so like a dream gone badly wrong – a nightmare of depression. I still keep hoping for someone to say it's all ok.

It is 3.35. I foolishly asked Al to say something I could remember – something nice about his BLJ. He stared silently away – and when I walked out called me back saying he thought the question 'was about level playing fields on the battlements'. But still no words of endearment – I long for some sign, but he is not really here so I must be content with a squeezed hand and not grumble.

He was so dear as I struggled to get him on to the bed and comfy saying I was angelic. I told him I couldn't let anyone else sit in the room and nurse him and he was so pleased and reassured. Being really ill, if you are a proud and private person, is so cruel it is only your loved ones you want round you at this moment.

Cool heavy rain, but sky blue, too   *Wednesday, 18 August*

Dr Chandrakumar came 12.30-ish – I like him. He does not go for the make-him-eat-drink-and-force-his-bowels-open stuff. Is really quite spiritual in that way – agrees the most important thing is to make sure there is no pain, which, thank goodness, is the situation now. Was v kindly worried about how I was coping and agreed to be my doctor and will put me on the NHS. Talked about what to do when he dies – I did not know and had asked him. I have to notify him if possible – no objection to him staying here and undertakers were always on 24-hours call. It's all essential information and I am calmer for knowing everything.

Earlier Stewart Coltart had come – he is nice too and did not rush us, but gave his time. He took a look at the rash and said it was Epanutin – his wife was a dermatologist and he telephoned her and she confirmed this – so at last we do have a culprit – ok to stop it tonight as still in blood for a bit so perhaps by the weekend it will start clearing. He does not complain of it, but it looks v uncomfortable, and is really everywhere, but face, hands and feet.

Crisp, windy, but fine   *Thursday, 19 August*

Gail, the quiet District Nurse came – do hope we can continue with her – and was very pleased with Al. Said to Lynn how different from Monday he was. She will collect the new anti-fit pill and drop it in at Lynn's. Al tinkled well and is so much better and more smiling – I'm aghast at the fact I was shovelling in that little green and white Epanutin pill every night and it was causing so much aggro to his blood/skin, poor darling. Late lunch as he dropped off – but he did have some soup and almost half an apple. Drinking quite a bit more. Have put on Gail's recommendation 1 Redoxon into one of his drinkers.

New anti-fit pill is a lovely violet colour!

Rang Mummy whose legs are still v bad – she goes tomorrow to have stitches out.

Crisp and fine today   *Friday, 20 August*

Poor dogs not walked as James did not want to be left to get Al on to commode. He is quite different from Andrew who is a genuine carer. J just like Al would be.

Watched while we had tea the boys and little boys and others playing on the lawn. It was fine and sunny and I cried tears for a future that Al was not to share. It is like a terrible dream and you wake and it's real and oh how I long for it to be not so. Al is not aware of my crying whereas tears would have upset him before – that too is hard – we are already apart yet still both alive and close. Strange.

Crisp and v fine, heavy dew   *Saturday, 21 August*

A quite good night after tinkling at 10 and then asking again at
11, but it was a blank. We cuddled instead, but he was not really
here – a strange faraway look on his face. He had left me and I
must realise this will happen more and more. He has always been
my other half, but the branch is nearly off and the scar will take
time to heal over. It is strange to see and feel him and yet know
he is fading away from me.

I am writing this on Sunday and only did the above and my
mind is a complete and utter blank as to what happened on
Saturday. I'm going mad, not Al. Talked to Nick [Jane's brother]
or was *that* yesterday. Shit, shit, shit. I am going completely gaga.

I know I wanted to go to the church, but a wedding was in
progress so that was out – and somehow it was hard to leave the
place.

Overcast day   *Sunday, 22 August*

Awake on and off but all seems well. Finally fall asleep as usual
after 6 and woken by Al throwing the duvet back and wanting
to 'dump'. Half asleep I shot round and helped him on to the
commode, but too late and I got it all down left leg of my
pyjamas and I later realised it was a little on floor so he trod that
in and all over front of commode legs tinkly etc and his pyjamas
too. A disaster for first thing and *most* tiring.

James came and popped him into the bed as I was going to
wash him – but before that he suddenly announced he wanted
to dump again so off we got and more produced. Tup came and
we got him back into bed and comfy.

Breakfast reduced one to tears of frustration – he had wanted
porridge, but when it came he refused to taste it. Toast and
honey minute little mouthfuls – 1st one spat out – and gagging
ensued. Coffee ½ a cup ok. Went and made Weetabix + warm

Complan milk. ¼ only but after 3 egg spoons Al was gagging and trying to retch, so hardly anything.

Started on 'the pills'. 2 D/M + anti-sickness, 1 anti-fit: difficult now as he will not swallow it in one go so it stays in his mouth dissolving. After the 2 D/M and anti-sickness, he said 'I must dump' so out of bed and on commode – just saw in time. He had got his tinkle out and pushed it back in – as more foul-smelling diarrhoea and large pee came. Back to bed (alone so back twingey). Put pyjama top on as it is colder although sun now out. Made hotty. I only managed a bit of toast and cold cup of coffee – am quite exhausted.

11.45 now and I am lying on the bed while Al sleeps 'Venice train'. He was dear though and said he was sorry about all this. I said I found it so hard that he no longer seemed to notice if I wept and I wished he would weep with me – are we in this together or not, I said – if you can't cry with me who can you cry with? He said he didn't want to give in and only to God could he cry, and we would look back on this and he would remind me of our conversation. Yesterday – I might have thought it possible – this morning I feel there isn't any hope. Everyone says it will be up and down, but oh it's so terribly cruel – when you are up you think all will be well, this nightmare will end, we have a future to share.

It is a horrible, horrible, horrible thing to watch someone you love and who has such an incredible brain slipping into Kafka rambling and yet suddenly lucidly ticking one off for not reading something properly.

12.10 I must go downstairs now, have been sitting writing this up or reading *Sunday Times*. Al is asleep still – his face is getting much thinner.

It is the silences I find so depressing. He just stares ahead. Does he hear? I think so but he can't answer. We talked about how I would miss politics. What fun this last year or so had been since getting back into H of C, fun for me for once as I could share some of it.

I asked if there was anyone he wanted to see – any messages to or for anyone – he just looks ahead or talks so quietly it is impossible to hear and he never repeats it as it is obviously an effort to answer at all.

Supper was lovely fried squid – done by Julie in a jolly good batter. Al asleep – but did not stir when I kissed him. His dear face as I look at him sideways is falling in – oh dear God what a foul and miserable thing you have sent us all on such a beloved husband and father – everything has a reason, but I do not know what this is.

Crisp and fine again   *Monday, 23 August*

8.30 Al still asleep. Made coffee and grapenuts for myself and a piece of toast. Al said, 'You have been crying – so have I.' He seems quite different again, more on the ball and not so muddled. Another cruel quirk of this awful cancer – another 'up' to give us hope before a steeper decline again to despair? He had coffee and noticed today I had put sugar in it! Liked the idea of grapenuts and had 3 spoonfuls (teaspoons) and then two small pieces of brown toast and marmalade – and more coffee (nearly 1 cup of coffee). Drank nearly ½ Redoxon. I stayed with him – carpet swept the room and polished about, talked – he said he felt a weakening of his grip, but I tested it and it is as strong as ever – found him the wrist-strengthener which he used while talking. Quite good form, some wires crossed.

Grey and overcast and light rain fell today   *Tuesday, 24 August*

He seemed good this morning – fell asleep late a.m. and slept over lunch, which is now the norm. I took up soup and yoghurt, but not wanted. Sat for a bit, but left a note and went downstairs to do some bills – red reminder from the telephone as had not done them. Heard a noise and went up to find Al half out of bed having had an accident – changed pyjamas, sheets etc and got him back into bed. James came to help. He is now so heavy and dead-limbed it is awkward to move him – his face is now so thin you can see the 'plate' where the operation was, and his ribs, backbone and hip bones plus legs are too depressing. He is bones with skin and v little flesh. We talked, but he is quite muddled now – will try the lavender anti-fit, but not the anti-sickness one.

Late now after 11.30 and Al thirsty – suspicious even of water so offer to get him a piece of melon – downstairs to find J.J. still up. Back upstairs and Al takes one look/smell of melon and starts to choke retch – frantic trying to get upright. I rushed for James who held him upright. He sat on the edge of the bed lucid compared to earlier and not keeling over. Drank some water and took Epilium – while we talked to him. Julie came through and he lay down and we sat with him and talked.

Wednesday, 25 August

Michael Howard telephoned. I rang him and told him all not well. He was shattered by news.

Thursday, 26 August

Quite a good night for both of us. No sign of Bromley so *hope* he/she will appear again. 2Boy fine and jolly.[1] Al asleep as I write – sleep now and v calm. Just woke him calling Bromley – but it was 2Boy on the window. Al said good morning to me on

---

[1] Two jackdaws.

coming round, but otherwise just stares out of the window or ahead – looking so dreadfully sad.

He has now lost so much weight he looks like a PoW. Slept on and off, is low today – Helen (hospice nurse) came. He was monstrous and grimaced crazily when I tried to lift him and then flatly refused to speak to her at all.

Had tea with him and we chatted. I asked if he'd like Reg or Michael †,[1] but he did not answer and when he did much later on being re-asked said no.

Up with Complan for supper. *Very* little – he became quite fussed and asked about it. Was it poisoned, as they were trying to poison him? Andrew with me and we tried to reassure him, but this accounts for the fact he will not eat or drink.

Fine, cloudy, cooler (windy now)   *Friday, 27 August*

Dr C and Gail came and we have organised everything for a drip should he need one – Gail returned with an enormous tin and bags of medicines, which I have locked away. Al woke and peed, but I was not there and although we were in the kitchen it is obvious that isn't any good. I or someone should be *in the room* from now on as he is not aware of anything today and does not know he has peed or remember to call out. It is a dreadful down day. He does not even speak much, but when I kiss him and tell him I am here he half smiles, which is lovely.

Made tea and upstairs Al asleep. Woken and I went round and he asked for a kiss so he could remember my taste. We talked about it all. If it was for a reason what was it? He said he knew what I was doing for him and thanked me. Stayed until 7-ish – half asleep holding each other's hands.

---

[1] Reg Humphriss and Michael Seed.

Heavy dew, but v fine and dry, few clouds   *Saturday, 28 August*

Bromley appeared at the window for food. 'You tried to spike him,' Al said. 'No', I said, 'I've just given him a biscuit.'

Up to church with Julie – had a good cry. Felt better for it. James came back with a paddling pool and choc ices. Al actually ate a bit.

Did Al's nails and massaged his feet, creamed his arms and hands. He spat out the fish and peas. Is in a non-speaking mood, which is irritating to say the least.

Out now to do poor dogs who have had no walk or supper and it's 7.35 – I only walk around the top woodland and upper terrace. Back, gave them supper and met James who had taken up lovely picture of swimming pool to Al. J said he was very lucid and loving so I should go up and be with him. Told him I had been there all afternoon and he was just pretty non-speakers to one and I was bloody fed up with him.

He was not loving and friendly so I left him and came down after changing for lovely dinner of squid. Bed 5 to 10. Al asleep, covered him up and kissed him goodnight – (no response).

Heavy dew, v fine early autumn   *Sunday, 29 August*

5 to 5 I leapt out of bed and ½ asleep got bottle ready etc, but he had in fact peed lightly – so changed pyjamas and pad. He did not say a word, just glared. I am going to find this phase *very* difficult and depressing.

It's now 12.30. He doesn't seem good at all – not a good colour and stays mainly asleep. He was dear, though, and kissed me and said I was his BLJ and thanked me when I sorted him out after Thompson.

The children and young have been sitting outside in the sun with paddling pool in use and general jolly chatter/tears etc. It's another world out there, inside here my world is crumbling and yes, I am frightened.

James sat with him for 45 mins, came down and was quite rude when we said supper – he said he was going out for a fag. I then said don't worry I'm going up to bed and went out to get dogs. Dear J came out too and totally broke down in tears: 'I'm nearly 40 and I'm crying. I love him so much.' We both agreed it was absolutely vile to watch someone you love so much being destroyed by such an awful thing. He had his fag and we went in, both calmer.

Dry, overcast, warm   *Bank Holiday Monday, 30 August*

Lost count of 'tinkling' 'dump' dramas. Sat in his room all afternoon as he dozed, but he is in a non-speak (to me) mood so it is really depressing. I might just as well have a nurse sitting in here and just go off outside. I sometimes wonder if he recognises me at all. – (yes, he does).

Staring into space, not talking – feel terribly low today. A lovely walk which restored me round the moat with the dogs and then with J J and A to see the combining. Bob kind and stopped the machine for Angus, but it is really so huge he was overcome. Bed late, too late.

Written at EMT, 7.40   *Tuesday, 31 August*

A fairly ghastly night. I am so overtired by everything and things rather came to a head by a call for peeing at 12.40 and then nothing done at all. I fell back into my side of the bed at 1.05 and then another call 10 mins later (or rather not a call, but a throwing off of the bedclothes). Held the pee bottle until gone 2, but had a row with God and tried to tell Al how tired I was by all this and that I would have to get nurse in if this carried on. You always think you can cope, but you can't.

Tiny pee done, but he was a dear and whispered he knew how much I was doing and he was sorry. We talked and I lay with my head on his dear bony chest while he tried to stroke my hair. Oh dear, darling Al. Oh God how I will miss you. I dread the future without my soulmate. I dread being really alone without his wisdom, strength, fun and companionship. For 41 years we have been together, through ups and downs. Can I live without him? For the children's sake I must remain strong – the 'Dowager Empress' he said I would be. I must not let him down.

Woke this morning dragged to the surface by light (6.45), turned to Al and found he had thrown back his side of the duvet and peed. Down, laundry on and out for my bathe, up again with EMT. Al asleep – breathing v shallow today. Like dear Tom, you look closely to see if it is so.

Helen came, said to reduce his Dexa by 1 so only on 2 pills a day. She came up and saw him as Andrew said he was awake having peed again. I stayed and changed him. Tup saw Helen out and J J and Tup had a chat to her. She is worried about *me*. So is Dr C who said I should have 24-hour nursing for him now. I simply wouldn't, not while he still is aware of what's happening and although sometimes he looks through me and glares he will suddenly smile and say 'I know what you're doing and you are incredible' – or tonight he said he loved the gentle look I gave him. How could I just let a stranger take over? It is my job and I will go on.

Seems cooler, but still dry, high cloud, heavy dew again   Wednesday, 1 September

It's now September, the whole summer has gone by in a surreal way. I look out at the changing season from afar lost in this high-intensity 'drama', which is taking place in the Summer

Bedroom. Cannot get him out of bed any more, now too risky.

All the family off this a.m. to Dymchurch, girls by car, boys in the little train. Went on the beach on the way home. They are back now, said beach was lovely. Angus bathed so is now wrapped in James's T-shirt.

Dry, fine day, no wind, heavy dew   *Thursday, 2 September*

Woke before 6 to strange noises, put out my hand, but no response at all. I panicked. He was 'drowning' in his phlegm. Tried to put another pillow under his shoulders – not wildly successful. By 6.15 I thought it was the end. Terrible noises and looking v v bad. I rushed down with dogs to see if Tup and Boy there – no sign. Back up, caught Tup going down so asked him to fetch James, who rushed out of room to 'go for a pee' the minute he came in. Poor James, he is only making it harder for himself.

Al still open-mouthed, open-eyed, twitched lower jaw – a very minor fit possibly as it later (1 hour) turned into a shaking of shoulders, arms and hands, so I unpicked my hand from his very firm grip and took a little pill out to pop under his tongue, quite difficult and it was still under his tongue when much later Tup and I moved him to my bed to change and wash him and put a fresh sheet on the bed.

No sign of Reg on telephone, so Tup drove up, but he is obviously away. Tup brilliantly thought of Norman so I went and rang. Patsy, his wife, answered and said he was doing a service, but could come up at 10. She would go and find him. She rang back and dear Norman was coming straight up. He is *so* nice, a truly good, holy man. Both boys came in and we said prayers and he was anointed with oil. Felt so much better for it, and in a way I was glad fate had decreed it was Norman. Although I like Reg, we have known Norman longer and he has been a good man to know. Feel *so* much better that someone came in time; I would have felt guilty before God if I had failed to have him blessed. Waves of calmness are there now.

11.45 Realised he had had *no* medication and so Andrew rang Helen (hospice). Gail will come to put in syringe driver. When??

In fact the syringe driver was put in after 7. Dr C came 6.30-ish and saw Al – confirmed he was in a coma and unconscious and we discussed S-D. James said a fit would be very distressing and so when we realised the S-D would not do anything, but peacefully end him we all agreed.

Dr C came back and Heather the twilight nurse, whose own mother had died of cancer, came to put it in. I could not stay for this as it somehow seemed to be wrong to violate the body. Andrew stayed. Everyone being really kind. Al had been in a coma, but could squeeze your hand until about lunchtime – his breathing so rasping through the mouth, eyes open, but not aware. Oh dear God what a waste, what a waste! It is this I mind so much, not just the fact I shall be losing my soul mate of 41 years, my lover, my friend, my companion, my dearest husband – oh *how* I shall miss him! What an empty horizon stretches ahead, so frightening I cannot think of it, so am blocking it out.

It is now 20 to 10. I am lying on the bed beside him, his breathing fast and noisy, his chest tight and violent in the breathing. I hold his hand, but no response, his eyes now closed. How long can his body hold on to life? I talk to him of what I will do, the office, the woodland walk, the brambles on the cistus bank as well as the woodland. Keeping the paperwork in order, the bank statements in order, my life in order, a Lady Dunn minus Beaverbrook. We were always such a good team and now I shall be leaderless. Still the faith he always had in me will be my inspiration. I must not let him down. The Dowager Empress shall reign.

Now v hot and sunny   *Friday, 3 September*

Sat on bed or lay on it beside Al most of the afternoon. Flies
bothersome. I am paranoid about them settling on Al. Do they
sense he will shortly be dead? Finally went for a walk round the
garden while Andrew sat with him. Several scares, but tonight
(10.20) he sleeps ok, head slightly on one side. Eyes sometimes
open and still clutching the crystal.

Sarah and Julie both come in and boys a lot. James (and Tup)
really worried about *men* bothering me – how *dear* of them. I
simply do not see it at all.

Rang Col tonight – Celly out and Fr Michael out too.

Hot and sunny   *Saturday, 4 September*

Not an impossible night, difficult for me to sleep, but Al seemed
to be sleeping quite peacefully – one or two hiccups, but then
restarted. Talked at 4 to him, was sure he knows. Then at 10 to
6 Hannah got on the bed, plus Lëhni. I put Al's hand out so they
could smell him and he opens his eyes and I *know* he senses they
are there – a lovely moment.

Later back from a bathe and making EMT I tell him I'm back
and have bathed and I love him etc and he squeezes my hand (I
had cleaned him up, he had 'dumped' a little and peed – so now
he is lying comfortably). Oh such magic moments, but cruel too
as you suddenly think perhaps it's stopped and all will be well.

Washed hair. Celly rang, was very sweet and sympathetic. Nick
rang worried about me. We both agreed Ma seemed perkier.

Back upstairs with bowl of cereal I had dashed down for –
now in bedroom with papers and mail. Cutting from Romeike
and Curtice from the *Express* saying Al thinking of standing
down and I was going to support his decision. Furious, *hate* the
papers. What untruths they can publish. I shall have nothing to
do with them after it all comes out.

Stayed in the room all day on and off. Lunch came up, lovely
cauliflower cheese. Father Michael telephoned, is coming down
this afternoon. I went and rested with Al – fell asleep so Fr M
had to wait – it was ok. Everyone gave him tea and talked. Then
he, Fr M, came upstairs. Tup came too. We said prayers and Fr M
anointed him with oil (been here before I thought). Downstairs
and Fr M and I to Red Study where he talked and he told me
Al *was* a Catholic. He had made him one on 10 July when he
was with him. He had written down notes of that day. Sarah
brought us tea. I was gasping for a cup, then I went back
upstairs, Tup had very kindly stayed with Al. I must say I could
have shaken Al. I felt quite hurt he had not told me he was made
Catholic on 10 July – he only said he had blessing for sick and
communion secretly. Why when we can't talk about it do I only
know – for a short minute I actually hate him for holding
something as major as this back. I had thought we shared all
these things. How could he exclude me of all people? In a way
it's quite good as I can now distance myself much more.

Tip came in surprised to see me sitting on *my* side of the bed,
not 'in the crack' by Daddy. Showed him the letter Fr Michael
had written for me. I was cheered up by the fact he didn't think
Fr Michael *had* given Daddy last rites. I thought it poor
compared to Norman Woods's which was v moving. This was
very much a Catholic priest saying something for someone *not*
a Catholic. Swing back. I do *not* think he was fully received.[1]

We talked about burying Daddy. I said he'd always wanted a
shroud, not a coffin. James has not managed to hire a Kubota
[mechanical digger].

---

[1] Jane's journal, Wednesday 8 September: 'A fax from Fr Michael. Long and
rambling, sticking to his tale of Al's conversion, but tonight while cleaning my
teeth I spotted Al's Day Diary which reminded me I had his journal in my drawer
– how silly of me, I could look and see what happened. As we suspected – only
the sacrament of the sick. Do you not feel Al would have written up at length
such a major thing as being received into the RC church? Of course he would.
He didn't, because he wasn't.'

Al died at 11.45   *Sunday, 5 September*

Slept fitfully and woke with a jolt at 3.20 (Al's time) as Al was breathing differently now, shorter, tighter rasping breaths – with sighs every so often. Lay awake beside him. He is incredibly hot, 'muck sweat', but his arms are very cold and body temp ok. V hot hands and face.

Jolted, no jarred by 2Boy and dogs at 6.45 so let them out and came back to bed. Tup up getting EMT for himself. Down a bit later for EMT and a bowl of cereal. No change from Al upstairs since then although shot down to have a word with Sue. Washing machine flooding the floor downstairs – wish to goodness J had left it alone. It's much worse than just being temperamental with spinning.

Upstairs all morning. Janice [nurse] came 11-ish to change the syringe driver. Al's breathing still bad – and I noticed when I changed his pads that blotches were appearing under his skin on his legs and knees, reddish purple, and on the soles of his feet. Janice says this is the body's way of shutting down. Lynn came up – looking very well after her break in Britanny – and saw Al.

While we were there, she was just leaving, Al's breathing changed and I said we must get the boys in. Luckily, really luckily they were both outside in the courtyard and came running up. Within 5 or 6 minutes Al had died. Silence, then gasp and a little breathing. More gasps and pulse now weaker. He just looked so peaceful and you really felt his soul and spirit had left on their journey, a wonderful calm feeling entered the room. We all stroked him and talked and kissed him. It was such a lovely ending. Then we all hugged each other. The end of an era. Rang SEDOC and a doctor came up. Rang everyone, Ma, Nick, Celly, Col etc etc.

Reg coming up at 3.30 – was very nice and calming. Quite happy to bury Daddy and will ask Norman to help. Rang the gravedigger who can do it and will come tomorrow, at one o'clock. Dr C came and checked Daddy, and was very kind and concerned about me.

Walked dogs. Was sure I felt Al above going towards Roman tower. Talked at length to Celly. Michael Howard telephoned. Was terribly upset by news. V kind.

A big stumbling block. We have to have Shepway's [local council] permission to bury Daddy in the grounds. I am quite shattered. Fear they will say no. It has all gone so well. I do pray that we can bury Al as a family without pressure and where we wanted to, *when* we want. Delay will inevitably mean he will have to leave to go somewhere cooler. To bed after a bit of a sibling outburst over the fact Norman and Reg cannot go ahead without Shepway's ok. Julie very kindly came in and had a chat.

Monday, 6 September

So-so night, only jarred by worrying about possible problems with Shepway. No worries about Al beside me. In fact it was lovely as I could talk to him still. Much nicer than an empty space, which will come tonight, perhaps?

Up 6.20 writing this and the first of many LISTS! Downstairs breakfast. Did I have any? No, don't think so, too tense. Reg telephoned at 9-ish with Shepway's number, a Sandra Francis. I dialled it. A really nice woman answered and it was Sandra. She was so sympathetic and I cried, but wonderfully it is all under control and she doesn't see any problems at all. Oh *what* a weight lifted off my shoulders. I feel so calm. Had got myself in a terrible state if the answer had been 'no, not possible'.

Immediately wheels set in motion. James doing base for shroud (wood base). Andrew organised to collect death certificate and have it registered. Sarah has gone back to Broomhayes with little 'fair-heads'. Gail came and took syringe away. Julie and I bought flowers at farm shop in Sellindge. Back and then Reg and Michael Marsh and his son arrived to dig grave. MM and son *really* nice couple. Reg very calming and we discussed placing of chairs and bier. Grave was dug in record time and looks very pleasing. Walked dogs and fed hens on return. Saw Graham who is coming, and Eddie, who is still terribly distressed. Picked bay and wild clematis and a few white sweet peas. Did some flowers for the Red Library – organised curtains for table after tea.

Andrew dressed Daddy, who, I must say, had made our room a tiny bit high and window had to be shut because of flies. We have prepared him in his Cuixmala t-shirt, white silk shirt, his favourite battered cords and his suede shoes, his blue necker-chief. He looked very nice. Tup had re-shaved him as well and sprayed him with Roger & Gallet. Downstairs with Tup – he seems to have got heavier somehow. Have all helped to wrap him in his shroud, beautifully done by Julie and Sarah, and he has taken with him a lot of softies: pricklepins, heart stone, Creaggan early heather, seaweed, markies for dogs, digestives, fruit cake, H of C miniature, Zermatt rock, 2 Swiss francs, his armband, his racing vintage goggles, his H of C pass and a travel warrant, 1 handkey.

Supper omelette in kitchen. James insisted on lasagne.

Bed very late 11.30, but feel so much better.

Tuesday, 7 September

Today is Al's funeral – the first overcast morning which was lovely. It rained the day he died and now a dull day. Up quite early and bathed and made EMT, took it and a bowl of cereal back upstairs to bed. Got up at 8 and downstairs, made some cake as nothing to offer people, then organised everyone and saw Al out of the house on to the Mehari and round on to the table in the Knight's Hall. A white damask tablecloth of Great Granpa's with Albany gold curtain over and then the shroud on its wooden base. Did the flowers, 2 large bowls. The white urns inside the blue pots – full of chrysanths, lilies, bay, rosemary, old man's beard and Russian vine and hops. We put our individual posies on Al – peace lilies from Hannah and Lëhni, mixed little bunches from all of us. Very pretty it looked.

Dashed up to wash hair and change at 5 to 11. Felt very shaky, but hope I looked ok for Al, black plain linen dress, black stockings, black shoes, hair clean and loose. Only jewellery my diamond cross Al had given me, and my sapphire rings.

Celly and Col had arrived, and Sue[1] joined me when I was doing the flowers – dear Sue she was so shattered. Lynn, Peggy, Eddie and Graham, and Canon Norman Woods and Reg Humphriss, resplendent in flowing robes. Julie looked lovely, and so did Sarah and both boys very dashing. I was so proud of them. It was the nicest funeral I have been to, intimate and personal and I do hope Al would have been pleased with me. Sue dear and kept saying how proud he would have been of you. The first part of the service over we went across the lawn to the grave. Reg blessed the grave and consecrated it and after a short prayer we lowered Al into it and I threw or rather shovelled 2 spades of earth on to him, the first one rather splendidly landing on his tinkey. All then to the Red Library for sandwiches, gossip and coffee/tea. Both Reg and Norman were so complimentary about it and said it was one of the nicest funerals they had done.

When everyone had gone Sue and all of us retired to the kitchen to thrash out the press releases. Kept to what Al had wanted – 'Suddenly at Saltwood on 5 September. He wanted it to be known he had gone to join Tom and the other dogs.' Good and zany. Informed the Queen first as he was a PC, then Press Association. Phones frantic after that and camera crews at the gate.

Just talked and watched TV and listened to radio. The coverage is absolutely fantastic. On and on it went.

At 9 bizarrely the new Discovery turned up and so James and

---

[1] Sue Line, AC's former secretary.

I went up to the layby by the M-way and swapped our old one for the smartest vehicle ever owned by me.[1] Back and into bed very tired, but so pleased it all went so well.

---

[1] Bizarre is no exaggeration. Ordered earlier in the summer from Macrae & Dick, it had been brought south from Scotland on a car transporter, but the driver's tachograph reading forced him to stop near the Dartford tunnel. The only solution was to go and collect it. But with press cameras still massed outside the castle gates, Jane realised that to drive out past them in her old Discovery on the day of her husband's funeral only to return an hour later in a spanking brand-new machine was to invite trouble. Headlines of 'the merry widow' variety might be the least of it. So Jane and James waited until early evening, when, with deadlines passing, the press began to drift away. By the time they returned with the new Discovery the castle gates were deserted. Phew!

ACKNOWLEDGEMENTS

This third volume of Alan Clark's diaries would not have been possible without Jane Clark's support. Having decided to give the go-ahead her help was unstinting, although I know how daunting, difficult and stressful she found the process at times. As well as giving me free range through Alan's journals, day diaries, indeed anything that might prove useful, she also painstakingly read my transcripts against Alan's originals, even to the extent of peering through a magnifying glass at enlargements of particularly intractable entries. We shared moments of triumph – and exasperation – at some of the reading tests AC left behind. But knowing as she did the background to so many of the entries proved an enormous help. Any errors are, though, mine, and I would be glad to hear from readers who wish to offer comments that should be taken into account for any future editions.

Jane was also the most generous of hosts. I am very grateful to her.

Let me also thank here James and Andrew Clark, who separately provided invaluable expert knowledge on Eriboll, cars and their father's official visit to Oman in 1992.

After seven years as Alan's publisher, my editorial involvement in these diaries had its origins in a conversation with Michael Sissons, who represented Alan as his literary agent for more than forty years. I appreciate his faith in my abilities as well as his wide general knowledge.

As with the work of editing the earlier volume of diaries I wish to acknowledge here the many supporters who responded to my calls for help, not least in compiling footnotes:

Antony Beevor, Nigel Nicolson (and not only for his masterly edition of Harold Nicolson's diaries), Graham Stewart, Andrew Roberts, Simon Heffer, Katie Campbell, Susie Dowdall, Nigel Reynolds, Matthew D'Ancona, Michael White, Katy Heslop, Michael Cockerell, Hugo Vickers, George Weidenfeld, Gerald Isaaman, Simon Jenkins, Bruce Anderson, Dean Godson, Alan Williams, Brian MacArthur, Tim Heald, Carol MacArthur, Robert Coucher, Ilsa Yardley, Douglas Matthews, Jane Birkett, Christopher Silvester, 'Google' and the staff of the London Library. For the paperback edition Shaun Woodward, Juliet Pannett, David Ruffley among others.

A number of books were invaluable aides: let me single out for a general and often precise understanding of the events of the governments of John Major that cover much of the period of these diaries, *Major* by Anthony Seldon (Weidenfeld & Nicolson), undoubtably the most comprehensive source. Not for the first time I doff my hat in acknowledgement to Anthony's talents as a contemporary historian. As readers of this volume will note the diaries of Chips Channon are frequently mentioned. Robert Rhodes James's edition (Phoenix Press) has been well-thumbed. I am grateful, also, to *Knee Deep in Dishonour: the Scott Report and Its Aftermath* by Richard Norton-Taylor, Mark Lloyd and Stephen Cook (Victor Gollancz). The lines from Keith Douglas's 'On a Return from Egypt' are quoted by permission of Faber & Faber.

My colleagues at Orion and Weidenfeld & Nicolson put up with my absences. I would like in particular to thank Anthony Cheetham, Peter Roche, Adrian Bourne, Bing Taylor, Katie White, my assistant Victoria Webb, and the ace Orion group production team headed by Richard Hussey, aided in particular by Erin Hussey, Helen Ewing and Iram Allam.

Finally, but not in the least, my gratitude to my wife Sue for her patience and understanding of the time I spent with the diaries in a year when we also twice moved house and home.

Ion Trewin

INDEX